LET'S GO

www.letsgo.com

SPAIN & PORTUGAL

researcher-writers
Ian Armstrong
Graham Lazar
Anthony Ramicone
Mark Warren

staff writers
Adeline Byrne
Alexander Jaffe
Mikia Manley
Mark Warren

research managers
Clémence Faust
Dorothy McLeod

editors
Mary Potter
Mallory Weiss

managing editors
Sarah Berlow
Mark Warren

CONTENTS

RESEARCHER-WRITERS

IAN ARMSTRONG. Though he never left the Iberian Peninsula, Ian hopped deftly from culture to culture and language to language. Between Castile, Asturias, Basque Country, Catalonia, Valencia, Andalucía, and Gibraltar (UK), Ian conquered the peninsula more thoroughly than anyone since the Umayyads, and grew a beard that would make Hemingway cry little-girl tears.

GRAHAM LAZAR. Along with his bougie alter ego Winston Shrewsbury, Graham attacked the streets of Madrid with an aplomb hitherto unheard of—at least, that's how Winston would say it. Overcoming such obstacles as solo-tackling the communal Spanish dinner, foodie Graham held every restaurant to the highest of gourmet standards and kept his copy sharp for the duration of his route.

ANTHONY RAMICONE. Upon arriving in Portugal, Anthony was out of his country but hardly out of his element. He took to the welcoming Portuguese culture like a fish to water—or, perhaps, a sardinha to a grill. During his travels he found the hippest hostels, the cheapest drinks, the sweetest eats, and a chapel made of bones—hardcore. Or maybe post hardcore.

MARK WARREN. A Let's Go veteran, Mark found most of his stay in Barcelona to be a cakewalk, especially since he speaks every language remotely related to the city. Easily handling even the parts of his visit that were decidedly not cakewalks—discovering local dives and dueling armed muggers—Mark is a posterboy for LG stardom.

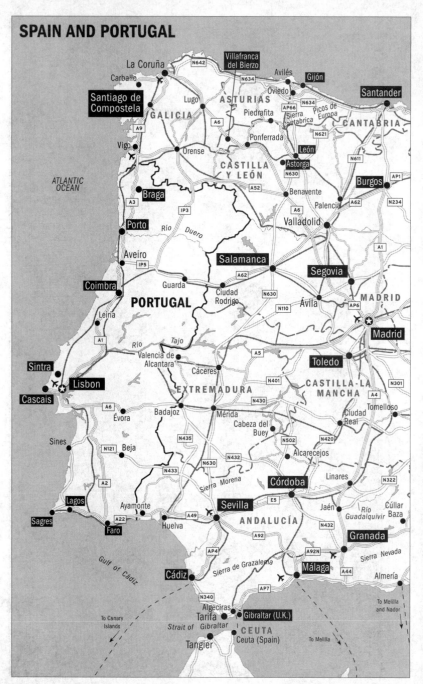

SPAIN AND PORTUGAL

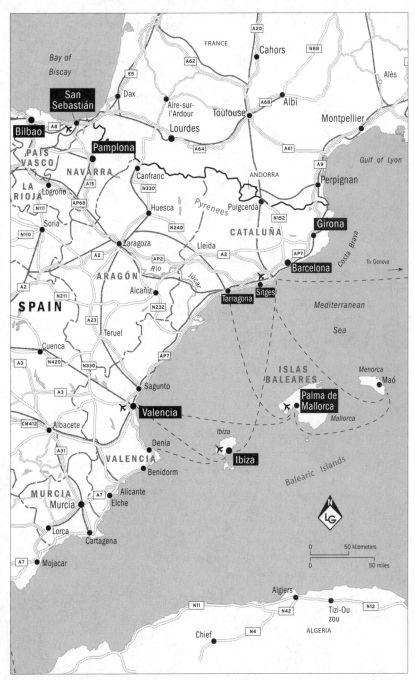

SPAIN & PORTUGAL

Forget *Lost* and its enchanted island—the Iberian Peninsula has seen more drama than ABC's entire Thursday night lineup. Isolated from Europe and Africa by mountain and sea, Spain and Portugal are themselves cultural mosaics. Despite being fiercely proud of their individuality, Spain's regions share a common rhythm (though they'd never admit it). The disappearance of the *sol* doesn't mean the disappearance of the soul. From the lull of afternoon siestas to the riotous tapas bars and *discotecas*, Spain harbors an invigorating lifestyle that galvanizes any traveler.

Portugal draws hordes of backpackers by fusing its timeless coastal towns and majestic castles with industrialized cities like Lisbon, whose graffiti-covered walls separate bustling bars from posh *fado* restaurants. It also helps that it's cheap, cheap, cheap—at least compared to the rest of Western Europe.

when to go

Summer is **high season** *(temporada alta)* for most of Spain and Portugal, when tons of tourists come to live *la vida loca*. Winter is high season for ski resorts in the Pyrenees and the Sierra Nevada. In many areas, high season begins during **Semana Santa** (Holy Week; March 24-30, 2013, April 13-19, 2014) and includes festival days like Pamplona's **Running of the Bulls** in early July (p. 390). July and August bring some serious heat, especially to the central plains and southern coasts. When the locals go on vacation in other parts of Europe in August, tourism peaks on the Iberian Peninsula. To be safe, make sure to book ahead if you plan to travel in June, July, or August.

Taking advantage of the **low season** *(temporada baja)* has many advantages, most notably lighter crowds and lower prices. Some lodgings drastically cut rates, and there's no need for reservations. Even as major cities and university towns exude energy during these months (due in part to study-abroad students), smaller coastal towns are empty, and discounts abound.

what to do

For the last two millennia, invaders ranging from hordes of European tribes to overzealous study-abroad students have swept over these countries, leaving their own mark on a culture already ripe with customs, tradition, history, and an undeniable fervor. Witness this excitement in Madrid's famous nightlife (p. 56), in the historic Alfama district in Lisbon (p. 452), or even in the beach-crazed town of Lagos (p. 532). There are countless ways to see Spain and Portugal: some tourists binge on sightseeing, getting through multiple churches and monuments every hour, while others spend weeks trekking through small towns, seeking authenticity and trying to blend in. Whatever your travel desires, these countries will not disappoint.

SMALL PLATES, BIG OPTIONS

We were always curious how Spaniards didn't get cranky waiting for their 9pm dinnertime—that is, until we tried the country's delectable tapas. Derived from the Spanish verb *tapar*, meaning "to cover," **tapas** are a ubiquitous treat flavored with garlic, chilies, and blends of spices like paprika and cumin. From cold vegetable medleys to roasted meat slathered in original sauces, these small plates

top five sweets for your sweetie

5. ASTORGA: Head to the Museo de Chocolate with your sweet pea for an informative and delicious adventure (heavy on the delicious).

4. SEVILLA: Impress your honey bun with sticky buns made by gifted nuns in the Santa Cruz district at El Torno bakery.

3. PORTO: Bring your love muffin to a Croft tasting tour to try some of the Douro region's best Port, a sweet dessert wine.

2. GRANADA: Fall in love with your *amorcito* one more time over some *pionono*, sugary cookies covered in baked cream at Pastelería Lopez Mezquita.

1. CÓRDOBA: Share the *hojas con chocolate*, a Spanish puff pastry longer than your forearm, at Pastelería-Cafetería San Pedro.

are a perfect sampling of regional and national cuisine. As a traveler, you can often tell your whereabouts with just one look at your plate. In Madrid and parts of Andalucía, tapas bars serve small tapas free with drinks, and certain areas like Leon's **Barrio Húmedo** are filled with finger-food havens dedicated to these tasty tidbits. In parts of northern Spain like País Vasco, chefs cook up *pinchos*, or tapas on toothpicks, that keep the snack from falling off its bread. Regardless of where you find yourself, don't miss out on a sampling of the nation's favorite little antipasto that could.

- **CASA ALBERTO:** Home to eclectic tapas like lamb's knuckles and pig's ears, this bar also serves up regional favorites like salted cod and oxtail. (Madrid, Spain; p. 46.)

- **TABERNA DE ANTONIO SÁNCHEZ:** Opened in 1830 by a Spanish bullfighter, this bar serves up piping hot *tapas calientes;* it's rumored that two of these bad boys together rival any dinner option in Madrid. (Madrid, Spain; p. 45.)

- **EL XAMPANYET:** While named after the house wine, this place should be named after its deliciously varied tapas selection. (Barcelona, Spain; p. 151.)

- **GATZ:** Despite sharing the surname of the famous Great Gatsby, this tapas bar is not a sham. With pinchos prizes lining its walls, Gatz serves up some seriously tasty dishes like fried *foie* and potato *pinchos* and salmon wrapped around cream cheese and capers. (Bilbao, Spain; p. 366.)

- **A FUEGO NEGRO:** *Let's Go's* choice for tapas with some 'tude, A Fuego Negro serves up some heavy rock and even heavier tapas plates. (San Sebastián, Spain; p. 378.)

student superlatives

- **BEST PLACE TO FULFILL YOUR PIPE DREAMS:** Head to Barcelona's Pipa Club, an unmarked bar and lounge specializing in tobacco products.

- **BEST ROCK AND SOL:** Come to Puerta del Sol, the "gateway of the sun" and soul of Madrid's shopping, people-watching, and partying.

- **BEST MIXTURE OF THE SACRED AND THE PROFANE:** Imbibe in all kinds of sin at Porto's Festa de São João in commemoration of St. John the Baptist.

- **BEST PLACE TO PARTY LIKE ITS 1755:** At Madrid's Palacio Real, you'll live like a king—at least until the end of the one-hour walking tour.

- **BEST PLACE TO RETIRE:** Even if your social security hasn't kicked in yet, head to Madrid's Parque del Retiro for rest and relaxation in the city's best green space.

FROM DUSK 'TIL DAWN

Taking the etymology of the term "nightlife" to its extreme, Spain and Portugal help make Iberia the peninsula that never sleeps. **Barcelona's** eat-late-but-party-later attitude creates an edgy nightlife that reflects the city's distinct sense of style. With intoxicating energy flowing from an array of discotecas and *tablaos*, **Madrid** has become internationally recognized as one of the greatest party cities in the world. Sevilla's **La Macarena** district is the perfect meeting ground for travelers looking to booze with locals, and **Ibiza** houses some of the world's largest clubs. Bring out your inner bro in the student-packed **Salamanca**, an international frat-star haven, or head out on the town in Portugal's **Lagos**, a city with more bars and backpackers per square meter than any other place in the world. Even if your days are already packed with doing a little dance and making a little love, be sure to leave time to get down tonight.

- **MADRID:** Find the next big discoteca in Madrid's Chueca district (p. 24), a nightlife sanctuary home to some of the trendiest and sleekest clubs and bars.

- **BARCELONA:** For alternative music and some of Spain's most eclectic party people, head to Barcelona's El Raval district to move to the beat of your own drum. (p. 105)

- **SALAMANCA:** Students and the young at heart don't think about heading to clubs until well after midnight in this party-'til-the-break-of-dawn university town. (p. 95)

- **LAGOS:** Turn your surfboard into a pong table by surfing the beaches until dusk and starting the night early in one of the city's bars dotting the coastline. (p. 532)

- **IBIZA:** Sand might not be the only thing you get in your pants after a night on this debauched island. (p. 244)

TAKE A HIKE

Don't get out of town, just get outdoors. Spain and Portugal offer a wealth of hiking opportunities whether in a garden or up a tower.

- **PARQUE NACIONAL DA PENEDA-GERÊS:** One of Portugal's best hiking destinations, this protected wilderness area boasts a number of trails and for all levels of outdoorsman. (p. 518)

- **THE ROCK OF GIBRALTAR:** This isn't a rock you could toss into a pond (unless, perhaps, you are a superhero...*Let's Go* understands that even Batman has a budget). The stairs up this rock can take up to two and a half hours to climb, but there is a cable car for the average human. (p. 350)

- **PARC DE COLLSEROLA:** With hiking trails and a cycling track along the ridge of the mountain range, this park outside of Barcelona will quench your thirst for nature. (p. 145)

BEYOND TOURISM

That last guided tour put you to sleep? Need to take a break from schlepping your baggage around cobblestone streets? Or maybe you're broke beyond belief and in need of some spare cash to prolong your trip? Whatever the case may be, use our Beyond Tourism section to discover how to study, work, or volunteer in these countries to spice up your trip and help you get closer to the local way of life.

- **NIKITAS LANGUAGE ABROAD:** With schools in Spain and Portugal, Nikitas Language Abroad offers courses for students with all levels of language ability. (p. 591)

- **BTCV:** Volunteer with this Portuguese conservationist group and focus on issues like combatting invasive plant (p. 592)

- **PLANET AU PAIR:** Enroll with this network and land a job taking care of Spanish *niños* for a few months. (p. 595)

suggested itineraries

BEST OF SPAIN AND PORTUGAL (1 MONTH)

Discover the Iberian Peninsula through Portugal and southern Spain.

1. LISBON: Visit Portugal's capital city, where hilltop castles and Roman arches overlook a modern metropolis.

2. PORTO: Imbibe the city's namesake wine along the impressive Douro River.

3. SALAMANCA: Rage with study-abroad students from around the world in this historic college town.

4. MADRID: The political and geographic center of the country, Madrid offers countless opportunities to partake in Spanish culture.

5. GRANADA: Play king of the hill for a day in the Alhambra, the crowning jewel of this city found at the foot of the Sierra Nevada.

6. SEVILLA: Dance flamenco late into the night in Spain's third-largest city.

7. CÁDIZ: Housing the Spanish Navy since the 1700's, this port city offers tourists breathtaking vistas and is arguably the oldest city on the Iberian Peninsula.

8. GIBRALTAR: Whether you want to sip a Guinness or swing with Barbary macaques, a daytrip to the UK's Mediterranean gem won't disappoint.

Best of Spain and Portugal

Get Your Toes Wet

FRANCE

■San Sebastián

4

PORTUGAL

Porto ■

3

SPAIN

5

Valencia ■

6

2

■ Lisbon

■Ibiza

1

Algarve ■

0   100 miles

0   200 kilometers

MOROCCO

ALGERIA

GET YOUR TOES WET (2 WEEKS)

Hang ten, and then four more. That's right, fourteen days of soaking up the sun like a loaf of bread soaks up water in a swimming pool (it's a long story).

1. ALGARVE: Head to the white-sand beaches of Lagos for year-round sunshine on Portugal's southern coast.

2. LISBON: Travel to the beaches of Cascais to shred some waves with the local surfing community.

3. PORTO: Be careful when mixing sun and sherry in this Portuguese paradise.

4. SAN SEBASTIÁN: A resort destination for the European bourgeoisie on holiday, this beach town comes equipped with kayaking and surfing lessons for all levels.

5. VALENCIA: With a vivacious energy often lost in a beach town, this beach town offers sun, sand, and paella up the Wazoo.

6. IBIZA: Get baked on Ibiza's warm sands in more ways than one before heading to its crazy clubs and downright dirty discos.

WINE NOT? (1 WEEK)

Cultured connoisseurs and crazy college kids alike will enjoy a week of wine tasting in the best regions of Spain and Portugal. Get ready to whiff, swish, spit, and swallow. There are tannins to be tasted!

1. SANTIAGO DE COMPOSTELA: This city is a great starting point for ⚐**wine-tasting** in the Galicia region known for its Albariño wine.

2. PORTO: With various international imposters attempting to steal its name, this city's port wine remains the original tawny dessert masterpiece.

3. BARCELONA: Grab a glass of traditional *cava* and enjoy Barcelona with bubbly in hand.

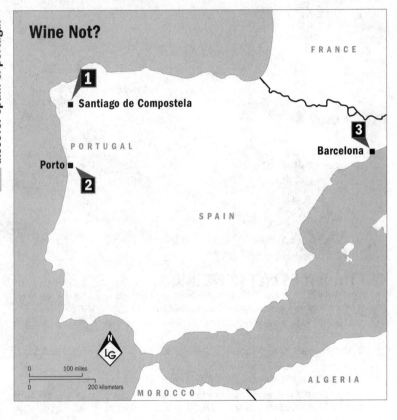

how to use this book

CHAPTERS

Let's Go Spain & Portugal begins in **Madrid,** Spain's capital in the center of the country. From there, we explore the nearby cities of **Central Spain,** then head east to **Barcelona** and the surrounding area of **Catalonia and Valencia.** After a brief island jaunt to the **Balearic Islands,** we continue down the coast to **Andalucía.** Next we head to **Basque Country** in the northeast, then across the rest of **Northern Spain** with Santiago de Compostela and the cities of the Camino de Santiago, as well as some coastal cities for your beach fix.

In Portugal, we start with **Lisbon,** the capital and largest city, followed by the nearby towns of **Cascais and Sintra.** We round out our coverage with chapters on **Northern Portugal** and **Southern Portugal.**

But that's not all, folks. We also have a few extra chapters for you to peruse:

CHAPTER	DESCRIPTION
Discover Europe	Discover tells you what to do, when to do it, and where to go for it. The absolute coolest things about any destination get highlighted in this chapter at the front of all *Let's Go* books.
Essentials	Essentials contains the practical info you need before, during, and after your trip—visas, regional transportation, health and safety, phrasebooks, and more.
Beyond Tourism	As students ourselves, we at *Let's Go* encourage studying abroad, or going beyond tourism more generally, every chance we get. This chapter lists ideas for how to study, volunteer, or work abroad with other young travelers in Europe to get more out of your trip.

LISTINGS

Listings—a.k.a. reviews of individual establishments—constitute a majority of *Let's Go* coverage. Our Researcher-Writers list establishments in order from **best to worst value**—not necessarily quality. (Obviously a five-star hotel is nicer than a hostel, but it would probably be ranked lower because it's not as good a value.) Listings pack in a lot of information, but it's easy to digest if you know how they're constructed:

ESTABLISHMENT NAME TYPE OF ESTABLISHMENT $$$$
Address ☎phone number website
Editorial review goes here.
➜ Directions to the establishment. i Other practical information about the establishment, like age restrictions at a club or whether breakfast is included at a hostel. $ Prices for goods or services. ⏰ Hours or schedules.

ICONS

First things first: places and things that we absolutely love, sappily cherish, generally obsess over, and wholeheartedly endorse are denoted by the all-empowering 👍**Let's Go thumbs-up.** In addition, the icons scattered at the end of a listing (as you saw in the sample above) can serve as visual cues to help you navigate each listing:

👍	*Let's Go* recommends	☎	Phone numbers	➜	Directions
i	Other hard info	$	Prices	⏰	Hours

OTHER USEFUL STUFF

Area codes for each destination appear opposite the name of the city and are denoted by the ☎ icon.

PRICE DIVERSITY

A final set of icons corresponds to what we call our "price diversity" scale, which approximates how much money you can expect to spend at a given establishment. For **accommodations,** we base our range on the cheapest price for which a single traveler can stay for one night. For **food,** we estimate the average amount one traveler will spend in one sitting. The table below tells you what you'll *typically* find in Spain and Portugal at the corresponding price range, but keep in mind that no scale can allow for the quirks of all individual establishments.

ACCOMMODATIONS	WHAT YOU'RE LIKELY TO FIND
$	Campgrounds and dorm rooms, both in hostels and actual universities. Expect bunk beds and a communal bath. You may have to provide or rent towels and sheets.
$$	Upper-end hostels and lower-end hotels. You may have a private bathroom, or a sink in your room with a communal shower in the hall.
$$$	A small room with a private bath. Should have some amenities, such as phone and TV. Breakfast may be included.
$$$$	Large hotels, chains, and fancy boutiques. If it doesn't have the perks you want (and more), you've paid too much.
FOOD	WHAT YOU'RE LIKELY TO FIND
$	Street food, fast-food joints, university cafeterias, and bakeries (yum). Usually takeout, but you may have the option of sitting down.
$$	Sandwiches, pizza, low-priced entrees, ethnic eateries, and bar grub. Either takeout or sit-down service with slightly classier decor.
$$$	A somewhat fancy restaurant. Entrees tend to be heartier or more elaborate, but you're really paying for decor and ambience. Few restaurants in this range have a dress code, but some may look down on T-shirts and sandals.
$$$$	Your meal might cost more than your room, but there's a reason—it's something fabulous, famous, or both. Slacks and dress shirts may be expected.

MAP LEGEND

You'll notice that our maps have lots of crazy symbols. Here's how to decode them.

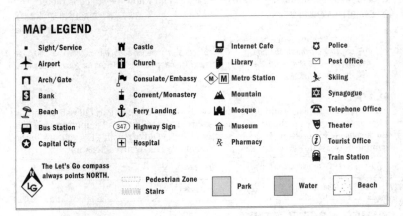

MAP LEGEND

- ■ Sight/Service
- ✈ Airport
- ⌐ Arch/Gate
- $ Bank
- 🐎 Beach
- 🚌 Bus Station
- ✪ Capital City

- ♜ Castle
- ✝ Church
- ⚑ Consulate/Embassy
- ☩ Convent/Monastery
- ⚓ Ferry Landing
- (347) Highway Sign
- ✛ Hospital

- 💻 Internet Cafe
- 📖 Library
- Ⓜ-M Metro Station
- ▲ Mountain
- ☪ Mosque
- 🏛 Museum
- ℞ Pharmacy

- ✪ Police
- ✉ Post Office
- ⛷ Skiing
- ✡ Synagogue
- ☎ Telephone Office
- ▮ Theater
- ⓘ Tourist Office
- 🚆 Train Station

The Let's Go compass always points NORTH.

⬡ LG

▩ Pedestrian Zone
▨ Stairs

☐ Park   ☐ Water   ⋮ Beach

SPAIN

MADRID

Welcome to Madrid, where the day starts later, the night ends later, and the locals look like Javier Bardem. Sound good? Well, there's more. Much more. Madrid is home to some of the biggest and baddest sights in the world, from museums filled with iconic art to discotheques packed with Spain's most beautiful. From Goya's *The Naked Maja* by day to the (almost) naked *madrileños* at night, Madrid insists that you stay on the move—in only the most laid-back style, of course. When it's time to recuperate, slow down, savor some of the best in Spanish cuisine, and lounge at one of the city's immaculate parks or gardens under the warm Spanish sun. Life is good. Madrid's plazas, gardens, and monuments tell the city's rich history. After Philip II made the city the capital of his empire in 1561, Madrid enjoyed centuries at the top of the heap. It served as Spain's artistic hub during the Golden Age, becoming a seat of wealth, culture, and imperial glory, whose legacy can still be felt in literary neighborhoods like Huertas, in the sumptuous interiors of royal estates like the Palacio Real, and in the bad-ass collections of the museums along the Avenida del Arte. So get some rest on the plane because from here on out it's all dinners at midnight, parties at three, marathon treks through museums the size of small countries by day, and chasing down Javier Bardem at high noon.

greatest hits

- **LIVE LIKE A KING.** No, not the Palacio Real—better! The amenities at the government-run **Albergue Juvenil Municipal Hostel** (p. 30) will make you feel like you're staying in a four-star hotel.

- **ACT THE AFICIONADO. Museo Nacional del Prado** can show only 10% of its gigantic collection at a time. (p. 35)

- **ANCIENT EATS. El Sobrino de Botín** is actually the oldest restaurant in the world. (p. 42)

- **SEVENTH HEAVEN. Kapital** offers seven floors of uniquely themed dance fun. (p. 60)

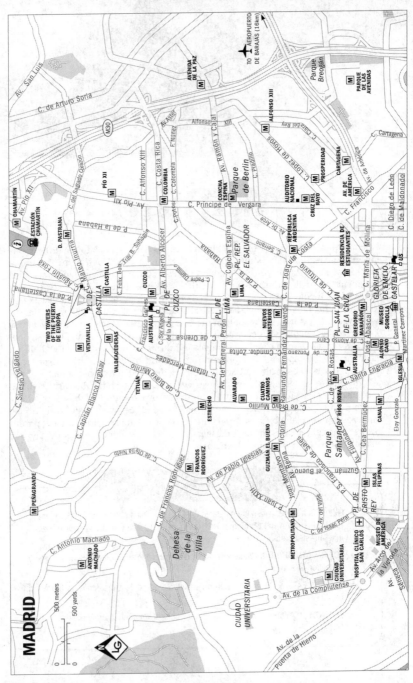

madrid

MADRID

500 meters
500 yards

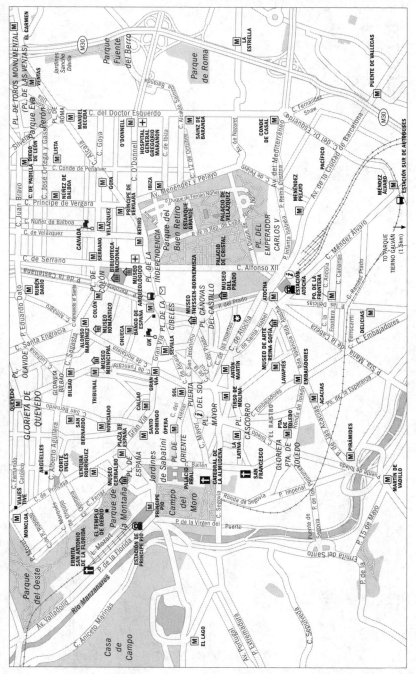

madrid

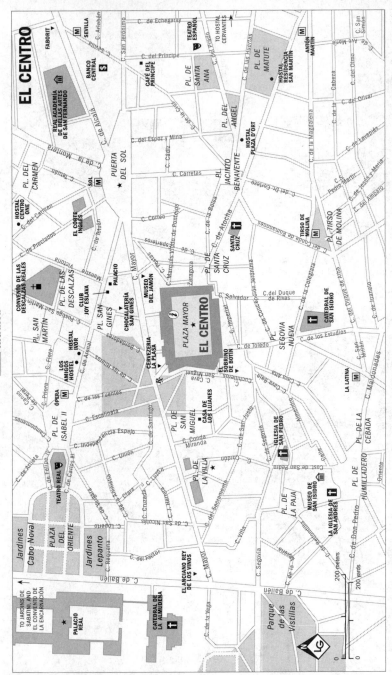

madrid

EL CENTRO

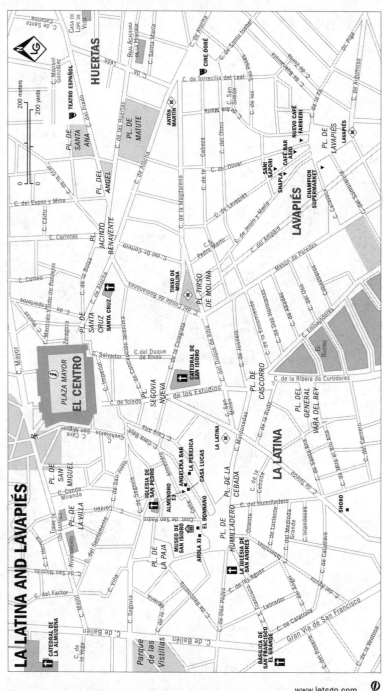

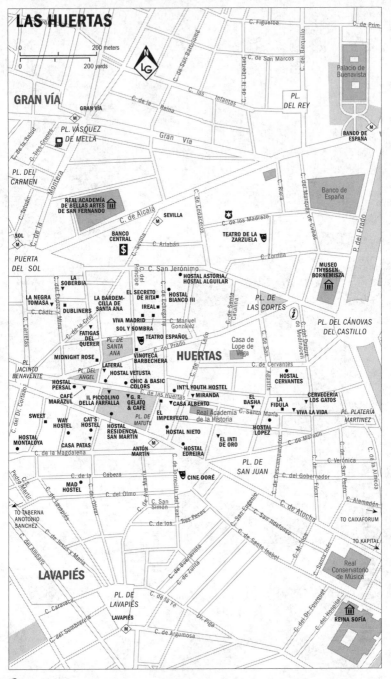

LAS HUERTAS

0 — 200 meters
0 — 200 yards

GRAN VÍA

GRAN VÍA

PL. VÁSQUEZ
DE MELLA

PL. DEL
CARMEN

REAL ACADEMIA
DE BELLAS ARTES
DE SAN FERNANDO

SEVILLA

SOL

BANCO
CENTRAL

PUERTA
DEL SOL

LA
SOBERBIA

LA NEGRA
TOMASA

DUBLINERS

FATIGAS
DEL
QUERER

MIDNIGHT ROSE

PL
JACINTO
BENAVENTE

HOSTAL
PERSAL

CAFÉ
MARAZUL

SWEET

WAY
HOSTEL

CAT'S
HOSTEL

HOSTAL
MONTALOYA

CASA PATAS

LA BARDEM-
CILLA DE
SANTA ANA

VIVA MADRID

PL. DE
SANTA
ANA

LATERAL

PL. DEL
ANGEL

IL PICCOLINO
DELLA FARFALLA

HOSTAL
RESIDENCIA
SAN MARTÍN

EL SECRETO
DE RITA

IREAL

SOL Y SOMBRA

TEATRO ESPAÑOL

VINOTECA
BARBECHERA

HOSTAL VETUSTA

CHIC & BASIC
COLORS

G. R.
GELATO
& CAFÉ

PL. DE
MATUTE

EL
IMPERFECTO

ANTÓN
MARTÍN

MAD
HOSTEL

HOSTAL ASTORIA/
HOSTAL ALGUILAR

HOSTAL
BIANCO III

C. Manuel
González

HUERTAS

INT'L YOUTH HOSTEL

MIRANDA

CASA ALBERTO

HOSTAL NIETO

HOSTAL
EDREIRA

CINE DORÉ

Casa de
Lope de
Vega

Real Academia
de la Historia

EL
BASHA

LA
FIDULA

EL INTI
DE ORO

PL. DE LAS CORTES

PL. DEL CÁNOVAS
DEL CASTILLO

HOSTAL
CERVANTES

CERVECERÍA
LOS GATOS

VIVA LA VIDA

HOSTAL
LÓPEZ

PL. PLATERÍA
MARTÍNEZ

PL. DE
SAN JUAN

TEATRO DE LA
ZARZUELA

Banco de
España

MUSEO
THYSSEN-
BORNEMISZA

Palacio de
Buenavista

PL.
DEL REY

BANCO DE
ESPAÑA

TO TABERNA
ANOTONIO
SÁNCHEZ

LAVAPIÉS

PL. DE
LAVAPIÉS

LAVAPIÉS

REINA SOFÍA

Real
Conservatorio
de Música

TO CAIXAFORUM

TO KAPITAL

madrid

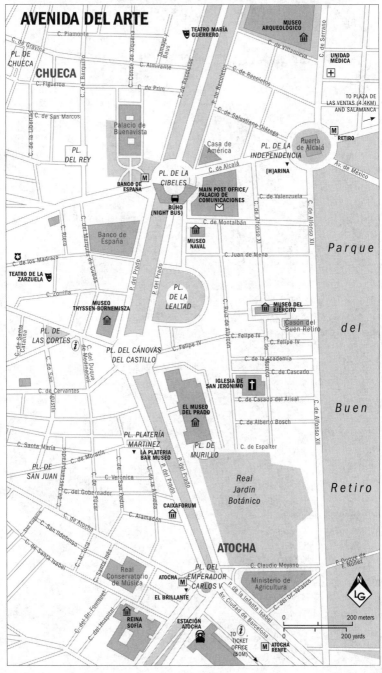

AVENIDA DEL ARTE

avenida del arte

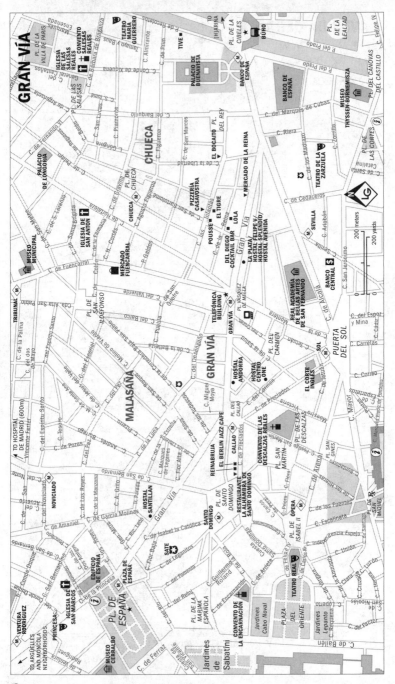

madrid

GRAN VÍA

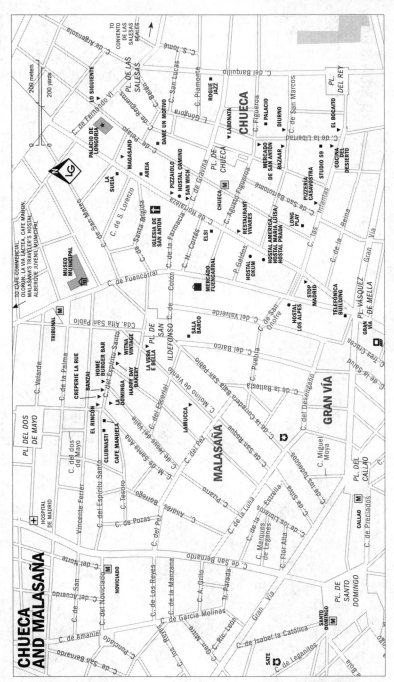

CHUECA AND MALASAÑA

C. de San Bernardo
C. del Norte
C. del Acuerdo

NOVICIADO Ⓜ

C. de San Andrés

HOSPITAL
DE MADRID

PL. DEL DOS
DE MAYO

C. del dos
de Mayo

TRIBUNAL Ⓜ

C. de la Palma

C. de Velarde

Vincente Ferrer

CREPERIE LA RUE ■
BANZAI ▼
HOME ▼
BURGER BAR
DOMINGA ▼
HAPPY DAY ▼
BAKERY

EL RINCÓN ■
CLUBNASTI ■
CAFÉ MANUELA ■

WITNA VINTAGE ■
LA VERA ▼
E BELLA

LAMUCCA ▼

C. del Espíritu Santo

C. del Tesoro

C. del Escorial

C. M. de Santa Ana

C. de San Vicente Ferrer

C. del Pez

C. de la Luna

C. de la Puebla

C. de San Roque

C. de la Corredera Baja de San Pablo

MALASAÑA

GRAN VÍA

C. de la Ballesta

C. del Desengaño

C. Miguel
Moya

PL. DEL
CALLAO

CALLAO Ⓜ

C. de Preciados

PL. DE
SANTO
DOMINGO

SANTO
DOMINGO Ⓜ

Gran Vía

SATE ✚

C. de Leganitos

C. de Isabel la Católica

C. de García Molinas

C. de Amaniel

C. Ponciado

C. de San Bernardo

C. de los Reyes

C. de la Manzana

C. A. Grilo

C. del Limón

C. de Pozas

C. del Tesoro

C. de Borbego

C. de la Palma

Andrés Borrego

C. del Pizarro

C. de la Estrella

C. de los Libreros

C. Marqués
de Leganés

C. de Jesús del Valle

C. de Pozas

C. de Flor Alta

C. Rico León

C. Mira

C. de San Bernardo

C. Parada

Gran Vía

TO CAFÉ COMMERCIAL,
OLOKUN, LA VIA LÁCTEA, CAFÉ MAHON,
MALASAÑA'S TRAVELER'S HOSTAL,
ALBERGUE JUVENIL MUNICIPAL

C. de San Mateo

PALACIO DE
LONGORIA ★

LG

LA
SUECA ■

C. de S. Lorenzo

C. de Santa Brígida

MUSEO
MUNICIPAL �📷

C. de Fuencarral

Cda. Alta San Pablo Ⓜ

PL. DE
SAN
ILDEFONSO

SALA
BARCO ■

C. del Barco

C. del Molino de Viento

C. de Fernando VI

LO SIGUIENTE ▼

PL. DE LAS
SALESAS

C. de las Salesas

C. de Regueros

C. de San Lucas

MAGASAND ■

AREIA ■

PIZZAIOLO ▼
DAME UN MOTIVO ●

IGLESIA DE
SAN ANTÓN ✝

PL. DE
CHUECA

CHUECA Ⓜ

C. de Gravina

C. de la Farmacia

C. H. Cortés

ELSI ■

C. de Argensola

C. de San Tomé
S. Tomé

TO
CONVENTO
DE LAS
SALESAS
REALES

PL. DE LAS
SALESAS

C. Piamonte

ROGUE
JAZZ ●

CHUECA

LABONATA ●
C. Figueroa
PALACIO ●
DIURNO ●

MERCADO
DE SAN ANTÓN ●
BAZAAR ▼

PL. DE
LAS
SALESAS

C. de San Marcos

EL BOCAITO ●

COCINA
DEL
DESIERTO ▼

STUDIO 59 ●

C. de la Libertad

PIZZERÍA
CASAVOSTRA ●

C. de San Bartolomé

C. de Augusto Figueroa

RESTAURANT
VIVARES ▼

LONG
PLAY ●

C. de las Infantas

C. de la Reina

HOSTAL AMÉRICA,
HOSTAL MARÍA LUISA,
HOSTAL PRADA ●

P. Galdós

HOSTAL
OKUM ●

MERCADO
FUENCARRAL ▪

C. del Valverde

C. de San Onofre

STOP
MADRID ●

HOSTAL
LOS ALPES ●

TELEFÓNICA
BUILDING

PL. VÁSQUEZ
DE MELLA

GRAN
VÍA Ⓜ

C. de Hortaleza

C. de Fuencarral

C. de Colón

Cda. Alta de San Pablo

HOSTAL DAMINO ●
HOSTAL SAN WICH ▼

C. de Gravina

PL. DE
CHUECA

CHUECA

C. de Barquillo

C. de las Infantas

Gran Vía

C. de la Salud

C. de Tres Cruces

C. de Hortaleza

PIZZAIOLO

200 meters
200 yards

chueca and malasaña

madrid

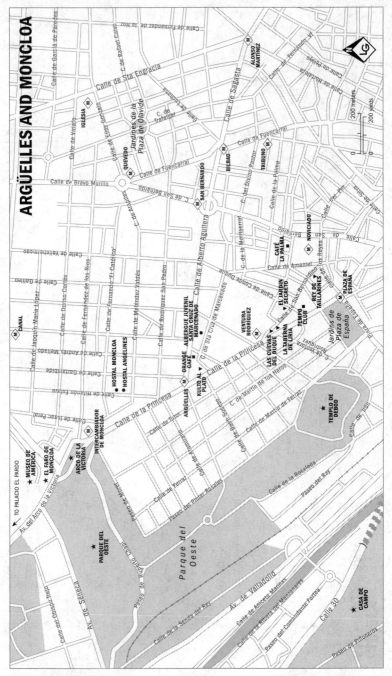

ARGÜELLES AND MONCLOA

orientation

EL CENTRO

Bordered by the beautiful Palacio Real in the west and the relaxing Parque del Retiro in the east, El Centro, the heart of Madrid, contains the city's most famous historical sites and modern venues. Churches, plazas, and winding cobblestone streets are set beside clubs and countless tapas restaurants. In the middle is **Puerta del Sol,** the "soul of Madrid," where thousands descend to ring in each New Year. By day, the area around Puerta del Sol is a commercial hub with plenty of name-brand stores and fast food chains. Branching off of Puerta del Sol is **Calle Mayor,** a main thoroughfare which leads west to **Plaza Mayor,** a vibrant square bordered by restaurants and filled with street performers and vendors. On the western side of Pl. Mayor is **Calle Bailén.** Here you will find El Centro's most famous sights, including the **Palacio Real,** and Madrid's most picturesque gardens in **Plaza de Oriente.** Finally, **Plaza Santa Ana** to the south of el Sol provides a popular meeting place where locals and tourists escape for drinks and tapas. While El Centro can be a bit chaotic, it is home to the city's most essential landmarks. El Centro is easily walkable and the Metro provides convenient and reliable access to the rest of the city. The main sights are deceptively close to one another. When in doubt, stick to the main streets—**Calle de Alcalá, Calle Mayor, Calle de las Huertas,** and **Calle de Atocha**—for adequate restaurants, nightlife, hostels, and cafes.

LA LATINA AND LAVAPIÉS

La Latina and Lavapiés lie toward the south of El Centro. These areas are young, hip, and distinctively *madrileño*. While accommodations are limited, these areas provide some of the finest dining and nightlife options in the city. Many unadventurous tourists will stick to the obvious food and drink options surrounding Puerta del Sol and Pl. Mayor, but the *tabernas* of **Calle Cava Baja** and **Calle Almendro** serve some of the city's best traditional Spanish cuisine. These narrow streets are packed with meal options and one rule is universal: quality matters. While Lavapiés is less active at night, it remains one the best neighborhoods for international cuisine, particularly along **Calle Lavapiés** with its many Indian restaurants; if you are sick of tapas, this is a great place to mix things up. Try to make it to the Sunday flea market **El Rastro**.

LAS HUERTAS

Las Huertas' walls are etched with quotes from writers like Cervantes and Calderón de la Barca, who lived in this literary neighborhood during its Golden Age. This is its claim to fame, meaning that today it is unmistakably a travelers' haunt, with cafes, bars, pubs, and clubs lining the narrow streets. Unlike El Centro, which is largely commercial and geared toward tourists, Las Huertas feels like a playground for 20-somethings, with small independent shops, cafes, *cervecerías*, bars, and clubs in every direction. **Plaza Santa Ana** and **Plaza del Ángel** are the vital centers of the area, but you will find a greater diversity of food and drink venues as you move outward, especially east down C. de Las Huertas, and to the north up C. de la Cruz. Huertas' northern boundary is C. Alcalá, the southern is C. Atocha, and the eastern is Paseo del Prado.

AVENIDA DEL ARTE

Bordering the eastern edge of the city, **Parque del Buen Retiro** is Madrid's Central Park. This is where the fast pace of cosmopolitan life breaks down, where *madrileño* families come to spend time together, where tourists can escape their hostel bunk beds. El Retiro is its own world of walkways, gardens, fields, and trees, and it is deceptively close to the city center. The Avenida del Arte just west of Retiro is the city's cultural endowment. While the city center is largely commercial (save the odd cathedral or convent), Avenida del Arte protects Spain's most prized cultural artifacts, from Picasso's *Guernica* to Goya's *Second* and *Third of May*. While the **Museo Nacional del Prado**, the **Reina Sofía**, and the **Museo Thyssen-Bornemisza** have become famous individually, it is their totality that makes the Avenida del Arte such a powerful showing of Spain's culture. The walk along the tree-lined **Paseo del Prado** has become a cultural phenomenon of its own, a celebration of the beauty and sophistication of this city.

GRAN VÍA

Calle Gran Vía is filled with all the stuff that tourists don't need to come to Europe to see: fast-food restaurants, chain stores, and traffic jams. While the main avenue tends to be crowded and commercial, the greater Gran Vía area should not be discounted. Running east to west from **Plaza de Cibeles** to **Plaza de España**, Gran Vía has a number of great restaurants, bars, clubs, and live music venues—you just have to look hard. On the southeastern boundary with Chueca, you will find the highest concentration of small restaurants, bars, and boutiques, particularly on **Calle de la Reina** and **Calle de las Infantas**. C. Gran Vía is nothing glamorous, but as you venture outward, you'll discover plenty of standout venues. They're not always obvious, but, they're there.

CHUECA AND MALASAÑA

Once the center of bohemian life in Madrid and the birthplace of a counterculture movement (La Movida) in the 1970s and early '80s, Malasaña is today something of a caricature of its former self. Within a few decades, Malasaña has become one of the most expensive and image-driven *barrios* of the city, with high-end cafes and international novelty restaurants like creperies and fresh juice stands. It is rumored that somewhere in this *barrio* there is a place that sells "Russian Tapas," which begs the question, "WTF?" (We couldn't find it.) Art supply stores can be found on every other block, meaning that there are either a lot of artists in this neighborhood or a lot of people who like to spend money on expensive paints. For the traveler, Malasaña is a total playground, with the city's best nightlife, live music, and dining. Chueca is no different. Malasaña's historically gay neighbor to the East (bordered by C. Fuencarral) is today a high-end *barrio* with great food and nightlife in every direction. In Chueca you will find plenty of art galleries, yoga studios, and boutique shops, but you will also run into the more insidious signs of the bourgeoisie, such as yoga studios that rent movies and video stores where you can practice yoga. Oh yeah, and a lot of sex shops.

ARGÜELLES AND MONCLOA

Argüelles and Moncloa are quiet residential areas spanning the western edge of the city from the Plaza de España to the city's northwest corner at Moncloa. While these areas are less geared towards tourists, they are great areas to explore *madrileño* life in its most simple and unpretentious manner. Plaza de España, Casa de Campo and Parque del Oeste provide the city's most expansive green spaces on the west side of Madrid, functioning as both sites of recreation and centers of culture. Outside of the major parks, in these neighborhoods you will find quiet streets with book stores, small shops, and uninspiring cafes. From Argüelles you can explore the odd and beautiful Templo de Debod to the west, and the great restaurants and nightlife options of neighboring Malasaña just south. Moncloa is dominated by the presence of Franco's Arco de la Victoria, and it is the best outpost to explore Parque del Oeste or journey by bus to the El Pardo palace. While accommodations are limited in this area, some tourists might find refuge staying in a quiet neighborhood a few stops removed from the chaotic city center.

SALAMANCA

Salamanca is primarily a high-end residential district filled with luxury shopping and fancy restaurants on the side streets of C. Castellano and C. de Serrano. While this area may seem posh, buried beneath all of the Gucci and Prada is a neighborhood very accessible to budget travelers. Salamanca is also deceptively close to the city center, just a 5min. walk north up Paseo de la Castellana from el Arco de la Victoria in Moncloa. Here you will find one of Madrid's most beautiful avenues, with a tree lined promenade running through the center. As you make your way north you will reach the **Biblioteca Nacional,** and, making your way further north, you will find two of the city's terrific, less visited art museums: the **Museo Sorolla** and the **Museo de Lázaro Galdiano**. A visit to either of these museums will inevitably take you down some of the city's most beautiful residential streets.

accommodations

Madrid has a range of affordable lodging options, from cheap hostels to boutique hotels, in almost every neighborhood. In El Centro, most backpackers' hostels are found close to Puerta del Sol; they offer cheap beds and shared bathrooms, and many have kitchens and common spaces. South of Puerta del Sol, a number of hostels offer slightly pricier private accommodations with ensuite bathrooms. Despite noise and pedestrian traffic, Gran Vía is also a deceptively good place to stay and is home to some of the city's best high-end hostels, where doubles offer some of the best value in the city (€50-70). If you're partying in Chueca and Malasaña, staying in the area at one of the fine private-roomed *hostales* (inexpensive hotels that sometimes offer dorm options) will eliminate the late-night odyssey back to your bed.

EL CENTRO

HOSTAL CERVANTES — HOTEL $$$

C. de Cervantes, 34 — ☎91 429 83 65 www.hostal-cervantes.com

Hostal Cervantes is located in a quiet residential corner of the city center. The rooms are bright, colorful, and somewhat of a relief from the drab accommodations that litter El Centro. The *hostal*'s desirable and affordable rooms have renovated private bathrooms and TVs, but the place is generally booked to capacity. The four rooms with balconies are particularly difficult to reserve in advance.

⇄ From the Museo Thyssen-Bornemisza, walk toward the Pl. Canovas del Castillo and make a right onto C. de Cervantes. ***i*** *Free Wi-Fi. Check the website for reservation info.* *[S] Singles €40-45; doubles €50-55; triples €65-70.*

HOSTEL IVOR HOTEL $$$

C. del Arenal, 24, 2nd fl. ☎91 547 10 54 www.hostal-ivor.com

Hostel Ivor offers clean, comfortable, and private rooms with flatscreen TVs and ensuite bathrooms away from the most hectic and noisy parts of El Centro. While Hostel Ivor lacks a kitchen and the common space of neighboring hostels, it gives the service and quality of a mid-range hotel at a competitive price. Perhaps most importantly, Hostel Ivor has free Wi-Fi everywhere! Enjoy Skyping your friends and family in the privacy of our own bathroom. What? That isn't socially acceptable?

From Puerta del Sol, walk down C. del Arenal a little bit past C. de las Hileras. ***i*** *Free Wi-Fi.* [$] *Singles €44; doubles €65.* ⏰ *Reception 24hr.*

LOS AMIGOS HOSTEL HOSTEL $

C. del Arenal, 26, 4th fl. ☎91 559 24 72 www.losamigoshostel.com

Los Amigos is a classic backpackers' hostel. Located on the top floor, Los Amigos is separated enough from the madness below that the rooms are surprisingly bright and tranquil. This is by far one of the city's most affordable options. Guests make use of the hostel's great communal spaces, which include a small TV lounge and a well-stocked kitchen that serves complimentary continental breakfast in the morning. Rooms are clean and comfortable, but, like any backpacker haunt, privacy comes at a price.

From Puerta del Sol walk down C. del Arenal until you pass C. de las Hilerias; Los Amigos will be on your right. ***i*** *Breakfast and linens included. Extra large lockers and towels available for a fee. Free Wi-Fi.* [$] *Dorms €17, with private bath €19; doubles €45-50.* ⏰ *Reception 8am-midnight.*

HOSTAL RESIDENCIA MARTIN HOTEL $$

C. de Atocha, 43 ☎91 429 95 79 www.hostalmartin.com

Hostal Residencia Martin is located between the bars and clubs of Puerta del Sol and the culture and museums of Paseo del Prado. Without any common spaces, it does not provide the social life of a youth hostel, but it does have the comfort and privacy of a small hotel. The rooms are clean, with white tiled floors, geriatric-looking furniture, and floral bedspreads. Though the *hostal*'s location on the major thoroughfare of C. Atocha may lack glamor, it is within walking distance of all the major attractions in downtown Madrid.

From [M]Antón Martín, walk straight down C. de Atocha. Right before you hit C. Cañizares the hostel will be on your right. ***i*** *Safes and towels included. Free Wi-Fi.* [$] *Singles €29; doubles €39; triples €49.*

HOSTAL CENTRO ONE HOSTEL $

C. Carmen, 16 ☎91 523 31 92

Hostal Centro One is a newly renovated backpackers' hangout in the center of the center (2 blocks from the center of the Spanish Kingdom). The communal kitchen, living room, and six internet-access computers keep people around well into the day. The *hostal* has hardwood floors, bright lights, new furniture, and a variety of room styles, all of which have clean, shared bathrooms. While the hostel is a four-floor walk-up in an old and tired building, the silver lining is that you are also four floors removed from the madness of C. Carmen.

From [M]Sol, take C. Carmen northwest 2 blocks. ***i*** *Kitchen and TV lounge. Free Wi-Fi.* [$] *8-bed dorms €23; 6-bed €25; 4-bed €28; doubles €30. Towels €1. Luggage storage €2. Cash only.* ⏰ *Reception 9am-10pm. Check-in noon. Check-out 10am.*

LAS HUERTAS

HOSTAL PLAZA D'ORT HOTEL $$

Pl. del Ángel, 13 ☎91 429 90 41 www.plazadort.com

Hostal Plaza d'Ort's location on Pl. del Ángel is its biggest attraction. The plaza is a tranquil place to stay, with sophisticated nightlife and none of the chain stores and tasteless bars that swamp so much of El Centro. Hostal d'Ort's private bedrooms are simple and unglamorous. The decor is old-lady-themed. Each room has a flatscreen TV, and some have private bathrooms. The *hostal* salon faces the plaza and has a large flatscreen and an espresso bar.

➡ From ⓂSol, walk south down C. de la Carretas and take a left on Pl. del Ángel. ℹ Safes included. Free Wi-Fi. A/C. $ Singles €35; doubles €55-65; triples €80-110. Cash only. ⏰ Reception 9am-10pm.

👍 **MAD HOSTEL** HOSTEL $

C. de la Cabeza, 24 ☎91 506 48 40 www.madhostel.com

From the first-floor bar to the rooftop terrace, Mad Hostel is a temple of fun made for student travelers. While it is located in a traditional Madrid apartment complex, everything about Mad Hostel feels new. The dorm-style rooms with bunk beds are quite simple, as are the shared bathrooms, but the real appeal here is a renovated bar always alive with travelers and a rooftop terrace that is used as a bar during the summer months. The downstairs bar has a pool table and a small stage where they bring in musical acts for evening parties, and there's even a small weight room available on the top floor.

➡ ⓂAntón Martín. From the metro, walk down C. de la Magdalena, then take C. Olivar (the 2nd street on the left). Walk until you see C. de la Cabeza and turn right. Look for the Mad Hostel sign on the left. ℹ Reservations must be made online ahead of time. Breakfast, safes, and linens included. Towels €5 deposit. Free Wi-Fi. Laundry machines available. €10 key deposit. $ Rooms €16-23. ⏰ Reception 24hr.

👍 **CAT'S HOSTEL** HOSTEL $

C. Cañizares, 6 ☎91 369 28 07 www.catshostel.com

Cat's Hostel is one of Madrid's most popular backpackers' choices for good reason. Dorm bunk beds are cheap, clean, and offer the safety of private lockers, but the main draw is the hostel's social life. A colorful bar area with beer barrel tables, the "Cat Cave" basement lounge, and a restored Moorish patio provide guests with plenty of space to mingle. The hostel owners go out of their way to bring guests together through organized events including a complimentary paella dinner for guests each Friday, tapas tours through Las Huertas, and late-night pub crawls. While all guests are automatically assigned to the large dorm-style rooms, there are a few double rooms available on request, but they can't be reserved in advance.

➡ From ⓂAntón Martín, walk 1 block down C. de la Magdalena and make a right onto C. Cañizares. Cat's will be on the left. ℹ All rooms must be reserved online ahead of time. Breakfast included. Laundry €5. $ Dorms €17-22; doubles €38-42. ⏰ Reception 24hr.

👍 **HOSTAL ASTORIA** HOTEL $$$

Carrera de San Jerónimo, 32, 5th fl. ☎91 429 11 88 www.hostal-astoria.com

While slightly more expensive than its neighbors, Hostal Astoria is worth it for the step up in quality. With hardwood floors, extra pillows, and linen changes available, these rooms are an exceptional value, not just for the neighborhood, but for all of Madrid. All rooms come with ensuite bathrooms, flatscreen TVs, and Wi-Fi. The location on Carrera de San Jerónimo is not picturesque but will offer quieter nights than the center of Las Huertas. As an added bonus, Astoria is on the fifth floor of the building, meaning you will be that much more removed from the stammering drunkards below.

➡ From Puerta del Sol, walk 100m east along Carrera de San Jerónimo toward Paseo del Prado. ℹ Reserve in advance online. $ Singles €40; doubles €60; triples €84. Cash only. ⏰ Reception 24hr.

WAY HOSTEL HOSTEL $

C. Relatores, 17 ☎91 420 05 83 www.wayhostel.com

Way offers the nicest rooms of all the backpacker hostels listed in this section. While all rooms are shared in four- to 10-person dorms, the hardwood floors and generous layout set Way apart. The spacious communal kitchen and large TV room feel like upscale college common rooms—perfect for your next beer.

➡ ⓂTirso de Molina. Walk toward the museum district and make a left up C. Relatores. The hostel will be on the right. ℹ Breakfast included. Reserve online. $ Rooms €18-24. ⏰ Reception 24hr.

HOSTAL AGUILAR HOSTEL $$$

Carrera de San Jerónimo, 32, 2nd fl. ☎91 429 59 26 www.hostalaguilar.com

With a huge lobby area, swipe access, modern furniture, and private bathrooms, Aguilar is more hotel than hostel. Rooms have tiled floors, old TV sets, and light pink bedspreads. The bathrooms are newly renovated. Don't expect the calm of a convent, but, compared to other hostels in the area, you will be paying a good price for a better night of sleep. The availability of four-person rooms is a plus for larger groups.

➜ From Puerta del Sol, walk 100m east along Carrera de San Jerónimo toward Paseo del Prado. $ Singles €40; doubles €50; triples €66, quads €84. ⏰ Reception 24hr.

HOSTAL MONTALOYA HOTEL $$$

Pl. Tirso de Molina, 20 ☎91 360 03 05 www.hostalmontaloya.blogspot.com

While pricier than dorm-style living, with comfortable beds, TVs, ensuite baths, and even desks in all rooms, Montaloya makes for a comfortable stay. Though the employees at the front desk speak only Spanish, the *hostal*'s proximity to restaurants, bars, and stores along the Pl. Tirso de Molina make it a convenient choice. For a weekend stay, you ask about interior rooms, as rooms facing the plaza are quite noisy.

➜ ⓂTirso de Molina. ℹ Call ahead for wheelchair-accessible accommodations. $ Singles €45; doubles €58; triples €80. ⏰ Reception 24hr.

INTERNATIONAL YOUTH HOSTEL HOSTEL $

C. de las Huertas, 21 ☎ 91 429 55 26 www.posadadehuertas.com

This is one of the best dorm-style hostels in the city. Located right on the drinking hub of C. de las Huertas, International Youth Hostel is ideal for groups of backpackers looking for other people to join their wolf packs. Guests generally take advantage of the great communal facilities: a TV room, a kitchen that serves complimentary breakfast, and free internet in the computer room. Don't expect much privacy, as all rooms are dorm-style with simple bunk beds and storage lockers. The large shared bathrooms are clean and separated by gender. While rooms are certainly bare-bones, cleanliness and bargain prices are a major draw.

➜ ⓂAntón Martín. Walk north up C. de León and make a right on C. de las Huertas. ℹ Breakfast included. Beds can be reserved in single-sex or co-ed rooms. Luggage storage. Free Wi-Fi. $ Dorms €16-22. ⏰ Reception 24hr.

HOSTAL PERSAL HOTEL $$$$

Pl. del Ángel, 12 ☎91 369 46 43 www.hostalpersal.com

Situated on Pl. del Ángel between Pl. Santa Ana and C. de las Huertas, Hostal Persal puts you in the perfect place to discover the best of Madrid's tapas bars and nightlife. The rooms here are of a similar size and decor as other hostels in the area with private rooms, but they are in far better condition. A full continental breakfast, which includes fresh fruit and sandwich fixings, is offered in the downstairs restaurant.

➜ ⓂAntón Martín. Walk south down C. del Olivar until you see Pl. del Angel on your right. 2min. from Pl. Santa Ana. $ Singles €60; doubles €84; triples €125. ⏰ Reception 24hr.

CHIC AND BASIC COLORS HOTEL $$$$

C. de las Huertas, 14 ☎91 429 69 35 www.chicandbasic.com

This chain hotel looks something like the lovechild of the chic boutique hotel and the conventional European hostel. Each room has a bold color scheme, contemporary furniture, and hardwood floors. This is a great place to stay if you like traveling in style and don't mind paying for it. A simple continental breakfast is available in the small common area, and there are snacks in the fridge, fruit, and an espresso machine. Check the website for various discounts and special offers.

➜ ⓂAntón Martín. From Pl. del Ángel, walk down C. de las Huertas toward the museum district. Chic and Basic Colors will be on the right. ℹ Ensuite bathrooms. Same company has a high-end hotel called Chic and Basic on C. Atocha, 113. $ Singles €60-70; doubles €80-90. ⏰ Reception 24hr.

GRAN VÍA

HOSTAL ANDORRA
B&B $$$

C. Gran Vía, 33, 7th fl.   ☎91 532 31 16 www.hostalandorra.com

Hostal Andorra is a legitimate bed and breakfast. Unlike many *hostales* where common spaces are an afterthought, Hostal Andorra does a terrific job with the solarium and breakfast room. High ceilings, hardwood floors, and natural light make for open and inviting common areas. This is actually a pleasant place to catch your breath and read a book. Rooms are spacious, modestly decorated, and come with ensuite bathrooms with clean towels. While €47 might be a bit expensive for a single, doubles are a great value.

✦ ⓜ*Callao. Walk east down C. Gran Vía.* ⓢ *Singles €47; doubles €62.* ⓩ *Reception 24hr.*

HOSTAL SANTILLAN
HOTEL $$

C. Gran Vía, 64   ☎91 548 23 28 www.hostalsantillan.com

Hostal Santillan offers a great value with simple and sizable rooms, modern furniture, and crisply painted walls. Rooms come with standard wood furniture, refurbished hardwood floors, and clean ensuite bathrooms with fresh towels. This *hostal* has no illusions of grandeur; it just makes sure to do all the little things that will make your stay comfortable. In a neighborhood that is often noisy, expensive, and uncomfortable, Hostal Santillan offers accommodations that are quiet, affordable, and pleasant, but if you are looking for a "unique" floral bedspread, this isn't the place to go.

✦ ⓜ*Plaza de España.* *i Laundry service. Ensuite bathrooms and daily room cleaning. Ask about scheduled excursions and complimentary luggage storage.* ⓢ *Singles €30-35; doubles €50-55; triples €70-75.* ⓩ *Reception 24hr.*

LA PLATA
HOTEL $$$

C. Gran Vía, 15   ☎91 521 17 25 www.hostal-laplata.com

The mismatched antique furniture of La Plata makes the decor tough to decipher, but the rooms are pleasant. This family-run *hostal* works hard to keep the rooms clean. Thanks to this place's incredibly helpful and friendly staff, *Let's Go* recommends this *hostal* out of all the options at C. Gran Vía.

✦ ⓜ*Gran Vía. Walk east; the building is on the right.* ⓢ *Singles €45; doubles €60; triples €85.* ⓩ *Reception 24hr.*

HOSTAL FELIPE V
HOTEL $$$

C. Gran Vía, 15, 4th fl.   ☎91 522 61 43 www.hostalfelipev.com

This *hostal* gets it—you don't book a budget *hostal* to sit in your room and look at the "antiques," you leave that to the Palacio Real. These accommodations are contemporary: rooms all come spacious and standard, with simple furniture, high ceilings, and private bathrooms. At the end of the day, you need a clean and comfortable place to crash, and that is precisely what this *hostal* offers.

✦ ⓜ*Gran Vía. Walk east; the building will be to the right.* *i Breakfast €4.50.* ⓢ *Singles €46; doubles €64; triples €78.* ⓩ *Reception 24hr.*

HOSTAL SPLENDID
HOTEL $$

C. Gran Vía, 15, 5th fl.   ☎91 522 47 37 www.hostalsplendid.com

If you're pinching euro pennies, Hostal Splendid offers rooms at €5-10 below the standard rate in the building. While most *hostals* on C. Gran Vía offer only suites with ensuite bathrooms, Hostal Splendid has a few individual rooms with shared bathrooms, and a few twin doubles that run smaller and cheaper than the norm.

✦ ⓜ*Gran Vía. Walk east; the building will be to the right.* *i TV. Wi-Fi. A/C.* ⓢ *Singles €25-35; doubles €45-60; triples €65-80.* ⓩ *Reception 24hr.*

accommodations

CHUECA AND MALASAÑA

👍 ALBERGUE JUVENIL MUNICIPAL — HOSTEL $

C. Mejía Lequerica, 21 ☎91 593 96 88 www.ajmadrid.es

This is one of only a handful of exciting budget accommodations in the city of Madrid. Albergue Juvenil Municipal is a state-of-the-art youth hostel built by the city government in 2007. The decor is more like that of a four-star city hotel with frosted glass, dark tiled floors, and Ikea-style furniture. Add the pool tables, cafeteria, laundry room, exercise room with stationary bikes, and media room with a computer lab, and you have a true paradise for budget travelers. The layout is spacious enough for you to jump out of bed and rollerblade around the bedroom for a morning workout. Most importantly, the hostel is situated perfectly between the nightlife of Chueca and Malasaña—close to the action but far enough from the busier streets that you're guaranteed a good night's sleep. With the subway just 2min. away, access to the major sights is a no-brainer, and the English-speaking staff will be happy to give you a free map and point you in the right direction. You may as well be sleeping in the Prado.

*➡ From Ⓜ Bilbao, follow C. de Sagasta 3 blocks west to C. Mejía Lequerica; the hostel is on the right. **i** Breakfast included. Laundry €3. Towels €3. 4- to 6-bed co-ed dorms. Book at least 5 days in advance. [$] Under age 25 €20 per person, 25-year-olds €22, over age 25 €27. Cash only. ⏰ Reception 24hr. Inform the staff if you must check in after 3pm.*

HOSTAL LOS ALPES — HOTEL $$

C. de Fuencarral, 17, 3rd and 4th fl. ☎91 531 70 71 www.hostallosalpes.com

Recently renovated, this is about as clean, cheap, and comfortable as *hostals* get in Madrid. Rooms in Los Alpes have new hardwood floors, nicely made beds, brightly painted walls, and simple drapes. Unlike many *hostales*, the decor doesn't look like it was selected by octogenarians. The look here is refreshingly simple, and all of the rooms come with basic amenities: a tiled bathroom, towels, and TV. While there aren't proper common areas to meet other guests, the reception area is nice and cheery. There's a computer available at no charge and Wi-Fi everywhere. While the *hostal*'s address on C. Fuencarral, one of Madrid's busiest shopping streets, might be hectic for some, its location just blocks from the centers of Chueca and Malasaña may be too good to pass up.

➡ Ⓜ Chueca. Make a right onto C. de Gravina and a right onto C. de Hortaleza. [$] Singles €34; doubles €50. ⏰ Reception 24hr.

MALASAÑA TRAVELER'S HOSTEL — HOSTEL $

C. Manuela Malasaña, 23 ☎91 591 15 79

With small dorm-style rooms and great common areas, this is a traveler's hostel through and through. The shared bathrooms and bedrooms aren't glamorous, but the private lockers will keep your valuables safe. The common areas are generally in use, particularly the six new computers in the lobby area. The kitchen in back is usually in use by some pajama-clad backpacker cooking up dinner to keep the budget low.

➡ From Ⓜ Bilbao, cross C. Fuencarral to C. Manuela Malasaña, and follow due west for 2½ blocks. [$] 2-bed dorms €24-36; 4-bed €19-27; 12-bed €16-21. Cash only. ⏰ Reception 24hr.

HOSTAL AMERICA — HOTEL $$$

C. de Hortaleza, 19, 5th fl. ☎91 522 64 48 www.hostalamerica.net

Located on the top floor, America is the best *hostal* in a building full of accommodation options. Rooms feature big windows, new furniture, spacious bathrooms, and paintings on the wall. Service is friendly, quick, and mostly English-speaking. Be sure to check out the view from the outdoor terrace.

➡ Ⓜ Chueca. Make a right on C. de Gravina and a right on C. de Hortaleza. [$] Singles €40-43; doubles €52-55; triples €67-70. ⏰ Reception 24hr.

ARGÜELLES AND MONCLOA

ALBERGUE JUVENIL SANTA CRUZ DE MARCENADO (HI)   HOSTEL $
C. de Santa Cruz de Marcenado, 28   ☎91 547 45 32

At only €12 per night for dorms, you'll be hard-pressed to find cheaper accommodations. While rooms are anything but private (guests should be prepared to spend the night on the top bunk), the owners place a premium on cleanliness. The TV lounge and dining areas are simply decorated with modern furniture. Rooms and common areas are also kept relentlessly clean, and secure metal lockers are available for use. Be sure to reserve well in advance, as rooms at this cheap hostel go quickly.

✠ ⓂArgüelles. Walk 1 block down C. de Alberto Aguilera way from C. de la Princesa, turn right onto C. de Serrano Jover, then left onto C. de Santa Cruz de Marcenado. *i* Free Wi-Fi. ⓢ Dorms €12. Discounts available for HI members. ⓠ Reception 9am-9:45pm. Curfew 1:30am.

HOSTAL MONCLOA   HOTEL $$$
C. de Hilarión Eslava, 16   ☎91 544 91 95 www.hostalmoncloa.com

The comfortable rooms at Hostal Moncloa are a bargain. Guests can count on the rooms being nice and quiet, with large ensuite bathrooms, but the lack of natural sunlight might be a mood killer. This is certainly not a honeymooners' hotel, but it is well-kept and well-situated in a quiet part of town. Rooms have flatscreen TVs and Wi-Fi.

✠ ⓂMoncloa. Walk south down C. de la Princesa and make a left onto C. de Romero Robledo. Keep walking until you reach Hilarión Eslava and then make a left. ⓢ Singles €45; doubles €50; triples €80. ⓠ Reception 24hr.

HOSTAL ANGELINES   HOTEL $$$
C. de Hilarión Eslava, 12   ☎91 543 21 52

If you want to escape the madness of El Centro, this is a great place to do it. Angelines offers simple singles and doubles with private bathrooms and small TVs. While Moncloa might look far from El Centro on the map, it is only a 15min. journey by Metro, and it's within walking distance of Argüelles, Malasaña, and Pl. de España. If you value comfort, sleep, and a clean, private bathroom, Angelines makes a good refuge.

✠ ⓂMoncloa. Walk south down C. de la Princesa and make a left on C. de Romero Robledo. Keep walking until you reach Hilarión Eslava, then make a left. *i* Free Wi-Fi. ⓢ Singles €40; doubles €45. ⓠ Reception 24hr.

sights

La Avenida del Arte is reason enough to come to Madrid. A trip down this historic path takes you along Madrid's most picturesque tree-lined avenue and through the canon of Western art. Other neighborhoods may not have world-class art on every block, but they still pack a punch. El Centro contains some of the city's most iconic sights, like the 18th-century Plaza Mayor. Chueca and Malasaña, Madrid's former bohemian centers, provide ample people-watching opportunities with their cafe- and shop-lined streets. Argüelles and Moncloa, crucial fighting grounds during the Spanish Civil War, are marked by the Arco de la Victoria, erected by General Franco and perhaps the most visible remnant of this haunting legacy in Madrid. The palace El Pardo, just north of Moncloa, offers a view into the dictator's private bunker. Argüelles and Moncloa are also home to the city's most anomalous historical sight, the Egyptian Templo de Debod.

EL CENTRO

▨ PALACIO REAL

PALACE

C. de Bailén   ☎91 454 88 00   www.patrimonionacional.es

The Royal Palace is the ultimate symbol of the Spanish Empire's wealth and power. The palace was constructed by King Philip V between 1738 and 1755 on the site of a ninth-century Muslim fortress and one thing is quite clear: Phil had a thing for marble. While the palace is still the official residence of the Spanish royal family, it is nevertheless totally accessible to the general public, and, for a meager entrance fee, you can view the orgy of artistry and craftsmanship 275 years in the making. The self-guided palace tour (1hr.) takes you through 15 rooms, each of which was curated by a different Spanish royal. The result is an eclectic mix in which artistry and wealth are the only constants. Flemish tapestries, exotic Orientalist frescoes, and Persian carpets are thrown together in a maze of opulence, sometimes to gratuitous effect. When Carlos IV purchased a set of instruments to be displayed in the Royal Palace, he traveled to Italy and bought the five violins that are displayed in the palace today. And that violin you are looking at ain't just any violin: it was made by Antonio Stradivari, the finest instrument maker the world has ever known. (When the Spanish royal family wants something, they get it.) If you're in town on the first Wednesday of the month between September and May, check out the changing of the guard ceremony, which takes place at noon.

✦ Ⓜ*Opera. Walk west down C. de Arrieta. Palacio Real is at the end of the road.* *i* *Come early to avoid long lines.* Ⓢ *€8, with tour €10; ages 5-16, students, and seniors €5.* ⚄ *Open Apr-Sept M-Sa 9am-6pm, Su 9am-3pm; Oct-Mar M-Sa 9:30am-5pm, Su 9am-2pm.*

madrid

PLAZA MAYOR

PLAZA

Pl. Mayor

Today Pl. Mayor is something of a vestigial structure in the bustling cosmopolitan center of Madrid. It may be about as useful as your appendix, but your appendix is probably a lot less awesome-looking. While the plaza itself has been around since the reign of Philip III, the buildings of today's plaza date to the late 18th century. During the Inquisition, the plaza was the site of public executions, but today the plaza is most known for the week long **Fiesta de San Isidro** (starts May 15th), during which the city celebrates its patron saint. The buildings around the plaza have also become entirely residential; 237 apartment balconies overlook one of the single most important sites in the city's history. While the presence of King Philip III is memorialized at the plaza's center, he doesn't seem to be able to keep the scam artists away. Costumed Elvis and Spiderman wander the plaza daily, looking like they may have both had a few too many *cervezas*. The **tourist office** in the plaza is quite helpful and offers free maps.

✚ ⓂSol or ⓂOpera. From Puerta del Sol, walk 2min. down C. Mayor toward the Palacio Real. Pl. Mayor will be to the left.

PUERTA DEL SOL

PLAZA

Puerta del Sol

Spain's *kilómetro cero*, the point from which all distances in Spain are measured, is located in Puerta del Sol. You certainly can't get more *"el centro"* than the center of the Spanish kingdom itself, but Puerta del Sol is something of a cultural wasteland. The plaza, memorialized in Goya's paintings The *Second* and *Third of May* which hang in the **Prado**, is today overrun by newsstands, billboards, scam artists, and street performers dressed like Mickey Mouse and Spongebob. If these are what brought you to Madrid, you may in fact find Puerta del Sol "soulful," but otherwise it is more of a quick stopping point before you venture further into the dynamic areas of El Centro, Las Huertas, La Latina, and Lavapiés. If you are visiting Madrid for the New Year, Puerta del Sol hosts the 12 Grapes Ceremony, during which the city celebrates the New Year by eating 12 good-luck grapes, one for each toll of the bell and for month of the new year. With the regional government situated on the southern end of the plaza, the Puerta del Sol has also been the site of major protests and political rallies.

✚ ⓂSol.

CATEDRAL DE LA ALMUDENA

CATHEDRAL
☎91 542 22 00

C. Bailén

The Catedral de la Almudena is in many ways a freak of history. While Madrid became the offical capital of the Spanish Kingdom during the reign of Philip II, it took many years for the Spanish Catholic church to recognize the city as a worthy religious center. Favoring the former capital of Toledo, the Church was just as resistant to the idea of building a new central cathedral in Spain. While the Catedral de la Almudena was concieved in the 16th century, construction did not begin until 1879 and was only completed in 1999. Located across from the Palacio Real, this monumental cathedral is little more than a happy accident: the Catholic church's "love child" with the city of Madrid. The architectural style reflects this precarious past; the roof is painted in bright, bold patterns that resemble the work of Henri Matisse, while the panes of stained glass recall Picasso and the Cubist tradition. In some ways, Catedral de la Almudena may seem like a run-of-the-mill cathedral: you walk into a cavernous space, it looks cool, it feels impressive, you feel insignificant, and then you leave. But if you pay close attention, you will notice that this church is quite peculiar and filled with red herrings. Don't let the exterior fool you—this is a truly modern cathedral.

✚ ⓂOpera. Walk west down C. de Arrieta, then left on C. Bailén at the Palacio Real. Ⓢ Free. ⏰ Open daily 10am-2pm and 5-8pm.

PLAZA DE ORIENTE PLAZA

Pl. de Oriente, 2

Across the way from the Palacio Real, Pl. de Oriente is a monument to the empire in its own right. Formal gardens, fountains, and manicured hedges accent the 20 marble statues of Spain's kings and queens. If the Pl. de Oriente can teach us anything, it's that to be a Spanish ruler you need an impressive bone structure, a grizzly beard, or both. Pl. de Oriente is a relaxing retreat where lovers, tourists, sunbathers, and sunbathing-tourist-lovers lounge midday to escape the streets of El Centro. What better place to practice the art of PDA than under the marble gaze of King Philip III?

↔ [M]Opera. Across from the Palacio Real. $ Free.

JARDINES DE SABATINI GARDEN

C. de Bailén, 9 ☎91 588 53 42

This maze of trees, hedges, and fountains stand on what used to be the stable grounds of El Palacio Real, originally designed by the Italian architect Francisco Sabatini. The immaculately kept trees, fountains, and hedges create a relaxing environment to take a break, breathe deep, look up at the palace, and feel helplessly poor and intimidated.

↔ [M]Opera. Right next to the Palacio Real. $ Free. ⏰ Open daily dawn-dusk.

PLAZA DE LA VILLA PLAZA

Pl. de la Villa, 5

Many of the neighboring plazas in El Centro are bigger, but it isn't size that really matters…right, ladies? In any case, Pl. de la Villa is easily overlooked, but very much worth a quick visit. The first major building on the plaza is the Casa de la Villa. Pl. de la Villa is also home to El Torre de Los Lujanes, the private family home of the Lujanes that was built in the 15th century. This is not only one of the oldest buildings in the square, but also one of city's best remaining examples of *mudéjar*, or Islamic-influenced architecture. Unlike Pl. Mayor, Pl. de la Villa is quiet, so you won't find yourself accosted by scam artists. And isn't it every traveler's dream to look at medieval architecture without being attacked by a guy in a cat suit singing "If You Like Piña Coladas"?

↔ [M]Opera. Off C. Mayor between the Palacio Real and Pl. Mayor. $ Free.

CONVENTO DE LA ENCARNACIÓN CONVENT

Pl. de la Encarnación, 1 ☎91 454 88 00

Every July 27th, it is said that the blood of St. Panthalon, held in a crystal orb, visibly liquefies. It is not entirely clear that St. Panthalon was in fact a living, breathing (and bleeding) person, but a crystal orb containing his alleged blood is on display at the Convento de la Encarnación. Convents are normally pretty exclusive: it doesn't matter how hot your friends are, you still aren't getting in. (That bouncer Sister Martha is such a witch!) This convent is a little different. While it was founded as an exclusive center of monastic life nearly 400 years ago, today it is accessible to the general public for a small entrance fee. The tour takes you through the formerly secluded chapel filled with artwork by European masters and into the famous reliquary, which contains thousands of Christian relics, most notably those blood-filled crystal orbs. Located close to the Palacio Real and Pl. de Oriente, the convent is an easy stop and a great opportunity to get some face time with ancient relics.

↔ [M]Opera. Take Pl. de Isabel II northwest to C. de Arrieta, turn right onto Pl. de la Encarnación. ℹ Tours conducted in Spanish every 30min. $ €3.60. ⏰ Open Tu-Th 10:30am-12:30pm and 4-5:30pm, F 10:30am-12:30pm, Sa 10:30am-12:30pm and 4-5:30pm, Su 11am-1:30pm.

AVENIDA DEL ARTE

⬛ MUSEO NACIONAL CENTRO DE ARTE REINA SOFÍA   ART MUSEUM

C. Santa Isabel, 52   ☎91 774 10 00 www.museoreinasofia.es

King Juan Carlos I named the Reina Sofía for his wife and declared it a national museum in 1988. The building itself is a masterpiece: what was once Madrid's general hospital in the 18th century has been gutted and transformed into a temple of 20th-century art. Two glass elevators at either end of the museum ferry visitors between the four floors of the collection. The second and fourth floors are mazes of permanent exhibits that chart the Spanish avant-garde and include galleries dedicated to Juan Gris, Joan Miró, and Salvador Dalí. The museum's main attraction is undoubtedly Picasso's *Guernica* in Gallery 206. This is truly a masterpiece, and the best way to make the most of your visit is to invest in an audio guide, which gives a full historical and critical account of the work. The basement and first floor exhibits focus on more contemporary artists.

✈ Ⓜ Atocha. Ⓢ €6, ages 17 and under and over 65 free Sa afternoon and Su. Temporary exhibits €3. Audio guides €4, students €3. 🕐 Open M 10am-9pm, W-Sa 10am-9pm, Su 10am-2:30pm.

⬛ MUSEO NACIONAL DEL PRADO   ART MUSEUM

C. Ruiz de Alarcón, 23   ☎91 330 28 00 www.museodelprado.es

El Prado is one of the greatest art museums in the world. Curated from the original collection of the Spanish royal family, El Prado celebrates the entirety of western art from Hellenistic Greek sculpture to Dutch altarpieces to Spanish and Italian Renaissance paintings. The museum really requires at least a day-long visit, but if you can't stay, be sure to put in some face time with the following masterpieces.

Diego Velázquez's ⬛**Las Meninas,** one of the most studied pieces of art in the world, captures a studio scene centered on the Infanta Margarita. Velázquez himself stares out from behind his easel in the left side of the painting. It may look like just another picture of wealthy Spaniards and their dwarves, but this piece has been praised as the culmination of Velázquez's career—a meditation on reality, art, illusion, and the power of easel painting.

Goya's side-by-side portraits *La Maja Vestida* and *La Maja Desnuda* portray a woman believed to be the Duchess of Alba in different states of undress. (The museum has yet to recover the third long-lost portrait, *La Maja Spread Eagla.*) The collection of his *Black Paintings* is alarmingly haunting but nightmarishly beautiful, and his emotional *Tres de Mayo, 1808* depicting the execution of Spaniards by Napoleon's invaders, can't be missed.

For a truly triptastic experience, be sure to check out the works of Hieronymous Bosch, including the famous ⬛**Garden of Earthly Delights.** Shake your head and judge, or smile and say, damn, that looks hella fun.

We'll skip the exhaustive list of amazing artists whose works are housed here and refer you to the free museum maps offered at the information kiosk. The English audio tour (€3.50) is an invaluable resource to learn the history of the 1500+ works on display. Evenings are free at the museum, but crowds do gather.

✈ Ⓜ Banco de España and Ⓜ Atocha. From Ⓜ Atocha, walk north up Paseo del Prado; the museum will be on your right, just past the gardens. *i* ⬛**Free entry** Tu-Sa 6-8pm, Su 5-8pm. Check the website for an up-to-date schedule. Ⓢ €8, students €4, under 18 and over 65 free. 🕐 Open Tu-Su 9am-8pm.

⬛ MUSEO THYSSEN-BORNEMISZA   ART MUSEUM

Paseo del Prado, 8   ☎91 369 01 51 www.museothyssen.org

The Thyssen-Bornemisza has a bit more of an international emphasis than either the Reina Sofía or the Prado. The museum is housed in the 19th-century Palacio de Villahermosa and contains the collection of the late Baron Henrich Thyssen-

Bornemisza. Today, the museum is the world's most extensive private showcase. Exhibits range from 14th-century Flemish altarpieces to an impressive collection of German avant-garde canvases from the early 20th century. Don't forget to explore the Impressionist, Fauvist, and early avant-garde pieces that paved the way to modern art as we know it today. To be honest, there are too many famous artists to name-drop—just come here to be wowed and won over by the gigantic collection.

[M]Banco de España and [M]Atocha. From [M]Atocha, walk north up Paseo del Prado; the museum is on the left at the corner of Carrera de San Jerónimo. $ €7, children under 12 free. ⏰ Open Tu-Su 10am-7pm.

CAIXAFORUM MUSEUM

Paseo del Prado, 36 ☎91 389 65 45

The Caixaforum is a visual magnet along Paseo del Prado. The 19th-century factory seems to float on one corner of the Avenida del Arte beside the museum's towering vertical garden. Designed by the same architects as London's Tate Modern, the Caixaforum is an architectural masterpiece and an incredible cultural resource. The interior has two floors of gallery space for art, design, and architecture exhibits, including major retrospectives of internationally renowned architects. The basement auditorium hosts anything and everything cool and relevant, from lectures by architects to dance performances to film screenings. The exterior vertical garden is a marvel of botany and urban design.

[M]Atocha. From the metro, walk north up Paseo del Prado; the Caixaforum will be on the left. $ Free. Some special events are ticketed. ⏰ Open daily 10am-8pm. Closed Dec 25, Jan 1 and 6.

PARQUE DEL BUEN RETIRO PARK

C. Alfonso XII, 48 ☎91 429 82 40 www.parquedelretiro.es

When a run-of-the-mill millionaire needs a break, he goes to a spa. When a Spanish monarch needs some time off, he just builds his own park. A former royal hunting ground, the Parque del Buen Retiro was reconstructed by Felipe IV in the 1630s as his lavish personal retreat. Outfitted with an artificial lake (Estanque Grande) and two palaces (Palacio de Velázquez and Palacio de Cristal), this 300-acre park was certainly a kingly getaway. More democratic times have rendered El Retiro a favorite escape of all *madrileños*, who use it for both relaxation and recreation thanks to some modern additions, including a running track and a sports complex. On weekends the promenades fill with musicians, families, and young lovers, amateur rowers go out onto the Estanque Grande, and exhibits and performances are showcased at the palaces. Try to avoid the park after dark if you're alone, as **shady characters** (not just trees) have been known to hang here at night.

[M]Retiro. Or, from [M]Atocha, past the roundabout north onto Calle de Alfonso XII. The park will be on the right. $ Free. Row boats M-F until 2pm €1.40, Sa-Su and holidays €4.55 ⏰ Open in winter daily 6am-10pm; in summer 6am-midnight. Estanque pier open daily July-Aug 10am-11pm; Sept-June 10am-45min. before sunset.

REAL JARDÍN BOTÁNICO GARDEN

Pl. de Murillo, 2 ☎91 420 30 17 www.rjb.csic.es/jardinbotanico/jardin

The Real Jardín Botánico is not just a garden, but a self-proclaimed "museum" of plant life. For our purposes, it's a garden. With beautiful trees, fountains, and exotic plant life, the Real Jardín is the perfect place to reflect on the countless pieces of art you cranially digested.

Next to the Prado. $ €2.50, students €1.25, groups €0.50. ⏰ Open daily Jan-Feb 10am-6pm; Mar 10am-7pm; Apr 10am-8pm; May-Aug 10am-9pm; Sept 10am-8pm; Oct 10am-7pm; Nov-Dec 10am-6pm.

stop worrying and love the nap

The afternoon nap is hardly an alien concept to the typical American college student, but out in the real world, dropping off for an hour or two in the middle of the day is a tough feat to pull off—if you live in the boring, nine-to-five US, that is. Spain, on the other hand, has it all figured out: after waking up to a big bowl of café con leche and heading off to work for four or five hours, the Spanish come back home around 1pm for lunch, immediately followed by that most glorious of Iberian traditions, the siesta. The *siesta* doesn't have to be a nap; it's quite common instead to just *tumbarse* (lie down) on the sofa and slip into a dazed stupor in front of one of the popular game shows that daily grace the Spanish airwaves (or the Spanish-dubbed *Los Simpson,* whose afternoon broadcast consistently ranks among the top-rated programs). Yes, there are still another few hours of work in the afternoon, but the break helps divide and conquer the workday in a way that makes those last few hours between siesta and fiesta manageable.

LAS HUERTAS

REAL ACADEMIA DE BELLAS ARTES DE SAN FERNANDO MUSEUM

C. de Alcalá, 13 ☎91 524 08 64 rabasf.insde.es

The oldest permanent art institute in Madrid, the Real Academia de Bellas Artes is a short walk away from bustling Puerta del Sol. This is the only museum dedicated exclusively to Spanish artists, and with a collection 1400 paintings, 15,000 drawings, and 600 sculptures, this should be your first stop if you couldn't get enough at El Prado. Particularly notable are the Goya paintings in Room 13, including two rare self-portraits. The museum also contains notable works by Rubens, Ribera, and Sorolla. The collection is certainly dwarfed by the Prado down the street, but the museum gives a concise tour of art history in Spain from the 17th century through 20th century.

⇄ From Puerta del Sol, walk east down C. de Alcalá. Real Academia de Bellas Artes will be on the left. $ €5; groups of 15-25, university students, teachers, under 18 and over 65 free. Free to all W. ⏰ Open Tu-Sa 9am-5pm, Su 9am-2:30pm.

LA LATINA AND LAVAPIÉS

BASILICA DE SAN FRANCISCO EL GRANDE CATHEDRAL

C. de San Buenaventura ☎91 365 38 00

This Roman Catholic church is one of the most distinctive structures in La Latina. The basilica was designed in a Neoclassical style in the second half of the 18th century and comes to life when lit up at night. The cathedral has three chapels, including the Chapel of San Bernardino de Siena, where Goya's magnificent painting of the chapel's namesake rests. Pay close attention to the picture and you will see that the figure looking down on the right is Goya himself. Don't forget to check out the adjacent gardens, which have spectacular views of western Madrid.

⇄ From Ⓜ La Latina, walk straight west down Carrera San Francisco. $ Free. Guided tours €3. ⏰ Open Tu-F 11am-12:30pm and 4-6:30pm, Sa 11am-noon.

LA IGLESIA DE SAN ANDRÉS   CHURCH
Pl. de San Andrés

One of the oldest parishes in Madrid, the Iglesia de San Andrés used to be *the* go-to church for La Latina local San Isidro Labrador, the patron saint of Madrid. Much of the original interior was destroyed during the Spanish Civil War, but the structure still showcases a Baroque style crafted by designer José de Villarreal. Pay specific attention to the 15th-century cupola stationed above the sanctuary of the San Andrés chapel.

☀ ⓜ*La Latina. Make a left onto C. de la Cava.* ⓢ *Free.*

CHUECA AND MALASAÑA

PALACIO LONGORIA   ARCHITECTURE
C. de Fernando VI, 6

This just might be the ugliest building in the city. Depending on who you are, you will either find Palacio Longoria to be an eyesore or a beautiful relic of *modernista* architecture. Whether you like it or not, you will probably run into it during your time in Chueca, and it is worth noting its peculiarity as the only true example of Catalan *modernisme* (à la Gaudí) in Madrid. Palacio Longoria was built in the early 20th century as a private residence for the banker Javier González Longoria. In 1950 it was converted into a private office building for the General Society of Spanish Authors and Editors. Unfortunately, the building is rarely open to the public, but its façade is a sight to behold along your way through Chueca. If you can't get enough and want to be all up inside of it, you're probably best off hopping on a plane to Barcelona (we have a guide for that, too).

☀ *From* ⓜ*Chueca, take C. Gravina 1 block west to C. Pelayo and follow 2 blocks north. The building is on the left.* *i The interior is only open to the public during National Architecture Week (2nd week of Oct).*

CONVENTO DE LAS SALESAS REALES   CATHEDRAL
C. Bárbara de Braganza, 1   ☎91 319 48 11 www.parroquiadesantabarbara.es

Conceived in 1748 by Barbara of Portugal, this monastery continues to function as a church, but for tourists in Chueca it's a great place to slow down, quit eating, and consume some culture instead. Originally designed by Francois Carlier, the church has since suffered a series of fires but still holds King Ferdinand VI and the convent's founder, Barbara of Portugal, in their tombs which were constructed by Francesco Sabatini and Francisco Gutierrez. The adjacent building of the convent is now the seat of the Supreme Court of Spain, so this would definitely not be the place to take your pants off and run around naked. (Not that we tried it or anything.)

☀ ⓜ*Colón. From Pl. Colón, go down Paseo de Recoletos and take a right onto C. de Bárbara de Braganza.* ⓢ *Free.* ⌚ *Open M-F 9:30am-1pm and 5:30-8pm, Sa 9:30am-2pm and 5-9pm, Su 9:30am-2pm and 6-9pm. Closed to tourists during mass.*

MUSEO DE HISTORIA   MUSEUM
C. Fuencarral, 78   ☎91 701 18 63 www.munimadrid.es/museodehistoria

This renovated 18th-century building constructed under Philip V now holds a collection of models, illustrations, and documents that showcase the history of Madrid. The building itself is a historical relic as one of Madrid's few lasting examples of Baroque architecture. While it was saved from destruction in 1919 by the Spanish Society of Friends of Art, only recently has the city decided to make this building a tourist destination. The façade is currently being renovated, and upon completion, the museum will have a totally new state-of-the-art facility to exhibit the history and culture of Madrid.

☀ ⓜ*Tribunal. Walk straight north up C. Fuencarral. The large pink building will be on the right.* ⓢ *Free.* ⌚ *Open Tu-Sa 10am-9pm, Su 11am-2:30pm.*

GRAN VÍA

⬛ PLAZA DE ESPAÑA
PLAZA

In a city filled with statues of Spanish royalty and Roman deities, Pl. de España is something of an anomaly. Located on the western edge of Gran Vía, Pl. de España is a monument to the father of Spanish literature, **Miguel de Cervantes.** The stone statue of Cervantes at the center of the plaza is surrounded by characters from his most celebrated work *Don Quixote.* The bronze statues immediately below Cervantes depict the hero Alonso Quixano and his chubby and slightly less heroic sidekick Sancho Panza. To the right and left are Quixano's two love interests, the peasant lady Aldonza Lorenzo and the woman of his dreams Dulcinea Del Toboso. Like every Spanish plaza, Pl. de España is a prime ⬛**makeout destination.**

✣ *The western end of C. Gran Vía, also accessible by* Ⓜ*Plaza de Espana.* Ⓢ *Free.*

PLAZA DE CIBELES
PLAZA

When Real Madrid fans want to party before a game or celebrate a victory they come to Pl. de Cibeles and proudly drape their flag on the central fountain. Commissioned by King Charles III, the fountain depicts the Greek goddess of nature, Cibele, on her morning commute, driving a chariot pulled by two lions. The daringly white **Palacio de Comunicaciones** on the edge of the plaza is the headquarters of Madrid's city government. This building is open to the general public, and it's a worthy stop before or after a day in El Retiro or along La Avenida del Arte. The palace's rooftop tower is open to the public and has one of the best free views of the city.

✣ Ⓜ*Banco de España. From the intersection of C. Gran Vía and C. Alcalá, walk 1 block east down C. Alcalá.* Ⓢ *Free.*

TELEFÓNICA BUILDING
LANDMARK

C. Gran Vía, 28

If you want skyscrapers, go to Dubai. If that's why you came to Madrid, you're in the wrong place. That said, the Telefónica Building is Madrid's most iconic 20th-century building. Completed in 1920, this was the first skyscraper in Madrid, and arguably the first in all of Europe. During the Spanish Civil War, the Telefónica Building was used as a lookout by the Republicans to scout Franco's advancing Nationalist troops. It became a target of enemy bombings, and reportedly housed Ernest Hemingway on several occasions. Today the building is used as an office headquarters for the telecom giant, but the lobby is open to the public and has a free museum of communications technology.

✣ Ⓜ*Gran Vía.*

ARGÜELLES AND MONCLOA

⬛ TEMPLO DE DEBOD
TEMPLE, PARK

Paseo del Pintor Rosales, 2   ☎91 366 74 15 www.munimadrid.es/templodebod

On a nice day, this is one of the most beautiful spots in Madrid. In the '60s, the rapid industrialization taking place in Egypt severely threatened its most precious archaeological remains, which Spain played a critical role in preserving. When the Egyptian government proposed the construction of a hydroelectric dam along the Nile that would have destroyed Egypt's ancient temple complex at Abu Simbel, a team of Spanish archaeologists intervened to rescue the national treasure. In appreciation, the Egyptian government shipped the Templo de Debod to Madrid's Parque de la Montaña, where you can now see a small archaeology exhibit inside. The original temple archways are even more impressive at night when lit up and reflected in the adjacent pool. The park surrounding the temple teems with families, runners, tourists, and locals lounging in the afternoon sun. Check out the lookout point behind the temple for one of the most beautiful views of western Madrid.

*＃ Ⓜ**Plaza de España**. Walk to the far side of Pl. de España, cross the street, and walk a couple of blocks right; it will be on the left. Ⓢ Free. ⓐ Open Apr-Sept Tu-F 10am-2pm and 6-8pm, Sa-Su 10am-2pm; Oct-Mar Tu-F 9:45am-1:45pm and 4:15-6:15pm, Sa-Su 10am-2pm. Rose garden open daily 10am-8pm.*

⬛ EL PARDO   PALACE

C. de Manuel Alonso   ☎91 376 15 00

Originally built in the 15th century as a hunting lodge for Henry IV, El Pardo is today most famous as the private residence of General Franco during his military dictatorship. While much of the palace seems excessively ornate and unremarkable, the tour (45min.) takes you through Franco's private quarters, which have remained untouched since his death in 1975. His wardrobe, prayer room, personal study, and bedroom (where he kept his most treasured personal possession, a relic of St. Teresa's silver-encrusted petrified arm) are all on display. The tour even takes you into Franco's bathroom, and, yes, he had a bidet. In addition to its function as a museum, El Pardo hosts important state galas and functions as the official hotel of foreign dignitaries.

*＃ Ⓜ**Moncloa**. Take bus #601 from the underground bus station adjacent to Moncloa. ⓘ Mandatory 45min. guided tour in Spanish; last tour leaves 45min. before closing. Ⓢ €4, students and over 65 €2.30. ⓐ Open Apr-Sept M-Sa 10:30am-5:45pm, Su 9:30am-1:30pm; Oct-Mar M-Sa 10:30am-4:45pm, Su 10am-1:30pm.*

CASA DE CAMPO   PARK

Av. de Portugal

Casa de Campo offers many excuses to leave downtown Madrid. While the expansive urban park is a bit removed—on the other side of the Mazanares river—Casa de Campo is a totally manageable destination for a morning or afternoon trip out of the city center. Bike trails crisscross the park, and kayaks and canoes are available for rent along the park lagoon. If you are looking for something more than a tranquil afternoon in the park, the **Parque de Atracciones** (☎91 463 29 00 www.parquedeatracciones.es) has rides that will jack your heart rate up without fail. No need to commit yourself to the all-day pass (€24); single and double ride tickets can be purchased on the cheap (single €7; double €12). The park also has Madrid's only zoo and aquarium (☎91 512 37 70 www.zoomadrid.com), but be prepared to shell out for an entrance pass (€19), and don't expect any particular Castilian flair from the monkeys; they're just regular monkeys. If you plan on visiting these various venues within the park, head to Casa de Campo on quieter weekdays when there aren't long lines.

*＃ Ⓜ**Lago, Batan, and Casa de Campo** are all within the park. To get there from the city center: ⓂBatan or bus #33 or 65. ⓘ Let's Go does not advise walking here after dark. Ⓢ Entrance to the park is free; venues and rentals are ticketed. ⓐ Parque de Atracciones open M-Sa 9am-7pm. Zoo Madrid open daily, but check website for hours as schedule changes.*

ARCO DE LA VICTORIA   MONUMENT

Near Parque del Oeste

This Neoclassical arch at the center of Moncloa was built in 1956 by order of General Franco to commemorate the rebel army's victory in the Spanish Civil War. Looking at the concrete arch, you'd think that Franco and his friends came to power stomping through the country Caesar-style, but that glorious horse and chariot at the top of the arch is actually a few centuries off the mark. The history of Franco's military dictatorship still touches a nerve with many *madrileños* who prefer to call the arch Moncloa Gate. Surrounded by traffic, the history of the Arco de la Victoria has faded somewhat within the fast pace of cosmopolitan life.

*＃ Ⓜ**Moncloa**.*

PARQUE DEL OESTE PARK

C. de Francisco y Jacinto Alcántara

Less crowded than el Retiro, the Parque del Oeste is a lush break from the concrete jungle of western Madrid. This vast wooded park, with rolling hills, soaring pine trees, and small lagoons feels more like a nature reserve than a city park. The dirt paths that cross through the park are great for an afternoon walk or jog, but exercise caution at night, as the park is more deserted after sunset. If you're parched, there are plenty of cafes along the nearby Paseo del Pintor Rosales.

✠ ⓂMoncloa. *i Let's Go does not advise walking here after dark.* Ⓢ *Free.* 🕒 *Open 24hr.*

MUSEO DE AMÉRICA MUSEUM

Av. de los Reyes Católicos, 6 ☎91 549 26 41 www.museodeamerica.mcu.es

In 1771, Carlos III started a collection that brought together ethnographic objects from scientific expeditions and pieces from the first archaeological excavations carried out in America. Today, the modern Museo de América holds a collection that encompasses American cultures from the tip of South America to the tundra of Alaska. Some of the most interesting artifacts are treasures from the pre-Columbian cultures conquered by Spain, including some Mayan hieroglyphic documents.

✠ ⓂMoncloa. Ⓢ *€3; EU citizens €1.50; under 18, over 65, and students free.* 🕒 *Open Tu-W 9:30am-3pm, Th 9:30am-3pm and 4-7pm, F-Sa 9:30am-3pm, Su 10am-3pm.*

SALAMANCA

🖼 **MUSEO SOROLLA** MUSEUM

C. General Martínez Campos, 47 ☎91 310 15 84 http://museosorolla.mcu.es

This museum will surprise you. While the Valencian painter Joaquim Sorolla (1863-1923) is not quite a household name like Picasso or Goya, he is nonetheless one of Spain's greats. The museum, which resides in Sorolla's former palace and studio, is a living monument to the artist. Sorolla's home has a fantastic bohemian vibe, with his studio preserved with simple wooden bookcases filled with rare books and esoteric objects, canvases framed on easels, and paint brushes tucked into ceramic vases around the room. A trip to this museum gives you a sense of Sorolla's importance in art history, and, more importantly, of his spirit.

✠ ⓂIglesia. Turn right on C. General Martínez Campos. Ⓢ *€3. Free on Su.* 🕒 *Open Tu-Sa 9:30am-8pm, Su 10am-3pm.*

MUSEO LAZARO GALDIANO MUSEUM

C. Serrano, 122 ☎91 561 60 84 www.fig.es

Museo Lazaro Galdiano holds the personal collections of Spain's great patron of art and literature—Jose Lazaro Galdiano. This 13,000 piece collection, housed in Galdiano's former residence, includes a number of significant works, such as Goya's *Witch's Sabbath*, and El Greco's *Portrait of St. Francis of Assisi*. While these works are certainly worth visiting, the real appeal of this museum is its assemblage of more unusual works of art, decorative objects, weapons, jewels, and rare books. Galdiano was an influential board member of the Prado, a publisher of art and literary periodicals, and throughout his life he collected everything from rare jewels and Renaissance paintings to ivory weapons.

✠ ⓂGregorio Marañón. Ⓢ *€4, students €3, EU citizens free.* 🕒 *Open M 10am-4:30pm, W-Su 10am-4:30pm.*

MUSEO DE CIENCIAS NATURALES MUSEUM

C. José Gutiérrez Abascal, 2 ☎91 411 13 28 www.mncn.csic.es

You probably went to a natural history museum like this on a fifth-grade field trip, but the great thing about Mother Nature is that she never gets old. This is a particularly great place to go if you enjoy zoos and wild animals but prefer to see them dead. El Museo de Ciencias Naturales, based on the original Cabinet of Curiosities of the Spanish royal family in the 18th century, has today grown into a vast collection of natural specimens, fossils, and minerals. Perhaps the most thrilling room is the public warehouse in the basement, which houses thousands of taxidermied animals in a cramped, dimly lit room. You name it, and you'll likely find it in this room: vultures of every kind, primates, cats, and foxes, all looking at you, ready for the kill (but not ready enough). Particularly notable are the preserved African elephant, the giant squid, and the snow leopard (of which there are only about 5,000 living specimens today).

From [M]Gregorio Marañón, walk 2 blocks north on Paseo de la Castellana. $ €5, students and ages 4-14 €3, under 4 free. Open Jan-June Tu-F 10am-6pm, Sa 10am-8pm, Su 10am-2:30pm; July-Aug Tu-F 10am-6pm, Sa 10am-2:30pm, Su 10am-2:30pm; Sept-Dec Tu-F 10am-6pm, Sa 10am-8pm, Su 10am-2:30pm.

BIBLIOTECA NACIONAL LIBRARY

Paseo de Recoletos, 20-22 ☎91 883 24 02 www.bne.es

This spartan building on Paseo de Recoletos is the flagship of Spain's national library system. While the main corridors of the library are closed to the public, the building hosts a number of temporary exhibits (usually on literary topics) and cultural performances. For many people, this won't be the most thrilling visit because, let's face it, books are a waste of time (especially those stupid guidebooks). Nonetheless, the Biblioteca is a major landmark in the Salamanca area. On your way out of the library, check out the adjacent **Jardines del Descubrimiento,** a grassy public plaza smattered with trees and (expensive) outdoor cafes that spans C. Castellano.

[M]Colón. $ Free. Exhibits open Tu-Sa 10am-9pm, Su 10am-2pm.

food

Affordable and delicious food is plentiful in Madrid, but you'll have to dodge the many tourist traps in order to find it. For instance, dining options in El Centro are best for a midday refreshment, and drinks are shockingly cheap, but bottled water and mediocre food come with a hefty price tag. Lavapiés is notable for its reasonably priced international fare and La Latina also has some of the city's best *tabernas.* Las Huertas' central plazas (Pl. Santa Ana and Pl. del Ángel) are packed with contemporary tapas bars, iconic 19th-century *tabernas*, and international restaurants. The southern boundary of Argüelles has spectacular bars, cafes, and *tabernas*, particularly on **Calle del Duque de Liria, Calle Conde Duque,** and **Calle San Bernardino.** Chueca and Malasaña are packed with gourmet options that will cost you an arm and a leg. For those on a tight budget, your best bet may be to grab a beer and *bocadillo*, which may cost as little as €2.

EL CENTRO

EL SOBRINO DE BOTÍN SPANISH $$$

C. de Cuchilleros, 17 ☎ 91 366 42 17 www.botin.es

The world's oldest restaurant, El Sobrino de Botín, reeks of roasted pig and illustrious history: Goya was a waiter here; Hemingway ate here and wrote about it. Step inside and you will quickly realize that this is a truly authentic historical landmark and protector of the *madrileño* culinary tradition. With oil still-life paintings, antique revolvers, and porcelain tiles on the walls, El Sobrino is what so many restaurants in the barren El Centro scene aspire to be. As you approach the winding wooden staircase, you will notice *"el horno,"* the nearly 300-year-old wood-fired oven that continues to roast the same traditional dishes. Try the infamous roast suckling pig (€22) that Ernest Hemingway memorialized in the final pages of *The Sun Also Rises.* While the food is not cheap at El Sobrino, even their simple dishes like the *sopa de ajo* (garlic soup with egg; €7.90) are far better than what you can expect from neighboring El Centro restaurants. Forget sitting outside in Pl. Mayor and getting accosted by street performers; this restaurant is timeless, if a bit touristy.

⚔ *From* Ⓜ*Sol, walk 6 blocks west down C. Mayor to C. Cava de San Miguel to C. de Cuchilleros.* Ⓢ *Dishes €6-30.* ⏰ *Open daily 1-4pm and 8pm-midnight.*

📖 CAFÉ DE CÍRCULO DE BELLAS ARTES   CAFE $
C. de Alcalá 42   ☎ 91 521 69 42 www.circulobellasartes.com

This is Madrid's cafe society at its best—a requisite visit for any connoisseur visiting Madrid. Located on the first floor of the Círculo de Bellas Artes, this cafe is part of an institution. The interior is truly grand with crystal chandeliers, columns stamped with Picasso-like figure drawings, and frescoed ceilings. The wicker chairs on the streetside terrace make for a comfortable place to relax and people-watch amidst the bustle of C. de Alcalá. While the cafe has a full menu, simple things like sangria (€5) and *bocadillos* (€5.80) are excellent and a reasonable price of admission into one of Madrid's finest cafes.

⚔ *From* Ⓜ*Sevilla, walk 2 blocks west down C. Alcalá.* Ⓢ *Coffee drinks €3-6. Wine €3-6. Sandwiches €5-8.* ⏰ *Open M-Th 9:30am-1am, F-Sa 9:30am-3am, Su 9:30am-1am.*

MERCADO DE SAN MIGUEL   MARKET $
Pl. de San Miguel, 2   ☎91 542 73 64 www.mercadodesanmiguel.es

This almost-open-air market sells fine meats, cheeses, flowers, and wine. It also contains a number of specialty *bodegas*, bars, and restaurants. Prices here are reasonable, especially compared to the expensive sit-down dining options in nearby Pl. Mayor. The partial air-conditioning makes it the locals' pit stop for a glass of wine (€2-3), a fresh oyster (€1.50-3), or more traditional tapas (€2-4). Just a few years old, this reinvention of the open-air market has already become hugely popular and is reliably packed night and day. While you can still get traditional market goods like fresh produce, fish, and poultry, the market is more popular as a midday and evening hangout.

⚔ *At the Pl. de San Miguel, off the northwest corner of Pl. Mayor right beside the cervecería.* Ⓢ *Prices vary.* ⏰ *Open M-W 10am-midnight, Th-Sa 10am-2am, Su 10am-midnight.*

CHOCOLATERÍA SAN GINÉS   CHOCOLATERÍA $
Pl. de San Ginés, 5   ☎91 366 54 31

After spending all day looking at 500-year-old buildings and pretending to care, it's okay to let loose. Sometimes this means treating yourself to a good dinner; sometimes this means ingesting unconscionable amounts of deep fried batter and melted dark chocolate. Since it was founded in 1894, Chocolatería San Ginés has been serving the world's must gluttonous treat: *churros con chocolate* (€4). San Ginés is an institution and an absolute late-night must for clubbers and early risers alike.

⚔ *From Puerta Del Sol, walk down C. Arenal until you get to Joy nightclub. Chocolatería San Ginés is tucked in the tiny Pl. de San Ginés.* Ⓢ *Chocolates from €4.* ⏰ *Open 24hr.*

MUSEO DEL JAMÓN   TAPAS $$
C. Mayor, 7   ☎91 542 26 32 www.museodeljamon.com

There is something very special about your first *bocadillo* in Madrid. Like the birth of your first child, you probably won't forget it, and you will likely be anxiously snapping pictures to capture the magic of it all. The *bocadillo* is the simplest but most satisfying meal you will have in Madrid, and Museo Del Jamón does right by this tradition: crispy Spanish baguettes, freshly sliced *jamón*, rich Manchego cheese, and dirt cheap prices (€1-2). Vegetarians beware: there is meat everywhere—cured pig legs dangle from the ceilings, and the window display brims with sausages. Fanny packs and cameras are plentiful, but nothing can take away from the satisfaction of this authentic and criminally cheap meal.

The upstairs dining room also offers more substantial entrees like paella (€12) and full *raciones* (€10-15) of *jamón* and *queso*.

✦ *From* ⓂSol, *walk 2 blocks west down C. Mayor.* 𝒊 *Several locations throughout El Centro.* Ⓢ *Sit-down menu €10-20.* 🕓 *Open daily 9am-midnight.*

EL ANCIANO REY DE LOS VINOS
SPANISH $$
C. de Bailén, 19   ☎91 559 53 32 www.elancianoreydelosvinos.es

Right across the street from the Catedral de la Almudena, this is a pit stop for an afternoon drink and snack. Founded in 1909, El Anciano Rey de los Vinos is a granddaddy in the world of tapas bars in El Centro (maybe not a great-granddaddy, but a granddaddy nonetheless). The cafe has fantastic views, particularly from the terrace tables, but C. de Bailén can get a bit noisy. While the menu is not particularly inventive, at a certain point beer is beer and chairs are awesome—especially after a long day of museum-going.

✦ ⓂOpera. *Walk south on C. de Bailén past the Palacio Real.* Ⓢ *Tapas €6-13. Beer €2. Wine €3.* 🕓 *Open daily 10am-midnight.*

CERVECERÍA LA PLAZA
TAPAS $$
Pl. de San Miguel, 3   ☎91 548 41 11

If you are looking to avoid the more expensive restaurants in Pl. Mayor, the nearby Cervecería la Plaza is a solid option. Locals and tourists come here to enjoy the simple tapas menu, cheap beer (€2) and pitchers of sangria (€13). With a canopy of trees above the large canvas umbrellas, Cervecería la Plaza offers one of the best outdoor drinking and dining options in the area, protected from both the sun and the noise of heavy pedestrian traffic in Pl. Mayor.

✦ ⓂOpera. *Off C. Mayor between Palacio Real and Pl. Mayor.* Ⓢ *Entrees and tapas under €10. Beer €3.* 🕓 *Open daily 7am-midnight.*

FABORIT
CAFE, FAST FOOD $
C. de Alcalá, 21   www.faborit.com

The Starbucks of Spain (except with richer coffee), Faborit, with its modern furniture and young, cool vibe, is near almost every major tourist sight in Madrid. Their *shakerettes*, or fresh juice mixes, are delicious. Try the orange and strawberry juice mix or go for an iced coffee frappe. If you can't wait for your next meal, grab a dessert or sandwich (€5).

✦ ⓂSol. *Walk down Alcalá. It will be on your left next to Starbucks.* 𝒊 *Free Wi-Fi at most locations.* Ⓢ *Juices, coffee drinks, desserts, and sandwiches €3-6.* 🕓 *Open M-Th 7:30am-10pm, F-Sa 7:30am-midnight, Su 7:30am-10pm.*

LA LATINA AND LAVAPIÉS

🏆 ALMENDRO 13
SPANISH $$
C. Almendro, 13   ☎91 365 42 52

While many *madrileño* restaurants serve pre-made tapas at an uncomfortably lukewarm temperature, everything at Almendro 13 is made hot and fresh to order. Everything comes straight from *la plancha* with enough grease to make your heart murmur "thank you." The restaurant is always packed, with most parties snacking on Almendro's specialty, *huevos rotos* (fried eggs served on top of fries with a variety of toppings; €6-9.50). If this feels gluttonous, just remember that when you split something with a friend, there are no calories. The cold gazpacho (€4) and fresh salads (€7-10) are a welcome vacation from the heavier entrees. While many of the *tabernas* in Latina are cramped and crowded, the location of Almendro 13 just off the main drag of C. Cava Baja makes for a quiet and pleasant setting.

✦ ⓂLatina. *Walk west on C. Plaza Cebada 1 block, take a right on C. del Humilladero, walk 1 block to C. Almendro, and walk up 1 block.* Ⓢ *Sandwiches, tortillas, and salads €6-8. Entrees €6-9. Beer, wine, and vermouth €3.* 🕓 *Open daily 1-4pm and 7:30pm-12:30am.*

CAFE BAR MELO'S

C. Ave María, 44

BAR $

☎91 527 50 54

This is an institution in Madrid for good reason. Bread, cheese, and meat, cooked together to perfection. What else do you want in life? A wife? A couple of kids? A home to call your own? Cafe Bar Melo's has mastered the art of the grilled *zapatilla* (grilled pork and cheese sandwich; €3) and subsequently has become a favorite destination for both locals and travelers. Don't expect glamorous decor: Cafe Bar Melo's looks something like a hot dog stand at a major league baseball park after seven innings of play: dirty napkins are littered on the ground, the wraparound wooden bar is covered in half empty beer glasses, and soccer games blast on the TV in the corner. This is all part of the magic.

⌖ ⓜLavapiés. Walk up C. Ave María 1 block. ⓢ *Sandwiches €2-5. Beer €1-3.* ☷ *Open Tu-Sa 9pm-2am.*

TABERNA DE ANTONIO SÁNCHEZ

C. del Mesón de Paredes, 13

TAPAS $$

☎91 539 78 26

Founded in 1830 by legendary bullfighter Antonio Sánchez, this *taberna* has had plenty of time to perfect its tapas. The menu hasn't changed much, with the standby matador-worthy favorites like the *morcilla a las pasas* (black pudding and raisins; €9). Everyone knows you don't feed a matador a leafy salad before sending him off to stab a bull in the neck in front of thousands of people: like vampires, these guys thrive on blood. The interior of this restaurant is every bit as famous as the bloody tapas, with walls covered with original murals by the 19th-century Spanish painter Ignacio Zuloaga and victory trophies from 19th-century bullfights. The dark wood interior may not be the most cheery place to spend an afternoon, but it is certainly a chance to step back in time. If all this carnage sounds a little much, they also offer traditional dishes like gazpacho (€4), *sopa de ajo* (garlic soup; €4), and plenty of Manchego cheese and *jamón ibérico* to keep you happy.

⌖ *From* ⓜ*Tirso de Molina, walk past Pl. de Tirso de Molina until you get to C. del Mesón de Paredes. Take a left (head south) on C. del Mesón de Paredes. The taberna is on the left.* ⓢ *Entrees €3-15.* ☷ *Open M-Sa noon-4pm and 8pm-midnight, Su noon-4pm.*

NUEVO CAFE BARBIERI

C. Ave María, 45

CAFE $

☎91 527 36 58

Nuevo Cafe Barbieri is nothing short of grand. The high molded ceilings and large windows give the cafe an open and breezy quality. While this may be Lavapiés's finest traditional cafe, it is also a buzzing nightlife hub on weekends. With its Cadillac-sized espresso machine and fine selection of alcohol, Barbieri specializes in mixed drinks like the Barbieri (coffee, Bailey's, and vanilla ice cream; €7.50).

⌖ ⓜLavapiés. Walk up C. Ave María 1 block. ⓢ *Desserts €4-7. Coffee drinks €2-5. Tea €2.50.* ☷ *Open M-W 4pm-12:30am, Th 4pm-1:30am, F-Su 4pm-2:30am.*

LAS HUERTAS

CERVECERÍA LOS GATOS

C. Jesús, 2

TAPAS $$

☎91 429 30 62

If you took one of the grandfather tapas bars of Las Huertas and gave it a healthy dose of Viagra, it would look and feel something like Cervecería Los Gatos. Sandwiched between the madness of Las Huertas and the quieter museum district, Los Gatos is a local hangout for young *madrileños* that most tourists haven't yet discovered. Los Gatos may be old, but it still has a sense of humor: the ceiling sports a version of Leonardo da Vinci's *The Creation of Man*, in which Adam gracefully holds beer. The decor is eclectic, with a crystal chandelier hanging from the ceiling across from an antique motorcycle. If ever there's a

food

place to snack on traditional tapas, this is it, with top-quality *raciones* including *jamón ibérico* (€18) and Manchego (€11). The house special is the *boquerones en vinagre* (anchovies soaked in olive oil, garlic, and vinegar; €10).

➡ Ⓜ Antón Martín. Take C. Atocha southeast ½ block to C. de Moratín. Take C. de Moratín 4 blocks east to C. Jesús. Turn left (heading north) onto C. Jesús and walk 2 blocks. $ Pinchos €2-4. Raciones €8-18. Cash only. ⏰ Open daily 1:30pm-2am.

👍 LA BARDEMCILLA DE SANTA ANA
SPANISH $$

C. Núñez de Arce, 3 ☎91 521 42 56 www.labardemcilla.com
C. de Augusto Figueroa, 47

If you're wondering what made Javier Bardem the tall, strapping, dazzling Spanish beauty he is today, look no further than La Bardemecilla. The Bardem family restaurant serves only family recipes like *huevos de oro estrellados* (eggs scrambled with *jamón iberico* and onions; €8.70). With two Madrid locations, Grandma and Grandpa Bardem are getting some long overdue street cred. The food here is definitely traditional, but each dish has a signature touch, like the *chorizo con los días contados* (Spanish sausage cooked in white wine and clove; €9). Just a few blocks from C. de las Huertas, this is a great spot to grab dinner before a big night out.

➡ From Pl. Santa Ana, take C. Núñez de Arce on the west side of the plaza north toward Puerta del Sol. Follow C. Núñez de Arce 1 block. The restaurant is on the right just before C. de la Cruz. $ Pinchos €2-4. Entrees €8-10. Cash only. ⏰ Open M-F noon-5:30pm and 8pm-2am, Sa 8pm-2am.

LATERAL
TAPAS $$

Pl. Santa Ana ☎91 420 15 82 www.cadenalateral.es

If the curators of the Reina Sofía were to make a tapas restaurant, it would look something like this, with its sparse interior, marble bar, and white leather bar stools. The obvious appeal here is that it's located directly on Pl. Santa Ana, but the restaurant delivers much more, with good service, reasonable prices, and a menu full of freshly prepared tapas. Menu items like the lamb crepe (€4.50) and the salmon sashimi with wasabi (€6.50) are a nice break from the traditional oxtails and sweetbreads. While Lateral's menu racks up major points for variety and quality, they don't offer substantial entrees, so either order a lot of tapas or have your mother pack you a PB and J.

➡ If you face the ME Madrid Reina Victoria Hotel in Pl. Santa Ana, Lateral is on the left. $ Tapas €3-8. Combination platters €10-20. ⏰ Open daily noon-midnight.

CASA ALBERTO
SPANISH $$

C. de las Huertas, 18 ☎91 429 93 56 www.casaalberto.es

Founded in 1827, Casa Alberto is one of Madrid's oldest taverns. Once upon a time, bullfighters came here for a "cup of courage" before they entered the bullring. Today it's a tourist favorite, and for good reason. The walls are lined with history, with photographs of famous matadors and celebrities who have visited, and the charm hasn't faded. Enter your own bullring of fear by trying tripe: what could be more carnivorous than putting another animal's stomach inside of your stomach? Maybe eating a pig's ear, another dish proudly served here. More popular, less adventurous dishes include Madrid-style veal meatballs, or the house special, *huevos fritos* (fried eggs; €12) served with garlic lamb sweetbreads and roasted potatoes.

➡ From Pl. del Ángel, walk down C. de las Huertas toward the Prado. Casa Alberto will be on your right. $ Entrees €5-20. ⏰ Open daily noon-1:30am.

FATIGAS DEL QUERER
SPANISH $$

C. de la Cruz, 17 ☎91 523 21 31 www.fatigasdelquerer.es

While it doesn't have the "history" or institutional status of some of Las Huertas's other tapas bars, Fatigas del Querer still serves great traditional fare. The large open interior is a nice alternative to the cramped elevator-style dining found throughout Madrid. Expect standard, freshly made tapas. The waitstaff is particularly attentive and they keep the turnaround quick. Dishes like the mixed seafood paella (€7) and calamari (€10) are fantastic and won't break the bank, unless, of course, you develop an addiction.

⇄ From Pl. del Ángel, go north up C. Espoz y Mina and bear right. The street becomes C. de la Cruz. 💲 Tapas €4-12. Cash only. ⏰ Open M-F 11am-1:30am, Sa-Su 11am-2:30 or 3am. Kitchen open until 1am.

LA FINCA DE SUSANA RESTAURANT MEDITERRANEAN $$

C. de Arlabán, 4 ☎91 429 76 78 www.lafinca-restaurant.com

Madrid is not cheap, but La Finca de Susana does its best to offer a gourmet dining experience (think white tablecloths set with silverware and wine glasses) at a reasonable price. Though the look and feel is formal, don't be dismayed: the menu has plenty to offer the budget-conscious. The Mediterranean-inspired menu offers greater variety than the traditional *taberna*, with popular dishes like *arroz negro con sepia* (stewed rice with cuttlefish; €11) and *cordero al horno* (roasted lamb; €12). While the setting may feel a bit corporate, the food is far from that: rich in flavor and affordable in price.

⇄ ⓂSol. Follow C. de Alcalá east and take a right (south) onto C. de Sevilla. Follow C. de Sevilla to C. de Arabal and take a left (heading east). 💲 Entrees €7-16. ⏰ Open M-W 1-3:45pm and 8:30-11:30pm, F-Sa 1-3:45pm and 8:30pm-midnight, Su 1-3:45pm and 8:30-11:30pm.

IL PICCOLINO DELLA FARFALLA ITALIAN, ARGENTINIAN $

C. de las Huertas, 6 ☎91 369 43 91

Forget the frou-frou thin crust: this small Italian restaurant serves cheap pizza loaded with cheese and toppings. The obvious choice here is the pizza served with any two toppings (€7.90), but staples like the *margarita* (€6.90) are perfectly satisfying. Split two ways, these pizzas make for a great budget dinner. While Il Piccolino might not be the most authentic Italian food in the city, it is certainly a step up from the pizza-by-the-slice sold throughout Las Huertas. If dessert is in the cards, the Argentine *alfajor* with *dulce de leche* (€4) is gluttonous in the best way possible.

⇄ From Pl. del Ángel, take C. de las Huertas east toward Paseo del Prado. Il Piccolino will be on the right. 💲 Salads €5-7. Pizzas and pastas €6-9. Desserts €3-5. Cash only. ⏰ M-Th 1-4:30pm and 8:30pm-2:30am, F-Su 1pm-2:30am.

MIRANDA INTERNATIONAL $$

C. de las Huertas, 29 ☎91 369 10 25

Miranda's burgers, burritos, salads, and other staples make it one of the best budget international menus in the area. While they offer typical bar snacks, items like the Cajun burrito with guacamole (€9.50) or the French burger with chèvre and caramelized onions (€10) are hard to come by in Madrid. While Miranda buzzes through the night, it is particularly popular among travelers for its hearty breakfast menu. The English Breakfast (coffee or juice, eggs, bacon, and toast; €5) is a good alternative to the meager complimentary breakfast at your hostel, and the full brunch (€12 per person) is a major quality-of-life enhancement: fresh orange juice, coffee, eggs, *raciones* of *jamón* and *queso*, and pastries.

⇄ From Pl. Santa Ana walk down C. de las Huertas toward Paseo del Prado. Miranda is on the left. 💲 Breakfast €4-12. Entrees €8-12. ⏰ Open daily 8am-2am.

LA SOBERBIA TAPAS $$

C. Espoz y Mina, 1 ☎91 531 05 76 www.lasoberbia.es

La Soberbia has struck the happy medium between cramped hole-in-the-wall and expansive contemporary tapas bar. La Soberbia isn't known for a chic interior or an ironic theme, just its well-priced traditional dishes like paella (€7) and better-than-average *tostados* served on warm baguette (€3-4).

⇄ From Pl. de Santa Ana head North on C. Espoz y Mina toward Puerta del Sol. 💲 Entrees €4-12. Cash only. ⏰ Open M-W 9am-1:30am, Th-Sa 9am-2:30am, Su 10am-1:30am.

CAFETERIA MARAZUL   SPANISH $

Pl. del Ángel, 11   ☎91 369 19 43

Las Huertas is loaded with places that try really hard; Cafeteria Marazul doesn't seem to give a damn and it's all the better for it. This is a typical *madrileño* cafeteria filled with typical *madrileños* in one of the city's most tourist-heavy plazas. Staples like *patatas bravas* (€6) and *bocadillos* (€4-5) are of standard quality and served on banged-up steel plates. This is also a great place to pick up a quick-and-dirty breakfast. The Marazul breakfast (€2.40) includes coffee and a plateful of *churros*.

✦ Ⓜ*Antón Martín. From the metro, walk right down C. Atocha, and make a right on C. Olivar. Walk until you see Plaza del Ángel on your left, right before Pl. Santa Ana.* ⓘ *Expect Cafeteria Marazul to charge extra for terrace seating.* Ⓢ *Meals €4-10.* ⓩ *Open daily 6:30am-3am.*

EL INTI DE ORO   PERUVIAN $$

C. Amor de Dios, 9   ☎91 429 19 58   www.intideoro.com

While plenty of people have tried ceviche in swank gourmet restaurants, few have had authentic Peruvian cuisine. El Inti de Oro is a good place to start, with a menu that is faithful to traditional recipes, using plenty of cilantro, fresh onion, lime, and pepper. Most stick to what they know on the menu, choosing from the selection of ceviches (€11-13), but the waitstaff is very helpful in suggesting other traditional dishes like *arroz con pato norteño* (duck garnished with cilantro, served with rice; €11). More daring visitors might consider Peruvian cocktails (€4-6), which use the traditional sweet brandy *pisco* mixed with lemon, sugar, and cream. If you're up for dessert, try the homemade fresh fruit gelato (€4.50).

✦ *Steps from* Ⓜ*Antón Martín down C. Amor de Dios.* Ⓢ *Entrees €5-15.* ⓩ *Open daily 1pm-midnight.*

AVENIDA DEL ARTE

EL BRILLANTE   TAPAS $

Pl. Emperador Carlos V, 8   ☎91 539 28 06

El Brillante provides quality budget eating in pricey Avenida del Arte. While its claims to have the best *bocadillo de calamares* (fried calamari sandwich; €6) in Madrid have not been substantiated, patrons don't seem to care, and they order the sandwich in abundance. If nothing else, the sandwich is as cheap and flavorful as anything in the immediate area, with the calamari piping hot from the deep-fryer. The restaurant has indoor bar seating and outdoor terrace seating near the Reina Sofía.

✦ Ⓜ*Atocha.* Ⓢ *Sandwiches €4-8. Cash only.* ⓩ *Open daily 9am-1am.*

LA PLATERÍA DEL MUSEO   TAPAS $$

C. de las Huertas, 82   ☎91 429 17 22

This upscale tapas bar has some of the best terrace seating along Paseo del Prado. They offer plenty of staples such as *gazpacho andaluz* (€4.50) and *croqueta de jamón* (€3) that are perfect as a post-museum snack. While entrees and daily specials are generally pricey, regular tapas and refreshments come at a standard price. More than anything, La Plateria del Museo stands out for its exceptional terrace seating and proximity to the three museums of Avenida del Arte. The wine selection changes daily but the sangria (€3.50) and cocktails (€5) stay the same.

✦ *From* Ⓜ*Atocha, follow Paseo del Prado 2 blocks to C. de las Huertas and turn left.* Ⓢ *Appetizers €2.50-8; entrees €8-14. Drinks €2-6.* ⓩ *Open daily 9am-2am.*

GRAN VÍA

[H]ARINA
CAFE $$

Pl. de la Independencia, 10   ☎91 522 87 85   www.harinamadrid.com

[H]arina stands out among the many cafes throughout Madrid that feel old and tired. It is one of those places where you will magically feel great after eating a big meal. The menu is made up of all the foods that you likely know and love—fresh salads, sandwiches, and paper-thin-crust pizzas—and the environment is hard to beat. The whitewashed wooden interior makes for a pleasant cafe setting, but the terrace seating overlooking Pl. de la Independencia stands out. Indoor and outdoor seating are both generally packed, particularly on weekends, and many patrons take their food to go from the bakery. The house special lemonade (€3) is made with fresh lemon juice and crushed mint leaves, and keeps people coming back.

♯ ⓂBanco de España. Walk 1 block east to Pl. de la Independencia; the restaurant is on the southwest corner. *i* Terrace seating requires a €1 additional charge. Ⓢ Salads €8. Sandwiches €6. Pizzas €9-11. ☼ Open daily 9am-9pm.

PIZZERÍA CASAVOSTRA
ITALIAN $$

C. Infantas, 13   ☎91 523 22 07   www.pizzacasavostra.com

Everything on Casavostra's menu is fresh—from the brick-oven pizzas to the traditional appetizers. While many of the restaurants between Gran Vía and Chueca try hard to break out of the tapas mold, Casovostra keeps things simple with a traditional Italian menu. The pizzas (€8.50-14) are fired in the brick oven and topped with ingredients like arugula, fresh mozzarella, and cherry tomatoes. The appetizer salads come in huge portions and are great to share for a first round (€5-10). They also offer a full selection of *burrata* (unpasteurized mozzarella) appetizers that are so good they'll make your mom's taste like steel wool.

♯ From ⓂGran Vía, walk east 1 block to C. Hortaleza and then 2 blocks north to C. de la Infantas. Follow C. de las Infantas. Ⓢ Appetizers €4-12; entrees €7-15. Drinks €2-4. ☼ Open daily 1:30-4pm and 10pm-midnight.

EL BOCAITO
TAPAS $$

C. de la Libertad, 6   ☎91 521 31 98   www.bocaito.com

Ever since Spain's most well-known filmmaker, Pedro Almodóvar, cited El Bocaito as one of his favorites in Madrid, it has been all the rage. El Bocaito is as traditional as tapas bars get, from the matador paraphernalia on the walls to the platters of *pinchos*. El Bocaito sticks to tradition and does it well. Its back-to-back bars and four small dining rooms in back are filled nightly with a mix of locals and tourists. While drinks (€2-4) and tapas (€2-5) won't cost much, a full sit-down dinner with a bottle of wine and entrees (€12-20) makes for a pretty expensive meal.

♯ From ⓂGran Vía, walk east 1 block to C. Hortaleza, 2 blocks north to C. de las Infantas, and then follow C. de las Infantas 4 blocks west to C. de la Libertad. Ⓢ Appetizers €2-5; entrees €10-20. Drinks €2-4. ☼ Open Jan-July M-F 1-4:30pm and 8:30pm-midnight, Sa 8:30pm-midnight; Sept-Dec M-F 1-4:30pm and 8:30pm-midnight, Sa 8:30pm-midnight.

MERCADO DE LA REINA
TAPAS $$

C. Gran Vía, 12   ☎91 521 31 98   www.mercadodelareina.es

Mercado de la Reina is one of the few exciting restaurants amid the dearth of options on C. Gran Vía. While the bar snacks are the standard pre-made *pinchos* (€2.50-5) you find elsewhere, the full dinner menu has some great options, including a winning gourmet burger served with a fried egg (€12). The tables in the back dining area are a bit more quiet and civil than the swarm up front. Mercado de la Reina is one of the better options for contemporary *taberna* food along C. Gran Vía, even though dishes like *patatas con huevos rotos* (€12-13) could be found elsewhere for less.

♯ From ⓂGran Vía, walk straight east down Gran Vía; the restaurant will be on your right. Ⓢ Entrees €10-20. ☼ Open M-Th 9am-midnight, Sa-Su 10am-1am.

food

CHUECA

▦ MERCADO DE SAN ANTÓN
MARKET $$

C. Augusto Figueroa, 24 ☎91 330 07 30 www.mercadosananton.com

This is Europe's fierce rebuttal to Whole Foods. What was once an open-air market in the middle of Chueca is now a state-of-the-art building filled with fresh produce vendors, *charcuterías*, *bodegas*, and a rooftop restaurant. Along with Mercado de San Miguel, this is a terrific place to get a sweeping tour of Spain's culinary landscape, from traditional delicacies to international fare. Prices might be a bit steep, but you can easily sample your way through a meal by visiting a few different shops.

✴ Ⓜ*Chueca. On the southern end of Pl. de Chueca.* ⓘ *For the rooftop terrace, make reservations in advance at* ☎91 330 02 94. *Visit www.lacocinadesananton.com for more on the restaurant.* Ⓢ *Varies greatly, but a full meal at the market costs around €10. Cash only.* ⌚ *1st fl. market open M-Sa 10am-10pm. 2nd fl. restaurants and bars open Tu-Su 10am-midnight. Rooftop restaurant open M-Th 10am-midnight, F-Sa 10am-1:30am, Su 10am-midnight.*

▦ SAN WISH
CHILEAN $$

C. de Hortaleza, 78 ☎91 319 17 76 www.san-wish.com

San Wish is a novelty bar and restaurant that looks like it will actually make it in Chueca. The power of their picture menu is magnetic, displaying a lineup of greasy, crispy traditional Chilean sandwiches like the *hamburguesa voladora* (chicken, tomato, lettuce, grilled cucumbers, melon chutney; €6.50) and the *clásica* (grilled steak, sweet pickle, tomato, and lettuce; €6.50). The list goes on, but, true to their name, they don't offer much that doesn't belong between two pieces of bread. This is as trendy as fast food gets, with all sandwiches made on pressed Chilean bread and served alongside traditional cocktails like the pisco sour (grape brandy, lemon juice, egg white, syrup, and bitter herbs; €4.50). The young and wealthy *madrileño* crowd can't seem to get enough of it. Seats are nearly impossible to snag, especially during peak weekend hours.

✴ *From* Ⓜ*Chueca, take C. Gravina 2 blocks east to C. de Hortaleza and then a right on C. de Hortaleza. The restaurant will be on your right.* Ⓢ *Sandwiches €5.50-8.90. Beer €1.50-3.50. Wine €2.50. Cash only.* ⌚ *Open M 8pm-midnight, Tu-Sa 1-4pm and 8pm-midnight, Su 1:30-4pm.*

BAZAAR
MEDITERRANEAN $$

C. de la Libertad, 21 ☎91 523 39 05 www.restaurantbazaar.com

You would expect this place to be prohibitively expensive, but, somehow, it isn't. This expansive two-story restaurant has the look and feel of a high-end place with white tablecloths and wine glasses waiting on the table, but they offer something completely different from dinky *pinchos* and lukewarm à la carte dishes with a menu of fresh pasta (think fettuccine with grilled chicken and sundried tomatoes; €7), salads, and meat dishes, with almost everything falling below the €10 mark. The upstairs and downstairs dining rooms are quite large, but partitioned into smaller, more intimate spaces by shelves filled with artisanal food displays. While the food is not necessarily daring, it is fresh, comes in great portions, and can be enjoyed in a relaxed but formal setting.

✴ Ⓜ*Chueca. Make a left on C. Augusto Figueroa and a right on C. de la Libertad.* Ⓢ *Entrees €7-10.* ⌚ *Open M-W 1:15-4pm and 8:30-11:30pm, Th-Sa 1:15-4pm and 8:30-midnight, Su 1:15-4pm and 8:30-11:30pm.*

LO SIGUIENTE
TAPAS $$

C. Fernando VI, 11 ☎91 319 52 61 www.losiguiente.es

With high bar tables, metal stools, and silver columns, Lo Siguiente has the feel of both a traditional tapas bar and a chic Chueca restaurant. While it may have a cool, polished aesthetic, Lo Siguiente is still an informal restaurant that

madrid

madrileños enjoy for precisely that reason. You can get all of the staples like the classic *huevos rotos* (a fried egg over pan-fried potatoes, garlic, and chorizo; €9.50), but don't be afraid to try the lighter Mediterranean items like tomato and avocado salad and ceviche served atop grilled vegetables.

From [M]Chueca, head 2 blocks northeast on C. San Gregorio and take a left onto C. Fernando VI. Lo Siguiente is on the right. $ Meals €10-15. Cash only. 🕐 Open M-Th 8:30am-1:30am, F-Sa 8:30am-2:30am, Su 8:30am-1:30am.

MAGASAND CAFE, SMOOTHIES $$

Travesía de San Mateo, 16 ☎91 319 68 25 www.magasand.com

The long list of gourmet sandwiches here makes the traditional *bocadillo* pale in embarrassment and inadequacy, and the upstairs dining area/library has every pretentious magazine you could imagine. All of the sandwiches are served on fresh bread, with greens, fancy condiments, and a wide selection of meat beyond the *jamón* that starts to taste like rubber after a few days in Madrid. For a bougie afternoon, order the *el rollito de Luisa* (tuna carpaccio, arugula, and bread pressed with tomatoes; €4), and then pick up the latest edition of *Monocle* upstairs. Magasand also serves fresh salads and a spectacular Saturday brunch (a selection of fresh-fruit smoothies, coffee, pastries, fried eggs, sandwiches, and crepes; €16).

[M]Chueca. Make a right on C. Augusto Figueroa, and another right on C. de Hortaleza. Turn right onto Travesía de San Mateo (a sign on C. de Hortaleza points you in the right direction). $ Sandwiches €5-8. Salads €4-7. 🕐 Open M-F 9:30am-10pm, Sa noon-5pm.

IL PIZZAIOLO ITALIAN $$

C. de Hortaleza, 84 ☎91 319 29 64 www.pizzaiolo.es

The appeal of Il Pizzaiolo is pretty clear: it's the cheap gourmet pizzas, made to order and baked super thin. The menu is full of simple crowd-pleasers, including Italian salads, antipasti, pizza, and pasta. The brightly painted murals of Italian landmarks on the walls are an afterthought. The *diavola* (tomato, mozzarella, spicy chorizo; €9.90) is a favorite on the long list.

[M]Chueca. Make a right on C. de Gravina and a right on C. de Hortaleza. The restaurant is on the right. $ Pizzas €8-10. 🕐 Open M-Th 1:30pm-midnight, F-Sa 1:30pm-12:30am.

STOP MADRID SPANISH $$

C. de Hortaleza, 11 ☎91 521 88 87 www.stopmadrid.es

Founded in 1929, this old-school tapas bar is one of the best in Chueca. *Raciones* of *queso, jamón ibérico*, and seafood are standard *taberna* fare, but the quality here is exceptional. They serve only *Ibérico de la Belota* (€21), the best quality *jamón* in the world, and the *manchego curado* (€10) is richer than most versions in Madrid. But what really sets Stop Madrid apart is its extensive wine list, with each option available by the glass. For better or worse, this old *taberna* feels a bit out of place in Chueca's clutter of posh cafes and shops selling "XXXleatherXXX."

From [M]Gran Vía, walk up C. de Hortaleza. $ Entrees €5-10. 🕐 Open daily noon-2am.

RESTAURANT VIVARES SPANISH $$

C. de Hortaleza, 52 ☎91 531 58 13 www.restaurantesvivares.com

You can't fake home-cooked food: either it is or it isn't. Restaurant Vivares is, and it may be the best meal in Chueca. The interior of the restaurant is unassuming, with a typical bar up front and tables in back, but during peak hours it's packed with locals. They offer not only a *menú del día* (entree, drink, bread, and dessert; €12), but also a *menú de la noche* (burger, drink, bread, and dessert; €9.60). For a more contemporary menu of salads, pasta, and vegetarian options, they have recently opened an annex restaurant, **Vivares 37**, across the street.

[M]Chueca. Head 1 block south on C. de Pelayo, make a right on C. Augusto Figueroa, and left onto C. de Hortaleza. $ Entrees €5-12. 🕐 Open daily 12:30-5:30pm and 8:30pm-1:30am.

DIURNO

CAFE, VIDEO RENTAL $

C. San Marcos, 37   ☎91 522 00 09 www.diurno.com

This combination cafe, gourmet shop, and DVD store is something of a novelty. At last, Spaniards seem to have figured out that eating a sandwich (try the chicken with pesto and mozzarella; €2.30) is that much better when you get the added pleasure of unwrapping it like a present. Diurno is open through the day for sandwiches and fresh smoothies (€2.50) and serves cocktails (€2-5) in the evening. Browse the DVD rentals on the way out.

✦ Ⓜ*Chueca. Make a left onto C. Augusto Figueroa and a right onto C. de la Libertad. Diurno is across from Bazaar.* Ⓢ *Salads €5-7. Sandwiches €2-4. Pasta €5-7. Coffee €1-2. Cocktails €2-5.* ☒ *Open M-Th 10am-noon, F-Sa 10am-1am, Su 11am-midnight.*

MALASAÑA

⬛ LA DOMINGA

SPANISH $$$

C. del Espíritu Santo, 15   ☎91 523 38 09 www.ladominga.com

Now with two locations (one in Chueca, one in Malasaña), La Dominga is making a name for itself as one of the best family-run *tabernas* in Madrid. Known primarily for traditional dishes like *rabo de toro* (oxtail stew; €14), it also caters to a younger clientele with plenty of contemporary dishes. Dishes like the beef carpaccio (served with parmesan and arugula; €13) are more refined than the heavier stewed and grilled meats that dominate traditional Spanish cuisine. The decor here is equally mixed, with high ceilings that make it feel more like a modern Malasaña restaurant than an old-time *taberna*. Reservations here are a must for prime weekend nights (10pm-1am), but many choose to forgo the sit-down menu in favor of the tapas, which include a platter of *croquetas* (€9.70) that critics have called the best in the city.

✦ Ⓜ*Tribunal. Go west on C. de San Vicente Ferrer, make a left on C. del Barco, and make a right on C. del Espíritu Santo.* Ⓢ *Entrees €10-15.* ☒ *Open daily 1-4:30pm and 8:30pm-midnight.*

⬛ LAMUCCA

INTERNATIONAL $$

Pl. Carlos Carbonero, 4   ☎91 521 00 00 www.lamucca.es

Lamucca covers the globe on its menu, and it does it quite well. While appetizers like cheese fondue and "Nachos de la Teki" might raise some eyebrows, these along with many other international dishes at Lamucca are executed with great sophistication. Dishes like Thai curried chicken with jasmine rice (€11) share the menu with Italian pizza and pasta as well as contemporary Spanish dishes. Lamucca has certainly stuck to the trends with exposed brick, mismatched furniture, and chalkboard menus, but, the food here is daring and covers plenty of terrain (from Texas to Switzerland).

✦ Ⓜ *Tribunal. Head south on C. Fuencarral a few meters and take a right (west) onto C. de la Palma, turn left on C. San Pablo and follow for 2 blocks. Take a right on C. Don Felipe and a quick left onto C. del Molino de Viento. Follow C. del Molino de Viento until you reach Pl. Carlos Carbonero. The restaurant is on the right.* Ⓢ *Appetizers €5-12; entrees €12-20. Pizza €10-15. Cash only.* ☒ *Open Tu-F 1:30pm-2am, Sa-Su 12:30pm-2:30am.*

HOME BURGER BAR

BURGERS $$

C. del Espíritu Santo, 12   ☎91 522 97 28 www.homeburgerbar.com

Home Burger Bar is one of many restaurants catching on to the fancy burger craze. This retro diner has dimly lit brown leather booths, plays American doo-wop and soul, and serves American-style burgers with fries. Portions here are large, but the emphasis is on quality, and all the meat is organic. They also serve a number of grilled chicken and vegetable club sandwiches, including a hugely popular *hamburguesa caprese* (sun-dried tomatoes, parmesan, and arugula; €14).

✦ Ⓜ*Tribunal. Go west on C. de San Vicente Ferrer, make a left on C. del Barco, and make a right on C. del Espíritu Santo. ℹ Other locations at C. San Marcos, 25 and C. Silva, 25.* Ⓢ *Burgers €10-13. Sandwiches €8-15.* ☒ *Open M-Sa 1:30-4pm and 8:30pm-midnight, Su 1-4pm and 8:30-11pm.*

CAFÉ MAHÓN
Pl. del 2 de Mayo, 4

CAFE $$

☎91 448 90 02

With a combination of international favorites, Mediterranean-inspired salads, and traditional entrees, Café Mahón is a great budget option on Malasaña's most tranquil plaza. Brightly colored metal chairs and odd tables make for a kooky setup, and the menu of international comfort foods is equally eclectic. Try the nachos with cheese and guacamole (€7), the hummus appetizer (€6), or the moussaka (€8). A menu of specialty teas (€2-3.50) and coffees keeps people coming throughout the day to enjoy the beautiful terrace seating (next to the local jungle gym), and the bar inside gets active post-dinner with locals enjoying cocktails and *chupitos* (shots; €3-4).

✻ From Ⓜ Tribunal, head west on C. de la Palma 2 blocks west to to C. San Andrés, take a right and follow until you reach the plaza. Cafe Mahon is at the northeast corner. Ⓢ Salads €7. Appetizers €6-9; entrees €7-12. ☾ Open daily July-Aug 3pm-2am, Sept-June noon-2am. Terrace open daily July-Aug 3pm-1am, Sept-June noon-1am.

BANZAI
C. del Espíritu Santo, 16

JAPANESE $$

☎91 521 70 81

Banzai is clearly a Malasaña take on Japanese food, with 1950s bebop playing in the background and rolls named after great American cities. Really? Albuquerque? Whatever—the hip picturebook menu with black etchings of all the dishes reveals great variety beyond standard sushi (€9-11). Dishes like the ground *iberico* burger (marinated in wasabi; €8.50) are unmistakably of Spanish influence, but they also have a selection of miso soups (€5), *gyoza* (dumplings; €7.50-9.50) and sautés (€6-13). While it's easy to rack up a big bill at Banzai, the generous *menú del día* (sushi, salads, and hot appetizers; €11) is a steal.

✻ Ⓜ Tribunal. Go west on C. de San Vicente Ferrer, make a left onto C. del Barco, and make a right onto C. del Espíritu Santo. Ⓢ Meals €10-20. ☾ Open Tu-Su 1-4:30pm and 8:30pm-midnight.

EL RINCÓN
C. del Espíritu Santo, 26

CAFE $$

☎91 522 19 86

El Rincón seems like a perfect caricature of bohemian Malasaña with its mismatched decor, baby-blue walls, and chalkboard menu. In truth, it's a very thoughtfully put-together cafe, from the simple five-item menu to the tasteful interior. With simple wood tables, and small Asian prints on the walls, the decor is sparse compared to the kitschy messes throughout the neighborhood.

✻ Ⓜ Tribunal. Go west on C. de San Vicente Ferrer, make a left onto C. del Barco, and make a right onto C. del Espíritu Santo. Ⓢ Sandwiches €5. Entrees €10. Cocktails €5-7. Wine €2.50. Coffee €2-3. ☾ Open daily 11am-2am.

LOLINA VINTAGE CAFE
C. del Espíritu Santo, 9

CAFE $

☎66 720 11 69 www.lolinacafe.com

Filled with '50s memorabilia like album covers and movie stills, mismatched armchairs, and vintage lamps, Lolina looks like it was assembled from a shopping spree at a Brooklyn thrift store, but it fits perfectly in trendy Malasaña. The intimate space attracts people at all times of the day, whether for morning tea or late-night cocktails. The food offerings are limited, with a selection of salads (€8), bratwurst sandwiches (€5), and open faced *tostas* like the *sobrasada* (sausage, brie, and honey; €4).

✻ Ⓜ Tribunal. Go west on C. de San Vicente Ferrer, make a left onto C. del Barco, then make a right onto C. del Espíritu Santo. Ⓢ Salads €8. Cocktails €6. Coffee and tea €2-5. ☾ Open M-Tu 9:30am-1am, W-Th 9:30am-2am, F-Sa 9:30am-2:30am, Su 9:30-1am.

OLOKUN CUBAN $$

C. Fuencarral, 105 ☎91 445 69 16

Olokun might not have the quirky decor and sophisticated garage-sale aesthetic of its Malasaña neighbors, but it has its own appeal with a menu of hearty Cuban dishes. While plenty of restaurants in the neighborhood try to fake different kinds of international cuisine, everything is actually Cuban at Olokun, right down to the dark mojito (made with black rum; €7). Traditional platters like *mi vieja Havana* (pork, fried plantains, black beans; €14) and *soroa* (chili, fried plantains, rice; €15) all come in large Cuban portions. With dark walls covered in the etched signatures of customers and a foosball table in the basement, it's pretty clear that Olokun doesn't take itself quite as seriously as many Malasaña restaurants, bars, and cafes; it's a good thing.

From [M]Tribunal, walk straight north up C. Fuencarral. The restaurant is on the left. [$] Entrees €10-15. ⏰ Open daily noon-5pm and 9pm-2am.

HAPPY DAY BAKERY, DESSERTS $

C. del Espíritu Santo, 11 ☎66 720 11 69

Andy Warhol would be proud. With walls of Pepperidge Farm cookies, Betty Crocker cake mix, Aunt Jemima syrup, and Goober peanut butter, this is much more than an American bakery—it's a museum of America's best traditions. (Try not to confuse it with the neighboring store, Sad Day, which sells polluted water, handguns, and junk mortgages.) While the cupcakes (€2), muffins (€2), and slices of cake (€3) all look great, the overpriced American imports, including bags of marshmallows (€4.50), are more intriguing. This is definitely a novelty experience, but they do offer a good selection of American desserts and Spanish gelato.

[M]Tribunal. Go west on C. de San Vicente Ferrer, make a left onto C. del Barco and a right on C. del Espíritu Santo. [$] Pastries €2-4. Ice cream €2-3. Packaged goods €2-6. ⏰ Open daily 9am-11:30pm.

CREPERIE LA RUE CREPERIE $

C. del Espíritu Santo, 18 ☎91 189 70 87

Creperie La Rue's small shop is filled with murals of Parisian street scenes, French music, and, most importantly, the aroma of crepes. Sweet and savory offerings here are fairly standard for a small creperie: goat cheese and grilled vegetables, *jamón* and Emmental, and sweet crepes like the *limón cointreau* (lemon, liqueur, and cinnamon) and chocolate and orange. Sweet crepes are large enough to share as a dessert, and savory crepes make a good late-night fix. All crepes are served on paper plates, as there are only a few seats in shop.

[M]Tribunal. Go west on C. de San Vicente Ferrer, make a left onto C. del Barco, and make a right onto C. del Espíritu Santo. [$] Crepes €4-8. ⏰ Open daily 11:30am-midnight.

LA VITA È BELLA ITALIAN $

Pl. de San Ildefonso, 5 ☎91 521 41 08 www.lavitaebella.com.es

La Vita è Bella looks and feels like a college-town pizza joint. With limited seating, most people order cheap and greasy Sicilian-style pizza by the slice (€2.50) or calzones (ham, mozzarella, and mushroom; €3.50). They also bake personal thin-crust pizzas made to order, like the Malasaña (tomato, mozzarella, bacon, egg, and parmesan; €8.50) and the La Vita è Bella (tomato, buffalo mozzarella, and basil; €8.50).

[M]Tribunal. Go west on C. de San Vicente Ferrer, make a left onto C. del Barco, and make a right onto C. del Espíritu Santo. [$] Entrees €2.50-5. ⏰ Open daily noon-2am.

ARGÜELLES AND MONCLOA

LA TABERNA DE LIRIA SPANISH $$$$

C. del Duque de Liria, 9 ☎91 541 45 19 www.latabernadeliria.com

Most of the items on the menu of Taberna de Liria have been staples for years. Head Chef Miguel López Castanier is a published authority on traditional Mediterranean cuisine and has led La Taberna de Liria through a very successful 23 years in Madrid. Dishes are simple and sophisticated, and the house specialty is the menu of foie gras appetizers (€11-14). While this is not a budget restaurant, it offers excellent food and a romantic setting for a special night in Madrid. Call ahead to make reservations, particularly on weekends.

[M]Ventura Rodríguez. Walk forward, then take the left fork in the road onto C. San Bernardino. [$] Appetizers €8-15; entrees €17-25. Full tasting menu €50. Open M-Sa 2-4pm and 9-11:45pm.

EL JARDÍN SECRETO CAFE $

C. de Conde Duque, 2 ☎91 541 80 23

Tucked away in a tiny street close to C. de la Princesa, El Jardín Secreto is, appropriately, Argüelles's best-kept secret. Walk into this eclectic cafe filled with beaded window coverings, wooden ceiling canopies, and crystal-ball table lamps to enjoy one of their dozens of coffees, hot chocolates, and snacks. For a real taste of what Secreto has to offer, try the *chocolate El Jardín*, served with chocolate Teddy Grahams and dark chocolate at the bottom of your cup (€6), or the "George Clooney" cocktail with *horchata*, crème de cacao, and Cointreau (€7.25).

[M]Ventura Rodríguez. Head left at the fork in the road onto C. San Bernardino. [$] Desserts €4.20. Coffee and tea €3-6. Cocktails €7.25. Open M-Th 6:30pm-1:30am, F-Sa 6:30pm-2:30am, Su 6:30pm-1:30am.

EL REY DE TALLARINES ASIAN $$

C. San Bernardino, 2 ☎91 542 68 97 www.reydetallarines.com

El Rey de Tallarines is a great option for noodles and dumplings in a land of tortillas and tostados; it has built a reputation as one of the best options for budget Asian food in Madrid. The specialty here is La Mian, the ancient art of the hand-pulled noodle. Everyday at 1 and 9pm the cooks prepare fresh noodles from scratch at the main bar of the restaurant. Dishes like La Mian with chicken and vegetables (€6) do not disappoint. The menu also has a number of meat dishes like the crunchy roast duck (€14), and the assorted dim sum (8 pieces; €9) is particularly popular for sharing with a small group.

[M]Ventura Rodríguez. Take the left fork in the road onto C. San Bernardino. [$] Entrees €8-15. Open daily 12:30-5pm and 7:30pm-midnight.

LAS CUEVAS DEL DUQUE SPANISH $$$$

C. de la Princesa, 16 ☎91 559 50 37 www.cuevasdelduque.galeon.com

What distinguishes Las Cuevas del Duque is its selection of big-game dishes like the stewed deer with mixed vegetables (€14). They offer a great selection of steaks and grilled fish; the filet mignon (€20) is a particularly popular choice. The basement location makes the restaurant feel a bit like a cave, but eating meat underground has its own appeal—ask any Neanderthal.

[M]Ventura Rodríguez. Take the left fork in the road onto C. San Bernardino; the restaurant will be on a tiny street to your right. [$] Entrees €15-30. Open daily 7-11pm.

KULTO AL PLATO SPANISH $$

C. Serrano Jover, 1 ☎91 758 59 46 www.kultoalplato.com

Kulto al Plato serves contemporary tapas in an upscale setting. While its location between El Corte Inglés and the neighboring hotel isn't thrilling, it's one of the best dining options near the Argüelles metro stop. Tapas dishes have a modern take, such as the mushroom ravioli with foie gras sauce (€13). The fish and meat entrees are grilled fresh. The roasted duck with seasoned pear is also a house specialty (€16).

☛ Ⓜ️Argüelles. Walk south down C. de la Princesa to C. Serrano Jover. Ⓢ Meals €12-20. ⌚ Open M-Th 8:30-11:30pm, F-Sa noon-1am, Su 8:30-11:30pm.

SALAMANCA

LA ÚRSULA
TAPAS $$

C. López de Hoyos, 17   ☎91 564 23 79 www.laursula.com

Across the street from the Museo Lazaro Galdiano, La Úrsula is an upscale tapas bar with terrace seating on a quiet side street off C. Serrano. The setting is fantastic and attracts a steady crowd of wealthy *madrileños*. La Úrsula offers particularly great lunch deals, including one of the city's best hamburger specials (€8)—a large burger with three tasty toppings of your choice (fried egg, manchego, sautéed peppers, etc.) and served with fries, a drink, and coffee or dessert.

☛ Ⓜ️Gregorio Marañón. Cross Paseo de la Castellana on C. de María de Molina. Follow C. de María de Molina for 3 blocks until you reach C. Serrano. Ⓢ Menú del día €7-11. Meals €14-20. Cash only. ⌚ Open daily 8am-noon.

MUMBAI MASSALA
INDIAN $$$

C. de los Recoletos, 14   ☎91 435 71 94 www.mumbaimassala.com

While Mumbai Massala is not a bargain, it is gourmet. Rather than the heaping portions you find at many Indian places, taste and quality are the focus of Mumbai Massala, which garnishes dishes with lemon, fresh parsley, and chopped onion. It has the typical stewed meat and vegetable dishes like *tikka masala* and *saag gosht*, and the traditional tandoor turns out spectacular charcoal-grilled entrees like Peshwari *gosht tikka* (lamb marinated in yogurt and spices; €14).

☛ Ⓜ️Colón. Walk 2 blocks south down Paseo de los Recoletos. Turn left (east) onto C. de Recoletos, and follow it for 1 block. Ⓢ Appetizers €8-12; entrees €10-16. Menú del día €15. Menú de la noche €25. Cash only. ⌚ Open daily 1:30-4:30pm and 9pm-midnight.

nightlife

If you came to Europe for the nightlife, you've chosen the right city. Not only does Madrid offer every type of nightlife experience known to man: thanks to the youth culture of *el botellón*, it offers one experience only known to sleepless teenaged zombies. La Latina and Lavapiés are home to some internationally recognized clubs, a spectrum of bars, *tabernas*, and late-night cafes. Meanwhile, the streets of Las Huertas are packed with *discotecas* that would have the old literati of the neighborhood pondering the great moral dilemma of the dance floor makeout. In Chueca and Malasaña, the nightlife scene is chameleon-like, with clubs and bars opening and closing at a rapid pace. Other neighborhoods, like Argüelles and Moncloa, are more laid-back and house some great live music venues. So pick your poison, get crazy, and stay hydrated.

EL CENTRO

PALACIO GAVIRIA
CLUB

C. del Arenal, 9   ☎91 526 60 69 www.palaciogaviria.com

Built in 1850 and inspired by the Italian Renaissance, Palacio Gaviria is a beautiful palace turned nightlife hotspot. Make your royal entrance by heading down the grand marble staircase onto the dance floor, which is powered by techno beats and electric dance moves. Be on the lookout for promoters of Palacio Gaviria in Puerta del Sol, as they will often have vouchers for free entry or drinks.

☛ From Puerta del Sol walk straight down C. del Arenal. Ⓢ Cover M-Th €10, F-Sa €15, Su €10. ⌚ Open 11pm-late.

CAFE DEL PRÍNCIPE BAR

Pl. de Canalejas, 5 ☎91 531 81 83

A 2min. walk from Puerta del Sol, this bar and restaurant offers the "best mojitos in Madrid" as well as a variety of entrees and beverages. Come to take a tranquil break from the noisy Sol without venturing too far from all the clubs.

Right at the corner of C. de la Cruz and C. del Príncipe. $ Mixed drinks €5-15. ⏰ Open M-Th 9:30am-2am, F-Sa 9:30-2:30am, Su 9:30am-2am. Kitchen open daily 9:30am-4pm and 8pm-2am.

JOY ESLAVA CLUB

C. del Arenal, 11 ☎91 366 37 33 www.joy-eslava.com

An old standby, this converted theater has stayed strong amid Madrid's rapidly changing nightlife scene. Number one among study-abroad students and travelers, Joy Eslava plays an eclectic mix of music and features scantily clad models of both genders dancing on the theater stage. Balloons and confetti periodically fall New-Year's-Eve-style from the ceiling.

$ Cover M-W €12, Th €15, F-Su €18. ⏰ Open M-Th 11:30pm-5:30am, F-Sa 11:30pm-6am, Su 11:30pm-5:30am.

GRAN VÍA

REINABRUJA CLUB

C. Jacometrezo, 6 ☎91 542 81 93 www.reinabruja.com

Reinabruja is not just a club, it is a futuristic fantasyland. In Reinabruja, the internationally renowned industrial designer Tomas Alia has created a world of endless light and sound. Every surface of this club—including the toilet seats—changes color using cutting-edge LED technology. Reinabruja is Madrid nightlife at its most creative and over-the-top. This subterranean world of phosphorescent lighting and stenciled pillars is hugely popular with tourists but hasn't lost its edge in the *madrileño* scene.

[M]Callao. $ Cover €12; includes 1 drink. Wine €7. Mixed drinks €9. ⏰ Open Th-Sa 11pm-6am.

EL TIGRE BAR

C. de las Infantas, 30 ☎91 532 00 72

The motto of El Tigre might as well be "don't f*@% with Spain." On a block with fusion restaurants, contemporary cuisine, and fancy cocktail lounges, El Tigre keeps everything Spanish: beer, mojitos, and sangria in towering glasses; bull heads on the walls; and taxidermied animals. We can only imagine the interior decorator's philosophy was "put the head on the wall and serve the rest as tapas." Drinks come with a plate of greasy fries, pork loin, and chorizo. This place is absolutely packed; it can be hard to make your way through the door. While the noise and crowds may be a turn-off for some, this is definitely a place where you can start your night off cheap, drunk, and greasy.

From [M]Gran Vía, walk north up C. de Hortaleza, then make a right on C. de las Infantas. $ Drinks €2-5. ⏰ Open daily 10:30am-1:30am.

EL PLAZA JAZZ CLUB MUSIC

C. Martín de los Heros, 3 ☎91 548 84 88 www.elplazacopas.com

People don't just come here because of the music, they come here because it's a dynamic environment. The nightly program of live sets is one of the best in the city for jazz, particularly the Wednesday night Dixie Jam. But the typically *madrileño* crowd comes here to drink, socialize, and lounge on comfortable couches, not just to listen to saxophone solos and pretend to understand every last note. El Plaza also occasionally screens films and hosts open mic nights and comedy performances.

[M]Pl. de España. Walk 1 block west to Martín de los Heros. $ Most events are free; some ticketed shows €5. Drinks €3-6. Cash only. ⏰ Open daily 7:30pm-2:30am.

nightlife

EL BERLÍN
MUSIC

C. Jacometrezo, 4   ☎91 521 57 52 www.nuevocafeberlinmadrid.webgarden.es

This is not only one of the best places for live music in Gran Vía, it is one of the best-known jazz clubs in all of Madrid. El Berlin attracts the city's most talented artists in jazz, blues, funk, and soul for its nightly sets and is most famous for its Tuesday jam sessions (10pm). The crowd is generally more middle-aged and the intimate venue isn't always packed, but El Berlin is a popular alternative to fussy and expensive clubs.

⚲ Ⓜ️Callao. Ⓢ Drinks €3-7. ⏱ Opens daily at 9pm. Sets begin at 10pm.

DEL DIEGO COCKTAIL BAR
BAR

C. de la Reina, 12   ☎91 523 31 06

Del Diego is an upscale one-room cocktail lounge that is quiet and spacious and has served the same classic cocktails for 20 years. Drinks are expensive, but Del Diego is one of the nicest cocktail lounges in the area and a better place for conversation than many of the standing-room-only tapas bars.

⚲ Ⓜ️Gran Vía. Walk north up C. de Hortaleza and make a right onto C. de la Reina. Ⓢ Cocktails €10. ⏱ Open daily 7pm-3am.

POUSSE
BAR

C. de las Infantas, 19   ☎91 521 63 01

With refurbished antique furniture alongside sleek leather loveseats and music from every decade, the ambience at Pousse is self-consciously eclectic. The cardboard and finger-paint art on the walls was made by either avant-garde artists or kindergarteners. (You never know—there are some pretty pretentious kindergarteners out there who really dig Abstract Expressionism.) The drink menu is every bit as mixed as the decor, with everything from all-natural fresh fruit milkshakes (€6) to gourmet cocktails made with premium liqueurs (€9-13).

⚲ Ⓜ️Gran Vía. Walk north up C. de Hortaleza, then make a right on C. de las Infantas. Ⓢ Drinks €6-13. ⏱ Open M-Sa 10pm-2am.

LOLA
BAR

C. de la Reina, 25   ☎91 522 34 83 www.lola-bar.com

Lola Bar is a cool but unpretentious cocktail bar. Groups of mid-20-something professional *madrileños* come here for their first drink of the night on a pub crawl through Gran Vía and Chueca. While this bar doesn't pack full, groups arrive as soon as work gets out around 7pm. Lola serves plenty of American favorites such as Coito a la Playa (Sex on the Beach), but they also keep things simple with Spanish wines by the glass (€2-4) and beer on tap (€3).

⚲ Ⓜ️Gran Vía. Walk north up C. de Hortaleza, then right on C. de la Reina. Ⓢ Cocktails €9-10. ⏱ Open M-Th noon-2am, F-Sa noon-2:30am.

MUSEO CHICOTE
BAR

C. Gran Vía, 12   ☎91 532 67 37 www.museo-chicote.com

A longtime favorite of artists and writers, this retro-chic cocktail bar maintains its original 1930s design. During the Spanish Civil War, the foreign press came here to wait out the various battles, and during the late Franco era it became a haven for prostitutes. Today Museo Chicote offers one of the best happy hours on Gran Vía (cocktails €5; 5-11pm), but things shift pretty quickly at midnight when the nightly DJ set starts. Located directly on C. Gran Vía, this isn't the most adventurous place, but it's a Madrid institution with a steady crowd.

⚲ Ⓜ️Gran Vía. Walk east on Gran Vía. Museo Chicote is on the left. Ⓢ Cocktails €7-9. ⏱ Open daily 8am-3am.

LA LATINA AND LAVAPIÉS

CASA LUCAS BAR

C. Cava Baja, 30 ☎91 365 08 04 www.casalucas.es

Props to Casa Lucas for making life seem simple and delicious. On a long block of successful restaurants, bars, and *tabernas* that thrive on gimmicks, Casa Lucas stands out by sticking to the basics: freshly prepared tapas and a premium wine list. The interior of the restaurant is bright, comfortable, and packed with locals. The tapas here are a notch above what you will find elsewhere. The chalkboard menu of wines changes nightly, and nearly everything is offered by the bottle or the glass.

[M]La Latina. Walk west down Pl. de la Cebada. Make a right onto C. de Humilladero and continue right on C. Cava Baja. $ Wine by the glass €2-4, by the bottle €16-25. Raciones €7-15. ⏰ Open M-Th 8pm-midnight, F-Sa 8pm-1am, Su 8pm-midnight.

LA PEREJILA TAPAS, BAR

C. Cava Baja, 25 ☎91 364 28 55

La Perejila feels something like the world's most inviting shoebox. The interior is filled with beautiful antiques from the golden age of flamenco, vintage photographs, oil paintings, and vases of flowers that make this place come alive. Live parakeets greet you at the door. While grabbing a table is tricky, patrons are happy to stick around anyway to enjoy some of C. Cava Baja's freshest *taberna* food, and the wine selection changes daily.

[M]La Latina. Walk west down Pl. de la Cebada. Make a right onto C. de Humilladero and continue right on C. Cava Baja. $ Cocktails €5-10. Tostados €5-7. Entrees €9-12. ⏰ Open daily 1-4pm and 8:15pm-12:30am.

ANGELIKA COCKTAIL BAR BAR

C. Cava Baja, 24 ☎91 364 55 31 www.angelika.es

Vintage DVD posters line the walls, projectors screen international films, and the walls are lined with DVDs for rent. Angelika has over 3,000 titles available to borrow from their library, and they also serve a mean mojito. We can't decide if this is the most cinema-friendly bar in Madrid, or the world's bougiest Blockbuster. Sure, it's a gimmick, but sometimes gimmicks are fun.

[M]La Latina. Walk west down Pl. de la Cebada. Make a right onto C. de Humilladero and continue right on C. Cava Baja. $ Cocktails €5-10. ⏰ Open daily 3pm-1am.

EL BONANNO BAR

Pl. del Humilladero, 4 ☎91 366 68 86 www.elbonanno.com

Located at the southern end of the bustling C. Cava Baja, El Bonanno makes a great place for the first stop of the evening or a last-minute drink before you hit the club. Because space is limited in the bar, people take their drinks to the sidewalk. El Bonanno serves the requisite tapas, but the cramped interior makes it better suited for a quick drink.

[M]La Latina. Walk 1 block west down Pl. de la Cabeza. Take a left onto Plaza del Humilladero. $ Cocktails €3-10. ⏰ Open daily 12:30pm-2:30am.

SHOKO CLUB

C. de Toledo, 86 ☎91 354 16 91 www.shokomadrid.com

With massive "bamboo" shoots that reach to the ceiling, a huge stage featuring internationally acclaimed acts, and a swanky VIP section that *Let's Go* wishes we could live in, Shoko is an Oriental-inspired *discoteca* that violates every last rule of feng shui. This is the big-time.

[M]La Latina. Head south down C. de Toledo. $ Cover €10-15. ⏰ Open daily 11:30pm-late.

LAS HUERTAS

KAPITAL
CLUB

C. de Atocha, 125 ☎91 420 29 06 www.grupo-kapital.com/kapital

This is the mothership of Madrid nightlife. Built in a gutted theater, Kapital is a seven-story temple of trashy fun. The first floor, which blasts house music, is where most of the action happens, but it keeps going, with separate dance floors for hip hop, reggae, and Spanish pop on the stories above. There is a little bit for everybody here: the third floor has a karaoke bar; the sixth floor screens movies; the seventh floor terrace has hookahs, pool tables, and killer views; and finally, on the yet-to-be-completed eighth floor, they hold live reenactments of the American Civil War (BYOB: bring your own beard). The good people of Kapital are rumored to be expanding upward at a rapid pace all the way to heaven itself. If you plan on making the pilgrimage, whatever you do, wear nice clothes—no sneakers or shorts. While Kapital doesn't get busy until around 2am, arriving early dressed in something nice will let you avoid the long wait.

✈ *2min. walk up C. de Atocha from ⓂAtocha. ⓈCover €15; includes 1 free drink. Drinks €10-15. ⓉOpen Th-Su 11:30pm-5:30am.*

SOL Y SOMBRA
CLUB

C. de Echegaray, 18 ☎91 542 81 93 www.solysombra.name

With thousands of LED lights on every last surface, Sol y Sombra might be the most high-tech thing ever to hit Madrid. Unlike the monster warehouse-style *discotecas* around the city, Sol y Sombra is surprisingly intimate. The walls shift in color to accent the bold patterns, while the music shifts between techno, jazz, funk, and hip hop. This is not a sloppy Eurotrash *discoteca;* it's a cool and innovative club. While you should expect a line out the door during prime weekend hours (midnight-3am), you won't be endlessly stranded: people tend to move in and out pretty quickly on their way to bigger *discotecas.*

✈ *Ⓜsol. From the metro, walk toward Paseo del Prado on Carrera de San Jerónimo and make a right onto C. de Echegaray. ⓈCover €10. Beer €5. Cocktails €7. ⓉOpen Tu-Sa 10pm-3:30am.*

CAFE LA FIDULA
JAZZ BAR

C. de las Huertas, 57 ☎91 429 29 47 www.myspace.com/lafidula

This jazz bar has been on the Las Huertas strip since long before the tourists started showing up. For more than 30 years, La Fidula has attracted some of the city's best jazz and blues musicians. While it's every bit as famous as Café Central and Café Jazz Populart, the setting is more intimate: built inside a 19th-century grocery store, the small stage encircled by tables puts you within spitting distance of the performers. While La Fidula isn't normally packed, this is precisely its appeal—a setting apart from the ebb and flow of Las Huertas where you can enjoy some of the city's most talented musicians. The performance schedule shifts nightly, with a combination of sets in the early evening from 8 to 10pm and jam sessions that carry on until the early hours of the morning.

✈ *ⓂAntón Martín. Take C. León north to C. Las Huertas. ⓘVisit the MySpace page for an up-to-date schedule, or call to inquire about late-night performances. ⓈCoffee €3-4. Beer €2-4. Cocktails €5-8. Cash only. ⓉOpen M-Th 7pm-3am, F-Sa 7pm-4am, Su 7pm-3am.*

EL IMPERFECTO
BAR

Pl. de Matute, 2 ☎91 366 72 11

El Imperfecto is unapologetically kitschy, with walls plastered with images from American film, music, and art, and decorations straight from the garage sale (would it be a crime if two stools matched?). This shoebox interior is always fun and upbeat with people sipping cocktails (€6-10) and milkshakes (€4-6). Ice-blended drinks are reasonably priced for Madrid (€7) and much better than

madrid

anything you'd find at a major club. Expect a crowd, and, on weekend nights, plenty of American study-abroaders, some friendly German accents, and some fanny packs. El Imperfecto is packed during weekend dinner hours (11pm-1am), so expect to stand at the bar.

[M]Antón Martín. Walk uphill until you reach Pl. de Matute. Make a right toward C. de las Huertas. El Imperfecto will be on the right. $ Drinks €4-10. Sangria €2 per glass; pitchers €11. ⏰ Open daily 3pm-2:30am.

EL SECRETO DE RITA BAR

C. de Echegaray, 10

El Secreto de Rita is a small bar that holds its own on a long block of *discotecas*. Dim lighting, soul revival music, and cheap cocktails are the major draw. While many bars need a critical mass to keep the energy alive, El Secreto de Rita is still fun even when it isn't packed. If conversation, eye contact, and interpersonal connection are things you value in life, you'll find El Secreto a good alternative to the flashing lights, onerous covers, and mind-numbing sound systems of so many clubs in the area. Bonus points to anyone who can figure out what's up with Rita—what's she hiding?

From Pl. Santa Ana, walk north up C. de Echegaray toward Puerta del Sol. Rita is on the left. $ Drinks €3-10. ⏰ Open M-W 6pm-2am, F-Sa 6pm-2:30am.

VIVA MADRID BAR

C. de Manuel Fernández y González, 7 ☎91 429 36 40

Viva Madrid has long been a favorite celebrity haunt; it's rumored that Ava Gardner and the bullfighter Manolete got handsy here in the '50s. While this might have once been an artists' hangout, today it's been adopted by young *madrileños* and internationals. The front terrace is in the thick of the pedestrian traffic of Las Huertas nightlife, but the interior feels dramatically removed, with a wood-carved ceiling and velvet drapes that look straight out of El Palacio Real.

[M]Sol. Walk toward Paseo del Prado on Carrera de San Jerónimo and turn right onto C. de Manuel Fernández y González. $ Beer €2.50-4. Cocktails €6-10. ⏰ Open daily noon-2am.

IREAL BAR

C. de Echegaray, 16

Gaga gets old. When you tire of American dance music, iReal is a good place to educate yourself in the latest Spanish discopop. Expect flashing lasers, disco balls, and pulsing Spanish pop brought to you by lyricists that make Rebecca Black sound like TS Eliot. Jump on the dance floor and get lost in the fun, or sit on the sidelines in ironic detachment. Drinks run a bit pricey with €5 beers and mixed drinks from €6, but iReal doesn't have a cover, so at the very least it's a good stop on the way to bigger and badder clubs on Las Huertas.

From Pl. Santa Ana walk up C. de Echegaray toward Puerta del Sol. $ Drinks €5-8. ⏰ Open daily 11pm-3am.

MIDNIGHT ROSE BAR

Pl. de Santa Ana, 14 ☎91 701 60 20 www.midnightrose.es

Swanky, bougie, euro-yuppie—these are all words that apply to Pl. de Santa Ana's top-dollar cocktail lounge in the ME Madrid Reina Victoria Hotel. Cocktails are expensive (€12-14), lights are dim, and the young and wealthy European clientele is predictably beautiful. The leather-cushioned penthouse terrace is a total fantasyland, if you can make it up there. It's open to the proletariats but requires a steep cover (€15) on weekend nights when the crowds arrive. The line can be long, so your best bet is to go for an early drink (7-10pm) when there's neither cover nor line.

It's the most prominent building on Pl. Santa Ana (lit purple at night). $ Cover for penthouse terrace €15 Th-Su. Cocktails €5-15. Cash only. ⏰ Downstairs lounge open daily 1:30-4pm and 10pm-2:30am. Penthouse terrace open daily 7pm-2:30am.

DUBLINERS BAR

C. Espoz y Mina, 7 ☎91 522 75 09

How many tiny *cañitas* does it take to get drunk? A lot. This is just one reason why so many come to Dubliners, a traditional Irish pub with traditional Irish pints (€3). While it's dark and loud, Dubliners has a fun international vibe and gets packed and crazy during major sports games. Ever seen grown men from around the world attempt their own drunken rendition of "We Are the Champions"? This is a great place to make friends, taunt enemies, and, when it's all said and done, come back the next morning for the Dubliner's Irish breakfast (€5.70).

➤ From Puerta del Sol walk south down C. Espoz y Mina. The bar is on the left. Ⓢ Beers €2-4. Cocktails €6-10. ⏰ Open M-Th 11am-3am, F-Sa 11am-3:30am, Su 11am-3am.

VINOTECA BARBECHERA BAR, RESTAURANT

C. del Príncipe, 27 ☎91 420 04 78 www.vinoteca-barbechera.com

Vinoteca Barbechera is a nationally successful chain that delivers premium Spanish and imported wines. Nearly everything on the menu is available by the glass. While Vinoteca Barbechera also offers a range of tapas and *pinchos* (€3-6), the appeal here is clearly the wine list. With over 300 domestic brands, this is a great place to test your palate or your bullshitting skills. The waitstaff can help you find a glass that suits your tastes, and the terrace seating on Pl. Santa Ana can't be beat.

➤ Pl. Santa Ana. Ⓢ Wine €2-8. Drinks €5-15. ⏰ Open M-Th noon-1am, F-Su noon-2am.

SWEET FUNK CLUB CLUB

C. del Doctor Cortezo, 1 ☎91 869 40 38 www.myspace.com/sweetfunkclub

While suspended cages, disco balls, and a daringly dressed clientele are staples of this hot club, leave your whip at home. Sweet is a self-proclaimed funk club that plays American auto-tuned hip hop to a primarily *madrileño* crowd. By 4am on weekends, the dance floor here is usually packed, and women with very little clothing keep things steamy with "suggestive" dances on the small circular stages throughout the club.

➤ ⓂAntón Martín. From the metro, walk uphill on C. de Atocha and make a left on C. del Doctor Cortezo. Ⓢ Cover €10-14; includes 1 drink. Beer €5. Cocktails €7. ⏰ Open F-Sa 11pm-sunrise.

CHUECA

👍 **BOGUI JAZZ CLUB** JAZZ CLUB

C. Barquillo, 29 ☎91 521 15 68 www.boguijazz.com

Bogui is one of Madrid's premier jazz venues and most happening weekend clubs. Nightly sets of live jazz (9 and 11pm) are a fantastic way to get plugged into the local music scene, and during weekend DJ sets (Th-Sa 1am), Bogui brings in some of Madrid's best-known jazz, funk, and soul DJs from Sala Barco. Bogui also caters to a Chueca crowd that likes to dance. The Wednesday midnight set is when musicians from around the city convene for a late-night jam session after a long night of gigs.

➤ ⓂChueca. Take C. Gravina 2 blocks west to C. Barquillo. The club is on the left. Ⓢ DJ sets Th-Sa free; concerts €10. Beer €4. Cocktails €7. €1 surcharge for all beverages Th-Su. ⏰ Open M-Sa 10pm-5:30am.

AREIA BAR, TAPAS

C. de Hortaleza, 92 ☎91 310 03 07 www.areiachillout.com

Areia calls itself a "chillout zone," which must sound *so* cool to native Spanish speakers. While to Americans this slogan seems to fit better in your teen rec center, this is one of the hippest spots in Chueca. The Moroccan-themed bar and lounge has a crimson-draped ceiling, low-lying tables, large cushion seats, and embroidered pillows where people snack on international tapas like pad thai (€6) and tandoori chicken (€6) as well as traditional Moroccan dishes like *tayin de cordero* (stewed lamb). Things stay pretty laid-back, even during the weekend DJ sets (11pm-late). Cocktails are set at standard prices (€6-8) and come served with fresh fruit. Music ranges from house to reggae.

[M]Chueca. Make a right onto C. Augusto Figueroa, then a right on C. de Hortaleza; bar will be on your right. $ Cocktails €6-9. ⏰ Open daily 1pm-3am.

DAME UN MOTIVO BAR

C. Pelayo, 58 ☎91 319 74 98

Dame un Motivo is a one-room bar with an outlook on nightlife that's refreshing in Chueca: strip it down to its essentials (good music, cheap drinks, and sparse decor). The idea here is to do away with all of the excess of Chueca nightlife—cover charges, overpriced sugary drinks, flashing lights, and loud music—and offer an alternative environment for people to hang out and converse. That Dame un Motivo is busy on the weekends with a primarily local crowd is a testament to its success. During the week, people come to enjoy the film and book library.

*From [M]Chueca, take C. Gravina 1 block west to C. Pelayo, follow north ½ a block. The bar is on the right. **i** Check out Dame un Motivo's Facebook page for event listings. $ Beers €1.30-2.50. Cocktails €5.50. ⏰ Open W-Th 6pm-2am, F-Sa 4pm-2:30am, Su 4pm-2am.*

LA SUECA BAR

C. de Hortaleza, 67 ☎91 319 04 87

The drag queen beauties behind the bar are a huge presence in this small cocktail lounge. They joyously shake martinis and mix fruit daiquiris for a young and beautiful *madrileño* crowd. Like many bars on the block, La Sueca is small, but it has enough white leather lounge seating to accommodate larger groups. The crystal chandeliers are a nice touch, but nothing out of the ordinary for Madrid's most flamboyant *barrio*.

[M]Chueca. Make a right onto C. Augusto Figueroa and a right onto C. de Hortaleza. $ Beer €3.50. Cocktails €8. ⏰ Open daily 8pm-3am.

STUDIO 54 CLUB

C. Barbieri, 7 ☎61 512 68 07 www.studio54madrid.com

You're going to see a lot of six packs at Studio 54, and we're not talking beer. With pulsing Spanish pop and sculpted bartenders wearing nothing but bowties, Studio 54 tends to attract a crowd of predominantly gay *madrileños* and American and European tourists. If you haven't spent a night dancing to ridiculous Spanish pop music yet, this is the place to do it, with crystal chandeliers and disco balls hanging above a violet dance floor, surrounded by mirrors and etched silhouettes of curvy women.

[M]Chueca. Walk straight south down C. Barbieri toward Gran Vía. The discoteca is on the right. $ Cocktails €8. After 1am, cover €10. ⏰ Open Th-Sa 11:30pm-3:30am.

EL51 BAR

C. de Hortaleza, 51 ☎91 521 25 64

EL51 is a posh single-room cocktail lounge with white leather chairs, crystal chandeliers, and mirrors lit with violet bulbs. Just steps from the center of Chueca's nightlife, they tend to pack people in during prime hours (midnight-2am), but they also attract a steady crowd with a two-for-one happy hour that includes mojitos, caipirinhas, martinis, and cosmopolitans. Spanish pop plays in the background, but, unlike other bars, they keep the volume low enough that you can still hold a conversation (if you're still sober enough, that is).

[M]Chueca. Make a right on C. Augusto Figueroa, then a right onto C. de Hortaleza. $ Cocktails €8-10. ⏰ Open daily 6pm-3am. Happy hour F-Sa 6-11pm, Su 6pm-3am.

LONG PLAY CLUB

Pl. de Vázquez de Mella, 2 ☎91 532 20 66 www.discotecalongplay.net

Clubs in Chueca come and go, but Long Play has been around to see it all. Once a venue of the early 1970s *madrileño* counterculture, today Long Play attracts a crowd of gay *madrileños*, European tourists, and American study-abroaders.

Things tend to start late at Long Play with the crowds descending en masse around 3am. The downstairs DJ plays a variety of international pop, and things get pretty sweaty on the upstairs dance floor, which plays strictly European house.

✦ Ⓜ️Gran Vía. Head north up C. de Hortaleza, make a right onto C. de las Infantas, and a left to Pl. de Vázquez de Mella. Ⓢ Cover €10 after 1:30am Th-F (includes 1 drink), all night Sa. Drinks €8. Ⓒ Open daily midnight-7am.

MALASAÑA

🏮 LA VÍA LÁCTEA
BAR

C. Velarde, 18   ☎91 446 75 81 www.lavialactea.net

This is a Spanish temple dedicated to rock, grunge, and everything '70s counterculture. La Vía Láctea was founded in the early years of Movida Madrileña, the youth-propelled revolution of art, music, fashion, and literature. Today it's more a relic of this past than a continuing force of change, with pop music memorabilia covering the walls from floor to ceiling, and a fine perfume of stale beer lingering in the air. The sentimentality of La Vía Láctea is unashamed and that seems to draw crowds of loyal *madrileños* and international tourists night after night.

✦ Ⓜ️Tribunal. Walk north up C. Fuencarral and make a left onto C. Velarde. Ⓢ Cover €10 after 1am; includes 1 drink. Beer €3-5. Cocktails €5-7. Ⓒ Open daily 7:30pm-3:30am.

CLUB NASTI
CLUB

C. de San Vicente Ferrer, 33   ☎91 521 76 05 www.nasti.es

Come to Club Nasti on Saturday nights for a hipster heaven of synth pop, electro beats, and punk jams. For a lighter touch, try Friday nights, when house DJs spin remixes of rock groups like The Strokes and The Arctic Monkeys. Now in its 12th year, Nasti is a neighborhood institution that remains hugely popular among locals. The small dance floor gets packed as the night progresses, and you might end up shimmying out of your sweaty plaid shirt to dance in your nevernudes. Don't say we didn't warn you: there's no PBR.

✦ Ⓜ️Tribunal. Walk south down C. de Fuencarral and make a right onto C. de San Vicente Ferrer. Ⓢ After 2am, cover €10; includes 1 drink. Beer €4-5. Cocktails €8-9. Ⓒ Open Th 2-5am, F 1-6am, Sa 2-6am.

BARCO
CLUB

C. del Barco, 34   ☎91 521 24 47 www.barcobar.com

With a full program of nightly concerts, late-night DJ sessions, and weekly jam sessions, this small venue covers plenty of musical terrain. While many bars and clubs in the area try to attract international bands, BarCo has made its name as a stalwart venue for local acts, with most bands drawing heavily on funk, soul, rock, and jazz. While the concert schedule is continually changing, the nightly DJ sets are given to a handful of veteran European DJs who have been spinning in Madrid for years. For those more interested in their live music events, the Sunday night jam session brings in some of the city's best contemporary jazz musicians. The cover charge changes with the act, so check online for updates.

✦ Ⓜ️Tribunal. Head south on C. de Fuencarral 3 blocks. Take a right onto C. Corredera Baja de San Pablo, walk 2 blocks, and take a left (south) onto C. del Barco. The bar is on the right. Ⓢ Cover €5-10. Beer €4. Cocktails €7. F-Sa €1 drink surcharge. Cash only. Ⓒ Open M-Th 10pm-5:30am, F-Sa 10pm-6am, Su 10pm-5:30am.

CAFÉ-BOTILLERÍA MANUELA
CAFE, BAR

C. de San Vicente Ferrer, 29   ☎91 531 70 37

Dark wood shelves filled with liquor, a white marble bar, and gilded columns make Café-Botillería feel like a five-star hotel lobby in miniature. The list of cocktails is standard for the late-night *madrileño* cafe, and so are the prices. Most people choose to imbibe rather than caffeinate, and many take advantage of the cafe's selection of board games, and the small tables and red-cushioned booths are nearly always full.

⚑ Ⓜ*Tribunal. Walk south down C. de Fuencarral and make a right onto C. de San Vicente Ferrer.* Ⓢ *Wine €2.50-3.50. Beer €1.50-3.50. Cocktails €8-12.* 🕐 *Open daily June-Aug 6pm-2am; Sept-May 4pm-2am.*

CAFÉ COMERCIAL
Glorieta de Bilbao, 7

CAFE, BAR
☎91 521 56 55

Founded in 1887, this remains a Malasaña institution. Once a meeting point for the anti-Franco Republican army during the Spanish Civil War, today Café Comercial remains a place for informal gatherings of tourists and locals of all ages. The downstairs dining room, with dark wood pillars, marble tables, and mirrored walls, makes the setting a bit less intimate than smaller tapas bars or *cervecerías* in the area, but that doesn't keep it from being packed. More than anything, it is convenience that keeps people coming to Café Comercial: it's a great place to park for a few cheap drinks before pub crawling through the more contemporary bars. There is a surcharge for table service (€0.25-1 per item), but it's small enough that most people don't seem to care.

⚑ Ⓜ*Bilbao.* Ⓢ *Beer €1-3. Wine €2-3. Cocktails €5-7. Internet access €1 per hr. Drinks and tapas €3-7.* 🕐 *Open M-W 7:30am-midnight, Th 7:30am-1am, F 7:30am-2am, Sa 8:30am-2am, Su 9am-midnight.*

ARGÜELLES AND MONCLOA

🏛 TEMPO CLUB
C. Duque de Osuna, 8

MUSIC
☎91 547 75 18 www.tempoclub.net

International or local, jazz or soul, Tempo Club does not discriminate so long as a rhythm section and horns are involved. Tempo is one of the premier spots in Madrid to catch great live funk, soul, rock, and hip hop, with all of their acts accompanied by a full live band. Even when the DJ takes over for the late night set, the rhythm section often sticks around. The venue is divided between a street-level cafe and cocktail area and the downstairs concert hall. This is a great alternative to large clubs and *discotecas* where lines are rampant and cover charges are onerous.

⚑ Ⓜ*Ventura Rodríguez. From C. Princesa follow C. del Duque de Liria south to the intersection with C. Duque de Osuna. Turn left onto C. Duque.* ℹ *Live performances Th-Sa.* 🕐 *No cover. Cocktails €5-8. Cash only.* Ⓢ *Open daily 6pm-late.*

CAFE LA PALMA
C. de la Palma, 62

MUSIC
☎91 522 50 31 www.cafelapalma.com

Cafe la Palma is in many ways a typical Malasaña rock club even though it is just outside of the *barrio*. Like many clubs in the area, La Palma strives for a lot—a cafe that people can enjoy during the day, a cocktail lounge at night, a concert venue late at night, and a full club with a live DJ set in the early morning. The musical acts La Palma attracts are every bit as eclectic as the venue itself. While they try to accomplish a lot within the three small rooms of the cafe, they don't spread themselves too thin. There is a drink minimum (€6) for some live sets, but this is a great alternative to forking over a fat cover charge.

⚑ Ⓜ*Pl. de España, follow C. de Los Reyes northeast 2 blocks, take a left onto C. Amaniel, and walk 2 blocks to C. de La Palma.* Ⓢ *Drink minimum for some events €6; check website for more info. Cocktails €6. Cash only.* 🕐 *Open M-Th 4pm-3am, F-Su 4pm-4am.*

ORANGE CAFE
C. Serrano Jover, 5

BAR, CLUB
☎91 542 28 17 www.soyorangecafe.com

Orange Cafe is a venue for local rock acts in the evening and a packed dance club later at night. If you are more interested in finding a local *madrileño* venue, this club might not be for you, as it normally fills with tourists and travelers looking for American pop music. Women should take advantage of free drinks and free entry Wednesday nights between 11:30pm and 12:30am. Check the website for a list of concerts and cover charges.

⚡ Ⓜ*Argüelles*. Ⓢ *Cover €10-15, depending on night*. 🕐 *Open F-Sa 11:30pm-6am.*

EL CHAPANDAZ   BAR
C. de Fernando, 77   ☎91 549 29 68 www.chapandaz.com

We'll be totally up front and say that this place is ridiculous. Not only is it designed to look like a 🔲**cave**, but it is a fully functional, lactating cave with stalactites hanging from the ceiling that periodically drip milk into glass pitchers. The house drink Leche de Pantera (panther's milk) is a combination of rum, cinnamon, and that special milk that drips from the ceiling. If you are suspicious (for perfectly good reasons), it also offers standard fare and a full menu of sweet, fruity, and colorful drinks. The bar is generally quiet until 11pm but fills up with a mostly international study-abroad crowd who stop in for the novelty before they head out clubbing.

⚡ *From* Ⓜ*Moncloa, get to the intersection of C. de Fernando and C. de la Princesa and walk east down C. de Fernando.* 𝒊 *International night Tu.* Ⓢ *Drinks €10.* 🕐 *Open daily 10pm-3am.*

arts and culture

With some of the best art museums, public festivals, and performing arts groups in the world, Madrid's arts and culture scene is thriving. From street performers in the Parque del Buen Retiro to Broadway musicals, you can find anything you're looking for in this metropolis.

CORRIDAS DE TOROS *Bullfights*

Whether you view it as animal cruelty or national sport, the spectacle of *la corrida* (bullfighting) is a cherished Spanish tradition. Although it has its origins in earlier Roman and Moorish practices, today bullfighting is considered Spain's sport, and some of the top *toreros* (bullfighters) are national celebrities. The sport has been subject to continuing protest in recent years by animal rights activists, and it's common to see demonstrations outside of stadiums, but many tourists come to observe the tradition nonetheless.

If you choose to go, it is important to know a little bit about the rituals of the sport. The bullfight has three stages. First, the *picadores*, lancers on horseback, pierce the bull's neck muscles. Then, *banderilleros* thrust colorfully decorated darts called *banderillas* into the bull's back to injure and fatigue it. Finally, the *matador* kills his large opposition with a sword between the bull's shoulder blades, killing it instantly. Animal rights activists call the rituals savage and cruel, but aficionados call it an art that requires quick thinking and skill.

The best place to see bullfighting in Madrid is at the country's biggest arena, **Plaza de Toros de las Ventas,** where you can buy tickets in *sol* (sun) or *sombra* (shade) sections. Get your tickets at the arena the Friday or Saturday before the bullfight, which takes place Sundays and holidays. (C. de Alcalá, 237 ☎913 56 22 00 www.las-ventas.com ⚡ Ⓜ Ventas. 🕐 Ticket office open 10am-2pm and 5-8pm.) You'll pay more to sit out of the sun, but either way you'll have a good view of the feverish crowds who cheer on the matador and wave white handkerchiefs after a particularly good fight. Rent a seat cushion at the stadium or bring your own for the stone seats. Exceptional performances by matadors are rewarded with prizes: one ear, two ears, or two ears and a tail. During the **Fiesta de San Isidro** in May, fights are held almost every day, and the top bullfighters come face to face with the fiercest bulls. People across Spain are bitterly divided about the future of the sport, so visitors should approach the topic with sensitivity.

MUSIC

By 10pm, bars across Madrid are filled with live music. For visitors unfamiliar with local bands and venues, this can seem daunting and difficult to navigate. The best way to tame this beast is to check out the citywide program *Madrid En Vivo* (www.madridenvivo.es; paper copy available at most bars). The calendar is organized by neighborhood, venue, and musical style. Most events require a cover of €5-10, which usually includes a drink.

EL CÍRCULO DE BELLAS ARTES DE MADRID   EL CENTRO
C. de Alcalá, 42   ☎91 360 54 00 www.circulobellasartes.com

El Círculo de Bellas Artes is a factory of culture. This Art Deco tower on the periphery of the city center provides first-rate facilities to support the visual and performing arts and is accessible to the general public. Located on the pulsing C. de Alcalá, this hub of innovation fiercely rejects the idea that art and culture are made in kitschy shops on winding, romantic European roads. The seven floors provide facilities for temporary visual arts exhibits, performing arts exhibitions, and film screenings. The building both celebrates Spain's rich cultural traditions and provides institutional support for emerging artists. Make sure to leave enough time to visit the rooftop terrace, which provides stunning panoramic views of the city. Also check out the streetside cafe—it's one of Madrid's finest. (See **Food**). This is where serious art happens in Madrid, and it's not to be missed.

⚲ Ⓜ*Sevilla. Walk 1 block northwest to the intersection of C. Gran Vía.* *i* *Check the website for ticket prices and event schedules. Free Wi-Fi.* Ⓢ *Rooftop access €2.* ⏰ *Open M 11am-2pm, Tu-Sa 11am-2pm and 5-8pm, Su 11am-2pm. Cafe open M-Th 9am-midnight, F-Sa 9am-3am.*

CAFÉ CENTRAL   LAS HUERTAS
Pl. del Ángel 10   ☎91 369 32 26 www.cafecentralmadrid.com

Since 1982, Café Central has been a premier venue for live jazz in Madrid. While plenty of cafes and bars of a similar breed have cropped up since then, Café Central continues to attract the best groups in the city. With its signature red façade along Pl. del Ángel and cool Art Deco interior, it stands out from the pack. Nightly concerts last from 10pm until midnight and feature primarily instrumental groups and the occasional vocalist.

⚲ Ⓜ*Antón Martín. From the Metro, take C. de León 1 block north to C. de las Huertas, follow for 3 blocks until it ends at Pl. del Ángel. The cafe is on the left.* Ⓢ *Cover €8-12.* ⏰ *Open M-Th 1:30pm-2:30am, F-Sa 1:30pm-3:30am, Su 1:30pm-2:30am.*

CLAMORES   MALASAÑA
C. de Alburquerque, 14   ☎91 445 79 38 www.salaclamores.com

Located just north of Malasaña, Clamores attracts a following of *madrileños* committed to the city's live music scene. While Clamores calls itself a jazz venue, it pushes the envelope with a program of pop, soul, funk, rock, and everything in between. Unlike some of the smaller jazz bars and cafes around Madrid, Clamores has a proper stage and better acoustics, which allows for more dynamic programming across musical genres.

⚲ Ⓜ*Bilbao. Walk north up C. de Fuencarral, and make a right on C. de Alburquerque.* Ⓢ *Cover €5-12. Beer €3-5. Cocktails €6-8.* ⏰ *Most shows 9, 9:30, or 10:30pm. Check the schedule online.*

CAFÉ JAZZ POPULART   LAS HUERTAS
C. de las Huertas, 22   ☎91 429 84 07 www.populart.es

Café Jazz Populart has a mixed program of American jazz, blues, and country for its nightly sets. While many jazz clubs in Madrid stick to traditional instrumental trios, quartets, and quintets, Café Populart features more vocalists and rowdier groups that get people out of their seats. The small room styled like an old-school *madrileño* cafe with musicians cramped onto a tiny stage creates the setting for one of the city's most enjoyable live music venues.

✦ ⓂAntón Martín. Walk north up C. de León and make a left onto C. de las Huertas. Ⓢ Cover €5; includes 1 drink. 🕐 Open M-Th 6pm-2:30am, F-Sa 6pm-3:30am, Su 6pm-2:30am. Sets daily 10:15 and 11:30pm.

HONKY TONK   SALAMANCA
C. de Covarrubias, 24   ☎91 445 68 86 www.clubhonky.com

Honky Tonk is where nostalgic *madrileños* come to hear cover bands play The Rolling Stones, The Beatles, and other classic '60s rock and roll. While Honky Tonk is open throughout the week and has live sets most nights, given its location in the quieter neighborhood of Chamberi (near Salamanca), things can be pretty quiet early in the evening. Honky Tonk is best on weekends, especially when the cover bands take the stage at 12:30am.

✦ ⓂAlonso Martínez. Go north up C. de Santa Engracia. Make a left onto C. de Nicasio Gallego and a right on C. de Covarrubias. Ⓢ Cover €10; includes 1 drink. Beer €3-5. Cocktails €9. 🕐 Open M-Th 9:30pm-5am, F-Sa 9:30pm-5:30am. Concerts M-Sa 12:30am.

FLAMENCO

Flamenco is a gypsy art dating back to 18th-century Andalucía that has become a 21st-century business in Madrid. Many flamenco clubs offer overpriced dinners combined with overdone music and dance spectaculars geared toward tourists. There are some clubs in Madrid that offer more traditional and soulful flamenco. You'll still pay a decent amount to see it, but it's a great way to learn about the art form.

🦪 CASA PATAS   LAS HUERTAS
C. de los Cañizares, 10   ☎91 369 04 96 www.casapatas.com

While Casa Patas certainly caters to tourists, it remains one of Madrid's best venues for traditional flamenco. Though it offers dinner, the real attraction is the flamenco stage in back, where some of Madrid's finest dancers perform for packed tourist audiences. Tickets aren't cheap, but they're worth every penny. Shows sell out night after night, particularly in the summer months. The restaurant and tapas bar up front serve the usual suspects: platters of *jamón y queso* (€19), fried squid (€13), and *albondigas de la abuela* (grandma's meatballs; €3). Who could turn down grandma's meatballs?

✦ ⓂAntón Martín. From the Metro, walk up C. de Atocha and turn left onto C. del Olivar. Casa Patas is on the right. Ⓢ Tickets €32; includes 1 drink. Entrees €10-25. 🕐 Open M-Th 1-4pm and 8pm-midnight, F-Sa 7:30pm-2am. Flamenco M-Th 8:30pm, F-Sa 9pm and midnight.

CARDAMOMO   LAS HUERTAS
C. de Echegaray, 15   ☎91 369 07 57 www.cardamomo.es

Cardamomo offers traditional flamenco that has a raw improvisational quality to it. The focus is more on rhythm and movement and less on the kitschy costumes that are usually synonymous with flamenco. You can expect to hear syncopated guitars and soulful old men crooning flamenco verse, with swift choreography. The nightly sets are short but intense (50min.) and a good way of seeing flamenco without dedicating an entire evening to it.

✦ ⓂSol. Walk east toward Pl. de las Cortes and make a right on C. de Echegaray. Ⓢ Tickets €25; includes 1 drink. Some accommodations offer discounts. 🕐 Shows daily 10:30pm.

THEATER

The obvious consideration for those interested in seeing live theater in Madrid is the language barrier. Madrid has a thriving theater scene, but much of it is inaccessible to those who don't speak Spanish. Madrid does host a number of international musicals like *Mamma Mia!*, which are written in the universal language of glee. Many theaters also host concerts, dance productions, and flamenco spectacles that don't require any language skills.

◼ TEATRO COLISEUM
GRAN VÍA

C. Gran Vía, 78 ☎91 542 30 35

Since C. Gran Vía is often referred to as the Broadway of Madrid, it makes sense that the sprawling Teatro Coliseum is located there. One of the largest theaters in the city, Teatro Coliseum has hosted some of Broadway's biggest international hits, like *Beauty and the Beast, Chicago, El Musical,* and *Mamma Mia!* Teatro Coliseum also hosts concerts featuring Spanish and international pop musicians.

⌖ Ⓜ*Pl. de España. From the plaza walk east down C. Gran Vía. The theater is on the left.* ⓘ *Purchase tickets online at www.arteria.com or at the box office.* Ⓢ *Tickets €10-40.* ⌚ *Box office open M-Th noon-8:30pm, F-Sa noon-10pm, Su noon-7pm. Check online for showtimes.*

TEATRO ESPAÑOL
LAS HUERTAS

C. del Príncipe, 25 ☎91 360 14 84

Funded by Madrid's municipal government, the Teatro Español features a range of classic Spanish plays and performances. This is Madrid's oldest stage; it dates back to a 16th-century open-air theater. Though the building has since been reconstructed many times, it has consistently played a critical role in the development of dramatic literature in Spain. The present building, which dates to the mid-1800s, has premiered works by Spain's most notable writers, including Benito Galdós and Antonio Vallejo, and played a critical role in the development of the literary culture of Las Huertas.

⌖ Ⓜ*Antón Martín. Walk uphill on C. de Atocha. Make a right at the 1st light and head north until you see Pl. Santa Ana. The theater is on the east side of the plaza.* ⓘ *Purchase tickets online at www. telentrada.com, by telephone, or at the box office.* Ⓢ *Tickets €3-20; ½-price on W.* ⌚ *Box office open Tu-Su 11:30am-1:30pm and 5pm-curtain.*

TEATRO HÄAGEN-DAZS CALDERÓN
LAS HUERTAS

C. de Atocha, 18 ☎90 200 66 17 www.teatrohaagen-dazs.es

Named for its recent takeover by Häagen-Dazs, this theater has a seating capacity of 2,000 and features musical, dance, and theater performances. Teatro Häagen-Dazs focuses on local Spanish musicals.

⌖ Ⓜ*Tirso de Molina. From the Metro, walk north up C. del Doctor Cortezo.* ⓘ *Purchase tickets online at www.arteriaentradas.com, by telephone, or at the box office.* Ⓢ *Tickets €25-60.* ⌚ *Shows begin most evenings at 8pm. Check online for up-to-date box office hours and showtimes.*

TEATRO BELLAS ARTES
EL CENTRO

C. del Marqués de Casa Riera, 2 ☎91 532 44 37 www.teatrobellasartes.es

Founded in 1961 by Jose Tamayo, the former director of the Teatro Español, this avant-garde theater was originally created to expose audiences to America's great playwrights of the 1950s, such as Arthur Miller and Tennessee Williams. Today Teatro Bellas Artes has a more diverse program with a mix of original Spanish productions and adaptations and translations of famous international works.

⌖ Ⓜ*Banco de España. Walk west down C. de Alcalá and make a left onto C. del Marqués de Casa Riera.* Ⓢ *Tickets €16-25.* ⌚ *Box office open Tu-Su 11:30am-1:30pm and 5pm-curtain.*

FÚTBOL *Soccer*

You might see churches in every city in Spain, but the national religion is **fútbol.** Matches are a beloved spectacle everywhere in Spain, but particularly in Madrid, home to **Real Madrid,** one of the world's best soccer clubs. On game days, from the end of August through the end of May, locals line the streets and pack bars to watch the match. Celebrations after games are common in public plazas and squares, probably helped by the fact that most matches fall on Saturdays. For Real Madrid, the victory party always takes place in **Plaza Cibeles.** *Fútbol* doesn't just happen on the field in Spain—it takes over city life, particularly on big game days. The other two major teams in Madrid are **Atlético** and **Getafe.**

Seeing a game live with 80,000 other fans can be an incredible experience, but often difficult logistically. Tickets are expensive and hard to come by. All teams sell a number of tickets through their stadium box offices and release a limited number online through their club website. If you are intent on going to a game, research ticket availability at least two weeks in advance. Tickets are also available from vendors outside the stadium, but these are often counterfeit or marked up well above face value. Tickets for Atlético and Getafe tend to be cheaper and more easily available than tickets for Real Madrid. Regardless of whether you make it to the stadium or not, it's at least worth going to a local tapas bar to watch.

👍 **ESTADIO SANTIAGO BERNABÉU** — NORTH OF CITY CENTER

Av. Cochina Espina, 1 ☎91 464 22 34 www.santiagobernabeu.com, www.realmadrid.com

Site of the 2010 European Final Cup, Estadio Santiago Bernabéu is also home to Real Madrid, named the greatest club of the 20th century by FIFA. Come watch a match and feel the tumultuous energy of the crowd as it cheers on its beloved home team. Tours of the stadium are also available and take you to its most hallowed grounds: from the trophy room to the visitors' dressing room to the pitch itself. Tickets to European club soccer games are notoriously very difficult to come by, and Real Madrid is no exception. Most tickets go to season ticket holders, and a limited number of tickets are released at the central stadium box office at Gate 40 located next to Tower A. Advance tickets can also be purchased at www.servicaixa.com, and remaining tickets are released on the club website at 11am the Monday before each game.

➜ ⓂSantiago Bernabéu. $ Tickets €30-300. Tours €16, under 14 €10. ⏰ Season runs from the beginning of Sept through the end of May. Check online for game schedules and tour times.

ESTADIO VICENTE CALDERÓN — SOUTH OF CITY CENTER

Paseo de la Virgen del Puerto, 67 ☎91 364 22 34 www.clubatleticodemadrid.com

Estadio Vicente Calderón is home to the Atlético *fútbol* club (red and white stripes). With a storied past that includes European Cups and international recognition, this Madrid-based club participates in the esteemed Primera División of La Liga. While they've had some big wins in the past, they are the perennial underdogs in the city rivalry with Real Madrid. This stadium may not be the city's biggest stage for football, but it's a good place to take part in the *madrileño* tradition. Tickets can be purchased at www.servicaixa.com or on the club website.

➜ ⓂPirámides. From the Metro, head west 1 block to C. de Toledo, follow 1 block south to Paseo de los Melancólicos. ⏰ Check the website for schedule.

COLISEUM ALFONSO PÉREZ — SOUTH OF CITY CENTER

Av. Teresa de Calcuta ☎91 695 97 71 www.getafecf.com

Coliseum Alfonso Pérez is home to the Getafe *fútbol* club. The club was founded in 1946 and merged with another local club in 1983. Despite offering spectators some great soccer, this club pales in comparison to local rivals. Tickets can be purchased in person at the stadium box office or online from www.entrada.com.

➜ ⓂVillaverde Alto. Stop is 1hr. from Puerta del Sol on the number 3 metro. From the Metro, walk 1 block east to Av. Real de Pinto. Take Av. Real de Pinto 4 blocks through the highway underpass and turn left on Av. Teresa de Calcuta. $ Tickets €40-80. ⏰ Check the website for schedule.

FESTIVALS

THREE KINGS PROCESSION   EL CENTRO
The one day Spaniards don't party too hard is Christmas. So they instead celebrate the Epiphany, the day when the three kings arrived in Bethlehem to view baby Jesus. During the Three Kings Procession, three Santa-like men parade through the center of the city with 30 carriages filled with 7000kg of sweets, making a pathway from the Parque del Buen Retiro to Pl. Mayor via Puerta del Sol. The kings and their helpers (not elves) shower sweets on the huge crowd in the streets, and local establishments host events for children.

✚ ⓂSol. ⌚ Jan 5 6:30pm.

MADRID CARNAVAL   CITY CENTER
http://carnaval.esmadrid.com/

Madrid celebrates the week before Lent with a citywide festival of theater, dance, and music, culminating in a grand parade on Saturday evening. The parade starts in the Parque del Buen Retiro and travels to Pl. Cibeles before ending at Pl. Colón. There's also a tradition called "The Burial of the Sardine," in which participants decked out in black cloaks and hats walk through the streets with a coffin containing an effigy of a dead sardine. Don't understand? Neither do we, but it's seriously awesome. You can download a full program of events at the festival website.

⌚ Feb 7-13, 2013. Grand Parade Sa 7pm.

MADRID EN DANZA   CITY CENTER
www.madrid.org/madridendanza

From mid-March to late April, Madrid plays host to a flurry of dance performances from around the world. From ballet to modern, there's something for everyone at this festival that celebrates movement, not Tony Danza.

ℹ Consult the festival website for a performance schedule. Ⓢ Tickets €5-20. Most tickets sold online at www.entrada.com. ⌚ Mar-Apr.

DOS DE MAYO   MALASAÑA
On May 2, 1808, the people of Madrid rose up against Joseph Bonaparte, Napoleon's brother, to fight for freedom from French rule. Among the mobs was Manuela Malasaña, a 17-year-old seamstress who died a brutal death defending Spain. Today she and the many other victims of the attacks are honored in Malasaña's biggest party. The center of the festivities is the Pl. Dos de Mayo, a major site of the uprisings. The gathering of young people in the plaza is one of the most infamous festival events of the calendar year, and the party carries on well into the night in the area's bars, cafes, restaurants, and clubs.

✚ ⓂTribunal. From the Metro, take C. de la Palma 2 blocks west to C. de San Andrés. Turn right and head north 1 block. ⌚ May 2.

FIESTAS DE SAN ISIDRO   CITYWIDE
www.esmadrid.com/sanisidro

This week-long festival takes over the city's streets and plazas to celebrate Madrid's patron saint, Isidore the Laborer. The primary stage is Pl. Mayor, where street performers, parades, and vendors selling *barquillos* (ice cream cones) take over. There are dance, theater, and music performances throughout the city, and fireworks along the banks of the Mazanares near San Isidro's home. The festivities culminate with a large procession across the Mazanares and a mass at the Basilica de San Isidro on May 15. While the festival is filled with pomp and circumstance, many *madrileños* celebrate more informally with picnics in the Parque del Buen Retiro and parties at bars, cafes, and clubs around the city. For bullfighting enthusiasts, this festival marks the beginning of a month of nightly bullfights at Plaza de Toros de las Ventas, which features the world's best fighters and most vicious bulls. Tickets for these bullfights are difficult to get, but check the stadium website www.las-ventas.com for schedules and ticket availability.

[M]Sol. i Consult the festival website for details on concerts and performances around the city. ⏰ May 8-15.

BOLLYMADRID LAVAPIÉS

www.bollymadrid.com

During the first week of June, Lavapiés features Bollywood dance performances, movies, and amazingly cheap Indian food. Get that henna facial tattoo you always wanted, grab a few samosas, and check out the mighty Sharukh Kahn in one of the open-air film screenings. Check online for an updated schedule of performances.

[M]Lavapiés. $ Performances free. Food €1-5. ⏰ 1st week of June.

DÍA DE LA MÚSICA SOUTH OF CITY CENTER

Paseo de la Chopera, 14 ☎91 517 95 56 www.diadelamusica.com

What was once the city's largest slaughterhouse is now home to one of Madrid's biggest music festivals. Within a few years, Matadero Madrid, with help from the city government, has been converted from an industrial wasteland into a vast multipurpose community art center with art installations, exhibition halls, and bandshells. This music festival brings in big name international artists like Janelle Monae and Lykke Li. Día de la Música is one of Matadero Madrid's biggest annual events, with great music and the latest in contemporary art and design.

[M]Legazpi. From the Metro station, walk 1 block northwest up Paseo de la Chopera. Matadero is on the left. i Tickets can be purchased online at www.entradas.com or in person. $ €15-24. ⏰ Mid-June. Concerts M-Tu 8pm-1am, Sa-Su 11am-1am.

ORGULLO GAY CHUECA

www.orgullogay.org

During Orgullo Gay, one of the biggest Pride parades in Europe, Madrid explodes with GLBT celebrations, parades, parties, and more. Chueca, Madrid's gay district, is packed, particularly on the last Saturday of the festival when the parade takes over the neighborhood.

[M]Chueca. ⏰ Last week of June.

PHOTOESPAÑA EL CENTRO

☎91 298 55 23 www.phe.es/festival

PhotoEspaña is a public photography exhibition that takes over the city center in early summer. From exhibits in the Reina Sofía to sidewalk installations, PhotoEspaña seeks to showcase the latest developments in still photography and video art. Each year the festival exhibits work of a common theme by dozens of artists from around the world. Plans of the exhibition are available at various public info points or online.

i Public info points at Real Jardín Botánico, C. de Alcalá, 31; Pl. de Murillo, 2; and Teatro Fernán Gómez Centro de Arte, Pl. de Colón, 4. $ Free. Exhibits in ticketed museums subject to normal admission fees. ⏰ June-July.

FIESTAS DE LA LATINA AND LAVAPIÉS LA LATINA AND LAVAPIÉS

This triumvirate of festivals in La Latina and Lavapiés celebrates the neighborhoods' respective patron saints. These days are typically a hot sweaty mess of tradition, with *madrileños* dressed in unseasonably warm 19th-century clothing and drinking sangria to cool off. The first festival takes place around August 7th, and celebrates San Cayetano in and around Pl. de Cascorro. The second festival (Aug 10), celebrates San Lorenzo near Pl. de Lavapiés. The final festival day (Aug 15) features a parade in which the city firemen carry an image of the Virgin of Paloma between the two neighborhoods as locals sing her praises.

[M]Lavapiés or [M]La Latina. ⏰ 2nd week of Aug.

To ring in the new year, thousands of *madrileños* gather at the city's version of Times Square, Puerta del Sol, to watch the ball drop from the clock tower. Instead of counting down, the clock chimes 12 times to represent the 12 upcoming months of the year, ending with a fireworks display. According to tradition, you're supposed to eat a grape at every toll and drink at midnight for good fortune.

✢ Ⓜ*Sol.* 🕐 *Dec 31.*

shopping

While areas like Puerta del Sol, Pl. Mayor, and Gran Vía are filled with name-brand chains, there are plenty of local boutiques, marketplaces, and flea markets that sell products unique to Madrid. **El Rastro** is undoubtedly the biggest shopping event in Madrid. This flea market, which takes place on Sundays in La Latina and Lavapiés, was once where thieves went to pawn goods. Today it offers antiques, clothes, books, and more. In the neighborhoods of Chueca and Malasaña you'll find the city's best upscale boutiques, many of which are prohibitively expensive for the budget traveler but always worth it for the window shopping. Salamanca is home to high-end European designers like **Gucci** and **Prada.** There, socks cost as much as a suit, and a suit costs more than a single family home.

Generally speaking, buying clothes in Europe isn't easy, it's often expensive, and it's not very feasible for the budget traveler. If you're shopping more out of necessity than impulse, department stores like **H &M** and **El Corte Inglés** offer the cheapest clothes on the continent. There are also a number of good Spanish chain stores like **Zara** that offer quality products at reasonable prices.

RETAIL STORES

ABC SERRANO   SALAMANCA

C. de Serrano, 61   ☎91 577 50 31 www.abcserrano.com

Located in the refurbished publishing headquarters of the ABC Newspaper, this complex houses upscale chains that sell everything from jewelry and cosmetics to art, housewares, and electronics. The location in the middle of Salamanca's high-end shopping district tends to attract *madrileños* from nearby. There's a rooftop terrace as well as a few cafes and dining options for when you need a quick break. While ABC Serrano might not be the most glamorous way to spend an afternoon in Madrid, it does conveniently bring all your errand destinations together under one roof.

✢ Ⓜ*Rubén Darío. From the Metro, walk 2 blocks east down C. de Juan Bravo (crossing C. de Castelló) and turn right onto C. de Serrano. The complex is on the left.* 🕐 *Open M-Sa 10am-9pm, Su noon-8pm.*

EL CORTE INGLÉS   EL CENTRO

C. de Preciados, 3   ☎91 379 80 00 www.elcorteingles.es

Many other locations around the city

Steps away from Puerta del Sol, El Corte Inglés is the most convenient department store in the city. Located in multiple buildings around the central plaza, El Corte Inglés sells clothing, cosmetics, shoes, books, and electronics. Some staff members speak English.

✢ Ⓜ*Sol. C. de Preciados is to the left of the fountain as you face north.* 🕐 *Open M-Sa 10am-10pm.*

ZARA   SALAMANCA

C. de la Princesa, 45   ☎91 541 09 02 www.zara.es

Other major locations: C. de la Princesa, 58 C. de las Infantas, 5 C. de Preciados, 18.

There is at least one Zara in every major shopping district in Madrid. Much like Banana Republic in the United States, Zara offers professional attire as well as

sportswear at reasonable prices. Men's and women's pants cost anywhere from €20 to €60, suits can be purchased for as little as €90, and women's dresses cost €20-60. Zara is a cheaper yet reliable alternative to boutique shopping.
 # [M]Argüelles. ⏰ Open M-Sa 10am-8:30pm.

EL RASTRO

El Rastro is the biggest thing in Madrid on Sundays. This open-air flea market takes over La Latina, beginning at **Plaza de Cascorro** off C. de Toledo and ending at the bottom of **Calle Ribera de Curtidores,** with rows of stalls set in the middle of the road between the city's infamous streetside pawnshops. Modern art, American comics, and Art Deco furniture can all be found throughout the market. Bargains are possible if you keep your eyes peeled and haggle. While El Rastro is hugely popular with tourists, it's still typical for local families to head to the market together and go out to brunch afterward in La Latina or Lavapiés (see **Food**). El Rastro starts at 9am sharp and ends at 3pm, with many of the better shops closing earlier. Large crowds tend to attract pickpockets, so use common sense and be aware of your surroundings.

BOUTIQUES

YUBE MADRID CHUECA

C. de Fernando VI, 23 ☎91 319 76 73 www.yubemadrid.com

European boutique shopping is unfortunately expensive and Yube is no exception. The carefully curated store in the middle of Chueca sells beautiful garments from international and local designers that are financial eons beyond reach for budget travelers. Menswear from designers like Paul Smith and women's blouses and dresses from French designer ba&sh are the very pinnacle of European style. While justifying the purchase might be difficult, this is a great place to check out the latest European trends.

 # [M]Alonso Martínez. From the Metro, take Pl. de Santa Bárbara south 2 blocks to C. de Mejía Lequerica. Follow C. de Mejía Lequerica 2 blocks southeast until it becomes C. de Fernando VI. i Check the website for info on seasonal sales. $ Men's shirts €100-200. Women's dresses €100-300. ⏰ Open M-Sa 9am-6pm.

POÈTE SALAMANCA

C. de Castelló, 32 ☎91 577 60 62 www.tiendapoete.com

Poète is one of Spain's finest boutique chains specializing in women's apparel. Originally started in Madrid, Poète has now expanded to 14 locations across the country. Poète models itself on the traditional French boutique, offering simple-patterned dresses and blouses. Poète also has more reasonable prices than other *madrileño* boutiques.

 # [M]Velázquez. Head east on C. de Goya 1 block and make a left onto C. de Castelló. $ Dresses and blouses €80-120. Shoes €100. Accessories €10-20.

MINI ARGÜELLES

C. del Limón, 24 ☎91 548 08 35 www.gruposportivo.com

Mini offers a collection of high-end menswear primarily from American upscale brands like Band of Outsiders, Universal Works, and Levi's Vintage, in addition to British brands like Fred Perry and Oliver Spencer. Mini's small boutique shop on C. del Limón is complemented by two sibling shops owned by Group Sportivo: **Duke,** which specializes in high-end shoes, and **Sportivo,** which focuses on American vintage. You can expect fairly standard European boutique prices at all three stores, with jeans and long-sleeved cotton shirts starting at €100.

 # [M]Ventura Rodríguez. From the Metro, head southeast on C. del Duque de Liria 2 blocks (just past El Jardín Secreto) and take a left onto C. del Limón. i Sportivo located at C. del Conde Duque, 20. Duke located at C. del Conde Duque, 18. $ Shirts €50-150. Pants €50-150. Shoes €100-200. ⏰ Open daily 10am-9pm.

☎63 989 15 18 www.madridinloveindustrial.com

Modeled on a concept that has taken Paris by storm, Madrid in Love is bringing the novelty of the "pop-up store" to Spain. Rather than owning a set retail space, Madrid in Love showcases a gallery of vintage decorative objects in various industrial spaces around the city. The company's owners travel through Europe carefully collecting, and every three to four months announce a two-week sale that attracts the city's hippest and most style-conscious. Though you may not have the chance to see this pop-up store in action, it's worth checking the website to see if there's an event while you're in town.

i Location changes; consult the website for latest events. Exhibitions and sales last 2 weeks and take place every 3-4 months.

OHMYGOD   SALAMANCA

C. de Serrano, 70   ☎34 914 354 412 www.ohmygod.com.es

Like, oh my God! Come to OhmyGOd boutique in upscale Salamanca for funky, chunky, one-of-a-kind jewelry. While you may not be able to take your eyes off these fancy baubles, keep in mind that they're about three times as much as a backpacker's daily budget. Internet buyers beware: make sure to type in the web address correctly or run the risk of ending up at a ◪**Russian bride site.**

⚑ Ⓜ*Serrano. Walk 4 blocks north up C. de Serrano.* Ⓢ *Items start at €100.* Ⓩ *Open M-Sa 10am-8:30pm.*

BOOKS

Finding English books in Madrid can be very difficult. If you're looking for an English title, the best bet is to head to mega-chain stores like **El Corte Inglés** or **Casa del Libro** that sell whatever is on the bestseller list in addition to a smaller library of classic literature. If you're just browsing, Madrid has plenty of small bookstores that sell secondhand paperbacks and art books. You'll find many of these stores in Malasaña on **Calle de la Palma** and **Calle del Espíritu**, and in Las Huertas on **Calle de las Huertas. Cuesta de Mayona** marketplace along the southern end of the Parque del Buen Retiro has interesting offerings every Sunday, though be prepared to dig around to find something in English.

CASA DEL LIBRO   GRAN VÍA

C. Gran Vía, 29   ☎90 202 64 02 www.casadellibro.com

Other locations at C. Fuencarral, 119 and C. de Alcalá, 96

This is the city's best bet for English titles. This Spanish equivalent of Barnes and Noble has three locations in Madrid—and many more across the country—each offering as substantial a foreign literature section as you will find. The location on C. Gran Vía has an entire floor of books in English and French where you can find everything from *Harry Potter* to Proust. They carry most bestsellers in English, and prices are reasonable, with paperbacks starting around €12.

⚑ Ⓜ*Gran Vía. Walk west down C. Gran Vía.* Ⓢ *Paperbacks €8-15. Hardcovers €20-30.* Ⓩ *Open M-Sa 9:30am-9:30pm, Su 11am-9pm.*

ARREBATO LIBROS   MALASAÑA

C. de la Palma, 21   ☎91 282 11 11 www.arrebatolibros.com

Arrebato Libros is a very typical Malasaña bookshop, featuring uncommon books of poetry, philosophy, art, and graphic novels. This two-room shop has plenty of titles in Spanish and a modest English selection, but they are best known for their collections of rare books salvaged from fairs around the city. Secondhand paperbacks run exceptionally cheap (€3-6), but rarer volumes and art books tend to be more expensive (€20). The shop is also involved in the local literary community, hosting weekly readings and lectures. Check the website for a schedule of upcoming events.

⚑ Ⓜ*Tribunal. From the Metro, head west down C. de la Palma.* Ⓩ *Open M-Sa 10:30am-2pm and 5-8:30pm.*

shopping

BERKANA LIBRERÍA GAY Y LESBIANA

CHUECA

C. Hortaleza, 64　　　　　　　　　　　　☎91 522 55 99　www.libreriaberkana.com

This Chueca bookstore features a large selection of books related to GLBT issues, from novels by famous gay writers like Truman Capote, Allen Ginsberg, and Tennessee Williams to comics like *El Kamasutra Gay*. It also has a wide collection of books about adolescence, education, religion, and philosophy. Prices here tend to be a bit above most bookstores. Berkana keeps a table of flyers and pamphlets about the latest GLBT happenings in and around the *barrio*.

✦ ⓂChueca. *From the Metro, turn around, make a right on C. Augusto Figueroa, and make another right onto C. Hortaleza.* Ⓢ *Paperbacks €10-25. DVDs €10-15.* ☑ *Open M-F 10am-9pm, Sa 11:30am-9pm, Su noon-2pm and 5-9pm.*

ALTAÏR

ARGÜELLES

C. de Gaztambide, 31　　　　　　　　　　　☎91 543 53 00　www.altair.es

Altaïr specializes in all books related to travel. They offer an extensive collection of English-language city and country guides as well as handy books of maps, photography, and travel writing. Altaïr's location in Argüelles won't be accessible by foot for most visitors to Madrid, but if you are need of anything travel-related, this is your best bet, as most bookstores in Madrid have very limited travel sections and mostly carry Spanish titles.

✦ ⓂArgüelles. *Walk north up C. de Hilarión Eslava, make a right onto C. de Meléndez Valdés and a left onto C. de Gaztambide.* ☑ *Open M-F 10am2pm and 4:30-8:30pm, Sa 10:30am-2:30pm.*

CUESTA DE MOYANO

AVENIDA DEL ARTE

If you're looking for Spanish books, head to Cuesta de Moyano, the book marketplace on the southern edge of Parque del Buen Retiro. Around 30 stalls set up shop every Sunday to sell secondhand finds and antique books. Come and browse the stalls to find some Spanish first editions before heading to an afternoon picnic in the park.

✦ ⓂAtocha. *Cross Paseo del Prado and walk uphill. The market is on the edge of the park on the right.* ☑ *Open Su 10:30am-sunset.*

essentials

PRACTICALITIES

- **TOURIST OFFICES:** The **Madrid Tourism Centre** in Pl. Mayor (☎91 588 16 36　www.esmadrid.com) is a good place to start; here you'll find city and transit maps as well as suggestions for activities, food, and accommodations. English is spoken at most tourist offices throughout the city. There are additional tourist offices and stands throughout the city; look for large orange stands with exclamation marks. Offices are located at: **Calle del Duque de Medinaceli, 2** (☎91 429 49 51 ☑ Open M-Sa 9:30am-8:30pm, Su and holidays 9:30am-2pm); **Estación de Atocha** (☎91 528 46 30 ☑ Open M-Sa 9:30am-8:30pm, Su and holidays 9:30am-2pm); **Madrid-Barajas Airport Terminal 1** (☎91 305 86 56); **Madrid-Barajas Airport Terminal 4** (☎90 210 00 07 ☑ Open daily 9:30am-8:30pm); and the **Madrid-Barajas Airport train station** (☎91 315 99 76 ☑ Open M-Sa 8am-8pm, Su 9am-2pm).

- **TOURS:** Different themed tours leave regularly from the Madrid Tourism Centre. For dates, times, and more info, visit **www.esmadrid.com.** Many youth hostels host tapas tours, pub crawls, and walking tours for reasonable prices. Check out **www.toursnonstop.com.** (Ⓢ Tapas and pub tours €10.) **LeTango Tours** is run by a Spanish-American husband-wife team, with tours that take you to local bars, give fun city facts, and explain Spanish traditions. (☎91 369 47 52 www.letango.com.) Run by historian and writer Stephen Drake-Jones, the **Wellington Society** (☎60 914 32 03 www.wellsoc.org) offers different themed tours of

Madrid and daytrips to Toledo and Segovia. Another option is **Madrid Vision** (☎91 779 18 88 www.madridvision.es), which runs the double-decker red buses that you see throughout the city. Choose between the *histórico* and *moderno* routes. Each route makes 15-20 stops around the city. ($ €17; discounts online.)

- **CURRENCY EXCHANGE:** The most convenient place to change your money—although not always the cheapest—is the airport. There are also currency exchanges in Puerta del Sol and Gran Vía (look for booths that say "change"), but try to use these as a last resort, as rates are bad and commission charges are high. Most hotels will also be able to change your money; rates vary by location. Another option is **Banco Santander Central Hispano,** which charges €12-15 commission on non-American Express Travelers Cheques (max. exchange €300). Wherever you go, be sure to bring your passport as identification.
- **LUGGAGE STORAGE:** You can store your luggage at the **Aeropuerto Internacional de Barajas.** (☎91 393 68 05 $ 1 day €3.70; 2-15 days €4.78 per day. ⏰ Open 24hr.)
- **POST OFFICES:** Buy **stamps** *(sellos)* from a post office *(correos)* or tobacco stand *(tabacos).* Madrid's **central post office** is at Pl. de Cibeles. (☎91 523 06 94; 90 219 71 97 ⏰ Open M-F 8:30am-9:30pm.) Mailboxes are usually yellow with one slot for "Madrid" and another for everywhere else.
- **POSTAL CODE:** 28008.

EMERGENCY

- **EMERGENCY NUMBERS: Medical emergency:** ☎061 or ☎112. For non-emergency medical concerns, go to **Unidad Médica Angloamericana,** which has English-speaking personnel on duty by appointment. (C. del Conde de Aranda, 1, 1st fl. ☎91 435 18 23 $ Open M-F 9am-8pm, Sa 10am-1pm.)
- **POLICE: Servicio de Atención al Turista Extranjero (SATE)** is a service that deals exclusively with tourists and helps with contacting embassies, reporting crimes, and canceling credit cards. (C. Legantos, 19 ☎91 548 85 27; 90 210 21 12 ⏰ Open daily 9am-midnight.)

GETTING THERE

By Plane

All flights come in through the **Aeropuerto Internacional de Barajas** (MAD; ☎902 404 704 www.aena.es). The **Barajas** metro stop connects the airport to the rest of Madrid ($ €2). To take the subway into the city center, take the #8 toward Nuevo Ministerios, transfer to the #10 toward Puerta del Sur, get off at Tribunal (3 stops), transfer to the #1 toward Valdecarros, and get off at Sol. The journey should take 45-60min. By bus, the **Bus-Aeropeurto 200** leaves from the national terminal T2 and runs to the city center through [M]Avenida de America. (☎90 250 78 50 ⏰ Every 15min., 5:20am-11:30pm.) **Taxis** ($ €35. ⏰ 30min.) are readily available outside of the airport. For more info on ground transport, visit **www.metromadrid.es.**

By Train

Trains (☎90 224 02 02 www.renfe.es) from northern Europe and France arrive on the north side of the city at **Chamartín.** (C. Agustín de Foxa ☎91 300 69 69; 91 506 63 29.) Trains to and from the south of Spain and Portugal use **Atocha.** Buy tickets at the station or online. There is a **RENFE** information office at the main terminal. (☎90 224 02 02 ⏰ Open daily 7am-7pm.) **AVE** trains offer high-speed service throughout Spain, including Barcelona, Salamanca, Segovia, Sevilla, and Toledo. Be sure to keep your ticket, or you won't be able to pass the turnstiles at the other end. Call **RENFE** for both international destinations and domestic travel. (☎902 24 34 02 for international destinations; ☎90 224 02 02 for domestic.) Ticket windows are open daily 6:30am-9pm; when they're closed, you can buy tickets at vending machines.

By Bus

If you prefer four wheels, many private bus companies run through Madrid, and most pass through **Estación Sur de Autobuses.** (C. Méndez Alvaro. ☎91 468 42 00 www.estacionautobusesmadrid.com ⏰ Info booth open daily 6:30am-1am.) National destinations include Algeciras, Alicante, Oviedo, and Toledo, among others. Inquire at the station, online, or by phone for specific information on routes and schedules.

GETTING AROUND

By Metro

The Madrid metro system is by far the easiest, cheapest way to get you almost anywhere you need to go in the city. Service begins Mondays through Saturdays at 6am and Sundays at 7am, and ends daily at around 1:30am. Try to avoid rush hours (daily 8-10am, 1-2pm, and 4-6pm). You can buy either a one-way ticket (€1), or, if you're making multiple trips, you can save by purchasing a combined **10-trip metrobus ticket** (€9.30). Trains run frequently, and green timers above most platforms show the next approaching train times. Be sure to grab a **free metro map** (available at any ticket booth or tourist office). **Abonos mensuales,** or monthly passes, grant unlimited travel within the city proper for €47.60, while **abonos turísticos** (tourist passes) come in various lengths (1, 2, 3, 4, or 7 days) and sell for €6-25 at the metro stations or online. For metro information, visit **www.metromadrid.es** or call ☎90 244 44 03.

By Bus

Buses cover areas that are inaccessible by the Metro and are a great way to see the city. The pamphlet "Visiting the Downtown on Public Transport" lists routes and stops. (*i* Free at any tourist office or downloadable at **www.madrid.org.**) Tickets for the bus and metro are interchangeable. The *Búho* (owl), or night bus, travels from Pl. de Cibeles and other marked routes along the outskirts of the city. (⏰ M-Th every 30min. midnight-3am, every hr. 3-6am; F-Sa every 20min. midnight-6am; Su every 30 min. midnight-3am.) These buses, marked on the essential **Red de Autobuses Nocturnos** (available at any tourist office) run along 26 lines covering regular daytime routes. For info, call **Empresa Municipal de Transportes** (☎90 250 78 50 www.emtmadrid.es). **Estación Sur** (C. Méndez Alvaro ☎91 468 42 00) covers mainly southern and southeastern destinations outside Madrid such as **Granada, Málaga, Sevilla,** and **Valencia.** Visit **www.avanzabus.com** for timetables and routes.

By Taxi

Registered Madrid taxis are black or white and have red bands and small insignias of a bear and *madroño* tree (symbols of Madrid). Hail them on the street or at taxi stands all over the city. A green light means they're free. The fare starts at €1.75 and increases by €1 every kilometer thereafter. To call a city taxi, dial ☎91 447 51 80.

By Moped and Bike

Biking in the city is ill-advised, but Casa de Campo and Dehesa de la Villa both have easily navigable bike trails. You can rent a bike from **Karacol Sport.** (C. Tortosa, 8 ☎91 539 96 33 www.karacol.com *i* Cash deposit of €50 and photocopy of passport required. $ €18 per day. ⏰ Open M-W 10:30am-3pm and 5-8pm, Th 10:30am-3pm and 5-9:30pm, F-Su 10:30am-3pm and 5-8pm.) **Motocicletas Antonio Castro** rents mopeds for €23-95 per day including unlimited mileage and insurance, but you'll need your own lock and helmet. You must be at least 25 years old and have a driver's license for motorcycles. (C. Clara del Rey, 17 ☎91 413 00 47 www.blafermotos.com ⏰ Open M-F 8am-6pm, Sa 10am-1:30pm.)

CENTRAL SPAIN

Within just a couple of hours from the peninsula's epicenter in Madrid lie some of Spain's most historic and beautiful cities. They make great daytrips, but they're just as good for a few nights—or an entire semester. Head to Toledo (much more scenic than its similarly named Ohio cousin) for churches, fortresses, and some seriously fine art. Hit up Salamanca and its student-fueled scene, for centuries home to one of Spain's best universities. And don't skip magical Segovia, home to the basis for Cinderella's Castle at Disney World and to an ancient Roman aqueduct that's as intimidating and as centrally located as you're ever likely to find. Enjoy the golden fields stretching across the Castilian plateau and tuck into that steaming plate of *cochinillo*.

greatest hits

- **ALCAZARS, ALL THE TIME.** Hit up Toledo's *alcázar* (p. 84), which looks like a real pain to besiege, and Segovia's (p. 91), which looks like a fairy princess should be trapped in its highest tower.

- **TWO CATHEDRALS ARE BETTER THAN ONE.** Check out Salamanca's twin cathedrals (p. 97) between classes and the bars.

- **DOMENIO...DOMEKINO...EL GRECO.** See the master's most masterful masterpiece in Toledo's Iglesia de Santo Tomé. (p. 84)

Salamanca, home to one of Europe's oldest universities, has been partying college-style since 1218, and it has the battle scars to prove it (seriously—bull's blood stains left by graduates). The club scene in this part of the peninsula isn't the best, but bar-hop to your heart's content. You're also likely to find plenty of study-abroad groups passing through historic **Toledo,** home to more sights than even the most avid art, history, or art-history buff could possibly know what to do with.

toledo ☎925

Known as La Ciudad de las Tres Culturas (the city of three cultures), this small city was home to Muslims, Jews, and Christians during the Middle Ages, and retains its vibrant heritage. Toledo was the adopted home and death place of the painter El Greco, and it has remained largely unchanged since the 16th century, when it inspired his famous *View of Toledo*, today in New York's Metropolitan Museum of Art. Walk through winding cobblestone streets to take in beautiful Gothic buildings and views of the surrounding river. The city center has become rather commercial, with souvenir shops selling knight's armor, Damascene swords (à la *Lord of the Rings*) and marzipan.

ORIENTATION

Toledo is a web of cobblestone streets that fork at every opportunity. A wrong turn is almost inevitable, but you'll find yourself back on the right path in no time; while Toledo is a reasonably large city of 80,000 people, the historic city center with all of the major landmarks is small and very walkable. On the eastern edge of the historic center you'll find the **Alcázar,** on the western edge there's the **Monasterio de San Juan de Los Reyes,** and at the city center is the **Catedral de Santa María de Toledo,** one of Spain's largest and most significant Gothic cathedrals. The best way to navigate from east to west through the city center is to follow **Calle de Comercio** from **Plaza de Zocodover.** This street turns into **Calle Hombre de Palo** and then **Calle de la Trinidad.** This path will take you from Pl. de Zocodover past the Cathedral. To get some of the best views of the countryside, follow **Calle de los Reyes Católicos** from Monasterio de San Juan de los Reyes for two short blocks to **Plaza Mirador Barrio Nuevo** on the southwestern edge of the city.

ACCOMMODATIONS

HOSTAL PALACIOS   HOTEL $$
C. Navarro Ledesma, 1   ☎92 528 00 83 www.hostalpalacios.net
Hostal Palacios delivers quality rooms with pastel walls, tiled floors, and balconies overlooking the street. The rooms are as clean as the guest room in your obsessive-compulsive family friend's house. The *hostal* is located in a beautiful building, with a restaurant and a nice common room with computer access. The standard continental breakfast is cheap (€2), and the hotel owners offer discounts on lunch and dinner as well.

✚ *From the cathedral, walk northeast up C. de Nuncio Viejo.* ⓘ *Breakfast €2. Free Wi-Fi.* Ⓢ *Singles €30-35; doubles €50.* Ⓐ *Reception 24hr.*

TOLEDO

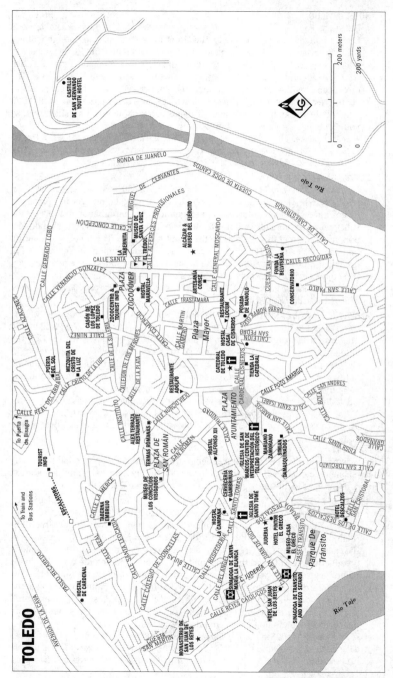

toledo

HOTEL IMPERIO HOTEL $$

C. Cadenas, 5 ☎92 522 76 50 www.hotelimperio.es

Long a budget favorite in Toledo, the Hotel Imperio has basic hotel amenities, friendly service, and an excellent location, just one block from Pl. de Zocodover and close to the Alcázar and Cathedral. Rooms feature well-made beds with crisp white sheets and large ensuite bathrooms with toiletries and fresh towels. The downstairs restaurant serves continental breakfast (€2-4) and there are plenty of quality restaurants nearby. The only drawback here is the temperamental Wi-Fi, which only works in the lobby. C. Cadenas is a reasonably quiet sidestreet, so you can count on a good night of sleep.

⇟ From the cathedral, head straight north. The hotel is next to the Iglesia San Nicolás. ℹ Free Wi-Fi. Groups of 3 or more should check availability and prices online. $ Singles €30; doubles €45, with extra bed €60. ⏰ Reception 24hr.

LA POSADA DE MANOLO HOTEL $$$

C. de Sixto Ramón Parro, 8 ☎92 528 22 50 www.laposadademanolo.com

La Posada de Manolo is as good as budget accommodations get in Spain. The rooms have medieval cottage decor (including old-school wooden tools on the wall), and they actually pull it off, successfully avoiding the saggy, abandoned-nursing-home feel that is so often the result elsewhere. The hotel is a beautiful building, with a central staircase leading to the salon dining room where a full breakfast buffet is served daily. The hotel also has a rooftop terrace where you can enjoy a drink with spectacular views of the town and countryside.

⇟ C. de Sixto Ramón Parro, a quiet street at the southeast edge of the cathedral. ℹ Free Wi-Fi. $ Singles €42; doubles €66. ⏰ Reception 24hr.

ALBERGUE JUVENIL CASTILLO DE SAN SERVANDO (HI) HOSTEL $

Subida al Castillo ☎92 522 45 54

This hostel is in a castle. Enough said. One of the dominant features on the Toledo skyline, this fortress gave refuge to the top-ranking Castilian general El Cid Campeador during his exile in 1080. Located 10-15min. uphill from the middle of town, the HI hostel features spacious common rooms, a pool with a panoramic view of the center of Toledo, and the lowest rates in the city. Be sure to join Hostelling International and then reserve far in advance if you wish to stay here.

⇟ From the city center, cross the river using Puente de Alcántara. You'll be able to see it from afar. It's the only castle in the area. ℹ Wi-Fi €1 per hr. $ Dorms €14. HI card required. ⏰ Lockout 11am-2pm.

SIGHTS

Toledo is packed with sights. If it all seems overwhelming, keep in mind that many of these sights can be visited quickly, cheaply, or simply admired from the exterior. Grab a **free map** of local sights from the tourist office (see **Essentials**).

★ MUSEO DEL GRECO MUSEUM

Paseo del Tránsito ☎92 522 36 65 http://museodelgreco.mcu.es

After a five-year renovation and much anticipation, El Museo del Greco has finally opened to the public, and it does not disappoint. Directly across from the quarters where El Greco lived and worked, this museum offers a unique perspective on El Greco the artist and Mr. Theotokópoulos the man. While his paintings grace the walls of museums around the world, this is one of the few collections dedicated specifically to his work. In a short 45min. tour through the museum, you can see the bizarre qualities of his art up close: the supernatural use of light and the elongated figures. The collection contains some absolute masterpieces, including a room of portraits of the 13 apostles.

⇟ From Monasterio de San Juan de los Reyes, follow C. de los Reyes Católicos southeast to Paseo del Tránsito. ℹ Free entry Sa 2-8pm, Su 2-3pm. $ €3, students and seniors €1.50. Cash only. ⏰ Open Oct-Mar Tu-Sa 9:30am-6:30pm, Su 10am-3pm; Apr-Sept Tu-Sa 9:30am-8pm, Su 10am-3pm.

🏛 MONASTERIO DE SAN JUAN DE LOS REYES — MONASTERY

C. de los Reyes Católicos, 17 ☎92 522 38 02 www.sanjuandelosreyes.org

Located on the western edge of the city, the Monasterio de los Reyes was commissioned by Ferdinand and Isabella to commemorate their victory in the Battle of Toro. While the building itself is impressive, with an intricately carved granite façade and stunning vaulted ceilings, what is most striking about the monastery is the tranquility of its cloister, with blooming fruit trees and beautiful gardens. This is another quick visit, but absolutely worth the nominal entry fee.

⇞ Located along the western edge of the city center. Follow the signs. $ €2.30, students and seniors €2. Cash only. ⏰ Open daily summer 10am-6:30pm; winter 10am-5pm.

CATEDRAL PRIMADA SANTA MARÍA DE TOLEDO — CATHEDRAL

C. del Cardenal Cisneros ☎92 522 22 41

Built between 1226 and 1493 on the former site of a mosque, the Catedral de Santa María de Toledo (Cathedral of Saint Mary of Toledo) is considered by many to be Spain's greatest Gothic cathedral. The grandeur of its naves and transepts—and the intricacy of its chapels and altarpieces—is the product of endless toil and craftsmanship. While €7 is a bit steep, if you're going to visit any of the churches in Toledo, this should be the one. If you're still too much of a cheapskate, at least walk around the outside. Particularly notable are the three intricately carved doorways on the front façade facing Pl. Ayuntamiento: the door of forgiveness (center), the door of the last judgment (right), and the door of hell (left).

⇞ From Pl. de Zocodover, take C. Comercio southwest to C. Hombre de Palo and take a left (south) onto C. de Nuncio Viejo. ℹ Purchase tickets and audio tours across the street in Pl. Ayuntamiento. $ €7. ⏰ Open M-Sa 10am-6:30pm, Su 2-6:30pm.

IGLESIA DE SANTO TOMÉ CHURCH

Pl. del Conde, 4 ☎92 525 60 98 www.santotome.org

This tiny 14th-century *mudéjar*-style church is charming from the outside, but the treasure within is what draws the tourists. A full wall of the church is covered with El Greco's masterwork *The Burial of the Count of Orgaz*, which depicts the eponymous count's funeral. The ceremony's guests include saints, angels, nobles, and the painter himself.

From the Cathedral, head west on C. de la Ciudad, bear right on C. El Salvador, left onto C. Santo Tomé, and left again onto Pl. del Conde. $ €2.30. 🕐 Open daily Mar 15-Oct 14 10am-6:45pm; Oct 15-Mar 14 10am-5:45pm.

IGLESIA DE SAN ILDEFONSO CHURCH

Pl. del Padre Juan de Mariana, 1 ☎92 525 15 07

Advertised as the "view from heaven," the lookout point from the top of Iglesia de San Ildefonso features some truly spectacular panoramic views that include the Cathedral and Alcázar. Fair warning: you'll have to hike up quite a few stairs. However, this is probably the best view in Toledo, so it's worth it. The church interior's bright white walls and columns make it stand out from the massive stone-carved Gothic churches throughout Toledo.

From the Cathedral, go north up C. de Nuncio Viejo. i No tours during mass or religious ceremonies. $ €2.30, students €2. 🕐 Open daily May-Aug 10am-6:45pm; Sept-Apr 10am-5:45pm.

ALCÁZAR AND MUSEO DEL EJÉRCITO MUSEUM, PALACE

C. General Moscardo, 4 ☎92 522 16 73

The Alcázar of Toledo has long been equated with the might of the Spanish Empire. Built atop a third-century CE Roman fortress, the Alcázar is best known today as one of the most important battlegrounds of the Spanish Civil War. Because of its symbolic value and historical importance to the Spanish Kingdom, Republican troops believed that a successful capture of the Alcázar would strengthen their image in the public eye. For two months, Republican forces struggled to capture the Alcázar from Nationalist militias, quickly depleting resources and artillery in the Seige of the Alcázar, now considered one of the Republicans' greatest military blunders. Evidence of this turbulent history is found in the Alcázar's collection of military equipment, which dates back to the Middle Ages. The collection includes firearms, uniforms, flags, and an informative exhibit on the history of the Alcázar.

From Pl. de Zocodover, walk 1 block south on Cuesta de Carlos V. The museum is the contemporary building labeled Museo del Ejército on your left. $ €4, under 9 free. Cash only. 🕐 Open daily June-Sept 10am-9pm; Oct-May 10am-7pm.

HOSPITAL DE TAVERA MUSEUM

C. de Cardenal Tavera, 2 ☎92 522 04 51

For our time-traveling readers, we would not recommend visiting this site 400 years ago: the beautiful Renaissance building was once filled with beds occupied by the deathly ill. Today, the former hospital is hardly recognizable; it's been converted into a museum dedicated to the first Duque de Lerma, the hospital's original benefactor. Deathbeds have been replaced by a significant collection of art and decorative objects, including a room of El Greco paintings commissioned by the hospital in the 16th century to give hope to the sick. Today the museum also includes the original hospital pharmacy and the administrative archives of the hospital. This building is owned by the descendants of the Duque de Lerma, and the basement is still used as the family crypt, just to maintain the creep factor.

Directly north of the city wall. From Puerta Nueva de Bisagra, go north up C. de Cardenal Taverna. $ €4.50. 🕐 Open M-Sa 10am-1:30pm and 3-5:30pm, Su 10am-1pm.

SINAGOGA DE SANTA MARÍA LA BLANCA — SYNAGOGUE

C. de los Reyes Católicos, 4 ☎92 522 72 57

Built in 1180, this converted synagogue (now owned by the Catholic Church) is considered one of the oldest Jewish centers of worship in Europe. Built by Moorish architects, it now houses an art gallery featuring religious art and landscapes of Toledo. While the interior is quite nice, the plain white columns and intricate stone details of the synagogue would be just as well appreciated from the exterior gardens without paying for admission.

From the Monasterio de San Juan de los Reyes on the western edge of the city center, walk east down C. de los Reyes Católicos. $ €2.30. Cash only. ⏰ Open daily 10am-2pm and 3:30-6pm.

MUSEO DE SANTA CRUZ — MUSEUM

C. Miguel de Cervantes, 4 ☎92 522 10 36 www.jccm.es

Built in 1504 by the Catholic Church, this former church is considered a great work of Spanish Renaissance architecture. Today, the two-story museum holds a sizeable permanent collection of archaeological artifacts dating back to the Roman Empire, Spanish Renaissance paintings and sculpture, and an impressive collection of El Grecos, including his *Immaculate Conception.*

From Pl. de Zocodover, take C. Santa Fé west and make a quick left to the museum entrance. $ Free. ⏰ Open M-Sa 10am-6:30pm, Su 10am-2pm.

FOOD

RESTAURANTE PALACIOS — SPANISH $$

C. Navarro Ledesma, 1 ☎92 522 34 97 www.hostalpalacios.net

Located below the Hostal Palacios, this restaurant is packed throughout the day with locals and budget travelers looking to eat well on the cheap. The most popular dishes here are traditional stewed meat dishes, many of which are unique to Toledo, such as *perdiz a la toledana* (stewed partridge; €9) and *carcamusas* (stewed pork loin; €10). Also popular are grilled meat dishes like *chuletón ternera* (grilled steak; €10) and *venado a la plancha* (grilled venison; €10). While roast suckling pig typically costs €20-25, here they offer a half portion for only €10. Don't be dismayed by the picture menu outside and the English flag stamped on the outside of the restaurant: there's a reason budget travelers keep coming back.

From the Cathedral, walk northeast up C. de Nuncio Viejo. i Discounts for guests of Hostal Palacios. $ Breakfast €2-5. Full meals €10-20. Cash only. ⏰ Open daily 8am-1am.

LA FLOR DE LA ESQUINA — SPANISH $$

Pl. Juan de Mariana, 2 ☎627 94 50 20 www.laflordelaesquina.com

The quaint decor of white-washed wood cabinetry and hand-painted ceramic wall tiles at this small cafe accent a fine menu of appetizers, salads, and sandwiches. The obvious choice is the house special burger (with bacon, Manchego, and grilled onions; €7.50). While most places in Spain offer wimpy mixed salads with shredded carrots and tomatoes, here the grilled chicken caesar (€7) is a substantial meal in itself. For something lighter, they offer small *bocaditos* (€2.50), miniature sandwiches made with far more love and care than those sloppy mammoths you see sitting behind so many lunch counters. This is one of the few places in town where you can ditch the picture menu and tourist prices and enjoy a quality meal. The terrace seating has some of the best views of the main cathedral.

With your back to the Iglesia de los Jesuitas, the restaurant will be on your left. $ Entrees €5-12. ⏰ Open daily noon-4pm and 6:30pm-midnight.

TABERNA ALFERITOS 24 SPANISH $$$

C. Alferitos, 24 ☎90 210 65 77 www.alfileritos24.com

Taberna Alferitos offers an original menu and atmosphere that doesn't break the bank. While you can certainly eat cheaply with items like the grilled chicken caesar (€9) or the venison burger (€7), the meat and fish entrees are a surprisingly good deal. Rather than serving a la carte like most traditional restaurants, they serve proper entrees with sides, including a *bacalao con espinaca* (cod served with sauteed spinach; €17) and *lomo de cerdo con manzanas asadas* (pork tenderloin with grilled apples; €18). Many restaurants in Toledo struggle to pull off the contemporary aesthetic, but Alferitos nails it with upstairs tables situated around the sky-lit courtyard and tucked into the intimate brick basement downstairs.

From Iglesia de San Nicolás, make a left onto C. Alferitos. The restaurant is on the left. $ Meals €10-25. Open M-Sa 10am-1am, Su 10am-midnight.

DAR AL-CHAI CAFE $

Pl. Barrio Nuevo, 6 ☎92 522 56 25 www.daralchai.es

Located on the western edge of the city, Dar Al-Chai is a picturesque cafe in a quiet part of town next to one of Spain's oldest synagogues. The interior resembles a dark hookah lounge, and a leafy canopy shades the outdoor terrace. The varied menu of loose-leaf teas, including specialty teas that will cure all sorts of ailments including indigestion and insomnia, and a great selection of crepes sweetens the deal.

From Monasterio de San Juan de los Reyes, walk south down C. de los Reyes Católicos. Pl. Barrio Nuevo is in a nook on the left. $ Coffee and tea €2-4. Open M-Th 9:30am-10pm, F-Sa 4pm-1am, Su 9:30am-10pm.

CAFÉ DEL FIN CAFE $$

C. Taller del Moro 1 ☎92 525 10 52 www.cafedelfin.com

Pop on to one of Café del Fin's comfortable couches and enjoy a coffee and surprisingly high-quality pizza and burgers. While the food might not compare with what you're used to back home, it's a good alternative to blowing your budget on overpriced tapas at an expensive sit-down restaurant. The *hamburguesa de la casa* is the specialty here (half ground beef, half pork, served with sauteed mushrooms, salad, and fries; €7), and they offer a number of classic pizzas like barbecue chicken (€10), margherita (€9), and the Hawaiian (€10).

From the monastery walk straight east down C. del Ángel and make a right onto C. Taller del Moro. i Free Wi-Fi. $ Entrees €6-14. Open M-W 8:30am-6pm, Th 8:30am-1am, F 8:30am-2am, Sa 9am-2am, Su 9am-12:30am.

LA ABADIA CERVECERÍA, TAPAS, SPANISH $$$

Pl. de San Nicolás, 3 ☎92 525 11 40 www.abadiatoledo.com

While the upstairs bar is fairly standard, the downstairs dining in small brick catacomb rooms offers a unique setting. La Abadia has the standard tapas, but it specializes in larger shared dishes such as the grilled lamb platter (€30), the sampling platter of grilled beef, pork, and lamb (€17), and grilled cod (€11). A tasty selection of European beers on tap (€2) beyond the standard Mahou and San Miguel also help to set this place apart.

From Iglesia de San Nicolás, walk straight north up C. de Núñez de Arce. The restaurant is on the right. $ Tapas €2-5. Entrees €10-20. Cocktails €4-9. Open daily 1:30-11pm.

NIGHTLIFE

CÍRCULO DE ARTE TOLEDO CAFE, MUSIC

Pl. de San Vicente, 2 ☎92 521 43 29 www.circuloartetoledo.org

The Círculo de Arte Toledo is a cafe, art gallery, and concert hall all housed in a renovated church. With modern paintings on the walls, Moorish arches, and white brick, it's a great place to grab an evening cocktail and check out a concert. Live music ranges from house to international pop, country, and folk. It really is a matter of luck here: if you come on the right weekend, you just might get to hear your favorite klezmer band!

Right next to Convento Agustinas Gaitanas. [i] Consult the monthly program (available at the entrance), as the schedule and cost of admission are subject to change. [$] Wine €1.80-2. Coffee and cocktails €4-8. Tapas €5. ⏰ Hours vary depending on performance times. Concerts tend to start 8-9pm or around midnight.

LA TABERNA DE LIVINGSTON COCKTAIL BAR

C. Alferitos, 4 ☎92 521 26 75

With zebra-print chairs, black and white pictures of Africa, hunting memorabilia, and British posters, this place screams colonialism. Despite the decor, the establishment is a good stop for a post-dinner coffee or cocktail. And with portraits of white colonial leaders and pictures of wild animals being slaughtered lining the walls, the place lets all you animal-poaching travelers finally sit back at ease. This is a joke: *Let's Go* does not condone animal poaching, unless it is done with a harpoon gun, in which case coolness outweighs cruelty.

From Iglesia de San Nicolás, make a left onto C. Alferitos. [$] Wine €2-3. Cocktails €6. Tapas and desserts €4-6. ⏰ Open M-Th 9:30am-midnight, F-Sa 9:30am-1am, Su 9:30am-midnight.

ENEBRO CAFE, BAR

Pl. de Santiago de los Caballeros, 1 www.barenebro.com

With three locations in tiny Toledo, Enebro is the go-to bar and nightlife stop for students in Toledo. Food here is limited to basic tapas, and the good selection of imported beers (Heineken, Budweiser, Foster's, Guinness; €2.50) is the real draw. While Enebro is primarily a spot for late-night mingling, there are occasional concerts and parties.

Right beside Museo de Santa Cruz. [i] 2nd location at Pl. San Justo, 9. Check online for concert schedule. [$] Drinks €4-6. ⏰ Open daily 1pm-2am.

PÍCARO CAFE TEATRO BAR

C. Cadenas, 6 ☎62 752 60 76

While Toledo is a fairly sleepy town, this is one of the few venues that keeps things going late. Just around the corner from Pl. de Zocodover, this club and cocktail lounge hosts DJ sets on weekends, playing loud techno beats well into the morning. Sometimes you can find a critical mass of Toledo's university students and tourists partying away, but on an off-night during low season, you'll be hard-pressed to find much activity. Pícaro's flashing lights and dance floor are a rarity in this town, but if you want them, they are there waiting for you.

From the Cathedral, walk straight north up C. de Tornerías. Veer right onto C. del Comercio. Make a left onto C. de la Plata and then a right onto C. Cadenas. [$] Mixed drinks €6. ⏰ Open M-Th 4pm-3am, F-Sa 4pm-6am.

ESSENTIALS

Practicalities

- **TOURIST OFFICES:** There is a tourist office located in the **train station** which provides indispensable free maps of Toledo in English and Spanish. Grab one on your way from the station to the city. Another option is the **tourist information office.** (Puerta de Bisagra ☎92 522 08 43 ⏰ Open M-F 9am-6pm, Sa 9am-7pm, Su 9am-3pm.) **Casa de Mapa** also provides free maps. (Pl. de Zocodover ⏰ Open daily 11am-7pm.)
- **CURRENCY EXCHANGE: Banco Santander Central Hispano** has a 24hr. ATM. (C. del Comercio, 47 ☎92 522 98 00 ⏰ Open Apr-Sept M-F 8:30am-2pm; Oct-Mar M-F 8:30am-2pm, Sa 8:30am-1pm.)

- **LUGGAGE STORAGE:** Lockers are available at the **bus station.** ($ €1.80-3 per day. ⏰ Open daily 7am-11pm.)
- **INTERNET ACCESS:** **Locutorio El Casco.** (C. de la Plata, 2 ☎92 522 61 65 ➔ Across from the post office. $ €1.50 per hr. ⏰ Open daily 11am-11pm.)
- **POST OFFICE:** C. de la Plata, 1. ☎92 528 44 37 ⏰ Open M-F 8:30am-2pm and 5-8:30pm, Sa 9:30am-2pm.

Emergency

- **LOCAL EMERGENCY NUMBER:** ☎092
- **NATIONAL EMERGENCY NUMBER:** ☎091.
- **LOCAL POLICE:** Av. Carlos III, 2. ➔ At the intersection of Av. de la Reconquista and Av. de Carlos III. ☎92 525 04 12.
- **NATIONAL POLICE:** Av. Portugal. ☎92 522 59 00.
- **HOSPITAL:** **Hospital Virgen de la Salud.** (Av. de Barber ☎92 526 92 00.)
- **PHARMACIES:** Pharmacies are located throughout the city; there's one at Pl. de Zocodover. (☎925 22 17 68 ⏰ Open daily 9:30am-2pm and 5-8pm.)

Getting There

BY TRAIN

The **RENFE** high-speed train from **Atocha** is the best way to get to Toledo from Madrid. ($ Around €11. ⏰ 30min.; 12 per day.) Student discounts are only available to EU residents. Consult **www.renfe.com** for details or pick up a pamphlet at the train station. If possible, buy your tickets one day prior as lines to buy tickets can be long and unpredictable. From the Toledo RENFE station (Paseo de la Rosa, 2 ☎92 522 30 99), a bus (€0.95) or a taxi (€10) can take you to the center of town. The bus stop is directly outside of the train station, 10m to the right. Take bus #5, 5D, 6.1, or 6.2 to get to Pl. de Zocodover.

BY BUS

Buses run from **Estación Sur** in Madrid ($ €5 ⏰ 1hr.; every 30min. M-F 6am-10:30pm, Sa 6:30am-10:30pm, Su 8am-11:30pm) and arrive at the **Avenida de Castilla-La Mancha** bus station (☎92 521 58 10 ⏰ Open 7am-11pm). To get from the bus station to center of town, take a 5min. bus ride on #8.1 or 8.2. To walk from the bus station, head south on Av. de Castilla-La Mancha, take a soft right (heading west) on C. de la Carrera at the first roundabout, and follow C. de la Carrera (5min.) until you reach the large medieval arch Puerta de Bisagra.

Getting Around

You will need a map to navigate this city. Streets are narrow, poorly marked, and often quite steep. Maps are available at the tourist office in the train station and at each of the locations throughout town. You will be able to access all parts of the historic center of Toledo quite easily by foot. Keep in mind that the city's many steep cobblestone streets may be difficult for visitors in wheelchairs to navigate. The most important **buses** are #8.1 and 8.2, which travel from the bus station to the center of town. Buses #1-7 leave from Pl. de Zocodover on various routes throughout town. ($ Day ticket €0.95, night €1.25.) For a mixture of transportation and touring, hop on one of the double-decker tour buses smattered throughout the city. For **taxis,** call Radio Taxi (☎92 522 70 70).

segovia ☎921

Set above rolling hills and country pasture just 60km from Madrid, Segovia is a true escape. The city's Roman aqueduct running through the center of town and its imposing cliffside medieval castle are undoubtedly its greatest attractions, and they don't fail to impress. The 2000-year-old granite aqueduct has stood virtually unchanged since Roman times and was even functional until recently. Meanwhile the 12th-century Alcázar remains intact and as fantastical as ever. But Segovia is more than any single monument: it's a sleepy, comforting town that calls to travelers when they tire of big-city life in Madrid. It is definitely a tourist destination, and you will see people who look just like your grandparents, but at a certain point, we're all tourists.

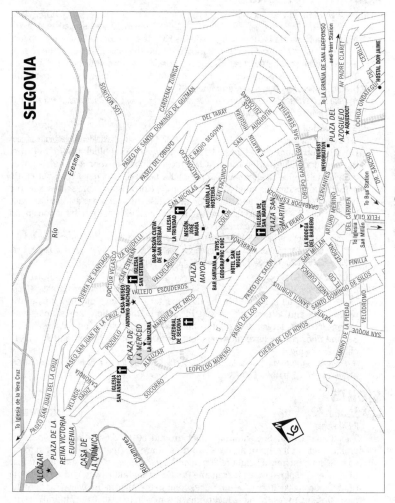

ORIENTATION

The best way to orient yourself in Segovia is to get a **free map** at the visitors' reception center (see **Essentials**); you'll need it to navigate the labyrinth of winding roads in the **old city.** To get to the visitors' reception center from the train station, take bus #8 to "Acueducto" (7min.). If you are arriving from the bus station you can also take bus #4 to "Acueducto" or take a short taxi ride (€4). The visitors' center is on the northwest corner of the Pl. del Azoguejo. The best way to navigate the old city is to follow the main street starting at the aqueduct, passing the Cathedral at **Plaza Mayor,** and ending at the Alcázar, known at various points as **Calle de Cervantes, Calle de Juan Bravo, Calle de Isabel "La Católica," Calle del Marqués del Arco,** and **Calle Daoíz.** The newer part of town lies to the south and east, to the right as you face the aqueduct at Pl. Azoguejo.

ACCOMMODATIONS

NATURA LA HOSTERÍA — HOTEL $$$

C. Colón, 5 and 7 ☎92 146 67 10 www.naturadesegovia.com

Natura La Hostería is located in Pl. de los Huertos, one of the few green spaces in the Old City. Many of the rooms look out onto the plaza, and all of the rooms, including the smaller singles, have queen-sized beds, air-conditioning, flatscreen TVs, and ensuite bathrooms. The downstairs Cafe Natura offers a simple breakfast (coffee, tea, toast, and juice; €4).

From Pl. Mayor take C. Cronista Lecea from the corner opposite the Cathedral, then right on C. Colón. [$] Singles €35-40; doubles €50-80.

HOSTAL DON JAIME — HOTEL $$

C. Ochoa Ondategui, 8 ☎92 144 47 87 hostaldonjaime@hotmail.com

Hostal "Don Jaime" is a pleasant family-run *hostal* one block up the hill from the aqueduct. They offer some of the most affordable rooms in old Segovia, with some singles as cheap as €20 per night. Located on a quiet road with little activity, Don Jaime is a great place to crash. The downstairs cafe serves a simple breakfast (juice, coffee, and toast; €3), and while the *hostal* has a computer with internet, at €0.50 for every 15 minutes, it can be an expensive habit if you spend all of your time in Segovia on Second Life.

From the tourist office in Pl. del Azoguejo, walk east through the aqueduct away from the Old City, and bear right onto C. de Ochoa Ondategui, walk uphill, and look for the "Don Jaime" sign. [$] Singles M-Th €20-30, F-Su €35; doubles M-Th €45, F-Su €50.

HOTEL SAN MIGUEL — HOTEL $$

C. Infanta Isabel, 6 ☎92 146 36 57 www.sanmiguel-hotel.com

Hotel San Miguel is located in the dead center of the city, one block from the restaurants and attractions around Pl. Mayor. Rooms here are simple, with queen-size beds, large private bathrooms with fresh towels, and flatscreen TVs. Second-floor rooms have nice balconies overlooking the street, and run €5-10 cheaper per night.

*From Pl. Mayor follow C. Infanta Isabel (opposite City Hall) for ½ a block. **i** Breakfast €3. [$] Singles €30-35; doubles €60-70.*

SIGHTS

AQUEDUCT — MONUMENT

Pl. Azoguejo

The Romans built Segovia's aqueduct around 50 BCE with 20,000 blocks of granite and not a drop of mortar. Two tiers of arches (that's 166 arches in total) span 813m, reaching a height of 29m near Pl. del Azoguejo. This spectacular feat of engineering piped water in from the Río Fuenfría, 14km away, and was capable of transporting 30 liters of water per second to the Alcázar. In disuse for only the past 60 years, today the aqueduct primarily pipes in tourists from Madrid.

👍 ALCÁZAR

PALACE

Pl. Reina Victoria Eugenia ☎92 146 07 59

Walt Disney reportedly modeled Disney World's Cinderella Castle on the Alcázar's spiral towers and pointed turrets; you may experience a magical sense of déjà vu. Alfonso X renovated the original 11th-century fortress in the 13th century, and successive monarchs only increased the grandeur; final touches were added for the coronation of Isabel I in 1474. Wander through the luxurious royal bedrooms and halls. The **tower of Juan II,** 152 steps up, offers incredible views of Segovia and the surrounding hills.

➡ From Pl. Mayor follow C. del Marqués del Arco past the Cathedral; continue straight as it becomes C. Daoíz and ends at the Alcázar. ℹ Buy tickets in the Real Laboratorio de Chimia, to the left of the Alcázar. $ Palace €4, seniors and students €3. Tower €2. Audio tours in English €3. ⏰ Open daily Apr-Sept 10am-7pm; Oct-Mar 10am-6pm. Tower closed Tu.

CATEDRAL DE NUESTRA SEÑORA DE LA ASUNCIÓN

CATHEDRAL

Pl. Mayor ☎92 146 22 05

In 1525, Carlos V commissioned a cathedral in Pl. Mayor to replace the 12th-century edifice that was destroyed in the Revuelta de las Comunidades, a political uprising against the crown from 1520 to 1521. When the cathedral was finally finished 200 years later, its impressive 23 chapels topped with stained glass earned Nuestra Señora de la Asunción the nickname "The Lady of All Cathedrals." The altar was designed by Sabatini, creator of the gardens in Madrid, and features the four saints of Segovia. The **Sala Capitular,** hung with 17th-century tapestries, displays an ornate silver-and-gold chariot. Off the cloister (moved from the Alcázar) is the **Capilla de Santa Catalina,** filled with crosses, chalices, and candelabra. A framed coin collection on the cloister wall has currency from the royal mint going back five centuries.

➡ Just off Pl. Mayor. $ €3, under 14 free. Guided tours leave from the entrance at 11am, 4:30, and 5:30pm. ⏰ Open daily Apr-Oct 9am-6:30pm; Nov-Mar 9:30am-5:30pm. Last entry 30min. before close. Mass M-Sa 10am, Su 11am and 12:30pm.

LA GRANJA DE SAN ILDEFONSO

PALACE

Pl. de España, 17, San Ildefonso ☎92 147 00 19

11km southeast of Segovia, La Granja is the most extravagant of Spain's royal summer retreats. Philip V, the first Bourbon king of Spain and grandson of Louis XIV, detested the Hapsburgs' austere Escorial palace. Nostalgic for Versailles, he commissioned La Granja in the early 18th century, choosing the site for its hunting and gardening potential. A fire destroyed the living quarters in 1918, but the structure was rebuilt in 1932. Today it houses the **Museo de Tapices,** one of the world's best collections of Flemish tapestries, which were all the rage in Spanish royal palaces. The usual marble clocks, East Asian porcelain, and paintings by Luca Giordano round out the palace's decor. French architect René Carlier designed the immense French-style **gardens** around the palace. Hedges surround impressive flowerbeds and lead to endless waterworks, including the decadent *cascadas nuevas,* an ensemble of illuminated fountains and pools that represents the continents and seasons. The **Baños de Diana** is a massive pool with a bronze statue of the goddess, backed by a wall meticulously inlaid with hundreds of seashells.

➡ La Sepulvedana (☎92 142 77 07) runs buses from Segovia's Estación Municipal de Autobuses (Paseo Ezéquiel González, 12 ☎92 142 77 07) to La Granja ($ €1.05 ⏰ 20min.; 9-15 per day M-Sa 7:40am-9:30pm, Su 10:30am-10:30pm). ℹ Tours in Spanish every 15min. $ €5; students and under 16 €3. ⏰ Palace open June 17-Aug 10am-9pm; Sept 10am-8pm; Oct 10am-6:30pm; Nov-Feb 10am-6pm; Mar 10am-6:30pm; Apr 10am-7pm; May-June 16 10am-8pm. Gardens open daily 10am-9pm. Baños de Diana open July 22-Sept 2 Sa 10:30am-11:30pm. Other fountains suspended due to lack of water.

CASA-MUSEO ANTONIO MACHADO   MUSEUM

C. de los Desamparados, 5   ☎92 146 03 77

Antonio Machado (1875-1939), literature professor, playwright, and, above all, poet, never made much money. The poet rented this small *pensión* from 1919 to 1932 for three *pesetas* per day while he taught French at the nearby university. A short, informative tour details major influences on Machado's poetry, including the 1909 death of his teenage wife and his affair with a married woman. The poet's room, filled with manuscripts and portraits (including one by Picasso), has been left untouched.

⚐ *From Pl. Mayor follow C. del Marqués del Arco past the Cathedral, then right on C. de los Desamparados.* ℹ *Mandatory guided tour in Spanish every 30min.* Ⓢ *M-Tu €1.50, W free.* ⌚ *Open daily M-Tu 4:30-7:30pm, W-Su 11am-2pm and 4:30-7:30pm.*

FOOD

The restaurants in the larger plazas cater to tourists and jack up their prices accordingly—steer clear of any menu printed on "parchment." *Sopa castellana* (soup with eggs and garlic), *cochinillo asado* (roast suckling pig), *ponche* (egg yolk pastry), and lamb dishes are regional specialties worth trying. There's a fresh fruit and vegetable market on **Plaza Mayor** on Thursdays and **Avenida de la Constitución** on Saturdays (9am-2:30pm). For basic groceries, head to **Día**. (C. Gobernador Fernández Jiménez, 3. ⚐ *Off Av. de Fernández Ladreda.* ⌚ Open M-Sa 9am-9pm.)

▨ **RESTAURANTE LA ALMUZARA**   MEDITERRANEAN, VEGETARIAN $$

C. Marqués del Arco, 3   ☎92 146 06 22

La Almuzara is a quiet, family-owned restaurant that specializes in vegetarian pizza and pasta. While many of the upscale restaurants throughout town go for the dark, wooden coffin-like interiors, La Almuzara keeps it cool and calm with pastoral murals on the walls and fresh flowers. The vegetarian specialties like vegetable lasagna (€9.50) and pizzas (€10-12), other Italian staples like *pasta bolognese* (€10), and local dishes like *sopa de ajo* (garlic soup with poached egg; €5) all make a nice meal on a budget.

⚐ *From Pl. Mayor take C. Marqués del Arco west just past the Cathedral.* Ⓢ *Salads €5-8. Entrees €9-14.* ⌚ *Open Tu 8-11:30pm, W-Su 12:45-4pm and 8-11:30pm.*

BAR-MESÓN CUEVA DE SAN ESTEBAN   SEGOVIAN $$

C. Valdeláguila, 15   ☎92 146 09 82

The owner knows his wines: he's still celebrating his 2002 victory in the national "nose of gold" competition, and he uses this schnozz to serve a stellar selection of wines. While Bar-Mesón serves Segovia specialties like suckling pig and roasted lamb, they also have a number of good options for budget travelers, such as the freshly prepared *tortillas*. The *tortilla con gambas fritas* (tortilla with fried prawns; €6.50) is particularly good. And with such a highly regarded connoisseur at the helm, there are always a number of great choices served by the glass (€2-4).

⚐ *From Pl. Mayor with the Cathedral behind you, take a left on C. Potro at the far side of the plaza. This quickly merges into C. Valdeláguila. Take C. Valdeláguilla ½ block down the narrow alley.* Ⓢ *Menú del día M-F €9, Sa-Su €10. Meat dishes €12-20.* ⌚ *Open daily 11am-midnight.*

RESTAURANTE-MESÓN JOSÉ MARÍA   SEGOVIAN $$$

C. Cronista Lecea, 11   ☎92 146 11 11 www.rtejosemaria.com

While this restaurant lacks the pomp and overdone interiors of so many *asadores* in town, Mesón José María is still a destination for local specialties like suckling pig (€23) and roasted lamb (€44). All of Mesón José María's best meat dishes come in mammoth servings made for two. For those less interested in shelling out for the most expensive entrees, Mesón José María is also known for *papas con huevas rotas* (€10) served with pork loin.

🪧 From Pl. Mayor with the Cathedral behind you, take C. Cronista Lecea from the far right corner for ½ block. 🕒 Open M-W and Su 1-4pm and 8:30-11pm, Th-Sa 1-4pm and 8:30pm-12:30am.

LA BODEGA DEL BARBERO — BAR $

Pl. Alhóndiga, 2 — ☎92 146 27 70

La Bodega del Barbero is an easy-to-miss wine bar with terrace seating just of C. Juan Bravo. The selection of wines changes daily, but you should always be able to get a decent glass at a reasonable price (€1.50-3). They also serve salads (€5.80-9), *bocadillos* (€4-8), and a *menú del día* for €10.

🪧 From Pl. Mayor, take C. de Isabel "La Católica," which becomes C. Juan Bravo, and follow it 2 blocks to Pl. Alhóndiga. Take a right down the small flight of stairs and look for the yellow awning. $ Food €5-10. Drinks €1.50-3. 🕒 Open Tu 11am-3:30pm, W-Su 11am-3:30pm and 7:30-11:30pm.

NIGHTLIFE

Segovia is a decidedly smaller city; if you came here to grab a stranger's ass on the dance floor, you are in the wrong place. (Madrid is just a short train ride away…) That said, if you are with a group of friends and looking for a place to hear live music or just get on a dance floor, there are a handful of options. The best bet is to head to **Calle de la Infanta Isabel** just off Pl. Mayor, or to **Paseo del Salón de Isabel II** (though the latter plays host to more locals' *botellones*). While there are a few other bars and clubs throughout the Old City, places shut down and streets get pretty quiet by midnight, so it's best to roll out with a posse.

BAR SANTANA — BAR, LIVE MUSIC

C. Infanta Isabel, 18 — ☎92 146 35 64

Santana is one of the few live music bars in town, drawing local acts every Friday. Tasty tapas and rock music bring in a casual older crowd, which loiters outside with drinks at the exterior bar. Photo and poetry exhibits line the back wall.

🪧 Down C. Infanta Isabel from Pl. Mayor. $ Beer €1.10. Mixed drinks €4.50. 🕒 Open Th-Sa 10:30pm-3:30am.

TOYS — CLUB

C. Infanta Isabel, 13 — ☎92 146 31 27

Toys looks something like your favorite trashy club in your favorite trashy college town. Drinks are cheap, the music is loud, and the room is **dark.** This is one of the few venues open late, along with neighbor Geographic Chic.

🪧 Down C. Infanta Isabel from Pl. Mayor. $ Beer €1. Mixed drinks €4.50-5.50. 🕒 Open daily 10pm-4am.

GEOGRAPHIC CHIC — CLUB

C. Infanta Isabel, 13 — ☎92 146 30 38

Mannequins line the windows and cherubs smile on the bar. Drinks are cheap and American pop is the norm. Come late if you choose to come at all; this place is often empty until 1am.

🪧 Down C. Infanta Isabel from Pl. Mayor. $ Mixed drinks €5. 🕒 Open W-Sa 10:30pm-4am.

ARTS AND CULTURE

Festivals

FIESTAS DE SAN JUAN Y SAN PEDRO — CITYWIDE

In the month of June, Segovia holds a fiesta in honor of San Juan and San Pedro, with free open-air concerts on Pl. del Azoguejo, a pilgrimage to the hermitage of Juarrillos (5km away), and dances and fireworks on June 29.

🪧 In Pl. del Azoguejo. 🕒 June 23-June 29.

FIESTAS DE SANTA ÁGUEDA — ZAMARRAMALA

The town of Zamarramala hosts the Fiestas de Santa Águeda. Women take over the town for a day and dress in period costumes to commemorate a 👍**sneak attack** on the Alcázar in which women distracted the castle guards with wine and song. The all-female local council takes advantage of its temporary authority to ridicule men, burning a male effigy at the festival's end.

🧭 In Zamarramala, 3km northwest of Segovia. As you face the Alcázar, head right on Paseo de San Juan de la Cruz, then left downhill. Follow C. de San Marcos across the river, then right just past the tiny Romanesque 👍**Iglesia de la Vera Cruz** *up Ctra. de Zamarramala. Stay right at the fork onto C. Real Alta, which leads to the center of Zamarramala. 🕐 1st Su in Feb.*

ESSENTIALS

Practicalities

- **TOURIST OFFICES: Regional office.** (Pl. Mayor, 10 ☎92 146 03 34 🕐 Open July-Sept 15 M-Th 9am-8pm, F-Sa 9am-9pm, Su 9am-8pm; Sept 16-June daily 9am-2pm and 5-8pm.) **Visitor's Reception Center.** (Centro de Recepción de Visitantes. Pl. del Azoguejo, 1 ☎92 146 67 20 🕐 Open M-F 10am-7pm, Sa 10am-8pm, Su 10am-7pm.)
- **CURRENCY EXCHANGE: Banco Santander Central Hispano.** (Av. de Fernández Ladreda, 12 🕐 Open Apr-Sept M-F 8:30am-2pm; Oct-Mar M-F 8:30am-2pm, Sa 8:30am-1pm.) **ATMs** and other banks, which also change cash, line Av. de Fernández Ladreda.
- **LUGGAGE STORAGE: Lockers** at the train station. (☎90 224 02 02 💲 €3 per day. 🕐 Open daily 6am-10:30pm.)
- **INTERNET ACCESS: Biblioteca Pública.** (C. Juan Bravo, 11 ☎92 146 35 33 ℹ Passport required. Max. 30min. 💲 Free. 🕐 Open Sept-June M-F 9am-9pm, Sa 9am2pm; July-Aug M-F 9am-3pm, Sa 9am-2pm.) **Locutorio Acueducto.** (C. San Francisco, 6 ℹ Off Pl. Azoguejo. 💲 €1 per hr. 🕐 Open daily noon-11pm.)
- **POST OFFICE:** Pl. Dr. Laguna, 5 ☎92 146 16 16 🧭 Up C. Cronista Lecea from Pl. Mayor. 🕐 Open M-F 8:30am-8:30pm, Sa 9:30am-2pm.
- **POSTAL CODE:** 40001.

Emergency

- **EMERGENCY NUMBERS:** ☎091. **Ambulance:** ☎112.
- **POLICE: City Police.** (C. Guadarrama, 24 ☎92 143 12 12.) **National Police.** (☎92 141 47 00.)
- **HOSPITALS: Hospital General de Segovia.** (C. de Ávila ☎92 141 91 00 🧭 Take Av. del Padre Claret from Pl. Azoguejo, then left at the second roundabout onto C. Cardadores.)

Getting There

BY TRAIN

The **train station** is at C. Obispo Quesada, 1 (☎90 224 02 02). There's a high-speed train (🕐 27min.; 8, 8:45am, every 1½hr. 2-8pm) and a regional train (💲 €5.90 🕐 every 2hr. M-F 5:55am-8:55pm, Sa-Su 8:55am-8:55pm) from Madrid. There's also a regional train from Villalba (💲 €3.90 🕐 1hr., 7-9 per day M-F 5:55am-8:55pm), with transfers to Ávila, El Escorial, León, and Salamanca.

BY BUS

The bus station, **Estación Municipal de Autobuses** (Paseo Ezéquiel González, 12 ☎92 142 77 07) offers two bus options. **La Sepulvedana** (☎92 142 77 07) runs buses from Ávila (💲 €4.25 🕐 1hr.; M-Sa 7:45am, 6pm.), La Granja (💲 €1.05 🕐 20min.; 9-15 per day M-Sa 7:40am-9:30pm, Su 10:30am-10:30pm), and Madrid (💲 €6.43 🕐 1hr.; M-F every 30min. 6:30am-10:30pm, Sa every 30min. 8am-10:30pm, Su every hr. 8am-10:30pm). **Linecar** (☎92 142 77 06) goes between Segovia and Valladolid. ($ €6.85. ⏰ 2hr.; M-F 12 per day 6:45am-9pm, Sa 8 per day 6:45am-9pm, Su 6 per day 9am-9pm.)

Getting Around

BY BUS

Transportes Urbanos de Segovia runs city buses, including the *búho* at night. (☎92 146 27 27 $ €0.80, discounted electronic passes available.)

BY TAXI

Taxi stands are located in the train and bus stations, in Pl. Mayor, and just beyond Pl. Azoguejo. **Radio Taxi** (☎92 144 50 00 ⏰ 24hr.) is a good bet.

salamanca ☎923

Dubbed Spain's "Golden City," Salamanca radiates with beautiful landmarks carved of yellow Villamayor stone. Pretty plazas and cathedrals aside, Salamanca is a college town at heart, famous for the **Universidad de Salamanca,** one of the oldest in Europe. Once a battleground between Muslims and Christians, Salamanca now worries less about rampaging armies and more about its over 30,000 raging students.

ORIENTATION

Salamanca is oriented around three key sights: the **university** at the city center, **Plaza Mayor** just to the north, and the **cathedrals** to the south. The historic Old City is accessible on foot and **Calle de Rua Mayor** is the major thoroughfare.

ACCOMMODATIONS

REVOLUTUM HOSTEL HOSTEL $

C. Sánchez Barbero, 7 ☎923 2176 56 www.revoltumhostel.com

This newly renovated backpackers' hostel is every bit as cool as the made-up word "Revolutum." The social hostel has a range of different commons areas: a "cafe-bar," a "living-cafe," a "chill out," a patio, and a shared kitchen-dining area. Bedrooms are mostly shared with simple bunks, clean white sheets, and a Granny Smith apple waiting for you. While the bedrooms are simple enough, all of the common areas have posh-club-VIP-room decor with low-lying banks of cushions, plastic egg-shaped chairs, and bright pillows. The location is as central as it gets, just a few meters from Pl. Mayor and close to plenty of restaurants. Private rooms are also available, but be sure to book in advance as they go quickly.

‡ From Pl. Mayor, exit through the south end toward C. de Rua Mayor and take a left onto C. Sánchez Barbero. $ Dorms €20; private rooms €30. ⏰ Reception 24hr.

HOSTAL CONCEJO HOTEL $$$

Pl. de la Libertad, 1 ☎923 21 47 37 www.hconcejo.com

With floral bed coverings, hardwood floors, and full baths, the modern rooms at the Hostal Concejo resemble those of a boutique hotel. Many of the rooms have balconies overlooking the beautiful gardens and cypress trees of Pl. de la Libertad. The *hostal* is in a peaceful, less tourist-ridden location just a few steps from Pl. Mayor.

‡ From Pl. Mayor, take C. Concejo (on the left facing north) 10m to Pl. de la Libertad. i Check online for discounts. $ Singles €45-49; doubles €56-69; triples €79-83. ⏰ Reception 24hr.

HOSTAL SARA HOTEL $$$

C. de Meléndez, 11 ☎923 28 11 40 www.hostalsara.org

Nicely decorated with simple bed coverings and light wood floors, Hostal Sara is a great option if you want to stay in the center of town. The location between Pl. Mayor and the university is convenient for those staying just one night, and the complimentary Wi-Fi is a rare privilege in Salamanca. Rooms are simple and include a mini-fridge and full bath. With a large elevator, the *hostal* is also easily wheelchair-accessible.

⚲ From the university, walk northeast up C. de Meléndez toward Pl. Mayor. [$] Singles €38; doubles €45-48; triples €78-85. ⏰ Reception 24hr.

HOSTAL LAS VEGAS HOTEL $

C. de Meléndez, 13 ☎923 21 87 49 www.lasvegascentro.net

This ain't the Bellagio. The closest thing you'll find to a million-dollar fountain in this hotel may be a bidet. Despite the name, the accommodations at Hostal Las Vegas are basic, with mismatched furniture and particularly small bathrooms. That said, it's cheap. The private rooms and bathrooms are clean and will be a welcome relief to those looking to avoid another night in the dorm. The location on C. de Meléndez puts you in the middle of the major sights, and close to restaurants and nightlife.

⚲ From the university, walk northeast up C. de Meléndez toward Pl. Mayor. [$] Singles €24; doubles €36-45; triples €60; quads €80. ⏰ Reception 24hr.

HOSTAL CATEDRAL HOTEL $$

C. de Rua Mayor, 46-48 ☎923 27 06 14

Located next to the cathedral, this *hostal* has the feel of a small guesthouse. The landlady is very attentive and keeps the rooms tidy, though you can expect the typical odds-and-ends decor of Spanish *hostales*. There are only a few rooms available so reservations are a must. The location across the plaza from the Cathedral is quiet, but you can expect plenty of nighttime activity just a block north along C. de Rua Mayor.

⚲ From Pl. de Anaya, facing north, approach C. de Rua Mayor. The hostal is the 1st building on the left. [$] Singles €30; doubles €45-48. ⏰ Reception 24hr.

SIGHTS

Salamanca is and always has been a college town. (And we mean **always.**) The Universidad de Salamanca remains the city's primary attraction, along with Pl. Mayor and the New and Old Cathedrals. In addition to these major sights, there are plenty of small museums with collections dedicated to everything from cars to Art Deco to film.

UNIVERSIDAD DE SALAMANCA UNIVERSITY

C. de los Libreros ☎923 27 71 00

The heart of Salamanca, this university is one of the most important buildings in the city and a jewel of the Spanish Renaissance. The storied school has been around pretty much forever: it was founded by Alfonso IX of León in 1218. Legend has it that if you can find the frog (perched atop a skull) in the façade without assistance, then you will receive good luck and marriage. Inside the university you can view the historical library, which holds 40,000 precious volumes including priceless manuscripts like *El Libro de Buen Amor* by the archpriest of Hita. You can also see the classroom where superstar academic Fray Luis de León used to teach. While you're here, look for the red marks covering the sides of the building—when students graduated, they used to stamp the walls with a mixture of bull's blood and oil.

Next to Pl. Mayor. [$] €4, students and over 65 €2, under 12 free. Free M morning. Cash only. Open Tu-F 10:30am-12:45pm and 5-7pm, Sa 9:30am-1:30pm and 3-7pm, Su 10am-1:30pm.

CATHEDRALS OF SALAMANCA CATHEDRALS

Pl. de Anaya ☎923 21 74 76

What could be cooler than a giant cathedral? How about **two giant cathedrals stuck together?** This was the attitude of the Spanish Catholic church in 1513 when it began constructing the massive New Cathedral right next to Cathedral Classic. Exactly when construction began on the original Cathedral is unclear, but records suggest sometime in the second half of the 12th century. Today the most artistically renowned part of the Old Cathedral is its altarpiece, which is made of 53 panels conveying the life of Jesus Christ in the style of the Florentine Renaissance. The New Cathedral isn't new by any measure—work started in 1513, and it took two centuries to build. While predominantly Gothic in style, it also incorporates Baroque and Renaissance ornament. When you enter, be sure to look for the astronaut and lion with an ice cream cone carved into the stone by mischievous artists during renovations in 1992. In the Old Cathedral, it is said that if you visit the Santa Bárbara chapel and place your feet on the tombstone of the bishop Juan Lucero, wisdom will surge from your feet to your head. Whether or not this will actually happen is questionable, but you're reading *Let's Go*, so chances are you're pretty wise already.

*From Pl. Mayor, exit south to C. de Rua Mayor and follow it south to Pl. de Anaya. The New Cathedral is on the plaza; the Old Cathedral is directly behind. **i** Purchase tickets to the Old Cathedral in the New Cathedral. [$] New Cathedral free. Old Cathedral €4.75, students €3.25. Tu 10am-noon free. Cash only. New Cathedral open daily 9am-8pm. Old Cathedral open daily 10am-7:30pm.*

PLAZA MAYOR PLAZA

Pl. Mayor is one of the most beautiful plazas in Spain. Built by Alberto de Churriguera in 1775, the plaza is a popular social hub that has historically been the center of Salamanca's political, economic, and religious activities. At different times in its history it has served as a market, concert hall, bullring, and theater. Today it is home to dozens of restaurants and tourist shops. Stop by in the early evening (8-9pm) when locals convene to chitchat before heading off to dinner.

From the New Cathedral, follow C. de Rua Mayor north. [$] Free.

CASA DE LAS CONCHAS LIBRARY, PALACE

C. Compañía, 2 ☎923 26 93 17

Built by Rodrigo Arias Maldonado at the end of the 15th century, the "House of Shells" is dotted with 365 shells on its facade, one for each day of the year. They represent Maldonaldo's love for his wife (her family symbol was the shell) and his dedication to the Order of Santiago (whose symbol is also a shell). Today the former palace is free to the public, but there's not much happening inside besides a nice courtyard. The building is now the city's public library.

Across the street from the university. From Pl. Mayor, exit south and take a right onto C. de Meléndez. This street dead-ends into the university building. Casa de las Conchas will be on your right. [$] Free. Open M-F 9am-9pm, Sa 9am-2pm and 3-7pm, Su 10am-2pm and 3-7pm.

MUSEO DE LA HISTORIA DE LA AUTOMOCIÓN MUSEUM

Pl. Mercado Viejo ☎923 26 02 93 www.museoautomocion.com

This museum showcases a car collection, most of which belong to Gomez Planche. With over 100 vehicles, thousands of parts, and scores of car accessories, the collection is an impressive ode to the car's place in history. The collection ranges from awkward-looking spoke-wheel contraptions to modern sports cars straight out of *2 Fast 2 Furious*.

➡ Just south of the Cathedral. From Pl. de Anaya, head east on C. de Tostado to C. San Pablo. Right on C. San Pablo to Paseo del Rector Esperabe, cross to the other side of the street and head to the right. $ €3, students and over 65 €2. Free 1st Tu of each month 5-8pm. ⏰ Open Tu-Su 10am-2pm and 5-8pm.

FOOD

Salamanca offers plenty of great budget options for travelers. Avoid the two major thoroughfares of **Plaza Mayor** and **Calle de Rua Mayor,** which offer picture menus, *menús del día* and alluring terrace seating, and follow our lead for the best local food.

👍 **ZAZU BISTRO** ITALIAN, MEDITERRANEAN $$

Pl. de la Libertad, 8 ☎923 26 16 90

Located in a restored townhouse along Pl. de la Libertad, the setting of Zazu Bistro cannot be beat. Unlike busy C. de Rua Mayor, Pl. de la Libertad remains calm through the night, which makes it more like dining in a sleepy European town than a major tourist destination. The menu draws heavily on traditional Italian fare, with dishes like pizza with goat cheese, tomato, basil, and bacon (€11) and Mediterranean-inspired salads and entrees. The top floor, with its vaulted ceilings and living room with couches, is a popular spot later in the evening for cocktails and dessert.

➡ From Pl. Mayor, walk north along C. Concejo (on the west side of plaza) to Pl. de la Libertad. The restaurant is on the south side of the plaza. $ Entrees €10-20. ⏰ Open daily 2-4pm and 8:30pm-midnight.

DELICATESSEN AND CAFE MEDITERRANEAN $$

C. de Meléndez, 25 ☎923 28 03 09

Located just a few steps from the university, Delicatessen and Cafe has figured out how to please its student clientele. The menu here is dominated by large portions of Mediterranean staples and the occasional stateside favorite, like "the Continental" (steak with fried eggs, salad, and homefries; €10). Simple pizzas (€10-12), pasta (€10), and risotto (€11) are popular, as are combination entrees like the *estudiante* (grilled chicken, grilled vegetables, salad, and potatoes; €10). The food isn't particularly inventive, but it's satisfying. The restaurant's heated outdoor terrace has large tropical plants and a massive dome glass roof. At night, local DJs spin pop tunes and music videos play on the big-screen projector.

➡ Exit Pl. Mayor through the southwest corner and walk past Iglesia de San Martín until you reach C. de Meléndez. The restaurant is just around the bend on the left. $ Entrees €10-15. ⏰ Open daily 10am-3am. Kitchen open 1-4pm and 8:30pm-midnight.

CAFE BAR MANDALA CAFE, BAR $

C. de Serranos, 9 ☎923 12 33 42

Cafe Bar Mandala is a popular student hangout right across from the university. The drink variety here is endless, with each of the six menus dedicated to a different kind of beverage: there is a menu exclusively for loose-leaf tea, regular tea, iced tea, Arabic coffee, milk shakes, and Italian sodas. If you are looking for the same variety in food, though, you just won't find it. The menu is limited to a simple selection of *bocadillos* (€2-4), salads (€4-6), and international staples like lasagna and quiche.

‡ From C. de Rua Mayor, walk west along the southern edge of the university to C. de Serranos. The restaurant is just past C. de los Liberos. $ Meals €5-10. Beverages €2-4. ⏰ Open daily 9am-1am.

NIGHTLIFE

Because of Salamanca's year-round student population, the city has a number of fairly steady nightlife options.

GATSBY BAR, CLUB

C. de los Bordadores, 16 ☎923 21 72 74

With old farming tools, tribal masks, and wooden chandeliers hanging from the ceiling, Gatsby is more Westphalia than West Egg. With a good mix of Spanish and American clientele and music, Gatsby is loved by everyone (except maybe Daisy). This club has been around since 1985 and continues to deliver on the same booze specials and themed parties. Deals like five shots for €5 sit well with university students, as do themed parties like "The Lollipop Party" and "The Galactic Party."

‡ From Pl. Mayor, walk west down C. del Prior and make a right onto C. de los Bordadores. $ Beer and mixed drinks €3-8. ⏰ Open M-Th 5:30pm-3:30am, F-Sa 5:30pm-5am.

CAMELOT BAR, CLUB

C. de los Bordadores, 3 ☎923 21 21 82 www.camelotsalamanca.es

Decorated like an ancient castle, Camelot is your best bet for a round table or Dark (Ages) dance floor. With a wrought-iron balcony, the second floor is a perfect place to party like its 1299. Occasional free flamenco shows get the crowd moving early in the night. They don't serve mead, so pretend your sangria is slightly less fruity and significantly more disgusting for the full medieval effect.

‡ From Pl. Mayor, walk west down C. del Prior and make a right onto C. de los Bordadores. $ Beer €3-4. Cocktails €6. ⏰ Open M-W 9pm-4:30am, Th 9pm-5:30am, F-Sa 9pm-6:30am, Su 9pm-4:30am.

ARTS AND CULTURE

Named a European Capital of Culture in 2002, Salamanca has plenty to offer visitors beyond traditional sights. As one of Spain's primary university cities, Salamanca has a thriving music, dance, theater, and film scene. Pick up the seasonal program of cultural events *Cultura Aquí* from the tourist office in Pl. Mayor (see **Essentials**) or check out nightly events at **www.salamancaciudaddecultura.org.** Like everywhere else in Spain, Salamanca is serious about tradition. Look out for seasonal festivals and bullfighting events taking place in Salamanca's famous **La Glorieta.**

PLAZA DE TOROS DE SALAMANCA "LA GLORIETA" BULLRING

Av. de San Agustín, 1 ☎923 22 12 99

The area around Salamanca is the most prominent bull-breeding territory in Spain, so you can expect some wicked fights and even wilder fans. Every June and September, the famous Plaza de Toros de Salamanca (also known as "La Glorieta") hosts the most famous matadors and fiercest bulls. Bullfights took place in Pl. Mayor until La Glorieta was completed in 1893. Today it holds up to 10,000 spectators and hosts cultural events and concerts when bullfighting isn't in season. If you happen to be in Salamanca during February, make the 45min. trip to **Ciudad Rodrigo,** where the Carnaval del Toro shakes the city up with street dancing, festivities, music, and bullfighting.

‡ A 15min. walk from Pl. Mayor. Exit the plaza through from the northwest corner onto C. del Concejo, which becomes C. del Zamora. Follow C. del Zamora north to Paseo del Doctor Torres

Villarroel and make a slight right at the roundabout. ℹ For more info on the Carnaval del Toro, visit www.aytociudadrodrigo.es. Buses leave for Ciudad Rodrigo every hr. from Estación de Autobuses de Salamanca.

MUSEO TAURINO MUSEUM

C. del Doctor Piñuela, 5-7 ☎923 21 94 25 www.museotaurinosalamanca.es

To learn more about this fierce sport, check out the bullfighting museum, Museo Taurino, where you'll find exhibits on everything from matador fashion to bullfighting in Spanish popular culture.

⇆ From Pl. Mayor, exit the plaza on the northwest corner and take C. del Toro north ½ block to C. del Doctor Piñuela. The museum is on the left. $ €3. ⏰ Open Tu-F 6-9pm, Sa noon-2pm and 6-9pm, Su noon-2pm.

TEATRO LICEO CLASSICAL MUSIC, THEATER

Pl. Liceo ☎923 28 06 19

Built on the ruins of the convent of San Antonio del Real, this theater was renovated in 2002 and has an impressive 565-person auditorium with the look and feel of Carnegie Hall. Teatro Liceo is the city's most impressive venue for classical and contemporary theater, dance, music, and Baroque opera. The space also hosts a popular film series throughout the year. Tickets vary in price, but most events do not exceed €15.

⇆ From Pl. Mayor, exit the northwest corner onto C. del Toro and walk 2 blocks north. The theater is on the left. ℹ For a performance schedule, consult the tourist office. Tickets can be purchased at the box office or through El Corte Inglés (☎902 40 02 22; www.elcorteingles.es). ⏰ Ticket office open M-F 11am-2pm, Sa noon-2pm. The ticket office also opens 2hr. before each performance.

TEATRO JUAN DE ENZINA THEATER

C. de Tostado, 2 ☎923 29 45 42

This university-sponsored theater offers some of the cheapest seats in all of Spain and focuses on contemporary theater, dance, and music performances.

⇆ From the Cathedrals, follow C. de Tostado just east of Pl. de Ayana. ⏰ Shows year-round.

Festivals

REYES MAGOS

Like most Spanish cities, Salamanca needs little excuse to party. Every year on January 5th, residents, students, and tourists celebrate the arrival of the Three Kings during the *Cabalgata de los Reyes Magos*, an evening parade that features dancing, music, and costumes. The day after is similar to Christmas Day in the United States, with feasts and the exchange of gifts.

⏰ Jan 5-6.

FACYL: INTERNATIONAL ARTS FESTIVAL OF CASTILLA AND LEÓN

www.facyl-festival.com

During the first two weeks of June, this arts festival takes over every cultural establishment in the city. Plazas, museums, and major performance spaces become venues for the latest in contemporary art, music, theater, and dance.

⏰ 1st 2 weeks of June.

CORPUS CHRISTI

On June 18th, the Corpus Christi celebration is in full force around the Old Cathedral. Salamanca residents celebrate with street performances and parties.

⏰ June 18th.

ESSENTIALS

Practicalities

- **TOURIST OFFICES:** The **Municipal Tourist Office** distributes free maps and pamphlets. (Pl. Mayor, 32 ☎923 21 83 42 ⏰ Open June-Sept M-F 9am-2pm and 4:30-8pm, Sa 10am-8pm, Su 10am-2pm; Oct-May M-F 9am-2pm and 4-6:30pm, Sa 10am-6:30pm, Su 10am-2pm.) The **Regional Tourist Office** also has free information. (C. de Rua Mayor ☎923 26 85 71 ⏰ Open July-Sept M-Th 9am-8pm, F-Sa 9am-9pm, Su 9am-8pm; Oct-June daily 9am-2pm and 5-8pm.) Look out for **DGratis,** a free listing of goings-on distributed every F, available at tourist offices and distributors in Pl. Mayor. For details, visit www.salamanca.es.
- **TOURS:** A **walking tour** departs from the tourist office in Pl. Mayor and covers Pl. Mayor, Casa de las Conchas, La Clerecía, Universidad Civil, and the Cathedrals. (☎653 75 96 02 *i* In English. Min. 10 people. $ €15; includes admission to sights. ⏰ 2hr., M and W.)
- **CURRENCY EXCHANGE: EuroDivisas** has ATMs and currency exchange. (C. de Rua Mayor, 2 ☎923 21 21 80 ⏰ Open M-F 8:30am-10pm, Sa-Su 10am-7pm.)
- **LUGGAGE STORAGE:** At the **train station.** ($ €3-4.50) and **bus station** ($ €2 ⏰ 7am-7:45pm).
- **LAUNDROMAT: Coin Laundry.** (Pasaje Azafranal, 18. ☎923 36 02 16 $ Wash and dry €4. ⏰ Open M-F 9:30am-2pm and 4-8pm, Sa 9:30am-2pm.)
- **INTERNET ACCESS:** The **Biblioteca Pública** offers free internet access. (Casa de Las Conchas, C. Compañía, 2 ☎923 26 93 17 ⏰ Open July-Aug M-F 9am-3pm, Sa 9am-2pm; Sept-June M-F 9am-9pm, Sa 9am-2pm.) **Cyber Place Internet** is busy, but has good rates for internet access. (Pl. Mayor, 10, 1st fl. $ €1 per hr. ⏰ Open M-F 11am-midnight, Sa-Su noon-midnight.) **Cyber Anuario** is another option. (C. Traviesa, 16 ☎923 26 13 54 $ €1.50 per hr. ⏰ Open M-Sa 11am-2:30pm and 4:30-11pm.)
- **POST OFFICE:** C. de la Gran Vía, 25-29. ☎923 28 14 57 ⏰ Open M-F 8:30am-8:30pm, Sa 9:30am-2pm.
- **POSTAL CODE:** 37001.

Emergency

- **EMERGENCY NUMBER:** ☎112.
- **POLICE:** Ayuntamiento, Pl. Mayor, 2. ☎923 26 53 11.
- **CRISIS LINES: Red Cross.** (C. Cruz Roja, 1 ☎923 22 22 22.)

Getting There

BY PLANE

Flights arrive at the **Aeropuerto de Salamanca.** (SLM; Ctra. Madrid, 14 km from the city. ☎923 32 96 00.)

BY TRAIN

Trains arrive at the **Vialia Estación de Salamanca** (Paseo de la Estación ☎902 24 02 02) from Lisbon ($ €47 ⏰ 6hr., 1 per day 4:51am) and Madrid ($ €18 ⏰ 2½hr., 6-7 per day 6am-7:53pm).

BY BUS

The **Estación de Autobuses de Salamanca** (Av. Filiberto Villalobos, 71 ☎923 23 67 17) has express buses to Madrid ($ €22 ⏰ 2½hr., every hr., 6am-9:30pm), and local bus routes to Madrid ($ €16 ⏰ 3hr., every hr. 7:30am-8:30pm).

Getting Around

Salamanca is easily walkable, and most sights are concentrated around Pl. Mayor. The trip from the train station to the city center is 15-20min. on foot or 5min. by taxi (**Radio Taxi** ☎923 25 00 00 $ €5). To walk from the Vialia Estación de Salamanca, walk southwest down Paseo de la Estación three blocks to Pl. de España and make a right onto Paseo de las Canalejas. Walk half a block and make a left onto C. del Toro (this street dead-ends into the northern end of the Pl. Mayor). To get to the city center from the bus station, exit the station and follow Av. de Filiberto Villalobos four blocks southeast. Cross Pl. de las Carmelitas, at which point Av. de Filiberto Villalobos becomes C. de Ramón y Cajal. Follow for two blocks, at which point this street becomes C. del Prior. This dead ends into the western edge of Pl. Mayor.

BARCELONA

Benvolgut a Barcelona! Welcome to a city more exquisite, more idiosyncratic, more bold, and more fun than you ever thought a city could be. There's a whole lot more to Barcelona than Gaudí's architecture and the incredible clubs, and *Let's Go* will show you the way—at the end of the day, you've always got Gaudí and the clubs to fall back on.

You'll find that the locals consider themselves Catalan first and Spanish a distant second. Barcelona is quite proud of its Catalan culture and language, which is the default and which you'll probably hear much more frequently than *castellano*. Everybody in Catalonia speaks Spanish—they just generally prefer not to—and even if your Spanish-language skills don't extend beyond *hola* and *cerveza*, you'll get by just fine.

Whether you're strolling through the broad tree-and-*modernista*-building-lined avenues of l'Eixample by day, bar-hopping beneath the walls of Gothic churches of the Ciutat Vella at night, or napping off that hangover in one of Gràcia's shady plazas, if you take a second to look around you'll be mesmerized by the city's ubiquitous charm. Oh, and did we mention there's also a 🏖beach? Save it for last, because once you head to the beach, you'll never see anything else.

greatest hits

- **A PALACE FIT FOR AN INDUSTRIALIST.** Live the hostel life in a converted *modernista* palace near Parc Güell at Mare de Déu de Montserrat Youth Hostel. (p. 126)

- **THE WALLS ARE MELTING, MAN.** Stand in awe before what Gaudí was able to do with stone at the Sagrada Família. (p. 136)

- **TAP DANCE.** Try Let's Go's favorite tapas in town: Bombeta's *bombas,* which are certainly *cojonudas.* (p. 160)

- **DANCE DANCE.** Just don't start a revolution when you hit up KGB. (p. 181)

orientation

Though a large and complex city, Barcelona's *barris* (neighborhoods) are fairly well-defined. The **Ciutat Vella** (old city) is the city's heart, comprised of **El Raval** (west of Las Ramblas), **Barri Gòtic** (between **Las Ramblas** and Via Laietana), **El Born** (between Via Laietana and Parc de la Ciutadella), and **La Barceloneta** (the peninsula south of El Born). Farther down the coast (to the left as you look at a map with the sea at the bottom) from the *Ciutat Vella* is the park-mountain **Montjuïc,** and the small neighborhood of **Poble Sec** between Montjuïc and Avinguda Paral·lel. Farther inland from the *Ciutat Vella* is the large, central, rigidly gridded zone of **l'Eixample,** and still farther away from the sea is **Gràcia.** The **Plaça de Catalunya** is one of the city's most central points, located where Las Ramblas meets the Passeig de Gràcia; it is essentially the meeting point of El Raval, Barri Gòtic, and l'Eixample.

BARRI GÒTIC AND LAS RAMBLAS

You will get lost in Barri Gòtic. Knowing this, the best way to properly orient yourself in the confusing neighborhood, where streets still follow their medieval routes, is to take a day to learn your way around. **Las Ramblas** provides the western boundary of the neighborhood, stretching from the waterfront to **Plaça de Catalunya. Via Laietana** marks the eastern border, running nearly parallel to Las Ramblas. The primary east-west artery running between Las Ramblas and V. Laietana is known as **Carrer de Ferran** between Las Ramblas and the central **Plaça de Sant Jaume,** and as **Carrer de Jaume I** between Pl. Sant Jaume and V. Laietana. Of the many plazas hiding in the Barri Gòtic, **Plaça Reial** (take the tiny C. de Colom off Las Ramblas) and Plaça de Sant Jaume are the grandest. The neighborhood is better known, though, for its more cramped spaces, like the narrow alleys covered with arches or miniature *placetas* in the shadows of parish churches. The **L3** and **L4** metro lines serve this neighborhood, with ⓜ**Drassanes,** ⓜ**Liceu,** and ⓜ**Catalunya** along Las Ramblas (L3), and ⓜ**Jaume I** at the intersection of C. Jaume I and V. Laietana.

EL BORN

El Born, which makes up the eastern third of the **Ciutat Vella,** is celebrated for being slightly less touristy than the Barri Gòtic and slightly less prostitute-y than El Raval. The neighborhood is renowned for its confusing medieval streets, whose ancient bends hide fashionable boutiques and restaurants both traditional and modern. The **Passeig del Born,** the lively hub of this quirky *barri*, makes for a good bar- and restaurant-lined starting point.

barcelona

EL RAVAL

There's no point beating around the bush: El Raval is one of Barcelona's more dangerous neighborhoods. By no means should you avoid it, just be careful and aware—even during the day—and be prepared to deal with persistent drug dealers and aggressive prostitutes. In particular, avoid **Carrer de Sant Ramon.** Clearly, El Raval does not lack character, and it is actually one of the city's most interesting neighborhoods. Everything tends to be significantly less expensive than on the other side of Las Ramblas, and a large student population supports a bevy of quirky restaurants and bars. Areas around the **Rambla del Raval** and the **Carrer de Joaquim Costa** hide small unique bars and late-night cafes frequented by Barcelona's alternative crowd. For daytime shopping, check out **Riera Baixa,** a street lined with secondhand shops that also hosts a flea market on Saturdays, or the ritzier neighborhood around **Carrer del Doctor Dou, Carrer del Pintor Fortuny,** and **Carrer Elisabets** for higher-end (though still reasonably priced) shops.

L'EIXAMPLE

In this posh neighborhood (pronounced leh-SHAM-pluh), big blocks, wide avenues, and dazzling architecture mean lots of walking and lots of exciting storefronts. *Modernista* buildings line **Passeig de Gràcia** (pronounced pah-SAYCH da GRAH-see-yuh), which runs from north to south through the neighborhood's center (Ⓜ️Diagonal, Ⓜ️Passeig de Gràcia, Ⓜ️Catalunya). **L'Eixample Dreta** encompasses the area to the east around the **Sagrada Família,** and **l'Eixample Esquerra** comprises the area closer to the **University,** uphill from **Plaça de la Universitat.** Though the former contains some surprisingly cheap accommodations for those willing to make the hike, l'Eixample Esquerra is somewhat more pedestrian-friendly and more interesting to walk around. While this neighborhood is notoriously expensive, there are some cheaper and more interesting options for accommodations and food as you get closer to Pl. Universitat. The stretch of **Carrer del Consell de Cent** west of Pg. de Gràcia boasts vibrant nightlife, where many "hetero-friendly" bars, clubs, and hotels give it the nickname **Gaixample.**

BARCELONETA

Barceloneta, the triangular peninsula that juts out into the Mediterranean, is a former mariners' and fishermen's neighborhood, built on a sandbank at the beginning of the 18th century to replace the homes destroyed by the construction of the *ciutadella.* The grid plan, a consequence of Enlightenment city planning, gives the neighborhood's narrow streets a distinct character, seasoned by the salty sea breezes that whip through the urban canyons. Tourists and locals are drawn to unconventional Barceloneta by the restaurants and views along the **Passeig Joan de Borbó,** by the 🏖️beaches on the other side along the **Passeig Marítim de la Barceloneta,** and by the *discotecas* at the **Port Olímpic.**

GRÀCIA

Gràcia is hard to navigate by Metro. While this may at first seem like a negative aspect, the poor municipal planning is actually a bonus. Filled with artsy locals, quirky shops, and a few lost travelers, Gràcia is a quieter, more out-of-the-way neighborhood, best approached by foot. Ⓜ️Diagonal will drop you off at the northern end of the Pg. de Gràcia; follow Pg. de Gràcia across Av. Diagonal and uphill as it becomes **Carrer Gran de Gràcia,** one of the neighborhood's main thoroughfares. Ⓜ️**Fontana** lies further up on C. Gran de Gràcia. If you're heading uphill on C. Gran de Gràcia, any right turn will take you into the charmingly confusing grid of Gràcia's small streets, of which **Carrer de Verdi,** running parallel to C. Gran de Gràcia several blocks away, is probably the most scenic. For bustling *plaças* both day and night, your best bets are **Plaça de la Vila de Gràcia** (more commonly known as Pl. Rius i Taulet), **Plaça del Sol,** and **Plaça de la Revolució de Setembre de 1868,** off of C. de Ros de Olano.

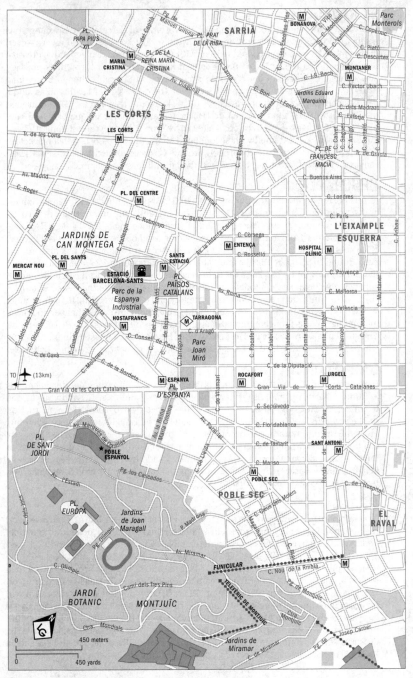

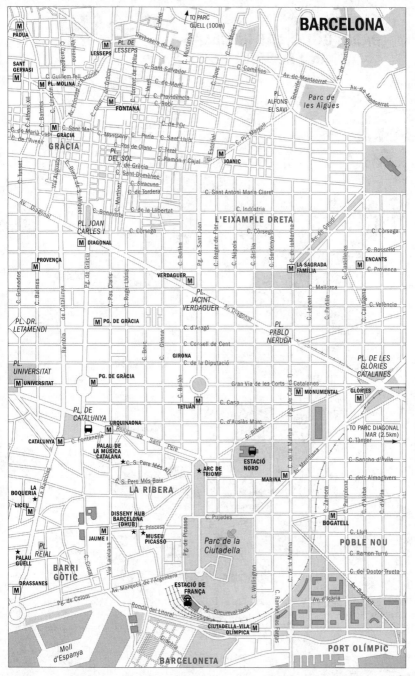

BARCELONA

TO PARC GÜELL (100m)

SANT GERVASI

PÀDUA

PL. DE LESSEPS

Travessera de Dalt

C. Montanya

C. de Mülel

Av. de Montserrat

Av. de Montserrat

SANT GERVASI

PL. MOLINA

C. Guillem Tell

C. de Zaragoza

C. Verdi

C. Sant Salvador

C. Camélies

C. de Sostres

C. Sant Salvador

PL. ALFONS EL SAVI

Parc de les Aïgües

FONTANA

C. Gran de Gràcia

C. Turbol de l'Ora

C. de Martí

C. Providencia

C. Roibí

GRÀCIA

C. Alfons XII

C. Balmes

C. Sant Marc

C. Montseny

C. Perla

C. Sant Lluís

C. de l'Or

GRÀCIA

C. de Maria Cubí

C. de l'Avenir

C. Tuss et

PL. DEL SOL

C. Ros de Olano

C. Terol

C. Ramon y Cajal

C. Sant Domènec

C. Siracusa

C. de Tordera

JOANIC

C. Esgloial

C. Pi i Margall

C. Sant Antoni Maria Claret

C. Industria

Av. de Gaudí

C. de la Libertat

C. Bonavista

L'EIXAMPLE DRETA

C. Còrsega

C. Còrsega

C. Còrsega

PL. JOAN CARLES I

Av. Diagonal

DIAGONAL

C. Bailen

Pg. de Sant Joan

C. Roger de Flor

C. Nàpols

C. Sicília

C. Sardenya

C. de la Marina

Av. de Gaudí

C. Rosselló

C. Provença

ENCANTS

PROVENÇA

C. Granados

C. Balmes

Pg. de Gràcia

C. Pau Claris

C. Roger Llùria

VERDAGUER

C. Castillejos

LA SAGRADA FAMÍLIA

C. Mallorca

C. Provença

PL. DR. LETAMENDI

Rambla de Catalunya

C. Bruc

C. Girona

PL. JACINT VERDAGUER

Av. Diagonal

C. d'Aragó

PL. PABLO NERUDA

C. Lleida

C. Padilla

C. Cartagena

C. València

PG. DE GRÀCIA

C. Consell de Cent

GIRONA

C. de la Diputació

PL. UNIVERSITAT

UNIVERSITAT

PG. DE GRÀCIA

C. Bailen

Gran Via de les Corts Catalanes

PL. DE LES GLÒRIES CATALANES

MONUMENTAL

GLÒRIES

PL. DE CATALUNYA

TETUÁN

C. Casp

C. d'Ausiàs Marc

C. Cardenal Casañas

TO PARC DIAGONAL MAR (2.5km)

C. Tànger

URQUINAONA

Ronda de Sant Pere

C. Ribes

C. Sancho d'Àvila

CATALUNYA

C. Fontanella

PALAU DE LA MÚSICA CATALANA

C. S. Pere Més Alt

ESTACIÓ NORD

Av. Meridiana

C. de la Marina

C. dels Almogàvers

LA BOQUERIA

LICEU

C. S. Pere Més Baix

ARC DE TRIOMF

MARINA

C. Zamora

C. de la Marina

C. Pamplona

C. d'Àlaba

C. d'Àvila

LA RIBERA

DISSENY HUB BARCELONA (DHUB)

C. Princesa

C. Pujades

BOGATELL

C. Llull

PALAU GÜELL

JAUME I

MUSEU PICASSO

Pg. de Picasso

Parc de la Ciutadella

POBLE NOU

C. Ramon Turró

C. del Doctor Trueta

BARRI GÒTIC

Via Laietana

C. Marquès de l'Argentera

ESTACIÓ DE FRANÇA

C. Wellington

Av. d'Icària

Av. Bogatell

DRASSANES

Pg. de Colom

Ronda del Litoral

CIUTADELLA-VILA OLÍMPICA

Ramblas Mas Fargas

PORT OLÍMPIC

Moll d'Espanya

C. Doble

BARCELONETA

orientation

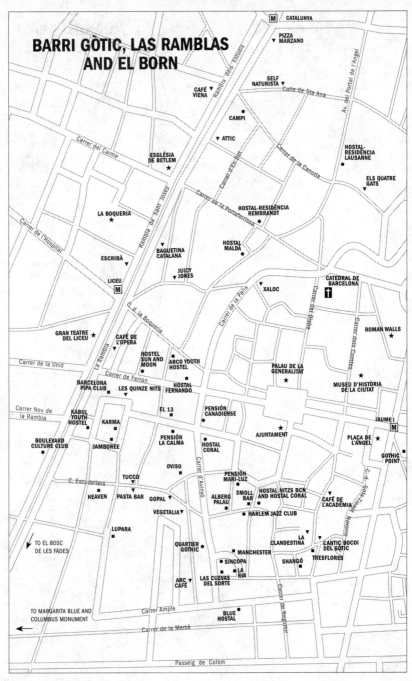

BARRI GÒTIC, LAS RAMBLAS AND EL BORN

barcelona

M CATALUNYA

▼ PIZZA MARZANO

CAFÉ ▼ VIENA

SELF NATURISTA ▼

Calle de Sta Ana

CAMPI ●

▼ ATTIC

Carrer del Carme

ESGLÉSIA DE BETLEM ●

Carrer d'en Bot

Carrer de la Canuda

HOSTAL-RESIDÈNCIA LAUSANNE ●

Carrer de la Portaferrissa

ELS QUATRE GATS ●

LA BOQUERIA ★

Carrer de l'Hospital

HOSTAL-RESIDÈNCIA REMBRANDT ●

BAGUETINA CATALANA ●

HOSTAL MALDA ●

ESCRIBÀ ▼

JUICY JONES ▼

XALOC ●

CATEDRAL DE BARCELONA ✝

LICEU M

C. d. la Boqueria

Carrer de la Palla

ROMAN WALLS ★

Carrer del Bisbe

GRAN TEATRE DEL LICEU ★

CAFÉ DE L'OPERA ●

Carrer dels Comtes

HOSTEL SUN AND MOON ●

ARCO YOUTH HOSTEL ●

PALAU DE LA GENERALITAT ●

Carrer de la Unió

Carrer de Ferran

BARCELONA PIPA CLUB ●

LES QUINZE NITS ●

HOSTAL FERNANDO ●

MUSEU D'HISTÒRIA DE LA CIUTAT ●

Carrer Nou de la Rambla

KABUL YOUTH HOSTEL ●

EL 13 ●

PENSIÓN CANADIENSE ●

JAUME I M

KARMA ■

AJUNTAMENT ★

PLAÇA DE L'ANGEL ★

BOULEVARD CULTURE CLUB ●

JAMBOREE ■

PENSIÓN LA CALMA ●

HOSTAL CORAL ●

GOTHIC POINT ●

C. Escudellers

OVISO ●

PENSIÓN MARI-LUZ ●

Carrer d'Avinyó

TUCCO ●

HEAVEN ■

PASTA BAR ■

GOPAL ▼

ALBERG PALAU ●

SMOLL BAR ■

HOSTAL NITZS BCN AND HOSTAL CORAL ●

CAFÉ DE L'ACADÈMIA ●

VEGETALIA ▼

HARLEM JAZZ CLUB ■

LUPARA ●

LA CLANDESTINA ●

LA ★

L'ANTIC BOCOI DEL GÒTIC ■

TO EL BOSC DE LES FADES

QUARTIER GOTHIC ●

MANCHESTER ■

SHANGÓ ■

TRESFLORES ■

SINCOPA ■

LA RIA ■

ARC CAFÉ ▼

LAS CUEVAS DEL SORTE ●

Carrer de Regomir

TO MARGARITA BLUE AND COLUMBUS MONUMENT

Carrer Ample

BLUE HOSTAL ●

Carrer de la Mercè

Passeig de Colom

Rambla dels Estudis

Rambla de Sant Josep

La Rambla

Av. del Portal de l'Angel

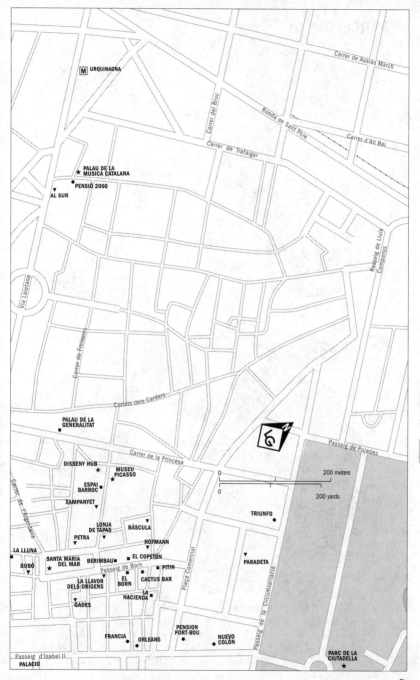

M URQUINAONA

Carrer de Ausiàs March
Carrer del Bruc
Ronda de Sant Pere
Carrer d'Ali Bei
Carrer de Trafalgar

★ PALAU DE LA MUSICA CATALANA
● PENSIÓ 2000
▼ AL SUR

Passeig de Lluís Companys

Via Laietana

Carrer de Freixures

Carrers dels Carders

■ PALAU DE LA GENERALITAT

Passeig de Pujades

Carrer de la Princesa

0   200 meters
0   200 yards

■ DISSENY HUB
★ MUSEU PICASSO
ESPAI BARROC ★
▼ XAMPANYET

Carrer de l'Argenteria

▼ TRIUNFO

LONJA DE TAPAS ▼   BÁSCULA ▼
PETRA ▼
HOFMANN ▼
LA LLUNA ▼
SANTA MARIA DEL MAR ★   BERIMBAU ▼   ● EL COPETÓN
BUBÓ ▼
Passeig de Born
PITIN ▼
▼ PARADETA
LA LLAVOR DELS ORIGENS ▼   EL BORN ▼   CACTUS BAR ▼
LA HACIENDA ▼
GADES ▼

Plaça Comercial

Passeig de la Circumval·lació

FRANCIA ●   ORLEANS ●   PENSION PORT-BOU ●   NUEVO COLON ●

Passeig d'Isabel II
PALACIO

PARC DE LA CIUTADELLA ★

orientation

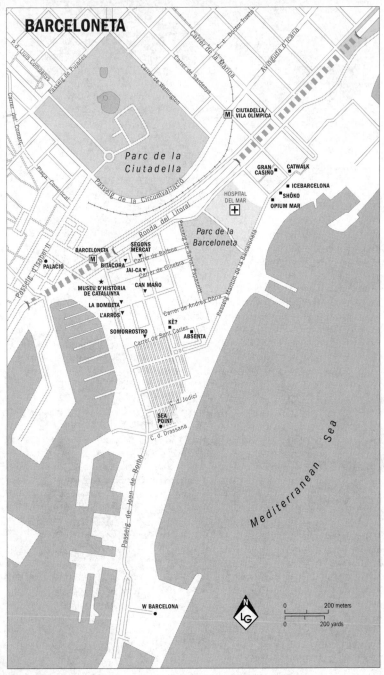

BARCELONETA

Carrer de la Marina

Carrer de C. u. Doctor Trueta

Carrer de Sardenya

Carrer de Wellington

Avinguda d'Icària

P. de Lluís Companys

Passeig de Pujades

Carrer del Comerç

Plaça Comercial

M CIUTADELLA/VILA OLÍMPICA

Parc de la Ciutadella

Passeig de la Circumval·lació

GRAN CASINO ■ ■ CATWALK

■ ICEBARCELONA

■ SHÔKO

HOSPITAL DEL MAR ✚

OPIUM MAR ■

Ronda del Litoral

Parc de la Barceloneta

Passeig de Salvat Papasseit

Passeig Marítim de la Barceloneta

Passeig d'Isabel II

BARCELONETA **M**

SEGONS MERCAT ▼

Carrer de Balboa

● PALACIO

BITÁCORA ▼

JAI-CA ▼

Carrer de Ginebra

★ MUSEU D'HISTÒRIA DE CATALUNYA

CAN MAÑO ▼

LA BOMBETA ▼

L'ARRÒS ▼

Carrer d'Andrea Dòria

SOMORROSTRO ●

KÈ? ■

Carrer de Sant Carles

ABSENTA ●

C. d. Judici

SEA POINT ●

C. d. Drassana

Passeig de Joan de Borbó

Mediterranean Sea

W BARCELONA ●

barcelona

N

LG

0 — 200 meters

0 — 200 yards

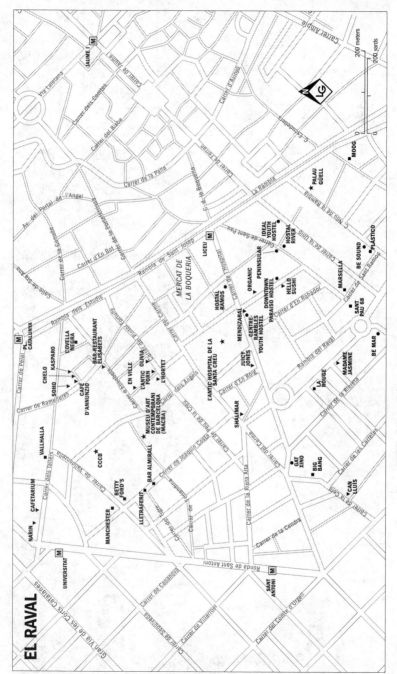

EL RAVAL

orientation

L'EIXAMPLE

GRÀCIA

DISTRITO DIAGONAL

L'EIXAMPLE

SANT ANTONI

PLAÇA DE GAUDÍ
PL DE LA SAGRADA FAMÍLIA
SAGRADA FAMÍLIA
SAGRADA FAMÍLIA
★ SAGRADA FAMÍLIA
HOSTAL GIMON
GRAFFITI BARCELONA URBANY HOSTEL
PL DE LA HISPANITAT
TO ELS ENCANTS VELLS AND TORRE AGBAR
EL MONUMENTAL
PLAÇA BRAUS MONUMENTAL
L'AUDITORI DE BARCELONA
MONUMENTAL

PLAÇA DE PABLO NERUDA
PLAÇA DE TETUAN
TETUAN

PL DE MOSSÈN JACINT VERDAGUER
VERDAGUER

Mercat Concepció
LA MUSCLERIA
FRIDA'S
DOU JONES
CAN CARGOL
TOPXI
EL RODIZIO
A-TIPIC
COLMADO DE SOL
BCN
SMOOKER BAR
GIRONA

CASA MILÀ (LA PEDRERA) ★
EL JAPONÈS
LIZARRAN
CAMPECHANO AND LES GENTS QUE J'AIME
LA RITA
PASSEIG LA GRACIA
MADRID-BARCELONA
CASA BATLLÓ
CASA AMATLLER
POINT CENTRIC
HOSTAL OLIVA
THAI GARDENS
TAPAC 24
PASSEIG DE GRÀCIA
TAPELA
CAFÈ BOOKSTORE
CAFÉ MUSSOL

FUNDACIÓ ANTONI TÀPIES
SANT JORDI HOSTEL ABRAO
LA PULPERIA
THE ROXY BLUE
NOMO'S BAR
HOSTAL RESIDÈNCIA NEUTRAL
HOSTAL SOMNIO
FUNDACIÓ FRANCISCO GODIA

MAUR
CERVESERIA CATALANA
KIRIN
MOON CAFÉ
GINZA
MOJITO CLUB

LE CYRANO
AIRE (SALA DIANA)
OMEIA
HOSTAL EDEN
EL GATO NEGRO (ESPIT CHUPITOS)
BAR CENTRIK
ROOMS4RENT
HOSTAL CENTRAL

LA FIRA
ESPIT CHUPITOS (ARIBAU)
CERVESERIA CATALANA YAMAMOTO
SON-HAO
AXEL HOTEL
ARAME
LA FLAUTA
UNIVERSITAT DE BARCELONA
UNIVERSITAT
PL DE LA UNIVERSITAT

ANTILLA
DIETRICH GAY CAFÉ
ZELTAS
EL RAIM
LA CHAPELLE
PLATA BAR
TO LISBOA AND CAFÉ CHAPULTEPEC

UNIVERSITAT INDUSTRIAL
HOSPITAL CLÍNIC
HOSPITAL CLÍNIC I PROVINCIAL
PL DEL DOCTOR FERRER I CAJIGAL
PL DEL DOCTOR LETAMENDI

Plaça de Catalunya
CATALUNYA

Carrer De Còrsega
Carrer De Provença
Carrer De Mallorca
Carrer De València
Carrer D'aragó
Carrer De Consell De Cent
Carrer De Diputació
Gran Via De Les Corts Catalanes
Ronda De La Universitat
Ronda De Sant Pere

Carrer D'en Grassot
Carrer De Sicília
Carrer De Nàpols
Carrer De Roger De Flor
Passeig De Sant Joan
Carrer De Bruc
Carrer Del Bruc
Carrer De Roger De Llúria
Carrer De Pau Claris
Rambla De Catalunya
Carrer De Balmes
Carrer D'enric Granados
Carrer D'aribau
Carrer De Muntaner
Carrer De Casanova
Carrer Del Comte D'Urgell
Carrer De Villarroel
Carrer De Roma

PL DE JOAN CARLES I
DIAGONAL
Diagonal
Avinguda Diagonal

TO SANT JORDI
TO ZAC CLUB
TO LUZ DE GAS

0 200 meters
0 200 yards

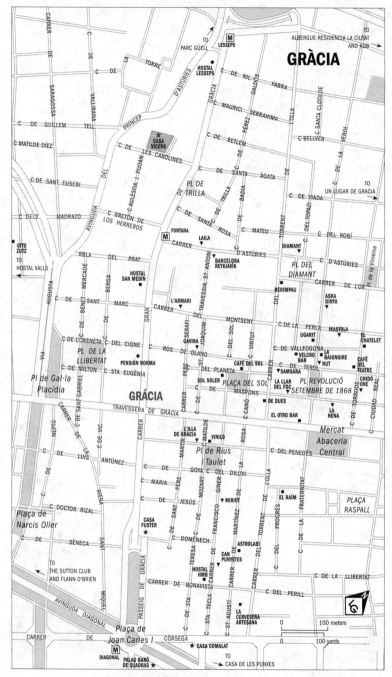

GRÀCIA

TO
ALBERGUE-RESIDÈNCIA LA CIUTAT
AND KGB

TO
PARC GÜELL

M LESSEPS

HOSTAL
LESSEPS

CASA
VICENS

PL DE
TRILLA

TO
UN LUGAR DE GRACIA

M FONTANA

LAILA

DIAMANT

PL DEL
DIAMANT

CARRER DE L'OR

BARCELONA
REYKJAVIK

BERIMPAU

HOSTAL
SAN MEDÍN

L'ARMARI

ASKA
DINYA

UGARIT

IKASTOLA

EL
CHATELET

GAVINA

VELCRO
BAR

LA
BAIGNOIRE

CAFÈ
DEL
TEATRE

PL DE LA
LLIBERTAT

NUT

CAFÉ DEL SOL

SAMSARA

CHIDO
ONE

PENSIÓN NORMA

SOL SOLER

PLAÇA DEL SOL

LA LLAR
DEL FOC

PL REVOLUCIÓ
SETEMBRE DE 1868

Pl de Gal·la
Placídia

MASPONS

GRÀCIA

TRAVESSERA DE GRÀCIA

EL OTRO BAR

LA
NENA

Mercat
Abaceria
Central

L'ILLA
DE GRÀCIA

VINILO

Pl de Rius
Taulet

EL RAÏM

PLAÇA
RASPALL

MIRIOT

CASA
FUSTER

ASTROLABI

CAN
PUNYETES

Plaça de
Narcís Oller

HOSTAL
HMB

TO
THE SUTTON CLUB
AND FLANN O'BRIEN

LA
CERVESERA
ARTESANA

0   100 meters

0   100 yards

Plaça de
Joan Carles I

M DIAGONAL

PALAU BARÓ
DE QUADRAS

CASA COMALAT

TO
CASA DE LES PUNXES

orientation

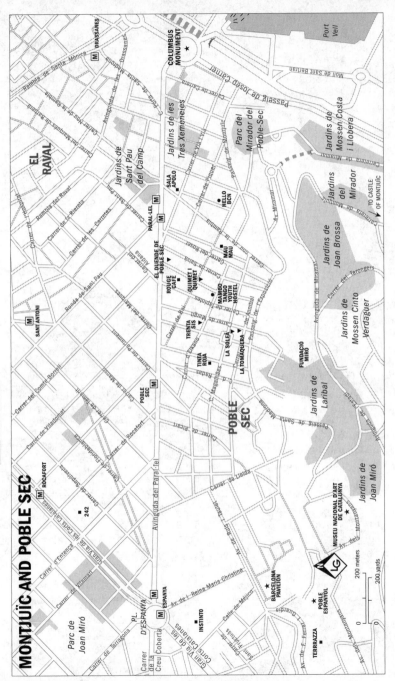

MONTJUÏC AND POBLE SEC

barcelona

MONTJUÏC AND POBLE SEC

Montjuïc, the mountain just down the coast from the old center of Barcelona, is one of the city's chief cultural centers. Its slopes are home to **public parks,** some of the city's best museums, theaters that host everything from classical music to pop, and a ⚔️**kick-ass castle** on its peak. Montjuïc (old Catalan for "mountain of the Jews," possibly for the Jewish cemetery once located there) also has some of the most incredible views of the city. Many approach the mountain from the **Plaça d'Espanya** (Ⓜ️Espanya) passing between the two towers to ascend toward the museums and other sights; others take the funicular from Ⓜ️Paral·lel.

The small neighborhood of **Poble Sec** (Catalan for "dry village") lies at the foot of Montjuïc, between the mountain and **Avinguda del Paral·lel.** Tree-lined, sloping streets characterize the largely residential neighborhood, with the **Plaça del Sortidor** as its heart and the pedestrian-friendly, restaurant-lined **Carrer de Blai** as its commercial artery.

accommodations

You can find accommodation in any of the neighborhoods that *Let's Go* lists, and they will all have their pros and cons. The main reasons to stay in the Barri Gòtic are its convenience (few sights are out of walking distance), its beauty, and the sheer preponderance of accommodations. However, if being surrounded by hordes of tourists is likely to annoy you, you may want to check out a less central neighborhood.

El Born's options are reasonably priced and varied, but be sure to scout out your hotel's location ahead of time, as this neighborhood's narrow streets can disorient even the most experienced traveler. Though El Raval is grittier than the other areas of the Ciutat Vella, its *hostals* and *pensions* generally cost as much as or more than their counterparts in Barri Gòtic and El Born. The pure abundance of accommodation options in L'Eixample means it's likely you'll end up staying there: however, the neighborhood is pricier and less pedestrian-friendly than others. If it's the beach you crave, you might think Barceloneta is your best bet: however, it's generally cheaper and easier to stay in El Born or Barri Gòtic if you want to be near the clubs and beaches of Barceloneta, as Barceloneta's options are few. Gràcia is a good choice if you anticipate getting sick of the tourists around Las Ramblas and want more of a neighborhood feel. Poble Sec, in the shadow of Montjuïc, doesn't offer much in the way of tourist attractions, but it does have a couple of backpackers' hostels close to the Metro that make good bases for exploring the rest of the city.

BARRI GÒTIC AND LAS RAMBLAS

The main reasons to stay in the Barri Gòtic are its convenience, its beauty, and the sheer preponderance of accommodations. If you can see through the tourist crowds to the neighborhood's true charm—or if you just want to blend in with the hordes—the Barri Gòtic is for you.

▨ **HOSTAL MALDÀ**   HOTEL $
C. del Pi, 5   ☎93 317 30 02 www.hostalmalda.jimdo.com
Hostal Maldà provides a dirt-cheap home away from home, complete with kitschy clocks, ceramics, confusing knick-knacks, and your grandmother's cat. A comfy lounge with books and a TV feels more like a living room than a dorm common space. Unlike many *hostals*, the prices don't change with the season, nor will Maldà be booked months in advance during the summer—knowing their audience and popularity, the owners only accept reservations for up to

60% capacity, so try stopping by if you're stranded or weren't quick enough to snag a room beforehand.

🧭 ⓂLiceu. Begin walking away from Las Ramblas past the building with the **dragon** *and take an immediate left onto C. Casañas. Stay on this street as it passes in front of the church and through the Pl. del Pi. Enter the Galeries Maldà (interior shopping mall) and follow the signs to the hostel.* ***i*** *Linens included. Luggage storage available. All rooms have shared bath; some have ensuite showers. $ Singles €15, with shower €20; doubles €30; triples €45; quads €60. Cash only. ⏰ Reception 24hr.*

👍 HOSTAL-RESIDÈNCIA REMBRANDT — HOTEL $$

C. de la Portaferissa, 23 ☎93 318 10 11 www.hostalrembrandt.com

Hostal-Residència has a variety of large rooms with great additions. Many include large windows or balconies looking out over the corner of the street or into the courtyard, and one triple even has a loft. For once, it's worth paying for an ensuite bathroom—they're big enough to spend an entire week relaxing in. The rooms are a real steal in the low season, and the location and charm are still worth it in the high season.

🧭 ⓂLiceu. Walk up Las Ramblas toward Pl. Catalunya and take a right onto C. Portaferissa; the hostal is on the left. ***i*** *Linens and towels included. Free Wi-Fi. Internet use on hostal computers €2 per 30min., €3 per hr. $ Singles €20-30, with bath €25-35; doubles €35-40; triples €60-75; quads €100. ⏰ Reception 9am-11pm.*

👍 HOSTEL SUN & MOON — HOSTEL $$

C. de Ferran, 17 ☎93 270 20 60 www.sunandmoonhostel.com

Though the prices may seem far too high given the crowded dorms and with rental linens, blankets, and towels, Hostel Sun & Moon is actually a pretty good deal for the neighborhood. More importantly, it has a popcorn machine (€1). Located on one of Barri Gòtic's main drags, the recently renovated hostel has an lively atmosphere thanks to its endless stream of young travelers. A deal with a nearby restaurant allows it to offer €4 meals as well. Watch out for the 10-bed dorm, though, in which 10 guests share a single bathroom.

🧭 ⓂLiceu. Walk toward the sea on Las Ramblas and take a left onto C. Ferran. ***i*** *Breakfast included. Linens €2. Towels €2. Blankets €3. Luggage storage €2. Free Wi-Fi. Full kitchen for guest use. $ Dorms €14-28; doubles (in another building across the street) €75; triples €85; quads €95. ⏰ Reception 24hr.*

KABUL YOUTH HOSTEL — HOSTEL $$

Pl. Reial, 17 ☎93 318 51 90 www.kabul.es

One of the biggest and most popular hostels in Barcelona, the Kabul Youth Hostel has hosted nearly one million backpackers since it opened in 1985. The hostel offers bare-bones dorms—many with balconies overlooking Pl. Reial—and a rooftop terrace. Lower-capacity rooms are often cramped and more expensive, but if you can get one with a balcony (just ask), it's worth the added expense. The common space boasts backpacker photo galleries, a pool table, foosball, music, and a never-ending swarm of chatty younger travelers who are genuinely excited to meet each other. Complimentary breakfast and dinner make these rooms a steal.

🧭 ⓂLiceu. Walk toward the sea on Las Ramblas and turn left onto C. Ferran. Take the 1st right and enter the Pl. Reial. Kabul Youth Hostel will be on the far left, with well-marked glass doors. ***i*** *Breakfast and dinner included. Linens €2. Lockers €15 deposit. Luggage storage and laundry facilities available. 20min. free internet per day. Guestlist access to local nightclubs. $ Dorms €15-29. ⏰ Reception 24hr.*

ALBERG PALAU — HOSTEL $$

C. del Palau, 6 ☎93 412 50 80 www.bcnalberg.com

Alberg Palau's clean dorms with pleasant views onto the street and courtyard below fit four to eight people. Rooms have cheerfully colored ceilings and wooden floors, and some include balconies—perfect for scoping out fellow travelers, restaurants, or the nearby souvenir shop. The common space provides a bright, if boring seating area in which to veg out in front of the TV, grab snacks from the vending machine, or meet fellow hostelmates over a board game.

✦ ⓜLiceu. Walk down C. Ferran and take a right onto C. Palau when you reach Pl. Sant Jaume. *i* Breakfast and lockers included. Linens €2. Free Wi-Fi. Kitchen open 7-10pm. Ⓢ 4- to 8-bed dorms €13-25; doubles €28-55. ⓩ Reception 24hr.

HOSTAL-RESIDENCIA LAUSANNE
HOTEL $$

Av. del Portal de l'Àngel, 24   ☎93 302 11 39   www.hostallausanne.es

A beautiful stairway (marble stairs, blue and gold tiles, stained glass at each landing) leads to equally impressive rooms. Each has an excellent view, but try to get one that faces the patio—the view is better and it will be quieter at night, so long as the other guests aren't total hooligans. Enjoy the view from your room; chat up some fellow travelers in the bohemian common space with free internet, microwave, and TV; or chill out on the back patio overlooking the neighboring rooftops.

✦ ⓜCatalunya. As you face El Corte Inglés, turn right onto Av. Portal de l'Àngel. *i* Towels, linens, and toiletries included. Fridge and luggage storage available. Ⓢ Singles €24-35, with bath €35-50; doubles €42-53/48-70; triples €60-75/69-95. Call for up-to-date rates. ⓩ Reception 24hr.

QUARTIER GOTHIC
HOSTAL $$

C. d'Avinyó, 42   ☎93 318 79 45   www.hotelquartiergothic.com

Flags from around the world and the hostel's own regalia deck the halls of Quartier Gothic. Rooms overlooking the courtyard have the nicest views and the least noise from the night-long cacophony of the Barri Gòtic. Though the private baths are more spacious than those in comparable hostels in the area, the shared bath is practically a room of its own (one at a time, please). This hostel shows up many in its price range in terms of amenities (some TVs and DVD players, a fairly impressive breakfast) while still being in a central location.

✦ ⓜDrassanes. Head toward Pl. Catalunya on Las Ramblas. Turn right onto C. Escudellers, then right onto C. Avinyó. *i* Breakfast €3. Linens included. Rooms have safes. Lockers available for day after checkout €2. Free Wi-Fi. Ⓢ Singles €16-29; doubles €28-45, with bath €42-62; triples €42-75. Discounts available online. ⓩ Reception 24hr.

HOSTAL FERNANDO
HOSTEL, B &B $$

C. de Ferran, 31   ☎93 301 79 93   www.hfernando.com

The *Alberg de Joventut* (Youth Hostel) portion of Hostal Fernando is comprised of big, clean, and bright dormitories with bunk beds. It offers the amenities you'd expect from a nicer hostel: comfortable common spaces, complimentary breakfast, and daily activities such as walking tours and discounts at clubs. The private rooms (the *pensió* part) are similarly modern but unremarkable.

✦ ⓜLiceu. From Las Ramblas heading toward the water, take a left onto C. Ferran. Hostal Fernando is on the left. *i* Breakfast and linens included. Towels €1.50. Lockers €1.50 per day; safes in private rooms. Free Wi-Fi in common area; internet €1 per 30min. Credit card required for 1st night reservation. Walking tour daily 10:45am. Ⓢ Dorms €18-25; singles €45-55; doubles €60-75; triples €75-95; 4- to 6-person family rooms €90-160. ⓩ Reception 24hr.

PENSIÓN CANADIENSE
HOTEL $$$$

Baixada de Sant Miquel, 1   ☎93 301 74 61

The nine rooms of Pensión Canadiense tempt the budget traveler with quiet rooms just seconds away from the bustling nightlife of the Barri Gòtic. Each room has a private bath that will make you feel like backpacking royalty as well as balconies for you to hold court. Expect to pay a pretty eurocent for these amenities, as prices are steeper than at nearby accommodations.

✦ ⓜJaume I. Walk down C. Ferran toward Las Ramblas. Turn left on C. Avinyó and take the 1st left onto Baixada de Sant Miquel. The hostel is on the left. Once inside, take the right stairwell. *i* Linens and towels included. Free Wi-Fi. Ⓢ Doubles €60-70; triples €95. ⓩ Reception 24hr. Min. stay 4 nights.

PENSIÓN LA CALMA HOTEL $$$

C. de la Lleona, 10 ☎93 318 15 21 www.pensionlacalma.com

Ask to see the rooms yourself to find the one with the most beautiful balcony view in all of the budget accommodations in the Barri Gòtic—one with hanging laundry, latticed gardens, terraced roofs, and all. A refreshing break from the boring private rooms in most *hostals* and *pensions*, Pensión La Calma instead promises linens that look like they date to the '70s, tiles straight out of the '80s, and paintings that would look at home in any Goodwill. If you're looking for a clean and convenient place with character, La Calma should be on your radar.

🪧 ⓂLiceu. Head toward the sea on Las Ramblas. Turn left onto C. Ferran and right onto C. Raurich. Take the 2nd left, C. Lleona. ***i*** *Towels and linens included. Free Wi-Fi. Microwave and fridge available. $ Doubles €40, with bath €50; triples €60/75. Cash only. ⏰ Reception 24hr.*

ARCO YOUTH HOSTEL (ALBERGUE ARCO) HOSTEL $

L'Arc de Santa Eulàlia, 1 ☎93 412 54 68

Offering rooms for six, eight, and 18 (!) people, the Arco Youth Hostel provides a bunk to crash in and breakfast to wake you up. Sunny Japanese-themed murals of cherry blossoms and **dragons** greet tired guests, and a full communal kitchen provides a stage for your own Iron Chef battles. The smaller common space has couches, books, and a TV—just hope that no one is using their "gym," a.k.a. the exercise bike squeezed along the wall. The prices are rock-bottom for this neighborhood, but be sure to abide by their extensive check-in and cancellation policies to avoid fees.

🪧 ⓂLiceu. Walk down C. Boqueria; L'Arc de Santa Eulàlia is the 3rd right. ***i*** *Breakfast included. Linens €1.70. Lockers €10 deposit. Free Wi-Fi and internet use. Kitchen available. Call ahead if arrival time is different than originally noted. Fee for canceled reservations with less than 48hr. in advance or no show; cancellations must be via email (not phone or fax). $ Dorms €20-23. ⏰ Reception 24hr.*

HOSTAL CAMPI HOTEL $$

C. de la Canuda, 4 ☎93 301 35 45 www.hostalcampi.com

Upon entering Hostal Campi, be prepared to navigate the labyrinth of well-lit, breezy social spaces—complete with balconies and sculptural bamboo shoots—to get to your room. Rooms are of average size for the price and neighborhood. The more people staying, the better the deal, and with extensive common space and all of the Barri Gòtic outside, there's no need to worry about being stuck with your bros in an overcrowded room.

🪧 ⓂCatalunya. Walk toward the sea on Las Ramblas and take a left onto C. Canuda. ***i*** *Towels and linens included. Wi-Fi in common room; internet €1 per hr. TV and computers available in living room. $ Singles €30-35; doubles €52-68, with shower €56-63, with full bath €60-69; triples €67-87. ⏰ Reception 24hr.*

PENSIÓN MARI-LUZ HOTEL, HOSTEL $

C. del Palau, 4 ☎93 317 34 63 www.pensionmariluz.com

The sign out front describes Pensión Mari-luz as a *pensió* for "youngsters," so geezers and old fogies better back off. Private rooms are sizable and modestly priced; small but livable shared dorms cost much less. The main drawbacks are the lack of common space or an elevator (it's on the third floor).

🪧 ⓂLiceu. Walk down C. Ferran to Pl. Sant Jaume and take a right onto C. Palau. ***i*** *Linens and towels included. Lockers in dorms; safes in private rooms. Free Wi-Fi. Kitchen, phone, and fax available. $ Dorms €15-23, with bath €16-24; doubles €50-60; triples €58-72; quads €60-92, with bath €64-96. ⏰ Reception 24hr.*

BLUE HOSTEL   HOTEL $$$$
C. Ample, 24   ☎65 321 75 98 www.bluehostelbcn.com

This hidden *hostal*—no signs anywhere, to keep the riff raff from stumbling in—is a true gem. Gorgeous, colorfully decorated rooms and an airy common space make this a perfect sanctuary in the heart of the old city. Be warned, though, this is a quiet retreat, *not* a raucous party hostel: the owners have had bad experiences in the past with unruly young travelers, so do the backpacking community proud and show this *hostal* just how laid-back you can be.

⚐ Ⓜ*Drassanes. With your back to the Columbus Monument, take C. Josep Anselm Clavé (the 1st right off Las Ramblas), which becomes C. Ample.* ⓘ *Linens, towels, and luggage storage included. Free Wi-Fi. Kitchen available. Online or email reservations required.* Ⓢ *Doubles €45-60. Cash only.*

EL BORN

Many accommodations in this area are found just off **Via Laietana** or concentrated on **Avinguda del Marquès de l'Argentera,** near Estació de França. Scout out your hotel's location ahead of time, as this neighborhood's narrow streets can disorient even the most experienced traveler.

GOTHIC POINT YOUTH HOSTEL   HOSTEL $
C. dels Vigatans, 5   ☎93 268 78 08 www.gothicpoint.com

This youth hostel's social life is as vibrant as its lime green walls, with a ping-pong table on the huge terrace for those nights when you just need to duke it out. The place is trying way too hard to be that one super-cool social hostel with the quirky-but-not-quite-kitschy decor and the lived-in college-hangout feel. Sometimes it succeeds, but generally it just comes off looking toolish. The chutes-and-ladders-esque bedrooms provide standard youth hostel fare with one significant improvement: beds come with curtains for a little bit of privacy on those steamy hostel nights. (BYO Barry White CDs.)

⚐ Ⓜ*Jaume I. Walk down C. Argenteria and take a left onto C. Vigatans.* ⓘ *Kitchen available. Inquire about working to pay for your stay. Linens €2. Towels €2.* Ⓢ *Dorms €15-25.* ⓩ *Reception 24hr.*

HOTEL TRIUNFO   HOTEL $$$
Pg. de Picasso, 22   ☎93 310 40 85 www.atriumhotels.com

The musty darkness of an apartment building's stairwell is shattered by the gleaming lights and colors of this sleek hotel. Chic but small rooms are a steal and boast curtains that actually match the covers, luxurious bathrooms with slick black tubs, and flatscreen TVs. Be sure to request a room with a window, as some have only a narrow slit facing the tiny, dark courtyard. A small common room with black leather couches, a bright white sculpture, and posters of art exhibitions from around the world provide the perfect place to prep before heading to the nearby Museu Picasso.

⚐ Ⓜ*Arc de Triomf. Walk down Pg. Lluís Companys through the arch and toward the Parc de la Ciutadella. Stay to the right once it meets the park to get on Pg. Picasso. Hotel Triunfo is on the right underneath the arcade.* ⓘ *All rooms have private baths.* Ⓢ *Singles €40-45; doubles €60-70; triples €90-100. Ask about discounts M-F.* ⓩ *Reception 24hr.*

HOSTAL ORLEANS   HOTEL $$$
Av. del Marquès de l'Argentera, 13   ☎93 319 73 82 www.hostalorleans.com

This large *hostal* (a good bet if other places are full) is a simple and comfortable option, though the hallway floors get a little Escher-esque in places—watch for unexpected steps and inexplicable inclines. The decor is humble but clean, and it just feels a little bit nicer than its competitors.

⚐ Ⓜ*Barceloneta. Walk on Pla del Palau away from the water and take a right onto Av. Marquès de l'Argentera. The hostal is on the left at the corner of C. Comerç.* Ⓢ *Singles €45, with private bath €55; doubles €60-70; triples €70-80.* ⓩ *Reception 24hr.*

HOSTAL RIBAGORZA

C. de Trafalgar, 39, 1st fl.   ☎93 319 19 68 www.hostalribagorza.com   HOTEL $$$

Simple rooms decorated with bland art and some ceramic knick-knacks make for an unexciting but perfectly pleasant stay. Let this place spoil you with clean rooms, balconies, and surprisingly large shared bathrooms.

✱ Ⓜ*Arc de Triomf. Stand on the side of the arch closest to the Metro stop with your back to the arch. C. Trafalgar is the 1st street on the left.* Ⓢ *Doubles €45, with bath €50-62; triples €60-€75.* ⏰ *Reception 24hr.*

HOSTAL DOS REINOS

C. de Trafalgar, 39, 4th fl.   ☎62 822 36 24 dosreinos@hotmail.com   HOTEL $$$

This accommodation is wholly unremarkable, simple, and inexpensive. The building's lobby has an old-world feel, with sculpted marble ornament and wrought iron, while the fourth-floor *hostal* just has an old feel, with finicky window shades you need to open just so or they'll come off the tracks. Once you do get the windows open, though, the views are lovely, and the rooms themselves perfectly passable.

✱ Ⓜ*Arc de Triomf. Stand on the side of the arch closest to the Metro stop with your back to the arch. C. Trafalgar is the 1st street on the left.* Ⓢ *Doubles €40; triples €60; quads €80. 10% additional fee for booking online, so call ahead to make reservations.* ⏰ *Reception 24hr.*

PENSIÓN PORT BOU

C. del Comerç, 29   ☎93 268 05 10 www.pensionportbou.com   HOTEL $$$

With no kitchen or Wi-Fi and a TV that will leave you feeling as if you stepped back into the '80s, Port Bou is a no-frills *pensió*. Clean, sometimes spacious accommodations provide a retro feel for those tired of glitz and glam. If renting a room with an ensuite bathroom, just be sure it's one you can fit inside. Luckily, rooms come relatively cheap, so this is an affordable option if you're just looking to crash.

✱ Ⓜ*Barceloneta. Walk on Pla de Palau away from the water and take a right onto Av. Marquès de l'Argentera. Take a left onto C. Comerç.* Ⓢ *Doubles €45, with private bath €55; triples €55/60.* ⏰ *Reception 24hr.*

PENSIÓN FRANCIA

C. Rera Palau, 4   ☎93 319 03 76   HOTEL $$

Rooms that range in size from spacious to minuscule sit just upstairs from the hip bodegas of el Born, a few blocks from the sunny beaches of Barceloneta, and right across the street from the limitless possibilities of the Estació de França. Many rooms have balconies that face onto the pleasant pedestrian plaza; others have views of the courtyard wall. We recommend the former.

✱ Ⓜ*Barceloneta. Walk away from the water, toward Pg. Isabel II. Take a right onto this street when you reach it (it's the big one) and then a left onto C. Rera Palau. It's on the pedestrian plaza across from the Estació de França train station.* Ⓢ *Singles with shared bath from €35; doubles with shower €50, with full bath €60; triples €65.*

HOSTAL NUEVO COLÓN

Av. del Marquès de l'Argentera, 19   ☎93 319 50 77 www.hostalnuevocolon.com   HOTEL $$

Newly renovated rooms provide motel-level charm without the underage drinkers partying in the room next door. Rooms vary greatly in size, so be sure to scope out the selection if you're claustrophobic—many are closet-sized and have air-shaft views. Shockingly quiet rooms guarantee a good night's sleep.

✱ Ⓜ*Barceloneta. Walk on Pla de Palau away from the water and take a right onto Av. Marquès de l'Argentera.* ⓘ *Computer use €1 per 30min.* Ⓢ *Singles with shared bath €35; doubles with shared bath €48, with private bath €65; triples €85.* ⏰ *Reception 24hr.*

EL RAVAL

[👍] HOTEL PENINSULAR
HOTEL $$$$

C. de Sant Pau, 34 ☎93 302 31 38 www.hotelpeninsular.net

Austere rooms—there used to be a monastery here—are situated off a sky-lit four-story-high atrium, with seating below, plants above, and mint-green paint everywhere (though no sign of a 1964 Buick Skylark). There's still a secret passageway connecting the former monastery to the church across the street, though its use has been quite infrequent since the building's conversion to a hotel for the 1888 Exposició Universal. Though at the higher end of the *Let's Go* pricing scale, this is your chance to get a taste of old-world grandeur for a reasonable rate.

 # [M]Liceu. Walk away from Pl. Catalunya on Las Ramblas. C. Sant Pau is on the right. **i** *Free Wi-Fi. Ensuite bathrooms.* *[$] Singles €50-60; doubles €65-80; triples €85; quads €100. Cash only.* *⏰ Reception 24hr.*

BE SOUND HOSTEL
HOSTEL $$

C. Nou de la Rambla, 91 ☎93 185 08 00 www.behostels.com/sound

This laid-back hostel deep in El Raval offers a range of amenities, fairly large dorm rooms, and a huge common room in the basement with foosball, leather sofas, and a flatscreen TV. When you're done watching TV, head out on one of the two free daily walking tours of the city, or just go up to the rooftop terrace (open daily 8am-11pm).

 # [M]Paral·lel. Follow Av. Paral·lel briefly toward the water and turn left on C. Nou de la Rambla. **i** *Linens and towels €2.50 each, €3.50 for both. Lockers included. Free internet and Wi-Fi. Kitchen available.* *[$] 6- or 8-person dorms in winter €16; in summer €29. Rates average €2 higher on weekends.* *⏰ Reception 24hr.*

BE MAR HOSTEL
HOSTEL $$

C. de Sant Pau, 80 ☎93 324 85 30 www.barcelonamar.com

The clean and cheerily painted Be Mar appears to be the livelier, more energetic cousin of Be Sound a couple of blocks away (it must be something in the complimentary breakfast). The dorms are large—some have 16 beds—but not cramped, and the common areas are similarly spacious.

 # [M]Paral·lel. From Av. Paral·lel, take Carrer de Sant Pau (not Ronda de Sant Pau). **i** *Breakfast and lockers included. Linens and towels €2.50 each, €3.50 for both. Free internet and Wi-Fi. Free walking tours daily. Kitchen for guests' use.* *[$] 6-, 8-, 10-, 14-, or 16-bed dorms in winter €14; in summer €29. Rates average €2 higher on weekends.* *⏰ Reception 24hr.*

IDEAL YOUTH HOSTEL
HOSTEL $$

C. de la Unió, 12 ☎93 342 61 77 www.idealhostel.com

An industrial-chic common space with foosball and amoeba-like couches hosts a revolving door of vibrant young backpackers. The bathroom facilities in this standard youth hostel smell soapy so you know they must be clean. The young staff will point you in the right direction and may even end up joining you to show you the ropes.

 # [M]Liceu. Walk toward the water on Las Ramblas and take a right onto C. Unió. **i** *Breakfast included. Safes available. 30min. free Wi-Fi.* *[$] Dorms €19-27; private rooms €27-32. €9.50 deposit. Cash only.* *⏰ Reception 24hr.*

DOWNTOWN PARAISO HOSTEL
HOTEL $$$$

C. de la Junta de Comerç, 13 ☎93 302 61 34

Beautiful, hip artwork covers the already colorful walls of this lively *hostal.* There's more turquoise and orange beneath the high ceilings than you're likely to see this side of Santa Fe, and the common room and sunny terrace are perfect for hiding from the madness of El Raval. Downtown Paraiso is not inexpensive, but it more than lives up to its rates.

 # [M]Liceu. Follow C. Hospital away from Las Ramblas, then left on C. Junta de Comerç. **i** *Linens included. Towels €2. Kitchen for guests' use. Free Wi-Fi and internet.* *[$] Singles €50-60, with bath €55-80; doubles €70-90.* *⏰ Reception 24hr.*

HOSTAL GAT XINO

HOTEL $$$$

C. de l'Hospital, 155   ☎93 324 88 33 www.gatrooms.es

The super-modern rooms have a white, black, and lime-green color code that will have you lining up to buy one of their T-shirts to blend into the colorful surroundings. The coherent color scheme runs throughout the building, extending (perhaps excessively) into the *hostal*'s cafe and bathrooms. If you end up craving a chromatic world beyond this souped-up checkerboard, head up to the comfy cushions on the massive roof terrace and take in the view over El Raval's rooftops.

� Ⓜ*Sant Antoni. Walk down C. Sant Antoni Abat, which runs diagonally from the corner of the plaça. Bear right onto C. Hospital at the fork.* *i* *Breakfast and towels included. Ensuite bathrooms.* Ⓢ *Singles €55-65; doubles €60-80; suites €95-105.*

CENTER-RAMBLAS YOUTH HOSTEL (HI)

HOSTEL $$

C. de l'Hospital, 63   ☎93 412 40 69 www.center-ramblas.com

Though you won't be aching to call this place home, the social atmosphere and clean rooms make it an attractive option for a few nights. Industrial metal walls filled with photo murals of Barcelona will persuade you to head into the city with newly made friends in tow.

✻ Ⓜ*Liceu. Walk down C. Hospital away from Las Ramblas.* *i* *Breakfast and linens included. Lockers €2. Towels €2. Laundry €2 wash, €2 dry. Free Wi-Fi and internet.* Ⓢ *Dorms July-Aug €25; Sep €22; Oct-Mar €17; Apr-June €22.* ⌚ *Reception 24hr.*

HOSTAL RAMOS

HOTEL $$$

C. de l'Hospital, 36   ☎93 302 07 23 www.hostalramos.com

Wind your way through the long carpeted corridors to find your homey Raval room—hopefully one with a terrace overlooking the busy and fascinating Pl. Sant Agustin below, though the rest of the rooms face a handsome atrium. Good-sized private baths, sleek TVs, and balconies make it a steal in the low season and worth the price in summer.

✻ Ⓜ*Liceu. Walk down C. Hospital away from Las Ramblas.* *i* *Safes included. Ensuite bathrooms. Free Wi-Fi.* Ⓢ *Singles €35-50; doubles €60-72; triples €90-105.* ⌚ *Reception 24hr.*

HOSTAL RIVER

HOTEL $$$

C. de Sant Pau, 15   ☎93 318 94 93

This no-frills *hostal* offers private rooms at pretty low prices for the neighborhood. Stop by if you can't find a place to stay—it doesn't take reservations, so during the high season you're more likely to find vacancies here than anywhere else. All the rooms are different, so try to take a look at a few before settling in.

✻ Ⓜ*Liceu. Walk away from Pl. Catalunya on Las Ramblas. C. Sant Pau is on the right.* Ⓢ *Doubles €50, with bath €55; triples €90; quints €100. Cash only.* ⌚ *Reception 9am-5pm.*

L'EIXAMPLE

▨ SANT JORDI: HOSTEL ARAGÓ

HOSTEL $$

C. d'Aragó, 268   ☎93 215 67 43 www.santjordihostels.com/hostel-arago

Kick back in the gloriously bright and homey kitchen and common room, or gather round on one of the couches and listen to hostelmates play covers of Bob Dylan and Andrew Bird on the communal guitar. Any hostel with quotes from Guy Debord, Wittgenstein, and Nietzsche on its board has to be a little different, and Hostel Aragó is—in only the best way. Modern wooden and steel bunks offer little more than a place to rest your head, but nightly outings and a solid community ensure you'll be spending little time in them.

✻ Ⓜ*Passeig de Gràcia. Walk up Pg. de Gràcia away from Pl. Catalunya and take a left onto C. Aragó.* *i* *Linens, lockers, and luggage storage included. Towels €2. Laundry available. Free Wi-Fi and internet.* Ⓢ *Dorms €18-35.* ⌚ *Reception 24hr.*

SANT JORDI: SAGRADA FAMÍLIA
HOSTEL $$

C. del Freser, 5   ☎93 446 05 17 www.santjordihostels.com/apt-sagrada-familia/

For those sick of dining on takeout, coffee, and beer, Sant Jordi's apartment-style lodging offers the chain's characteristic laid-back style, communal guitars, employees dedicated to organizing nightly parties, and social hostelmates guaranteed to be as cool as you. Each apartment includes a private bath, stylish and comfy living room, free washing machine, and stocked kitchen, with the added benefit of hostel-style sociability. With rooms for one, two, or four people, you can pick your privacy without *pensión*-style isolation. If you long for that traditional hostel feel, they also have air-conditioned six-, eight-, 10-, and 12-person dorms in the next building, whose common areas include Seussian wall niches and a small halfpipe on the terrace.

✦ ⓂSant Pau/Dos de Maig. Walk downhill on C. Dos de Maig toward C. Còrsega. Take a left onto C. Rosselló and stay left as the road splits to C. Freser. *i* Lockers and linens included. Free Wi-Fi. Ⓢ 4-bed dorms €16-28; singles €20-38; doubles €36-64. Hostel dorms €16-35. ⓩ Reception 24hr. Quiet hours after 10pm.

HOSTAL OLIVA
HOTEL $$$

Pg. de Gràcia, 32   ☎93 488 01 62 www.hostaloliva.com

If you think the interior view of Oliva's sunlit atrium from the period wooden elevator is impressive, ask for a room facing the street. Large windows facing the grandiose Pg. de Gràcia offer peep shows of the architectural orgasm of the Mansana de Discòrdia. Though lacking the fantastic views, interior rooms make up for their shortcomings with more space. Huge rooms with marble floors and the view of Gaudí's Casa Batlló make this *hostal* well worth the few extra euro.

✦ ⓂPasseig de Gràcia. Walk up Pg. de Gràcia away from Pl. Catalunya; Hostal Oliva is on the right at the corner of C. Diputació and Pg. de Gràcia. *i* Free Wi-Fi. Ⓢ Singles €39; doubles €68-87; triples €120. Cash only.

ROOMS4RENT
HOSTEL $

Gran Via de les Corts Catalanes, 602 ☎93 317 01 49, 68 634 28 68 www.rooms4rentbcn.com

This hostel isn't easy to spot—no sign marks its door, and you'll have to look for its sticker on the buzzer. Inside, you'll find a near-blinding assortment of primary colors that match an equally vibrant and young clientele. Plenty of cozy common space fills out this charming old place, complete with turn-of-the-century doorways with stained glass and original fixtures.

✦ ⓂUniversitat. Facing the university, walk to your right along Gran Via de les Corts Catalanes. Look for the name on the buzzer. *i* Breakfast and linens included. Kitchen available for guests' use. Free Wi-Fi. Ⓢ Dorms €17-25; doubles €50. Private rooms available to rent for €300 per month. ⓩ Reception 24hr.

HOSTAL CENTRAL
B &B $$$

Ronda de la Universitat, 11   ☎93 302 24 20 www.hostalcentral.net

Hostal Central has large, slightly quirky rooms between Pl. Universitat and Pl. Catalunya. Some rooms use their sunny enclosed porches for lazy mornings, while in the more crowded rooms these areas become fanciful sleeping spots, complete with lace curtains for a dose of privacy.

✦ ⓂUniversitat. Facing the university, walk to the right, parallel to Gran Via de les Corts Catalanes, to exit the plaza. Ronda Universitat runs diagonally to the right. *i* Breakfast included. Free Wi-Fi. Ⓢ Singles €25-38, with bath €40-55; doubles €35-45/50-62. Extra bed €15. ⓩ Reception 24hr.

EQUITY POINT CENTRIC
HOSTEL $$

Pg. de Gràcia, 33   ☎93 215 65 38 www.equity-point.com

Equity Point's location can't be beat, especially for the price. Though the sheer number of rooms and the gargantuan reception area in this *modernista* building

accommodations

might intimidate you, the hostel website would prefer you think of it as "a cuckoo that's muscled into the very plushest of nests." Great views from the dorms and a ton of amenities, including a terrace and bar, provide the perfect escape if for some reason you don't feel like spending the day on Pg. de Gràcia.

🪧 Ⓜ Passeig de Gràcia. Walk along Pg. de Gràcia away from Pl. Catalunya. Equity Point is on the corner of C. Consell de Cent and Pg. de Gràcia. ℹ Linens €2. Lockers available. Free Wi-Fi; computers with internet free for 20min. $ Dorms €19-32. ⏰ Reception 24hr.

GRAFFITI HOSTAL HOSTEL $

C. d'Aragó, 527 ☎93 288 24 99

True to its name, this hostel is covered in graffiti, which ranges from impressive works of art spanning entire walls to mundane scratchings by drunk hostelmates. An unmarked door (on C. d'Aragó, next to Bar Giralda) hides some of the cheapest rooms in Barcelona, complete with lockers (BYO padlock), two outdoor terraces, and a common room with computers and a TV. It's got a much less clean-cut feel than the other hostels you're likely to find in Barcelona, but what else would you expect from a place with a name like Graffiti Hostal?

🪧 Ⓜ Clot. Facing the rocket-shaped Agbar Tower, head to the right along C. Aragó. Or, Ⓜ Encants: walk along C. Dos de Maig toward the Agbar Tower and take a left onto C. Aragó. ℹ Linens €2. Free Wi-Fi. $ Dorms €15-20. ⏰ Common areas closed midnight-8am.

BARCELONA URBANY HOSTEL HOSTEL $$

Av. Meridiana, 97 ☎93 503 60 04 www.barcelonaurbany.com

Young people swarm this hostel, guaranteeing an exciting Barcelona experience. The free gym and pool access and nightly clubbing outings simply heighten this potential. Rooms are super-modern, but you'll probably spend most of your time on the terrace bar sipping cheap beer and sangria.

🪧 Ⓜ Clot. Walk along Av. Meridiana toward the rocket-shaped Agbar Tower. Urbany is on the right, on the corner of Av. Meridiana and C. Corunya. ℹ Breakfast included. Luggage storage and laundry available. $ Dorms €20-31. Women-only dorms €23-34. Singles and doubles €68-94. ⏰ Reception 24hr.

HOSTEL SOMNIO HOSTEL, HOTEL $$

C. de la Diputació, 251 ☎93 272 53 08 www.somniohostels.com

This ultra-sleek *hostal* offers the best of both worlds—beautifully decorated private rooms and cost-efficient dorms. Wooden floors and modern decor will leave you expecting higher rates, but, thankfully, both the dorms and the private rooms are remarkably cheap for the neighborhood.

🪧 Ⓜ Passeig de Gràcia. Walk down Pg. de Gràcia toward Pl. Catalunya and turn right on C. Diputació. ℹ Breakfast €2. Linens and locker included. Free Wi-Fi. $ Dorms €26; singles €44; doubles €78, with bath €87. ⏰ Reception 24hr.

BARCELONETA

👍 **PENSIÓN PALACIO** HOTEL $

Pg. d'Isabel II, 10 ☎93 319 36 09 www.pensionpalacio.com

This refreshingly colorful and inexpensive *pensió* with a deceiving laundry list of rules and fees (they're actually laid-back, we promise) is just a 5min. walk from the hip neighborhood of El Born and the sandy beaches of Barceloneta. Balconies overlook the pleasant and breezy Pg. d'Isabel II.

🪧 Ⓜ Barceloneta. With your back to the water, walk to the left on Pg. Isabel II. Pensión Palacio is under the arcade on the left. ℹ Safes included. Laundry wash €5, dry €2. Kitchen €1 per day. Free Wi-Fi. Internet computers available. $ Rooms €13-25 per person. ⏰ Reception 24hr. Computer room open 8am-11pm.

SEA POINT   HOSTEL $

Pl. del Mar, 1-3   ☎93 231 20 45 www.equity-point.com

Sea Point is just seconds from the beach, making it the only youth hostel on
the water. Tumble out of one of the solid metal bunk beds (no annoying
midnight squeaks here) and onto the sand. Though clean, bright, and lively, the
accommodations here aren't as spiffy as other Barcelona hostels in the chain.

⚐ ⓂBarceloneta. Follow Pg. Joan de Borbó until Pl. del Mar (near the beach) and enter the hostel
through the cafe on the right side of the building. *i* Breakfast included. Lockers €3. Linens €2.
Luggage storage. Free 20min. internet access. Kitchen available. Ⓢ Dorms €15-25.

GRÀCIA

▨ ALBERGUE-RESIDENCIA LA CIUTAT   HOSTEL $

C. de ca l'Alegre de Dalt, 66   ☎93 213 03 00 www.laciutat.com

This large (room for 180), busy, and cheerfully decorated hostel is a little off the
typical tourist's path—but we don't see this as a negative in the least. The simple,
brightly painted dorms are some of the cheapest beds in the area, and it's close
enough to the lively heart of Gràcia for you to enjoy the neighborhood, while still
far enough away that its revelers won't keep you up at night (unless you bring
one back). Complimentary breakfast should give you the energy to make it to
the Metro in order to explore the rest of the city.

⚐ ⓂJoanic. Walk along C. Escorial for 5-10min., passing through the plaza. Take a right onto
C. Martí before the clinic and take the 1st left onto C. ca l'Alegre de Dalt. *i* Towels and linens
€1.80. Lockers €1.50 per day, €5 deposit. Free Wi-Fi and internet computers. Kitchens and shared
bathrooms on each floor. Ⓢ 4- to 10-bed dorms €17-20; singles €35-50; doubles €52-60. 1st
night deposit required for online booking. ⚏ Reception 24hr.

HOSTAL SAN MEDÍN   HOTEL $$

C. Gran de Gràcia, 125   ☎93 217 30 68 www.sanmedin.com

Big beds and rooms make San Medín feel more like a bed and breakfast than
a budget *hostal*. Pictures of Barcelona's famous architecture cover the newly
papered walls, and bright chandeliers add some sparkle to your sleeping space.
Snag a room with a balcony; otherwise you'll be looking onto a drab (though
quiet) scene: the classic light well.

⚐ ⓂFontana. Take a left onto C. Gran de Gràcia. San Medín is 1 block down on the right, just after
Rambla de Prat. *i* Free Wi-Fi. Ⓢ Singles €32, with bath €45; doubles €50/65; triples €70/80.

PENSIÓN NORMA   HOTEL $$

C. Gran de Gràcia, 87   ☎93 237 44 78

Meticulously maintained rooms in an unbeatable location provide a relaxing
place to return to after a night of marching the *modernista*-studded Pg. de Gràcia
nearby. A few pieces of "art" give the somewhat bland rooms a splash of color
and ease you out of the overwhelming artistry of the city beyond the *pensión's*
walls. If traveling with lots of luggage, be warned: it's a third-story walk-up.

⚐ ⓂFontana. Take a left onto C. Gran de Gràcia. Pensión Norma is a few blocks down on the right.
i Linens included. Ⓢ Singles €30; doubles €45, with bathroom €50; triples €66. ⚏ Reception 24hr.

HOSTAL HMB   HOTEL $$$

C. Francisco Giner, 5   ☎93 368 20 13 www.hostalhmb.com

Definitely the most modern-looking accommodation in the area, this *hostal*
has large, boring, reasonably priced rooms in one of Gràcia's most charming
locations just down the street from the gorgeous but touristy Pg. de Gràcia. Grab
a business card on your way out to explore—they have a useful map of the Metro
on the reverse.

⚐ ⓂDiagonal. Follow Pg. de Gràcia uphill across Av. Diagonal. Take a right onto C. Bonavista and
then a left onto C. Francisco Giner. *i* Free Wi-Fi. Ⓢ Singles €48; doubles €63. ⚏ Reception 24hr.

accommodations

HOSTAL VALLS HOTEL $$$

C. Laforja, 82 ☎93 209 69 97 www.hostalesbarcelona.eu

A smattering of Greek columns and sculptures spruce up the comfortable, sunlit common spaces and surprisingly large rooms. Be prepared for a trek back to your place, though—the surrounding area offers nothing in the way of sights or nightlife, and just finding the closest Metro can be a bit of a pain.

➡ FGC: Muntaner. Walk 4 blocks downhill on C. Muntaner and turn left onto C. Laforja. i Luggage storage. Free Wi-Fi. Some rooms have shared bath. $ Singles €35-45; doubles €45-55, with bath €60-70; triples €65-75; quads €75-90. ⏰ Reception 8am-11:30pm.

MONTJUÏC AND POBLE SEC

HELLO BCN HOSTEL HOSTEL $$

C. de Lafont, 8-10 ☎93 442 83 92 www.hellobcnhostel.com

This hostel has a huge common area for those who want to relax, and a gym—unusual for hostels—for those who want to bring the energy up a level. Hello BCN's brightly painted common spaces and four-, six-, and eight-bed dorms have served the Barça backpacker community well, and they keep travelers coming back.

➡ [M]Paral·lel. Follow C. Nou de la Rambla up into Poble Sec past the Apolo Theater and turn left on C. Vilà i Vilà, then right onto C. Lafont. i Breakfast, linens, and lockers included. Towels €3. Key deposit €10. Free Wi-Fi and internet. Kitchen and gym available. $ Dorms €13-30; doubles €75-90. ⏰ Reception 24hr.

MAMBO TANGO YOUTH HOSTEL HOSTEL $$

C. del Poeta Cabanyes, 23B ☎93 442 51 64 www.hostelmambotango.com

Colorful rooms and even more vibrant bedding make for the most vivid hostel in town. A common area with the plushest sofas you've ever seen make it tough to leave, but the fun-loving staff will make sure you do.

➡ [M]Paral·lel. Follow Av. Paral·lel away from the water past the small plaza on the left and turn left up C. Poeta Cabanyes. i Linens and lockers included. Towels for rent. Free Wi-Fi and internet. Kitchen for guests' use. $ Dorms €15-30. ⏰ Reception 24hr.

FARTHER AFIELD

👍 **MARE DE DÉU DE MONTSERRAT YOUTH HOSTEL (HI)** HOSTEL $

Pg. de la Mare de Déu del Coll, 41-51 ☎93 483 83 63 www.xanascat.cat

Once a bourgeois country home, this renovated *modernista* palace near Parc Güell is now owned and operated by the government. Basic rooms offer huge lockers for all of your hiking gear, but the real draw is the breathtaking stained glass and neo-Moorish detail in the foyer and common rooms; it's worth the visit even if you're staying elsewhere.

➡ Buses #28, 92, and N5 stop across the street. Behind Parc Güell. i Breakfast, linens, and luggage storage included. Lockers and safes available. Laundry €4.50. Free internet. $ Dorms €17-22; singles, doubles, and triples with ensuite bathrooms €20-25 per person. ⏰ Reception 24hr.

sights

Sights in Barcelona run the gamut from cathedrals to *casas* to museums and more. Here's a brief overview of what each neighborhood has to offer. **El Gòtic** is Barcelona's most tourist-ridden neighborhood: despite the crowds of foreigners, however, the Gothic Quarter is filled with alley after alley of medieval charm.

Beginning along the sea and cutting straight through to Pl. de Catalunya, **Las Ramblas** is Barcelona's world-famous tree-lined pedestrian thoroughfare that attracts thousands of visitors daily. The *ramblas*, in order from Pl. de Catalunya to the Columbus Monument are: **La Rambla de les Canaletes, La Rambla dels Estudis,**

La Rambla de Sant Josep, La Rambla dels Caputxins, and La Rambla de Santa Mònica. El Born is a sight in itself, with ancient streets surrounded by sloping buildings and crumbling arches suddenly opening onto secluded *placetes*. El Raval has its own beauties, from the medieval Hospital de la Santa Creu i Sant Pau to the present day artwork housed in the modern buildings of MACBA and CCCB. L'Eixample's sights are mostly composed of marvelous examples of *modernista* architecture; Sagrada Família and Casa Batlló are must-sees. Barceloneta is filled with Catalan pride, from the *senyeres* (Catalan flags; four red stripes on a yellow field) hanging on apartment balconies to the museum devoted to Catalonia and its history. Gràcia contains the epic mountain-*modernista*-retreat Parc Güell, as well as a few independent examples of this historic Barcelonan style. Finally, Montjuïc—you know, that big hill with the castle on it that you can see from just about anywhere in Barcelona—is home to some phenomenal museums, a model Spanish village, and, of course, that castle.

BARRI GÒTIC AND LAS RAMBLAS

Barri Gòtic

El Gòtic is Barcelona's most tourist-ridden neighborhood. Despite the crowds of foreigners, the Gothic Quarter is filled with alley after alley of medieval charm. The neighborhood is so convoluted that some areas still manage to remain largely unsullied by tourists; good luck finding them!

⬛ MUSEU D'HISTÒRIA DE LA CIUTAT   MUSEUM, ROMAN RUINS
Pl. del Rei   ☎932 56 21 00 www.museuhistoria.bcn.es

If you thought the winding streets of the Barri Gòtic were old-school, check out the Museu d'Història de la Ciutat's Roman ruins, hidden 20m underneath Pl. del Rei. Beneath the medieval plaza lie the archaeological remains of ancient Barcino, the Roman city from which Barcelona evolved; get into the elevator/time-machine that's so cheesy it's awesome (who needs a DeLorean?) and go back in time as you descend in altitude. Once under the plaza, a massive ruin lies before you, with elevated walks allowing you to pass through the entire site. One thing has remained the same since Roman times—the people of Barcelona love their booze, and huge ceramic wine vats can be seen dotting the intricate floor mosaics in the strikingly well-preserved ruins dating from the first to sixth centuries CE. The second part of the museum features the comparatively new Palau Reial Major, a 14th-century palace for Catalan-Aragonese monarchs, built in part using materials from the fourth-century CE Roman walls. Inside the palace, the expansive and impressively empty Gothic Saló de Tinell (Throne Room) is the seat of legend: here Columbus was received by Ferdinand and Isabella after his journey to the New World. The Capilla de Santa Àgata avoids the fame of kitschy tales and goes right for the goods, hosting rotating exhibits about modern Barcelona.

⚑ Ⓜ*Jaume I.* ⓘ *Free multilingual audio guides.* Ⓢ *Museum and exhibition €7, students and ages 16-25 €5, under 16 free.* ⌚ *Open Apr-Oct Tu-Sa 10am-7pm, Su 10am-8pm; Nov-Mar Tu-Sa 10am-5pm, Su 10am-8pm.*

⬛ AJUNTAMENT DE BARCELONA (CITY HALL)   GOVERNMENT
Pl. de Sant Jaume, enter on C. Font de Sant Miquel   ☎934 02 70 00 www.bcn.es

The stolid 18th-century Neoclassical facade facing the Pl. de Sant Jaume hides a more interesting 15th-century Gothic one, located at the old entrance to the left of the building (where the tourist office is on C. Ciutat). You can only get into the City Hall building on Sundays 10am-1:30pm, or if you get voted in (municipal elections are usually held in May), but once you're inside, it's marvelous. The lower level of this bureaucratic palace is home to many pieces of sculpture by modern Catalan masters, while the upper level showcases elaborate architecture, vivid stained glass, and lavish rooms like the *Saló de Cent*, from which the *Consell de Cent* (Council of One Hundred) ruled the city from 1372-1714.

✈ Ⓜ Jaume I. Follow C. Jaume I to Pl. Sant Jaume; City Hall is on your left. *i* Tourist info available at entrance. To enter, take alley to the left of City Hall and take a right onto C. Font de Sant Miquel. Ⓢ Free. ☒ Open Su 10am-1:30pm. Tours every 30min. in Spanish or Catalan.

CATEDRAL DE BARCELONA
CATHEDRAL

Pl. de la Seu ☎ 933 42 82 60 www.catedralbcn.org

Behold: la Catedral de la Santa Creu i Santa Eulàlia (the Cathedral of the Holy Cross and Saint Eulalia, or *La Seu*, for short) and its ever-present construction accoutrements. This is Barcelona's only cathedral and it is a marvel of beauty and perseverance. The impressive scaffolding rig and skeletal spire drawing attention away from the Gothic façade are actually signs of what you'll see advertised with the "Sponsor a Stone" campaign in the interior—costly renovations began in 2005 and are racing at a snail's pace to beat the construction on the Sagrada Família. The cathedral is no stranger to drawn-out construction projects, though. Work on the cathedral began in 1298, but the main building wasn't finished until 1460, the front façade until 1889, and the central spire until 1913.

Once you've been funneled through the scaffolding and into the main interior, almost all signs of construction disappear. Soaring vaulted ceilings mark the nave, and decadent chapels—28 in all—line the central space. Don't miss the crypt of St. Eulàlia, located at the bottom of the stairs in front of the altar.

To the right of the altar is the entrance to the cloister, a chapel-laden courtyard enclosing palm trees and 13 white ducks meant to remind visitors of St. Eulalia's age at the time of her martyrdom. Here you will find the cathedral's museum, which hides various religious paintings and altarpieces in various stages of restoration; a very gold monstrance (used during communion); and, in the Sala Capitular, Bartolomé Bermejo's *Pietà*. If you only have a couple of euro to spend, take the lift to the terrace instead—you'll get up close and personal with one of the church's spires and find yourself with a churchbell's-eye view of the city.

✈ Ⓜ Jaume I. From the Metro, go left onto Via Laietana and then left onto Av. de la Catedral. Ⓢ Cathedral free. Museum €2. Elevator to terrace €2.50. ☒ Cathedral open M-F 8am-12:45pm and 5:15-7:30pm, Sa 8am-12:45pm and 5:15-8pm, Su 8am-1:45pm and 5:15-8pm. Inquire about guided visit to museum, choir, rooftop terraces, and towers, as hours vary.

PALAU DE LA GENERALITAT
GOVERNMENT

Pl. de Sant Jaume ☎ 902 40 00 12 www.gencat.cat

Facing the Pl. de Sant Jaume and the Ajuntament, the Palau de la Generalitat provides a second reason for this plaza's incredible popularity with protestors and petitioners. The 17th-century exterior conceals a Gothic structure that was obtained by the Catalan government in 1400. Although the majority of visitors will be stuck admiring its wonderfully authoritative feel from the exterior, with a bit of magic in the way of good timing and advance planning, it's possible to see the interior. There, visitors will find a Gothic gallery, an orange tree courtyard, St. George's Chapel, a bridge to the house of the President of the Generalitat, many historic sculptures and paintings, and the **Palau's carillon,** a 4898kg instrument consisting of 49 bells played on holidays and during special events.

✈ Ⓜ Jaume I. Take C. Jaume I after exiting the station. Once in Pl. Sant Jaume, the Palau de la Generalitat is on your right. Ⓢ Free. ☒ Open to the public on Apr 23, Sept 11, and Sept 24, and on 2nd and 4th Su of each month from 10am-2pm. Make reservations online at least 2 weeks in advance.

GRAN TEATRE DEL LICEU
THEATER

Las Ramblas, 51-59   ☎934 85 99 00 www.liceubarcelona.com

Though Las Ramblas itself is one of Europe's grandest stages, the highbrow Liceu specializes in opera and classical music. The Baroque interior of the auditorium will leave you gawking at the fact that it dates to 1999, when it was reconstructed following a 1995 fire—you can't say they don't make 'em like they used to. A 20min. tour provides a glimpse of the ornate *Sala de Espejos* (Room of Mirrors), where Apollo and the Muses look down upon opera-goers during intermission, and the five-story auditorium, where, if you're lucky, you may catch a director yelling furiously during a rehearsal. For a more in-depth tour that won't leave you spending half of your time looking at stackable chairs in the foyer or being told about the donors list (though it does include the venerable Plácido Domingo), come for the 1hr. tour at 10am, arrange a behind-the-scenes tour with the box office, or attend a performance in person.

✣ ⓂLiceu. *i* Discounted tickets available. Ⓢ 20min. tour €4, 1hr. tour €8. ⓩ Box office open M-F 2-8:30pm. 20min. tours start every 30min. daily 11:30am-1pm; 1hr. tour daily at 10am.

PLAÇA DE L'ÀNGEL
SQUARE

Where C. de la Princesa meets Via Laietana

The square immediately surrounding the ⓂJaume I station may now seem like nothing but a place to catch the Metro or grab a good pastry, but in the days of Roman Barcino this spot was the main gate into the city. To revel in some of this seemingly absent history, simply walk parallel to **Via Laietana**, the busy street forming one side of the square's border. For a more contemporary piece of history (though still dating from the triple digits CE), look no further than the statue of an angel pointing to her toe. This sculpture commemorates the event for which the plaza was named—according to legend, the caravan carrying the remains of St. Eulalia to the cathedral from the church of Santa Maria del Mar stopped here. Suddenly, the remains became too heavy to carry, and when the caravan members set them down, an angel appeared and pointed to her own toe, alerting the carriers that one of the church officials had stolen St. Eulalia's little digit. If you see St. Eulalia's toe, please contact the appropriate authorities.

✣ ⓂJaume I. Ⓢ Free.

ROMAN WALLS
RUINS

Scattered throughout the Ciutat Vella, Roman ruins are marked clearly with informative orange and black plaques provided by the city, and it's hard not to run into at least one. For those history buffs looking for the most bang for their buck, walk down **Carrer Tapineria** (follow C. Jaume I one block and take a right), a narrow street connecting Pl. de l'Àngel and Pl. Ramon Berenguer. This street holds the most concentrated number of fourth-century CE wall remains, though they may be hard to spot, as they are entirely incorporated into the base of the 14th-century Palau Reial Major. The second area of interest is the **Plaça de la Seu** in front of the cathedral, which you can reach by following C. Tapineria and taking a left onto Av. de la Catedral. To the left of the cathedral is the only remaining octagonal tower, and to the right are a reconstruction of the Roman aqueduct and other smaller remains. Still hankering for more? The information placards at each site carry a map listing all of the visible Roman ruins in Barcelona.

✣ ⓂJaume I. Ⓢ Free.

sights

Las Ramblas *Les Rambles*

Beginning along the sea and cutting straight through to Pl. de Catalunya, Las Ramblas (spelled *Les Rambles* in Catalan, though pronounced the same as in Spanish) is Barcelona's world-famous tree-lined pedestrian thoroughfare that attracts thousands of visitors daily. Marked by shady trees, cafes, tourist traps, human statues, beautiful buildings, animal vendors, and ever-present 🐀**pickpockets,** the five distinct promenades combine seamlessly to create the most lively and exciting pedestrian area in Barcelona—perhaps in all of Europe. The *ramblas*, in order from Pl. de Catalunya to the Columbus Monument are: **La Rambla de les Canaletes, La Rambla dels Estudis, La Rambla de Sant Josep, La Rambla dels Caputxins,** and **La Rambla de Santa Mònica.**

COLUMBUS MONUMENT   MONUMENT, VIEWS
Portal de la Pau   ☎933 02 52 24

The *Mirador de Colom*, at the coastal end of Las Ramblas, offers a phenomenal view of the city and a heart attack for those afraid of heights, small spaces, or tourists. The 60m statue was constructed 1882-88 for Barcelona's 1888 World's Fair, in order to commemorate Christopher Columbus meeting in Barcelona with King Ferdinand and Queen Isabella upon his return from the New World. Though some say the 7.2m statue at the top of the tower points west to the Americas, it actually points east, supposedly to his hometown of Genoa. Reliefs around the base of the column depict the journey, and bronze lions are guaranteed to be mounted by tourists at any given hour.

⚑ Ⓜ*Drassanes. Entrance located in base facing water.* Ⓢ *€4, seniors and children €3.* ⏲ *Open daily May-Oct 9am-7:30pm, Nov-Apr 9am-6:30pm.*

LA RAMBLA DE LES CANALETES   PROMENADE
The head of Las Ramblas when walking from Pl. de Catalunya to the water, this *rambla* is named after the fountain that marks its start: the Font de les Canaletes. Surprisingly unceremonious, the fountain is not a spewing spectacle of lights and water jets but instead a fancy drinking fountain with four spouts, rumored to make those who drink its water fall in love with the city. These days the fountain has (amusingly) run dry, so you'll have to fill your Nalgene elsewhere, sans love potion.

⚑ Ⓜ*Catalunya.*

LA RAMBLA DELS ESTUDIS   PROMENADE
Named for the university that was once located here, the path is now closer to a lesson in animal taxonomy than more philosophical topics. Known colloquially as "La Rambla dels Ocells" (literally, "of the birds"), the shops along this stretch of pavement sell everything from rabbits to guinea pigs, iguanas to turtles, ducks to parrots, and much more. Here's your chance to pick up a pigeon, and, with some good training, you may soon be able to sidestep Spain's postal service. This area has understandably become a target for Barcelona's active and outraged animal rights proponents, but there seems to be no indication that La Rambla dels Estudis will be any less furry, fluffy, feathery, or adorable anytime soon.

⚑ Ⓜ*Catalunya. Walk toward the water.*

LA RAMBLA DE SANT JOSEP   PROMENADE
If you're looking for a bouquet for that special someone, or you've just decided that your hostel bed could really benefit from a few rose petals, La Rambla de Sant Josep is your place. Flower shops line this stretch of the pedestrian avenue, giving it the nickname "La Rambla de les Flors." The **Boqueria** market is also found along this stretch, along with the once grand but now practically gutted

Betlem Church. The end of this promenade is marked by Joan Miró's mosaic in the pavement at Pl. Sant Josep.

✢ ⓂLiceu. *Walk toward Pl. Catalunya.*

LA RAMBLA DELS CAPUTXINS
PROMENADE

La Rambla dels Caputxins boasts access to ⓂLiceu and a straight shot to the Pl. de Sant Jaume via C. Ferran, which runs directly through the center of the Barri Gòtic. Cafes and restaurants line this portion of Las Ramblas, and eager business owners will try desperately to pull you into their lair—if "tapas" and specials listed in English and 10 other languages don't do it first. Littered with eye candy such as the **Casa Bruno Cuadros** (corner of C. Boqueria and Las Ramblas, the one with the 🐉dragon in front), Teatre Liceu, and a mosaic by Joan Miró, this portion of Las Ramblas is often the busiest.

✢ ⓂLiceu. *Walk toward the sea.*

LA RAMBLA DE SANTA MÒNICA
PROMENADE

Ending at the feet of Christopher Columbus himself, La Rambla de Santa Mònica leads the promenade to the waterfront. This portion of the path is the widest and, unlike its saintly name would suggest, the most packed with vices and temptation. Filled with artists peddling their takes on Miró, your face, or dolphins in the shape of letters during the day, at night the area becomes thick with aggressive prostitutes. In the same debaucherous spirit, Santa Mònica is also the go-to *Rambla* for peep shows.

✢ ⓂDrassanes.

ESGLÉSIA DE BETLEM
CHURCH

Las Ramblas, 89

Constructed between 1680 and 1729 on the site of an earlier church dating from 1553, "Our Lady of Bethlehem" served as an important nucleus for the Jesuit school in Barcelona until the order's expulsion from Spain in 1767. Today, Església de Betlem's fortification-like façade looming over La Rambla de Sant Josep is hard to miss. The church does have a softer side, though—facing the C. Carme is a Baroque wall flanked by sculptures of Jesuit saints Ignacio de Loyola and Francisco de Borja, both by Catalan sculptor Andreu Sala. Also stretching over the entrance is a representation of the Nativity by Francesc Santacruz.

With such an intriguing exterior, the interior of the church is bound to disappoint. Once considered one of the most beautiful churches in Spain, the unadorned single nave and sparsely populated surrounding chapels leave knowledgeable visitors wondering just what happened to its former glory. Though the edifice itself has been largely restored, the church's simple interior remains a victim of the Spanish Civil War, when a fire started by Leftists (the Church allied itself with Franco) caused the entire vaulting system to collapse, destroying the interior. Some chapels have been refurbished using altarpieces from other churches and private collections, with some of the more beautiful and elaborate pieces located in the chapels along the left side of the nave. Betlem currently functions as a parish church and offers daily mass in both Spanish and Catalan.

✢ ⓂLiceu. *Walk on Las Ramblas toward Pl. de Catalunya. Betlem is on the left after the Boqueria.* ⓢ *Free.* 🕐 *Open daily 8:30am-1:40pm and 6-9pm. Masses in Catalan M-F 8am, 1:15, and 8pm; Sa 8, 9, 11am, 1:15, 8:15pm; Su 9:30am, noon, 7pm. Masses in Spanish M-F 11am; Su 11am, 1, and 8:15pm.*

sights

EL BORN

👍 PALAU DE LA MÚSICA CATALANA — THEATER

C. del Palau de la Música, 4-6 ☎90 244 28 82 www.palaumusica.org

Home to both Barcelona's Orfeó Choir and the Catalan musical spirit, the Palau is Barcelona's most spectacular music venue. But forget about saving up for a live concert—the building itself is the sight to behold. Lluís Domènech i Montaner, contemporary of Gaudí and architect of the **Hospital de Sant Pau**, **Casa Fuster**, and the 👍**Castell dels Tres Dragons** crafted this awe-inspiring *modernista* masterpiece from the humble materials of brick, ceramic, stone, iron, and glass. True to the *modernista* movement's principles, the building (1905-08) is covered inside and out with natural motifs. It's hard to get a good view of the outside because of the narrow width of the streets flanking the structure, but the stunning interior more than makes up for this shortcoming. The breathtaking inverted dome of the stained-glass ceiling and the tall stained-glass windows make the luminous interior shimmer. Columns pose as abstracted trees, while intricate ceramic flowers decorate the ceiling. Behind the stage, angelic muses emerge from the walls, part flat ceramic tiles, part stone sculpture. Above and around the stage, angels interact with trees, flying Valkyries, and musicians such as Wagner and Beethoven. Back in commission after a 30-year hiatus, the Palau's 3,772-pipe organ stands front and center in the upper portion of the hall. The Palau offers reduced-admission concerts regularly, but if you're dying to hear the legendary acoustics, just ask your tour guide—chances are they'll play a pre-programmed song on the organ for your group.

🪧 ⓂJaume I. On Via Laietana, walk toward the Cathedral for about 5min. and then take a right onto C. Sant Pere Més Alt. Palau de la Música Catalana will be on the left. ℹ Schedule of events and ticketing info on website. $ Guided tours €12, students €10. ⏰ Guided tours 50min. daily 10am-3:30pm, with English every hr. and Catalan and Spanish every 30min. Aug and Easter week tours 10am-6pm. Box office open 9am-9pm.

👍 MUSEU PICASSO — MUSEUM

C. de Montcada, 15-23 ☎93 256 30 00 www.museupicasso.bcn.es

Tucked away among the *bodegas* and medieval charms of the old city is the Museu Picasso—five beautiful connected mansions dedicated to showcasing Picasso's entire career, not just the funky faces with eyes in all the wrong places. Works from his early years are organized chronologically, providing insight into his development. Paintings from his time in Paris and afterward show the French influence, while several works from his Blue and Rose periods help to—literally—paint a picture of his past. The museum also contains a work whose title (unclear whether it was Picasso's or added later) represents the greatest disjunction between image and description yet encountered by *Let's Go:* a small but graphic depiction of two women *in flagrante*—and in ecstasy—is dubbed *Two Women and A Cat.* The highlight of the collection is easily the room of the artist's 58 renditions of Velázquez's *Las Meninas*, where the iconic work is spiked and contorted into a nightmarish landscape of typically Picasso forms. Temporary exhibits highlight the work of Picasso's contemporaries, providing some context for the permanent collection. Expect a long wait along the crowded Carrer de Montcada any day of the week, but especially on Sundays when the museum is free. To beat the throngs, try hitting up the museum early or waiting until the later hours.

🪧 From ⓂJaume I, walk down C. Princesa and turn right onto C. Montcada. $ Admission €10, 16-24 and retirees €6, under 16 and teachers free. 1st Su of each month free, other Su free after 3pm. ⏰ Open Tu-Su 10am-8pm. Last entry 30min. before close.

PARC DE LA CIUTADELLA — PARK, MUSEUMS

Between Pg. de Picasso, C. de Pujades, and C. de Wellington

Once the site of a Spanish fortress built in the 18th century to control the rebellious Catalan city, the park was transformed into its current state after the revolution of 1868, and remodeled again in preparation for the Universal Exhibition of 1888. The sprawling grounds designed by Josep Fontserè include plenty of green space as well as various *modernista* buildings. Points of architectural interest are located in two areas: the old fortress holds the governor's palace (now a medical school), the arsenal (today home of the **Parlament de Catalunya**), and chapel, while the 1888 Exhibition area showcases century-old gems. Many of these are still in use today: the steel and glass **Hivernacle,** a greenhouse-turned-civic-space near the Pujades entrance, maintains its original function as well as its newer one as a concert venue. The **Natural History Museum** (Museu de Ciències Naturals ☎93 319 69 12 ⏰ Open Tu-F 10am-7pm, Sa-Su 10am-8pm) continues to educate crowds and complete conservation work. The **Museu Martorell** functions as a geology museum, and the 📷**Castell dels Tres Dragons,** designed by Lluís Domènech i Montaner (of Palau de la Música Catalana and Hospital de Santa Creu fame) houses the **Zoological Museum.** The **Barcelona Zoo** (☎90 245 75 45 www.zoobarcelona.cat $ €17 ⏰ Open daily May 16-Sep 15 10am-7pm; Sep 16-Oct 29 10am-6pm; Oct 30-Mar 26 10am-5pm; Mar 27-May 15 10am-6pm) is at the end farthest from the Arc de Triomf. The extravagant **Cascada Monumental** fountain, designed in part by Antoni Gaudí, still provides a spectacle. Though a newer addition, the 📷**mastodon** near the fountain makes for an excellent photo op.

For those just looking to use the park as, well, a park, bike trails run around the exterior walls, and dirt pedestrian paths break up the lush grass and tree-shaded pockets. Expect to see nearly every corner covered in picnickers during the summer months, and be sure to stop by and join the locals for a bath in the fountain. The typical pigeons are often joined by quite atypical green parrots.

*⇄ [M]Arc de Triomf. Walk through the arch and down the boulevard to enter the park. **i** Free Wi-Fi available at the Geological Museum, Parliament building, and Zoological Museum. $ Park free. Museums €4.10-7, Su 3-8pm free. ⏰ Park open daily 10am-dusk.*

SANTA MARIA DEL MAR CHURCH

C. dels Canvis Vells, 1 ☎93 319 23 90

El Born is dominated by this church's stoic presence, but it's nearly impossible to get a good glimpse from the outside. Nearby streets allow remotely satisfactory views of the exterior from the Fossar de les Moreres at the end of Pg. del Born. The Pl. de Santa Maria, located at the west entrance of the church, holds the best outside views of the church's impressive rose window (which dates to 1459) and the intricate relief and sculptural work of the main entrance. The best view of the stained glass, of course, is from inside on a sunny day.

Constructed between 1329 and 1838, this church exemplifies the Catalan Gothic style—tough on the outside, light and airy on the inside, like a Twinkie you've left out for a day or two. The inside is spacious and open, with tall, slim octagonal pillars lining the main nave and no constructed boundaries between the nave and the altar. Despite the beautiful architecture, the interior has limited decoration (apart from the stained glass, of course), due to a fire that gutted the church in 1936 during the Spanish Civil War.

⇄ [M]Jaume I. Walk down C. Argenteria. $ Free. ⏰ Open M-Sa 9am-1:30pm and 5:30-8:30pm, Su 10am-1:30pm and 5:30-8:30pm.

DISSENY HUB BARCELONA (DHUB) MUSEUM

C. de Montcada, 12 ☎93 256 23 00 www.dhub-bcn.cat

Split over two buildings nearly a town apart, Disseny Hub Barcelona showcases Barcelona's cutting edge contemporary art with a commercial twist through historical displays, video supplements, and a creative laboratory that fosters the budding designer in even the least creative visitor. The **Montcada branch,** located across from the Museu Picasso, houses temporary exhibitions of design and fashion. Just across town, its sister museum in the Palau de Pedralbes hosts the

Museu de les Arts Decoratives and the **Museu Tèxtil i d'Indumentària** (Av. Diagonal, 686 ☎932 563 465 ⚲ Ⓜ️Palau Reial 🕐 Open Tu-Su 10am6pm), both of which highlight the evolution of art objects and fashion from the Romanesque to the Industrial Revolution with enough quirky artifacts and period dress to make it worth the trek. Currently, DHUB's ground-floor exhibition space on Carrer de Montcada is free while the Pedralbes branch costs €5 (free 1st Su of month, other Su 3-6pm), but look for both to be housed under the same roof in the near future as the primary home of the Disseny Hub Barcelona is finished in Pl. de les Glòries Catalanes. There's currently a model of DHUB's future home on display, and, when it opens, it will be one handsome museum.

⚲ *From Ⓜ️Jaume I, walk down C. Princesa and turn right onto C. Montcada.* ⓘ *New combined museum due to open in 2013 in Pl. de les Glòries.* Ⓢ *Free.* 🕐 *Open Tu-F 11am-7pm, Su 11am-8pm.*

ARC DE TRIOMF   MONUMENT
Pg. de Lluís Companys

For a proper greeting from the city of Barcelona, be sure to get out of the Metro at the Ⓜ️Arc de Triomf station, to be welcomed by the incredible neo-*mudéjar* Arc de Triomf. At first glance you'll know that this is most definitely not Paris' Arc de Triomphe; the differences between the two encapsulate why Paris is Paris and Barcelona is awesome. Situated at the beginning of the wide pedestrian boulevard leading to the **Parc de la Ciutadella,** the arch frames the palm tree- and *modernista*-building-lined road and its incredible terminus. The arch was designed by Josep Vilaseca i Casanovas and constructed for the 1888 Universal Exhibition, when it served as the main entrance to the main fairgrounds in the Parc de la Ciutadella. Today the arch serves as little more than a historical artifact, but it's worth a look if you're in the area.

⚲ *Ⓜ️Arc de Triomf.* Ⓢ *Free.*

EL RAVAL

Barcelona's historically immigrant neighborhood contains sights ranging from the medieval to the ultra-modern. For one of the oldest and most beautiful, check out the striking Romanesque church of **Sant Pau del Camp,** whose founding date is unknown but likely lies in the late ninth century CE; the cloister dates back to the 12th. (C. Sant Pau, 101 ☎93 441 00 01 ⚲ Ⓜ️Paral·lel. Ⓢ Free. Cloister €3. 🕐 Open M 5-8pm, Tu-F 10am-1:30pm and 5-8pm, Sa 10am-1:30pm. Mass Sa 8pm and Su noon.)

⬛ PALAU GÜELL   ARCHITECTURE
C. Nou de la Rambla, 3-5   ☎93 472 57 75 www.palauguell.cat

Commissioned by Eusebi Güell, the wealthy industrialist of Parc Güell fame, Güell Palace was designed by Antoni Gaudí and completed in 1888. The Palau Güell holds the distinction of being the only building that Gaudí himself completed, and it hasn't been significantly altered since, though it just reopened in May 2011 after being closed for restoration. Palau Güell represents an early phase in Gaudí's career in which he began to develop his own architectural style. Its roots in the Islamic-Hispanic architectural tradition are visible in many of the windows, which look like Moorish horseshoe arched windows that have been elongated and smoothed out with a typical Gaudí twist. Be sure to look up in the Saló Central to see another example of this influence: tiny holes in the conical ceiling allow in rays of light, reminiscent of an Islamic bath. The rooftop is perhaps the most impressive aspect of the palace, with its colorful, typically Gaudían ceramic-tiled chimneys and its views of the city.

⚲ *Ⓜ️Liceu. Walk toward the water on Las Ramblas and take a right onto C. Nou de la Rambla.* ⓘ *Rooftop closed when raining.* Ⓢ *€10, students €8. Free 1st Su of month. Audio tour free.* 🕐 *Open Tu-Su Apr-Sept 10am-8pm; Oct-Mar 10am-5:30pm. Last entry 1hr. before close.*

barcelona

📖 MUSEU D'ART CONTEMPORANI DE BARCELONA (MACBA)   MUSEUM
Pl. dels Àngels, 1   ☎93 412 08 10 www.macba.cat

If the teeny art galleries and student-studded restaurants around El Raval have struck your fancy, consider checking out the culture hub that helped spawn them. Bursting out of the narrow streets and into its own spacious plaza, American architect Richard Meier's bright white geometric building has made an indelible mark on the land by turning the area into a regional cultural and artistic center. The stark, simple interior displays an impressive collection of contemporary art, with particular emphasis on Spanish and Catalan artists, including a world-renowned collection of the interwar avant-garde and a selection of works by Miró and Tàpies. With its prime location near the Universitat and its undeniable appeal to local youth, MACBA prides itself on hip happenings, so check the website to see if there are any evening events coming up. As if these weren't enough, the museum completely transforms during Barcelona's **Sónar** music festival every year, converting into the Sónar Complex stage and denying admittance to those without a festival ticket.

♯ Ⓜ*Universitat. Walk down C. Pelai, take the 1st right and then turn left onto C. Tallers. Take a right onto C. Valldonzella and a left onto C. Montalegre.* 𝒊 *Admission includes English-language tour.* Ⓢ *Entrance to all exhibits €7.50, students €6. Temporary exhibits €6, students €4.50. 1-year pass €12.* ☒ *Open June 24-Sept 24 M 11am-8pm, W-F 11am-8pm, Sa 10am-8pm, Su 10am-3pm; Sept 25-June 23 M 11am-7:30pm, W-F 11am-7:30pm, Sa 10am-8pm, Su 10am-3pm.*

CENTRE DE CULTURA CONTEMPORÀNIA DE BARCELONA (CCCB)   MUSEUM
C. Montalegre, 5   ☎93 306 41 00 www.cccb.org

The Centre de Cultura Contemporània de Barcelona boasts everything from art exhibits to lectures on Gilles Deleuze to theater to literature to help in trying to figure out what the hell public and private space really *means.* Three exhibition galleries host large and involved temporary exhibits. Two lecture halls, an auditorium, and a bookstore fill out the striking architectural complex, which includes an early 20th-century theater turned supersleek glass annex. Paired with the thought-provoking collections of nearby MACBA, the CCCB offers everything you'll need to inspire your next existential crisis.

♯ Ⓜ*Universitat. Walk down C. Pelai, take the 1st right, and then turn left onto C. Tallers. Turn right onto C. Valldonzella and left onto C. Montalegre.* 𝒊 *Guided visits in Spanish Tu 6pm, Th 6pm, Sa 11:30am.* Ⓢ *1 exhibition €5, ages 15-24 €3, under 15 free; 2 or more exhibitions €7/5/free. W €3, Th 8-10pm €3, 1st W of month and Su 3-8pm free.* ☒ *Open Tu-W 11am-8pm, Th 11am-10pm, F-Su 11am-8pm. Last entry 30min. before close.*

L'ANTIC HOSPITAL DE LA SANTA CREU   ARCHITECTURE
C. de l'Hospital, 56

L'Antic Hospital de la Santa Creu (or the Old Hospital of the Holy Cross) is a 15th-century Gothic building located in the middle of El Raval. The main core no longer functions as a hospital, but its interior courtyard is now open as a park. The operating theater has a rotating marble dissection table, and the archives hold records of the admittance of famous Catalan architect Antoni Gaudí to the hospital before his death in 1926. At that time, the hospital was used to treat the poor, and Gaudí was mistaken for a homeless man and brought to the premises after being hit by a tram. The former hospital also houses the stunning 1.5 million-volume library of the 📖**Biblioteca de Catalunya,** a truly splendid space sure to please any bibliophile (☎93 270 23 00 www.bnc.cat), and an art museum that hosts temporary exhibitions in the Gothic chapel, **la Capella** (☎93 442 71 71).

♯ Ⓜ*Liceu. Walk down C. Hospital.* 𝒊 *Free Wi-Fi in courtyard.* Ⓢ *Free.* ☒ *Open daily 10am-dusk. Biblioteca open M-F 9am-8pm, Sa 9am-2pm. La Capella open Tu-Sa noon-2pm and 4-8pm, Su 11am-2pm.*

L'EIXAMPLE

CASA BATLLÓ — ARCHITECTURE

Pg. de Gràcia, 43 ☎93 216 03 06 www.casabatllo.es

From the spinal-column stairwell that holds together the scaly building's interior to the undulating **dragon's** back curve of the ceramic rooftop to the skull-like balconies on the façade, the Casa Batlló will have you wondering what kinds of drugs Gaudí was on and where one might go about acquiring them (though the Rambla del Raval is a good bet). This remarkable building has hardly a right angle inside or out; every surface—stone, wood, glass, anything—appears soft and molten. This architectural wonderland was once an apartment complex for the fantastically rich and is now the busiest of the *modernista* marvels on the **Mansana de la Discòrdia** block on Pg. de Gràcia. A free audio tour lets you navigate the dreamlike space at your own pace, so be sure to spend some time with the curved wood and two-toned stained glass of each of the doors (from both sides—the glass changes color), the soft scaled pattern of the softly bowed walls, and the swirly light fixture that pulls at the entire ceiling, rippling into its center. Gaudí's design ranges from the incredibly rational to the seemingly insane, including a blue lightwell that passes from deep navy at the top to sky blue below in order to distribute light more evenly.

[M]Passeig de Gràcia. On Pg. de Gràcia near the intersection with C. Aragó, on the left as you face uphill. i Tickets available at box office or through TelEntrada. Admission includes audio tour. $ €18.15, students €14.55. Open daily 9am-8pm.

SAGRADA FAMÍLIA — CHURCH, ARCHITECTURE

C. de Mallorca, 401 ☎93 208 04 14 www.sagradafamilia.cat

If you know Barcelona, you know the Sagrada Família—its eight completed towers and fanciful forms befitting its Gaudí nametag have been plastered on tourist magazines, featured in movies, and included in every panorama of the city ever photographed in the modern era. And 131 years of construction have made the cranes surrounding the Sagrada Família complex as iconic as the church itself.

Although still very much a work in progress, Sagrada Família's construction began way back in 1882. The super-pious, super-conservative Spiritual Association for Devotion to Saint Joseph (or the Josephines) commissioned the building as a reaction to the liberal ideas spreading through Europe in the decades prior. It was intended as an Expiatory Temple for Barcelona in commemoration of the sacred family—Mary, Jesus, and Joseph. The Josephines originally picked Diocesan architect Francisco de Paula del Villar, but the relationship quickly soured, and one year later, after the Gothic foundations had already been laid, the church replaced Villar with Gaudí.

At the time of his employment, Gaudí was just 30 years old, and he would continue to work on the building until his death over 40 years later. Modest private donations funded the construction of the church in the beginning, but after the completion of the **crypt** in 1889, the church received an incredibly generous private donation that allowed Gaudí to step up his game. This extra cash gave birth to the design that would make the building both the most ambitious and the most difficult to complete in Barcelona. After building the **Nativity Façade,** a drop in private donations slowed construction, and in 1909 temporary schools were built next to the church for workers' children. Gaudí set up shop on-site a few years later, working next to his incomplete masterpiece until his brutal death by tram just outside of the church's walls in 1926. He was buried inside the **Carmen Chapel** of the crypt.

Gaudí's bizarre demise marked the start of a tragic period for the temple. The Civil War brought construction entirely to a halt, and in 1936 arsonists raided Gaudí's tomb, smashed the plaster models of the site, and burned every document in the workshop, effectively destroying all records of the architect's design. Since then, plans for the church's construction have been based on the few remaining reconstructed plaster models, and, more recently, on computer analyses of Gaudí's complex mathematical methodologies. Currently, the building remains under the auspices of the Josephines, and architect **Jordi Bonet,** whose father worked directly with Gaudí, is in charge of the overall direction.

The neo-Cubist **Passion Façade** faces Pl. Sagrada Família, and was completed by Josep Maria Subirachs in 1998. Its angular and abstracted forms are a far cry from Gaudí's 1911 plans for the façade and provide a stark contrast to his more traditional Nativity Façade on the other side. The first mass was held inside the then-gutted church in 2000 to celebrate the millennium, and the interior was completed in 2010; on November 7, 2010, Pope Benedict XVI consecrated the Sagrada Família as a basilica.

If all goes well, the projected completion date is 2036, but we wouldn't bet on it. The final structure will look radically different from what you see today: there will be two more façades of four towers, five even taller towers in the middle, and one massive tower in the center that will be almost twice as tall as those already standing. Until that glorious and perhaps apocryphal day arrives, drawings and projections of the completed building can be seen in the adjacent museum, and an exhibit dedicated to the mathematical models lets you imagine the completed building.

⚑ Ⓜ*Sagrada Família.* *i Towers closed during rain.* Ⓢ *€13, students €11, under 10 free. Elevator €2.50. Audio tour €4. Combined ticket with Casa-Museu Gaudí (in Parc Güell) €15, students €14.* ⓩ *Open daily Apr-Sept 9am-8pm; Oct-Mar 9am-6pm. Last elevator to the tower 15min. before close. Guided tours in English May-Oct at 11am, 1, 3, and 4pm; Nov-Apr at 11am and 1pm.*

CASA MILÀ (LA PEDRERA) ARCHITECTURE

Pg. de Gràcia, 92 entrance at C. Provença, 261-265☎93 484 59 00 www.lapedreraeducacio.org

No, this building's façade didn't melt in the Barcelona sun, though it has garnered some equally unflattering theories. Its nickname "La Pedrera" literally means "the quarry," and stems from popular jokes, criticism, and caricatures about the house upon its construction a century ago. Wealthy businessman Pere Milà hired Gaudí after being impressed by his nearby Casa Battló, but his wife began to loathe this building as construction progressed and eventually refused to let the costly venture proceed. Not one to let a difficult couple have the last word, Gaudí sued the rich pair over fees and gave his winnings from the suit to the poor. The couple then looked elsewhere to complete their home's interior, making La Pedrera the only house designed by Gaudí that isn't graced by his furniture.

La Pedrera still functions as a home for the rich, famous, and patient—the waitlist for an apartment is over two decades long—as well as the offices of the Caixa Catalunya bank. Many portions of the building are open to the public, including an apartment decorated with period furniture (true to the house, not designed by Gaudí) and the main floor. The attic, a space known as **Espai Gaudí,** boasts a mini-museum to the man himself, including helpful exhibits explaining the science behind his beloved catenary arches and what exactly it means for the architect to be "inspired by natural structures." Up top, a terrace holds the perfect photo op, whether it be with the desert-like sculptural outcroppings or of the view overlooking Barcelona to the Sagrada Família. During the summer, the terrace lights up with jazz performances on Friday and Saturday nights in a series known as *Nits d'Estiu a La Pedrera.*

⚑ Ⓜ*Diagonal. Walk down Pg. de Gràcia away from Av. Diagonal; La Pedrera is on the left.* *i Purchase tickets to Nits d'Estiu a La Pedrera online via Telentrada at www.telentrada.com.* Ⓢ *€14, students and seniors €10. Audio tour €4. Nits d'Estiu a La Pedrera €25; includes access to Espai Gaudí.* ⓩ *Open daily Mar-Oct 9am-8pm; Nov-Feb 9am-6:30pm. Last entry 30min. before close. Concerts mid-June to late Aug, some F and Sa 8:30pm.*

sights

CASA AMATLLER
ARCHITECTURE

Pg. de Gràcia, 41 ☎93 496 12 45 www.amatller.org

The more rational—but no less whimsical—counterpart to Gaudí's neighboring acid-trip Casa Batlló, Casa Amatller was the first in the trio of buildings now known as the **Mansana de la Discòrdia.** In 1898, chocolate mogul Antoni Amatller commissioned **Josep Puig i Cadafalch** to build his palatial home along Pg. de Gràcia, and out popped a mix of Catalan, Neo-Gothic, Islamic, and Dutch architecture in a strict geometric plane. A carving of Sant Jordi battling that pesky dragon appears over the front door, accompanied by four figures engaged in painting, sculpting, and architecture. The building's entrance hall is free to see—note the ornate lamps and amazing stained-glass ceiling in the stairwell, created by the same artist that did the ceiling of the Palau de la Música Catalana. The rest of the building is even more spectacular and is well worth the €10 tour; unfortunately it is closed for renovations, but is expected to reopen in 2013.

✠ ⓂPasseig de Gràcia. On Pg. de Gràcia between C. Aragó and C. Consell de Cent, on the left as you face uphill. *i* Reservation by phone or email required for tour. **Closed for restoration; expected to reopen 2013.** Ⓢ Tours €10. ⌚ Guided tours M-F at 10am, 11am, noon, 1, 3, 4, 5, and 6pm.

HOSPITAL DE LA SANTA CREU I SANT PAU
ARCHITECTURE

C. de Sant Antoni Maria Claret, 167 ☎90 207 66 21 www.santpau.es

Considered the most important piece of *modernista* public architecture, this hospital's practice is anything but *nouveau.* Dating back to 1401, the Hospital de la Santa Creu i Sant Pau is the newer embodiment of the medical practice formerly housed in the Antic Hospital de la Santa Creu in El Raval. Wealthy benefactor Pau Gil bequested funds for the building with strict instructions, including the name appendage. Construction then began in 1902 under the direction of Lluís Domènech i Montaner, who, in almost Gaudían fashion, died before its completion. His son saw the work to fruition, giving the hospital 48 large pavilions connected by underground tunnels and bedazzled with luxurious modern sculptures and paintings. Although the hospital still functions as a world-class medical facility, you won't need to break a leg to appreciate its beauty. Guided tours (€10) are offered daily as a part of Barcelona's Ruta de Modernisme, or you can just waltz in and have a look around. Much of the complex is currently closed for renovation, but it's still worth a visit.

✠ ⓂGuinardó/Hospital de Sant Pau. Walk down C. Sant Quintí and turn right onto C. Sant Antoni Maria Claret. Ⓢ Free. Tours €10. ⌚ Guided tours in English daily at 10, 11am, noon, and 1pm. Information desk open daily 9:30am-1:30pm.

FUNDACIÓ ANTONI TÀPIES
MUSEUM

C. d'Aragó, 255 ☎93 487 03 15 www.fundaciotapies.org

Housed in a building by *modernista* architect Lluís Domènech i Montaner, the Fundació Antoni Tàpies is unmissable thanks to its mess of wire and steel atop the low brick roofline. Made by the museum's namesake, Antoni Tàpies, it's actually a sculpture entitled *Núvol i Cadira (Cloud and Chair,* 1990) that supposedly shows a chair jutting out of a large cloud. Once inside, the lowest and highest levels are dedicated to temporary exhibitions on modern and contemporary artists and themes—recent shows have included work by Eva Hesse and Steve McQueen—while the middle floors hold Tàpies' own work. Start upstairs and work your way down, watching the descent from Surrealistic-Symbolist beauty into a misshapen chaos of not so well-seeming forms.

✠ ⓂPasseig de Gràcia. Facing uphill on Pg. de Gràcia, turn left onto C. Aragó. Ⓢ €7, students €5.60. Free May 18 and Sept 24. ⌚ Open Tu-Su 10am-7pm.

FUNDACIÓ FRANCISCO GODIA   MUSEUM

C. de la Diputació, 250   ☎93 272 31 80 www.fundacionfgodia.org

The next time you start making NASCAR the butt of a redneck joke, consider the Fundació Francisco Godia. Though Godia was a successful businessman by trade, his two true loves are the focus of this museum: art collecting and Formula One racing. The museum reflects these disparate interests—a front room filled with the "gentleman driver's" racing trophies and riding goggles opens into the foundation's more culturally respected holdings, including his collection of paintings, sculptures, and drawings. Due to Godia's broad collecting interests, the permanent collection features everything from stunning 12th- and 13th-century wooden sculptures to medieval paintings to modern works by Santiago Rusiñol, Joaquim Mir, and Gutiérrez Solana. In fact, the foundation continues to acquire contemporary pieces, and temporary exhibits (€3) attempt to fit somewhere into the framework of the diverse collection.

✠ Ⓜ*Passeig de Gràcia. As you face uphill on Pg. de Gràcia, turn left onto C. Diputació.* *i Guided tours in Spanish and Catalan free Sa and Su at noon.* Ⓢ *€6.50, students €3.25. Temporary exhibits €3.* ❑ *Open M 10am-8pm, W-Su 10am-8pm.*

BARCELONETA

MUSEU D'HISTÒRIA DE CATALUNYA   MUSEUM

Pl. de Pau Vila, 3   ☎93 225 47 00 www.mhcat.cat

If you've had "Catalonia is not Spain" pounded into your head without a proper explanation of what that could possibly mean, stop by the impressive, if slightly proselytizing, Museu d'Història de Catalunya. Located on the threshold between the Old City and Barceloneta, this informative museum doubles as regional propaganda, attempting to inform anyone and everyone about Catalonia's history, politics, and culture in a way that is both patriotic and informative. Hands-on and 3D displays, complete with English captions and vivid dioramas, recount the city's history and shed light on the layers of ruins that you've seen throughout the city. But this museum is more than a mere supplement to *Let's Go*'s Barcelona coverage: it's an introduction for the uninitiated and for Catalans alike to the unique identity of the region. The museum recounts Catalonia's history from prehistoric flint tools to the birth of the Catalan language (the first written use of the term is traced to the 12th century) to Franco's crackdown on the region, followed by Catalonia's subsequent resurgence after the Generalíssimo's demise. Don't be surprised if you walk out of this museum wrapped in the *senyera* (Catalonia's flag).

✠ Ⓜ*Barceloneta. Museum is located along the water on Pg. Joan de Borbó.* Ⓢ *€4, students and under 18 €3, college students free with ID. 1st Su of month free.* ❑ *Open Tu 10am-7pm, W 10am-8pm, Th-Sa 10am-7pm, Su 10am-2:30pm. Last entry 30min. before close.*

GRÀCIA

Some of the most defining features of Gràcia's cityscape are the cafe-lined **places** that seem to appear out of nowhere around every corner. The **Plaça de la Vila de Gràcia** (also known as Plaça de Rius i Taulet) is one of the largest and most beautiful, with a massive 19th-century clocktower (Ⓜ Fontana; take a left down C. Gran de Gràcia and then a left onto C. Sant Domènec). With your back to the powder-blue municipal building, head up the street running along the right side of the plaza, and in a few blocks you'll get to the **Plaça del Sol,** the neighborhood's most lively square, especially at night. Two blocks east of that (follow C. Ramon i Cajal) is the **Plaça de la Revolució de Setembre de 1868,** a long, open square with the word "Revolució" engraved in the pavement. Head up C. Verdi from Pl. Revolució de Setembre 1868 and take a left at the third intersection, which will bring you to the shady **Plaça del Diamant,** while a right will bring you to the true gem that is the ▨**Plaça de la Virreina.**

sights

PARC GÜELL

Main entrance on C. Olot

Now a mecca for countless tourists and outdoor- or architecture-loving locals, Parc Güell was originally intended for the eyes of a select few. Catalan industrialist, patron of the arts, and all-around man of disgusting wealth Eusebi Güell called upon his go-to architect Antoni Gaudí in 1900 to collaborate on a project completely unlike previous commissions. The patron envisioned a luxurious community of 60 lavish homes enclosed by an English-inspired Eden overlooking Barcelona—rich, elite, and pleasantly removed from the city and its riffraff. Unfortunately for Güell and his endeavor, other members of Barcelona's upper class weren't convinced; they weren't about to abandon the amenities of the city for a cut-off hunk of grass dotted by Gaudí's seemingly deranged buildings, which at the time lacked even basic luxuries. Construction came to a halt in 1914, with only two homes completed: Güell's and Gaudí's. In 1918 the Barcelona City Council bought the property and made it into a park. It was opened to the public in 1923 and has since been declared a UNESCO World Heritage Site. Buses bring flocks of visitors directly to the **Palmetto Gate,** a structure flanked by a giftshop and guardhouse-turned-museum—the one that looks like a gingerbread house on LSD ($ €2, students €1.50; free Su after 3pm and 1st Su of month ⏰ Open daily Apr-Oct 10am-8pm; Nov-Mar 10am-4pm). Musicians in the acoustically remarkable alcove across from the guardhouse provide ethereal soundtracks for most visits. Those with sturdy shoes and no fear of heights often choose to take the Metro and climb the escalators to the nature-clad side entrance. (➜ From [M]Vallcarca, exit onto Av. República Argentina, walk downhill, and go left on C. Agramunt, which becomes the steep Baixada de la Glòria.)

The park's main attractions are the brightly colored *trencadís* mosaics and fountains, such as the colorful 📷**drac** (dragon) fountain just across from the Palmetto Gate. The pillar forest of the **Hall of One Hundred Columns (Teatre Griego)**—dotted with sculptural pendants by Josep Maria Jujol, musicians, and vendors peddling fake handbags—has today come close to its intended purpose as Güell's garden-city's marketplace. The intricate vaults of the hall support the **Plaça de la Nauturalesa,** which is enclosed by the winding serpentine bench decked out in colorful ceramics, including 21 distinct shades of white that were castoffs from the **Casa Milà.** If you catch yourself wondering how a ceramic bench can be so comfortable, thank the woman rumored to have sat bare-bottomed in clay for Jujol to provide the form.

Paths to the park's summit provide amazing views, and one in particular showcases what the park has to offer aside from the spectacular entrance: walk to the right when facing the 📷**dragon** fountain from its base. Follow the wide path and veer right toward the shaded benches, continuing uphill to come across the **Casa-Museu Gaudí** (C. Olot, 7 ☎934 57 22 84 www.casamuseugaudi.org $ €5.50, students €4.50 ⏰ Open daily Apr-Sept 10am-8pm; Oct-Mar 10am-6pm) where the architect lived for about two decades. As you continue, another original building of the complex, Juli Batllevell's **Casa Trias** lies inconspicuously ahead, still privately owned by the Domènech family. Continuing on the long, winding route, **El Turó de les Tres Creus** greets visitors at the top of the path. This, the park's highest point with appropriately incredible views, was originally intended to be the residents' church and now serves instead to mark the end of the ascent—or the beginning of the descent, if you arrive from the Baixada de la Glòria.

Although the main areas of the park are regularly full during the dog days of summer, it's possible to ditch the toddlers and fannypacks by showing up at or before the park's opening—chances are they won't turn you away, and, even if you have to wait, at least there's an incredible view to enjoy while you do so.

✠ ⓂLesseps. *Walk uphill on Travessera de Dalt and take a left to ride escalators. Or* ⓂVallcarca: *Walk down Av. República Argentina and take a left onto C. Agramunt, which becomes the partially be-escalatored Baixada de la Glòria. Bus #24 from Pl. Catalunya stops just downhill from the park.* ⓢ *Free.* ⌚ *Open daily May-Aug 10am-9pm; Sept 10am-8pm; Oct 10am-7pm, Nov-Feb 10am-6pm; Mar 10am-7pm; Apr 10am-8pm.*

CASA VICENS
C. de les Carolines, 24

Built in the 1880s for wealthy industrialist Manuel Vicens, this house is Antoni Gaudí's first major work. Though lacking the fluid forms that would characterize his later projects, Casa Vicens hardly lacks his typical exuberance: colored tiles, made in Vicens' factory, cover the eclectic neo-Moorish façade. While you can't visit the interior, this private residence is up for sale—the asking price at time of writing is rumored to be around €27 million. So you can always pretend to be a Russian oil magnate and try to get the real estate company to give you a tour.

✠ ⓂLesseps. *Follow C. Gran de Gràcia downhill from Pl. Lesseps, then right on C. Carolines.*

CASA FUSTER
Pg. de Gràcia, 132

The last building Lluís Domènech i Montaner built in Barcelona, the Casa Fuster (1908-11) was a gift from the incredibly wealthy Mariano Fuster to his wife. (Guys, step it up.) The *modernista* aspects of the building are a bit understated from the outside, but the interior, now a luxury hotel, is all *modernisme*. Check out the lobby if you get a chance; if not, it's still a great sight from the street.

✠ ⓂDiagonal. *Follow Pg. de Gràcia across Av. Diagonal.*

CASA COMALAT
Av. Diagonal, 442 rear façade C. Còrsega, 316

No, it's not so hot out that the building started to melt; it's just *modernisme*. The Casa Comalat (1909-11), built by architect Salvador Valeri i Pupurull, clearly owes much of its form (curving façades, parabolic arches, ceramic mosaics) to the work of contemporary Gaudí. Nevertheless, it is a fantastic example of the *modernista* style; the rear façade in particular, with its irregular wooden galleries, showcases Valeri's inventiveness.

✠ ⓂDiagonal. *Take a right on Av. Diagonal. To see the rear façade, cross Av. Diagonal and take a right on C. Còrsega.*

CASA DE LES PUNXES
Av. Diagonal, 416

Josep Puig i Cadafalch's Gothic castle in the middle of Av. Diagonal, was initially residential. The building, also called Casa Terrades after the original 1905 owners, exemplifies *modernisme* in its quirkiness, its dissociation of façade from function, and its nationalistic Catalan motifs, which include regional symbols on the ceramic panels.

✠ ⓂDiagonal. *Take a right onto Av. Diagonal and follow it for 2 blocks.*

PALAU BARÓ DE QUADRAS
Av. Diagonal, 373 rear façade on C. Roselló

Another one by Puig i Cadafalch, Palau Baró de Quadras sports an incredible *modernista* façade on C. Roselló and an ornate façade on Avda. Diagonal that is oddly reminiscent of a northern European Baroque palace. The house is a treat for the eyes, even if you're not an architecture-lover: you could spend a good 20min. staring at just the intricate carvings around the windows above the Av. Diagonal entrance.

✠ ⓂDiagonal. *Take a right on Av. Diagonal.*

sights

MONTJUÏC AND POBLE SEC

[🏛] FUNDACIÓ MIRÓ MUSEUM

Parc de Montjuïc ☎93 443 94 70 www.fundaciomiro-bcn.org

From the outside in, the Fundació serves as both a shrine to and a celebration of the life and work of Joan Miró, one of both Catalonia and Spain's most beloved contemporary artists. The bright white angles and curves of the Lego-esque Rationalist building were designed by **Josep Lluís Sert,** Miró's close friend who also designed his studio in Mallorca. Since it first opened, the museum has expanded beyond Miró's original collection to include pieces inspired by the artist. A collection of over 14,000 works now fills the open galleries, which have views of the grassy exterior and adjacent **Sculpture Park.** The collection includes whimsical sculptures, epic paintings, and gargantuan *sobreteixims* (paintings on tapestry) by Miró as well as works by Calder, Duchamp, Oldenburg, and Léger. Have fun gazing at Calder's politically charged **mercury fountain,** which was exhibited alongside Picasso's *Guernica* at the 1937 World's Fair in Paris. Like much of Barcelona, the foundation refuses to be stuck in its past—although an impressive relic of a previous era, Fundació Miró continues to support contemporary art. Temporary exhibitions have recently featured names such as Olafur Eliasson, Pipllotti Rist, and Kiki Smith, while the more experimental **Espai 13** houses exhibits by emerging artists selected by freelance curators. Overwhelmed? You should be. This is one of the few times we recommend paying for the audio tour (€4).

➜ Ⓜ Paral·lel. From the Metro, take the funicular to the museum. $ €9, students €6, under 14 free. Temporary exhibits €4, students €3. Espai 13 €2.50. Sculpture garden free. ⏰ Open July-Sept Tu-W 10am-8pm, Th 10am-9:30pm, F-Sa 10am-8pm, Su 10am-2:30pm; Oct-June Tu-W 10am-7pm, Th 10am-9:30pm, F-Sa 10am-7pm, Su 10am-2:30pm. Last entry 15min. before close.

MUSEU NACIONAL D'ART DE CATALUNYA (MNAC) MUSEUM

Palau Nacional, Parc de Montjuïc ☎93 622 03 76 www.mnac.cat

This majestic building perched atop Montjuïc isn't quite as royal as it first appears. Designed by Enric Catà and Pedro Cendoya for the 1929 International Exhibition, the Palau Nacional has housed the Museu Nacional d'Art de Catalunya (MNAC) since 1934. The sculpture-framed view over Barcelona from outside the museum can't be beat, and more treasures await on the inside. Upon entrance you'll be dumped into the gargantuan colonnaded **Oval Hall,** which, though empty, gets your jaw appropriately loose to prepare for its drop in the galleries. The wing to the right houses a collection of Catalan Gothic art, complete with paintings on wood panels and sculptures that Pier 1 would die to replicate. To the left in the main hall is the museum's impressive collection of Catalan Romanesque art and frescoes, removed from their original settings in the 1920s and installed in the museum—a move that was probably for the best considering the number of churches devastated in the Civil War just a decade later. More modern attractions grace the upstairs, with modern art to the left, numismatics (coins, for you non-collectors) to the near right, and drawings, prints, and posters to the far right. For those intoxicated by the quirky architecture of the city, Catalan *modernista* and *noucentista* works dot the galleries, from Gaudí-designed furniture to Picasso's Cubist *Woman in Fur Hat and Collar.* The collection, which spans the 19th and early 20th century, includes an impressive selection from the underappreciated Joaquim Mir, and a couple of large, fascinating works by the more renowned José Gutiérrez Solana. If art isn't your thing, check out the currency collection—though beauty may be in the eye of the beholder, this 140,000-piece brief in the history of Catalan coins will have hardly any detractors.

⚡ Ⓜ*Espanya. Walk through the towers and ride the escalators to the top; the museum is the palace-like structure.* Ⓢ *Permanent exhibits €8.50, students €6, under 16 free. Annual subscription (permanent and temporary exhibits) €14. Combined ticket with Poble Espanyol €15. Audio tour €3.10. 1st Su of each month free.* 🕐 *Open Tu-Sa 10am-7pm, Su 10am-2:30pm. Last entry 30min. before close.*

POBLE ESPANYOL   ARCHITECTURE
Av. de Francesc Ferrer i Guàrdia, 13   ☎93 508 63 00 www.poble-espanyol.com

One of the few relics of the 1929 International Exhibition that still dot the mountain, the Poble Espanyol originally aimed to present a unified Spanish village. Inspired by *modernista* celebrity Josep Puig i Cadafalch, the four architects and artists in charge of its design visited over 1,600 villages and towns throughout the country to find models to copy in constructing the village's 117 full-scale buildings, streets, and squares. Though intended simply as a temporary arts pavilion, the outdoor architectural museum was so popular that it was kept open as a shrine (or challenge) to the ideal of a united Spain that never was. It's perfect for those traveling only to Barcelona but want to get some idea of what the rest of the country looks like—the "Barri Andaluz" truly feels like a Sevillian street with whitewashed walls and arches. Nowadays, artists' workshops peddle goods along the winding roads, spectacles take place during the day, and parties rage at night, particularly at La Terrrazza.

⚡ Ⓜ*Espanya. Walk through the towers, ride the escalators, and take a right.* Ⓢ *€9.50, students €6.60, at night €5.50. Combined visit with National Art Museum of Catalonia €15. Audio tour €3.* 🕐 *Open M 9am-8pm, Tu-Th 9am-2am, F 9am-4am, Sa 9am-5am, Su 9am-midnight. Last entry 1hr. before close. Workshops and shops open daily in summer 10am-8pm; in fall 10am-7pm; in winter 10am-6pm; in spring 10am-7pm.*

BARCELONA PAVILION   ARCHITECTURE
Av. de Francesc Ferrer i Guàrdia, 7   ☎93 423 40 16 www.miesbcn.com

Though the original Barcelona Pavilion was dismantled when the International Exhibition ended in 1930, this faithful 1986 reconstruction recreates the original feel perfectly. **Ludwig Mies van der Rohe's** iconic 1929 structure of glass, steel, and marble reminds us that "less is more." The open interior is populated by the famous Barcelona chair and a reflecting pool with a bronze reproduction of Georg Kolbe's *Alba*. This pavilion—simple, tranquil, sleek—changed modern architecture, modern design, and the way we look at both, whether we realize it or not.

⚡ Ⓜ*Espanya. Walk through the towers and take the escalators up Montjuïc. Barcelona Pavilion is on the 1st landing to the right—follow the signs.* Ⓢ *€4.60, students €2.50, under 18 free.* 🕐 *Open M 4-8pm, Tu-Su 10am-8pm.*

CASTLE OF MONTJUÏC   CASTLE
Ctra. Montjuïc, 66   ☎93 256 44 45 www.bcn.cat/castelldemontjuic

Built in 1640 during the revolt against Philip IV, this former fort and castle has been involved in its fair share of both Catalan and Spanish struggles. The fortress first saw action in 1641 against Castilian forces and continued its function as a military post until 1960 when it was ceded to the city and refurbished as a military museum by Franco. Despite being handed to the city, the fort was controlled by the army until 2007, when its direction was finally handed to the Barcelona City Council. Since then, Barcelona has really enjoyed having a castle—maybe a little too much. A current exhibition named "Barcelona té castell!" (Barcelona has a castle!) explores and celebrates the possibilities for the space, while the castle itself remains, well, a castle. Incredible views of the harbor and city as well as a moat-turned-beautifully-manicured-garden await those that make the hike (or shell out for the gondola to the top). Bring your own cannonballs and help guard the city!

⚡ Ⓜ*Espanya. Montjuïc telefèric on Av. Miramar.* Ⓢ *Free.* 🕐 *Open daily Apr-Sept 9am-9pm; Oct-Mar 9am-7pm.*

the great outdoors

Let's talk 🏖**platges**—that's beaches in Catalan (pronounced PLOT-juss). There are a number of beaches within Metro-distance from the city, and just about everyone should be able to find one that tickles his or her fancy. For basic information on all of the city beaches, contact the **city beach office.** (☎932 21 03 48 http://ves.bcn.cat/platja ⏰ Lifeguards on duty at all beaches June-Sept daily 10am-7pm; Mar-June Sa-Su 10am-7pm.) Barcelona is also not lacking in park space: in addition to the world-famous **Parc Güell** and the downtown **Parc de la Ciutadella**, Barcelona has some parks along more traditional but no less glorious lines.

BEACHES

Tents, motorcycles, loud music, littering, and dogs—though we've seen plenty of the latter two—are all prohibited. Showers, bathrooms, police, first aid, and basic info are available at each beach (June-Sept 10am-7pm). Lockers are available at the police station during certain hours. For gym rats and juice heads, almost all beaches have some sort of outdoor workout facility.

PLATJA DE SANT SEBASTIÀ — BARCELONETA

Pl. del Mar to end of Barceloneta peninsula

The slightly more remote nature of this beach makes it a better bet in your quest to find a square foot of sand during the packed summer weekends. All the way at the end of the peninsula of Barceloneta, this is where most local Barcelonans who choose to stay in the city come for their tanning. Bathe in sea and sun under the shimmering auspices of the new W Hotel, designed by Ricardo Bofill and nicknamed *la vela* ("the sail") for obvious reasons.

➡ Ⓜ Barceloneta. Take bus #17, 39, or 64 all the way down Pg. Joan de Borbó to Pg. Escullera. $ Free. ⏰ Open 24hr. Wheelchair-accessible bathing services available daily from July to early Sept 11am-2pm; June and late Sept Sa-Su and holidays 11am-2pm.

PLATJA DE SANT MIQUEL — BARCELONETA

Pl. del Mar to C. Almirall Aixada

Walk through Barceloneta parallel to Pg. Joan de Borbó, and you'll eventually hit this beach, at the urban area's southernmost tip. This is where city meets sea, with some beautiful beach in between. The beach is the site of the now iconic *Homenatge a la Barceloneta* monument by German artist Rebecca Horn (the one that looks like a skyscraper after a mild earthquake) and is one of the most crowded spots in Barcelona in the summer.

➡ Ⓜ Barceloneta. Take bus #17, 39, or 64 down Pg. Joan de Borbó to Pl. del Mar. $ Free. ⏰ Open 24hr.

PLATJA DE LA BARCELONETA — BARCELONETA

Pg. Marítim de la Barceloneta, from C. Almirall Aixada to Parc de la Barceloneta

The most popular (read: crowded) beach in Barcelona, Platja de la Barceloneta attracts a vibrant mix of visitors, tourists, and brave locals regardless of the weather. Good luck finding a place to sunbathe—even when there's no sun to be seen. If you're looking for a little exercise, pick-up volleyball games abound on the public courts.

➡ Ⓜ Barceloneta. Buses #35, 45, 57, 59, or 157 to Pg. Marítim. $ Free. ⏰ Open 24hr.

PLATJA DEL SOMORROSTRO — BARCELONETA

Pg. Marítim de la Barceloneta, Parc de la Barceloneta to Port Olímpic

Once the site of a 15,000-person shantytown, Somorrostro is now one of the busiest beaches at all hours. Come during the day to take advantage of the *biblioplatja* (beach library) and athletic facilities, or stumble out of the clubs at 3am for a late-night swim; you'll be in good company.

➡ Ⓜ Barceloneta or Ciutadella/Vila Olímpica. Buses #36, 45, 57, 59, or 157 to Pg. Marítim/C. Trelawny. ℹ Book rental. Volleyball courts, gym, and sports areas available. $ Free. ⏰ Open 24hr.

PLATJA DE LA NOVA ICÀRIA
POBLENOU
From Port Olímpic to Bogatell Pier

This short stretch of coastline marks the beginning of the less touristy, more modern neighborhood of Poblenou, but it still boasts a fair number of non-locals. Evidence of domestic living has started to creep into the vacationer's paradise, so expect to see happy families and jolly athletes taking advantage of this calmer beach's great location.

 Ⓜ*Ciutadella/Port Olímpic.* *i* *Ping-pong tables and volleyball courts available.* Ⓢ *Free.* ⏰ *Open 24hr. Wheelchair-accessible bathing services available daily from July to early Sept 11am-2pm; June and late Sept Sa-Su and holidays 11am-2pm and 4-7pm.*

PLATJA DEL BOGATELL
POBLENOU
From Bogatell Pier to Mar Bella Pier

A rock wall protects a portion of Platja del Bogatell from the sea's sometimes perilous waves, but the sport of choice is marathon sunbathing on sand that resembles kitty litter when it gets wet. This beach tends to draw an older crowd; those with a little more energy usually head to beaches slightly farther afield in search of better sand and fewer fogies. The adjacent Parc del Poblenou also offers a pleasant haven for those few that have grown tired of sand and waves, though we're not sure how that is possible.

 Ⓜ*Poblenou or* Ⓜ*Llacuna. Or buses #14, 36, or 41.* *i* *Volleyball courts and ping-pong tables available.* Ⓢ *Free.* ⏰ *Open 24hr.*

PLATJA MAR BELLA
POBLENOU
From Mar Bella Pier to Bac de Roda Pier

Past the Bogatell naval base, rocky outcroppings provide cover for Barcelona's only designated nude beach. Beyond this short stretch of plentiful skin is a gay beach, marked by a rainbow flag flying at the beachside restaurant. Mostly frequented by younger and local people, the two sections provide a perfect place to shed some inhibitions (among other things).

 Ⓜ*Poblenou. Bus #41.* *i* *Ping-pong tables, skating area, biblioplatja (beach library), and basketball courts available.* Ⓢ *Free.* ⏰ *Open 24hr.*

PLATJA NOVA MAR BELLA
POBLENOU
Bac de Roda Pier to Selva de Mar Pier

One of urban Barcelona's most distant beaches and consequently the least crowded, Platja Nova Mar Bella is the stomping ground of local teenagers and students. Still easily accessible by Metro, this beach boasts a more relaxing alternative to the tourist-shoving death-match of Platja de la Barceloneta, especially on weekends.

 Ⓜ*Selva de Mar. Bus #41.* Ⓢ *Free.* ⏰ *Open daily from July to early Sept 11am-6pm. Wheelchair-accessible bathing services available from June to late Sept Sa-Su and holidays.*

PARKS

In addition to the world-famous **Parc Güell** and the downtown **Parc de la Ciutadella**, Barcelona has some parks along more traditional but no less glorious lines.

PARC DE COLLSEROLA
OUTSKIRTS
Ctra. de l'Església, 92   ☎93 280 35 52 www.parccollserola.net

On Barcelona's outskirts lies the world's largest metropolitan park—though that distinction gives its urban counterparts short shrift, as the Parc de Collserola is really more of a suburban forest than anything else. The park stretches along the **Collserola mountain range** from the **Besòs River** to the **Llobregat River,** between Barcelona and **Sant Cugat del Vallès** farther inland. Although the park is easily accessible by public transportation, few non-Barcelonans visit, so don't expect information in English.

the great outdoors

The park's 31 sq. mi. include diverse flora and fauna, like wild boars and badgers and such naughtily named birds as woodpeckers, whitethroats, and the small but perky blue tits. For a greatest-hits showcase of the park's variety, the 13km trail from **Parc del Laberint d'Horta** (ⓂMundet) to **Sant Cugat** is highly recommended. Collserola is a good place to work off those tapas with a ton of hiking trails and the **Carrertera de les Aigües** (Water Highway), a cycling track that follows the ridge of the mountain range and has stunning views of the city to the south and the valley to the north.

For those who do not find never-ending delight in nature alone, the park is littered with places to eat, benches to relax on, and historic architecture and ruins to mentally digest. History buffs will want to check out the 12th-century *ermitas* (dwellings) of **Sant Adjutori** and **Sant Medir,** while those interested in the modern should be sure to stop at the **Collserola Tower,** a telecommunications tower designed by architect Norman Foster for the '92 Olympics. Although the games have long past, the 10th-floor observation deck and unbeatable location on Vilana Hill make it an ideal place to look out over Barcelona, Montserrat, and, if the day is clear, the Pyrenees.

✈ *FGC: Baixador de Vallvidrera for Information Center (S1, S2), FGC: Peu de Funicular (S1, S2), FGC: Les Planes (S1, S2), FGC: La Floresta (S1, S2, S5, S55), or ⓂMundet (L3).* ℹ *Tourist information center, museum, and restaurant near FGC: Baixador de Vallvidrera entrance. Other museums and restaurants scattered throughout; see website for full list.* Ⓢ *Free.* 🕐 *Tours daily 10am-2pm. Info center open daily 9:30am-3pm.*

PARC DE LA GUINEUETA
NOU BARRIS

Pl. de Llucmajor
www.bcn.cat/parcsijardins

This narrow but beautiful park, though a bit out of the way, draws visitors from all over the city; it's surprisingly busy considering its distance from the center. Occupying a natural gully, the lower part of the park offers isolation, while a large plaza at the park's summit serves as a popular place for meetings, demonstrations, and *sardanes* (traditional dances).

✈ *ⓂLlucmajor. Follow Pg. Verdum toward Pl. Llucmajor.* Ⓢ *Free.* 🕐 *Open daily 10am-dusk.*

PARC DEL GUINARDÓ
EL GUINARDÓ

Pl. del Nen de la Rutlla
www.bcn.cat/parcsijardins

This diverse park—meticulously landscaped gardens in parts, rugged forest in others—is surrounded by the city but feels worlds away. Head to the peak (or take the #28 bus) to be reminded that the city's still there, though it seems to recede into the sea from your stunning vantage.

✈ *ⓂGuinardó/Hospital de Sant Pau. With the hospital behind you, head right on Ronda Guinardó, left up C. Telègraf, and right onto Av. Mare de Déu de Montserrat. Buses #39 and 117 also go to Pl. Nen de la Rutlla. From Pl. Catalunya, bus #28 goes to the highest point of the park (C. de la Gran Vista stop).* Ⓢ *Free.* 🕐 *Open 24hr.*

JARDINS DEL TURÓ DEL PUTGET
VALLCARCA

C. de Manacor
www.bcn.cat/parcsijardins

Just across the valley from the architectural madness of tourist-ridden Parc Güell, el Turó del Putget is a sanctuary in the heart of the city. Scale the peak for some incredible views of the city, or stay down below and play some *botxes* (bocce) with the geezers.

✈ *ⓂVallcarca. Follow Av. República Argentina downhill and turn right onto C. Agramunt, which becomes C. Manacor; the park's entrance is 3 blocks up on the right. Alternatively, ⓂVallcarca. Follow Av. República Argentina uphill 1 block, head left up the escalators, and turn right. Take a left onto C. Marmellà; the park entrance is on the left.* Ⓢ *Free.* 🕐 *Open 10am-dusk.*

food

Given the cosmopolitan character of Barcelona, you can find just about whatever sort of food you crave. The cheapest options are chain supermarkets (Dia, Caprabo, and Spar, to name a few), and local groceries that tend to run a few eurocents cheaper still; in terms of prepared food, **kebab** restaurants are some of the cheapest and most plentiful. Local **Catalan cuisine** is varied and includes food from land and sea: some of the most traditional dishes are *botifarra amb mongetes* (Catalan pork sausage with beans), *esqueixada* (cod with tomato and onion), *llonganissa* (a kind of salami), and *coques* (somewhere between a pizza and an open-faced sandwich; singular *coca*). The simplest and most prevalent dish is **pa amb tomàquet** (bread smeared with tomato, garlic, olive oil, salt, and pepper). Note also that the Catalan for "salad" is *amanida*; this bears no relation to the word in English or Spanish, which confuses some travelers poring over a menu in search of *ensalada*.

BARRI GÒTIC AND LAS RAMBLAS

Avoid the tourist traps along Las Ramblas and let *Let's Go* show you the ones worth going to, both on and off the beaten path.

👍 LA BOQUERIA (MERCAT DE SANT JOSEP) — MARKET

Las Ramblas, 89

If you're looking for the freshest tomatoes, leeks the size of a well-fed child's arm, fruit prickly enough that it could second as a *shuriken*, a whole sheep's head (eyes included), or maybe just some nuts, the Boqueria has you covered in the most beautiful way—just look for the stained-glass archway facing Las Ramblas. Though each neighborhood in Barcelona has its own *mercat*, the Mercat de Sant Josep is not only the biggest and most impressive in the city, it's the largest open air market in all of Spain. As a consequence, though, be ready to fight your way through wildebeest-like hordes to get to those cherished lychees (or whatever exotic fruit you might fancy) for your beach picnic. If filling your stomach from the glowing rows of perfectly arranged, perfectly ripe produce doesn't satisfy your famished gut, restaurants surrounding the market offer meals made from produce straight from the nearby vendors.

➡ ⓂLiceu. Walk on Las Ramblas toward Pl. Catalunya and take a left onto Pl. Sant Josep. ⏰ Open M-Sa 8am-8pm, though certain vendors stay open after 9pm.

👍 ATTIC — CATALAN, FANCY $$$

Las Ramblas, 120 — ☎93 302 48 66 www.angrup.com

After a long day along Las Ramblas, Attic provides a soothing and incredibly orange world away from the performers, pickpockets, and never-ending construction. It serves fresh, delectable food at downright reasonable prices for the quality and the presence of cloth napkins. Attic has no dress code, but you should probably change out of that pit-stained T-shirt and the Tevas. Sit on the rooftop terrace overlooking Las Ramblas at dinner for a truly memorable experience.

➡ ⓂLiceu. On Las Ramblas, on the right as you face Pl. Catalunya. $ Appetizers €4.50-12; meat entrees €8-14, fish €10-13. ⏰ Open daily 1-4:30pm and 7pm-12:30am.

ESCRIBÀ — SWEETS $

Las Ramblas, 83 — ☎93 301 60 27 www.escriba.es

Grab a coffee and ogle the stained-glass peacock or one of the impressive works of art waiting to be devoured in the front display case. With tarts, croissants, cakes, and lifelike rings made of caramel, Escribà is waiting to tempt you from every corner of its beautiful *modernista* store. If you're not in the mood for sweets, try a savory dish, such as the croissant with blue cheese, caramelized apple, and walnuts (€4.50) or the "bikini" bread mold with ham and brie (€3.50).

[M]Liceu. Walk toward Pl. Catalunya. Escribà is on the left. [S] Sandwiches €3.50. Salads €3. Menú €5.90. Sweets €3-5. i Open daily 8:30am-9pm. Kitchen open M-Th noon-5pm and 8-11pm, F-Sa noon-5pm and 8pm-midnight, Su noon-5pm.

ARC CAFÉ ASIAN $$

C. d'en Carabassa, 19 ☎93 302 52 04 www.arccafe.com

Down the narrow C. d'en Carabassa, Arc Café is easy to miss. For this reason, it's a great stop when you're sick of the fanny packs and sneakers that crowd Las Ramblas—it's virtually guaranteed to be tourist-free. The restaurant boasts a vegetarian-friendly menu that rotates every three months as well as popular Thai nights on Thursdays and Fridays (regular menu still available). Luckily, their curries are always available—choose between chicken, or tofu, with jasmine rice (€11-12)—just be sure to order a mojito with Malibu to cool off (€6) if you're brave enough to go for spice. There's also a cheaper midday menu daily (€9.60).

[M]Drassanes. Walk toward the sea on Las Ramblas and take a left onto C. de Josep Anselm Clavé. Walk 5min. as the road becomes C. Ample. Take a left onto C. Carabassa. Arc Café is on the right. i Reservations recommended on weekends. Free Wi-Fi. [S] Appetizers €4.50-6.90; entrees €8.50-12. Wine €2. Beer €2-3. ⏰ Open M-Th 10am-1am, F 10am-3am, Sa 11am-3am, Su 11am-1am.

L'ANTIC BOCOI DEL GÒTIC CATALAN $$$

Baixada de Viladecols, 3 ☎93 310 50 67 www.bocoi.net

Enter the lair of L'Antic Bocoi del Gòtic, where walls of rustic stone and exposed ancient brick surround diners in cave-like intimacy. The restaurant specializes in Catalan cuisine with fresh, seasonal ingredients and prides itself on bringing new ideas to traditional food. The staff recommends the selection of cheeses and their own take on the *coques de recapte*, a regional dish made of a thin dough with delicious fresh produce and thickly layered meats (€8.50-9). This fancy joint fills up quickly after opening, so make reservations.

[M]Jaume I. Follow C. Jaume I toward Pl. Sant Jaume, then left onto C. Dagueria, which becomes C. dels Lledó, which becomes Baixada de Viladecols. i Reservations recommended. [S] Appetizers €7-10; entrees €10-21. ⏰ Open M-Sa 8:30pm-midnight.

CAFÈ DE L'ACADÈMIA CATALAN $$$

C. dels Lledó, 1 ☎93 319 82 53

This Barri Gòtic staple on Pl. de Sant Just has been a local favorite since it opened some 30 years ago, and has remained a locals' secret—until now. The high-quality food at surprisingly reasonable prices draws everyone from businessmen and government bureaucrats from the *ajuntament* up the street to more casual groups of friends out for a bite. Sit in the dark, cellar-like interior, or in the summer months enjoy the *plaça* outside in one of the least touristy corners of the Barri Gòtic. This place has such disdain for tourists that they close on the weekends and for most of August.

[M]Jaume I. Follow C. Jaume I toward Pl. Sant Jaume, then left onto C. Dagueria, which becomes C. dels Lledó. i Reservations recommended. [S] Entrees €14-30. Menú €15, at the bar €10. ⏰ Open M-F 1:30-4pm and 8:30-11:30pm. Closed 3 weeks in Aug.

CAFÉ VIENA SANDWICHES, CAFE $

Las Ramblas, 115 ☎93 317 14 92 www.viena.es

This incongruously named cafe—it has nothing to do with the Austrian capital—has earned much renown for a fulsome 2006 *New York Times* article whose author raved for several paragraphs about Viena's *flauta ibèric* (Iberian ham sandwich; €6.60), calling it "the best sandwich I've ever had." The sandwich's secret, which the article's author almost figured out but couldn't quite pin down, is that the *flauta* comes on *pa amb tomàquet*, the staple of the Catalan kitchen that involves smearing tomato on bread before seasoning with salt, pepper, olive oil, and garlic. And it is a damn good sandwich, the sort that melts in your mouth with each bite, though *Let's Go* isn't sure that ham is supposed to do that.

☞ Ⓜ*Catalunya. Follow Las Ramblas toward the sea; it's on the right.* Ⓢ *Sandwiches €2.40-9.30 (most under €4). Coffee €1.30-2.40.* ☑ *Open M-Th 8am-11:30pm, F-Sa 8am-12:30am, Su 8am-11:30pm.*

JUICY JONES (BARRI GÒTIC)   VEGAN, VEGETARIAN, INDIAN $$
C. del Cardenal Casañas, 7   ☎93 302 43 30

Juice bar and vegan haven, Juicy Jones serves a variety of veggie-stuffed sandwiches, vegan pizzas and lasagnas, daily specials, and a *menú* (appetizer, entree, dessert, and wine; €8.50). If you have a strong stomach, chill out in the back seating area, where it looks like a kaleidoscope full of acid exploded in a 1950s diner. Keep an eye out for "Turtle Jones" chillin' on a wall. Otherwise, sit among dreadlocked locals at the fruit-filled bar in the front and sip on one of the freshly made delicious juice combinations or milkshakes; the adventurous can create their own (€3-5).

☞ Ⓜ*Liceu. From the Metro, walk down C. de La Boqueria. Take a left onto C. del Cardenal Casañas.* Ⓢ *Tapas €3.50. Sandwiches €4.50. Salads €5. Thali €6. Plate of the day €6.25. Juice €2.50-5. Cash only.* ☑ *Open daily 10am-midnight.*

PASTA BAR   PASTA $$
C. dels Escudellers, 47

Assemble your own steaming bowl of fresh pasta, made to order right in front of you. Pick a pasta and a sauce, add ingredients (cheese is free), and take your pasta to go or eat it under one of the chic hanging lamps made from wine bottles. Most *Let's Go* readers will understand the value of refueling with lots of inexpensive carbohydrates after an exhausting day of sightseeing; Pasta Bar is a delicious and convenient stop to do just that.

☞ Ⓜ*Liceu. Walk on Las Ramblas toward the water. Take a left onto C. Escudellers.* Ⓢ *Pasta €3.90-7.90 depending on sauce; extra ingredients €0.30-2 each. Pasta of the week €5.90. Desserts €3.90. Menú €9.90.* ☑ *Open daily noon-1am.*

TUCCO PASTAS FRESCAS   PASTA $
C. de n'Aglà, 6   ☎93 301 51 91 www.tuccopastasfrescas.com

True to its name, Tucco "fresh pasta" offers just that—a selection of fresh pastas topped with your choice of sauce and cheese (€3.95). The limited seating in the teeny store serves as a revolving door for hip, young locals and internationals wandering far off the beaten path. If pasta isn't your thing, a selection of wallet-friendly sandwiches, pizzas, salads, and snacks loaded with veggies attempts to fill the nutritional void that a meal of carbs creates. Don't expect to sit if you come at mealtime; instead, take your plasticware and hit the road.

☞ Ⓜ*Liceu. Walk on Las Ramblas toward the water. Take a left onto C. Escudellers. Left onto C. d'Aglà.* Ⓢ *Pasta €3.95. Pizza from €9.* ☑ *Open M-F 1-11:30pm, Sa 1-6pm.*

LA CLANDESTINA   TEA, SANDWICHES $
Baixada de Viladecols, 2B   ☎93 319 05 33

A hidden—dare we say, clandestine?—tea house with the most relaxed atmosphere in all the Barri Gòtic. An artsy feel is nearly as pervasive as the thick air, fragrant from the freshly brewed tea and occasionally from smoking hookahs. The cavernous *teteria* makes for a great place to take a short (or long) reprieve from the frenetic pace of the Gothic Quarter.

☞ Ⓜ*Jaume I. Follow C. Jaume I toward Pl. Sant Jaume, then left onto C. Dagueria, which becomes C. dels Lledó, which becomes Baixada de Viladecols.* *i* *Free Wi-Fi.* Ⓢ *Sandwiches €4.20-4.40. Teas €2.50-6; pots €10-15. Juices €2.70-3.60. Cash only.* ☑ *Open M-Th 10am-10pm, F-Sa 10am-midnight, Su 11am-10pm.*

food

ČAJ CHAI

TEA $

C. Sant Domènech del Call, 12   ☎61 033 47 12 www.cajchai.com

Pronounced "Chai Chai" and named after *čaj* (Czech for tea), Čaj Chai gives off more of a pseudo-Japanese zen vibe than any eastern European bohemian affectation. Beg the waitstaff to help guide you through their overwhelming list of teas from around the globe, and be sure to ask if there are any teas that are particular to the season. A variety of Arabic, Indian, and Japanese pastries (€1.50-2) provide the perfect complement to the international array of teas. Luckily, all teas come in a personal pot, so you'll have an excuse to lounge a while longer. Morning specials for chai and pastries are also available.

✠ Ⓜ *Jaume I. From the Metro, take C. Jaume I through Pl. Sant Jaume. After the square, the road becomes C. Ferran. Walk briefly down C. Ferran and take a right onto the narrow C. Sant Domènech del Call.* Ⓢ *Snacks €1.50-2. Tea €2.50-7; pots for 4 €12-15. Cash only.* Ⓩ *Open M 3-10pm, Tu-Su 10:30am-10pm.*

LES QUINZE NITS

MEDITERRANEAN $$$

Pl. Reial, 6   ☎93 317 30 75 www.lesquinzenits.com

Despite the restaurant's white tablecloths, leather chairs, and fabulous view of Pl. Reial, the line outside of Les Quinze Nits is enough to make any weary and impatient traveler looking for a classy meal reconsider their priorities. But don't be discouraged—it's worth the wait. Where else can you woo your most recent romantic acquisition on a backpacker's budget? Try the duck confit with pesto sauce (€10) or the leek pie with tomato and arugula (€6.40). Expect a 30min. wait if you come early; the line reportedly diminishes around 9pm.

✠ Ⓜ *Liceu, walk down Las Ramblas toward the sea and turn left on C. Colom to enter Pl. Reial. The restaurant is in the far left corner as you enter Pl. Reial.* *i* *No reservations.* Ⓢ *Bread €0.90. Appetizers €3-6; entrees €5.70-11.20.* Ⓩ *Open daily 1-3:45pm and 8:30-11:30pm.*

CAFÉ DE L'OPERA

CAFE $$

Las Ramblas, 74   ☎93 317 75 85 www.cafeoperabcn.com

Beginning in the 18th century as a boarding tavern and later a chocolate shop, the cafe assumed its current form in 1929, adopting the amusing mix of *modernista* curves, Grecian women, and pastel paint that can be seen today. Don't be scared away by the fancy Parisian cafe front or the impressive historical pedigree—although famous as a post-opera institution, Café de l'Opera offers affordable fare and a wide list of beers (including "Cannabis Club," which purportedly tastes like, well...), wines, drinks, and tapas.

✠ Ⓜ *Liceu. On the left side of Las Ramblas as you face the water.* *i* *Credit card min. €30.* Ⓢ *Tapas €2-4. Sandwiches €3-6.70. Entrees €6.70-14. Specials €11-13.* Ⓩ *Open M-Th 8:30am-2:30am, F-Sa 8:30am-3:30am, Su 8:30am-2:30am.*

VEGETALIA

ORGANIC, VEGETARIAN $$

C. dels Escudellers, 54   ☎93 317 33 31 www.restaurantesvegetalia.com

Vegetalia delivers delicious organic, natural, and environmentally conscious foods at reasonable prices. Relax at the bar and chat with the staff about the ironic history of the Pl. de George Orwell, or experience the square for yourself after ordering at their walk-up window. Try one of the pizzas (€9.50) and top it off with the vegan carob chocolate cake (€4.50), or gorge yourself on the daily *menú* (€10). A range of organic foods, teas, and coffees is located in the back of the store.

✠ Ⓜ *Liceu. Walk down Las Ramblas toward the sea and take a left onto C. dels Escudellers.* *i* *Organic store in the rear. Free Wi-Fi.* Ⓢ *Appetizers €5.50-5.90; entrees €6.20-8.90. Menú €9.90.* Ⓩ *Open M-Th 1-4:30pm and 8-11:30pm, Sa-Su 1-11:30pm.*

ELS QUATRE GATS

C. Montsió, 3

CATALAN, HISTORIC SITE $$$$
☎93 302 41 40 www.4gats.com

Named after a *hostal* that served as a vital grounds for the artistic and literary community in Barcelona in the 1890s, Els Quatre Gats now attracts the tourist hordes as much for its historic affiliations as for the quality of its offerings. Hand-painted tiles, drawings from the period, and a rustic wooden interior remind patrons of Barcelona's days of yore, even if the whole shtick is entirely constructed. The sheer beauty of the Casa Figuras (the building that houses the restaurant) itself justifies a visit, and, considering the prices are only very inflated (as opposed to outrageously inflated), the experience is well worth the money.

✦ Ⓜ*Catalunya. Follow Av. Portal de l'Àngel from Pl. Catalunya, then take a left onto C. Montsió.* i *Live piano daily 1-4pm.* Ⓢ *Appetizers €8-18; entrees €13-26. Menú M-F 1-4pm €16; Sa 1-4pm €24; Su 1-4pm €16.* ☼ *Open daily 10am-1am.*

EL BORN

This chic neighborhood is full of restaurants of nearly every genre imaginable, from traditional Catalan food to Basque *pintxos* to meat fondue and crunchy vegetarian co-ops.

▩ EL XAMPANYET

C. de Montcada, 22

TAPAS $$
☎93 319 70 03

This is as authentic as it gets, with sheepskin wine bags, an overwhelming selection of *cava*, and crunchy old locals spilling out the door and onto the street at all hours. Inside it's a museum of casks, blackened bottles, and kitschy bottle openers displayed against handpainted ceramic tiles. We recommend you try the cask-fresh *cervesa* (€3.50) or the house wine *xampanyet* (€2), and pad your stomach with some of the delicious tapas.

✦ Ⓜ*Jaume I. Walk down C. Princesa and take a right onto C. Montcada, toward the Museu Picasso. Xampanyet is on the right before the Placeta Montcada.* Ⓢ *Tapas €1.10-13. Beer €3.50. Wine and cava from €2.* ☼ *Open Tu-Sa noon-4pm and 7-11pm, Su noon-4pm.*

▩ PETRA

C. dels Sombrerers, 13

MEDITERRANEAN $$
☎93 319 99 99

With dark wood, stained glass, Art Nouveau prints, menus pasted onto wine bottles, and chandeliers made of silverware, Petra's eccentric decor will have you expecting an expensive meal. Luckily, the lively bohemian feel is matched by bohemian prices. Pasta dishes like the rich gnocchi with mushrooms and hazelnut oil (€5.20) and entrees such as the duck with lentils (€7.90) are easy on the wallet, as is the midday *menú* of a main course (varies daily), salad, and wine for €6.60—a true steal.

✦ Ⓜ*Jaume I. Walk down C. Princesa and take a right onto C. Pou de la Cadena. Take an immediate left onto C. Barra de Ferro and a right onto C. Banys Vells. Petra is located where C. Banys Vells ends at C. Sombrerers.* Ⓢ *Menú €6.50. Appetizers €4.90-7.10; entrees €7.90.* ☼ *Open Tu-Sa 1:30-4pm and 9-11:30pm, Su 1:30-4pm.*

▩ LA BÁSCULA

C. dels Flassaders, 30

CAFE, VEGETARIAN $$
☎93 319 98 66

This working cooperative serves vegetarian sandwiches, *empanadas*, salads, and more—the menu changes daily. Doors laid flat serve as communal tables, and a mixture of art, environmentally friendly sodas, and protest flyers set this restaurant apart. Though discretely robed in the same antique exterior as more expensive places, Báscula provides a more reasonably priced alternative to the upscale eateries. Hours and seating availability may change as the restaurant fights for its right to serve in-house, but takeout is available no matter the outcome.

✦ Ⓜ*Jaume I. Walk down C. Princesa and take a right onto C. Flassaders.* Ⓢ *Entrees and salads €7-9. Sandwiches and soups €4-5. Piadinas €6. Cash only.* ☼ *Open W-Sa 1pm-midnight, Su 1-8pm.*

food

LA PARADETA

SEAFOOD $$$

C. Comercial, 7 ☎93 268 19 39 www.laparadeta.com

For the highest quality seafood, this hybrid fish market/restaurant is where Barcelona goes. The line often stretches down C. Comercial, but it's worth the wait to walk into the simple interior and pick out fresh fish to be cooked to your liking. When they call your number, head up and grab your meal, then sit back down and enjoy.

⌖ ⓂJaume I. Follow Carrer Princesa all the way to C. Comerç, then right, then left at C. Fusina (just before the market), then right on C. Comercial. Ⓢ Market prices. ☒ Open Tu-Th 1-4pm and 8-11:30pm, F-Sa 1-4pm and 8pm-midnight, Su 1-4pm.

HOFMANN PASTISSERIA

SWEETS $$

C. dels Flassaders, 44 ☎93 268 82 21 www.hofmann-bcn.com

Pastry school meets storefront in this Seussian mindbender. Drift through the door, take a deep breath, and let that wonderful smell of freshly baked sweets fill your lungs. Watch artisans work on delectable goods ion the surreal spiral staircase above, while glass cases and wooden cabinets wait below filled with adorable gelatos (€3.50), precious marmalade jars (€8), and a selection of not-so-sickeningly-cute-but-utterly-delectable tarts and cakes wait below.

⌖ ⓂJaume I. Walk down C. Princesa and take a right onto C. Flassaders. You'll see Hofmann right before crossing Pg. del Born. Ⓢ Croissants €1-1.50. Gelato €3.50. Marmalades €8. Chocolates €1-5. Coffee €1.20-1.50. ☒ Open M-Th 9am-2pm and 3:30-8pm, F 9am-2pm and 3:30-8:30pm, Sa 9am-8:30pm, Su 9am-2:30pm.

LA LLAVOR DELS ORIGENS

CATALAN $$

C. de la Vidrieria, 6 ☎93 453 11 20 www.lallavordelsorigens.com

La Llavor dels Origens serves traditional Catalan fare with a picture menu that lets you see your meal in painstaking detail before you eat it, with even more excruciatingly specific written descriptions of each dish—these guys take food seriously. Seasonal menus change every two months, while the regular menu changes every six, ensuring that there will always be something new to try (and maybe cook yourself—all recipes are available on the website). Drawings from customers young and not-so-young deck the walls, undermining the sleek decor.

⌖ ⓂJaume I. Walk down C. Princesa and take a right onto C. Montcada. Upon crossing Pg. del Born, C. Vidrieria is the street directly in front of you. ⓘ Organic meat available on request. Ⓢ Entrees €6-11. Beer €3. Wine €3.50. 15% discount for takeout. 10% surcharge for sitting outside. ☒ Open daily 12:30pm-1am.

GADES FONDUES

FONDUE $$$

C. de l'Esparteria, 10 ☎93 310 44 55 www.gadesfondues.com

For those who just can't get enough of sticking food in other food, Gades Fondues steps up to fill an oft-neglected role. A choice of chocolate, meat, or cheese fondues (€15-24 per person, min. 2 people) lets you pick it and stick it in a much classier setting than the phrase would imply. Salads, carpaccio, and a selection of other dishes round out the menu for those who prefer a less interactive meal. Bring a friend and try one of the set menus: salad, basil cheese fondue, fruit skewer with molten chocolate, wine or sangria, and coffee (€21), or the same deal with meat (beef, turkey, and *botifarra*—Catalan sausage; €22).

⌖ ⓂJaume I. Walk down C. Princesa and take a right onto C. Montcada. Cross Pg. del Born and follow C. Vidrieria until you reach C. Esparteria. Ⓢ Fondues €15-24 per person. Tapas €6-12. Entrees €10-18. Menú (min. 2 people) €21-22 per person. ☒ Open M-Th 8:30pm-midnight, F-Sa 8:30pm-1am.

AL SUR CAFE $

C. de Sant Pere Més Alt, 4 ☎93 310 12 86 www.alsurcafe.com

Directly across from the Palau de la Música Catalana, Al Sur whips up cheap and tasty *bocadillos* and *empanadas* that please empty pockets. Free Wi-Fi, an iBar with Apple TV, and a small but comfy loft-lounge encourage you to kick back and relax, while hot, filling sandwiches are perfect for on-the-go diners. The baristas can put together a mean coffee, too—look for lunch combos that include a sandwich or *empanadas*, a drink, and a coffee for just a handful of euro.

✦ ⓂUrquinaona. Walk down C. Jonqueres and take a right onto C. Sant Pere Més Alt. Al Sur is directly across from the Palau de la Música Catalana. 𝒊 Free Wi-Fi. Ⓢ Combo food and drink specials €4.10-6.50. ⓩ Open M-Th 8:30am-1:30am, F 8:30am-3am, Sa 10am-3am, Su 10am-1:30am.

BUBÓ BAKERY, BAR $$

C. de les Caputxes, 6 (bar) and 10 (bakery)☎932 68 72 24 (bakery), 933 10 57 73 (bar) www.bubo.es

Whether you're chilling in the outdoor seating with an up-close-and-personal view of the massive, elegant Santa Maria del Mar or just gazing at the bakery display case, Bubó is sure to delight the eyes. Heartier fare includes reasonably priced sandwiches from its "world sandwich tour," while the perfectly glazed tarts and rainbow of macaroons whipped up by decorated pastry chef Carles Mampel tempt any sweet tooth.

✦ ⓂJaume I. Exit to C. de l'Argenteria and walk down C. de l'Argenteria away from Via Laietana. At the plaça surrounding the church, take an immediate right onto C. dels Sombrerers and the 1st left onto C. Caputxes. Ⓢ Menú (1 drink, 6 tapas, dessert; for 2 or more) €16 per person. Sandwiches €3.30-4. Desserts €1-3.50. Cakes €20-30. Cocktails €4-8. ⓩ Open M-Th 9am-1am, F-Sa 9am-2am, Su 9am-1am.

EL RAVAL

Kebab is a major food group in El Raval, and it's always a good, cheap option. For those looking for more of a traditional Barcelonan meal, though, El Raval has much to offer.

▨ CAN LLUÍS CATALAN $$$

C. de la Cera, 49 ☎93 441 11 87

Can Lluís? Yes he can! (Just kidding: *can* is Catalan for *chez*). This crowded restaurant has been an El Raval staple since its founding in the 1920s, when this neighborhood was Barcelona's Chinatown. It's stayed in the family for three generations and today it looks today like many of the customers have been around since the early days, too—try to get there when it opens, as the usual suspects have dibs on most of the tables. Don't be intimidated by the fact that everyone already knows each other, or by the fact that you'll almost certainly be spoken to in Catalan. Just remember: "Què vols?" ("What do you want?") is your cue to order.

✦ ⓂSant Antoni. Follow Ronda Sant Antoni toward Mercat de Sant Antoni, bear left on Ronda Sant Pau, and then head left on C. Cera. Ⓢ Appetizers €4.90-15; entrees €9.90-24. Lunch menú €9.30. ⓩ Open M-Sa 1:30-4pm and 8:30-11:15pm. Closed 3 weeks in Aug.

▨ SOHO PITAS, HOOKAH $

C. de les Ramelleres, 26

A welcome recent addition to the neighborhood, Soho serves cheap and simple with meat and vegetarian options (€2) without rushing you out of the place. It feels very impromptu, with everything written by hand and a lot of exposed plywood, but, at prices this low, it's definitely here to stay. Low-slung seats around low wooden tables in a simple dining room make for a no-frills dining experience, while smaller, intimate rooms are perfect for test-driving a hookah (€10) from the impressive wall of smoking paraphernalia.

✦ ⓂUniversitat. Walk down C. Tallers and take a right onto C. Ramelleres. Ⓢ Pita and drink €3.50. Cash only. ⓩ Open M-Sa 1pm-midnight.

[icon] JUICY JONES (EL RAVAL) VEGETARIAN, INDIAN $$

C. de l'Hospital, 74 ☎93 443 90 82 www.juicyjones.com

The big brother of the Juicy Jones in the Barri Gòtic, this version of the vegetarian eatery fits into its surroundings more appropriately—daily specials of Indian *dahl* and curries that seemed a bit out of place in la Gòtic fit right into El Raval's culinary landscape. If you've ever wondered what MC Escher's art would have looked like if he used more color and took more 'shrooms, the interior will satisfy your curiosity.

➜ [M]Liceu. Walk down C. Hospital. Juicy Jones is on the right at the corner of C. Hospital and C. Roig, before Rambla del Raval. [$] Daily thali plate €6. Tapas €2-3.50. Sandwiches €3.90-4.50. Menú €8.50. 🕐 Open daily 1-11:30pm.

NARIN MEDITERRANEAN $

C. dels Tallers, 80 ☎93 301 90 04

Sitting discreetly among the shops and cafes of C. Tallers, Narin is hiding the best baklava (€1) in Barcelona as well as equally scrumptious falafel, shawarma, and kebabs. If you can't stand the heat, get out of the kitchen—the inside resembles a sauna with wooden walls and sweaty customers. Luckily, beers come cold and cheap (€1.80) for those looking to brave the bar, and a tiled dining room provides a reprieve from the buzz of the electric shawarma shaver.

➜ [M]Universitat. Walk down C. Tallers. [$] Pitas €2.90-4. Durums €3.50-4.50. Main dishes €6.50-7.40. 🕐 Open M-Th 11am-2am, F-Sa 11am-3am, Su 11am-2am.

HELLO SUSHI JAPANESE $$

C. de la Junta de Comerç, 14 ☎93 412 08 30 www.hello-sushi.com

The large, semi-industrial interior, decorated with both modern and traditional Japanese art, offers a relatively cheap daily *menú* (€8.50) and sushi platters at reasonable prices, luring a young clientele into its dark, pillow-padded lair. Dine at the bar, grab a table, or sit on the floor in the foyer and admire the paintings while the smell of tempura and teriyaki tempt you to stay for another round.

*➜ [M]Liceu. Walk down C. Hospital and take a left onto C. Junta de Comerç. **i** Sometimes hosts live music; check website for schedule. [$] Entrees €8-14. Sushi rolls €4-8; combos €12-32. 🕐 Open Tu-Sa 12:30-4:30pm and 8:30pm-12:30am, Su 8:30pm-12:30am.*

SHALIMAR PAKISTANI, INDIAN $$

C. del Carme, 71 ☎93 329 34 96

Shalimar serves authentic Pakistani and Indian dishes tandoori style. Generous portions and delicious meat-based curries (€7-9) punctuate a menu that would make any vegetarian happy. Hand-painted tiles and warm lighting perk up the simple interior, and lace curtains block out the busy streets of Raval.

➜ [M]Liceu. Walk down C. Hospital and take a right onto C. Roig, then a left onto C. Carme. Shalimar is on the left before the fork. [$] Appetizers €2-8; entrees €6.80-9.20. Beer €2. 🕐 Open M-Tu 8pm-midnight, W-Su 1-4pm and 8pm-midnight.

MADAME JASMINE CAFE $$

Rambla del Raval, 22

Allow yourself to be seduced by either the hip 19th-century French-brothel-chic interior or the scrumptious *bocadillos* (€5.50). Orange and red lighting sets the mood, incense fills the nostrils, and a selection of sultry Latin, electro, and lounge music may just convince you to partake in the less legal red-light activities lining the streets of Raval.

➜ [M]Liceu. Walk down C. Hospital and take a left onto Rambla del Raval. Madame Jasmine is on the right nearly ¾ of the way down. [$] Salads €7. Cocktails €5. Beer €2-3. 🕐 Open M-F 5:30pm-2:30am, Sa-Su 1:30pm-2:30am. Kitchen open daily until 12:30am.

MENDIZABAL SANDWICHES $

C. de la Junta de Comerç, 2

A crowd of young, artsy students out front and vibrant multicolored tiles in the back make this otherwise inconspicuous foodstand hard to miss. Take your cheap eats to go, or grab a seat on the terrace in the neighboring *plaça* for an extra 10% (look for the coordinating chairs). Some veggie-friendly options are available—we recommend the tomato, brie, and avocado sandwich (€3.60).

‡ [M]Liceu. Walk down C. Hospital. Mendizabal is on the left at the corner of C. Hospital and C. Junta de Comerç. [$] Bocadillos €3-4. Beer €2.50. Cocktails €4.50. Cash only. ⏰ Open daily 8:30am-1am.

RITA ROUGE INDIAN $$$

C. del Carme, 33 ☎93 481 38 86 www.ritarouge.com

This thin, seemingly neverending restaurant stretches from C. Carme and spills its outdoor seating into Pl. Gardunya behind the Boqueria; some days you may even have to enter from Pl. Gardunya. Red walls, mirrored columns, and gold curtains interspersed with inexplicable pictures of Hawaii and saucy ladies will have you ready to spice up the night with one of the curries (€10-19).

‡ [M]Liceu. Walk on Las Ramblas toward Pl. Catalunya and take a left onto C. Carme. [$] Tapas €4.10-6.10. Salads €6.10-13. Menú €11-14. ⏰ Open M-Sa noon-2am, Su 6pm-2am.

KASPARO CAFE $$

Pl. de Vicenç Martorell, 4 ☎93 302 20 72

You'll only find a handful of seats inside—seriously, there are so few you might be able to hold them with one hand—but the real appeal is the outdoor seating under the arched colonnade or out on the Pl. Vicenç Martorell. Sit on the metal-clad seating of the terrace to partially escape the clatter of dishes and silverware inside, and grab one of the veggie-friendly *platos del día* (€4.60-8.50) or just a beer (€2.70-3.40) to satisfy whichever appetite you've mustered.

‡ [M]Catalunya. When facing Las Ramblas, take C. Pelai, on the right, along the plaça. Turn left onto C. Jovellanos at the end of the plaça. Follow C. Jovellanos as it becomes C. Ramelleres; Pl. Vicenç Martorell is on the left. [$] Tapas €2.60-12. Appetizers €1.40-5.30; entrees €4.60-8.50. Sandwiches €3.40-5.70. Cash only. ⏰ Open Tu-Sa 9am-midnight.

L'ANTIC FORN CATALAN $$$

C. del Pintor Fortuny, 28 ☎93 412 05 86 www.lanticforn.com

White tablecloths and an unremarkable interior hide high-quality, reasonably priced Catalan cuisine. The dining room is bright and airy during the day, with the crowd getting younger and the lighting sultrier as the night progresses. Order the artichokes (€6.50) or grilled goat (€9) as you get prepared for a rowdier end to your night elsewhere.

‡ [M]Catalunya. Walk toward the sea on Las Ramblas and take a right onto C. Pintor Fortuny. i Reservations recommended on weekends. [$] Tapas €4.90-6.50. Appetizers €4.50-11; entrees €8.10-17. Daily menú €9.50-11. ⏰ Open M-Sa 1-5pm and 7:30pm-midnight.

ORGANIC CAFE, MEDITERRANEAN $$

C. de la Junta de Comerç, 11 ☎93 301 09 02 www.antoniaorganickitchen.com

For once, you won't have to worry about space for seating—Organic has enough room to fit an entire youth hostel and their luggage. A vegan buffet (€7) surprises and delights with croquettes, pasta, and salad fixings, while all-vegetarian Mediterranean dishes will please even the most outspoken carnivores. Be sure to say thanks to Mother Earth as you leave—she'll be on your left looking down on you approvingly, surrounded by peas, earth, and fire.

‡ [M]Liceu. Walk down C. Hospital and take a left onto C. Junta de Comerç. [$] Vegan salad buffet €7. Pizza €9. Menú €9.50-12. ⏰ Open daily 12:30pm-midnight.

EN VILLE
FRENCH $$$

C. del Doctor Dou, 14 ☎93 302 84 67 www.envillebarcelona.es

En Ville is a typical French-style bistro, with brick ceilings, dim lighting, and mirrors everywhere. Located on the most Parisian-looking of El Raval streets, En Ville is decked with marble-topped tables, terra-cotta floors, wicker chairs, and lamps that mimic the posts in the neighborhood, bringing the outside in, while waiters bring out impressive dishes like the roasted pig with melon and cantaloupe tartare (€15). Actual outdoor seating is available as well, if that's your thing, but be sure to sit inside on Tuesday and Wednesday nights to be serenaded by live flamenco, jazz, or bossanova.

 # [M]Liceu. Walk toward Pl. Catalunya on Las Ramblas. Take a left onto C. Carme and a right onto C. Doctor Dou. [$] Tapas €3.50-20. Appetizers €6.90-12; entrees €13-20. ⏰ Open M 1-4pm, Tu-Sa 1-4:30pm and 8-11:30pm.

L'HORTET
VEGETARIAN $$

C. del Pintor Fortuny, 32 ☎93 317 61 89

An upscale vegan and vegetarian restaurant for when a side salad just won't cut it. Red faux-leather tablecloths and abstract paper lights that only vaguely resemble produce will leave you guessing where its allegiances lie. Come hungry during the day when only the *menú* is available, or for lighter fare at night and on Sunday.

 # [M]Catalunya. Walk toward the sea on Las Ramblas and take a right onto C. Pintor Fortuny. i A la carte items only available at night and on Su midday. [$] Menú M-F €9.80, Sa €13, Su €15. ⏰ Open M-Th 1-4pm, F-Sa 1-4pm and 8-11:30pm, Su 1-4pm.

BIOCENTER
VEGETARIAN $$

C. del Pintor Fortuny, 25 ☎93 301 45 83 www.vegetarianobarcelona.com

White walls and a modular grid make the perfect gallery-like setting for Biocenter's rotating selection of paintings, sculptures, and dusty antique books. Relaxing piano music contributes to the feel, and an entirely vegetarian menu specializing in healthy and environmentally friendly cuisine will please your inner yuppie.

 # [M]Catalunya. Walk toward the sea on Las Ramblas and take a right onto C. Pintor Fortuny. [$] Appetizers €5-9; entrees €7.50-13. Dish of the day €6.50. Menú (Sa 1-5pm) €10. Desserts €4.30. ⏰ Open M-Sa 1-11pm, Su 1-5pm.

OLIVIA
CAFE $

C. del Pintor Fortuny, 22 ☎93 318 63 80

Brightly furnished with lacquered wooden tables and booths, this tiny corner cafe will draw you in with its sweet aromas and keep you with its sweeter pastries and inexpensive sandwiches. Big windows provide a good people-watching venue in the poshest section of El Raval.

 # [M]Catalunya. Walk toward the sea on Las Ramblas and take a right onto C. Pintor Fortuny. [$] Pastries €1.40-3.60. Sandwiches €2.80-4.70. Cash only. ⏰ Open M-Sa 8am-9pm.

BAR RESTAURANT ELISABETS
BAR, RESTAURANT $

C. d'Elisabets, 2-4 ☎93 317 58 26

A hopping local bar by night, this resting place for decrepit radios—they line the restaurant's walls—offers a daytime *menú* of cheap sandwiches and lighter fare (€2.40-3.50) as well as heavier homemade dishes (€6-12) and cheese and meat platters (€9-10). No matter what you eat, be prepared to get cozy with a younger crowd.

 # [M]Universitat. Walk down C. Tallers and take a right onto C. Elisabets. [$] Appetizers €2.40-3.50; entrees €6-12. Lunch menú €8.50. Beer €1.40-2.20. Mixed drinks €5-7. Cash only. ⏰ Open M-F 7:30am-2am, Sa 7:30am-11pm.

CHELO CAFE $$

Pl. de Vicenç Martorell, 4 ☎93 302 40 95

Gold and silver couches and painted cherry trees are a shabby-chic twist for this little cafe, but the real scene is outside on the terrace in Pl. Vicenç Martorell, where it's part of the trifecta of cafes lining this side of the courtyard. With cheap breakfasts like the *tosta* with brie and tomato (€3.50) and *bocadillos* like salmon and cream cheese (€4.90), the food at this cafe is the best of the bunch.

🧭 [M]Catalunya. When facing Las Ramblas, take the road to your right, C. Pelai, along the plaça. Turn left onto C. Jovellanos at the end of the plaça. Follow C. Jovellanos as it becomes C. Ramelleres; Pl. Vicenç Martorell is on the left. [$] Breakfast €1.90-4.20. Sandwiches €4.60-5.60. Salads €5.80-7. Cash only. ⏰ Open daily 10am-midnight.

CAFÉ D'ANNUNZIO CAFE $$

Pl. de Vicenç Martorell, 5 ☎93 302 40 95

Rainbow stickers mark the glass doors of the last of the three cafes that line the arcade of the Pl. Vicenç Martorell. Pictures of Venice and sculptures of Roman heads dress up the otherwise generic interior that sells delicious coffee (€1.50-3.90) supplied by Café del Dog. Sit inside to enjoy the anachronistic '80s alternative hits playing over the stereo.

🧭 [M]Catalunya. When facing Las Ramblas, take the road to the right, C. Pelai, along the plaça. Turn left onto C. Jovellanos at the end of the plaça. Follow C. Jovellanos as it becomes C. Ramelleres. Pl. Vicenç Martorell is on the left. [$] Appetizers €1.60-4. Sandwiches €3.30-8. Platters €10-15. Beer €2.70-3. ⏰ Open M-Sa 10am-10pm.

CAFETARIUM CAFE $$

C. dels Tallers, 76 ☎66 764 01 11 www.cafetarium.com

Much classier and less horror-movie-esque (the Sharktopus of cafes?) than the name would imply, Cafetarium serves a mix of cheap sandwiches and more filling *platos del día* for when *bocadillos* and coffee just can't cut it. For those missing the greasy comforts of home, a double hamburger (€5.20) will remind your arteries of the good old days. Quirky frames and vintage chandeliers make those creature comforts just hip enough to stomach.

🧭 [M]Universitat. Walk down C. Tallers. [$] Sandwiches €3.30-5.20. Tapas €4.10-6.10. Main courses €7.50-11. Menú €7.50. ⏰ Open M-Sa 8am-1am.

TALLERS 76 VALENCIAN $$

C. dels Tallers, 76 ☎93 318 89 93 www.tallers76.com

A modern, lilac interior covered in mirrors lets you peep at your fashionable self (or at your date, if you don't happen to be a complete narcissist). Valencian rice dishes are the house specialty, so be prepared to dig into a huge platter of paella. Tapas and meat dishes round out the menu for those looking to avoid a carbohydrate-induced coma.

🧭 [M]Universitat. Walk down C. Tallers. [$] Tapas €3.50-6.50. Entrees €9-11. Lunch menú €11-13. Dinner menú €15-18. Cocktails €3.50. ⏰ Open daily 9am-11:30pm.

L'EIXAMPLE

★ LA RITA CATALAN $$

C. d'Aragó, 279 ☎93 487 23 76 www.laritarestaurant.com

La Rita serves traditional Catalan dishes with a twist, like potatoes and black sausage in mushroom sauce, and duck with apples, raspberry *coulis*, and mango chutney. Though the price is dirt-cheap given the quality and quantity of food, the interior is anything but—expect an upscale but relaxed ambience (think piano music) that will make you wish you had changed out of that sweaty T-shirt.

🧭 [M]Passeig de Gràcia. Walk up Pg. de Gràcia away from Pl. Catalunya and turn right onto C. Aragó. [$] Appetizers €5-7.50; entrees €7-12. ⏰ Open daily 1-3:45pm and 8:30-11:30pm.

LISBOA
PORTUGUESE $$

C. del Comte Borrell, 145   ☎93 451 00 27 www.lisboaenbarcelona.com

Incredibly rich and delicious Portuguese fare will make anyone who's been to Portugal nostalgic—and will make anyone who hasn't book a ticket for the next flight to Lisbon. The only traditional Portuguese restaurant in Barcelona, Lisboa serves the expected *bacalhau* (cod) dishes as well as *alheira* (chicken sausage; €11), which is nearly impossible to find outside of Portugal. Wash it all down with a shot of Lisbon's classic liqueur, sour cherry *ginja* (€2).

⚲ ⓜUrgell. *With your back to the rocket-shaped Agbar Tower, walk along Gran Via de les Corts Catalanes and take a right onto C. Comte Borrell.* Ⓢ *Entrees €9-16. Lunch menú Tu-F €9.90* ⓩ *Open Tu-Sa 1-4pm and 8-11pm, Su 1-4pm.*

OMEÍA
MIDDLE EASTERN $$

C. d'Aragó, 211   ☎93 452 31 79 www.omeia.es

When you're tired of cheap shawarma stands, stop into Omeía for some authentic Middle Eastern fare. Start off with their roasted red pepper soup (€6.50), then fill up with one of the traditional Jordanian dishes (€11-13). Pick something you haven't got a chance of pronouncing correctly and hope for the best!

⚲ ⓜUniversitat. *Walk up C. Aribau to the left of the University building and turn right onto C. Aragó.* Ⓢ *Appetizers €6.30-7; entrees €7.50-13. Lunch menú €7.50.* ⓩ *Open daily 10am-4pm and 8pm-1am.*

CAMPECHANO
GRILL $$

C. de València, 286   ☎93 215 62 33 www.campechanobarcelona.com

If you've ever wondered what it's like to picnic at a Barcelonan *merendero* (outdoor bar and lunch area), Campechano may not quite satisfy your curiosity—but it will try. The restaurant offers *carnes a la brasa* (grilled meat) beside a courtyard campfire. Peek through the painted trees to peep mountainside campers and prepare to chow down on delicious, relatively cheap eats.

⚲ ⓜDiagonal. *Head downhill on Pg. de Gràcia and turn left onto C. València.* Ⓢ *Salads €4-6. Entrees €8.50-18. Lunch menú €10.* ⓩ *Open M 1-4pm, Tu-F 1-4pm and 8:30-midnight, Sa 1:30-4pm and 8:30-midnight.*

EL JAPONÉS
JAPANESE $$$$

Passatge de la Concepció, 2   ☎93 487 25 92 www.grupotragaluz.com

This sushi may cost more than your hostel bunk, but if you appreciate quality, it's worth the splurge. Bulk up on noodles or rice and order a mixed sushi platter (€20) for a slightly more economical—though by no means cheap—alternative. Trendy hardly begins to describe the clients and the interior; definitely leave the backpack in your hostel.

⚲ ⓜDiagonal. *Walk down Pg. de Gràcia and turn right onto Passatge de la Concepció, which is the 1st narrower road on the right.* Ⓢ *Appetizers €6-10; entrees €8-16. Sushi €5-10.* ⓩ *Open M-W 1:30-4pm and 8:30pm-midnight, Th 1:30-4pm and 8pm-midnight, F-Sa 1:30-4pm and 8pm-12:30am, Su 1:30-4pm and 8:30pm-midnight.*

CAFÉ CHAPULTEPEC
MEXICAN $$

C. del Comte Borrell, 152   ☎93 451 92 85 www.cafechapultepec.com

Cheap burritos (€4.30-5.40) and other Mexican dishes, along with free internet, make this cafe a pleasant retreat from generally overpriced l'Eixample. Grab some *chilaquiles de pollo* (€6), or try one of the flavored hotcakes with ham or bacon (€4.80).

⚲ ⓜUrgell. *With your back to the rocket-shaped Agbar Tower, walk along Gran Via de les Corts Catalanes and turn right onto C. Comte Borrell.* Ⓢ *Appetizers €3.60-5.90; entrees €4.30-8.50.* ⓩ *Open Tu-F 10am-4pm and 7-11pm, Sa 12:30-4:30pm and 7-11pm, Su 12:30-4:30pm.*

MUSSOL
C. de Casp, 19

CATALAN $$

☎93 301 78 10

Mussol serves delicious and inexpensive traditional fare in a massive den filled with businessmen, families, and 10 ft. wine casks. With tchotchkes lining the wall and *faux-bois* decor, it doesn't quite achieve a down-home feel, but the prices are remarkably low.

⚑ Ⓜ*Catalunya. Head up Pg. de Gràcia and turn right onto C. Casp.* Ⓢ *Appetizers €4.60-10; entrees €5.80-17 (most under €12). Daily specials €4-10.* ⚂ *Open M-F 7:45-noon and 1pm-1am, Sa 1pm-1am, Su 1pm-midnight.*

FRIDA'S
C. del Bruc, 115

MEXICAN $$

☎93 457 54 09

Renowned as the most authentic Mexican restaurant in l'Eixample, Frida's serves anti-Tex-Mex quesadillas, *tostadas*, and a range of traditional dishes including *cochinita pibil* (€12) and *michoacan carnitas* (€12). Kick back with a margarita (€5.70) at the bar under a portrait of Frida Kahlo, or take your food to-go for a picnic along nearby Pg. de Gràcia.

⚑ Ⓜ*Girona. Walk down C. Girona past C. Aragó and take a left onto C. Mallorca. Frida's is on the corner of Mallorca and Bruc.* 𝒊 *5 tacos €9 on Th and F.* Ⓢ *Tostadas and quesadillas €3. Entrees €7.80-12. Lunch menú €11.* ⚂ *Open Tu-Sa 1-4pm and 8:30pm-midnight.*

GINZA
C. de Provença, 205

JAPANESE $$

☎93 451 71 93

Ginza is a tastier and cheaper alternative to the multitude of all-you-can-eat Japanese restaurants in the area. Fresh, delicious dishes are served amid paper lamps and woodblock prints. Look up at the photograph of sumo wrestlers under blossoming cherry trees as you sip miso soup (€3), fill up on *teppanyaki* (€6-12), and wash it all down with a cup of sake.

⚑ Ⓜ*Diagonal. Walk away from Pg. de Gràcia on C. Rosselló. Take a left onto C. Balmes and a right onto C. Provença.* Ⓢ *Appetizers €3-9.60; entrees €6-12. Sushi €6.50.* ⚂ *Open daily 1-4pm and 8pm-midnight.*

MAURI
Rambla de Catalunya, 102 and 103

SWEETS, SANDWICHES $$

☎93 215 10 20 www.pasteleriasmauri.com

This tripartite pastry-deli-dessert shop has something to satisfy any craving, whether sweet or savory. Dine on little sandwiches, croquettes, croissants, and more cakes than you've seen in one place at Rambla Catalunya, 102, or order something from the deli next door and dine in the wood and plaster salon. Across the street, you'll find Mauri's *bomboneria* and tearoom, which sells gift baskets perfect for wooing cute hostelmates.

⚑ Ⓜ*Diagonal. Walk away from Pg. de Gràcia and take a right onto Rambla Catalunya. The pastisseria is on the right; the tea shop on the left.* Ⓢ *Pastries and snacks €1.50-2.50. Tapas €3.20-8. Sandwiches €2-3. Lunch menú €13.* ⚂ *Open M-Sa 9am-9pm, Su 9am-3pm.*

LAIE BOOKSTORE CAFÉ
C. de Pau Claris, 85

CAFE, CATALAN $$

☎93 302 73 10 www.laie.es/restaurante/pau-claris/8

Perfect for the bibliophilic foodie—or just anyone looking for a cafe to chill with her copy of *Let's Go.* Head to the sunny yellow back room with palm trees and burlap shades, or chill out on the couches hovering around the bookstore's entrance. A veggie-friendly snack bar with gourmet mini-sandwiches and pastries provides snacks during the odd hours, while a full-on restaurant serves inexpensive dishes come mealtime.

⚑ Ⓜ*Catalunya. Follow Pg. de Gràcia away from Pl. Catalunya and turn right onto C. Casp and then left onto C. Pau Claris.* 𝒊 *Internet €1 per 15min.* Ⓢ *Coffee and snacks €1.40-4.50. Food €7-10. Beer €2.60. Wine €1.60-3. Lunch menú M-F €14, Sa-Su €17.* ⚂ *Open M-F 9am-10pm, Sa 10am-10pm.*

food

TAPAÇ 24 TAPAS $$

C. de la Diputació, 269 ☎93 488 09 77 www.tapas24.net

Climb down the stairs and into this den of delicious tapas. Chef Carles Abellán serves food that you can actually afford (in small portions, at least) at this alternative to his acclaimed Comerç 24. Marble countertops and colorful paintings spruce up this cafeteria-esque alcove. Try a plate of *patatas bravas* (€3.80) with either a glass of *cava* (€3) or the house sangria (€3.80), or see what looks good on the daily tapas menu.

➡ *[M]Passeig de Gràcia. Tapas, 24 is on the corner of C. Diputació and Pg. de Gràcia.* [$] *Tapas €2.50-14. Raciones €9-12.* ⏰ *Open daily 9am-midnight.*

BARCELONETA

Barceloneta is surrounded by the Mediterranean on three sides, so it's no surprise that its cuisine involves an abundance of seafood, ranging from the homeliest tapas bars to the swankiest restaurants, with everything in between.

👍 **LA BOMBETA** TAPAS $$

C. de la Maquinista, 3 ☎93 319 94 45

Take heed of the warning scrawled above the bar, "*No hablamos inglés, pero hacemos unas bombas cojonudas*"—or, for the non-Spanish speaking set, "We don't speak English, but we make *bombas* that are out of this world." The retro facade is plastered with menu listings, and a no-frills dining room inside offers typical Spanish fare like *tostadas*, tortillas, and tapas, but really—just get the *bombas* (fried potato balls with spicy ground beef inside; €3.50 for 2).

➡ *[M]Barceloneta. Walk down Pg. Joan de Borbó (toward the beach) and take a left onto C. Maquinista.* [$] *Appetizers €3-9.50; entrees €5-18.* ⏰ *Open M-Tu 10am-midnight, Th-Su 10am-midnight.*

👍 **SOMORROSTRO** SEAFOOD $$$

C. de Sant Carles, 11 ☎93 225 00 10 www.restaurantesomorrostro.com

This extraordinary restaurant assembles a new menu every day based on selections from the catch of the day that the young chefs have selected—though "artists" might be a more appropriate term—Jordi Limón and Andrés Gaspar. Somorrostro is not cheap—its rotating menu of seafood dishes, paella, curries, and other dishes runs about €13-20 per entree, but the nighttime *menú* (€15-17) of the chefs' gastronomical experiments is the real treat. The kitchen is in full view right behind the bar, so you can watch the masters at work and ask them questions like, "How the hell did you manage to make a solid bar of gazpacho?"

➡ *[M]Barceloneta. Walk on Pla del Palau over Ronda del Litoral, following the harbor. After crossing Ronda del Litoral, take the 5th left onto C. Sant Carles.* [$] *Weekday lunch buffet €13 per kg. Appetizers €6-14; entrees €13-20. Dinner menú €15-17. Wine €3-5.* ⏰ *Open M 8-11:30pm, W-Sa 8-11:30pm, Su 2-4pm and 8-11:30pm.*

L'ARRÒS PAELLA $$$

Pg. de Joan de Borbó, 12 ☎93 221 26 46 www.larros.es

At first glance, L'Arròs ("Rice") appears to be a typical tourist trap along Barceloneta's main drag, but don't let the uninspired decor and multilingual menu of this *arrosseria* fool you. What the restaurant lacks in atmosphere it makes up for with its paella, which Barcelona natives claim is some of the best in town.

➡ *[M]Barceloneta. Walk on Pla del Palau over Ronda del Litoral and follow Pg. Joan de Borbó.* [$] *Appetizers €8-17; entrees €14-20.* ⏰ *Open daily noon-11:30pm.*

BAR JAI-CA TAPAS, SEAFOOD $$

C. de Ginebra, 13 ☎93 268 32 65

This unassuming tapas bar serves fresh seafood and local flavor to swarms of locals. Ceramic jars and houses line the shelves, while signed photographs of FC Barcelona legends look down from overhead. Grab a single *bomba* (fried potato ball with spicy ground beef; €1.40) or wash down a plateful of crunchy sea critters (€3-6) with some cheap beer (€1.80).

✦ ⓂBarceloneta. Walk on Pla del Palau over Ronda del Litoral to follow the harbor. After crossing Ronda del Litoral, take the 2nd left onto C. Ginebra. *i* Credit card min. €10. Ⓢ Tapas €1.30-8. ⓒ Open Tu-Sa 9am-11:30pm, Su 9am-10:30pm.

BAR BITÁCORA
TAPAS $

C. de Balboa, 1   ☎93 319 11 10

During the summer months, the giant neon eyeball of this establishment looks onto a small terrace full of young people who flock from the beach like pigeons to a tasty chunk of bread. The 10% surcharge to sit in the courtyard terrace is worth every cent, though a simple interior offers plenty of seating for those looking to get out of the sun, with a cheap but filling daily *menú* (entree with salad and *patatas bravas*, bread, a drink, and dessert; €5).

✦ ⓂBarceloneta. Walk down Pg. Joan de Borbó (towards the beach) and take the 1st left after Ronda del Litoral onto Carrer Balboa. Ⓢ Tapas €2.50-8. Sangria €3. Menú del día €5-7. ⓒ Open M-W 9am-midnight, Th-F 9am-2am, Sa 10am-2am, Su noon-midnight.

CAN MAÑO
SEAFOOD $$

C. del Baluard, 12 ☎93 319 30 82

This no-frills joint has been serving fresh seafood for rock-bottom prices to a never-ending crowd of locals for years. Tile floors, white paint, and a random assortment of old framed newspaper clippings provide a refreshing break from those restaurants that actually attempt interior decoration.

✦ ⓂBarceloneta. Walk on Pla del Palau over Ronda del Litoral to follow the harbor. Take the 1st left after crossing Ronda del Litoral, onto C. Balboa. Take the 2nd right onto C. Baluard. Ⓢ Meat and fish dishes €3-10. Combination plates €6.50-8. Cash only. ⓒ Open M 8am-11pm; Tu-F 8-11am, 12:15-4pm, and 8-11pm; Sa 8-11am and 12:15-4pm.

SEGONS MERCAT
SEAFOOD $$$

C. de Balboa, 16   ☎933 10 78 80 www.segonsmercat.com

On the aging streets of Barceloneta, this sleek and clean restaurant stands apart. The menu and prices vary each day, as the name (*segons mercat* is Catalan for market price) suggests. Dine in the shiny interior with businessmen on their lunch breaks and other diners who appreciate the best seafood, even if they have to shell out (get it?) a little extra.

✦ ⓂBarceloneta. Walk on Pla del Palau over Ronda del Litoral to follow the harbor. Take the 1st left after crossing Ronda del Litoral, onto C. Balboa. Ⓢ Tapas €4-7.50. Entrees €7.90-17. Wines €2.50-4. ⓒ Open M-F 7:30am-1:30am, Sa-Su 1pm-midnight.

GRÀCIA

Gràcia's pedestrian *places* and cute streets are home to some of Barcelona's most vibrant cafes. Almost every establishment will have tapas, even if they aren't the house specialty, but don't miss out on the more traditional meals that Gràcia has to offer.

🔖 UN LUGAR DE GRÀCIA
CATALAN $$

C. de la Providència, 88   ☎93 219 32 89

Un Lugar de Gràcia has the best-priced and most ample lunch special in the neighborhood by far: any two dishes from the midday *menú*—no distinction between first and second courses, so the very hungry may essentially order two main courses at no extra cost—bread, water or wine, and dessert cost €9.50. For that amount of food at that price, you'd expect mediocre fare in a depressing bar, but this is a brightly colored and lively meeting place, with locals returning often for the great food and company.

✦ ⓂJoanic. From the Metro, follow C. Escorial uphill and take a left onto C. Providència. Ⓢ Entrees €6-11. ⓒ Open M 8:15am-4:30pm, W-Th 8:15am-4:30pm and 7:30pm-midnight, F 8:15am-4:30pm and 7:30pm-2am, Sa 11am-4:30pm and 7:30pm-2am, Su 11am-4:30pm. Also open for all 🔖FC Barcelona matches.

food

SAMSARA
C. de Terol, 6
TAPAS $$
☎93 285 36 88

Samsara has a long regular menu with some of the best tapas in the neighborhood as well as about a half dozen "novetats": daily tapas specials listed on the chalkboard. The restaurant's feel would be date-like, were it not for the often communal tables: low wooden tables surrounded by even lower cushioned ottomans accommodate as many as can squeeze in, so be prepared to make new friends.

✢ ⓜFontana. Head downhill on C. Gran de Gràcia, then turn left on C. Ros de Olano, which becomes C. Terol. ⓢ Tapas €4.40-7.50. Beer €2-3.20. Wine €3-4. ⓩ Open M-W 8:30pm-1am, Th 8:30pm-2am, F-Sa 8:30pm-3am, Su 7:30pm-1am.

LA NENA
C. de Ramón y Cajal, 36
CAFE $
☎93 285 14 76

La Nena has an extensive menu of gourmet chocolates, ice creams, crepes, sandwiches, and quiches at ridiculously low prices. Don't try ordering a cold beer to beat the heat, though—the huge banner overhead alerts visitors that this may be the only spot in Barcelona that doesn't serve alcohol. This is a *xocolateria*, and as such, it specializes in that thick and excellent Spanish hot chocolate (€2.50-3.50). For a more savory treat, try one of the *tostadas*, like the goat cheese with tomato and mushroom, which will have you wishing you, too, had an extra stomach for more room.

✢ ⓜFontana. Follow C. Astúries away from C. Gran de Gràcia and take a right onto C. Torrent de l'Olla. Walk a few blocks and take a left onto C. Ramón y Cajal. ⓢ Sandwiches €3-6. Quiches €5.50. Pastries €1.80-2.50. Cash only. ⓩ Open M-W 9am-2pm and 4-10pm, Th-Su 9am-10:30pm.

GAVINA
C. de Ros de Olano, 17
PIZZA $$
☎93 415 74 50

Gavina is Gràcia's most heavenly pizzeria: winged cherubs above the door welcome you, and a further host of angels and saints watches benevolently as you eat, while a giant plastic hand of God scoops through the wall, about to pick you up. The big draw, though, is not the impressive kitsch but the gigantic, delicious pizzas (€6.50-14). Try the namesake Gavina (potatoes, ham, onion, and mushrooms; €12) or the pizza of the day—but be sure to bring friends or an otherworldly appetite.

✢ ⓜFontana. From the Metro, walk downhill on C. Gran de Gràcia and take a left onto C. Ros de Olano. ⓢ Pizza €6.50-14. Midday menú €10. ⓩ Open M-Th 1pm-1am, F-Sa 1pm-2am, Su 1pm-1am.

IKASTOLA
C. de la Perla, 22
BAR, CAFE $

If you don't like the specials, just write your own on the chalkboard menu—but don't expect the cook to take heed. Every night young locals gather at Ikastola (Basque for "nursery school") to chat, pound out tunes on the upright piano, and scribble everything from love notes to apartment listings on the walls of this cafe. Lively and quick with cheap and famous *bocatas* (sandwiches made with the fresh bread; €4.50) on view behind the bar, Ikastola is the perfect place to start the night before embarking on more mature shenanigans.

✢ ⓜFontana. Follow C. Astúries away from C. Gran de Gràcia, then take a right onto C. Torrent de l'Olla and left onto C. Perla. ⓢ Salads €7. Beer €1.70-2.30. Wine €2. Cash only. ⓩ Open M-Th 7pm-midnight, F-Sa 7pm-1am, Su 7pm-midnight.

CHIDO ONE
MEXICAN $$

C. de Torrijos, 30 ☎93 285 03 35 www.chidoone.es

If the colorful Oaxacan wooden animals lining the walls don't tip you off that this place means business, the *mole* (spicy chocolate-based sauce) will. The tacos, served in tiny flour tortillas, are the best on this side of the Atlantic, and the *mole*-drowned enchiladas "Santa Rosa" (€12) are absolutely divine. Grab a Mexican beer (€2-4) to wash it all down.

✦ ⓂFontana. Follow C. Astúries away from C. Gran de Gràcia to Pl. Virreina. In the middle of the right side of the plaza, take a right down C. Torrijos. Ⓢ Appetizers €8.50-9.50; entrees €10-13. Cash only. ⏰ Open M-Th 1-5pm and 7pm-1am, F-Su 1pm-2am.

LA LLAR DE FOC
CATALAN $$

C. Ramón y Cajal, 13 ☎93 284 10 25

Colorful chalkboard menus outside show graphic depictions of the restaurant's *carns a la brasa* in a way that's more comic book than carnal. The dishes are straight-up Catalan home cooking, from *torrades* (€4.50-10) to *canelons* (€5.20). If you want meat, they've got it. They also offer a range of pasta dishes in a traditional interior that reminds *Let's Go* of grandma's outdated lake cabin.

✦ ⓂFontana. Follow C. Astúries away from C. Gran de Gràcia and take a right onto C. Torrent de l'Olla. Walk a few blocks and take a left onto C. Ramón y Cajal. Ⓢ Appetizers €5-6.50; entrees €6-15. Pasta €5-6. Daily specials €5-9.50. ⏰ Open daily 1-4pm and 8:30pm-midnight.

L'ILLA DE GRÀCIA
VEGETARIAN $$

C. de Sant Domènec, 19 ☎93 238 02 29 www.illadegracia.com

A haven for vegetarians, this modern eatery just off the Pl. Vila de Gràcia serves meatless meals worlds away from the cheese *bocadillos* you've been trying to enjoy while your friends savored their delicious ham. The restaurant offers vegetarian versions of Catalan classics, including spinach *canelons* and seitan dishes served in personal crocks (€5-8).

✦ ⓂFontana. From the Metro, head downhill 5 blocks on C. Gran de Gràcia and turn left onto C. Sant Domènec. Ⓢ Salads €5-6. Entrees €3.70-8. ⏰ Open Tu-F 1-4pm and 9pm-midnight, Sa-Su 2-4pm and 9pm-midnight.

CAFÈ DEL TEATRE
CAFE, BAR $

C. de Torrijos, 41 ☎93 416 06 51

This corner cafe's name is a bit misleading: don't come here expecting stuffy old-world pomp, because you're going to find a cool little bar with lots of shiny black surfaces and its name boldly stated in lime-green translucent plastic. The only hint of anything classic is found in the colorfully updated interpretations of vintage wallpaper. Drop by for the cheap *menú* (€6.40-6.90) and the even cheaper beer (€1-3).

✦ ⓂFontana. Follow C. Astúries away from C. Gran de Gràcia to Pl. Virreina. In the middle of the right side of the plaza, take a right down C. Torrijos. Ⓢ Entrees and sandwiches €4.90-6.50. Menú €6.40-6.90. Beer €1-3. Cash only. ⏰ Open daily 11am-3am.

MIRIOT
MEDITERRANEAN $$

C. de Francisco Giner, 54 ☎93 368 26 05 www.miriot.com

Miriot serves delicious Catalan and Mediterranean food, often with a bit of a twist (for example, the duck *canelons* €8). The place itself approaches the level of swanky but it stays quite within the budget traveler's reach thanks to the incongruously low prices. The decor is simple—plain brick walls punctuated by the obligatory photographs of Gaudí buildings—but the effort not spent on elaborate design has been put into the food.

✦ ⓂDiagonal. Follow Pg. de Gràcia uphill across Av. Diagonal. Take a right onto C. Bonavista and then a left onto C. Francisco Giner. Ⓢ Salads €6-10. Entrees €9.20-17. Menú M-F €10, Sa €13. Credit card min. €15. ⏰ Open M-Sa 1-4pm and 9pm-midnight.

food

CAN PUNYETES

CATALAN $$

C. de Francisco Giner, 8-10   ☎93 217 79 46

Can Punyetes is a cavernous Catalan *taberna* with simple but welcoming decoration and simple but delicious food. For those sick of stumbling across bohemian veggie establishments, this is the perfect chance to embrace Catalunya's meat-loving culture in a traditional atmosphere.

✚ ⓂDiagonal. Follow Pg. de Gràcia uphill across Av. Diagonal. Take a right on C. Bonavista and then a left onto C. Francisco Giner. Ⓢ Torrades €4.70-9.50. Appetizers €3.20-8.70; entrees €5.50-15. Cash only. ⌚ Open daily 1-4pm and 8pm-midnight.

L'ARMARI

FRENCH $$

C. del Montseny, 13   ☎93 368 54 13

The menus facing the street are not printed or handwritten but rather glazed onto a set of ceramic plates—cuter than a box full of baby alpacas. The food is modern, French, and a bit on the snazzy side (cod carpaccio, anyone?), but the prices don't reflect the *haute cuisine* you'll find here. The €4 cocktails before 10pm make sure this bistro leans away from straight-laced suppers and ever so slightly toward debaucherous fun.

✚ ⓂFontana. Walk downhill on C. Gran de Gràcia and turn left onto C. Montseny. Ⓢ Sandwiches €3.50-9. Tapas €4-7. Entrees €6-12. Daily menú €15. Cocktails after 10pm €5.50. ⌚ Open daily 6pm-2:30am.

BARCELONA REYKJAVÍK

BAKERY $

C. d'Astúries, 20   ☎93 302 09 21 www.barcelonareykjavik.com

This bakery is perfect for the discerning backpacker who's tired of white bread and those sugary, mass-produced *magdalenas*. Barcelona Reykjavík bakes mind-blowing breads—if you've been in Spain long enough, you'll find the sourdough a godsend—as well as delicious muffins, brioche, and other baked goods. Ingredients and potential allergens for each are listed, making the lives of those with dietary restrictions a little easier, if only for a second before they venture back out into the world of meat, cheese, sugar, and gluten. Be prepared to eat on your feet or save it for later—this little storefront has no seating.

✚ ⓂFontana. Follow C. Astúries away from C. Gran de Gràcia. Ⓢ Items sold by weight. Breads normally €3-5. Baked goods €1-2. ⌚ Open M-Sa 10:30am-9:30pm, Su 10:30am-8pm.

ASKA DINYA

MIDDLE EASTERN $$

C. de Verdi, 28   ☎93 368 50 77 www.askadinya.es

Garden views abound from the painted-crumbling-rock walls of this oasis—Aska Dinya holds nothing back in going for an "authentic" Middle-Eastern feel. Pesky cats peer from overhead as an intoxicating smell of incense fills your nostrils. Afraid of a feline messing with your meal? Well, don't fear—it's all a painted ruse (or at least the cats are), but the serious quality of the food isn't. Aska Dinya bakes all of its own bread, and loads of Palestinian-inspired options fill the menu, including *ozzi*, a dish of rice and ground spicy veal that is one of the most delicious creations known to man.

✚ ⓂFontana. Follow C. Astúries away from C. Gran de Gràcia, cross C. Torrent de l'Olla, and turn right onto C. Verdi. Ⓢ Appetizers €6.50-8.50; entrees €9-14. Ozzi €12, plus chicken €13. Menú €9. ⌚ Open daily noon-2am.

MONTJUÏC AND POBLE SEC

The neighborhood of **Poble Sec** hides a number of good, inexpensive restaurants and bars—perfect for those who don't feel like breaking the bank to eat at a museum cafe up on Montjuïc, or for those looking to explore a lovely neighborhood a bit off the beaten track.

🔲 QUIMET I QUIMET
C. del Poeta Cabanyes, 25

TAPAS, BAR $$
☎93 442 31 42

This pocket-sized tapas bar has walls lined with alcohol going all the way up to its very high ceiling, a crowd spilling out onto the street at tapas time, and the best tapas in Poble Sec—possibly in the entire city. Push your way through to the bar, order whatever looks good, and get the dark house beer if you're getting sick of Estrella Damm.

ⓣ Ⓜ*Paral·lel. Follow Av. Paral·lel away from the water past the small plaça on the left, then head left up C. Poeta Cabanyes.* Ⓢ *Tapas €1.90-5.50. Beer €2-4. Cash only.* ⓘ *Open M-F noon-4pm and 7-10:30pm, Sa noon-4pm.*

TRENTA SIS
C. de Margarit, 36

BAR $$
☎93 505 87 97

The meals at Trenta Sis are fancy but not at all expensive. As advertised outside, Trenta Sis is *"rico y baratito"*—delicious and very cheap. The handwritten specials on the chalkboard outside change frequently, but they generally don't break the €7 barrier, and the midday lunch *menú* (Tu-F) is just €6.

ⓣ Ⓜ*Poble Sec. Follow Av. Paral·lel toward the water and turn right on C. Margarit.* Ⓢ *Entrees €3.80-6.90. Cash only.* ⓘ *Open Tu-Th 1pm-2am, F-Sa 1pm-3am, Su 1pm-2am.*

LA TOMAQUERA
C. de Margarit, 58

CATALAN $$$

Though not Poble Sec's most affordable option, La Tomaquera is an informal neighborhood joint with a casual vibe and the constant buzz of locals catching up over lunch. Red-and-white checkered tablecloths and a dim interior make it feel like your local Italian place back home, but the cuisine here is staunchly Catalan.

ⓣ Ⓜ*Poble Sec. Follow Av. Paral·lel toward the water, then right on C. Margarit.* Ⓢ *Appetizers €5.90-11; entrees €7.30-20. Cash only.* ⓘ *Open Tu-Sa Jan-July 1:30-3:45pm and 8:30-10:45pm, Sept-Dec 1:30-3:45pm and 8:30-10:45pm.*

EL DUENDE DE POBLE SEC
C. del Poeta Cabanyes, 11

SPANISH $$
☎93 600 59 00

The glass floor with a minuscule fairy world underneath (*duende* is Spanish for a kind of fairy) is a huge hit with the kids, and the inexpensive but delicious Spanish cuisine keeps the grown-ups coming back. Fake ivy and new brick trying to look old envelop diners in the humble restaurant whose real attraction is the food. And the fairies.

ⓣ Ⓜ*Paral·lel. Follow Av. Paral·lel away from the water past the small plaça on the left, then left up C. Poeta Cabanyes.* Ⓢ *Salads €5.90-7.80. Tapas €2.80-6.90. Entrees €7.50-19. Menú €9.90. Cash only.* ⓘ *Open Tu-Sa 1-4pm and 8pm-midnight, Su 1-4pm.*

LA SOLEÁ
Pl. del Sortidor, 14

CAFE $$
☎93 441 01 24

La Soleá is a very small cafe—only two tables and a bar inside—with lots of seating on the quieter Pl. Sortidor, the heart of Poble Sec. Regardless, the midday *menú* (Tu-F €8.50) is quite popular. Snag one of the four chairs inside among the orange tiles of various shades and the activist posters or order some tapas for a nice excuse to sit out on the *plaça*.

ⓣ Ⓜ*Poble Sec. Follow Av. Paral·lel toward the water, then right up C. Blasco de Garay to Pl. Sortidor. La Soleá is on the far side of the plaça.* Ⓢ *Tapas €4.50-6.90. Entrees €8.50-17. Cash only.* ⓘ *Open Tu-Su noon-midnight.*

food

nightlife

Nightlife in Barcelona is ubiquitous and hardcore, though there are plenty of bars and pubs for those less likely to make it to dawn. The **Barri Gòtic's** dark corners and confusing lattice of streets hide many quirky and colorful bars that you're not likely to come across unless you know they're there—even then, your chances of finding them aren't great. **El Born's** nightlife involves hopping from bar to bar, past medieval churches and Baroque palaces, in what is sure to be one of the most beautiful nights out you've ever experienced. Given the outrageously lewd (and often illicit) nature of **El Raval** during daylight hours, it's no surprise that this *barri* gets wild at night. **L'Eixample** is known colloquially as "Gaixample," and this is why: a majority of the nightlife spots in this neighborhood are geared toward the GLBT community. **Barceloneta's** clubs are on the beach, and that's about all you need to know. **Gràcia's** strong neighborhood vibe and effectively pedestrian-only streets make it a natural hotbed of nightlife and bar culture. The nightlife of **Poble Sec** is of high quality but limited quantity, and it's often hard to find unless you know to go down empty streets and into barely marked doorways. Some of the nightclubs are a little more obvious, and the few to be found here are among the city's most popular. **Tibidabo** isn't really a neighborhood but a mountain, and a mountain that houses some fine clubs at that. You'll probably have to take a cab, but it will be worth it.

BARRI GÒTIC AND LAS RAMBLAS

🏴 BARCELONA PIPA CLUB   BAR

Pl. Reial, 3   ☎93 302 47 32 www.bpipaclub.com

With pipes from four continents, smoking accoutrements decorated by Dalí, and an "ethnological museum dedicated to the smoking accessory," the only pipe-related article missing from this club—albeit somewhat appropriately—is René Magritte's *Ceci n'est pas une pipe*. Despite its cryptic lack of signage and the furtive ambience of a secret society, the combination bar, pool room, and music lounge boasts a surprisingly high number of travelers. The dark wood, low lights, and provincial furnishings make for a perfect place to transport yourself away from the more collegiate nightlife of the Pl. Reial, even if your previous smoking experience amounts to time spent with a candy cigarette.

⚲ Ⓜ*Liceu. Walk on Las Ramblas toward the water and turn left onto C. Colom to enter Pl. Reial. Pipa Club is an unmarked door to the right of Glaciar Bar. To enter, ring the bottom bell.* **i** *Rotating selection of tobacco available for sale. Special smoking events. Tango and salsa lessons M and Th 8:30-10:30pm. Jazz jam session Su 8:30pm.* Ⓢ *Beer €4-5. Wine €4-5. Cocktails €7.50-9. Cash only.* 🕐 *Open daily 6pm-6am.*

🏴 HARLEM JAZZ CLUB   LIVE MUSIC, BAR

C. de la Comtessa de Sobradiel, 8   ☎93 310 07 55 www.harlemjazzclub.es

With live performances nightly and often a drink included in the cover (check the schedule), this is a budget-conscious music lover's paradise. A performance schedule online and at the door lets you choose whether you'll drop in to hear lovesick English crooning or a little saucier Latin flavor. Acts range from Bossa Nova to gypsy punk and the crowd is just as eclectic.

⚲ Ⓜ*Liceu. Walk toward the water on Las Ramblas and take a left onto C. Ferran, a right onto C. Avinyó, and a left onto C. Comtessa de Sobradiel.* **i** *Live music usually begins at 10 or 11pm. Calendar of events available online or at the door.* Ⓢ *Cover €5-6; sometimes includes 1 drink. Beer €3.80. Cocktails €7.80. Cash only.* 🕐 *Open M-Th 8pm-4am, F-Sa 9pm-5am, Su 9pm-4am.*

🏴 SINCOPA   BAR

C. d'Avinyó, 35

At night this music-themed bar—rumored to have once been owned by none other than Manu Chao—plays host to as many nationalities as it has currencies and secondhand instruments on its walls. Of Barri Gòtic's bars, Sincopa has some of the most colorful decor and clientele. One night the crowd might be baked and chilling to *Dark Side of the Moon*, and the next they'll all be salsa dancing.

[M]Liceu. Walk on Las Ramblas toward the water and take a left onto C. Ferran and a right onto C. Avinyó. $ Beer €2-3. Cocktails €7. Juices €2.50. Cash only. ⏰ Open M-Th 6pm-2:30am, F-Sa 6pm-3am.

MANCHESTER (BARRI GÒTIC) BAR

C. de Milans, 5 ☎66 307 17 48 www.manchesterbar.com

The names of the drinks posted on the front door—Joy Division, The Cure, Arcade Fire, The Smiths, and many, many more—let you know what you're in for once you enter. After passing the spinning turntable when you walk in, you'll find a dark, red-lit world of intimate seating, band references, and people chatting and drinking the night away. The happy hour with €1.50 Estrella Damms will have you crooning "This Charming Man" before the evening's up.

[M]Liceu. Walk toward the water on Las Ramblas and head left on C. Ferran, right on C. Avinyó, and left onto C. Milans, before C. Ample. Manchester is at the bend in the street. $ Beers €2-4; happy hour €1.50. Shots from €2.50. Cocktails €6. Cash only. ⏰ Open M-Th 7pm-2:30am, F-Sa 7pm-3am, Su 7pm-2:30am. Happy hour daily 7-10pm.

LAS CUEVAS DEL SORTE BAR

C. d'en Gignàs, 2 ☎68 776 50 83

The eponymous caves (accentuated by miniature stalactites on the ceiling) are filled with alcohol and revelers. Exquisite mosaics crop up in the most unexpected places, including the bathrooms. Downstairs, small tables and another bar surround a be-disco-balled dancefloor.

[M]Liceu. Walk toward the water on Las Ramblas and head left on C. Ferran, right onto C. Avinyó, and left on C. Gignàs. $ Cocktails €6-7; before 10pm €4.50. ⏰ Open M 7pm-2am, W-Th 7pm-2am, F-Sa 7pm-3am, Su 7pm-2am.

EL 13 BAR

C. de la Lleona, 13

If you can fight your way through the crowd of international 20-somethings into this pocket-sized hangout, Trece offers the self-proclaimed and *Let's Go*-confirmed best mojitos in Barcelona (€6). Exposed brick walls show off local artwork and an assorted selection of vinyl and dismembered mannequin body parts, including a set of legs that stick out over the restroom door and a torso that serves as the primary light source. Hits from the '80s abound, and a projector plays a selection of music videos and YouTube clips over the heads of the clientele. Watch out for the vintage porn over the bar and door.

[M]Liceu. Walk toward the sea on Las Ramblas and head left onto C. Ferran, right onto C. Avinyó, and left on C. Lleona. $ Beer €2-3. Cocktails €6-7. Shots €2.50. ⏰ Open M-Th 7pm-3am, F-Sa 7pm-5:30am, Su 7pm-3am.

SHANGÓ BAR

C. d'en Groch, 9 ☎66 210 51 65

Tucked down a poorly lit alley, Shangó's bright black-and-yellow door provides a warm, sunny beacon that beckons revelers throughout the night. Free salsa lessons and a neverending supply of spicy Latin tunes complement cheap mojitos (€4.50) and beer. Meanwhile, the comfortably full upper level of chairs and couches provides a relaxing place to grab a drink, meet some strangers, and soak in the sensation of being inside a big, sugary lemon.

*[M]Jaume I. Walk down Via Laietana toward the water. Take a right onto C. Gignàs and right onto C. Groch. **i** Free salsa lessons Tu-W 11pm-midnight. $ Beer €1.50-3. Mojitos €4.50. Cocktails €6; M and Su €4. ⏰ Open daily 9pm-3am.*

OVISO

CAFE, BAR

C. d'Arai, 5 ☎63 758 92 69 www.barnawood.com

Ancient Roman villa meets bohemian dive bar at Oviso. Frescoes adorn the walls, depicting peacocks, mythology, and a curious scene in which a man appears to be putting the moves on a lion. Benches and larger tables invite clients to continue the period theme and lounge at their discretion like a drunken Bacchus. Oviso serves a delicious variety of food and juices during the day, while at night the bar fills up quickly with locals from the Pl. Trippy (actual name Pl. de George Orwell, a theme picked up on by the live video feed of the bar visible on the website).

✦ ⓂLiceu. Walk toward the water on Las Ramblas and head left onto C. Ferran, right onto C. Avinyó, and right onto C. Arai. Oviso is on the right as you enter the plaça. Ⓢ *Beer €3. Cocktails €7. Cash only.* Ⓩ *Open M-Th 10am-2:30am, F-Sa 10am-3am, Su 10am-2:30am.*

SMOLL BAR

BAR

C. de la Comtessa de Sobradiel, 9 ☎93 310 31 73

The chic, updated '60s decor and friendly, burly bartenders combine to please an ever-present hip, gay-friendly, and young crowd. When there's room at the bar, squeeze in tight and try one of over 25 cocktails or a signature shot. The Rasmokov (vodka shot with a lime wedge topped in sugar and espresso; €2.50) will leave you caffeinated, sugar-buzzed, and full of fuzzy, extroverted feelings.

✦ ⓂLiceu. Walk toward the water on Las Ramblas. Take a left onto C. Ferran, a right onto C. Avinyó, and a left onto C. Comtessa de Sobradiel. Ⓢ *Beer €3.50. Cocktails €5.60. Cash only.* Ⓩ *Open M-Th 9:30pm-2:30am, F-Sa 9:30pm-3am.*

LA RIA

BAR

C. de Milans, 4 ☎93 310 00 92

A bright white interior, upright seating, and an entirely local clientele make for cheap booze, cheap food, and a refreshing—albeit grittier—alternative to the dressed up places in Pl. Reial. Order from the street and hang outside if the noisy sounds of Catalan from within intimidate you.

✦ ⓂJaume I. Walk on Via Laietana toward the water and take a right onto C. Gignàs. La Ria will be on the corner of C. Gignàs and C. Milans. Ⓢ *Beer €1-2.50. Wine €1.50-1.80. Tapas €4-12. Menú €6.50. Cash only.* Ⓩ *Open M-Th 10am-1am, F 10am-3am, Sa 6pm-3am.*

JAMBOREE

JAZZ CLUB

Pl. Reial, 17 ☎93 319 17 89 www.masimas.com/jamboree

A hall-of-fame assortment of jazz musicians on the walls of the lower level will leave you with no guesses as to where this club's allegiances lie, even when its grotto-like halls are filled with Americans singing Aaliyah. The club offers nightly jazz and blues performances and welcomes a younger set after the shows end at midnight. After this witching hour, be prepared for everything from hip hop to Shania Twain.

✦ ⓂLiceu. Walk on Las Ramblas toward the water. Left on C. Colom to enter Pl. Reial. ⓘ *Calendar of events and concerts on the website. Flyers provide discounts.* Ⓢ *Dance club cover €10. Event tickets €4-12. Tarantos (upstairs, mostly flamenco) cover €6. Beer €5. Cocktails €9-10.* Ⓩ *Dance club open M-Th 12:30pm-5am, F-Sa 12:30pm-6am, Su 12:30pm-5am. Music club open daily 9pm-1am, shows at 9 and 11pm. Tarantos open daily 8-11pm.*

MARGARITA BLUE

BAR

C. de Josep Anselm Clavé, 6 ☎93 412 54 89 www.margaritablue.com

Surprisingly, Margarita Blue has margaritas and—surprise number two!—they're blue (€4). They're also basically tequila plus blue food coloring, so be careful. Mexican platters complement the vaguely Mexican drink selection as colorful paintings of musicians paired with a mirrored wall keep loving watch over the bar. For those who need less supervision, a bright blue daisy wall in the back offers fluorescent cheer.

✦ ⓂDrassanes. Walk toward the water on Las Ramblas and take a left onto C. Josep Anselm Clavé. ⓘ *Magic show W and Su 10pm.* Ⓢ *Food €5.80-9. Cocktails €7-8.* Ⓩ *Open M-W 7pm2am, Th-Sa 7pm-3am, Su 6pm-2am.*

HEAVEN BAR

C. dels Escudellers, 20

€1 shots. Any questions?

🪧 [M]Liceu. Walk toward the water on Las Ramblas and take a left on C. Escudellers. $ Shots €1. Cocktails €4. Cash only. ⏰ Open M-Tu 8pm-2:30am, Th 8pm-2:30am, F-Sa 8pm-3am, Su 8pm-2:30am.

EL BORN

👍 **EL CASO BORN** BAR

C. de Sant Antoni dels Sombrerers, 7 ☎93 269 11 39

This is a quieter alternative for those too cool to bother with the packed houses and inflated prices of nearby Pg. del Born. Cheap drinks tempt travelers, while relaxed seating, a chill crowd, and a drinks menu with cocktails named for the Bourne movies (the name is a pun on *El Caso Bourne*, the Spanish title of *The Bourne Identity*) provide ample reasons to start the night here.

🪧 [M]Jaume I. Walk down C. Princesa and take a right onto C. Montcada. Upon entering Pg. del Born, take a right onto C. Sombrerers and then take a right again onto the 1st street on your right, C. Sant Antoni dels Sombrerers. $ Cava €1.80. Beer €2. Cocktails €5-7. ⏰ Open Tu-Th 6pm-2:30am, F-Sa 6pm-3am.

👍 **ESPAI BARROC** BAR

C. de Montcada, 20 ☎93 310 06 73 www.palaudalmases.com

Nobody wants to pay €12 for a cocktail, but consider it a €6 drink with a €6 entrance fee. The space is what you're really paying for anyway. Espai Barroc is in the courtyard and ground floor of the Palau Dalmases, a 17th-century palace whose simple facade hides one of the most beautiful patios in existence, with a jaw-dropping carved staircase and an overall elegance that makes this an obligatory stop. Get the cheapest drink you can find (if €6 of the drink price is for the setting, the beer is just €1!), relax, and drink like royalty.

🪧 [M]Jaume I. Walk down C. Princesa and take a right onto C. Montcada. $ Beer €7. Cocktails €12. ⏰ Open Tu-Th 8pm-2am, F-Sa 8pm-3am, Su 6-10pm. Flamenco M and W 9:30pm (€20; includes 1 drink), live opera Th 11pm, piano and jazz Su 9pm.

👍 **LA LUNA** BAR

C. dels Abaixadors, 10 ☎93 295 55 13 www.lalunabcn.com

Another of Barcelona's most beautiful bars, La Luna sits under timeless vaulted brick arches, with dim lighting and mirrors behind the bar making it seem even larger. Comfortable lounge seating in front makes the front a good place to camp out and take in the bar's beauty. The tropical mojito (with coconut rum; €7) and the *mojito de fresa* (€7.30), which replaces the lime with strawberries, are both quite popular.

🪧 [M]Jaume I. Take C. Argenteria to Santa Maria del Mar, then take a sharp right onto C. Abaixadors. $ Beer €2-3. Mixed drinks €6-8. ⏰ Open M-W 6pm-1:30am, Th-F 6pm-2:30am, Sa 1pm-2:30am, Su 1pm-1:30am.

LA FIANNA BAR

C. dels Banys Vells, 15 ☎933 15 18 10 www.lafianna.com

A glass partition divides the restaurant and bar, but be prepared to push your way through on weekend nights no matter where you choose to wine or dine. Unlike at other places in the area, finding a seat at the bar is a distinct possibility; getting a spot on one of the comfy couches, where patrons kick off their shoes and settle in, is another story altogether. Patience pays off with large mojitos (€7) made with special bitters.

🪧 [M]Jaume I. Walk down C. Princesa and take a right onto C. Montcada. Upon entering Pg. del Born, take a right onto C. Sombrerers and then another right onto C. Banys Vells. ℹ All cocktails €4.50 M-Th 6-9pm. Discounted tapas M-Th 7pm-12:30am, F-Sa 7pm-11:30pm, and Su 7pm-12:30am. $ Tapas €2-4.80. Beer €2.50-3.40. Shots €4. Cocktails €6-7. ⏰ Open M-W 6pm-1:30am, Th-Sa 6pm-2:30am, Su 6pm-1:30am.

EL BORN
BAR

Pg. del Born, 26 ☎93 319 53 33

Shed the themes and pretense and stop at El Born for a straight-up bar—no more, no less. Marble tables and green decor provide gametime seating for those brave enough to claim it. With cheap beer (€2-2.50) and ambient music, it's no wonder this place is always full.

*➜ [M]Jaume I. Walk down C. Princesa and take a right onto C. Montcada. Follow until you hit Pg. del Born and take a left. **i** Free Wi-Fi. $ Beer €2-2.50. Mixed drinks €6. ⏰ Open Tu-Su 10am-2:30am.*

EL COPETÍN
BAR, LATIN

Pg. del Born, 19 ☎60 720 21 76

This dance floor just won't quit: Latin beats blare all night long, attracting a laid-back, fun-loving crowd that knows how to move. A narrow, tightly packed bar up front provides little reprieve for those who need a drink, as the waitstaff will probably be too busy dancing anyway to tend to your every beck and call.

➜ [M]Jaume I. Walk down C. Princesa and take a right onto C. Montcada. Follow to Pg. del Born. $ Mixed drinks €7. Cash only. ⏰ Open M-Th 6pm-2:30am, F-Sa 6pm-3am, Su 6pm-2:30am.

BERIMBAU
BAR, BRAZILIAN

Pg. del Born, 17 ☎64 600 55 40

This *copas* bar, reportedly the oldest Brazilian bar in Spain (founded 1978), offers a range of drinks you won't easily find this side of the Atlantic. Try the *guaraná* with whiskey (€8), an orange and banana juice with vodka (€9), or the tried and true (and damn good) caipirinha (€7). Samba and Brazilian electronic music fill the room with a *brasileiro* feel, and the wicker furniture and stifling heat complete the scene.

➜ [M]Jaume I. Walk down C. Princesa and take a right onto C. Montcada. Follow to Pg. del Born, then left. $ Cocktails €7-10. Beer €2.50-3. ⏰ Open daily 6pm-2:30am.

CACTUS BAR
BAR

Pg. del Born, 30 ☎93 310 63 54 www.cactusbar.cat

Cactus Bar is renowned along Pg. del Born for its phenomenally delicious, large, and potent mojitos (€8). If you can get a bartender's attention over the clamor, you generally don't need to specify which drink you want: just use your fingers to indicate how many mojitos it'll be. The constant stream—or devastating flood, perhaps more accurately—of customers means the bartenders work as a team, creating a mojito assembly line that churns out over a dozen of the minty beverages at a time. Get your drink in a plastic cup to go and enjoy it on the (slightly) less crowded Pg. del Born.

*➜ [M]Jaume I. Walk down C. Princesa and take a right onto C. Montcada. Follow until you hit Pg. del Born, then take a left. **i** DJs M and W. $ Beer €3. Cocktails €8. Breakfast €1.50. Sandwiches €2.50-3.70. Tapas €1.80-6.50. ⏰ Open daily 4pm-2:30am.*

NO SÉ
BAR

Pg. del Born, 21 ☎67 148 59 87

This "Milanese" cocktail bar aims for a sleek look and calls itself an "artbar" for the artwork that covers the walls of both floors. Loud electronic music makes for an upbeat dance floor on weekday nights when there's actually a little room to breathe.

➜ [M]Jaume I. Walk down C. Princesa and take a right onto C. Montcada. Follow until you hit Pg. del Born. $ Beer €3. Mixed drinks €8-10. ⏰ Open daily 7pm-2:30am.

EL RAVAL

The nightlife in El Raval is mostly centered on the bars on and around **Rambla del Raval** and **Carrer de Joaquín Costa,** though there are a few **music clubs** dotting the rest of the neighborhood as well.

▨ MARSELLA BAR
BAR

C. de Sant Pau, 65   ☎93 442 72 63

Walls lined with antique mirrors, cabinets, old advertisements, and ancient liquor bottles that have probably been there since the age of *modernisme* will have you just waiting to witness your first saloon brawl. Luckily, the crowd is genial and friendly, even after a few absinthes (€5)—not that there's room to fight in this crowded place anyway. Paint falling from the ceiling and fuzzy chandeliers will have you feeling every month of the bar's 190 years of business.

⚑ ⓜ*Liceu. Follow C. Sant Pau from Las Ramblas.* Ⓢ *Beer €3. Mixed drinks €5-6.50. Cash only.* 🕒 *Open M-Th 11pm-2am, F-Sa 11pm-3am.*

▨ MOOG
CLUB

C. de l'Arc del Teatre, 3   ☎93 319 17 89   www.masimas.com/moog

One of Europe's premier clubs for electronic music, Moog—named for the synth that is the backbone of electronic music—caters both to electrotrash aficionados and lost souls just trying to find a place to dance. Come on Wednesdays and weekends for the biggest crowds, or drop in earlier in the week for house DJ sets. If you're looking for older hits or just want to get away from the throbbing mass on the dance floor, check out the upstairs, which plays a mix of older electro, disco, and techno.

⚑ ⓜ*Drassanes. Walk away from the water on Las Ramblas and left onto C. Arc del Teatre.* *i* *Discount flyers often available on Las Ramblas.* Ⓢ *Cover €10.* 🕒 *Open M-Th midnight-5am, F-Sa midnight-6am, Su midnight-5am.*

▨ PLÁSTICO BAR
BAR

C. de Sant Ramon, 23   ☎93 894 13 33   www.myspace.com/plasticobar

This tiny but hip bar, hidden on one of El Raval's seediest back streets, will accommodate as many people as are cool enough to enter. Dark paisley walls with a green-lit bar usher you in, but squeeze through to the back portion where the real life awaits. The upper level is for lounging, while the scratchy sound system of the lower portion pumps a mix of modern indie and '60s rock to a dance-ready crowd.

⚑ ⓜ*Liceu. Walk on Las Ramblas toward the sea. Take a right onto C. Nou de la Rambla and right onto C. Sant Ramon.* Ⓢ *Shots €3. Beer €3-3.50. Mixed drinks €6. Cash only.* 🕒 *Open Tu-Th 7pm-2:30am, F-Sa 7pm-3am.*

the botellón

The alfresco method of Spanish socializing, the *botellón* has lately gotten a lot of negative attention from older generations of Spaniards. The word basically means a giant, public pregame, in which the youths of Spain buy cheap alcohol, bags of ice, and plastic cups and then drink in the street. Many people believe the tradition arose because of the steep drink prices in bars and the former lack of real open container laws in Spain. However, another possible cause is the Spanish custom of not inviting guests over to the home just to get wasted, which does seem to make pregaming a necessarily public activity. However, the *botellón's* noisiness and (some would say) moral questionability have led the government to take extreme measures: some cities have considered passing laws forbidding any drink to be consumed in the street.

BAR BIG BANG

C. de Botella, 7

The back room attracts a collegiate crowd who watch free nightly jazz, standup, and vaudeville-esque theater. Out front, customers are serenaded by big band favorites—both local and national—from the stereo and black-and-white projector screen. Outsider art and vintage photographs line the walls, adding a little something extra to the sensory overload.

✦ ⓂSant Antoni. Walk down C. Sant Antoni Abad and take a right onto C. Botella. *i* Schedule of performances and special events on website. Variety show on Tu, DJ on F and Sa at midnight. Ⓢ Shots €3. Beer €3-4. Cocktails €6.50. All cheaper before 11pm. Cash only. ⌚ Open Tu-Su 9:30pm-2:30am.

BETTY FORD'S

C. de Joaquín Costa, 56

BAR
☎93 304 13 68

This ain't your dad's Betty Ford's. During the earlier hours of the evening, this bar and restaurant stuffs the crowds of local students coming in with relatively cheap and famously delicious burgers (€6.50). Happy hour (6-9pm) provides cheap drinks, and later in the night the place gets packed with a young, noisy crowd.

✦ ⓂUniversitat. Walk down Ronda Sant Antoni and take a slight left onto C. Joaquín Costa. Ⓢ Beer €3. Mixed drinks €5-6; happy hour €4. Burgers €6.50. Shakes €3.50. Cash only. ⌚ Open M 6pm-1:30am, Tu-Th 11am-1:30am, F-Sa 11am-2:30am. Happy hour M-Sa 6-9pm.

LLETRAFERIT

C. Joaquín Costa, 43

BAR, BOOKSTORE
☎93 301 19 61

A haven of calm in the frenetic, off-beat nightlife of C. Joaquín Costa, Lletraferit (Catalan for "bookworm") offers a little bit of literature to accompany your alcohol binge. Chill up front with a cocktail (€6-7.50) in comfy leather armchairs or head around to the back, where a cozy library and bookstore awaits. Settle in with a good book and watch the schwasted passersby while smugly sipping a drink.

✦ ⓂUniversitat. Walk down Ronda Sant Antoni and take a slight left onto C. Joaquín Costa. Ⓢ Cocktails €6-7.50. Cash only. ⌚ Open M-Th 4pm-1:30am, F-Sa 4pm-3am, Su 4pm-1:30am.

VALHALLA CLUB DE ROCK

C. dels Tallers, 68

BAR, CLUB, LIVE MUSIC

Be prepared to see burly men air-guitaring Slayer in the area where you'd usually find a dance floor. A concert hall some nights, this dark and industrial nightclub is a haven for those looking for something a little more metal after all the flashing lights and throbbing techno. Free entry on non-show nights means you can use the cash you save to try the entire selection of *chupitos del rock*, specialty shots named after bands from Elvis to Whitesnake (€1).

✦ ⓂUniversitat. Walk down C. Tallers. *i* Search for Valhalla Club de Rock on Facebook to find a calendar of concerts and special events. Ⓢ Shots €1-2. Beer €1.50-2.50, after 10pm €2.50-5. Mixed drinks €6-7. Cash only. ⌚ Open daily 6:30pm-2:30am.

SANT PAU 68

C. de Sant Pau, 68

BAR
☎93 441 31 15

Sant Pau 68 is an absurdist bar with an identity crisis. The wall of ears—be careful what you say, the walls here literally have ears—and gas-tank-inspired lights and a metal chandelier with circuit board cutouts cast geek-chic patterns of light across the stairwell. If you're looking to get away from the crowd, grab a Bloody Mary (€6) and head upstairs to scrawl your regards on the graffiti wall.

✦ ⓂLiceu. Follow C. Sant Pau away from Las Ramblas. Ⓢ Beer €2.20. Mixed drinks €6-7. ⌚ Open M-Th 8pm-2:30am, F-Sa 8pm-3:30am, Su 8pm-2:30am.

barcelona

LA ROUGE
BAR

Rambla del Raval, 10 ☎93 329 54 45

Push your way through the packed bar area to lounge in the dark seating in back, or look down on the masses from the loft. No matter where you stand, be sure to check out the chandelier made of tiny liquor bottles hanging above the entrance—just don't expect to drink them for free. Cocktails start at €5, while the house shot *chupito la rouge* will cost you €3.50. Electronic dance music plays over the stereo to please the younger crowd.

➡ [M]Liceu. Follow C. Hospital and take a left onto Rambla del Raval. La Rouge will be on the right. $ Beer €2.50. Cava €4. Cocktails €5-6. Tapas €1.50-6.50. Cash only. ⏰ Open M-Th 8pm-2am, F-Sa 8pm-3am.

L'OVELLA NEGRA
BAR

C. de Sitges, 5 ☎93 317 10 87 www.ovellanegra.com

Think **Viking beer hall** without the funeral pyre burning into the night. Cheap beer flows freely, which makes stomaching the kitsch—anyone care to take a picture with the drunken black sheep cutout?—possible. Split-log benches and a selection of foosball, pool tables, and TVs provide all the charm of a frathouse in Valhalla.

➡ [M]Catalunya. Walk toward the sea on Las Ramblas, take a right onto C. Tallers, and then a left onto C. Sitges. i Second location at C. Zamora, 78. $ Shots €3. Beer €1.20-3.60. Tapas €1.50-4. Drinks cheaper before 11pm. Cash only. ⏰ Open M-F 9am-3am, Sa-Su 7pm-3am.

MANCHESTER (EL RAVAL)
BAR

C. de Valldonzella, 40 ☎66 307 17 48 www.manchesterbar.com

Compared to the Manchester in Barri Gòtic, El Raval's incarnation stays surprisingly cool and unpretentious in spite of some serious music memorabilia. Whether you're into the overexposed pictures on the walls or the drones of Ian Curtis, or maybe you just stumbled in, Manchester provides a relaxed atmosphere in which anyone can feel indie cool, regardless of musical inclination.

➡ [M]Universitat. Walk on Ronda Sant Antoni and take a left onto C. Valldonzella. i Live music some nights; check website for calendar. $ Beer and wine €2.50. Mixed drinks €6. Cash only. ⏰ Open M-Th 7pm-2:30am, F-Sa 7pm-3am, Su 7pm-2:30am.

BAR ALMIRALL
BAR

C. de Joaquín Costa, 33 ☎93 304 13 68

With its rough yellow walls, cafe-style seating, and a *modernisme*-inspired wooden bar, Almirall is undoubtedly one of the best bars in which to pretend you've gone a century back in time. The clientele, though, probably isn't as well-dressed as it would have been at the turn of the century.

➡ [M]Universitat. Walk down Ronda Sant Antoni and take a slight left onto C. Joaquín Costa. $ Beer €2.40. Mixed drinks €5-6. Cash only. ⏰ Open M-Th 7pm-2:30am, F-Su 7pm-3am.

L'EIXAMPLE

LES GENTS QUE J'AIME
BAR

C. de València, 286B ☎93 215 68 79

Come down the stairs into this sultry red-velvet underworld, redolent of gin and *modernisme*, where you'll be transported back some hundred years into a *fin-de-siècle* fiesta. Black-and-white photographs, cool jazz, and vintage chandeliers set the mood for you to partake of sinful pleasures. Not sure where to head for the rest of the night? Cozy up next to the palm-reader or have your tarot cards read to avoid making the decision yourself.

➡ [M]Diagonal. Head downhill on Pg. de Gràcia and turn left onto C. València. Les Gents Que J'Aime is downstairs, just past Campechano. i Palm reading and tarot M-Sa. $ Wine €3. Beer €3.50. Cocktails €7. Palm reading €30. Tarot €25. ⏰ Open M-Th 7pm-2:30am, F-Sa 7pm-3am, Su 7pm-2:30am.

LA FIRA

C. de Provença, 171 ☎93 323 72 71

Decorated entirely with pieces from the old Apolo Amusement Park in Barcelona, this club is that creepy carnival from Scooby Doo, but with a bar instead of a g-g-g-ghooooost. Spend a little extra time in the Mystery Machine before entering, and this club will be one of Barcelona's most memorable. Chill with a drink and the carousel horses, or dance until you just can't handle this place anymore.

✦ ⓜHospital Clínic. Walk away from the engineering school along C. Rosselló and take a right onto C. Villarroel. Take the 1st left onto C. Provença; La Fira is a few blocks down. *i* Often hosts shows or parties, sometimes with entrance fee or 1-drink min. ⓢ Cover sometimes €10; includes 1 drink. Beer €5. Cocktails €8. Cash only. ⌚ Open W-Sa 11:30pm-3am.

LA CHAPELLE

BAR, GLBT

C. de Muntaner, 67 ☎93 453 30 76

A wall of devotional figurines, crosses, and paintings with mostly nude men in front allows La Chapelle to show a gayer side of the sacrament. Solemn red lighting mixed with modern bubble lights cut through the veil of testosterone—apparently debaucherous religious imagery is bait for bears, or maybe it's the video of naked male models on the flatscreen. Get a little closer to God while getting a lot closer to some grizzly guys.

✦ ⓜUniversitat. Face the University building and walk left on Gran Via de les Corts Catalanes. Turn right onto C. Muntaner; La Chapelle is 2 blocks up. ⓢ Beer €2.50. Mixed drinks €5. ⌚ Open daily 4pm-2:30am.

LE CYRANO

BAR

C. d'Aribau, 154 ☎93 231 79 09

Don't you just hate it when you watch the bartender pour your drink, and you're all like, okay, enough, that's good, really, ENOUGH? And then you're forced to sip the drink you just paid way too much for and could have done a better job making yourself? Well, this is the bar for you—for no more than €5 (usually €4) you get an empty glass and get to make your own cocktail, ranging from a 95%-Coke Cuba Libre to the *Let's Go* pregame special: vodka with a splash of juice. Free popcorn keeps you busy while you wait some 40min. for the ever-packed bar to clear so you can get your next round.

✦ ⓜDiagonal. Facing downhill on Pg. de Gràcia, head right on C. Rosselló 3 blocks, then right up C. Aribau. ⓢ All drinks €4-5. ⌚ Open Th-Sa 11pm-3am.

DOW JONES

BAR

C. del Bruc, 97 ☎93 476 38 31 www.bardowjones.es

During the day this bar has enough TV screens to keep every *futbol* fan happy, no matter his or her allegiance. At night, the bar lights up with raucous foreigners (mainly American, British, and Irish) trying desperately to order their favorite drink before the price spikes—like the stock market, drink prices here vary based on their popularity throughout the day. Wait for the prices to crash if you're craving a winner, or keep buying low and be glad the staff speaks English for when you start slurring your Spanish (or your English).

✦ ⓜGirona. Follow C. Consell de Cent 1 block toward Pg. de Gràcia and turn right up C. Bruc. ⓢ Beer €2-5.50. Cocktails €4-7. Food €2.80-7.50. Prices vary by demand. ⌚ Open M-F 7am-2:30am, Sa-Su noon-3am.

ÁTAME

BAR, GLBT

C. del Consell de Cent, 257 ☎93 434 92 73 www.facebook.com/bar.atame

Dietrich Gay Teatro Café's life partner, Átame's simple, dark interior, accented by sparkly rainbow flags, pulses with '80s hits and a mostly male crowd that loves to sing along (and encourages you to sing with them). The dance floor in back is crowded when drag shows aren't in session, while the front of the bar provides a pack of men lying in wait for unsuspecting newcomers.

✈ ⓂUniversitat. Face the University building and walk left on Gran Via de les Corts Catalanes. Turn right onto C. Aribau, walk 2 blocks, and turn left onto C. Consell de Cent; Átame is 1 block down.

i Drag shows and other events Tu-F and Su. Call for more info. Ⓢ Mixed drinks €5, happy hour €4.

🕐 Open M-Th 6:30pm-2:30am, F-Sa 7pm-3am, Su 6:30pm-2:30am Happy hour daily until 11pm.

AIRE (SALA DIANA)   CLUB, GLBT FRIENDLY
C. de València, 236   ☎93 454 63 94 www.arenadisco.com/aire.htm

If you're looking for a gay party spot that isn't overwhelmingly male (read: the rest of L'Eixample), check out Aire for all of the female company the neighborhood seemed to be lacking. This huge club is packed almost as soon as its doors open and continues to party with a mix of pop hits, R and B, and electronica well into the night. You generally don't even need to pay the cover to meet someone, as the party spills out onto C. València. Don't worry about feeling left out—no matter your gender or orientation, the club is, as the owner says, "for her and her male friends."

✈ ⓂPasseig de Gràcia. Head uphill toward Av. Diagonal and turn left onto C. València; Aire is 2½ blocks down on the left. Ⓢ Cover €5-10; includes 1 drink. 🕐 Open Th-Sa 11pm-3am.

LUZ DE GAS   CLUB, LIVE MUSIC
C. de Muntaner, 246   ☎93 209 77 11 www.luzdegas.com

One of the most renowned clubs in the city, and for good reason. Red velvet walls, gilded mirrors, and sparkling chandeliers will have you wondering how you possibly got past the bouncer, while the massive purple-lit dance floor surrounded by bars will remind you what you're here for. Big-name jazz, blues, and soul performers occasionally take the stage during the evening hours, while after 1am it turns into your typical *discoteca* (only better dressed). Ritzy young things dance to deafening pop from Outkast to Nancy Sinatra in the lower area, while the upstairs lounge provides a much-needed break for both your feet and ears.

✈ ⓂDiagonal. Take a left on Av. Diagonal and a right on C. Muntaner after a few blocks. *i* For show listings and times check the Guía del Ocio or the club's website. Ⓢ Cover €18; includes 1 drink. Beer €7. Cocktails €10. 🕐 Open daily 11:30pm-5:30am.

PLATA BAR   BAR
C. del Consell de Cent, 233   ☎93 452 46 36

Flatscreens over two floors play a simulcast of jacked models, and the chic interior is spiced up with rainbow flags and colored lights. Order a mojito (€9.50) from one of the ripped bartenders, and settle into this upmarket gay bar before heading over to shake a tailfeather elsewhere.

✈ ⓂUniversitat. Face the University building and walk to the left up C. Aribau for 2 blocks. Turn left onto C. Consell de Cent; Plata Bar is 2 blocks down. Ⓢ Beer €3.50. Cocktails €9.50. 🕐 Open daily 7pm-3am.

ANTILLA   LATIN CLUB
C. d'Aragó, 141   ☎93 451 45 64 www.antillasalsa.com

Be careful when entering—this Latin bar and dance club is so full of energy that dancers often dance right out the door. Little Cuban *maracas*, bongos, and cowbells are littered along the sandy bar, and painted palm trees dot the walls. For those intimidated by the frantic shimmying, salsa lessons are offered before the club opens to the public (Tu-Sa 5-11pm) so you can shake it like a pro—or at least make it look like you know a bachata from a rumba.

✈ ⓂUrgell. Walk along Gran Via de les Corts Catalanes and take a right up C. Comte d'Urgell. Walk 3 blocks and take a left onto C. Aragó. *i* W-Th 1-drink min. Ⓢ Cover F-Sa €10; includes 1 drink. Beer €6. Cocktails €8. 🕐 Open W 11pm-4am, Th 11pm-5am, F-Sa 11pm-6am, Su 7pm-1am.

nightlife

ESPIT CHUPITOS (ARIBAU)   BAR
C. d'Aribau, 77   www.espitchupitos.com

If you want shots, they've got 'em—580 different delectable little devils will let you party as if you'd gone to Cancún instead of Barcelona. Be prepared for a little more than just drinking, though, as most involve fire. Spectacle shots such as the *Harry Potter* literally light up the night, while others have the bartenders getting down and dirty. For a good laugh, order the *Monica Lewinsky* for somebody else, and thank us later.

✦ ⓂUniversitat. Walk up C. Aribau to the left of the university building; Espit Chupitos is 4 blocks uphill.
⑤ Shots €2-4. Cocktails €8.50. ☒ Open M-Th 8pm-2:30am, F-Sa 8pm-3am, Su 8pm-2:30am.

ZELTAS   BAR, GLBT
C. de Casanova, 75   ☎93 450 84 69

Like a story lifted from a sultry romance novel about an all-male harem with impeccable taste, Zeltas pleases the eyes in more ways than one. An all-black interior accented with blue lighting sets the tone, while chic white couches and a bar seemingly built for those looking to dance shirtless sets the mood. Musky cologne floats through the air, and beefy male dancers in tight black spankies make the air somehow thicker.

✦ ⓂUniversitat. Face the University building and walk left on Gran Via de les Corts Catalanes. Turn right onto C. Casanova; Zeltas is 2 blocks up. i Male dancers nightly. ⑤ Beer €5. Cocktails €7.50. ☒ Open daily 11pm-6am.

MOJITO CLUB   LATIN CLUB
C. de Rosselló, 217   ☎65 420 10 06 www.mojitobcn.com

A salsa-inspired club for the younger set, Mojito can't be as easily defined as its Latin-beat-blasting counterparts. Low leather couches and semi-private alcoves dot the foyer, while the dance floor pulses to everything from hip hop to rumba, depending on the night. Stop by during the day to take a salsa lesson from the **Buenavista Dance Studio** (☎93 237 65 28) or just come to the Brazil party on Wednesday nights, when free samba lessons start at 11:30pm.

✦ ⓂDiagonal. Facing down Pg. de Gràcia toward Pl. Catalunya, C. Rosselló is to the right. Mojito is near the intersection of C. Balmes, on the far side. i Salsa night on Th, salsa on F-Sa until 1:30am. Check the website for special events. ⑤ Cover F-Sa €12; includes 1 drink. Th and Sa 1-drink min. Beer €7. Cocktails €9. ☒ Open daily 11pm-5am.

DBOY/LA MADAME/DMIX   CLUB, GLBT
Ronda de Sant Pere, 19-21   ☎93 453 05 82 www.matineegroup.com

Three clubs in one, this spot hosts a downright confusing variety of nightlife options depending on the night. **DBoy** is men-only, with a young and lively gay crowd dancing in a laser-lit mosh pit. **La Madame** is geared toward women, but that doesn't deter the DBoy regulars from getting their groove on. **DMix** supplies just like what it promises—a crowd of both genders, with some straighter action going on as well. Check the website to see what you can expect on a given night.

✦ ⓂUrquinaona. Head along Ronda Sant Pere away from Pl. Catalunya and toward Arc de Triomf. Follow it a few short steps and look for the LED sign. ⑤ Cover €10-15. ☒ DBoy open in summer F-Sa midnight-6am. La Madame open in summer Su midnight-5am. Demix open Sept-July F-Su midnight-6am.

DIETRICH GAY CAFÉ   BAR, GLBT
C. del Consell de Cent, 225   ☎93 451 77 07 www.facebook.com/dietrichcafe

Rainbow flags, a cheery staff, and an unquestionably classy—but overly graphic—portrait of a fishnet-clad Marlene Dietrich greet you as you walk in the door. Despite the lighthearted atmosphere at the bar in front, a serious dance floor waits in back, complete with a Bacardi-cooler-turned-sculpture presiding. Some nights are hit-or-miss—the house is packed during their special events but can be an echoing shell on nights off. If the bar seems too empty for your tastes, hop next door to the club's other portion, Átame, for a guaranteed full house.

✚ ⓂUniversitat. Face the University building and walk left on Gran Via de les Corts Catalanes. Turn right onto C. Aribau, walk 2 blocks, and turn left onto C. Consell de Cent. *i* Drag shows, acrobatics, and dancers on some nights. Check for event schedule. Ⓢ Beer €3.50. Mixed drinks €4.50 before 1:30pm, after €5.50-7.50. ⓸ Open from Oct to mid-July F-Sa 10:30pm-3am, from mid-July to Sept daily 10:30pm-3am.

EL GATO NEGRO (ESPIT CHUPITOS) BAR
C. del Consell de Cent, 268 ☎69 977 36 74 www.espitchupitos.com

All of the shocking variety of Espit Chupitos, but now with half-hearted attempts at a spooky theme (look for the black cat in the corner). Luckily, this bustling bar is a favorite for lively young travelers (read: wasted Americans), and the atmosphere (paired with the cheap, often incredibly amusing, shots) makes up for the decor. Check out the original Espit Chupitos just down the street if the pocket-sized bar gets too packed for your refined tastes.

✚ ⓂUniversitat. Face the University building and walk left on Gran Via de les Corts Catalanes. Turn right onto C. Aribau, walk 2 blocks, and take a right onto C. Consell de Cent; El Gato Negro is 1 block down on the right. Ⓢ Shots €2-4. Beer €1.60-2. Cash only. ⓸ Open M-Th 10pm-2:30am, F-Sa 10:30pm-3am.

SNOOKER BAR BAR, POOL HALL
C. de Roger de Llúria, 42 ☎93 317 97 60 www.snookerbarcelona.com

With award-winning interior decor in the bar and an equally impressive pool hall in back, Snooker is like what your smoky bowling-alley-slash-pool-hall back home would look like after an episode of "Pimp My Smoky Bowling-Alley-Slash-Pool-Hall." Sit back in one of the custom-designed red velvet chairs with one of Snooker's many scotches and wait for some sucker to challenge you foolishly to a round of what the English call "the beautiful game."

✚ ⓂPasseig de Gràcia. Facing Pl. Catalunya, head left on Gran Via de les Corts Catalanes for 2 blocks and turn left onto C. Roger de Llúria. *i* Singles night W 8pm. Salsa dancing Th 6:30 and 7:30pm, Su 6 and 7pm. Ⓢ Mixed drinks €8. Beer €3-4. ⓸ Open M-Th 7pm-2:30am, F-Sa 7pm-3am, Su 7pm-2:30am.

THE ROXY BLUE CLUB
C. del Consell de Cent, 294 www.roxyblue.es

A star-studded interior with twinkling blue lights matches the ritzy young clientele that pack its three dance rooms. Hope you look good in blue—true to the club's name, the lighting is all blue, all the time, except when it's just straight-up strobe-colored. Fences reminiscent of police barricades keep the dancers on the floor, while people chill on the couches around the edges. The music spans from Latin beats to soul and R and B to electronica, so check the website if you're looking for a particular groove.

✚ ⓂPasseig de Gràcia. Facing uphill, turn left onto C. Consell de Cent; Roxy Blue is on the left just after Rambla Catalunya. Ⓢ Cover €15. Beer €5. Cocktails €10. ⓸ Open Th midnight-5am, F-Sa midnight-6am, Su 11:30pm-5am.

MOMO'S BAR BAR
C. del Consell de Cent, 319 ☎93 487 33 14

A dark interior lit with old Victorian lanterns and a string of rainbow-colored lights around the bar provides the setting for drinks such as the "afrodisiaco" (blackberry liqueur, mint, cinnamon) and its companion for later in the night, the "orgasmo." Candles along the bar warm the place up, while low couches along the back provide ample seating for the young crowd that trickles in later during the night. Don't come here expecting a rager—a calm and sparse clientele keeps it classy.

✚ ⓂUniversitat. Facing the University building, C. Aribau is on the left. Follow it for 2 blocks and turn right onto C. Consell de Cent. Ⓢ Beer, wine, and shots €2-3. Mixed drinks €6-7. Cocktail of the day €5. Cash only. ⓸ Open M-Th 8pm-2:30am, F-Sa 8pm-3am, Su 8pm-2:30am.

nightlife

BARCELONETA

👍 ABSENTA BAR

C. de Sant Carles, 36 ☎93 221 36 38 www.kukcomidas.com/absenta.html

Not for the easily spooked, Absenta is like an episode of the Twilight Zone if you were trapped inside the TV looking out and were also experiencing a touch of that wormwood hallucination. Staticky TV sets with flickering faces dot the walls, and vintage proscriptions against the consumption of the vivid green liquor scold you from above the bar while you sinfully sip the eponymous absinthe (€4-7). A young crowd brings this *modernisme*-inspired beauty up-to-date in an appropriately artsy manner.

➔ [M]Barceloneta. Walk down Pg. Joan de Borbó toward the beach and take a left onto C. Sant Carles. $ Beer €2.30. Mixed drinks €7. Absinthe €4-7. ⏰ Open M 11am-2am, Tu 6pm-2am, W-Th 11am-2am, F-Sa 11am-3am, Sa-Su 11am-2am.

¿KÉ? BAR

C. del Baluard, 54 ☎93 224 15 88

Plop down on a cushioned keg chair or the comfiest barstool you'll ever experience. This small bar attracts internationals and provides a calm alternative to the crowded beaches and throbbing bass of the *platja*. Shelves doubling as upside-down tables, fruit decals along the bar, and a playful group of faces peering down from overhead will have you wondering "*¿Ké?*" as well.

➔ [M]Barceloneta. Walk down Pg. Joan de Borbó toward the sea and take a left onto C. Sant Carles. Take a left onto C. Baluard once you enter the plaça. $ Beer €2.50. Cocktails €6. ⏰ Open M-Th 11am-2:30am, F 11am-3am, Sa noon-3am, Su noon-2:30am.

CATWALK DISCOTECA

C. de Ramon Trias Fargas, 2-4 ☎93 224 07 40 www.clubcatwalk.net

One of Barcelona's most famous clubs, Catwalk has two packed floors of *discoteca*. Downstairs, bikini-clad dancers gyrate to house and techno in neon-lit cages while a well-dressed crowd floods the dance floor. Upstairs, club-goers attempt to dance to American hip hop and pop in very close quarters. Dress well if you want to get in—really well if you want to try to get in without paying the cover—and don't bother trying to get the attention of a bartender at the first bar upon entering; there are about six others, and they're all less busy.

*➔ [M]Ciutadella/Vila Olímpica. **i** No T-shirts, ripped jeans, or sneakers permitted. Events listing on website. $ Cover €15-20, includes 1 drink. Beer €7. Mixed drinks €12. ⏰ Open Th midnight-5am, F-Sa midnight-6am, Su midnight-5am.*

OPIUM MAR CLUB, RESTAURANT

Pg. Marítim de la Barceloneta, 34 ☎90 226 74 86 www.opiummar.com

Slick restaurant by day and even slicker club by night, this lavish indoor and outdoor party spot is a favorite in the Barça nightlife scene. Renowned guest DJs spin every Wednesday, but the resident DJs every other night of the week keep the dance floor sweaty and packed, while six bars make sure the party maintains a base level of schwasty.

*➔ [M]Ciutadella/Vila Olímpica. **i** Events listing on website. $ Cover €20; includes 1 drink. ⏰ Restaurant open daily 1pm-1am. Club open M-Th midnight-5am, F-Sa 1-6am, Su midnight-5am.*

SHÔKO CLUB, RESTAURANT

Pg. Marítim de la Barceloneta, 36 ☎93 225 92 00 www.shoko.biz

The younger, cheaper, raunchier sister of the Port Olímpic club scene. Entrance won't cost you a dime (though you'll still need to dress to impress), and, when it comes to dancing, the utilitarian black floors and wooden platform are only gritty when compared to ritzier clubs nearby. For prime booty-shaking time, drop in after 2am, or come by for Sexy Sundays.

✇ ⓂCiutadella/Vila Olímpica. *i* No sneakers, beach clothes, or lame shirts. Ⓢ No cover. Beer €6. Mixed drinks €10. ⌚ Restaurant open daily 7pm-midnight. Club open daily midnight-3:30am.

ICEBARCELONA
C. de Ramon Trias Fargas, 2
BAR
☎93 224 16 25 www.icebcn.com

You don't have to be in Barcelona long before you tire of the sticky humidity and the even sweatier *discotecas*. Fortunately, there's an alternative: adjacent to the beach and to the other Port Olímpic clubs is Icebarcelona, a bar made entirely of ice, whose temperature hovers between -2° and -10°C. Your €15 cover includes winter wear, so you can sip your ice-cold drink while sitting on a chair made of ice, sitting at a bar made of ice, gazing at sculptures made of ice, in a room made entirely of ice. And if you think this place is just too cool for you, chill outside on the beach terrace, which requires neither cover nor overcoat.

✇ ⓂCiutadella/Vila Olímpica. *i* Reservations recommended for weekends after midnight. Ⓢ €15 cover; includes 1 drink, coat, and gloves. No cover for beach terrace. Beer €4. Mixed drinks €8. ⌚ Open daily June-Sept noon-3am, Oct-May noon-2:30am.

GRÀCIA

▦ EL RAÏM
C. del Progrès, 48
BAR
www.raimbcn.com

It may be a little far from Gràcia's roaring plazas, but this confused time capsule is well worth the short trek. A mix between a Catalan bodega and '50s Cuban bar, this traditional winery has been in business since 1886, when it served as the diner for the factory across the street. Since then, the owner has transformed the place into a shrine to Cuban music and memorabilia that consistently attracts down-to-earth locals with its rum drinks, like the incredible mojitos (€6).

✇ ⓂFontana. Walk downhill on C. Gran de Gràcia and make a left onto C. Ros de Olano. Walk for about 4 blocks and take a right onto C. Torrent de l'Olla. Take the 4th left onto C. Siracusa; El Raïm is on the corner at the intersection with C. Progrès. Ⓢ Beer €2.30-3. Wine €2. Shots €2-3.50. Mixed drinks €5.50. ⌚ Open daily 8pm-2:30am.

▦ VINILO
C. de Matilde, 2
BAR
☎66 917 79 45

Those expecting a fetish club—whether for LPs or something a little kinkier—may be disappointed. Though this is certainly no shrine to a musical era past (or present), the warm lighting and comfy pillows make it the perfect place to kick back and watch the movie of the day in the orange neon light. Feel free to geek out over their giant phonograph or the Velvet Underground song playing over the speakers—chances are the hip clientele will understand.

✇ ⓂFontana. Head downhill on C. Gran de Gràcia, turn left on Travessera Gràcia, and take the 2nd right onto C. Matilde. Ⓢ Beer €3-3.50. Mixed drinks €5. ⌚ Open in summer M-Th 8pm-2am, F-Sa 8pm-3am; in winter M-Th 8pm-2am, F-Sa 8pm-3am, Su 8pm-2am.

▦ EL CHATELET
C. de Torrijos, 54
BAR
☎93 284 95 90

A cozy corner bar lit by candles, tiny hanging paper lamps, and dim but sparkly chandeliers, El Chatelet serves drinks so big and so strong they'll have you climbing the walls—look up and to your right as you come in to see previous revelers' footsteps. Sit at the bar under the auspices of the funky painted lizard on the wall behind you, or move to the back, where big windows provide excellent views of the partiers along C. Torrijos and C. Perla.

✇ ⓂFontana. Head downhill on C. Gran de Gràcia and turn left onto C. Montseny. Follow it as it turns into C. Perla and turn right onto C. Torrijos. Ⓢ Beer €2-3. Mixed drinks €6. ⌚ Open M-Th 6pm-2:30am, F-Sa 6pm-3am, Su 6pm-2:30am.

ASTROLABI
BAR, LIVE MUSIC

C. de Martínez de la Rosa, 14

You might need to break out your astrolabe to find this place, but once there, it's worth the voyage. Maps, clocks, and miniature ships help to explain away your drunk dizziness as "seasickness." Drop in early in the night for some entertainment, with a small and dedicated following cram into the watering hole to watch underground and up-and-probably-never-quite-coming acoustic acts croon over lost loves and anachronisms. If you need an ear to listen, shrunken heads dangle over the bar for your disposal.

✦ ⓂDiagonal. Head uphill on Pg. de Gràcia, cross Av. Diagonal, and turn right onto C. Bonavista before Pg. de Gràcia becomes C. Gran de Gràcia. Take a left onto C. Martínez de la Rosa. i Live music daily 10pm. Ⓢ Beer €2.50-3. Wine from €1. Mixed drinks €6. Cash only. ⓩ Open M-Th 8pm-2:30am, F-Sa 8pm-3am, Su 8pm-2:30am.

LA CERVESERA ARTESANA
BAR, BREWERY

C. de Sant Agustí, 14 ☎93 237 95 94 www.lacervesera.net

No matter what vows you've taken with PBR, when you visit the only pub in Barcelona that makes its own beer, you better order the house brew. With a huge variety—dark, amber, honey, spiced, chocolate, peppermint, fruit-flavored, and more—there's literally something for any beer-lover. If beer isn't your thing, come for the *fútbol* that perpetually plays on the flatscreen TVs.

✦ ⓂDiagonal. Head uphill on Pg. de Gràcia and take a right onto C. Còrsega at the roundabout where Pg. de Gràcia meets Av. Diagonal. C. Sant Agustí is the 3rd left. Ⓢ House brews €4.80-5. Other beers €3-4.50. ⓩ Open M-Th 6pm-2am, F-Sa 6pm-3am, Su 6pm-2am.

VELCRO BAR
BAR

C. de Vallfogona, 10 ☎61 075 47 42

Though Velcro Bar is a bit of a walk from Gràcia's popular plazas, its screenings of nightly movies attract a young and hip clientele that ends up paying little attention to the screen. Politically charged poster-style art covers the wall opposite the bar, where the real discussions take place. Though somewhat hokey, the bar's name represents the tight (and sometimes noisy) connections made by its patrons.

✦ ⓂFontana. Follow C. Astúries and turn right onto C. Torrent de l'Olla. Walk 3 blocks and turn left onto C. Vallfogona. Ⓢ Beer €2. Mixed drinks €6. ⓩ Open daily 7pm-2:30am.

DE DUES
BAR

C. del Torrent de l'Olla, 89 ☎93 416 14 96 www.dedues.es

Cheap beer, free bar snacks, daily specials served until 2am, and incredible super-fruity cocktails (for as little as €4) please the young, hip crowd. Whether you're looking for a late-afternoon drink or a nightcap in this snazzy floral-clad cocktail bar, you'll find yourself satisfied. Drop by with a new friend during weekday evenings (M-Th 9-11pm) to grab two cocktails with natural fruit juice for €8—though they're so good that you may want to ditch that friend and keep them both.

✦ ⓂFontana. From the Metro, walk down C. Astúries and turn right onto C. Torrent de l'Olla; walk 5½ blocks down C. Torrent de l'Olla. Ⓢ €1 beers daily 4-7pm. Cocktails €4-6. Sandwiches €1.80-4. Food €3-4. ⓩ Open M-Th 4pm-2:30am, F 4pm-3am, Sa 6pm-3am.

OTTO ZUTZ
CLUB

C. de Lincoln, 15 ☎93 238 07 22 www.ottozutz.com

Like a layer cake with an impeccably designed party inside (or maybe a recreation of Dante's *Inferno*, depending on the night), three floors of dancing and drinks await. At least four different DJs pound out a huge variety of music for a chic and shiny crowd. Watch out—during the summer this heaven gets hellishly hot.

✦ ⓂFontana. Walk along Rambla de Prat and take a left as it dead-ends into Via Augusta. Take the 1st right onto C. Laforja and the 1st right again onto C. Lincoln. Ⓢ Cover €10-15; includes 1 drink. Beer €6. Mixed drinks €6-12. ⓩ Open M midnight-6am, W-Sa midnight-6am.

barcelona

THE SUTTON CLUB CLUB

C. de Tuset, 13 ☎93 414 42 17 www.thesuttonclub.com

To get into the swankiest club this side of Diagonal, be sure to put on your finest duds (that's what nice clothes are called, right?), slick back your hair, and affect the snootiest air you can muster. Once you're in the door, though, all bets are off; four bars provide mass quantities of alcohol to a dance floor that gets sloppier as the night goes on.

➜ [M]Diagonal. Turn left on Av. Diagonal, walk about 4 blocks, and turn right on C. Tuset. $ Cover €12-18; includes 1 drink. Beer €5. Mixed drinks €8-12. ⏰ Open W midnight-5am, Th midnight-5:30am, F-Sa midnight-6am, Su 10:30pm-4am

KGB CLUB

C. de ca l'Alegre de Dalt, 55 ☎93 210 59 06

In Soviet Russia, the club hits you! But seriously, folks—the only indications of the Eastern Bloc are the KGB posters hanging from the walls and the sheer austerity of the decorations—expect lots of black, lots of metal, and little sparkle. Scrappy youth join the bartenders and live DJ and VJ in a sweaty countdown to get down. Entrance is free with a flyer; otherwise you'll ironically pay €12-15 to join this Party.

➜ [M]Joanic. Walk along C. Pi i Maragall and take the 1st left. $ Cover with 1 drink €12, with 2 drinks until 3am €15; free with flyer. Beer €4. Mixed drinks €9. Cash only. ⏰ Open F-Sa midnight-6am and for musical performances.

CAFÉ DEL SOL CAFE, BAR

Pl. del Sol, 16 ☎93 237 14 48

One of the many tapas bars lining the Pl. del Sol, the Cafe del Sol offers cheap and delicious eats in an ambience well-suited to the square's unbeatable outdoor cafe nightlife. Botero-esque figures line the wall along the bar, while a back room provides a cozy shelter for those looking for respite from the square.

➜ [M]Fontana. Walk downhill on C. Gran de Gràcia, make a left onto C. Ros de Olano, and turn right onto C. Virtut. $ Beer €2.20-2.80. Mixed drinks €6-7. Tapas €3.50-7.50. Entrees €3.50-5.80. ⏰ Open daily 12:30pm-3am.

SOL SOLER BAR, CAFE

Pl. del Sol, 21-22 ☎93 217 44 40 www.myspace.com/solsolertapas

Push your way through the forest of dreadlocks (you may need to bring a machete) as you yell over the clamor to order beer and tapas. If the bustling interior—big, but so crowded that fitting into a table often feels like human Tetris—is too claustrophobic and sticky for you, spill out onto the plaza with the rest of Gràcia's masses.

➜ [M]Fontana. Walk down C. Gran de Gràcia, turn left onto C. Ros de Olano, and make a right onto Pl. Sol. $ Wine €2. Beer €2. ⏰ Open M-W noon-1:30am, Th-Su noon-3am.

BAR CANIGÓ BAR

C. de Verdi, 2 ☎93 213 30 49

A longtime hometown haunt with all the affected tradition to match. Antique mirrors with vintage champagne and booze advertisements glint over a student crowd excitedly huddled around cafe-style tables. Despite the high ceilings, still expect a dull roar—bright and lively, this bar stays busy well past cafe-appropriate hours.

➜ [M]Fontana. Walk down C. Gran de Gràcia and make a left onto C. Ros de Olano. C. Verdi is about 6 blocks down. $ Beer €1.50. Mixed drinks €4.50. ⏰ Open M-Th 8pm-2am, F-Sa 8pm-3am, Su 8pm-2am.

BERIMPAU BAR, BRAZILIAN

C. del Torrent de l'Olla, 140 ☎63 419 42 57

A tiny new Brazilian bar, Berimpau serves some of Gràcia's most creative cocktails: if you can think of a fruit, chances are they can make you a *caipiroska* with it (€5). Not to be confused with the more traditional Berimbau (with a b) in El Born, Berimpau is lively in a much less geriatric way.

➜ [M]Fontana. Follow C. Astúries away from C. Gran de Gràcia and turn right onto C. Torrent de l'Olla. $ Caipirinhas and fruit caipiroskas €5. Mojitos €6. ⏰ Open M-Th 7pm-2am, F-Sa 7pm-3am, Su 7pm-2am.

MONTJUÏC AND POBLE SEC

ROUGE CAFÉ
BAR

C. del Poeta Cabanyes, 21
☎93 442 49 85

When you walk into a sultry red-lit lounge—think oversized photo darkroom—decked in leather chairs and a cavalcade of vintage decor (including a shoddy copy of Jan van Eyck's *Arnolfini Wedding*), you know you're doing something right. Luckily, a crowd of hip, friendly locals is there to join you. The prettiest drinks in the city are some of the most delicious, so try the melon Absolut Porno (€6) or the syrupy vodka-based Barcelona Rouge (€6.50).

⚓ Ⓜ*Paral·lel. With Montjuïc to your left, walk along Av. Paral·lel. Take a left onto C. Poeta Cabanyes. Rouge Café is on the left before Mambo Tango Youth Hostel. ⓈBeer €2-3.50. Wine €2.50-4. Cocktails €6-8. ☼ Open daily in summer 7pm-3am; in winter 8pm-3am.*

MAU MAU
BAR

C. d'en Fontrodona, 35
☎934 41 80 15 www.maumaunderground.com

The epicenter of Barcelona's underground, Mau Mau is best known for its online guide to art, film, and other hip happenings around the city, but the real-life bar is worth the trip up C. Fontrodona. Mau Mau takes its gin and tonics (from €8) very seriously—with 20 gins and nine brands of tonic water, the list takes some time just to read, let alone drink. The bartenders can also throw together a mean dark and stormy (€8) as well as its proletarian counterpart, the Moscow Mule (dark and stormy with vodka instead of rum; €8). Expect to see artsy 20-somethings reclining on this cool warehouse-turned-lounge's comfy white couches before and after concerts at the nearby Sala Apolo, or maybe for a Herzog screening (movies Th-Sa at 10pm).

⚓ Ⓜ*Paral·lel. Facing Montjuïc, walk right along Av. Paral·lel and take a left onto C. Fontrodona. Follow the street as it zigzags; Mau Mau is just a few blocks down. Ⓢ 1-year membership (includes discounts at Mau Mau and at various clubs, bars, and cultural destinations around the city) €12. No cover for visitors. Beer €2.50-3. Mixed drinks from €6. ☼ Open Th-Sa 10pm-2:30am and other days of the week for special events.*

SALA APOLO
CLUB

C. Nou de la Rambla, 113
☎93 441 40 01 www.sala-apolo.com

Looking to party, but lamenting the fact that it's Monday? Sulk no more—for a number of years, Sala Apolo has been drawing locals to start the week off right with Nasty Mondays, featuring a mix of rock, pop, indie, garage, and '80s. In fact, the night is so popular that it has spawned Crappy Tuesdays (indie and electropop), which take over after the American one-woman show *Anti-Karaoke*. Stop by later in the week when just about anybody and everybody is around, and check the website to see which of the latest big-ish-name indie groups may be rolling through.

⚓ Ⓜ*Paral·lel. Walk along Paral·lel with Montjuïc to your right. Take a right onto C. Nou de la Rambla. Not to be confused with Teatre Apolo, which is on Av. Paral·lel. Ⓢ Anti-Karaoke €8. Nasty Mondays €11. Crappy Tuesdays €10-12. Other tickets €15-23. Cover usually includes 1 drink. Beer €5. Mixed drinks from €8. ☼ Open daily midnight-6am and for concerts and events earlier in the evening; check website for schedule.*

LA TERRRAZZA
CLUB

Av. de la Marquès de Comillas, 13
☎68 796 98 25 www.laterrrazza.com

One of the most popular clubs in Barcelona, La Terrrazza lights up the Poble Espanyol after the artisans and sunburned tourists call it a day. The open-air dance floor gets packed early with everyone from the does-Spain-enforce-the-drinking-age young to the does-this-club-even-have-bouncers old, and

barcelona

everything in between, but nobody really cares because the Ibiza-style nightclub is so remarkable.

✈ ⓜEspanya. Head through the Venetian towers and ride the escalators. Follow the signs to Poble Espanyol. *i* Free bus from Pl. Catalunya (Hard Rock Café) to club every 20min. 12:20am3:20am; free bus from Terrrazza to Pl. Catalunya non-stop 5:30am-6:45am. Ⓢ Cover €18, with flyer €15; includes 1 drink. Beer €6. Mixed drinks €8-10. ☒ Open Th 11pm-5am, F-Sa midnight-6am.

TINTA ROJA
BAR

C. de la Creu dels Molers, 17 ☎93 443 32 43 www.tintaroja.net

Named after the 1941 tango "Tinta Roja," this cafe-bar mixes literal Latin flavor with the flair of the theater. Argentine drinks are the specialty, ranging from a little boost of mate (€4.80) to a full range of the country's liqueurs and beer. A ceramic basset hound on the bar greets you upon entering, while a back stage decorated with overwhelming amounts of modern art hosts popular tango classes on Wednesday nights at 9pm. Don't mind the mannequins looking down at you—chances are they're just admiring your footwork.

✈ ⓜPoble Sec. With Montjuïc to the right, walk along Av. Paral·lel. Take a right onto C. Creu dels Molers; Tinta Roja is on the left. *i* Tango classes W 9-11:30pm. Ⓢ Beer €2.30-4. Wine €2.50-3.70. Argentine liqueurs €5.50-6. Mixed drinks €7. ☒ Open Th 8:30pm-2am, F-Sa 8:30pm-3am.

242
CLUB, AFTER-HOURS

C. d'Entença, 37 ☎932 28 90 73 www.myspace.com/club242

You know that feeling of utter disappointment when that prudish club shuts down at the way-too-soon hour of 6am? If you're one of the select few who can party harder than Barça's discotecas, the best remedy is an "after"—a club that opens once the rest close down. One of the longest running afters in Barcelona, 242 opens at 6am, which means you never have to come down off your partying buzz. Once the other clubs close, a crowd trickles in to enjoy drinks and some serious underground electronica that would impress at any hour.

✈ ⓜEspanya. Walk away from Montjuïc on Gran Via de les Corts Catalanes and take a right onto C. Entença. 242 is just before the intersection with C. Sepúlveda. Ⓢ Cover €15; includes 1 drink. Beer €5. Mixed drinks €10. ☒ Open F-Su 6am-whenever the party stops.

INSTINTO
CLUB

C. de Mèxic, 7-9 ☎93 424 83 31

This small warehouse that's been converted into a two-floor dance club is packed entirely with locals who know how to party with stunning execution. Themed nights bring a dedicated throng of regulars to move to a mix of hip hop, drum and bass, and Latin beats—don't be surprised if you come across salsa line-dancing more insanely coordinated than you ever knew was possible.

✈ ⓜEspanya. Walk along Gran Via de les Corts Catalanes toward Montjuïc and take the 1st left onto C. Mèxic. Ⓢ Cover €12. Beer €5. Mixed drinks €8-10. Cash only. ☒ Open Th-Sa midnight-6am.

TIBIDABO

Tibidabo—the mountain that rises behind Barcelona—is easily reached by a combination of FGC and tram during the day, but a seriously long uphill hike once trams stop running at 10pm. A cab from ⓜLesseps to Pl. Doctor Andreu is about €8; from Pl. Catalunya, it's about €13. Once you figure out a safe way to get home, head here for a night of incredible views that seem to twinkle more with every drink.

▨ MIRABLAU
BAR, CLUB

Pl. del Doctor Andreu ☎93 418 56 67 www.mirablaubcn.com

With easily the best view in Tibidabo—and arguably the best in Barcelona—Mirablau is a favorite with posh internationals and the younger crowd, so dress well. It also happens to be near the mountain's peak, so we only recommend walking up here if you prefer to sip your cocktails while drenched in sweat.

nightlife

The glimmering lights of the metropolis and the bar's quivering candles create a dreamlike aura that earns Mirablau a *Let's Go* thumbpick. If the club is more your style, head downstairs where pretty young things spill out onto the terrace to catch their breath from the crowded dance floor.

⇞ L7 to FGC: Avinguda de Tibidabo. Take the Tramvia Blau up Av. Tibidabo to Pl. Doctor Andreu. i Th-Sa credit card min. €4.70. Drinks discounted M-Sa before 11pm, Su before 6pm. $ Beer and wine €1.80-6. Cocktails €7-9.50. ⏰ Open M-Th 11am-4:30am, F-Sa 11am-5:30am.

MERBEYÉ BAR

Pl. del Doctor Andreu, 2 ☎93 417 92 79 www.merbeye.net

Merbeyé provides a dim, romantic atmosphere on an outdoor terrace along the cliff. With the lights in the lounge so low that seeing your companion may be a problem, Merbeyé is the perfect place to bring an unattractive date. Smooth jazz serenades throughout, and with just one Merbeyé cocktail (cava, cherry brandy, and Cointreau; €9-10), you'll be buzzed real quick.

⇞ L7 to FGC: Avinguda de Tibidabo. Take the Tramvía Blau up Av. Tibidabo to Pl. Doctor Andreu. $ Beer €2.50-4. Cocktails €9-10. Food €2-7.60. ⏰ Open Th 5pm-2am, F-Sa 11am-3am, Su 11am-2am.

ATLÀNTIC CLUB

C. de Lluís Muntadas, 2 ☎93 418 20 18 www.atlanticdisco.com

If the neon sign and phalanx of bouncers in suits outside this mountainside villa weren't enough to trigger your posh alarm, then just try getting inside. Though reserved for private parties early in the night, the club opens to the public—of course, a relative term—after the clock strikes midnight. A sea of shiny tops and white suits litter the couches outside, while multiple bars provide social lubrication to get bodies moving on the small dance floor.

⇞ Take the L7 to FGC: Avinguda de Tibidabo. Walk up the mountain on Av. Tibidabo and take a right onto C. Lluís Muntadas. Alternatively, take the Tramvia Blau to Pl. Doctor Andreu. Walk down Av. Tibidabo and veer left onto C. Lluís Muntadas. C. Lluís Muntadas meets Av. Tibidabo at roughly number 65 on Av. Tibidabo. $ Cover €10; includes 1 drink. Beer €4-5. Cocktails €8-12. ⏰ Call ahead for hours and private reservations.

ARTS AND CULTURE

There's no doubt that Barcelona is one of world's capitals of culture. Hopefully you were looking forward to this, but even if you just came for the beaches and clubs, you'll discover that the artistic side of Barcelona life is pretty inescapable. Just look at the banners hanging from lampposts throughout the city—the variety of concerts and theater productions can be overwhelming. Every week, it seems, there's another festival, from the small (indie comic books) to the massive (Sónar music festival). Whatever genre of music you're into, the big names generally pass through Barcelona at some point, so check those concert schedules like a fiend. Theater options are more limited for those who speak only English, though no less fascinating or entertaining. Various public festivals dot the annual calendar; they close down stores and restaurants during the day but turn into phenomenal fiestas at night. And of course, there's always FC Barcelona, the *futbol* club that is Barcelona's pride and joy; on game days, FCB fever grips the city—or, at least, its bars.

MUSIC AND DANCE

For comprehensive guides to large events and information on cultural activities, contact the **Guía del Ocio** (www.guiadelociobcn.com) or the **Institut de Cultura de Barcelona (ICUB).** (Palau de la Virreina, Las Ramblas, 99 ☎93 316 10 00 www.bcn.cat/cultura ⏰ Open daily 10am-8pm.) If you're able to glean basic information from Catalan websites, check out **www.butxaca.com,** a comprehensive bimonthly calendar with film, music, theater, and art listings, or **www.maumabarcelona.com,** which lists local music news, reviews, and events.

The website **www.infoconcerts.cat/ca** (available in English) provides even more concert listings. For tickets, check out **ServiCaixa** (☎90 233 22 11 www.servicaixa.com) at any branch of the Caixa Catalunya bank, **TelEntrada** (☎902 10 12 12 www.telentrada.com), or **Ticketmaster** (www.ticketmaster.es).

Although a music destination year-round, Barcelona especially perks up during the summer with an influx of touring bands and music festivals. The biggest and baddest of these is the three-day electronic music festival **Sónar** (www.sonar. es), which takes place in mid-June. Sónar attracts internationally renowned DJs, electronica fans, and partiers from all over the world. From mid-June to the end of July, the **Grec** summer festival (http://grec.bcn.cat) hosts international music, theater, and dance at multiple venues throughout the city, while the indie-centric **Primavera Sound** (www.primaverasound.com) at the end of May is also a regional must-see. *Mondo Sonoro* (www.mondosonoro.com) has more information, and lists musical happenings across the Spanish-speaking world.

Classical and Opera

PALAU DE LA MÚSICA CATALANA   EL BORN
C. de Sant Francesc de Paula, 2   ☎90 244 28 82 www.palaumusica.org
Although the Bach- and Verdi-studded stage still hosts primarily classical concerts, this *modernista* structure welcomes a surprising variety of musical acts almost every night. Over 300 performances of choral and orchestral pieces, pop, acoustic, jazz, and flamenco grace the *palau*'s stage every year, including those from its very own Orfeo Català (Catalan choir), for which the building was constructed. If you're just looking for an excuse to see the breathtaking *Secret Garden*-esque interior without a tour (or you just really like giant air-driven instruments), drop by for one of the cheap and frequent organ performances.

✦ ⓂUrquinaona. *Follow Via Laietana toward the water and take the 1st left onto C. Sant Francesc de Paula.* **i** *Check the Guía del Ocio (www.guiadelociobcn.com) for listings.* Ⓢ *Tickets €8-175.* ☒ *Box office open M-Sa 10am-9pm, Su 2hr. before curtain. No concerts in Aug.*

L'AUDITORI   POBLENOU
C. de Lepant, 150   ☎93 247 93 00 www.auditori.com
Built in 1999 by world-renowned architect Rafael Moneo, this auditorium is now home to the Symphonic Orchestra of Barcelona. Glass, steel, and concrete reverberate with various highbrow genres of music, including classical, chamber, and jazz. In addition to the regular program, a number of festivals are held here throughout the year, including the World Music Festival, International Percussion Festival of Catalonia, Festival of Old Music of Barcelona, and even the electronic Sónar.

✦ ⓂMarina. *Walk down Av. Meridiana toward Pl. Glòries and turn left onto C. Lepant.* **i** *Tickets available by phone, at the box office, or through ServiCaixa or TelEntrada.* Ⓢ *Tickets €4-40.* ☒ *Box office open M-Sa noon-9pm, Su 1hr. before curtain.*

GRAN TEATRE DEL LICEU   LAS RAMBLAS
Las Ramblas, 51-59   ☎93 485 99 13 www.liceubarcelona.com
A Barcelona institution since its founding in 1847, the Gran Teatre del Liceu has been actively reclaiming its role as the premier venue for upscale performances after a fire closed it down in 1994. Classical, opera, and ballet grace the stage of its impressively restored auditorium, while a smaller reception room hosts smaller events and discussions about the pieces. Drop in for a tour and you may catch a sneak-peak of the rehearsal for the night's performance.

✦ ⓂLiceu. *Walk 1 block toward the water; the theatre is on the right.* **i** *Tickets available at box office, online, or through ServiCaixa.* ☒ *Box office open M-F 1:30-8pm.*

Pop and Rock

RAZZMATAZZ POBLENOU

C. de Pamplona, 88 ☎93 272 09 10 www.salarazzmatazz.com

This massive labyrinth of a converted warehouse hosts popular acts from reggae to electropop to indie to metal. The massive nightclub complex spans multiple stories in two buildings, connected by industrial stairwells and a rooftop walkway—definitely not intended for the navigationally challenged. The big room packs the popular draw (with bands like Motörhead, Alice in Chains, and Gossip), while the smaller rooms hide up-and-comers like The Pretty Reckless (we see you, *Gossip Girl*), up-and-cames like MGMT, never-made-its like Casiotone for the Painfully Alone, and has-beens-making-comebacks like Face to Face and Skunk Anansie. If there isn't a concert, you can still find a young crowd pulsing to the beat of one of the nightly DJs.

⇆ [M]Bogatell. Walk down C. Pere IV away from the plaza and take the 1st slight left onto C. Pamplona. Razzmatazz is on the right. i Tickets available online through website, TelEntrada, or Ticketmaster. $ Tickets €12-22.

SALA APOLO POBLE SEC

C. Nou de la Rambla, 113 ☎93 441 40 01 www.sala-apolo.com

Sala Apolo hosts major indie acts (think Crystal Castles and The Pains of Being Pure at Heart) as well as hip hop and electronica artists. A regular rumba club on Wednesday nights features a different band every week, and popular Nasty Mondays (cover €11) and Nasty Tuesdays (€10-12) shake up weeknights.

⇆ [M]Paral·lel. With Montjuïc to your right, walk along Av. Paral·lel and take a hard right onto C. Nou de la Rambla. Not to be confused with Teatre Apolo, which is on Av. Paral·lel. i Purchase tickets online. $ Rumba tickets €6-10. Other concert tickets €15-23. Beer €5. Mixed drinks from €8.

SIDECAR FACTORY CLUB BARRI GÒTIC

Pl. Reial, 7 ☎93 317 76 66 www.sidecarfactoryclub.com

Though bigger indie bands may tour here from time to time, Sidecar's real specialty is the local fare that you haven't heard of yet. Pop, rock, punk, and alternative acts grace the small stage downstairs in a setting that's more intimate than other Barcelona clubs of the same caliber.

⇆ [M]Liceu. Walk down Las Ramblas toward the water and turn left onto C. Colom to enter Pl. Reial. Sidecar is in the back left corner of the plaça. i Tickets available through Ticketmaster, via the club's website, or at www.atrapalo.com. $ Tickets from €6.

Folk and Jazz

JAMBOREE BARRI GÒTIC

Pl. Reial, 17 ☎933 19 17 89 www.masimas.com

The black and white portraits of jazz musicians lining the walls hint at Jamboree's reputation. The club has been hosting jazz acts for more than 50 years and manages to mix this rich history with a surprising dose of relevant contemporary artists—expect to hear a Billie Holiday tribute one night and the Markus Strickland Quartet the next. If you're looking for something a little less predictable, their WTF Jam Sessions are popular with local musicians and cost only €4.

⇆ [M]Liceu. Walk down Las Ramblas toward the water and turn left onto C. Colom to enter Pl. Reial. i Tickets available through TelEntrada. $ Jazz tickets €10-25. Su jam session €4. Flamenco €6. Beer €5. Cocktails €9-10. 🕐 Jazz performances Tu-Su 9 and 11pm; check site for exact times. WTF Jam Sessions M 9pm-1:30am. Tarantos (upstairs) holds flamenco shows daily 8:30, 9:30, and 10:30pm.

HARLEM JAZZ CLUB BARRI GÒTIC

C. de la Comtessa de Sobradiel, 8 ☎93 310 07 55 www.harlemjazzclub.es

With live performances nightly and a drink often included with the cover (check the schedule), this is a paradise for thin-walleted music lovers. A performance schedule online and on the door lets you choose whether you'll drop in to hear lovesick English crooning or something with a saucier Latin flavor. With acts ranging from Bossa Nova to gypsy punk, blues to funk, and soul to salsa, Harlem Jazz club attracts a crowd as eclectic as the lineup.

⚡ ⓂLiceu. Walk down Las Ramblas toward the water and turn left onto C. Ferran. Turn right onto C. Avinyó and left onto C. Comtessa de Sobradiel. *i* Live music usually begins 10 or 11pm. ⓈCover €5-6; sometimes includes 1 drink. Beer €3.80. Cocktails €7.80. Cash only. 🕐 Open M-Th 8pm-4am, F-Sa 9pm-5am, Su 9pm-4am.

CENTRE ARTESÁ TRADICIONÀRIUS   GRÀCIA
Travessia de Sant Antoni, 6-8   ☎93 218 44 85 www.tradicionarius.com

This mini-convention center serves as a one-stop shop for traditional Catalan music in a relaxed setting. Whether you're looking to drop in for a Barcelonan singing to a ukulele, or just to track down the next outdoor rumba session or Catalan folk festival, CAT can provide. Each winter the center helps to organize the Festival Tradicionàrius, which highlights a smorgasbord of Catalan music, dance, and art from January to March.

⚡ ⓂFontana. Head down C. Gran de Gràcia and turn left onto C. Montseny. Take a left onto Travessia Sant Antoni. *i* Events often located elsewhere in the city; check website for details. Ⓢ Events €6-20. 🕐 Box office open M-F 11am-2pm and 5-9pm.

Flamenco
Flamenco isn't really native to Barcelona—it's an Andalusian tradition—but there's a large enough tourist population to support a flamenco scene.

PATIO ANDALUZ   GRÀCIA
C. d'Aribau, 242   ☎93 209 33 78

Rumba, flamenco, *sevillano*—Patio Andaluz provides dinner and an authentic show, no matter which flavor you choose. Entrance includes your choice of drink, tapas, or a full *menú*, whether you come for the earlier show, which lasts about 1hr., or the 2hr. later show. Sick of sitting by the sidelines? Performers often encourage diners to try their luck on the floor, so be sure to wear your dancing shoes and most eager expression.

⚡ ⓂDiagonal. Take a left onto Av. Diagonal and walk for 10min., then take a right onto C. Aribau. Patio Andaluz is on the 1st block. *i* Call 9am-7pm for reservations or buy tickets at www.flamencotickets. com. Ⓢ Show and 1 drink €30; show and menú €54-67. 🕐 Shows daily 8 and 10pm.

THEATER
TEATRE LLIURE   MONTJUÏC
Pl. de Margarida Xirgu, 1   ☎93 289 27 70 www.teatrelliure.com

Established in 1976 by the artsy inhabitants of Gràcia, the Teatre Lliure has become known for presenting works in Catalan, including contemporary pieces and classics from around the globe as well as many original pieces birthed from its own theater cooperative. The theater has been at the foot of Montjuïc since 2001 but still maintains the feel of its bohemian homeland in Gràcia. Most tickets are reasonably priced, and many include a discussion after the show with the crew and theater critics.

⚡ ⓂEspanya. Facing Montjuïc, turn left onto Av. Paral·lel. Take a right onto C. Lleida and a left through the gate to enter the plaça. *i* Tickets available at box office or via ServiCaixa. Language of performance listed on website. Ⓢ Tickets €16-27. Student discounts available.

TEATRE GREC   MONTJUÏC
Pg. de Santa Madrona, 36   ☎93 316 10 00 grec.bcn.cat

No, this theater isn't left over from the good ol' days, no matter what its name may imply. This open-air Grecian theater dates to 1929, when it was carved out of an old stone quarry for the International Exhibition, which gave birth to many of Montjuïc's spectacles. The theater hosts a range of theater, opera, dance, and music performances during the summer and is the main venue of the city's annual **Festival Grec,** which takes place from mid-June to early August. Teatre Grec also hosts free events such as Montjuïc de Nit, a full night of music (10pm-4am) at the beginning of July.

✦ Ⓜ*Espanya. Head through the 2 bell towers marking the entrance to Montjuïc and follow the escalators to the top. Facing the palatial art museum, walk along the street to the left and stay left as it splits. Teatre Grec is on this road (Pg. Santa Madrona) just after the Ethnological Museum.* i *Tickets available at Tiquet Rambles (Las Ramblas, 99 ☎93 316 11 11) or via Telentrada or ServiCaixa. Most theater performances in Catalan or Spanish.* Ⓢ *Tickets €10-70, under 25 25% discount. Some events free.* ☒ *Tiquet Rambles open daily 10am-8:30pm.*

TEATRE NACIONAL DE CATALUNYA   POBLENOU
Pl. de les Arts, 1   ☎933 06 57 00 www.tnc.es

This modern structure designed by Ricardo Bofill is a questionable steel and glass nod to the Parthenon. It manages to pull this off at night, but, during the day, not so much. Inaugurated in 1997 on September 11, the National Day of Catalonia, it has since been promoted as the next cultural hub of Barcelona. An adjacent auditorium with a capacity of 36,000 is slated to be completed in the near future and a new Disseny Hub Barcelona is set to open across the Pl. de les Glòries Catalanes. The two performance halls of the main building host contemporary Catalan and foreign plays as well as traditional Catalan dance and music, while the second building of the complex houses workshops. Take advantage of youth, if you have it—tickets for shows start at €12 for those under 25.

✦ Ⓜ*Glòries. Facing the rocket-shaped Torre Agbar, take the 1st right onto Avda. Meridiana. Teatre Nacional de Catalunya is on the right.* i *Tickets available through TelEntrada, ServiCaixa, Tiquet Rambles (Las Ramblas, 99 ☎93 316 11 11), and box office.* Ⓢ *Tickets €15-32, under 25 from €12.* ☒ *Box office open W-F 3-8pm, Sa 3-9:30pm, Su 3-6pm. Tiquet Rambles open daily 10am-8:30pm.*

CINEMA

CINEMA VERDI   GRÀCIA
C. de Verdi, 32   ☎93 238 79 90 www.cines-verdi.com/barcelona

This is Barcelona's first theater to run movies in their original language. The cinema, along with its annex a few streets over on C. Torrijos, makes for a cinephile's mecca in Gràcia, with 10 screens featuring independent and foreign films. It's perfect for any aspiring Ebert—or just a lonely American longing for English.

✦ Ⓜ*Fontana. Walk down C. Astúries and turn right onto C. Verdi.* i *Schedule available on website.* Ⓢ *Tickets €5.50-8.*

FESTIVALS

For a full list of what's going on during your visit, stop by the tourist information office. As a teaser, here are a few of the biggest shindigs:

DIADA DE SANT JORDI   CITYWIDE

A more intelligent, civil alternative to Valentine's Day, this festival both celebrates St. George (the 🐉dragon-slayer and patron saint of Barcelona) and commemorates the deaths of Shakespeare and Cervantes. On this day, Barcelona gathers along Las Ramblas in search of flowers and books to give to lovers.

☒ *Apr 23.*

FESTA DE SANT JOAN   BARCELONETA, POBLENOU
Beaches

These days light a special fire in every pyromaniac's heart as 🎆**fireworks,** bonfires, and 🔥**torches** light the city and waterfront in celebration of Saint John and the coming of summer.

☒ *Night of June 23; June 24.*

BARCELONA PRIDE

Parade ends at Av. Maria Cristina, behind Pl. Espanya

This week is the biggest GLBT celebration in the Mediterranean, and Barcelona is no exception. Multiple venues throughout the region take active part in the festival, which culminates with a parade through "Gaixample" and a festival.

🗓 *Last week of June.*

FESTA MAJOR DE GRÀCIA
GRÀCIA

Pl. de Rius i Taulet (Pl. de la Vila de Gràcia)

The Festa Major is a community festival in Gràcia in which the artsy intellectuals put on performances and fun happenings in preparation for the Assumption of the Virgin. Expect parades, concerts, floats, arts and crafts, live music, dancing, and—of course—parties.

🗓 *End of Aug.*

DIADA NACIONAL DE CATALUNYA
EL BORN

Fossar de les Moreres

Catalunya's national holiday celebrates the end of the Siege of Barcelona in 1714 as well as the reclaiming of national—whoops, we mean regional—identity after the death of Franco. Parties are thrown, flags are waved, and Estrella Damm is imbibed—🍺lots of Estrella Damm.

🗓 *Sept 11.*

LA MERCÈ
CITYWIDE, BARRI GÒTIC

Pl. de Sant Jaume

This massive outpouring of joy for one of Barcelona's patron saints (Our Lady of Mercy) is the city's main annual celebration. More than 600 free performances take place in multiple venues. There is also a 🎪castellers competition in the Pl. Sant Jaume; competitors attempt to build *castells* (literally "castles"; here, human towers) several humans high, which small children clad in helmets and courage attempt to climb.

🗓 *Weeks before and after Sept 24.*

FUTBOL *Soccer*

Although Barcelona technically has two *futbol* teams, **Futbol Club Barcelona** (usually known as **"Barça"** or **FC Barcelona**) and the **Real Club Deportiu Espanyol de Barcelona (Espanyol)** you can easily go weeks in the city without hearing mention of the latter. It's impossible to miss the former, though, and for good reason. Besides being a really incredible athletic team, Barça lives up to its motto as "more than a club."

During the Franco years, FC Barcelona was forced to change its name and crest in order to avoid nationalistic references to Catalonia, and thereafter became a rallying point for oppressed Catalan separatists. The original name and crest were reinstated after Franco's fall in 1974, and the team retained its symbolic importance; it's still seen as a sign of democracy, Catalan identity, and regional pride.

This passion is not merely patriotic or altruistic, though—Barça has been one of the best teams in the world in recent years. In 2009 they were the first team to win six out of six major competitions in a single year; in 2010 they won Spain's Super Cup trophy; in 2010 and in 2011 FCB took Spain's La Liga trophy; in 2011 they beat Manchester United to win the UEFA Champion's League and won the FIFA Club World Cup, cementing their place as the world's best soccer club. This was followed up in 2012 with a Copa del Rey victory, though they ceded their La Liga and Champions League titles. Their world-class training facilities (a legacy of the 1992 Olympics) supply many World Cup competitors each year, leaving some Barcelonans annoyed that Catalonia is not permitted to compete as its own nation, much like England, Wales, and Scotland do in the United Kingdom. In fact, Spain's 2010 World Cup victory disappointed many hardheaded Barça fans (known as *culers*).

nightlife

Because Barça fervor is so pervasive, you don't need to head to their stadium, the Camp Nou, to join in the festivities—almost every bar off the tourist track boasts a screen dedicated to their games. Kick back with a brew and be sure not to root for the competition.

shopping

Whether you're gawking at the high fashion on the Pg. de Gràcia or enjoying less mainstream shopping in the backstreets of El Raval, you'll find whatever it is that you're looking for and probably a good deal more. El Born is where you're most likely to stumble across cute boutique and vintage shops (pause for squeals), particularly on and around **Carrer dels Flassaders;** rapidly gentrifying Gràcia is another good place to look for the same. El Raval is the best for vintage and secondhand shopping, particularly on and around **Carrer de la Riera Baixa** (where there is also a weekly flea market on Saturdays) and **Carrer dels Tallers;** slightly more upscale shopping can be done around **Carrer del Pintor Fortuny** and **Carrer del Doctor Dou.** More tourist-oriented and overpriced shopping fills the Barri Gòtic, though it's hardly a complete wasteland, and you can find your Gucci (along with more affordable Zara and Desigual) on the **Passeig de Gràcia** in **l'Eixample.**

BOOKS

LA CENTRAL DEL RAVAL
EL RAVAL
C. d'Elisabets, 6   ☎90 288 49 90 www.lacentral.com
A massive bookstore and cafe set in the 17th-century Casa de la Misericòrdia, selling a wide selection of titles in different languages. This expansive bookstore is as close to Carlos Ruiz Zafón's Cemetery of Forgotten Books as you'll get.
⚎ ⓂCatalunya. Follow Las Ramblas away from Pl. Catalunya and turn right onto C. Elisabets. ⌚ Open M-F 9:30am-9pm, Sa 10am-9pm.

HIBERNIAN BOOKS
GRÀCIA
C. del Montseny, 17   ☎93 217 47 96 www.hibernian-books.com
This secondhand, English-language bookstore is a godsend for bibliophiles. With an alarmingly broad selection, Hibernian is the perfect place to stock up on cheap paperbacks for a long flight home.
⚎ ⓂFontana. Head downhill on C. Gran de Gràcia and turn left onto C. Montseny. ⌚ Open Jan-July M 4-8:30pm, Tu-Sa 10:30am-8:30pm; Aug Tu-Sa 11am-2pm and 5-9pm; Sept-Dec M 4-8:30pm, Tu-Sa 10:30am-8:30pm.

COME IN LLIBRERIA ANGLESA
L'EIXAMPLE
C. de Balmes, 129   ☎93 453 12 04 www.libreriainglesa.com
Out of English books? Don't worry, it happens to all of us. Don't cave and get an e-reader—head to the English-language bookstore. And while you're there, request that they order large shipments of *Let's Go.*
⚎ ⓂDiagonal. From Pg. de Gràcia facing downhill, turn right onto C. Rosselló. Come In is 2 blocks down. ⌚ Open M-Sa 10am-2pm and 4:30-8pm.

DOCUMENTA
BARRI GÒTIC
C. de Cardenal Casañas, 4   ☎93 317 25 27 www.documenta-bcn.com
For the last 35 years this Barri Gòtic staple has helped feed Barcelona's ravenous literary appetite. This bustling bookstore just steps from Las Ramblas has a good selection of English-language novels.
⚎ ⓂLiceu. From Las Ramblas, facing the building with umbrellas and a ◪dragon, walk to the plaza in front of the building, and then turn left around it onto C. Cardenal Casañas. ⌚ Open M-F 9:30am-8:30pm, Sa 10am-8:30pm.

barcelona

CLOTHING

Boutiques

CLINK
GRÀCIA

C. de Verdi, 14 ☎93 302 88 68

C. Verdi is home to many a cute boutique, but Clink stands out with its collection of brightly colored dresses (€20-30) with distinct prints and fabrics. Clink also has an excellent selection of women's hats and a variety of accessories.

✦ ⓂFontana. Follow C. Astúries away from C. Gran de Gràcia, then right down C. Verdi. ⓘ Open M-Sa 10am-10pm.

INSTINTO
GRÀCIA

C. d'Astúries, 15 ☎93 217 92 99

This women's clothing store has clothes in exuberant colors, made of exceptionally soft fabrics. It's a great place to pick up a present to take home to your mom—and who knows? You might luck out and find something that you like, too.

✦ ⓂFontana. Follow C. Astúries away from C. Gran de Gràcia. ⓘ Open M-F 10:30am-2:30pm and 5-9pm, Sa 11am-2:30pm and 5-9pm.

EL PIANO TINA GARCIA
GRÀCIA

C. de Verdi, 20 ☎934 15 51 76

This boutique has an offbeat selection of distinctive garments for women. The menswear version, **El Piano Man,** is across the street at C. Verdi, 15.

✦ ⓂFontana. Follow C. Astúries away from C. Gran de Gràcia, then right down C. Verdi. ⓘ Open M-Sa 10am-9:30pm.

OLOKUTI
GRÀCIA

C. d'Astúries, 36 ☎93 217 00 70 www.olokuti.com

If you like to think of yourself as a conscientious consumer, head to this eco-friendly shop selling "world" books, music, scarves, underwear, and more. Shop 'til you drop and feel good about yourself doing it.

✦ ⓂFontana. Follow C. Astúries away from C. Gran de Gràcia. ⓘ Open M-Th 10am-9:30pm, F-Sa 10am-10pm.

SOMBRERIA MIL
BARRI GÒTIC

C. de Fontanella, 20 ☎93 301 84 91

Sombreria Mil is great excuse to say the word "milliner." It's also a great place to try on hats and take funny pictures. Maybe you'll even buy a handsome fedora—we've leave that up to you.

✦ ⓂCatalunya or ⓂUrquinaona. On C. Fontanella between Pl. Catalunya and Pl. Urquinaona. ⓘ Open M-Sa 9:30am-8:45pm.

Major Chains

EL CORTE INGLÉS
LAS RAMBLAS

Pl. de Catalunya, 14 ☎93 306 38 00 www.elcorteingles.es

El Corte Inglés is an enormous, upscale department store—think Macy's, but with an even more powerful brand presence—that sells just about anything you can think of. Need a nice bathing suit before hitting Barceloneta? No problem. Or an engagement ring for your traveling companion with whom you've fallen madly in love? Done.

✦ ⓂCatalunya. You can't miss it. ⓘ Open M-Sa 10am-10pm, Su 11am-10pm.

shopping

DESIGUAL

LAS RAMBLAS, L'EIXAMPLE

Las Ramblas, 136 ☎93 304 23 23 www.desigual.com

Pg. de Gràcia, 47 ☎93 467 62 87

One of the most popular Spanish designer brands, Desigual emphasizes an eclectic mixture of bright colors and clashing patterns that many Spaniards find works for them. Will it work for you too? Find out.

⚡ ⓂCatalunya; ⓂPasseig de Gràcia. ⏰ Open M-Sa 10am-9:30pm.

MANGO

L'EIXAMPLE

Pg. de Gràcia, 8-10 ☎93 412 15 99 www.mango.com

Pg. de Gràcia, 65 ☎93 215 75 30

A competitor of stores like H&M and Topshop, this Spanish chain is renowned for giving fashionable passersby whiplash as they walk past the window displays.

⚡ ⓂPasseig de Gràcia. ⏰ Open M-Sa 10:15am-9pm.

ZARA

L'EIXAMPLE

C. de Pelai, 58 ☎93 301 09 78 www.zara.com

A popular Spanish women's clothing chain. The clothing usually falls in the center on a spectrum of "classic" to "trend-of-the-week."

⚡ ⓂUniversitat or ⓂCatalunya. On C. Pelai between Pl. Universitat and Pl. Catalunya, though closer to Catalunya. ⏰ Open M-Sa 10am-10pm.

BLANCO

L'EIXAMPLE, EL RAVAL

C. de Pelai, 1 ☎93 318 23 40 www.blanco.com

Blanco's relatively affordable clothing is usually true to the season's styles. It's comparable to Old Navy, though undoubtedly more European and stylish.

⚡ ⓂUniversitat or ⓂCatalunya. On C. Pelai between Pl. Universitat and Pl. Catalunya, though closer to Universitat. ⏰ Open M-Sa 10am-9:30pm.

Secondhand

🏵 GALLERY

GRÀCIA

C. del Torrent de l'Olla, 117 ☎93 551 01 91

Gallery sells vintage clothing of all shapes, sizes, and colors. It's the sort of place you want to save for the end of the day, because you won't be able to leave.

⚡ ⓂFontana. Head downhill on C. Gran de Gràcia, then left on C. Montseny, then right on C. Torrent de l'Olla. ⏰ Open M 5-9pm, Tu-Sa 11am-2pm and 5-9pm.

LOISAIDA

EL BORN

C. dels Flassaders, 42 ☎93 295 54 92 loisaidabcn.com

Hip Loisaida has secondhand and vintage clothing inspired by New York's Lower East Side, along with new international brands and clothes of its own label.

⚡ ⓂJaume I. Follow Pg. Born to the end farthest from the church, and take a left near the end up C. Flassaders. ⏰ Open M-Sa 11am-9pm.

MARKETS

🏵 MERCAT RAVAL

EL RAVAL

Rambla del Raval www.mercatraval.com

A clothing, art, and design market with booths of colorful, funky dresses, designer T-shirts, and trendy accessories. Almost as odd and alternative as its locale.

⚡ ⓂLiceu. Follow C. Hospital and take a left onto Rambla del Raval. ⏰ Open Sa-Su 11am-9pm.

LA BOQUERIA (MERCAT DE SANT JOSEP)

LAS RAMBLAS

Las Ramblas, 89

Barcelona's main food market is an absolute treat to browse. See **Food**.

⚡ ⓂLiceu. Walk toward Pl. Catalunya on Las Ramblas and take a left onto Pl. Sant Josep. ⏰ Open M-Sa 8am-8pm, though certain vendors stay open after 9pm.

barcelona

MERCAT GÒTIC

BARRI GÒTIC

Pl. de la Catedral   www.mercatgotic.com

This flea market in front of the Catedral de Barcelona sells just about anything you're looking for, from vintage clothing to antique jewelry to postcards for Mom and Dad.

🚇 Ⓜ*Jaume I. Follow Via Laietana away from the water and turn left onto Av. Catedral.* ☑ *Open Th 10am-9pm, sometimes more frequent; check website for schedule.*

RIERA BAIXA

EL RAVAL

C. de la Riera Baixa

A street lined with secondhand shops, Riera Baixa is a mecca for any bargain or vintage shopper. The main attraction happens on Saturdays when clothes, records, trinkets, cameras, and an unfathomable amount of other ▧stuff combine with El Raval's large student population to give birth to the most exciting flea market in the city.

🚇 Ⓜ*Liceu. Walk down C. Hospital and take a slight right onto C. Riera Baixa.* ☑ *Flea market open Sa 11am-9pm.*

FIRA DE FILATÈLIA I NUMISMÀTICA

BARRI GÒTIC

Pl. Reial

The vendors at this flea market specialize in stamps and coins—some so old that the market can feel like a museum. That last hanging clause was referring to the coins, not the vendors. You'll be able to find many other knick-knacks and souvenirs as well as old watches and vintage jewelry.

🚇 Ⓜ*Liceu. Walk toward the water on Las Ramblas, then left on C. Colom to Pl. Reial.* ☑ *Open Su 10am-2:30pm.*

MUSIC

CD DROME

EL RAVAL

C. de Valldonzella, 3   ☎93 317 46 46 www.cddrome.com

This hip record store with an underground feel specializes in electronica and house. DJ your own personal dance party at the vinyl listening stations.

🚇 Ⓜ*Universitat. From Pl. Universitat, take C. Tallers and turn right onto C. Valldonzella.* ☑ *Open M-Sa 10:30am-8:30pm.*

WAH WAH RECORDS

EL RAVAL

C. de la Riera Baixa, 14   ☎93 442 37 03 www.wah-wahsupersonic.com

Wah Wah carries an eclectic mix of vinyl and CDs with a specialty in '60s garage and psychedelia. The store also runs its own record label, which re-releases forgotten gems across a variety of genres.

🚇 Ⓜ*Liceu. From Las Ramblas, follow C. Hospital, then right up C. Riera Baixa.* ☑ *Open M-Sa 11am-2pm and 5-8:30pm.*

essentials

PRACTICALITIES

- **TOURIST OFFICES: Plaça de Catalunya** is the main office, offering free maps and brochures, last-minute booking service for accommodations, currency exchange, and box office. (Pl. de Catalunya, 17S. ☎93 285 38 34 www.barcelonaturisme.com 🚇 ⓂCatalunya, underground, across from El Corte Inglés. Look for the pillars with the letter "i" on top. ☑ Open daily 8:30am-8:30pm.) **Plaça de Sant Jaume.** (C. Ciutat, 2. ☎93 270 24 29 🚇 ⓂJaume I. Follow C. Jaume I to Pl. Sant Jaume. Located in the Ajuntament building on the left. ☑ Open M-F 8:30am8:30pm, Sa 9am-7pm, Su and holidays 9am-2pm.) **Oficina de Turisme de Barcelona** (Palau Robert,

Pg. de Gràcia, 107. ☎93 238 80 91, toll-free in Catalunya ☎012 www.gencat.es/probert ⚧ ⓂDiagonal. ⏰ Open M-Sa 10am-7pm, Su 10am-2:30pm.) **Institut de Cultura de Barcelona (ICUB)** (Palau de la Virreina, Las Ramblas, 99. ☎93 316 10 00 www.bcn.cat/cultura ⚧ ⓂLiceu. ⏰ Open daily 10am-8pm.) **Estació Barcelona-Sants.** (Pl. Països Catalans. ☎90 224 02 02 ⚧ ⓂSants-Estació. ⏰ Open June 24-Sept 24 daily 8am8pm; Sept 25-June 23 M-F 8am8pm, Sa-Su 8am-2pm.)

- **TOURS:** Self-guided tours of Gothic, Romanesque, *modernista*, and contemporary Barcelona available; pick up pamphlets in tourist offices. A wide variety of guided tours also exist, check the brochures at the tourist office. The **Plaça de Catalunya tourist office** hosts its own walking tours of the Barri Gòtic and has info about bike tours. (☎93 285 38 32. ⚧ ⓂCatalunya, underground across from El Corte Inglés. Look for the pillars with the letter "i" on top. Ⓢ €12, ages 4-12 €5. ⏰ English tours daily 10am, Spanish and Catalan Sa noon.) **Picasso tours** of Barcelona are given in English, Spanish, and Catalan and include entry to **Museu Picasso.** (☎93 285 38 32 ⚧ ⓂCatalunya Ⓢ €19, ages 4-12 €7. ⏰ Tu, Th, Sa 4pm in English; Spanish or Catalan available Sa 4pm with booking in advance.)

- **LUGGAGE STORAGE: Estació Barcelona-Sants.** (ⓂSants-Estació. Ⓢ Lockers €3-4.50 per day. ⏰ Open daily 5:30am-11pm.) **Estació Nord.** (ⓂArc de Triomf. *i* Max 90 days. Ⓢ Lockers €3.50-5 per day.) **El Prat Airport.** (Ⓢ €3.80-4.90 per day.)

- **GLBT RESOURCES: GLBT tourist guide,** available at the Pl. de Catalunya tourist office, includes a section on GLBT bars, clubs, publications, and more. **GayBarcelona** (www.gaybarcelona.net) and **Infogai** (www.colectiugai.org) have up-to-date info. **Barcelona Pride** (www.pridebarcelona.org/en) has annual activites during the last week of June. **Antinous** specializes in gay and lesbian books and films. (C. Josep Anselm Clavé, 6. ☎93 301 90 70 www.antinouslibros.com ⚧ⓂDrassanes. ⏰ Open M-F 10:30am2pm and 5-8:30pm, Sa noon-2pm and 5-8:30pm.)

- **INTERNET ACCESS:** The **Barcelona City Government** (www.bcn.es) offers free Wi-Fi at over 500 locations, including museums, parks, and beaches. **Easy Internet Café** has decent rates and around 300 terminals. (Las Ramblas, 31. ☎93 301 75 07 ⚧ ⓂLiceu. Ⓢ €2.10 per hr., min. €2; day unlimited pass €7, week €15, month €30. ⏰ Open daily 8am-2:30am.) **Easy Internet Café.** (Ronda Universitat, 35. Ⓢ €2 per hr.; day pass €3, week €7, month €15. ⏰ Open daily 8am-2:30am.) **Navegaweb.** (Las Ramblas, 88-94. ☎93 318 90 26 nevegabarcelona@terra.es ⚧ ⓂLiceu. Ⓢ Calls to USA €0.20 per min. Internet €2 per hr. ⏰ Open M-Th 9am-midnight, F 9am1am, Sa 9am-2am, Su 9am-midnight.) **BCNet (Internet Gallery Café).** (C. Barra de Ferro, 3 ☎93 268 15 07 www.bornet-bcn.com. ⚧ ⓂJaume I. Ⓢ €1 per 15min., €3 per hr., 10hr. ticket €20. ⏰ Open M-F 10am11pm, Sa-Su noon-11pm.

- **POST OFFICE:** Pl. Antonio López. ☎93 486 83 02 www.correos.es. ⚧ⓂJaume I or ⓂBarceloneta. ⏰ Open M-F 8:30am-9:30pm, Sa 8:30am-2pm.

- **POSTAL CODE:** 08001.

EMERGENCY

- **EMERGENCY NUMBERS:** ☎112. **Ambulance:** ☎061.

- **POLICE: Local police:** ☎092. **Mossos d'Esquadra (regional police):** ☎088. **National police:** ☎091. **Tourist police:** Las Ramblas, 43 ☎93 256 24 30 ⚧ ⓂLiceu. ⏰ Open 24hr.

- **LATE-NIGHT PHARMACY:** Rotates. Check any pharmacy window for the nearest on duty or call **Informació de Farmàcies de Guàrdia** (☎010 or ☎93 481 00 60 www.farmaciesdeguardia.com).

- **MEDICAL SERVICES: Hospital Clínic i Provincial.** (C. Villarroel, 170. ☎93 227 54 00 ⚧ ⓂHospital Clínic. Main entrance at C. Roselló and C. Casanova.) **Hospital de la Santa Creu i Sant Pau.** (☎93 291 90 00; emergency ☎91 91 91 ⚧ ⓂGuinardó-Hospital de Sant Pau.) **Hospital del Mar.** (Pg. Marítim, 25-29. ☎93 248 30 00 ⚧ ⓂCiutadella-Vila Olímpica.)

GETTING THERE

By Plane

There are two possible airports you may use to reach Barcelona. The first, **Aeroport del Prat de Llobregat** (BCN; Terminal 1 ☎93 478 47 04, Terminal 2 ☎93 478 05 65), is located slightly closer to the city, though both necessitate bus rides. To get to Pl. Catalunya from the airport, take the **Aérobus** in front of terminals 1 or 2. (☎92 415 60 20 www.aerobusbcn.com $ €5.30, round-trip ticket valid for 9 days €9.15. ⏰ 35-40min.; every 5-20min. to Pl. Catalunya daily 6am-1am; to airport 5:30am-12:10am.) To get to the airport, the **A1** bus goes to Terminal 1 and the **A2** goes to Terminal 2. For early morning flights, the NitBus **N17** runs from Pl. Catalunya to all terminals. ($ €1.45. ⏰ From Pl. Catalunya every 20min. daily 11pm-5am, from airport every 20min. 9:50pm-4:40am.) The **RENFE Rodalies** train is cheaper and usually a bit faster than the Aérobus if you're arriving at Terminal 2. (☎90 224 34 02 www.renfe.es $ €1.45, free with T10 transfer from Metro. ⏰ 20-30min.; every 30min., from airport 5:40am-11:38pm, from Estació Sants to airport 5:10am-11:09pm.) To reach the train from Terminal 2, take the pedestrian overpass in front of the airport (with your back to the entrance, it's to the left). For those arriving at Terminal 1, there's a shuttle bus outside the terminal that goes to the train station.

The **Aeroport de Girona-Costa Brava** (GRO; ☎90 240 47 04 www.barcelona-girona-airport.com) is located just outside of Girona, a city about 85km to Barcelona's northeast. However, **Ryanair** flights arrive at this airport, so it may be your best bet for getting to Barcelona on the cheap. The **Barcelona Bus** goes from the airport in Girona to Estació d'Autobusos Barcelona Nord. (☎90 236 15 50 www.barcelonabus.com ℹ Buses from the airport to Barcelona Nord are timed to match flight arrivals. Buses from Barcelona Nord arrive at Girona Airport approximately 3hr. before flight departures. $ €12, round-trip €21. ⏰ 1hr. 10min.)

By Train

Depending on the destination, trains can be an economical choice. **Estació Barcelona-Sants** (Pl. Països Catalans 🚶 ⓂSants-Estació) serves most domestic and international traffic, while **Estació de França** (Av. Marqués de l'Argentera 🚶 ⓂBarceloneta) serves regional destinations and a few international locations. Note that trains often stop before the main stations; check the schedule. **RENFE** (reservations and info ☎ 90 224 02 02; international ☎90 224 34 02 www.renfe.es) runs to Bilbao (€65); Madrid (€118); Sevilla (€143); Valencia (€40-45); and many other destinations in Spain. Trains also travel to Milan (€135, via Girona, Figueres, Perpignan, and Turin); Montpellier (€60); Paris (€146); and Zurich (€136.) via Geneva and Bern. There's a 20% discount on round-trip tickets, and domestic trains usually have discounts for reservations made more than two weeks in advance. Call or check website for schedules.

By Bus

Buses are often considerably cheaper than the train. The city's main bus terminal is **Estació d'Autobusos Barcelona Nord.** (☎90 226 06 06 www.barcelonanord.com 🚶 ⓂArc de Triomf or #54 bus.) Buses also depart from **Estació Barcelona-Sants** and the airport. **Sarfa** (ticket office at Ronda Sant Pere, 21 ☎90 230 20 25 www.sarfa.es) is the primary line for regional buses in Catalunya, but **Eurolines** (☎93 265 07 88 www.eurolines.es) also goes to Paris, France (€80) via Lyon and offers a 10% discount to travelers under 26 or over 60. **Alsa** (☎90 242 22 42 www.alsa.es) is Spain's main bus line. Buses go to Bilbao (€43); Madrid (€29-34); Sevilla (€79-90); Valencia (€26-31); and many other Spanish cities.

By Ferry

Ferries to the Balearic Islands (Ibiza, Mallorca, and Minorca) leave daily from the port of Barcelona at **Terminal Drassanes** (☎93 324 89 80) and **Terminal Ferry de Barcelona** (☎93 295 91 82 ⚓ ⓜDrassanes) The most popular ferries are run by **Trasmediterránea** (☎90 245 46 45 www.trasmediterrana.es) in Terminal Drassanes. They go to Ibiza (ⓢ €90 ⌚ 9hr. 30min.) and Mallorca. (ⓢ 8hr. ⌚ €83.)

GETTING AROUND

By Metro

The most convenient mode of transportation in Barcelona is the **Metro.** The Metro is actually comprised of three main companies: **Transports Metropolitans de Barcelona** (TMB ☎93 318 70 74 www.tmb.cat), whose logo is an M in a red diamond; **Ferrocarrils de la Generalitat de Catalunya** (FGC ☎93 205 15 15 www.fgc.cat), whose logo is an orange square; and **Tramvia de Barcelona** (Tram ☎90 070 11 81 www.trambcn.com), whose logo is a green square with a white T. The TMB lines are likely the ones you will use most. Thankfully, all three companies are united, along with the bus system and Rodalies train system, under the **Autoritat del Transport Metropolità** (www.atm.cat), which means that you only need one card for all forms of transport, and that you get free transfers. Most Metro lines are identified with an L (L1, L2, etc.), though some FGC lines begin with S, and all Tram lines begin with T. (ⓢ 1 day €6.20, 10 rides €8.25, 50 rides €33.50, 1 month €51. ⌚ Trains run M-Th 5am-midnight, F 5am-2am, Sa 24hr., Su 5am-midnight.)

By Bus

For journeys to more remote places, the bus may be an important complement to the metro. The **NitBus** runs 🌙**all night long** after the Metro closes; these bus lines begin with an N. Barcelona's tourist office also offers a **tourist bus** (http://bcnshop. barcelonaturisme.com ⓢ 1 day €23, 2 days €30) that hits major sights and allows riders to hop on and off. Depending on how much you plan to use the route, a pass may be a worthwhile investment.

By Bike, Motorcycle, and Scooter

Motocicletas (scooters, and less frequently motorcycles; *motos* for short) are common in Barcelona, and **bicycles** are also becoming more popular. Many places rent *motos*, but you need a valid driver's license recognized in Spain to rent one. Many places offer bike rental, but if you're around for a while you can buy a bike secondhand (try **www.loquo.com**) or register for **Bicing** (☎90 231 55 31 www.bicing.cat), the municipal red and white bikes located throughout the city.

By Taxi

When other cheaper and more exciting options fail, call **Radio Taxi** (☎93 225 00 00). Taxis generally cruise at all hours; when the green light is on, the cab is free.

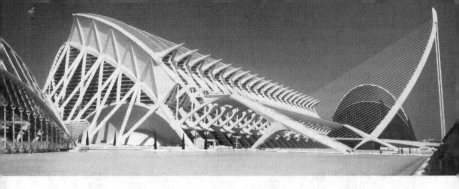

CATALONIA AND VALENCIA

The fiercely independent regions of Catalonia *(Catalunya)* and Valencia are among Spain's most incredible—though they might not consider themselves part of Spain at all. As you leave Barcelona and head to the countryside, you'll hear still less *castellano* and more and more Catalan; Girona is truly Catalonia's heartland. Meander through the medieval streets and stuff yourself with *botifarra*. To the south of Barcelona, you'll find the GLBT capital of Sitges, lined with beach after beach and gay bar after gay bar. Farther along the coast is Tarragona, chock-full of Roman ruins and medieval charm, and still farther south (past beach after beach after beach) is Valencia, the metropolis that anchors the Costa Blanca. Forget about Spain: you're in the *Comunitat Valenciana* and the *Generalitat de Catalunya* now. Stuff yourself with paella, throw back an Estrella Damm, and enjoy the land of the Catalans.

greatest hits

- **CALL ME MAYBE.** Or don't. But *el call*, Girona's old Jewish quarter, is pretty crazy. (p. 198)

- **SIT-GAYS.** Actually, Sitges's *Carrer del Pecat* is way crazier. (p. 214)

- **TARRAGOING, TARRAGOING, TARRAGONA.** Reenact Roman gladiatorial games in the amphitheater's ruins by the sea. (p. 221)

- **IS THAT A WHALE'S SKELETON?** Make your own conclusions about Calatrava's Ciutat de les Arts i les Ciències in Valencia. (p. 232)

For student life in this corner of Spain, your best bet is to head to Barcelona—but that doesn't mean you won't find any in the area around it. The Universitat de Girona ensures that the small city is full of students during the term, and the Universitat de València keeps the youth scene there vibrant and sipping *agua de Valencia* well into the night.

girona *gerona* ☎972

This oft-besieged city (pop. 97,000) has been invaded over the years by Romans, Visigoths, Moors, Charlemagne, and Napoleon. These days, however, many of the invaders are of the stag party variety, arriving at the budget airline hub of the Aeropuerto de Girona before speeding off to Barcelona. They're missing out on this spirited Catalan provincial capital with its picturesque *barri vell* (old town), a great place to share a romantic night with a date or a tasty evening with a *botifarra* (Catalan sausage) amid an atmosphere rich in history. The Count of Barcelona incorporated the city into his countship in 878, which we would go ahead and file under "Very Boring" if he didn't have the awesomely honest name of Count Wilfred the Hairy. Beginning in the 12th century, Girona had one of the most prominent Jewish communities in Catalonia, and its rabbis played an important role in the development and spread of a mystic Jewish school of thought called Kabbalism. It's a good thing Madonna wasn't around in 1492 (wait, was she?), since in that year all of Girona's—and Spain's—Jews were expelled, Kabbalist or not. Visitors can still wander the maze-like streets and steep staircases of the medieval Jewish neighborhood, *el call*, one of the best preserved in Europe. Girona is only a medium-sized city, but that makes it easy to get to know and love. And don't worry, this ain't no sleepy provincial backwater—the many students from the Universitat de Girona fill it with energy.

ORIENTATION

Most travelers arrive in Girona at the bus or train station, located next to each other at the Plaça d'Espanya, on the western edge of the small city center. The **Riu Onyar** divides Girona somewhat asymmetrically in two. The smaller eastern bank is the pedestrian **barri vell,** bordered by the river on the west and the medieval walls on the east. The *barri vell*'s main thoroughfares are the **Rambla de la Llibertat,** by the river, and the hilly **Carrer de la Força,** which runs through the center of the neighborhood. The *barri vell* also contains most of the city's major sights, including **el call** (the old Jewish quarter), the **Cathedral,** and most of the city's museums. The larger neighborhood to the west of the river is the new part of town, but it's not without areas of interest to tourists: the Museu del Cinema and many bars can be found here, as can the bus and train stations. The focal points of this part of town are the **Plaça de la Independència** and the pedestrian **Carrer de Santa Clara.** Getting from one side of the river to the other is easy, as bridges cross every few streets. The most scenic of these bridges are the **Pont de Pedra,** just north of **Plaça de Catalunya,** and the red, iron **Pont de les Peixateries Velles,** designed by Gustave Eiffel 12 years before a certain tower in Paris would be built.

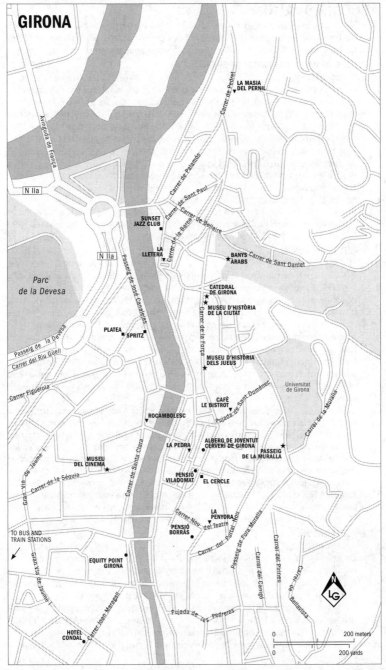

GIRONA

N IIa

N IIa

**LA MASIA
DEL PERNIL**

Avinguda de França

Carrer de Pedret

Carrer de Palamós

Carrer de Sant Paul

Carrer de Bellaire

**SUNSET
JAZZ CLUB**

Carrer de la Barca

**LA
LLETERA**

**BANYS
ÀRABS**

Carrer de Sant Daniel

Passeig de José Canalejas

Parc
de la Devesa

**CATEDRAL
DE GIRONA**

**MUSEU D'HISTÒRIA
DE LA CIUTAT**

PLATEA **SPRITZ**

Carrer de la Força

Passeig de la Devesa

Carrer del Riu Güell

**MUSEU D'HISTÒRIA
DELS JUEUS**

Universitat
de Girona

Carrer Figuerola

Carrer de la Muralla

Pujada de Sant-Domènec

**CAFÈ
LE BISTROT**

ROCAMBOLESC

Gran Via de Jaume I

**MUSEU
DEL CINEMA**

Carrer de la Séquia

Carrer de Santa Clara

LA PEDRA

**ALBERG DE JOVENTUT
CERVERÍ DE GIRONA**

**PASSEIG
DE LA MURALLA**

**PENSIÓ
VILADOMAT** **EL CERCLE**

Carrer Nou

LA PENYORA
del Teatre

Carrer del Fort-Nou

**PENSIÓ
BORRÀS**

TO BUS AND
TRAIN STATIONS

Gran Via de Jaume I

Carrer Joan Maragall

**EQUITY POINT
GIRONA**

Passeig de Fora Muralla

Carrer de la Bellavista

Carrer del Camí

Carrer del Primet

N
LG

Pujada de les Pedreres

**HOTEL
CONDAL**

| 0 | | 200 meters |
| 0 | | 200 yards |

girona

ACCOMMODATIONS

Most of Girona's accommodations are located either in or a short walk from the *barri vell;* the free map given out at the tourist office lists all of the city's accommodations. During the summer, it's best to make reservations at least a week in advance.

ALBERG DE JOVENTUT CERVERÍ DE GIRONA HOSTEL $

C. dels Ciutadans, 9 ☎97 221 80 03 www.xanascat.cat

A great place to meet fellow travelers, whether in the cafeteria-style dining room that serves all three meals or in the TV room fully stocked with 👍**VHS tapes.** From Sept 15-June 30, the place is half university dorm and half hostel, but in summer the place fills up with tourists looking for the cheapest bed in town. The 2- to 8-bed dorms are simple and clean and all cost the same, so you don't need to pay any extra to decrease your number of roommates and thus the chance that one of them snores like a nocturnal jackhammer.

➡ From the east end of the Pont de Pedra, cross Rambla de la Llibertat into Pl. Vi, then turn left and continue straight through the plaza onto C. Ciutadans. ℹ Free Wi-Fi. Computers with internet access €1 per hr. Laundry machines available. Lunch and dinner €7 each. Locks for sale €5. Towels for sale €5. Bicycle rental €6 per 3hr., €8 per 5hr., €10 per 8hr. [$] 2- to 8-bed dorms 29 and younger with breakfast €16, with breakfast and either lunch or dinner €22.65, with all 3 meals €28.10. 30 and older €18.80/26.70/33. ⏰ Reception 24hr.

EQUITY POINT GIRONA HOSTEL $$

Pl. de Catalunya, 23 ☎97 241 78 40 www.equity-point.com

It's hard not to socialize at this friendly hostel whose common spaces, including a wooden rooftop terrace with amazing views of the city and a TV room with couches and beanbags, are among its main draws. Once you've made your new friends, play one of the board games kept at the front desk; have a drink at the terrace bar (summer only); and if any particular friendship seems to be blossoming into something more, buy a condom (€1). Even the anti-social will find something to like about this hostel, whose 4- and 6-bed dorms with private bath are uncharacteristically spacious for hostel dorms; the 6-bed dorms with shared bath have somewhat more traditional proportions. Social and anti-social alike will unite to agree that it would be nice if the doll-sized showers and sinks were a little bigger.

➡ From the bus and train stations, cross the parking lot, turn right onto C. Barcelona, then left onto C. Bisbe Lorenzana; then take the 2nd left onto C. Joan Maragall, which will lead to Pl. Catalunya. The hostel is on the left. Or, from the barri vell, proceed along Rambla de la Llibertat with the river on your right. At Pl. Catalunya (with big Catalan flag), cross the plaza diagonally. ℹ Breakfast and linens included. Towel rental €2. Free Wi-Fi in lobby and on top floor. Computers with internet access first 20min. free, then €0.50 per 15min. Kitchen available. Lockers free; locks €3. Umbrellas €3. Condoms €1. Toiletry bag €5. Flip-flops €5. [$] 6-bed mixed dorms with hallway bath July-Sept €20; Apr-June €17; Oct-Mar €16. 6-bed dorms (mixed and female) with ensuite bath €22/19/18; 5-bed mixed dorms with ensuite bath €23/20/19; 4-bed mixed dorms with ensuite bath €24/22/20. Triple with private bath €78/69/63. Double with private bath €62/48/44. ⏰ Reception 24hr.

PENSIÓ VILADOMAT HOTEL $$

C. dels Ciutadans, 5 ☎97 220 31 76 www.pensioviladomat.cat

On this *barri vell* street close to the Pont de Pedra, solo travelers can find comfortable singles (with shared bath); they're fairly standard except for enough outlets to set up a tiny electronics business and small but pleasant balconies from which to hawk your wares. Don't try this on the higher floors, though, as we're pretty sure those teensy balconies are decorative. Doubles and triples with private bath have a little bit more space per person, and also include a TV and minifridge. Travelers whose main workout consists of spreading *alioli* on their *botifarra* but who still need to do whatever it is you do in Farmville will have a tough decision to make: only the top two floors of the five-floor walk-up have Wi-Fi.

*From the east end of the Pont de Pedra, cross Rambla de la Llibertat into Pl. Vi, then turn left and continue straight through the plaza onto C. Ciutadans. **i** Free Wi-Fi on the 3rd and 4th fl. [$] Single with shared bath €23; double with shared bath €40, with private bath €50; triple with private bath €75. ⏰ Reception 9am-12:30am.*

PENSIÓ BORRÀS HOTEL $

Tv. Auriga, 6 ☎97 222 40 08 www.pensionesperezborras.blogspot.com.es

Even if you brought along a small traveling circus on your backpacking trip, you'll fit into the enormous rooms of this *pensió*. (Okay, the elephants might need a second room.) The cheap individual rooms (all with shared bath) are an incredible bargain for the massive amount of empty space. The interior rooms here are all windowless, though, and cannot be recommended for claustrophobics or members of kingdom *Plantae*. Doubles, some with private baths and balconies overlooking a less-than-scenic interior patio, are a bit more varied. No matter what room you end up in, they're all really big, pretty cheap, and conveniently located a few anonymous blocks away from the Plaça del Vi.

From the east end of the Pont de Pedra, cross Rambla de la Llibertat into Pl. Vi, turn left, and then immediately take the 1st right onto C. Nou del Teatre, then the next right into the Pl. Bell-lloc. From the small plaza, turn left onto a nameless street and take the first right onto another; at the end of this street, turn left onto Tv. Auriga. [$] Singles €22; doubles with shared bath €37, doubles with private bath €42. ⏰ Reception 10am-8:45pm.

HOTEL CONDAL HOTEL $$$$

C. de Joan Maragall, 10 ☎97 220 44 62 www.hotelcondalgirona.com

The perfect place to recharge after a trying week of shared bathrooms and snoring bunkmates, this comparatively cheap hotel provides comfortable (if not enormous) rooms, private bathrooms, and a polished hotel feeling. Ask for a room with a view of the *centro* rather than a view of the back end of another building, unless that's your thing.

*From the Pl. Catalunya, with the river on your left and the giant Catalan flag behind you, turn right onto C. Joan Maragall, which extends diagonally from the plaza. **i** Free Wi-Fi. TV available. Breakfast €3.50 at nearby cafeteria. [$] Singles €41-50, doubles €69. ⏰ Reception 24hr.*

SIGHTS

Most of Girona's sights are in the *barri vell* on the east bank of the Riu Onyar. The city has many excellent museums; in addition to the ones listed here, the **Museu d'Arqueologia** (C. Santa Llúcia, 8 ☎97 220 26 32 www.mac.cat From Pl. Catedral with the cathedral on your right, proceed straight until the end of the street, then turn right. [$] €2.30, students €1.61, under 16 and over 65 free. Free admission last Su of month. ⏰ Open June-Sept Tu-Sa 10:30am-1:30pm and 4-7pm; Oct-May Tu-Sa 10am-2pm and 4-6pm, Su and holidays 10am-2pm) and the **Museu d'Art** (Pujada de la Catedral, 12 ☎97 220 38 34 www.museuart.com [$] €2, students and seniors €1.50. ⏰ Open May-Sept Tu-Sa 10am-7pm, Su and holidays 10am-2pm; Oct-Apr Tu-Sa 10am-6pm, Su 10am-2pm) are worth a look if you have time. If you're planning to go to more than one of the city-run museums, ask for a Ticket M-5 at the first one you visit; it'll get you 50% off any subsequent museums. The main religious sights, the **Catedral** and the **Església de Sant Feliu,** the oldest church in Girona (Pujada de Sant Feliu, 29 ☎97 220 14 07 From Pl. Catedral with the cathedral on your right, walk 1 block and turn left. [$] Free. ⏰ Open M-Sa 10am-12:30pm and 4-6:30pm, Su and holidays 10am-noon and 4-6:30pm) are both worth visiting but aren't the must-sees of the city. In fact, it's hard to pinpoint any one superstar sight; some of the great pleasures of Girona include simply admiring the painted houses lining the Riu Onyar and getting lost in the staircases and maze-like streets of *el call*.

CATEDRAL DE GIRONA
Pl. de la Catedral

CHURCH, MUSEUM

☎97 242 71 89 www.catedraldegirona.org

It's hard not to be awed by your first glimpse of the Catedral de Girona, perched atop a seemingly endless set of stairs like a shining temple in the sky. Most of the building was constructed in the 14th century, but its façade says it was finished in 1733, which in the world of Spanish cathedrals is sort of like flashing your boy-scout ID to get into the hottest underground club in town. Despite its youth, this cathedral has a pretty bad-ass accomplishment to brag about to that cute Italian *cappella* it has its eye on: it has the widest Gothic nave in the world (St. Peter's could cockblock; its nave is 3m wider, but not Gothic). Inside that nave are some impressive artworks like a gilded silver altarpiece depicting 16 scenes from the life of Christ and the Chair of Charlemagne, an 11th-century marble bishop's chair that originally sat in the site's earlier Romanesque church. Sadly, the positioning of these treasures behind the altar and a locked gate makes them difficult to get a good look at, and looking at the images displayed on nearby TV screens just isn't the same. It's easy to miss the treasury, whose entrance is opposite the ticket desk, but it's definitely worth a visit to see its famous 11th-century **Tapís de la Creació** (Tapestry of the Creation), which depicts scenes from Genesis, and a collection of documents like the cheerful illuminated manuscript *Comments on the Apocalypse.*

✦ *At the top of the hill. From the east end of the Pont de Pedra, cross Rambla de la Llibertat into Pl. Vi, then turn left and continue straight through the plaza onto C. Ciutadans, which becomes C. Bonaventura Carreras Peralta and then C. Força; the Cathedral is up the steps to the right.* Ⓢ *Nave, treasury and cloister €5, students and seniors €3, under 7 free (audioguide in Catalan, Spanish, or English included). Treasury and cloister alone (during mass) €3/2/free. Free admission Su, audioguide €1.* Ⓐ *Open daily Apr-Oct 10am-8pm; Nov-Mar 10am-7pm. Last entry 30min. before close. Mass M-F 8-10am, Sa 8-10am and 4:30-8pm, Su and holidays 8am-2pm; only the cloister and treasury can be visited during these times.*

MUSEU D'HISTÒRIA DELS JUEUS
C. de la Força, 8

MUSEUM

☎97 221 67 61 www.girona.cat/call

Rising above the site of Girona's medieval synagogue, this museum explores the tumultuous history of Girona's Jewish community in *el call*, the hilly area of C. Força and the streets to the east. In addition to the wide-ranging collection of artifacts, including Torah scrolls, tefillin, and illuminated religious books, the museum also squeezes in some Judaism 101 that will be useful to those whose Seder invites always seem to get lost in the mail. Even if you're Jewish, from New York, or otherwise know a minyan from a mezuzah, the explanatory notes on the mikvah (ritual bath) will explain at least one mystery: apparently all the water for the baths came from the Riu Onyar. So that's where it all went!

✦ *From the east end of the Pont de Pedra, cross Rambla de la Llibertat into Pl. Vi, then turn left and continue straight through the plaza onto C. Ciutadans, which becomes C. Bonaventura Carreras Peralta and then C. Força.* Ⓢ *€4, students and seniors €2, 16 and under free. Audioguide in Catalan, Spanish, English, French, and Hebrew €6 (includes admission). Free 1st Su of the month. Guided tours €6.* Ⓐ *Open July-Aug M-Sa 10am-8pm, Su and holidays 10am-2pm; Sept-June M 10am-2pm, Tu-Sa 10am-6pm, Su and holidays 10am-2pm. Guided tours Apr-Nov at noon (€6), bilingual Spanish-English.*

MUSEU DEL CINEMA
C. de la Sèquia, 1

MUSEUM

☎97 241 27 77 www.museudelcinema.cat

We're not really sure what Girona has to do with the film industry, but it had the good fortune to be the birthplace of one amateur filmmaker who was an avid collector of all things related to the development of cinema. His collection, now housed in this museum, traces the long history of the moving image, from Chinese shadow theater and the *camera obscura* to Thomas Edison and the

Lumière brothers. For those worried about getting bored (even in a museum as low-brow and fun as this one) there are plenty of hands-on exhibits, including several 19th-century wheels that create simple moving images when spun. The museum ends chronologically in the golden age of Hollywood, with a room covered with black-and-white photographs of bygone movie stars, each more depressingly perfect-looking than the last.

➔ From the left bank side of the Pont de Pedra, with your back to the bridge, turn right onto C. Santa Clara, then take the 1st left onto C. Perill, then left onto C. Sèquia. $ €5, students and seniors €2.50, under 16 free. ⏰ Open July-Aug daily 10am-8pm; May-June and Sept Tu-Sa 10am-8pm and Su 11am-3pm; Oct-Apr Tu-F 10am-6pm, Sa 10am-8pm, Su 11am-3pm. Guided tours (1¼hr.) in Catalan Sa 6pm and Su noon. Free film screenings usually 1 Th per month.

PASSEIG DE LA MURALLA VIEWS, RUINS

East of *barri vell*

This Great Wall of Girona, dating in some sections all the way back to Charlemagne, marks the eastern border of the *barri vell.* Climb the (many) stairs to the top and walk along the surprisingly narrow wall to enjoy spectacular views of the city below; go up to the top of any of the many towers for even better views. When the heat of the sun overpowers the prettiness of the panoramas, there are several places from which to come down; a great place to do so is the staircase next to the peaceful **Jardins d'Alemanys,** where vines grow on the medieval walls and a canopy of leaves provides merciful shade and muffles the shouts of kids playing soccer.

➔ Entrances/exits (from north to south): Jardins de la Francesa, behind the cathedral and the Banys Àrabs; Jardins d'Alemanys, at the end of C. Alemanys between the Museu d'Art and the university, off of Pl. Josep Ferrater i Mora; and off Pl. General Mendoza, 2 blocks inland from the Passera de l'Alferes Huarte. $ Free. ⏰ Open daily 7am-10pm, though not all entry/exit points follow this schedule rigidly.

BANYS ÀRABS HISTORIC SIGHT

C. del Rei Ferran el Catòlic ☎97 219 07 97 www.banysarabs.cat

Ever noticed that most ancient bath ruins look deceptively like nondescript piles of rock? Well, it's nice to finally see some baths with the walls intact, even if they were constructed just yesterday in bath years (1294). The architecture incorporates both Romanesque and Moorish elements in the four rooms of the ancient *baño completo.* If you're looking for an in-depth learning experience, go on one of the guided tours—there isn't any information posted, and the pamphlet from the front desk lists the names of the rooms but little else.

➔ With the cathedral on your right, proceed out of Pl. Catedral and take the 1st right onto C. Rei Ferran el Catòlic. $ €2; students, under 16, and over 65 €1. ⏰ Open Apr-Sept M-Sa 10am-7pm, Su and holidays 10am-2pm; Oct-Mar daily 10am-2pm.

MUSEU D'HISTÒRIA DE LA CIUTAT MUSEUM

C. de la Força, 27 ☎97 222 22 29 www.girona.cat/museuciutat

Near the top of C. Força (sorry, weary calves), this museum traces the history of Girona from its Roman infancy (childhood nickname: Gerunda) through its Muslim childhood and awkward medieval adolescence (so much drama with the Jews) to its eventual blooming into Catalonia's second city. There are some great artifacts, like the model of the city's army during its ill-fated 18-month resistance against Napoleon, which apparently included a regiment of monks packing heat, and a touching series of 10-year-olds' drawings from 1937 depicting the carnage of the Spanish Civil War. On the whole, though, it's hard to follow much of the history without being able to read the Catalan-only signs.

➔ From the east end of the Pont de Pedra, cross Rambla de la Llibertat into Pl. Vi, then turn left and continue straight through the plaza onto C. Ciutadans, which becomes C. Bonaventura Carreras Peralta and then C. Força. $ €4, students and M5 ticket holders €2, under 16 and seniors free. Free 1st Su of the month. ⏰ Open Tu-Sa 10am-2pm and 5-7pm, Su 10am-2pm.

FOOD

Girona's restaurants run the gamut from cheap self-service cafeterias with €7 set *menús* to **El Celler de Can Roca** (tasting menu €130), which one foodie magazine named the second-best restaurant in the world. There are lots of great, cheap restaurants in between on both sides of the river; **Carrer de Cort-Reial** and the streets around it have many relatively budget-friendly restaurants. Though common throughout Catalonia, **botifarra amb mongetes** (Catalan sausage with beans) is one of Girona's specialties, and no carnivore should miss it. There are tons of places to eat on the **Rambla de la Llibertat** and the **Plaça de la Independència,** but many of these are tourist-oriented and overpriced. Those looking to save some money can buy groceries at the small supermarket **Pròxim** (C. Ciutadans, 7 🧭 Off Pl. Vi. ⏰ Open M-Sa 9am-9pm, Su 9am-2pm), though it's better to buy produce at **Colmado L'Estuca.** (Pujada Sant Feliu, 13 ☎97 242 77 16 🧭 Walk out of Pl. Sant Feliu with the river on your right and the big hill on your left. ⏰ Open M-F 9am-8:30pm, Sa 9am-2:30pm and 4-8:30pm, Su 10am-2pm.)

👍 LA MASIA DEL PERNIL — CATALAN $

C. de Pedret, 28-30 — ☎97 222 29 57

Tired of Castilian tapas and craving some true Catalan cuisine? This intimate restaurant serves cheap, filling Catalan specialties Th-Su nights in a rustic little two-story house. Though you might have some trouble deciphering the Catalan-only menu, it's hard to go wrong with most of the simple but delicious traditional dishes. The *pam i mig de botifarra de sal i pebre* (roughly a foot and a half of *botifarra; "un pam "* is the distance between your thumb and pinky with your hand outstretched), curves halfway around the large plate and is so meaty and rich that the palate-cleansing efforts of the large pieces of toast and tomato are largely in vain. Vegetarians won't be overwhelmed with choices, but the sausage-averse can happily take comfort in the cheese assortment (€7) or the "La Masia" salad (includes anchovies, €4.50). Stay far away from the very pricey bread (€2), but run into the welcoming arms of the decent house *vi negre* (red wine), a small pitcher of which will set you back a mere €1.80.

🧭 Follow C. Força to its northernmost end, through the giant arch. Left at C. Bellaire, then right through Pl. Sant Pere, and continue straight along C. Pedret from the far end of the plaza. ℹ Prices do not include IVA (8%). 💲 Entrees €5-16. Desserts €2-4.50. Menús available only for groups €16-25. ⏰ Open Th-Su 8pm-12:30am.

LA PEDRA — CATALAN, TAPAS $$

C. dels Mercaders, 18 — ☎69 017 32 21

If the profound schizophrenia of this around-the-clock awesome bar is any sign, anti-psychotic meds must not be a *plat típic* of Girona. During the afternoon, the tables lining the picturesque, narrow C. Mercaders fill with camera-clutching international tourists marveling at the quality of the traditional Catalan dishes of the cheap *menú del dia* (€9.50, €10.50 outside). At night, the vibe changes completely as the small street echoes with the Catalan chatter of energetic young locals enjoying a beer and a smoke outside, often accompanied by some of the *tapes del dia* (€3.50). Try not to get too attached to any of the dishes, though, since the lineup changes almost every day; your favorite salad with warm goat cheese from lunch today could easily be in the big salad bowl in the sky tomorrow.

🧭 From the east end of the Pont de Pedra, cross Rambla de la Llibertat into Pl. Vi, turn left and cross the plaza, then take the 1st left onto C. Abeuradors, then the 2nd right onto C. Mercaders. ℹ Menú del dia (M-Sa 1-3pm) always includes at least 1 vegetarian option for each course. Menu in Catalan but waiters speak English. 💲 Menú del dia €9.50. Tapas €3.50-4. Beer €2. Mixed drinks €5.50-7.50. €1 terrace surcharge. ⏰ Open M-Sa 10am-3pm and 7:30pm-1am.

LA LLETERA ICE CREAM $

C. de la Barca, 1 ☎97 241 24 19

Melted Ferrero Rocher chocolates, Nutella, and fresh kiwi—no, this isn't heaven's *menú del dia;* it's proof that dreams really do come true in Girona—at least ice cream dreams (come on, we know Let's Go isn't the only one who has these). At this *gelateria* with outdoor seating in the buzzing Pl. Sant Feliu, you can put any two of these or a display case's worth of other sauces, jams, and nuts on your cup of deliciously tart frozen *iogurt* (€3). The popular fruit *granissats* (slushies) from the line of machines on the wall will make you permanently turn away from 7-Eleven's soda-based monstrosities, though hopefully not in the direction of those nauseating, slowly rotating hot dogs.

With the river on your left, follow Rambla de la Llibertat, which becomes C. Argenteria; at the end, turn right and then immediately left onto C. Ballesteries, which turns into C. Calderers and leads to Pl. Sant Feliu. La Lletera is on the far side of the plaza, on the left. $ Frozen yogurt and 2 toppings €3. Ice cream cones €1-4, cups €2-4. Additional toppings €0.50. Granissats €2-6. Water €1. Soda €2. ⏰ Open M-Th 11am-midnight, F-Sa 11am-3am, Su 11am-midnight.

LA PENYORA CATALAN, INTERNATIONAL $$$

C. Nou del Teatre, 3 ☎97 221 89 48

We know travel partners don't always agree on everything, but thanks to this restaurant, they can put the switchblades away during the conversation about where to have dinner; this restaurant excels in both Catalan dishes and inventive international cuisine. You can mix and match with the affordable *menú del dia;* try starting with the Thai noodles, followed by the juicy *pollastre rostit amb prunes i pinyons* (roasted chicken with prunes and pine nuts, €8 à la carte). *Menú* pros will be pleasantly surprised to hear that both wine and water are included and that the silverware is replaced between courses.

From the east end of the Pont de Pedra, cross Rambla de la Llibertat into Pl. Vi, turn left, and then immediately take the 1st right onto C. Nou del Teatre. $ Menú del dia €15 (served 1-4pm). Appetizers €7-16. Entrees €10-20. ⏰ Open M 1-4pm and 8:30-11:30pm, W-Sa 1-4pm and 8:30-11:30pm, Su 1-4pm.

ROCAMBOLESC GELATERIA ICE CREAM $

C. de Santa Clara, 50 ☎97 241 66 67 www.rocambolesc.com

Run by the three brothers behind El Celler de Roca, the snazziest restaurant in town (and maybe in all of Spain), this *gelateria* serves up thick, creamy soft-serve ice cream made with the same eye for detail that made the brothers' restaurant an international star. There are six pre-set combinations of flavors and toppings, so you don't have a lot of say in what ends up in your cup, but it's hard to go wrong. The sheep's-milk ice cream with guava jam, caramelized sheep's milk, and gourmet cotton candy (oxymoron, anyone?) is the specialty, but other options like the decidedly un-plain Tahitian vanilla and brown sugar ice cream with flourless chocolate cake pieces, chocolate sauce, and caramel chips are equally inventive and satisfying.

On C. Santa Clara, the street closest to the river on the west side, between Pl. Independència and the red, iron Pont de les Peixateries Velles. From east side of the river, cross Pont de les Peixateries Velles (the red bridge) and turn right onto C. Santa Clara. i Large tubs of ice cream available. $ Cone €2.75. Cone with toppings €3.30. Cup with toppings €3.75. ⏰ Open Tu-F 11am-1:30pm and 4-9pm, Sa-Su and holidays 11am-9pm.

CAFÈ LE BISTROT CAFE $$$

Pujada de Sant Domènec, 4 ☎97 221 88 03 www.cafelebistrot.com

Let's be frank: there are better lunch *menús* out there for €14. This impossibly romantic restaurant is at its best at night anyway, and is best enjoyed with a cutie (or two, we won't judge) on your arm. The sophisticated interior's pink walls, wicker chairs, and understated lighting are romantic enough, but it's the seats on the terrace outside that will make that special someone gaze into your eyes with a look that will clear your mind of all thoughts, let alone bitter ones about the 10% night terrace surcharge.

✈ From the east end of the Pont de Pedra, cross Rambla de la Llibertat into Pl. Vi, turn left and continue straight through the plaza onto C. Ciutadans, which leads into Pl. Oli. Turn right onto Pujada de Sant Domènec and walk up the hill. i Menu in Catalan but waiters speak English. Ⓢ Menú del dia M-F €12-14, Sa-Su €20. Entrees €7-17. Ⓒ Open M-Th 1-4pm and 7pm-1am, F-Sa 1-4pm and 7pm-2am, Su 1-4pm and 7pm-1am.

NIGHTLIFE

Girona's nightlife is fairly spread out, though much of it can be found in the pedestrian areas on both sides of the river. Any of the bars on the **Plaça de la Independència** and the streets around it, especially the **Passeig de José Canalejas**, can be good places to start the evening, though you'll often find students drinking beer or *calimotxo* early in the evening on the steps leading from the Pl. Oli up to the university. Outside of the pedestrian areas, **Carrer de Pedret**, north of the *barri vell*, has several bars and clubs, though these tend to be somewhat pricey.

SUNSET JAZZ CLUB
JAZZ CLUB

C. de Jaume Pons i Martí, 12   ☎87 208 01 45 www.sunsetjazz-club.com

This welcoming jazz club is a great place to have a relaxed drink, listen to dizzying jazz, and perfect your foot-tapping skills any night of the week. Live jazz concerts four days a week bring in musicians from Spain and abroad. There's usually a €5-10 cover, but it can be avoided by coming on Monday when concerts are free, or on Tuesday and Wednesday when videos of jazz concerts are projected onto a large screen; that way you can save your money for one of the cocktails made with the bar's large selection of gins and vodkas.

✈ From the west side of the river, cross the Pont de Sant Feliu and turn left onto C. Jaume Pons i Martí. Or, from the east side, follow Rambla de la Llibertat, which becomes C. Argenteria, C. Ballesteries, and C. Calderers before leading to the Pl. Sant Feliu; cross the plaza diagonally onto C. Jaume Pons i Martí. i Free Wi-Fi for customers. Ⓢ Concert prices vary, but generally M free, Th €5, Sa €7-8, Su €3. Concert videos Tu-W free. Beer €3. Cocktails €6.50. Ⓒ Open June-Sept daily 6:30pm-3am; Oct-May daily 9pm-3am. Concerts dates and times vary, but generally M and Th 10pm, Sa 11pm, Su 8pm or 8:30pm; call or check online for exact details. Concert videos Tu-W 9:30pm.

EL CERCLE
BAR

C. dels Ciutadans, 8   ☎97 222 45 29

Cheap beers, fancy cocktails, and plenty of secluded areas with romantic purple lighting (trust us on this one) mean that if you can't score with the hostel hottie after a night out here, you must be doing something wrong. Hey, maybe it's not your fault—maybe they just don't like drinking or listening to the blues. Keep telling yourself that.

✈ From the east end of the Pont de Pedra, cross Rambla de la Llibertat into Pl. Vi, then turn left and continue straight through the plaza onto C. Ciutadans. i Occasional live music. Ⓢ Beer €1-1.50. Cocktails €6. Menú del dia €10 (served 1-4pm). Ⓒ Open M-Sa 8:30am-4pm, 7pm-1:30am.

SPRITZ
BAR

Pg. de José Canalejas, 1   ☎66 749 45 23

Rock 'n' roll, soul, and funk energize this bar popular with students and 20-somethings looking for a reasonably priced beer or a carefully prepared cocktail. The eponymous spritz is the obvious choice, but the mojitos and gin and tonics are also highly recommended. In the morning, the lights come on and coffee, not caipirinhas, is the drink of choice, though David Bowie's mug shot sticks around 24/7.

✈ From the intersection of Pl. Independència and C. Santa Clara, cross the plaza diagonally onto Pg. José Canalejas. Or, from the east side of the river, cross the Pont d'en Gómez and turn right onto Pg. José Canalejas. i Breakfast and sandwiches served during the day. Ⓢ Beer €2. Cocktails €5.50-6.50. Ⓒ Open M-Th 8am-2pm and 6pm-2am, F-Sa 8am-2pm and 6pm-3am, Su 8am-2pm and 6pm-2am.

girona

LOCAL PLATEA CLUB, LIVE MUSIC

C. de Jeroni Real de Fontclara, 4 ☎97 241 19 02 www.localplatea.com

Here's your chance to tell your friends back home that you danced on stage in front of a packed theater in Spain, and have it be sort of true. This *discoteca* was once a theater, and today's revelers get down on the former stage amid theatrical remnants like curtains and scenery. On Thursday and Friday, the place styles itself as "Sala Tourmix" and hosts concerts ranging from punk rock to reggae. The crowd tends to be on the younger side of 30, though on Saturday nights there are some older folks reliving the proms and frat parties of yesteryear courtesy of the '70s, '80s, and '90s music played alongside house remixes of current pop hits. The drinks are so pricey you'd think the place was still a theater, but at least there's no cover on Saturdays.

🧭 From the corner of the Pl. Independència leading to the Pont de Sant Agustí, cross the plaza diagonally and turn left; after the post office, turn right onto C. Jeroni Real de Fontclara. $ Cover occasionally Th and F €8-10. Beer €3.50. Cocktails €6-10. ⏰ Open Th-Sa midnight-6am.

FESTIVALS

TEMPS DE FLORS CITYWIDE

www.gironatempsdeflors.cat

Every May, Girona—especially the *barri vell*—converts itself into one giant botanical garden with enough flowers to overwhelm even the most hippie of botanists. The city's monuments, pedestrian streets, shop windows, parks, balconies, and even the courtyards of its private houses (opened to the public) are adorned with colorful and creative flower arrangements. Visitors from all over Europe and around the world eagerly snap photos to share with friends back home—then again, they might just be competing in the photo contest (prizes €100-380).

⏰ 2nd week in May.

FIRES DE SANT NARCÍS CITYWIDE

www.girona.cat/fires_sant_narcis

This religious festival honors Sant Narcís, the patron saint of Girona, who is supposed to have both freed the city from a plague of locusts and have chased away invading French soldiers when they entered the Església de Sant Feliu by sending a cloud of mosquitoes after them. Nevertheless, these *fires* (Catalan for *fiestas*) are happily insect-free. They begin with a mass in the chapel of the Església de Sant Feliu, containing the saint's remains, before the city erupts with parties and free concerts, mostly centered around the Parque de la Devesa. On the last night, there's a dazzling fireworks display; go to the other side of the Riu Ter for the best views.

⏰ Oct 28 to 1st Su of Nov.

ESSENTIALS

Practicalities

- **TOURIST OFFICES:** The **municipal tourist office** has maps of the city that include a comprehensive list of the city's accommodations and information on the city and province of Girona. (Rambla de la Llibertat, 1 ☎97 222 65 75 www.girona.cat/turisme 🧭 From the east end of the Pont de Pedra with your back to the bridge, it's the 1st building on the left. ⏰ Open M-F 9am-8pm, Sa 9am-2pm and 4-8pm, Su 9am-2pm.) The **regional tourist office** has much of the same information about the city and province of Girona as well as information about the rest of Catalonia. (C. Joan Maragall, 2 ☎87 297 59 75 www.girona.cat/turisme 🧭 From Pl. Espanya, with the bus station behind you, turn right onto C. Barcelona, left onto C. Bisbe Lorenzana, then 2nd left onto C. Joan Maragall. ℹ Catalan, Spanish, English, French, German, and Italian spoken. ⏰ Open May-Oct M-F 9am-8pm, Sa 9am-4pm, Su and holidays 9am-2pm; Nov-Apr M-F 9am-8pm and Sa 9am-4pm.)

- **TOURS: Turisme Imaginari** runs the tourist office-sponsored "Girona Walks," a guided walking tour of the city that includes the *barri vell* and a visit to the Museu d'Història dels Jueus. (Leaves from Punt de Benvinguda; C. Berenguer Carnicer, 3 ☎97 221 16 78 www.puntdebenvinguda. com ⚓ On C. Berenguer Carnicer, the 2nd left from the western end of the Pont de Sant Feliu. *i* Bilingual tours in English and Spanish. ⓢ €10, under 14 free. ⌚ 2hr., Apr-Nov Tu-Su 10:30am.)

- **CURRENCY EXCHANGE: La Caixa** exchanges major foreign currencies. (C. Santa Clara, 9-11 ☎97 224 76 50 www.lacaixa.es ⚓ At the west end of the Pont de Pedra. ⌚ Open May-Sept M-F 8:15am-2pm; Oct-Apr M-W 8:15am-2pm, Th 8:15am-2pm and 4:30-7:45pm, F 8:15am-2pm.)

- **LUGGAGE STORAGE:** There is no luggage storage in the bus or train stations, but **Equity Point Girona,** a hostel, offers luggage storage to the public. (Pl. Catalunya, 23 ☎97 241 78 40 www.equity-point.com ⚓ On the western side of Pl. Catalunya. ⓢ €5 per day. ⌚ Open daily 6am-midnight.)

- **INTERNET ACCESS:** Free Wi-Fi is difficult to come by in Girona, but is available in most hotels and many cafes. The regional tourist office has computers with 20min. free internet access. The **Alberg de Joventut Cerverí de Girona** offers computers with paid internet access for everyone, including non-guests. (C. Ciutadans, 9 ☎97 221 80 03 www.xanascat.cat ⚓ From Pl. Vi, with the river on the left, walk straight onto C. Ciutadans. ⓢ €1 per hr. ⌚ Open 24hr.)

- **POST OFFICE:** Av. de Ramon Folch, 2 ☎97 248 32 72 www.correos.es ⚓ From the corner of the Pl. Independència leading to the Pont de Sant Agustí, cross the plaza diagonally and exit; it's on the right-hand side of the traffic circle. ⌚ Open M-F 8:30am-8:30pm, Sa 9:30am-2pm.

- **POSTAL CODE:** 17001

Emergency

- **EMERGENCY NUMBER:** ☎112

- **POLICE: Municipal Police.** (C. Bernat Bacià, 4 ☎092 or ☎97 241 90 92 www.girona.cat/policia ⚓ From Pl. Catalunya, walk 1 block on C. Joan Maragall, then take the 1st right onto Gran Via Jaume I, then the 1st left onto C. Bernat Bacià.) **Regional Police.** Mossos d'Esquadra (Gran Via Jaume I, 57 ☎088 or ☎97 218 16 00 ⚓ From Pl. Catalunya, walk 1 block on C. Joan Maragall, then take the 1st right onto Gran Via Jaume I). **National Police.** (C. Rajolers, 7 ☎091 or ☎97 248 60 01 ⚓ Entrance on C. Sant Agustí, at intersection with C. dels Rajolers.)

- **MEDICAL SERVICES:** The private **Clínica Bofill** has English-speaking doctors and translators. (Ronda de Sant Antoni Maria Claret, 20 ☎97 220 43 50 www.clinicabofill.net ⚓ From Pl. Catalunya, go 2 blocks on C. Joan Maragall, then turn right onto Ronda de Sant Antoni Maria Claret. ⌚ Open 24hr.) The largest nearby hospital is **Hospital de Girona Dr. Josep Trueta.** (Av. França ☎97 294 02 00 www.gencat.cat/ics/trueta ⚓ Bus #2 from train station, Pl. Catalunya, or near the post office.)

- **PHARMACY:** Pharmacies are located throughout the *barri vell* and the rest of the city; one conveniently located one is at the intersection of Rambla de la Llibertat and C. Germans Busquets. (☎97 220 01 91 ⌚ Open M-F 9:15am-1:30pm and 4:30-8:30pm, Sa 9:15am-2pm.) Outside of regular pharmacy hours, check a local newspaper or the window of any pharmacy for a list of the pharmacies with extended hours that day.

Getting There

Since Barcelona is one of Spain's main transportation hubs, many bus and train lines terminate there and do not continue north to Girona. Therefore, most trips to Girona involve a change of bus or train in Barcelona; it's actually often easier to get direct service from France than from Spain.

girona

BY TRAIN

The train station (Pl. Espanya ☎90 224 02 02 ⇆ From Pl. Catalunya, walk 3 blocks on C. Joan Maragall, then right onto C. Bisbe Lorenzana. Or bus #2, 4, 7, 8, or 10) is located in the southwest part of the modern city on the Pl. Espanya, right next to the bus station. The cheapest way to get to Girona from Barcelona is by a **RENFE** regional or *media distancia* train ($ €11 ⏰ 1½hr.; M-F 24 per day 5:56am-9:16pm, Sa-Su and holidays 19 per day 6:46am-9:46pm). Direct overnight trains run from Madrid ($ €48 ⏰ 10½hr., daily 10:50pm) and Paris (*i* Book well in advance on weekends $ €174 ⏰ 10¼hr., daily 8:23pm).

BY BUS

The platforms of the bus station (Pl. Espanya ☎97 2201 591 ⇆ From Pl. Catalunya, walk 3 blocks on C. Joan Maragall, then right onto C. Bisbe Lorenzana. Or bus #2, 4, 7, 8, or 10) are located in front of the train station, while the ticket windows are located in a building to the right of the train station. **Barcelona Bus** operates the most frequent buses to Girona from Barcelona Nord ($ €12.50 ⏰ 1½hr.; M-F 5 per day 6:30am-7pm, Sa 4 per day 6:30am-7pm, Su 3 per day 6:30am-7pm) and Figueres ($ €5.50 ⏰ 1hr.; M-F 5 per day 7:45am-6:30pm, Sa 2 per day 11am and 3:45pm, Su 3 per day 7:45am-6:15pm). **ALSA** and its partners provide direct service from: Madrid ($ €43 ⏰ 9½hr., daily 10:30pm); Zaragoza ($ €27 ⏰ 5½hr., daily 2:35am); Nice ($ €58-61 ⏰ 8-10hr.; M, W, F, and Su 5:15pm; Tu, Th, and Sa 3:15am); Paris ($ €83 ⏰ 14hr., M-Sa 2:45pm); and Perpignan ($ €29-39 ⏰ 1½-2¼hr.; M and Th 6 per day 6am-2:15am, Tu-W and F 5 per day noon-2:15 am, Sa 6 per day 8am-12:50am, Su 4 per day noon-1:30am).

BY PLANE

The **Aeropuerto de Girona-Costa Brava** (GRO; ☎90 240 47 04 www.aena.es), located 8mi. outside of the city of Girona, is one of budget airline **Ryanair's** major hubs; the airline operates flights to Girona from 17 European countries and Morocco. **Barcelona Bus** operates buses between the bus station in Girona and the airport ($ €2.60, round-trip within 30 days €5 ⏰ 30min.; from airport to Girona 19 per day 5:30am-12:30am, from Girona to airport 19 per day 5am-midnight).

Getting Around

Walking is the easiest way to get around Girona. The city isn't particularly big, and the area of interest to most visitors can be walked end to end in 15min. Furthermore, much of the *barri vell* is closed to vehicles.

BY BUS

Transports Municipals del Gironès (TMG) operates the city's bus system (☎97 224 50 12 www.girona.cat/bus $ €1.30), which is rarely used by tourists. Bus #11 (really more of a van) is the only line that runs through the *barri vell;* buses #2, 4, 8, 7, and 10 go to the bus and train stations.

BY BIKE

Girona isn't quite as bike-friendly as many other Spanish cities; it lacks extensive designated bike lanes, and large parts of the *barri vell* are difficult to maneuver on a bike. Nevertheless, bikes are available for rental (including by non-guests) at the **Alberg de Joventut Cerverí de Girona.** (C. Ciutadans, 9 ☎97 221 80 03 www.xanascat.cat ⇆ From Pl. Vi with the river on your left, walk straight onto C. Ciutadans. $ €6 per 3hr., €8 per 5hr., €10 per 8hr. ⏰ Open 24hr.)

BY TAXI

Taxi stands are located near Pl. Independència (on Av. Ramon Folch, in front of the post office), near Pl. Catalunya (on C. Joan Maragall), and in front of the bus and train stations; if you're not near any of these call **Taxi Girona.** (☎97 222 23 23 or ☎97 220 33 77 www.taxigirona.es ⏰ Open 24hr.)

sitges ☎938

There's a reason the population of this tiny coastal town (pop. 27,000) inflates in the summer like Harry's awful Aunt Marge. Situated just 50km south of Barcelona, the sandy beaches of Sitges (pronounced "SEAT-jess") serve as a refuge for those fleeing the metropolis for the day to find turquoise waters, 300 days of sun, and rocky alcoves. Sitges is much more than a sandy second to Barcelona, though. Its architecture tells the story of a time of farming and fishing long past, while the lush interiors of its museums hint at its rise to prominence in the late 19th century as a center of *modernisme*. Sitges is also one of Europe's premier gay resort destinations.

ORIENTATION

Most people arrive in Sitges by train or bus, and both methods of transportation let off at spots along **Avinguda d'Artur Carbonell/Passeig de Vilanova**—buses at the intersection of Pg. de Vilanova and Pg. de Vilafranca, and trains at the station a couple of blocks east on Av. d'Artur Carbonell. Going left along Av. Artur Carbonell from the bus stop or right from the train station (both with the train tracks behind you), turn onto **Carrer de Sant Francesc** and walk for 5min. to find the heart of the Old Town, the **Plaça Cap de la Vila,** where C. de les Parellades meets C. Major. Follow **Carrer Major** to get to the historic center. Any downhill street off **Carrer de les Parellades** (which runs parallel to the beach) will lead to the waterfront, with **Passeig de la Ribera** wrapping around the closest (and most popular) beaches.

ACCOMMODATIONS

Most visitors to Sitges make it a daytrip from Barcelona, but those looking to take full advantage of the town's nightlife will probably want a place to crash after hitting the clubs. The **tourist office** lists the town's accommodations on a free map, but in the summer it's best to book a couple of weeks in advance.

▦ HOSTAL PARELLADES   HOTEL $$
C. de les Parellades, 11   ☎93 894 08 01

Ceilings that reach to the sky cover rooms just big enough to move around in comfortably. The singles are the cheapest in the area, and the sunny terrace with a shaded arcade overlooking the street provides a nice place to curl up with a book if you didn't get enough reading done on the beach, which is a block away. For the musically inclined, a piano awaits in the sunny common room.

⚒ *On C. Parellades between C. Sant Pere and C. Sant Pau.* ℹ *Linens and towels included. Free Wi-Fi. Singles and some doubles have shared baths.* ⓢ *Singles €35; doubles €65; triples €80.*

HOSTAL BONAIRE   HOTEL $$$
C. del Bonaire, 31   ☎93 894 53 26 www.bonairehostalsitges.com

With the beach in full view just down the street, chances are you won't want to spend too much time lounging in your room in front of the TV. If you do, though, or if you prefer air-conditioning, or even a terrace, just ask—the hostal contains a mix-and-match assortment of amenities that fit its relaxed feel.

⚒ *From C. Parellades, walk toward the beach on C. Bonaire.* ℹ *Free Wi-Fi.* ⓢ *Singles €25-50; doubles €35-70; triples €65-90. Cash only.*

HOSTAL ESPALTER   HOTEL $$$$
C. d'Espalter, 11   ☎93 894 28 63 www.pensionespalter.com

Nestled inside the Sauna Sitges behind a door framed by rainbows, this *hostal* offers cheap rooms near the heart of Sitges's gay nightlife. The rooms are big and newly painted, and those that don't have balconies have a fullblown patio-size terrace.

⚒ *From the train station, take a right onto Av. Artur Carbonell and a left onto C. San Francesc at the roundabout. Take a right onto C. Espalter. Reception is in the Sauna Sitges.* ℹ *Free Wi-Fi. Each room has a fridge and ensuite bathroom.* ⓢ *Doubles €45-60.*

HOTEL EL CID HOTEL $$$$

C. de Sant Josep, 39 ☎93 894 18 42 www.hotelsitges.com

With reasonable rates for luxurious amenities—swimming pool, terraces, TV, air-conditioning, safes—Hotel El Cid allows you to play El Cid and conquer Sitges for yourself. Have breakfast like a conquistador in the massive *comedor* that's more feasting hall than dining room. All rooms have terraces overlooking either the street or the pool. Wi-Fi is only available in the lower level, which is decked out with enough leather couches, stone pillars, and iron fixtures to make it worth your time.

 # From the train station, take a right onto Av. Artur Carbonell, pass the roundabout, and take the 4th left onto C. Sant Josep. $ Singles €50-60; doubles €68-79; triples €99-115. ⏰ Open May-Oct.

SIGHTS

CAU FERRAT MUSEUM, MARICEL MUSEUM, ROMANTIC MUSEUM ART MUSEUMS

C. del Fonollar C. de Sant Gaudenci, 1 ☎938 94 03 64

Although Sitges's museums may not all be housed under one roof, the city couldn't have made visiting them any easier: they all have the same hours and ticket prices, and the combination ticket that grants admission to all three is a deal. Overlooking the waterfront by the church, on C. Fonollar, the **Cau Ferrat Museum** is the former home of *modernista* big shot Santiago Rusiñol (1861-1931) and provides a snapshot into the area's artistic, star-studded past with works by Picasso, Ignacio Zuloaga, Ramon Casas i Carbó, and more.

The **Maricel Museum,** a palace built in 1910 for the American millionaire Charles Deering, is next door. True to the American way, the interior is sumptuous, with incredible halls and rooftop terraces. Art from medieval to modern decks the walls, and the museum also provides a chronology of Catalan art and influences from the Romantic period onward for those willing to make the mental leap. Cau Ferrat and Maricel are undergoing renovations, so you should call ahead or visit the website to check opening information.

The **Romantic Museum** is located a bit further inland at C. Sant Gaudenci, 1, off C. Parellades, and provides a literal snapshot of the town's past where the other museums only hint at it. This perfectly preserved 19th-century house is filled with ceramics, music boxes, and furniture. The special collections boast over 400 antique dolls from around the world and over 25 intricate, though somewhat creepy, dioramas of 19th-century life in Sitges.

i **Cau Ferrat Museum and Maricel Museum closed while undergoing renovations.** *Guided tours every hr. in Museu Romàntic. $ Single tickets €3.50, students and seniors €2; combined ticket for all museums €6.50/4. ⏰ Open July-Sept Tu-Sa 9:30am-2pm and 4-7pm, Su 10am-3pm; Oct-June Tu-Sa 9:30am-2pm and 3:30-6:30pm, Su 10am-3pm.*

BEACHES

Over a dozen beaches and more than 3km of Mediterranean coast along the city center make Sitges a clear alternative to Barcelona's crowded shores. That said, don't expect to find your own spot near the popular beaches close to downtown—**Platja de la Ribera** and **Platja de la Fragata**—during the peak summer months. To flee the crowds, try the hipper **Platja de la Barra** and **Platja de Terramar** a couple of kilometers down the coast, where you'll find rocky islands and a more interesting crowd. Walk about 20min. or take the L2 bus ($ €1.45 ⏰ Every 30min. 9am-9pm) from the train station to the stop next to Hotel Terramar, and walk for a few minutes back toward the city center.

Sitges also boasts a number of gay beaches. **Platja de la Bassa Rodona** is the most popular and just a short walk from downtown, though in the past years its tight bronzed bodies and little Speedos have been infiltrated by a more mixed crowd. If you like clear water and naked old dudes, or if you are a naked old dude yourself and want company, head to **Platja dels Balmins.** To get there, take a left (as you face the water) and pass the church and the restaurant-lined, family-frequented **Platja de**

Sant Sebastià. Go around the first restaurant you come to and take the dirt walkway between the coast and walls of the cemetery—the beach is the quiet cove before the port right after the little hill. For surfing (or to pick up surfers), your best bet is the far end of **Platja de l'Estanyol,** just past Platja de la Bassa Rodona.

If tan lines aren't your thing, try one of Sitges's many renowned nude beaches—the farther out they are, the less likely you are to get your picture snapped by a tourist aiming for the church. A 1hr. hike to the right along the seafront past Terramar, rocks, and a golf course (or, alternatively, taking a cab to Club l'Atlàntida and walking 15min.) will get you to **Platja de l'Home Mort;** the small cove itself is located just behind the hills where the train tracks run along the coast. This cove also houses Sitges's only exclusively gay beach, with a neighboring forest known for its debauchery.

FOOD

Affordable dining in Sitges is difficult to come by, unless you consider dropping €25 "affordable." You're probably better off stopping at any of the town's many supermarkets and picking up a picnic for the beach; try **Gust Bo.** (C. Jesús, 42 ☎93 811 24 55 🕐 Open M-Sa 9am-9pm, Su 9am-2pm.)

IZARRA — BASQUE, TAPAS $$

C. Major, 24 — ☎93 894 73 70

Izarra offers some of the best Basque food this side of Pamplona with surprisingly reasonable prices, especially for wallet-busting Sitges. Small stools line the walls and bar, but show up early if you want to get a seat. Order from its daily *menú* or snag a plate from the back and pile on the tapas yourself.

➜ Walk down C. Major from C. de les Paralledes. Izarra is on the left. $ Tapas €3-11. Entrees €6.80-17. 1-course menú €8.50; 2-course €13. 🕐 Open M-F 1-11pm, Sa-Su noon-midnight. Menú available 1:30-4pm and 8:30-11pm.

ELS ARCS — CATALAN $$

C. de les Parellades, 50 — ☎93 811 20 26

The food itself isn't remarkable, but backpackers with empty stomachs and empty wallets take note: in terms of sheer quantity, Els Arcs will give you the biggest bang for your euro. €9 will get you a *menú* of three ample courses, bread, and a good-sized carafe of wine. Perfect for those times when your gut screams, "Screw quality. GIVE ME FOOD."

➜ Follow C. Parellades away from Pl. Cap de la Vila. $ Pizzas €7. Paellas €15. Menú €9. 🕐 Open M-W noon-4pm and 8:30pm-midnight, F-Su noon-4pm and 8:30pm-midnight.

CAFÉ DEL MÓN — CAFE, BAR $

C. de l'Illa de Cuba, 43 — ☎93 811 11 04

Café del Món serves inexpensive food like "bikini" sandwiches (€2.30) in a cheery cafe setting, with paint handprints on the walls. At night, the bar livens up with loud music, cheap drinks, and a young crowd. If you're heading back into Barcelona for the night, it's a good stop for a bite and a drink before catching your train at the station down the street.

➜ Walk along C. Parellades away from Pl. Espanya and veer left to stay on C. Jesús. Turn left onto C. Illa de Cuba. $ Sandwiches €2.30-4. Salads €4.50. Entrees €3.80-7. Beer €1.80-3. Cocktails €4.50. Cash only. 🕐 Open M-F 7:30am-midnight, Sa 9:30am-1am, Su 7:30am-midnight.

ALFRESCO — MEDITERRANEAN $$$$

C. d'en Pau Barrabeig, 4 — ☎93 894 06 00 www.alfrescorestaurante.es

There's no avoiding it: Sitges is outrageously expensive. If you're going to splurge, this stylish candlelit restaurant is the place to do it. Pull up a white bowl stool under ultra-modern glass sculptures and geometric tile, or relax in the airy courtyard.

➜ Walk down C. Major from C. Parallades. Alfresco will be down C. Barrabeig on your right. $ Appetizers €15; entrees €16. 1-course menú €22, 2-course €35. 🕐 Open July-Oct daily 8:30-11:30pm; Nov-June Tu-Su 8:30-11:30pm.

NIGHTLIFE

Many visitors to Sitges just make it a daytrip from Barcelona, but others stick around for more. Sitges's nightlife is predominantly geared toward the gay community, though most establishments are straight-friendly. The heart of the nightlife scene is the legendary **Carrer del Pecat** or "Street of Sin" (officially C. del Primer de Maig; follow C. de les Parellades away from Pl. Cap de la Vila and take a left on C. del Marquès de Mont-roig)—the entire street and the one that intersects it are lined with bars and clubs. Nearby **Carrer del Bonaire** and **Carrer de Sant Pau,** parallel to each other between the water and C. de les Parellades, are also hot nightlife streets. As far as hetero nightlife goes, most say **Ruta 66** is the place to be. (C. Bonaire, 12 ☎93 894 51 12 www.r66sitges.com ⏰ Open F-Sa midnight-6am.)

TRAILER — CLUB, GLBT

C. d'Àngel Vidal, 36 — ☎93 814 65 75 www.trailerdisco.com

Shed those heavy clothes, shoes, and inhibitions for Trailer's incredibly popular Wednesday and Sunday foam parties, and don't be surprised if you see fellow revelers (or pairs of revelers) with nothing to hide. Check your clothes upon entering and throw on your trunks—or not. One of the oldest gay dance clubs in Spain, Trailer boasts nearly 30 years in the game and it's easy to see why. Though you're unlikely to see many women here most nights, this club is nothing but men on Thursdays—during "After Dark," the colored lights are flipped off and anything goes.

🚏 From Pl. Cap de la Vila, follow C. d'Àngel Vidal. ℹ Foam parties on W, Su; After Dark on Th. $ Cover €15; includes 1 drink. Use a flyer for free admission. ⏰ Open May-Sept daily 1-6am; Oct-Apr Sa 1-6am.

L'ATLÀNTIDA — CLUB

Platja de les Coves — ☎93 894 26 77 www.clubatlantida.com

This expansive beach-bar and nightclub has it all—beautiful sand, chic lighting, and a crowd that's not afraid to take it all off. Sweaty bodies slide past each other to electro hits during the summer months, spilling into the open air in an attempt to cool down. There are frequent themed nights—check the events schedule to see which way the night swings.

🚏 A free bus runs from Calipolis Hotel in Sitges center. ℹ Listing of events on website. VIP list available on L'Atlàntida's Facebook page. $ Cover €15-20. ⏰ Open June-Sept M-Th midnight-5am, F-Sa midnight-6am.

ARTS AND CULTURE

Festivals

In the 19th century, Sitges was a hangout of *modernisme* artists ranging from Santiago Rusiñol i Prats to Picasso; however, you won't need to visit the Cau Ferrat Museum to be reminded of this influence. Ignasi Mas i Morell's **Modernista Clocktower** (corner of C. Parellades and C. Sant Francesc), for instance, looms over the city. The **Sitges Music Festival** (July and August) and **Sitges Film Festival** (October) attract thousands to its sandy shores every year. For almost nearly as long as Sitges has been known for the arts, it has also been known as a gay mecca. The **Sitges Gay Pride** festival (mid-July) attracted over 60,000 people from across the world in its first year in 2010, packing the beaches and over 20 gay bars in the city. True to its (arguably) Spanish roots, the annual **Corpus Christi** celebration (early June) blankets the streets with flowers, while the **Festa Major** (last week in August) unites the city under flames and fireworks to celebrate Sitges's patron saint, Sant Bartolomé. The city's **Carnaval** (first week of Lent; mid-February in 2013) celebrations are some of the most famous in the region. True to Mediterranean fashion, Sitges is also proud of its booze—September brings the

Festa de la Verema, or grape harvest, where competitors fight to squash grapes along the beach. Despite its small size, Sitges knows how to party.

Since 1968, sci-fi geeks, horror buffs, and really famous people have flocked to the sandy shores of Sitges in early October to catch the world's foremost fantasy and horror film festival, the **Festival Internacional de Cinema Fantàstic de Catalunya** (☎93 894 99 90 www.sitgesfilmfestival.com). This 10-day extravaganza has seen special screenings of movies from *Final Fantasy VII* (2005) to *Hellraiser* (1987), *The Bourne Identity* (2002) to *Aliens* (1986), and *Kill Bill* (2003) to *Mulholland Drive* (2001). The year's best is awarded the Midnight X-Treme Award. Besides being a fantastic place to catch a flick, the festival also attracts a star-studded crowd of directors, actors, and producers ready to receive awards, known as Marias, for the best of their categories, as determined by international jury. Like a doomsday scene from one of the movies being screened, the city is swarmed with a sea of the living undead during the festival's annual **Zombie Walk.**

When the somber legacy of Lent threatens to take away revelry for 40 days, a giant, ridiculous party ensues. Boasting one of the biggest and baddest **Carnavals** in all of Europe, the small town of Sitges fills with over 250,000 visitors for the week's festivities, held the seven days preceding Lent each February. The week kicks off with *Dijous Gras* (Fat Thursday) when the King of the Carnaval marks the start of the party. Other highlights of the week include Sunday's **Rua de la Disbauxa** (Debauchery Parade), which includes over 40 floats and 2,500 participants. Masquerade festivities continue throughout the week, with Tuesday's **Rua de l'Extermini** (Extermination Parade) solemnly marking the end of the party week, with drag queens dressed in black to mourn the death of the King of the Carnaval. After nearly a full week of revelry, Carnaval is symbolically put to rest with Wednesday's **Burial of the Sardine,** where a large effigy of the little fish is buried along the beach to mark the end of debauchery and the start of more somber days. Get your hotel reservations early if you prefer not to sleep on the beach—this is predictably the local hotel industry's busiest time of year.

ESSENTIALS

Practicalities

- **TOURIST OFFICES:** The **Sitges tourist office** helps book accommodations and distributes a monthly calendar of events, *Sitges Agenda,* and a free map. (Pl. Eduard Maristany, 2 ☎93 894 42 51 www.sitgestur.cat ⇄ Immediately to your left exiting the train station. *i* Additional branches at Pl. Ajuntament and near the beach, below the church. ⏰ Open M-F 9am-2pm and 4-8pm, Sa 10am-2pm and 4-8pm, Su 10am-2pm.)
- **LAUNDROMATS: Net i Sec.** (Av. Artur Carbonell, 8 ☎93 894 98 11 ⇄ From the train station, take a right onto Av. Artur Carbonell. Net i Sec is on the left. ⏰ Open daily 7am-midnight.)
- **INTERNET: Internet Espalter.** (C. Espalter, 20 ☎93 811 03 29 ⇄ From the train station, turn right onto Av. Artur Carbonell and take the 3rd left onto C. Sant Francesc, then first right onto C. Espalter. $ €0.50 per 15min., €0.70 per 30min., €1 per hr. Day-pass €6. Wi-Fi €1. ⏰ Open daily 11am-11pm.)
- **POST OFFICES:** Pl. Espanya. ☎938 94 70 63 www.correos.es ⇄ Exit the train station and take a right onto Av. Artur Carbonell. Continue through the roundabout as it turns to Pg. de Vilanova and take a left onto C. Europa. Follow as it takes a slight right and take a slight right onto C. Espalter to enter the plaza. ⏰ Open M-F 8:30am-2:30pm, Sa 9:30am-1pm. No package pickup Sa.
- **POSTAL CODE:** 08870.

Emergency

- **EMERGENCY NUMBERS:** ☎112 or ☎061.
- **POLICE: Local police.** (Pl. Ajuntament. ☎938 11 00 16 or 938 10 97 97.) **Mossos d'Esquadra** (regional police) ☎088.
- **MEDICAL SERVICES: Hospital Sant Camil.** (Ronda De Sant Camil ☎938 96 00 25 www.hrsantcamil.es)

Getting There

BY TRAIN

Cercanías RENFE trains, known in Catalunya as **Rodalies** (☎90 224 02 02 www.renfe.es/cercanias) run from Estació Barcelona-Sants, Estació Passeig de Gràcia, and Estació de França in Barcelona to Sitges (*i* Line 2 toward St. Vicenç de Calders or Vilanova i la Geltrú $ €3 ⏰ 45 min., every 25-40min. 7:05am-10:21pm) and from Sitges to Barcelona ($ €3 ⏰ Every 25-40min. 6:15am10:54pm). Trains also run from Sitges to Cambrils via Tarragona. ($ €5.70. ⏰ 1hr.)

BY BUS

Mon Bus (☎93 893 70 60 www.monbus.cat) connects the Barcelona airport to Pg. de Villafranca in Sitges. ($ €3. ⏰ M-F every hr. 7:40am-11:40pm.) Late-night buses operate from Pg. de Vilafranca to Ronda de la Universitat in Barcelona and back. ($ €3 ⏰ Every hr. 12:13-3:13am.)

BY TAXI

You can also take a taxi between Barcelona and Sitges, though it'll set you back a pretty penny. (☎93 894 13 29 $ €50-60.)

Getting Around

Sitges is first and foremost a walking city, with major sights just 5-10min. from each other. If you're looking to venture outside the center, Sarbus operates the **Bus Urbà** within the city. All three lines depart the train station and travel outward. The **L1** travels north; **L2** travels west to Platja del Cellerot, Platja de Terramar, and Platja de la Barra; and **L3** travels east to Platja de Sant Sebastià and Platja dels Balmins. (☎93 814 49 89 $ €1.45. ⏰ Every 30min. M-F 7am-9pm, Sa-Su and holidays 9am-9pm.)

Taxis provide a safe ride home for tired feet and drunken bodies. (☎938 94 35 94 or ☎93 894 13 29.)

tarragona   ☎977

¿Cómo se dice Rome? We're no experts, but we're pretty sure it sounds something like Tarragona. Founded in 218 BCE at the height of the Punic Wars as a military base for Roman troops in between elephant-killing sprees, Tarragona grew up into a fashionable seaside resort. The city served as a sort of Rome away from Rome for patricians and for Augustus Caesar himself, who wintered here during his Spanish military campaigns. It was made the capital of Hispania Citerior, which comprised a large chunk of the Iberian Peninsula including all of modern-day Catalonia. Though Barcelona has long since stolen Tarragona's tourist thunder and its capital status, Tarragona retains something that the flashy city can't boast: the best-preserved Roman ruins in Spain and some of the best anywhere outside of Italy (as well as a trippy flag that looks like the Catalan one after a few *copas*). For most of Tarragona's visitors, the Roman ruins are the biggest draw, but Carthaginians, Milanese, and anyone else looking to avoid all things Roman can still have a good time here by visiting the pleasant courtyard of the *Catedral* or engaging in the Tarragonian pastime of *anar a tocar ferro:* walking, watching, and gossiping the evening away alongside the iron railings of the seaside Balcó del Mediterrani.

ORIENTATION

The **Plaza de la Imperial Tarraco,** home to the bus station and some giant flags, is the center of Tarragona's modern *centro*. **Rambla Nova,** the city's main thoroughfare, runs east from Pl. Imperial Tarraco all the way to the Mediterranean Sea, which forms the eastern and southern boundaries of the city. Most major tourist sights, including most of the Roman ruins and the cathedral, are located uphill from Rambla Nova in the *casco antiguo* north of **Rambla Vella,** commonly called the *parte alta* (because of its higher altitude) and centered around the **Plaça de la Font** and **Carrer Major.** A few blocks south of Rambla Nova the altitude drops sharply again, so much so that there is an escalator on C. Pau del Protectorat leading to the nightlife-filled *parte baja* that stretches almost to the sea. The areas of interest bordering the sea are, from west to east, **El Serrallo,** the fishermen's neighborhood with many restaurants; **the Port Esportiu,** with a great deal of the city's nightlife; and the **Platja del Miracle,** a beach that forms the eastern border of the city.

ACCOMMODATIONS

Tarragona's *parte alta* might look like the other *cascos antiguos* you know and love, but look closely and you'll see there's a crucial difference: the lack of signs heralding cheap *pensiones*. There aren't very many affordable accommodations in Tarragona, though there are a few in the Pl. Font, in the *parte baja* near the train station, and around Pl. de la Imperial Tarraco near the bus station.

PENSIÓ FORUM   HOTEL $
Pl. de la Font, 37   ☎97 723 17 18

These incredibly cheap rooms with private baths in the center of the Pl. Font just might be the best deal in town. There's a pretty wide difference in quality (though none in price) between the well-lit, high ceilinged rooms overlooking the plaza and the rooms with much lower ceilings in the back, though even the latter are an incredible deal for the price. There is no difference, however, in the size of the private bathrooms—they're all miniscule. Solo travelers with a soft spot for plaza views will be glad to hear that, unlike in most hotels, both single and double rooms get a piece of the plaza action.

With your back to the Ajuntament, the hotel is on the right side of the Pl. Font. From the bus station, take the 3rd right off of Pl. Imperial Tarraco onto Rambla Nova, then take the 7th left onto C. Comte de Rius, which will lead to the Pl. Font; turn right immediately upon entering the plaza. Or, from the train station, turn right onto Passeig d'Espanya and continue as it turns into Vial de William J. Bryant. Turn left (uphill) at the fork and turn left at the traffic circle onto Rambla Vella, then take the 2nd right onto C. Portalet, which leads to the Pl. Font; turn left immediately upon entering the plaza. ***i*** *Free Wi-Fi.* [$] *June-Oct 15 singles €18, doubles €30; Oct 16-May singles €20, doubles €35.* ⏰ *Reception 24hr.*

RESIDÈNCIA UNIVERSITÀRIA SANT JORDI HOSTEL $$

Rambla del President Lluís Companys, 5 ☎97 763 52 00 www.resa.es

If you're traveling alone or just looking to meet fellow travelers, this place is your best bet—but it's only open in July and August, when the students who live there during the year have gone home. Make friends during the three meals served in the cafeteria-style dining room or over a game of pool in the game room before going back to your single or double room, available with private bath.

Entrance on C. Marqués de Guad-El-Jelú. Upon exiting the bus station in Pl. Imperial Tarraco, turn left onto Rambla del President Lluís Companys (at about 10 o'clock), then take the 2nd right onto C. Marqués de Guad-El-Jelú. Or, from the train station, cross the Pl. Pedrera and proceed along the street to the right (C. Orosi), then take the 2nd right onto C. Pau del Protectorat. Take the escalator up the hill and continue straight, and turn left onto Rambla Nova and walk to the end; at Pl. Imperial Tarraco, cross through the plaza straight onto Rambla del President Lluís Companys, then take the 2nd right after the plaza onto C. Marqués de Guad-El-Jelú. ***i*** *Open July-Aug only. Breakfast included. Single rooms with shared bath, double rooms available with private and shared bath. Common area with TV and games. Gym available. Washer €2, dryer €2. Lunch and dinner each €10.10.* [$] *Singles or doubles with shared bath €21.85; doubles with private bath €24.85; doubles with private bath, TV, and A/C €29.50.* ⏰ *Reception 24hr.*

HOSTAL NORIA HOTEL $$

Pl. de la Font, 53 ☎97 723 87 17

Conveniently located on one of the city's main squares, this *hostal* is one of the few affordable options for those who want to be close to both the major sights and to the restaurants and nightlife of the Pl. Font. The rooms are hardly massive, but there's plenty of space to lay down your pack and stride comfortably over to your private bathroom or your balcony, some of which have an impressive view onto the plaza and an equally impressive ruckus on warm evenings as the restaurants' terraces fill. If you're going out late at night, you better hope that the night watchman got his z's during the day, or you may have to rouse him to let you in and out of the building.

At the opposite end of the Pl. Font from the Ajuntament. From the bus station, take the 3rd right off of Pl. Imperial Tarraco onto Rambla Nova, then take the 8th left onto C. Sant Agustí, which leads to the Pl. Font; the hotel is on the right. Or, from the train station, turn right onto Passeig d'Espanya and continue as it turns into Vial de William J. Bryant. Turn left (uphill) at the fork and turn left at the traffic circle onto Rambla Vella, then take the 2nd right onto C. del Portalet; the hotel is on the right. ***i*** *Reception in the cafe on the ground floor. Free Wi-Fi in the cafe downstairs reaches the rooms on the 1st floor. Private bath available. Catalan, Spanish, English, French, and Russian spoken.* [$] *Singles €24-31; doubles €38-49.* ⏰ *Reception 7am-11:30pm. Outside of these hours, the door to the street is locked (both ways), and guests only receive keys to their rooms. The door to the street can be opened by the night watchman who stays in the cafe overnight.*

HOSTAL EUROPA HOTEL $$

C. del General Contreras, 10 ☎97 724 05 61

With decor somewhere between minimalist art gallery and boutique hospital, this newly opened *hostal* provides a slightly sleeker, more upscale alternative to the cheaper accommodations nearby without sacrificing proximity to the train station and the nightlife of the *parte baja* and Port Esportiu. It's a study in contradictions: the double beds are enormous and the two single rooms could easily be the biggest in Catalonia, but the sinks are so tiny that rinsing your toothbrush seems to pose a threat to the building's existence.

➜ Entrance on C. Orosi. From train station, cross Pl. Pedrera; C. Orosi leads away from the right side of the plaza. Or, from the bus station, take the 3rd right onto Rambla Nova, then the 6th right onto C. Méndez Núñez, then proceed straight, go down the stairs, and walk 1 block along C. Pau del Protectorat and take the 1st left onto C. Orosi. ***i*** *Private bath. Free Wi-Fi (weaker on 2nd floor).* [$] *Singles €30-35; doubles €40-45. Extra bed €10-17.* ⏰ *Reception 24hr.*

PENSIÓ LA PILARICA HOTEL $

C. de Smith, 20, 2nd fl. ☎97 724 09 60

The kindly old woman (and self-styled "mother of the guests") who runs this *pensió* rents out rooms in the *parte baja* of Tarragona, close to much of the city's nightlife. Though she doesn't seem like a hipster, she must have been using euros before it was cool; the rock-bottom prices haven't changed, she says, in twenty years. Many of the rooms are rented on a long-term basis, so call ahead to reserve one of the few rooms set aside for short-term tourists.

➜ From train station, cross Pl. Pedrera and proceed along C. Orosi (on the right side of the plaza) for 3 blocks, go down the stairs, proceed straight along C. Cartagena for 3 more blocks, then turn left onto C. Nou de Santa Tecla; the hotel is at the end of the street. Or, from the bus station, take the 3rd right onto Rambla Nova, then the 6th right onto C. Méndez Núñez, then proceed straight, go down the stairs, proceed 1 block along C. Pau del Protectorat, take the 1st right onto C. Orosi, go down the stairs, proceed straight along C. Cartagena for 3 blocks, and turn left onto C. Nou de Santa Tecla; the hotel is at the end of the street. [$] *High season €18; low season €15.* ⏰ *Reception 24hr.*

HOSTAL ALHAMBRA HOTEL $$

Av. d'Estanislau Figueres, 51 ☎97 721 64 85 www.hostalalhambratarragona.com

This *hostal* just off the Pl. Imperial Tarraco has rooms with either private or shared bath and is a great place to stay if you arrive on the last bus of the night and don't want to make the trek down the Rambla Nova. However, unless your idea of a relaxing night is ringing a doorbell in vain, don't head straight to the *hostal*—the reception is located in Hotel Cosmos, on the same street but closer to the bus station; be sure to tell them you want a room in the *hostal* to avoid a nasty surprise when the bill comes.

➜ Just off the Pl. Imperial Tarraco on Av. Estanislau Figueres. Upon exiting the bus station, take the 4th right onto Av. Estanislau Figueres. Or, from the train station, cross the Pl. Pedrera and proceed along the street to the right (C. Orosi), then take the 2nd right onto C. Pau del Protectorat, take the escalator up the hill and continue straight, and turn left onto Rambla Nova and walk to the end; at Pl. Imperial Tarraco take the next right onto Av. Estanislau Figueres. ***i*** *Breakfast €3. Free Wi-Fi in lobby. Catalan, Spanish, English, French, German, Dutch, and Arabic spoken.* [$] *June 15-Sept 15 singles with bath €27, without bath €24; doubles €36/27; triples €54/40.50. Sept 16-Dec 22 and Jan-June 15 singles with bath €24, without bath €21; doubles €30/24; triples €45/36. Dec 23-Jan 7 singles with bath €27, without bath €24; doubles €36/ 27; triples €54/40.50.* ⏰ *Reception 24hr. in Hotel Cosmos (C. Estanislau Figueres, 57; closer to Pl. Imperial Tarraco).*

SIGHTS

You can't walk five minutes in Tarragona without stumbling across a tall red sign that heralds yet another Roman ruin. Unfortunately, many of the most impressive, like the **Arc de Berà** honoring Augustus Caesar and the Pedrera del Mèdo, the Roman quarry, are located outside of the city and can only be reached by car; thankfully, the most impressive of them all, the **Pont del Diable aqueduct,** can be reached by bus. For those looking for a respite from 2000-year-old stone, check out the free **Museu d'Art Modern.** (C. Santa Anna, 8 ☎97 723 50 32 ➜ From the Pl. Rei, facing the Pretori, turn left onto C. Santa Anna. [$] Free. ⏰ Open Tu-F 10am-8pm, Sa 10am-2pm and 5-8pm,

Su 11am-2pm.) The Museo de Història de Tarragona, which oversees many of the Roman sites, includng the Amfiteatre Romà, the Circ Romà, the Pretori Romà, and the Passeig Arqueològic, sells a global ticket that includes admission to all their sites, though many of the included sights can be seen just fine for free from the street. (*i* Available at all MHT ticket windows. Ⓢ €10.55, students and seniors €5.25.)

PONT DEL DIABLE (AQUEDUCTE DE LES FERRERES) ROMAN RUINS
N-240 to Lleida, 4 km. from Tarragona

The centerpiece of Tarragona's array of ruins is not to be missed, despite its distance from the city center. You truly get a sense of how long the aqueduct is by walking up to the end and staring down the length of it; you can pretend to be the Río Francolí and walk across all 650ft. of the aqueduct, though it's a bit of a squeeze and you'd be missing the only thing to see in the area. Those who have been to the other UNESCO World Heritage Site aqueduct in the neighborhood, the Pont du Gard in Nîmes, might be a little disappointed by the fact that there are only two tiers of arches (not three) and that there's no river to swim in underneath, but they'll get over it when they see how isolated and peaceful this site is, miles away from the nearest gift shop and with the chirping of the birds as your only audioguide.

✈ *From the side of Pl. Imperial Tarraco directly opposite the bus station, take bus #5 (dir.: San Salvador) to Pont del Diable, the 3rd stop. After getting off the bus, turn around and walk along the highway against traffic for 30 seconds, then take a sharp left up the hill and follow the yellow signs. When returning to Tarragona, use the same bus stop and stay on the bus as it goes to its final destination and then circles back around to Tarragona.* Ⓢ *Free; bus each way €1.30.* ⏱ *1st bus leaves Pl. Imperial Tarraco M-F 6:14am, Sa 6:16am, Su 7:49am; last bus leaves Pont del Diable M-F 9:08pm, Sa 9:26pm, Su 9:27pm.*

catalonia and valencia

MUSEU NACIONAL ARQUEOLÒGIC DE TARRAGONA — MUSEUM

Pl. del Rei, 5 — ☎97 723 62 09 www.mnat.cat

Lest the rest of Tarragona's sights make you think that stone blocks were the be-all and end-all of Roman civilization, this museum presents a more balanced picture of life in Romanized Tarragona. Push on past the first room, which focuses on architecture, to the rooms with artifacts like sculptures, mosaics, and objects from everyday life. The most impressive mosaic in the museum is also probably the smallest: the Mosaic of the Medusa, with miniscule tiles so lifelike that *Let's Go* would like to state that we cannot claim any responsibility for readers who turn to stone, just to be on the safe side. On the stairs to the top floor is another, less skillfully made, mosaic that depicts 47 different species of Mediterranean marine fauna, accompanied by a macabre *menú del dia*-type panel that describes which fish is which.

#From the hill leading up to C. Major, turn right onto C. Nau, which leads into the Pl. Rei; the museum is on the opposite side of the plaza. ***i*** *Signs in Catalan only, booklets available in each room with translations of that room's signs into Spanish, English, and French.* $ *€2.40, students €1.20, under 18 and over 65 free.* ⏰ *Open June-Sept Tu-Sa 9:30am-8:30pm, Su 10am-2pm; Oct-May Tu-Sa 9:30am-6pm, Su 10am-2pm.*

AMFITEATRE ROMÀ — ROMAN RUINS

Parc del Miracle — ☎97 724 25 79 www.museutgn.com

Constructed during the early second century CE, this amphitheater once held gladiatorial contests and other public spectacles. Today, after much of the stone was scavenged for other purposes, the only fights it holds are ones that break out among students from school groups; and you can bet that the angry teacher isn't sparing any lives. In fact, at times so many groups fill the stands that if you pretend really hard, you can imagine the arena on the day of a gladiator fight, although we hope the crowd gave a bigger hand to the gladiators than the marginally polite one that students give their tour guides. Part of the amphitheater's charm is how un-isolated it is from the modern world around it: you can see freight ships from the tiered seating, and right behind its ancient arches, the RENFE train clanks along by. In fact, it's so integrated that you can skip the admission fee and observe the whole thing from just outside the gates.

#Walk toward the sea on Rambla Vella, then turn left at the flags and take the 1st right down the stairs. The entrance is inside the park to the right. ***i*** *MHT global ticket sold here. Bathrooms available.* $ *€3.15, students and seniors €1.60, under 16 free.* ⏰ *Open Easter-Sept M-Sa 10am-9pm, Su 10am-3pm; Oct-Easter M-Sa 9am-7pm, Su 10am-3pm.*

CATEDRAL DE TARRAGONA — CHURCH

Pl. de la Seu — ☎97 723 86 85 museu.diocesa.arquebisbattarragona.cat

While lacking the high-octane wowing power of some other Spanish cathedrals, the Catedral de Tarragona is an incredibly pleasant place to visit. The Museu Diocesà has the standard collection of Madonnas, reliquaries, and sarcophagi, but nothing as memorable as the alabaster altarpiece depicting scenes from the bad-ass life of St. Tecla, the patron saint of Tarragona, including a dramatic scene in which she is about to be torn apart by wild animals (we won't ruin the ending). The cloister is unusually large, unusually landscaped, and open for exploring.

#From C. Major, walk up the stairs leading to the cathedral, but instead of walking towards the cathedral, turn left onto C. Escrivanies Velles, then right onto C. Mare del Déu del Claustre. ***i*** *Audioguide (€0.50) available in Catalan, Spanish, English, French, German, and Italian.* $ *€3.80 (includes audioguide), students and seniors €2.80, ages 7-16 €1.20, under 7 free.* ⏰ *Open Mar 16-Oct 15 M 3-6pm, Tu-Sa 10am-6pm; Oct 16-Mar 15 M-Sa 10am-2pm. Mass M-F 11:30am; Sa 7:30pm; Su and holidays 9:30, 11am, and 12:30pm.*

MAQUETA DE TARRACO MODEL

Pl. del Pallol ☎97 725 37 59 www.museutgn.com

Unless you had room in your backpack for your toga, this scale model of Tarragona at its second-century peak is the best way to prepare for a day of seeing the Roman sights of Tarragona. It's also a chance to see some of the sights that you might not get to see without a car.

 # At the top of the hill leading from Pl. Font to C. Major, turn left onto C. Cavallers, which leads to Pl. Pallol. i Signs in Catalan and Spanish only. $ Free. ⏰ Open Easter-Sept M 9am-3pm, Tu-Sa 9am-9pm, Su and holidays 9am-3pm; Oct-Easter M 10am-3pm, Tu-Sa 9am-7pm, Su and holidays 10am-3pm.

CIRC ROMÀ ROMAN RUINS

Rambla Vella ☎97 724 22 20 www.museutgn.com

Less impressive than the amphitheater but still worth a visit, this circus once held chariot races attended by 25,000 spectators. Only a small portion remains; to give you an idea of how big it was, there's a bit of it to the left of the hill that goes from the Pl. Font to C. Major. After entering from the end of Rambla Vella, you will face three arches (there were once 56), one of which is completley original. The best views of the ruins are actually from the street on C. Sant Oleguer. There, you get a full view of what's left of the circus; to the left is a painted image of a hypothetical complete building that orients you far better than the wordy informational panels inside ever could.

 # Proceed along Rambla Vella toward the sea; just before the end, take the diagonal left towards the big Roman ruin. i MHT global ticket sold and accepted. $ €3.15, students and seniors €1.60, under 16 free. ⏰ Open Easter-Sept Tu-Sa 10am-9pm, Su 10am-3pm; Oct-Easter Tu-Sa 9am-7pm, Su 10am-3pm.

FOOD

The *parte alta* is filled with restaurants that are mostly tourist-oriented, although on the quieter streets away from the main sights there are a few pricier restaurants for locals. There are also many cafes along the Rambla Nova and on the streets leading from the *parte alta* to the Rambla Nova, especially C. Méndez Núñez. The fishermen's neighborhood, El Serrallo, in the southwest of the city, has many seafood restaurants along C. Trafalgar.

EL TIBERI BUFFET, SPANISH $$$

C. d'en Martí d'Ardenya, 5 ☎97 724 28 96 www.eltiberi.com

Bring your appetite to this all-you-can-eat buffet of Catalan and Spanish specialties. Try not to bring too much thirst, though—the sticker price doesn't include drinks, and the staff doesn't look very kindly upon fans of *agua del grifo* (tap water). The buffet in the center of one of the two surprisingly elegant dining floors groans under the weight of the periodically refreshed hot and cold dishes. Since some of the hot dishes can end up out there for a while, sit near the buffet so you can see what's freshest and swoop in. Despite the considerable scale of the operation, many of the dishes are prepared quite well, including a seafood paella that doesn't discriminate against solo travelers and a *botifarra* so juicy you could get sausage juice in your eye upon cutting it (theoretically, of course). Try and save room for the impressive array of desserts.

 # From the Pl. Font, facing the Ajuntament, turn left onto the street closer to the Ajuntament and continue straight. 3 blocks after Rambla Nova, go down the hill to the right of the escalator. i Drinks not included. $ Buffet Tu-Sa 1-4pm €11.25, Tu-Sa 8-11:30pm €12.25, Su 1-4pm €12.50. Water €1.85. 8% IVA not included. ⏰ Open Tu-Sa 1-4pm and 8-11:30pm, Su 1-4pm.

THE BURGER BAR SANDWICHES $

C. de Sant Fructuós, 5 ☎97 789 36 36

Great for a quick, cheap meal in the *parte alta*, The Burger Bar serves giant burgers and sandwiches (€3.50-4) just off the main square of the old town. For those who can't bring themselves to say the dreaded words "*una hamburguesa, por favor*," The Burger Bar also serves the much more Spanish-sounding (and arguably better) *lomito de ternera* (€4), a veal sandwich that takes an all-of-the-above approach to what should join it between the bread (lettuce, tomato, onion, ham, cheese, and a fried egg are all welcome).

Off of the Pl. Font. Facing the Ajuntament, turn left onto the street closest to the Ajuntament. Or, from the Rambla Nova, facing the sea, turn left onto C. Comte de Rius, which will lead to C. Sant Fructuós after Rambla Vella. $ Burgers and sandwiches €3.50-4. Tapas €1. Beer €1. Open daily 9am-11:30pm.

TALLER DE CUINA CATALAN $$$

C. de la Merceria, 34 ☎97 723 94 21 www.tallerdecuina.es

One of the few marginally affordable restaurants in the *parte alta* with more locals than tourists, this restaurant rings with the sound of crystal glasses clinking together and other sounds equally as foreign as the Catalan greetings of the waitstaff. You probably can't afford this place except during lunchtime, and then only by reaching deep into your pockets, but it's worth it—the menu changes weekly based on what's fresh, and the fruits and vegetables taste like it; you'll half expect the waitress to come out with dirt on her apron from the garden in the backyard. Budget travelers will largely be confined to what's on the *menú del dia*, but pray to St. Tecla, patron saint of Tarragona, for the *ensalada de naranjas y frutos secos* (salad with orange and dried fruit)—or just resign yourself to a dinner of bread and water and order it à la carte (€12). It will forever redefine how good a salad can be, although recovering chocolate addicts should note that this probably has as much to do with the chocolate in the vinaigrette as with the divinely sweet orange slices.

From the base of the stairs leading from C. Mayor to the cathedral, facing the cathedral, turn right onto C. Merceria and left at the Pl. Forum. $ Lunch menú M-F €15.50, Sa-Su €18. Dinner menú M-F €25. Menú degustación Sa-Su (all day) €33. Open June-Oct Tu-Sa 1:15-4pm and 8:30-11pm; Nov-May Tu 1:15-4pm, W-Sa 1:15-4pm and 8:30-11pm, Su 1:15-4pm.

L'ANCORA SEAFOOD $$

C. de Trafalgar, 25 ☎97 724 28 06

Whether in the classroom, at the movie theater, or (especially) on the bus, people tend to spread out as much as possible. El Serrallo, Tarragona's fishermen's neighborhood, seems to have the power to negate those basic instincts. Instead of spreading out over the dozens of restaurants lining the sea-facing C. Trafalgar, everyone seems to pack in under the terrace of L'Ancora for fresh seafood, from the shrimp cocktail (€7.40) to more filling dishes like the grilled salmon (€11.90) and the *paella de mariscos* (€12). Eat inside the ship-like interior, complete with portholes, for a less overwhelmingly loud setting and a peek at the fryer and all those other kitchen tools used to churn out delicious seafood dishes for hundreds of hungry tourists.

From Pl. Imperial Tarraco, proceed along C. Pere Martell (to the right of the bus station) for 10-15min., then turn right onto C. Trafalgar. $ Seafood dishes €3.50-21.50. Open daily 12:30-5:30pm and 7:30pm-12:30am.

LES VOLTES SPANISH $$

C. del Trinquet Vell, 12 ☎97 723 06 51 www.restaurantlesvoltes.cat

When was the last time you had lunch in a UNESCO World Heritage Site? Dine under the vaults of the Roman circus at this restaurant. The *menú del dia* includes both wine and water (make it clear you want both) and the Roman delicacy of potato chips. The food is fine, though certainly nothing special, and is clearly secondary to the dramatically lit setting. The cringe-worthy attempts at spicing the place up a little (chariot races painted on front wall, statue of a Roman soldier decked out in shiny plastic armor) do their best to detract from the incredible atmosphere, but can't quite do it (it can't hurt to face the other way, though). The service isn't exactly subtle—the waitresses' heads pop up behind a curtain like a Whac-A-Mole to see if you've finished your course—but in a setting like this, who cares?

➜ From the end of Pl. Font opposite the Ajuntament, turn right at the base of hill leading up to C. Major. $ Menú del dia (served M-F 1-3:30pm) €10.80. Menús available daily at both lunch and dinner €18 and €24. Entrees €7-19. ⏰ Open Tu-Th 1-3:30pm and 8:30-10:30pm, F-Sa 1-3:30pm and 8:30-11pm, Su 1-3:30pm.

NIGHTLIFE

In the *parte alta*, the restaurants of the Pl. de la Font double as bars at night. After these close, the party moves out to the pubs and clubs of the *parte baja* and the Port Esportiu, a port with a dozen clubs of different shapes, sizes, music, and clientele.

SALA GOLFUS CLUB

Port Esportiu

This club, regally overlooking the rest of the Port Esportiu, draws a young crowd enthusiastic about Top 40, house, and reggaetón—and even more enthusiastic about the insanely cheap drinks. There's no cover, except during the periodically hosted rock and hip-hop concerts and whenever a big-name DJ from Barcelona rolls into town. The place doesn't fill up until 3am, but if you come early, you'll get a chance to say hello to the friendly yellow lab before they put him away for the night.

*➜ From the Pl. Font, facing the Ajuntament, turn left onto the street closer to the Ajuntament and proceed straight and down the stairs as it turns into C. Pau del Protectorat; follow this street to the end, and turn left after the train tracks. **i** Sometimes closed for private events. $ Beer €2-2.50. Cocktails €3-4. Shots €1. Cover €5 (includes 1 drink) when important DJ spins. ⏰ Open June-Sept Th-Sa midnight-6:45am, Oct-May Th-Sa midnight-6am.*

LES GOLFES CLUB CLUB

C. de la Pau del Protectorat, 5 www.lesgolfesclub.com

With an indie rock playlist and a more alternative vibe than the clubs of the Port Esportiu, this club is one of the highlights of the *parte baja* nightlife scene. Foreign exchange students seem to dig it and are a frequent presence on regular nights (no cover), as well as the two monthly concerts and the two Fridays a month when prominent DJs from Barcelona spin under the club's sky-high ceilings.

*➜ From the Pl. Font, facing the Ajuntament, turn left onto the street closer to the Ajuntament and proceed straight and down the stairs as it turns into C. Pau del Protectorat; the club is on the right. **i** Cover during concerts or when there's a prominent DJ from Barcelona. $ Beer €3. Cocktails €6-9. ⏰ Open Th-Sa midnight-5am.*

SALA EL CAU BAR, CLUB

C. del Trinquet Vell, 2 ☎97 723 98 12 www.elcau.net

Bread and circuses may have satisfied the Romans, but to keep the modern Tarragona visitor happy, we all know what's really necessary—👍**mojitos** and circuses. Enjoy a mojito or a host of other cocktails under a vault of the old Roman circus at this bar to a different soundtrack every night of the week. The pub also hosts frequent concerts and the occasional magic show.

*➜ From the end of Pl. Font opposite the Ajuntament, turn right at the base of hill leading up to C. Major. **i** M house music, Tu reggae, Th nu-disco, F-Sa indie rock, Su electronic. $ Beer €3. Cocktails €6. ⏰ Open daily 11pm-5am. Opens at 9pm on nights with concerts.*

24 BAR

C. Major, 24 ☎97 724 12 49

A great place for a nightcap during the week after the Pl. Font has quieted down, this bar has more than 100 types of gin. It feels like a lounge during the week, with intimate seating areas in the back, but on the weekend a DJ spins pop hits and music from the '80s and '90s—and the dance floor sees some action.

🚶 From the end of Pl. Font opposite the Ajuntament, proceed up the hill onto C. Major. $ Beer €3. Cocktails €7-15. ⏰ Open M-Th 10pm-3am, F-Sa 10pm-5am, Su 10pm-3am.

GIOCONDA BAR, CLUB

Port Esportiu

This pub gets going a little earlier than much of the other nightlife in the Port Esportiu, though later than the club packed with teenagers across the street. A crowd of mixed ages sips cocktails and moves their hips on the dance floor under the over-the-top light show as countless (okay, fine, 15) reproductions of the Mona Lisa look on either approvingly or disapprovingly—we're not sure which.

🚶 From the Pl. Font, facing the Ajuntament, turn left onto the street closer to the Ajuntament and proceed straight and down the stairs as it turns into C. Pau del Protectorat; follow this street to the end, and turn left after the train tracks. $ 1-drink minimum. Beer €3. Cocktails €3-8. ⏰ Open daily 12:30am-6am.

ARTS AND CULTURE

FESTES DE SANTA TECLA CITYWIDE

http://santatecla.tarragona.cat

In theory a festival in honor of Santa Tecla, the patron saint of Tarragona, these *festes* are really a tribute to traditional dances, farcical theater, and ★**human towers,** or *castells*. Tarragona is known worldwide in the human tower community (there's one of those, right?) for its enormous human castles and the final day's awesome *pilar caminant* (walking pillar), an epic 15min. parade of four-person high towers from the Pl. de la Seu up stairs and down steep hills that finishes up in front of the Ajuntament in the Pl. de la Font. Even if you're not in town during the festival, you can see artifacts and learn about its history at the **Casa de la Festa** (Via Augusta, 4 ☎977 22 00 86 🚶 Follow Rambla Vella towards the sea and turn left at the traffic circle onto Via Augusta $ Free ⏰ Open F 5-9pm, Sa 10am-2pm and 5-9pm, Su 10am-2pm) and get a taste of the scale of the human tower spectacles from the statue on the Rambla Nova.

⏰ Sept 15-24.

ESSENTIALS

Practicalities

- **TOURIST OFFICES:** The main **municipal tourist office** is located on C. Major, right before the cathedral, and provides information on the city and province of Tarragona (C. Major, 39 ☎97 725 07 95 www.tarragonaturisme.cat 🚶 At the end of C. Major next to the cathedral. From the bus station, take the 3rd right off of Pl. Imperial Tarraco onto Rambla Nova, then take the 8th left onto C. Sant Agustí, which leads to the Pl. Font; cross the plaza diagonally and walk up the steep hill, which turns into C. Major. Or, from the train station, turn right onto Passeig d'Espanya and continue as it turns into Vial de William J. Bryant. Turn left (uphill) at the fork and turn left at the traffic circle onto Rambla Vella, then take the 2nd right onto C. Portalet and continue straight onto a steep hill, which turns into C. Major. *i* Catalan, Spanish, English, French, German, and Italian spoken. ⏰ Open June 23-Sept 24 M-Sa 10am-8pm, Su 10am-2pm; Sept 25-June 22 M-Sa 10am-2pm and 3-5pm, Su 10am-2pm); **satellite offices** are located on Rambla Nova (🚶 at the intersection with C. Sant Francesc/C. Unió ⏰ Open M-Sa 10am-2pm and 4-7pm, Su 10am-2pm) and the Camp de Mart. (⏰ Open Sa-Su 10am-2pm.) The **regional tourist office** has much of the same information about the city and province of Tarragona, as well as information about the rest of Catalonia. (C. Fortuny, 4 ☎97 723 34 15 www.catalunya.com ⏰ Open M-F 9am-7pm, Sa 9am-2pm.)

- **TOURS:** The tourist office does not organize tours but gives out a helpful "Guided Visits and Routes" guide that summarizes the many tours offered by private companies. Two of the biggest companies are **Àgora Tarraco** (☎97 724 88 66 www.turismotarragona.com) and **Itinere.** (☎97 723 96 57 www.turismedetarragona.com.) These companies and others offer themed tours, including Roman Tarragona, medieval Tarragona, and night-time Tarragona, that are usually on weekends, last around 1-2hr., and cost around €10.
- **LUGGAGE STORAGE:** Luggage storage is not available at the bus or train stations, though some travelers report that the main municipal tourist office on C. Major is willing to let tourists leave their bag there during office hours if they ask nicely.
- **CURRENCY EXCHANGE: La Caixa** exchanges major foreign currencies (Rambla Nova, 100 ☎97 719 06 40 www.lacaixa.es ➜ From Pl. Imperial Tarraco, proceed along Rambla Nova 2 blocks; it's right after the intersection with Av. Ramón y Cajal ⏰ Open May-Sept M-F 8:15am-2pm; Oct-Apr M-W 8:15am-2pm, Th 8:15am-2pm and 4:30-7:45pm, F 8:15am-2pm), as do most of the banks along Rambla Nova.
- **INTERNET ACCESS:** The **Biblioteca Hemeroteca Municipal,** next door to the tourist office, has free Wi-Fi and computers with internet access. (C. Major, 39 ☎97 725 18 61 ➜ At the end of C. Major next to the cathedral, next door to the tourist office. ⏰ Open June-Sept 10am-3pm, Oct-May 10am-7pm.) **Cyber Tarraco** has Wi-Fi and computers with internet access. (C. Major, 34 ☎87 705 12 52 ➜ Across the street from the library and tourist office. $ €0.25 per 15min. ⏰ Open daily 10am-11pm.) Ask at the tourist office for a list of all public places with free Wi-Fi.
- **POST OFFICE:** The central post office is located in the Pl. Corsini, near the Mercat Central. (☎97 725 19 46 www.correos.es ➜ From Pl. Font, facing the Ajuntament, turn left onto either street, then turn right onto Rambla Nova, then turn left onto C. Canyelles and walk 2 blocks. ⏰ Open M-F 8:30am-8:30pm, Sa 9:30am-2pm.)
- **POSTAL CODE:** 43001

Emergency

- **EMERGENCY NUMBER:** ☎112
- **POLICE: Municipal Police.** (Av. Prat de la Riba, 37 ☎092 or ☎97 724 03 45 ➜ From Pl. Imperial Tarraco, proceed 1 block along Av. Prat de la Riba.) Regional Police: **Mossos d'Esquadra.** (C. Doctor Mallafré Guasch, 7 ☎97 763 53 00 ➜ From Pl. Imperial Tarraco, proceed along Rambla del President Lluís Companys, which will turn into Rambla del President Francesc Macià; at the traffic circle, turn right onto C. Doctor Mallafré Guasch. Or, bus #8 from Rambla Vella.) **National Police.** (Pl. Orleans ☎091 or ☎97 724 98 44 ➜ From Pl. Imperial Tarraco, proceed along Rambla del President Lluis Companys and take the 2nd left onto C. President Josep Irla, which leads to Pl. Orleans.)
- **HOSPITAL: Hospital Universitari de Tarragona Joan XXIII** (C. Doctor Mallafré Guasch, 4 ☎97 729 58 00 www.hj23.org ➜ From Pl. Imperial Tarraco, proceed along Rambla del President Lluís Companys, which will turn into Rambla del President Francesc Macià; at the traffic circle, turn right onto C. Doctor Mallafré Guasch. Or, bus #8 from Rambla Vella.)
- **PHARMACY:** Pharmacies are located throughout Tarragona; one is conveniently located at Rambla Nova, 55. (☎97 722 14 30 www.farmaciaferminsanz.com ➜ At intersection with C. Comte de Rius. ⏰ Open M-F 8am-10pm, Sa 9am-2pm and 4-9pm.) Outside of regular pharmacy hours, check the window of any pharmacy, a local newspaper, or www.coft.org/guardies for a list of pharmacies with extended hours that day.

Getting There

Tarragona is well served by both buses and trains, since it lies on the routes from many major cities to Barcelona. Depending on where you're coming from, either the bus or the train could be cheaper—be sure to check out all your options.

BY BUS

The bus station is located in the Pl. Imperial Tarraco. (☎97 722 91 26 ➜ At the end of Rambla Nova farthest away from the old town and the sea.) **ALSA** (☎90 242 22 42 www.alsa.es) runs buses from: Barcelona ($ €8.10 ⏰ 1½hr., 8 per day 9am-9:30pm); Bilbao ($ €40 ⏰ 7½hr.; M-F 9:30am, Sa at 6:30am and 9:30am, Su 9:30am); Girona ($ €21 ⏰ 4¾hr., daily 8:45am); Madrid ($ €37 ⏰ 7hr., at 12:30pm and 11pm); Sevilla ($ €85 ⏰ 14hr., daily 4:15pm); and Valencia ($ €21-24 ⏰ 4hr., 8 per day 7am-4:30am).

BY TRAIN

Tarragona has two train stations. The train station in the city center (Passeig d'Espanya ☎90 243 23 43 www.adif.es ⏰ Open 5am-midnight), behind the beach and next to the Port Esportiu, receives regional and national trains, while the Camp de Tarragona station, 8mi. outside of the city center, receives faster but more expensive high-speed trains. If you are buying tickets on RENFE's website, be sure to select "Tarragona (*)" from the drop-down menu to ensure that you will be shown trains arriving at both stations. **Empresa Plana** (☎97 721 44 75 www.empresaplana.es) runs buses between the Camp de Tarragona train station and Tarragona in both directions. ($ €1.55. ⏰ 20-25min.; from train station to Tarragona M-F 28 per day 6:20am-11:19pm, Sa 22 per day 6:20am-11:19pm, Su 19 per day 8:20-11:24pm; from Tarragona to train station M-F 24 per day 6am-11:05pm, Sa 21 per day 6am-10:05pm, Su 19 per day 7:50am-11:10pm.) **RENFE** (☎90 232 03 20 www.renfe.es) trains arrive at the **Tarragona** train station from: Barcelona ($ €7.40-21 ⏰ 1hr.; M-F 18 per day 7am-10:20pm, Sa 16 per day 7am-10:20pm, Su 17 per day 8:30am-10:20pm); Girona ($ €20-28 ⏰ 2-3hr., at 10:42am and 8:42pm 10:50pm); Madrid ($ €38-49 ⏰ 7½hr., at 8:17am and 10:50pm); Sevilla ($ €67 ⏰ 10hr., daily 9am); and Valencia ($ €31-38 ⏰ 2-2¾hr.; M-F 15 per day 5:10am-7:55pm, Sa 13 per day 5:10am-7:55pm, Su 14 per day 7:53am-11:04pm). Trains arrive at the **Camp de Tarragona** train station from: Barcelona ($ €16-36 ⏰ 30min.; M-F 29 per day 6:05am-10:10pm, Sa 27 per day 6:05am-10:10pm, Su 27 per day 7:35am-10:10pm); Madrid ($ €90 ⏰ 2½hr.; M-F 9 per day 5:50am-8:25pm, Sa-Su 9 per day 7:30am-8:25pm); and Sevilla ($ €63-125 ⏰ 4¾hr., 2 per day 9am and 4pm).

BY PLANE

The closest airport is the **Aeropuerto de Reus,** located 8mi. outside of the city (REU; Autovía Tarragona-Reus ☎91 321 10 00 or ☎90 240 47 04 www.aena.es), which receives flights from the UK, Ireland, Germany, and Belgium, although many routes are seasonal. **Hispano Igualadina** (☎90 229 29 00 www.igualadina.com) runs buses between the Tarragona bus station and the airport in both directions. ($ €3 ⏰ 15min., coordinated with flight schedules.)

Getting Around

The cheapest and easiest way to get around Tarragona is to **walk.** The city's bus system (www.emtanemambtu.cat $ €1.30) is mainly used by tourists to get to the Pont de Diable, served by bus #5. Taxis are available at the taxi stands on Rambla Vella near the Pl. Font, on Rambla Nova at C. Sant Francesc, and at the train and bus stations; or call **Taxis Tarragona** (☎97 722 14 14).

valencia *valència* ☎96

With the energy of Madrid, the warmth of Sevilla, and the artsy spunk of Barcelona, Valencia is a smaller city that combines the best of its neighbors through a mix of extremes. Layers of history unfold with a short walk through the city, whether from the almost year-round extravagant costumes and sword-slinging of the Moor-and-Christian celebrations or from the menus dotted with regional language Valencià, both of which are remnants from the clash of Moorish invaders and Catalan crusaders that left an indelible mark both on the city's culture and architectural landscape. Old city gates overlook the plethora of church belltowers scattered throughout the city, while incredible ever-changing street art and quirky architecture like the Art Deco theater shake up the antique charm of plazas in the **Ciutat Vella.** Winding around the northern boundary of the old city is the lush **Jardín del Turia,** and it's hard to believe that not long ago these grassy paths were instead the Río Turia, diverted after the river flooded the city with 2m of water in 1957. Located along its former banks is a mix of the best of the old city's artistic treasures, a young and hip university area bustling with student life, and the ultramodern, ultra-contrasting architectural marvel of Calatrava's **City of Arts and Sciences.** Despite its beauty and respectable pedigree, the town is anything but a reliquary of heartwarming buildings. Cuisine and culture are matched with incredible beaches, and the oranges and Valencian tomatoes will have any produce-lover in rapture for weeks. Sticky paella dots nearly every table in town (as it should—Valencia is its birthplace), while flamenco fills even the smallest clubs.

ORIENTATION

The most convenient way to enter the city is via the Ⓜ**Xátiva** or Ⓜ**Calle Colon** Metro stations, or by the train to **Estación del Norte. Avenida Marqués de Sotelo** runs from the train station and the **Plaza de Toros** through the **Plaza del Ayuntamiento,** the center of town. Take a slight right once you get to the end of this triangle-shaped plaza to walk along **Calle San Vicente Mártir,** which leads you to the most bustling areas of town, including the center of architecture, restaurants, and tourism, the **Plaza de la Reina.** To the left upon entering this plaza is a land of shops and pedestrians around **Plaza Doctor Collado,** and continuing inward will take you past the **Mercat Central** into the old city. Plan on bringing a map if you'll be spending time on these confusing streets. To the right upon entering Plaza Reina is **Calle de la Paz,** a big and bright road leading to impressively ritzy architecture and higher-end shops. Continuing straight to the end of the Plaza Reina, past the cathedral, will eventually get you to the old riverbed-turned-park **Jardín del Turia,** and with a right and a 3km walk (or bike or bus ride) you'll make your way along the university area to the modern marvel of the **City of Arts and Sciences.**

ACCOMMODATIONS

▨ **RED NEST HOSTEL**   HOSTEL $
    C. de la Paz, 36   ☎96 342 71 68 www.nesthostelsvalencia.com
Bright and vibrant, this hostel is so popular—and rightfully so—that it has two locations within a 5min. walk of each other. A mix of large private and dormitory-style rooms features modern decor, windows with beautiful views to the street, and guests so social you'll be juggling 15 names in your head five minutes after arriving. The inside of the hostel is decorated like a cheery Rubik's cube, only with copious bathrooms and a fully stocked kitchen. A/C in the rooms is sometimes spotty, but a huge fifth-floor lounge and bar keeps things chilly for those afraid of melting away.
    ✈ *From the train station, walk along Av. Marqués de Sotelo and follow it as it takes a slight right and turns into C. San Vicente Mártir, which leads to the Pl. Reina. From the plaza, turn right onto C. Paz; it's a 5-10min. walk to the hostel.* ℹ *Breakfast included. Sheets included. Free (though spotty) Wi-Fi. Towel and padlock deposit €5 each. Kitchen available.* ⑤ *High season dorms €17-26; doubles €60-65; low season €12-16/19.50.* ◩ *Reception 24hr.*

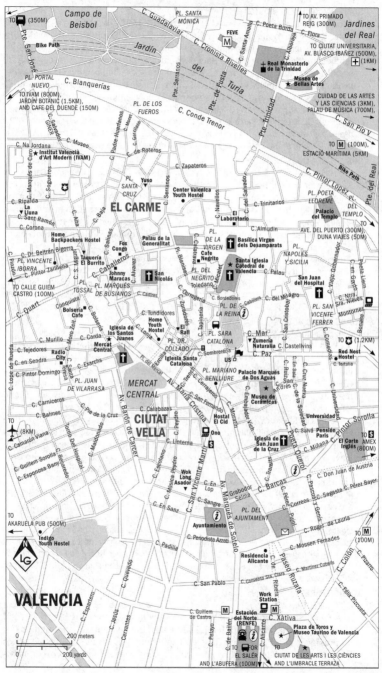

valencia map

HOME BACKPACKERS HOSTEL HOSTEL $

Pl. de Vicente Iborra, 46 ☎96 391 37 97 www.homehostelsvalencia.com

Four floors of rooms range from cozy six-person dorms to massive double-vaulted 16-person airplane hangars. The social life centers around the equipped kitchen and the sunny terrace. Backpackers are drawn by the low prices, vibrant social scene, and pop-art murals that link it to its slightly more mature older brother, Home Youth Hostel. It's also very close to the raging nightlife of C. Caballeros—so feel free to let out your inner party animal.

‡ From Pl. Tossal, proceed along C. San Miguel to Pl. Vicente Iborra, then cross the plaza diagonally. i Sheets €2, towels free. Earplugs €0.20. Lockers in rooms free; daytime luggage storage €2-8 depending on size and for how long you store it. Spanish, English, French, German, and Italian spoken. $ 16-bed dorms €9-14; 6-, 8-, and 12-bed dorms €11-20. ⏰ Reception 24hr.

HOME YOUTH HOSTEL HOSTEL $$

C. de la Lonja, 4 ☎96 391 62 29 www.homehostelsvalencia.com

All the perks of a *pensión* (large, private rooms and no need to climb up to the top bunk) with the perks of a youth hostel (a crowd that's actually fun, an equipped kitchen, and punchy decor that will amuse rather than lull you to sleep). Young and social clientele populate the funky leather chairs of the pop-art-clad living room. Rooms facing outward offer an incredible in-your-face view of the Baroque La Lonja across the street.

‡ From the train station, walk along Av. del Marqués de Sotelo and take a slight right onto C. San Vicente Mártir, then take the third left onto C. Derechos; the hostel is in the plaza. i Mixed and female dorms available. Free Wi-Fi and computers with internet access. Sheets €2, towel included. Washer and dryer €3.50. Kitchen. Free lockers in rooms. Extend stay until 6pm on checkout day (Su-Th only) €5. $ 3- to 4-bed dorms €14-20; doubles €18-28. ⏰ Reception 24hr.

INDIGO YOUTH HOSTEL HOSTEL $

C. de Guillem de Castro, 64 ☎96 315 39 88 www.indigohostel.com

A place to meet fellow travelers and save money where raging is the exception rather than the rule, this hostel draws a young crowd more relaxed and less party-hardy than what you'll find at many of Valencia's other cheap accommodations. Guests still socialize on the orange couches of the common area, but you're more likely to see them dutifully chatting about how long they've been in Valencia and where to get good paella than to see massive groups flooding out at dusk and trickling back at dawn. If that one conversation is of a highly stimulating nature and you find yourself planning to get freaky-freaky, avoid the squeaky-squeaky by dropping a few extra euro on a 4-bed dorm, which is gloriously bunk bed-free. But easy there, tiger—don't wear yourself out too much, since the only air conditioning comes from fans and there's no breakfast to replenish all those calories in the morning. Also, your dormmates will hate you.

‡ From the train station, turn left onto C. Xàtiva and continue as it becomes C. Guillem de Castro and curves to the right. Or, from the bus station, turn left onto Av. Menéndez Pidal and cross the next bridge, then take a diagonal right onto C. Guillem de Castro. i Free Wi-Fi and computers with internet access. All rooms with shared bath. Female-only 8-bed dorm. Kitchen with free tea and coffee. Common area with TV. Sheets included, towel rental €1. Laundry service €5.50. Key deposit €5. Padlock deposit €10. Max. stay 10 days. Under 40 only, under 18 must be accompanied by adult. $ 10-bed dorms €12.50-18; 8-bed dorms €13.50-19; 4-bed dorms €15.50-22. Doubles €40-52; triples €54-72. ⏰ Reception 24hr.

PENSIÓN PARIS HOTEL $$

C. de Salvá, 12, 1st fl. ☎96 352 67 66 www.pensionparis.com

"It's a girl!" scream the pink walls of this *pensión*, while the baby-blue doors and sheets respectfully beg to differ. Regardless of the outcome, congratulations!—on picking a hotel where you'll sleep like a baby (minus the crying, we hope) in large, immaculately kept rooms. Quiet rooms with some huge corner suites (think two balconies) are perfect for those looking for a calm, cheap, and private refuge from the city while still being in the middle of it all.

✈ *From the train station, turn right and proceed along C. Xàtiva, take a slight left at the fork onto C. Cristóbal Colón, then take the 1st left onto C. Pasqual i Genis, then the 3rd right onto C. Pintor Sorolla, then take the 1st left and immediately turn left again onto C. Salvá; the hotel is on the left.* **i** *Free Wi-Fi. Free coffee and tea 8:30-10am.* Ⓢ *Singles with sink €23; doubles with sink €34, with shower €40, with bathroom €42; triples with sink €50, with shower €54.* Ⓠ *Reception 8am-midnight.*

CENTER-VALENCIA YOUTH HOSTEL
HOSTEL $

C. de Samaniego, 18   ☎96 391 49 15 www.center-valencia.com

Get out your smoking jacket and practice your Charleston—prohibition is alive and well at Center-Valencia Youth Hostel, which forbids drinking alcohol anywhere in the hostel, from the bunk beds of the compact mixed dorms to the loungy white couches of the common room. Thankfully, eating is still allowed—at least the included breakfast of muffins, tostadas, and cereal. Those bummed out about not getting to trip and stumble in the bathroom need not despair; some of the bathrooms have floors so uneven and bumpy they call the builder's adherence to hostel temperance rules into serious doubt. There's a rooftop terrace, but unless you like ugly terraces and hanging out next to washing machines, not even harder drugs could make it very appealing.

✈ *From the bus station, turn left onto Av. Menéndez Pidal and cross the 3rd bridge (Pont de Serrans), then proceed straight along C. Serrans (behind the building facing the bridge) and take the 2nd left onto C. Samaniego and follow it as it takes a hard left.* **i** *Breakfast included. Free Wi-Fi and computers with internet access. A/C. Washer €3, dryer €3. Sheets free, towel rental €2. Lockers and kitchen available. Key deposit €5.* Ⓢ *12-bed dorms €9-15; 8-bed €12-22; 6-bed €12-22; 4-bed €14.50-22. Doubles €35-60.* Ⓠ *Reception 24hr.*

RESIDENCIA ALICANTE
HOTEL $$

C. de Ribera, 8   ☎96 351 22 96 www.hostalicante.com

Standard *hostal*-style rooms with TV close to the train station. The rooms with private bath have air conditioning as opposed to fans, but you run the risk of having to climb over the toilet to get to the shower.

✈ *From the train station, walk along C. Marqués de Sotelo and take the 1st right onto C. Convento de Santa Clara. Take a left onto C. Ribera—it's next to a busy cafe.* **i** *Free Wi-Fi. All rooms with sink and TV.* Ⓢ *Singles €25-35; doubles €35-45; triples €50-60.* Ⓠ *Reception 24hr.*

HOSTAL EL CID
HOTEL $$$

C. de Cerrajeros, 13   ☎96 392 23 23 hostalelcid.blogspot.com

Besides the charming tiled staircase leading to reception, nothing in this quaint, stylish pension is befitting of the rustic plaster and dark-wood imagery that the name provokes. Homey doubles with big beds are cooled by fans during the summer.

✈ *From the train station, walk along Av. Marqués de Sotelo and follow it to take a slight right onto C. San Vicente Mártir, then take the 2nd left onto C. Cerrajeros.* **i** *Linens and towels included.* Ⓢ *Doubles €38-43, with bath €45-52; triples €45-50/55-60.* Ⓠ *Reception 9am-7pm.*

SIGHTS

Old buildings, modern buildings, free museums, really-darn-expensive museums, beaches—sight-wise, it seems like Valencia's got it all. The old city and the area around the **Plaza de la Reina** are filled with beautiful old buildings; Gothic architecture fans shouldn't miss the **Torres de Quart**, the twin towers of the former wall that defended the city (C. Guillem de Castro, 89 ☎96 352 54 78 ✈ From Pl. Tossal, proceed along C. Quart Ⓢ €2, students and seniors €1, under 7 free; free Sa-Su and holidays Ⓠ Open Tu-Sa 10am-2pm and 4:30-8:30pm, Su and holidays 10am-3pm) and the **Lonja de la Seda**, a Gothic silk market and UNESCO World Heritage Site (Pl. Mercat, ☎96 352 54 78 ✈ From Pl. Reina, proceed along C. San Vicente Mártir and take the 5th left onto Av. María Cristina Ⓢ €2, students and seniors €1, under 7 free; free Sa-Su and holidays

⏰ Open summer M 10am-3pm, Tu-Sa 10am-2pm and 4:30-8:30pm, Su 10am-3pm; rest of year closed M). There's also proof aplenty that currently functioning buildings can be pretty too, and free: the main **post office** is beautiful inside and out (Pl. Ayuntamiento, 24 ☎96 351 23 70 www.correos.es 🚏 Across the plaza from the Ayuntamiento ⏰ Open M-F 8:30am-8:30pm, Sa 9:30am-2pm), and the **Estació del Nord,** with (fake) Valencian oranges decorating its gorgeous Art Nouveau façade, is one of the prettiest train stations in Spain (C. Xátiva, 24 ☎96 352 02 02 ⏰ Open daily 4:45am-1am). The city has numerous museums, many of which are free; of those not listed here, the **Museu de Belles Arts** (C. San Pío V, 9 ☎96 387 03 00 www.museobellasartesvalencia.gva.es 🚏 On the other side of the Jardines del Turia, across the Puente de la Trinidad. $ Free ⏰ Open M 11am-5pm, Tu-Su 10am-7pm) and the **Museo Histórico Municipal** (Pl. del Ayuntamiento, 1 ☎96 352 54 78 🚏 Enter through main façade of Ayuntamiento $ Free ⏰ Open M-F 9am-2pm) might be worth the lost beach time.

CIUTAT DE LES ARTS I LES CIÈNCIES ARCHITECTURE, MUSEUM

Av. Autopista del Saler, 1 ☎90 210 00 31 www.cac.es

Rising from perfectly blue reflecting pools like a Roger Moore-era Bond villain's lair, the futuristic blue and white structures of the City of the Arts and Sciences feel a world away from the winding streets, shaded plazas, and antique charm of the rest of Valencia. Designed almost entirely by world-renowned Spanish architect **Santiago Calatrava,** this 350,000 sq. m artistic, scientific, and cultural complex is a mini-city entirely of its own. When the center's first building, the **Palau de les Arts,** isn't busy serving as Boba Fett's headgear, it hosts opera, dance, and musical performances (and is only accessible with tickets to a performance or through a guided tour). Next is the eye-shaped **Hemisfèric,** the largest movie theater in Spain, which shows IMAX movies and laser shows and doubles as a planetarium. After this, on the left is the dinosaur-resembling and highly enjoyable **Museu de les Ciències Príncep Felip,** while on the right is the expansive white spine of the **Umbracle,** innocuous by day, but springing into a thriving club at night. Last but not least (especially from your wallet's perspective) is Spain's largest aquarium, **L'Oceanographic,** with over 45,500 aquatic creatures. Though prices for admission to the ocean complex are steep, the dolphin shows are top-notch.

🚏 Bus #35 from C. Xàtiva, across the street from the Plaza de Toros. Or, bus #95 from Torres de Serranos. $ Museu de les Ciènces €7.85, seniors and under 12 €6.10; special exhibits may cost extra. L'Hemispheric tickets €7.85, seniors and under 12 €6.10. L'Oceanographic €24.90, seniors and under 12 €18.80. Combination tickets €32.90, seniors and under 12 €25. 15% student discount. Tickets can be bought at box office or at municipal tourist office branches. ⏰ Museu de les Ciènces open daily July-Sept 16 10am-9pm; Sept 17-June 10am-7pm. L'Hemisphéric runs shows daily on the hr. (except 2pm and sometimes 3pm) May-June 11am-9pm, July-Sept 11am-10pm, other months call for showtimes. L'Oceanographic open July 13-Aug daily 10am-midnight; Sept 1-Sept 15 daily 10am-8pm; Sept 16-Sept 30 M-F 10am-7pm, Sa 10am-8pm, Su 10am-7pm; Oct-June 17 M-F 10am-6pm, Sa 10am-8pm, Su 10am-6pm; June 18-June 28 M-F 10am-7pm, Sa 10am-8pm, Su 10am-7pm; June 29-July 12 daily 10am-8pm. Guided tours of Palau de les Arts Sept-July 15 daily 11:30am and 1pm.

SANTA IGLESIA CATEDRAL DE VALENCIA CHURCH

Pl. de la Reina ☎96 391 81 27 www.catedraldevalencia.es

Though many bell towers dot the skyline of Valencia, the Catedral's 70m **Micalet** (cathedral tower) is the biggest and baddest of them all. For €2 you can make the 202-stair trek to the top and see the view from above—Victor Hugo once counted 300 bell towers from the city, and if you stick around until the top of the hour then you will get to hear them in surround sound. The building dates back all the way to 1238, after the original cathedral was replaced by a mosque during Muslim rule in the eighth century. Though stepping inside is free, getting an up-close view of the ornate Gothic **Capilla de Sant Caliz** will cost you—but €4.50 is a small price to pay for getting up close and personal with a chalice purported to be the **Holy Grail** used by Christ at the Last Supper; hell, we'd pay thirty pieces of silver for that.

⇞ From Pl. Ayuntamiento, with the Ayuntamiento behind you, proceed along C. Marqués de Sotelo, then take a slight right onto C. San Vicente Mártir, which leads into the Pl. Reina; the church is at the opposite end. ℹ Audioguide in Spanish, Valencian, English, French, German, Italian, and Japanese. $ €4.50 (includes audioguide and museum), children and seniors €3; 5:30-6pm free. Tower €2, under 14 €1. ⏰ Museum open Apr-Oct M-F 10am-4:30pm and 5:30-6pm, Sa 10am-5:30pm, Su and holidays 2-5:30pm; Nov-Mar M-Sa 10am-5:30pm; last tickets sold 1hr. before close. Tower open daily 10am-7:30pm.

MUSEO NACIONAL DE CERÁMICA Y ARTES SUNTUARIAS MUSEUM

C. del Poeta Querol, 2 ☎96 351 63 92 mnceramica.mcu.es

If you've ever been dissatisfied by the percentage of exhibits in Spanish museums devoted to ceramics, don't worry—this museum is devoted entirely to ceramics. And this isn't your sleepy regional museum's endless array of identical clay plate fragments; it's a far more impressive, informative, and entertaining collection of sculptures, painted ceramic panels, architectural motifs, and, yes, some (gilded) bowls and plates. The pieces on display come mostly from Valencia, including a terrific collection of Moorish ceramics, though there are works from as far afield as Greece and China. Try not to get caught behind one of the many private tour groups, which can cramp the museum's small galleries and your style. Downstairs from the ceramics museum are the restored rooms of the Palacio de Dos Aguas, a former marquis's palace converted into a sort of My First Versailles.

⇞ From. Pl. Reina, on the opposite end from cathedral and with your back to it, proceed along C. San Vicente Mártir, take the 2nd left onto C. Ababia, and walk 2 blocks; the museum is at the intersection with C. Poeta Querol. ℹ Printed guide €3. $ €3, under 18 and EU and Latin American students and seniors free. Free admission Sa 4-8pm and Su. ⏰ Open Tu-Sa 10am-2pm and 4-8pm, Su 10am-2pm.

PLAZA DE TOROS AND MUSEO TAURINO DE VALENCIA MUSEUM

Pasaje del Doctor Serra, 10 ☎96 388 37 38 www.museotaurinovalencia.es

You won't graduate with a Doctorate in Tauromachy, but this museum offers an entertaining, if brief, look inside Valencian bullfighting. Articles in the permanent collection range from bullfighters' embroidered suits to a set of terrifying-looking branding irons to a life-sized stuffed bull ready to spring into action. Look for the multilingual briefs on the history, traditions, and methods of the sport, from the training of a young *picador* to the path of a bull from birth to (possible) pardoning in the ring. If you're not planning on attending a show, sneak peeks of the ring are also offered approximately every hour.

⇞ From C. Xàtiva, facing the Plaza de Toros, turn left and proceed along C. Xàtiva, then turn right into a covered area; the museum is halfway down to the right. ℹ Signs in Valencian, Spanish, and English. $ €2, students €1. ⏰ Open Tu-Su 10am-8pm. Guided tours of bullring 11am, noon, 1, 4:30, 5:30, 6pm (depends on event schedule).

MERCAT CENTRAL MARKET

Pl. del Mercat ☎www.mercadocentralvalencia.es

Home to the Mercado de Valencia, one of the biggest and oldest markets in Europe, this gorgeous modernist building has impressive ceramic ornamentation on its outside walls and an even more impressive dome inside. Get lost in the mazes of vendor stalls and the smells of fresh fruit, spices, and meats. The seafood portion of the market may be the most eye-catching (and smelly) part; not only does it have giant octopuses and live eels, it also has a smaller dome of its own.

⇞ From Pl. Reina, proceed along C. San Vicente Mártir and take the 5th left onto Av. María Cristina to Pl. Mercat. ⏰ Open M-Sa 7:30am-3pm.

INSTITUT VALENCIÀ D'ART MODERN (IVAM) MUSEUM

C. de Guillem de Castro, 118 ☎96 386 30 00 www.ivam.es

Come see a huge amount of contemporary art for less than you'd pay to rent a towel at your hostel. Permanent galleries house a famed collection of abstract works by 20th-century sculptor Julio González and artist Ignacio Pinazo, while temporary exhibits fill the remaining galleries with avant-garde works from the 20th and 21st centuries, including sculpture, painting, video, and architectural works. Even if only a few galleries are open during your visit (which may happen—this museum's exhibits are constantly in flux), it's well worth the trip.

⇄ From the Pl. Virgen (behind the cathedral), turn left onto C. Caballeros until it passes through the Pl. Tossal and becomes C. Quart. Walk under the Torres de Quart and turn right onto C. Guillem de Castro; the museum is on the right. Or, bus #5 from Pl. Ajuntament. ℹ Free Wi-Fi. $ €2, students €1; free on Su. ⏰ Open Tu-Su 10am-8pm. Library open M-Th 10am-2pm, F 10am-3pm.

THE GREAT OUTDOORS

Beaches

Chances are if it's summer and you're in Valencia, then your hostel will empty out midday as beach bums make the pilgrimage to the city's shores. The cream-colored sand fills with white umbrellas during the peak season, with sunbathers and outdoor enthusiasts splashing in the azure water and walking, biking, and running along the boardwalk that creeps along the expansive beach. If you're planning on walking or biking to the beach, **Avenida del Puerto** runs from the riverbed to the port, after which the beach is just a few blocks north; otherwise, bus #19 from the Pl. Ajuntament or buses #1, 2, 13, 15, 20, 23, 31, or 32 will drop you off seaside. **Las Arenas** is the most popular beach and is connected by the boardwalk to **La Malvarossa,** which provides water to the sea creatures of L'Oceanographic in the **City of Arts and Sciences.** Although you won't get any alone time by heading the 14km south to **Salér,** the view will be much more attractive, including a beautiful pebbled beach, white sand dunes, and a calm lagoon. **Autocares Herca** (☎96 349 12 50 www.autocaresherca.com) runs buses to **Salér** (⇄ 15th stop on the bus to El Perello. $ €1-1.10, depending on destination ⏰ 30min., daily every hr. 7am-9pm) from the intersection of Gran Vía de Germanías and C. Sueca. To get to the bus stop, exit the train station and take a right down C. Xàtiva, then turn right onto C. Ruzafa to Gran Vía. Look for a yellow MetroBus post. The ride to Salér can be jammed on weekends, and be sure to leave an entire day to make it worth the trip. For those adventurers seeking the beauty of Salér without the crowds, continue 10min. further on the bus for Salér and walk for another half hour along the shore—the undeveloped **La Devesa** sports a luxurious beach with a nudist section, as well as an incredible forest and lake. However, don't expect the beach bars and capitalist comforts of the city beaches—be sure to bring your own food, and be prepared to use the forest to take care of business. When looking for the return bus, head toward the intersection of the main road and the beginning of the forest trail.

Parks

JARDÍN DEL TURIA

Jardín del Turia is easy to stumble upon, wrapping around the northern portion of the old city where the river once flowed before it flooded one too many times and was diverted around the city. Lined with lush grass, pedestrian paths, and dogs off the leash, this park is now a favorite with joggers, bike tours, and locals out for a *paseo.*

⇄ North of the casco antiguo. From the Pl. Virgen (behind the cathedral), walk straight away from the cathedral on C. Navellos and follow it until the end.

JARDINES DEL REAL

Near the Museo de Bellas Artes and off of C. Sant Pío are the Jardines del Real, whose maze-like pathways smell sweetly of the fruit of the many orange trees and are dotted with nude sculptures both classical and modern. Kids will get a kick out of the playground, zoo, and hedge maze.

 # From the Pl. Virgen, proceed along C. Salvador (behind the basilica, the building to your right if the cathedral is behind you) to the end, then cross the Puente de la Trinidad and turn right onto C. Sant Pío V and enter just past the museum. ⏰ Open Apr-Oct 7:30am-9:30pm; Nov-Mar M-F 7:30am-8:30pm, Sa-Su and holidays 7:30am-9:30pm. Some doors may close earlier; the last to close is the one on Av. Blasco Ibáñez.

JARDÍ BOTÀNIC

C. de Quart, 80 ☎96 315 68 17 www.uv.es/jardibotanic

Jardí Botànic, run by the Botany School of the Universitat de València, is the most impressive of Valencia's parks, though it sadly has a price to match. The gardens are home to over 43,000 kinds of plants from a wide variety of climates. Budding horticulturists should be sure to bring along your dichotomy chart, while others can simply kick back and relax under the shade on one of their many benches. If you're swinging by after a long day of sightseeing, or you exhaust yourself by spending too much time in the heat of the Tropical Greenhouse, reward yourself with an in-depth study of the beans of the cacao tree—fermented, roasted, mixed with milk, and found inside the vending machines near the exit.

 # From Pl. Tossal, proceed along C. Quart through the Torres de Quart. Don't be fooled by your map, the C. Quart entrance is the only one. [$] €2, students and seniors €1, under 7 free. Free Jan 31, May 18, May 22, June 5, Nov 20. ⏰ Open daily May-Aug 10am-9pm, Apr and Sept 10am-8pm, Mar and Oct 10am-7pm, Nov-Feb 10am-6pm.

FOOD

Paella, paella, paella, *agua de Valencia.* These are the words that will be pounded into your skull as you trek the paths of the city, with large black pans of yellow rice and seafood splayed out on nearly every table and jars of the area's famed alcoholic drink being offered at every bar. If you're looking for something lighter, try grabbing some fresh fruits and veggies from the **Mercat Central,** (Pl. Mercat ☎96 382 91 00 # From Pl. Reina, proceed along C. San Vicente Mártir and take the 5th left onto Av. Maria Cristina to Pl. Mercat ⏰ Open M-Sa 7:30am-3pm); for other groceries try the supermarket in the basement of the department store **El Corte Inglés.** (C. Colón, 27 ☎96 315 95 00 # From Pl. Reina, proceed along C. Paz, then turn right onto C. Bonaire and walk 4 blocks. ⏰ Open daily 10am-10pm.)

LA LLUNA VEGETARIAN, VALENCIAN $$

C. de San Ramón, 23 ☎96 392 21 46

A taste of traditional Valencia, *sin carne.* This tucked-away vegetarian eatery serves cheap, delicious seafood-less paella, gazpacho, *crema catalana,* and more to a pack of dedicated locals and map-carting travelers. The ceramic-tiled, dark-raftered interior is splattered with moon memorabilia and packs in enough tables that you can't help but be impressed with the single waiter, who keeps the three courses and dessert of the *menú del día* (€7.70) coming at an unusually quick pace. That wonderfully cheap *menú* is an incredible bargain in terms of quality, though we'd be happy to pay a little more for a little more food.

 # From the intersection of the Pl. Tossal and C. Caballeros, proceed downhill along the street and turn left at the fork onto C. Alta, then turn left onto the Pl. Mossén Sorell, right after the glass building, and left onto C. San Ramón. [$] Menú del día €7.70. Tasting menu €19. Entrees €3.50-7.25. Dessert €3.70-4.50. ⏰ Open M-Th 1:30-4pm and 8pm-midnight, F-Sa 1:30-4pm and 8pm-1am.

WOK LONG ASADOR BUFFET, CHINESE $$

C. de Garrigues, 4 ☎96 394 19 56

For the homesick and the hungry, there's no better place to have a cheap, filling lunch than this all-you-can-eat Chinese buffet that serves up great takeout-style

Chinese food. The old favorites are all there—egg rolls, fried rice, chicken in a sickeningly sweet sauce—alongside a few headscratchers ranging from the inaccurate (e.g. sushi) to the divine (e.g. chocolate fountain); eat them with chopsticks to wow the exclusively fork-wielding locals around you. The prepared dishes in the buffet alone will more than fill you up, but budding chefs can assemble dishes of their own with raw fish, meat, and vegetables before handing it over to the pros to cook. After such a large meal, ordering dessert certainly won't do wonders for your beach bod, but go ahead and play a dangerous game of ice cream roulette with the unmarked ice cream bars in the freezer, or play it safe with cake or fruit.

From Pl. Reina, on the end opposite the cathedral and with your back to it, proceed along C. San Vicente Mártir and turn right at the Ayuntamiento onto C. Sangre, which will turn into C. Garrigues. **i** *Menú includes buffet and 1 drink.* $ *Menú M-F lunch €9.95; M-Th dinner €11.95; F dinner, Sa-Su, and holidays €12.95.* ⏰ *Open daily 1-4:30pm and 8:30pm-midnight.*

EL RALL VALENCIAN $$$

C. de Tundidores, 2 ☎96 392 20 90 www.elrall.es

This popular paella restaurant has a lively crowd that takes over the secluded nearby plaza and the even more secluded alleyway behind the restaurant. *Paella valenciana* (with chicken and rabbit), *paella de marisco* (with cuttlefish, shrimp, prawns, and mussels) and other stickily delicious rice dishes are brought out in pans based on the size of the group, though parties of one aren't invited to the paella party and are stuck with the meat and fish entrees. If the passing guitar players and the candles on the tables aren't properly setting the mood, intimate seating is also available inside.

From the Mercat Central, walk up the stairs to the right of Lonja de la Seda onto C. Pere Compte and continue along as it becomes C. Estamenyeria Vella and leads to a plaza; the restaurant is across the plaza, on the right. **i** *Reservations recommended.* $ *Appetizers €8.50-15. Meat and fish entrees €13-16. Paella €12-15 per person (min. 2 people). Desserts €3-5.50.* ⏰ *Open daily 1-3:30pm and 7-11:30pm.*

ZUMERÍA NATURALIA CAFE $

C. del Mar, 12 ☎96 391 12 11

Is there anything better than fresh-squeezed Valencian orange juice? Yep—fresh-squeezed Valencian orange juice with **whiskey.** This cheerfully-colored cafe is a great place for a light dinner of crepes or *bocadillos*, but the real stars of the show are the more than 50 fresh fruit drinks, with and without alcohol, served in huge crystal goblets that scream Holy Grail.

From Pl. Reina, on the opposite end from cathedral and facing it, take the 2nd right onto C. Mar; the cafe is on the right. $ *Juices €3.50-4.50, with alcohol €6-6.50.* ⏰ *Open M-Th 5pm-1am, F-Sa 5pm-3am, Su 5pm-midnight.*

YUSO VALENCIAN $$$

C. de la Creu, 4 ☎96 315 39 67

Tough day of sightseeing got you down? Looking for a *menú* that actually, completely, unequivocally leaves you full? Check out this local favorite's filling three-course *menú* that doesn't leave off the restaurant's best dishes, though at the hefty price, it would be hard to justify doing so. The *ensalada templada de calamares* is a tasty tango of lettuce and squid and could be a (small) meal on its own. Vegetarians feeling left out from the paella-fest will love the vegetable paella with zucchini, pepper, eggplant, and other veggies they'll be too busy gobbling up to take note of. Those who forgot to leave their caffeine addictions at home will rejoice upon hearing that a post-meal coffee is included, while those who are avid fans of substances both more and less addictive (wine and water, respectively) will be devastated to hear that you'll have to pay for these. If all this sounds good but perhaps not worth €20, be sure not to miss the *menú* served Friday afternoon, half the price but almost identical other than the lack of the unremarkable first course.

⇟ From Pl. Virgen (behind cathedral), turn left onto C. Caballeros and take the 2nd right, which will turn into C. Creu. [$] Menú €17 always served (drinks not included). Very similar menu €8 (F 1-4pm). Salads €6-9. Paellas €10. Other entrees €8-15. ⏰ Open F-Su 1:30-4pm and 8:30pm-midnight.

TAQUERÍA EL BURRITO MEXICAN $

C. Alta, 12 ☎96 113 36 08

We'll let this taco and burrito joint speak for itself: "I want YOU to eat a burrito! Right now! In Taquería El Burrito! Fight in the Mexican Revolution!" Actually, that doesn't make a whole lot of sense. If you heed Uncle Sancho's advice regardless, take up not only a freshly made burrito, but also the rest of the *menú combi* (€5.90), which includes nachos and a large fruit juice, with a wide selection including kiwi, melon, papaya, mango, guava, pineapple, lime, strawberry, and tamarind juices. If you simply can't choose between them, go for a Corona instead. There isn't much seating, so you might have to get your *revolución* to go.

⇟ From the intersection of the Pl. Tossal and C. Caballeros, proceed downhill along the street and turn left at the fork onto C. Alta. ℹ Delivery on €10+ orders €2. [$] Menú €5.90. Burritos €3.50-7.50. Tacos €4-9. Quesadillas €4.50-7. Nachos €2.50-4. Beer €2.50. Fruit juice €1.50. ⏰ Open M-F 8am-midnight, Sa-Su 1-5pm and 8pm-12:30am.

NIGHTLIFE

There is a reason why hostels are lousy with midday siesta-revelers. Valencia's nightlife starts off late, with bars and pubs not hitting their stride until around midnight. Check the pedestrian areas around **Plaza de la Virgen** and **Calle de Caballeros** for big, bright places and crowds of fellow travelers to start off the night with the region's famed *agua de Valencia.* The old city hides a plethora of smaller, quirkier pubs and nightclubs, especially around **Plaza del Tossal** and along C. Caballeros, which attract hordes of club-hopping locals and tourists. **Dance clubs** remain painfully empty until 1 or 2am and become packed shortly thereafter. For calmer destinations, check around plazas in the old quarter, and for some more intense action, scout out the university area around **Avenida de Blasco Ibáñez.** For a list of events, check out *Valencia City* (€0.50), available at newsstands and tourist offices, and the free monthly *24/7 Valencia* available at internet cafes, tourist booths, and some hostels.

👍 CAFÉ DEL DUENDE BAR, FLAMENCO

C. del Turia, 62 ☎63 045 52 89 www.cafedelduende.com

This intimate, upbeat local (and tourist) favorite gives the best deal in town, bringing flamenco so close you can touch the performers, a crowd that knows how to clap and sing along, and beer, all for just €7. Show up early to get a seat; otherwise, stand, stomp, and join the show. Please don't yell, though—that's what the singer is there for.

⇟ From the Pl. Tossal, proceed along C. Quart and turn right onto C. Turia at the Jardí Botànic. Café del Duende is at the far end of the garden. ℹ Flamenco Th-Sa 11:30pm, Su 8pm. Distributes "Alma 100" and "Flama," free monthly publications about flamenco. Schedule of performances on website. [$] Flamenco show €7; includes 1 drink. ⏰ Open Th 10pm-2:30am, F-Sa 10pm-3:30am, Su 6-11pm.

👍 RADIO CITY CLUB

C. de Santa Teresa, 19 ☎96 391 41 51 www.radiocityvalencia.com

One bar up front and two on the dance floor keep the youth moving to alternative American pop like Gnarls Barkley and Gorillaz with cheap mini-mojitos flowing freely. Kitschy painted tiles cover the ceiling, and a small border running around the club gives free kama sutra lessons for those of you looking to pick up some moves even steamier than your dancing.

 # From the Pl. Tossal, with C. Caballeros on your left and C. Quart on your right, cross the plaza and take the slight right onto C. Moro Zeit and walk 3 blocks. i Flamenco Tu 11pm. $ Beer €2.50-4. Cocktails €6. ⏰ Open daily 11pm-3:30am.

L'UMBRACLE TERRAZA CLUB, BAR

Av. del Saler, 5 ☎67 166 80 00 www.umbracleterraza.com

Nestled right next to the dazzling white and geometric, modern architecture of the City of Arts and Sciences, the open-air L'Umbracle Terraza offers dazzling views of the city's unnaturally striking (and illuminated) setting. The nightclub is more than just a place to do some sightseeing—swanky white tables and chairs dot the patio, while lower couch-beds invite bedazzled guests to kick back, relax, take in some hookah, and prepare for the move to **Mya,** the bustling nightclub below.

 # Bus #35 from C. Xàtiva, across the street from the Plaza de Toros. Or, bus #95 from Torres de Serranos. Located in outside garden parallel to Av. Saler, up a flight of stairs. i List of events available on website. $ Cover €15 Th-Sa from 11:30pm on for both L'Umbracle and Mya. ⏰ L'Umbracle open May-Sept Th-Sa 6pm-7:30am. Mya open year-round daily Th-Sa 1am-7:30am.

JOHNNY MARACAS BAR, CLUB

C. de Caballeros, 39 ☎96 391 52 66 www.johnnymaracas.es

A Havana-chic atmosphere that's more classy than kitschy provides a chill alternative to the often-suffocating bar dance floors elsewhere. Order one of the killer mojitos, and place it on the sparsely populated fish tank underneath the glass bar, whose empty clam shells might look mighty familiar from your paella and whose goldfish swim happily along—for now. The maracas and miniature bongos lining the bamboo walls aren't just for show; you might hear a beat from the bartenders if the feeling is right. Latin beats and American pop play every night of the week, and don't be surprised if you stumble across a salsa lesson.

 # From the Mercat Central, follow C. María Cristina past the church and take a slight right onto C. Bolsería. At the plaza, turn right onto C. Caballeros; Johnny Maracas is almost immediately on the right. i Flyer for 1 free drink before 12:45am. $ Beer €5. Cocktails €8-9. Shots €3. ⏰ Open M-Th 7pm-3:30am, F-Sa 7pm-4am, Su 7pm-3:30am.

CAFÉ BAR NEGRITO BAR

Pl. del Negrito, 1 ☎96 391 42 33

A popular cafe and even more popular late-night hangout, Negrito welcomes a younger crowd inside its faux industrial metal walls. Hostellers keep the place alive even early in the week, and the wide selection of reasonably priced drinks keeps things interesting. If you get chatting with the bartender, the half-liter of *agua de Valencia* (€8) comes with a highly entertaining story about the time a Japanese MTV crew came to film the bartender prepare the drink and insisted that all of the oranges had to be exactly the same size (maybe you had to be there); another specialty is the slushy-like mojito (€6). If you arrive early, grab one of their silver tables out in the calm courtyard, but if you show up late, plan to fight for a spot to even stand.

 # From Pl. Virgen (behind cathedral), turn left onto C. Caballeros and left onto C. Calatrava. $ Beer €2-4. Cocktails €5-12. Agua de Valencia €8. ⏰ Open daily 4pm-3:30am.

AKUARELA CLUB, BAR

Pub: C. de Juan Llorens, 48 disco: C. de Eugenia Viñes, 152 ☎96 385 93 85 www.akuarela.es

Located along Malvarrosa Beach, Akuarela isn't an easy stumble from your hostel—plan on paying for a ride to get to the party. Once you arrive on your magical steed, plan to stay the night (and morning). During the summer this party center boasts a pub, club, and a beachside party zone. Four floors of dancing with remarkably classy decor, complete with bars and plush seating at each level, make for a hard-core but tasteful night, with a huge rooftop terrace on which to catch a breather. Expect a mix of every danceable music imaginable, with a focus on Spanish styles—from Valencia's own artists to electronica, R and B, and salsa.

 # Taxi to Plaza Malvarrosa (€15). ℹ Flyer gains free entrance until 3am and €3 discounts on drinks after 3am. ⏰ Free entrance to club with €7 purchase at pub; otherwise Th-Sa €15 cover (includes 1 drink). ⏰ Pub open Tu-Sa 6pm-3:30am. Club open Sa midnight-7:30am. Beach club open Th-Sa in summer midnight-7:30am.

FOX CONGO CLUB

C. de Caballeros, 35 ☎61 770 74 22 www.foxcongo.com

Hop up onto the back benches and shimmy your hips to get the night started off right. Fox Congo fills up quickly and early for those looking to get into their groove before others have stopped their bar-hopping. Chemically lit marble and metal walls set the stage while dance-beat pop plays to an open, international crowd of hostelers and locals moving to equally diverse rhythms.

 # From the Pl. Virgen (behind the cathedral), with the cathedral behind you, take the 1st left onto C. Caballeros. ℹ Frequent themed parties. $ Beer €3-4. Cocktails €5-8. When full or special DJ, cover €8 (includes beer). ⏰ Open daily 7pm-3:30am.

BOLSERÍA CAFE BAR

C. Bolsería, 41 ☎96 391 89 03

This is without a doubt one of the swankiest bars around the Pl. del Tossal—expect button-up shirts, shiny tops, and dismissal at the door if you're wearing a threadbare, ratty T-shirt. Come early in the night for the free *agua de Valencia* and stick around as it fills to bursting and as that ✓**free liquor** starts to liberate the crowd's dance moves, especially in the nautical-themed steel back room with roses hanging from the ceiling (huh?).

 # From the Pl. Virgen (behind the cathedral), with the cathedral behind you, take the 1st left onto C. Caballeros and follow it to Pl. Tossal; the bar is situated diagonally across the plaza. ℹ Free agua de Valencia before 1:30am. $ Beer €4-5. Cocktails €8-9. ⏰ Open daily 5pm-3:30am.

EL LABORATORIO BAR

Pl. dels Cors de la Mare de Déu, 3 ☎96 392 61 93

A great place to start the night before heading next door to the more intense pubs and clubs of C. Caballeros, this bar lacks both dance floors and the inflated prices that accompany them. The cheap beers, wines, and cocktails, including the €4 *cocktail del día*, are served in a chic but unpretentious space off of the Pl. Virgen.

 # From the end of Pl. Virgen farthest away from the cathedral, turn right onto C. Almudín. $ Beer €1.50-2. Wine by the glass €1.50-4. Food €2.50-8. ⏰ Open daily 6pm-1:30am.

valencia

FESTIVALS

✓ **LA TOMATINA** BUÑOL

Pl. del Pueblo www.tomatina.es

The food fight to end all food fights, La Tomatina, in the nearby town of Buñol, draws locals and travelers from around the world for a 1hr. no-holds-barred tomato-pelting free-for-all. It all starts at 10am with the *palo jabón*, as participants try to climb a greased pole to snatch the ham on top. We don't really get that part, but it's important because once someone succeeds, the trucks filled with 150,000 cheap, poor-quality tomatoes grown especially for La Tomatina start to make their way into the Pl. Pueblo. At 11am, a shot is fired and the hour-long squishy red chaos begins (don't forget your goggles.) When it's all over, juice and pulp-drenched participants lay down their tomatoes and are hosed down by the fire department. After a quick change of clothes, reward your exertions with a nice glass of gazpacho, or scoop an improvised glass from the street (please don't actually do this).

 # Train to Buñol from Estación del Norte. ⏰ Last W in Aug.

LAS FALLAS CITYWIDE

www.fallas.com

Be glad that your hostel isn't made of wood—Valencia is full of pyromaniacs. Though they have to surpress their urges during the year, during Las Fallas, a week-long festival in March, it's burn, baby, burn. Reportedly inspired by the tradition of local 16th-century carpenters burning scrap wood on the eve of the day of their patron San José, Valencia's citizens spend months building elaborate *fallas* (huge wooden cardboard and papier-mâché figures) across the city with the eventual goal of burning them down. The *Fallera Mayor*, the so-called "queen of Las Fallas," officially opens the festival the last Sunday in February just outside of the Torres de Serranos (though the main events occur March 15-19.) Every day for the rest of Las Fallas, she can be found on the balcony of the Ayuntamiento at 2pm ordering the beginning of the daily *mascletà*, a fireworks display, by saying *"Senyor pirotècnic, pot començar la mascletà!"* ("Mr. Pyrotechnic, you may begin the *mascletà!*"). Nightly showers of light illuminate the Turia Gardens, culminating in the appropriately named Nit del Foc (night of fire) on March 18 and the burning of the *fallas* at midnight, ringing in San José's day with a fiery bang.

🕐 *Last Su in Feb to Mar 19. Most events Mar 15-19.*

FESTIU DE JULIOL CITYWIDE

www.feriadejulio.com

Originally a flower and produce fair devised in 1871, the Feria de Julio (July Fair) has come a long way from old ladies yelling at you for touching their fruit. Concerts and open-air cinema dot the city's gardens and the Palau de la Música, while regular events on beaches and parties keep the festivities rolling well into the night. Bullfights occur daily, and the festival concludes with a float-filled parade along Paseo de la Alameda and the 120-year-old *batalla de flores* (battle of the flowers), in which young girls shower the crowd with flowers from their stately carriages.

🕐 *July.*

ESSENTIALS

Practicalities

- **TOURIST OFFICES:** The **municipal tourist office** (www.turisvalencia.es) has several branches; the biggest is in the Pl. Reina (Pl. Reina, 19 ☎96 315 39 31 ➡ Facing the cathedral, on the right side of the plaza 🕐 Open M-Sa 9am-7pm, Su 10am-2pm), but there are also branches in the Pl. Ayuntamiento (☎96 352 49 08 🕐 Open M-Sa 9am-7pm, Su 10am-2pm), the beach (Paseo de Neptuno, 2 ☎96 355 58 99 ➡ Opposite the Hotel Neptuno 🕐 Open during Formula One (mid-June) M-F 10am-7pm, Sa-Su 10am-6pm; after Formula One to 1st week of Sept M-Sa 10am-5pm, Su 10am-2pm), at the Joaquín Sorolla train station (C. San Vicente, 171 ☎96 380 36 23 ➡ Free shuttle bus from Estación del Norte. 🕐 Open M-F 9am-8pm, Sa-Su 10am-6pm), and on the arrivals floor at the airport (☎96 153 02 29 🕐 Open July-Sept M-F 8:30am-9:30pm, Sa-Su 9:30am-9:30pm; Nov-Feb M-F 8:30am-8:30pm, Sa 9:30am-5:30pm, Su 9:30am-2:30pm; Mar-Oct M-F 8:30am-8:30pm, Sa-Su 9:30am-5:30pm). All municipal tourist offices sell the **Valencia Tourist Card,** which entitles the bearer to free public transportation and discounts on tourist attractions (☎90 070 18 18 www.valenciatouristcard.com ℹ Can also be purchased at 24hr. vending machine on arrivals floor of airport $ 24hr. €15, 48hr. €20, 72hr. €25) and can help book accommodations, tours, and visits to popular attractions like the Ciutat de les Arts i les Ciències. The **regional tourist office** (C. Paz, 48 ☎96 398 64 22 www.comunitatvalenciana.com ➡ From Pl. Reina, on the side opposite the cathedral while facing it, turn right onto C. Paz 🕐 Open M-F 9am-8pm, Sa 10am-8pm, Su 10am-2pm) has more limited services but provides information about the entire region of Valencia.
- **CURRENCY EXCHANGE: BBVA.** (Pl. Ayuntamiento, 9 ☎96 388 03 50 www.bbva.com ➡ Diagonally across the Pl. Ayuntamiento from the Ayuntamiento. 🕐 Open M-F 8:30am-2:15pm.)

- **LUGGAGE STORAGE:** Luggage storage is available at both the Estación del Norte and the Estación de Joaquín Sorolla train stations (Ⓢ 24hr. €3-5, depending on size ☒ Estación del Norte 8am-9pm, Estación de Joaquín Sorolla 9am-9pm) and at the bus station (☎96 346 62 66 Ⓢ 24hr. €3-4, depending on size ☒ Open 24hr.).

- **INTERNET ACCESS:** Free Wi-Fi is available in public places denoted on the tourist office map with a Wi-Fi symbol, including the Jardines del Real and the Jardines del Turia near the Palau de la Música. Free Wi-Fi and free computers with internet access are also available at the **Biblioteca Pública de Valencia Central.** (C. Hospital, 13 ☎96 256 41 30 www.portales.gva. es/bpv ✚ From Pl. Reina, walk away from cathedral on C. San Vicente Mártir, then turn right onto C. Garrigues, which will turn into C. Hospital. ☒ Open M-F 9am-2pm and 5-8:30pm.)

- **POST OFFICE:** Valencia's main post office is so beautiful it's worth checking out even if you're all set with stamps. (Pl. Ayuntamiento, 24 ☎96 351 23 70 www.correos.es ✚ Across the plaza from the Ayuntamiento. ☒ Open M-F 8:30am-8:30pm, Sa 9:30am-2pm.)

- **POSTAL CODE:** 46002

Emergency

- **EMERGENCY NUMBERS:** ☎112

- **POLICE:** Municipal Police (Av. Cid, 37 ☎092 ✚ Ⓜ Av. del Cid.)

- **PHARMACY:** **Late-night pharmacies** rotate by night—check listings in local paper *Levante* (€1.10) or the *farmacias de guardia* schedule, posted outside any pharmacy around the Pl. Reina and Pl. Virgen.

- **HOSPITAL/MEDICAL SERVICES: Hospital General Universitari.** (Av. Tres Cruces, 2 ☎96 197 20 00 ✚ Bus #3.)

Getting There

BY BUS

Buses arrive at the bus station across the riverbed. (Av. Menéndez Pidal, 13 ☎96 346 62 66 ✚ Bus #8 runs between the bus station and the Pl. Reina and the Pl. Ayuntamiento. Or, from Pl. Virgen, with cathedral behind you, turn left onto C. Caballeros and continue through Pl. Tossal as it becomes C. Quart, then turn right at the towers onto C. Guillem de Castro, cross the Puente de las Artes, and turn left onto Av. Menéndez Pidal.) **ALSA** (☎90 242 22 42 www.alsa.es) runs buses from: Alicante (Ⓢ €20 ☒ 2½-5½hr.; M-F 23 per day 6:30am-4:30am, Sa 22 per day 7am-4:30am, Su 23 per day 6:30am-4:30am); Barcelona (Ⓢ €27-33 ☒ 4-4½hr.; M-F 9 per day 7am-1am, Sa 22 per day 7am-4:30am, Su 23 per day 6:30am-4:30am); and Málaga (Ⓢ €55 ☒ 9½-11½hr.; 4 per day 8am-1am). **Auto-Res,** a subsidiary of Avanza Group (☎90 202 00 52 www.avanzabus.com) provides service from Madrid. (Ⓢ €28-35. ☒ 4-4½hr.; M-F 14 per day 7am-1am, Sa 13 per day 7am-1am, Su 13 per day 8am-1am.)

BY TRAIN

Valencia has two train stations: the beautiful **Estación del Norte,** which receives regular domestic trains (C. Xàtiva, 24 ☎90 243 23 43 ✚ At intersection of C. Marqués de Sotelo and C. Xàtiva ☒ Ticket windows open daily 8:45am-10:10pm) and the **Estación de Joaquín Sorolla,** which receives high-speed and international trains. (C. San Vicente Mártir, 171 ☎90 243 23 43 ✚ Shuttle bus from Estación del Norte. ☒ Ticket windows open daily 7am-10pm.) Free shuttle buses run between the two stations. **RENFE** (☎90 232 03 20 www.renfe.es) runs trains to the Estación del Norte from: Alicante (Ⓢ €19-27 ☒ 2hr.; M-F 8 per day 7:21am-7:44pm, Sa 6 per day 7:21am-6:45pm, Su 7 per day 8:01am-7:44pm); Barcelona (Ⓢ €29-41 ☒ 3-5hr.; M-F 9 per day 8am-9:30am, Sa-Su 8 per day 8:30am-9:30pm); Granada (Ⓢ €51-53 ☒ 6¾-7½hr.; M at 8:55am and 10:15pm, Tu-W 10:15pm, Th at 8:55am and 10:15pm, F 10:15pm, Sa at 8:55am and

10:15pm, Su 10:15pm); and Madrid ($ €79 🕐 7hr.; daily 7:30am). High-speed trains run to the Estación de Joaquín Sorolla from: Barcelona ($ €27-45 🕐 3hr.; M-F 7 per day 7am-8:30am, Sa 6 per day 7am-6pm, Su 5 per day 10am-8:30pm); Madrid ($ €32-80 🕐 1½-2hr.; M-F 17 per day 7:10am-9:10am, Sa 11 per day 8:40am-9:10pm, Su 14 per day 8:40am-9:10pm); and Sevilla ($ €42-104 🕐 4½hr.; M-F 3 per day 8:45am-5:22pm, Sa 8:45 am, Su 3 per day 8:45am-5:22pm).

BY PLANE

Flights to the Valencia area land in the **Aeropuerto de Valencia,** also known locally as the Aeropuerto de Manises (VLC; ☎91 321 10 00 www.aena.es), 8km. from the city. Getting between the airport and the city center is fairly straightforward: city bus #150 runs between the airport and the bus station ($ €1.35 🕐 45min.; to Valencia M-F every 15min. 5:25am-11:10pm, Sa every 20min. 5:20am-11:10pm, Su and holidays every 20min. 6:25am-11:10pm; to airport M-F every 15min. 5:45am-11:50pm, Sa every 20min. 5:20am-11:40pm, Su and holidays every 20min. 6:25am-11:45pm) and Metro lines #3 and 5 go between the airport and C. Xàtiva, near the train station. A taxi from the airport to the city center will a bit faster and a lot pricier.

BY FERRY

Trasmediterránea offers ferry service to Valencia from Palma de Mallorca, Mahón, and Ibiza. (Muelle de Poniente ☎90 245 46 45 www.trasmediterranea.es ➡ Bus #4 from Pl. Ayuntamiento or #1 or #2 from the bus station.) Reserve through a travel agency or accept the inconvenience—and risk of a "Sold Out" sign—of buying tickets at the port of departure.

Getting Around

For complete information and routes for Valencia's public transportation, contact the **Municipal Transport of Valencia (EMT) Office.** (Pl. Correo Viejo, 5 ☎96 315 85 15 www.emtvalencia.es ➡ From Pl. Reina facing cathedral, turn left onto C. Correjería, then right onto C. Calatrava, then left onto C. Valencians. 🕐 Open M-F 8am-9pm, Sa 9am-1pm and 4-7pm.)

BY BUS

EMT operates more than a hundred city buses. Many buses run through the Pl. Ayuntamiento. Tourists most often use the buses to get to the Ciutat de les Arts i les Ciències (buses #35 and 95) and to the beaches (buses #1, 2, 14, 15, 19, 20, 23, 31, and 32) during summer. Buy individual tickets on the bus ($ €1.50) or a pass for unlimited travel on buses and Metro zone A (close to the city center) at a newsstand. ($ 1 day €3.70, 2 days €6.30, 3 days €9.10.) There is limited late-night bus service.

BY METRO

The Metro (☎90 046 10 46 www.metrovalencia.es) is mainly used to get from the city to the suburbs and is usually a worse option for tourists than buses. Perhaps the only stop tourists will see during their stay in Valencia is ⓂXàtiva, near the train station and the Pl. Toros; it also goes to the airport. Buy tickets from machines in any station. (ℹ Prices depend on distance traveled. $ €1.45-3.75, 10-journey card €6.85-19.05.)

BY TAXI

Contact **Radio Taxi Valencia** (☎96 370 33 33), **Tele Taxi** (☎96 357 13 13), **Onda Taxi** (☎96 347 52 52) or **Buscataxis** (☎90 274 77 47) for pickup and rates.

BY BIKE

Valencia has tons of bike-rental places, including **Orange Bikes.** (C. Editor Manuel Aguilar, 1 ☎96 391 75 51 www.orangebikes.net ➡ With the Mercat Central on your left, proceed along Av. Barón de Cárcer and turn right onto C. Editor Manuel Aguilar. $ Bikes €9-12 per day, €45-55 per week. 🕐 Open M-F 9:30am-2:30pm and 4:30-7:30pm, Sa 10am-2pm and return only 7-7:30pm.)

BALEARIC
ISLANDS

Time for a little island-hopping. These Mediterranean paradises just off the Spanish coast have some of the country's best beaches and nightlife—and, yes, a bit of culture to go along with it. You may find yourself hearing more German and Italian than Spanish and Catalan during the summer, as these islands are popular destinations for tourists from other European nations, but they don't lose too much of their charm—and everyone's here to tan and party, anyway.

greatest hits

- **DON'T YOU FORGET ABOUT ME.** Though you probably won't remember too much from your night at Amnesia. (p. 253)
- **BEST DEAL IN TOWN.** Eat all the paella for almost none of the money at Bon Profit in Ibiza Town. (p. 251)
- **STUDIO ART.** See Miró's paintings *in situ* at the Fundació Pilar i Joan Miró on Mallorca. (p. 259)

The nightlife on these islands is packed with students, both Spanish and international. From Sant Antoni's Sunset Strip to Platja d'en Bossa to Palma de Mallorca, these islands at time feel made for the student appetite for alcohol—though perhaps not for the student budget.

ibiza *eivissa* ☎971

We won't tell mom and dad, but we know why you're making the trip to Ibiza. You want the whitest sands, the clearest waters, the hottest sun, and ▨**the sexiest clubs.** This small, Mediterranean island has a rich history of settlement and exploration, but it's modern status is the real draw. You'll be wearing as little clothing at the beach as is acceptable, stuffing your face with the delicious selection of international eats, and reaping the benefits of the commercial tourist industry.

This is where the young and beautiful come to get tanner and more beautiful on their summer vacations. Take that summer designation seriously—this packed party scene turns into a quaint and empty island during the winter months, so work hard all year to save the cash for this trip. You'll be encountering pricey accommodations, ridiculous covers, and expensive *mojitos*, but memories (assuming you can remember all that goes down on this debauchery-filled island) are priceless. Test your limits and see how many nights straight you can go beaching by day and clubbing by night. You're in for a ride!

ORIENTATION

Ibiza town, or **Eivissa,** is on the southeast part of the island of Ibiza can be traversed with just a short walk. The main avenues running across the western, newer part of the city are **Avinguda d'Isidor Macabich,** home to the town's main **bus station,** and **Avinguda d'Espanya,** where you'll find a slew of markets, restaurants, internet cafes, and inexpensive shops. The **Passeig de Vara de Rei** branches off the eastern end of Avda. Espanya, and the restaurant-lined **Plaça del Parc** is one block away. The commercial shopping area is most developed on and around **Avinguda Bartolomé Rosselló** and **Carrer Comte de Rosselló,** and the most interesting (though expensive) restaurants line the port along **Avinguda Andanes** and **Avinguda Santa Eulària des Riu.** The historical center—and prettiest part of Ibiza town—is the World Heritage Site **Dalt Vila,** the quiet walled city above the busy town below.

The island's other hub is Sant Antoni de Portmany (or **Sant Antoni**), on the western shore. The bus station is on the eastern edge of town, and most accommodations are away from the water to the north, but the entire town is very walkable. Head out of the city along the water to the left to hit the **beach.** Cafes and raucous nightlife can be found all along the water, from the **Sunset Strip** at the far western end of **Carrer Vara de Rey** and along **Passeig del Mar** on the shore. The wildest nightlife is on **Carrer de Santa Agnès** and its side streets.

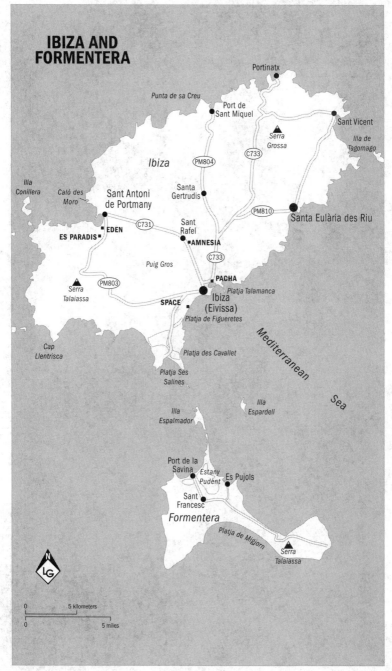

IBIZA AND FORMENTERA

Portinatx

Punta de sa Creu

Port de Sant Miquel

Sant Vicent

Serra Grossa

Illa de Tagomago

Ibiza

PM804

C733

Illa Conillera

Caló des Moro

Sant Antoni de Portmany

Santa Gertrudis

ES PARADIS ■

■ **EDEN**

C731

Sant Rafel

PM810

Santa Eulària des Riu

■ **AMNESIA**

C733

Puig Gros

PACHA ■

■ *Serra Talaiassa*

PM803

Platja Talamanca

SPACE ■

Ibiza (Eivissa)

Platja de Figueretes

Mediterranean

Cap Llentrisca

Platja des Cavallet

Platja Ses Salines

Sea

Illa Espardell

Illa Espalmador

Port de la Savina

Estany Pudent

Es Pujols

Sant Francesc

Formentera

Platja de Migjorn

Serra Talaiassa

N

LG

0	5 kilometers
0	5 miles

ibiza

IBIZA TOWN

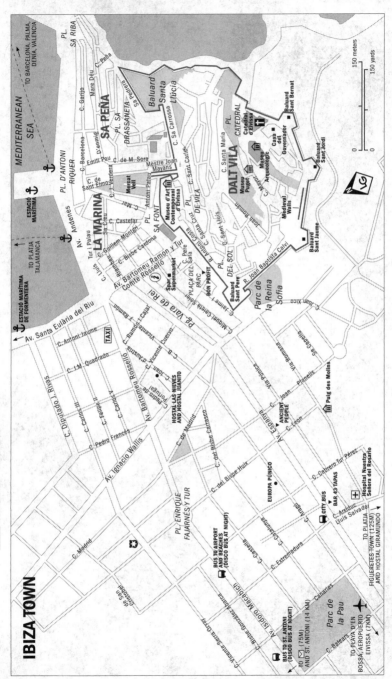

ACCOMMODATIONS

Accommodations in **Ibiza town** are generally pricey, though there are a few budget options. If you're coming to the island to party and don't need to have culture or history close at hand, **Sant Antoni de Portmany** may be your best bet. Sant Antoni's hotels and *hostales* are generally less expensive, plus you're right on the beach and in a prime location close to some of the hottest clubs and the **Sunset Strip.** Keep in mind that rates will be significantly higher in summer, and that some places may even close at the end of September.

Ibiza Town

HOSTAL GIRAMUNDO HOSTEL $$

C. de Ramon Muntaner, 55 ☎64 011 69 64 www.hostalgiramundoibiza.com

Possibly the only true hostel on the island, Giramundo has large, internationally themed dorms as well as brightly colored private rooms (a better bet if you're hoping to bring someone back from the club). The slightly more expensive private rooms and dorms have terraces, which make for excellent pre- and post-gaming, while the tropically decorated common rooms are filled with incense and built for relaxation. If you find the blacklit psychedelic murals on the top floor a little too trippy, head to the ground floor for a cheap meal (€9.50 midday menu) or a drink at the restaurant. The location is great, too: Giramundo is just a few minutes uphill from the beach and a 20min. walk from the center of town.

*‡ From the airport, take bus #10 to Av. Espanya. Walking away from the roundabout, turn right down C. Ramon Muntaner; the hostel is around the bend on the left. **i** Breakfast, linens, and towels included. Lockers €10 deposit. Free Wi-Fi. $ Dorms €15-28; private rooms €22-40, with private bath €30-55. ⏰ Reception 24hr.*

HOSTAL LAS NIEVES AND HOSTAL JUANITO HOTEL $$

C. de Juan de Austria, 17 and 18 ☎97 119 03 19 www.hostalibiza.com

Located in the middle of the city center, just a short walk from the historic Dalt Vila and history-making Platja d'en Bossa, this *hostal* pair gives you some freedom in deciding how much you're going to spend. Simply put, Hostal Juanito has some of the cheapest rooms you'll find in Ibiza proper—you'll enjoy a spacious and clean room but will have to sleep through the heat with no air-conditioning. Las Nieves, on the other hand, provides some ventilation and the possibility of ensuite bathrooms. The couple that owns these two *hostals* is one of the nicest you'll encounter on the island, and they're more than willing to help plan your trip.

‡ From the main Ibiza bus stop, take Av. Isidor Macabich toward the city center, turn right onto Av. Ignaci Wallis and left onto C. Juan de Austria. ⏰ Juanito singles €25; doubles €50. Nieves singles €30; doubles €60, with bath €75; triples €90/95. ⏰ Reception M-Sa 9am-1pm and 4-8pm, Su 9am-1pm and 5-8pm.

EUROPA PÚNICO B &B $$$$

C. d'Aragó, 28 ☎97 130 34 28 www.hostaleuropapunico.com

This quiet and peaceful *hostal*, conveniently located near the Parc de la Pau and Avda. Espanya, may be one of the best deals in Ibiza town (and believe us, accommodation deals are few and far between). Simple rooms have wood floors, bright white sheets, and sizable windows. Some even have a small balcony, while some others have air conditioning. Pile your plate high at the breakfast buffet, and take your meal out to the lush patio.

*‡ From the main Ibiza bus stop, with your back to Parc del Pau, take C. Extremadura to the right until you reach C. Aragó. **i** Breakfast, linens, and towels included. Free Wi-Fi. ⏰ Singles €36-66; doubles €45-120; triples €60-150. $ Reception 24hr.*

Sant Antoni de Portmany

HOTEL OROSOL HOTEL $$$$

Camí General, 1 ☎97 134 07 12 www.orosolhotel.com

For these prices (especially if you're traveling with a group), Hotel Orosol's luxury is unbelievable. This larger hotel recently received three stars and is stacked with all those fine facilities that you've missed while hostel-hopping. Your massive room's TV and balcony are just the tip of the iceberg—the full continental breakfast buffet, big pool, and bright, modern lobby add to the luxury. The welcoming receptionists will provide you with information on local happenings and give you tons of activity suggestions—need a bike? Want a discount club ticket? Care to visit Formentera? They'll organize it all at no extra cost, so just take it easy and relax.

 # From the bus station, head down C. Ramón y Cajal and take the first right onto Camí General. i Breakfast, linens, and towels included. Laundry €7 wash, €4 dry. Free Wi-Fi; internet access in lobby €0.50 per 15min. $ Singles €29-60; doubles €44-100; triples €60-141; quads €76-180. ⏰ Reception 24hr.

HOSTAL VALENCIA HOTEL $$$$

C. de València, 23 ☎97 134 10 35 www.ibizahostalvalencia.com

Hostal Valencia looks more like a home than a *hostal*—and a dream home at that. From the comfy couches and warm living room to the full cafeteria-restaurant to the porch-patio and lush garden, this is one little oasis that you won't want to leave. Should you get sick of Sant Antoni's beach life, hit Hostal Valencia's pool instead. The whole complex is a short walk from the beach and nightlife but feels completely secluded from the town's notoriously sloppy party scene.

 # From the bus station, take C. Ramón y Cajal to the right to the roundabout and turn left onto C. Soledad. Take the 4th right onto C. València; the hostal is at the end of the street. i Linens and towels included. Free Wi-Fi. $ Singles €25-70; doubles €40-80; triples €54-105. ⏰ Reception 24hr.

HOSTAL MONTAÑA B &B $$$

C. de Roma, 8 ☎97 134 04 90 www.montanamarino.com

Hostal Montaña knows how to help you make the most of your stay in Sant Antoni—the friendly staff will point out the best beaches, direct you to the pool at Montaña's sister *hostal*, **Hostal Marino,** sell you discount tickets to the hottest clubs, and organize a ferry trip to Formentera. If that night of partying has you sleeping through the complimentary breakfast, fight that hangover by grabbing a snack in the cafeteria-bar and join a game of foosball between *bocadillos*. The rooms come equipped with a mini-fridge (store the mixers), full closet (unpack the stilettos), small balcony (toast the sunset), and clean, comfy beds (get some…sleep, that is).

 # From the bus station, take C. Ramón y Cajal to the right past the roundabout and turn left onto C. Roma. i Breakfast, linens, towels, and safes included. Free Wi-Fi. $ Singles €17-45; doubles €28-64; triples €42-96. €3 extra per person for air-conditioning. ⏰ Reception 24hr.

HOSTAL ROSALIA HOTEL $$

C. de Santa Rosalia, 5 ☎97 134 07 09 www.hostalrosalia.com

This inexpensive *hostal* is packed with partying beachgoers. The white walls and gray tiles of the simple rooms get a nice splash of life from the colorful sheets and big windows. You can lounge around the pool and enjoy the TV in the cafeteria during the day, or take the 10min. walk down to the beaches and port. And if the walk seems too long, Rosalia can get you there faster—the *hostal* runs **Top Moto** out of the lobby and offers discounts for guests.

 # From the bus station, take C. Ramón y Cajal to the right and turn left onto C. Soledad at the roundabout. Turn right up C. Vicente Ramón and left onto C. Santa Rosalia. i Breakfast €3. Free Wi-Fi. Internet available on lobby computer. $ €20-50 per person. ⏰ Reception 24hr.

SIGHTS

The most historic part of Ibiza town is ⊠**Dalt Vila** ("upper town"), the walled old city that UNESCO has named a World Heritage Site. Climb the small, winding streets to make your own way past the major attractions, or follow one of the designated routes described in pamphlets available at the information offices. The **bastions** surrounding Dalt Vila are the perfect lookout points and impressive sights in their own right. As of the time of research, museums closed while undergoing renovations include the **Museu d'Art Contemporani d'Eivissa** (modern art) and **Museu Arqueològic** (archaeological museum) in Dalt Vila, and the **Museu i Necròpolis de Puig des Molins** (Phoenecian ruins) just outside the walls; some of the ruins in this last museum are visible from the street.

CATEDRAL D'EIVISSA
CHURCH

Pl. de la Catedral, 1

In 1234, a group of Catholic monarchs sat down and realized what Ibiza was missing—a cathedral dedicated to the Virgin Mary. Plans for this Gothic cathedral began, and construction continued all the way until the 16th century. The Catedral d'Eivissa takes particular pride in its collection of 14th- and 15th-century artwork and its 16th- and 17th-century bells, which are still rung today. The small museum on the side of the cathedral holds paintings and sculptures from Ibiza's religious history.

✦ *Follow signs to Dalt Vila; once inside the walls, follow signs to the Catedral.* ***i*** *Information available in English and Spanish.* Ⓢ *Catedral free. Museum €1.* Ⓩ *Open in summer Tu-Sa 9:30am-1:30pm and 5-8pm; in winter Tu-Sa 9:30am-1:30pm and 4-7pm. Mass Su 10:30am.*

MUSEU PUGET
MUSEUM

C. Major, 18
☎97 139 21 47

The Museu Puget is dedicated to Narcís Puget Viñas (1874-1960) and his son Narcís Puget Riquer (1916-83), two local artists from the island who amassed quite the body of work. The permanent exhibition is composed of 130 pieces by this talented pair, including Viñas' drawings and oil paintings and Riquer's watercolors. If this isn't enough island pride for you, the building itself has been a point of interest on the island since the 15th century. This classic Ibizan house passed through the hands of some of the island's most powerful families over the years before becoming a museum in 2007. Temporary exhibits downstairs also generally have a local flavor.

✦ *From Pl. Catedral, follow C. Major downhill. The museum is on the right.* ***i*** *Information available in English and Spanish.* Ⓢ *Free.* Ⓩ *Open May-Sept Tu-F 10am-1:30pm and 5-8pm, Sa-Su 10am-1:30pm; Oct-Apr Tu-F 10am-1:30pm and 4-6pm, Sa-Su 10am-1:30pm.*

MUSEU ARQUEOLÒGIC
MUSEUM

Pl. de la Catedral, 3
☎97 130 12 31

You think Ibiza rakes in international visitors today? It's had three millennia of practice. The Archaeological Museum takes you through six major periods in Ibiza and Formentera's history: prehistoric, Phoenician, Punic, Early Roman, Late Roman and Late Antiquity, and Islamic Medieval. Each exhibit provides maps, images, and a clear timeline as well as ceramics, statues, and currency.

✦ *Next to the information office. Follow signs upon entering Dalt Vila.* ***i*** *Information available in English and Spanish.* Ⓢ *€2.40, students €1.20.* Ⓩ *Open Apr-Sept Tu-Sa 10am-2pm and 6-8pm, Su 10am-2pm; Oct-Mar Tu-Sa 9am-3pm, Su 10am-2pm.*

ibiza

BEACHES

There are at least 50 beaches encircling the island of Ibiza, all with predictable pros and cons. You can enjoy the biggest parties on the beaches—and deal with the biggest crowds—closer to Ibiza town, or you can battle the bus schedule to reach Ibiza's nature reserves and smaller coves. No matter what you choose, you'll be under that same Mediterranean sun, sipping (more or less) the same mojitos.

PLATJA DE SES SALINES

Parc Natural de Ses Salines d'Eivissa i Formentera

There's a reason Platja de Ses Salines is one of Ibiza's most popular (though not most crowded) beaches. In the Ses Salines Nature Reserve, you'll find soft sand and clear waters. You'll see tourists and locals wading out into the calm sea to test their skills at paddle ball or just floating around on an inflatable tube. While Ses Salines is the perfect place to relax and work on that tan, it's also home to some of the biggest, most well-established beach restaurants on the island. **The Jockey Club** and **Malibu** will bring cocktails right to your lounge chair, spray you with their mist machines, and have their DJs spinning hot tunes all day long.

Take bus #11 from Ibiza town to Ses Salines. i First aid available. $ Lounge chair and umbrella rentals €6-10. ⏰ Lifeguard on duty daily July-Sept 11am-7pm; early Oct noon-6pm; from mid-May to June noon-6pm.

CALA BASSA

If you say its name fast enough, "Cala Bassa" may remind you of the *Teenage Mutant Ninja Turtles'* trademark "cowabunga!" While you can definitely enjoy pizza and sea creatures (and a life free of bad guys) at this small cove getaway, there's way more to the Cala Bassa than any '80s cartoon can provide. Leap off the rocky cliffs into the clear waters below, play some paddle ball on the shore, or just stretch out on the sand under the shade of the trees. Cala Bassa is also the perfect place to test your wits at some water sports—**Ski Portmany** offers waterskiing (€20), banana-boating (€10), and tubing (€15), and **Phoenix Dive Center** (☎97 180 63 74 www.phoenixdive.de) offers snorkeling (from €15) and scuba diving (€34). Both companies work best with walk-ins, so just show up and hop in!

Near Sant Antoni de Portmany; take bus #7 from Sant Antoni. i Showers and bathrooms available. Camping prohibited. $ Chair rentals €4. ⏰ Lifeguard on duty daily July-Sept 11am-7pm; early Oct noon-6pm; from mid-May to June noon-6pm. Ski Portmany open in summer daily 11am-7pm. Phoenix Dive Center open in summer daily 10am-6pm.

PLATJA D'ES CAVALLET

Parc Natural de Ses Salines d'Eivissa i Formentera

Platja d'es Cavallet's free-spirited vibe stems from a few factors: groups of locals frequently make the switch from swimsuits to birthday suits, masseuses perform aggressive and artistic massages right on the sand, and the few restaurants along the beach (like the huge **Chiringay**) play calmer tunes than the average Ibizan beach bar. Tourists who arrive via public transit must walk 30min. through the Platja de Ses Salines to arrive at this peaceful paradise. Along the coast you'll find locals looking for some private tanning in the rocky coves and the 15th-century **Torre de Ses Portes** at the point.

From Ibiza town, take bus #11 to Ses Salines and walk about 30min. along the coast to Platja d'es Cavallet. i First aid available. Nudity permitted. ⏰ Lifeguard on duty daily July-Sep 11am-7pm; early Oct noon-6pm; from mid-May to June noon-6pm.

PLATJA D'EN BOSSA

Lounging around Platja d'en Bossa, you'll hear bottles popping, lighters clicking, and the repeated "Amigo, what's your plan for tonight?" of promoters offering free and discounted club tickets. While you may not find the pristine cleanliness of the more distant nature reserve beaches here, you'll get lines of huge hotels, tall palm trees, and Ibiza's biggest seaside parties. Major beach bars like the legendary **Bora Bora** and **Ushuaia Beach Hotel** serve drinks and food all day before turning into raging discos after dark. One block inland, you'll find tons of bars, pubs, supermarkets, internet cafes, gyms, and restaurants.

⇋ Take bus #14, summer bus #10B, or the discobus to Platja d'en Bossa. ℹ First aid, showers, and lockers available. Jet ski and banana boat rentals. On-beach massages. $ Lockers €3 per 10hr. Lounge chairs €7.

FOOD

Supermarkets and convenience stores abound in Ibiza town, as do cheap pizzerias and sandwich shops, especially along **Avinguda d'Espanya.** Don't waste your time wandering around Dalt Vila looking for eats, as the few restaurants there tend to be pricey.

👍 BON PROFIT — CATALAN $

Pl. del Parc, 5

The prices look too good to be true, but yes, you can get a full plate of delicious paella for **👍€3.80** any day of the week, and no, there's no catch. Other daily specials run between €3.80 and €9, and no meal here is complete without fresh *pa amb alioli* (bread with garlic spread; €1.40). Any selection from the lengthy wine list costs only €1.90 per glass. The small restaurant doesn't have many tables, so you may have to wait a few minutes for some of the ancient locals to relinquish their seats.

⇋ On the side of Pl. del Parc closest to Dalt Vila. $ Desserts €1.20-2.70. 🕐 Open daily 1-3pm and 8-10pm.

👍 BAR 43 TAPAS — TAPAS, INTERNATIONAL $$

Av. d'Espanya, 43 — ☎97 130 09 92 www.ibiza-43.com

The international tapas here are the perfect size for sharing (2 *racions* per person is generally plenty), so grab a group to try some Spanish *albondigas* (meatballs) in mustard sauce (€5), a Mexican quesadilla (€4.50), Hungarian goulash (€5), or some Indian chicken curry (€6.50). You can add to the party by tasting one of the refreshing cocktails, like the tropical "Ibiza 43" that mixes rum, apricot brandy, and blackberry liqueur (€7).

⇋ From the main Ibiza bus stop, with the Parc de la Pau behind you, follow C. Extremadura to the right and turn left onto Av. Espanya. ℹ Free Wi-Fi. $ Salads €7.50-9.50. Beer €1.50-3.50. 🕐 Open Tu-Su 1-5pm and 8pm-1am.

BAR SAN JUAN — SEAFOOD, CATALAN $$

C. de Guillem de Montgrí, 8 — ☎97 131 16 03

A family establishment, this Ibiza classic has been passed down through three generations over 60 years. It may not look too exciting from the outside, but the moment you walk in and see the massive portions passing under your nose, you'll understand why you're completely enveloped in the sound of bustling conversation and clinking glasses. The menu includes a slew of fresh seafood options including cuttlefish (€5-11), six different types of tortillas (€3.50-5), and a hefty paella (€4.80) as well as a long list of daily options.

⇋ From Av. Espanya, walk down Pg. Vara de Rei to C. Comte de Rosselló. On the far side of the street, take a slight right down C. Bisbe Torres and walk 2 blocks. $ Appetizers €5-8; entrees €5-12. Wine €1-1.70. 🕐 Open M-Sa 1-3:30pm and 8:30-11:30pm.

ANCIENT PEOPLE — INDIAN $$

Av. Espana, 32 — ☎97 130 66 87 www.ancientpeopleibiza.com

This Indian restaurant and tea shop overflows with the smell of classic spices and the sound of booming conversation. Take a seat among cushions, pillows, colors, and startlingly colorful drapery on one of the elevated platforms. You'll find all those classics you've missed while traveling Spain: one part of the menu allows you to select chicken, lamb, or prawns and match that up with a preparation of your liking, whether it be *korma*, *kashmiri*, or *vindaloo*. The real deal is the delicious three-course lunch menu, which is just €9.50.

➡ From the main Ibiza bus stop, with the Parc de la Pau behind you, follow C. Extremadura to the right and turn left onto Av. Espanya. $ Appetizers €4-5.80; entrees €9-12. Vegetarian dishes €5.50-6.80. ⏰ Open M-Th 1pm-midnight, F-Sa 1pm-2am, Su 6pm-midnight.

KE KAFE INTERNATIONAL $$

C. del Bisbe Azara, 5 ☎97 119 40 04 www.kekafe-ibiza.com

Ke Kafe is truly international—you'll find a menu full of Mediterranean, Spanish, Moroccan, Indian, and Thai classics—but, more importantly, it understands the universal appeal of good eats. Whether you're in the mood for warm couscous with veggies, chicken, or lamb (€11-14), or a refreshing "7 Pekados" salad (€7) with fresh strawberries, goat cheese, nuts, and a fruity vinaigrette, Ke Kafe will soothe your cravings. It will also soothe your mind with a mellow soundtrack, Tibetan prayer flags, and the warm glow of spherical orange lamps.

➡ From Av. Espanya, walk down Pg. Vara de Rei. Turn right onto C. Comte de Rosselló and then left on C. Bisbe Azara. $ Appetizers €6-7; entrees €10-15. 3-course daily menú €10. Dish of the day €6.50. ⏰ Open M-Sa 1-4pm and 9pm-midnight.

LA CANELA BAKERY $

C. d'Aragó, 54 ☎97 130 50 40

If the sweet aroma of this bakery hasn't lured you in from the other side of the island already, let us guide you there. Behind the glass case, you'll find shelf upon shelf of glistening tarts, colorful mousses, and flaky *empanadas*. La Canela serves 22 varieties of homemade savory treats, and 24 types of fresh, tempting sweets. You'd be foolish to leave this island without trying the traditional Ibizan *flaó* (€2), a sweet tart made with three fresh cheeses and mint, or *greixonera* (pronounced gray-show-NEH-ra; €1.70), a pudding-like cake.

➡ From the main Ibiza bus stop, with your back to Parc de la Pau, follow C. Extremadura to the right and turn left onto C. Aragó. $ Pastries €0.70-3.50. Cakes €14-19 per kg. ⏰ Open M-Sa 7am-9pm.

NIGHTLIFE

Nightlife is Ibiza's raison d'être. Whether you're an Ibiza virgin or a proud vet, the enormous *discotecas* will never cease to shock and impress. The covers and drinks are exorbitant, but you can find discounts from the street promoters, along the beaches, and at many hostel receptions. The major clubs are generally located outside the cities. Ibiza has made club transport particularly convenient with the **discobus** (€3), which runs from midnight to 6:30am, dropping you right in front of the major clubs. There are also options for some less expensive partying. **Sunset Cafe** by the waterfront and smaller clubs along **Carrer de Santa Agnès** in Sant Antoni are island favorites, and there are late-night bars all over Ibiza town below Dalt Vila.

👍 SPACE IBIZA CLUB

Platja d'en Bossa ☎97 139 67 93 www.spaceibiza.com

You may be wondering how they came up with the name Space—it might be because with four dance floors, there's so much of it, or maybe the nightlife here is simply out of this world. This top Ibiza disco, consistently ranked among the best in the world, draws just about everybody, from Spanish teenagers to middle-aged British bachelorette parties. Space is ready to rage any night of the week, but be sure to check out the always popular "We Love Sundays" party and DJ Carl Cox's hard techno beats every Tuesday.

➡ Take the discobus from the Ibiza port, or, during the day, bus #14 to Platja d'en Bossa. $ Cover usually €35-50. Beer €10. Mixed drinks €13-17. ⏰ Open M 10pm-6am, Tu 8pm6am, W 10pm6am, Th 8pm-6am, F-Sa 10pm-6am, Su 4pm-6am.

👍 AMNESIA
CLUB

Ctra. d'Eivissa-Sant Antoni de Portmany, km. 5 ☎97 119 80 41 www.amnesia.es

Two enormous rooms compete to see which can rage harder, as dueling DJs make the dance floors shake at this electronic music mecca. The most popular nights tend to be "Tonight" on Tuesdays and 👍**"Cream"** on Thursdays, with a 2011 lineup that included such major names as Calvin Harris, Paul van Dyk, and Above & Beyond. Dance as hard as you like, and wait for the jets to blast down icy fog from the ceiling to cool you off. Don't expect to have much room to move, though; you're lucky if you have room to breathe.

🧭 Take the discobus from the Ibiza port to Amnesia. $ Cover €30-50. Beer €10. Mixed drinks €15-20. ⏰ Open daily midnight-6am.

👍 PACHA
CLUB

Av. del Vuit d'Agost ☎97 131 35 00 www.pacha.com/ibiza

Pacha is one of Ibiza's more expensive clubs (and that's saying something). An Ibiza staple for some 40 years—and a global club empire with branches all over the world—Pacha brings in the hottest names and throws the wildest parties, including David Guetta's "F*** Me I'm Famous" on Thursdays and 👍**Swedish House Mafia's** "Masquerade Motel" on Mondays. Located on the edge of Ibiza town in a slightly smaller space than some of the other clubs, the feel is less "mega-club" and more "sweet-ass party."

🧭 Walk to the Ibiza town port and then go left along the water for 20min., or take the discobus. $ Cover usually €45-70. Beer €10. Mixed drinks €15-20. ⏰ Open daily midnight-6am.

EDEN
CLUB

C. de Salvador Espriu, 1 ☎97 134 02 12 www.edenibiza.com

This debaucherous garden of Eden could only have been created by the party gods—in this multi-level warehouse, massive flatscreens play the hottest music videos, and the VIP list is stacked with some of the world's most famous DJs and celebs. ☐**Eden** is all about temptation, and the glistening red apples all over the dance floor just remind you of all those things that you're dying to have, from those pricey spirits behind the bar to that sexy dancer across the room. The apple's just sitting there—take a bite.

🧭 Take the discobus. Alternatively, take bus #3 to Sant Antoni; follow C. Ramón y Cajal to the roundabout on the left and follow C. Dr. Fleming. $ Cover €20-55. Beer €10. Mixed drinks €14. ⏰ Open daily midnight-6am.

ES PARADIS
CLUB

C. de Salvador Espriu, 2 ☎97 134 66 00 www.esparadis.com

The title doesn't lie—you have found Ibiza's party paradise. Step inside this enormous pyramid of party glory to find various dance floors and stages decorated with sparkling disco balls. The fog and strobe lights will get you lost in the line-up of house and electronic hits, but the real draw is Es Paradis' signature dance-floor-turned-pool at the twice-weekly "Fiesta del Agua," the sloppiest, sexiest party on the island.

🧭 Take the discobus to Sant Antoni. Alternatively, take bus #3 to Sant Antoni; follow C. Ramón y Cajal to the roundabout on the left and follow C. Dr. Fleming. ℹ Fiesta del Agua on Tu and F. $ Cover €30-45. Beer €6-7. Mixed drinks €11-12. ⏰ Open daily midnight-6am.

CAFÉ DEL MAR
BAR

C. de Lepant, 4, Sant Antoni ☎97 134 25 16

With an all-white decor accented by blue tiles, Café del Mar is more Santorini than Sant Antoni. While Café del Mar's packed patio may be a laid-back alternative to the Ibiza club scene before the sun goes down, it's also a popular pre-clubbing spot come nightfall.

🧭 Sunset Strip. Take C. Vara de Rey in Sant Antoni all the way to the water. $ Beer €4.50-7.50. Wine €5.50. Cocktails €10-11. ⏰ Open daily 10am-5am.

SAVANNAH BEACH CLUB CAFE, BAR, CLUB

C. del General Balançat, 38, Sant Antoni ☎97 134 80 31 www.savannahibiza.com

In Ibiza, your priorities are likely clubbing, tanning, drinking, and eating—and Savannah has you covered on all counts. The hot pink drapes, white globe lamps, and pink bar make this chic cafe-bar-club impossible to miss. Once you've filled up on the delicious meals and watched the Ibiza sunset from the outdoor patio, the DJ's mellow tunes turn into commercial dance beats, and the club in back starts pulling in the Sant Antoni boardwalk crowd.

🧭 Sunset Strip. Take C. Vara de Rey in Sant Antoni down to the water and turn left. $ Wine €4. Mixed drinks €8. Appetizers €8.50-11; entrees €13-22. ⏰ Cafe open daily 11am-midnight. Club open daily midnight-6am. Check website for schedule.

SOUL CITY CLUB

C. de Santa Agnès, 2 ☎97 134 05 09 www.digitalibiza.com/soulcity

We're about to have your wallet jumping for joy—it's possible to party like crazy in Ibiza without dropping more on a cover than on your hotel. Soul City will let you in for free, provide the hottest dance beats for free, and even project movies all over their flatscreen TVs and projection screens for—you guessed it—free. Ibiza's original exclusive hip hop and R and B club has DJs spinning songs that are guaranteed to get you moving. Though smaller than some of Ibiza's other *discotecas*, Soul City packs the same number of people onto its dance floor to achieve the same steamy, party-animal effect.

🧭 Take the discobus to Sant Antoni; C. Santa Agnès runs down to the port. $ Beer €3-4. Spirits €5-6. Cocktails €7. Cash only. ⏰ Open daily 10pm-6am.

TEATRO PEREYRA LIVE MUSIC

C. del Comte de Roselló, 3 ☎97 130 44 32èwww.teatropereyra.com

We don't want to knock the talent and popularity of the international DJs that spin at the hottest Ibiza clubs, but there's definitely something special about seeing and hearing non-electronic music live in a great venue. Teatro Pereyra prides itself on providing live international music every night. The drinks are pricey, but the shows and entry are free.

🧭 From the end of Pg. Vara de Rei farthest from Av. Espanya, take C. Comte de Rosselló toward Dalt Vila. $ Wine €8. Beer €8-9. Cocktails €13. ⏰ Open in summer daily 8am-4am; in winter M-Sa 8am-4am. Concerts around 11:30pm; check website for schedule.

ESSENTIALS

Practicalities

- **TOURIST OFFICES:** There are **information offices** (www.ibiza.travel) all around the island, including at the **port** (C. Antoni Riquer, 2 ☎97 119 11 95 ⏰ Open Apr-Oct M-Sa 9:30am-6pm, Su 10am1pm; Nov-Mar M-F 9:30am-3:30pm, Sa 9:30am-2:30pm) and the **airport.** (☎97 180 91 18 ⏰ Open May-Oct M-F 9am8pm, Sa 9am-7pm; Nov-Apr M-F 9am-3pm, Sa 8am-1pm.) There are multiple offices in **Ibiza town,** including at **Passeig de Vara de Rei** (Pg. de Vara de Rei, 1 ☎97 130 19 00 info@ibiza.travel ⏰ Open Apr-Oct M-Sa 9am8pm, Su 9am-3pm; Nov-Mar M-F 9am-7pm, Sa 10am-6pm, Su 10am-2pm), in **Dalt Vila** across from the Catedral (Pl. Catedral ☎97 139 92 32 ⏰ Open June-Sept M-Sa 10am2pm and 5-9pm, Su 10am-2pm; Oct-Mar M-Sa 10am-3pm), and at **Parc de la Pau** (Av. Isidor Macabich ⏰ Open Apr-Oct M-Sa 10am-1:30pm and 5-8pm, Su 10am-2pm; Nov-Mar M-Sa 10am-2pm). There are also offices in **Sant Antoni de Portmany** (Pg. Ses Fonts ☎97 134 33 63 ⏰ Open May-Oct M-F 9:30am8:30pm, Sa 9am-1pm, Su 9:30am1:30pm; Oct-Apr M-F 9:30am-2:30pm, Sa 9:30am-1:30pm), **Santa Eulària des Riu** (C. Caria Riquer Wallis ☎97 133 07 28 ⏰ Open May-Oct M-F 9:30am-1:30pm and 5-7:30pm, Sa 9:30am-1:30pm; Nov-Apr M-F 9am-2pm, Sa 9am-1:30pm), and beaches **Cala Llonga** (⏰ Open May-Oct daily 9:30am2pm and 3:30-8pm) and **Es Canar** (⏰ Open May-Oct daily 9:30am-2pm and 3:30-8pm).

- **INTERNET:** The **public library** in the Espacio Cultural Can Ventosa has free Wi-Fi. (Av. Ignaci Wallis, 26 ⚲ Open M-F 8am-3pm.) **Telecentro** offers internet for €1 per hour and printing and copying for €0.20 per page. (C. Castella, 10 ☎97 139 42 69 ⚲ Open daily 10am-11:30pm.)

- **LAUNDROMATS: Wash and Dry Ibiza** also has ironing services and internet access (Av. Espanya, 53☎97 139 48 22).

- **POST OFFICE:** The central **post office** of Ibiza town also has an ATM and copying and fax services. (Av. Isidor Macabich, 67 ☎97 139 97 69 ⚲ Open M-F 8:30am-8:30pm, Sa 9:30am-2pm.)

Emergency

- **EMERGENCY NUMBER:** ☎112. National Police: ☎091. Local Police: ☎092.

- **POLICE: National Police** (☎97 139 88 31). **Local Police** (☎97 131 58 61 for Ibiza town).

- **HOSPITALS: Can Misses** (C. Corona, 32 ☎97 139 70 00).

- **LATE-NIGHT PHARMACIES: Pharmacies** in each city take turns staying open 24hr. Visit any pharmacy during the day to see the late-night schedule. Within Ibiza town, there are pharmacies at **Parc de la Pau, Passeig de Vara de Rei,** along **Av. Espanya,** and near the border of **Dalt Vila.**

Getting There

BY PLANE

The **Ibiza airport** (☎97 180 99 00), is located 7km from Ibiza town. Over 50 airlines connect through the airport including Air Berlin (☎90 232 07 37 www.airberlin. com); Air Europa (☎90 240 15 01 www.aireuropa.com); British Airways (☎90 211 13 33 www.britishairways.com); Aer Lingus (☎95 210 54 88 www.aerlingus.com); Iberia (☎90 240 05 00 www.iberia.com); Ryanair (www.ryanair.com); SpanAir (☎97 191 60 47 www.spanair.com); and Vueling (☎80 700 17 17 www.vueling.com). There is also Wi-Fi access throughout the airport. From the airport, city bus line **#9** runs to Sant Antoni de Portmany. (Ⓢ €3.20. ⚲ From mid-June to mid-Sept every hr. 7am-2am; from late Sept to early June 12 per day 7am-11:30pm.) **Bus #10** (Ⓢ €3.20 ⚲ Apr-Oct every 15-20min. 6am-midnight; Nov-Mar every 30min. 7am-11:30pm) and **#10B** run to Ibiza town. (Ⓢ €3.20. ⚲ July-Aug every hr. 12:30-5:30am.) Alternatively, **Radiotaxi** runs cabs. (☎97 180 00 80 Ⓢ €1.50 airport fee plus €0.90 per km during the day; €1.10 per km overnight.) Cabs from the airport to Sant Antoni generally cost €25-€30, and to Ibiza town €15-€20.

BY FERRY

You can get to Ibiza by boat from the Spanish mainland or from other islands in the Mediterranean. **Acciona-Trasmediterránea** (☎90 245 46 45 www.trasmediterranea. es) can take you from Barcelona (Ⓢ €49 ⚲ 8hr.; Tu 10:30pm, Th noon, F-Sa 9:30am) and Valencia (*i* Arrives at Sant Antoni. Ⓢ €25-67 ⚲ 3½hr., daily 2pm). **Baleària Eurolínies Marítimes** (☎90 216 01 80 www.balearia.com) can also take you to Ibiza from Barcelona (Ⓢ €63 ⚲ 8½hr.; M midnight, W midnight, Sa 11pm), Valencia (Ⓢ €55-€78 ⚲ 3-4hr.; M 9:45pm, W 9:45pm, F 9:45pm, Sa 9:45pm, Su 9pm) and Mallorca (Ⓢ €54. ⚲ 2-3hr.; M 8 and 10am, Tu 8 and 10:45am, W 8am and noon, Th 8 and 10:45am, F 8am and noon, Sa 8 and 10:45am, Su 8, 9, and 9:30am), and also offers ferries to Formentera. (Ⓢ€25. ⚲ 30min., approximately 20 per day 7:30am-9pm.)

ibiza

Getting Around

BY BUS

The main bus company, **Ibizabus** (www.ibizabus.com), runs 34 lines across the island. Bus **#9** runs to the airport from Sant Antoni; **#10** and **#10B** run to the airport from Ibiza town. Bus **#45** circles Ibiza town. (🕑 June-Sept M-Sa every hr. 7:45am-10:45pm, Su 8:45am, 12:45pm, and every hr. 4:45-8:45pm. Oct-May M-Sa every hr. 7:45am-1:45pm and 4:45-8:45pm, Su 8:45am, 12:45pm, and every hr. 4:45-7:45pm.) Line **#3** connects Ibiza town and Sant Antoni. (🕑 From June to mid-Oct every 15min. 7am-11:30pm; from late Oct to May every 30min. 7am-10:30pm.) Fares vary, but generally range between €1 and €2.50. The main **bus stop** in Ibiza town is located on Av. Isidor Macabich, near the Parc de la Pau. There's no bus station, just a three-block-long bus stop; buy tickets at windows along this stretch. As far as nightlife travel goes, the summer **Discobus** runs four lines that stop at Ibiza's major clubs, including **Space, Pacha, Amnesia,** and **Privilege.** (☎97 131 34 47 www.discobus.es Ⓢ €3. 🕑 June-Sept approximately midnight-6:30am.)

BY TAXI

There are also multiple **taxi companies** on the island, including Radio Taxi Ibiza (Ibiza town; ☎97 139 84 83) and Radio Taxi Sant Antoni (☎97 134 37 64). There are taxi stands in Ibiza town along the **port,** near **Parc de la Pau,** off **C. Galicia,** and off **Av. Bartomé Rosselló.** However, taxis are often difficult to come by late at night anywhere except outside clubs, and dispatchers often stop answering the phone at around 1am. Many travelers avoid preposterously long taxi queues by taking unlicensed cabs, which generally charge only a couple of euro more, though *Let's Go* does not recommend engaging in illegal activity.

BY BIKE OR RENTAL CAR

You can rent a **motor scooter** or **bike** from **Extra Rent A Car** in Ibiza town. (Av. Santa Eulària des Riu ☎90 050 60 13 www.extrarent.com *i* Driver's license required. Ⓢ Scooters €30-40 per day. Bikes €6-10 per day.) **Top Moto** in Sant Antoni also rents scooters. (C. Santa Rosalia, 5 ☎97 134 42 66 Ⓢ €24-29 per day.)

mallorca ☎971

If you come to Palma (the capital of Mallorca) expecting a sleepy beach town, you'll be disappointed. The 12th-largest city in Spain, Palma is a frenetic metropolis with a beautiful historic core. The upscale main streets of the center are geared toward wealthy tourists, but if you wander through the side streets, you'll find plaza after plaza of shaded calm. The enormous Catedral and neighboring Palau de l'Almudaina both tower over the waterfront, serving as reminders to beach-goers that this city's got culture, with monuments ranging from the medieval Castell de Bellver to the artwork of illustrious resident Joan Miró. Mallorca is a nice break from Barcelona: it's a bit less intense, and the number of sights and things to do is more manageable. But that won't stop you from partying along the shore until 6am, leaving the clubs only as the sun rises over the Catedral.

ORIENTATION

The **historic center** of Palma can be incredibly confusing to navigate without a map; be sure to stop by one of the tourist offices to grab one. The **Passeig Marítim (Avinguda Gabriel Roca)** follows the waterfront; **Avinguda d'Antoni Maura** leads up from the water to **Plaça de la Reina.** With your back to the water from Pl. Reina, a left takes you to Pl. Llotja and Pl. Drassana, a right takes you uphill to the **Catedral** and the **Palau de l'Almudaina,** and heading straight brings you to the **Passeig des Born.** At the end of Pg.

Born is **Plaça del Rei Joan Carles I;** to the left, upscale shops line **Avinguda de Jaume III,** while to the right lie the very touristy **Carrer Unió, Plaça Mercat, Plaça Weyler,** and **Plaça Major.** From Pl. Major, **Carrer Sant Miquel** takes you to the transit hub of **Plaça d'Espanya,** while the store-lined **Carrer del Sindicat** leads to one of the prettiest parts of old Palma.

West along the harbor (to the right as you face the water), the **waterfront** of the newer neighborhood of **El Terreno** is lined with nightclubs and bars. Uphill from the clubs is the Castell de Bellver, while a bit farther away from the center along the water is the Fundació Pilar i Joan Miró.

ACCOMMODATIONS

While Palma is definitely the island's hub, it doesn't exactly cater to budget travelers. There are a few cheap options in Palma, but many choose to stay in the nearby beach town and ostensible German colony of **s'Arenal,** a 40min. bus ride out of the city along the Playa de Palma.

Palma

TERRAMAR — HOSTEL $

Pl. de la Mediterrània, 8 — ☎97 173 99 31 www.palma-hostales.com

Possibly Palma's only true backpacker hostel, Terramar's rock-bottom prices make it worth the 10min. bus ride to get to the old city. Plus, it's only 5min. from the clubs lining the waterfront below El Terreno. The private rooms are simple and the dorms are even less remarkable, but you'll probably spend most of your hostel time on the small, shady patio with fellow travelers.

 # Bus #3 or #46 to Pl. Gomila. As you face the water, cross to the far side of the plaça and follow C. Germans Schembri, the small street that branches off to the right. Terramar is on the right at the small Pl. Mediterrània. i Linens and towels included. Free Wi-Fi in common areas. $ Dorm €18-20; singles €30-35, with bath €40-45; doubles €40-44/46-50. ⏰ Reception open 8am-9pm.

HOSTAL RITZI — B &B $$

C. dels Apuntadors, 6 — ☎97 171 46 10 www.hostalritzi.com

Hostal Ritzi is a budget traveler's dream—s'Arenal prices just steps away from one of Palma's main plazas. Despite the basic, no-frills *hostal* rate, the place is on the whole incredibly comfortable, from the worn but plush green sofas to the Oriental rugs carpeting just about every square inch of common space. Enjoy a full breakfast in the bright dining room or on the cheerfully decorated patio before hitting the town.

 # C. Apuntadors branches off Pl. Reina. i Breakfast, linens, and towels included. Dinner €6-7. Free Wi-Fi in common areas. $ 4-bed dorms €20; singles €30; doubles €55, with private bath €70. Cash only. ⏰ Reception 8:30am-10pm.

HOSTAL APUNTADORES — HOTEL $$

C. dels Apuntadors, 8 — ☎97 171 34 91 www.palma-hostales.com

Although the rooms are a bit more expensive than Ritzi next door, it's worth the splurge for access to the rooftop terrace, which has some of the most amazing views of the city. Grab a coffee or snack from the first-floor cafe and enjoy it on the leather couch down there, or take the elevator up eight stories to sip and chat while enjoying the harbor and Catedral views. The air-conditioned rooms have basic amenities.

 # C. Apuntadors branches off Pl. Reina. i Linens and towels included. $ Singles €35, with bath €50; doubles €50/55; triples €70. ⏰ Reception 24hr.

HOSTAL REGINA — HOTEL $$

C. de Sant Miquel, 77 — ☎97 171 37 03 www.hostalreginapalma.com

You'll get a good night's sleep at this comfortable *hostal*, conveniently located near Pl. Espanya and Pl. Major. Bright pink walls decorated with tasteful paintings guide you to your quiet room, where floral sheets and wooden furniture will probably remind you of granny's house (now we just need to find some warm chocolate chip cookies and milk).

♯ *From Pl. Espanya, take C. Joan March to C. Sant Miquel and turn left.* ℹ *Linens and towels included. Laundry €10. Free Wi-Fi.* Ⓢ *Singles €35, with bath €50; doubles €60/70; triples €90. Bike rental €10 per day.* ☒ *Reception 24hr.*

S'Arenal

HOSTAL TIERRAMAR
C. de Berlín, 9

HOTEL $$

☎971 26 27 51 www.hostaltierramar.com

One of the most popular accommodations in s'Arenal (and that's saying something—the town is pretty much all hotels), Hostal Tierramar provides a comfortable stay for beach-goers. About 100 ft. away from the water and just as close to the bus stop, Tierramar is about as cheap and convenient as s'Arenal gets. The rooms are huge, and the ground-floor reception area doubles as a cafe and triples as a pool hall. The rooms can be sweltering though, so consider springing for one with air-conditioning.

♯ *Take bus #21 from the airport or bus #15 or #25 from Palma to Playa de Palma. Backtrack 2 blocks toward Palma to C. Berlín.* ℹ *Breakfast, linens, and towels included. Free Wi-Fi in common spaces.* Ⓢ *Singles €22-33, with bath €24-38, with bath and air-conditioning €26-41; doubles €32-48/36-55/38-60; triples with bath €48-72.* ☒ *Reception 24hr.*

SOL DE MALLORCA
C. d'Amílcar, 5

HOTEL $$$

☎97 126 83 73 www.hotelsoldemallorca.com

Another of s'Arenal's cheapest options, Sol de Mallorca offers little more than a bed and good location just up the street from the beach. Well, there's also a condom dispenser at reception; Sol de Mallorca's got you covered for your return from s'Arenal's nightlife. Prices jump as much as €15 in July, so come in June and be the early bird that gets the triple for only €55.

♯ *Take bus #21 from the airport to the last stop at Playa de Palma. Backtrack 3 blocks toward Palma and take a right onto C. Amílcar.* ℹ *Breakfast, linens, and towels included.* Ⓢ *July-Aug singles €30-40; doubles €60; triples €70; quads €80. Sept-June singles €25-30; doubles €28-45; triples €36-55; quads €40-65.* ☒ *Reception 24hr.*

tooth mouse

Most countries have some tradition involving children's baby teeth. In America, we're used to a tooth fairy replacing them with coins as we sleep. However, in Spain (and other Spanish-speaking countries like Argentina), the agent of tooth-to-coin transformation is actually a mouse! His name, in the legend, is Ratoncito Pérez. Ratoncito translates to "cute little mouse," and Pérez is a generic last name (think Smith). The tooth-mouse story came into being—allegedly—when the royal Prince Alfonso XIII lost one of his first baby teeth. The royal parents, in an effort to reassure him, asked a certain priest to formulate some sort of nice story for the toothless prince. So, as he didn't have much of a choice, the priest wrote a book about a boy, Bubi (the prince's nickname), who loses a tooth but is later rewarded by a mouse. It probably had a bunch of priestly morals thrown in there as well, but what really stuck was the idea of a mouse swapping teeth for presents. You might think it's a bit of a one-sided deal, but rumor has it that Ratoncito Pérez is actually building a modernist mansion out of all the baby teeth.

SIGHTS

FUNDACIÓ PILAR I JOAN MIRÓ MUSEUM

C. de Joan de Saridakis, 29 ☎97 170 14 20 http://miro.palma.cat

Missed the Fundació Miró in Barcelona? Not to worry. While you can see Miró's works in museums the world over, Mallorca's Fundació is the only place to see them *in situ*, displayed in the very studios where they were created. Miró had a deep connection to Mallorca: he spent his childhood summers here with his grandmother, escaped to the island during the Nazi invasion of France, and permanently moved to Palma in 1956, where he lived and worked until his death in 1983. His entire studio space—the 18th-century Son Boter building and the newer studio designed by Miró's friend Josep Lluís Sert—and much of his collection were then donated to Palma. Along with the thousands of pieces by Miró (and a few by other artists as well), you can visit the artist's studios: the Sert studio is a fascinating work of architecture, and the Son Boter still has Miró's graffiti covering the walls.

 # Take bus #46 toward Can Tàpera to Saridakis and walk uphill 1 block. Or, take bus #3 to Marivent and walk to the right as you face the coast. Take a right up C. Infanteria de la Marina, then a right onto C. Bernat de Santa Eugènia and a left up C. Saridakis. i Information in English and Spanish. $ €6, ages 16-18 €3, under 16 free. Free on Sa and on May 18, June 24, and Dec 19. ⏰ Open May 16-Sept 15 Tu-Sa 10am-7pm, Su 10am-3pm; Sept 16-May 15 Tu-Sa 10am-6pm, Su 10am-3pm.

CATEDRAL DE MALLORCA CHURCH, MUSEUM

Pl. de l'Almoina ☎90 202 24 45 www.catedraldemallorca.org

The Christian community of Palma built the massive Catedral you see today, which was begun in the 14th century when Christian kings retook the city from Muslim rulers. Centuries of wear and tear—and an earthquake in 1851—meant that a facelift was in order and in 1904, Antoni Gaudí installed the stunning canopy, which hangs above the altar, glowing with lanterns. In 2007 another renovation took place: the Chapel of the Holy Sacrament (just to the right of the altar) was completely taken over by a trippy undersea-themed art installation by Mallorcan artist Miquel Barceló—not at all what you'd expect from a Gothic cathedral.

 # Take the steps leading up from Pl. Reina (to the left as you face the harbor). i Informational pamphlets in English and Spanish. $ €4. ⏰ Open June-Sept M-F 10am-6:15pm, Sa 10am-2:15pm; Oct M-F 10am-5:15pm, Sa 10am-2:15pm; Nov-Mar M-F 10am-3:15pm, Sa 10am-2:15pm; Apr-May M-F 10am-5:15pm, Sa 10am-2:15pm. Open for worship only M-F 8-9:45am, Sa 8-9:45am and 6:30-7:45pm, Su 8:30am-1:45pm and 6:30-7:45pm.

CASTELL DE BELLVER CASTLE

C. de Camilo José Cela, 17 ☎97 173 50 65

Bellver is your ordinary moat-surrounded, turreted, mountaintop, parapeted castle with amazing views of the city and sea—in other words, it's a whole lot of awesome. Built as a vacation home for visiting Catholic kings, this structure has actually spent much of its history serving as a heavily fortified high-security prison. Wander the grounds and tour the stone building, which houses the museum of Palma's history and an exhibit about one of the castle's most famous prisoners, Gaspar Melchor de Jovellanos, the Enlightenment thinker locked up for simply being "different." While it's quite a hike to the main gates (unless you take the double-decker tour bus, which drops you at the doorstep)—we promise it's worth the trek.

 # Take bus #3 or #46 to Pl. Gomila and take C. Bellver to the top. The tour bus (#50) takes you directly to the sight. i Information in English and Spanish. $ €2.50, students €1. Free Su. ⏰ Open Tu-Su Nov-Feb 10am-5pm; Mar-Apr 10am-6pm; May-Aug 10am-7pm; Sep-Oct 10am-6pm.

PALAU DE L'ALMUDAINA
C. del Palau Reial   PALACE

☎97 121 41 34   www.patrimonionacional.es

This massive stone structure on the shores of Mallorca belonged to Muslim royalty during the 10th century until James II's arrival turned the tables. The first Catholic monarch of the island left a few remnants of the Moorish construction, although he did place a cross-bearing angel on top of the **Torre de l'Angel**—it was clear that no one would be praying toward Mecca anymore. The palace has separate residences, orchards, and chapels for the Spanish Queen and King, all decorated with pointed ceilings, colorful tapestries, and period furniture. Shudder with envy at the Queen's corner office views, and don't miss the phenomenal **⚑dragon** helmet in the Saló de Reis. Visitors can also wander through the original Arab baths, used more for luxury than hygiene.

✦ *From Pl. Reina walk up the steps and take a right. The entrance is between the palace and the Catedral.* *i* *Information in English and Spanish.* ⓢ *€9, students €4. Free Apr-Sept W-Th 5-8pm; Oct-Mar W-Th 3-6pm.* ☼ *Open Apr-Sept M-F 10am-5:45pm, Sa 10am-1:15pm; Oct-Mar M-F 10am-1:15pm and 4-5:15pm, Sa 10am-1:15pm.*

BEACHES

You're on a Mediterranean island—chances are you're going to want to hit the beach at some point. The closest beach to the center (and, therefore, the most crowded) is the **Platja de Can Pere Antoni;** as you face the water from the city center, walk to the left past the Parc del Mar and the end of the old city wall. Hidden in a small cove and a short bus ride away from the center in the other direction is **Cala Major,** a short but lovely beach under the royal auspices of the Marivent Palace; take bus #3 to Cala Major. A bit farther afield and packed with German tourists, **Platja de Palma** is the largest beach in the area. It's located in the town of **s'Arenal** (bus #15, 21, or 25).

FESTIVALS

Most of the events held in Palma are music and art festivals. However, one of the most popular is the **Fira del Ram** in March and April, which brings the newest, most high-tech amusement park rides to the city. The most historical event of the year (in fact, one of the most historical in all of Spain) is the **Festa de l'Estendard,** or Banner Day, which honors King Jaume I's conquest of the island in 1229. The Ajuntament publishes pamphlets and also has an online calendar detailing the city festivities, with a special calendar for the **Festa de Sant Sebastià.**

FESTA DE SANT SEBASTIÀ
PALMA

This annual festival is Palma's biggest party of the year. It honors the patron saint of the city, Sant Sebastià, who took on his honorable role as the plague ended in 1524. Millions of people were suddenly no longer dying—there has to be someone to thank, right? Taking over all the city's major plazas, including the **Plaça Major, Plaça del Rei Joan Carles I,** and **Plaça d'Espanya,** this celebration consists of concerts and performances, bike and foot races, guided tours, and—of course—parties. Festivities begin on January 16 with bonfires, barbecues, and the procession of dancing devils through the streets and culminate on January 20th, the day good ol' Sebastià was actually made a saint. A grand mass is held in the **Catedral,** major artistic and musical awards are presented at the **Teatre Principal,** competition brews at the *diada* cycling race, and a spectacular fireworks display is set off in the evening.

FOOD

Mallorcan restaurants are as international as the tourist population they serve. Traditional Mallorcan dishes include *mallorquí* (fried offal, potatoes, tomatoes, and onions), vegetable *trumbet* (eggplant, peppers, potatoes, tomatoes, and onions), toasty *pa amb oli* (bread topped with tomato and cheese, fish, or meat), and savory *sabrosada* (pork and pepper pâté).

ECO-VEGETARIA VEGETARIAN $

C. de la Indústria, 12 ☎97 128 25 62

Budget-friendly Eco-Vegetaria may be the best destination in Palma for a creative and delicious meal that even carnivores will appreciate. While your only option is the incredibly well-priced *menú*, which changes daily, you get some freedom of selection with the appetizer, two entrees, and dessert (€6.80, F-Sa night €10). Plus, there's fresh bread and air-conditioning—what more could you ask for?

Follow Av. Jaume III away from Pl. Rei Joan Carles I (at the end of Pg. Born opposite Pl. Reina). Cross the bridge and bear right toward the windmills on C. Catalunya, which becomes C. Indústria. Open M-Th 1:15-4pm, F-Sa 1:15-4pm and 8:30-11pm.

REINA MORA INTERNATIONAL $$

C. de Sant Magí, 53 ☎97 145 27 54

Reina Mora's sophisticated dishes of the day (€10) are the kind you'd expect in those restaurants where you always feel underdressed no matter how nice you look. While those places tend to serve tiny food on big plates, Reina Mora offers ample portions. The decor is quirky and cool, with plenty of odd trinkets lining the walls to distract you from your date. The handful of small tables outside are perfect for breezy evenings and smokers, while the farther back you go inside, the dimmer and more romantic it gets.

From the old city, face the water and walk to the right along the harbor. Turn right up Av. Argentina and then left onto C. Sant Magí. $ Appetizers €6-10; entrees €8-9.80. Open M 12:30-4pm, Tu-Sa 12:30-4pm and 7pm-midnight.

CAFÉ SET CAFE $$

C. de Sant Nicolau, 7

Café Set's menu isn't extensive—or expensive—and meals come with the added benefit of sitting in the shadow of the pretty Church of Sant Nicolau. The decor is chic, with whitewashed walls accented with stylized flowers, and the shaded terrace is furnished with white banquettes and white wicker chairs. Order a sandwich (€4) and sangria (1L; €13) or make a bigger meal out of one of the tasty pasta dishes (€7.50)—and you know, still marvel at the beauty of the setting.

From Pl. Rei Joan Carles I, follow C. Jovellanos 1 block, turn left onto C. Paraires, and take a right onto C. Sant Nicolau. $ Tapas €4-7.50. Pizza €7.50-8.50. Salads €7.50. Open M-Sa 8:30am-9:30pm.

BAR COTO INTERNATIONAL, MALLORCAN $$

Pl. de Drassana, 12 ☎63 609 61 26 www.bar-coto.com

Bar Coto certainly knows how to be bold—think hot pink exterior, massive flowers, fiery red interior, golden tables, and giant Frida Kahlo paintings. Yet the decor isn't the only thing that makes a statement at this cute patio-cafe. The international menu provides a wide array of homemade options to cure any craving, as Indian dishes like the eggplant tomato curry (€8.50) and Sri Lankan soups (€5.50) transport you around the globe. If you'd prefer some local flavor, go for the classic Mallorcan *pa amb oli* (€6.50) or a tapas tasting platter (small €8; large €15). Freshly baked desserts like the warm apple strudel make the daily *menú* (€10) even more appealing.

From Pl. Reina, take C. Apuntadors and make the 3rd left into the plaza. $ Entrees €7.50-9.50. Sandwiches €3-4. 0.5L of sangria €7.50. Cash only. Open M-F 8am-1am, Sa-Su 9am-1am.

SAMBAL THAI $$$

Pl. de Progrés, 15 ☎97 122 01 22 www.restaurantesambal.com

This isn't the cheapest option on the island, but if you like Thai food, you shouldn't miss it. Choosing from three styles of curry with five options of meat and veggies (€13-19) can cause quite the existential crisis, so if you need guidance, meditate before the golden Siddhartha sitting cross-legged in the corner. For what it's worth, *Let's Go* recommends the red duck curry (€18), which is among the most heavenly dishes in Palma—and has surprise lychees.

Take bus #3 to Pl. Progrés. $ Appetizers €5.90-9.90; entrees €9.90-19. Thai iced tea €3.50. Lunch menú €9.90. Open M-F 11am-4pm and 8-11:30pm, Sa 8-11:30pm.

NOODLE BAR JAPANESE $$

Pl. del Coll, 10 ☎97 171 77 97 www.noodlebar.es

Huge bowls of noodles—udon, soba, or ramen—with various toppings are the perfect fuel after a hike up to the castle. The portions may even be big enough to share, especially if you pair them with an appetizer like the shrimp tempura (€5.50). The restaurant's look is shiny and modern, and the outdoor seating on the pleasant Pl. Coll will have you ordering dessert just for the excuse to stay a little longer.

Pl. Coll is at the very end of C. Sindicat, near Pl. Major. $ Appetizers €4-10. Sushi €7.50-8.20. Open M-Sa 1pm-1am.

SAZÓN MALLORCAN, GERMAN $$

C. Apuntadors, 4 ☎971 72 08 17

The German influence at Sazón is most notable in the beer selection (€2.20-4.50) and desserts such as the *apfelstrudel* (€4.50). The rest of the menu is mostly traditional Spanish and Mallorcan, with a curry or two thrown in for good measure. The huge space is not the most intimate, but the food is sure to distract from the occasionally empty feel.

Just off Pl. Reina. $ Tapas €3.50-10; 6-tapas menú €15. Entrees €6.50-16. Lunch menú €9.50. Open M-F 1-4pm and 7pm-1am, Sa 7pm-1am.

THE GUINNESS HOUSE CAFE, BAR $$

Parc de la Mar

Disclaimer: we understand that The Guinness House is innately touristy and that the menu isn't exactly creative—but the location and ambience are unbeatable. Located right on the waters of the Parc de la Mar, and with the city's best view of the Catedral, The Guinness House is the best spot in Palma for an afternoon snack. The cafe is busiest during the opening hours of the Catedral but it also draws a crowd on summer evenings with open-air movies. For all you beer connoisseurs, The Guinness House lives up to its name with a lengthy list of international *cervesas* on tap or by the bottle (€2.60-4.60), served at the outdoor patio bar or in the even larger tavern indoors.

In Parc de la Mar across from the Catedral. i Open-air movie screenings July-Aug 9pm. $ Sandwiches €4.85-5.90. Entrees €6.70-13. Open daily 8am-2am.

NIGHTLIFE

You'll find a few mellow bars around the streets of old Palma, near the main plazas and city center, but the city forces most of them to close at a relatively early hour. The real nightlife is concentrated down the coast toward El Terreno, along the **Passeig Marítim (Avinguda Gabriel Roca).** Take a stroll along the water and about 15min. away from the Catedral things will start to heat up; the entire waterfront is lined with club after club (with some drunk-food places interspersed). Pro-tip: early in the evening (around 1:30-2am) promoters outside the bars and clubs along the water will often offer **free shots** to get you to come to their establishments.

MOJITO SOUL BAR, CLUB

Pg. Marítim (Av. Gabriel Roca), 27

The DJ spins a mix of soul and R and B hits—overlaid with some heavy electronic beats, of course—to entertain the young crowd as they try to answer the eternal question—another daiquiri (€8) or another dance? Judging by the viscous consistency of the floor and the heavy smell in the air, most have answered "both." While it's difficult to find a bar or club in Spain that *doesn't* specialize in mojitos and caipirinhas, this one truly deserves the distinction. You can try seven varieties of each of these drinks (€8), whether in their classic forms or with a fruity twist like strawberry, peach, or passion fruit.

From the center of Palma as you face the water, head to the right along the water. Open daily in summer 9pm-4am; in winter 10pm-3am.

THE SOHO BAR

Av. Argentina, 5 ☎97 145 47 19

This eclectic bar claims to have a '60s theme, but the decor is more catch-all vintage. Old wooden TV sets contrast with the indie rock blasting over the sound system, while the young crowd orders drinks like the "Woodstock 1969" and "Audrey Hepburn." Bring a student ID on Tuesdays to grab a €5 cocktail, or just show up on Thursdays for the €1.50 beers.

From Pg. Marítim, with the water to your left, head to the right up Avda. Argentina; Soho is on the left. i Credit card min. €10. $ Beer €2-4.80. Cocktails €7. Shots €3; shot of the day €2. Open M-Th 6:30pm-2:30am, F-Sa 6:30pm-3am, Su 6:30pm-2:30am.

GIBSON BAR

Pl. del Mercat, 18 ☎97 171 64 04

Gibson is one of the livelier nightlife spots in this neck of the woods, and with good reason: they serve tall, strong drinks at excellent prices. Mirrors covered with eclectic drawings decorate the inside, but most people wait for one of the terrace seats on Pl. Mercat on nice nights. Try the Don Draper-approved Old Fashioned (€7), which will probably hold you for at least an hour.

Pl. Mercat is between Pl. Rei Joan Carles I and Pl. Weyler. $ Mixed drinks €6-7. Beer €2. Open daily 8am-2am.

SA RIBELLETA BAR, CAFE

C. de Boteria, 1 ☎97 172 24 89

Though Pl. Llotja is almost entirely taken up by restaurant and bar seating, it is one of Palma's most beautiful places to sip a drink alfresco. The Llotja, a former fish market that resembles a medieval church, presides over its namesake plaza, which is frequented mainly by tourists. Sip a *hierba* (a powerfully sweet Mallorcan liqueur; best to hold your nose and just throw it back) and let yourself be entranced by your table's candle flickering in the harbor breezes that cool the plaza.

On Pl. de la Llotja. From Pl. Reina facing the water, head right down C. Apuntadors, then left, and then right. $ Beer €2.50-4.80. Wine €3. Hierbas €4. Cocktails €7-8. Cash only. Open daily 11am-midnight.

JAZZ VOYEUR CLUB JAZZ BAR

C. dels Apuntadors, 5 ☎97 172 07 80 www.jazzvoyeur.com

This small, dark club lined with photos of jazz greats is a fixture of the live music scene in Palma. In addition to holding concerts almost nightly (the pricey drinks allow the music to remain free), it also runs the annual jazz and music festival in July and over the course of November and December. You can find any type of music at Jazz Voyeur—Thursdays are jam sessions, Wednesdays are Cuban and blues nights, and the rest of the lineup fills up with jazz, reggae, funk, soul, and cover bands. The crowd is all over the place, from young music-lovers to middle-aged tourists calling for that soul band to play a little Marvin.

✚ *C. Apuntadors branches off Pl. Reina; the club is on the left.* ℹ️ *Jam session on Th 8-10pm. €5 drink minimum F-Sa.* Ⓢ *Beer €3.50. Wine €4. Cocktails €10.* 🕐 *Open Tu-Th 9pm-1am, F-Sa 9pm-2:30am, Su 9pm-1am. Music theoretically begins at 11pm.*

MISTRAL
                                                                    BAR, CLUB
Pg. Marítim (Avda. Gabriel Roca), 28   ☎97 145 21 45

You'll know just from walking by and scoping out the attractive locals on the outdoor patio that Mistral has the crowd you want to be dancing with. The navy walls, accented by two silver bars, may evoke the night sky, but this doesn't signal bedtime—it signals a long night of nonstop clubbing to blasting mash-ups of commercial hits. Prismatic cocktails and colorful strobe lights will keep your energy up all night; you may even want to bring sunscreen to keep from getting burned on the walk home.

✚ *From the center of Palma, as you face the water, head to the right along the shore.* Ⓢ *Beer €4. Mixed drinks €7.* 🕐 *Open daily 10pm-5am.*

ESSENTIALS

As in Barcelona, the official language of Mallorca is **Catalan**, not Spanish, though Catalan is much less common in Palma than on the mainland. Street signs and many establishment names are in Catalan, but everyone speaks Spanish and many speak English as well.

Practicalities

- **TOURIST OFFICES:** There are 4 main tourist offices in Palma. The Mallorca Tourist Information service has 2 locations: the head office at **Parc de les Estacions** near Pl. Espanya and the more centrally located **Casal Solleric Office** (Pg. Born, 27 ☎90 210 23 65 palmainfo@a-palma.es). The Ajuntament de Palma also has 2 tourist information offices, one at Plaça de la Reina, 2 (☎97 171 22 16) and one at the airport (☎97 178 95 56).

- **TOURS:** The **Ajuntament** runs walking tours from Pl. Cort. (☎97 172 07 20 ℹ️ In English, Catalan, Spanish, or German, depending on the day. 🕐 Daily at 10, 10:30am; some days at 4:30pm as well. Check schedule at tourist office). **Palma on Bike.** (☎971 71 80 62 www.palmaonbike.com 🕐 3½hr.; daily 10am from Av. Gabriel Roca, 10:30am from Av. Antoni Maura, 10. Ⓢ €25.) There are also **taxi tours.** (✚ Look for designated signs on city cabs. Ⓢ €30 per hr.) The **tourist bus** picks up from 16 stops all over the city. (Ⓢ €13. 🕐 1½hr., every 20min. Mar-Oct 10am-8pm; Nov-Feb 10am-6pm.)

- **CURRENCY EXCHANGE:** There's an office just off the water on Av. Antoni Maura. (Av. Antoni Maura, 28 🕐 Open M-F 10am-5pm, Sa-Su 10am-4pm.)

- **INTERNET:** Free city Wi-Fi is available at **Plaça del Rei Joan Carles I,** in the **Parc de Llevant, s'Escorxador,** and the **Cultural Centre Flassaders.** It can be accessed in 30min. increments by activating your computer's Bluetooth. Many restaurants and cafes offer Wi-Fi with more forgiving time limits. The **public library** also has Wi-Fi. (C. Palau Reial, 18 ☎97 171 11 22 🕐 Open M 9:30am-2pm, Tu 4-8pm, W 9:30am-2pm, Th 4-8pm, F 9:30am-2pm.)

- **POST OFFICE:** C. Constitució, 6 ☎90 219 71 97 www.correos.es 🕐 Open M-F 8:30am-8:30pm, Sa 9:30am-2pm.

Emergency

- **POLICE: Local police.** (Av. Sant Ferran, 42 ☎97 122 55 00 www.palmademallorca.es) **National police.** (C. Ruiz de Alda, 8 ☎97 122 52 00 www.policia.es)

- **LATE-NIGHT PHARMACY:** You'll find pharmacies all over the city. **Bagur** is open 24hr. (C. Aragó, 70 ☎97 127 25 01)

- **MEDICAL SERVICES: Hospital General de Mallorca.** (Pl. Hospital, 3 ☎97 121 20 00 www.gesma.org)

Getting There

BY PLANE

The **Aeroport de Son Sant Joan** (PMI; ☎97 178 90 00) is located 11km southeast of Palma and serves many international and domestic carriers including Air Berlin (☎90 232 07 37 www.airberlin.com), Easy Jet (www.easyjet.com), Iberia (☎90 240 05 00 www.iberia.com), Lufthansa (☎+49 696 960 www.lufthansa.com), Ryanair (www.ryanair.com), Spanair (☎97 191 60 47 www.spanair.com), and Vueling Airlines (☎80 700 17 17 www.vueling.com). As many of the flights are short and run very consistently, prices vary immensely. The **Empresa Municipal de Transportes (EMT)** runs airport bus line **#1** ($ €2 ⏰ M-F 6am-1:50am, Sa-Su 6am-1:10am; every 12-15min) directly to Palma. Bus **#21** (€1.25) goes from the airport to s'Arenal.

BY FERRY

You can also travel to Mallorca on a boat from the Spanish mainland or between islands. **Acciona-Trasmediterránea** (☎90 245 46 45 www.trasmediterranea.es) runs to Palma from Barcelona ($ €49 ⏰ 7½-8hr.; M-W 12:35 and 11pm, Th-Sa 11pm, Su 12:35 and 11pm) and Valencia ($ €49 ⏰ 8hr.; M-Sa 11pm) on the mainland, as well as from Ibiza ($ €43 ⏰ 4hr.; F-Sa 6:45pm) and Minorca ($ €43 ⏰ 5½hr., Su 5:30pm). **Baleària Eurolínies Marítimes** runs ferries to Mallorca from Ibiza. (☎90 216 01 80 www.balearia.com $ €38-67. ⏰ 3½hr.; M 4am and 8pm, Tu 2:30am and 8pm, W 3:15am and 8pm, Th 2:30am and 8pm, F 3:15am and 8pm, Sa 2:30am and 8pm, Su 3:15, 5am, and 8pm.)

Getting Around

BY TRAIN

If you're interested in exploring the interior of the island, **TIB** runs trains from Palma to Sa Pobla and Manacor via Inca. (⏰ M-F 5:45am-10pm, Sa-Su 6:05am-10pm.) **Tren de Sóller** runs trains from Pl. Espanya to Sóller, a scenic route enjoyed by tourists and locals alike. (☎97 175 20 51 www.trendesoller.com $ €10. ⏰ 8am-7:30pm.)

BY BUS

Public buses within the city of Palma are run by the **EMT Urbanas de Palma de Mallorca.** (C. Josep Anselm Clavé, 5 ☎97 121 44 44 www.emtpalma.es $ €1.25; 10 rides €8.) There are 35 lines that run daily 6am-2am. **Line #50** runs a circular route that stops at many tourist sights. (⏰ Every 20min. May-Oct 9:30am-7pm, Nov-Apr 10am-4:40pm.) **Line #41** is the night bus. ($ €1. ⏰ Every 15min. F-Sa 11:45pm-7am.) **Line #15** ($ €1.25 ⏰ Every 10min. 5:45am-1:20am) and the faster **line #25** ($ €1.25 ⏰ Every 10-13min. M-F 6:25am-9:25pm, Sa-Su 6:30am-9:30pm) run to Playa de Palma and s'Arenal. **Lines #3** ($ €1.25 ⏰ Every 9-10min. 5:45am-12:35am) and **#46** ($ €1.25 ⏰ Every 20-35min. M-Sa 6:30am-11:10pm, Su 7:18am-11:30pm) travel through El Terreno and stop just downhill from the Castell de Bellver and at the Fundació Pilar i Joan Miró.

To get to parts of Mallorca beyond Palma, **Transport de les Illes Balears** (TIB ☎90 017 77 77 http://tib.caib.es), runs five bus lines (#100, 200, 300, 400, and 500) from Palma that go clockwise around the island (i.e., #100 covers the westernmost part, #500 goes to the southeast). They are notoriously late, and their timetables are variable, but they are scheduled to run 6am-11pm.

BY TAXI

For a taxi, call **Taxi Palma Radio** (☎97 175 54 40) or **Radio Taxi** (☎97 175 54 14). There are taxi stands at **Plaça Weyler, Plaça Forti, Avinguda de Jaume III, Plaça de la Reina,** and **Passeig de Sagrera.**

BY BIKE

Palma is a major center for bike tourism. For wheels, head to **Palma On Bike.** (Av. Antoni Maura, 10 and Av. Gabriel Roca, 15 ☎97 191 89 88 www.palmaonbike.com $ €14 per day for 1-2 days; cheaper rates for longer rentals. In-line skate rental €10 per day. Kayak rental singles €30 per day; doubles €50 per day.)

ANDALUCÍA

This sun-beaten region is home to some of Spain's best beaches, quirkiest towns, most prominent Islamic heritage, and most tongue-pleasing tapas—not to mention a minuscule British territory chilling next door. It seems as though every cathedral was once a mosque, and a synagogue before that, and probably a church before that. And maybe even a Roman temple before that, or a Phoenician settlement (we see you, Cádiz). The diachronous layering of nations and ages has left Andalucía with its characteristically heterogeneous culture: Granada's Middle Eastern-style tea houses sit in the shadow of the Alhambra; Córdoba's cathedral is filled with Moorish arches stretching to eternity; Sevilla's flamenco dancers and bullfighters move gracefully beside the waters of the river that launched Columbus. And Gibraltar has some very silly monkeys. There are a lot of layers of history here: it's up to you to experience them all.

greatest hits

- **GET CLAPPING.** See flamenco at its best in Sevilla (p. 286). Yes, her voice is supposed to sound like that.

- **BE A MENSCH.** Visit the synagogue (p. 296) and Casa de Sefarad (p. 296) in Córdoba.

- **MONKEY BUSINESS.** Stand atop the Rock of Gibraltar, a macaque on your back and the African coast in the distance. (p. 350)

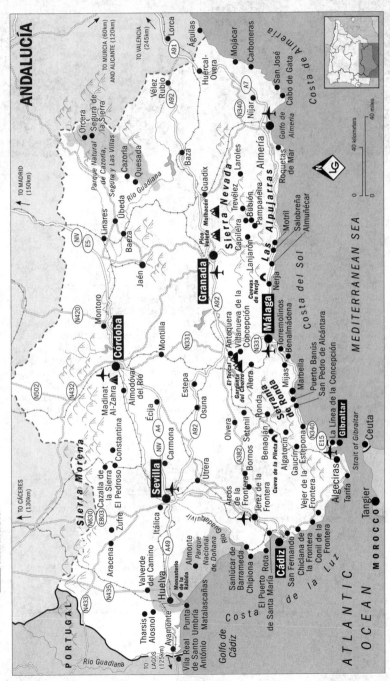

ANDALUCÍA

sevilla ☎95

Welcome to Sevilla, capital of Andalucía and hub of culture for the last millennium running. Flamenco, bullfighting, and great food bring Sevilla up to Madrid's and Barcelona's level, though its smaller size means it probably won't keep you as long. Stroll, explore, gawk, and get clapping—it's flamenco time.

ORIENTATION

Sevilla can be divided into a few loosely separated neighborhoods. Apart from the prominent geographic feature of the canal, which divides the city center from Triana, there are few absolute barriers between Santa Cruz, El Centro, and La Macarena. As a general rule, the area immediately surrounding the **Alcázar** and **Catedral** is regarded as Santa Cruz, the **Alameda de Hércules** is the heart of La Macarena, and the dominant shopping trio of **Calle Sierpes, Calle Cuna,** and **Calle de Velázquez** hold strong in El Centro. The divisions aren't merely geographic—Santa Cruz is tourist-filled, El Centro is commercial, La Macarena is a mix of religious and reckless, and Triana is slow-paced and mellow. Ultimately, Sevilla is a small, walkable city, making it easy to move from one *barrio* to the next without even noticing.

Santa Cruz

Santa Cruz is the historic center of Sevilla, featuring its two most exceptional historic landmarks, the **Cathedral** and the **Alcázar.** There's an array of narrow streets that radiate outward lined with kitschy tourist shops and ice-cream stands, but also many of the city's classic restaurants, bars, and *bodegas*. This area can be difficult to navigate, so stop by the tourist office to pick up a free map. Beyond this nucleus of tightly wound meandering streets you'll find the **University** and **Plaza de España** just a 5min. walk south of the *barrio*. Santa Cruz is also close to the Prado de San Sebastián park, 5min. east across Av. de Menéndez Pelayo.

El Centro

Sevilla's commercial center, El Centro is crossed by the trio of **Calle Cuna, Calle Sierpes,** and **Calle de Velázquez,** which all run parallel from north to south and are packed with international chain stores like Zara and H&M. While perhaps not the most charming part of town, these streets are a great way to navigate from Santa Cruz to the north of the city. The cultural center of El Centro is the **Plaza de la Encarnación.** If Sevilla had a Pl. Mayor, this would be it, but this is one of the few cities in Spain that seems to have avoided this lazy naming habit. Pl. de la Encarnación is the site of political protests as well as outdoor concerts and cultural programs sponsored by the city. To the west of El Centro you will find **Estación de Autobuses Plaza de Armas,** where buses from within the province of Andalucía arrive.

sevilla

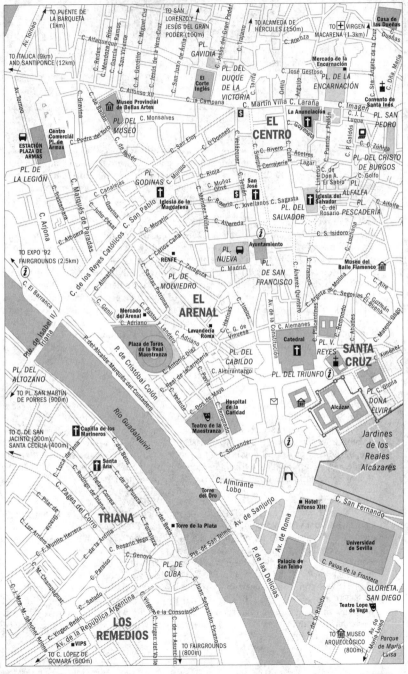

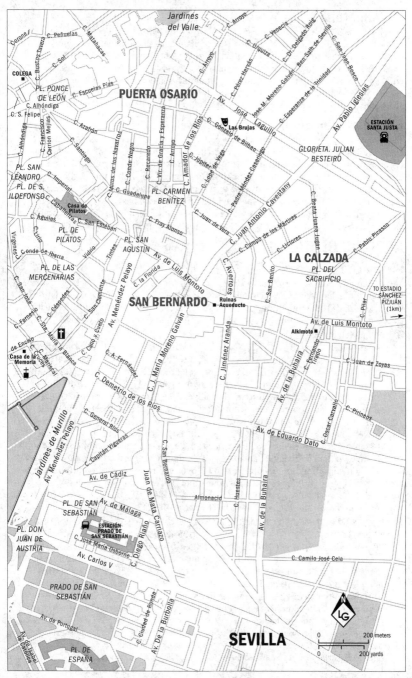

sevilla

La Macarena

La Macarena's biggest landmark is the **Alameda de Hércules,** a center for eating, drinking, and clubbing. Radiating outward you'll find a residential neighborhood with simple shops, markets, the occasional bar, and neighborhood tapas joints. **Calle Feria** runs from north to south, lined with a number of good restaurants and bars. While La Macarena is quite active at night, the neighborhood is best known as a religious center, with a number of small convents, monasteries, and churches. **Avenida Torneo** and **Calle Resolana** border La Macarena at the west and north, respectively.

El Arenal and Triana

These two neighborhoods sandwich the canal between the **Puente de San Telmo** and **Puente de Triana.** On the eastern side of the canal, El Arenal's main street is **Paseo de Cristóbal Colón,** and its main center is the **Plaza de Armas,** at the base of the Puente de Triana. Making your way to the "other side of the tracks," you'll find the neighborhood of Triana. While the main streets, **Avenida de la República Argentina** and **Calle San Jacinto** are useful landmarks, the layout of Triana is generally much less confusing compared to the rest of Sevilla. **Calle Betis** along the water is home to some of the best seafood restaurants and bars in Sevilla, and **Calle de Salado** is lined with inexpensive ethnic restaurants.

ACCOMMODATIONS

Santa Cruz

More than any other *barrio*, Santa Cruz caters to tourists. Home to Sevilla's major historic sights, hardly a block remains unmarked by some kind of accommodation. Because of this stiff competition, many places go above and beyond to attract guests, offering great amenities, newly renovated facilities, and competitive rates.

SAMAY SEVILLA HOSTEL HOSTEL $

Av. Menéndez Pelayo, 13 ☎95 521 56 68 www.samayhostels.com

One of the nicest hostels in Santa Cruz, Samay provides all the essentials at great rates. Upon entering the hostel, you'll be welcomed by an English-speaking staff member (or three) ready to help you to your room. While the retro wallpaper and furniture might be a bit loud, these decor decisions are worth overlooking. The shared bedrooms are clean, comfortable, and larger than those at competing hostels. They come equipped with electronically coded security lockers, fresh towels, and clean ensuite bathrooms with large showers, all of which make life just a little bit easier. The top floor terrace hosts a steady night crowd who lounge on the hammocks. Samay also offers newly renovated common areas, a kitchen with modern appliances, and an overwhelming slew of entertainment, including free walking tours, tapas tours, and flamenco and *discoteca* nights.

‡ 7min. up Av. Menéndez Pelayo from Prado de San Sebastián. ***i*** *Lockers and towels included.* *$ 8-bed dorm €15; 6-bed €18; 4-bed €20.* *🕐 Reception 24hr.*

SEVILLE BACKPACKER HOSTEL PICASSO HOSTEL $

C. San Gregorio, 1 ☎95 421 08 64 www.sevillebackpacker.com

This small, inexpensive hostel, just minutes from the Cathedral and Alcázar, draws backpackers with an authentic Spanish feel, created by colorful Moorish-style tiles and hanging plants around the central stairwell. Shared bedrooms have simple wood bunks, fresh linens, large windows and small balconies. The hostel offers plenty of common spaces, including a canopied roof terrace, computer lounge, communal kitchen, and a dining area, where a complimentary breakfast is served in the mornings.

‡ From Puerta Jérez, follow C. San Gregorio 1 block to the hostel. If you're facing the cathedral from Puerta Jérez, C. San Gregorio is to the right of Av. de la Constitución. ***i*** *Breakfast included. Free Wi-Fi. Women-only rooms available.* *$ 4- and 6-bed dorms €18; doubles €22.*

HOSTAL FLORIDA   HOTEL $$

Av. Menéndez Pelayo, 27   ☎95 442 25 57 www.hostalfloridasevilla.com

The appeal here is simple private bedrooms, ensuite baths, and hotel
amenities like towel service, TVs, free Wi-Fi, and toiletries. While clean and
comfortable, the rooms tend to be smaller, and the lack of common spaces
renders Florida less social than nearby backpackers' hostels. But if quiet
and privacy are important to you, Hostal Florida definitely offers both at an
affordable rate.

✦ *10min. up Av. Ménendez Pelayo from Prado de San Sebastián. i Safes included. Ⓢ Singles
€25-30; doubles €40-45; triples €65-70.*

El Centro

While El Centro may not offer the same historic feel of Santa Cruz, the quiet side
streets and alleyways that feel removed from the bustle of the city and yet are
within walking distance of most sights and attractions provide equally reasonable
accommodations.

▨ OASIS BACKPACKERS' HOSTEL   HOSTEL $

Pl. de la Encarnación, 29, 1-2   ☎95 429 37 77 www.hostelsoasis.com

From a rooftop pool (more of a pond, but in the Sevillian heat, any body
of water is appreciated) and a happy hour (two beers, wines, sangrias, or
shots for €2) to bike rentals and Spanish lessons, Oasis has it all. The bright
shared rooms have simple wooden bunks mad up with clean bedspreads,
and, most importantly, individual electronically coded safes. The location
can't be beat: Oasis is just a few meters from the Pl. de la Encarnación in
the heart of El Centro. The hostel has three buildings; try to get a room in
the building with the reception, as it also houses the pool and the kitchen
where breakfast is served. If you are also considering Oasis's sister hostel
Hostel Palace Seville, beware that it has neither a reliable Wi-Fi connection
nor lockers.

✦ *At the corner of Pl. de la Encarnación. Facing #29, turn right into the alley; the entrance is on the
left where the alley curves. i Breakfast included. Ⓢ 8-bed dorms €15; 6-person €18; 4-bed €21.
Doubles from €44. ⏰ Reception 24hr.*

HOSTEL NUEVO SUIZO   HOSTEL $$$

C. del Azofaifo, 7   ☎95 422 91 47 www.nuevosuizo.com

Housed in a renovated historic Sevillan building on a quiet corridor off C.
Las Sierpes, Hostel Nuevo Suizo feels more like a fine boutique hotel than a
backpackers' hostel. The most private rooms, just off a skylit courtyard, are
adorned with hanging plants and twisting wood-carved beams. The rooms
may be simple in decor, but they have all the backpacker essentials like air-
conditioning, Wi-Fi, and large windows overlooking the narrow streets below.
The hotel feel extends to the somewhat lackluster social scene, but that's
not for lack of common spaces and amenities, including the courtyard lounge
(where complimentary breakfast is served daily), a great rooftop terrace
with hammocks, and new computers on each floor. The small staff speaks
English and is very helpful in pointing guests to Sevilla's best in food, drink,
and entertainment. The hostel's private single, double, and triple rooms are
pricier than a cheap bunk in a backpackers' hostel, but for those who value
privacy, there's no greater budget accommodation in Sevilla.

✦ *In a small alley off C. las Sierpes right by C. Vargas Campos. Ⓢ Singles €31-39; doubles €48-54;
triples €69-74. ⏰ Reception 24hr.*

Triana

Triana is a terrific alternative to staying in the busy city center. Adjacent to the canal, Triana offers plenty of traditional restaurants, bars, and *bodegas*, but has a more small-town feel. Most of Triana's accommodations are just a 10min. walk from the center of Sevilla.

TRIANA BACKPACKERS HOSTEL $

C. de Rodrigo de Triana, 69 ☎95 445 99 60 www.trianabackpackers.com

This peaceful, traditional-looking hostel takes on the true Triana spirit—from the hammocks and hot tub on the terrace to the board games in the lounge and the Spanish radio playing in the halls. Located in a renovated townhouse across the river, Triana Backpackers plays up the Sevillian aesthetic, with rooms along a light-flooded corridor with Spanish wall tiles and potted plants. While Triana Backpackers provides plenty of common spaces, you won't find the same hustle and bustle of many hostels across the river. The hostel even offers a full program of hostel activities such as bike tours to Cartuja (€5) and Italica (€6), and flamenco outings in the evening.

From Puente de Triana, take C. de San Jacinto and make a left onto C. de Rodrigo de Triana; the hostel is on the left. i Breakfast and lockers included. Free Wi-Fi. Women-only suites available. $ 10-bed dorms €15-18; 6-bed €16-19; 4-bed €17-20. Doubles €50. ⏰ Reception 24hr.

LA POSADA DE TRIANA HOTEL $$$

C. de Pagés del Corro, 53 ☎95 433 21 00 www.laposadadetriana.com

Within a recently renovated 19th-century building lies this small, welcoming hotel. The friendly older woman at the desk will use her best English to greet you, and then lead you to your small but colorfully decorated room with closet space, a (very) compact bathroom, and a fan. There are no bells and whistles—just a simple place to sleep in a great location.

From Puente de Triana, take C. de San Jacinto and make a right onto C. de Pagés del Corro; the hotel is on the right. $ Singles €40-45; doubles €60; triples €70. ⏰ Reception 24hr.

Outside the Center

If you are traveling to Sevilla to stay in close proximity to restaurants, historical sights, and nightlife, it would be unthinkable to stay outside of the city center, which has plenty of cheap and convenient accommodations. The following listings may be of interest to those more interested in hanging around the rec room than snacking, sightseeing, and drinking their way through Sevilla.

CAMPING VILLSOM CAMPGROUND $

Autovía Sevilla-Cádiz, km 554.8, Ctra. de Isla Menor ☎95 472 08 28

Camping Villsom is the closest campground to Sevilla. It has well-kept facilities and all of the essentials: hot showers, clean bathrooms, charcoal grills, laundry facilities, a multilingual staff, and neat spaces for your tent, car, or RV. It also has a number of additional amenities to make your stay easy and relaxing, including a TV room, ping-pong tables, and a large, palm-shaded pool. The mini-mart and cafeteria can keep you fed with breakfast (€2.40) and drinks (€1.20-€3.90).

Take bus #132 from Av. de Portugal. i Pool. Pets allowed. Mail service. $ €4.80 per person; €4.82 per site; €5.05 per car; €5.24 per trailer. ⏰ Security 24hr.

ALBERGUE INTURJOVEN SEVILLA (HI) HOSTEL $$

C. de Isaac Peral, 2 ☎95 506 55 00 www.inturjoven.com

What the Albergue Inturjoven Sevilla lacks in convenience (it's a bus ride away from the city), it makes up for with modern facilities and large, bare rooms with ensuite bathrooms and ample closet space. The generous size of the facilities and the convenient meal service attract both vacationing families and groups of college-aged backpackers. The price is the same whether or not your room has a balcony and ensuite bath, so do your best to score one of the nicer rooms.

Take bus #34 from C. del Cid to "Isaac Peral." i Breakfast included. Other meals €8. Wi-Fi €1 per hr., €6 per day. Laundry €2.50 wash, €2 dry. $ €29; under 26 €23. HI members discount €3.50. ⏰ Reception 24hr.

SIGHTS

Santa Cruz

PLAZA DE ESPAÑA HISTORIC SITE, MONUMENT

Av. de Isabel "la Católica"

Constructed for the Ibero-American Exposition of 1929, this is one of the most impressive examples of neo-*mudéjar* architecture anywhere, a tribute to Spain and its architectural history. Anachronism is a common theme for the Pl. de España; George Lucas filmed part of *Star Wars Episode II: Attack of the Clones* on the bridges of the site. The plaza was built as an apology to the nations of the world who had fallen to the violence of Spanish colonialism and takes on this request for forgiveness in full force—the plaza itself is constructed in the shape of a heart. The details of the plaza are the perfect Spanish history study guide: the seating surrounding the main area is decorated with colorful, handmade tiles, with each booth honoring one of Spain's principal cities of Spain and all major Spanish leaders are preserved in statue form.

Directly across Av. de Portugal from the Prado de San Sebastián. $ Free. ⏰ Open daily 7am-11pm.

CATEDRAL DE SEVILLA CHURCH

Entrance by Pl. de la Virgen de los Reyes ☎95 421 49 71 www.catedraldesevilla.es

This isn't just any old church—La Catedral happens to be the world's largest Gothic building and the third-largest cathedral. The city restricts any construction project from exceeding 100m to ensure that **la Giralda,** the Cathedral's tower, remains Sevilla's highest point. La Giralda had been the minaret of the mosque that formerly occupied the site, and was the only portion to survive an earthquake in 1365. The stained-glass windows and gold-plated religious scenes that line the interior of the Cathedral are worth checking out, as they have a Moorish-Catholic flair that traditional Renaissance churches lack. La Catedral is perhaps best known for holding the remains of Christopher Columbus. The adorned tomb is suspended in the air by four pallbearers representing Spain's four kingdoms: Castile, León, Aragon, and Navarre. The bones of the world's most famous explorer have traveled the world since his death, moving from Spain to Santo Domingo to Havana, and finally to their resting place in Sevilla in 1902. Only recently, however, have the bones been verified as his by DNA tests. As you leave the Catedral, watch out for the ambush of "religious" palm readers at the exit: they'll grab you, tell you about all the money that you'll never make, all the ugly kids you'll have, and how many divorces it'll take before you find true love—six isn't bad, is it?—and then they'll guilt you into tipping.

Located off Av. de la Constitución next to the Alcázar. $ €8.50, students €2. ⏰ Open July-Aug M-Sa 11am-5pm, Su 9:30am-4pm; Sept-June M-Sa 11am-5pm, Su 2:30-6pm.

ALCÁZAR DE SEVILLA HISTORIC SITE, FORTRESS

Patio de Bandera ☎95 450 23 23 www.patronato-alcazarsevilla.es

Don't stress about getting your black tie back from the dry cleaners before visiting the Alcázar. While it does double as the summer palace for Spanish royalty, you aren't likely to run into them—just backpackers like you. After the Romans originally constructed the walls to protect the city, the Moors then expanded them into an all-out fortress to protect against enemy advances on Sevilla. Once the Catholics took over, they converted the fortress into a palace, and overcame the awkwardness of being Christian monarchs residing in a Muslim palace. The incredible architecture and overwhelming ornament is truly impressive. More than anything, though, it is the palace gardens, filled with towering banyan, cypress, and palm trees, that make the Alcázar much more than a quick museum visit. These wonderful gardens are shared by shade-seeking tourists, families of wild peacocks, and ducks that have full roaming privileges around the grounds.

 # Located off the back corner of La Catedral, off Pl. Triunfo. $ €8.50, students 17-25 with ID €2. ⏰ Open Apr-Sept M-Sa 9:30am-7pm; Oct-Mar daily 9:30am-5pm.

UNIVERSIDAD DE SEVILLA UNIVERSITY

C. San Fernando, 4 ☎95 455 10 00 www.us.es

If every college in the world looked like this, we'd probably have far more productive young people. The Universidad de Sevilla is the second-largest building in all of Spain and uses every square inch to saturate you with impressive architecture. While the library and computers are only available to students and university personnel, the stone courtyards lined with statues of religious and historic Spanish figures are open to all those who wish to read, write, or take a siesta there. If you think you're too cool for school, consider the university's rebellious history. Originally built as a tobacco factory, the establishment once employed the "deadly sexy" Carmen, namesake of the opera. And if you're interested in picking up some knowledge while spending time in Sevilla, the university offers extension classes.

 # Down the block from Prado de San Sebastián. $ Free. ⏰ Open M-Sa 7am-9:45pm.

El Centro

MUSEO DEL BAILE FLAMENCO MUSEUM

C. de Manuel Rojas Marcos, 3 ☎95 434 03 11 www.museoflamenco.com

This museum is the one-stop shop for all things flamenco. Walking through the halls of this high-tech museum, you'll be bombarded by movies, photography, and artifacts explaining the rich history of the art form in Sevilla. For a piece of hip-shaking history, be sure to check out the dress worn during the opening ceremonies of the 1992 Barcelona Olympics. While

the second floor of the museum is the main attraction, it's worth visiting the 300-year-old, underground Moorish gallery that holds classic flamenco photographs. The museum offers live flamenco performances in the evenings and, if you're not too shy, you can try your hand at some dancing with the professionals.

⇞ From La Catedral, take C. Argote de Molina, turn left onto C. Estrella, and then left onto C. de Manuel Rojas Marcos; the museum is on the right. ℹ Exhibits in English and Spanish. Performers teach a 20min. class that is open to the public. $ €10, students €8. Flamenco performances M-Th €15, students €12; F-Sa €23/20. Classes €10, students €8. ⏰ Museum open daily 10am-7pm. Flamenco performances M-Th 7pm, F-Sa 7pm. Flamenco classes M-Th 6:30pm.

MUSEO DE BELLAS ARTES MUSEUM

Pl. del Museo, 9 ☎95 478 65 00 www.museodeandalucia.es

The most user-friendly art museum you'll ever encounter, the Museo de Bellas Artes is organized chronologically. Starting in the medieval period and progressing to the 20th century, the museum devotes entire rooms to its favorite artists, including Bartolomé Esteban Murillo, Valdés Leal, and Francisco de Zurbarán. Sevilla is not quite the art museum superpower that Madrid and Barcelona are, but Museo de Bellas Artes is a great place to get a taste of Spanish art if the other cities aren't on your itinerary. The building, which dates back to 1603, is centered on three beautiful courtyards.

⇞ At intersection of C. de Alfonso XII and C. San Vicente. ℹ Lockers €1. $ €1.50, EU citizens free. ⏰ Open Tu 2:30-8:30pm, W-Sa 9am-8:30pm.

La Macarena

On paper, La Macarena looks like churches on churches on churches (with maybe a convent or basilica thrown in for variety), and that's just what you'll find. With some exploration, you'll come away with a much better understanding of **Semana Santa** and **Feria de Abril,** two of Sevilla's most important festivals.

BASÍLICA DE SANTA MARÍA DE LA ESPERANZA MACARENA AND HERMANDAD DE LA MACARENA MUSEUM CHURCH, MUSEUM

C. Bécquer 1 and 3 ☎95 490 18 00 www.hermandaddelamacarena.es

While the 20th-century Basílica de la Macarena isn't terribly overwhelming after seeing the main event of Spanish Catholicism in downtown Sevilla, this small church has played an important role in the local history of the religion. The small church is the home of the Hermandad de la Macarena, a 400-year-old Catholic brotherhood that dresses in ominous black robes and leads an annual procession through the city of Sevilla during **Semana Santa** (holy week), just before Easter. This semi-secret brotherhood has had a fraught history with the Catholic church and was denied legitimacy for centuries. With the popularization of Semana Santa in the 20th century, the brotherhood's procession through the streets of Sevilla on the eve of Good Friday is one of the most anticipated events of the year. While the basilica itself may underwhelm, the clear attraction here is the museum next door, which gives you a full history of Semana Santa and the peculiar story of this secret brotherhood. Perfectly preserved documents, books, tapestries, and ancient flags line the museum halls. The massive, decorated floats used during Semana Santa nearly a century ago will leave you with an appreciation for the magnitude of the historic festival.

⇞ At the intersection of C. San Luis and C. Resolana; the entrance is on C. Resolana. ℹ La Macarena should not be confused with "The Macarena," a festive dance that you mastered at the age of 10. $ Basilica free. Museum €5, under 16 €4. ⏰ Basilica open M-Sa 9am-2pm and 5-9pm, Su 9am-2pm and 5-9:30pm. Mass M-F 9, 11:30am, 8, 8:30pm; Sa 9am, 8pm; Su 10:15am, 12:15, 8pm. Museum open daily 9am-1:30pm and 5-8:30pm.

BASÍLICA DE SAN LORENZO Y JESÚS DEL GRAN PODER CHURCH

Pl. de San Lorenzo, 13 ☎95 491 56 86 www.gran-poder.es

This church combo is one of the most ornate and impressive around. When facing the duo, the Basílica de San Lorenzo is on the left, filled with frescoes, gilded artwork, and glistening altars. The Basílica de Jesús del Gran Poder stays true to its name—it's one powerful place. The entirely marble, circular main room pales in comparison to the massive altar in the center. The tall golden statue of Jesus adorned with purple robes and carrying the cross is the basilica's main attraction. People from all over line up to pass behind the statue, kissing its ankle and saying a quick prayer—just make sure not to leave any lipstick stains.

 # From Alameda de Hércules, take C. Santa Ana and turn left onto C. Santa Clara; the plaza and churches are on the right. $ Free. ⏰ Basilica open M-Th 8am-1:30pm and 6-9pm, F 7:30am10pm, Sa-Su 8am-2pm and 6-9pm. Mass M-F 9:30, 10:30am, 7:30, 8:30pm; Sa 9:30, 10:30am, 1:15, 7:30, 8:30pm; Su 9:30, 11am, 12:30, 1:30, 7:30, 8:30pm.

CONVENTO DE SANTA PAULA MUSEUM, CONVENT

C. Santa Paula, 11 ☎95 453 63 30 www.santapaula.es

While you may feel like you're sneaking into the land of Oz when you ring the doorbell at the tiny, brown door toward the right corner of the convent, the sight of the nuns instead of munchkins will bring you back to Earth. You can visit the small museum (€3) and browse the collection of artifacts stored in this 15th-century establishment. While none of the items are labeled, a nun will guide you on a private tour through the three museum rooms, pointing out all of her favorites. This is the kind of attention you just don't get at that Gothic beast downtown. Your friendly nun-guide may take you to the gift shop downstairs where they sell homemade marmalade.

 # Located near C. Siete Dolores de Nuestra Señora, beside Pl. Santa Isabel and Iglesia San Marcos. $ Tour €3. Small marmalade €3; large €4.40. ⏰ Museum open Tu-Su 10am-1pm. Shop open Tu-Su 10am-1:30pm and 4:30-7pm.

El Arenal and Triana

PLAZA DE TOROS DE MAESTRANZA MONUMENT

Paseo de Cristóbal Colón, 12 ☎95 421 03 15 www.realmaestranza.com

Constructed between 1761 and 1881, the Maestranza is one of the oldest bullfighting rings in the world. The Maestranza offers a tour of the ring, stables, and museum (conducted in both English and Spanish) that will leave you feeling like a true master of almost three centuries of bullfighting history. The bullfights themselves, occurring on Sundays between April and October, are a true taste of Sevilla's culture. Aside from the **Feria de Abril,** when the best matadors are in town, you should be able to grab a ticket the day or even hours before the fight. Visit www.plazadetorosdelamaestranza.com or buy in person at the stadium ticket window before the fight.

 # Off Paseo de Cristóbal Colón between Pl. de Armas and Torre de Oro. $ Tours €6.50, students €4. Tickets €15-150. Cash only. ⏰ Museum open daily May-Oct 9:30am-8pm; Nov-Apr 9:30am-7pm. 40min. tours every 20min. Bullfights Apr-Oct select Su 7, 7:30pm.

TORRE DE ORO MUSEUM, VIEW

Paseo de Cristóbal Colón ☎95 422 24 19

While it may no longer be filled with gold (sorry to burst your bubble), the Torre de Oro is still worth a visit. The maritime museum takes no more than 20min. to visit and it's free for students. But even if you come for some history, you'll stay for the views. Climb the spiraling marble stairs to the top of the tower (yes, you should go all the way to the top) and you'll be able to see all of Triana to one side of the canal and great views of La Catedral and Alcázar toward Santa Cruz.

 # On the canal side of the street at the intersection of Paseo de Cristóbal Colón and C. Almirante Lobo. $ €2, students and Tu free. ⏰ Open Tu-F 9:30am-1:30pm, Sa-Su 10:30am-1:30pm.

Near Estación Plaza de Armas

CENTRO ANDALUZ DE ARTE CONTEMPORÁNEO MUSEUM

Av. Américo Vespucio, 2 ☎95 503 70 70 www.caac.es

Embedded in the grounds of **Monasterio de la Cartuja de Santa María de las Cuevas** lies this oasis of contemporary Spanish art. And that's quite a pairing—the classic, Moorish-style monastery grounds provide a sharp contrast to the bright white walls and multi-media art collection found in the hallways of the museum. The small permanent collection primarily features Andalusian artists of the last 50 years, while the temporary exhibits feature prominent artists from around the world. The museum's aim is to connect local movements in Andalusian art to the international scene. From projected films and slideshows to simple audio installations, the museum features an incredible diversity of artistic mediums. While the museum looks far away on the map, it's really just a short walk from the city center.

About 10min. from Estación Pl. de Armas. Cross Puente de la Cartuja and make a right. Alternatively, take bus #C1 or C2. ***i*** *Tours available; reserve a spot in advance by phone (☎95 503 70 96) or email (educ.caac@juntdeandalucia.es).* $ *Museum €1.80; free all day Tu, W 7-9pm, Th 7-9pm, F 7-9pm, all day Sa. Cash only.* ⏰ *Open Tu-Sa 11am-9pm, Su 11am-4pm. Tours Su 12:30pm.*

THE GREAT OUTDOORS

While many visitors get their fill of the outdoors in the gardens of the Alcázar and Pl. de España, those more serious about the outdoors should consider a daytrip to nearby Parque Doñana, which offers hundreds of square miles of untouched Andalucian coastal habitats.

PARQUE NACIONAL DE DOÑANA NATIONAL PARK

A-483, km. 37.5 ☎95 943 04 32 http://reddeparquesnacionales.mma.es

One of the largest national parks in all of Europe, Parque Doñana covers a significant portion of the coastal territory of Andalucía. The park itself is bordered by three cities (Huelva, Cádiz, and Sevilla) and is composed of three main ecosystems: forest, marshland, and beach. The national park offers a sweeping tour of these ecosystems in a 4x4 jeep which can be described as "safari lite"—you're probably not going to see that stampede of buffalo get mauled by those lions the way you always wanted to, but you will absolutely see some stunning natural habitats and one of Spain's only stretches of untouched coastland. The tour guides will likely provide the disclaimer that you might not see any animals, but we'd be shocked if you went the whole tour without seeing anything with a heartbeat. Common species include red deer, African migratory birds, and pink flamingos. While few visitors get the chance to see the elusive Iberian lynx or eagle, both of which are endangered, this excursion will take you through the highlight reel of the park. If you're more independently minded, they also allow free entry for unguided hiking routes through the park.

From Estación Pl. de Armas, take a 1½hr. bus to Matalascañas (€6.70), and then take a 20min. bus to El Rocío/El Almonte (€1.20) and get off at "El Rocío." The visitor center for excursions to the park is to the left of the main church at El Rocío. ***i*** *Tours in Spanish. Advanced reservations are required and can be made online (www.donanavisitas.es) or by phone (☎95 942 04 32).* $ *Excursion through the park by van and bus €26. Cash only.* ⏰ *Open from May to mid-Sept M-Sa 8:30am-5pm; from mid-Sept to Apr Tu-Su 8:30am-5pm. Excursion 4hr.*

FOOD

There are plenty of local specialties to try, including different varieties of *bacalao* (cod). Look out for items like *bacalao con tomate* (with stewed tomatoes), *bacalao al horno* (oven roasted), or *pavia de bacalao* (fried). Many restaurants serve elaborate platters of fried seafood including *chocos* (squid), *calamares* (calamari), *gambas* or *langostinos* (shrimp), and *boquerones* (anchovies). Pay close attention to the *cocina casaras* (home cooking) section of the menu, where you will find a variety of traditional Andalusian stewed meats and vegetables, such as *espinacas con garbanzos* (spinach with chickpeas) and *solomillo al whisky* (pork tenderloin stewed in whiskey). While it is easy enough to eat cheaply in Sevilla, your best bet for groceries is **El Corte Inglés** in El Centro, with locations at Pl. del Duqe de la Victoria, 13 (☎95 459 70 00) or at Pl. Magdalena, 1 (☎95 459 70 10).

Santa Cruz

TABERNA COLONIALES — ANDALUSIAN, TAPAS $$

Pl. Cristo de Burgos, 19 — ☎95 450 11 37 www.tabernacoloniales.es

The biggest complaint to make about this place is that it's just too busy for its own good. Taberna Coloniales has made its name by sticking to the basics: cheap Andalusian tapas like *pollo con salsa de almendras* (chicken with almond sauce; €2.50) and fried cod (€2) as well as traditional country bread platters called *tablas* (€5.10-11). Each helping is like tapas on steroids, piled onto a slice of toast and topped with traditional cheeses, meats, and spreads. Luckily Taberna Coloniales has added two new locations to ease the congestion, but if you can, it's worth it to check out the original on the beautiful Pl. Cristo de Burgos, shaded by granddaddy banyan trees.

*⇟ On the southwest corner of Pl. de Burgos. From Pl. de la Encarnación head south and turn left on C. Imagen. Stay on C. Imagen for 3 blocks to Pl. Cristo de Burgos. **i** Other locations at C. Fernández y Gonzáles, 36-38 and C. Chaves Nogales, 7. $ Plates €1.60-3.60. Tablas €5.10-11. ⏰ Open daily 1:30-4:30pm and 8:30pm-12:15am.*

HORNO DE SAN BUENAVENTURA — SPANISH, CAFE $$

C. Carlos Cañal, 28 — ☎95 422 35 42

Between the heat and the general fatigue of sightseeing in Santa Cruz, it's good to have a convenient place like Horno de San Buenaventura to cool off. This restaurant/cafe/bakery claims to have been established in 1385, making it only slightly younger than the world's largest Gothic building across the street. They provide any and all midday refreshments from gelato (€2-3) to gazpacho (€4.50). While prices for full meals at Horno de San Buenaventura are a bit expensive (half *raciones* from €10, full *raciones* from €15), they have plenty of treats, and affordable takeaway goods for a picnic. This is also a hugely popular breakfast spot for tourists and locals alike, who wake up for the fresh-baked, thick-cut bread loaded with toppings (with coffee; €3.60).

⇟ Across Av. de Constitución from the cathedral. $ Tapas €2.30-4.50. Sandwiches €3.50-8.50. Ice cream €1.10. ⏰ Open daily 7:30am-11pm.

El Centro

★ **EL RINCONCILLO** — ANDALUSIAN, TAPAS $$

C. Gerona, 40 — ☎95 422 31 83 www.elrinconcillo.es

Opened in 1670, El Rinconcillo is the oldest tapas bar in Sevilla, and the tiled walls and warm lighting are clear relics of this historic past. El Rinconcillo's staff serves so many people that they manage to keep tabs chalked on the bar without getting a speck of white powder on their uniforms. Ask anyone for the house special and they'll tell you to try the *pavia*—deep fried *bacalao* (cod) served straight from the fryer. The gazpacho is cheap, fresh, and served straight like a smoothie (cup €2, bowl €3). The other clear favorite is the *espinacas con garbanzos* (spinach stewed with chickpeas; €2). Surprisingly, even El Rinconcillo's signature grilled entree dishes come at reasonable prices, including the lamb chops (€13) and steak (€14.) The real attraction is the bar, where you can try the best and oldest Andalusian tapas recipes in the city.

From Pl. de Ponce de León, C. Gerona is a tiny street behind Iglesia Santa Catalina. [$] Tapas €1.80-2.80. ⏰ Open daily 1pm-1:30am.

LA BODEGA DE LA ALFALFA ANDALUSIAN, TAPAS $$

C. Alfalfa, 4 ☎95 422 73 62

La Bodega offers the tastiest traditional tapas around, serving them practically before you have time to pick a table. Located just off Pl. de Alfalfa, locals are constantly pouring in and out (mainly in). The Andulusian favorite "grandma-style cod" (€2.20) is as good as any in the city. There's formal seating in the back, but try to blend in with the mob of locals at the bar.

Located right off Pl. de Alfalfa at the base of C. Alfalfa. [$] Tapas €1.80-2.20. Entrees €6-10. ⏰ Open daily 12:30-4pm and 8pm-midnight.

HABANITA INTERNATIONAL, VEGETARIAN $$

C. Golfo, 3 ☎60 671 64 56 www.habanita.es

Habanita is the budget traveler's alternative to traditional Sevillian cuisine. With a wide selection of dishes, from spaghetti bolognese to couscous to ratatouille, it's hard to tell if Habanita has a case of healthy variety or culinary identity crisis. Popular with budget travelers, Habanita offers one of the few menus you will see in Spain that is color-coded for vegan and vegetarian dishes. What is a colorblind vegan to do?

From Pl. Alfalfa, exit the far right corner and follow the L-shaped bend and make a quick left onto C. Pérez Galdós. Follow C. Pérez Galdós for a few meters; C. Golfo is on the right. [$] ½ portions €4.20-8.30. Entrees €6-14. Cocktails €4.50-5.80. ⏰ Open daily 12:30-4:30pm and 8pm-12:30am.

CONFITERIA LA CAMPAÑA BAKERY $

C. Sierpes, 1-3 ☎95 422 35 70 www.confiterialacampana.com

If you've got a sweet tooth, we've found your kryptonite. Opened in 1885, La Campaña has mastered dessert. The *cervantinas* are must-try classics. The *ingleses* (€2.20), the bakery's most popular dessert, provide a sweet flan-like flavor without the gooey texture. It also sell meringues, eclairs, truffles, cakes, and tarts, if you want something more familiar. While there are a few savory items, if you're looking for something substantial you might need to tame that sweet-toothed beast inside of you and come back after a proper meal. This place deals in sugar—pounds and pounds of it.

From the Ayuntamiento, walk down C. Sierpes; Confiteria la Campaña is on the right. [$] Pastries €1.80-2.20. ⏰ Open daily in summer 8am-11pm; in fall, winter, and spring 8am-10pm.

La Macarena

ESLAVA TAPAS $$

C. Eslava, 5 ☎95 490 65 68 www.restauranteeslava.es

Though just over 20 years old, Eslava is already a city institution. Beloved by young locals, Eslava offers exquisite food at totally reasonable prices. While the narrow baby-blue corridor of the restaurant is totally packed afternoon and night, it's worth it to squeeze in and place an order. The menu is rooted in traditional Andalusian recipes, but the chefs are willing to experiment. Dishes like the over-easy egg (served on top of a mushroom cake with mushroom emulsion and honey; €2.20) have brought serious accolades to the restaurant, including the 2010 Best Tapa of the Year. Other menu items are wonderfully simple, such as the *costillas a la miel* (pork ribs barbequed in honey; €2.20) and a good selection of market-fresh seafood (€12-17). The sit-down restaurant in back is a bit more pricey, but it is easy to eat on the cheap at the bar where all tapas cost €2-3.

Take C. Santa Ana from the Alameda de Hércules and turn left onto C. Santa Clara. The restaurant is in back of the church of Santa Clara. [$] Drinks €1-2. Restaurant open daily 1-4pm and 9-11pm. Bar open daily 12:30-4:30pm and 8pm-midnight.

CASA PACO ANDALUSIAN $$

Alameda de Hércules, 23 ☎95 490 01 48

While Casa Paco serves an array of classic Sevillian dishes from *salmorejo* (a chilled soup similar to gazpacho; €2.50) to *carrillada* (pig's cheek; €3.50), its general ambience is a nice break from the typical dark, dive-y tapas bar. The prices are a little higher than the competition, but house specialties are clearly worth it. The best dishes come *gratinado*, straight from the oven, such as the *queso de cabra* (goat cheese; €4) and the *solomillo al mostaza* (pork tenderloin roasted in mustard; €3.50), and the house specialty of *bacalao gratinado* (cod baked with artichoke, peppers, lemon, and olive oil; €4). The alfresco seating along Alameda de Hércules is fantastic, though occasionally an accordion player will wander over to make things sound "European."

On the southwest corner of Alameda de Hércules. [$] Tapas €2.50-4. Entrees €7-12. Wine and beer €1.50-2.50. Open daily 1:30-4:30pm and 8:30pm-midnight.

El Arenal and Triana

FARO DE TRIANA ANDALUSIAN, SEAFOOD $$$

Puente Isabel II (Puente de Triana) ☎95 433 61 92

You may get a bit discouraged walking down C. Betis and seeing restaurant after restaurant offering fresh seafood at painfully expensive prices. What's a backpacker to do? Faro de Triana. Though not cheap, Faro provides slightly lower prices without any loss of quality. You can keep it casual and still get the freshest fish around. Like most of the restaurants along the canal, Faro specializes in its fried and whole grilled fish (€15-18). The heaping half portions are large enough to fill you up and maybe even take you out of commission for your next meal. While this is unquestionably a seafood restaurant, one of the most popular platters is the *solomillo de cerdo con pimientos* (pork tenderloin grilled with peppers; €15).

Immediately to the left once you cross Puente de Triana. Open M-Sa 8am-midnight.

BLANCA PALOMA TAPAS, ANDALUSIAN, SEAFOOD $$

C. San Jacinto, 49 ☎95 433 36 40

Blanca Paloma is an unassuming locals' bar just a few blocks down San Jacinto from the canal, where you can find all of the same seafood as at canal-side restaurants. While the seafood can be a bit pricey, plenty of the traditional Andalucian dishes use market seafood but don't break the bank. Dishes like the platters of *boquerones fritos* (fresh anchovies fried with lemon and olive oil; €6) are cheap and popular, as are the *revueltos* (eggs scrambled with market seafood; €10). The setting is not quite as picturesque as the restaurants along the water, but Blanca Paloma is where the locals of Triana come to dine.

At the intersection of San Jacinto and C. Pagés del Corro. On the far right corner if coming from Puente de Triana. [$] Tapas €1.80-3, ½ portions €5.40-9, full €9-15. Open M-F 8:30am-5:30pm and 7pm-midnight, Sa 12:30-4:30pm and 8:30pm-12:30am, Su 8:30am-4:30pm and 7pm-midnight.

MERCADO DE TRIANA MARKET $$

Intersection of C. San Jorge and Pl. del Altozano

Mercado de Triana is one of the cleanest, best-organized, most air-conditioned marketplaces in Sevilla. It has the feel of a local market, selling the freshest breads, produce, cheese, meat, and fish. **Bar La Muralla** (Mercado de Triana, 72

☎95 434 43 02 ⏰ Open M-Sa 6:30am-3pm), in the back of the market, uses all the products offered in the marketplace to serve lunch and breakfast to enthusiastic local customers. You'll get laughed at if you ask for a menu (they don't have any). Just ask for a recommendation and they'll tell you about all the fresh products that have come in that day (tapas €2.20-3). La Muralla is also a good place to grab a breakfast of *churros con chocolate* or a lunch to go.

⇞ On the right-hand side at the base of the Puente de Triana. ⏰ Open M-Sa 6:30am-3pm. Hours for specific vendors vary.

NIGHTLIFE

Santa Cruz

While not necessarily the party capital of Sevilla, Santa Cruz still has some nice spots to drink, snack, and get the night off to the right start. By day, much of Santa Cruz is overrun with fanny packs, but, by night, the locals return. Popular destinations in Santa Cruz include the tree-filled **Plaza de Alfalfa** and the surrounding streets at the north end of the *barrio*, and near **Calle Mateos Gago** just west of the cathedral. If you want a sure-fire way to pick out the locals, look to the tables snacking on *caracoles*—snails are generally not for tourists.

BAR ALFALFA BAR

C. Candilejo, 1 ☎95 422 23 44 baralfalfa@hotmail.com

The plaza's namesake bar does not disappoint. With the feel of a traditional tavern, Bar Alfalfa continues to attract Sevilla's 20-somethings for early evening drinks and tapas. The food and drink here is a joint Spanish and Italian effort with an extensive list of wines from both countries and tapas that use the best Iberian and Mediterranean ingredients. The menu is limited, but classic. Bar Alfalfa also serves simple cocktails and has a strong list of affordable wines by the glass.

⇞ At the tip of Pl. Alfalfa, off C. Alfalfa. $ Drinks €1.60-€2.80. Bruschetta €2.30-€2.90. ⏰ Open daily noon-4pm, 8pm-12:30am.

ANTIGÜEDADES BAR

C. Argote de Molina, 40 www.tapearensevilla.com

Stepping into Antigüedades, you may be a little confused as to whether you're in a bar or a Halloween shop. With mannequins dressed as clowns draping the walls and fake bloodied hands and feet adorning the ceiling, this bar is for the happy drunk. And if the decor isn't enough to get you on your toes, maybe the Spanish covers of American '80s hits (*Vídeo mató a la estrella de radio*, anyone?) or mashups between classic Spanish songs and American hip hop will freak you out. In any case, the calm terrace seating just north of La Catedral is a welcome refuge for an evening drink.

⇞ Just north of the cathedral. From Pl. Virgen de los Reyes, take C. Placentines to C. Argote de Molina; the bar is on the left. $ Wine and beer €2. Cocktails €6. Pitchers €12. ⏰ Open daily 5pm-3am. Terrace seating closes at 1am.

La Macarena and West

La Macarena and the area further west may be the best place to set out for an evening in Sevilla. You'll find everything from open-patio dining to relaxed bars and hip clubs with nightly DJ sets.

★ THEATRO ANTIQUE CLUB

C. Matemáticos Pastor y Castro ☎95 446 22 07 www.antiquetheatro.com

Twenty-five hundred sq. m, a 1400-person capacity, three outdoor bars, and a swimming pool? We don't want to get you all flustered with the math, but the full magnitude of Theatro Antique can't be comprehended without a visit. This upscale club is the place to see and be seen, catering to a few famous faces and thousands of trendsters looking for the snazziest evening around. You'll hear the booming music from all the way across the river, putting some of the smaller clubs along the Torneo to shame. In the summer, take relaxation to a whole new level by sitting around the pool on the Aqua Antique patio in your personal cabana, hanging with friends and sipping your caipirinha (€8). This is a high end-European club, so dress accordingly: lose the muscle tank and throw on some slacks, a going-out shirt, and a good pair of shoes. Without proper attire, you may have trouble getting in.

From Alameda de Hércules, take C. Calatrava and cross the bridge; the club is on the left. $ Call in advance to determine cover. Beer €4. Sangria €6. ⏰ Open in summer Tu-Su midnight-7am; in winter Th-Sa midnight-7am.

BODEGA VIZCAÍNO BAR

C. Feria, 27 ☎95 438 60 57

Bodega Vizcaíno is unapologetic about its dive-bar status. You can expect the tiled floor to be littered with crushed peanut shells and dirty napkins, but the local clientele doesn't seem to care. The interior has a few spare stools and tables, but most take their cheap drinks and drift out onto the sidewalk to enjoy the cooler Sevilla evenings. While the place is usually buzzing with a younger crowd come 9:30pm, if you stop by at midday you can expect plenty of scruffy middle-aged men catching a break from the heat with a cold beer. Drinks are as cheap as they get in the city with beer (€1.10) and house wine (€1.30) served straight out of the barrels behind the bar.

Near the intersection of C. Feria and C. Correduría. $ Cash only. ⏰ Open M-Sa 8am-11:30pm.

JACKSON CLUB

C. Relator, 21

From the front door, Jackson may not look like much—it lurks in a dark corner with a cheesy icon as a sign—but don't pass judgment just yet. At 2am on weekend nights, much of the young late-night drinking crowd from the bars of the Alameda de Hércules drift to this nearby *discoteca* and club that specializes in '80s funk and groove. If you take a break from dancing, you will notice the namesake cartoon of the bar "Jackson," a perhaps uncomfortably caricatured cartoon of a black male. While the cartoon is disturbingly 1880s, the music is definitely 1980s, with Prince, Michael Jackson, and the like. While Jackson advertises a closing time of 3am, locals describe the schedule as "11pm through the rest of the week." So grab a beer (€2-3), and rely on that next morning's *cortado* to wake you up after a night of hip-shaking (and drunkenly trying to figure out who this Jackson guy is and why they've made a bar in his honor).

Off the right corner of the Alameda de Hércules from El Centro. Take C. Relator a ½ block west; the bar is on the left. $ Beer €2-3. Cocktails €6-7. Cash only. ⏰ Open daily 11:30pm-3am.

BOSQUE ANIMADO BAR

C. Arias Montano, 5 ☎95 491 68 62

Escape the noisy, crowded patios of the Alameda de Hércules and experience the relief of this fairytale cave, filled with Sevilla's most attractive men. With your *cubata* (rum or whiskey and Coke; €6) in hand, grab any seat at the bar aside from the one at the corner—it's permanently occupied by a gnome statue, Bosque Animado's signature denizen. Surrounded by a mix of 20- and 30-something locals, this is a great place to enjoy mellow music in the early evening before moving onto one of La Macarena's few late-night options.

On the left-hand side of a small street branching off the Alameda de Hércules between C. Recreo and C. Santa Ana. $ Beer €1.50-2.50. Cocktails €6. ⏰ Open daily 4pm-2am.

El Arenal and Triana

KUDÉTA CAFE CHILLOUT DISCOTECA (BUDDHA) — CLUB

Pl. de la Legión ☎95 408 90 95 www.kudetasevilla.es

If you ask a local how to get to Kudéta, they'll likely shrug their shoulders. But if you drop the name Buddha, you'll get an immediate sly smirk—they've probably been there, and they've probably had some crazy nights there, too. Located in the historic Pl. de Armas train station, Kudéta is one of Sevilla's largest, most well-known clubs. They know they'll fill up, so they have no problem with less-than-ascetic prices. While the first floor remains pretty mellow (how can you not be mellow with pictures of Siddhartha on every wall and silky pillows and drapes everywhere?), offering hookah and a selection of wines and beers, things get rowdy on the upstairs dance floor and outdoor terrace. Thursday nights are reserved for enormous study-abroad student parties of about 1,000 visitors. While the club is quieter early in the week, the outdoor terrace, which sits directly under the wrought-iron facade of the Pl. de Armas, is a fantastic place to sit, with cool white leather seating and large shaded palms that will make you feel like you are living in your favorite music video.

‡ In the Centro Comercial de Pl. de Armas, in the portion closest to Av. de la Expiración. ***i*** *Roof terrace open May-Oct.* $ *Beer €4. Cocktails €7.50.* ⏰ *Open in summer daily 3pm-6am; in winter M-W 3pm-4am (lounge only), Th-Sa 3pm-6am, Su 3pm-4am (lounge only).*

ISBILIYYA — GLBT, BAR, CLUB

Paseo de Cristóbal Colón, 2 ☎95 421 04 60

With a canal-front terrace absolutely packed on any summer night and a booming dance floor year-round, Isbiliyya may be Sevilla's best hotspot for GLBT nightlife. Cross the Puente de Triana and be welcomed by the friendly staff, as open and congenial as the crowds of locals (young and old) ready to meet and mingle. Enjoy the cafe during the evening, the bar a bit later (discounted drinks until 1am: beers €2; cocktails €4), and the party until the early morning. The combo of house and '80s dance music can't be beat. Did we mention the pride of Isbiliyya? The bar holds a drag show Mondays through Saturdays on its main stage, bringing out some of the most colorful and creative costumes that the city has ever seen. If you're intrigued, they also host an "after-hours" drag show on Sunday.

‡ On Paseo de Cristóbal Colón at the base of Puente de Triana. $ *Beer €3-4. Cocktails €7.* ⏰ *Open daily 8pm-4am. Drag show M-Sa 1:30am.*

ARTS AND CULTURE

As the capital of **Andalucía,** Sevilla attracts the best and brightest from the artistic and cultural scene. Sevilla's got the money, motivation, and spirit of possibility flowing through the streets. Traditional flamenco, opera, dance, and performance are far from provincial, with international artists and companies routinely passing through the city's major venues. While **bullfighting** has become taboo in parts of Spain like Catalonia, in Andalucía the culture is as alive as ever. Sevilla's **Plaza de Toros** is one of the country's oldest and most prestigious arenas and continues to attract the best fighters and strongest bulls around. If you have the stomach for the sport, fights run Sundays from the end of April to September. Tickets can be purchased online or by phone. (☎95 450 13 82 www.plazadetorosdelamaestranza.com $ Tickets €15-100.) While Real Madrid and FC Barcelona are the international stars of club soccer, Sevilla has a number of well-respected teams, including **Real Betis,** which competes in La Liga. Tickets can be purchased on the club website. Home games are held in Estadio Benito Villamarín. (Glorieta Plus Ultra ☎954 61 03 40 www.realbetisbalompie.es $ Tickets €30-100. ⏰ Season runs early Sept-early May.) Make no mistake, this is a serious soccer town with fans every bit as committed as those in Madrid and Barça; the same cannot be said for the team, though.

Theater

Theater culture in Sevilla caters to those looking for the big and extravagant as well as smaller, more intimate performances. Apart from the listings below you can find indie and alternative concerts at **Sala Fun Club** (Alameda de Hércules, 86 ☎95 421 80 64 www.funclubsevilla.com 🕐 Open Th-Sa 9:30-10pm), or folk and blues shows at **Cafe Lisboa** (C. de la Alhóndiga, 43 ☎98 329 16 15 🕐 Open M-Sa 3pm-3am, Su 1pm-3am)or **El Hobbit.** (C. Regina, 20 🕐 Jazz Th 10pm; folk Sa 10pm.) If you want to catch a flick, **Avenida 5 Cines** (C. Marqués de Paradas, 15) shows international films with Spanish subtitles for €5.50, while **Cinesa** (Pl. de la Legión, 8 ☎90 233 32 31) in the mall at Pl. de Armas, shows flicks dubbed in Spanish (€6.50) and 3D movies (€9.50).

TEATRO LOPE DE VEGA SANTA CRUZ

Av. María Luisa ☎95 547 28 28 www.teatrolopedevega.org

Teatro Lope de Vega is the main stage in Sevilla, and it fits any stereotype you'd hold of a classic theater, including red velvet chairs and curtains with golden trim. Located just behind the Universidad de Sevilla, the theater is run by the city government. Tickets can be purchased in person at the box office, online at www.generaltickets.com/sevilla, or by phone.

➜ Off Parque María Luisa near the Universidad and the Pl. de España. $ Tickets €4-21. 🕐 Box office open Tu-Sa 11am-2pm and 6-9pm, Su 11am-2pm. Shows usually start at 9pm.

TEATRO DE LA MAESTRANZA ARENAL

Paseo de Cristóbal Colón, 22 ☎95 422 33 44 www.teatrodelamaestranza.es

Teatro de la Maestranza holds operas, flamenco shows, dance performances, and piano recitals. Maestranza regularly welcomes acts from around the world in dance and music, including major European ballet companies, symphony orchestras, and distinguished solo acts. This is one of the premier stages in the south of Spain, and you can expect ticket prices to reflect that. The theater thanks Mozart for including the city of Sevilla in his *Marriage of Figaro* through the character Barbaro with a statue of the composer out front.

➜ Next to the Pl. de Toros on Paseo de Cristóbal Colón. i Tickets can be purchased at the box office or by phone at ☎95 422 65 73. $ Opera tickets €40-100. Concerts €15-42. Dance shows €25-50. 🕐 Shows Th-F 8:30pm. Box office open M-F 10am-2pm and 5:30-8:30pm.

Flamenco

TARDES DE FLAMENCO EN LA CASA DE LA MEMORIA SANTA CRUZ

C. Ximénez de Enciso, 28 ☎95 456 06 70 www.casadelamemoria.es

The stage is located in the central courtyard of an 18th-century house, with beautiful plants hanging from the skylit ceiling and a few wood chairs centered around the stage. Tardes de Flamenco knows how to set the scene and pack the seats of this intimate venue. The nightly show is performed by four artists, all of whom couldn't be older than 25. Try not to scrape your chin on the floor when your jaw drops—these kids know their stuff. Running through two centuries of flamenco, they layer on the components, starting with just a guitar before adding in the male and female dancers one at a time. The dancers aren't the only ones getting their heart rate up—you'll get so sucked into the drama that you'll feel your chest pounding. This is hands-down the best deal around for classic flamenco and the setting can't be beat. Buy tickets in advance and arrive at least 30min. early, as shows sell out.

➜ From Pl. de la Virgen de los Reyes, facing the cathedral, take a slight left onto C. Mateos Gago (passing the bar El Giraldo), follow C. Mateos Gago west a few meters past C. Ángeles, take a right on C. Mesón del Moro, follow for 1 block until this street ends at C. Ximénez de Enciso. $ €15, students €13. 🕐 Daily shows 9 and 10:30pm. Arrive at least 30min. early to get a seat.

TABLAO EL ARENAL ARENAL

C. Rodo, 7 ☎95 421 64 92 www.tablaoelarenal.com

Tablao el Arenal requires an investment of time and money but it's rumored to be some of the best flamenco in town. If you don't want to take our word for it, even *The New York Times* called it the best place in the world to experience flamenco. The show is about 1½hr. long and ticket prices range €37-72 depending on how much you want to eat and drink with the performance. Keep in mind that if you do buy the expensive dinner with the first performance, dinner is served on the early side at 7pm before the first show. Call ahead to make reservations and arrive 30min. early so that you snag a good seat close to the performers.

➡ Between the bullring and Hospital de Caridad. $ Show with 1 drink €37; with tapas, drink, and dessert €59; with full dinner €72. ⏰ Shows daily 8 and 10pm.

EL PATIO SEVILLANO ARENAL

Paseo de Cristóbal Colón, 11A ☎95 421 41 20 www.elpatiosevillano.com

One of the oldest flamenco bars in town, El Patio Sevillano provides another classic flamenco performance with a meal included at a steep price. Compared to Tablao del Arenal (whose prices are about the same), you're getting a shorter show at a less famous establishment. That said, the colorful, cool, underground dining room sets the tone for some traditional Spanish performances. El Patio Sevillano is one of Sevilla's largest flamenco venues, with a capacity of 300, but it still sells out during weekends and the high season. Reservations can be made in advance online at their website or by telephone.

➡ On Paseo de Cristóbal Colón, only meters from the bullring. ℹ Discounts may be negotiated for small groups. Call the box office in advance or send an inquiry through their online reservation system. $ Show €38, with tapas €60, with full dinner €72. ⏰ Shows daily 7 and 9:30pm.

Festivals

SEMANA SANTA CITYWIDE

www.semana-santa.org

Semana Santa, or **Holy Week,** takes place during the last week of Lent, between Palm Sunday and Easter Sunday. During these seven days, all 57 religious brotherhoods of the city don hooded robes and guide two candlelit floats honoring Jesus and the Virgin Mary along the tiny, winding streets of Sevilla. As they make their way to La Catedral, they grab the attention of around one million spectators year after year. You don't need to be religious to be awed by the history and spectacle of Semana Santa. If you're going to stay for the end of the week, you may also consider extending your trip until **Feria de Abril** (below)—after this, you may be due for a shift from pious patron to partier. Semana Santa is the busiest week for tourism in Sevilla, so reserve rooms well in advance and beware the spike in rates. Also note that accommodations may be slightly less full during the first part of the week, as Semana Santa culminates on **Good Friday.** The city tourist offices are well equipped to answer any questions about accommodations and dining during this busy time. You can also visit the museum at the **Basílica de la Macarena** to learn more about the history of the festival.

⏰ Usually falls in the 1st 2 weeks of April.

FERIA DE ABRIL SOUTH OF TRIANA

Los Remedios district www.feriadesevilla.andalunet.com

Following the holy week of Semana Santa each year, Feria de Abril is the time for Sevilla to let its hair down and celebrate its rich culture and history. Started in 1847 as a cattle trade expo in the Prado de San Sebastián, this week of festivities has made great strides since then, though hardly less animalistic. The Feria today takes up one million sq. m of Sevillian territory, where celebrations take place in three main parts: the 15-block **Real de la Feria,** the colorful amusement park at **Calle de Infierno,** and the main entrance, or **Posada.** The Real is the heart of the Feria—the asphalt is covered in golden sand to match the bullring, the sidewalks are lined with *casetas* (canvas houses where you can spend the week drinking and eating with friends and family), and horse-drawn carriages and flamenco dancers pass through the streets. Each day, six bulls are set into the ring at **Plaza de Toros de la Maestranza** to face off against Spain's most famous matadors. Tickets sell out way in advance, so call the ticket office (☎95 421 03 15) for reservations.

From the moment thousands of Chinese-style lanterns light up the city in unison at midnight on the first night, to when Sevilla cuts to black at the closing of the festivities at midnight on the last, you're in for a treat. As far as suggestions for rooms, turn to the **information offices** throughout the city or the **kiosks** located on the Feria grounds. Special direct buses run from the Prado and Charco de la Pava to the Real, and the #C1, C2, and 41 bus lines run throughout the day (€1.50). Both ends of Metro Line 1 are located smack in the middle of the excitement.

⏰ *Usually falls between the last 2 weeks of Apr and 1st week of May.*

ESSENTIALS

Practicalities

- **TOURIST OFFICES: Centro de Información de Sevilla Laredo.** (Pl. de San Francisco, 19 ☎95 459 52 88 www.sevilla.org/turismo ⏰ Open M-F 9am-7:30pm, Sa-Su 10am-2pm.) **Turismo de la Provincia** also has tourist info and gives out special discounts at some of the newer and more popular restaurants in the area. (Pl. del Triunfo, 1-3 ☎95 421 00 05 www.tourismosevilla.org ⏰ Open daily 10:30am-2:30pm and 3:30-7:30pm.)
- **LAUNDROMAT: Vera Tintoreria.** (C. Aceituna, 6 ☎95 453 44 95 $ Self-serve wash and dry €10. ⏰ Open M-F 9:30am-2pm and 5:30-8pm, Sa 10am-1:30pm.) 2nd location at C. Menéndez Pelayo, 11. (☎95 454 11 48 $ Self-serve wash and dry €10. ⏰ Open M-F 9:30am-2pm and 5:30-8pm, Sa 10am-1:30pm.)
- **INTERNET : Internetia.** (C. Menéndez Pelayo, 43-45 ☎95 453 40 03 $ €2.20 per hr.)
- **POST OFFICE:** The main post office has a bank and also helps with international cell phones. (Av. de la Constitución, 32 ☎95 422 47 60 www.correos.es.)
- **POSTAL CODE:** 41001.

Getting There

BY TRAIN

The train is the best way to get to Sevilla. The main train station, **Estación Santa Justa** (Av. de Kansas City ☎90 224 02 02) offers luggage storage, car rentals, and an ATM. Trains depart from Madrid's **Puerta de Atocha** via the high speed service **AVE** ($ €84 ⏰ 2½hr., every 30min. daily 6:15am-9:45pm) or via the **Alvia** train. ($ €66. ⏰ 2¾hr., 2 per day.) There are also daily services from and to Barcelona via AVE ($ €143 ⏰ 5½ hr.; daily 9am and 4pm) or via **ARCO.** ($ €64.30. ⏰ 12½hr., daily 8am.) A full list of train times and routes leaving from Estación Santa Justa is available at tourist offices.

If you have a foreign credit card, tickets can be purchased online at **www.renfe.com** only once you have made a purchase in person from a RENFE office and verified your card with proper ID like a passport or driver's license. Return tickets can be purchased in Sevilla in person at the Renfe Office in the city center just off Pl. Nuevo. (C. Zaragoza, 29 ☎95 421 14 55 ⏰ Open M-F 9:30am-2pm and 5:30-8pm, Sa 10am-1:30pm.)

To get to the city from Estación Santa Justa, the best bet is to take a **taxi** (€10); the station is a 25min. walk from the city center that can be grueling under the Sevilla sun. **Bus #32** (€1.70) will take you to Pl. Ponce de León, which is still a considerable walk from many hostels. To catch the #32, exit the bus station and walk to the left of the parking lot 100m to Av. de José Laguillo.

BY BUS

There are two regional bus stations in Sevilla: Estación Plaza de Armas and Estación Prado de San Sebastián. **Estación Plaza de Armas** (Av. Cristo de la Expiración ☎95 490 77 37 ⏰ Open daily 5am-1:30am) serves all destinations outside of Andalucía, including daily routes to Madrid operated by **Socibus** (www.socibus.es $ €20 ⏰ 6hr., 10 per day 8am-1am) and to Granada operated by **Alsa.** (www.alsa.es $ €20. ⏰ 2¾hr., 9 per day 8am-11pm.) Pl. Nueva is a 10min. walk or a 5min. taxi ride (€5).

Estación Prado de San Sebastián serves destinations within the province of Andalucia. (Pl. de San Sebastián, 1 ☎95 441 71 11 ⏰ Open daily 5:30am-1:30am.) There are three major lines from which to choose: **Los Amarillos** (☎90 221 03 17 www.touristbuses.es), **Alsina Graells** (☎90 242 22 42 www.alsa.es), and **Transportes Comes** (☎90 219 92 08 www.tgcomes.es). Estación Prado de San Sebastián is also a Metro, bus, and tram stop. To get to the city center from Estación Prado de San Sebastián take the **tram** T1 ($ €1.30 ⏰ 5min.) or a taxi ($ €5 ⏰ 5min.) to Pl. Nueva.

Getting Around

BY BUS

Tussam buses blanket the city and run frequently. (www.tussam.es $ €1.30.) The best way to navigate this system is to pick up a transit map from a tourist office. The **C3** and **C4** buses, running every 10min., are particularly helpful, as they circle the border of the city clockwise and counterclockwise, respectively.

BY METRO

The **Metro** is very limited, with only one line running currently, but it can be useful nonetheless. **Metro Line 1** ($ 1-way €1.30, day pass €4.50 ⏰ Open M-Th 6:30am-11pm, F 6:30am-2am, Sa 7:30am-2am, Su 7:30am-11pm) ends in Ciudad Expo and Olivar de Quintos, making stops in Prado de San Sebastián, San Bernardo, Gran Pl., and Parque de los Príncipes.

BY BIKE

You'll quickly notice that the locals are all about biking. You'll find lines of **Sevici** (www.sevici.es) bicycles around the city. Set up a week- or year-long subscription ($ €10/25) at any of the kiosks around the city. The system is convenient, but comes with many rules. Once you sign up for the service, you can check out a bike for 30min. for free, after which they charge a fee for additional use (€1 per hr.; €2 per hr. thereafter). There's a €150 safety deposit at sign up. Consult a tourist office for more information and a map of kiosk locations.

BY TAXI

City officials recommend **Radio Taxi** (☎95 458 00 00) and **Tele Taxi** (☎95 462 22 22).

córdoba   ☎957

Forget it, Rome; wait your turn, Constantinople; get in line, Paris; get outta here, New York. During the Middle Ages, Córdoba was the undisputed center of Western civilization and the most populous city in the world. While it's been 1,000 years since the peak of its glory as the capital of the Umayyad Caliphate (932-1031), this justifiably proud Andalusian city retains an exceptional ability to teach, entertain, and inspire like few other cities in the world. You'll experience thousands of years of history and learn about Islamic, Christian, and Jewish culture (and Córdoba's characteristic combination of the three) as you walk through the narrow streets of the old city. Though the Cordoban summer sends temperatures flying up to feverish levels and beyond, you'll find refuge among the plants and gurgling fountains of the city's traditional patios while feasting on typical dishes like the refreshing *salmorejo*, a cold tomato soup. You'll sip infused teas in an Arab bath before making your way over to the city's modern section to sip decidedly non-Islamic things with a little more punch. Córdoba is no longer the capital of the world, nor even of Andalucía, but its unparalleled mix of fascinating medieval history and thoroughly modern splendor make it one of the most unforgettable cities in Spain.

ORIENTATION

Most travelers arrive in Córdoba at the bus and train stations, located in the modern, easy-to-navigate northern part of the city. As soon as you get off the city bus in the *casco antiguo*, though, you'll be in a spaghetti-like mess of streets courtesy of good old (read: bad old) medieval street planning; pick up a map at the tourist office at the train station if you want to have any hope of finding your hotel. Most of the historic sights are packed in and around the narrow streets of **La Judería,** including the **Mezquita** and the **Alcázar de los Reyes Cristianos.** Behind these monuments flows the **Río Guadalquivir,** crossed by bridges including the Puente Romano, though you're unlikely to find yourself needing to cross the river. From the river, C. San Fernando runs uphill to C. Claudio Marcelo, the street that connects the two main plazas of the *centro,* **Plaza de la Corredera** and **Plaza de las Tendillas.** The former has lots of restaurants and bars, while the latter is full of shopping, banks, and pharmacies, as well as a tourist office. Heading north from Pl. Tendillas leads to ever-more modern areas of the city, plus the nightlife of **Avenida del Gran Capitán** and **Avenida del Brillante.**

ACCOMMODATIONS

Córdoba is absolutely covered in accommodations. Whether in or out of La Judería, you won't need to take more than a few steps to find a sign pointing you to at least three or four hostels and hotels. You can pick up an accommodations guide at the tourist office, though it includes few hotels suitable for budget travelers. Even more than most Spanish cities, Córdoba's hotel prices vary greatly based on season, sometimes by as much as €35. The exact definitions of the season change from place to place, but the high season generally includes Semana Santa, weekends in April, and all of May; the low season is the rest of the year. Unlike many other cities, July and August fall in the low season because it's so incredibly hot and there is nary a beach in sight.

🏠 FUNKY CÓRDOBA   HOSTEL $
C. Lucano, 12   ☎95 749 29 66 www.funkycordoba.com

The hostel so nice they named it thrice—depending on who you ask, this place is called Funky Córdoba, Terrace Backpackers, or Pensión El Pilar del Potro. Don't be confused—no matter what you call it, this hostel is the perfect stop for any young traveler on the go. It's impossible not to feel upbeat when entering the lobby and seeing every wall painted a different bold color and covered with fun

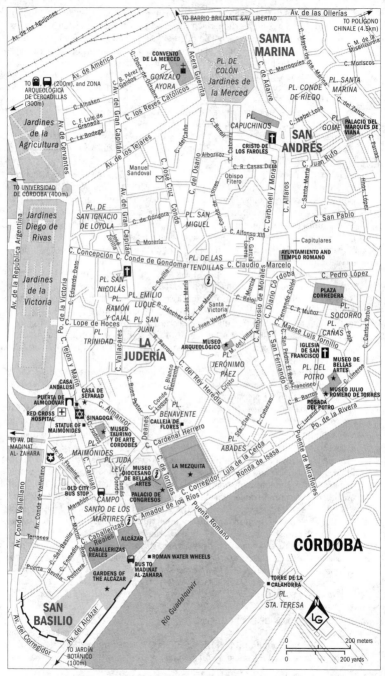

facts and interesting star-shaped lamps. If you're too exhausted after a long trip to head out to the tourist office, the information posted on the walls will spoon-feed you all the info you need. The chalkboards around the hostel provide the daily weather report, tips for local discounts, and maps pointing out the hottest restaurants and clubs. You'll have to get a little active to climb up to the small rooftop terrace, with a comfy seating area to meet fellow travelers, but you can regain all those lost calories with the help of the breakfast buffet (€2) and the shared kitchen.

*➡ From the bus and train stations, take bus #3 to San Fernando, proceed in the direction of the bus, and take the 3rd left onto C. Lucano. **i** Free Wi-Fi (doesn't reach some rooms) and computers with unlimited free internet access. Female-only dorms available. Kitchen available. Sheets included. Towels €2. Laundry €5. $ Dorm €12-28; double €26-28. ⏰ Reception 24hr.*

👍 BED AND BE HOSTEL $$

C. de José Cruz Conde, 22 ☎95 710 14 86 www.bedandbe.com

Given the neo-hippie imperative in its name, it should come as no surprise that Bed and Be is the coolest place to stay in Córdoba. "Be" your heart out at this brand new accommodation halfway between a hostel and a boutique hotel, whose understated, hip interior design comes courtesy of José—backpacker, former sustainable-tourism grad student, amateur design enthusiast, owner, and sole employee. It's quieter than most hostels, but there are plenty of opportunities to meet fellow travelers over breakfast in the eclectic collection of chairs in the living room, while cooking dinner in the shared kitchen, or over a beer (€1) at one of the periodic parties on the rooftop *azotea* (terrace). The cheapest option for solo travelers is the sole four-bed dorm with wood-framed bunk beds and extremely high ceilings, while those traveling in pairs will be happy to hear that all the doubles, including a truly massive one that takes up almost an entire floor, all cost the same. While it's a bit far from the sights and can get quite pricey during the high season, there aren't many places to stay in Córdoba with this much character.

*➡ From the bus and train stations, take bus #3 to Gran Capitán, proceed in the same direction as the bus, turn left onto Ronda de los Tejares, and then take the 2nd right onto C. José Cruz Conde; the hostel is on the left. **i** Breakfast included. Spanish and English spoken. A/C. Lockers free, but are too small for large backpacks. Sheets and towels included. Bike rental €15 per day; guests €15 per 2 days. $ 4-bed dorms €20-35; doubles €40-90. ⏰ Reception 24hr.*

PENSIÓN TRINIDAD HOTEL $

C. del Corregidor Luis de la Cerda, 58 ☎95 748 79 05

This *pensión* near the Mezquita is unusual, though not because it lacks a plant-filled interior patio and ceramic-lined staircase; it if didn't have these, it would cause a tear in the fabric of space-time in these parts. What makes it remarkable are its cheap, comfortable private rooms close to the sights of the old city. Everything is pretty straightforward (bed, towels, table, dresser) except for the fact that the doors to some rooms do not open directly into a bedroom, but rather into a small anteroom with a sink—that's actually a bit of a headscratcher.

*➡ From the bus and train stations, take bus #3 to San Fernando, proceed in the same direction as the bus, and take the 1st right onto C. Cardenal González, which will turn into C. Corregidor Luis de la Cerda; the hotel is on the right. Or, from the rear side of the Mezquita on C. Corregidor Luis de la Cerda (across from the Puente Romano), with your back to the Mezquita, turn left; it's on the left. **i** All rooms have sink and shared bath. A/C. $ May and Semana Santa singles €25, doubles €50; Mar-Apr and June-Oct €20/40; Nov-Feb €18/36. ⏰ Reception 7am-10pm.*

ALBERGUE INTURJOVEN DE LA CREATIVIDAD (HI) HOSTEL $

Pl. de Judá Leví ☎95 735 50 40 www.inturjoven.com

This bright, airy, and enormous HI hostel is the closest budget accommodation to the Mezquita, which means you're likely to find not just solo backpackers but also penny-pinching families and study-abroad students in town from Salamanca for the weekend. Pass through the sliding glass doors that are so big you'll mistake them for a window and enter the massive, high-ceilinged lobby that looks like the love child of a spa and an airport departure gate. Make your way through the large, shady outdoor patio on your way to your fairly spacious but not air-conditioned room with ensuite bathroom; make sure to request a non-bunk bed. The free Wi-Fi only reaches the lobby, which is kind of frustrating, since Andalucía's logo, plastered all over the hostel, looks exactly like the Wi-Fi symbol.

*From the bus and train stations, take bus #3 to San Fernando. With your back to the river, turn left onto C. Julio Romero de Torres, left at Pl. Jerónimo Páez onto C. Horno de Cristo, then right onto C. Rey Heredia, and immediately left onto C. Encarnación. Then turn right at the end of the street onto C. Cardenal Herrero and proceed straight as the street becomes C. Judería and curves slightly to the left to become C. Manríquez; the hostel is in a small plaza on the right. **i** Breakfast included. Free Wi-Fi in lobby. Sheets included, towels €2. [$] High-season dorms €19, over 26 years old €25; low-season dorms €14/20. €3.50 discount with HI card. ⏰ Reception 24hr.*

HOSTAL FONDA LA CORREDERA HOTEL $$

C. de Rodríguez Marín, 23 ☎95 747 05 81 www.hostallacorredera.com

Seeing as this is Andalucía we're talking about, we should probably break the bad news right up front: this *hostal*'s rooms have no air-conditioning. Once you've accepted the fact that you'll probably spend the night getting more intimate with the floor fan than with your significant other, these are some of the best centrally located private rooms you'll find without breaking the bank; plus, if it gets too hot, you can always find relief in the air-conditioned living room with couches and a TV. The doubles with twin beds and triples with balconies overlooking the busy Pl. Corredera are fairly spacious; the singles and doubles with double beds are far less roomy but have sinks. The bathrooms are in the hallway, and the shower and toilet are gloriously separate, so the vanity and/or constipation of your neighbors shouldn't delay the start to your day.

*From the bus and train stations, take bus #3 to San Fernando, proceed in the same direction as the bus, take the 1st left onto C. San Francisco, then the 1st left onto C. Armas, which turns into C. Sánchez Peña before leading to the Pl. Corredera. Cross the plaza diagonally to the left and start going up the hill; the hotel is on the right. **i** Free Wi-Fi. Shared baths, some rooms with sinks. [$] May, Semana Santa, and long weekends singles €30, doubles €50, triples €70; Mar 15-Apr €27/47/68; June-Aug €25/36/55; Sept-Oct €27/47/68; Nov-Mar 14 €25/36/55. Parking €12-15. ⏰ Reception M-Th 9:30am-2:30pm, F-Sa 10:30am-3pm and 5-8:30pm, Su 9:30am-2:30pm; after 5pm M-Th and Su by phone.*

HOSTAL SÉNECA SENSES Y COLOURS HOTEL $$

C. del Conde y Luque, 7 ☎95 749 15 44 www.hostalsenecasensescolours.com

Sitting on the bend of an especially picturesque street in La Judería, Hostal Séneca provides more of a homey, lived-in atmosphere than some of the neighborhood's other accommodations. The shaded rooftop terrace with cushioned benches and views of the Mezquita is a great place to have a drink at night, maybe with a new friend you made in the kitchen, the plant-covered patio, or from sleeping rather close to him in the bed-packed, tapestry-lined dorms. The four-bed dorms are bunk-free and have extra-long and extra-wide (and extra-close together) beds; the six-bed dorms have bunks, but one of them also has an ensuite bathroom.

*From the bus and train stations, take bus #3 to San Fernando. With your back to the river, turn left onto C. Julio Romero de Torres, turn left at Pl. Jerónimo Páez onto C. Horno de Cristo, then turn right onto C. Rey Heredia, take the 3rd left onto C. Blanco Belmonte, which leads to Pl. Benavente, and walk straight across the plaza onto C. Conde y Luque; the hotel is on the left. **i** Breakfast €4. Free Wi-Fi. A/C. Sheets €2, towels €2, both €3. Kitchen available. [$] 6-bed dorms from €12; 4-bed from €13.75. Singles from €25; doubles from €33; triples €45-80. ⏰ Reception 8am-midnight.*

HOSTAL MAESTRE

C. de Romero Barros, 16

HOTEL

☎95 747 53 95

This *hostal* has comfortable private rooms, traditional Andalusian decor, and a central location equidistant from the Mezquita and the Pl. Corredera. The internal skylit patio, decorated with plants and ceramic plates, looks more pleasant than most, though that advantage is quickly erased by the patio's lack of air-conditioning (the rooms all have A/C). The private bathrooms have all the fan favorites, plus the always-useful bidet and hair dryer.

⚑ *From the bus and train stations, take bus #3 to San Fernando, proceed in the same direction as the bus, and take the 2nd left onto C. Romero Barros; the hotel is on the right.* ⓘ *Breakfast €5. Free Wi-Fi. A/C.* ⑤ *Singles €25-45; doubles €30-52; triples €35-60.* 🕐 *Reception 24hr.*

HOTEL BOSTON

C. de Málaga, 2

HOTEL $$$

☎95 747 41 76 www.hotel-boston.com

This hotel, right in the center of the action of the Pl. Tendillas, is a wicked sweet deal during the low season (when many international tourists are in town) and completely unaffordable on weekends during the high season. Don't mistake the super-high May prices for incredible luxury, though—the spacious yellow rooms decorated with painted flowers are pleasant, and the private bathrooms with personalized towels will feel incredibly decadent after a week or two of hostel showers and towel deposits, but it's a simple hotel that provides a peaceful stay at reasonable prices.

⚑ *From the Pl. Tendillas, with your back to the front of the equestrian statue, cross the plaza diagonally to the left; the entrance is around the corner on C. Málaga, on the right.* ⓘ *Breakfast €2.20-4.75. Free Wi-Fi. A/C. Safe available.* ⑤ *Singles €25-45, doubles €35-60, triples €45-75; weekends in May €60/105/120.* 🕐 *Reception 24hr.*

HOSTAL LA FUENTE

C. de San Fernando, 51

HOTEL $$

☎95 748 78 27 www.hostallafuente.com

The *fuente* (fountain) that gives this *hostal* its name may not be as impressive as you expected, but its shaded patio with hanging plants and marble tables is one classy hangout. Once you get into the hallways, you don't lose even an ounce of class. You'll find tasteful paintings of flowers on the walls, fancy couches, and giant wood-framed mirrors as you make your way up this four-story building. The red-and-white-striped matching comforters and curtains shoot for Mezquita chic but land somewhere between gourmet candy cane and high-end clown.

⚑ *From the bus and train stations, take bus #3 to San Fernando. From the bus stop, you will see the hotel's sign.* ⓘ *Free Wi-Fi. Private bath with hair dryer. A/C. TV and safe available.* ⑤ *Mar-Nov singles €35; doubles €50; triples €75; quads €90. Dec-Feb €30/45/65/80. Prices may be higher during holidays and long weekends. IVA not included.* 🕐 *Reception 24hr.*

SIGHTS

Córdoba has a quantity of sights befitting the former cultural capital of the West. Luckily, most of the city's many sights are concentrated in and around La Judería and are easily within walking distance of each other and of most accommodations. The remaining columns of the **Templo Romano** stand like 11 marble middle fingers to those who have forgotten the glory of Rome and Córdoba's role as capital of Hispania Baetica amid all the medieval fanfare. (C. Claudio Marcelo ⚑ At intersection with C. Capitulares.) Pick up a list of major sights and their hours and prices at the tourist office, and make sure to check schedules ahead of time, as many are closed on Mondays, have unusual weekend hours, or have certain days or times when they can be visited for free. A bit farther afield, 8km. to the west of the city, is the magnificent **Conjunto Arqueológico de Madinat al-Zahra,** the ruins of a vast 10th century palace complex. (☎95 735 28 60 www.juntadeandalucia.es/cultura/museos/CAMA ⚑ Bus from Glorieta de la Cruz Roja or Paseo de la Victoria opposite the Mauseolo

Romano; bus tickets must be purchased in advance at a tourist office. $ €1.50, EU citizens free. Round-trip bus fare €7, under 12 €3.50, under 5 free. ⏰ Open Tu-Sa 10am-8:30pm, Su 10am-2pm. Buses depart Córdoba summer Tu-Sa 10:15am and 5pm, Su and holidays 9:30am and 10:15am; winter Tu-Sa 10:15am and 3pm, Su and holidays 9:30am and 10:15am. Buses depart Madinat al-Zahra Tu-Sa 1:45pm and 8:30pm, Su 1pm and 1:45pm.) Also, *Let's Go* is not your mother, but please wear sunscreen and bring a water bottle—Andalusian afternoons in summer are no joke.

LA MEZQUITA-CATEDRAL DE CÓRDOBA CHURCH, MUSEUM

C. del Cardenal Herrero ☎95 747 05 12 www.catedraldecordoba.es

No matter how many times you've seen pictures of its red brick and white stone striped arches stretching away to infinity, the inside of the Mezquita will still take your breath away. Boasting one of the most beautiful interior spaces in the world, the Mezquita is the most dramatic and awe-inspiring witness to—and participant in—the complex centuries-long dance between Christianity and Islam in the Iberian Peninsula. On this site originally stood the Visigoths' Christian Church of San Vicente, but when the Moors came to town in 758 CE they knocked it down and constructed a mosque in its place. When complete, the Mezquita turned Córdoba into the hottest thing this side of Baghdad; it was the most important Islamic structure in the West and the second largest mosque in the world, second only to Mecca's. When Córdoba fell once again to the Christians, King Ferdinand III and his successors set about Christianizing the structure, most dramatically adding the bright, pearly white Renaissance nave where mass is held every morning. A visit doesn't come cheap (€8), but you can get in for free between 8:30-10am any day except Sunday, though you'll have to do without the audioguide (€3.50); almost all of the cathedral is open during this time except the nave, which opens after Mass concludes at 10am. Beware the gypsies outside, especially on C. Cardenal Herrero and C. Torrijos, yelling *"Toma!"* (Take!) and thrusting an herb toward you; things quickly devolve into fortune-telling and then begin to involve money—a firm *"No, gracias"* should help you avoid getting into any situations you want to avoid.

⇞ From the Pl. Tendillas, with your back to the front of the equestrian statue, turn left onto C. Jesús y María, which becomes C. Ángel de Saavedra and C. Blanco Belmonte, which leads to the Pl. Benavente. Cross the plaza and take a slight left onto C. Céspedes, which leads straight to the main façade of the Mezquita. From the main entrance on C. Cardenal Herrero, the ticket offices are to the right, near the base of the bell tower. ℹ *Audioguide available 10am-5pm in Spanish, English, French, German, and Italian.* $ *€8, under 14 €4, under 10 and M-Sa 8:30am-10am free (only individual visits allowed). Audioguide €3.50. El Alma de Córdoba nighttime tour €18; students, seniors, and under 10 €9; under 7 free but do not receive audioguide.* ⏰ *Open Mar-Oct M-Sa 8:30am-7pm, Su 8:30am-10:30am and 2-7pm; Nov-Feb M-Sa 8:30am-6pm, Su 8:30-10:30am and 2-6pm. Mass M-Sa 9:30am, Su 11am and 1pm.*

ALCÁZAR DE LOS REYES CRISTIANOS MUSEUM

C. de las Caballerizas Reales ☎95 742 01 51 www.alcazardelosreyescristianos.cordoba.es

Originally constructed in 1328 as a palace, the Alcázar has been home to far more interesting things than fussy royal dinners over the years: it served as a planning headquarters for the discovery of America and the reconquest of Granada, as well as the seat of the local Inquisition. Today, it's back to being filled with people wearing funny costumes, except the royal ruffs have been replaced with the fanny packs of the tourists that pour into this castle, museum, and garden complex. Climb one of the towers (some are original, while others were added in the 15th, 18th, and 20th centuries) or explore the collections of second- and third-century Roman mosaics discovered in the Pl. Corredera. Perhaps most impressive are the Jardines del Alcázar, a wide expanse of pools, flowers, and immaculately trimmed hedges. Try to arrive early in the morning: not only is it free during the week from 8:30-10:30am, but after that the sun can get oppressively hot, when instead of appreciating the bubbling fountains you'll just stare at them angrily and curse the water for not being potable.

⇞ From the main entrance to the Mezquita on C. Cardenal Herrero, with your back to the Mezquita, turn left and proceed straight as the street becomes C. Judería, then curves slightly to the left to become C. Manríquez, then curves slightly to the left again to become C. Tomás Conde; continue past the small park and enter the right-hand side of the large building at the end of the street. $ €4.50, students €2.25, free Tu-F 8:30-10:30am. ⏰ Open June 16-Sept 15 Tu-Sa 8:30am-2:30pm, Su and holidays 9:30am-2:30pm; Sept 16-June 15 Tu-F 8:30am-7:30pm, Sa 9:30am-4:30pm, Su 9:30am-2:30pm. Last entry 30min. before close.

SINAGOGA SYNAGOGUE

C. de los Judíos, 20 ☎95 729 06 42 www.turismodecordoba.org

Built all the way back in 5075 (1315, for all you *goyim*), this synagogue has come a long way over its 700 years. When the Jews were expelled from Spain in 1492, all but three synagogues in the entire country were destroyed, and just one survived in Andalucía—you guessed it, the Sinagoga de Córdoba. Although it wasn't knocked down, it was repurposed into a hermitage and into a hospital for rabies patients. It wasn't until 1884, when a piece of falling plaster revealed the rich artistic design hidden in the ceiling, that the building was converted into a national monument and the careful restoration began. Visitors can now enjoy the historic beauty of the main prayer room's walls, engraved with Hebrew biblical inscriptions from the Book of Psalms and translated on posters around the museum.

⇞ From the main entrance to the Mezquita on C. Cardenal Herrero, with your back to the Mezquita, turn left and proceed straight as the street becomes C. Judería and curves slightly to the left to become C. Manríquez. Turn right onto C. Tomás Conde, which leads to the Pl. Maimónides; cross the plaza diagonally and proceed along C. Judíos; the synagogue is on the left. ℹ Signs in Spanish and English. $ Free. ⏰ Open Tu-Su 9:30am-2pm and 3:30-5:30pm. Last entry 10min. before close.

CASA ANDALUSÍ MONUMENT

C. de los Judíos, 12 ☎95 729 06 42 www.lacasaandalusi.com

Sure, maybe they only bathed once a year, but the people of the 12th century definitely knew how to relax. Come experience a glimpse of the high life of the caliphs in this preserved house's patio, where you can enjoy the quiet sound of tranquil fountains and the sweet smell of fresh flowers. It's a bit of an environmental jump to the room with a replica of a 10th-century Arab paper factory, but just go with it—the model and the old Arabic books are pretty cool. Don't miss the Andalusian coin collection in the traditional tea room—and if you get bitten by the tea bug, pay a visit to the affiliated **tea parlor.** (C. Buen Pastor, 13 ☎95 748 79 84 ⇞ Walk toward the Sinagoga on C. Judíos and continue to Pl. Maimónides, then turn left onto C. Cardenal Salazar, right onto C. Romero, left onto C. Deanes, and left onto C. Buen Pastor. $ Tea €3.30-6.50. ⏰ Open daily 11am-11pm.)

⇞ From the main entrance to the Mezquita on C. Cardenal Herrero, with your back to the Mezquita, turn left and proceed straight as the street becomes C. Judería and curves slightly to the left to become C. Manríquez; then turn right onto C. Tomás Conde, which leads to the Pl. Maimónides. Cross the plaza diagonally and proceed along C. Judíos; the monument is on the left, just after the Sinagoga. ℹ Information available in English and Spanish. $ €2.50. ⏰ Open daily 10am-7pm.

CASA DE SEFARAD CULTURAL CENTER, MUSEUM

C. de Averroes, 2 ☎95 742 14 04 www.casadesefarad.es

For those a little miffed at how empty the Sinagoga is, this museum and cultural center will more than fulfill your craving for all things Sephardi. Right across the street from the Sinagoga (in fact, the two were once connected by a tunnel), the Casa de Sefarad will guide you through the history of the Sephardi Jews in Córdoba prior to their expulsion in 1492, the history-changing event of that year that had nothing to do with the ocean blue. The crash course on holidays and kosher dining is par for the course, but the recently added upstairs exhibits on the Spanish Inquisition and Maimonides—the rabbi, author, doctor, and golden boy of Sephardi Judaism—are unique and fascinating. As this is a cultural center and not just a museum, there's always room for some more interactive fun: Casa de Sefarad holds frequent evening activities like concerts, music workshops, storytelling, and seminars. If you like your cultural experiences a little more edible, don't miss **Casa Mazal,** the delicious affiliated restaurant (see **Food**).

From the main entrance to the Mezquita on C. Cardenal Herrero, with your back to the Mezquita, turn left and proceed straight as the street becomes C. Judería and curves slightly to the left to become C. Manríquez; then turn right onto C. Tomás Conde, which leads to the Pl. Maimónides. Cross the plaza diagonally and proceed along C. Judíos; it's on the right at the intersection with C. Averroes. i Signs in Spanish and English. $ €4, students €3. ⏰ Open M-Sa 11am-7pm, Su 11am-2pm.

CAPILLA MUDÉJAR DE SAN BARTOLOMÉ CHURCH

C. de Averroes ☎90 220 17 74 www.turismodecordoba.org

After the Reconquista of Córdoba by the Castilian king in 1236, Muslims and Jews were initially allowed to remain, until a little thing called the Inquisition came to town. This small chapel is one of Córdoba's finest examples of Mudéjar art, a style combining Christian and Muslim artistic traditions that developed during this period of coexistence under Christian rule; the word Mudéjar comes from the Arabic word *mudayyan*, meaning "bad-ass interior decorator" (as well as "he who has been allowed to remain.") This free chapel is definitely worth a brief visit to admire its *zócalos*, the zig-zag decorative motifs on the walls; the colorful geometric ceramic tile patterns considerably more authentic-looking than what you'll find in the lobby of every single Cordoban restaurant and hotel; and the stylized Arabic script praising Allah. The free pamphlet, whose author appears to still fear the Inquisition, assures us the praise is for decorative purposes only.

From the main entrance to the Mezquita on C. Cardenal Herrero, with your back to the Mezquita, turn left and proceed straight as the street becomes C. Judería and curves slightly to the left to become C. Manríquez. Turn right onto C. Tomás Conde, which leads to the Pl. Maimónides. At the plaza turn right onto the unmarked street and take the 1st left; the church is immediately on the right. i Signs in Spanish and English; pamphlets in Spanish, English, French, German, and Italian. $ Free. ⏰ Open Jun 15-Sept 14 M 5:30pm-8:30pm, Tu-Sa 10:30am-1:30pm and 5:30pm-8:30pm, Su 10:30am-1:30pm; Sept 15-June 14 M 3:30-6:30pm; Tu-Sa 10:30am-1:30pm and 3:30-6:30pm, Su 10:30am-1:30pm.

TORRE DE LA CALAHORRA AND MUSEO VIVO DE AL-ANDALUS MUSEUM

Puente Romano ☎95 729 39 29 www.torrecalahorra.com

The Museo Vivo de al-Andalus takes you back in time to the period between the ninth and the 13th centuries, when Córdoba was the cultural center of the world and more than one million people walked its streets. Passing through the museum's rooms, you'll encounter many points of pride in Cordoban heritage, including the advanced surgical technology of Abulcasis, whose methods were still being cited until the 20th century, or the musical stylings of the *rebab*, a wooden string-and-bow instrument that produces traditional tunes. In the hall of thinkers, medieval wisdom gets beamed into your futuristic wireless audioguide: Alfonso X will tell you about opening the world's first school where Jews, Christians, and Muslims studied together, while Ibn Arabi will tell you about the power of love and the importance of individual thought. If this is all a little heavy for you, head upstairs for the scale models of the Mezquita and the Alhambra and learn about the daily life in Córdoba during its heyday, or head all the way up to the top of the Torre de la Calahorra for views of the old city.

From the rear side of the Mezquita on C. Corregidor Luis de la Cerda, cross the Puente Romano. i Audioguide available in English, Spanish, French, and German; text of audioguide available in Italian, Japanese, and Dutch. $ €4.50, students €3. ⏰ Open daily May-Sept 10am-2pm and 4:30-8:30pm; Oct-Apr 10am-6pm.

CASA MUSEO ARTE SOBRE PIEL MUSEUM

Pl. de la Agrupación de Cofradías, 2 ☎95 705 01 31 www.artesobrepiel.com

This is the world's premiere collection of *guadamecíes omeya*, embossed leather artworks popular in the 10th-century Caliphate of Córdoba. Actually, it's pretty much the world's only collection of *guadamecíes omeya*—this lost art is no longer practiced or taught, except by Ramón García Romero, who dedicated his life to this curious art of leather colored, gilded, and adorned almost beyond recognition to create beautiful patterns. His works now fill this small museum. We could do without the €3 entrance fee given the museum's size, but it's not every day that you discover an entirely novel medium and see works by its only practitioner in 1,000 years.

From the main entrance to the Mezquita on C. Cardenal Herrero, with your back to the Mezquita, proceed straight along C. Céspedes, which leads to the Pl. Agrupación de Cofradías; it's to the right as soon as you enter the plaza. ***i*** *Free pamphlet available in Spanish, English, French, and German.* $ *€3, seniors €2.* ⏰ *Open Tu-Sa 11am-2pm and 4:30-8pm, Su 11am-2pm.*

MUSEO DE LA INQUISICIÓN MUSEUM

C. de Manríquez, 1 ☎95 747 45 08 www.museodelainquisicion.com

The Museo de la Inquisición is about the Spanish Inquisition in the same way porn is about pizza delivery men—it's just a premise. In this case, the real subjects are the stomach-churningly brutal tortures used on those suspected of heresy during the centuries-long Catholic-orthodoxy-and-execution fest of the Spanish Inquisition. Six dimly lit rooms are filled with familiar instruments of torture like the iron maiden, the rack, and the headcrusher, as well as ones you'd previously lived in blissful ignorance of, like the Heretic's Fork, which we assure you does not get stuck in food, and Judas's Cradle, which *Let's Go* does not recommend as a baby shower gift. In case there was any confusion about how these large metal machines worked, drawings and pictures illustrate their proper use; in case there was any confusion about the end result, the skeletons in several of the rooms should provide some clarity. The clunky English translations make the descriptions of the vile tortures sound so matter-of-fact that it would be funny if it weren't all so horribly gruesome. This place is not for the squeamish, and not for anyone after lunch, but it'll give you a visceral feeling of how the religious cooperation for which medieval Córdoba is so celebrated fell apart: violently, completely, and perhaps irreversibly.

From the main entrance to the Mezquita on C. Cardenal Herrero, with your back to the Mezquita, turn left and proceed straight as the street becomes C. Judería, then curves slightly to the left to become C. Manríquez; the museum is on the left. ***i*** *Signs in Spanish, English, French, German, and Italian.* $ *€3, under 10 free.* ⏰ *Open daily 10:30am-8:30pm.*

MUSEO ARQUEOLÓGICO MUSEUM

Pl. de Jerónimo Páez, 7 ☎95 735 55 17 www.museosdeandalucia.es

There's so much to see in Córdoba that it's hard to get excited about what at first appears to be yet another Paleolithic-to-present museum of spear tips, column capitals, and makeup paraphernalia. Nevertheless, the history of Córdoba is so rich that there are a few things that make this newly renovated museum stand out (a bit) from the rest, including an archaeological site of the old Roman theater in the basement and a collection of coins, dishes, gravestones, an XXXL chamber pot, and other artifacts from Córdoba's golden age during the Caliphate (929-1031). It should by no means be at the top of your sightseeing list, but it will provide a little more detail for your mental images of Roman and medieval Córdoba; furthermore, it's cheap, well air-conditioned, and open during the *siesta*.

From the main entrance to the Mezquita on C. Cardenal Herrero, with your back to the Mezquita, turn right, take a slight left onto C. Encarnación, and proceed until the end of the street. Turn right onto C. Rey Heredia and immediately left onto C. Horno de Cristo, which leads to the Pl. Jerónimo Páez; it's across the plaza. ***i*** *Signs in Spanish and English.* $ *€1.50, EU citizens free.* ⏰ *Open Tu 2:30-8:30pm, W-Sa 9am-8:30pm, Su 9am-2:30pm.*

MUSEO DE BELLAS ARTES MUSEUM

Pl. del Potro, 1 ☎95 735 55 50 www.museosdeandalucia.es

At the Museo de Bellas Artes, you'll get a quick trip through 15th- to 20th-century Spanish and Cordoban culture courtesy of a sizeable collection of drawings, paintings, and sculptures. While the museum includes artists from all over Spain, it especially prides itself on its extensive representation by Cordoban artists. The massive pieces in the Baroque chapel-like space will stun you with their bold colors and powerful subject matter, and the bright contemporary sculptures will leave you perplexed and intrigued. It's not what Córdoba is famous for, but if you're looking for a little fine art, swing on by—it's free for EU citizens and cheap for everyone else.

🚏 From the Pl. Corredera, proceed along C. Sánchez Peña, which will turn into C. Armas before leading to Pl. Potro; the museum is on the left. ℹ Pamphlets available in English but exhibits only in Spanish. $ €1.50, EU citizens free. ⏰ Open June 16-Sept 15 Tu-Sa 8:30am-2:30pm, Su and holidays 9:30am-2:30pm; Sept 16-June 15 Tu-F 8:30am-7:30pm, Sa 9:30am-4:30pm, Su and holidays 9:30am-2:30pm.

MUSEO JULIO ROMERO DE TORRES MUSEUM

Pl. del Potro, 1 ☎95 776 02 69 www.museojulioromero.cordoba.es

By your 15th birthday, how many internationally acclaimed paintings had you produced? We don't want to hurt your self-esteem, but Julio Romero de Torres had several works under his belt before he was old enough to see an R-rated movie. After this celebrated Cordoban painter's premature death at the age of 56, his wife and children collaborated with the city government to establish this museum dedicated to all things Torres. If you aren't too put off by the sky-high price-to-size-of-museum ratio, you'll likely enjoy this small museum full of portraits, ravishing female nudes, and other artists' depictions of the devilishly handsome Torres himself.

🚏 From the Pl. Corredera, proceed along C. Sánchez Peña, which will turn into C. Armas before leading to Pl. Potro; the museum is on the left. ℹ Audioguide in Spanish and English free (€20 deposit). $ €4.50, students €2.25; free Tu-F 8:30-10:30am. ⏰ Open Tu-F 8:30am-7:30pm, Sa 9:30am-4:30pm, Su 9:30am-2:30pm.

FOOD

There are few moments of complete faith in man's ability to develop the perfect solution to any obstacle in his way like your first sip of *salmorejo* on a scorching Cordoban afternoon. In addition to this cold tomato-based soup topped with ham and honey, specialties of the Cordoban kitchen include the *flamenquín*, a deep-fried rolled log of ham, and the *pastel cordobés*, a thin, flaky, pumpkin jam-filled cake. All these can be tried at any of the touristy restaurants suffocating the narrow streets of La Judería, though the farther away you get from the Mezquita the more likely you are to find good food at affordable prices. To save money, buy groceries at **Maxi Dia Supermercado.** (C. Sevilla, 4 🚏 From the Pl. Tendillas, with your back to the front of the equestrian statue, proceed straight ahead along C. Conde de Gondomar and take the 1st left onto C. Sevilla. ⏰ Open M-Sa 9:30am-9:30pm.)

[✓] TABERNA SALINAS CORDOBAN $$

C. de Tundidores, 3 ☎95 748 01 35 www.tabernasalinas.com

This welcoming, traditionally decorated restaurant's menu is a veritable who's who of Cordoban specialties, each more delicious than the last. Start off with the first, cheapest, and most refreshing thing on the menu: a glass of *gazpacho* served with a single ice cube. After that, it's hard to know what to recommend: the refreshing *salmorejo* might be the only good reason not to order the pretty similar *gazpacho;* the *flamenquín* is as much of a crispy guilty pleasure as fried ham ought to be; and the melt-off-the-bone *rabo de toro* (oxtail), served with french fries, is tender and flavorful. The plates are big enough that one will fill you up just fine, but you'll probably end up trying more than one during your stay in Córdoba—the food is so cheap and so good that few travelers can resist a return trip.

🍴 *From the Pl. Corredera, with your back to C. Sánchez Peña, cross the plaza diagonally to the left, walk up the hill, and take the 1st left onto C. Tundidores.* 🍽 *Menu in Spanish, English, French, German, Italian, and Japanese.* Ⓢ *Raciones €6.40-6.90. Desserts €2.60.* 🕐 *Open Sept-July M-Sa 12:30-4pm and 8-11:30pm. Closed Aug.*

▨ CASA MAZAL   SEPHARDI $$$
C. de Tomás Conde, 3   ☎95 794 18 88 www.casamazal.com

Let's Go Spain and Portugal 1013, painstakingly handwritten by monks, might not have recommended Casa Mazal, since its traditional Sephardi food wouldn't have stood out in La Judería during medieval times. However, since we're in the 21st century, and the Sephardi Jews are long gone from Córdoba, Spain, and most of Europe, *Let's Go Spain and Portugal 2013* heartily recommends this unique and delicious cultural experience. Treat yourself to one of the house specialty couscous dishes with chicken and citrus fruits, duck confit, or suckling lamb (€17-19) and a glass of red wine. (Those who've visited the Casa de Sefarad will remember that the latter has been called "the best and most exquisite of foods.") The patio is picturesque, but few of the tourists who make up the bulk of the restaurant's clientele have the willpower to turn down a table in the air-conditioned interior.

🍴 *Just off of the Pl. Maimónides in La Judería. From the main entrance to the Mezquita on C. Cardenal Herrero, with your back to the Mezquita, turn left and proceed straight as the street becomes C. Judería, then curves slightly to the left to become C. Manríquez. Turn right onto C. Tomás Conde; the restaurant is on the right.* 🍽 *Menu in English available.* Ⓢ *Appetizers €5.50-8. Entrees €7.50-19. Desserts €5.70-6.90.* 🕐 *Open daily 12:30-4:30pm and 8-11:30pm.*

LA FLOR DE LEVANTE   ICE CREAM $
Pl. de las Tendillas, 3   ☎95 747 40 04

Where were you in 1934? While our guess would be that you were still two generations of boy-meets-girl away from existence, this Cordoban institution was already serving up deliciously thick ice cream from its small storefront in the Pl. Tendillas. The homemade *turrón* (nougat) and *trufa* (truffle) ice creams are incredibly rich but not too sweet, and the underrated *fresa* (strawberry), *coco* (coconut), and other fresh fruit flavors are just as refreshing. If you just can't decide between a cup or a cone, leave them both for an ice cream sandwich (€2.30-2.40); if you don't want ice cream at all, the *granizada de limón* (lemon slushie, €1.90) does wonders on a hot day (i.e., any day in summer).

🍴 *From the Pl. Tendillas, with your back to the rear end of the equestrian statue, cross the plaza diagonally to the right.* Ⓢ *Ice cream cones €1.10-2.90, cups €2.75-5. Ice cream sandwiches €2.30-2.40. Mixed drinks €4.50. Table service €0.10-0.30 extra.* 🕐 *Open Mar-Oct daily 10am-2am, often later on F-Sa.*

PASTELERÍA-CAFETERÍA SAN PEDRO   BAKERY $
C. del Escultor Juan de Mesa, 10   ☎95 747 44 82

With all of Córdoba's delicious specialty dishes, it can sometimes be hard to save room for dessert. *Let's Go* understands, but this bakery off of the Pl. Corredera is out for revenge: its pastries and desserts are so big that after eating one you probably won't be able to even look at another *flamenquín* until tomorrow at the earliest; the *hojas con chocolate* (puff pastries dipped in dark chocolate, €1.30) are longer and thicker (and tastier) than Barry Bonds's forearm. This is also a great place to try the traditional *pastel cordobés* (€1.50), a thin, flaky, sweet cake with a jam-like pumpkin filling. If you're looking for something a little more savory, look no further than the empanadas (€1.35)—though it's not like you have a choice, since they're so enormous they block everything behind them from sight.

🍴 *From the Pl. Corredera, with your back to C. Sánchez Peña, turn right and exit the plaza into the Pl. Socorro, then proceed straight and take a slight right onto C. Escultor Juan de Mesa; the bakery is on the right.* Ⓢ *Desserts €1.30-1.50. Ice cream €1.25-2.15. Empanadas €1.35.* 🕐 *Open daily 8:30am-8:30pm.*

EL ARBOLITO
CAFE $

C. de San Fernando, 84 ☎95 794 10 85

Take some lusciously juicy orange slices and fresh-off-the-boat pineapples, throw in a cheap menu of sandwiches and salads, top it all off with a sprig of free Wi-Fi, and toss everything in the blender—the refreshing, soothing, delicious mixture you end up with is El Arbolito. Invigorate yourself for a day of sightseeing with this cafe's breakfast of cereal, yogurt with fruit, fresh fruit juice, and tea or coffee (€6.50), or, after your last museum of the afternoon, drag your dehydrated, exhausted self here for a glass of mixed fresh fruit juices or a fruit milkshake (€3) before your well-deserved *siesta*. Despite its proximity to the touristy restaurants around the Mezquita, it's a local favorite and is far less concerned with mimicking traditional Cordoban decor than with churning out mouth-wateringly fresh antidotes to the heat of the Andalusian afternoon.

⇶ From the rear side of the Mezquita on C. Corregidor Luis de la Cerda (across from the Puente Romano), with your back to the Mezquita, turn left and proceed straight as the street becomes C. Cardenal González, then take the 5th left onto C. San Fernando; the cafe is on the left.
i Free Wi-Fi. Ⓢ Juices €3. Milkshakes €3. Breakfast €6.50. Coffee, tea, and hot chocolate €1.50. Sandwiches €1.50. Salads €3.50. ⚄ Open daily 10:30am-8pm.

RESTAURANTE FEDERACIÓN DE PEÑAS
CORDOBAN $$

C. del Conde y Luque, 8 ☎95 747 54 27 www.federaciondepeñas.com

If you really must have a *menú del día* in La Judería, this calm restaurant run by a cultural association is one of the best affordable options. There's better food, lower prices, and prettier patios scattered across the neighborhood, but few places have a better combination of the three. Since most of the customers are tourists too exhausted to talk, you'll be able to appreciate the quiet gurgle of the fountain and the mood-setting recorded guitar music. A handful of different cheap *menús* are offered during lunch (€8-13.50, IVA not included), though be warned that while all but the cheapest include a drink, bread, and dessert, the breadstick-like crackers aren't really bread and fruit isn't really dessert, no matter what Michelle Obama wants us to believe.

⇶ From the main entrance to the Mezquita on C. Cardenal Herrero, proceed straight along C. Céspedes, then turn left at the plaza onto C. Conde y Luque; the restaurant is on the right.
i €8 menú does not include drinks, bread, or dessert. Ⓢ Menús €8-13.50. Appetizers €4.25-12. Entrees €6-15.40. 8% IVA not included. ⚄ Open daily 12:30-4pm and 7:30-11pm.

LA ESTRELLA
SPANISH $$

Pl. de la Corredera, 14 ☎95 747 42 60

Walking into Pl. Corredera on a summer evening, it's impossible to miss the large territory marked by La Estrella's metallic tables and blue chairs emblazoned with spray-painted gold stars. A great place to try Cordoban classics outside once the sun goes down and the city cools down a bit, all the favorites are here, like *patatas bravas*, *flamenquín*, and their mouth-watering *salmorejo*. You can either get a hefty bowl of this seasoned, chilled, honey- and ham-topped soup on its own (€5), or pair it with fried eggplant (€6) or a slice of *tortilla española* (€4.50). Surrounded by mostly 20-somethings looking for a relaxed evening, you'll also find quite a few couples of any age enjoying a casual, outdoor date.

⇶ From the Pl. Corredera, with your back to C. Sánchez Peña, walk straight across the plaza.
Ⓢ Appetizers €3.50-9. Meat and fish entrees €6-12. ⚄ Open daily May-Sept noon-4pm and 7pm-2am; Oct-Apr noon-4pm and 7-11pm.

NIGHTLIFE

We know you've spent your entire afternoon navigating the small streets of La Judería, but when the sun goes down, it's time to make your way out of there. Córdoba is a city that's always down for a good time and out for a long time. In the area near the **Plaza de la Corredera** and **Calle de Alfaros,** you'll find smaller cafe-bars open day and night, catering to a young, mellow clientele. Following **Avenida del Gran Capitán** away from the city center, the bars and clubs keep getting bigger and more extravagant. By the time you hit **Avenida de América** and farther outward, it's massive establishment after massive establishment packed with glowing lights, pricey drinks, and a flashy crowd. During the school year, the Ciudad Jardín neighborhood on the other side of the Jardines de la Victoria is where the students tend to hang out, especially around C. Alderetes, but this area is much less lively during the summer. If it's 4am and you're still going hard, take a taxi up to the large clubs of the **Polígono Industrial de Chinales,** to the north-east of the city.

BAMBUDDHA — BAR, CLUB

Av. del Gran Capitán, 46 — ☎957 40 39 62

You've seen the synagogue. You've seen the cathedral-mosque. And while this ain't no Buddhist temple, those down for a good time should pay a visit to this Buddha-themed pub as well. The first thing that will catch your eye as you approach is the exclusive-looking terrace, hidden under low-draped white sheets glowing with green and red lights. On a hot summer evening, though, you'll probably want to head inside to the air-conditioned interior, complete with a few Eastern touches like faux-paper lanterns above the bar. Enjoy the air-conditioning while you can, though, since on weekends the temperature rises sharply around 2am as the bar fills up and the cocktails start coaxing out the dance moves.

From the Pl. Tendillas, with your back to the front of the equestrian statue, proceed straight ahead along C. Conde de Gondomar, then take the 2nd right onto the wide pedestrian Av. Gran Capitán and walk 10-15min.; it's right after the park, at the intersection with Av. Libertad. $ Beer €1.50-3. Cocktails €6-7. ⏰ Open July-Aug M-W 6pm-3am, Th-Sa 6pm-4am, Su 6pm-3am; Sept-June M-W 3pm-3am, Th-Sa 3pm-4am, Su 3pm-3am.

JAZZ CAFÉ CÓRDOBA — BAR, LIVE MUSIC

C. de la Espartería — ☎957 48 14 73

The perfect place for a one- or two-drink night out with friends, this centrally located jazz club right off of the Pl. Corredera has less of a smoky back-room vibe than most. It also has a more varied program, including not only jazz but also stand-up, magic shows, blues jam sessions, and even classic disco recordings on Saturdays. If Gloria Gaynor groupies and Woody Allen wannabes can both find a home here, surely so can you.

From the Pl. Corredera, with your back to C. Sánchez Peña, cross the plaza diagonally to the left and walk up the hill; the bar is on the left. ℹ Live music Tu-Th at 10 or 11pm (Tu jazz; W miscellaneous concerts, monologues, or magic shows; Th blues jam sessions). Sa disco after midnight. Free Wi-Fi. $ Beer €2-3. Cocktails €5.50. All drinks €1 more during concerts. ⏰ Open daily summer 9am-2pm and 10pm-4am; winter 9am-2pm and 5pm-4am.

SOJO RIBERA — BAR

Paseo de la Ribera, 1, 3rd fl. — ☎957 49 21 92 www.cafesojo.es

Despite sharing a building with a parking garage, Sojo Ribera is one of the swankiest places to have a drink in Córdoba near the major tourist sites of the old city. A crowd of all ages sips surprisingly cheap drinks in the well air-conditioned, vaguely Arabian interior, while couples get cozy around a candle in the romantic outdoor area. Live rock music (often '80s covers) on Thursdays at 10pm draws an especially large crowd, though the Thursday night barbecue probably has something do with that as well.

✝ *From the rear side of the Mezquita on C. Corregidor Luis de la Cerda (across from the Puente Romano), with your back to the Mezquita, walk toward the Puente Romano and turn left onto Ronda de Isasa, which will turn into Paseo de la Ribera; the bar is on the left, through the glass doors with the parking sign. Take the elevator to the 3rd fl.* ℹ *Live rock music Th 10pm.* Ⓢ *Beer €2.50-3.50. Cocktails €7-18.* 🕐 *Open M-Th 8:30am-3am, F 8:30am-4am, Sa 11am-4am, Su 11am-3am.*

AUTOMÁTICO MUZIK BAR   CAFE, BAR, CLUB
C. de Alfaros, 4

Automático can be best described as a mullet: business in the front, party in the back. The front of Automático is a cafe area, with a bar equipped with a cappuccino and latte machine that can muster up any caffeinated drink you can think of. As you make your way farther into this late-night hangout, you'll find yourself at the modern bar and elevated dance floor, glistening under the disco ball and jamming to dance beats. Whether these tunes are part of the Thursday night live shows (10pm) or the DJ-produced weekend parties, you'll definitely want to get moving with the young, casual crowd into the early morning.

✝ *From the Pl. Corredera, with your back to C. Sánchez Peña, cross the plaza diagonally to the left and walk up the hill and proceed straight as the street becomes C. Capitulares and then C. Alfaros; it's on the right.* ℹ *Free Wi-Fi. Concerts some Th 10pm.* Ⓢ *Tea €1.50. Coffee €1.90. Beer €1.20-2.50. Cocktails €5-6.* 🕐 *Open July-Aug daily 9pm-4am; Sept-Apr M-Th 5pm-3am, F 5pm-4am, Sa 1pm-4am, Su 1pm-3am; May-June M-W 5pm-2am, Th 5pm-3am, F-Sa 5pm-4am, Su 5pm-2am.*

LA POSADA DE BABYLONIA   BAR, CLUB
C. de Fernando de Córdoba, 8   ☎662 35 23 89 www.laposadadebabylonia.com

Forget al-Andalus—this large club justifies its vaguely Middle Eastern decor with reference to Babylon, thank you very much. You won't hear any tranquil guitar music here, but you'll hear just about everything else, including Top 40, house, reggaetón, and anything the DJ feels like that evening. The club is pretty large for the side of Av. América closer to the *centro*, but on the weekends it fills up with a crowd in their young 20s and is the rowdiest place on a street with two other clubs and a sex shop.

✝ *From the Pl. Tendillas, with your back to the front of the equestrian statue, proceed straight ahead along C. Conde de Gondomar, then take the 2nd right onto the wide pedestrian Av. Gran Capitán. Take the 5th left onto C. Alhakén II and the 2nd right onto C. Fernando de Córdoba; the bar is on the right.* Ⓢ *Cover Th-Sa €8, includes 1 drink. Beer €3. Cocktails €6-16.* 🕐 *Open M-Th 4pm-6am, F-Sa 4pm-7am, Su 4pm-6am.*

MIÚ GARDEN   CLUB
Av. del Brillante, 18

On your trek up Av. Brillante, you will come across a white castle on your right and think to yourself, "If only I lived in a castle." After you've explored the artistically decorated, two-story interior with three bars, a spacious dance floor, and a top floor equipped with three living-room hangouts that look like the snazziest bachelor pads you've ever seen, you'll be thinking, "If only I lived in *this* castle." Then you'll realize that every weekend has a special guest performer to get the crowd dancing, followed by a DJ dropping the hottest beats from every country across the globe, and you'll exclaim, "I'm never leaving this castle!" You may find that you're in the younger half of the clientele, but trust us when we say that the dance floor's hot.

✝ *From Pl. Tendillas, with your back to the front of the equestrian statue, proceed straight along C. Conde de Gondomar, take the 2nd right onto Av. Gran Capitán, and walk 15-20min. as the street eventually turns into Av. Brillante; the club is on the right.* Ⓢ *Beer €2-3. Mixed drinks €6-9. Cover on concert nights, but no regular cover.* 🕐 *Open July-Aug W-Th 9pm-3am, F-Su 10pm-4am; Sept-June F-Sa 10pm-4am.*

córdoba

ARTS AND CULTURE

While perhaps the most traditionally Cordoban experience, flamenco shows aren't the only live performances on the city's cultural menu. For those looking for other options, the three theaters run by the Instituto Municipal de las Artes Escénicas de Córdoba (www.teatrocordoba.org), including the picturesque **Gran Teatro,** have diverse programming, including theater, dance, and music productions (Av. Gran Capitán, 3 ☎95 748 02 37 ⇞ From the Pl. Tendillas, with your back to the front of the equestrian statue, proceed straight along C. Conde de Gondomar and take the 2nd right onto Av. Gran Capitán; the theater is on the left). Classical music fans should check out the **Orquesta de Córdoba.** (C. José Cruz Conde, 13 ☎95 749 17 67 www.orquestadecordoba.org ⇞ From Pl. Tendillas, with your back to the front of the equestrian statue, turn right onto C. José Cruz Conde.) For a rare fusion of cultural experience and window shopping, visit the **Zoco** crafts market, which sells artisanal ceramics, metalwork, and leather products in a two-story building surrounding a pleasant patio. (C. Judíos ☎95 720 40 33 www.aretensiadecordoba.com ⇞ From the Sinagoga, proceed along C. Averroes and follow it as it twists and turns; the market on the right. ⏰ Open daily 10am-8pm.) For those needing a peaceful respite from the seemingly endless list of sights and cultural experiences, the relaxing Arab baths await.

Baths

Though they'll cost you the equivalent of two and a half *menús del día*, Córdoba's Arab baths will reinvigorate you after even the toughest day of sightseeing. Hammam al-Andalus is bigger and has a student discount during the low season, but hygiene-conscious and sweet-toothed travelers might prefer the **Baños Árabes de Córdoba,** where provided sandals and bathing caps are required and tea and pastries are included. (C. Almanzor, 18 ☎95 729 58 55 www.arabbath.com ⇞ From the main entrance to the Mezquita on C. Cardenal Herrero, with your back to the Mezquita, turn left and proceed straight as the street becomes C. Judería, then turn right at the fork onto C. Deanes and then immediately left onto C. Romero Barros, which becomes C. Almanzor. *i* Bathing suit and bathing cap are required and available for rent. Sandals must be rented. $ May and July-Oct 15 baths €26, with 15min. massage €33; Oct 16-Apr and June €23/28. ⏰ Open daily 10am-2am.)

HAMMAM AL-ANDALUS

C. del Corregidor Luis de la Cerda, 51 ☎902 33 33 34 www.hammamalandalus.com

For those willing to pay a little more for a relaxing cultural experience, these medieval-style Arab baths, the biggest in Europe, provide a taste of old-school Andalusian luxury. Visits to the baths (€23) last 90min. and include access to a warm bath, a hot bath, and a cold bath; you can switch between the three at your leisure, perhaps taking a quick break from the water to sip a free mint-infused tea. For those looking to relax even more, a variety of massages are available, ranging from a standard 15min. relaxing massage to an elaborate 30min. "al-Andalus ritual." The exotic architecture and dim lighting make this place pretty romantic, which is great for couples; individual travelers and "just friends," however, should be warned that they might be sitting next to a spectacle of things even steamier than the hot bath. Bring your bathing suit (or rent one—eek!), but leave your sandals at home—entrance to the baths is barefoot.

⇞ From the rear side of the Mezquita on C. Corregidor Luis de la Cerda (across from the Puente Romano), with your back to the Mezquita, turn left; the bath is on the right. i Spanish and English spoken. Reservations recommended 1-2 days in advance during Apr-May, July-Oct, Dec, and on weekends; can usually be made same day otherwise. Bathing suit required; rental €1.50. Bathing caps not required. Sandals permitted in the locker room but not in the bath areas; disposable latex sandals are available upon request. $ Bath alone €23, with 15min. massage €33. Jan-Mar, June, Nov M-F 10am-4pm and midnight bath with 15min. massage €28, students €23. ⏰ Bath (and massage, if purchased) lasts 1.5hr. Time slots daily every 2hr. 10am-midnight.

Flamenco

Flamenco in Córdoba is much more reasonably priced than in other cities in Andalucía, such as Sevilla. While Tablao Flamenco Cardenal is the most prominent spot, there are multiple options around the city that offer their own spin on this classic Andalusian experience. **Perol Flamenco** combines a flamenco show with a hearty, traditional dinner. (C. Velázquez Bosco, 10 ☎64 771 12 66 ⇞ From the main entrance to the Mezquita on C. Cardenal Herrero, with your back to the Mezquita, turn right and then left onto C. Velázquez Bosco. $ €20. ⏰ Show daily at 8:30pm.) Prices drop as you get farther away from La Judería; **La Bulería** is another excellent option. (C. Pedro López, 3 ☎95 748 38 39 ⇞ From the Pl. Corredera, with your back to C. Sánchez Peña, cross the plaza diagonally to the left, walk up the hill, and take the 1st right onto C. Pedro López. *i* Show includes 1 drink. $ €12. ⏰ Show daily at 10:30pm.)

TABLAO FLAMENCO CARDENAL

C. de Torrijos, 10 ☎957 48 33 20 www.tablaocardenal.com

In an atmosphere as Cordoban as they come, across the street from the Mezquita, Tablao Flamenco Cardenal puts on six 2hr. shows a week (10:35pm) featuring renowned guitarists, singers, and dancers. You'll get a taste of many different types of flamenco from different time periods and regions of Spain including *sevillanas*, *alegrías*, *seguilladas*, and *bulerías*. Whether you're looking for the classic show or some modern variations, Tablao Flamenco Cardenal will give you a taste of everything for €20, with a drink thrown in as well.

⇞ From the main entrance to the Mezquita on C. Cardenal Herrero, with your back to the Mezquita, turn left and then take the 1st left onto C. Torrijos. $ Show €20, includes 1 drink. ⏰ Open M-Sa 10:35pm-12:20am.

Festivals

FESTIVAL INTERNACIONAL DE MÚSICA SEFARDÍ

Real Jardín Botánico de Córdoba, Av. de Linneo, 1 www.turismodecordoba.org

You've seen their crafts at the Casa de Sefarad, you've visited their place of worship at the Sinagoga, you've noshed on their noms at Casa Mazal—now rock out (sort of) to Sephardi jams at this festival of Sephardi music and more in Córdoba's beautiful botanical garden. Cheap nightly concerts and music and dance workshops (€5) are the centerpieces of the festival, featuring musicians from across Spain and Europe. In addition to the music events, there are the occasional cooking workshops and wine tastings—be sure to reserve ahead for these.

⇞ From the rear side of the Mezquita on C. Corregidor Luis de la Cerda (across from the Puente Romano), with your back to the Mezquita, walk toward the Puente Romano and turn right onto Ronda de Isasa, which turns into Av. Alcázar; the entrance to the Real Jardín Botánico is at the far end of the traffic circle. i Tickets sold at Real Jardín Botánico beginning 1 week before the festival and continuing throughout the festival. Pamphlet with information and schedule available at tourist office. $ Concerts and workshops €5; discounts available for attending multiple events. ⏰ June.

LAS CRUCES DE MAYO

Citywide www.turismodecordoba.org

Cordobans may seem friendly and welcoming, but their competitive streak runs wild during this May festival. Every spring, Catholic brotherhood organizations and neighborhood associations expend all their creative ammunition on decorating enormous 10ft. crosses with flowers in a competition for the best-decorated cross in town, and tourists are happily caught in the distinctive, pretty, and sweet-smelling crossfire. The crosses are beautiful during the day, but walking around the city and seeing them illuminated at night is an unforgettable experience. There's more to these days than just the crosses, though—organizations set up bars next to their crosses, and free flamenco music by day and rock by night can be heard throughout the city. Be sure to pick up a map from the tourist office that shows the location of all the crosses.

i Map of crosses available at tourist office. $ Free. ⏰ End of Apr to beginning of May.

FESTIVAL DE LA GUITARRA

Various locations throughout Córdoba ☎57 480 644 www.guitarracordoba.com

Though it's hard to believe after you've been traveling for a while, there's more to guitar music than hostel strumming and dinnertime busking. Held for two weeks every July, the Festival de la Guitarra is one of the biggest events of the summer in Córdoba. The festival celebrates the music, history, and culture of the guitar in Spain, and in recent years has gained international exposure. While the focus of the festival is the flamenco guitar, classical, jazz, and rock guitar also make appearances, sometimes in the hands of internationally famous artists like Jethro Tull's Ian Anderson. The festival is also an educational program, as professional musicians and dancers give classes on classical and flamenco guitar playing and flamenco dancing, singing, and choreography. The other main component of the festival is the series of concerts held at indoor and outdoor venues across the city; tickets range from free to €55 and can be purchased online (service charge applies) or at any of the participating theaters' box offices. As if the workshops and concerts weren't enough, the city also hosts lectures, interviews, book and CD signings, and instrument exhibitions to make sure no guitar-related string is left un-plucked.

i Pamphlet with information and schedule available at tourist office. Register online on the festival's website for classes; classes are open but limited in size, so you should apply early. $ Music lessons €60-200, discounts available for multiple lessons. Concerts up to €55, some free. ⏰ Early July.

ESSENTIALS

Practicalities

- **TOURIST OFFICES:** The **Consorcio de Turismo de Córdoba** operates several tourist information points that serve as both municipal and provincial tourist offices (☎95 720 17 74 www.turismodecordoba.org.) The main office is actually the least useful for tourists, since it has the most limited hours and does not make tour bookings (C. Rey Heredia, 22 ⇞ From the main entrance to the Mezquita on C. Cardenal Herrero, with your back to the Mezquita, turn right, take a slight left onto C. Encarnación and proceed until the end of the street, then turn right onto C. Rey Heredia. ⏰ Open M-F 8:30am-2:30pm); more services and longer hours are found at the branches in the **Plaza de las Tendillas** (*i* Spanish, English, and French spoken. ⏰ Open daily 9am-2pm and 5:30-8pm), across the street from the **Alcázar de los Reyes Cristianos** (C. Campo Santo de los Mártires ⇞ From the rear side of the Mezquita on C. Corregidor Luis de la Cerda, with your back to the Mezquita, turn right onto C. Amador de los Ríos; it's in the park on the right. *i* Spanish, English, and French spoken. ⏰ Open daily 9am-2pm and 5-7:30pm), and at the **train station.** (Glorieta de las Tres Culturas ☎90 220 17 74 ⇞ Next to the exit onto Av. Libertad. *i* Spanish, English, and French spoken. ⏰ Open daily 9am-2pm and 5-7:30pm.) The **regional tourist office,** in the magnificent Palacio de Congresos, does not make tour bookings but provides a much easier-to-read map than the municipal tourist office. (C. Torrijos, 10 ☎95 735 51 79 www.andalucia.org ⇞ From the main entrance to the Mezquita on C. Cardenal Herrero, with your back to the Mezquita, turn left and then take the 1st left onto C. Torrijos. ⏰ Open M-F 9am-7:30pm, Sa-Su and holidays 9:30am-3pm.)
- **TOURS:** The municipal tourist office offers a "Córdoba Monumental" guided tour of the city that includes visits to the Mezquita, the Alcázar de los Reyes Cristianos, the Sinagoga, La Judería, the Puente Romano, and other sights of the old city; the tour begins at the tourist office opposite the Alcázar de los Reyes Cristianos. (⇞ Departs from tourist office opposite the Alcázar de los Reyes Cristianos. *i* Tours in Spanish and English; Tu, Th, and Sa also in

French. Includes admission to monuments. $ €33, under 8 free. 5% discount if purchased online. ⏰ 3½hr., Tu-Sa 10:30am.) The tourist office-chaperoned fun doesn't stop at night: it also runs **"Paseos por Córdoba, "** a nighttime guided tour of the *casco antiguo* that includes tapas and a drink (➜ Departs from tourist office in the Pl. Tendillas. *i* Tours in Spanish, English, and French. $ €16, under 12 €8, under 5 free. ⏰ 2hr.; July-Sept 15 W, F, and Sa 9:30pm; Sept 16-Nov 15 W, F, and Sa 8:30pm; Nov 16-Mar F and Sa 7:30pm; Apr-June F and Sa 9:30pm; no tours during Semana Santa) and **El Alma de Córdoba,** a nighttime tour of the Mezquita involving light and sound effects. (www.elalmadecordoba.com ➜ Departs from the main entrance to the Mezquita on C. Cardenal Herrero. *i* Tours in Spanish, English, French, German, Italian, Portuguese, Japanese, and Arabic. $ €18; students, seniors, and under 10 €9; under 7 free. ⏰ June-July W-Sa 9:30pm and 11pm; Aug M-Sa 9:30pm and 11pm; Sept M-Sa 9pm and 10:30pm; Oct M-Sa 8pm and 9:30pm; Nov-Feb F-Sa 8pm and 9:30pm; Mar 1-Mar 15 W-Sa 9pm and 10:30pm; Mar 16-May M-Sa 9pm and 10:30pm.) Reservations for most tourist office tours can be made in person at any branch of the municipal tourist office (except the one at C. Rey Heredia), by phone (☎90 220 17 74), online (www.reservasturismodecordoba.org), or through travel agencies and some hotels; El Alma de Córdoba has a different website (www.elalmadecordoba.com) and can also be booked at the Mezquita ticket office.

- **ATMS AND CURRENCY EXCHANGE:** Modern Córdoba is as filled with ATMs as any city, but there are very few ATMs in La Judería. The few **ATMs** are found near the Mezquita; try the Caja Rural ATM on C. Judería (➜ From the main entrance to the Mezquita on C. Cardenal Herrero, with your back to the Mezquita, turn left and proceed straight as the street becomes C. Judería) or one of the Caja Sur ATMs on C. Torrijos, preferably the one inside, since that street can get very crowded and you never know who's out there. (➜ From the main entrance to the Mezquita on C. Cardenal Herrero, with your back to the Mezquita, turn left and then take the 1st left onto C. Torrijos.) The **Caja Sur** branch (C. Medina y Corella ☎95 747 53 01 www.cajasur.es ➜ At intersection with C. Torrjios. ⏰ Open M-F 8:30am-2:30pm) also exchanges major foreign currencies, as does **Banco Santander** (Pl. Tendillas, 5 ☎95 749 79 00 www.bancosantander.es) and many of the banks along **Avenida Gran Capitán.**
- **LUGGAGE STORAGE:** Lockers are available in the **train station** (Glorieta de las Tres Culturas ☎90 243 23 43 $ €1.75 per 60min. or less, regardless of size; €3-6 per 24hr., depending on size. ⏰ Open daily 9:30am-10:30pm) and the **bus station.** (Av. Libertad ☎95 740 40 40 www.estacionautobusescordoba.es $ €4 per day. ⏰ Open daily 5:30am-1am.)
- **INTERNET ACCESS:** The **Biblioteca Provincial de Córdoba** has free Wi-Fi and computers with 1hr. free internet access. (C. Amador de los Ríos ☎95 735 55 00 ➜ From the rear side of the Mezquita on C. Corregidor Luis de la Cerda, with your back to the Mezquita, turn right onto C. Amador de los Ríos; it's on the right. ⏰ Open June 16-Sept 15 M-F 9am-2pm; Sept 16-June 15 M-F 9am-9pm, Sa 9am-2pm.) Outside of the library's limited hours, some travelers report having no trouble using the free Wi-Fi in the lobby of the **Albergue Inturjoven de la Creatividad,** even if they are staying elsewhere. (Pl. Judá Leví ☎95 735 50 40 www.inturjoven.com ➜ From the main entrance to the Mezquita on C. Cardenal Herrero, with your back to the Mezquita, turn left and proceed straight as the street becomes C. Judería and curves slightly to the left to become C. Manríquez; it's in a small plaza on the right. ⏰ Open 24hr.)
- **POST OFFICE:** The main post office is also the most conveniently located. (C. José Cruz Conde, 15 ☎95 749 63 42 www.correos.es ➜ From Pl. Tendillas, with your back to the front of the equestrian statue, turn right onto C. José Cruz Conde and walk 2 blocks; it's on the left. ⏰ Open M-F 8:30am-8:30pm, Sa 9:30am-2pm.)
- **POSTAL CODE:** 14001.

Emergency

- **EMERGENCY NUMBERS:** General Emergencies ☎061
- **POLICE: Local Police.** (Av. Custodios ☎092 or 95 745 53 00 ➡ From the rear side of the Mezquita on C. Corregidor Luis de la Cerda, walk toward the Puente Romano and turn right onto Av. Alcázar, then turn right at the traffic circle onto Av. Corregidor, then take the 2nd left onto Av. Custodios.) **National Police.** (Av. Doctor Fleming, 2 ☎091 or 95 759 45 00 ➡ From the Alcázar de los Reyes Cristianos, proceed along Av. Doctor Fleming, on the left side of the park.)
- **FIRE:** ☎080 or 95 745 54 95
- **HOSPITAL: Hospital Universitario Reina Sofía.** (Av. Menéndez Pidal ☎95 701 00 00 www.juntadeandalucia.es/servicioandaluzdesalud/hrs2 ➡ From the rear side of the Mezquita on C. Corregidor Luis de la Cerda, walk toward the Puente Romano and turn right onto Av. Alcázar, then turn right at the traffic circle onto Av. Corregidor, then take the 1st left onto Av. Menéndez Pidal.)
- **PHARMACY:** There are many pharmacies in the Pl. Tendillas, but they all keep regular business hours. The most centrally located of Córdoba's three 24hr. pharmacies is the nearby **Farmacia El Globo.** (C. Mármol de Bañuelos, 4 ☎95 747 40 24 ➡ From the Pl. Tendillas, with your back to the rear end of the equestrian statue, turn left onto C. Diego León, then at the fork turn left and then immediately right. ⏰ Open 24hr.) Complete information on all pharmacies open outside of regular pharmacy hours is available at www.cofco.org or in the window of any pharmacy.

Getting There

BY BUS

The cheapest way to get to Córdoba, from cities near and far, is almost always the bus. Buses arrive at the bus station in the modern part of the city northeast of the *centro histórico* (Av. Libertad ☎95 740 40 40 www.estacionautobusescordoba.es ➡ Bus #3 to RENFE-Estación de Autobuses from the Glorieta de la Cruz Roja.) **Secorbús,** a subsidiary of Socibus (☎90 222 92 92 www.socibus.es) provides most long-distance bus service to Córdoba, with buses from: Bilbao ($ €42 ⏰ 10¾hr., at 9:15am and 9:30pm); Burgos ($ €33 ⏰ 8hr., at 12:05pm and 12:30am); Cádiz ($ €9.40 ⏰ 3¾hr., 3 per day 8:40am-9:10pm); Jerez de la Frontera ($ €8.25 ⏰ 3¼hr., 2-3 per day 9:20am-9:50pm); Madrid ($ €16 ⏰ 4¾hr., 6 per day 9am-1am); and San Sebastián ($ €48 ⏰ 12hr., 2 per day 8am and 8pm).

Alsina, a subsidiary of ALSA (☎90 242 22 42 www.alsa.es), runs buses from other cities in Andalucía, including: Granada ($ €14-16 ⏰ 2½-4hr., 8 per day 8:30am-8pm); Málaga ($ €14 ⏰ 2½-3½hr., 4 per day 9am-7:30pm); and Sevilla ($ €12 ⏰ 1¾-2¼hr., 7 per day 8am-10pm). **ALSA** also provides service from Barcelona ($ €71-82 ⏰ 12¾-14¼hr., at 4:30pm and 9:30pm). To get from the bus station to the *centro histórico*, catch the #3 bus ($ €1.15) to San Fernando, the fifth stop—but grab a map from the tourist office across the street in the train station first.

BY TRAIN

Relative to buses, trains to Córdoba are usually either a little faster and a little more expensive (regular trains) or much faster and much more expensive (high-speed trains), though sometimes cheap fares are available on www.renfe.es. Both high-speed and regular trains arrive at the Estación de Córdoba in the modern part of the city northeast of the *centro histórico*, across from the bus station. (Glorieta de las Tres Culturas ☎90 243 23 43 ➡ Bus #3 to RENFE-Estación de Autobuses from the Glorieta de la Cruz Roja.) **RENFE** (☎90 232 03 20 www.renfe.es) trains arrive from: Barcelona ($ €66-138 ⏰ 4½-9½hr., 4 per day 8:30am-3:50pm); Cádiz ($ €24-40

🚊 2½-3½hr.; M-F 10 per day 5:35am-7:05pm, Sa-Su 8 per day 6:35am-7:05pm); Granada (💲 €22-36 🚊 2½hr., at 9:10am and 6:05pm); Madrid (💲 €28-69 🚊 1¾-2hr.; M-F 34 per day 6:30am-9:35pm, Sa 28 per day 8am-9:30pm, Su 29 per day 8:30am-9:35pm); Málaga (💲 €19-46 🚊 1hr.; M-F 19 per day 6:20am-8:30pm, Sa 14 per day 7:55am-8:30pm, Su 15 per day 7:55am-9:05pm); and Sevilla (💲 €13-34 🚊 45min.-1½hr.; M-F 40 per day 6:15am-9:35pm, Sa 30 per day 7:15am-9:35pm, Su 32 per day 7:15am-9:35pm). To get from the train station to the *centro histórico*, catch the #3 bus across Av. América from the train station (💲 €1.15) to San Fernando, the fifth stop—but grab a map from the tourist office next to the exit on your way out.

BY PLANE

There are no passenger flights to Córdoba; the nearest airports are in Sevilla (88mi.) and Málaga (100mi.), both of which have regular bus and train service to Córdoba.

Getting Around

The main way to get around Córdoba, and especially La Judería, is on foot. There is a city **bus** system, operated by **Aucorsa** (www.aucorsa.net); the only bus you'll probably ever need to worry about is bus #3, which will take your tired feet and heavy pack from the train and bus stations to the *centro* and La Judería. (💲 €1.15.)

Bikes are available for rental at **Duribaik** (C. Sevilla, 13 ☎95 778 84 76 www.duribaik.com ✚ From the Pl. Tendillas, with your back to the front of the equestrian statue, turn left onto C. Jesús y María, then take the 2nd right onto C. Rodríguez Sánchez; it's at the end of the block, on the left. 💲 €5 per 5hr., €8 per 24hr., €20 for F-Su 🕐 Open M-F 10:30am-2pm and 5:30-8pm, Sat 10:30am-2pm) and **SóloBici.** (C. María Cristina, 5 ☎95 748 57 66 or 62 031 83 70 ✚ From Pl. Tendillas, with your back to the rear end of the equestrian statue, proceed straight ahead along C. Claudio Marcelo and take the 3rd left onto C. María Cristina. 💲 €6 per 3hr., €10 per 5hr., €15 per 24hr. 🕐 Open M-F 9:30am-2pm and 6-9pm, Sa 10am-2:30pm.)

Taking a **taxi** is an expensive way to get to sights outside the city and the only way to get to the clubs of the Polígono Industrial de Chinales; taxi stands are located in Pl. Tendillas and on Av. Gran Capitán at the intersection with Ronda de los Tejares, and near the train station on Av. América. In the unlikely event you find yourself very far from one of these, call **Radio Taxi Córdoba.** (☎95 776 44 44 www.radiotaxicordoba.com.)

granada ☎858 or 958

So it's 15th-century *House Hunters*. You're the queen of Spain and you can live anywhere in the kingdom. Where do you choose? If you're Isabella, the Spanish queen who, with the help of her far-less-powerful husband, Ferdinand, gobbled up the Iberian Peninsula for the sake of the kingdom and the Church, then Granada it is. By 1492, Granada had spent centuries under Moorish rule. Boabdil, the last sultan on the peninsula, clung to his city as his brethren fell left and right. With a little persuasion (and a lot of gold), Isabella took control of Granada without a drop of bloodshed, and made the Moorish royal settlement of the Alhambra her own. This princely paradise of gardens and palaces was considered the most sophisticated example of Moorish architecture and design. While the Spanish royal family added a number of Renaissance palaces and chapels to the grounds, they largely preserved the original complex, and the additions were designed to complement the original Moorish palaces and gardens, making the Alhambra an amusement park of wealth, design, and craftsmanship.

Today, the Alhambra is one of Spain's most visited sites, and it offers visitors a theme-park experience of art history, design, and craftsmanship. But Granada is far from a one-stop destination. The city retains strong elements of this cross-cultural

granada

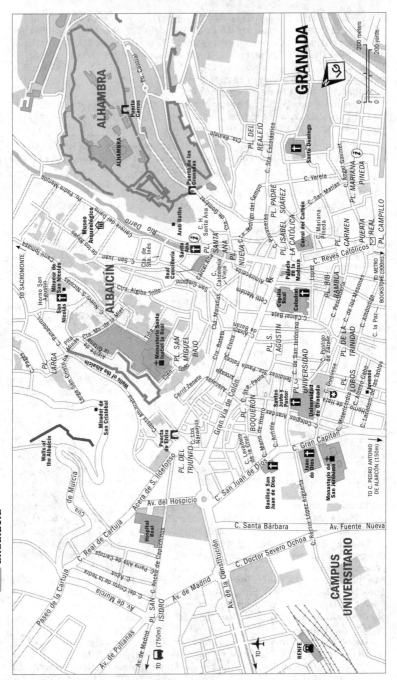

GRANADA

ALHAMBRA

ALBAICÍN

CAMPUS UNIVERSITARIO

history, from the remnants of the original city walls built by Boabdil, to the timeless gypsy *barrio* of Sacromonte and the Arabic neighborhood of El Albaicín. This is one of Spain's most ethnically diverse cities with cuisine that blends Mediterranean, Moroccan, and traditional Spanish ingredients, and flamenco, the traditional Spanish dance developed by the gypsies. With a population of only 250,000, Granada manages to be cosmopolitan, bustling with activity and bursting with history.

ORIENTATION

Plaza Nueva and City Center

Plaza Nueva is the tourist and commercial center of the city. Located just before the opening of the **Darro River,** Pl. Nueva is only a short distance from the historically ethnic neighborhoods of El Albaicín and Sacromonte. Just west of Pl. Nueva, **Cuesta de Gomérez** leads to the Alhambra. **Calle de los Reyes Católicos** runs from Pl. Nueva south to the *ayuntamiento* (city hall) and the tourist office at **Plaza del Carmen.** Just east of Pl. del Carmen, along **Calle Navas,** you'll find the city's signature tapas restaurants. West of C. Reyes Católicos, **Calle Cría Nueva** and **Calle Calderería Vieja** are part of a confusing network of narrow streets lined with ambiguously ethnic bars, restaurants, and clothing shops.

Sacromonte and el Albaicín

El Albaicín and Sacromonte lie to the north of the city center. Immediately north of Pl. Nueva, the ancient Moorish quarter **El Albaicín** is a tangle of streets that snake around churches and plazas. Many sights in this neighborhood, including the **Convento de Santa Isabel la Real** and the **Iglesia de San Nicolás,** were built by the Church on the sites of mosques, which once dominated the neighborhood. At the center of the neighborhood, popular **Plaza de San Nicolás** and **Mirador de San Nicolás** are filled with bars and restaurants, some with incredible views of the Alhambra and the city's tiled roofs.

On the north side of **Cuesta del Chapiz,** the *barrio* of **Sacromonte** is most easily navigated along its namesake **Camino del Sacromonte.** Running north to south through the *barrio*, this street is considered one of the major sites in the development of flamenco. Small restaurants and bars in traditional white stucco dwellings dot the road. If stray cats and poor lighting at night give you the creeps, you might want to take a friend along.

Cathedral and University

South of **Calle Gran Vía,** the streets become much more organized. The dominant feature, in case you couldn't guess, is the Catedral de Granada, which is surrounded by a number of small plazas. **Plaza Trinidad** and **Plaza Bib-Rambla** are lined with restaurants and small shops. South of Pl. Trinidad, the student presence is palpable in the neighborhood's many bookstores and cafes. While the Universidad de Granada is nearby, it isn't much of a tourist attraction. The greater university area does contain some of the city's best parks, including the student favorite **Parque Fuente Nueva. Parque Federico García Lorca** is located south of Pl. Trinidad, down C. Tablas.

ACCOMMODATIONS

We recommend staying in Granada proper in one of the city's many budget *hostales*. If you'd prefer to stay outside the city and commute, government-run **Albergue Inturjoven Granada (HI)** is a reliable option, with clean, secure facilities and complimentary breakfast. (C. Ramón y Cajal, 2 ☎95 800 29 00 www.inturjoven.com ✢ A 30min. walk south of the university. Take the circular bus #11, 21, or 23 to Camino del Ronda 10 and turn right on C. Ramón y Cajal. $ Ages 25 and under €16-19; ages 26 and over €22-25. ⏰ Reception 24hr.)

Plaza Nueva and City Center

OASIS GRANADA HOSTEL $$

Placeta Correo Viejo, 3 ☎95 821 58 48 www.oasisgranada.com

The Oasis chain has backpacker dwelling down to a science. This hostel, just a few blocks from Pl. Nueva, is no exception, with top-notch facilities including a massive cafeteria (and complimentary breakfast), full bar (with happy hour nightly and a free drink upon arrival), and a rooftop terrace to soak up the sun. If you can bring yourself to leave, Oasis will help you get acquainted with the city. Check the welcome board in front for a daily list of activities, including themed tours. There are also frequent dinner parties and tapas outings. The only drawback of Oasis is that you won't be alone—this busy hostel floweth over with partiers on the weekends.

 # From Pl. Nueva, take C. de Elvira on the western edge of the plaza 3 blocks north, turn right onto C. de la Calderería Nueva, and take the 1st left onto C. del Correo Viejo. i Breakfast included. Towels €1. Security locks €3. $ Dorms €15-19. ⏰ Reception 24hr.

PENSIÓN BRITZ HOTEL $$

Cuesta de Gomérez, 1 ☎95 822 36 52

High-quality backpackers' hostels can be found all around Granada, but they're not for everyone. Steps from Pl. Nueva, Pensión Britz provides a quiet alternative for the more selective voyager. There are no common spaces in the *pensión*, but the rooms are clean and comfortable, with mismatched furniture and bedspreads. Some even overlook the plaza, which can be either a blessing or a curse, depending on what's going on below. Rooms with ensuite bathrooms are pricier, but they're also larger and brighter.

 # Cuesta de Gomérez branches off Pl. Nueva to the southeast; the hostel is the 1st building to the left as you head out of the plaza. i Laundry available. $ Singles €17-25, with bath €33-38; doubles €30-36/40-48; triples €45-48/51-57; quads €50-55/60-68. ⏰ Reception 24hr.

Cathedral and University

FUNKY BACKPACKERS HOSTEL $

C. del Conde de las Infantas, 15-17 ☎95 880 00 58 www.funkybackpackers.hostel.com

Funky Backpackers describes itself as Granada's "multicultural" hostel. You'll find murals from around the world, nightly dinners of international cuisine (€4-5), and a full activity agenda that includes salsa dancing, flamenco shows, and jam sessions. There's a schedule of daily hostel events and suggestions posted in the lobby. Whether in the downstairs courtyard or the rooftop lounge and terrace, you're bound to meet a new group of friends. Rooms have simple bunks and closets with locks. If this is just one stop on a grand tour of Spain, Funky Backpackers also offers a 10% discount for stays at Picasso's Corner in Málaga and Terrace Backpackers in Córdoba.

 # C. del Conde de las Infantas intersects Pl. Trinidad. The hostel is halfway down the block. i Breakfast included. Laundry available. Women-only dorms available. $ 7-bed dorm €15; 6-bed €17; 4-bed €18. Doubles €38-42. €50 credit card min. ⏰ Reception 24hr.

HOSPEDAJE ALMOHADA HOTEL $$

C. Postigo de Zárate, 4 ☎95 820 74 46 www.laalmohada.com

With a central courtyard filled with hanging plants, and cool concrete walls detailed with hand-painted ceramic tiles, Hospedaje Almohada feels like a boutique hotel, and it somehow manages to pull off bohemian without looking ramshackle. The private rooms are decorated with simple pastel furniture, and, at just €20, the singles are as good a value as any in the city. Common spaces are limited, but there's a kitchen and a nice patio. The location just off of Pl. Universidad is close to the Catedral de Granada but quieter than the heavily trafficked Pl. Nueva.

 # From Pl. Trinidad, take C. Trinidad to the T intersection and make a right onto C. Postigo de Zárate. i Towels and linens included. $ Singles €20; doubles €36; triples €51. Cash only. ⏰ Reception 9:30am-3pm and 4:30-9:30pm.

SIGHTS

Granada's sights are best explored by grabbing a map and wandering around the historic *barrios* of the city. You'll find a unique vibe in **El Albaicín** and **Sacromonte**, get a taste of Spanish history around the **Catedral**, and find yourself in complete awe as you make your way around the **Alhambra.**

Alhambra

In 1238, **Sultan Al-Ahmar** of the Nasrid Dynasty took a look around Granada and realized that he had an opportunity to make something of the old Alcazaba in the Albaicín, a centuries-old fortress with foundations constructed by the Romans. Al-Ahmar wanted to transform this city wall into a palace retreat for Moorish royalty and top government officials. Over the next two centuries, the descendants of Sultan Al-Ahmar built up an earthly paradise of palaces and gardens that exhibited the highest achievements of Islamic architecture and design. By 1491, though, Moorish influence on the Iberian Peninsula was declining and so was the Alhambra. Spain's Catholic monarchs had long been eyeing the Moorish stronghold, and in 1492 the Spanish army, under Ferdinand and Isabella, finally seized the Alhambra, thereby ending the *Reconquista*, the 780-year-struggle between Christians and Muslims for control of Iberia. Despite the change of hands from the Islamic to Catholic royalty more than 500 years ago, the palaces and gardens of the Alhambra remain remarkably similar to their original design under the Nasrid sultans.

Now a UNESCO World Heritage Site, the Alhambra is the government's biggest moneymaker—Gaudí's Sagrada Família in Barcelona has a higher income but loses tons of money to ongoing construction (due to be completed in 2036). And the Alhambra is more than just a single sight—it's a fortified city full of gardens, museums, towers, and baths. Be prepared to devote at least 3½hr. to your visit.

There are a few ways to get tickets. It is recommended that you purchase them in advance, particularly for visits in June and July. The official online ticket vendor is **ServiCaixa**, which sells tickets online at www.servicaixa.com. ($ €14; handling fee €2.) Tickets purchased from ServiCaixa can be collected at the automated ticket collection terminals at the Alhambra on the day of your visit, or in advance at ServiCaixa ticket terminals located in many La Caixa banks and ATMs throughout Spain, including at **Tienda de la Alhambra** (C. Reyes Católicos, 40 ☎90 288 80 01 www.alhambra-tickets.es). Tickets can also be purchased in person at the Alhambra Ticket Office. (C. Real ☎90 244 12 21 www.alhambra-patronato.es $ €12. ⏰ Open daily from 8am until 1hr. before close.) Many hostels will also book tickets for you for an additional charge of €2.

The general daytime tickets ($ €12) allow access to all sights on the grounds—either in the morning (⏰ Daily 8:30am-2pm) or afternoon (⏰ Daily Mar 15-Oct 14 2-8pm; Oct 15-Mar 14 2-6pm). There are also limited tickets that give you access to the Generalife and Alcazaba but not the Nasrid Palaces ($ €8). An evening ticket includes access to the Generalife or Nasrid Palaces, but not both. ($ €12. ⏰ Open Mar 15-May 31 Th-Sa 10-11:30pm; Sept 1-Oct 14 Th-Sa 10-11:30pm; Oct 16-Nov 14 F-Sa 8-9:30pm.) These later visits allow you to see the Alhambra grounds lit up against the night sky.

Audio tours are available in Spanish, English, French, German, Italian, and Portuguese, but they are quite expensive. ($ Nasrid Palaces €4, entire grounds €6; security deposit €20.) The guide focuses more on the aesthetics and design of the gardens and palaces than on the site's history.

NASRID PALACES PALACES

The Nasrid Palaces are definitely the place to be at the Alhambra. In fact, they're so popular that you have to schedule a specific time slot for your visit when purchasing tickets to the Alhambra. You're limited to 1hr. of exploration, and there's a ton to see, so be ready for quite the journey. Famous sights include the

Sala de la Barca (the boat room), known for its ornately carved roof shaped like the hull of a ship. The **Salon de Embajadores** is also notable as the place where Christopher Columbus reportedly received Ferdinand and Isabella's approval to travel the New World. The Nasrid Palace is known just as well for its exterior courtyards as it is for its interior chambers. The **Patio de los Arrayanes** (Court of Myrtles) features a narrow deep-green pool of water surrounded by aromatic bushes of—you guessed it—myrtle. The Nasrid's most iconic feature is the **Patio de los Leones,** which has a large water basin suspended on the backs of 12 marble lions. The fountain is known as a feat of both design and craftsmanship: it uses a complex system of gravity-powered aqueducts and pipes to keep the water in continuous circulation. The creativity and technical prowess blew the conquering Catholic royalty right out of the water. (Yeah, we took it there.)

GENERALIFE
GARDENS

The Generalife was definitely built for a king—or should we say a sultan? Constructed between the 12th and 14th centuries, this maze of gardens, patios, and fountains was intended to be a restful place for the royal family. If you feel like you may be in heaven—don't worry, that's perfectly normal. In fact, this paradise of lush greenery, long promenades, vegetable gardens, and interior courtyards was designed to make you feel that way. As you enter the Generalife you will immediately see the **royal amphitheater** to your right, which is still used for the annual **Festival Internacional de Música y Danza.** Next up are the **Lower Gardens,** which feature thick sculptural bushes of myrtle and trellised gardens with hanging vines. The villa attached to the Generalife feels like a quiet summer residence, with more modest decor than the Nasrid palaces. The last portion of the Generalife is perhaps most intriguing, featuring the **escalera de agua,** a staircase lined with laurel trees and streams of water running down either handrail. As you move through the Generalife, be sure to enjoy the stunning views of the Alhambra below.

ALCAZABA
FORTRESS

The survival of the sight you're enjoying today is largely thanks to the Alcazaba. This fortress was definitely hard to get by (especially wearing cloth sandals and traveling by donkey), and it protected the Alhambra for centuries. Today you can easily go where all those would-be conquerors wanted to be. Climb the **Torre del Cubo, Torre del Homenaje,** and **Torre de la Vela** to survey your kingdom: you'll be lost in the panoramic views of Granada, snapping pictures of the hundreds of thousands of tiled rooftops extending toward the horizon.

PALACIO DE CARLOS V
PALACE

Museo de Bellas Artes ☎95 889 54 30 www.museosdeandalucia.es
Museo del Alhambra ☎90 244 12 21 museo.pag@juntadeandalucia.es

While the Palacio de Carlos V is often referred to as the "unfinished" or "forgotten" palace, there are definitely memories to be made here. At this 16th-century Renaissance palace, not only is there a striking circular courtyard with two stories of marble columns, but it is also home to not one but two museums. The museum is Granada's main art museum and the oldest public museum in Spain. The exhibitions begin in the historic year of 1492—yes, yes, it's the year when Columbus sailed the ocean blue, but it's also the year when Granada came under Catholic control. The Museo de Bellas Artes all but ignores this Islamic past; it's known for its large collection of Catholic art dating to La Desamortización (1835-37), during which monasteries and convents across Spain were closed and privatized. The collection also places heavy emphasis on Andalusian artists, including a large number of works by **Alonso Cano,** the godfather of Renaissance painting in Granada. The collection also features 20th-century Granadan artists like **Manuela Rivera** who have finally managed to move beyond Jesus and the apostles.

andalucía

The Museo de Bellas Artes also hosts a number of temporary exhibitions in the crypt and chapel of Palacio de Carlos V. These generally explore the relationship of Granada's local artists to international 20th-century trends, with such recent exhibits as a Matisse retrospective highlighting the influence of Granada on his artistic development.

The **Museo del Alhambra** contains objects from—you guessed it!—the Alhambra. Luckily, since Ferdinand and Isabella moved in during the 15th century, the decorations, building elements, and possessions of the royal couple have been preserved. The museum, in development since 1940, now houses one of the world's best collections of Spanish-Moorish and Nasrid art.

Ⓢ *Museo de Bellas Artes €1.50, EU students free. Museo del Alhambra free. ⚄ Palacio box office open daily Mar-Oct 8am-8pm; Nov-Feb 8am-5pm. Museo de Bellas Artes open Mar-Oct Tu 2:30-8pm, W-Sa 9am-8pm, Su 9am-2:30pm; Nov-Feb Tu 2:30-6pm, W-Sa 9am-6pm, Su 9am-2:30pm. Museo del Alhambra open Tu-Su 8:30am-2pm.*

Sacromonte

Let's look at those monthly bills: rent, electricity, plumbing, heat. It adds up. You know what would be cheaper? Digging yourself a cave in the mountains across from the Alhambra. That must have been the thought process (more or less) of the gypsies who dug into the mountainside when they arrived on the Iberian Peninsula in the 15th century. While small groups had been living there comfortably for centuries along the Darro, the boom came when the lower classes packed their bags for Sacromonte between the late 19th and mid-20th century—by 1950 there were 3,682 known cave dwellings along the mountainside.

But a genius for economical living wasn't the only talent these gypsies had. Walking the **Camino del Sacromonte,** you'll come across flamenco bar after flamenco bar, all ready to present the gypsy *zambra* style of this famous dance. You can also stop in at the museum honoring *zambra* and one of its top performers, **Cueva María la Canastera** (Camino del Sacromonte, 89 ☎95 812 11 83 cuevacanastera@yahoo.es). Sacromonte is accessible by buses #34 and #35, which depart Pl. Nueva, but most people find the 15min. walk through the Albaicín and up Camino del Sacromonte to be one of the most distinctive experiences of the trip to Granada.

🏛 MUSEO CUEVAS DE SACROMONTE   MUSEUM, CAVES
Barranco de los Negros   ☎95 821 51 20 www.sacromontegranada.com

This museum contains restored cave dwellings that look surprisingly comfortable considering their location. They're certainly no Batcave, but you'll see stables, bedrooms, kitchens, and workplaces, all constructed in the ingenious manner used by the gypsies who came to Granada up until the 1950s. The museum also features exhibits on the influence of gypsy culture on the development of flamenco in Sacromonte as well as small gardens and displays on the ecology of the Darro river valley.

🚶 *Barranco de los Negros is off Camino del Sacromonte. From Pl. Nueva, follow the stream north up Carrera del Darro for 5min. Take a left on Cuesta del Chapiz and the 1st right onto Camino del Sacromonte. Follow Camino del Sacromonte 10min. to Barranco de los Negros. Head straight to a path that leads up the mountain. Take this path and follow signs. Alternatively, you can take bus #35 from Pl. Nueva (every 40min.), but it takes longer than walking, and you'll miss some of the best parts of Sacromonte, which are only accessible on foot. Ⓢ €5. ⚄ Open daily Apr-Oct 10am-2pm and 5-9pm; Nov-Mar 10am-2pm and 4-7pm.*

ABADÍA DEL SACROMONTE   MUSEUM
On Mt. Valparaiso, 2.5km uphill from Camino del Sacromonte   ☎95 822 14 45

The origin of the name Sacromonte, or "holy mountain," has several legends attached to it. The holiest of these myths centers on the appropriately named **Holy Cave.** In 1594, two men exploring the cave discovered a mysterious pile of ashes alongside a series of lead plates written in Arabic. The tablets suggested that the patron saint of Granada, San Cecilio, was actually of Arabic and not Spanish descent. This caused huge problems for the Church—so much so that the pope condemned the tablets in 1682. We've since learned that the pope was kind of right: the tablets are bogus, written by a Moorish scholar. That hasn't kept the Museum of the Abadía del Sacromonte from putting them on display. The museum requires a brief tour that takes you through the abbey's collection of relics and local religious art, including Alonso Cano's *Dead Christ Supported by an Angel.* The tour also brings you to the Holy Cave where the tablets were first discovered. On the first Sunday in February each year, a procession is held up Camino del Sacromonte to Mt. Valparaíso honoring San Cecilio.

⇟ The abbey and museum are located 2.5km uphill from Camino del Sacromonte. It's a 40min. ride on bus #35 or a 25min. walk from Pl. Nueva. $ €3.50; includes mandatory guided tour. ⏰ Open Tu-Sa 10am-1pm and 4-6pm, Su 11am-1pm and 4-6pm. Tours (in Spanish; English or French by request) every 45-60min.

El Albaicín

Some say the *barrio*'s name comes from the Arabic for "the miserables," but there's nothing "miserable" about it. It's the oldest, most historic part of Granada, where the city's first Muslim court was established in the 11th century. Spanish rulers have made some alterations over the years, stacking churches into and on top of mosques, but El Albaicín's narrow winding streets and terrific views of the Alhambra will still transport you to the area's Moorish past.

OLD MUSLIM BARRIO — NEIGHBORHOOD

Carrera del Darro, C. de San Juan de los Reyes, Cuesta del Chapiz

The old Muslim *barrio* begins at **Iglesia de Santa Ana** just north of Pl. Nueva. Built on the former grounds of the **Almanzora Mosque,** this church is just one of many converted sites of Muslim worship in the Albaicín. Many of the churches retain mosque-like architectural flourishes, like the Moorish arches of Iglesia de Santa Ana and the original brick minaret that was converted into the belfry. Farther down Carrera del Darro, you'll find **Los Bañuelos,** the Arab baths. (☎95 802 78 00 $ Free. ⏰ Open Tu-Sa 10am-2pm.) Continuing north toward **Cuesta del Chapiz,** you'll pass one of Granada's finest plazas, Paseo de los Tristes, which is right next to the Darro. As you go, explore the **carmens,** or classic patio-gardens of the wealthy, at **Casa del Chapiz** and as you then head west down Cuesta del Chapiz, you'll come to the **Iglesia El Salvador,** which stands atop what was once Granada's principal mosque. Making your way down Ronda de los Panaderos behind Iglesia El Salvador you will reach Pl. Larga, the *barrio*'s former marketplace and home of the **Puerta de Pesa.** Notice the weights that still hang from this entryway—they were once used as a warning to merchants that consequences awaited if they were to cheat the customers of the marketplace. While a few remain to remind slippery merchants, most of the weights have today been moved to the Albaicín's **Archeological Museum,** which displays many other artifacts from Granada's history. ($ €1.50, EU citizens free. ⏰ Open Tu 2:30-8:30pm, W-Sa 9am-8:30pm, Su 9am-2:30pm.) Just south of Pl. Larga along **Cuesta de Acahaba** stand on the original city walls that once protected Sultan Boabdil's five Granadan castles. Finish off a day of wandering through El Albaicín with a stop at **Mirador de San Nicolás,** a plaza at the center of the *barrio* with fantastic views of the Alhambra.

Cathedral and University

CATEDRAL DE GRANADA — CHURCH

C. Gran Vía, 5 — ☎95 822 29 59

Queen Isabella grew up in a convent, so it makes sense that she'd put one heck of a church in her favorite city. The Catedral de Granada, formerly connected to the Royal Chapel where Isabella is actually buried, is a massive circular building lined with 13 golden chapels, which are all overshadowed by the Capilla Mayor in the center. This sanctuary, surrounded by multiple organs and thick marble pillars (you'd need at least three people to give them a good hug), was definitely made for presentation's sake. It looks more like a theater than a church—two levels of balconies and stained-glass windows are the backdrop for an enormous red-carpeted altar.

✱ *Entrance on C. Oficios.* ⓘ *Information in Spanish only.* Ⓢ *€3.50. Audio tour €3.* Ⓒ *Open M-Sa 10:45am-1:30pm and 4-8pm, Su 4-8pm. Last entry 15min. before close.*

PARQUE FEDERICO GARCÍA LORCA
MUSEUM, PARK

C. Virgen Blanca ☎95 825 84 66 www.huertadesanvicente.com

Probably one of Granada's best spots for a picnic or a morning jog, the entire Parque Federico García Lorca smells of the roses that line its paths. Whether you want to chill by the duck pond or try one of the two restaurants in the park, don't leave without stopping at the main event. The **Casa-Museo Federico García Lorca** was the summer home of the famous Spanish poet, playwright, and director who was assassinated in the opening months of the Civil War. He is now honored in the home where he found some of his greatest inspiration. You can tour his kitchen and scope out his grand piano, writing desk, and even his high-school diploma, which reveals his barely passing grades.

✱ *Take the circular bus to the intersection of C. Recogidas and Camino de Ronda and follow the signs.* ⓘ *Tours available in English and Spanish.* Ⓢ *€3, students €1. W free. Cash only.* Ⓒ *Open Tu-Su Apr-June 10am-12:30pm and 5-7:30pm; July-Aug 10am-2:30pm; Sept 10am-12:30pm and 5-7:30pm; Oct-Mar 10am-12:30pm and 4-6:30pm.*

FOOD

Food in Granada comes in three main forms: Spanish-Granadan (think bold—*tortilla sacromonte* is scrambled up with marrow, brains, and bull's testicles), North African, and Mediterranean. Everyone will have their favorite falafel spot or *tetería* (Arabic tea shop), which are usually packed with people sitting on cushions and puffing hookah rings. But it's Granada's free tapas that will really make you want to stick around—order a drink at any tapas bar, and they'll bring it out with a selection of free small plates. While the bars and restaurants in the city center are great, it's worth a trip up **Camino del Sacromonte,** where you'll find traditional Andalucian food and terrace seating overlooking the city and the Alhambra.

Plaza Nueva and City Center

CASA LOPEZ CORREA
TAPAS $$

C. de los Molinos, 5 ☎95 822 37 75

You might be caught off guard in Casa Lopez Correa. You will be hard-pressed to find any locals or tourists. And yet it's generally quite full of people. Are they aliens? Are they robots? Are you living in a dream world "incepted" by Leonardo DiCaprio and Joseph Gordon-Levitt? Well, no. Casa Lopez Correa is the go-to expat bar in Granada, popular with Aussies, Brits, Kiwis, and Americans. The half-Italian, half-British chef and owner has cooked across Europe and ended up here, packing Italian, Spanish, and British cuisine onto a single menu. Particular favorites from the home-cooked selection include the beef lasagna (€8.50) and the British-style barbecued ribs (€6). The restaurant is busiest and most fragrant at midday when the expats show up for the *menú del día.* The extensive cocktail selection keeps 'em coming into the night with mojitos, caipirinhas, and margaritas made with fresh fruits and quality booze.

✱ *From Pl. de Isabel La Católica, take C. Pavaneras (to the left of the fountain) 3 blocks until it becomes Pl. del Realejo. At the intersection with C. de los Molinos, follow the pink street that reads "La Alhambra" down C. de los Molinos for ½ block. The restaurant's bright blue façade is on the left.* Ⓢ *Appetizers €3.50-7.50; entrees €7.50-9.50. 2-course menú €10; 3-course €12. Beer €1.70. Wine €2.10.* Ⓒ *Open M-Th noon-5pm and 8pm-1am, F-Sa noon-5pm and 8pm-2am, Su 1-5pm.*

LOS DIAMANTES TAPAS $$

C. Navas, 26 ☎95 822 70 70

On a block lined with expensive sit-down tourist joints, Los Diamantes is the local favorite. This one-room bar along C. Navas is unapologetically loud and littered with napkins and olive pits—and it's all the better for it. At night, the simple stainless steel counter swarms with local patrons, drinking cheap beer (€1.70) and snacking on a menu of almost exclusively fried tapas. Traditional seafood platters include fried calamari, shrimp, and cod, and there are a few popular vegetarian options like grilled eggplant (€6) and deep-fried vegetables (€9). Los Diamantes is by no means cheap, but, compared to other places on a block where the typical entree costs €15, the large shared platters will please the budget-conscious.

#From C. Reyes Católicos, walk through Pl. Carmen to C. Navas. [$] ½ platter tapas €6-8, full €10-14. ⏰ Open daily 12:30-4pm and 8:30pm-midnight.

Sacromonte and el Albaicín

CASA JUANILLO ANDALUSIAN $$

Camino del Sacromonte, 81-83 ☎95 822 30 94 casajuanillosacramonte@hotmail.com

Casa Juanillo may be a hike up Camino del Sacromonte, but it's worth every step. The charm of this family-run restaurant is hard to resist—a few chairs and tables grace a traditional dining room with fantastic views of the Darro river valley and Alhambra. The menu is simple, with just a dozen or so family recipes of regional specialties. *Bacalao con tomate* (cod with tomatoes; €5) and the lamb chops (€13) are favorites. Casa Juanillo is also in close proximity to many of the city's best flamenco bars, making it a popular after-show destination.

#From Pl. Nueva, follow the stream north up Carrera del Darro (5min.) to Cuesta del Chapiz and take a left. Take the 1st right onto Camino del Sacromonte and follow it until you reach Barranco de los Negros. Casa Juanillo is the one with a small terrace, umbrellas, and chairs. Alternatively, bus #35 runs up Camino del Sacromonte from Pl. Nueva. i Make reservations in advance. [$] Entrees €7-14. Beer €1.80. Wine €2-3. Free tapa with drink. ⏰ Open Tu-Sa noon-4:30pm and 8pm-midnight, Su noon-4:30pm.

EL HUERTO DE JUAN RANAS ANDALUSIAN, BAR $$$

C. de Atarazana, 8 ☎95 828 69 25 www.restaurantejuanranas.com

With an expansive terrace at the edge of Sacromonte, El Huerto de Juan Ranas offers unbeatable views of the Alhambra and the Darro River valley. Though the food is expensive, Juan Ranas is a perfect destination for a more formal dinner. The menu offers traditional Andalusian dishes, while the downstairs restaurant experiments with more expensive contemporary gastro-pub cuisine. To enjoy the setting without breaking the bank, stop in for cocktails (€8) or dessert (€6) and watch the sun set over the Alhambra.

#Located just off of the Mirador de San Nicolás. From Pl. Nueva, take bus #32 to Aljibe de Tomasas. After 8 stops, the bus drops you in front of a stone stairwell called Cuesta de Cabras. Take the stairwell up to C. de Atarazana; the restaurant is on the left. If you pass the Mirador you've gone too far south. [$] Terrace entrees €12-20; downstairs €20-35. Beer €3. Wine €3. Sangria €4.50. ⏰ Open daily noon-1am.

BAR KIKI TAPAS, BAR $$$

Pl. de San Nicolás, 9 ☎95 827 67 15

The booming conversation you can hear from Pl. de San Nicolás is coming from Bar Kiki. The huge patio out front is always packed with locals, who come for the creative menu that uses fresh ingredients from the local market. Kiki's massive portions are easily split between two people. The specialty, *solomillo nacional*, celebrates Granada's Moorish roots by topping a hefty slab of tenderloin with almonds, apples, dates, raisins, and a sweet Pedro Ximénez wine reduction (€20).

#Located right behind Pl. de San Nicolás. [$] Plates €14-20. Beer €2. Wine €3. ⏰ Open M-Tu 10am-midnight, Th-Su 10am-midnight.

MEKNES RAHMA   MOROCCAN $$
  C. Peso de la Harina, 1   ☎95 822 74 30 www.restaurantemeknes.com
  It might look like just another hookah lounge, but Meknes Rahma offers
  superior Moroccan cuisine, including couscous (€11-13) and baked *tajins* (rice
  with stewed meat and vegetables; €7.50-10) made with traditional ingredients. In
  addition to sweet and savory combos like *tajin de cordero* (lamb stewed with
  plums and almonds) the menu features plenty of lighter options; from the shrimp
  and avocado salad (€6) and eggplant salad (€4) to traditional Moroccan soups
  (€3-5). The dark and cool interior of this restaurant is a perfect escape from the
  heat and intense sun of Sacromonte. Hookahs (€10) are also particularly popular
  come nighttime.
  ⌗ *At the corner of Cuesta del Chapiz and Camino del Sacromonte.* Ⓢ *Salads €3-4. Entrees €7.50-*
  13. Teas €2.50. ⌚ *Open daily noon-midnight.*

Cathedral and University

POE   TAPAS, INTERNATIONAL, BAR $
  C. de Verónica de la Magdelena, 40   www.barpoe.com
  Poe is not fine dining. In fact, it might be the cheapest meal in Granada, so pull
  up a seat at the traditional bar, order a cheap half-pint of beer (€1.50), and let
  Matt, the gracious bartender and owner, take your tapas order. All drinks come
  with a free tapas, served piping hot in a small ceramic pot. Matt's wife, Ana,
  cooks up a menu focused on stewed chicken, pork, and fish dishes, which range
  from chicken in sweet-and-spicy Thai sauce to a traditional Brazilian black
  bean and pork stew. Both Matt and Ana are quick to strike up a conversation
  with customers from the other side of the bar, so don't be surprised if you stick
  around for at least two rounds. The price is right, and the environment is far
  friendlier than you will find in the tourist center around Pl. Nueva, where bars
  and restaurants hustle customers for every last crumb.
  ⌗ *From Pl. de la Trinidad, take C. de la Alhóndiga and turn right onto C. de la Paz.* ***i*** *Vegetarian*
  options available. Ⓢ *Beer €1.50-4. Wine €1.50-2.70. Extra tapas €1.50; ½-plate €3.50, full*
  €6.50. Cash only. ⌚ *Open Tu-Th 8pm-2am, F-Su 8pm-3am.*

LA CAMPERERÍA   BAR $$
  C. Duquesa, 3   ☎95 829 41 73
  Walking down C. Duquesa, it's impossible to miss the sleek, metallic sign
  denoting La Camperería in all-bold caps—that, and the crowd of loud and social
  students overflowing through the front door. The restaurant-bar specializes in
  camperos, or round, pressed sandwiches sliced up pizza-style. These absolutely
  enormous sandwiches are easily shared between two or three people, and they
  come in endless varieties, including the Mare (fried calamari, pureed tomatoes,
  lettuce, and aioli; €7) and Granada (*jamón serrano*, *queso ibérico*, avocado,
  and olive oil; €6). Campereria's bright lights and cheap drinks make it a popular
  late-night destination.
  ⌗ *From Pl. Trinidad, follow C. Duquesa ½ block. The restaurant is on the left.* Ⓢ *Entrees €11-14.*
  Menú €9.50. Beer €1.90. Wine €2.50. Mixed drinks €4. ⌚ *Open M-Th 8am-2am, F-Sa 8am-3am,*
  Su 8am-1am.

NIGHTLIFE

Like every big city in Spain, Granada has its share of flashy clubs with nightly DJ sets
and packed dance floors. But Granada is in no way the city of house or techno; it's
the city of flamenco. The birthplace of flamenco, Sacromonte may now thrive on the
tourist throngs, but it still offers a uniquely Granadan brand of nightlife, with informal
concerts, dance performances, and jam sessions occurring into the morning. Did we
mention the backdrop of the Alhambra?

Plaza Nueva and City Center

GRANADA 10 CLUB, THEATER

C. de la Cárcel Baja, 10 ☎61 021 99 10 www.granada10.com

Granada 10 has got the double-life thing down better than Clark Kent; it's a movie theater and cabaret by day and a hot dance club by night. When Granada 10 is packed (pretty much every night after 2am), partiers fill up the huge theater space that's converted into the dance floor. It's hard to believe that they screen local films here in the evening. The decadent marble bar and golden couches keep it classy, and a fancy light show gets the energy going. The only simple thing about this spot is the drink menu: just beer (€3), soda (€2), and cocktails (€6). While you can't expect tons of locals, you'll be hanging with an enthusiastic, reckless, college-age crowd any night of the week.

From C. Gran Vía, turn onto C. de la Cárcel Baja; the club is on the right. **i** *Ladies' night on W. Student special on Th. Salsa on Su.* $ *Cover varies. Movie ticket €4.* 🕐 *Open daily noon-6am. Movie screenings in the early evening.*

Sacromonte and el Albaicín

Along Camino del Sacromonte, you'll find bar upon bar offering cheap drinks, inexpensive flamenco performances, and live jazz. **Pena las Cuevas de Sacromonte** (Camino de Sacromonte, 21 ☎62 018 26 63 www.erasmusgranada.com) has free shows weekend nights at 11pm featuring a quartet of dancers and guitarists, and they often have informal music and dance until 4am. Throughout July and August, **Museo Cuevas del Sacromonte** has flamenco shows on Wednesdays and open-air screenings of independent films on Thursdays. (Barranco de los Negros, 5 ☎95 821 51 20 $ Films €3. Flamenco €12. 🕐 Films and flamenco start at 10pm.)

LA BULERÍA BAR, FLAMENCO

Camino de Sacromonte, 55 ☎61 704 88 64

This is one of the few remaining local favorites on Camino de Sacromonte. La Bulería is an after-hours bar where residents of the *barrio* come when the tourists vacate. The owner (and neighborhood legend) performs nightly guitar around 1am, and, if you come to the outdoor terrace around midnight, you can usually catch him warming up (think Jack and a cigarette, not calisthenics). The concerts can be quite memorable, but even if you miss them, the setting alone makes La Bulería a great watering hole.

From base of Cuesta del Chapiz, walk up Camino de Sacromonte (5min.); the bar is up a flight of stairs just past the club El Comborio. $ *Beer €2. Wine €3. Mixed drinks €5.* 🕐 *Open Tu-Sa 11pm-4am.*

Cathedral and University

CLUB AFRODISIA CLUB

C. Almona del Boquerón www.afrodisiaclub.com

Each week Club Afrodisia plays enough R and B, funk, and soul music to make James Brown roll over in his grave and shake his bony butt. They mix in a bit of hip hop on Tuesdays and reggae on Wednesdays, but the norm here is music straight from the soundtrack of a 1970s Blaxploitation film. The nightly concerts at 11pm offer a mix of live cover bands, original local acts, and DJs spinning in the leopard-curtained booth. Go for a simple beer (€3) or take the Afrodisia route and just mix anything with Red Bull (€4.50). If you find your groove at Afrodisia, you might also consider trying **Booga Club** (C. Santa Bárbara, 3; www.boogaclub.com) which is owned by the same people and plays similar music.

From C. Reyes Católicos, follow C. Gran Vía 9 blocks northwest. C. Almona del Boquerón branches off to the left, and the bar is just past the small flight of stairs from C. Gran Vía. $ *Shots €2.50. Mixed drinks €5-5.50.* 🕐 *Open Tu-Th 11pm-3am, F-Sa 11pm-4am.*

PERRA GORDA CLUB

C. Almona del Boquerón s/n www.facebook.com/laperragorda

Perra Gorda is Granada's go-to rock and roll bar, blasting loud '60s-'80s rock well into the early morning. This dark, windowless club centers on a massive bar ringed by posters for local concerts and TVs playing nostalgic videos of Mick Jagger, Gene Simmons, and other music greats. Whether you are enjoying the mixed drinks (€3), the house special (three Buds for €5), or the happy hour (two mixed drinks for €3), you can count on a cheap night out. The bar offers plenty of entertainment, including a pool table, dartboard, and foosball. On Wednesday nights at midnight, the bar hosts live acoustic rock sets. For the rowdiest crowd, come around 3am on the weekends.

 # From C. Reyes Católicos, follow C. Gran Vía 9 blocks northwest. C. Almona del Boquerón branches off to the left, and the bar is just past the small flight of stairs from C. Gran Vía. $ Shots €1-2. Beer €1.20-2.50. Mojitos €3. Mixed drinks €4. Cash only. ⏰ Open M-Th 10pm-3am, F-Sa 10pm-4am, Su 10pm-3am. Happy hour 10pm-midnight.

SALA VOGUE CLUB

C. Duquesa, 35 ☎69 152 72 42 www.salavogue.es

Sala Vogue is a double-trouble student favorite: you've got two dance floors, two DJs, and two absolutely massive bars surrounding each dance floor. *Sala 1* will be spinning indie, pop, rock, and '80s hits, while *Sala 2* can soothe your cravings for electronica and house. While you may have to pay a little extra for the guest DJs, they offer plenty of drink specials to keep the bill down: during the week it's 3 beers for €5, and on the weekends the cover charge includes one mixed drink or two beers. This is not the place to meet a Spanish lover on the dance floor—locals steer clear of Sala Vogue and let the American and European tourists do their thing.

 # On C. Duquesa between C. Gran Capitán and C. Horno de Abad. $ Cover Th-Sa €6; includes 1 mixed drink or 2 beers. Beer €3. Mixed drinks €5. Cash only. ⏰ Open M-Th midnight-6am, F-Sa midnight-7am, Su midnight-6am.

ARTS AND CULTURE

Flamenco and Jazz

VENTA EL GALLO SACROMONTE

Barranco de los Negros, 5 ☎95 822 84 76 www.ventaelgallo.com

Though pricier than many of the flamenco-jazz dive bars around Granada, Venta el Gallo is known to offer some of the highest-quality traditional Granadan flamenco. The restaurant and bar is situated in a typical Andalusian house with an arched clay stage decorated with hanging pots and pans. The shows here routinely sell out, and the roughly 100-person audience gives the performance a fantastic energy; you can hear the applause down the block. The venue offers a convenient pickup and drop-off service (€6), but it's accessible by a short 15min. walk from downtown that takes you through Sacromonte, with fantastic night views of the Alhambra.

 # From Pl. Nueva, follow Carrera del Darro beside the river north to Cuesta del Chapiz (8min.). Take a left and follow Cuesta del Chapiz 3 blocks to Camino de Sacromonte. Take a right and head north for 10min. Just past the terrace seating of Casa Juanillo, take the flight of stairs to the left to reach Venta el Gallo. Alternatively, take city bus #34 or #35 to the base of Camino del Sacromonte and follow the walking directions above. ℹ Reservations can be made in advance by telephone or email at ventaelgallo@hotmail.com. $ Show with drink €22; with dinner €52. ⏰ Doors open at 8pm. 1st show 8:30pm. 2nd show 10:45pm.

LE CHIEN ANDALOU PLAZA NUEVA AND CITY CENTER

Carrera del Darro, 7 ☎61 710 66 23 www.lechienandalou.com

Le Chien Andalou is only two years old, but it has already made a name as one of the best flamenco shows in Granada. Across from the Darro and just north of

Pl. Nueva, this is a great place to catch a quick evening show without making the trek up to Sacromonte. Nightly sets feature the city's younger talent, typically in a simple trio of guitarist, singer, and solo dancer. The traditional, cave-like performance space in the back creates an intimate setting, with the performers cramped up front and the audience packed close together. For only €6, Le Chien Andalou offers traditional flamenco at an incredible value. While the space always fills up, it doesn't book completely in advance, so it is easy enough to stop by 30-45min. before the show to grab a seat. They also offer a solid selection of tapas (€5-10).

➡ *From Pl. Nueva, walk due north up C. del Darro. The bar is to the left just past Iglesia de Santa Ana.* $ *Tickets €6. Beer €2-3. Wine or sangria €3. Mixed drinks €5.* ⏰ *Open M-Th 7-3am, F-Su 4pm-3am.*

Festivals

👍 CORPUS CHRISTI — CITYWIDE

While this festival is technically intended to celebrate the presence of Jesus Christ in Holy Communion, Corpus Christi has become more debaucherous than religious. The Catholic monarchs brought the festivities to Granada hoping to win over the large Muslim and Jewish populations—some say that the royalty even urged the local government to invest huge sums of money in order to make the celebrations as crazy and fun as possible. You'll be glad to know that these instructions were taken seriously. In its entirety, the festival lasts from the *encendido* (lighting of all the city lights Monday at midnight) until the **fireworks** extravaganza the following Sunday. The **Corpus Christi Parade** is held on Thursday and is the most important day of the festival when the throne created by Miguel Moreno is carried through the streets. Over the course of the week, *casetas* (booths) and a fair are set up on the outskirts of the city in **Almanjáyar,** just a short bus ride on the #19 or #43 from the city center. (Gran Vía $ €1.40. ⏰ Runs Tu-Sa until 4am.) In **Plaza Bib-Rambla,** kitty-corner to the Cathedral, you will also find live music, dance, and *carocas*, short satirical plays depicting the events of the past year. Every night there are bullfights held in the **Plaza de Toros** (Av. del Doctor Oloriz www.plazadetorosdegranada.com). Tickets can be purchased online in advance or at the stadium just before the 7:30pm fights. If you're not interested in the bullfights, the bars and restaurants surrounding Pl. de Toros are a popular destination for locals seeking to avoid the congestion of the city center during the festival. Accommodations tend to fill up early for Corpus Christi, so book in advance.

⏰ *60 days after Easter (generally sometime between late-May and mid-July).*

FESTIVAL INTERNACIONAL DE MÚSICA Y DANZA — CITYWIDE

☎95 822 18 44 granadafestival.org

The Festival Internacional de Música y Danza is one of Granada's most prized events. Now in its 60th year, this summertime festivity brings together a wide variety of music and dance, including flamenco, piano, *zarzuela*, orchestral, and vocals. Performances are held all over the city, including in such awe-inspiring spots as the outdoor theater of the Generalife and the Palacio de Carlos V. This festival is far from provincial with performances by internationally touring operas, symphonies, and ballet companies, including Spain's National Ballet. Tickets are available online, from venue box offices, or in advance from **Ticketmaster** (☎90 215 00 25 www.ticketmaster.es/granadafestival). While tickets can be quite expensive, the festival offers a generous 50% discount for those under 26 or over 65 for all events in the Generalife Amphitheater and in the Palacio de Carlos V.

ℹ *The festival program is available in print at tourist offices.* $ *Prices vary, usually €10-50.* ⏰ *From mid-June through mid-July.*

ESSENTIALS

Practicalities

- **TOURIST OFFICES:** There are over 25 tourist offices in the greater Granada area. The primary offices are in **City Hall** (el Ayuntamiento) in Pl. del Carmen (☎95 824 82 80 www.granadatur.com), at the **airport** (☎95 824 52 69 iturismo.aeropuerto@dipgra.es), and in the **Alhambra** (Av. Generalife ☎95 854 40 02 www.andalucia.org).
- **TOURS:** The tourist bus line for Granada runs English-language tours that stop at 10 major sights. (www.citysightseeing-spain.com/html/es/tour $ €10. ⏰ 1¼hr., every 15min.) You can also join the free walking tour, run by **Oasis Granada,** which departs from the fountain in Pl. Nueva. ($ €3-5 tip recommended. ⏰ Daily 11am.)
- **CURRENCY EXCHANGE: Interchange** is a money-exchange office that provides services for all major credit cards, including American Express. (C. Reyes Católicos, 31 ☎95 822 46 44 ⏰ Open M-Sa 9am-10pm, Su 11am-3pm and 4-9pm.)
- **INTERNET: Biblioteca de Andalucía** has 8 computers that you can use for free for up to 1hr. (C. Profesor Sáinz Cantero, 6 ☎95 857 56 50 www.juntadeandalucia.es/cultura/ba ⏰ Open M-F 9am-2pm.) **Idolos and Fans** has photocopying, fax, scanning, Wi-Fi, and even a PlayStation 3. (Camino de Ronda, 80 ☎95 826 57 25 $ €1.80 per hr., €9 per 6hr., €12 per 10hr. ⏰ Open daily 10am-midnight.)
- **POST OFFICE: Puerta Real.** (Intersection of C. Reyes Católicos and Acera del Darro ☎95 822 11 38 ⏰ Open M-F 8:30am-8:30pm, Sa 9:30am-2pm.)
- **POSTAL CODE:** 18005.

Emergency!

- **EMERGENCY NUMBERS: Municipal police:** ☎092. **National police:** ☎091.
- **LATE-NIGHT PHARMACIES:** You'll find a few 24hr. pharmacies around the intersection of C. Reyes Católicos and Acera del Darro, including **Farmácia Martín Valverde** (C. Reyes Católicos, 5 ☎95 826 26 64).
- **HOSPITALS/MEDICAL SERVICES: Hospital Universitario Vírgen de las Nieves.** (Av. de las Fuerzas Armadas, 2 ☎95 802 00 00.) **Hospital San Juan de Dios.** (C. San Juan de Dios ☎95 802 29 04.) For an **ambulance,** contact a local emergency team (☎95 828 20 00).

Getting There

BY PLANE

Aeropuerto Federico García Lorca (GRX; ☎95 824 52 69) is located about 15km outside the city in Chauchina. The airport has daily flights to and from Barcelona, Madrid, Mallorca, and Sevilla as well as weekly flights to and from Paris' Orly and Rome's Fiumicino airports. Air Europa, Iberia, Spanair, Ryanair, and Vueling Airlines all fly through Granada and offer connecting flights to and from cities across Europe.

A taxi will take you to the city center (€25) or directly to the Alhambra (€28). Call **Radio Taxi** in advance at ☎60 605 29 25 or wait in line at the airport. The bus company **Autocares José González** offers a direct service between the airport and the city center. (☎95 839 01 64 www.autocaresjosegonzalez.com $ €3. ⏰ Every hr. 5:20am-8pm.)

BY TRAIN

The main **train station** (☎95 827 12 72) is at Av. de los Andaluces. **RENFE** trains (www.renfe.es) run to and from Barcelona ($ €63 ⏰ 11½hr.; daily 8am and 9:30pm), Madrid ($ €70 ⏰ 4½hr.; daily 9:05am and 6:05pm), Sevilla ($ €24 ⏰ 3hr., 4 per day

8am-9pm), and many other smaller cities. To get from the station to the city center, you can take a short taxi ($ €5 🕐 5min.) or bus #3, 6, 9, or 11 ($ €1.20), which will take you to C. Gran Vía de Colón in the city center.

BY BUS

The bus station is at Carretera de Jaén (☎95 818 50 10). **Alsa** buses (www.alsa.es) run within Andalucía (☎95 818 54 80) and connect to the Madrid (☎95 818 54 80) and Valencia-Barcelona (☎90 242 22 42) lines. Buses run to and from Cádiz ($ €31 🕐 5hr., 4 per day 9am-9pm), Madrid ($ €17 🕐 5hr., 15 per day 1am-11:30pm.), Málaga ($ €10 🕐 1½hr., 15 per day 7am-9:30pm), Sevilla ($ €20 🕐 3hr., 10 per day 8am-11pm), and many other destinations. **Autocares Bonal** (☎95 846 50 22) also runs a direct route to and from **Sierra Nevada** ski resorts in winter. (🕐 25min.; M-F 3 per day, Sa-Su 4 per day.) City buses #3 and 33 on **Transportes Rober** run regular services between the station and the city center.

Getting Around

Transportes Rober runs almost 40 bus lines around the city as well as smaller direct buses to the Alhambra, the Albaicín, and the Sacromonte. (☎90 071 09 00 www.transportesrober.com $ €1.20; 7 rides €5.) The **tourist lines** are #30, 31, 32, and 34. The **circular lines** (#11, 21, and 23) make full loops around the city. Rober also runs a special Feria line ($ €1.40). When most lines stop running at 11:30pm, the **Búho lines** pick up the slack. ([i] #111 and 121 $ €1.30. 🕐 Daily midnight-5:15am.)

málaga ☎95

Málaga may be located right on the water, but don't show up looking for puka shells, ukuleles, or any Muppets singing "Kokomo." The second-largest city in Andalucía and the sixth-largest in Spain, culture-rich Málaga cringes at the thought of being just another beach town, styling itself not just "Capital of the Costa del Sol" but also "City of Museums." You'll enjoy the waves, but you'll also enjoy turning your back to them and plunging yourself into the student-filled bars of the *centro histórico*'s narrow streets, the shade of the palm tree-lined avenues, and the excellent international cuisine on plazas that keep crowds until long after the sun mercifully goes down. While the city's rich Phoenician, Roman, and Moorish history may not be quite as evident as in its fellow provincial capitals of Granada and Córdoba, this means that the *centro* doesn't feel quite as tourist-choked. And you'll still have the typical Andalusian experience of turning a corner only to see an imposing Moorish fortress on one side of you and the remains of a Roman theater on the other. Málaga's cultural clock doesn't switch off after the Reconquista, though—Pablo Picasso was born here, and there are several sights and references to Málaga's favorite Cubist, despite the dirty little secret that he left town as a young boy and last visited the city when he was 19. Perhaps the reason Picasso never made it back was that it would have been so hard to leave again—with famous beaches, a lively student scene, cheap restaurants, lots of shopping, and a long lineup of great sights, Málaga's got it all.

ORIENTATION

Málaga is divided by the often dry **Río Guadalmedina.** The only place you'll probably visit on the western bank is the bus or train station; the eastern bank has the beaches and the **centro histórico,** bordered by the river to the west, **Alameda Principal** to the south, the **Alcazaba** and **Catedral** to the east, and the **Plaza de la Merced** to the north. The main street, Alameda Principal, separates the *centro histórico* from the port;

it intersects with the shop- and bank-filled C. Marqués de Larios at the Pl. Marina, where the main tourist office is located. Lots of restaurants, bars, and clubs, often with a younger crowd, are centered around the Pl. Merced and Pl. Uncibay. To the east of the *centro histórico* are the popular Playa de la Malagueta and the slightly quieter, more family-oriented Playa de Pedregalejo.

ACCOMMODATIONS

Most of Málaga's affordable accommodations are located in the *centro histórico*, especially around the Pl. Merced and along C. Carretería. There is a wide variety of cheap hostels, ranging from the supremely chill to the somewhat swanky. Most of the hostels even offer private single rooms, often with private baths.

PICASSO'S CORNER BACKPACKERS HOSTEL HOSTEL $

C. San Juan de Letrán, 9 ☎95 221 22 87 www.picassoscorner.hostel.com

The name is only kind of a tourist ploy—this backpackers' getaway is tucked into a small street off of the nightlife-filled Pl. Merced, just a 1min. walk from Picasso's house and a 5min. walk from the Picasso Museum. It reps good ol' Pablo with bunk bed-filled dorms, some more cramped than others, named after his paintings; some of the rooms even have balconies overlooking the small, bar-filled street. You can make like a chef on the rooftop barbecue or in the communal kitchen, or just let the pro take over and try the excellent homemade lunches and dinners (€5).

From the main exit of the bus station (across the street from the train station), turn right onto Paseo de los Tilos and continue through the large plaza to your left as the street curves slightly to the left and becomes Callejones del Perchel. Turn right at the next roundabout (Glorieta de Albert Camus) onto Av. Aurora, cross the bridge, and immediately turn left onto Pasillo de Santa Isabel. Proceed 10min., then at the 5th bridge, take a slight right onto C. Carretería, which leads to the Pl. Merced; upon reaching the plaza, turn left and take the 2nd left onto C. San Juan de Letrán. ***i*** *Breakfast and sheets included. Free Wi-Fi and computers with free internet access. Female-only dorms available. Kitchen available. Lunch and dinner €5 each. Towels €2. Laundry €3. Luggage storage available. Make a booking at the reception desk for a Funky Hostel in Córdoba, Granada, or Fez and get a 10% discount.* [$] *6-bed dorms €14-17; 4-bed dorms €16-18; doubles €36-40.* ⏰ *Reception 24hr.*

PINK HOUSE BACKPACKERS HOSTEL $

C. Carretería, 2 ☎95 221 00 66

Relaxed without being hippie, Pink House's large, colorful dorms are some of the best bargains in town. Perhaps more importantly, there are a few perks that make a world of difference to the tired traveler: it's a bit closer to the bus and train stations than most of the hostels, and it has glorious, glorious **air-conditioning.** Breakfast isn't included, but you can make yourself something in the communal kitchen and eat it upstairs in the common area, which feels less like a hostel common room and more like a cool, well-traveled middle-age couple's living room.

From the main exit of the bus station (across the street from the train station), turn right onto Paseo de los Tilos and continue through the large plaza to your left as the street curves slightly to the left and becomes Callejones del Perchel. Turn right at the next roundabout (Glorieta de Albert Camus) onto Av. Aurora, cross the bridge, and immediately turn left onto Pasillo de Santa Isabel. Proceed 10min.; the hostel is across from the 5th bridge. ***i*** *Free Wi-Fi and computers with free internet access. A/C. Kitchen available. Sheets included. Towels €1.50.* [$] *9-bed mixed dorm €10-12; 8-bed mixed dorm €10-12; 8-bed female-only dorm with ensuite bath €10-12. Singles €30; doubles €36-40, with bath €44-48; triples with bath €51-57; quads with bath €72. Prices may rise up to €30 more during Semana Santa and Feria de Agosto.* ⏰ *Reception 9am-10pm.*

CASA BABYLON HOSTEL $
C. de Pedro de Quejana, 3 ☎95 226 72 28 www.casababylonhostel.com

Though it's a bit farther from the sights, food, and nightlife than most of Málaga's accommodations, Casa Babylon is an unabashedly laid-back mellow-fest perfect for the free-spirited backpacker who just needs to put his feet up in a hammock and throw back a beer. Shirtless staff, psychedelic murals, and a "chill out" zone are all par for the course here, and yes, there are actually hammocks out front perfect for a little time just for you and the shade, perhaps punctuated with visits from the big, friendly dog. The dorm rooms, cooled only by portable fans, are standard-issue hostel fare, although they're even more colorful than most places (we hope you like purple).

From the main exit of the bus station (across the street from the train station), turn right onto Paseo de los Tilos and continue through the large plaza to your left as the street curves slightly to the left and becomes Callejones del Perchel. Turn right at the roundabout (Glorieta de Albert Camus) onto Av. Aurora, cross the bridge, and immediately turn left onto Pasillo de Santa Isabel. Proceed 10min., then at the 5th bridge take a slight right onto C. Carretería, which leads to the Pl. Merced. Cross the plaza diagonally and turn left onto C. Victoria and proceed for 5min. until the street forks into 3, then turn right onto C. Ferrándiz, take the 1st left onto C. Hurtado de Mendoza, and take the 1st right onto C. Pedro de Quejana; the hostel is on the left. ***i*** *Breakfast and sheets included. Free Wi-Fi and computers with free internet access. Outdoor terrace with bar. Kitchen available. Towel rental €1. Luggage storage €1 per day. Laundry €3. Pick-up service from airport €25.* [$] *July 15-Aug 31 8-bed dorms with bath €14; 6-bed €13; 5-bed €14; 4-bed with bath €15; doubles €40. Sept 1-July 14 €12/10/12/13/36.* ⏰ *Reception 24hr.*

HOSTEL BABIA HOSTEL $
Pl. de los Mártires, 6 ☎95 222 27 30 www.babiahostel.com

Sometimes even the smallest of conveniences can brighten your day—isn't it nice to have a full restaurant at your feet, a foosball table in your giant living room, and some friendly Spaniards offering to take you snorkeling (€25)? What Hostel Babia's colorful dorm rooms, named after continents, lack in A/C (yep, even Antarctica is boiling hot in summer), they make up for in high ceilings, small balconies, and tall bunk beds with so much space between top and bottom that you might need to MacGyver a tin-can telephone to communicate with the person below you. Don't even think of trying to check in during a big soccer game, when a wall-to-wall crowd between the door and the reception desk is glued to the giant TV screen.

From the main exit of the bus station (across the street from the train station), turn right onto Paseo de los Tilos and continue through the large plaza to your left as the street curves slightly to the left and becomes Callejones del Perchel. Then turn right at the next roundabout (Glorieta de Albert Camus) onto Av. Aurora, cross the bridge, and immediately turn left onto Pasillo de Santa Isabel. Proceed 10min., then at the 5th bridge take a slight right onto C. Carretería, then take the 2nd right onto C. Andrés Pérez, which leads to the Pl. Mártires. ***i*** *Breakfast, towels, and sheets included. Female-only dorms available. Lockers (too small for big backpack) available. Free luggage storage.* [$] *10-bed dorms €10; 8-bed (female-only) €11; 6-bed €14. Doubles €30.* ⏰ *Reception 24hr.*

CASA AL SUR HOSTEL $
C. Molinillo del Aceite, 5 ☎95 113 24 29 www.casa-al-sur.com

Málaga's poshest hostel has fairly large four- and six-bed dorms with well-spaced beds, but it really distinguishes itself by a few comforts and pay-to-play perks you don't normally see in hostels. Need some alone time with Señor Suds? The small shared bathrooms have full bathtubs. Sick of bread and jam for breakfast? Start your day off right with a more elaborate buffet that includes **waffles** (€4). Had enough watery beers in saggy hostel leather couches to last a lifetime? Sip fine wines in a tasting organized by the owner, a former sommelier with a passable American accent, in the small, elegant bar (€10, min. 2 people).

Looking for rooms with A/C? Come on, we said it was posh, we didn't say it was the Ritz-Carlton!

From the main exit of the bus station (across the street from the train station), turn right onto Paseo de los Tilos and continue through the large plaza to your left as the street curves slightly to the left and becomes Callejones del Perchel. Then turn right at the next roundabout (Glorieta de Albert Camus) onto Av. Aurora, cross the bridge, and immediately turn left onto Pasillo de Santa Isabel. Proceed 10min., then at the 5th bridge take a slight right onto C. Carretería, then take the 4th right onto C. Molinillo del Aceite. i Breakfast €4. Free Wi-Fi. Towels and sheets included. Kitchen available. Bar and rooftop terrace. Washer €3, dryer €3, both €5. In-room 30min. massage €15. Beach towel rental €2. $ Apr and holidays 4- and 6-bed dorms €17; doubles €36. May-Sept €15/32. Oct-Mar €12/30. ⏰ Reception 9am-10pm.

THE MELTING POT HOSTEL $

Av. del Pintor Joaquín Sorolla, 30 ☎95 260 05 71 www.meltingpothostels.com

For those whose interests are a little less Picasso and a little more *playa*, this social hostel across the street from the Playa de la Malagueta (but far from everything else) is an ideal choice to proudly proclaim your beach bum pride. You'll have plenty of new friends to share it with—between the 24hr. bar in the lounge and the flower-filled terrace, there are plenty of places to have a drink or even share a hookah (€6) with fellow sand lovers. After a long day of lounging around, cook yourself dinner in the communal kitchen or just let the owner's dad grill you up some hamburgers (€3), then return to the comfort of your large dorm room with ensuite bath, and recharge for another strenuous day at the beach.

Right behind the Playa de la Malagueta. From bus or train station, take any bus that goes to Alameda Principal. Continue in the direction of the bus along Alameda Principal past the Pl. Marina; just before the roundabout there will be bus stops for bus #11 and 34. Take either of these buses to Av. Pintor J. Sorolla (Bellavista) and take the 1st right. i Breakfast included. Free Wi-Fi and computers with free internet access. 8-bed female-only dorm available. Linens included. Towels €1, beach towels €1.50. Ensuite bathrooms. $ June-July 10-bed dorms €18; 8-bed €20; 4-bed €21; doubles €48. Aug €23/25/27/60. Sept €18/20/21/48. Oct-Mar €12/14/17/40. Apr-May €16/18/19/44. Prices €4 higher during Semana Santa. ⏰ Reception 24hr.

SIGHTS

Although Málaga is famous for its beaches, there's definitely more to this city than sun and sand. Like any self-respecting Andalusian city, Málaga has a healthy array of ruins reflecting its Roman, Phoenician, and Moorish heritage. It also capitalizes on its claim to fame as the birthplace of Pablo Picasso, with two excellent museums dedicated to the artist. Once you've had your fill of Picasso, there are plenty of other museums; Málaga is known (mainly by the city government) as the City of Museums. There is a wide variety of excellent museums, ranging from the **Museo Carmen Thyssen,** a museum of 19th century Andalusian art (C. Compañía, 10 ☎902 30 31 31 www.carmenthyssenmalaga.org Off of Pl. Constitución $ €6, students and seniors €3.50; temporary exhibition €4/2.50; combined ticket €8/4.50; under 12 free ⏰ Open July-Aug M-Th 10am-8pm, F-Sa 10am-9pm; Sept-May Tu-Th 10am-8pm, F-Sa 10am-9pm, Su 10am-8pm; June Tu-Th 10am-8pm, F-Sa 10am-9pm, Su 10am-2pm) to the delightfully funky **Museo Casas de Muñecas (Doll's House Museum).** (C. Álamos, 32 ☎952 21 00 82 www.museocm.com From the Pl. Merced, with your back to the plaza, turn right onto C. Álamos; the museum is on the left. $ €5, children €3. ⏰ Open Tu-Su 11am-1pm.)

MUSEO DE PICASSO MUSEUM

C. San Agustín, 8 ☎95 212 76 00 www.museopicassomalaga.org

While you can feel the presence and history of Pablo Picasso throughout Málaga, there is no better place to truly capture the aura of this artist than the museum dedicated to the man himself. The building's pale marble floors and white walls allow the creative and wonderful collection to speak for itself. The rooms are organized in chronological order, allowing you to trace the changes and stages of the artist's style to better understand his passionate views on politics, education, the human body, bullfighting, and (of course) women. You'll find Picasso's quotes along the walls almost as thought-provoking as his paintings, sculptures, and ceramics. Aside from the main collection, you can explore the permanent basement archaeological site of Phoenician, Roman, and Moorish ruins (which has nothing to do with Picasso, in case you were wondering), or enjoy the temporary exhibitions that hone in on single aspects of Picasso's work and juxtapose his art with the works of his contemporaries or of modern artists.

From Pl. Merced, with your back to the plaza, proceed along C. Granada (on the left) and turn left onto C. San Agustín. $ Permanent collection €6, students and seniors €3. Temporary exhibition €4.50/2.25. Combined ticket €9/4.50. Under 18 free. ⏰ Open Tu-Th 10am-8pm, F-Sa 10am-9pm, Su 10am-8pm.

ALCAZABA FORTRESS

C. Alcazabilla, 2 ☎63 093 29 87

If you've been to Granada, you'll probably view the Alcazaba as a smaller version of the Alhambra. From the views to the gardens to the fountained passageways, there's no doubt that this building is another flavor of Moorish fortress. But even if you've seen the Alhambra, Málaga's Alcazaba is still worth a visit. Follow the path in your free pamphlet to encounter sights like the **Puerta de las Columnas** (Gate of the Columns), a picturesque example of Arab additions to Roman structures. In the **Nazareth Palace,** built between the 11th and 14th centuries, you'll see three main courtyards, including the marble column-filled **Torre de Maldonado.** If you have good walking shoes (and are immune to heat), you can make the trek up to the **Gibralforo,** the additional hideout and viewpoint used by Moorish royalty. Follow the route on your pamphlet or risk getting hopelessly lost, although this can be a rewarding experience as well.

From Pl. Merced, with your back to the plaza, turn left and take the 1st right onto C. Alcazabilla. Or, from Pl. Marina, with your back to the water, proceed straight along C. Molina Lario, then after the cathedral turn right onto C. Santa María, which will turn into C. Cister, which leads to the entrance. $ €2.20; students, seniors, and under 16 €0.60. Free Su after 2pm. Combined ticket with Gibralforo €3.55. ⏰ Open daily in summer 9:30am-8pm; in winter 8:30am-7pm.

MUSEO DEL VINO MUSEUM, WINE TASTING

Pl. de los Viñeros, 1 ☎95 222 84 93 www.museovinomalaga.com

Displaying an uncanny ability to make boring the drink that makes boring people interesting, this museum is passionate about wine—the history of Malagan wine regulatory organizations, that is. To be fair, there are a few more fun things to see in this propaganda-fest for the local wine industry, like a large collection of colorful 19th-century wine labels. But if you're like us, you'll spend exactly as much time in the museum upstairs as you feel is necessary to avoid being embarrassed when you return downstairs for the **wine tasting.** The two wines included with admission can be supplemented with additional tastings (€1) if you just can't get enough of the excellent Malagan wines a world away from what you've been getting with your *menú del día.*

From the Pl. Merced, proceed against the traffic on C. Álamos, which curves to the left to become C. Carretería, and take the 8th right onto C. Biedmas, which leads to the small Pl. Viñeros. i Admission includes 2 wine tastings. $ €5, students and seniors €3, under 18 free (does not include tasting). Additional tastings €1. ⏰ Open M-F noon-2:30pm and 4:30-7:30pm.

CATEDRAL DE MÁLAGA CHURCH

C. Molina Lario ☎95 222 84 91

Sacrilege alert!—all Spanish cathedrals start to look the same after a while. However, it should be clear from your first glance at the largely pink Baroque

andalucía

façade's **squiggly columns** that this won't be regular ol' Joe Catedral. Built in 1528, it's also remarkable for having only one tower, leading locals to affectionately call it the "one-armed lady." If you doubted the Catedral de Málaga's uniqueness, your uncertainty will surely be erased by the red Hulk-like statue hugging a cross and mooning everyone as they approach the ticket window. The inside isn't quite as out-there, but unlike many cathedrals, you can step inside the spectacular choir loft, overlooked by a pair of very green organs.

From Pl. Merced, with your back to the plaza, proceed along C. Granada (on the left) and follow it as it curves to the right, then take a slight left onto C. Molina Lario. Or, from Pl. Marina, with your back to the sea, proceed straight on C. Molina Lario. **i** *Audioguide in English, Spanish, French, German, or Italian included in ticket price.* $ *€5, under 13 free.* ⏰ *Cathedral open M-F 10am-6:45pm, Sa 10am-5:45pm; last entry 45min. before close. Choir open M-Sa 10am-2pm.*

CENTRO DE ARTE CONTEMPORÁNEO DE MÁLAGA (CAC MÁLAGA) MUSEUM

C. de Alemania ☎95 212 00 55 www.cacmalaga.org

Walking through the high-ceilinged, white-walled rooms of this one-story art museum, you'll start to wonder if there are any meaningful subjects not addressed by CAC Málaga's permanent collection of contemporary paintings, photographs, and sculptures. Violence? Check out the giant wooden gun cut-out smothered with skulls, lungs, hearts, cartilage, and bones. Beauty? Try 46 photographs of dead buzzards arranged in increasing order of attractiveness. Racism in the snowman community? If three jet-black stacked spheres don't open your eyes to this long-standing problem, then nothing will. A series of three-month rotating exhibits by international artists also crash the thought-provoking party—and unlike most parties, this one's best with a chaperone; guided tours offered twice a week will help Spanish speakers make sense of this rewardingly confounding museum.

From Pl. Marina with the port on your left, proceed along Alameda Principal to the river, then turn left at the river onto Av. Comandante Benítez; the museum is on the left. **i** *Free 30min. guided tours in Spanish July-Aug W and F 12:15pm, Sept-June Tu and Th 6pm and 7pm.* $ *Free.* ⏰ *Open July-Aug Tu-Su 10am-2pm and 5-9pm; Sept-June Tu-Su 10am-8pm.*

MUSEO CASA NATAL DE PABLO RUIZ PICASSO MUSEUM

Pl. de la Merced, 15 ☎95 206 02 15

If you weren't already jealous of Picasso for his artistic vision, his painting skills, and his general genius, be jealous of his family's sweet real estate—Picasso was born and spent the first three years of his life in this building right on the Pl. Merced. The museum that currently occupies the building is less of a re-creation than most childhood-home museums; you'll find just one room dolled up 19th-century style and just one of Picasso's childhood garments, his umbilical girdle (okay, we take back a little of that jealousy). That leaves most of the museum free to display a small collection, mostly of ceramics, and rotating exhibits of pieces from the collection of the Fundación Picasso. There's nothing major on display, but the man's genius is still readily apparent; he somehow could make even ceramic plates interesting, which, as anyone who has visited pretty much any archaeological museum in Spain can attest, is no easy feat. This museum's modest collection is nothing like the Museo Picasso's, but it's a godsend for those who like their Picasso in small (and cheap) doses.

On the opposite end of Pl. Merced from the traffic, on the left-hand corner. **i** *Audioguide in English, Spanish, French, German, or Italian.* $ *€1; students, seniors, and under 17 free. Audioguide €1.* ⏰ *Open daily 9:30am-8pm. Last entry 15min. before close.*

MUSEO DE ARTES Y COSTUMBRES POPULARES MUSEUM

Pasillo de Santa Isabel, 10 ☎95 221 71 37 www.museoartespopulares.com

Forget your floaties and your friendly YMCA swim teachers—this museum takes a sink-or-swim approach to teaching about life in 19th-century Málaga. To learn about the blacksmith industry, what better way than to cram half of the iron in the Costa del Sol into a tiny room of this former 17th-century inn? Make your way through the 18 artifact-packed rooms, each covering a different aspect of Malagan society, from fisheries to the wine industry to the life of the bourgeoisie—it's all vaguely reminiscent of Clue, except the only thing dead at the end is your enthusiasm for clay figurines.

From Pl. Marina with the port on your left, proceed along Alameda Principal to the river, then turn left onto C. José Manuel García Caparrós, which will turn into Pasillo de Santa Isabel; it's across from the 3rd bridge (Puente de la Trinidad). Or, from Pl. Merced, proceed against the traffic on C. Álamos, which curves to the left to become C. Carretería and then Pasillo de Santa Isabel; it's across from the 2nd bridge (Puente de la Trinidad.) $ €2, seniors €1, under 14 free. ⏰ Open in summer M-F 10am-1:30pm and 5-8pm, Sa 10am-1:30pm; in winter M-F 10am-1:30pm and 4-7pm, Sa 10am-1:30pm.

BEACHES

While the beaches closest to the city center are generally very crowded and not very picturesque, you'll find more peaceful terrain and better photo-ops as you move east along the coast. Once you get out there, show off your washboard abs before a few too many meals at one of the fresh seafood restaurants lining the boardwalk hide them away for good. For more information about Málaga's beaches, pick up a pamphlet at a tourist office or contact the beach office (☎95 192 69 14 http://playas.malaga.eu).

PLAYA DE PEDREGALEJO

While it may require a little extra travel to get here, the long walk or quick bus ride is definitely worth the trip down to Playa de Pedregalejo. This lengthy, 1200m strip of beach has finer sand and finer views than what you'll find back in the *centro*, and its small, W-shaped mini-coves make the beach feel smaller than it is. Buy some produce at **SuperSol** (Av. Juan Sebastián Elcano, 30 Walk up one of the side streets away from the beach ⏰ Open M-Sa 9:15am-9:15pm) for a cheap picnic lunch, even though it'll be hard to resist the restaurants packing the boardwalk that grill up fresh fish out of old tin boats converted into fire pits. Whether lunch is apples and bread or fried calamari, be sure to leave plenty of time after lunch to join a pickup soccer game on one of the enclosed sand pitches.

Take bus #11 or 34 to Av. Juan Sebastián Elcano and turn right onto any side street down to the beach. i Showers and bathrooms available. Information kiosk on C. Bolivia, after the first long stretch of restaurants. $ Free. ⏰ Lifeguards on duty 11am-8pm.

PLAYA DE LA MALAGUETA

This 1200m beach stretching from the harbor and curling into a cove may not be the most picturesque pairing of sand and sea, but it's definitely Málaga's most popular and convenient spot to laze around. You're steps from the busy city streets, 10min. from Pl. Merced, and a tentative wade away from some Mediterranean relaxation. The Playa de la Malagueta sucks in tourists and locals alike, whether they're lounging under a rented umbrella (€8 with 2 chairs), exploring the rock bar at the end of the *caleta* (cove), resting under a palm tree on a grassy knoll, or curling up in one of the stone letters of the statue spelling out the name of the beach (the lowercase "L" probably isn't your best choice). You can grab a bite at one of the many restaurants right on the sand or cool off with an ice cream bar from one of the many kiosks along the boardwalk.

From Pl. Merced, with your back to the plaza, turn left and walk through the tunnel, then proceed along Paseo de la Farola, which will take you to the western end of the beach. i Showers, bathrooms, and playgrounds available. Information kiosk near intersection of Pl. Malagueta and Paseo Marítimo Pablo Ruiz Picasso. $ Free. ⏰ Lifeguards on duty 11am-8pm.

FOOD

Málaga's restaurants are numerous, diverse, and spread out across the city. Fresh seafood is a staple of Malagan cuisine, whether you're looking for an expensive grilled tuna steak or a half-portion of fried calamari. For the more culinarily adventurous (or those allergic to omega-3 fatty acids), there are also tons of international and fusion restaurants serving creative modern cuisine. Many restaurants are located in the *centro histórico*, but there is also a non-stop lineup of seafood restaurants on the boardwalk behind the Playa de Pedregalejo serving up fried seafood from grills made from converted boats. You can eat well for less here than in many other Spanish cities, so no matter your preferences, dig in. *Buen provecho.* In the unlikely event you're feeling industrious despite the heat and the allure of nearby beaches, buy your own groceries at the **Mercado Central de Atarazanas** (C. Atarazanas, 8 ⇄ From Alameda Principal, facing the river, turn right and walk 2 blocks ⏰ Open M-Sa 8am-3pm) or **Eroski Aliprox** (C. Carretería, 105 ⏰ Open M-Sa 9am-2pm and 5:30-8:30pm).

☑ TAPERÍA PEPA Y PEPE TAPAS, TRADITIONAL $

C. de la Calderería, 9

It's hard to imagine any place named Pepa y Pepe could focus on serving food, since the chefs' and waiters' natural instincts would be to coo all day over the cuteness of their establishment's name. Nevertheless, this *tapería* somehow manages to serve up a large menu of delicious *raciones* (€3-7.50) and cheap drinks to the large crowd of tourists and regulars filling the small, traditional interior and the barrels-turned-tables on the street. The menu of fried seafood is so long that it's hard to know what to choose; the fried octopus (€5.50, ½ portion €3.80) is a good choice, but if you really can't decide, just order the Pepa y Pepe, which sounds like a teddy bear and a puppy, but is actually an assortment of fried fish (€4.80, ½ portion €2.90). Vegetarians sad that their diet generally means lower risk of heart disease can drown their sorrows in fried mushrooms (ration €4.80, ½ portion €2.90). Amid the fried food-fest, don't miss out on other star dishes—the *dátiles con bacon* (dates wrapped in bacon; €4.80, ½ portion €2.90) could easily be the best food on a toothpick in Málaga.

⇄ From C. Méndez Núñez, cross Pl. Uncibay and proceed 1 block along C. Calderería. [$] Raciones €3-7.50; ½ raciones €1.80-3.80. Beer €1-1.60. Wine €1.20-1.90. ⏰ Open daily noon-12:30am.

☑ VEGETARIANO EL CALAFATE VEGETARIAN $$

C. Andrés Pérez, 6 ☎95 222 93 44

It's not quite Lubavitchers serving up pork loin, but the contrast between this restaurant's beefy waiters and its dainty vegetarian dishes is pretty striking. Though everything's pretty affordable, the best choice for the budget traveler is the *menú*, served all day during the week. Gazpacho groupies looking to branch out will love their choices for the first course, a variety of tasty, refreshing cold soups: the *ajoblanco con uvas* and the *sopa de melón* are especially tasty. For a meatier dish (figuratively speaking—there's no meat on the menu), try the *berenjena rellena de setas* (eggplant stuffed with mushrooms, €8.90) or the *lasaña de espinacas* (spinach lasagna, €11.90). Even the bread tastes like little slices of heaven.

⇄ Just off Pl. Mártires. From Pl. Merced, proceed against the traffic on C. Álamos, which curves to the left to become C. Carretería, and take the 8th left onto C. Andrés Pérez. [$] Menú del día €9 (M-Th 1:30-4pm and 8:30-11pm, F 1:30-4pm; drink not included). Appetizers €4.50-8.50. Entrees €8.50-12. ⏰ Open M-Sa 1:30-4pm and 8:30-11pm.

CLANDESTINO INTERNATIONAL $$$

C. Niño de Guevara, 3 ☎95 221 93 90 www.clandestinomalaga.com

If you've been getting bored with the usual suspects on the Andalusian menu, Clandestino will take that boredom, mix it up with ricotta cheese and orange peel, stuff it into ☑**chocolate ravioli,** and serve it all with mint sauce (€11.90).

A local crowd fills the warmly decorated interior and the handful of tables outside to try the scrumptious and inventive international dishes, paired with a pitcher of sangria (€9.90) or one of the mixed drinks (€4-5) on the long beverage list. Most of the food isn't cheap when ordered à la carte, but the pasta dishes are delicious and comparatively affordable, and the lunchtime *menú del día* is a steal.

⇞ From the Pl. Uncibay, with the cafes on your right, proceed along C. Méndez Núñez and turn left onto C. José Denis Belgrano, then take the 1st right onto C. Niño de Guevara; the restaurant is on the right. ***i*** *Free Wi-Fi. $ Appetizers €10-15.30. Salads €9.70-11.40. Pasta €10.20-14.50. Meat and fish entrees €14-19. Desserts €4.50-6. Menú del día €8.90. ⏰ Open daily 1pm-1am. Menú del día available M-F 1:30-5pm.*

ASAKO ASIAN FUSION $$$

C. Carretería, 96 ☎95 221 40 60 www.restauranteasako.com

There are fusion restaurants and then there are confusion restaurants. Is Asako's food completely Japanese (sushi platters €17.50-26.50), sorta Japanese (tuna fish tataki with soft wasabi foam, €21.50), or not-at-all Japanese (tandoori chicken and couscous salad €12.50)? The sushi chefs dress in traditional Japanese garb but are as Spanish as the *siesta*. Chopsticks are often brought out, but they're quickly followed by rubber bands to help the often perplexed locals and European tourists. And in case you weren't totally disoriented along the Spanish-Japanese axis, Asako throws a whole other dimension into the mix with a soundtrack of golden oldies sung by Perry Como, Andy Williams, and other singers your parents barely remember. If you're looking for a similar kind of food but for a little less than Asako's cheap weekday *menú del día* (€8.90), check out **Tapadaki,** the affiliated tapas restaurant, which serves a *plato del día* and drink for €6.50 on weekday afternoons.

⇞ From Pl. Merced, with your back to the plaza, turn right onto C. Álamos, which curves to the left to become C. Carretería; the restaurant is just around the curve, on the left. $ Menú del día €8.90 (M-F 1:30-4:30pm, does not include drink). Appetizers €4.50-16. Salads €12.50-13.50. Entrees €12.50-21.50. Desserts €7-8. Beer €1.60. Wine by the glass €2.50. ⏰ Open daily 1:30-4:30pm and 8:30pm-midnight.

NAMASTE INTERNATIONAL $$

Paseo Marítimo del Pedregal, 74 ☎95 229 29 96

In places it seems like the Playa de Pedregalejo has more restaurants than grains of sand, but most of them serve basically the same thing: fish—fried, grilled, and paella'd. This eclectic international restaurant has a refreshingly different take on beachside food, as well as a *menú del día* (€10), practically unheard of on the boardwalk. The *ensalada marroquí* with chicken, couscous, and goat cheese dressing (€7.50) is filling without being heavy, and the lamb hamburger with caramelized onion, brie, and barbecue sauce might make you rethink the beef burger status quo. Wash it all down with some *tinto de verano* (sangria's cheaper cousin, €2) and views of the sea.

⇞ On the boardwalk behind Playa de Pedregalejo. $ Menú del día M-F 1-5pm €10. Appetizers €5-12. Salads €7-8. Entrees €7-16. Desserts €4. Beer €1.80-3.50. Wine by the glass €2.50-3. Tinto de verano €2. Cocktails €5.50. ⏰ Open daily 1-5pm and 7pm-midnight.

NIGHTLIFE

Nightlife in the *centro histórico* is largely confined to the area between C. Méndez Núñez and C. Álamos, near Pl. Merced, but that doesn't mean your options are limited. You'll find a wide selection of student-populated bars and clubs, each with their own styles of music and clientele. If you're still out by the Playa de Pedregalejo after dark on the weekend, check out the handful of bars and clubs on Av. Juan Sebastián Elcano and C. Bolivia.

[icon] ANDÉN CLUB

Pl. de Uncibay, 7 ☎95 221 35 36 www.discotecaanden.com

For those sick of schlepping to city outskirts to dance until dawn, Andén is a centrally located godsend, right in the center of Málaga's nightlife. Coming here means you'll rub shoulders (and maybe more) with the best-looking, best-dressed 20-somethings in town, so leave that "I Heart Granada" shirt at the hostel or risk a surly turn-away at the door. Once past the rope, make your way through the smoke (stay low and go!) and lasers to one of the four bars and sample a pricey mixed drink (€7) to prepare for a long night dancing to pop and reggaetón. Avoid the cover by entering before 2am—this place gets a crowd earlier than most *discotecas*, so coming that early isn't quite as lame as it sounds.

⇆ From Pl. Merced, with the plaza behind you, turn right onto C. Álamos, then take the 4th left onto C. Cárcer and turn left at the plaza. $ Cover €8 (includes 1 drink), free before 2am. Beer €4. Mixed drinks €7. ⏰ Open Th-Sa 11:30pm-7am.

BUNKER BAR BAR

C. Mariblanca, 9

You don't need to duck and cover to enter this bunker, but you should be ready for something a little rougher around the edges. Walk into this small bar and club and lean up against the metal siding on the walls and funky, dark murals in the corners. Bunker says they play a little bit of everything from anywhere in the world, but they maintain a strict policy against commercial pop or anything that could be heard at a middle school dance. Instead, Bunker is the place to rock out to some alternative beats and grab a beer (€2-4) with a mix of tourists and local students. You can go hard when the DJs spin on the weekend or come chill out during the Tuesday movie nights.

⇆ From Pl. Merced, with the plaza behind you, turn right onto C. Álamos and take the 2nd right onto C. Mariblanca. $ Beer €2-4. Mixed drinks €5-6. Discounts 11pm-2am. ⏰ Open Tu-Sa 11pm-4am. Movies Oct-May 9pm.

SHAM COPAS BAR

C. de Juan de Padilla, 24

Who needs decor when you have €1 shots? Sham Copas lacks much of the pretension of its neighbors on the nightlife-packed C. Juan de Padilla, focusing less on glowing lights and more on glowing faces. The crowd is largely overdressed 20-somethings fueling up for a long night at bigger and better places, but this place draws pretty much anyone looking for some of the cheapest shots (€1), *jarras* of beer (€1.50), and cocktails (€2.50-4) in town.

⇆ From the Pl. Uncibay, with the plaza on your left, proceed along C. Méndez Núñez and take the 1st right onto C. Juan de Padilla; the bar is on the right. $ Shots €1. Beer €1-1.50, 0.5L €2. Cocktails €2.50-4. ⏰ Open F-Sa 10:30pm-3am.

BAR YURI GAGARIN BAR

C. Álamos, 21

Bourgeois local 20-somethings, decadent Western tourists, and heroes of the Soviet Union alike all enjoy themselves at this small Russian bar that feels like more of a last stop than many of the flashier bars south of C. Álamos. While Comrade Gagarin may have been the first man in space, you certainly won't be the first to relish the novelty of the 12 brands of Russian beer or the 30 brands of Russian vodka at his namesake. Grab a seat at one of the tables next to the window, since the bar area could well be smaller than Vostok 1, and without the compensation of space ice cream.

⇆ From the Pl. Merced, with the plaza behind you, turn right onto C. Álamos. $ Imported beers €3. M-Th beer and vodka shot €3. ⏰ Open M-Th 8pm-2am, F-Sa 8pm-3am, Su 8pm-2am.

SHOPPING

From the moment you get off your train, you'll see how big shopping is in Málaga—the train station is an afterthought in a building that also houses a large American-style shopping mall. (🕐 Open M-Sa 10am-10pm, Su noon-8pm.) Just outside the stations is an even bigger mall, the **Centro Comercial Larios Centro** (Av. Aurora, 25 ☎95 236 93 93 www.larioscentro.com ✈ Proceed along Alameda Principal to the river, turn left, cross the next bridge, and proceed straight along Av. Aurora 🕐 Open M-Sa 10am-10pm), which has familiar Spanish stores like Zara and Mango as well as cafes, restaurants, and a supermarket. The all-encompassing and omnipresent Spanish chain **El Corte Inglés** has its Málaga store a block to the north on Av. Andalucía. (Av. Andalucía, 4-6 ☎95 207 65 00 www.elcorteingles.es ✈ Follow Alameda Principal across the river. 🕐 Open daily 10am-10pm.) For those looking for shopping in a little more of a Malagan setting, the wide C. Marqués de Larios is filled with medium- to high-end international stores, although if you're just looking to replace your smelly white T-shirt, the European retail giant **C &A** has a cheap store off a side street. (C. Liborio García, 10 ✈ From C. Marqués de Larios, with your back to Alameda Principal, turn left. 🕐 Open M-Sa 10am-9:30pm.)

RAYUELA IDIOMAS   BOOKS
Pl. de la Merced, 17   ☎95 222 48 10 www.libreriarayuela.com

Whether you're casually looking for a beach read, desperately searching for a copy of the Norton Anthology of American Literature, or just feel like browsing, this independent bookstore right next to Picasso's house has a decent-sized selection of books in English (and French and Italian). Most of the store is devoted to language learning books, although many of the materials act upon the assumption that you already know Spanish. If you do, in fact, read Spanish, be sure to check out the sister bookstore, the larger **Librería Rayuela**. (✈ From Pl. Merced, with plaza behind you, turn right onto C. Álamos and left onto C. Cárcer. 🕐 Open M-Sa 10am-8:30pm.)

✈ *On the opposite end of Pl. Merced from the traffic, on the left-hand corner.* 🕐 *Open M-Sa 10am-8:30pm.*

ESSENTIALS
Practicalities

• **TOURIST OFFICES:** Málaga is covered with tourist offices. The **municipal tourist office** has offices and kiosks throughout the city as well as an excellent website (www.malagaturismo.com) with PDF copies of all the pamphlets at the tourist offices. The main office in the Pl. Marina might not be the closest to your hotel, but it provides the most extensive services, including registration for city Wi-Fi and audioguides for self-guided tours (Pl. Marina, 11 ☎95 192 60 20 ✈ At the intersection of Alameda Principal and C. Marqués de Larios. 🕐 Open Mar-Sept daily 9am-8pm, Oct-Feb daily 9am-6pm). Other locations include the **Centro de Recepción de Visitantes Ben Gabirol** (C. Granada, 70 ☎95 221 33 29 🕐 Open daily 10am-2pm and 3-6pm) and **branches** near the Alcazaba (Pl. Aduana 🕐 Open daily 9am-2pm and 3-6pm), across the river near the post office (Av. Andalucía, 1 🕐 Open daily 10am-2pm), at the Playa de Malagueta (Paseo Marítimo de Pablo Ruiz Picasso, 1 ✈ Across from the western end of the beach, near the intersection with C. Fernando Camino. 🕐 Open June-Sept 10am-2pm and 3-7pm), at the Playa de Pedregalejo (C. Bolivia, 260 ✈ Across from the center of the beach, near the intersection with Paseo de las Acacias. 🕐 Open June-Sept 10am-2pm and 3-7pm), and at Terminal 3 of the airport. (🕐 Open M-F 9:30am-2pm and 2:30-6pm, Sa-Su 10am-2pm.) The **regional tourist office** provides information about the city of Málaga as well as Sevilla, Córdoba, Granada, Cádiz, and the other provincial capitals of Andalucía. (Pasaje de Chinitas, 4 ☎95 130 89 11 ✈ From Pl. Constitución, proceed along C. Marqués de Larios and take the 1st left. 🕐 Open M-F 9am-7:30pm, Sa-Su and holidays 9:30am-3pm.)

- **TOURS:** The municipal tourist office organizes **Málaga with 5 Senses,** a guided walking tour of the city that comments on the exteriors of the city's major sights. (☎66 239 79 61 guiasdemalaga@yahoo.es ✦ Departs from next to the main municipal tourist office in the Pl. Marina. *i* Bilingual tours in Spanish and English; call ahead for French, German, or Italian. Min. group of 5. Ⓢ €5. Ⓣ 1½hr., M-Sa and holidays 11:30am.) Free audioguides and pamphlets are available at the Pl. Marina tourist office for eight different **themed self-guided tours**, such as Traditional Málaga, Religious Málaga, Picasso's Málaga, and Contemporary Málaga. (*i* Available in Spanish, English, French, German, Italian, Japanese, Chinese, Arabic, and Russian. Credit card information and photocopy of passport required as deposit for audioguide. Ⓣ Pl. Marina tourist office open Mar-Sept daily 9am-8pm, Oct-Feb 9am-6pm.) **Málaga Bike Tours** offers a tour around the city that includes a drink. (C. Trinidad Grund, 4 ☎60 697 85 13 www.malagabiketours.eu ✦ Departs from next to the main municipal tourist office at Pl. Marina. *i* Tours in English. Bicycles and helmets included. Reservations recommended at least 24hr. in advance. Ⓢ €24. Ⓣ 4hr.; daily 10am, though other start times can be arranged in advance.) **bike2málaga** offers rickshaw tours of the city of varying lengths that leave from in front of the cathedral. (Ⓢ €10-30, depending on route. Ⓣ 20min.-1¾hr., available 10am-8pm.)

- **CURRENCY EXCHANGE: Banco Santander** (C. Marqués de Larios, 9 ☎95 221 37 97 www.bancosantander.es Ⓣ Open M-F 8:30am-2:30pm) exchanges major foreign currencies, as do several of the banks along C. Marqués de Larios, especially near Alameda Principal. Outside of regular bank hours, head across the river to El Corte Inglés and go to the Customer Service (Servicio de Atención al Cliente) desk on the 1st floor. (Av. Andalucía, 4-6 ☎952 07 65 00 www.elcorteingles.es ✦ Follow Alameda Principal across the river. Ⓣ Open daily 10am-10pm.)

- **LUGGAGE STORAGE:** Lockers are available in both the bus station (Ⓢ €3.20 per day Ⓣ Open daily 6:30am-midnight) and the train station. (*i* Luggage goes through security screening. Ⓢ €3-5 per day, depending on size. Ⓣ Open daily 7am-11pm.)

- **INTERNET ACCESS:** Free public Wi-Fi is available at Pl. Marina and along C. Marqués de Larios, but first you have to sign up for an account at the main branch of the municipal tourist office. Free Wi-Fi and computers with 1hr. of free internet access are also available at the **Biblioteca Provincial Cánovas del Castillo,** northwest of the Pl. Merced (C. Ollerías, 34 ☎95 213 39 36 ✦ From Pl. Merced, proceed against traffic on C. Álamos, which curves to the left to become C. Carretería, then take the 4th right onto C. Ollerías. *i* Ask at the information desk for a Wi-Fi password, valid for 24hr. Ⓣ Open July-Sept 15 M-F 9am-2pm, Sept 16-June M-F 9:30am-8pm. Closed Semana Santa.) For Wi-Fi and computers with internet access outside of library hours, try **TelSat.** (C. Gómez Pallete, 7 ☎95 222 77 84 ✦ From Pl. Merced, with your back to the traffic, take the 3rd left onto C. Gómez Pallete. Ⓢ Internet access €1 per hr. Ⓣ Open daily 10am-1:20am.)

- **POST OFFICE:** The main post office is just across the river from the centro histórico. (Av. Andalucía, 1 ☎95 236 43 80 www.correos.es ✦ Follow Alameda Principal across the river; it's on the left. Ⓣ Open M-F 8:30am-8:30pm, Sa 9:30am-2pm.)

- **POSTAL CODE:** 29002.

Emergency

- **EMERGENCY NUMBER:** ☎112.

- **AMBULANCE AND EMERGENCY HEALTHCARE:** ☎061. Red Cross: ☎95 222 22 22.

- **INFORMATION:** ☎010.

- **FIRE:** ☎080.

- **POLICE: Local Police** (Av. Rosaleda, 19 ☎092 or ☎95 212 65 52 www.policiademalaga.com ✦ From Alameda Principal, walk to the river, turn right, and walk 12min.) **National Police** (C. Ramos Marín, 4 ☎091 or ☎95 204 62 00 www.policia.es ✦ From Pl. Merced, with your back to traffic, take the 2nd left onto C. San Juan de Letrán, then turn right at the end of the street.)

- **HOSPITAL: Hospital Regional Universitario Carlos Haya de Málaga** (Av. Carlos de Haya ☎95 129 00 00 www.carloshaya.net 🚌 Bus #8, 21, or 23 from Alameda Principal.)
- **PHARMACY:** There is a 24hr. pharmacy on Alameda Principal, near Pl. Marina. (Alameda Principal, 2 ☎95 221 28 58.)

Getting There

BY BUS

Buses from destinations across Spain arrive at the **Estación de Autobuses de Málaga.** (Paseo de los Tilos ☎95 235 00 61 www.estabus.emtsam.es 🚌 Bus #4 goes from the station to Alameda Principal.) **Daibus** (☎91 652 00 11 www.daibus.es) provides service from Madrid. ($ €24-25. ⏰ 6-7¼hr. July-Aug 12 per day 7:30am-midnight; Sept-June M-Th 8 per day 7:30am-midnight, F 10 per day 7:30am-midnight, Sa 8 per day 7:30am-midnight, Su 10 per day 7:30am-midnight.) **Alsina,** a subsidiary of ALSA (☎90 242 22 42 www.alsa.es) runs buses from other cities in Andalucía, including Córdoba ($ €14 ⏰ 2½-3hr., 4 per day 8:30am-5pm), Granada ($ €11-13 ⏰ 1½-2hr.; M-Th 16 per day 7am-9:30pm, F 17 per day 7am-10pm, Sa 16 per day 7am-9:30pm, Su 16 per day 7am-10pm), and Sevilla ($ €17-22 ⏰ 2½-4hr.; 6 per day 7am-8:30pm). **ALSA** also provides service from Barcelona. ($ €83. ⏰ 16-17hr., 5 per day 7am-6:20pm.)

BY TRAIN

Trains to Málaga run to the **Estación de Málaga-Maria Zambrano,** across the street from the bus station. (C. Explanada de la Estación ☎90 224 02 02 www.adif.es 🚌 Bus #1, 3, 9, or 10 goes from the station to Alameda Principal. ⏰ Open daily 5am-12:45am.) **RENFE** runs trains from: Barcelona ($ €58-70 ⏰ 5½-12hr.; 3 per day 8:30am-3:50pm); Córdoba ($ €19-46 ⏰ 45min.-2½hr.; M-Th 17 per day 7:40am-11:29pm, F 18 per day 7:40am-11:29pm, Sa 14 per day 10:10am-8:40pm, Su 15 per day 10:10am-11:29pm); Madrid ($ €36-88 ⏰ 2¼-2¾hr.; M-Th 11 per day 7:35am-9:35pm, F 13 per day 7:35am-9:35pm, Sa 9 per day 7:39am-8:35pm, Su 11 per day 9:35am-9:35pm); Sevilla ($ €23-44 ⏰ 2-2½hr.; M-Th 11 per day 6:50am-8:05pm, F 12 per day 6:50am-8:05pm, Sa 9 per day 7:40am-8:05pm, Su 10 per day 7:40am-8:05pm); Valencia ($ €61-107 ⏰ 4-8¾hr.; M-F 3 per day 8:15am-4:10pm, Sa 2 per day 8:15am and 11:58am, Su 2 per day at 11:58am and 4:10pm).

To get to the *centro histórico* and its many accommodations from the train station, exit the train station onto C. Héroes de Sostoa (on the other side of the station from the bus station), turn right, take the 1st left onto C. Góngora, and take the 1st right onto C. Ayala; from the bus stop, take bus #1, 3, 9, or 10 to Alameda Principal.

BY PLANE

The **Aeropuerto de Málaga-Costa del Sol,** located 5mi. outside the city, is the second-biggest airport in Andalucía. (AGP; Av. Comandante García Morato ☎90 240 47 04 www.aeropuertodemalaga-costadelsol.com.) It receives domestic and international flights from across Europe from a variety of airlines, including budget carriers **easyJet** (www.easyjet.com), **Ryanair** (www.ryanair.com), and **Vueling Airlines** (☎80 700 17 17 inside Spain, ☎93 151 81 58 outside Spain www.vueling.com.) There are several ways to get between the airport and the *centro histórico.* The cheapest option, bus #19, runs between the airport and the Pl. General Torrijos, at the end of Paseo del Parque farthest from Pl. Marina, in both directions ($ €1.20 ⏰ From airport to *centro* every hr. 8:03am-10pm; from *centro* to airport every hr. 7:35am-9:30pm). Bus A Express (bus #75), an express airport shuttle, cuts the journey to 15min. but is more expensive. ($ €2. ⏰ From airport to *centro* every 30min. 7am-midnight; from *centro* to airport every 30min. 6:25am-11:30pm.) RENFE Cercanías train C-1 runs between the airport and the Málaga Centro-Alameda station. ($ €1.60. ⏰ 12min.; from airport to *centro* every 20min. 5:42am-10:42pm; from the *centro* to airport every 20min. 6:20am-11:20pm.) A taxi from the airport to *centro* costs €25-30.

Getting Around

The *centro histórico*'s narrow streets are best navigated on **foot.** In fact, walking can get you pretty much anywhere you need to go in Málaga; even the trip from the bus and train stations to Pl. Merced is only a 20min. walk. Empresa Municipal de Transportes (☎90 252 72 00 www.emtmalaga.es) operates the city's bus lines, practically all of which stop along Alameda Principal. The most useful of these are bus #11 and 34, which run to the streets parallel to the Playa de la Malagueta and the Playa de Pedregalejo, and bus #36 (really more like van #36), which squeezes through the small streets of the old quarter; a limited number of late-night lines provide service throughout the night.

Bicycles are available for rent from **Málaga Bike Tours** (C. Trinidad Grund, 4 ☎60 697 85 13 www.malagabiketours.eu ⇞ Just off Pl. Marina; C. Trinidad Grund runs parallel to Alameda Principal. $ €5 per 4hr., €10 for 24hr., €26 for 3 days, €50 for 7 days ⏰ Open daily 10am-2pm and 4-8pm) and **Málaga Custom Bikes.** (C. Álamos, 42 ☎63 441 38 70 www.malagacustombikes.com ⇞ From Pl. Merced, with your back to the plaza, turn right onto C. Álamos. *i* Credit card information and photocopy of passport required as deposit. $ Standard bikes €5 per half day, €10 per day; tandem bikes €15/25. ⏰ Open daily 10am-2pm and 4-8pm.)

If you need a **taxi,** call **Unitaxi** (☎95 200 00 00 or ☎95 233 33 33 www.unitaxi.es) or **Taxi-Unión** (☎95 204 08 04 or ☎95 204 00 90 www.taxi-union.es).

cádiz ☎956

On paper, Cádiz shouldn't really care if you visit its turf or not. In fact, it should probably be sick of visitors—has been hosting them since 1104 BCE, when the Phoenicians established the trading outpost of Gadir, and in all those years, someone is bound to have clogged the toilet. Nevertheless, this candidate for oldest city in Europe retains a very medieval feeling in its *casco antiguo* and still welcomes visitors from around the world, especially during its world-famous Carnaval. The city is on a peninsula jutting into the Atlantic Ocean, which made it an important naval base during Roman times and during the Age of Exploration. What that means for you is endless beaches and ocean breezes. This relaxing city will welcome you with an Andalusian smile and a glass of *manzanilla.*

ORIENTATION

Cádiz is located on a peninsula, with the Atlantic Ocean to the west and north and the Bahía de Cádiz to the east. The city can be broadly divided into the *centro histórico*, at the northern tip of the peninsula, and the modern part of the city, to the south. The *centro histórico* is home to most budget accommodations, sights, restaurants, tapas bars, and nightlife; your only ventures into the modern city will probably be on your way to the beaches. Buses and trains arrive in the Pl. Sevilla, in the eastern part of the city next to the port. With the water on your right, walking along the Av. Puerto to the end of the peninsula will bring you to **Plaza de España,** while walking three blocks and then turning left will bring you to the **Plaza de San Juan de Dios;** continuing along C. Pelota will lead to **Plaza de la Catedral.** These are the three major plazas of the old city, though smaller plazas are scattered throughout. The *centro histórico* is divided up into several *barrios* that look similar but feel somewhat different, including the touristy Barrio del Pópulo, in between the Pl. Catedral and the Pl. San Juan de Dios; the slightly less busy Barrio de Santa María, at the southern end of the *centro histórico;* and the quiet, authentic Barrio de la Viña near the Playa de la Caleta.

ACCOMMODATIONS

The *casco antiguo* is filled with hostels and *pensiones* with reasonable rates for most of the year that climb steeply during summer (usually July-Sept) and even higher during Carnaval. Be sure to reserve ahead or you could easily find yourself walking from *completo* sign to *completo* sign.

👍 CASA CARACOL — HOSTEL $

C. Suárez de Salazar, 4 ☎95 626 11 66 www.hostel-casacaracol.com

The best hostel in Cádiz, the social Casa Caracol oozes the genuine quirkiness that other hostels try to imitate. Nick, the English owner and amateur carpenter, always seems to have a hammer in hand, sadly not to beat up the snorers but rather to make improvements to the hostel, like the wooden non-squeaking bunk beds he built himself and the recently-installed, blue-tiled rooftop shower (thankfully not the only shower option). Social space was previously limited to the small kitchen and the hammock-filled rooftop terrace but has recently been expanded to include a giant living room with a TV after the hostel annexed the building next door, the last brothel in the *casco antiguo*. If you're inspired to action of your own by the history of the place, it's best to ask for a private double or, if you're as cheap as you are horny, one of the dorms with wooden beds, which have tons of space between top and bottom bunk and don't squeak at all. If you really want to save money, the cheapest option is spending the night in a hammock on the roof, though it can get pretty cold at night, even during the summer.

➡ From Pl. Sevilla (with bus and train stations), with the water to your right, proceed along Av. Puerto and turn left into Pl. San Juan de Dios. Cross the plaza and take the 2nd left onto C. Sopranis, then take the 2nd left onto C. Suárez de Salazar. ***i*** *Breakfast included. Free Wi-Fi and computer with internet access. Kitchen available. Sheets included. Towels €1. Laundry €5. Lockers available. Luggage storage €2. Dinner €5.* [$] *July-Sept 15 4- to 6-bed dorms €20; doubles €45. Sept 16-June €16-17/40. Carnaval €26/52. Semana Santa €22/44. Outdoor hammocks €10-12.* 🕐 *Reception 10am-1am.*

CÁDIZ INN BACKPACKERS — HOSTEL $

C. de la Botica, 2 ☎95 626 23 09 www.cadizbackpackers.es

There's definitely something that draws an energetic down-to-party crowd to this popular hostel. Perhaps it's the social atmosphere or maybe the weekend pub crawls at 11:11pm—make a wish (includes 5 drinks, €10)—or maybe it's just the hookah (€7). The 6-bed dorms are spacious and unusually furnished with a small couch and table, although there's only one small fan insufficient for cooling a pretty big room. The 4-bed dorms aren't worth the extra €2, unless you're a female traveler looking for a female-only dorm, whether for personal comfort reasons or to have free reign to gossip about the hunks in the dorm down the hall.

➡ From Pl. Sevilla (with bus and train stations), with the water on your left, proceed along Av. Puerto and take the 2nd right onto C. Goleta, then turn right and take the 1st left onto C. Botica. ***i*** *Breakfast included. Free Wi-Fi and computers with internet. Female-only dorm available. Sheets €2. Towels €1. Kitchen available. Free luggage storage. Laundry €8.* [$] *July-Sept 6-bed dorms €20; 4-bed dorms €22; doubles €50. Oct-June €13/15/30-40. Call for prices during Carnaval.* 🕐 *Reception 8am-midnight.*

HOSPEDERÍA MARQUÉS — HOTEL $$

C. Marqués de Cádiz, 1, 1st fl. ☎95 628 58 54 www.hospederiamarques.es

This *pensión* is proof that you don't have to shell out gobs of money for comforts like high ceilings, fans, Wi-Fi, an ensuite sink, and a bathroom shared in some cases with just one other room. However, it's also a reminder of the obscene price tag of a private bathroom, which can tack on an extra €30 per night for an otherwise similar room. Most of the rooms are very spacious; many have red sheets, tasteful photographs of flowers, and handsome wooden closets. The walk down the hall to the shared bathroom takes you around the light-filled central atrium, so be sure to cover up well or risk being fodder for *pensión* gossip.

⚑ *From Pl. Sevilla (with bus and train stations), with the water to your right, proceed along Av. Puerto and turn left into Pl. San Juan de Dios. Cross the plaza and continue straight on C. Pelota, to the right of the Ayuntamiento, then take the 1st right onto C. Marqués de Cádiz.* ℹ *Free Wi-Fi. TV available. Free luggage storage.* Ⓢ *July-Sept and Carnaval singles €30; doubles €50, with bath €70; triples €60, with bath €90. Oct-June singles €25; doubles €35/45; triples €45/70. Discounts often available if reservation made by phone.* 🕐 *Reception 24hr.*

THE MELTING POT
HOSTEL $

C. de Rosario Cepeda, 14 ☎95 607 02 07 www.meltingpothostels.com

Though the social side of this hostel might not be quite as pronounced as at the other two hostels in town, you'll definitely see people grabbing a beer from the rooftop bar before all the common areas shut down at midnight, at which point about half the hostel hits the hay and the other hits the bars and clubs. Since the dorms have 10 beds, you'll probably have a snorer, but you might also be lucky enough to have someone with the balls to wake up the snorer and tell him to close his mouth. The ceilings are low by Cádiz's standards, so the rooms don't feel particularly spacious, although the ensuite bath is a welcome convenience.

⚑ *From Pl. Sevilla (with bus and train stations), with the water to your right, proceed along Av. Puerto and turn left into Pl. San Juan de Dios. Cross the plaza and continue straight on C. Pelota, to the right of the Ayuntamiento, which turns into C. Compañia; at the Pl. Flores, turn right onto C. Columela, then take the 1st left onto C. Sacramento, then the 4th right onto C. Rosario Cepeda.* ℹ *Breakfast included. Free Wi-Fi.* Ⓢ *10-bed mixed dorms €14-19.* 🕐 *Reception 8am-midnight.*

PENSIÓN INMA
HOTEL $$

C. Pelota, 14, 3rd fl. ☎95 627 79 00

While dealing with the humorless Inma herself can be a little intimidating even for Spanish-speakers, this *pensión* right around the corner from the Pl. San Juan de Dios and the Pl. Catedral has plenty of other things going for it. The beds are comfortable, the rooms are spacious and come with sinks, and the dark green ceilings seem literally twice as high as most American ceilings, though if you were planning on perfecting your bed jumping skills, it's best to check with Inma first (no points for guessing what she'll say).

⚑ *From Pl. Sevilla (with bus and train stations), with the water to your right, proceed along Av. Puerto and turn left into Pl. San Juan de Dios. Cross the plaza and continue straight on C. Pelota, to the right of the Ayuntamiento.* ℹ *Shared bath, sinks in room.* Ⓢ *July-Sept and Carnaval singles €35; doubles €55. Oct-Dec €25/30. Jan-June €28/30.* 🕐 *Reception 24hr.*

SIGHTS

All of Cádiz's sights are in the *casco antiguo* and are within easy walking distance of each other and of most budget accommodations. You don't need to pay admission fees or even step inside to see some breathtaking sights in Cádiz: an evening walk along one of the seaside *paseos* during one of the beautiful sunsets is a truly memorable experience.

MUSEO DE CÁDIZ
MUSEUM

Pl. de Mina, 11 ☎95 620 33 68 www.museosdeandalucia.es/cultura/museocadiz

When the purple-wearin', amphora-bearin', sea-farin' Phoenicians dropped anchor at Cádiz, little did they know that three millennia hence we would be gawking at their bronze statues and perfume bottles. The Phoenician artifacts are definitely the highlight of the archaeological part of the museum; the most impressive items are the giant male sarcophagus, whose discovery in 1887 led to the creation of the museum, and the equally large female sarcophagus next to it discovered in 1980, which seems practically brand new (for a sarcophagus). In addition to the Paleolithic, Phoenician, Roman, and Islamic

cádiz

artifacts in the archaeological museum on the bottom floor, upstairs there is a less impressive museum of fine arts.

From Pl. San Juan de Dios, walk down C. Pelota (to the right of the Ayuntamiento), which turns into C. Compañía; at Pl. Flores, turn right onto C. Columela, then take the 6th left onto C. Rosario, which turns into C. Tinte before leading to Pl. Mina. [i] *Free guided tours of permanent exhibition Tu noon, meet in reception 15min. before.* $ *€1.50, EU citizens free.* ⏰ *Open Tu 2:30-8:30pm, W-Sa 9am-8:30pm, Su 9:30am-2pm.*

TORRE TAVIRA VIEWS, MUSEUM

C. del Marqués del Real Tesoro, 10 ☎95 621 29 10 www.torretavira.com

In New York or Shanghai, a 150ft. tower would give you admirable views of the building across the street and little else, but in two- and three-story Cádiz, that modest height is enough to command spectacular panoramic views of the city and the surrounding waters. There's a helpful compass on the ledge, compassionately placed to save people from having to ask which of the two bodies of water is the Atlantic Ocean. In addition to the great views from the top, a visit to the Torre Tavira also includes a fun 15min. virtual guided tour of Cádiz with the help of a knowledgeable guide and a camera obscura, which uses mirrors to reflect live images of the city with spectacular resolution onto a screen in a dark room. This is a great place to come your first day in Cádiz, since it will get you oriented and will help you figure out which of the city's sights actually interest you, or whether you'd rather just join all those ant-sized humans on the never-ending beaches.

From Pl. San Juan de Dios, walk down C. Pelota (to the right of the Ayuntamiento), which turns into C. Compañía; at Pl. Flores, turn right onto C. Columela, then take the 1st left onto C. Sacramento, then the 3rd right onto C. Marqués del Real Tesoro. [i] *Calling ahead for reservations recommended, especially in summer.* $ *€5, students and seniors €4.* ⏰ *Open May-Sept daily 10am-8pm, Oct-Apr daily 10am-6pm. 15min. camera obscura sessions approx. every 30min. Last camera obscura starts 30min. before close.*

CATEDRAL DE CÁDIZ AND MUSEO CATEDRALICIO CHURCH, MUSEUM

Pl. de la Catedral ☎95 628 61 54 www.catedraldecadiz.com

Pl. de Fray Félix (museum) ☎95 628 66 20

Neoclassical architecture can't be beat when it comes to libraries and post offices, but it rarely makes for the most exciting of cathedrals. Compared with Spain's endless lineup of haunting Gothic and ornate Baroque cathedrals, the largely colorless Neoclassical interior of the Catedral de Cádiz comes off as a little vanilla, especially due to the conspicuous absence of stained glass. There's plenty of eye-catching stuff on a smaller scale, though—the gilded pulpits will have you wondering if it's too late to join the priesthood, and the massive silver monstrance (receptacle for the host) is probably about the same size as the room in your last *pensión*. The low-ceilinged crypt downstairs, dramatically lit with candle-style light bulbs, has the tombs of former bishops and famous *gaditanos*, as well as a statue of Jesus that looks from a distance like Augustus Caesar on a diet. The separate but nearby museum has mostly mediocre paintings but also a large collection of bronze religious medals that will leave you both wondering who won the gold and salivating, since the largest medal is reminiscent of a giant M&M-filled cookie.

From Pl. San Juan de Dios, proceed along C. Pelota (to the right of the Ayuntamiento), which leads to Pl. Catedral. To get to the museum, upon exiting the cathedral, turn right and go up the stairs, then turn left onto C. Piratas, which leads to Pl. Fray Félix; cross the plaza diagonally. [i] *Free pamphlet in Spanish and English.* $ *Combined entry €5, students and seniors €3. Cathedral entry free Su 11:30am-12:30pm, but does not include museum admission.* ⏰ *Cathedral and museum open M-Sa 10am-6:30pm, Su 1:30-6:30pm.*

ORATORIO DE LA SANTA CUEVA CHURCH

C. del Rosario, 10 ☎95 622 22 62

At the Oratorio de la Santa Cueva, you get two beautiful chapels for the price of one, with some lovely Goya paintings thrown in for hard bargainers. The Capilla Baja, downstairs, is unusually barren and solemn, and every Good Friday holds a service reflecting on the Seven Last Words of Christ, accompanied by the work of the same title by Haydn commissioned by this church. For an unusual perspective on the sculpture of the Passion, head one flight up to an intermediate level with a window overlooking the altar of the Capilla Baja, as well as vestments, candlesticks, and reproductions of portraits of Church bigwigs. The highlight of the church is the Capilla Alta, with its marble reliefs and its three Goya paintings of scenes from the Bible. Ironically, if you go on Sunday, you could easily have the place to yourself.

🚏 From Pl. San Juan de Dios, walk down C. Pelota (to the right of the Ayuntamiento), which turns into C. Compañía; at the Pl. Flores, turn right onto C. Columela, then take the 6th left onto C. Rosario. $ €3, students and seniors €1.50. ⏰ Open June 18-Sept 17 M 10:30am-1pm and 5-8pm, Tu-F 10am-1pm and 5-8pm, Sa-Su 10am-1pm; Sept 18-June 17 Tu-F 10am-1pm and 5-8pm, Sa-Su 10am-1pm.

IGLESIA DE SANTA CRUZ CHURCH

Pl. de Fray Félix ☎95 628 77 04

There's no question that size matters, at least when it comes to cathedrals. The modest size of this small but pretty church, Cádiz's former cathedral, makes it clear why the insecure city felt the need to open the big boy next door in 1838. Though the rounded arches might remind those who have visited Córdoba of the Mezquita, the building lacks significant direct Islamic influence; these arches are characteristic of the 16th- and 17th-century Mannerist style of the rest of the building.

🚏 From Pl. Catedral, facing the cathedral, walk up the flight of stairs to the left and turn left onto C. Piratas, which leads to the Pl. Fray Félix; cross the plaza diagonally. $ Free. ⏰ Open M 5:30-7:45pm, Tu-Sa 10am-1pm and 5:30-7:45pm, Su 10am-noon and 6:15-7:30pm.

BEACHES

✓ PLAYA DE LA VICTORIA

Paseo Marítimo

The most popular beach in Cádiz, the endless Playa de la Victoria somehow manages to get crowded on a hot summer day despite being a long walk from the old town. Wider than the Playa de la Caleta and with slightly nicer sand, this 2mi.-long beach is the best beach to get away from it all, whether that means relaxing under a beach umbrella (€5) with a beer from one of the walking vendors or playing a sweaty pickup game of beach volleyball. On Saturday nights in July and August, once the brilliant colors of the sunset have faded to black and the umbrellas are folded up for the night, the city screens newly out-of-theaters movies for free on the beach.

🚏 Bus #1 from Pl. España to San Felipe or any subsequent stop, then turn right and walk down any side street to the beach. i Toilets and showers available. Beach umbrellas €5. $ Free. ⏰ Lifeguard on duty Apr-May M-F noon-5pm, Sa-Su noon-6pm; June 1-June 15 noon-7pm; June 16-June 30 11am-7pm; July-Aug 11am-8pm; Sept 1-Sept 15 11am-7pm; Sept 16-Sept 30 noon-7pm. Movies July daily 10:30pm, Aug daily 10pm.

PLAYA DE LA CALETA

Av. de Duque de Nájera

The small but popular Playa de la Caleta, the only beach in the *centro histórico*, doubled as Havana in the James Bond movie *Die Another Day* (don't blame it for the rest of the movie, though). You are (sadly) unlikely to see Halle Berry rising seductively from the water, but you'll see plenty of young tourists and locals of all ages swimming and relaxing on the beach. While working on your tan is free (though your dermatologist may disagree), beach umbrellas cost €5—though crafty beach-lovers can snag a bit of free shade under the white building in the center of the beach.

➔ From Pl. San Juan de Dios, follow C. Obispo Félix Soto (to the left of the Ayuntamiento) to the end, then turn right onto Av. Campo Sur. Follow this to the end, then turn right onto Av. Duque de Nájera. ℹ Toilets and showers available. Beach umbrellas €5. $ Free. ⏰ Lifeguard on duty Apr-May M-F noon-5pm, Sa-Su noon-6pm; June 1-June 15 noon-7pm; June 16-June 30 11am-7pm; Jul-Aug 11am-8pm; Sept 1-Sept 15 11am-7pm; Sept 16-Sept 30 noon-7pm.

FOOD

It should come as no surprise that this peninsula is a fish town; fresh fish and seafood feature prominently on most menus in Cádiz. A popular local drink is sherry, from the dry *fino* to the sweet *Pedro Ximenez* to the *manzanilla*—the Spaniards know how to do booze. Tapas are so popular here that it can a bit trickier to find *menús del día* than in many other Spanish cities, especially on the weekends. Restaurants in Cádiz are considerably less concentrated than in many other Spanish cities, although you'll find plenty of restaurants along C. Compañía and on side streets off of C. Columela; the restaurants in the Pl. San Juan de Dios and the Pl. Catedral are mostly tourist-oriented.

👍 BURGER LA HUELLA FAST FOOD $

C. Plocia, 11 ☎95 626 41 17

A favorite among locals looking for a cheap bite, Burger La Huella's filling salads, sandwiches, burgers, and chicken (in both nugget and finger form) will leave your stomach smiling and your wallet jumping for joy. The burgers, flipped on the spotless grill behind the bar, are rather thin by American standards, but the *hamburguesa completa* (€3.70) packs in enough tomato, onion, ham, cheese, and fried egg that you'll barely notice. A standard glass of beer or *tinto de verano* is pretty cheap, but go for the better deal, the considerably larger *jarra*—don't worry, we won't tell.

➔ From Pl. San Juan de Dios, with your back to the Ayuntamiento, proceed straight ahead and take the 1st right onto C. Plocia; it's the 1st building on the right. $ Sandwiches €1.80-4. Burgers €2.20-3.70. Beer €1.50-2.80. Tinto de verano €1.80-3. ⏰ Open daily 1-4:30pm and 8pm-12:30am.

CASA TINO SEAFOOD $$

C. de la Rosa, 25 ☎85 607 01 25

Despite being a 5min. walk from the water, which in Cádiz is basically equivalent to being landlocked, Casa Tino serves fresh, reasonably-priced seafood dishes that you'll love whether you like your seafood fried, grilled, or swimming in a sticky sea of rice in *paella* for two. The black-and-white photographs from the restaurant's opening in 1948 add a touch of class which is immediately counteracted by a horrible black plastic mat draped over the table in lieu of a tablecloth. The menu is available in English but has at least one particularly cringe-worthy translation: though translated as "heartburn," the *acedías* (sole, €10) won't give sensitive tummies acid reflux—that'll be the venison stew in a *manzanilla* sauce (€10).

➔ From Pl. Catedral, facing the cathedral, walk down C. Arquitecto Acero (to the right of the cathedral), then immediately turn right onto C. San Juan; at the fork, take a slight right onto C. Desamparados, which turns into C. María de Arteaga and then C. Rosa. ℹ ½ portions available for ½ price plus €1. $ Menú del día (served M-F noon-5pm) €9.90. Appetizers €3-9. Entrees €6-15. Tapas €2. ⏰ Open Tu-Th noon-5pm and 8pm-midnight, F-Sa noon-5pm and 8pm-1am, Su noon-5pm 8pm-midnight.

BALANDRO SPANISH $$$

Alameda de Apodaca, 22 ☎95 622 09 92 www.restaurantebalandro.com

This restaurant's dishes taste as fancy as their lengthy descriptions sound, yet aren't quite out of reach for a budget traveler looking to splurge on an upscale meal. Even the cheapest of the long list of hot and cold appetizers creatively combine foods you don't normally see together; the *jamon ibérico*, foie gras, and jam (€5) will be one of the most deliciously odd combinations that ever tops your tapas. Since the restaurant is just steps from the water, it's no surprise that the many fish dishes on the menu are varied, fresh, and not too expensive, though the pasta dishes are equally delicious and even cheaper options. As long as you're planning to spend the few extra euro to come here, call ahead for a reservation and ask for a table on the ground floor—its interior is very design-conscious (though we're not sure about the barcode-like columns) and the views of the Bahía de Cádiz are spectacular, especially during the jaw-dropping sunsets.

From Pl. Mina, with the museum on your right, proceed straight ahead on C. General Menacho and turn right onto Alameda de Apodaca. $ Appetizers €3.50-15. Entrees €9.50-20. Desserts €4.50. ⏰ Restaurant open daily 1-4pm and 8-11:15pm. Bar open daily 1-4:30pm and 8-11:45pm.

CAFETERÍA LAS CORTES DE CÁDIZ CAFE $

C. San Francisco, 9 ☎95 622 04 89 www.hotellascortes.com

The salads that begin €9 *menús* are usually lettuce-and-tomato-only affairs, but here you'll see more complex dressings and warm goat cheese as well. Affiliated with a three-star hotel, this cafeteria serves two-and-a-half star food at one-and-a-half-star prices, all served by waiters dolled up in bowties—an unusual sight for budget travelers. The airy interior is nice, but the seats outside under the awning are an even nicer place to watch the world (mostly tourists and elderly Spanish ladies, actually) go by.

From Pl. Catedral, with your back to the cathedral, turn left onto C. Compañía and turn right onto C. Columela at the Pl. Flores, then take the 7th left onto C. San Francisco. $ Menú del día €9. Tapas €2.50-3. Raciones €5.50.8. Sandwiches and burgers €2.50-4.50. ⏰ Open daily 9am-11pm.

NIGHTLIFE

Home to lots of students (thanks to the University of Cádiz) and lots of tourists (thanks to the beaches), Cádiz is the kind of town where there's always something to do after the sun goes down. The area around C. Beato Diego de Cádiz has the most centrally located nightlife, but for the massive clubs open until dawn, make the short walk out to the Punta de San Felipe.

CAFÉ NAHU BAR, CLUB

C. Beato Diego de Cádiz, 8 ☎85 607 00 70 www.nahucadiz.es

If you're looking for an authentic, local-filled bar, you will certainly not find it here. But if you're looking for a fun, student-oriented bar that gets a crowd almost every day of the week, this African-themed bar will be your go-to nightlife spot in Cádiz. Everyone is between 18 and 25, and almost everyone is either an international student or a Spanish student who wants to hang out with international students, perhaps to giggle at their vastly clumsier dance moves. The bar happily caters to all these young people with lots of fun events, like weekly belly dance classes, salsa classes, themed parties, and lots of cheap drinks, including a €1 beer night on Wednesdays and free cocktails for ladies on Fridays. This bar is busiest during the school year, when the most students are in town, though tourists and students studying abroad keep it lively during the summer as well.

From Pl. San Juan de Dios, on the side opposite the Ayuntamiento and with your back to it, turn left onto C. Nueva, which turns into C. San Francisco; take the 11th right onto C. Beato Diego de Cádiz. i M free belly dance classes, Tu free salsa classes and €1 shots, W €1 beers, Th international student party, F free cocktails for ladies, Sa live music, Su reggae night and €2.50 cocktails. $ Beer €1.50. Cocktails €3.50-5. Frequent drink specials. ⏰ Open May-Sept 15 M-Th 9:30pm-3am, F-Sa 9:30pm-4am, Su 9:30pm-3am; Sept 16-Apr M-Th 5pm-3am, F-Sa 5pm-4am, Su 5pm-3am.

C. de Manuel Rances, 1 ☎69 715 10 05

Café Nahu's main competition for the student crowd, M-2 isn't quite as popular, though it does manage to draw a bit of a more varied crowd. There are plenty of ways to enjoy your night out here, whether it's ordering the "pablito," with Bailey's, amaretto, chocolate, and whipped cream, over and over again; playing a friendly (or brutally competitive) game of foosball; or taking everyone back to the '90s, courtesy of your spot-on *NSYNC-era Justin Timberlake impersonation on Tu karaoke night. You can sit with friends in the cushioned seating area, but not on Wednesdays—it folds out into a stage for rock, reggae, and flamenco concerts.

⚑ *From Pl. San Juan de Dios, on the side opposite the Ayuntamiento and with your back to it, turn left onto C. Nueva, which turns into C. San Francisco; take the 11th right onto C. Beato Diego de Cádiz.* ⓘ *Tu karaoke, W live music, Th international student party, Su movies.* Ⓢ *Beer €1.50. Cocktails €4. Shots €1.50.* ⓩ *Open M-Th 10pm-3am, F-Sa 10pm-4am, Su 8pm-1am.*

MEDUSSA

BAR

C. Beato Diego de Cádiz, 10

You've got to give it to Medussa—how many places can be so thoroughly unpretentious while still sporting artsy photographs of Paris as decor? This solitary holdout of rock in a neighborhood filled with commercial pop draws a long-haired clientele thanks to its long-haired rock-heavy playlist. It's less hectic, less crowded, and less touristy than the sleeker establishments nearby.

⚑ *From Pl. San Juan de Dios, on the side opposite the Ayuntamiento and with your back to it, turn left onto C. Nueva, which turns into C. San Francisco; take the 11th right onto C. Beato Diego de Cádiz; the entrance is on C. Manuel Rances, the 1st left.* Ⓢ *Beer €2. Mixed drinks €4-6.* ⓩ *Open M-Sa 10pm-4am.*

IMAGINA JARDÍN BAR

CLUB

Punta de San Felipe

One of the hottest clubs on the *discoteca*-filled Punta de San Felipe, Imagina is a good-looking club for good-looking people. The outdoor bar has bar-like, lounge-like, and club-like areas interspersed with plants under big white tents. A young but mature crowd in their 20s and early 30s fills up the outdoor dance floor by 3:30am, and earlier on the frequent nights with special concerts. Most of the crowd comes fairly well dressed, but you usually don't have to dress to the nines to get in. Imagina isn't the cheapest place to dance in Cádiz, but it's the Punta de San Felipe at its finest.

⚑ *From Pl. España, proceed toward the water on C. Fernando "El Católico" and continue straight onto C. Nuevo Mundo, which leads to the Punta de San Felipe.* Ⓢ *Cover €8 (includes 1 drink), though there are sometimes coverless nights. Beer €3. Mixed drinks Th €5-7, F-Sa €6-8.* ⓩ *Open Th midnight-6am, F-Sa midnight-7am.*

ARTS AND CULTURE

CARNAVAL

You know this carnival is a big deal if the Church forgives those who can't attend Mass due to the festivities. One of the biggest and most famous carnivals in Spain, the Carnaval de Cádiz is a boozy two-week barrage of costumes, jokes, and songs. Apart from its sheer scale, what really makes this Carnival stand out from the rest is the acidic wit of the *chirigotas*, groups that unsparingly sing satirical songs about prominent figures and current events. Walking through the streets of the *centro histórico*, especially around Pl. Flores, you'll also encounter the *coros*, groups of fancily dressed singers with guitars who sing a comical repertoire, the *cuartetos*, groups accompanied by nothing more than a kazoo, and the *comparsas*, who sing about tragedy and are, frankly, kind of downers. A giant competition between all the performers takes place at the Gran Teatro Falla, with the winners announced the first Saturday of Carnival.

ⓩ *Begins 43 days before Easter Sunday.*

ESSENTIALS

Practicalities

- **TOURIST OFFICE:** The municipal tourist office's main branch is on the end of the Paseo de Canalejas closest to the **Pl. San Juan de Dios** (☎95 624 10 01 ⛳ From Pl. Sevilla with bus and train stations, with the water on your right, proceed along Av. Puerto; the Paseo de Canalejas is on the right. ⏰ Open June-Sept M-F 9am-7pm, Sa-Su and holidays 9am-5pm; Oct-May M-F 8:30am-6:30pm, Sa-Su and holidays 9am-5pm); there are **branches** in the modern part of the city (Av. José León de Carranza ☎95 628 56 01 ⛳ At intersection with Av. Coruña. ⏰ Open June-Sept M-F 9am-3pm and 5-7pm, Sa-Su and holidays 9am-5pm; Oct-May M-F 8:30am-3pm and 4:30-6pm, Sa-Su and holidays 9am-5pm), at the **Playa de la Victoria** (Paseo Marítimo ☎95 625 04 26 ⛳ Near the center of the beach, in the Módulo Central. ⏰ Open daily May 15-May 31 noon-6pm, June 1-June 15 noon-8pm, June 16-Sept 15 11am-8pm, Sept 16-Sept 30 11am-7pm), and at the **Playa de la Caleta** (Av. Duque de Nájera ⛳ Near the center of the beach and the white building. ⏰ Open July-Aug 10am-8pm; Sept M 9am-7pm, Tu-W 9am-3pm and 5-7pm, Th-Su 9am-7pm; Oct-May M-Th 8:30am-3pm and 4:30-6pm, F 8:30am-6pm, Sa-Su 9am-5pm; June M 9am-7pm, Tu-W 9am-3pm and 5-7pm, Th-Su 9am-7pm). The **regional tourist office** has information about the city and province of Cádiz as well as the major cities in the rest of Andalucía. (Av. Ramón de Carranza ☎95 620 31 91 www.andalucia.org ⛳ Just off the side of Pl. San Juan de Dios opposite the Ayuntamiento, on the left if facing the water. ⏰ Open M-F 9am-7:15pm, Sa-Su and holidays 10am-2:45pm.)
- **TOURS:** The municipal tourist office has a free "4 Walks Through Cádiz" pamphlet that outlines four themed walks: the Medieval District and Puerta de Tierra, Castles and Bastions, Shippers to the Indies, and Cádiz and the Constitution. The path for each walk is painted that walk's color on the street. A more structured tour is available through Amaría Alcanter, which offers a tour of the *centro histórico* and a visit to the Torre Tavira. (☎95 687 14 06 www.amaria-alcanter.es ⛳ Departs from Pl. San Juan de Dios, at the intersection with C. Nueva. $ €10, under 17 €5; 10% discount online ⏰ 2½hr.; M, W, F, and Sa 11:30am).
- **CURRENCY EXCHANGE: Banco Santander** changes major foreign currencies (C. Columela, 13 ☎95 622 55 09 www.bancosantander.es ⏰ Open M-F 8:30am-2:30pm).
- **LUGGAGE STORAGE: Urban Bike** stores luggage in its store in the *centro histórico* (C. Marqués de Valdeiñigo, 4 ☎85 617 01 64 www.urbanbikecadiz.es $ €5 per day. ⏰ Open June-Sept M-F 10:30am-2pm and 6-9pm, Sa 10:30am-1:30pm; Oct-May M-F 10am-1:30pm and 5:30-8:30pm, Sa 10am-1:30pm). There is no luggage storage at the bus or train station.
- **INTERNET ACCESS:** Free Wi-Fi and computers with internet access are available at the **Biblioteca Pública Provincial de Cádiz** (Av. Ramón de Carranza, 16 ☎95 620 33 24 ⛳ From the Pl. España, on the side opposite the Pl. Hispanidad and with the monument on your left, proceed straight along Av. Ramón de Carranza. ⏰ June 16-Sept 15 M-F 9am-2pm, Sept 16-June 15 M-F 9am-9pm, Sa 9am-2pm.)
- **POST OFFICE:** The **main post office** is in the Pl. Topete, colloquially known in Cádiz (and on your tourist map) as Pl. Flores (Pl. Topete ☎95 621 05 11 www.correos.es ⛳ From the Pl. San Juan de Dios, walk down C. Pelota (to the right of the Ayuntamiento), which turns into C. Compañía and leads to the Pl. Topete. ⏰ Open July-Aug M-F 8:30am-2:30pm, Sa 9:30am-1pm; Sept-June M-F 8:30am-8:30pm, Sa 9:30am-2pm). The branch at El Corte Inglés has longer hours but provides fewer services (Av. Cortes de Cádiz, 1 ☎95 625 34 98 www.correos.es ⛳ From Pl. Sevilla, with the water on your left, turn left onto Av. Astilleros, then turn left at the fork onto Av. Cortes de Cádiz. ⏰ Open M-Sa 10am-10pm.)
- **POSTAL CODE:** 11001 (Pl. Topete), 11012 (El Corte Inglés).

Emergency

- **EMERGENCY:** ☎112

- **POLICE: Local Police.** (Pl. San Juan de Puerto Rico ☎092 or ☎95 624 11 00 ⚓ From the *centro histórico*, proceed along Av. Andalucía and turn left at the Estadio Ramón de Carranza.) **National Police.** (Av. Andalucía, 28 ☎091 or ☎95 629 75 00 www.policia.es ⚓ From the Pl. Constitución, with your back to the Puerta de Tierra, proceed straight 3 blocks along Av. Andalucía.)

- **HOSPITAL: Hospital Universitario Puerta del Mar.** (Av. Ana de Viya, 21 ☎95 600 21 00 www.hupm.com ⚓ From the *centro histórico*, proceed along Av. Andalucía, which will turn into Av. Ana de Viya).

- **PHARMACY:** Farmacia Herbos (C. Columela, 2 ☎95 621 12 48 ⚓ From the Pl. San Juan de Dios, walk down C. Pelota to the right of the Ayuntamiento, which turns into C. Compañía; at Pl. Flores, turn right onto C. Columela. ☑ Open M-Sa 9am-10pm.)

Getting There

BY BUS

The cheapest way to get to Cádiz is by bus. Most buses to Cádiz are operated by **Transportes Generales Comes** (☎90 219 92 08 www.tgcomes.es) and arrive at the provisional bus station next to the train station (⚓ From Pl. San Juan de Dios, walk away from the Ayuntamiento and turn right onto Av. Puerto), including buses from: Granada (Ⓢ €33 ☑ 5-5½hr.; 4 per day 10am-3am); La Línea de la Concepción, the Spanish city across the border from Gibraltar (Ⓢ €13.09 ☑ 2½-2¾hr., 2 per day at 7am and 8pm); Málaga (*i* Service offered in association with Portillo. Ⓢ €25 ☑ 4hr., 4 per day 7:30am-8pm); and Sevilla (Ⓢ €12.20 ☑ 1¾hr., M-Sa 9 per day 7am-10pm, Su 10 per day 7am-10pm). **Secorbús**, a subsidiary of Socibus (☎90 222 92 92 www.socibus.es) provides service from Córdoba (Ⓢ €9.40 ☑ 3¼-3¾hr., 3 per day 8:20am-6:50pm) and Madrid (Ⓢ €26 ☑ 8hr., 6 per day 9am-11:59pm), though these buses leave from a different location. (Av. José León de Carranza, 20 ⚓ Proceed along Av. Andalucía, which runs parallel to Playa de la Victoria and turns into Av. Ana de Viya, Av. Cayetano del Toro, and Av. José León de Carranza.)

BY TRAIN

Trains to Cádiz arrive at the Estación de Cádiz (Pl. Sevilla ☎90 243 23 43 ⚓ From Pl. San Juan de Dios, walk away from the Ayuntamiento and turn right onto Av. Puerto, which leads to Pl. Sevilla. ☑ Open 5:20am-11:45pm). **RENFE** (☎90 232 03 20 www.renfe.es) runs trains from: Barcelona (Ⓢ €144 ☑ 7¾hr., daily 3:50pm); Córdoba (Ⓢ €28-41 ☑ 2½-3½hr.; M-F 18 per day 8:53am-8:52pm, Sa 13 per day 8:53am-8:30pm, Su 14 per day 8:53am-8:52pm); Jerez de la Frontera (Ⓢ €5.60-14.50 ☑ 40min.; M-F 16 per day 7:42am-10:49pm, Sa 13 per day 8:46am-10:49pm, Su 12 per day 9:56am-10:49pm); Madrid (Ⓢ €73-89 ☑ 4½hr.; M-F 11 per day 7am-7pm, Sa 7 per day 8:30am-6:35pm, Su 8 per day 8:30am-7pm); Sevilla (Ⓢ €15-36 ☑ 1¾hr., 16 per day 6:35am-9:45pm); Valencia (Ⓢ €108 ☑ 6¼hr., M-F 8:15am).

BY PLANE

The nearest airport is the **Aeropuerto de Jerez,** located 5mi. outside of Jerez de la Frontera and 30mi. from Cádiz. (☎91 321 10 00 www.aena.es) Flights arrive from across Spain and across Europe, although many of the routes only operate during the summer. To get from the airport to Cádiz, you can either take the bus (Ⓢ €3.40 ☑ 1¼hr.; M-F 9:30am, Sa-Su and holidays 2 per day at 12:30pm and 4:30pm) or the train (Ⓢ €3.80-5 ☑ 45min.-1hr.; M-F 4 per day 7:20am-7:20pm, Sa-Su and holidays 4 per day 8:20am-7:20pm). To get from Cádiz to the airport, you can also take the bus (Ⓢ €3.40 ☑ 1¼hr.; M-F 2 per day at 8am and 3pm, Sa-Su and holidays 11am and 3pm) or the train (Ⓢ €3.80-5 ☑ 45min.-1hr.; M-F 4 per day 6:10am-6:10pm, Sa-Su and holidays 4 per day 7:10am-6:10pm).

andalucía

Getting Around

The only way to get around most of the *centro histórico* is to walk. On the few traffic-friendly streets, you can **bike** as well; bikes are available for rental at **Urban Bike.** (C. Marqués de Valdeiñigo, 4 ☎85 617 01 64 www.urbanbikecadiz.es ⇞ From Pl. San Juan de Dios, walk down C. Pelota (to the right of the Ayuntamiento), which turns into C. Compañía, turn left onto C. Obispo Urquinaona, then take the 6th left onto C. Rosario and the 1st right onto C. Marqués de Valdeiñigo. *i* Must be 18 and over, show ID, and leave €50 deposit. $ €8 per 3hr., €12 for 1 day between 10am-8:30pm, €14 per 24hr., €24 per weekend. ⏰ Open June-Sept M-F 10:30am-2pm and 6-9pm, Sa 10:30am-1:30pm; Oct-May M-F 10am-1:30pm and 5:30-8:30pm, Sa 10am-1:30pm.) The city **bus** system is largely used to get around the modern city, but can also be useful for getting between the *centro histórico* and the modern areas. Most buses stop in the Pl. España; the bus of most interest to tourists is probably bus #1, which runs from Pl. España past the bus and train stations and continues along Av. Andalucía, a short walk from the Playa de Santa María del Mar and the Playa de la Victoria. **Taxi** stands are located in Pl. San Juan de Dios, Pl. Palillero, Pl. Hispanidad, across from the Playa de la Caleta, and in front of the train station; alternatively, call **Radiotaxi Cádiz** (☎956 21 21 21).

gibraltar ☎350

Gibraltar is surely one of the strangest settlements on Earth, an odd little gift from the ancient hand of geology and the canon of the British Empire to the curiosity and wonder of future generations. Originally, this Little Peninsula that Could more or less followed the standard Andalusian script, dutifully shuttling between Phoenician, Carthaginian, Roman, Vandal, Moorish, and Catholic control. The ubiquitous Union Jacks and the pervasive oily smell of fish and chips, however, are testaments to the fact that Gibraltar's path was set in 1704, when Anglo-Dutch forces occupied the city during the War of the Spanish Succession. Following the war, while the rest of Andalucía remained under Spanish control, Spain ceded the Rock to Britain "in perpetuity," and even threw in the cute Barbary macaques to sweeten the deal. Ever since, Gibraltarians have developed a fierce loyalty to Britain, so much so that at times the city can feel like a bit of an over-the-top theme park with all its pubs, bobbies, and red phone booths. Nevertheless, "Gib" still has a distinctive Mediterranean culture—most Gibraltarians are of Mediterranean descent, and almost all are bilingual, often conversing among one another in Llanito, a combination of British English and Andalusian Spanish. Don't mistake this familiarity with Spanish for a desire to be part of Spain, though—a 2002 referendum asking voters if they wanted joint sovereignty between the UK and Spain received a 98-and-a-half-percent ass-whuppin' at the polls. It appears as if this strange outpost of Britishness at the southern end of Europe will continue to march to its own, monkey-filled drum.

papers, please

You will need your passport to enter Gibraltar! You probably won't have it stamped, or even closely inspected, but attempting to cross from Spain into the British territory of Gibraltar sans documentation will get you turned back by border guards long before the monkeys have an opportunity to drive you out.

ORIENTATION

Gibraltar is a small peninsula jutting into the Strait of Gibraltar, the narrow strip of water that separates the Atlantic Ocean from the Mediterranean Sea and Europe from Africa. The western half of the peninsula has the small city of Gibraltar, while the eastern half is taken up by the enormous Rock of Gibraltar. Whether you arrive over land from Spain or by air, you'll physically enter the main part of the city in a wonderfully weird and unforgettable way: **walking across a live airplane runway.** Once safely on the other side, proceed straight along the left side of Winston Churchill Ave. (cross at the pedestrian bridge past the traffic circle, if necessary), following the signs for the city center, to get to **Casemates Square,** Gibraltar's restaurant-filled main square. Branching off of Casemates Sq. is **Main Street,** home to most of Gibraltar's restaurants, banks, pharmacies, and stores, although Irish Town, which runs parallel to Main St., also has lots of restaurants and pubs, as do some of the perpendicular side streets. The old part of Gibraltar largely turns its back to the sea, but newer marinas, like Ocean Village, to the west of Casemates Sq., combine luxury residences, restaurants, and nightlife into seafront complexes. Following Main St. to the end leads to the Trafalgar Cemetery; going up the hill to the left and turning right puts you on Europa Rd., which twists and turns as it leads to Europa Point, the southern tip of Gibraltar and the closest point in Europe to Africa, just 14mi. away.

ACCOMMODATIONS

Everything in Gibraltar is expensive, but it's the accommodations that will really make your wallet cry little wallet tears. The only hostel and only budget hotel in Gibraltar are both far more expensive than what you'd pay for identical accommodations in most of Spain, though they remain the best options for travelers looking to remain close to all of the action without blowing half their remaining cash on an incredibly expensive (and not necessarily luxurious) hotel. Travelers on a tight budget should strongly consider staying across the border in the Spanish city of La Línea, where prices are a bit lower; pick up a *guía de alojamientos* from the La Línea tourist office. If you're looking for a hotel as wacky as Gibraltar as a whole, check out **Con Dios,** a permanently moored boat turned into a small hotel (Marina Bay ☎200 50755 www.condios.co.uk ⇄ After entering Gibraltar, turn right immediately after Victoria Stadium and turn right into the marina. *i* Breakfast £2.50-5.75. Free Wi-Fi. Sink and toilet ensuite; no showers, but free 24hr. showers located nearby. Beach towel rental £2.50. No children under 11. $ Rooms can be doubles or singles; £25-35 per person. ⏰ Reception 9am-8pm, call ahead if arriving outside of these hours.)

PENSIÓN LA ESTEPONERA HOTEL $

C. Carteya, 10, La Línea ☎95 617 66 68

By far the best deal on either side of the border, and probably one of the best of your trip, this *pensión* has simple but comfortable private rooms for nearly half what you'd pay for a sweaty bunk bed across the runway. The dirt-cheap prices conjure up images of grim converted prison cells and shifty organ harvesters, but all of the pleasant rooms have colorful bedspreads and standard comforts like TVs, sinks, and fans. Most guests share bathrooms with large bathtubs, but many rooms with sizeable private baths are also available. While the free Wi-Fi doesn't reach the rooms upstairs, you can use it in the large living room downstairs, if you're not watching TV on one of the plump couches or getting your pool shark on at the billiards table. Though it's a 10-15min. walk to the border, you'll save enough money every day for at least an order of fish and chips and a pint or two—it's worth it.

From the La Línea bus station, turn right onto Av. Europa, then walk across the park and proceed along C. Doctor Villar until the end, then turn left onto C. Isabel la Católica and take the 2nd right onto C. Carteya. ***i*** *Cash only. Common area with free Wi-Fi, couches, TV, microwave, refrigerator, and pool table.* [S] *Singles €13.50, with bath €22; doubles €24, with bath €31.* ⏰ *Reception 24hr.*

EMILE HOSTEL HOSTEL $$

Montagu Bastion, Line Wall Rd., Gibraltar ☎200 51106

This hostel's sunburned Gibraltarian owner looks nothing like a dashing mustachioed robber baron, but when it comes to hostels, he is Gibraltar's very own Mr. Monopoly. At first, when you hear that you're being asked to pay £18 for a bunk bed with a comically thin mattress in a dorm without air-conditioning or fans (breakfast not included), you'll probably decide to look elsewhere—especially if communal (though gender-separated) showers aren't really your thing. Then you'll come to terms with the fact that it's the only hostel in town and £12 cheaper than Gib's next cheapest option for a solo traveler, feel as frustrated and helpless as if you'd been told to pay a poor tax of $15, and succumb to a stay at this Baltic Ave. house at Boardwalk hotel prices.

Just up the hill from the southeast corner of Casemates Sq. After entering Gibraltar, proceed straight along the left side of Winston Churchill Ave. and follow it as it curves slightly to the left, then walk through the 2 sets of tunnels, which lead to Casemates Sq. Cross the square diagonally and walk up the hill; Emile Hostel is across the street. ***i*** *Free Wi-Fi. Cash only. Sheets included. Towels €1. Washers €5, dryers not available.* [S] *4-bed and 6-bed dorms £18; singles £25; doubles £40.* ⏰ *Reception 8:30am-11pm.*

HOSTAL CARLOS I HOTEL $$$

C. de los Carboneros, 6, La Línea ☎95 676 21 35 www.hostalcarlos.es

A 10min. walk from the border and a 25min. walk from Casemates Sq., this *hostal* provides what Gibraltar apparently can't: affordable private rooms with air-conditioning. The rooms are compact but have enormous closets for you to store all those duty-free cigarettes you *haven't* smuggled past the less-than-vigilant Spanish border officials. All rooms have Wi-Fi, private bath, and no need for that UK electrical adapter you totally forgot you would need.

From the La Línea bus station, turn left, then immediately turn left onto C. Focona, then left onto Av. 20 de Abril (with the shops), then proceed to the end, cross to the other side of the plaza, and take the 2nd left onto C. Carboneros. ***i*** *Free Wi-Fi. TV available. Private bath. A/C.* [S] *July-Sept 15 singles €35; doubles €45. Sept 16-June singles €28; doubles €36. Extra bed €12.* ⏰ *Reception 24hr.*

CANNON HOTEL HOTEL $$$

9 Cannon Ln., Gibraltar ☎200 51711 www.cannonhotel.gi

If you want comfortable hotel-style accommodations in Gibraltar, this is your best bet. The ceilings are high, the beds are large, and there's a sink in every room, but you'd still expect a good deal more luxury at these prices in Spain. Still, once you accept the inevitable Gibraltarian markup, you'll appreciate that it's right off of Main St., it includes a full English breakfast, and it's a full ATM withdrawal cheaper than most of the other hotels.

After entering Gibraltar, proceed straight along the left side of Winston Churchill Ave. and follow it as it curves slightly to the left, then walk through the two sets of tunnels, which lead to Casemates Sq. Cross the square and proceed straight along Main St., then turn left onto Cannon Ln. ***i*** *Full English breakfast included. Free Wi-Fi reaches most rooms. All rooms with sink, some with private bath. Fans.* [S] *Singles £30; doubles £42, with private bath £53; triples £52.50, with private bath £60.* ⏰ *Reception 8am-midnight.*

SIGHTS

The Rock of Gibraltar

The cheapest way to get to the top of the Rock is to walk up the Mediterranean Steps off of Europa Rd., but this walk is too strenuous for many (⏰ 1½-2½hr). The best option is the cable car which leaves from Red Sands Rd. (☎200 70052 ⇆ Proceed along Main St. until the end, then make a slight right onto Rosia Rd., then a slight left onto Red Sands Rd. ℹ Does not stop at middle station Apr-Sept. ⏰ 6min.; Mar 26-Oct every 15min. daily 9:30am-7:15pm, last return trip 7:45pm; Nov-Mar 25 every 15min. daily 9:30am-6:15pm, last return trip 6:45pm.) Tickets can be purchased for the cable car alone, but travelers interested in seeing the sights of the Rock beyond the lookout area and the monkeys should buy the combination ticket with the Nature Reserve, which includes entry to St. Michael's Cave, the Great Siege Tunnels, the City Under Siege exhibition, and the Moorish Castle. The best way to see the sights is to purchase a one-way cable car ticket to the top and then walk between the sights and back down into town, all of which takes about 3hr. (💲 Cable car alone round-trip £9.75, under 12 £5; cable car and Nature Reserve ticket £18, under 12 £12). A slightly more expensive and less independent alternative is to take a tour with a taxi, which generally requires a minimum of four people, although if you are traveling in a smaller group, the taxi driver will usually find other tourists to fill up the taxi. The standard four-stop tour includes the Great Siege Tunnels, views from the Upper Rock, St. Michael's Cave, and the Pillars of Hercules; the extended six-stop tour does not stop at the Pillars of Hercules but adds the Moorish Castle, the 100 Ton Gun, and Europa Point. To get a taxi, just walk toward the cable car station; you'll be accosted outside the station, if not before, by an eager taxi driver (☎200 70052 ℹ Available in English, Spanish, French, and German. 💲 4-stop tour £12; 6-stop tour £20. £10 Nature Reserve ticket not included. ⏰ 4-stop tour 1½hr., 6-stop tour 2¼hr.)

👍 ST. MICHAEL'S CAVE

The handiwork of millions of years of rainfall on the soluble limestone of the Rock, the massive St. Michael's Cave is the most impressive sight on the Rock. Walking through the forest of stalactites and stalagmites is an awesome experience that will make you understand why it was once thought to hold the gates to the underworld. A subtle sound-and-light show

enhances rather than cheapens the experience; the quiet cello sonatas are a better soundtrack than tourists' chatter, and the understated lights are better than the old lighting method, where soldiers sat on top of stalagmites with torches.

$ Included in Nature Reserve ticket. ⏰ Open Mar 26-Oct daily 9:30am-7:15pm; Nov-Mar 25 9:30am-6:15pm. Last entry 30min. before close.

GREAT SIEGE TUNNELS

Built during the Great Siege of 1779-1783, these tunnels were dug in order to advantageously place British cannons, though today you're more likely to see informative history signs than cannon-fire. Nevertheless, the patriotic songs will get you so pumped up that you'll want to defend the Rock yourself, as long as your cannon works better than the faulty motion sensor that triggers a recording of a soldier saying "Halt! Who goes there?" that gets very old very quickly.

$ Included in Nature Reserve ticket. ⏰ Open Mar 26-Oct daily 9:30am-7:15pm; Nov-Mar 25 9:30am-6:15pm. Last entry 30min. before close.

MOORISH CASTLE

The Moorish Castle, with its proudly waving Union Jack, is one of the most eye-catching sights on the Rock from town. Once you get up close and personal, though, it seems much smaller and not quite as impressive, though it is pretty old (built in 1333) and durable (a veteran of 10 sieges).

$ Included in Nature Reserve ticket. ⏰ Open Mar 26-Oct daily 9:30am-7:15pm; Nov-Mar 25 9:30am-6:15pm. Last entry 30min. before close.

The Town of Gibraltar

EUROPA POINT SCENIC VIEW

Southern tip of Gibraltar

Few places on Earth feel like the end of the familiar world quite like Europa Point, the southernmost tip of Gibraltar. Faintly in the distance across the freight ship-filled Strait of Gibraltar, you can see the coast of North Africa seductively beckoning you toward a new land. The fact that the three main buildings in the vicinity are a church, a mosque, and a lighthouse give the area a sort of frontier outpost feel, a last stop before venturing onward to new adventures. There are expansive, near-360-degree views, as well as a certain you-are-here feeling that's diluted by the bird's-eye perspective from the top of the Rock. Even if you don't like dramatic views, come for the breezes alone, whipping in refreshingly from sea, straits, and ocean.

🚌 Bus #2 from Main St. at Convent Pl. to the last stop. ℹ Binocular use £1 or €1. $ Free. ⏰ Europa Point open 24hr.

THE ALAMEDA: GIBRALTAR BOTANIC GARDENS BOTANICAL GARDENS

Red Sands Rd. ☎200 41235 www.gibraltargardens.gi

The iconic British red phone booths sprinkled among the flowers, bushes, and trees of these excellent botanical gardens are an odd but thoroughly Gibraltarian touch. The extensive collection of plants from around the world and the ample seating and shade would make these gardens stand out anywhere, but the picturesque views of the straits and the in-your-face views of the Rock add extra dramatic flair. Be careful while exiting: one wrong turn and you'll find yourself gingerly stepping through a maze of angry cacti that doesn't lead anywhere.

🚌 Proceed along Main St. until the end, then make a slight right onto Rosia Rd., then a slight left onto Red Sands Rd. ℹ Free guided tours one Sa a month at 10:30am. $ Botanic gardens free; wildlife park £2, under 12 £1.50. ⏰ Botanic gardens open daily 8am-sunset; wildlife park open daily 10am-4:45pm.

GIBRALTAR MUSEUM MUSEUM

18-20 Bomb House Ln. ☎200 74289 www.gibmuseum.gi

Gibraltar's long and wonderfully strange history saves this museum from being just another city museum. You'll still get the Stone Age-to-present treatment, though in the excellent 15min. introductory video you'll actually start a little further back, with cartoon dinosaurs, a geological history of the Rock, and a discussion of the Neanderthal remains found in Gibraltar, believed to be the last outpost of Neanderthals. The downstairs has familiar Phoenician, Greek, and Islamic artifacts; upstairs, things take a sharp turn for the British, including a hagiographic exhibit on Lord Nelson containing his shoe buckle and other quasi-relics.

➜ From Main St., take a slight right at the cathedral onto Bomb House Ln.; the entrance is through the courtyard on the right. $ £2, under 12 £1, under 5 free. ⏰ Open M-F 10am-6pm, Sa 10am-2pm. Last entry 30min. before close.

TRAFALGAR CEMETERY CEMETERY

Trafalgar Rd.

This small but beautiful cemetery at the south end of Main St. is dedicated to the memory of the sailors who were wounded in the Battle of Trafalgar and later died of their injuries. It's a touching place, filled with butterflies, trees, shade, and the poignantly fading gravestones of young men who died far from home.

➜ Proceed along Main St. until the end, then make a slight left under the stone gate; the cemetery is on the left. $ Free. ⏰ Open daily 8:30am-sunset.

FOOD

Say goodbye to *pimientos rellenos de bacalao* at the border—the only cod here is battered, fried, and served with chips (french fries). Most of Gibraltar's food is pointedly and perhaps exaggeratedly British, though there are also a few Indian and Moroccan restaurants hidden away on side streets. **Casemates Square** has many places to eat, including several fish and chip shops; tourist-oriented restaurants also line **Main Street** (especially the southern end) and **Irish Town.** For pricier fare, head out to the seaside Ocean Village or Queensway Quay complexes. Food prices generally aren't quite as exorbitant as hotel prices, but the cost of eating out in Gibraltar is certainly higher than in Spain, a difference exacerbated by Gibraltar's general lack of *menús del día.* Nevertheless, quintessentially British dining experiences need not lay siege to your budget—for a quick lunch on the go, stop off for a pre-packaged sandwich from **Gibraltar Confectionery.** (232 Main St. ⏰ Open M-F 8:30am-6pm, Sa 9:30am-1:30pm.) For an affordable taste of colonial era-luxury (and divine clotted cream), climb up to **The Rock Hotel's** Barbary Bar for afternoon tea, served on a beautiful shaded terrace with panoramic views of the straits. (3 Europa Rd. ☎200 73000 ➜ From the southern end of Main St., turn left at Trafalgar Cemetery and follow the hill as it curves to the right; after a short walk the hotel is up a steep driveway on the left. *i* Bar open to the public. No dress code, though beach attire may raise some eyebrows. $ Tea £1.70. Scones £2.25. ⏰ Bar open noon-midnight.) While there's no free food in Gibraltar (unless you're a Barbary macaque), shopping for groceries at Morrison's, a British supermarket chain, is probably about as close as you can get. (Westside Rd. ☎200 41114 www.morrisons.co.uk ➜ From Casemates Sq., exit through the arches to the right of the tourist office and proceed straight along Waterport Rd., then turn left at the 2nd traffic circle onto Europort Rd., then take the 2nd right onto Westside Rd. ⏰ Open M-Sa 8am-10pm, Su 8am-8pm.)

MUMTAZ INDIAN $

20 Cornwall's Ln. ☎200 44257

This Indian hole-in-the-wall is as much a take-out joint as a restaurant, so don't expect a fine dining experience—just expect large, steaming-hot plates of delicious Indian dishes at some of the best prices on the Rock. The wide variety of chicken, lamb, fish, and vegetarian dishes, including delicious old standbys like vegetable curry (£3.25) and chicken korma (£5), is a welcome relief for anyone who finds themselves pretending to like over-priced British cuisine during their stay in Gibraltar. Sweet and spicy dishes alike go down easy with a bottle of beer from the unusually extensive selection of international beers, unpacked cases of which are the main source of decoration in the small, functional interior.

From Casemates Sq., proceed along Main St., then turn left onto Bell Ln.; at the top of the hill, turn right and go down the hill on the right. ***i*** *Halal meat. Take out £1.50 (minimum order £15).* *[$] Appetizers £0.30-0.80. Naan £1.25-4.50. Vegetarian dishes £3.25-5. Chicken and lamb dishes £3.25-6. Fish dishes £4.50-10.* ⏰ *Open M-Th 11am-3pm and 6pm-midnight, F-Sa 11am-3pm and 6pm-2am, Su 11am-3pm and 6pm-midnight.*

ROY'S COD PLACE FISH AND CHIPS $$

Casemates Sq. ☎200 76662

Eating fish and chips in Gibraltar is sort of like taking a moonlit stroll in Paris after a rough break-up—it might not be good for your heart, but as long as you're there, you might as well do it anyway. This unassuming fish and chips shop in Casemates Sq. is one of the best and most authentic of Gibraltar's twenty gazillion places to eat this classically British dish. Fish and chips are the unquestioned highlight of the streamlined menu; your main choice will not be what dish to order but whether to order that dish with the traditional cod or the bit more flavorful haddock. No matter your choice of fish, douse it in salt and vinegar and wash it down with an ice-cold beer—though the only beer on tap is Spanish standard San Miguel, whose quality would make a beer-loving Brit blush, and not in the good way.

On the left side of Casemates Sq. if entering from Main St. ***i*** *Free Wi-Fi.* *[$] Fish and chips £6.50, £7.75, or £14. Other dishes £4.25-8. Beer £3.25-3.50.* ⏰ *Open M-Sa 10am-10pm.*

BISTRO MADELEINE FRENCH $$$

256 Main St. ☎200 65696

You'd be forgiven for not expecting much from a French bistro run by Brits on Main St. of a tourist town, but this intimate restaurant's tasty French and fusion dishes will make you forget that you're in a British Overseas Territory, even if you won't exactly think you're in Lyon either. Unusually for Gibraltar, Bistro Madeleine offers a *menú del día* (£12), and unusal for anywhere, it's served at both lunch and dinner, every day of the week. Before you can even start feeling sheepish about indulging in a fillet with bleu cheese sauce (£15) in fish-and-chips country, the owner will come out and welcome you in his wonderfully thick British accent. Get him talking and he may give you an inadvertent lesson in Llanito, the local dialect that combines British English and Andalusian Spanish, as he talks about how he gets all his veg from *fincas* (farms) whose owners he personally knows.

Just before Cathedral Sq. if coming from Casemates Sq. *[$] Menú del día (served all day) £12. Entrees £10-15.* ⏰ *Open M-Sa 10am-10pm, Su noon-10pm.*

THE CLIPPER PUB $$

78B Irish Town ☎200 79791 www.theclipper.gi

This nautical-themed pub is a tasty introduction to those traditional British dishes you've always heard about but never actually understood exactly what they were. The chicken and mushroom pie (£7) keeps all of regular pie's yumminess but swaps sweet for savory, and the jacket potatoes (baked potatoes, £4-5.45) come with toppings as normal as cheese, as wacky as tuna salad, and as bagelicious as smoked salmon and cream cheese. No matter when you come, you'll find a mix of vacationing families frantically eating and local old-timers calmly setting up shop at the bar with their newspaper; you'll also always have the chance to try the wonderfully filling English breakfast (£5.45), served all day.

From Casemates Sq., proceed along Main St., then take the 1st right onto Cooperage Ln., then take the 1st left onto Irish Town. **i** *Free Wi-Fi. ½ portions available for under 12 and seniors. Take-out available. Full menu on website.* $ *Breakfast platters £5.45-6. Appetizers £2-3.45. Sandwiches and toasties £2.70-4.70. Entrees £7.* ⏰ *Open M-Sa 9:30am-10pm, Su 10:30am-10pm.*

NIGHTLIFE

Since most college student-aged Gibraltarians head to the UK for university, nightlife in Gib tends to cater to a crowd either a shade younger or a great deal older, though plenty of young tourists supplement the ranks of the city's bars, pubs, and clubs. On "Wild Wednesdays" during the summer, many of the city's nightlife establishments compete for the business of Gibraltar's young people with an arms race of drink specials, guest DJs, and open bars. Nightlife in Gibraltar generally gets going an hour or two earlier than in Spain.

SAVANNAH BAR, CLUB, RESTAURANT

27 Leisure Island, Ocean Village ☎200 66666 www.savannah.gi

Seven's main competition for Gibraltar's limited clubbing population, this swanky cocktail bar turns into a house-pumping club on Wednesdays during the summer and on Fridays year-round. It has a lot more fancy lights (especially of the strobe variety) than Seven, and the crowd is either a little older or a little better at seeming older. It's also bigger, which means it's not quite as easy to fill. Don't miss their Wild Wednesday promotion, an open bar with unlimited beer, *tinto de verano*, house spirits with mixer, and shots for £10; or the nights approximately once a month with special DJs from Madrid or Ibiza.

From Casemates Sq., exit through the arches to the right of the tourist office, then turn right into the Ocean Village; Savannah is at the far end of the complex. **i** *Happy hour 5-8pm with 2-for-1 cocktails.* $ *Cover £5 with guest DJ, cover when open bar £10. Beer £3. Cocktails £4.50-5.50.* ⏰ *Restaurant and bar open daily noon-10:30pm. Club open W (summer) and F (year-round) midnight-5am.*

FRESH BAR

5 Waterport Rd.

A forgettable restaurant by day and a memorable bar by night, this is the first stop of the evening for young tourists and slightly younger Gibraltarians. You may feel a bit odd since the young Gibraltarians all know one another, but that means they're so happy to see new faces that you may find yourself on the receiving end of a free detox (vodka, peach schnapps, and grenadine, £2.20) or one of the other specialty shots. Everything's served up with a patient smile by Sandra, the bartender, middle-aged mother figure to all of Gib's boozing teens, and the only person more outraged than you about the drinking age in the United States.

From Casemates Sq., exit through the arches to the right of the tourist office; Fresh is on the left. **i** *Happy hour specials 9-11pm.* $ *Beer £1-2. Shots £1.50-3.* ⏰ *Open M-Th 9am-1am, F-Sa 9am-2am, Su 9am-1am.*

ALL'S WELL BAR

Unit 4, Casemates Sq. ☎200 72987 www.sologib.com/allswell.html

This pub in the heart of Casemates Sq. is a favorite with Gibraltar's surprisingly small middle-aged nightlife-seeking population. The music selection caters to them with lots of '80s music. If you don't think Bon Jovi nailed "You Give Love a Bad Name," show him how it's done on karaoke nights (M and W, 10pm). If you want the experience of drinking in class without any of the negative consequences, order a pint of one of the nine beers on draft and drink it while inspecting the captioned murals depicting the history of Gibraltar on the wall opposite the bar.

☏ *On the side of Casemates Sq. opposite Main St.* ℹ *Karaoke M and W 10pm.* Ⓢ *Beer £3.50. Mixed drinks £3.* ☺ *Open M 1pm-midnight, Tu-Th noon-1am, F 10am-3am, Sa 1-5pm and 10pm-3am, Su 1pm-midnight.*

SEVEN CLUB

Line Wall Rd.

If you're looking for Seven, just follow the trail of varyingly intoxicated 19-year-olds walking up the small hill at the south end of Casemates Sq. This club fills up early; there are lines on the street outside at the same time that Spaniards across the street in La Línea are just sitting down to dinner. A young crowd of restless Gibraltarians and fun-seeking tourists gets down to house music in this straightforward, unadorned club, though there's barely any room to get down or get much of anywhere since it's so packed, especially on the student-filled Wild Wednesdays during the summer.

☏ *Walk up the hill at the intersection of Main St. and Casemates Sq.* Ⓢ *No regular cover. Beer and mixed drinks £3.* ☺ *Open W midnight-late, F-Sa midnight-late.*

THE GREAT OUTDOORS

🏞 THE ROCK OF GIBRALTAR HIKE

Your first sight of the Rock of Gibraltar combines the awe of nature inspired by the Grand Canyon and the instant sense of place of the Eiffel Tower—not bad for a 1400ft. hunk of limestone. Though humans have done interesting things on the Rock over the years (read: war), nature is really the star of the show here, whether it's the mind-blowing St. Michael's Cave, the birds weekending on the Rock during their seasonal migrations between Europe and Africa, or the 250 adorable 🐒**Barbary macaques** that call the Upper Rock home. In order to protect the Rock's flora and fauna, the entire Upper Rock, approximately 40% of Gibraltar's territory, has been named a nature reserve. There are a few great ways to explore the Upper Rock Nature Reserve. The **Royal Anglian Way** (600m) is the shortest and easiest walk, and passes by a Barbary macaque feeding station; go in the early morning or late evening to see a (legal) feeding. (☏ Follow the normal path down the rock of St. Michael's Cave and take the 1st hard left, which leads to the starting point. ☺ 20-30min). The **Inglis Way** (1200m) is a bit trickier but passes by some of the most flora- and fauna-rich areas of the Rock; keep your eye out for the Barbary partridge, Moorish gecko, and yellow-bee orchid, which mimics female yellow-bees since it relies on male yellow-bees for pollination. (☏ Follow the normal path down the rock from St. Michael's Cave and turn right at the fork onto Queen's Rd.; the hike starts just after Charles V Wall. ☺ 1-1½-hr.) The hardest walk, up the **Mediterranean Steps** (1400m), is a grueling but rewarding hike not recommended for those afraid of heights or startled by the sudden takeoff of Barbary partridges; go early in the morning before it gets too hot or in the late afternoon, when there's a bit more shade. (☏ From the southern end of Main St., turn left at the Trafalgar Cemetery and follow the hill as it curves to the right to become Europa Rd., after a long walk, take a slight left onto Windmill Hill Rd., which leads to Jews' Gate, where the hike starts. ☺ 1½-2½hr). Download a guide to the Upper Rock Nature Reserve from the Gibraltar Ornithological and Natural History Society at www.gonhs.org/documents/UpperRockGuide.pdf.

CATALAN BAY BEACH

Gibraltar's second-largest beach is immensely popular with residents and tourists alike, and with good reason. The surroundings are impossibly scenic, with the pastel colored restaurants and fishermen's houses providing the only separation between the seashell-filled sand and the sheer cliff of the Rock. A bus stops right next to the beach, but the 20min. walk there is half the fun, since you get to see another side of the Rock, both literally (it's on the eastern side) and figuratively (you pass establishments like Maritime and Commercial Waste Collection headquarters).

➜ Bus #4 or #6 from Trafalgar Cemetery or Line Wall Rd. Or, after crossing the runway, take the 1st left onto Devil's Tower Rd. and follow it as it curves around the corner, then walk down the hill on the left which leads to the beach. ℹ Toilets and showers available. First aid available. $ Free. ⏰ Lifeguard on duty M-F 11am-7pm and Sa-Su 10:30am-7:30pm.

ESSENTIALS

Practicalities

- **TOURIST OFFICES:** Gibraltar is small enough that you're never likely to be far from one of the several offices of the **Gibraltar Tourist Board** (www.visitgibraltar.gi). If entering by land from Spain, the first office you'll encounter is just after you clear Gibraltarian passport control (☎200 50762 ⏰ Open M-F 9am-4:30pm); if entering by air, there's an office in the arrivals terminal (⏰ Hours coordinated with arriving flights.); if entering by sea, there's another office at the cruise terminal. (☎200 47671 ⏰ Hours coordinated with arriving cruises.) Once you get into town, you'll find the **main tourist office** in Casemates Sq. (☎200 45000 ➜ On the right of the square if entering from Winston Churchill Ave. ⏰ Open M-F 9am-5:30pm, Sa 10am-3pm, Su 10am-1pm) and a satellite branch at **Europa Point** (☎200 64809 ⏰ Open M-F 9am-4:30pm). If you're thinking of staying in La Línea, go to the regional tourist office for a map and a guide to accommodations (Av. Ejército ☎95 678 41 35 www.andalucia.org ➜ From the La Línea bus station, turn left, then immediately turn left onto C. Focona, then left onto Av. 20 de Abril (with the shops). Or, from Gibraltar, after crossing the border proceed straight along Av. 20 de Abril. it's just in front of the intersection with the first big street, on the right. ⏰ Open M-F 9am-7:30 pm, Sa-Su and holidays 9:30am-3pm.)
- **TOURS:** Most tours in Gibraltar focus exclusively on the Rock and not on the city. The most popular tour of the Rock is offered by the **Gibraltar Taxi Association** (see **Sights**); ask at the tourist office for a complete list of tour operators.
- **CURRENCY EXCHANGE AND ATMS:** Gibraltar mints its own currency, the Gibraltar pound, whose value is pegged at a 1:1 ratio to the British pound. Gibraltar pounds and British pounds are both universally accepted in Gibraltar; euro are accepted practically everywhere except the post office, though paying in pounds often saves you money. With so many currencies floating around, Gibraltar has almost as many places to change currency as it has fish and chip shops, especially along Main St. Bear in mind that you may get a better rate by withdrawing pounds from an ATM than by exchanging euro or US dollars. Gibraltar pound notes are completely useless anywhere outside of Gib, so unless you want them as a souvenir, make sure to change them back into British pounds before you leave (most shops will do this for you for free). If you want to avoid getting Gibraltar pounds in the first place, use the right-hand ATM at Barclays on Main St., which only dispenses British pounds. (84/90 Main St. ⏰ ATM 24hr.)
- **LUGGAGE STORAGE:** Luggage storage is currently only available at the departures terminal of the airport ($ £2-5, depending on size. ⏰ Open daily 8:15am-9:30pm or until the last flight departs), although there are plans to open a left-luggage office in the new arrivals terminal as well.
- **INTERNET ACCESS:** Free Wi-Fi and computers with free internet access (unenforced 1hr. limit for computers) are available in the library on the second floor of John Mackintosh Hall (308

Main St. ☎200 78000 ⇟ From Casemates Sq., proceed until just before the end of Main St.; it's inside the complex on the right, on the top floor. ⏰ Open M-F 9:30am-7:30pm); if the library is closed, the courtyard of John Mackintosh Hall also has free Wi-Fi and is often open a little later. (⏰ Open M-F 9:30am-10pm, though it might close earlier if there are no events.) Late at night and during the weekends, try to get Wi-Fi from a cafe or hotel, or be prepared to spend exorbitant amounts at Café Cyberworld (14-16 Ocean Heights Gallery, Queensway ☎200 51416 *i* Wi-Fi, computers with internet access, ethernet cables, and drinks. Cash only. $ £2.50 per 30min., £4.50 per hr. Printing £0.30 per page. Beer £2.80. ⏰ Open daily noon-midnight.)

- **POST OFFICE:** The main post office on Main St. has an attached shop that sells stamps, coins, and postcards. (104 Main St. www.gibraltar.gov.gi/postal-a-philatelic *i* Cash only; British or Gibraltar pounds only. $ Letters and postcards to the UK £0.42; EU and Morocco £0.44; elsewhere £0.51. ⏰ Post office open mid-June to mid-Sept M-F 9am-2:15pm, Sa 10am-1pm; mid-Sept to mid-June M-F 9am-4:30pm, Sa 10am-1pm. Stamp shop M-F 9:30am-3pm, Sa 10am-1pm.)

Emergency

- **GENERAL EMERGENCY NUMBER:** ☎112.
- **FIRE/AMBULANCE NUMBER:** ☎190.
- **POLICE:** The Royal Gibraltar Police's headquarters are on Rosia Rd., past the end of Main St. (☎199 or 112 (emergencies) or ☎200 72500 (general enquiries) ⇟ Proceed along Main St. until the end, then make a slight left under the stone gate, cross the street, walk up the hill, and then take a slight right onto Rosia Rd.)
- **HOSPITAL:** The recently constructed St. Bernard's Hospital is Gibraltar's only hospital (Europort Rd. ☎200 79700 www.gha.gi ⇟ From Casemates Sq., proceed along Main St., then take the 1st right onto Cooperage Ln., pass through the tunnels, and turn left onto the Queensway, then take the 1st right onto Europort Rd.)
- **PHARMACY:** Gibraltar is filled with pharmacies, especially along Main St. For information on pharmacies open outside of regular pharmacy hours, go to www.gha.gi and select "St. Bernard's Hospital" and "Pharmacy on Duty," or look at the sign in the window of any pharmacy.

Getting There

The most important thing to remember about entering Gibraltar by land is that you are leaving Spain and entering a territory of the United Kingdom. Do not forget your passport! You will be required to show it to Spanish and Gibraltarian authorities every time you cross the border, though often they will wave you through without examining it. You can't technically get to Gibraltar directly from Spain except on foot; the closest the Spanish transportation gets is La Línea de la Concepción, the Spanish city directly across the border.

BY BUS

A slew of different bus companies provide service to the La Línea bus station (Polígono San Felipe ☎95 617 00 93 ⇟ After crossing the border, proceed straight along Av. 20 de Abril and turn left onto C. Focona; the bus station is on the right. ⏰ Open daily 6am-10:30pm). It can be confusing, but there will be someone who can get you there from just about anywhere. If you're coming from outside Andalucía, you will likely to have to connect in a provincial capital. **Alsina,** a subsidiary of ALSA (☎90 242 22 42 www.alsa.es) runs buses to La Línea de la Concepción from Córdoba ($ €26 ⏰ 5¾hr.; daily 8:30am) and Granada ($ €23 ⏰ 5¼hr., daily 2pm). **Portillo** runs buses from Málaga ($ €15 ⏰ 3hr.; 4 per day 7am-4:30pm, Su 5 per day 7am-7:15pm). **Transportes Generales Comes** (☎90 219 92 08 www.tgcomes.es) runs buses from the rest of Cádiz province, including Cádiz ($ €13.09 ⏰ 2¾hr., 2 per day 10:15am and 4:30pm), and Sevilla ($ €23 ⏰ 4-4¼hr., 4 per day 9:30am-8pm). The **Consorcio de Transporte Metropolitano del Campo de Gibraltar** (☎90 245 05 50 www.ctmcg.com *i* Tickets can be purchased on the bus) operates shorter routes from Algeciras (*i* Line M-120 $ €2.25 ⏰ 30-60min.; M-F 35 per day 7am-10:30pm, including 4 direct buses at 7, 8:30am, 1:30, and 3pm; Sa 21 per day 7am-10:30pm; Su 20 per day 8am-10:30pm) and San Roque, the city with the nearest train station. (*i* Line M-230 $ €1.25 ⏰ 15min.; M-F 27 per day 7:30am-10:30pm, Sa-Su 15 per day 7:30am-10pm.) To get from the bus station to the border, upon exiting, turn left, then immediately turn left onto C. Focona, then take the first right onto Av. 20 de Abril, which leads to the border.

BY PLANE

Flights currently operate to Gibraltar (GIB) only from the United Kingdom. **EasyJet** (www.easyjet.com) is the largest carrier operating from the airport, with 11 flights per week from London Gatwick and three per week from Liverpool. **Monarch** (☎08719 40 50 40 from UK, ☎800 09 92 60 from Spain, ☎200 41169 from Gibraltar www.monarch.co.uk) flies from London Luton five times per week and Manchester twice per week. British Airways (☎0844 493 0787 from UK, ☎902 11 13 33 from Spain, ☎34 902 111 333 from Gibraltar www.ba.com) flies daily from London Heathrow. Check airline websites for prices, which can vary widely.

Getting Around

Gibraltar is a small town and it's easy to walk pretty much anywhere you need to go, although if you're staying in La Línea the 20-30min. back-and-forth between your hotel and Casemates Sq. can get old after a while. Despite Gibraltar's comparatively small size, **Gibraltar Bus Company** (☎200 47622 www.gibraltarbuscompany.gi) operates a municipal bus system of six lines; you are most likely to encounter bus #2, which goes to Europa Point, buses #4 and 6, which go to Catalan Bay, and bus #5, which stops in front of the airport ($ £1, under 18 £0.80. Unlimited day pass £1.50/1.20.) **Bicycles** can be rented from **Cycle Centre.** (Corral Rd. ☎200 76903 www.cyclecentre.gi ➜ From the airport, proceed along Winston Churchill Ave. and take a slight left at the 2nd traffic circle as if you were going to Casemates Sq., then take a slight right and follow the curve. *i* Includes bike, helmet, and lock. $ £15 for 1 day, £25 for 2 days, £8 after 2nd day. ⏰ Open M-F 10am-6pm.) The one place walking, buses, and bikes will not get you is the Upper Rock, which is normally reached by **cable car** or by **taxi.** If you need a taxi to the Rock, many are found next to the cable car station; if you need one in any other context, call the radio taxi service (☎200 70027).

BASQUE COUNTRY

Though the ETA terrorist organization has been quiet lately, the *País Vasco* is yet another region of Spain that considers itself an oppressed nation prevented from independence. You probably won't hear as much Basque as you will Spanish—at least in the major cities—but the local culture is evident in street signs, posters, and the written word everywhere, including the distinctive Basque typeface (check out those funky *a*'s). Even with all those Basque words (funny-looking as they are), the local cuisine nevertheless defies description. Delicious tapas are speared with toothpicks and known as *pintxos*, served throughout the region, and San Sebastián has some of the freshest seafood around.

Of course, no introduction to the Basque Country would be complete without a nod to the world-famous Running of the Bulls, held every year in Pamplona. For a week the city parties harder than any, forgoing sleep for adrenaline-fueled wine-guzzling sessions and, of course, running in front of bulls.

greatest hits

- **THE BILBAO EFFECT.** See the Museo Guggenheim Bilbao, which singlehandedly kicked off the industrial city's gentrification. (p. 363)

- **TAPAS WITH A 'TUDE.** Stuff yourself at the trendy tapas bar A Fuego Negro in San Sebastián's *parte vieja*. (p. 378)

- **A LOAD OF BULL.** Run in front of the bulls in Pamplona during *los Sanfermines*. We suggest doing so in winter, when you can beat the bulls to the finish line by several months. (p. 390)

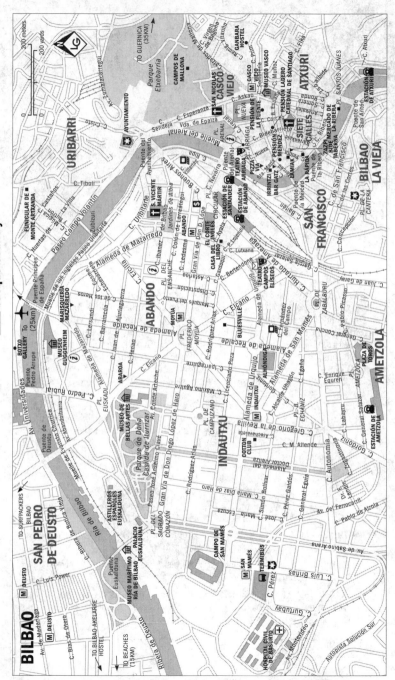

The best places to look for student-oriented nightlife are the grittier neighbor-hoods: Indautxu in Bilbao and Egia in San Sebastián. In Pamplona, the area west of the Ciudadela fills up with students during the school year, though it's quieter in summer—except during *los Sanfermines,* when the whole city becomes one giant rager.

bilbao *bilbo* ☎944

Bilbao (pop. 350,000) is, for the most part, a modern city that has not forgotten its historic roots. The city thrived during the Middle Ages, as it was on both a major ◢**sea route** and on the **Camino de Santiago.** After a couple of fairly quiet centuries, nearby lucrative mineral deposits were discovered in the 19th century, and the city grew as both a seaport and an **industrial center;** it soon became a major producer of steel and the Basque country's economic hub. In the late 20th century, the steel industry declined, and Bilbao began to experience some urban decay; it was lovingly known as **"the Pittsburgh of Spain."** Over the last couple of decades, however, Bilbao has been thoroughly revitalized, due mostly to the transformation of its industrial zones into parks and cultural spaces like Frank Gehry's architecturally marvelous **Guggenheim Museum.** The "Guggenheim Effect" has propelled Bilbao back to the top of the proverbial heap as a tourist destination.

bilbao

ORIENTATION

The **casco viejo,** or old quarter, sits on the east side of the city, to the east of the Río Nervión, which makes a sort of upside-down "U" as it cuts through the city. The *casco viejo* contains the cathedral, the **siete calles** (the city's original seven streets), and the highest concentration of bars and accommodations. Across the river from the *casco viejo* are the neighborhoods of **Abando** to the north (where the museums are), **Indautxu** further south (where the nightlife rages on past 2am), **Basurtu** to the southwest (where the bus terminal is located), and **Deusto** all the way west across the river.

ACCOMMODATIONS

Bilbao has several recently opened hostels, but most are far from the major sights of the city. Closer to the center of things, the *casco viejo* is brimming with cheap *pensiones*, most on the upper floors of residential buildings; walking down the street, look for a "pensión" sign on the side of a building, and ring up to ask for a room. In the high season (approximately June-Aug), however, it's better to reserve a place in advance. *Pensiones* outside the *casco viejo* tend to be quieter and less expensive. Rates may be higher during *Aste Nagusia* (mid- to late August).

GANBARA HOSTEL	HOSTEL $
C. de Prim, 13B	☎94 405 39 30 www.ganbarahostel.com

This hostel's quirky decor might just be artsy enough to earn it a place in the Guggenheim out in Abando, but the building itself is right in the center of things in the *casco viejo*. The dorms in the neighborhood's only hostel are an excellent option for travelers looking to save money without sacrificing location; many of Bilbao's other hostels are a tram ride or a long walk from the museums, restaurants, and bars of the *casco viejo*. The larger dorms have ensuite bathrooms, which sounds great until about the third flush of the night.

Even if you've rolled into town solo, there's a good chance you won't need to go out to the numerous nearby bars alone—the large common area downstairs and TV lounge upstairs promote a social atmosphere.

✻ ⓜCasco Viejo (Pl. Unamuno exit). Cross to the corner of Pl. Unamuno diagonally across from the Metro exit. Without crossing any streets, turn around the corner on the left; you will be on C. Prim, and the hostel is up the hill. *i* Breakfast included. Kitchen and 2 common areas with TV and Nintendo Wii. Free Wi-Fi and computers. Washer €2.50, dryer €1.50. Free lockers and locks (€3 deposit for lock). English and Spanish spoken. ⓢ 8-bed dorms with bath €17.50; 6-bed with bath €19; 4-bed €21. ⓩ Reception 24hr.

PENSIÓN MÉNDEZ I   HOTEL $$
C. de Santa María, 13, 4th fl.   ☎94 416 03 64 www.pensionmendez.com

Though not quite as comfortable as the affiliated Pensión Méndez II downstairs (€15-20 more per night), these austere but good-sized rooms are located five stories above one of the busiest tapas- and bar-hopping streets in the *casco viejo*. In the center of one of the liveliest spots in town, be careful when you open the front door to leave on a weekend evening—you might trip over (or, better yet, get invited to) a *botellón* taking place on the doorstep.

✻ EuskoTran: Arriaga. Walk with the river on your right for 1 block, then turn left onto C. Santa María. Or take the Metro to ⓜCasco Viejo (Pl. Unamuno exit) and follow C. Sombrerería before making a left at C. Santa María. ⓢ Singles €20-25; doubles €30-35; triples €45-50. ⓩ Reception 24hr.

SURFPACKERS BILBAO   HOSTEL $
C. de Luzarra, 18, bajo   ☎94 475 42 14

Bilbao's newest hostel is also its gnarliest, dude. Yes, Bilbao is 16km from the ocean, and no, this surf-themed hostel doesn't care. Those who forgot to check the map before hopping on the plane could easily fit their surfboards into the spacious common area and kitchen; they could probably even get it into the long but narrow 12-bed dorm. It's out in Deusto, fairly far from the major sights of the city, but it's just a hop and a skip away from the Metro stop.

✻ ⓜDeusto (Lehendakari Aguirre exit). Cross Av. Lehendakari Aguirre (the street to your left upon exiting the station), then turn right and cross the 2 little streets. Walk up the stairs to your left and turn right onto C. Luzarra. *i* Breakfast included. Shared bath. Common area with TV, PlayStation, and computer. Free Wi-Fi. Bicycles for rental. ⓢ 12-bed dorms €15-18; 10-bed €17-21; 8-bed €18-22; 6-bed €20-24. ⓩ Reception 24hr.

BILBAO AKELARRE HOSTEL   HOSTEL $
C. de Morgan, 4-6   ☎94 405 77 13 www.bilbaoakelarrehostel.com

Akelarre means "meeting of witches" in Basque, and even a witch would enjoy her stay at this hostel, as long as she isn't warded off by the crisp sheets in the simple but clean dorms. She might be a little put off by its distance from most of the city's major sights, but she can store her broom in one of the free lockers, since it's only a 5min. walk from the Metro station and a 10min. walk from the Euskotren. She could also fill the pockets of her robe with the individually packaged muffins served at breakfast before heading out for the day—or night. Muffins are, after all, a witch's favorite food.

✻ ⓜDeusto (Iruña exit). Follow C. Iruña downhill, then turn right onto C. Morgan (the last street before the bridge). Or take EuskoTran tram to Euskalduna, then walk across the Puente Euskalduna (the bridge that curves to the left) and turn left onto C. Morgan (the 1st street after the bridge). Or take Bilbobus #11 (dir. Deusto) to the last stop, Madariaga/Basabe, and turn left onto C. Morgan. *i* Breakfast included. Shared bath. Lockers available. Free Wi-Fi and access to computer with internet. Common area with TV and kitchen (8am-midnight). Spanish, English, French, and Italian spoken. ⓢ 12-bed dorms €17.50, 8-bed €18.50, 6-bed €19.50 (with private bath €20); doubles €42. ⓩ Reception 8am-midnight. Guests receive keycards with 24hr. access.

PENSIÓN LADERO   HOTEL $$
C. de la Lotería, 1, 4th fl.   ☎94 415 09 32

This family-run *pensión* has well lit rooms with balconies in the center of the *casco viejo*. There are two enormous triples (which can become quadruples for an extra €10), as well as several smaller doubles. Get a room on the bottom of the two floors—though the narrow spiral staircase in the corner may look cool, the bump(s) on your head probably won't.

⚲ ⓂCasco Viejo (Pl. Unamuno exit). Follow C. Cruz south 1 block, then turn left onto C. España, which becomes C. Lotería. *i* Shared bath. TV. Ⓢ Singles €25; doubles €35; triples €50. Extra bed €10.

BOTXO GALLERY   HOSTEL $
Av. de las Universidades, 5   ☎94 413 48 49 www.botxogallery.com

Right across the river from the Guggenheim, this hostel's common areas have even better views than those you'll get standing right next to it. Both of the dorms house so many people that you're bound to have snorer or two, and the triple-bunk beds are a little cramped, but the views and the proximity to the museum are major draws.

⚲ EuskoTran: Guggenheim. Cross through the park, left over Puente Pedro Arrupe bridge, then turn right onto Av. Universidades. *i* Breakfast and linens included. Shared bath with hair dryers. Free Wi-Fi and laptops for borrowing. Towel and blanket rental €2 each. Bicycle rental €7 per day. Ⓢ 21-bed and 15-bed dorms €16.50-19.20. ⌚ Reception 8:30am-2pm and 3:30pm-8pm.

PENSIÓN DE LA FUENTE   HOTEL $
C. de la Sombrerería, 2, 2nd fl.   ☎94 416 99 89 www.hostaldelafuente.com

This *pensión* boasts some of the *casco viejo*'s lowest rates for private rooms as well as a convenient location just steps from the Metro stop. The carpeted hallways are dark, but all the rooms are filled with light streaming in from either a balcony or a window facing an interior patio. Despite the law against smoking in hotels, there is an ashtray in every room.

⚲ On C. Sombrerería just off Pl. Unamuno and 1 block from ⓂCasco Viejo (Pl. Unamuno exit). *i* Shared bath. TV. Free Wi-Fi. Laundry service €7. Reservations by phone or by email. Ⓢ Singles €20-22; doubles €30-32, with bath €42. Extra bed €10. ⌚ Reception 24hr.

SIGHTS

🖼 MUSEO GUGGENHEIM BILBAO   MUSEUM
Av. de Abandoibarra, 2   ☎94 435 90 80 www.guggenheim-bilbao.es

It is hardly an exaggeration to say that **Frank Gehry** put Bilbao on the map. Since the Guggenheim opened in 1997, Bilbao has become an internationally known cultural center—a far cry from its former reputation as "the Pittsburgh of Spain"—and there is no doubt that this is a result of the building, not just the artwork it houses. While the art should certainly not be overlooked—**Richard Serra's** installation, *The Matter of Time*, is truly a sublime experience that undermines perceptions of space and context, and **Jeff Koons's** *Puppy* is enormously adorable. Everybody interprets the enormous titanium, limestone, steel, and glass building differently, but perhaps more impressive is how different it appears from each angle and location at different times of the day; Monet would have had a field day with this place.

⚲ EuskoTran: Guggenheim. *i* Audio guide (available in English) €2. Ⓢ €13, students and seniors €7.50, under 12 free. Bono Artean, which provides admission to both the Guggenheim and the Museo de Bellas Artes, can be purchased for €13.50. ⌚ Open July-Aug daily 10am-8pm; Sept-June Tu-Su 10am-8pm. Guided tours in Spanish daily at 11am and 5pm (inquire at information desk for other languages). Cafe open Tu-Su 9:30am-8:30pm. Restaurant open Tu-W 1-3:15pm, Th-Sa 1-3:15pm and 8:30-10:30pm, Su 1-3:15pm.

MUSEO DE BELLAS ARTES
Pl. del Museo, 2 ☎94 439 60 60 www.museobilbao.com
MUSEUM

While this museum's building is an interesting one—a century-old brick structure sheathed in a modern renovation—the main attraction here is the actual artwork. Some 33 rooms house a collection that's essentially a basic survey course in Western European art history since the Middle Ages. Don't let the lack of name recognition turn you away. Though there are works by well-known artists such as El Greco (born Doménikos Theotokópoulos—say that five times fast), Ribera, Zurbarán, Goya, and Cassatt, many of the works that catch your eye may be by artists you're discovering for the first time. Spanish and Basque artists are particularly well-represented.

✦ *From casco viejo, take Puente de Arenal bridge across the river and follow Gran Vía Don Diego López de Haro to Pl. Moyua; turn right and follow C. Elcano to Pl. Museo. Or, Ⓜ Moyua, and follow C. Elcano to Pl. Museo.* Ⓢ *€6, students and seniors €4.50, under 12 free; free on W. Audio tour €1. Bono Artean, which provides admission to both the Guggenheim and the Museo de Bellas Artes, €13.50.* ☒ *Open Tu-Su 10am-8pm; guided tours Su at noon.*

BIBLIOTECA DE BIDEBARRIETA
C. de Bidebarrieta, 4 ☎94 415 09 15 www.bilbao.net/bibliotecas
LIBRARY

Even the radiators are gilded at this proud and tastefully ornate central branch of Bilbao's municipal library. The books upstairs are mostly in Spanish, but don't worry: they've got a few in Basque (and English), too. Come for a peek at the architecturally eclectic interior, stay for the free Wi-Fi, and leave because you're a little freaked out by the separatist graffiti in the bathroom.

✦ *EuskoTran: Arriaga. Walk toward the Teatro Arriaga and turn right onto the 1st street, C. Bidebarrieta. The library is almost immediately on the right.* ⓘ *Free Wi-Fi in the reading room on the ground floor, free access to computers with Internet in the basement.* Ⓢ *Free.* ☒ *Open M 2:30-8:30pm, Tu-F 8:30am-8:30pm, Sa 10am-2pm.*

MUSEO MARÍTIMO RÍA DE BILBAO
Muelle de Ramón de la Sota, 1 ☎94 608 55 00 www.museomaritimobilbao.org
MUSEUM

The same place where you went tapas-hopping last night was once home to sailors even saltier than your *tacos de bacalao*. Bilbao was once a thriving port, and this museum won't let you forget it. If you like ship models, you will feel heavenly bliss here. If you don't like ship models, you will be in some kind of maritime purgatory, though you might find it interesting to recognize the *casco viejo* in old maps and photographs. The ships on the dry docks outside the museum also give a taste of what the city was like for the hundreds of years before Guggenheim & Co. came to town.

✦ *EuskoTran: Euskalduna. Walk toward the bridge on the right and cross the street that feeds onto the bridge. There will be a flight of stairs on the right; the museum is at the bottom of these stairs, on the right.* Ⓢ *€5; students, seniors, and unemployed €3.50; under 6 free.* ☒ *Open high season Tu-Su 10am-8pm; low season Tu-F 10am-6pm, Sa-Su 10am-8pm.*

EUSKAL MUSEOA BASQUE MUSEUM
Pl. de Miguel de Unamuno, 4 ☎94 415 54 23 www.euskal-museoa.org
MUSEUM

The centerpiece of the Basque Museum is the Mikeldi idol, an ancient Basque sculpture of a male hog that sits at the center of the cloister. The museum around it is uneven, with some eye-catching artifacts like the giant room-sized scale model of the Basque Country and other less engaging sections, like the floor that consists entirely of nearly identical ceramics.

✦ Ⓜ *Casco Viejo. On the opposite side of Pl. Unamuno.* ⓘ *Signs only in Spanish and Basque.* Ⓢ *€3, students €1.50, seniors and under 10 free. Free Th.* ☒ *Open Tu-Sa 11am-5pm, Su 11am-2pm.*

FOOD

The **casco viejo** is the best place to go **tapas-hopping; Calle Santa María** and **Calle Barrenkale** are two of the most crowded streets with some of the best bars. There are also a number of good, affordable restaurants in the **Abando** neighborhood, which has flourished with the opening of the Guggenheim Museum and the subsequent boost to the neighborhood's economy.

👍 GATZ
TAPAS $

C. de Santa María, 10 ☎94 415 48 61 www.bargatz.com

The Great Gatsby (born James Gatz) may have been a sham, but this place is the real deal. Its numerous *pintxo* prizes are displayed on the wall behind the bar, and any diner would agree that they are well deserved. Though the average price is a few cents higher than the neighboring bars, this place is a cut above the rest. The fried foie and potato *pintxo* (€1.60) is so rich you won't have to eat another meal for the rest of the day, and the smoked salmon wrapped around cream cheese and capers (€1.60) is perfect for anyone pining for a nice nova and shmear.

➜ On C. Santa María in the casco viejo, between C. Jardines and the river. $ Pintxos €1.60. Beer €2. ⏰ Open M-Th 1-3pm and 7-11pm, F-Sa 1-3pm and 7pm-midnight, Su 1-4pm.

ZAZPI BIDE TABERNA
TAPAS $

C. de Barrenkale Barrena, 18B, 2 ☎94 479 58 17

This bar in the *siete calles* ("seven streets") district of the *casco viejo* has one of the liveliest atmospheres and some of the most reasonable prices of any establishment in town (one assumes these two factors go hand-in-hand). It takes its name from its menu: *zazpi* means "seven" in Basque and *bide* means "euro fewer than you would have spent for the same food in San Sebastián."

➜ From the Catedral de Santiago, walk down C. Torre towards the river, and turn left onto C. Barrenkale Barrena. $ Pintxos €1.70. Beer €2.20. Mixed drinks €3.50. ⏰ Open M-Th noon-4pm and 7-11pm, F-Sa noon-4pm and 7pm-1am, Su noon-4pm.

PIZZA VIA
PIZZA $

C. de Santa María, 1 ☎94 479 42 32 www.pizzavia.net

This *casco viejo* pizzeria complements the standard pizza toppings with a variety of more adventurous options like "Hot," which features anchovies, spicy sausage, and chili peppers. Vegetarians (and cheese lovers) will appreciate the "4 Quesos," with mozzarella, emmental, gorgonzola, and brie. It's best to order one of the personal pizzas (€7-9), since the selection of individual slices is limited. The cute pictograms on the menu should give you a general idea of what you're ordering even if you don't speak Spanish (or Basque).

➜ ⓂCasco Viejo. Follow C. Sombrerería to C. Victor to C. Jardines, then right on C. Santa María. ℹ Another location at C. Somera, 36. $ Slice €2.50. Personal pizza €7-9. ⏰ Open M 6:30-11:30pm, Tu-Th 6:30-11:30pm, F-Sa 1-3:30pm and 6:30pm-1am, Su 1-3:30pm and 6-11:30pm.

ABAROA
BASQUE $$$

Pl. del Museo, 3 ☎94 424 91 07 www.abaroa.net

This restaurant is a tad pricier than the *pintxos* bars in the *casco viejo*, but the incredibly rich food helps to take away the sting. The peppers stuffed with *bacalao* (cod) or *carne* (beef) taste like they should cost much more than the €7 you'll pay for them, and the *arroz con pollo y pato* (rice with chicken and duck; €10.50) is done perfectly. If you're feeling bold, try the regional *chipirones en su tinta* (cuttlefish in their own ink; €12.50) or *sapito a la plancha* (grilled toad; €16.50).

➜ Up C. Elcano from Pl. Museo, just across from the Museo de Bellas Artes. $ Dishes €7-18. Menú del día €10.80. ⏰ Open M-Th 1-4pm and 8:30-11:30pm, F-Sa 1-4pm and 8:30pm-midnight, Su 1-4pm and 8:30-11:30pm.

MARISQUERÍA MAZARREDO SEAFOOD $$

Alameda de Mazarredo, 49 ☎94 423 08 18 www.marisqueriamazarredo.com

Though this seafood restaurant is just around the corner from the Guggenheim, you're far more likely to eat alongside various workers from the neighborhood than a Swiss tour group. Despite the incredibly two-dimensional paintings on the walls, it feels very much like a cafeteria; nevertheless the filling *menú del día* (€10) is a bargain.

With the Guggenheim on your left, proceed along Av. Abandoibarra. Turn right and cross the street onto Alameda de Mazarredo. $ Menú del día €10. 🕒 Open M-Th 7:45am-midnight, F-Sa 7:45am-2am.

NIGHTLIFE

The nightlife in Bilbao is simple: most revelers do a fairly standard **bar crawl** in the **casco viejo** until every place closes down, then head over to the clubs in the newer part of town. The main spots are **Calle Licenciado Poza,** particularly around **Calle Aranzadi, Calle Simón Bolívar,** and **Calle Manuel Allende** farther west. There are also a few clubs on **Calle Dos de Mayo** and **Calle Hernani,** closer to the *casco.*

BLUESVILLE BAR

C. de Telesforo Aranzadi, 1 ☎94 443 70 56 www.bluesvilledisco.net

If little girls dream of castles, big girls dream of castles filled with bottles of liquor, like the ones behind the bar at this popular medieval-themed spot. Queen Bartender will be happy to share her bounty with you (i.e., a cocktail) for a small tribute (€6-7.50), so try one—or a few. Don't worry, the centaurs and **dragons** on the wall won't judge you—they've seen much worse (especially at the annual Halloween party.)

[M]Moyua. Walk to the plaza on your right, walk 1 block on C. Marqués del Puerto, turn right onto C. Rodríguez Arias and left onto C. Telesforo Aranzadi. $ Beer €2.30-4. Mixed drinks €6-7.50. 🕒 Open M 9am-11pm, Tu-Th 9am-4am, F 9am-5am, Sa 5pm-5am, Su 5-11pm.

IRRINTZI BAR

C. de Santa María, 8 ☎94 416 76 16 www.irrintzi.es

This is a good place to begin your night of hopping from bar to bar in the *casco*, sampling *cervezas*, *sidras*, and whatever other type of *bebida* suits you; maybe even a *pintxo* or two, as well. Make what you will of the slightly hipster faux-ironic Japanese manga-anime theme, but the establishment calls itself a "bar emblemático de Bilbao."

[M]Casco Viejo. Follow C. Sombrerería to C. Victor to C. Jardines, then right on C. Santa María. $ Pintxos €1.50. Beer €2.10. Cider €1.10. 🕒 Open M-Th 9am-11pm, F 9am-12:30am, Sa 10:30am-12:30am, Su 11:30am-10pm.

COTTON CLUB BAR

C. de Gregorio de la Revilla, 25 ☎94 410 49 51 www.cottonclubbilbao.es

This place may be a little hard to find, but once you see it, you'll know—it's the one with the **animatronic polar bears** in the window. The walls are covered with tens of thousands of bottle caps and the dance floor with dozens and dozens of partiers. The place is packed on Friday and Saturday nights and occasionally has live music with bands from Spain and farther afield; it's a bit calmer during the week.

[M]Indautxu. Exit to the right through the shopping area, then make a right at the elevator. Once outside, make an immediate left; entrance is on C. Simón Bolívar. i Around 6 concerts per month on F and Sa at 8:30pm. $ Beer €2.50. Mixed drinks €6. 🕒 Open M-Th 8:30pm-3am, F-Sa 6:30pm-6am.

LAMIAK BAR, GLBT

C. de la Pelota, 8 ☎94 415 96 42

A cafe/bar in the *casco viejo* that's lively on the weekends and a bit quieter during the week, Lamiak welcomes people of all sexual orientations in an open, lounge-style atmosphere. There's more seating than in most bars, with lots more upstairs in a trendy area that looks down onto the bar. Make sure to get your *pintxo* beforehand, though, since they aren't served here.

 # Between C. Santa María and the river. $ Beer €3.50. ⏰ Open M-Th 4pm-midnight, F-Sa 3:30pm-2am, Su 4-11:30pm.

BULLITT GROOVE CLUB DANCE CLUB

C. de Dos de Mayo, 3 ☎94 416 30 36 www.bullittgrooveclub.com

For those bored with barhopping in the *casco viejo*, try Bullitt, just across the river in Abando. A little trendier and with a bit more bass, Bullitt is a good midway point between the more typical bars of the *casco viejo* and the clubs that stay open later in Indautxu.

 # From the casco viejo, cross Puente de la Merced bridge, make a right on C. Naja, and take a left up C. Dos de Mayo. $ Beer €2. Mixed drinks €6. ⏰ Open Th 10pm-1am, F 10pm-3am, Sa 6am-noon and 10pm-3am, Su 6am-noon.

FESTIVALS

ASTE NAGUSIA (SEMANA GRANDE) PL. ARRIAGA

☎94 420 42 00 www.astenagusia.com

Nine beloved and anticipated days of fireworks, music, theater, and bullfights in late August. It's nothing on the scale of Pamplona's *San Fermín*, but it begins with a *txupin* (rocket) all the same and takes over the city for more than a week. Aste Nagusia came in first in a competition of Spain's best intangible cultural treasures. Get a *Bilbao Guide* from the tourist office for a schedule and more information.

 # Events centered on Pl. Arriaga, but the festival is located throughout the whole city. $ Free. ⏰ Begins the 1st Sa after Aug 15.

INTERNATIONAL FESTIVAL OF DOCUMENTARY AND SHORT FILMS OF BILBAO CITYWIDE

☎94 424 86 98 www.zinebi.com

The Festival Internacional de Cine Documental y Cortometraje de Bilbao began as a documentary film competition in 1959, then started screening short films as well in 1971. It managed to survive Generalísimo Franco, a complete lack of money, and controversy (the true sign of good art) to become one of Spain's leading film festivals. The main festival is the last week in November, but there is related programming earlier in the month and an affiliated fantasy film festival at the beginning of May.

ZINEGOAK CITYWIDE

☎94 415 62 58 www.zinegoak.com

Zinegoak, the Bilbao international gay, lesbian, and transgender film festival, runs for a week from the end of January through the beginning of February (so, if you can't find a bar to watch the Super Bowl, here's an alternative). Its opening ceremony is in the iconic Teatro Arriaga, and screenings are held in a variety of theaters across the city.

i Check website or tourist office for venues and schedule. $ Opening ceremony €6, screenings €5 or €20 for 6 screenings. ⏰ Late Jan to early Feb.

LOS DULCES DEL CONVENTO CASCO VIEJO

Pl. de la Encarnación, 9B ☎94 432 01 25

During the last weekend in May, the Diocesan Museum of Religious Art houses a sweets fair in its usually quiet cloister. All the *dulces* are made by cloister nuns and monks, mostly with raw materials they grow themselves. The fair draws approximately 10,000 visitors annually.

 # In the casco viejo, follow C. Ribera to C. Atxuri, or take the Euskotren to Atxuri and walk 1 block back along the track, then make a right. $ Free. Sweets €2-12. ⏰ Last weekend in May F-Su 10:30am-8pm.

ESSENTIALS

Practicalities

- **TOURIST OFFICES:** The tourism office's main branch is in **Abando,** (Pl. Ensanche, 11 ☎94 479 57 60 www.bilbao.net/bilbaoturismo. 🚇 [M] Moyua. Between C. de Henao and C. de Colón de Larreategui. ⏰ Open M-F 9am-2pm and 4-7:30pm) but that branch is not open on weekends; instead, go to the branch at **Teatro Arriaga** in the *casco viejo* (Pl. Arriaga 🚇 EuskoTran: Arriaga. ⏰ Open daily June-Sept 9:30am-2pm and 4-7:30pm; Oct-May M-F 11am-2pm and 5-7:30pm, Sa 9:30am-2pm and 5-7:30pm, Su 9:30am-2pm) or the branch at the **Guggenheim Museum** (Alameda Mazarredo, 66 🚇 EuskoTran: Guggenheim. ⏰ Open June-Sept M-Sa 10am-7pm, Su 10am-6pm; Oct-May Tu-F 11am-6pm, Sa 11am-7pm, Su 11am-3pm).
- **TOURS:** Guided walking tours ($ €4.50 per person ⏰ 1½hr.) leave from the Guggenheim tourism office daily at noon for the tour of Ensanche and Abandoibarra and from the Arriaga Theater daily at 10am for the tour of the *casco viejo.*
- **CURRENCY EXCHANGE: El Corte Inglés** (Gran Vía, 7-9 ☎94 425 35 00 ⏰ Open daily 10am-9pm) or any of the banks along the Gran Vía, such as **Caja Laboral** (Gran Vía, 2 🚇 in the Plaza Circular. ☎94 331 90 21 ⏰ Open June-Sept M-Th 8:30am-2:15pm and 4:15-7:45pm, F 8:30am-2:15pm; Oct-May M-F 8:30am-2:15pm and 4:15-7:45pm, Sa 8:30am-1:15pm).
- **LUGGAGE STORAGE:** Lockers are available in the **Termibús** bus station near the information booth. (🚇 [M] San Mamés. $ €1. ⏰ Open M-F 7am-9:45pm, Sa 8am-8:45pm, Su 9am-9:45pm.)
- **POST OFFICE:** The main post office is in Abando, but there are branches all over the city. (Alameda Urquijo, 19 ☎94 470 93 38 🚇 [M] Abando. Walk one block away from the river on the Gran Vía, then turn left. ⏰ Open M-F 8:30am-8:30pm, Sa 9:30am-2pm.)
- **POSTAL CODE:** 48001-48015

bilbao

Emergency!

- **MUNICIPAL POLICE:** ☎092 (C. de Juan Carlos de Cortázar, 3 🚇 EuskoTran: Ribera. Walk with the river to your left and cross the next bridge and continue straight on C. de Don Claudio Gallastegui, then turn right onto Av. de Askatasuna, then left at the traffic circle onto C. de Juan Carlos de Cortázar.)
- **MEDICAL SERVICES: Hospital de Basurto** (Av. Montevideo, 18 ☎112 🚇 EuskoTran: Basurto.)

Getting There

BY BUS

The **Termibús** bus station (C. Gurtubay, 1 ☎94 439 50 77 www.termibus.es 🚇 [M] San Mamés) is on the west side of Bilbao and has connections to the EuskoTran, Metro, and city bus. **Buses** arrive from: Barcelona ($ €44 ⏰ 8hr., at least 6 per day 10am-10:50pm); Burgos ($ €12 ⏰ 2-3hr.; M-Sa 7-10 per day 6:45am-7:30pm, Su 7 per day 11am-8pm); Madrid ($ €29 ⏰ 5hr.; M-Sa 16-21 per day 7am-1:30am, Su 18 per day 9am-1:30am); and Santiago de Compostela ($ €54 ⏰ 9-12hr.; M-Th and Sa 4 per day 6am-11:15pm, F and Su 5 per day 6am-11:15pm).

BY TRAIN

Bilbao has three train stations: **EuskoTren** (not to be confused with the EuskoTran tram that runs solely within Bilbao. ☎90 254 32 10 www.euskotren.es) arrives at **Estación de Atxuri,** just east of the *casco viejo;* **FEVE** trains (☎94 424 45 12 www.feve.es) arrive at **Estación de Santander,** across the river from the *casco viejo;* and **RENFE** trains (☎90 210 94 20 www.renfe.es) arrive at **Estación de Abando.** The **EuskoTren** runs to Bilbao from San Sebastián. ($ €6.20. ⏰ 1¼hr.; M-F 30 per day 6:18am-10:30pm, Sa-Su 21-33 per day 24hr.) **FEVE** arrives at Bilbao from León. ($ €22. ⏰ 7½hr., daily 2pm.) **RENFE** goes to Bilbao from: Barcelona ($ €40 ⏰ 6½hr.; M-Sa 2 per day 7:30am and 3:30pm, Su 3:30pm); León ($ €30 ⏰ 5hr., daily 3pm); Logroño ($ €13 ⏰ 2½hr.; M-Sa 11:24am and 7:25pm, Su 7:25pm); Madrid ($ €25-49 ⏰ 5hr.; M-F 8am and 4pm, Sa 8am, Su 4pm); and Salamanca ($ €19-32 ⏰ 6hr., daily 10:30am).

BY PLANE

Bilbao Airport (BIO; www.aena.es) has about 25 flights per day from Barcelona, Madrid, and other flights from all over Europe. The airport is about 10km from Bilbao; **BizkaiBus** ($ €1.35 ⏰ 25min. from airport to Bilbao, summer every 20min. 6:20am-midnight; winter every 30min. 6:15am-11:15pm. From Bilbao to airport, summer every 20min. 5:20am-10pm; winter every 30min. 5:25am-9:55pm) goes between **Pl. Moyúa** and the airport, and **taxis** to and from the airport usually run about €25 (€27 at night).

Getting Around

While walking is always the cheapest way to get around, Bilbao is not a small city, and getting from the *casco viejo* to the Guggenheim on foot can be a schlep. Fortunately, Bilbao has some very convenient alternatives. If you're going to be in Bilbao for longer than a day, get a **Creditrans** card, which cuts the price of all public transportation nearly in half.

By Light Rail

The **EuskoTran** (☎90 254 32 10 www.euskotren.es/tranviabilbao $ €1.25), a futuristic light rail line, runs along the river. Its stops include the Termibús bus terminal, Guggenheim Museum, *casco viejo*, and Atxuri EuskoTren station. Make sure to validate your Creditrans card at the stop before boarding.

By Metro

The brand-new Metro system (☎94 425 40 00 www.metrobilbao.net $ €1.40) is more suited for travel between the city center and the suburbs, but it's a quick way to get from one side of town to the other, too. Stops include Deusto, San Mamés (bus terminal), Indautxu, Moyua, Abando, and Casco Viejo. Don't lose or throw away your ticket, as you'll need it to exit.

By Bus

The **Bilbobús** (☎94 479 09 81 www.bilbao.net $ €1.20, €0.60 with Creditrans card) goes all over the city; check their online map for route information. **BizkaiBus** (☎90 222 22 65) goes between Bilbao and the airport and to some other suburbs.

By Taxi

Taxi services include TeleTaxi Bilbao (☎94 410 21 21 www.teletaxibilbao.com) and Radio Taxi Bilbao (☎94 444 88 88 www.taxibilbao.es). Taxi stands can be found in the *casco viejo* at the Puente de Arenal and Puente de San Antón bridges as well as at the northwest and southeast corners of the *casco.* On the other side of the river, stands can be found at the Museo de Bellas Artes, Museo Guggenheim, and various points throughout the city.

san sebastián *donostia* ☎943

Formed by combining three Basque fishing and whaling towns along the bay into one mega-port city, San Sebastián (pop. 180,000) thrived and became a major seaport before being burned to the ground in 1813 by Anglo-Portuguese forces. And so, instead of a *casco antiguo* filled with medieval buildings, San Sebastián's historic center is the **parte vieja,** whose older constructions come from the late-19th-century Beaux-Arts and Art Nouveau styles. Even the cathedral is new (relatively speaking—it's from the 1890s), and the narrow streets of the old quarter are basically on a grid. This newly built city attracted tourists from all over Europe, with its sunny beaches (made popular by Queen Isabel II) helping it to become the tourist-friendly resort town that it is today. There are still neighborhoods (particularly on the east side of the river) where one can escape the occasionally overwhelming feel of turn-of-the-century opulence, but the beaches are free, so even those traveling on a budget can bask in the sunny luxury of San Sebastián.

ORIENTATION

San Sebastián's relatively tiny but bustling **parte vieja** ("old part") is only about eight blocks by eight blocks in size and sits at the northern end of the central part of the city. The *parte vieja* is bordered by **La Concha** bay to the west, **Monte Urgull** to the north, **Río Urumea** to the east, and the broad **Alameda del Boulevard** to the south. South of that is **El Centro,** a newer district that is the city's center for shopping and business and contains the **Catedral.** To the east, across the **Río Urumea,** lies the **Gros** neighborhood, which has a **surf beach (Playa de Zurriola)** and tends to be slightly trendier and cheaper than the *parte vieja.* On the other side of the tracks, south of Gros, is **Egia,** where you're not likely to find any tourists but where you are likely to find a whole lot of cool. To the west of El Centro is the **Playa de la Concha,** which is not nearly as exciting as the Zurriola surf beach but enjoys a longer and richer history as a resort hangout.

ACCOMMODATIONS

Though San Sebastián is hardly limited to its **parte vieja** and **El Centro** neighborhoods, these locales tend to be the hub of the city's hotels and hostels. Thankfully, it's a small city and easy to walk, so the limited range of location options shouldn't hold you back.

HOSPEDAJE KATI GUESTHOUSE $$

C. de Fermín Calbetón, 21, 5C ☎94 343 04 87 www.hospedajekati.com

The elderly couple who rent rooms in this guesthouse do a great good-cop, bad-cop routine: Kati comes in to say good-night, then Luis follows to scold you for using the overhead light (six bulbs) instead of the single-bulb lamp by the bed. In addition to two rooms crammed with 13 beds, there is a large, lovely terrace just off the bedroom. During the high season, the place is full; during the low season, you may find yourself in the largest, cheapest single in town.

*⇟ From Alameda del Boulevard, walk 3 blocks on C. San Juan, then turn left onto C. Fermín Calbetón. **i** Free Wi-Fi. TV and shared bath. [$] July-Aug dorms €30-35, double €60; Sept-May €15-18/44; June €22-25/40. ⏰ Reception 24hr.*

PENSIÓN AMAIUR HOTEL $$$

C. del 31 de Agosto, 44 ☎94 342 96 54 www.pensionamaiur.com

Situated on one of the *parte vieja*'s main tapas-bar streets, this little *pensión* is colorfully cozy. The beds are big, the rooms clean with lots of closet space, and the shared kitchens well stocked with tea and coffee. Lovely views through flowery balconies onto the street below are available in the exterior rooms,

basque country

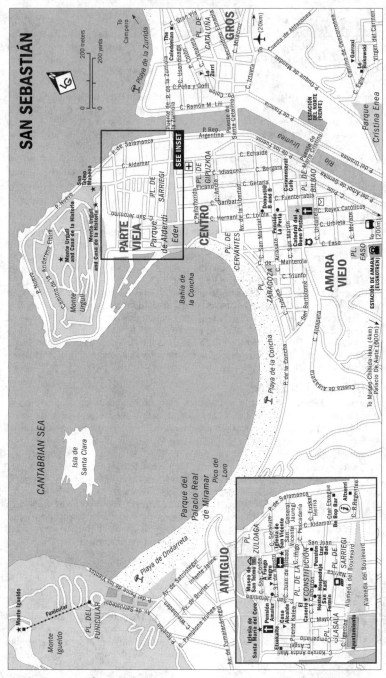

SAN SEBASTIÁN

CANTABRIAN SEA

Isla de
Santa Clara

Monte Igueldo

Funicular

PL. DEL
FUNICULAR

Monte
Igueldo

Parque del
Palacio Real
de Miramar

Pico del
Loro

Playa de Ondarreta

Bahía de
la Concha

MONTE URGULL and CASA DE LA HISTORIA
Monte Urgull
Camino de Andereño Elbira
P. Nuevo
Monte Urgull and Casa de la Historia
San Telmo Museoa

PARTE
VIEJA

Parque
de Alderdi
Eder

SEE INSET

CENTRO

P. de la Concha

ANTIGUO

GROS

ESTACIÓN
DEL NORTE
(RENFE)

Parque
Cristina Enea

BILBAO

AMARA
VIEJO

PL. DE
EASO

ESTACIÓN DE AMARA
(EUSKOTREN)

To Museo Chillida-leku (4km)
Palacio de Aiete (800m)

www.letsgo.com

372

though if you're staying in one of the cheaper interior rooms you can always cop your views from the communal balcony off the hallway.

From Alameda del Boulevard, take C. San Juan (next to the tourist office), then take the 7th left onto C. 31 de Agosto. **i** *Free Wi-Fi. Shared bath. Computer with internet access €1 per 18min. TV and kitchen available.* [$] *July-Sept and Semana Santa singles €45; interior doubles €54, exterior doubles €65; triples €85; family room €100. June and Oct €42/50/60/75/90. Apr and May €34/44/52/69/84. Nov-Mar €30/42/50/66/75.* ⏰ *Reception 8am-10:30pm.*

PENSIÓN IZAR BAT HOTEL $$$

C. de Fermín Calbetón, 6, 1st fl. ☎94 343 15 73 www.pensionizarbat.com

This *pensión*'s prices tend to get a little steep during the *temporada alta* (July-Aug), but this place is great if you're looking for a clean, cheery room and need a break from shared bathrooms. Just steps from the Alameda del Boulevard, Izar Bat is easily spotted due to its flowering balconies overlooking the start of C. de Fermín Calbetón.

From Alameda del Boulevard, take C. San Juan (next to the tourist office), then take the 3rd left onto C. Fermín Calbetón. **i** *5% discount with up-to-date copy of Let's Go. TV and fridge available. Private bath with hair dryer. Reservations strongly recommended July-Aug.* [$] *July-Aug singles €56, doubles €70; June and Sept €52/65; Oct-May €25/30-35.* ⏰ *Reception 24hr.*

HOSTEL SAN FERMÍN HOSTEL $$

C. de Fermín Calbetón, 23 ☎94 342 54 91 www.hostelsanfermin.com

This hostel offers no-frills, dormitory-style lodging at some of the *parte vieja*'s lowest rates. Unfortunately, it costs an arm and a leg during the high season and lacks many normal hostel conveniences like a kitchen, a common area, and breakfast. In spite of these shortcomings, this place still attracts a fun, youthful crowd that is always down to party. The staff is young and helpful, and they often go out with the guests to show them the best nightlife and hidden restaurants.

From Alameda del Boulevard, take C. San Juan (next to the tourist office), then take the 3rd left onto C. Fermín Calbetón. **i** *Free Wi-Fi. Lockers available. Discounts at 2 nearby bars.* [$] *Dorms July-Aug €40-55, Sept-June €19-38.* ⏰ *Reception 8am-midnight.*

PENSIÓN LA PERLA HOTEL $$$

C. Loiola, 10, 1st fl. ☎94 342 81 23 www.pensionlaperla.com

This *pensión*'s rooms are small, but its beds are big and comfy, and the spaces are quite bright during the day. Sandwiched between a modern shopping center and the cathedral, there's something here for devout Catholics and capitalists alike (those who fall in the center of that Venn diagram will be on cloud nine).

On the street in front of the main façade of the cathedral, on the right. **i** *Free Wi-Fi. Private bath. TV and laundry service available. Some rooms with fridge, some rooms with microwave.* [$] *June 21-Sept 30 singles €50, doubles €65, triples €80; Oct-May €33-40/42-52/55-62; June 1-21 €40/52/62.* ⏰ *Reception 24hr.*

DONOSTI@ B&B B&B $$$$

C. de San Marcial, 33, 5AB ☎94 342 85 03 www.donostiahostel.com

This B&B has a great location (close to the beach, the *parte vieja*, the cathedral, and inter-city transportation), but the real draw is that classic B&B attention you were looking for. Their full American breakfast even comes with eggs—an unheard-of amenity in these parts. Donosti@ for the win.

With your back to the main façade of the cathedral, proceed straight ahead on C. Loiola for 2 blocks, then turn right onto C. San Marcial. **i** *Free Wi-Fi and computer with internet access. Breakfast included. Shared bath. Laundry service available. Safety deposit boxes.* [$] *July-Sept singles €64, doubles €90, triples €135; May-June and Oct €50/70/105; Nov-Apr €45/64/90.* ⏰ *Reception 24hr.*

CAMPING IGUELDO   CAMPING $$

Paseo del Padre Orkolaga, 69   ☎94 321 45 02 www.campingigueldo.com

For those looking to escape the extortion of San Sebastián's urban accommodations during the high season, this campground offers a cheaper, more rustic alternative. It's also great if you have an RV, since those can be really hard to park in the city.

🚌 *Take bus #16 from the Pl. Gipuzkoa to the last stop, "Camping."* ℹ️ *Free Wi-Fi. Washers and dryers €5. Showers. Bar and restaurant.* 💲 *Parcels (70 sq. m for 2 people and room for RV and tent; includes water and electricity) June 16-Sept 15 €33.20, extra person €5.40; June 1-15 and Sept 16-30 €29.30/4.90; Oct-May €22.10/4.30. 20 sq. m parcels without water or electricity €8-15 cheaper. Family-sized bungalows July-Aug €85-115 (5-night min. stay); Sept-June €54-103 (2- to 3-night min. stay).* 🕐 *Reception 24hr.*

SIGHTS

MONTE URGULL AND CASA DE LA HISTORIA   MUSEUM, HISTORICAL SITE

Castillo de la Mota de Urgull   ☎94 342 84 17

Monte Urgull, the big mountain next to the *parte vieja* with the **Jesus statue** on top, is not a strenuous enough walk to make it into the hiking listings. The trek is still a lovely escape from the city, despite being just meters away—up, up, and away, of course. As you ascend, you'll pass castle after castle and be rewarded for your shin splints with breathtaking views of the city and bay (though the breathtaking part could also be chalked up to the climb). At the very top is the **Castillo de la Mota**, which houses the **Casa de la Historia** and a comprehensive exhibit on San Sebastián's history. When you're done there, limbo your way back down the dark, low-ceilinged stone stairs and take the north side of the mountain down to see the small, hauntingly beautiful 1837 **English Cemetery,** whose headstone carvers must not have been English, as names that are memorialized include misspelled ones like "Whiliam."

🚶 *Head uphill to the left of Iglesia de Santa María on C. 31 de Agosto. Or, bus #39 to "Urgull" (lazyhead).* ℹ️ *Free audioguides (leave ID as deposit).* 💲 *Free.* 🕐 *Monte Urgull open daily May-Sept 8am-9pm; Oct-Apr 8am-7pm. Casa de la Historia open daily May 2-Sept 14 11am-8pm; Sept 15-30 11am-7:30pm; Oct-Apr Tu-F 10am-2pm and 3-5:30pm, Sa-Su 10am-5:30pm. Castillo de la Mota open daily May-Sept 8am-8pm; Oct-Apr 8am-6pm.*

SAN TELMO MUSEOA   MUSEUM

Pl. de Zuloaga, 1   ☎94 348 15 80 www.santelmomuseoa.com

At the northeast corner of the *parte vieja*, there's a stately building with a handsome Neo-Renaissance façade over whose door is carved "Museo Municipal." Once the impressive entrance and accordingly pricey admission fee are behind you, you can dive into the enjoyable collection of Basque artifacts that tell some surprising stories. For example, married and widowed Basque women used to wear headdresses with stiff crests that indicated their place of origin, their economic class, and, most importantly, their marital status. Widows wore hats without a crest to indicate that they no longer had a husband. This may inspire only harmless giggles in the kids (and *Let's Go* researchers) who visit the museum, but the Church was less amused by the phallic imagery and put the kibosh on the tradition. Other highlights include the exhibits on traditional Basque music and the sport of *pelota vasca* (*euskal pilota*, in Basque). On the top floor there's a small fine arts collection that squeezes five centuries of art history into a few small rooms; it's kind of like your intro art history class, except there's nothing famous and your feet are tired.

🚶 *In the plaza at the end of C. San Juan.* ℹ️ *Signs in Basque and Spanish, with only section titles also in English and French.* 💲 *€5, students and seniors €3, under 18 free. Free admission Tu. Audioguide €2.* 🕐 *Open Tu-Su 10am-8pm. Guided tours Sa-Su 11am (English), 1 and 6:30pm (Spanish); call to arrange a tour by the previous F.*

IGLESIA DE SAN VICENTE CHURCH

C. de Narrica, 26

This massive church is one of the city's oldest remaining structures, built in the early 16th century. There's a considerably newer addition on the outside wall of the church facing C. San Vicente: a small but affecting Pietà sculpture made in 1998 by a Basque sculptor. The interior is gorgeous and often redolent of the lilies by the altar. You can also walk up to the balcony for a better view of the church and the stained glass, though *Let's Go* does not assume any responsibility for pierced eardrums resulting from extreme proximity to the organ.

From Alameda del Boulevard, walk up C. Narrica. [$] Free. ⏰ Open M-Sa 9am-1pm and 5-8pm.

MONTE IGUELDO VIEWS

☎94 321 35 25 www.monteigueldo.es

Take the rickety wooden funicular to the top of the mountain on the far western end of town for amazing views and creepy-looking carnival rides. Mostly for the views, though.

Funicular leaves from Pl. Funicular, 4 (accessible by bus #16) every 15min. M-F 11am-8pm, Sa-Su and holidays 10am-10pm. [$] Free. Round-trip funicular ticket €2.80, under 7 €2.10. Bathrooms €0.20. ⏰ Park open June 1-Sept 15 M-F 11am-2pm and 4-8pm, Sa-Su and holidays 11am-2pm and 4-9:30pm; Sept 15-Nov 1 Sa-Su and holidays 11:30am-2pm and 4-8pm; Nov 1-Mar 19 Sa-Su and holidays 11:30am-2pm and 4-7pm; Mar 19-June 1 Sa-Su and holidays 11am-2pm and 4-8:30pm.

CATEDRAL DEL BUEN PASTOR CHURCH

Pl. del Buen Pastor

This Neo-Gothic cathedral in the newer part of town dates from the last years of the 19th century and has a direct view of the Baroque Iglesia de Santa María del Coro, up the long street and into the *parte vieja*. The 250ft. belfry towers over San Sebastián and is visible from most of the city and bay. It was built as a mere church, but it got called up to the big leagues in 1949 when the diocese of San Sebastián was formed and it became a cathedral. If you go at just the right time in the early evening, you'll get a few awe-inspiring minutes as the cathedral fills with multi-colored light passing through the stained-glass windows.

From Alameda del Boulevard, take C. Hernani south from the western end; the Cathedral is at the end. [$] Free. ⏰ Open M-Sa 8:30am-12:30pm and 5-8pm. Mass M-F 9, 10, 11am; Sa 8pm; Su 9, 11am, noon, 1:30, 6pm.

IGLESIA DE SANTA MARÍA DEL CORO CHURCH

C. del 31 de Agosto, 46 ☎94 342 31 24

Stand for 5min. at the corner of C. Mayor and any street crossing it, and you'll hear more than one "Oh, my gosh" or "*Ahú* " as tourists round the corner and spot the magnificent Baroque façade of Santa María del Coro rising at the end of the street. Above the ornately curvaceous entrance (how sexy does this church sound?) is a sculpture of San Sebastián's martyrdom. Note also the ship, the city's symbol, at the highest part of the façade.

From the Alameda del Boulevard, turn right onto C. Mayor; it's the giant stone church at the end.
i Free pamphlets in English. [$] Free. ⏰ Open M-Sa 10:15am-1:15pm and 4:45-7:45pm. Mass M-F 11:30am, Sa 5pm, Su 11:30am.

THE GREAT OUTDOORS

Hiking

TXINDOKI

This peak in the Aralar range stands at just over 4400ft. and is considered one of the best hikes around. It's challenging but requires no particular expertise. The only problem is that it's difficult to reach without a car; some travelers say that hitchhiking (which *Let's Go* does not recommend) is an option, but renting a car is always safer.

➡ Best reached by car. Take the A-8 to the E-5, then take exit 431 onto the GI-2131 toward Alegia, and follow signs toward Amezketa. $ Free. 🕐 Don't start later than noon if you want to make it to the peak and back before dark.

CAMINO DEL NORTE

The second stage of the Camino del Norte, which runs from Irún to Santiago de Compostela, goes from San Sebastián to Zarautz and is about 14mi. Take the highway up Monte Igueldo and then follow the signs; turn back whenever you feel like it, since there's no pressure to make it all the way to Zarautz, unless you're making a pilgrimage of your own to its pristine surf beaches.

➡ Keep walking west along the bay until you see signs for the Camino.

Beaches

PLAYA DE ZURRIOLA

This is the surf beach, located to the east of the river and along the Gros neighborhood. Though not exclusively for surfing, this beach tends to draw a much younger crowd than its more historic neighbor to the west; in the evening, students (and their beer cans) line the stone ledges surrounding the beach. Bikini tops optional; bikini bottoms encouraged.

➡ East of Río Urumea, on the waterfront. $ Free. 🕐 Open dawn-dusk.

PLAYA DE LA CONCHA

This is the beach around which San Sebastián cultivated its reputation as a resort town for the vacationing European bourgeoisie; today it tends to be frequented mostly by an older crowd (and their grandchildren).

➡ Just west of the parte vieja and El Centro; it's the big strip of land with sand and water—you can't miss it. Or bus #5, 16, 18, 25, 33, or 40 to La Perla. $ Free. 🕐 Open dawn-dusk.

PLAYA DE ONDARRETA

Just to the west of Playa de la Concha but east of Monte Igueldo, this beach is a little less crowded, simply by virtue of its slightly greater distance from the center of town. During the high season, though, it's as packed as the rest of the beachfront.

➡ Bus #16 to Satrustegi. Or from El Centro, proceed along the Paseo de La Concha with the water on your right; it's after the Playa de La Concha. ℹ Lockers, showers, and toilets available. $ Free. 🕐 Open dawn to dusk.

PLAYA DE ZARAUTZ

About 30min. from San Sebastián via EuskoTren is **Zarautz,** a tiny town with a huge beach, almost completely tourist-free and home to some gnarly waves. Pukas surf shop (see: Surfing) rents boards and gives lessons.

➡ From the EuskoTren station, take the train (dir.: Zumaia) to Zarautz. Once there, head toward the water. $ Free. 🕐 Open dawn-dusk.

Kayaking

ALOKAYAK

Playa de Ondarreta ☎64 611 27 47 www.alokayak.com

This stand is set up on the Playa de Ondarreta during the high tourist season (June 15-Sept 15) and rents kayaks for solo and family excursions in the bay and surrounding area.

➡ From El Centro, proceed along the Paseo de La Concha with the water on your right; the Playa de Ondarreta is after the Playa de La Concha. It's the shack that says "alo-KAYAK." $ 1-person kayaks €6 per 30min., €10 per hr., €16 per 2hr; 2-person €10/15/25; 3-person €12/18/30. 🕐 Open June 15-Sept 15 daily 9am-8pm.

Surfing

⚜ PUKAS

Av. de Zurriola, 24   ☎94 332 00 68 www.pukassurfeskola.com

This is the Playa de Zurriola's go-to spot for surf gear, rentals, and lessons; in a world of slackers, these guys are pros. Try to get three other novices and go for a 3hr. group lesson over a weekend (€53), or if you're more experienced, rent a board for a day (€25).

⌖ *On Av. Zurriola across from the surf beach.* ⓘ *Passport and credit (not debit) card required for rentals. Other locations in the parte vieja at C. Mayor, 5, and in Zarautz.* Ⓢ *Surfboards €10 per hr., €15 per 2hr., €17 per 4hr., €25 per day. Wetsuit rental €5 per hr., €7 per 2hr., €8 per 4hr., €12 per day. Private surf lessons €52 per hr. (includes surfboard, wetsuit, and insurance). Optional accident insurance €2.50.* ⏲ *Open M-F 10:30am-2pm and 4-8pm, Sa 10am-2pm and 4-8pm, Su 10am-2pm.*

FOOD

Foodies the world over know San Sebastián for its outstanding culinary reputation. But you don't have to go to **Arzak** (average price €175 per person) to have some of the best meals of your life, albeit in very small portions. The city's best **tapas bars** are all reasonably affordable and are mostly found in the *parte vieja*, especially along **Calle del 31 de Agosto** and **Calle de Fermín Calbetón.** Many restaurants tend to be concentrated in this area as well, but for better prices (and, often, better food) check out the restaurants in **Gros** to the east of the river, particularly on Paseo de Colón. Those looking to do some exploring can search for hidden gems in the not-yet-gentrified **Egia** neighborhood.

⚜ GARRAXI   VEGETARIAN $$

C. de la Tejería, 9   ☎94 327 52 69

While omnivores will have no issues eating their way through San Sebastián's incredible culinary offerings, some vegetarians may feel a bit left out amid all the *jamón* and *mariscos*. For those adventurous enough to trek away from the Cantabrian coast and into the Egia neighborhood, there's a vegetarian option that's right up there with the best of the restaurants in the *parte vieja* and Gros. The inexpensive food at this laid-back restaurant is so delicious that even the most ardent meat eater won't notice its absence. The *bolitas de patatas y cebollas* (potato and onion balls, €6.50) are the best-tasting misshapen *latkes* you'll ever eat, and they're served in a curry sauce that gives them a little kick that will send you straight to veggie heaven.

⌖ *From the parte vieja, cross the Puente de Zurriola into the Gros neighborhood and turn right onto Paseo Ramón María Lili, then at the Pl. Euskadi take the far left onto C. Iztueta, which bends to the right and becomes Paseo Duque de Mandas. Next, turn left at C. Egia, then take a left again onto C. San Cristóbal for 1 block.* Ⓢ *Menú del día (M-F 1-3:30pm) €11, without dessert €8.50; menú degustación (weeknights and weekends) €15.50 per person. Entrees €4-9.* ⏲ *Open M-W 1-3:30pm and 8-10:30pm, Th-F 1-3:30pm and 8:30-11pm, Sa 1:30-3:30pm and 8:30-11pm, Su 1:30-3:30pm and 8-10:30pm.*

LA ZURRI   BASQUE $$

C. de Zabaleta, 9   ☎94 329 38 86

Spend too much time in the *parte vieja* and you might start to think that the two languages of bilingual San Sebastián are French and English, and that locals subsist solely on *pintxos*. This restaurant across the river in Gros will prove you wrong on both counts; there are plenty of locals here chatting away in Spanish or reading their Basque newspapers while chowing down on the cheap but well prepared *menú del día* that reads like a who's who of traditional Basque cuisine. Solo travelers take note: the place can get so busy that they might put you at a table with another rando flying solo.

⌖ *From Pl. Euskadi in Gros, with your back to the river, turn left onto the Paseo Colón, then take the 2nd left onto C. Zabaleta.* Ⓢ *Menú del día €10.80.* ⏲ *Open M-Sa 1-3:30pm.*

san sebastián

A FUEGO NEGRO TAPAS $$$

C. del 31 de Agosto, 31 ☎65 013 53 73 www.afuegonegro.com

This place knows how to do tapas with some 'tude. The young owner fancies himself a bit of a gastronomic bad boy, having trained at elite cooking schools but spurning the city's fancy restaurant scene to bring haute cuisine to the people. At this calculatedly edgy bar, funk, reggae, and rebellious hip hop rule the night. Despite the owner's noble intentions, the *pintxos* are still a bit pricier than elsewhere (€3.20-3.70), but they are completely worth it. The half-dollar-sized "MakCobe" served with banana chips (€3.70) is probably the best hamburger you'll ever have, if certainly the smallest; the olives with vermouth and the rabbit with garlic are also highly recommended. The youthful energy draws a young crowd of locals and tourists, some of whom are willing to shell out for the *degustación* menus (€35-45) but most of whom are just looking for a place to have a drink and a *pintxo* or two. *Let's Go* recommends leaving the beer for another night; the mouth-watering tapas go down best with *txakoli*, a Basque white wine.

➜ From Alameda del Boulevard, turn right onto C. Mayor, then take the 4th right onto C. 31 de Agosto. Ⓢ Pintxos €3.20-3.70. Wine by the glass €1.80-3.80. Cider by the bottle €6. Cocktails €7. ⏰ Bar open Tu-Th and Su 11:30am-12:30am, F-Sa 11:30am-1:30am. Kitchen open Tu-Su 12:30-4pm and 8-11pm.

CASA ALCALDE TAPAS $$

C. Mayor, 19 ☎94 342 62 16

This bar proves that even in the priciest part of an expensive town like San Sebastián, there can be good, affordable *pintxos*. The bar is so covered with plates you'll be surprised it's still standing; ask the bartender for a plate of your own (a clean one, mind you) and start hunting for the tapas with *champiñones y queso* (mushrooms and cheese) or *txangurro* (crab). The walls of the often noisy bar are lined with turn-of-the-century bullfighting posters.

➜ From Alameda del Boulevard, turn right onto C. Mayor Ⓢ Pintxos €1.75-2.50. Beer €2.30. ⏰ Open daily 11am-11pm.

CAMPERO SANDWICHES $

Paseo de José Miguel Barandiarán, 8 ☎94 327 14 95

Come here for inexpensive, filling sandwiches right across from the Playa de Zurriola. If you're all tuckered out from a day of surfing or sunscreen-applying, leave your dictionary on the beach and just order by number. The "Campero" sandwich (ham, cheese, lettuce, sautéed onions, tomato, *alioli;* €3.50) will fill you up for the whole afternoon. They also have burgers, pasta dishes, and traditional sides like *patatas bravas.*

➜ At the edge of the Playa de Zurriola farthest away from the parte vieja, across the street from the basketball courts. ℹ Terrace supplement €0.50. Dogs welcome. Ⓢ Sandwiches €3-6.50. ⏰ Open M-Th 12:30-11pm, F-Sa 12:30pm-midnight, Su 12:30-11pm. Bar open M-F 9am and Sa-Su 11am.

CARAVANSERAI CAFE CAFE $$

Pl. del Buen Pastor ☎94 347 54 18

If you're in the neighborhood and need something quick (or just miss good french fries), stop in at this cafe next to the cathedral. They also have a whole page of vegetarian options, and their open-all-day kitchen is a rare source of nutrition when the city becomes a barren food wasteland during the *siesta.*

➜ In Pl. Buen Pastor, to the right of the cathedral. ℹ Free Wi-Fi. Terrace supplement €0.70. Ⓢ Entrees €6-13. Beer €2.45-3. Wine by the glass €1.35-2. ⏰ Open M-Th 8am-midnight, F-Sa 8am-1am, Su 10:30am-midnight.

EL CASERIO BASQUE $$

C. de San Jerónimo, 16 ☎94 342 15 93 www.restaurantecaserio.com

Yes, like most moderately affordable sit-down restaurants in the *parte vieja*, this place is pretty touristy, but that decent all-day *menú* is a godsend for the ravenous traveler looking to fill up on the cheap during the evening without going through the ritual of tapas hopping. Based on the speed of the service, it sometimes feels like the wait staff is hitting up a few bars in between courses, but when each course finally comes, you're likely to be satisfied. If you've been putting off trying the Basque specialty of *txipirones en su tinta* (cuttlefish in their own ink), this is a great place to go for it; the meaty cuttlefish in their pitch-black ink are served alongside perfectly white rice (no prizes for guessing which color wins when you mix the two.)

� From Alameda del Boulevard, turn into the parte vieja onto C. San Jerónimo. Ⓢ Menú del día €15 (served all day). Entrees €8-20. ☑ Open daily 12:30-4pm and 7:30-11pm.

NIGHTLIFE

The most tourist-frequented nightlife scene in San Sebastián is unsurprisingly in the **parte vieja,** where the bars that served noisy tapas in the afternoon become bars that serve even noisier drinks at night. Each bar is pretty much the same as the next, but a few have their own distinct character. Some of the most prominent (and tourist-filled) nightclubs are located near the beaches, on Paseo de Zurriola and Paseo de La Concha. The nightlife options listed here are a little less obvious to the average tourist and are slightly farther off the beaten track.

▓ **ETXEKALTE**   BAR, CLUB
C. de Mari, 11   ☎94 342 69 25
This popular nighttime hotspot on the western limit of the *parte vieja* has two completely different sides. The ground floor, where most of the action (though there's not that much of it) tends to take place during the *entre semana* (midweek), has a pub-like feel and plays jazz. The place explodes on Thursday through Saturday nights, however, when there's a DJ spinning in the basement club, and the party doesn't end until just before dawn.

✝ Take Alameda del Boulevard west to the bay, then turn right onto C. Mari. Ⓢ Beer €2.20. Vino tinto €2.50. Mixed drinks €6-9. ☑ Open Tu-Th 6pm-4am, F-Sa 6pm-5am, Su 6pm-4am.

LE BUKOWSKI   BAR, CLUB
C. Egia, 18   www.lebukowski.com
Six or seven years ago, this was the center of San Sebastián's punk scene. It's unclear whether the punks have disappeared or simply migrated to still warmer climes, but today it's more of a hipster hangout, with live music Friday and Saturday nights most of the year.

✝ From the parte vieja, cross the Puente de Zurriola into the Gros neighborhood and turn right onto Paseo Ramón María Lili, then at the Pl. Euskadi take the far left onto C. Iztueta, which bends to the right and becomes Paseo Duque de Mandas. Turn left onto C. Egia. ⓘ Live music Sept-June. Ⓢ Beer €2. Cocktails €6-7. ☑ Open M-Th 7pm-2am, F-Sa 8pm-4am.

ALTXERRI   BAR, LIVE MUSIC
C. de la Reina Regente, 2   ☎94 342 16 93 www.baraltxerri.blogspot.com.es
One of the more relaxed places to spend a weekend evening in San Sebastián, this bar's bread and butter is jazz concerts, though you'll also hear soul, funk, and folk from time to time, and—if you're lucky—an ▓**erotic poetry reading.**

✝ On C. Reina Regente in the parte vieja, just off of the Puente de Zurriola from Gros. Ⓢ Cover free to €12. Beer €2.50. ☑ Open Tu-Th 5pm-2am, F-Sa 5pm-3am, Su 5pm-2am.

THE CALEDONIAN   BAR
Paseo de Colón, 27   ☎94 328 20 16
Although this bar's Scottish decor is a far cry from a traditional Basque vibe, it's one of the liveliest and biggest bars in the Gros neighborhood, filled with locals and tourists alike. There is a pool table, darts, and a wide selection of beers,

and despite being across the river, it's easily within stumbling distance from the bars and hotels of the *parte vieja*.

From the parte vieja, cross the river and proceed along Av. Zurriola, turn right onto C. Gran Vía, and then turn right onto Paseo Colón. $ Beer €2.50-4. Mixed drinks €6.50. ⏰ Open M-Th 2pm-4:30am, F-Sa 2pm-6:30am.

BE BOP BAR BAR, CLUB

Paseo de Salamanca, 3 ☎94 342 98 69

Before 2am, the place is not terribly thrilling, but once the *parte vieja* competition closes, the place fills up with tourists and a few locals (usually at 2:15am sharp). A few nights a month there are jazz and blues concerts, but the music is normally commercial, with some old favorites as well. Word to the wise: stand clear of the Alabaman tourists when "Sweet Home Alabama" comes on if you don't want two and a half beers knocked on your lap in unbridled excitement.

*On the Paseo Salamanca in the parte vieja, along the river. **i** Live jazz/blues concerts every 1-2 weeks. Bouncer may not let you in if it's too crowded and you don't look like the type of person he wants to let in (i.e., female), so get there before it fills up. $ Beer €2.20. Cocktails €6.50-7. ⏰ Open M-Th 3:30pm-5am, F-Sa 3:30pm-6am, Su 3:30pm-5am.*

basque country

FESTIVALS

INTERNATIONAL FILM FESTIVAL GROS

Av. de Zurriola, 1 www.sansebastianfestival.com

For a week in September every year since 1953, the international film scene has descended on San Sebastián for its annual film festival. Directors from around the world submit their films in competition for the Golden Shell, the festival's top prize. You can shell out the big bucks to attend the festival, or just admire the celebrities from afar. Better yet, get a couple of friends to crowd around you and take pictures, and see how long it takes before the real paparazzi start calling your name and stealing shots of you.

Ticket sales and most events at the Kursaal (Av. de Zurriola, 1). $ Most screenings €6.30-8; tickets for awards ceremonies and galas €60-250. ⏰ Sept.; exact dates change annually.

JAZZALDIA CITYWIDE

Select venues throughout the city ☎94 348 19 00 www.heinekenjazzaldia.com

San Sebastián's annual jazz festival takes place in late July, with performances at venues including the Teatro Victoria Eugenia, the Plaza de la Trinidad, and Kursaal Auditorium. Concerts at the historic Pl. Trinidad have an amazing atmosphere (especially at night) and shouldn't be missed; those with street-side rooms at Pensión Amaiur (see **Accommodations**) have a particularly impressive view.

The Teatro Victoria Eugenia is the opulent building off of the parte vieja side of the Puente de Zurriola; the Pl. Trinidad is at the far north end of the parte vieja; Kursaal Auditorium is the large, modern, silver building just across the Puente de Zurriola in Gros. $ Tickets for 3-4 shows €29-104. ⏰ Late July.

SEMANA GRANDE CITYWIDE

www.donostia.org

This week of festivities occurs during the third week of August and is marked by spectacular displays of fireworks and 15ft. tall puppets.

i *See schedule at www.donostia.org for times and locations.*

ESSENTIALS

Practicalities

- **TOURIST OFFICE:** The only tourist office is located just outside the parte vieja (Alameda del Boulevard, 8 ☎94 348 11 66 www.sansebastianturismo.com *i* Spanish, Basque, English, and French spoken. ⏰ Open June 18-Sept 23 M-Sa 9am-8pm, Su and holidays 10am-7pm; Sept 24-June 17 M-Th 9am-1:30pm and 3:30-7pm, F-Sa 10am-7pm, Su and holidays 10am-2pm.
- **TOURS:** The tourist office offers three walking tours. **San Sebastián Esencial** visits major sights of the city. (*i* Bilingual tours in Spanish and English; tours also available in Spanish only and Spanish and French. $ €10, under 12 free. ⏰ 2hr., Spanish-English tours July-Aug daily 4:30pm; Sept-June first F of month and most Sa 4:30pm, Su 11:30am.) **Flavors of San Sebastián** visits three *pintxo* bars and includes three *pintxos* and three drinks. (*i* Bilingual tours in Spanish and English. $ €18. Oct-Apr 50% discount for second person. ⏰ 2hr., July-Aug Tu and Th 11:30am; Sept-Jan and Apr-June approximately every other Sa 11:30am.) **San Sebastián: A Film City** visits cinema-related sights and includes a *pintxo* and a drink. (*i* Bilingual tours in Spanish and English. $ €14. Oct-Apr 50% discount for 2nd person. ⏰ 2hr., July-Aug W and F 11:30am; Sept-June 2-4 per month, call for dates.) Tour reservations can be made by calling ☎94 321 77 17 or at www.sansebastianreservas.com.
- **CURRENCY EXCHANGE: Banco Santander** exchanges major foreign currencies. (Av. Libertad, 31 ☎94 341 58 00 www.bancosantander.es 🚶 From end of Alameda del Boulevard closest to the Ayuntamiento, turn left onto C. Hernani; the bank is at the intersection with Av. Libertad. ⏰ Open M-F 8:30am-2:30pm.)
- **LUGGAGE STORAGE:** There is no luggage storage at the bus or train stations, but some *locutorios* will store suitcases, including **Locutorio Navi.net.** (C. Fermín Calbetón, 11 ☎94 344 00 66 🚶 In the *parte vieja,* between C. Narrica and C. San Juan. $ Less than 5 hr. €3, more than 5hr. €5 per day. ⏰ Open M-Th 10am-10pm, F 10am-midnight, Sa 11am-midnight, Su 10am-10pm.)
- **INTERNET ACCESS:** Computers with 45min. of free internet access are available at the **Biblioteca Municipal Central.** (Parque de Alderdi Eder ☎94 348 14 88 🚶 Down the flight of stairs in front of the Ayuntamiento. $ Wi-Fi €1 per day. ⏰ Library open M-F 10am-8:30pm, Sa 10am-2pm and 4:30-8pm. Computers login desk open M-Sa 10am-2pm and 4-8pm.)
- **POST OFFICE:** The main post office is right behind the Cathedral. (C. Urdaneta, ☎94 344 68 26 www.correos.es ⏰ Open M-F 8:30am-8:30pm, Sa 9:30am-2pm.)
- **POSTAL CODE:** 20006

Emergency

- **EMERGENCY NUMBERS:** General ☎112. Fire ☎080.
- **POLICE:** Municipal police. (C. Easo, 41 ☎092 or ☎94 345 00 00 🚶 Walk on Av. Libertad toward the beach and turn left at the end of the street onto C. Easo.)
- **MEDICAL SERVICES: Hospital Donostia.** (Paseo Dr. Beguiristain ☎94 300 70 00 www.hospitaldonostia.org 🚶 Bus #28, 31, 35, or 37.)
- **LATE-NIGHT PHARMACY:** Look in the window of any pharmacy for a list of pharmacies open outside of regular pharmacy hours.

Getting There

BY BUS

The easiest and cheapest way to get to San Sebastián from any nearby city is by **bus.** The bus station (C. Arquitectos Kortázar, 1 🚶 Between Pl. Pío XII and the river) is essentially an unstaffed parking lot; the ticket offices are located a block away along Avenida de Sancho "El Sabio." It's a decent walk from the center of town, on the south side of the city, but the #21, 26, and 28 buses run from the bus station to Alameda del Boulevard. **Vibasa** (www.vibasa.com) runs buses from Barcelona. ($ €31-36 ⏰ 5½-7hr.; M-F 4 per day 7am-10:15pm, Sa 3 per day 7am-10:15pm, Su 4 per day 7am-11:15pm.) **ALSA** (☎90 242 22 42 www.alsa.es) runs buses to San Sebastián from: Bilbao ($ €6.20 ⏰ 1-2hr.; M-F 11 per day 5:15am-10pm, Sa 10 per day 5:15am-10pm, Su 8 per day 5:15am-10pm); Burgos ($ €17 ⏰ 2½-3½hr.; M-Sa 8 per day 6:45am-3:15am, Su 6 per day 10:30am-3:15am); Gijón ($ €27-53 ⏰ 5¼-8hr., 6 per day 7:15am-12:14am); Madrid ($ €34-49 ⏰ 5¼-6hr.; M-Th 10 per day 7:30am-12:30am, F 12 per day 7:30am-12:30am, Sa 9 per day 7:30am-12:30am, Su 11 per day 7:30am-12:30am); Pamplona ($ €7.30 ⏰ 1-2hr.; M-Th 12 per day 7am-9:15pm, F 16 per day 7am-9:15pm, Sa 12 per day 7am-9:15pm, Su 14 per day 7am-9:15pm); Salamanca ($ €33 ⏰ 7-8½hr.; M-Sa 2 per day noon and 2:45pm, Su 3:30pm); Santander ($ €13-27 ⏰ 2½-3¾hr.; M-Sa 10 per day 6am-3:45am, Su 9 per day 7am-3:45am); and Santiago de Compostela ($ €61 ⏰ 12¾-13½hr., 2 per day 8:30am and 6pm).

BY TRAIN

San Sebastián has two train stations: the regional **EuskoTren station** on the western bank of the Río Urumea (Pl. Easo, 9 ☎90 254 32 10 ⇞ From the beach, walk 8 blocks on C. Easo) and the long-distance **RENFE station** on the eastern bank (Paseo de Francia, 22 ☎90 243 23 43 ⇞ Across the Puente de María Cristina). EuskoTren (☎90 254 32 10 www.euskotren.es) runs trains from Bilbao. ($ €5.10. ⏰ 2½hr.; M-F 31 per day 6am-10:30pm, Sa-Su 18-23 per day 7am-8:34pm.) RENFE (☎90 210 94 20 www.renfe.es) has trains from: Barcelona ($ €38-63 ⏰ 5½hr., 2 per day 7:35am and 3:30pm); Burgos ($ €15-29 ⏰ 3hr., 6 per day 10:23am-3:19am); Madrid ($ €27-76 ⏰ 5½-7½hr., 6 per day 7:30am-4:05pm); Salamanca ($ €36 ⏰ 6hr., 4 per day 7:25am-12:35am); and Zaragoza ($ €19-31 ⏰ 3½hr., 2 per day 9:34am and 5:29pm).

BY PLANE

Flights arrive at the **Aeropuerto de San Sebastián** in Hondarribia (EAS; ☎91 321 10 00 www.aena.es), 15mi. east of San Sebastián, from Madrid and Barcelona year-round and from other destinations like Palma de Mallorca during the summer. Ekialdebus (☎94 349 18 01 www.ekialdebus.net) buses #20, 21, 23, 27, 28, and 77 run from the airport to San Sebastián approx. every 30min. ($ €1.40-1.95). A taxi to the airport costs about €30.

Getting Around

BY BUS

The best way to get around San Sebastián is to **walk,** though for really long trips the **city bus system** (☎94 300 02 00 www.dbus.es $ €1.45) is fast and efficient. Buses #21, 26, and 28 go from the bus station to the Alameda del Boulevard next to the *parte vieja*. There is a second bus system, **Lurraldebus** (☎94 300 01 17 www.lurraldebus.net $ €1-4), whose routes go to the smaller towns outside San Sebastián.

BY BIKE

Bikes are another popular way to get around, and there are many designated bike lanes. Rent one at **Bici Rent Donosti.** (Av. Zurriola, 22 ☎63 901 60 13 www.bicirentdonosti.es ⇞ Across from the Playa de Zurriola. $ €4 per hr., €13 per 4hr., €17 per day. ⏰ Open daily 9:30am-8:15pm.)

BY TAXI

The **taxi** companies are Taxi Donosti (☎94 346 46 46 www.taxidonosti.com) and Vallina Teletaxi (☎94 340 40 40 www.vallinagrupo.com).

pamplona *iruña* ☎948

If people know one thing about Pamplona (pop. 200,000), it's the **Running of the Bulls.** If they know two things about Pamplona, they are the **Running of the Bulls** and the **earth-shattering week of partying** that accompanies it. Hemingway may have made this town famous in *The Sun Also Rises*, but Pamplona has had no trouble keeping itself in the headlines. The week of *los Sanfermines* (July 6-14) fills the city to the gills with revelers, and the high demand leads to skyrocketing prices.

Pamplona gets its name from the Roman general Pompey, who is said to have founded the town in the first century BCE, after which it grew and developed under the Romans and later the Visigoths. Despite its Roman history, though, Pamplona has a strong sense of its **Basque heritage:** almost all public signage in Pamplona (*Iruña* in Basque) is in both *castellano* and Basque (*euskera*). Heavily fortified Pamplona has

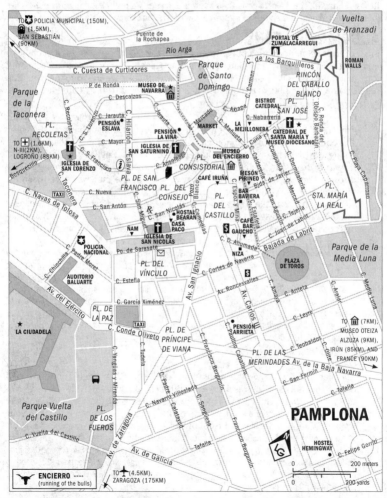

been a border city since the eighth century, caught between various Iberian kingdoms, France, and Spain. Since the Middle Ages, the Camino de Santiago has connected Pamplona with the rest of Europe across the Pyrenees and has kept it economically and culturally prosperous. The *casco antiguo* and nearby areas are largely tourist-oriented, but are still heavily frequented by locals, especially in the low season.

ORIENTATION

Most of the action in Pamplona takes place to the south and west of the Río Arga and to the east of the city's large parks (**la Ciudadela** and Parque de la Taconera). At the north end of this action-packed area is the *casco antiguo*, the old quarter, which has narrow streets lined with shops, bars, and plazas. The **Catedral** is in the *casco*'s northeast corner; the massive ✓**Plaza del Castillo** is in the center at the south end. The wide, pedestrian Av. Carlos III runs from the southern end of the Pl. Castillo to the **segundo ensanche,** an urban zone certainly newer than the *casco*, but not without its own charm. The **Avenida de la Baja Navarra** is the city's main thoroughfare and cuts east-west through the *segundo ensanche*, with the **bus station** at its western end.

ACCOMMODATIONS

Most of the accommodations in Pamplona are in the *casco antiguo*, though cheaper and quieter places can be found in the **segundo ensanche.** There's no need to fret about long distances; the city's small enough so that no matter where you stay, you'll be bar-hopping and tripping over cobblestones in the *casco antiguo* in no time.

✓ **HOSTEL HEMINGWAY** HOSTEL $

C. Amaya, 26, 1st fl. ☎94 898 38 84 www.hostelhemingway.com

Traveling alone and looking for a group to go tapas-tasting or bar-hopping with? The communal spaces at Pamplona's only hostel create instant bonds among the young crowds that stay here, facilitated by the fact that English was Hemingway's *lingua franca.* The hostel was opened in 2009 by three young friends traveling through Pamplona who realized there wasn't a hostel in town save those for pilgrims and decided to open their own. The shared bedrooms aren't exactly spacious, and it's in the *segundo ensanche*, a short walk from the *casco antiguo*, but the free breakfast and camaraderie among guests and hosts more than make up for it. Sandwiched in between two supermarkets, it's easy for budget travelers staying here to cook their own food in the communal kitchen.

 # Upon exiting the bus station, turn left and walk ½ block to Pl. Paz, then turn right and proceed along Av. Conde Oliveto, which will become Av. Baja Navarra. The street will pass through 2 traffic circles; after the 2nd circle (Pl. Merindades), take the 1st right onto C. Amaya. Or, from the train station, take bus #9 to C. Amaya, 22. ***i*** *Breakfast included. Laundry €3 wash, €4 dry. Kitchen available. All rooms with shared bath. Computers with internet €0.50 per 15min., €1.50 per hr. €10 deposit for key.* [$] *6-bed dorms €19, 4-bed €20; singles €35; doubles €42-44. M-Th and Su €15 for pilgrims with accreditation. During los Sanfermines (July 6-14), 6-bed dorms €65, 4-bed €70; doubles €150-160. Bike rental €3 per 2hr., €5 per 4hr.* ⏰ *Reception 8am-midnight.*

PENSIÓN LA VIÑA HOTEL $

C. de Jarauta, 8, 1st fl. ☎94 821 32 50

The blue of the walls and the linens subtly evoke the €20 bill you'd normally shell out for rooms as spacious as the ones at this *pensión* on a relatively quiet street in the *casco antiguo*. Though most of the rooms share a bath, the hotel has one of the best space-to-price ratios in all of Pamplona. If you're looking to keep up with your *telenovela*, though, you might be out of luck—only some of the rooms have TVs.

 # Upon exiting the bus station, turn left onto C. Yangüas y Miranda. Take the 3rd right after the traffic circle (Pl. Paz) onto the Paseo de Sarasate, then the 1st left onto C. San Miguel. Cross the Pl. San Francisco and walk 2 blocks on C. Eslava, then turn right onto C. Jarauta. ***i*** *Some rooms with TV. Shared bath.* [$] *Singles €15; doubles €30, with private bath €35. During los Sanfermines (July 6-14), €50 per person per day.* ⏰ *Reception 24hr.*

PENSIÓN ESLAVA
HOTEL $

C. de Hilarión Eslava, 13, 1st fl.   ☎94 822 15 58 www.pensioneslava.es

This cheap *pensión* has rooms that provide the basics and not much else: beds, closets, and windows. Some rooms come with a sink, while others have balconies looking onto one of the few relatively quiet streets in the *casco antiguo*. The old woman running the place might seem unfriendly at first, but get her talking about Navarra's wine fountain and she'll soften up in no time. There aren't many rooms, so be sure to reserve in advance during the summer.

✚ *Upon exiting the bus station, turn left onto C. Yangüas y Miranda. Take the 3rd right after the traffic circle (Pl. Paz) onto the Paseo de Sarasate, then the 1st left onto C. San Miguel. Cross the Pl. San Francisco and walk 2 blocks on C. Eslava. It's at the end of the block, on the left.* **i** *Shared baths.* ⑤ *Singles €15; doubles €30. During los Sanfermines (July 6-14), singles €50-80; doubles €100-160.* ⌚ *Reception 8am-midnight. During los Sanfermines (July 6-14) 24hr.*

PENSIÓN ARRIETA
HOTEL $$

C. de Arrieta, 27, 1st fl.   ☎94 822 84 59 www.pensionarrieta.net

Though it's located a few blocks out of the *casco antiguo* in a more modern part of town, this *pensión* is close to both the wide pedestrian Av. Carlos III and the bus station. The rooms are fairly large and the white walls amplify the light that comes in from the windows, so it's best to close the shades during your daytime *siesta*.

✚ *Upon exiting the bus station, turn left and walk ½ block to Pl. Paz, then turn right and proceed along Av. Conde Oliveto, which will become Av. Baja Navarra. After the traffic circle (Pl. Príncipe de Viana), take the 2nd left onto C. Paulino Caballero, then the 1st right onto C. Arrieta. Or, from Pl. Castillo, proceed 3 blocks along Av. Carlos III, then turn right onto C. Arrieta.* **i** *Free Wi-Fi. TV. Shared bath.* ⑤ *Singles €30; doubles €40-45, with private bath €50; triples €55. During los Sanfermines (July 6-14), singles not available; doubles €145; triples €195.* ⌚ *Reception 24hr.*

HOSTAL BEARAN
HOTEL $$$$

C. de San Nicolás, 25   ☎94 822 34 28

This *hostal* is a touch pricey, but you're paying for the convenient location in the heart of the *casco antiguo*, one block from Pl. Castillo and on the bar-packed C. San Nicolás. For those considering sleeping a little on the weekend, the spacious double with a couch facing a quiet interior patio might be a better choice, especially considering the alternative: a double with a balcony overlooking the busiest street in town after the sun goes down.

✚ *Upon exiting the bus station, turn left onto C. Yangüas y Miranda. Take the 4th right after the traffic circle (Pl. Paz) onto C. San Gregorio, which will turn into C. San Nicolás.* **i** *Free Wi-Fi. Private bath with hairdryer. TV. Bicycle storage. Safe deposit box rental €2 per day.* ⑤ *July 1-July 15 singles €116, doubles €130, triples €180; July 16-Sept 30 singles €45, doubles €50, triples €65; Oct 1-June 30 singles €38, doubles €45, triples €55.* ⌚ *Reception 9am-9pm.*

CAMPING EZCABA
CAMPING $

Carretera Pamplona-Irún   ☎94 833 03 15 www.campingezcaba.com

If you're willing to camp out and take a bus or bike, consider camping north of town to avoid Pamplona's exorbitant prices during *los Sanfermines* (July 6-14). The lodging is cheap, and the views of the hills that separate the campsite from Pamplona are stunning. Despite its distance from the *plaza de toros*, the festive atmosphere of *Las Fiestas de San Fermín* makes it all the way out to Ezcaba.

✚ *Take city bus 4V (20min.) from Pl. Merindades (intersection of Av. Baja Navarra and Av. Carlos III, the side farther away from Pl. Castillo) to Oricáin, the last stop. Walk along Ctra. Irún (N-121a) about ½mi., then turn left onto Ctra. Berriosuso (NA-4210) another ½mi.; entrance is up the hill on the right. Taxis approx. €15 each way.* **i** *Showers, laundry service, pool, restaurant, game room. Reservations not accepted.* ⑤ *€5.75, children €5; electricity €5. During los Sanfermines (July 6-14), €12.50, children €11; electricity €11.* ⌚ *Reception 8am-midnight, but can arrive at any time.*

SIGHTS

Pamplona's *casco antiguo* is home to most of the city's sights. The northeast corner of the *casco*, by the cathedral, is one of the most beautiful areas of the town. Don't miss the **Pl. Consistorial,** with its unbelievably florid **city hall,** from whose balcony a rocket is fired to signal the beginning of *los Sanfermines.*

CATEDRAL DE SANTA MARÍA Y MUSEO DIOCESANO CHURCH

C. Dormitalería, 3-5 ☎94 821 25 94 www.catedraldepamplona.com

This Gothic cathedral was built over the course of the 15th century on and around the ruins of its 12th-century Romanesque predecessor, whose pantry still stands. The dining room next door is devoid of eats but full of artwork from the 12th to 19th centuries; look at the left side of the Flemish altarpiece at the end of the room to see a priest rocking some awesome 15th-century specs. The two-story cloister is considered one of Europe's most beautiful, though it hides a dark secret: the numbers on the massive stones that make up the floor correspond to the tombs beneath them.

From Pl. Castillo, with your back to the Palacio del Gobierno (with the flags), turn right onto C. Bajada de Javier, then take the 3rd left onto C. Dormitalería. ***i*** *Free information pamphlet with helpful map and lots of pictures, available in English.* $ *€5, pilgrims €3, under 7 free. Free access to the cathedral 9:30-10:30am during mass.* ⏰ *Open Mar 15-Nov 15 M-Sa 10:30am-6pm, Nov 16-Mar 14 M-Sa 10:30am-5pm.*

LA CIUDADELA PARK, HISTORIC SITE

Av. del Ejército ☎94 842 09 75

What would you do if you had an unused medieval fortress half the size of the *casco antiguo* just sitting around? If you were Pamplona, you'd make it a public park. *La Ciudadela*'s towering stone fortifications are now bombarded not with cannonballs, but with soccer balls headed into them from pickup games on the park's expansive grassy fields. It's a great place to lounge during the *siesta,* and unlike many public parks, the bathrooms are not fodder for future nightmares; they're actually probably cleaner and more luxurious than the bathroom at your *hostal.*

From Pl. Castillo, take Paseo de Sarasate to C. Taconera, then left onto C. Chinchilla; the entrance is on the other side of Av. Ejército. $ *Free.* ⏰ *Park open M-F 7:30am-9:30pm, Sa 8am-9:30pm, Su and holidays 9am-9:30pm. Rotating art exhibits open June-Sept Tu-F 6:30-9pm, Sa noon-2pm and 6:30-9pm, Su noon-2pm; Oct-May Tu-F 6-8:30pm, Sa noon-2pm and 6-8:30pm, Su and holidays noon-2pm.*

MUSEO DE NAVARRA MUSEUM

C. de Santo Domingo, 47 ☎84 842 64 92 www.cfnavarra.es/cultura/museo

Art-lovers beware: do not try to come to this museum during the Running of the Bulls, or you'll be in for a rude shock—namely, the bulls charging up a hill at you as you take out your camera for a snapshot of the museum's 16th-century Plateresque façade. This museum, perched atop a hill on the street that marks the first stretch of the *encierro*, is most proud of its Goya portrait and a small but microscopically detailed Muslim ivory chest from 1004. The fairly well-preserved Gothic murals, especially the magnificent *Pasión de Cristo* (1330) are worth visiting as well; once you've seen them, head upstairs for a 16th-century Hispano-Flemish triptych of the same scene. On the same floor, pay no attention to the still life of dead fish in the room otherwise filled with saints, angels, and God (Father and Son).

 # From Pl. Castillo, with your back to the Palacio del Gobierno (with the flags), cross the plaza diagonally and proceed 1 block on C. Chapitela, then turn left into the Pl. Consistorial. Proceed down C. Santo Domingo (to the left of the Casa Consistorial); the museum is at the end of the block. ***i*** *Signs in Spanish only. Lectures open to the public most Tuesdays. Temporary exhibits change every few months.* $ *€2; students €1; under 18, over 65, and pilgrims free. Free admission Sa 5-7pm and Su.* ⏰ *Open Tu-Sa 9:30am-2pm and 5-7pm, Su and holidays 11am-2pm.*

IGLESIA SAN LORENZO CHURCH

C. Mayor, 74 ☎94 822 53 71

It's easy to forget amongst the constant flow of alcohol and adrenaline, but *la Fiesta de San Fermín* is a religious festival, and the Capilla de San Fermín at the Iglesia San Lorenzo is where it all begins. This is the starting point of the procession in honor of San Fermín, whose 16th-century effigy can be found in a chapel inside.

 # From Pl. Castillo, with the Palacio del Gobierno (with the flags) on your left, proceed straight along the Paseo de Sarasate, then take the 4th right onto C. Taconera. Church entrance will be at the intersection with C. Mayor. ***i*** *Be sure to be quiet while entering, as religious services may be taking place.* $ *Free.* ⏰ *Open M-Sa 8am-12:30pm and 5:30-8:30pm, Su 8:30am-1:45pm and 5:30-8pm; during los Sanfermines (July 6-14), open daily 8:30am-1:30pm and 5-9pm.*

MUSEO DEL ENCIERRO MUSEUM

C. de los Mercaderes, 17 ☎94 822 54 13 www.museoencierro.com

Once you embrace how touristy it all is and stomach the hefty admission price, this museum dedicated to the Running of the Bulls can be pretty fun. The light-up scale model of the path of the *encierro*, the stuffed bulls from years past, and the history section are all fine, but they're pretty clearly just filler for the simulator, where, with the help of 3D video-game-like graphics, a treadmill, and a lively imagination, you, too, can run with the bulls. Thankfully, the worst that can happen here is a temporary inversion of the screen.

 # From Pl. Castillo, with the Palacio del Gobierno (with the flags) on your left, turn right onto C. Bajada del Javier, then take the 1st left onto C. Estafeta; at the end of the street, turn left onto C. Mercaderes. ***i*** *Mandatory guided tours in Spanish, English, French, and Italian; groups must call ahead.* $ *€8; students, pilgrims, and 65+ €6; under 5 free. Call for prices during los Sanfermines (July 6-14).* ⏰ *Open July-Sept Tu-Sa 10am-2pm and 4-8pm, Su 10am-2pm; Oct-June Tu-Sa 11am-2pm and 4-7pm, Su 11am-2pm; during los Sanfermines (July 6-14), Jul 6 closed, Jul 7-14 open daily 10:30am-3pm and 4-6:30pm.*

FOOD

CAFÉ BAR GAUCHO CAFE, BAR $$$

Travesía Espoz y Mina, 4 ☎94 822 50 73 www.cafebargaucho.com

This bar claims to serve "the great cuisine of Navarra in miniature," and its award-winning *pintxos* are so good you'll wish they'd scrap the "miniature" part. You'll pay a bit more here than at most of the nearby establishments, but it's worth it for a taste of the *crêpe de espinacas y gambas* (crepe with spinach and shrimp) or the *anguila ahumada con gelatina de tomate* (smoked eel with gelatinized tomato). At night, the fairly small bar's seats fill up and many people take their *pintxos* into the narrow street outside, often with a glass of wine or the house drink, a generously poured gin and tonic (€6). If you just can't get enough of the tasty food, the recipe book is available for purchase (€20), but Cup-a-Soup cooks need not apply—they don't call these complicated delicacies *pintxos de autor* for no reason.

⇆ From the Pl. Castillo, with the Palacio de Gobierno (with the flags) on your right, proceed along the plaza and take the 2nd right onto Travesía Espoz y Mina. $ Pintxos €2-3. Bocadillos €1.90. Beer €2. Wine by the glass €1.70. 🕒 Open M-Th 7am-3:30pm and 6pm-midnight, F-Sa 8am-3:30pm and 6pm-2:30am, Su 10am-3:30pm and 6pm-midnight. Bar does not close in the afternoon. During los Sanfermines (July 6-14), open 24hr.

LA MEJILLONERA TAPAS $

C. de la Navarrería, 12 ☎94 822 91 84

This tapas bar is a favorite among locals who come to enjoy the *mejillones* (mussels, €2.90) from which the bar takes its name. "Shrine to mussels" might be a more apt description than "tapas bar"; mussel shells are laid as offerings (or just dropped) at the foot of the bar, an entire wall is covered with a ceramic mural depicting mussel fishing, and the mollusks themselves are served up just about any way you'd like (breathe easy, mayonnaise lovers). The drinks cost about half what you could expect to pay a couple of blocks away at the Pl. Castillo—€1.20 for a caña of beer, €1.50 for a sangria.

⇆ From Pl. Castillo, with your back to the Palacio del Gobierno (with the flags), turn right onto C. Bajada de Javier, then take the 2nd left onto C. Calderería, then the 2nd right onto C. Navarrería. ℹ Standing room only. $ Mussels €2.90. Beer €1.20. Sangria €1.50. 🕒 Open M 6:30-10:45pm, Tu-Th 11:30am-2:30pm and 6:30-10:45pm, F-Sa 11:30am-2:45pm and 6:30pm-midnight, Su 11:30am-2:45pm and 6:30-10:45pm. During los Sanfermines (July 6-14), open 21hr. (closed 3hr. in the morning to prepare the mussels).

MESÓN PIRINEO TAPAS $$

C. de la Estafeta, 41 ☎94 820 77 02

This bar serves up great *pintxos* at some of the lowest prices around. The *pintxos* with *bacalao* (cod) and *pulpo* (octopus) are especially popular, but don't make the hams hanging three-deep over the bar feel left out—go ahead and try the tasty *pintxo* with mushrooms and ham, too.

⇆ From the Pl. Castillo, with your back to the Palacio del Gobierno (with the flags), turn right onto C. Bajada de Javier, then left onto C. Estafeta. $ Pintxos €1.80-2.20. Menú del día €12. Beer €1.80. 🕒 Open M-Th 10:30am-5pm and 7-11pm, F-Sa 10:30am-5pm and 7pm-1am, Su 10:30am-5pm and 7-11pm. During los Sanfermines (July 6-14), open daily 11am-6am.

CAFÉ IRUÑA CAFE $$$

Pl. del Castillo, 44 ☎94 822 20 64 www.cafeiruna.com

This cafe, a staple of Pamplona's central square since 1888, is a great place to sit outside, enjoy a drink, and people-watch. That's what Ernest Hemingway did back in the day, and just in case you've forgotten, his face and the quote from *The Sun Also Rises* that mentions the cafe appear on literally every page of the menu. Despite the famous surroundings and the multilingual menu, the *menú del día* (€13.50) is reasonably affordable and worth the price—though it's only served in the opulent, mirror-filled dining room. If you'd prefer to sit outside, the tasty *bocadillos* (€5.60-7.10) will help make that drink go down a little easier. Don't channel Hemingway so much that you order his favorite drink, the mojito—they don't serve cocktails.

⇆ In the Pl. Castillo, on the opposite side from the Palacio del Gobierno (with the flags); underneath a large white awning with the name of the cafe. $ Entrees €7.50-16. Menú €13.50 (€22 Sa night). Bocadillos €5-7. Beer €2-2.55. Mixed drinks €5.30-8. 🕒 Open M-Th 8am-10pm, F-S 8am-2am. Menú available daily 1-3:30pm and 8-9pm. During los Sanfermines (July 6-14), bar open daily 8am-6am.

CASA PACO RESTAURANT $$$

C. del Rincón de San Nicolás ☎94 822 51 05

The *menú* (€14), served day and night, is the only game in town at this restaurant. Thankfully, that doesn't mean your options are limited—the large number of dishes to choose from for each of the two courses, as well as dessert, means you're sure to find something you like (or understand). The dishes aren't particularly innovative or complex, but all the old favorites like *paella* and *chuletas de cordero* (lamp chops) are done well. Sit outside for the ambience, the fresh air and the normal chairs—the doll-sized wooden chairs inside look like they were made in a high-school woodshop.

 # From Pl. Castillo, with your back to the Palacio del Gobierno (with the flags), take the 2nd left onto C. San Nicolas. Walk for 1½ blocks, then at the Iglesia San Nicolás, take a left so hard you're almost completely reversing direction onto C. Rincón de San Nicolás. ***i*** *Cash only. $ Menú €14 (served all day). Beer €2. ⏰ Open M-Th 9:30am-4pm, F-Sa 9:30am-4pm and 8pm-12:30am, Su 10:30am-4pm; July 6 9:30am-5pm and 7:30pm-midnight, July 7-14 daily 8am-5pm and 7:30pm-midnight.*

ÑAM CAFE, BAR $$

Paseo de Sarasate, 26 ☎94 822 05 49 www.namrestaurantes.com

A small bar and restaurant on the Paseo de Sarasate, Ñam has far and away one of the coolest names to pronounce in Pamplona. It also has excellent *bocadillos* (€5-6) and cheap *pintxos de la semana* (€0.90). The weekend *menú* (€20) is more expensive than those at some of the other establishments in the area, but the selection is wider and the dishes are more complex and of higher quality; during the week, the *menú* costs €12, but bargain-hunters can get the "Express" *menú*, with one *plato* instead of two, for €8. A young crowd takes over this restaurant's bar Friday and Saturday after 10pm.

 # From Pl. Castillo, with the Palacio del Gobierno (with the flags) to your left, proceed straight along Paseo Sarasate; the cafe is on the right. $ Menú €8-12, weekend menú €20 available F night-Su afternoon. Bocadillos €5-6. Pintxos €1.70-2.40. ⏰ Open M-Th 8am-11pm, F 8am-1:30am, Sa 9am-1:30pm, Su 10am-11pm. During los Sanfermines (July 6-14), open 24hr.

pamplona

NIGHTLIFE

The claustrophobic streets of the *casco antiguo* are the main arteries of the Pamplona nightlife scene. Most of the bars are more or less the same, and after a couple of minutes of wandering around to find one with the kind of crowd you're looking for (younger, older, loud, mellow—they often change from weekend to weekend and vary by night), head in and order. The main locales for this type of bar-hopping are C. San Nicolás, C. San Gregorio, C. Caldereriá, C. Navarrería, and C. San Agustín, but **following the shouts** echoing down the streets can also help you start your night. In the wee hours of the weekend, the party moves out to the *discotecas* in the San Juan neighborhood, a 20-30min. walk from the *casco antiguo*. Fair warning: things are dead around here on Sunday and Monday nights. But of course, during *los Sanfermines* (July 6-14), the party practically never stops.

NIZA BAR

C. del Duque de Ahumada, 2 ☎94 822 00 55

A little bigger, a little louder, and with a little more booty-shaking than most bars in the *casco antiguo*, on weekends Niza packs a big crowd onto its large floor a block from the Pl. Castillo. The only thing better looking than the bartenders is the price of the beers (€2), which you can sip amongst the crowd of all ages downstairs or on the small second-floor indoor balcony.

 # From Pl. Castillo, proceed 1 block along Av. Carlos III and take the 1st left onto C. Duque de Ahumada. $ Beer €2. Wine €1.50-2. Menú del día served 1-4pm M-F €13.50, Sa-Su €16.50. ⏰ Open M-W 8am-midnight, Th 8am-2am, F 8am-2:30am, Sa 10am-2:30am, Su 10am-midnight. During los Sanfermines (July 6-14), open daily 10:30am-7:30am.

OZONE CLUB

C. del Monastero del Velate, 5 ☎94 826 15 93 www.ozonepamplona.com

Like most of the city's *discotecas*, this club is in San Juan, a 20-30min. evening stroll from the bars of the *casco antiguo*. The distance from the *casco antiguo* is more than physical; out here, there are no more quaint wooden entrances—this club's street-level entrance looks like a glowing radioactive tuna can. Downstairs, students from the nearby university dance to house music on and off the octagonal dance floor in the main room; a smaller room plays more alternative music.

#From the Pl. Castillo, proceed along Av. Carlos III for 5 blocks, then at the traffic circle, turn right onto Av. Baja Navarra. Continue as it becomes Av. Ejército and pass by the stone walls of La Ciudadela; at Pl. Juan XXIII, continue straight onto Av. Bayona and walk 3 blocks, then turn right at the fork onto C. Monasterio del Velate. $ Cover Th €8, F €10, Sa €12, includes 1 drink. Beer €5. Mixed drinks €7. ⏰ Open Th-Sa 12:30am-6:30am. Closed during los Sanfermines.

BISTROT CATEDRAL BAR, LOUNGE

C. de la Navarrería, 20 ☎94 821 01 52 www.bistrotcatedral.com

This bar and lounge near the cathedral tries to be a little trendier than it actually is—the super-hip decor is a couple of notches cooler than its newly middle-aged clientele—but it's still a good change of pace from its neighbors. Though there isn't much seating, it has somewhat of a lounge atmosphere; there's more casual holding-of-drinks-and-chatting than actual drinking.

#From Pl. Castillo, with your back to the Palacio del Gobierno (with the flags), turn right onto C. Bajada de Javier and take the 4th left onto C. Dormitalería; it's on the corner of C. Navarrería. $ Beer €2.40. Mixed drinks €6-9. ⏰ Open M-W noon-1am, Th noon-2am, F-Sa noon-3am, Su noon-1am.

BAR BAVIERA BAR, CAFE

Pl. del Castillo, 10 ☎94 822 20 48

Find yourself looking to grab a drink late at night early in the week, but noticed that every place in the *casco antiguo* closes around midnight? Bar Baviera is open until 2am and is a convenient alternative to wandering around an otherwise dead part of town. It's a little pricey (€2 for a *caña*), but that's the Pl. Castillo for you.

#With the Palacio del Gobierno (with the flags) behind you, on the right of the Pl. Castillo. $ Beer €2. Mixed drinks €5.50. ⏰ Open M-Th 11am-2am, F-Sa 11am-2:30am, Su 11am-2am. During los Sanfermines (July 6-14), open M-Th 11am-5am, F-Sa 11am-6am, Su 11am-5am.

LAS FIESTAS DE SAN FERMÍN

La Fiesta de San Fermín, also known as **los Sanfermines,** is considered by many the greatest, **wildest week of partying in Europe** (or anywhere, for that matter). The nine-day festival encapsulates two crucial facets of Navarre's culture: millennia-old religious conservatism and a fervent desire to **party like it's going out of style.** The festival celebrates the third-century Saint Fermin *(San Fermín)* of Amiens, Navarre's patron saint and first bishop of Pamplona, whose mentor, Saint Saturninus, was martyred by being dragged to death after having his feet tied to a bull. The religious components of the *fiesta* take place alongside the nonstop debauchery of the red-scarved revelers, and despite the city's relatively small size, the two manage to coexist.

Los Sanfermines begins the morning of July 6, when the entire city of Pamplona and visitors from around the world gather at the Pl. Consistorial. At noon (though the plaza is too crowded to get into by 10am), the mayor appears amid shouts and traditional *San Fermín* cheers and songs, such as the famous "*Uno de enero, dos de febrero, tres de marzo, cuatro de abril, cinco de mayo, seis de junio, siete de julio, ¡San Fermín! A Pamplona hemos de ir, con una media, con una media, a Pamplona hemos de ir, con una media y un calcetín.* " ("January 1, February 2, March 3, April 4, May 5, June 6, July 7, *San Fermín!* To Pamplona we must go, with a stocking, with a stocking, to Pamplona we must go, with a stocking and a sock!") The mayor then fires a rocket from his balcony and yells in Spanish and Basque, "People of Pamplona! Long live *San Fermín!*" Whatever can be found (food, clothing, trash, small animals) is then thrown up in the air and rains down on the partiers, as the *fiesta* begins and everyone fans out from the Pl. Consistorial to fill the streets of the *casco antiguo*, which won't empty again for another nine days. The religious side of the festival makes an appearance with the **procession of San Fermín** at 10am on July 7, when church and city officials march the 16th-century statue of *San Fermín* from its home in the **Iglesia de San Lorenzo** through the *casco antiguo*, in the hope that it will protect the runners in return for their extravagant adulation.

THE RUNNING OF THE BULLS
Encierro route

The most famous component of *los Sanfermines* is the *encierro*, the running of the bulls each day July 7-13 at 8am. The *encierro*'s roots lie in the Middle Ages, when the bulls would be driven at dawn from the *corralillos* outside the city walls to certain death at the *plaza de toros*. At some point, young men began a tradition of running in front of the bulls during this daily routine, an act of lunacy and courage much like riding on top of subway cars today. Though the authorities tried to stop this dangerous ritual for the first couple of centuries after its establishment, they eventually decided to embrace it. In 1776, the Pamplona City Council passed a law requiring that fences be put up along the whole route, and thus began the centuries-old tradition. The route used for the *encierro* today has been in place since 1927. At exactly 8am the first *txupinazo* (rocket, pronounced and sometimes spelled *chupinazo*) is set off and the *encierro* begins. The first segment is a steep uphill section that is quite dangerous, as the bulls handle the incline much better than the bipedal humans. Once all the bulls are in the street, the second *txupinazo* is set off. The runners—who have just finished praying for San Fermín's blessing—and bulls then go through the Pl. Consistorial, past the *Ayuntamiento* (town hall), and make a left turn and then a 90° right turn. At this last turn, the Mercaderes bend, the speeding bulls tend to skid and pile up against the wall; the runners who aren't pinned use this brief distraction to get away. After another few hundred yards, they all enter the bullring (cue *txupinazo* number three), where the bulls are rounded up and put into holding pens (final *txupinazo*) for bullfights later in the day. For those who think about running with the bulls and hear their mother's voice unbidden in the back of their heads shrieking, **"You're going to do WHAT?"** the *encierro* can be watched from a safe distance, in the bullring or behind the fences. Those who wish to watch the spectacle at the *plaza de toros* should arrive no later than 6:30am, as tickets (€4.50-6) go on sale at 7am at the bullring box office. There is a free section, but the danger of suffocation and trampling is significantly higher. To watch from behind the fences, arrive as early as you can get up (or as late as you can stay up, as the case may be)—around 6am to get a decent spot. If you want to see one of the bullfights (Jul 7-13, 6:30pm), chances are pretty slim that you'll get in, as only a few tickets are on sale each day; the rest belong to season ticket-holders. Some travelers report that the easiest way to procure tickets is to buy them from scalpers (usually €50 or higher; lower as the start of the fight approaches).

THE PARTY
Plaza del Castillo

Seriously. This is The Party, capital T, capital P. Nine days of chaos, shenanigans, fireworks, dancing, singing, music, drinking, and just about anything else you can think of adding to make things crazier. Sleeping often occurs (when it does occur, that is) in streets, parks, or any free square inch that can be found in the packed city. Many of the bars are open 23hr. per day—they are legally obligated to close 1hr. each day to clean up a bit or at least to give the drunken masses a second to breathe between beers. The Pl. Castillo, in the heart of the *casco antiguo* but close to the *segundo ensanche,* is the center of this orgiastic glory. The plaza becomes one massive 24hr. *discoteca,* with the ever-swelling sea of partiers dressed in white with red *fajas* (sashes; about €6) and *pañuelos* (handkerchiefs; €2-5), which can be bought at stands throughout Pamplona. At midnight on July 14, the festival officially ends, as the revelers that remain sing the *Pobre de mí: "Pobre de mí, pobre de mí, que se han acabado las Fiestas de San Fermín"* ("Woe is me, woe is me, *San Fermín* has ended").

ESSENTIALS

Practicalities

- **TOURIST OFFICE:** The regional tourist office is open year-round and has excellent maps and information on the city of Pamplona, as well as on the region of Navarra and *camino*-specific sights. It also offers an essential **San Fermin Fiesta Programme** guide, with just about everything you would want to know about the *encierro* and festivals. Ask about guided tours. (Av. Roncesvalles, 4 ☎84 842 04 20 ⇄ From Pl. Toros de Pamplona, take Av. Roncesvalles. ⏰ Open July-Aug M-Sa 10am-7pm and Su 10am-2pm; Sept-May M-Sa 10am-2pm and 4-7pm, Su 10am-2pm; during *los Sanfermines* (July 6-14) daily 9am-2pm and 3-5pm.) During the summer, there is a municipal tourist office as well. (Pl. Consistorial, ☎64 678 08 97 ⇄ From Pl. del Castillo, take Calle de Chapitela until Pl. Consistorial. ⏰ Open Mar 30-Apr 15 10am-8pm, Apr 16-July 3 10:30am-2pm and 4:30-8pm, July 16-Sept 9 10am-8pm; closed during *los Sanfermines* (July 6-14).)
- **CURRENCY EXCHANGE: Banco Santander Central Hispano:** (Pl. Castillo, 21 ☎94 820 86 00 www.bancosantander.es ⏰ Open M-F 8:30am-2:30pm; during *los Sanfermines* (July 6-14) M-F 9:30-noon.)
- **LUGGAGE STORAGE:** At the bus station, small lockers are available for €4 per day and larger ones for €5 per day (Open daily 6:30am-11pm, including during *los Sanfermines* (July 6-14). During *los Sanfermines* (July 6-14), storage is also available at the Escuelas de San Francisco, across the Pl. San Francisco from the library. (☎94 821 24 80 *i* ID required. $ €4.40 per day ⏰ Open 24hr. from July 4 8am to July 16 2pm.) During *los Sanfermines* (July 6-14), there is more likely to be room for large backpacks at the Escuelas de San Francisco. No storage at train station.
- **INTERNET ACCESS:** Free Wi-Fi and computers with internet access are available at the **Biblioteca General de Navarra.** (Pl. San Francisco, ☎84 842 77 97 ⏰ Open June-Aug M-F 8:30am-1:45pm; Sept-May M-F 8:30am-8:45pm, Sa 8:30am-1:45pm. During *los Sanfermines* (July 6-14) open M-F 12:15-1:45pm.)
- **POST OFFICE:** The **post office** is just a couple minutes' walk from the Pl. Castillo (Paseo de Sarasate, 9 ☎94 820 72 17 ⏰ Open M-F 8:30am-8:30pm, Sa 9:30am-2pm.
- **POSTAL CODE:** 31002.

Emergency

- **EMERGENCY NUMBERS: Municipal police.** (C. Monasterio de Irache, 2 ☎092 or ☎94 842 06 39 ⇄ From Pl. Castillo, take C. Chapitela and turn left onto C. Mercaderes. Turn right onto Cuesta de Santo Domingo and continue as it curves to the left becoming Aldapa Portual Nuevo, then Cuesta de Curtidores, then Curtidores Aldapa. Turn right onto Av. Guipúzcoa. At the circle, continue onto Cuesta de la Reina. Turn right onto C. Monasterio de Irache.) **National police.** (C. General Chinchilla, 3 ☎091 or ☎94 829 97 00 ⇄ From Pl. Castillo, take C. San Nicolás and continue as it becomes C. San Gregorio. Go up the stairs and cross the street onto C. General Chinchilla.)

- **PHARMACY: Farmacia Yangüas** is located opposite the bus station. (C. Yangüas y Miranda, 17 ☎94 824 50 30 www.farmayanguas.com ⏰ Open 24hr.)
- **MEDICAL SERVICES:** The **Hospital de Navarra** is at the corner of C. Irunlarrea and Av. Pío XII (C. Irunlarrea, 3 ☎112 (emergencies) or ☎84 842 22 22.) During *los Sanfermines,* (July 6-14) the **Red Cross** sets up stations at the bus station, along the *corrida,* and at various points in the *casco antiguo.*

Getting There

BY BUS

The cheapest way to get to Pamplona is by bus. Most buses to Pamplona are run by carriers other than ALSA. The bus station is located along the edge of La Ciudadela closest to the *segundo ensanche* (C. Yangüas y Miranda ☎94 820 35 66 www.estaciondeautobusesdepamplona.com), and is served most directly by city bus **#16,** though many city buses stop at the nearby Pl. Príncipe de Viana. Buses arrive from: Barcelona (Vibasa ☎90 210 13 63 www.vibasa.com $ €25-32 ⏰ 6½hr.; M-Th at 7am and 10:15pm, F 4 per day 7am-10:15pm, Sa at 7am and 10:15pm, Su 3 per day 7am-3:15pm); Bilbao (La Burundesa ☎94 822 17 66 www.laburundesa.com $ €14 ⏰ 2hr.; M-Sa 5 per day 7am-8:30pm, Su 5 per day 8:30am-8pm); Irún (La Burundesa 8am; La Baztanesa 5 pm ☎94 858 01 29 www.labaztanesa.com $ €8 ⏰ 2hr.; M-Sa at 8am and 5pm, Su 8am); Logroño (La Estellesa ☎94 822 22 23 www.laestellesa.com $ €9 ⏰ 1-2hr.; M-Th 8 per day 7am-8pm, F 9 per day 7am-8pm, Sa 7 per day 7:45am-8pm, Su 5 per day 10am-8pm); Madrid (PLM ☎90 214 41 74 www.plmautocares.com $ €21-28 ⏰ 5-6hr.; M-Th and Sa-Su 16 per day 7am-1:15am, F 19 per day 7am-1:15am); and San Sebastián (La Baztanesa ☎94 858 01 29 www.labaztanesa.com $ €8 ⏰ 1-2hr.; M-F 16 per day 7am-9:30pm, Sa-Su 12 per day 7am-8:30pm).

BY TRAIN

The **RENFE** train station (Pl. Estación, 1 ☎90 232 03 20 ⏰ Open M-Sa 6am-11:30pm, Su 8am-11:30pm) is a bit far away from the *casco antiguo,* but is served by bus **#9** (€1.10), which goes to the center of town in about 15min. Trains arrive from Barcelona ($ €36-59 ⏰ 3¾hr.; M-F 4 per day 7:35am-6:40pm, Sa 4 per day 7:35am-3:30pm, Su 4 per day 7:35am-6:40pm) and Madrid ($ €35-58 ⏰ 3hr.; M-F 4 per day 7:35am-7:35pm, Sa 3 per day 7:35am-3:05pm, Su 3 per day 11:35am-7:35pm).

BY PLANE

Aeropuerto de Pamplona-Noáin (PNA; ☎90 240 47 04 www.aena.es), about 4mi. out of town, is served by bus **#21** (€1.10). **Air Nostrum** (☎90 240 05 00 www.airnostrum.es) operates flights to and from Madrid and Barcelona-El Prat; check their website for prices and schedules, as they vary.

Getting Around

Walking is the easiest way to get around Pamplona. The *casco antiguo* is tiny, and the *segundo ensanche* is not so big that you can't walk from one end to the other in 10min. There is a **bus** system. (☎90 150 25 03 www.infotuc.es $ €1.10, with *tarjeta monedero* €0.56; free transfers.) The #16 bus stops right next to the **bus station** (buses #2, 3, 4, 5, 11, 15, and 21 stop nearby as well), bus #9 goes to the **train station,** and bus #16 goes to the **Aeropuerto de Pamplona-Noáin. Taxi** stands are located all over the city, including at Hotel 3 Reyes (C. Navas de Tolosa, 25), C. Amaya between Av. Baja Navarra and C. Teobaldos, and outside the bus and train stations. Alternatively, call Teletaxi San Fermín (☎94 823 23 00 or ☎94 835 13 35).

NORTHERN SPAIN

From the arid Castilian plateau to the verdant Cantabrian coast to the rainy hills of Galicia, the northern part of Spain is dotted with disgustingly picturesque villages (see Villafranca del Bierzo), similarly picturesque cities (see Burgos), and some sweet beaches (see Santander). One of the least touristy chunks of the Iberian Peninsula, this is where you can explore Spanish (sorry—Castilian, Asturian, Cantabrian, Leonese, and Galician) culture far from the crowds of tourists that bring high prices and mediocre establishments. You might have to dust off your phrasebook (or use ours), but it's worth it. Ancient churches, backwards meals, and a lighthouse at the end of the world await.

greatest hits

- **HIT THE CAMINO.** The Camino de Santiago pilgrimage route runs through every city in this chapter before ending at the Catedral de Santiago de Compostela. (p. 399)

- **REST YOUR WEARY FEET...** Recharge from your long pilgrimage with some of Santiago's best food at O Dezaseis. (p. 401)

- **...OR KEEP GOING.** Some pilgrims just don't want to stop; keep on going until you run out of land at Cabo Finisterre. (p. 400)

SANTIAGO DE COMPOSTELA

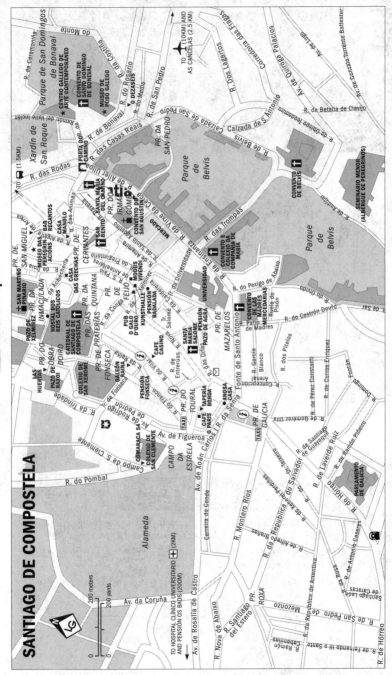

student life

In Santiago de Compostela your best bet for student hotspots is the area around the university, in the new part of town near Pr. Roxa. Most of the other cities in this chapter don't see too many tourists, so if you hit the nightlife centers in their oldest parts, you'll be sure to stumble across these cities' partying youth; León's *barrio húmedo,* for instance, is legendary.

santiago de compostela ☎981

If you've made it to Santiago after finishing the Camino, congratulations. Kick back with some local *tinto* or white *albariño* and give those tired pilgrim's feet a rest. If you flew here, give your stiff neck a rest and *Let's Go* will keep the congratulations. Santiago de Compostela was simply wilderness for centuries, until a monk discovered the remains of St. James in the area. This prompted the building of the Cathedral and the population swelled as thousands of pilgrims and new residents descended on what would become the third most important city in all of Christendom. The Cathedral, which houses the remains of the city's namesake St. James, is the main attraction, and much of the city—from the be-crossed almond cakes to the multilingual *menús*—is geared toward its visitors. Pilgrims are at the core of Santiago's identity, to be sure, but look beyond the surface and you will see it has much more to offer. It is a thriving city in the heart of Galicia, and the Galego lifestyle is everywhere, manifesting itself in nationalist flags, bagpipes, and a unique language (*galego*, for the uninitiated). So whether you are a pilgrim or not, take the time to discover what lies beyond the Cathedral; what you find might surprise you.

ORIENTATION

As soon as you arrive in Santiago, be sure to get a map, since the streets are very poorly marked. The main thoroughfares of the old city are **Rúa do Franco, Rúa do Vilar,** and **Rúa Nova,** which run (with some name changes, at times) from the **Praza do Obradoiro** and the **Catedral de Santiago de Compostela,** the old city's hub, to the **Praza de Galicia,** which sits between the old and new parts of town. The **bus station** (Pr. Camilo Díaz Baliño ☎98 154 24 16 🕐 Open daily 6am-10pm) is to the northeast of the old city. To get to Pr. Galicia, take bus #2 or 5 ($ €1) or head right on R. Ánxel Casal, then left at the roundabout onto R. Pastoriza. Because this area is a life-size IQ test, this street subsequently turns into R. Basquiños, then R. Santa Clara, and finally R. San Roque. Next, turn left onto R. Rodas which turns into R. Aller Ulloa, R. Virxe da Cerca, R. Ensinanza, and Fonte de Santo Antonio before reaching Pr. Galicia. The **train station** (R. Hórreo ☎90 224 02 02) is on the south end of the city; take bus #6 to get to Pr. Galicia or walk up the stairway across the parking lot from the main entrance and take R. Hórreo uphill about seven blocks.

ACCOMMODATIONS

✓ PENSIÓN FONSECA — HOTEL $$

R. de Fonseca, 1, 2nd fl. ☎64 693 77 65 www.pensionfonseca.com

The modern decor of this *pensión*'s bright, high-ceilinged rooms contrasts with the ancient façade of the Cathedral, a literal stone's throw across the street. So when your Camino is finished and you just want to collapse (try not to do that in the Cathedral), the walk here will only be an extra 10 yards. The rooms aren't anything special, but they come at just about the best prices you're going to find in the old city, and you couldn't dream of a better location.

➡ Take R. Franco toward Pr. Obradoiro, then turn right just before the Cathedral (1 block past the little plaza) onto R. Fonseca. Pensión Fonseca is on R. Fonseca, NOT Pr. Fonseca or Tv. Fonseca, which are all within 2 blocks of each other. ***i*** *All rooms have shared bath. 💲 July-Sept singles €20-23; doubles €36. Oct-Jun €15-18 per person. ⏰ Reception 8:30am-11pm.*

ANOSA CASA HOTEL $$$

R. de Entremurallas, 9 ☎98 158 59 26 www.anosacasa.com

This family-run *pensión*'s comfortable rooms overlook a narrow, quiet street in the old town and are located a few blocks from the Cathedral and one block from the old city's main bus stop. The owners are more helpful and knowledgeable when it comes to Santiago than the tourist office, and they serve up a mean home-cooked breakfast every morning (€3)—the sense of community here is much stronger than in a typical *pensión*. The street is nearly impossible to find, so be sure to bring a street map or a wand to tap on the bricks for the more magically inclined.

➡ From main bus stop, look up R. Entremurallas. ***i*** *Breakfast €3. Laundry service available. All rooms with private bath. 💲 Singles €28-37; doubles €40-55; triples €53-71. ⏰ Reception 8am-10:30pm.*

PENSIÓN PAZO DE AGRA HOTEL $$$

R. da Caldeirería, 37 ☎98 158 90 45 www.pensionpazodeagra.com

The rooms are not quite as palatial as the "Agra" part of the name might suggest (Agra is the Taj Mahal's hometown, people), but feel free to address your subjects from your room's balcony over the old city. Or ignore the plebes and just bask while taking in the glorious view. The bathrooms are private, but for singles they're outside the room across a narrow hallway, so you'll still need to cover up after a shower since exhibitionism is probably discouraged.

➡ From Pr. Galicia, take R. Orfas into old city; it becomes R. Caldeirería after 3 blocks. The hotel is on the right after 1 more block. 💲 June-Sept singles €32; doubles €45. Oct-May €26/36. ⏰ Reception 24hr.

PENSIÓN BADALADA HOTEL $$$

R. de Xelmírez, 30 ☎98 157 26 18 www.badalada.es

The rates are nearly as steep as the cobblestone street out front, but you could literally roll down the street to the Cathedral if you were so inclined (get it?). The rooms are also a bit tiny for the price, but if you don't come to this religious city believing in miracles, this might change your mind: every room has a real private bath, not some MacGyvered stall in the corner.

➡ 2 blocks up R. de Xelmírez from Pr. Praterías. ***i*** *Private bath. TV available. 💲 Singles €35-39; doubles €47-59. ⏰ Reception 8:30am-11pm.*

AS CANCELAS CAMPING $

R. do 25 de Xullo, 35 ☎98 158 02 66 www.campingascancelas.com

Guests at this campsite can make the pilgrimage to Santiago de Compostela every day: the final 2km of the Camino runs just a couple blocks from the campsite toward the Cathedral, so guests can make the easiest and most brag-worthy part of the pilgrimage whenever they'd like. The site is far enough from the city center to get away from it all and feel the true camping experience. While As Cancelas is a campsite, it's hardly roughing it: there's a fancy restaurant and bar, and a 5min. bus ride to the center of town is just a couple blocks away. Tents are obviously allowed, but bungalows can also be rented: although they end up costing the same per person as a room in a *pensión*, it is nice to have your own space.

➜ Bus #4 (M-F every 30min., Sa-Su every hr.) runs from R. Senra stop just west of Pr. Galicia to As Cancelas. Or a 2km walk from old town north on R. San Roque to Pr. Paz to R. San Caetano to Pr. España, then right onto R. Cancelas and right onto R. 25 de Xullo. ***i*** *Supermarket, cafeteria, restaurant, pool, and laundry service available.* [$] *Sept-June €5.20 per person, under 12 €3; €5.20 per car; €5.20 per tent; 4-person bungalow €50, 5-person €60. July-Aug €6.70/5.10/7/7/80/96.* ⏰ *Reception 9:30am-11:30pm.*

PENSIÓN OS BAOS — HOTEL $$$

R. de Rosalía de Castro, 106 — ☎98 159 14 87

If you're the kind of person who's in bed by 2am, this *pensión* is perfect for you, because you're not getting back in if you're out any later. Once inside, the tiny paintings on the walls and the narrow halls make it feel like you are living in the house of the little old lady who runs the place. It's in the university part of town, a 15min. walk from the Cathedral and right near the restaurants and nightlife off the Pr. Roxa—just make sure to enjoy the nightlife early.

➜ Bus #1 runs to Senra; bus #2 to bus station; from south side of old town, go past the park along Av. Xoán Carlos I, which becomes R. Rosalía de Castro. [$] *Rooms €30-36.* ⏰ *Open daily 8:30am-2am.*

SIGHTS

★ CATEDRAL DE SANTIAGO DE COMPOSTELA AND MUSEUM — CHURCH, MUSEUM

Pr. das Praterías — ☎98 158 11 55 98 156 93 27 www.catedraldesantiago.es

Pilgrims have arrived at this site for more than a millennium, walking here by following the well-trodden Camino de Santiago in order to gain personal fulfillment and a healthy feeling of superiority from the Church. The Cathedral's towers, speckled with mosses, lichens, and flowers, rise from the center of the city, making the enormous holy site look as though it is ruled by Poseidon. It has been above water the whole time, though (unless you count the frequent Galician rains), and the site has been a destination for pilgrims since the **relics of James the Apostle** were discovered here in the ninth century. Work on the ancient Romanesque cathedral began in 1075 and was completed in 1211, though the cloister was added during the Spanish Renaissance and most of the façades are 17th- to 18th-century Baroque. Today, pilgrims and tourists line up to embrace the jewel-encrusted statue of the Apostle and see the silver coffer that contains his remains. Entrance is free, but after walking by multiple signs asking for donations, so is the guilt. The *botafumeiro*, the massive silver-plated censer (a.k.a. the thing that makes you choke annually at Christmas mass) swung across the altar to disperse thick clouds of incense in the Cathedral's most famous spectacle, is usually used during the noon service, though the schedule varies and is not made public. The Cathedral's bells are older than the Cathedral itself, taken to Córdoba in 997 by invading Moors. However, the reconquering Christians had the last laugh when they took Córdoba in the 13th century and made their prisoners carry the bells all the way back to Santiago. The **museum** includes the peaceful cloister, the library (the books that line the shelves are ancient, but many of those on display are facsimiles), and the crypt. That funky smell in the crypt is caused by the humidity, not by human remains—or at least that's the official line.

➜ Enter Cathedral on Pr. Praterías; the museum entrance is inside on the left. [$] *Cathedral free. Museum €5; students, seniors, and pilgrims €3.* ⏰ *Cathedral open daily 7am-9pm. Museum open June-Sept M-Sa 10am-2pm and 4-8pm, Su 10am-2pm; Oct-May M-Sa 10am-1:30pm and 4-6:30pm, Su 10am-1:30pm.*

[icon] HOSTAL DOS REIS CATÓLICOS — HOSPITAL, MUSEUM, HOTEL

Pr. do Obradoiro, 1 ☎98 158 22 00 www.paradores-spain.com/spain/pscompostela.html

Making the pilgrimage to Santiago used to be dangerous business, and pilgrims would arrive in the city battered and sick. After picking up one too many dead bodies off the floor of the Cathedral, the Catholic Monarchs ordered a hospital to be built in 1499. Fast forward to today and the building is now a luxury hotel, but the integrity of the original structure is still very much intact, and visitors can walk through all four of the former hospital's courtyards. Plaques posted along the walls give an insightful and surprisingly interesting history of the hospital through the years, and the serene courtyards, with their fountains, wells, and **gargoyles,** are picturesque spots away from the madness outside of the Cathedral. Hidden gems show the builders' senses of humor: one bent-over human gargoyle is aptly dubbed **"the male contortionist."**

On the left side of Pr. Obradoiro, facing the cathedral. $ €3. ⏰ May-Oct M-F, Su noon-2pm and 4-6pm; Nov-Apr open daily noon-2pm and 4-6pm.

MUSEO DAS PEREGRINACIÓNS — MUSEUM

R. de San Miguel dos Agros, 4 ☎98 158 15 58 www.mdperegrinacions.com

This 14th-century palace has three stories of artifacts and historical information pertaining to pilgrimages of worldwide faiths going back to prehistory, but there is a predictable and understandable emphasis on Catholicism and the Camino de Santiago route. The museum takes its job seriously: you will have to leave your bag at the front desk so you don't smuggle out any of the goods. Bandits were common in the olden days of the Camino, so any attempted robbery could be framed as bringing realism to the exhibit. Upstairs, there is an 18th-century map of Santiago de Compostela (try to map your own pilgrimage back to your hotel) and a room of artwork depicting James the Apostle slaying Moors like it's his job.

Follow R. Preguntoiro through Pr. Cervantes as it becomes R. Algalia de Arriba, then turn left onto R. San Miguel dos Agros. $ Free. ⏰ Open Tu-F 10am-8pm, Sa 10:30am-1:30pm and 5-8pm, Su 10:30am-1:30pm.

GREAT OUTDOORS

[icon] CABO FINISTERRE (CABO FISTERRA) — CAPE

For some pilgrims, walking from the Pyrenees (or beyond) to Santiago is just not enough. The route continues beyond the Cathedral and keeps going until there's not another foot of dry land left to walk at **Cape Finisterre**—literally "the end of the earth," once believed to be just that. The wind-battered cape sticks out into the Atlantic, reaching toward the New World from the infamous **Costa da Morte** ("Coast of Death"; *Costa de la Muerte* in Spanish), so called because of its treacherously jagged shores and those made queasy by long, winding bus rides. The tiny town of **Fisterra** has narrow, winding alleys down to a lively port with restaurants lining the boardwalk and exhausted backpackers sunning themselves on the rocks.

It's a 1hr. walk uphill along the road to the **lighthouse** at the end of the cape (follow signs for the *faro*), the very end of the Old World. Stunning views of the town, ocean, and nearby coastline are the prize at the end of the trail, and the route runs past the ruins of an 18th-century fortress near the edge of town. Forty-five minutes in the other direction from Fisterra are the town's best beaches, though the water's usually chilly and the weather is rarely sunny. To get there, walk the 3mi. along the road back to Santiago or take the bus and ask to stop at the beaches. A 1hr. hike inland takes you up **Monte San Guillermo,** a surreal spot where pilgrims burn their clothes, couples having trouble conceiving make love on the bed-shaped fertility rocks, and weaklings and strongmen alike move boulders by rolling **As Pedras Santas** (the round rocks move effortlessly when pushed in the right spot).

The **Albergue de Peregrinos** (C. Real, 2 ☎98 174 07 81 ⏰ Open June-Aug daily 1-10pm, Sept-May M-F 11am-2pm and 5-10pm) has tourist information.

*➡ The bus stop is near the Albergue de Peregrinos, a couple of blocks uphill from the water. **i** Castromil/Monbus runs buses from Santiago to Fisterra. $ Buses €12.20; round-trip €23. ⏰ Last bus 7pm.*

☑ O CASTRO DE BAROÑA BEACH, RUINS

An hour's bus ride to the sea and another 30min. on a local bus down the coast takes you to **O Castro de Baroña,** a beautiful, out-of-the-way site that holds the ruins of a **fifth-century Celtic fortress** and a small but pristine crescent beach. Walk the rocky trail to the piece of land jutting out into the middle of the ocean and experience the history that radiates from the soil. All that remain of the 1500-year-old structures are their foundations and low walls, but the site is great to explore and enjoy the views of the sea as well as to reenact your favorite scenes from *Braveheart.* And if your favorite scene includes Mel Gibson and Co. flashing their enemies, you are in luck, because at the beach below clothing is technically *prohibido.* However, many beachgoers remain bathing-suited, especially on cooler days, and hostility toward the clothed is limited. There's little there beyond the fort, beach, and a bar, but a 45min. walk or 5min. bus back toward Noia (to the left as you face the road from the bar) is Porto do Son, which has inexpensive restaurants and accommodations near the bus stop.

➡ To reach O Castro, you'll need to change buses in Noia. Castromil/Monbus runs buses from Santiago to and from Noia. (€3.50, round-trip €6.45). From Noia, Hefsel runs buses that stop at O Castro de Baroña (in front of Café-Bar O Castro) en route to Ribeira (€2) and return to Noia from the same stop. Check at the bar for the most up-to-date information and schedules, and take note of the last bus for each day. Be sure to tell the bus driver where you're going, as the stop for O Castro is easy to miss. From the bus stop, follow the signs to the fortress, downhill toward the water: at the fork with the two signs, the fortress is to the right, the beach to the left.

FOOD

☑ O DEZASEIS GALICIAN $$$

R. de San Pedro, 16 ☎98 156 48 80 www.dezaseis.com

Naming itself after its address, this restaurant isn't banking on winning over any new customers with its cleverness, but if you're willing to shell out **(☑mollusk joke)** just a few more euro, you can get a serious step up in quality. This basement restaurant has an earthy feel and delicious regional cuisine at very affordable prices, and to make things even better, it is far enough away from the pilgrim madness to have a mostly local clientele. The classics like *tortilla española* (€5.80) are superb, and if you want a dish that Santiago himself would approve of, try the *vieira a galega* (a huge scallop served in its own shell, like the ones that line the Camino; €4.50). If you keep the shell, clean it, paint a cross on it, and sell it to a pilgrim, the dish will nearly pay for itself.

➡ Take R. Virxe da Cerca along the edge of the old city, then turn onto R. San Pedro away from old city. $ Menú del día €12. Raciones €3.50-13.50. Entrees €14-16. ⏰ Open M-Sa 2-4pm and 8pm-midnight.

☑ TAPERÍA BOROA TAPAS $$

R. dos Bautizados, 5-7 ☎98 157 30 32

The automatic sliding glass door in the front of the restaurant is there to give you a heads up: the theme is modern. If you didn't get it at the door, you will most certainly understand once you see the all-black furnishings, all with straight edges. However, the SpongeBob episodes running on the TV in the back let you know they don't take themselves too seriously. There are *tapas* (naturally), but the best deal is the *menú,* which includes some amazingly high-quality options for the price (€12).

➡ From Alameda Park, cross the street and head down R. Bautizados. The restaurant is on the right. $ Menú del día €12. ⏰ Open M-Sa 2pm-midnight.

CAFE CASINO CAFE, CAFE-CONCERT $$

R. do Vilar, 35 ☎98 157 75 03

This cafe is located in a grandiose room that looks like it came straight out of turn-of-the-century Paris. The gold gilding of the decor combined with the grand piano (no touching!) will make you feel like a proper aristocrat in no time. Sink into a plush armchair and enjoy a rich coffee (think caramel, whipped cream, alcohol, and a dash of coffee; €2.50-4) and a local *tarta de Santiago* (a not-sweet almond cake with a cross on it; €3.50).

➜ On R. Vilar, toward the Cathedral from Pr. Toural. $ Coffee €2.50-4. Desserts €3.20-5. ⏰ Open M-Th 8:30am-2am, F-Sa 9am-3am, Su 9am-2am. Dinner daily 7:30-11pm.

BAR RECANTOS TAPAS $$

R. de San Miguel dos Agros, 2 ☎98 157 25 44

Don't let its location in the old city fool you; this bar offers modern decor and tries new takes on old *tapas* favorites, combining ingredients and flavors you wouldn't even dream of—unless you usually dream about chorizo and raspberry sauce. They also have an impressive list of alcoholic coffees and hot chocolates, although the Irish coffee milkshake (€3.50) is next level.

➜ Follow R. Preguntoiro through Pr. Cervantes as it becomes R. Algalia de Arriba, then turn left onto R. San Miguel dos Agros; it's across from the Museo das Peregrinacións. $ Tapas €1.50-3. ⏰ Open M-Th 8am-midnight, F 8am-2am, Sa 9:30am-2am, Su 9:30am-midnight.

CASA MANOLO SPANISH $$

Pr. de Cervantes ☎98 158 29 50 www.casamanolo.es

The modern cafe art and hardwood floors make this restaurant feel like a two-story Starbucks or perhaps a trendy restaurant with small portions. None of these assumptions end up coming true, though, because the coffee is minimal and the portions are massive. The *chipirones* (cuttlefish), in particular, is adventurous but tasty, and many of the other options are just okay. However, the peckish and the penniless aren't complaining: massive quantities of food at a great price sounds right on the money, so to speak.

➜ From Pr. Obradoiro facing the Cathedral, go up through the arch to the left of the Cathedral and straight across Pr. Inmaculada, along R. Acibechería, and across Pr. Cervantes (the one with the column in the middle). $ Menú del día €9. ⏰ Open M-Sa 1-4pm and 8-11:30pm, Su 1-4pm.

GALEÓN RAÍÑA LATE-NIGHT $

R. da Raíña, 17B ☎98 193 55 95 www.galeonraina.com

Open till the wee hours of the morn, this restaurant serves up cheap *bocadillos* that are the size of your face. The perfect drunk food, these heavenly carbs will fill you up after a long night at the bars surrounding (ironically enough) the Cathedral. The place has a nautical theme, with fun-loving, scurvy-suffering pirates adorning the walls. If you want to continue the motif, you have plenty of options, including a greasy and delectable *bocadillo de chipirones* (fried cuttlefish sandwich, €2.80).

➜ From Pr. Obradoiro, facing the Cathedral, take R. Fonseca (on the right side) and take the 1st right. $ Bocadillos €2-4. ⏰ Open daily 10am-2:30am.

COMARCA 54 VEGETARIAN, HIPPIE-LIBERALS $$

R. de San Clemente, 11-12 ☎98 111 45 56

If you are against the needless slaughtering of animals or really into the needless slaughtering of plants, this restaurant is just for you. Everything here is vegetarian and organic (and probably vegan, fair-trade, and only grown at the local commune where they read bedtime stories to the plants so they can flourish into wonderful individuals). Pictures of nature adorn the walls, just to make sure you know how in touch with it they are here. The food is high quality although a tad pricey, but that's the price you pay for being trendy, you neo-Bohemian, you.

✚ *Just across the street from the Alameda (big park next to the old city); from Pr. Galicia, follow R. Senra to the left as you're facing the old city, then stay along the right side of the park down the hill, and turn right at the fork.* Ⓢ *Menú del día €12.* Ⓓ *Open Tu-Sa 9:30am-11pm, Su 9:30am-4pm.*

LAS HUERTAS
SPANISH $$$

R. das Hortas, 16 ☎98 156 19 79 www.lashuertas.pagina.de

Even the Top-40 pop music playing in the dining room can't kill the traditional, at-home feel of this welcoming restaurant down the street from the Cathedral. The location means that it isn't exactly a hotspot for locals, but the food is tasty enough to warrant a visit anyway. The deliciously rich *paella de mariscos* for two (€30) has fresh seafood and comes with a cool *albariño* (a local white wine).

✚ *From Pr. Obradoiro, take R. Costa do Cristo down the stairs (to the right of the Ayuntamiento with your back to the Cathedral), which becomes R. Hortas.* Ⓢ *Menú del día €15. Entrees €10-18 per person.* Ⓓ *Open daily 1-4pm and 8:30-11pm.*

NIGHTLIFE

Most of Santiago's nightlife is in the **old town** scattered around the **Cathedral**, but the area around the **Praza Roxa** has a more student-oriented scene.

CASA DAS CRECHAS
BAR, LOUNGE, LIVE MUSIC

R. da Via Sacra, 3 ☎98 157 61 08 www.casadascrechas.com

Take a quick walk up the steps behind the Cathedral and descend into a Celtic witch's den that provides ample seating and beer. Don't worry, though, no one will cast a spell on you…unless you can't speak *galego*, in which case all bets are off. If you want to get a feel for Galicia and its unique culture, this is the perfect place to start. There are frequent jazz and Galician folk performances, so call ahead or check the website for the schedule; impromptu *foliadas* usually pop up on Wednesday evenings, but you generally just have to be there when the right group of enthusiastic musicians comes in.

✚ *From Pr. Quintana with the Cathedral to your left, head up the stairs and to the right, then turn left onto R. Via Sacra.* Ⓢ *Beer €2.50.* Ⓓ *Open daily in summer noon-4am; in winter 4pm-3am.*

MODUS VIVENDI
BAR, LOUNGE

Pr. de Feixó, 1 ☎98 157 61 09 www.pubmodusvivendi.net

Welcome to the heart of Santiago's bohemia. Just about everyone in town will drop in at some point in the evening to mingle at the packed bar or push their way through to the more laid-back lounge. This place definitely did not start out as a bar, which you can see from the old stone arches in the back as well as the scary coffin-like slab that doubles as a coffee table. The trendy art and psychedelic lighting draw an eclectic crowd; the younger groups tend to gravitate to the back, so don't get scared off by all those graying male ponytails in front.

✚ *From Pr. Quintana, with the Cathedral to your left, head out to the far left corner of the plaza, then turn left onto R. Conga and bear left.* Ⓢ *Beer €2. Mixed drinks €4.50-6.* Ⓓ *Open July-Sept M-W 6:30pm-3:30am, Th-Su 6:30pm-4:30am; Oct-June M-W 4:30pm-3am, Th-Su 6:30pm-4:30am.*

CAFE O PARIS
WINE BAR

R. dos Bautizados, 11 ☎98 158 59 86

Maybe you feel like sticking your pinky out for a night. Or perhaps you are starting to feel guilty about that beer gut you have developed over the course of your trip. Whatever the reason you decide to go out for wine, this is the best place in the city to do it, hands-down. What at first seems like a narrow, cramped interior with pastel colors opens up in the back to a lounge area where you can chat with friends all night. Finally, you can go into a wine bar

santiago de compostela

without feeling like you've entered Cougartown: the crowd is all young people rather than divorcées in their mid-40s.

🍴 *From Alameda Park, cross the street and head down R. Bautizados. The bar is on the right.*
Ⓢ *Wine €1.80-2.40.* Ⓩ *Open M-Sa 9am-1am, Su 11am-1am.*

KUNSTHALLE BAR
R. da Conga, 8 ☎98 157 51 70

The scars that have been left on the Ikea Generation are quite visible here: minimalist interior with fluorescent lighting over a Swedish-looking hardwood floor. But once you are done feeling cheap-yet-sophisticated upstairs, head downstairs to enter another world. On weekdays, it's a dark room with a few people swaying more awkwardly than soccer moms at an Enya concert. But during the weekend, brace for carnage: the dance floor is a maelstrom packed with young adults who want to feel upscale but still pay less than €2 for their beer.

🍴 *From Pr. Quintana with the Cathedral to your left, head out to the far left corner of the plaza, then left onto R. Conga and bear left.* Ⓢ *Beer €1.80.* Ⓩ *Open M-Th 8am-1am; F-Sa 8am-2pm, Su 8am-1am.*

PUB O GALO D'OURO PUB, BAR
R. da Conga, 14-15 ☎98 158 21 80

Loaded with kitsch ranging from old newspapers to beer ads, this pub feels comfortable and unpretentious. Prices are a bit high, but everyone is here. The bar gets completely packed around midnight and the seating area in the back isn't much quieter. Although it is a strange practice for a place that calls itself a pub, there is no tap; beer is only served in bottles. This is probably done to secretly encourage bar fights.

🍴 *From Pr. Quintana with the Cathedral to your left, head out to the far left corner of the plaza, then turn left onto R. Conga. The bar is on the right.* Ⓢ *Beer €3.* Ⓩ *Open daily 8pm-2am.*

ARTS AND CULTURE

Festivals

APÓSTOLO

Santiago de Compostela celebrates its patron saint's feast day for a full two weeks known as **Apóstolo.** The party kicks off about a week before **el Día de Santiago** (St. James' Day, July 25—especially holy when it falls on a Sunday, which occurs next in 2021), the peak of the festivities. Programming changes from year to year, but daily musical performances, parades featuring grotesque and (thankfully) fake large heads known as *cabezudos*, and more take place throughout the city. On the night of the 24th, **las Vísperas de Santiago,** fireworks and *gaitas* (traditional Galician-Celtic bagpipes) fill the Pr. Obradoiro in front of the Cathedral, while the *botafumeiro* (a giant incense-burner) swings within. July 25 is also Galicia Day (*Día de la Patria Galega*) and is filled with traditional music and dance, because festivals just aren't any fun without nationalistic overtones.

Ⓩ *Apóstolo July 16-31; Día de Santiago July 25.*

ASCENCIÓN

Las Fiestas de la Ascención, which begins 40 days after Easter Sunday, is one of the city's biggest festivals, with events and revelry spreading to every corner of Santiago. *Ascención* lasts a week and draws much of its excitement from the participation of university students who have just finished their exams. The main highlights are cattle markets, equestrian exhibitions, concerts, and a food fair (specializing in octopus) at the Santa Susana grove in the Alameda.

Ⓩ *Usually in May.*

NOITE DE SAN XOÁN

The festival of **San Xoán** (pronounced *"hwan"*—it's the Galego equivalent of Juan, which is the Spanish equivalent of John) is essentially one massive peninsula-wide party, celebrated throughout Iberia with World Cup-worthy vigor. In Santiago, the festival is marked by daredevils jumping over bonfires lit throughout the town on the night of June 23. Scaredy cats can scarf down fish grilled by the hundreds as well as various other local street foods as they gawk. The Cathedral naturally holds religious services, although there aren't any bonfires inside.

⏰ *June 23-24.*

Traditional Music and Dance

Thought bagpipes were limited to the British Isles and St. Patty's Day parades? Not so. The **gaita** is a traditional **Galician bagpipe,** left by the Celts during their migration, and it's just as irritating as its Highland cousin. Often heard on Santiago's streets, particularly around the Pr. Obradoiro (the archway to the left of the Cathedral is a popular spot), in the Alameda park, and haunting you in your sleep, these bad boys are inescapable during every major festival. The **hurdy gurdy** (that's the technical term), a string instrument played by cranking a wheel, also makes occasional appearances. Full-fledged ensemble performances are a bit harder to come by, but only in the sense that you won't randomly run into them on the street. The best chance to dive into the Galician music scene is **Festival del Mundo Celta de Ortigueira** (www.festivaldeortigueira.com), a massive folk festival held every July in tiny Ortigueira. Throughout July, the **Via Stellae Festival de Música** (www.viastellae.es) takes place in Santiago and surrounding towns along the Camino; free music of all genres occurs at various venues throughout the city.

Traditional **Galician dance** is loud and lively and also reflects its Celtic origins—it looks sort of like a castanet-filled cross between an Irish jig and an Andalusian flamenco. Demonstrations can be seen at the festivals and sometimes at the **Teatro Principal.** (R. Nova, 21 ☎98 154 23 47)

ESSENTIALS

Practicalities

- **TOURIST OFFICE: Oficina Municipal de Turismo** has maps and thorough information on accommodations as well as a 24hr. interactive information screen outside. (R. Vilar, 63 ☎98 155 51 29 www.santiagoturismo.com ⇞ On R. Vilar 1 block toward Cathedral from Pr. Toural. *i* English, French, German, Portuguese, Italian, Galician, and other languages spoken. ⏰ Open daily 9am-9pm.) **Oficina de Turismo de Galicia** has information on the rest of Galicia, and on festivals. (R. Vilar, 30 ☎98 158 40 81 www.turgalicia.es ⇞ On R. Vilar between Pr. Toural and Cathedral, on opposite side of street from Municipal Tourism Office but closer to Cathedral. ⏰ Open M-F 10am-8pm, Sa 11am-2pm and 5-7pm, Su 11am-2pm.) **Oficina del Xacobeo,** in the same building, provides information on the Camino de Santiago. (R. Vilar, 30 ☎98 158 40 81 ⏰ Open M-F 10am-8pm.)

- **CURRENCY EXCHANGE:** Banco Santander has **Western Union** services and a 24hr. **ATM** outside, and cashes American Express Travelers Cheques commission-free. (Pl. Galicia, 1 ☎98 158 61 11 ⇞ On right side of Pl. Galicia with your back to the old town. ⏰ Open Apr-Sept M-F 8:30am-2pm; Oct-Mar Sa 8:30am-1pm.)

- **INTERNET ACCESS: Ciber Nova 50** has fast computers and pay phones. (R. Nova, 50 ☎98 156 41 33 ⇞ On R. Nova 1 block toward the Cathedral from Pr. Toural. $ €0.45 for 12min., €2 per hr. ⏰ Open M-F 9am-midnight, Sa-Su 10am-11pm.)

- **ENGLISH-LANGUAGE BOOKS: Libraria Couceiro** has several shelves of books in English. (Pr. Cervantes, 6 ☎98 156 58 12 ✈ From Pl. Galicia, take R. Orfas into old city; it becomes R. Caldeirería, then R. Preguntoiro, and the bookstore is immediately to the left on Pr. Cervantes. ⌚ Open M-F 10am-noon and 4-9pm, Sa 10am-noon and 5-9pm.)

- **POST OFFICE: Correos** has a *Lista de Correos* and fax. (R. Orfas ☎98 158 12 52 www.correos.es ✈ Take Cantón do Toural from Pr. Toural 2 blocks to R. Orfas. ⌚ Open M-F 8:30am-8:30pm, Sa 9am-2pm.)

Emergency

- **POLICE: Policía Local.** (Pr. Obradoiro, 1 ☎98 154 23 23 ✈ On Pr. Obradoiro across from Cathedral.)

- **MEDICAL SERVICES: Hospital Clínico Universitario** has a public clinic across from the emergency room. (Tr. Choupana ☎98 195 00 00 ✈ Take bus #1 from R. Senra toward Hospital Clínico. ⌚ Clinic open M-Sa 3-8pm, Su 8am-8pm.)

- **PHARMACY: Farmacia R. Bescansa** has been around since 1843—stop in to gawk at the classic 19th-century decor, even if you don't need anything. (Pl. Toural, 11 ☎98 158 59 40.)

Getting There

BY BUS

ALSA (☎91 327 05 40 www.alsa.es) runs buses from: Astorga (Ⓢ €21-25 ⌚ 5hr., 4 per day 4:15am-7:30pm); Barcelona (Ⓢ €72-86 ⌚ 17hr., 3 per day 10am-10:50pm); Bilbao (Ⓢ €49 ⌚ 9-11hr., 4 per day 10:30am-1:45am); Burgos (Ⓢ €40 ⌚ 8½hr., daily at 1:15pm); León (Ⓢ €28 ⌚ 6hr., daily at 4:45pm); Madrid (Ⓢ €44-64 ⌚ 8-9hr.; M-Th 5 per day 7:30am-12:30am, F-Sa 4 per day 7:30am-12:30am); Salamanca (Ⓢ €26-31 ⌚ 6-7hr.; M-F 3pm and 1:10am, Sa 5pm and 1:10am, Su 3pm and 1:10am).

BY TRAIN

RENFE (www.renfe.es) trains arrive from: A Coruña (Ⓢ €7-15 ⌚ 40min.; M-F 20 per day 5:35am-10:15pm, Sa 18 per day 6:55am-9:55pm, Su 17 per day 6:55am-9:55pm); Bilbao (Ⓢ €48 ⌚ 11hr., daily at 9:15am); Burgos (Ⓢ €42 ⌚ 8hr., 2 per day at 12:12 and 3:25pm.); Madrid (Ⓢ €47-53 ⌚ 7-9hr. 3 per day 3-10:30pm).

BY PLANE

Ryanair (www.ryanair.com) has flights to Santiago's **Lavacolla Airport** (SCQ; ⌚ 30min. bus from bus station or city center) from: Alicante, Barcelona (El Prat), Madrid, Málaga, Reus, Frankfurt (Hahn), London (Stansted), and Rome. **Iberia** (www.iberia.es) flies to Santiago from Bilbao, Sevilla, and Valencia.

Getting Around

Most of the old city is closed off to all but foot traffic, so the easiest way to get around is to walk. For those venturing farther afield, **buses** (€1, with *bono* €0.55) are a good way to get around, though not particularly frequent on weekends. Bus #2 and 5 go to the bus station; bus #6 goes to the train station. **Freire** (☎98 158 81 11) runs buses (Ⓢ €3 ⌚ 30min.) from R. Doutor Teixeiro and the bus station to the airport. There are **taxi** stands at the bus and train stations and at Pl. Galicia and Pr. Roxa. Otherwise, call **Radio Taxi** (☎98 156 92 92) or **Eurotaxi** (☎67 053 51 54).

león

León (pop. 165,000) is the last major city along the Camino de Santiago before the final stop at Santiago de Compostela. Though the old city retains vestiges of the Romans and the Middle Ages, the modern city that surrounds it has broad avenues and a cosmopolitan feel. The city's name (originally *Legio* in Latin, it changed over time to *León*) means "lion," and its inhabitants, who are appropriately proud of their city and identity, have been known to take down the occasional gazelle. The Roman walls still stand in part today, and the once heavily fortified city was a launching point for the knights of the *Reconquista*. The city is best known for its spectacular cathedral and its infamously boisterous nightlife.

ORIENTATION

León's **bus station** and **RENFE train station** are located on the west side of the Río Bernesga, while the rest of the city is to the east. The **Avenida de Ordoño II** runs directly east from the river until the **Plaza de Santo Domingo,** after which it becomes **Calle Ancha,** the main street of the mostly pedestrian **casco antiguo.** To the north of C. Ancha is the walled part of the city, with the **Cathedral** and **Basílica de San Isidoro.** To the south is the **barrio húmedo,** the main nightlife area, which centers around the **Plaza Mayor** and **Plaza de San Martín.**

ACCOMMODATIONS

León has a fair number of inexpensive *hostales* and *pensiones* located between the old town and the river, especially around Av. de Roma, Av. de Ordoño II, and Av. de la República Argentina. They tend to fill up very quickly from June-Sept, so try to reserve rooms in advance, especially on weekends.

PENSIÓN BLANCA B & B $

C. de Villafranca, 2, 2nd fl. ☎98 725 19 91 www.pensionblanca.com

No matter what your favorite color is, odds are there will be a matching room in this bargain of a *pensión*. Even if your tastes lie outside the Crayola palette, it's hard to say no to these cheap, cheerful, and colorful rooms. With high ceilings, clean wooden floors, and a location just steps from the main street between the river and the *casco antiguo*, this bargain is enough to make you color outside the lines. The free breakfast is icing on the cake (figuratively, alas—it's toast and cereal), and daily newspapers will keep you up-to-date on current events in Spain and abroad—if you can find them under the stack of gossip magazines.

From Pl. Santo Domingo, walk 3 blocks on Av. Ordoño II and turn left onto C. Villafranca. ***i*** *Breakfast included. Kitchen available. Free Wi-Fi and computer with internet access. Pets allowed. Laundry €7.* [$] *Singles €22, with bath €27-30; doubles €35/43; triples €55. Extra bed €12.* 🕘 *Reception open daily 9am-11pm.*

HOSTAL CASCO ANTIGUO HOTEL $

C. del Cardenal Landázuri, 11 ☎98 707 40 00 www.h-cascoantiguo.com

Right around the corner from the cathedral, this *hostal* charges steep prices for its private rooms but also has some of the lowest rates in the city for beds in its lone four-bed dorm. The dorm is essentially a double room with the two twin beds swapped out for bunk beds. Despite the fact that you're sleeping in a shared room, the place is pretty much a hotel; there are no lockers, breakfast, kitchen, or common areas, so please don't start soulfully strumming your guitar in one of the comfortable leather couches in the lobby.

From Pl. Regla walk with the Cathedral on your right to the end of the plaza, then turn right onto C. Cardenal Landázuri. Follow it as it takes a full left turn; the hotel is on the left. ***i*** *Free Wi-Fi. Reservations recommended.* [$] *4-bed mixed dorms €15-18; singles €29-49; doubles €39-76.* 🕘 *Reception open M-Tu 9am-8pm, W 9am-6pm, Th-Sa 9am-8pm, Su 9am-6pm.*

HOSTAL DON SUERO HOTEL $$

Av. del Suero de Quiñones, 15 ☎98 723 06 00 www.hostaldonsuero.es

This *hostal*'s size (eight floors of rooms complete with two elevators) means it's your best shot if you're rolling into town without a reservation. That said, *Let's Go* does not advise rolling into town without a reservation. Don't forget to bring your bubbles—both the normal-sized bathrooms in the doubles and the closet-sized bathrooms in the singles have relatively spacious bathtubs.

➡ From Pl. Santo Domingo, follow Av. Padre Isla 7 blocks, then turn left onto Av. Suero de Quiñones. i All rooms with private bath. TV available. Free Wi-Fi. Cafe downstairs. [$] Singles €24; doubles €40. ⏰ Reception 24hr.

PENSIÓN PUERTA SOL GUESTHOUSE $

C. de la Puerta del Sol, 1, 2nd fl. ☎98 721 19 66 www.pensionpuertasol.com

This inexpensive *pensión* sits right on the Plaza Mayor—which means scenic views during the day and early in the week but lots of drunken commotion on weekend nights. If you choose to stay here, though, you're more likely to be singing in the *plaza* than looking for earplugs, since the main reason to stay here is the proximity to the nightlife in the *barrio húmedo*. Be sure to change out of your slutty sailor or risqué robot costume before returning home for the night—guests get keys to the door on the street and to their room, but must ring the doorbell to be let into the apartment.

➡ From Pl. Mayor, take C. Santa Cruz from southwest corner of the plaza 1 block, then turn left onto C. Puerta del Sol. i Shared bath. [$] Singles €20; doubles €28. ⏰ Reception 24hr.

HOSTAL OREJAS HOTEL $$

C. de Villafranca, 8 ☎98 725 29 09 www.hostal-orejas.es

This mixed-bag *hostal* has three floors with rooms of all sizes, though mostly the same color (i.e., pale yellow) and shape (i.e., rectangular). The cheapest option is a single room with a shared bathroom directly across the hallway, though most of the rooms have large beds and private bathrooms. Make sure to book a room away from the seasonal construction directly across the street.

➡ From Pl. Santo Domingo, walk 3 blocks on Av. Ordoño II and turn left onto C. Villafranca. There is also an entrance at Av. República Argentina, 28. i Breakfast €3. All rooms have sink. TV available. Free Wi-Fi and computer with internet access. Laundry service available. [$] Singles €15-30, with bath €25-45; doubles €25-45/€40-60. Triples (with bath) €50-75. ⏰ Reception 24hr.

SIGHTS

In addition to its must-see religious sights, the **Catedral** and the **Basílica de San Isidoro,** León has several interesting museums. You can also see the beautiful **Casa Botines,** one of Gaudí's few buildings outside of Catalonia (at the far end of C. Ancha closest to the Pl. Santo Domingo; now a bank), and the **Convento de San Marcos,** a gorgeous Renaissance building in the Pl. San Marcos that has been used as everything from a veterinary school to a concentration camp and is now a luxury hotel.

CATEDRAL DE LEÓN AND MUSEO CATEDRALICIO CHURCH, MUSEUM

Pl. de la Regla ☎98 787 57 70 www.catedraldeleon.org

This 13th-century cathedral in the middle of the old town is one of the finest examples of Gothic architecture you're likely to see anywhere. The stained-glass windows are impressive at any hour of the day, but try to get there at 9:30am for the best show, as the sun's rays intensify the colors of the windows and illuminate the interior with an eerie blue glow. The tremendous façade facing the Plaza de la Regla displays a rowdy group of demons enjoying a *menú del día* of damned souls.

⇄ From Pl. Santo Domingo, proceed along C. Ancha; the cathedral is on the left. ℹ Cathedral admission includes free audioguide in Spanish or English. $ Cathedral admission (includes cloister) €5, students and seniors €4, under 12 free. Full museum and cloister €5 (€3 with cathedral admission ticket), partial visit (museum from Baroque to 20th century and cloister) €3, cloister €2. ⏰ Cathedral open May-Sept M-F 9:30am-1:30pm and 4-8pm, Sa 9:30am-noon and 2-6pm, Su and holidays 9:30-11am and 2-8pm; Oct-Apr M-Sa 9:30am-1:30pm and 4-7pm, Su 9:30am-2pm. Museum open May-Sept M-F 10am-1:30pm and 4-8pm, Sa 10am-noon and 2-7pm, Su and holidays 10-11am and 2-8pm; Oct-Apr Tu-F 9:30am-1:30pm and 4-7pm, Sa 9:30am-1:30pm. Mass M-Sa 9am, noon, 1, 6pm; Su and holidays 9, 11am, noon, 1, 2, 6pm.

REAL COLEGIATA DE SAN ISIDORO CHURCH

Pl. de San Isidoro, 4 ☎98 787 61 61 www.sanisidorodeleon.net

The Basílica de San Isidoro is beautiful inside and out, but the real attraction here is the **Panteón Real,** dating back to the 11th century and housing some of the original **Kings of Leon.** The museum and library upstairs have an impressive collection of reliquaries, other religious artwork, and massive religious books, while the tombs downstairs are the final resting place of 23 kings and queens, 12 *infantes*, and nine counts, watched over by 12th-century Romanesque paintings on the ceiling. While the basilica offers a guided tour, we recommend picking up a pamphlet at the information counter, giving yourself a tour, and saving a ton of time.

⇄ From C. Ancha, turn left onto C. Cid to Pl. San Isidoro. $ Basílica free. Museum €5, free Th afternoon. ⏰ Open July-Aug M-Sa 9am-8pm, Su 9am-2pm; Sept-June M-Sa 10am-1:30pm and 4-6:30pm, Su 10am-1:30pm. Hourly guided tours in Spanish.

MUSEO DE LEÓN MUSEUM

Pl. de Santo Domingo, 8 ☎98 723 64 05 www.museodeleon.com

The oldest museum in León examines the history, art, and ethnography of the city and the province from Paleolithic times to the present day. The "Conquest and Romanization" section has some particularly beautiful artifacts, like the central fragment of a mosaic that once measured 16 sq. m but was badly damaged during the Spanish Civil War, and some particularly unique pieces, like the winged phallus necklace (sadly, not available in the gift shop). Don't stop when you get to modern day, though, or you'll miss the top floor, which has a splendid panoramic view of some of the city's most important buildings.

⇄ On Pl. Santo Domingo, at the intersection with Av. Ramón y Cajal. ℹ Free audioguide. $ €1.20, students, under 18, and over 65 free. Free on Sa and Su. Temporary exhibits always free. ⏰ Open July-Sept Tu-Sa 10am-2pm and 5-8pm, Su and holidays 10am-2pm; Oct-June Tu-Sa 10am-2pm and 4-7pm, Su 10am-2pm.

MUSEO DE ARTE CONTEMPORÁNEO DE CASTILLA Y LEÓN (MUSAC) MUSEUM

Av. de los Reyes Leoneses, 24 ☎98 709 00 00 www.musac.es

Its acronym evokes thoughts of elevator music, but MUSAC is anything but bland. Rotating exhibits (sometimes quite literally) send the visitor on a total trip, and the free admission on Sunday evenings is a lot cheaper and more legal than most hallucinogens. Every six months, new exhibits fill the cavernous galleries with paintings, sculptures, photographs, and videos; most of the museum's permanent collection is also displayed every two years.

⇄ Bus #7, 11, 12, or 13. Or, walking from Pl. Santo Domingo, follow Av. Padre Isla about 10 blocks, then turn left onto Av. Álvaro López Nuñez, then slight right at the roundabout onto Av. Reyes Leoneses. Walk 4 blocks: the museum is the big multi-colored building on the right. ℹ Cafe available. $ €5, students, seniors, and under 16 €2, under 8 free. Free admission Su 5-9pm. ⏰ Open Tu-F 10am-3pm and 5-8pm, Sa-Su and holidays 11am-3pm and 5-9pm. Guided tours in Spanish Sa noon and 7pm; Su noon, 5:30, 7pm.

FOOD

The *casco antiguo* is packed with restaurants, bars, and cafes, especially around the **Plaza Mayor** and **Plaza de San Martín.** Outside the *casco*, there are plenty of restaurants along **Calle de Renueva,** the pedestrian **Calle de Burgo Nuevo** and **Plaza de la Pícara Justina,** and **Avenida de los Reyes Leoneses.** In most Leonese bars, you'll receive some free tapas with your drink, so many people just bar-hop instead of ordering a *menú*.

👍 **JAMÓN JAMÓN** TAPAS $

C. Cardiles, 1 ☎61 682 29 25

If you thought traffic jams were only for cars, think again—on most nights, pedestrian traffic on the narrow C. Cardiles in the *casco antiguo* slows to a standstill, blocked by half of León's residents crowding inside and outside this popular tapas bar. If you're looking to cut across the *casco* in a hurry, find another route, but if you're looking for a great atmosphere, reasonably priced drinks, and delicious tapas, then stick around. Even if it takes you a while to squeeze over to the handsome brick bar, you can feast your eyes on the array of hams and sausages hanging from the ceiling that will soon be yours: drinks come with a generous serving of free *tapas* that includes ham, sausage, and cheese.

➡ From Pl. Santo Domingo, walk 4 blocks on C. Ancha and turn right onto C. Varillas. Turn right at the fork onto C. Cardiles. [$] Raciones €5-8 (½ portions €3.50-5). Beer €1.10-2.40. Wine by the glass €1.10-2.20. ⏰ Open M and W-Su noon-4pm and 7pm-1am.

CENADOR RÚA NOVA LEONESE $$$

C. de Renueva, 17 ☎98 724 74 61 www.cenadorruanova.com

This lively bar and restaurant filled with businessmen out for a leisurely lunch is on the restaurant-lined C. Renueva, just two blocks from the Basílica de San Isidoro and the *casco antiguo*. The *menú* (€13) is the best way to try this restaurant's delicious food without breaking the bank; the two courses and dessert are exceptionally complex and sophisticated for such a reasonable price. If you've missed the *menú*, you'll pay more, but a taste of the *lubina rellena de Bechamel de gambas y mejillones* (sea bass stuffed with white sauce, prawns, and mussels; €16.50) or the *ración* of *jamón asado* (grilled ham; €12) is probably worth it anyway. The bar and large interior are pleasant, but the expansive terrace in the back, complete with discrete lights and fans, is the best place to sit on a warm summer night.

➡ From Pl. Santo Domingo, follow Av. Padre Isla 7 blocks, then turn right onto C. Renueva. [$] Menú €13. Entrees €16-22. ⏰ Open Tu-Sa 1:30-3:45pm and 9-11:30pm, Su 1:30-3:45pm.

EL LLAR LEONESE $$

Pl. de San Martín, 9 ☎98 725 42 87

El Llar serves traditional Leonese food both at the overwhelmingly wooden bar inside and on the open terrace that looks out onto Pl. de San Martín. Try to eat here on the early side, as the terrace gets chilly and the *plaza*'s street vendors come looking for customers.

➡ From C. Ancha, turn right onto C. Varillas, turn right at the fork onto C. Cardiles, which becomes C. Platerías, then turn right onto C. Plegaria and left onto Pl. San Martín. [$] Beer €1.50. Raciones €3-7. Entrees €5-14. ⏰ Open daily 1-3:30pm and 7pm-midnight.

EL VALENCIANO DINER $

Pl. de Santo Domingo ☎98 723 71 39

Perfectly located on the Pl. Santo Domingo, where Av. Ordoño II becomes C. Ancha, El Valenciano leads a double life. Around lunchtime, the *cafetería* in the back serves up cheap *bocadillos* to those looking for a quick bite. In the afternoon, traffic abruptly shifts to the *confitería* in the front, whose delicious-looking pastries would tempt even those still riding a *menú del día* high, and where the many customers seeking ice cream have to ponder really important questions, like "How does the brain give rise to the mind?" and "White chocolate with chocolate-covered peanuts or Kinder Egg?"

➹ On the south side of Pl. Santo Domingo. $ Coffee €1.50. Ice cream €1.90-4. Bocadillos and other lunch foods €2-6. ⏰ Open daily 8am-11pm.

NIGHTLIFE

León's best nightlife can be found in the *casco antiguo*, mainly around **Plaza de San Martín** and **Plaza Mayor** in the neighborhood known as the **barrio húmedo** ("the wet neighborhood," for all the alcohol there), south of C. Ancha, where almost every establishment seems to be a restaurant, bar, or club. The other side of C. Ancha tends to be a little more laid-back, but Spaniards do take a walk on the wild side around **Plaza de Torres de Omaña, Calle de Cervantes,** and **Calle del Cid.**

GARDEN CLUB

Pl. de San Martín

Conveniently located in the Pl. San Martín for your stumbling convenience, this club packs in one of the *barrio húmedo*'s youngest, most energetic crowds so tightly it's hard to make your way to the bar—probably a good thing, since the beers are among the priciest in the neighborhood. It gets busy a little earlier than nearby clubs; by 3am, when other nearby establishments are still taking out the trash, well-hydrated partiers here are already dancing on tables and couples are already making not-so-surreptitious use of the couches in the back.

➹ From C. Ancha, turn onto C. Varillas, turn right at the fork onto C. Cardiles, which becomes C. Platerías, then turn right onto C. Plegaria, and left onto Pl. San Martín. $ Beer €3.50. Mixed drinks €5.50. ⏰ Open Tu-Su 11pm-5am.

MOLOKO BAR

C. de la Paloma, 7 www.molokoleon.com

Cheap drinks in large quantities draw students to this bar. The management thinks the music videos playing on the large screen have something to do with it, but you'll probably be too busy with your liter of *calipiña* (white wine and pineapple juice, €2.50) to notice. If you're in town on Tuesday, don't miss the all-you-can-drink special, with unlimited beer, *calimocho* (red wine and Coke), and *calipiña* for €8.

➹ From the Pl. de Santo Domingo, walk 5 blocks on C. Anche and turn right onto C. Paloma. Or, from the Cathedral, cross C. Ancha and proceed along C. Paloma. $ Beer €1.50 (liter €4). Shots €1. Mixed drinks €4-5.50 (liter €7.50). ⏰ Open Tu and Th-Sa 11pm-4:30am.

DELICATESSEN BAR, CLUB

C. de Juan de Arfe, 1

The broken glass on the stairs up to this second-floor club makes it clear that this Delicatessen doesn't deal in pastrami on rye or root beer. Even if a sandwich-seeker makes it upstairs unfazed, he's unlikely to be disappointed with this club, one of the few spots in the *barrio húmedo* with alternative music. Speakers pulsing with indie rock and electronic music, fans to cool off the young dancing crowd, and old-fashioned advertisements for all your favorite vices (whiskey, cigarettes, etc.) hang from the exposed wooden ceilings. The small space to the left of the bar serves as the dance floor, while the lounge area to the right and the patio outside are geared to more subdued socializing.

➹ From the southwest corner of Pl. San Martín, proceed along C. Juan de Arfe. $ Beer €3. Mixed drinks €6. ⏰ Open Tu 11pm-5am, Th-Sa 11pm-5am.

NOX CLUB

C. de Matasiete www.noxleon.com

It doesn't get more *barrio húmedo* than this—even the floor is often soaked with the freely flowing alcohol. Open until 6am, leave your sandals at home if you plan to party until the break of dawn; if you're going to go really hard, it's probably best to stay away from the uncovered window facing the street, lest you startle the passing owner of your *pensión* with your provocative dance moves.

From the Pl. San Martín, walk toward the Pl. Mayor on C. Matasiete. $ Beer €3. Mixed drinks €6. ⏰ Open Th-Sa 11:30pm-6am.

CAFE-BAR GALA BAR

C. del Cid, 20 ☎98 723 60 24

Gala is a great place to start your night, especially if there's a *fútbol* game on, when an eager crowd squeezes into the bar to watch the match on the **127in. television.** If there's not a *fútbol* game on the big screen, hopefully you won't mind seeing the **Godzilla-sized** face of Barbara Walters during the next re-run of *The View*.

From the Pl. Santo Domingo, walk through the Pl. San Marcelo (toward C. Ancha) and take the 1st left onto C. del Cid. $ Beer €1.60. ⏰ Open daily 8am-1am.

ESSENTIALS

Practicalities

- **TOURIST OFFICES:** The **municipal tourist office** is located in the Ayuntamiento, across the street from the Casa Botines. (Pl. San Marcelo ☎98 787 83 36 ⏰ Open daily 9:30am-2pm, 5-7:30pm.) The **regional tourist office** is directly across from the Cathedral. (Pl. Regla, 2 ☎98 723 70 82 www.turismocastillayleon.com ⏰ Open July 1-Sept 13 and Semana Santa daily 9am-8pm; Sept 14-June 30 M-Sa 9:30am-2pm and 4-7pm, Su 9:30am-5pm.)
- **CURRENCY EXCHANGE: Banco Santander** (Pl. Santo Domingo, 6 ☎98 722 07 44 ⏰ Open M-F 8:30am-2pm) or any of the banks along Av. Ordoño II.
- **LUGGAGE STORAGE:** Storage available at the bus station. ($ €3 ⏰ Open M-F 9am-8pm, Sa 9am-2pm.)
- **INTERNET ACCESS:** The municipal library provides free Wi-Fi and computers with internet access. The main branch is across the river, but there is a more centrally located branch on Av. Padre Isla. (Av. Padre Isla, 57 ☎98 723 21 10 ⇆ 10 blocks down Av. Padre Isla from the Pl. Santo Domingo. ⏰ Open June 15-Aug 31 M-F 9am-2pm, Sept 1-Sept 15 M-F 9am-3pm, Sept 16-June 14 M-F 9am-8:30pm.) **Locutorio La Rua** (C. Varillas, 3 ☎98 721 99 94 ⇆ In the *barrio húmedo,* just off of C. Ancha. $ €2 per hr. ⏰ Open M-F 9:30am-9:30pm, Sa 10:30am-2:30pm and 5:30-9pm) is open on weekends.
- **POST OFFICE: Oficina de Correos** (Jardín de San Francisco, 2 ☎98 787 60 81 ⏰ Open M-F 8:30am-8:30pm, Sa 9:30am-2pm.)
- **POSTAL CODE:** 24004

Emergency

- **EMERGENCY NUMBER:** ☎112
- **POLICE: Municipal police.** (Paseo del Parque ☎092 or ☎98 725 55 00 ⇆ With the river on your right, proceed along Av. Facultad de Veterinaria; the Paseo del Parque begins on the other side of the Plaza de Toros.)
- **MEDICAL SERVICES: Hospital San Juan de Dios.** (Av. San Ignacio de Loyola, 73 ☎98 723 25 00 ⇆ With the river on your right, proceed along the Paseo de Salamanca on the western bank of the river, then turn left onto C. Río Valdueza.)

Getting There

BY BUS

Buses arrive at the bus station (Av. Ingeniero Sáenz de Miera ☎98 721 10 00 ⇆ Follow Av. Ordoño II to the river, cross the bridge, and turn left) across the river from: Astorga ($ €3.60 ⏰ 50min., M-F 20 per day 7am-10:30pm, Sa 8 per day 8:30am-7:30pm, Su 6 per day 11:50am-9:30pm); Barcelona (€48-59 10½hr., 2 per day 9am and 10pm); Bilbao (€26 5½hr., M-Sa at 9:15am); Burgos (€15 2-3hr.; M-Sa 3 per day 6:35am-5:25pm, Su 2 per day 6:35am-5:25pm); Logroño (€19-21 4hr., 2 per day 4:35am and 3:15pm); Madrid (€23-40 3½-5¼hr.; M-F 21 per day 9am-12:30am, Sa-Su 14 per day 9am-11:30pm); San Sebastián (€31 7hr., M-Sa at 7:40am); and Santiago de Compostela (€28 6hr., daily at 8am).

BY TRAIN

León has two train stations, the **RENFE station** (C. Astorga ☎90 224 02 02), on the other side of the river next to the bus station, and the **FEVE station** (Av. Padre Isla, 48 ☎98 727 12 10). RENFE trains arrive from: Barcelona (€71-92 7¾-8¾hr.; 3 per day 9:20am, 8:20, 9:10pm); Bilbao (€31 4¾hr., daily at 9:15am); Burgos (€21-39 2hr., 4 per day 12:14pm-3:42am); Madrid (€33-45 2¾-4½hr.; M-F 10 per day 7:30am-10:30pm, Sa 8 per day 7:30am-8:20pm, Su 8 per day 11am-10:30pm); San Sebastián (€35 5hr., daily at 9:02am); and Santiago de Compostela (€33 5¾hr., daily at 9:25am). FEVE trains arrive from Bilbao (€24 7½hr., daily at 2:30pm).

BY AIR

The **Aeropuerto de León,** located 6mi. outside the city, has incoming domestic flights year-round from Alicante, Barcelona, Málaga, Palma de Mallorca, and Valencia; additional summer service arrives from Gran Canaria, Ibiza, Jérez, Menorca, Reus and Tenerife. Shuttle buses (€3, round-trip €4.15) make the 30min. trip between the *centro* and the airport. Since there are so few flights, service is tailored to the flight schedule; buses arrive at the airport one hour before a flight leaves and depart the airport 30min. after a flight arrives.

Getting Around

The easiest and cheapest way to get around León is to walk. The city also has a **bus** system; bus #14 goes to the bus station, while #4 and 10 go to the RENFE train station. **Taxi stands** can be found at the Pl. Santo Domingo and along Av. Ordoño II; otherwise call Radio Taxi (☎98 726 14 15). The municipal tourist office rents **bicycles** (€5 per day, ½ day €3).

astorga ☎987

Rising over the surrounding plain, Astorga (pop. 12,000) is the last major stop for Santiago-bound pilgrims before they hit the mountains like a caravan of steamrollers. Astorga has always been a crossroad for silver-trading routes during Roman times, pilgrimage trails during the Middle Ages, and the A-6 and AP-71 today. The small **old city** is the renowned home of one of the few Gaudí buildings outside of Catalonia and also boasts a staggering ratio of chocolate shops to square feet. In fact, Astorga may be the only city in Spain with more sweets shops than churches, and we bow down to its greatness. Those up to the challenge can walk the picturesque, narrow streets of the old city in a quest to try to eat one sugary treat from every store in town. C'mon. We double-dog dare you.

ORIENTATION

Astorga is a small city with Roman and medieval historic sights situated around the edges of its old city. The **Camino de Santiago** cuts through the center of town, passing the **Plaza de España** (also referred to as the Pl. Mayor), the city's main square, at the eastern end and the **Plaza de Eduardo de Castro** at the northwest corner. The **bus station** (Av. Murallas, 52 ☎98 761 91 00) is just outside the northwest corner of the old city, and the **train station** (Pl. Estación ☎98 761 64 44) is about a 15min. walk northeast. Many accommodations are located a short walk west of the old city, about 15min. west of the bus station along **Avenida de las Murallas,** which becomes **Avenida de Ponferrada.**

ACCOMMODATIONS

Inexpensive lodging is tough to come by in Astorga; most of the old city's accommodations are pricey hotels, though there are a couple of cheap accommodations within the city walls. There are several more at the intersection of Av. de Ponferrada and the Carretera Madrid-Coruña, about a 15min. walk west of the historic center, and more still farther along the Carretera Madrid-Coruña. Most *hostales* and *pensiones* are affiliated with cafes or restaurants and don't have a designated reception area; just find a bartender or waiter and let them know you'd like a room, and he will instantly put on his receptionist hat.

PENSIÓN GARCÍA HOTEL $

Bajada del Postigo, 3 ☎98 761 60 46

One of the only affordable accommodations in the old city itself, this *pensión* sits on a sloping street in the southeast corner of town, where several sights and most of the city's nightlife are located. The rooms are spacious enough for dressers, sinks, and wide, comfortable beds, and are filled with the delicious aromas that waft up from the affiliated restaurant below. Make sure to note the location of the light switches during the day, otherwise your nighttime walk across creaky floorboards to the shared bathroom might be a little spooky.

⇞ From Pl. España, take C. Bañeza (to right of Ayuntamiento); the hotel is across from the playground. ℹ Free Wi-Fi. All rooms have a sink and shared bath. Reservations recommended. Ⓢ Singles €20; doubles €30. ⏰ Reception 9am-4pm and 8-11pm.

HOSTAL GALLEGO HOTEL $$

Av. de Ponferrada, 80 ☎98 761 54 50

About a 15min. walk from the old town, this *hostal*'s rates are much lower than you'll find for comparable rooms closer to the center of town. The singles are the same size as the fairly spacious doubles but have just the one (bigger) bed, thus making them feel even larger. The bathrooms in every room are compact, but there's room to move around even if your circumference increases from eating at the affiliated restaurant and bar downstairs.

⇞ From the bus stop, take a right onto Av. Murallas, which passes through Pl. Aljibe and becomes Av. Ponferrada. ℹ Reception in the bar. All rooms with private bathroom. No Wi-Fi. Ⓢ Singles €30; doubles €40. Extra bed €10. ⏰ Reception 24hr.

CASA SACERDOTAL HOTEL $$

C. de los Hermanos La Salle, 6 ☎98 761 56 00

This *hostal*'s rooms aren't exactly becoming, unless you have a soft spot for linoleum floors and plastic furniture, but they're the cheapest you'll find with private bathrooms in the old town. The doubles' two beds are spread over a large suite-like room that seems smaller than it is because of all the furniture tucked into the corners; some of the one-room singles have balconies overlooking an unremarkable street. If WWJD guides your hotel selection, look no further—there are pictures of Him everywhere, with a crucifix over every bed.

⇞ From Pl. Eduardo de Castro, with the Palacio Episcopal on your left, turn right onto C. Doctoral. Continue through Pl. Libertad and turn right onto Pl. Obispo Marcelo. Walk 1 block alongside the park and turn left onto C. Hermanos La Salle. ℹ Free Wi-Fi. Ⓢ Singles €30; doubles €50. ⏰ Reception 9am-10pm.

HOSTAL SAN NARCISO HOTEL $$

Ctra. Madrid-Coruña, km 325 ☎98 761 50 01

About a 15min. walk from the old town, this *hostal* has some huge rooms (as well as a few normal-sized ones) at very reasonable prices, especially considering the private (though almost comically small) bathrooms. Apparently the builders were so set on making the rooms as big as possible, they made the walls as thin as they could to maximize living space, so you'd better hope your neighbors don't snore, smoke, or watch TV.

From the bus stop, take a right onto Av. Murallas, which passes through Pl. Aljibe and becomes Av. Ponferrada. Follow Av. Ponferrada 5 blocks, then turn left before the gas station; the hostal is across the street. $ Singles €25; doubles €39. Reception 24hr.

SIGHTS

Most of Astorga's must-see sights are located within the small old city, where monumental **Roman walls** still surround some of the town. The partially excavated **Roman forum and baths** are in the southeast corner, and the **Museo Romano** is just a couple of blocks away by the **Plaza de España.** The monumental **Cathedral** and **Palacio Episcopal** are in the northwest corner.

PALACIO EPISCOPAL AND MUSEO DE LOS CAMINOS — MUSEUM, HISTORICAL SITE

Pl. de Eduardo de Castro ☎98 761 68 82

From outside, the Palacio Episcopal (one of the few buildings outside of Catalonia designed by architect **Antoni Gaudí**) looks like a quirky medieval castle perched above the Roman wall. The magnificent interior feels so weightless it almost seems to float toward heaven; many of the columns are almost impossibly thin, and in certain places the walls are made more of glass than stone. Though originally intended to house the bishop of Astorga, he never actually moved in; since 1963, the palace has instead housed the **Museo de los Caminos,** whose collection contains artifacts from Astorga's Roman past, religious artworks, and a collection of processional crosses. The top floor is less architecturally flashy than the others, and its permanent exhibit of contemporary Leonese art is not worth a detour, but there's a great view down onto the ceramic-lined arches and stained glass windows of the particularly impressive chapel.

Across the Pl. Eduardo de Castro from the Cathedral. $ €3, €5 combined ticket available for Palacio Episcopal and Cathedral Museum. Open Mar 20-Sept 19 Tu-Sa 10am-2pm and 4-8pm, Su 10am-2pm; Sept 20-Mar 19 Tu-Sa 11am-2pm and 4-6pm, Su 11am-2pm.

CATEDRAL DE ASTORGA AND MUSEO CATEDRALICIO — CHURCH, MUSEUM

Pl. de la Catedral ☎98 761 58 20

This cathedral, built between the 15th and 18th centuries, rises over the city with an imposing amalgamation of Gothic, Renaissance, and Baroque motifs that reflect the periods over which the church was constructed—there are even a few Modernist touches, if you count the red plastic chairs (extra seating for mass) and the flatscreen TVs (for those with obstructed views). The large room for the choir at the center of the nave (with a sign that says "Here is the Choir" in Latin) has intricate wooden carvings above every seat and a massive 24hr. clock above the main entrance. The **Museo Catedralicio** has a phenomenal collection of manuscripts and documents from as early as 934 CE; look for one from the king of León during the 12th century that sports an awesome hand-drawn lion. If it seems like you've stumbled into a T.J. Maxx circa 1150, you've found the highly enjoyable room with bishops' robes, jewel-studded miters, and shoes from the 12th to 16th centuries.

From Pl. Eduardo de Castro, with your back to the Palacio Episcopal, turn right onto C. Santa María; the unimposing entrance is through the gates, directly ahead. $ €3, €5 combined ticket available for Cathedral Museum and Palacio Episcopal. Cathedral side door open M-Sa 9-10:30am, Su 11am-1pm. Museum with Cathedral visit included open Tu-Sa 10am-2pm and 4-8pm, Su 10am-2pm. Mass M-Sa 10am, Su 10am and noon.

MUSEO ROMANO — MUSEUM

Pl. de San Bartolomé, 2 ☎98 761 69 37

The *Ergástula,* an arched hallway made of Roman concrete that serves as the entrance to this museum of artifacts from Asturica Augusta (the Romans' name for Astorga) was once a jail for slaves. Skip the sappy 12min. video they project onto its northern wall or you'll feel pretty enslaved yourself. If you get bored with the gravestones in the Roman portion of the building, head two flights up to the floor with the rest of the museum's small collection of assorted artifacts like thimbles, dice, jewelry, and coins. Keep an eye out for the shiny gold *áureo* of Emperor Tiberius, though it's hard to miss next to the pile of coins that look like well-oxidized pennies.

⇆ From Pl. España, take C. Padres Redentoristas (to left of Ayuntamiento), then take 1st left onto Pl. San Bartolomé. $ €2.50. €3 combined ticket for Museo Romano and Museo del Chocolate. €5 combined ticket for Museo Romano and Ruta Romana tour. ⏰ Open Tu-Sa 10:30am-2pm and 4-6pm, Su 10:30am-2pm.

FOOD

Astorga is famous for its **cocido maragato,** a traditional meal eaten by farmers to prepare themselves for a hard day of physical labor (or, in your case, sightseeing). Its three courses are served in reverse order: the meat comes first, followed by the garbanzos and vegetables, and finally the soup. Dessert still comes at the end, though, and this is a town that knows its sweets: dubbed the 👍**chocolate capital of Spain,** there have been chocolate factories in Astorga since the 17th century, including as many as 50 in 1914. Shops selling chocolate and other locally produced sweets line the streets of the old town today.

🍴 RESTAURANTE LAS TERMAS — ASTORGAN $$$$

C. de Santiago, 1 ☎98 760 22 12 www.restaurantelastermas.com

We hoard our tiny little €0.01 *monedas* like they were gold coins, but we would gladly give away all the gold in Fort Knox (and certainly €20) to feast on the *cocido maragato* in this gem of a restaurant. The husband (waiter) and wife (chef) who own the restaurant have perfected every part of the traditional Astorgan meal: all twelve meats are cooked to tender perfection, the locally grown garbanzos with cabbage are sublimely flavorful, and the soup is somehow delicious even if you're already stuffed out of your mind by the time it arrives. If you like anything—or, more likely, everything—just say the word and your waiter, Santiago, will bring you more. The food on its own will have you smiling (and not eating) for the rest of the day, but the bottomless glass of the excellent house red wine certainly helps as well. After dessert and a futile *digestivo*, Santiago will warmly shake your hand—in the unlikely case that you haven't already been eagerly moved to shake his.

⇆ From Pl. Eduardo de Castro, with the Palacio Episcopal on your left, turn right onto C. Doctoral and left onto C. Santiago. Or, from Pl. España, follow C. Pio Gullón, which turns into C. Postas and then C. Santiago. $ Cocido maragato €20. Menú del día €13 (weekends only). ⏰ Open Tu-Su 1-4pm.

🍴 MUSEO DE CHOCOLATE — DESSERT, MUSEUM $

C. de José María Goy, 5 ☎98 761 62 20

The Museo de Chocolate falls somewhere between the world's most delicious museum and the world's most informative desserterie. Redolent of fresh chocolate throughout, the museum begins with artifacts from Astorga's historic chocolate industry. After you've seen the small collection, don't miss the video on the chocolate-making process; it's in Spanish, but if the appeal of watching a joyful artisan scooping handfuls of soft chocolate out of a vat isn't universal, what is? The video will have you chomping at the bit for the grand finale, a tasting of free samples of dozens of different types of chocolate. If you're looking to impress that cute tourist, roll your eyes, sigh, and tell him/her that in a traditional chocolate *degustación*, chocolates are eaten in order of increasing cocoa content. It'll work, we promise.

⇆ From Pl. Eduardo de Castro, with the Palacio Episcopal on your left, proceed 3 blocks along C. Sitios to Pl. Obispo Alcolea, then turn right onto C. José María Goy. $ €2, under 18 and over 65 €1, under 10 free. ⏰ Open May-Sept Tu-Sa 10:30am-2pm and 4:30-7pm, Su 11am-2pm; Oct-Apr Tu-Sa 10:30am-2pm and 4-6pm, Su 11am-2pm.

CAFÉ BAR GAUDÍ CAFE $

Pl. de Eduardo de Castro, 1 ☎98 761 78 47

This bustling little cafe may be right in between the Cathedral and the Palacio Episcopal, but it's no tourist trap. The *bocadillos* are enormous, and the *tostas* (like toasted, open-faced sandwiches, only better) are fresh out of the oven and delicious. If the crowd watching the soccer game on the TVs downstairs gets a little too loud, there's a quieter area upstairs, but the calm can be shattered by a lively game on the *futbolín* (foosball) table or one of the periodic concerts. On a nice day, you can gawk at Gaudí's handiwork and chomp on *churros* at the same time at the terrace across the street, but be warned—there's an extra charge.

⇟ On Pl. Eduardo de Castro, on the corner closest to the Cathedral. [$] Bocadillos €3.50-4.50. Tostas €5. ⏰ Open daily 10am-midnight.

RESTAURANTE SERRANO ASTORGAN $$$

C. de la Portería, 2 ☎98 761 78 66 www.restauranteserrano.es

Discover the cooking of the Astorgan grandmother you never knew you had at this traditional Astorgan restaurant on a quiet street close to the cathedral. Park yourself on a comfortable seat in one of the two dining rooms and enjoy the simple yet flavorful local specialties. The excellent *garbanzos con pulpo* (chick peas with octopus, €12) come in an understated sauce of olive oil and pepper that lets the earthiness of the chick peas and the subtle saltiness of the octopus take center stage. If you're a little hungrier, the *cecina con foie* (cured beef with foie, €16) is so rich that it hijacks all your taste buds; it's best to have a big hunk of bread nearby to help calm things down.

⇟ Take C. Portería from Pl. Catedral. [$] Menú €12. Cocido maragato €18 (served 12:30-4pm only). Entrees €8-22. ⏰ Open Tu-Su 12:30-4pm and 8:30-11:30pm.

NIGHTLIFE

Astorga is known for many things, but nightlife is decidedly not one of them. What little nightlife there is can be found on the east side of the old city, on **Calle de Gabriel Franco** and **Calle de Rodríguez de Cela.**

BBT BAR

C. de Gabriel Franco, 10 www.bbtastorga.es

Sure, there's a small dance floor, but sorry, show-off with the moves—the real stars of the night here are the 500 €1 *chupitos* (shots). If you're fortunate enough to have a Spanish name, you can order the shot named after you; if not, just make like a pilgrim and order the *Santiago* (gin and vermouth). Even if you set a limit for yourself at the beginning of the night, the *tentación* (Parfait Amour, cinnamon liqueur) of the cheap, sweet shots might be too great. They're not very strong, but that doesn't mean you should go overboard—not only will you kill off some cells in your *cerebro* (peach liqueur, granadina, Bailey's), but you might have to take an *aspirina* the next morning (as in Advil, not the anisette and crème de menthe).

⇟ From Pl. España, proceed along C. Pietro de Castro (on the side of the plaza opposite the Ayuntamiento, on the left), then take the 1st left onto C. Gabriel Franco. [$] Shots €1. Beer €2. Mixed drinks €4.50. ⏰ Open Th-Sa 10:30pm-4:30am.

SIEMPRE CLUB, BAR

C. de Gabriel Franco, 8

Weary from walking here through the Pyrenees or just plain tired after the bus ride? Drown your pilgrim sorrows in a massive cocktail made from seemingly random amounts of seemingly random liquors, topped off with a dash of 7-Up—just don't do so if you want to be competitive in the darts games early in the night.

⇟ From Pl. España, proceed along C. Pietro de Castro (on the side of the plaza opposite the Ayuntamiento, on the left), then take the 1st left onto C. Gabriel Franco. [$] Beer €1.50. Cocktails €4.50. ⏰ Open Th-Sa 11:30am-5:50am.

ESSENTIALS

Practicalities

- **TOURIST OFFICE: Oficina Municipal de Turismo** has detailed maps of the city and schedules for all major sights, buses, and trains. (Pl. Eduardo de Castro, 5 ☎98 761 82 22 www.ayuntamientodeastorga.com ➡ From bus station, cross the street, walk through the small park and up the stairs; go between the Cathedral (the massive building to the right) and the Palacio Episcopal (the massive building to the left). Turn left; the office is on the right, across the street. ⏰ Open Tu-Sa 10am-1:30pm and 4-6:30pm, Su 10am-1:30pm.)
- **TOURS:** The tourist office offers **Ruta Romana** tours of Roman Astorga (www.astorica.com $ €4, combined ticket with Museo Romano €5 ⏰ 1¾hr., Tu-Sa 11am and 5pm, Su 11am) that leave from in front of the tourist office. Call to book at least one week in advance.
- **CURRENCY EXCHANGE: Banco Santander** is right down the street from the tourist office, Cathedral, and Palacio Episcopal. (P. Obispo Alcolea, 10 ☎90 224 24 24 ➡ From Pl. de Eduardo de Castro follow C. de los Sitios east. ⏰ Open M-F 8:30am-2:30pm.)
- **LUGGAGE STORAGE:** The **bus station** has luggage storage available. (Av. Murallas, 54 ☎98 761 91 00 ➡ From Pl. de Eduardo de Castro, facing the Palacio Episcopal, turn left, go down the stairs to the right, cross the park, and cross the street. $ €1. ⏰ Open M-F 8:30am-2:30pm.)
- **INTERNET ACCESS:** The **Biblioteca Municipal** offers free Wi-Fi and computer with internet access. (C. Luis Braille ☎98 761 86 90 www.bibliotecaspublicas.es/astorga ➡ From Pl. de España, take C. de la Bañeza (to right of Ayuntamiento), at the playground turn left onto C. Jardín and a left onto C. Luis Braille. The entrance is inside a courtyard. ⏰ Open M-F 10am-9pm.) **Ciberastor** offers internet access and printing. (C. Manuel Gullón, 2 ☎98 761 80 17 www.ciberastor.com ➡ From Pl. de España, take C. Pietro de Castro 1 block. The entrance is on C. Pietro de Castro. $ Internet access €2 per hr. ⏰ Open daily 10am-2pm and 4-10pm.)
- **SUPERMARKET: Gadis** (Pl. Santocildes, 6-7 ☎90 242 34 72 ➡ From Pl. España, with your back to the Ayuntamiento, proceed along the right side of the plaza, which will lead to Pl. Santocildes. ⏰ Open M-Sa 9am-9pm.)
- **POST OFFICE: Correos** (C. Correos, 3 ☎98 761 54 42 ➡ From Pl. de España, walk 1 block on C. del Sr. Ovalle and turn right onto C. Correos. ⏰ Open M-F 8:30am-2:30pm, Sa 9:30am-1pm.)

Emergency

- **EMERGENCY NUMBERS:** Police: ☎092.
- **MUNICIPAL POLICE: Policía Municipal** (Pl. Arquitecto Gaudí, 6 ☎987 61 60 80 ➡ From Pl. de España, walk 1 block on C. del Sr. Ovalle, then cross the street; it's on the right.)
- **MEDICAL SERVICES: Centro de Salud** (C. de Alcalde Carro Verdejo, 11 ☎987 61 66 88 ➡ From bus station, turn right onto Av. Murallas, then turn right at the roundabout onto C. Alcalde Carro Verdejo.)

Getting There

BY BUS

ALSA runs **buses** from: Bilbao ($ €30.28 ⏰ 6½hr., daily 10:45am); Burgos ($ €16 ⏰ 3½hr., daily 3:50am); Barcelona ($ €52 ⏰ 12hr., daily at 7pm); Gijón ($ €14 ⏰ 2½-3hr., 3 per day 8am-6:30pm); León ($ €3.60 $ 50min.; M-F 20 per day 6am-9:30pm, Sa 8 per day 7:30am-8:30pm, Su 6 per day 10:30am-8:30pm); Madrid ($ €23-32 ⏰ 4-5hr.; M-F 10 per day 9:30am-12:30am, Sa-Su 8 per day 9:30am-12:30am); Santiago de Compostela ($ €20 ⏰ 4½-5½hr., 5 per day 8am-11:15pm); and Sevilla ($ €38.40 ⏰ 9½hr., daily 11:20pm).

BY TRAIN

Trains arrive from: Bilbao (Ⓢ €32.70 🕓 5¾ hr., daily 9:15am); Burgos (Ⓢ €24-44 🕓 2½hr, 3 per day noon-2:49am); Barcelona (Ⓢ €72-94 🕓 8-9hr., 2 per day 9:20am and 8:20pm); León (Ⓢ €5-22 🕓 30-45min.; M-F 8 per day 7:16am-5am, Sa 7 per day 2:18pm-5am, Su 6 per day 2:18pm-5am); San Sebastián (Ⓢ €37 🕓 5-6hr., daily at 9am); and Santiago de Compostela (Ⓢ €30 🕓 5hr., daily 9:25am).

BY PLANE

The nearest **airport** is in León; see **León: Getting There**.

Getting Around

Astorga is a small city, and you can **walk** from one end to the other in under 30min. There is also a **taxi stand** at Pl. Obispo Alcolea (☎98 761 60 00).

villafranca del bierzo   ☎987

The tiny but beautiful town of Villafranca del Bierzo lies on the Camino de Santiago, hidden in the mountains and valleys of Spain's rugged northwest. Villafranca is beyond "cute." English does not have an adjective that adequately describes how adorable this village is. A little under 2hr. by bus from Astorga, Villafranca is full of ancient churches, narrow, cobblestone streets, and plazas from which you can see the town's medieval buildings silhouetted against the dramatic mountains that surround the village.

ACCOMMODATIONS

Try not to miss the last bus out of town, as cheap accommodations in Villafranca are practically non-existent. If you have to stay the night, **Hostal Burbia** is on a quiet street just a couple of blocks from the tourist office and has rooms from €35 (C. Fuente de Cubero, 13 ☎98 754 26 67 www.hostalburbia.com).

SIGHTS

The **Iglesia de San Francisco,** founded by St. Francis of Assisi himself according to legend, towers over the town with its 13th-century Romanesque doorway. (⚶ Take the stairs from the southeast corner of Pl. Mayor. Ⓢ Free. 🕓 Open Tu-Su 10am-1:30pm and 4-7pm.) Up the hill at the southeast corner of town are the **Castillo de Villafranca** (you can't go in, but hey, a castle's a castle) and the 12th-century Romanesque **Iglesia de Santiago** (⚶ From Pl. Mayor take C. Campairo from southwest corner 4 blocks to C. Salinas, then left up the hill Ⓢ Free. 🕓 Open daily 11am-1:30pm and 4:30-8:30pm) whose Puerta del Perdón is the Camino's end for those too ill to make it to Santiago de Compostela. From the Iglesia de Santiago, you can **follow the Camino** along the postcard-like **Calle de Ribadeo** and across the **Puente Medieval,** a majestic old bridge that takes westward pilgrims over the Río Burbia and on to Santiago.

FOOD

Restaurants and bars line the town's plazas and streets, especially **Plaza Mayor.** For something a little bit off the beaten track (in case Villafranca itself was too on-the-beaten-track for you), **El Padrino** has a €12 menú and a local feel. (C. Doctor Aren, 17 ☎98 754 00 75 ⚶ From Pl. Mayor take C. Doctor Aren from northwest corner 1 block. Ⓢ Cash only. 🕓 Open daily 1-3:30pm and 8-11pm.)

ESSENTIALS

Before exploring Villafranca, pick up a map at the **tourist office;** the town is small, but its winding streets are very confusing. (Av. Bernardo Díaz Ovelar, 10 ☎98 754 00 28 www.villafrancadelbierzo.org ⚶ From bus stop cross highway and follow Av. Calvo

Sotelo, which becomes C. Campairo and goes to Pl. Mayor, then follow Travesía de San Nicolás from far right corner of Pl. Mayor, and slight right onto Av. Bernardo Díaz Ovelar. *i* English and French spoken. ⏰ Open daily 10am-2pm and 4-8pm.)

Getting There

Buses leave from Astorga ($ €6.60 ⏰ 2hr.; 4 per day 4:15am-5:15pm, Su also 11:20am and 6:20pm; return 3 per day M-Sa 8am-1pm, Su 10am-3pm). Many find it more convenient to change buses in Ponferrada, which allows for visits to Villafranca that don't have to end before 1pm. Buses leave for Ponferrada from Astorga ($ €5.20 ⏰ 1hr.; M-F 14 per day 6:50am-10:20pm, Sa 6 per day 8:20am-9:10pm, Su 6 per day 11:10am-9:10pm), and for Villafranca del Bierzo from Ponferrada ($ €1.55 ⏰ 30min.; M-F 11 per day 9:30am-8:30pm, Sa 4 per day 9:30am-5:30pm, Su 5 per day 9am-9:30pm; return M-F 11 per day 8am-7pm, Sa 4 per day 8am-5pm, Su 5 per day 10am-9pm). Buses arrive in front of Hostal La Charola on Ctra. Madrid-Coruña; to get to the center of town from bus stop, cross the highway and follow Av. Calvo Sotelo, which becomes C. Campairo and leads to Pl. Mayor. Most buses leave from the same stop, but some buses leave from in front of tourist office on Av. Bernardo Díaz Ovelar; check with tourist office for bus locations.

burgos ☎947

Burgos (pop. 180,000) has one of the most spectacular city entrances anywhere, and the breathtaking first impression accurately introduces this northern gem. After walking through the large and ornate **Arco de Santa María** to the mind-bogglingly massive **Catedral** on the Pl. del Rey San Fernando, it doesn't take much imagination to understand why this was a favorite seat and burial place of Castilian and Leonese royalty. Though the Catedral is undoubtedly Burgos's centerpiece, the city is filled with dozens of other churches, from the ninth-century *Castillo* up the hill to the medieval monasteries on the city's outskirts. In the evening, plazas fill with friends and families enjoying their *paseos*, and as the clock strikes midnight they buzz with partiers on their way to the bars along the Camino de Santiago and the *discotecas* in the shadow of the Catedral.

ORIENTATION

Burgos is a simple city, but finding your way through the *centro histórico*'s jumbled streets can be quite complicated. Before traversing this area, pick up a map from the tourist office (the regional tourist office's map is better than the municipal tourist office's). The **bus station, post office, Museo de la Evolución Humana, Museo de Burgos,** and **Monasterio de las Huelgas** are pretty much the only important things south of the east-west-running **Río Arlanzón.** Most of the *centro histórico* is to the north of the river, with the **Catedral** on the west end, the **Castillo** up the hill to the north, and various winding streets and **✓magnificent, open plazas** throughout the city. The **Plaza de España,** a hub for most city buses, is east of the *centro*, and the **train station** is outside of the city to the northeast.

ACCOMMODATIONS

✓ HOSTAL GARCÍA HOTEL $

C. de Santander, 1, 3rd fl. ☎94 720 55 53

"Rooms Cheap," declares the sign on this *hostal*'s front door. It seems like a sign that might open a horror movie, but the rooms inside are quite peaceful, spacious, and slasher-free despite its super-central location a 2min. walk from the Pl. Mayor. The exposed light bulbs won't win it any design awards, but during the day it won't matter, as light inundates the rooms from the massive windows. Even better, they get how the strains of traveling and daily *menús del día* make you out of shape, and so have put the *hostal* on the fourth floor and the bathroom at the far end of the hall.

🚏 From Pl. del Mío Cid with your back to the river, walk along C. Santander; the hotel is on the left. ℹ Free Wi-Fi. Shared bath. $ Singles €20; doubles €30; triples €40. ⏰ Reception 10am-10pm.

HOSTAL CARRALES HOTEL $$

C. del Puente Gasset, 4 ☎94 720 59 16 www.hostalcarrales.com

A couple of blocks from the *centro histórico* and about 15min. on foot from the bus station, this quiet *hostal* has basic rooms, full baths, and a very affectionate cat who lives in the reception area (on a different floor than the rooms, allergy sufferers).

🚏 From Pl. del Mío Cid with the river to your right, walk 4 blocks along C. Vitoria, then turn right onto C. Puente Gasset. ℹ Free Wi-Fi. TV. Private baths available. $ Singles €25-40; doubles €40-55. ⏰ Reception 8am-11pm.

PENSIÓN VICTORIA HOTEL $

C. de San Juan, 3, 2nd fl. ☎94 720 15 42

This sunny *pensión* sits smack dab on the Camino de Santiago. Affordable rooms have balconies over the pilgrimage route and are a few blocks down the road from the Catedral and the nightlife. Before tired pilgrims rejoice too much, they should note that on the weekend, the doubles facing C. de San Juan can get pretty noisy.

🚏 From Pl. Rey San Fernando with the cathedral on your left, proceed 4 blocks along C. Virgen de la Paloma, then turn right onto C. San Juan. ℹ Shared bath, but some rooms have sinks. $ Singles €20; doubles €32. ⏰ Reception 8am-11pm.

CAMPING FUENTES BLANCAS CAMPING $

Ctra. Fuentes Blancas, km. 3 ☎94 748 60 16 www.campingburgos.com

Located in the Fuentes Blancas park, a 10min. bus ride from the *centro*, Camping Fuentes Blancas is a beautiful municipal campsite. Campers can save money with this cheaper overnight option, and outdoorsy backpackers can explore the many hiking trails—you can even walk here along a scenic river from Burgos itself.

🚏 #27 bus leaves from northwest side of Pl. España and runs to Fuentes Blancas ("Camping" stop), 4 per day 9:30am-7:15pm, returns to Pl. España 4 per day 9:45am-7:30pm. #26 bus runs only June 29-Aug 31 and leaves from the same stop, 10 per day 11am-9pm, returns to Pl. España, 10 per day 11:15am-9:15pm. ℹ Shop, supermarket, restaurant, bar, lounge, pool, mini-golf, common showers. $ €4.65 per person, ages 2-10 €3.20, €3.72-7.55 per tent, €4.65 per car. Bungalows with private bath €35-85.

SIGHTS

Turn any corner in Burgos's *centro histórico* and you're likely to stumble across a 14th-century church or the building where Ferdinand and Isabella met with Columbus upon his return from his second voyage to the New World. The **Catedral** is the city's main attraction, but Burgos has dozens of other sites that shouldn't be missed.

CATEDRAL DE BURGOS CHURCH

Pl. del Rey San Fernando ☎94 720 47 12 www.catedraldeburgos.es

The **Catedral,** a UNESCO World Heritage Site, is one of the most impressive churches in the world. Whether you first approach it from behind, by following the Camino de Santiago, or from the front via the magnificent Arch of Santa María, its incredible size and intricate detail will overwhelm you. What began in the early 13th century as a Romanesque church has been transformed over the intervening centuries into a Gothic marvel, and recent restorations (which some considered a bit excessive) have returned its original vivid colors and gilded finish. The Capilla de los Condestables, a little cathedral within the cathedral, has its own choir and organ; be sure to look up at the intricate eight-pointed star skylight, and look to the right as you walk in for carved 👍**dragons.** Just off the stained-glass-enclosed upper cloister (built 1260-1280) is the Capilla de Santa Catalina, whose walls are covered floor to ceiling with chronologically arranged portraits of the bishops of Burgos, and which houses the Visigothic Bible of Cardeña (c. 915) and El Cid's nuptial documents (1074); **El Cid** himself is in the transept. The museum's extensive collection includes reliquaries containing the remains of many saints as well as an artist's rendition of a stunningly handsome El Cid that looks more like the cover of a romance novel than anything else.

🧭 Walk through the Arco de Santa María with your back to the river. Or, from the Pl. Mayor, walk 1 block on C. Cardenal Segura (with your back to the Ayuntamiento, the second street on the left), then turn left onto C. Virgen de la Paloma and walk 1 block. ***i*** *Admission includes audioguide available in Spanish, English, French, German, or Portuguese. $ €7, seniors €6, students under 28 €4.50, pilgrims €3.50, children 7-14 €1.50. ⏰ Open daily Mar 19-Oct 31 9:30am-7:30pm, Nov 1-Mar 18 10am-7pm. Last entry 1hr. before close.*

MONASTERIO DE SANTA MARÍA LA REAL DE LAS HUELGAS CHURCH

C. de los Compases ☎94 720 16 30 www.patrimonionacional.es

Built in 1187 by King Alfonso VIII, the Monasterio de las Huelgas was a summer palace for Castilian kings and a Cistercian convent for princesses and nobles. Though the Cistercians preferred a no-frills attitude toward interior decorating, the monastery's royal status allowed it to break some of the order's strict rules against signs of opulence. The Romanesque cloister dates all the way back to the monastery's founding in the 12th century, and the colors on the ceiling of the Capilla de Santiago (which looks like it belongs more in the Alhambra of Granada than in a Castilian monastery) are original and from the 13th century. The museum contains the **Pendón de las Navas de Tolosa,** the Moors' flag captured by the re-conquering Castilians in 1212, which you can also see depicted on the far right of the huge 17th-century mural in the first room. That's one of the main draws of the museum, unless you have a passion for the fading pillows of 13th-century Spanish royalty.

🧭 Bus #5, 7, or 39 from Pl. España to Barrio de Las Huelgas. Or, from the Arco de Santa María, cross the Puente de Santa María and turn right onto C. Merced, which will turn into Av. Palencia. Turn left at the gas station onto Av. Monasterio de Las Huelgas and follow it until the end, then turn right; the entrance is on the left. ***i*** *Tours mandatory. $ €7, students under 25 and seniors over 65 €4. Free admission for citizens of EU and Latin America W-Th 4-5:30pm. ⏰ Open Tu-Sa 10am-2pm and 4-6:30pm. Last entry 1hr. before close.*

MUSEO DE LA EVOLUCIÓN HUMANA MUSEUM

Paseo de la Sierra de Atapuerca ☎90 202 42 46 www.museoevolucionhumana.com

A heavy dose of science complements Burgos's many religious sights at this beautiful, glass, modern museum filled with natural light across the Río Arlanzón. It addresses evolution from every possible angle, from the 500,000-year-old bones found in the nearby Sierra de Atapuerca to the development of tools to the life and work of Darwin. The details can get pretty technical sometimes, but you're bound to have a good time even if you've forgotten the difference between DNA and DUI. The drawing of a comparison of human life before and after the invention of tools will have your belly laughs echoing throughout the enormous museum (to wit: do not try and pick up and eat a porcupine with your bare hands).

🧭 From Arco de Santa María, cross the Puente de Santa María and turn left onto C. Valladolid. It's the large, modern building on the right, after the next bridge (Puente de San Pablo). ***i*** *Audioguide €3 (Spanish, English, French). Signs in Spanish and English. $ €6; students, seniors, under 16, and pilgrims €4; under 8 free. Free admission W 4:30-8pm. ⏰ Open July-Aug Tu-Su 10am-8pm; Sept-June Tu-F 10am-2:30pm and 4:30-8pm, Sa-Su and holidays 10am-8pm.*

MUSEO DEL LIBRO — MUSEUM

Tv. del Mercado, 3 ☎94 725 29 30 www.museofdb.es

Sorry, art heist enthusiasts—Burgos's Museo del Libro didn't secretly raid the Louvre. Almost everything at this private museum, owned by a publisher specializing in facsimile editions of old books, is a well-crafted copy of an original work housed in one of the world's greatest museums. While this small four-story building one block from the Pl. Mayor does not share this illustrious company, it is a pleasant, brief, air-conditioned alternative to extending your siesta to 9pm and dealing with the guilt that follows. The collection traces the history of writing and the book from cuneiform tablets to e-books, with stops aplenty in monasteries and German printers' shops along the way. You've seen most of this stuff before, but it's nice to see it all next to each other.

From the Pl. Mayor, with your back to the Ayuntamiento, take the 1st right out of the Pl. Mayor onto Tv. Mercado. Immediately turn left; the entrance is halfway down the block, on the right. $ €2.50, students €2, under 14 free. ⏰ Open summer Tu-Su 10:30am-2pm and 5-8:30pm; winter Tu-Sa 10:30am-2pm and 5-8:30pm, Su 10:30am-2pm.

CENTRO DE ARTE CAJA DE BURGOS (CAB) — MUSEUM

C. Saldaña ☎94 725 65 50 www.cabdeburgos.com

An island of modern art floats in Burgos's sea of old-school art and architecture; CAB showcases works by modern artists in its modern home. To keep things fresh, the exhibitions change every four months, but the vending machine on the top floor with free water is (we hope) forever.

From Pl. Santa María (to the left of the cathedral), go up steps and turn right onto C. Fernán González, then take the 1st left up a long, narrow flight of stairs. $ Free. ⏰ Open Tu-F 11am-2pm and 5:30-8pm, Sa 11am-2:30pm and 5:30-9pm, Su and holidays 11am-2:30pm. Tours Sa 1 and 8pm, Su 1pm.

FOOD

Morcilla (blood sausage) and *queso de Burgos* are staples of the Burgalese kitchen and can be found throughout the *centro histórico,* mainly near the Catedral. **C. San Lorenzo,** off the Pl. Mayor, is overflowing with tapas bars.

CERVECERÍA MORITO — BAR, RESTAURANT $

C. Porcelos, 1 ☎94 726 75 55

No sooner do the doors to this *cervecería* swing open than people start to crowd in for the deliciously cheap food and some of the cheapest drinks in town. The place rings with the sounds of friends laughing over sangria (€2) poured from the giant bowl on the bar and sizzles with the sound of the busy bartenders cooking up *revueltos* (scrambled eggs, €5.70) on the grill behind the bar. Those looking to save a bit of cash will no doubt be pleased to hear that a glass of the house *vino tinto* is cheaper than a small bottle of water.

From Pl. Rey San Fernando (in front of cathedral), proceed right along C. Virgen de la Paloma for 1 block, then turn right onto C. Porcelos. There is also an entrance on C. Sombrerería. $ Raciones €1.40-8.50. Sandwiches €3.40-4.30. Beer €1. Wine by the glass €0.50-2. Sangria €2. ⏰ Open daily noon-3:30pm and 7pm-midnight. Kitchen open daily 1-3:30pm and 7pm-midnight.

LA TAPERÍA DEL CASINO — CAFE, RESTAURANT $$

Pl. Mayor, 31 ☎94 727 81 56

Right on the Plaza Mayor, this place offers traditional Spanish food, from *morcilla con pimientos* (blood sausage with peppers, €5.70) to *patatas bravas* (€1.70). There's a €0.40 surcharge for everything served outside on the plaza, but it's worth it by day for the shaded seating area and by night to see the beautiful plaza glow gold with the light of the setting sun.

In the Pl. Mayor, to the left of the Casa Consistorial. $ Appetizers €1.30-2. Raciones €5.70-15.70. Salads €7.70-9.70. Sandwiches €4. Pizza €9.70. Beer €2.50. Menú del día M-F €12, Sa-Su €17. ⏰ Open daily 9am-midnight.

VINOTECA CORDÓN RESTAURANT, BAR $$

C. de la Puebla, 3 ☎94 727 72 79

Bargain *menú*-hunters rejoice! This restaurant isn't right next to any major tourist sites, but the few extra blocks from the Catedral means a precipitous drop in price for the same—if not better—two courses, dessert, bread, and wine. You're also more likely to see business papers or family photos on the table than maps or cameras.

From the Pl. del Mío Cid with the river to your right, walk 1 block on C. Victoria, then take the 1st left onto the street which will become C. Puebla as it curves to the right. $ Menú del día €10 (€16 and €25 menús also available). Drink and pincho €1.60. ⏰ Open M-Sa 10am-4pm and 8-11pm, Su 10am-4pm.

LA POSADA TAVERN $$$

Pl. de Santo Domingo de Guzmán, 18 ☎94 720 85 13

This welcoming tavern on a smaller plaza off Pl. Mayor is full of local *burgalese* and bullfighting paraphernalia (including the very menacing head of a bull behind the bar). La Posada has a different vegetable specialty for every day of the week—even Sunday, a rarity in these parts—and a *menú del día* (€16) that changes more quickly than a chameleon in a kaleidoscope.

From the Pl. Mayor with your back to the Casa Consistorial, cross the plaza diagonally to the right into Pl. Santo Domingo de Guzmán. $ Entrees €7-20. Menú €16. ⏰ Bar open M-Sa 8am-12:30am, Su 10am-midnight. Restaurant open daily 1-4pm and 8-11pm.

NIGHTLIFE

Locals start off the night with tapas and *tinto* in the crowded bars along **C. de San Lorenzo,** then head to the bars along **C. de San Juan** and **C. de la Puebla** for some liquid courage before hitting the **discotecas** on **C. del Huerto del Rey** and **C. de Fernán González** behind the Catedral.

TÍN-TÍN BAR

C. del Huerto del Rey, 15 ☎64 826 72 90

In the center of one of Burgos's busiest nightlife streets, this bar's cheap drinks draw in a young crowd—though not as young as its boy-reporter namesake. Come with friends or make some here to take advantage of the 9pm-midnight five bottles of beer for €5 special that would make even Captain Morgan put down the rum. The house shots (€1) are very sweet and not very strong.

With the cathedral on your left, proceed 1 block along C. Virgen de la Paloma, then take the 1st left onto C. Cardenal Segura, followed by the 1st right, onto C. Huerto del Rey. The bar is on the right. $ Beer €2. Cocktails €5. Shots €1. Five beers (before midnight) €5. ⏰ Open Th-Sa 9pm-2:30am.

EL BOSQUE ENCANTADO BAR

C. de San Juan, 31 ☎94 726 12 66

For a delightfully weird experience, head to this bar along the busy C. de San Juan, where trance music floats around strangely placed dollhouses—yeah, we don't get it either. The establishment takes its name from the enormous fake tree that sits at the bar, illuminated by lighting reminiscent of a high school theater production. No matter how kitschy this bar may sound, it offers a great deal on teas (€1.50-2.50).

From the Pl. Rey San Fernando with the cathedral on your left, walk 4 blocks along C. Virgen de la Paloma, then turn right onto C. San Juan. $ Tea €1.50-2.50. Beer €1.70-2.50. ⏰ Open M-W 5pm-2am, Th-Sa 5pm-4am, Su 5pm-2am.

TRASTOS CLUB

C. del Huerto del Rey, 9 ☎94 720 52 40

The electronic music here is so loud that even El Cid's bones in the nearby cathedral rattle a little. Partiers, in their late teens and early twenties, don't fill up the dance floor until later in the night, but that means early in the night you can test out your new moves while the TVs projecting the dance floor capture every pop, lock, and break.

✠ *With the cathedral on your left, proceed 1 block along C. Virgen de la Paloma, then take the 1st left onto C. Cardenal Segura, followed by the 1st right, onto C. Huerto del Rey. On the right.* Ⓢ *Beer €2.50. Cocktails €6. Shots €2.* Ⓩ *Open Th-Sa 8pm-4am.*

EL PEREGRINO CLUB
C. de Fernán González, 48 ☎60 001 50 96

Situated just behind the Catedral on the Camino de Santiago, this bar (whose name means "the pilgrim") draws a young crowd that knows how to party. It's less Euro-pop than the clubs on C. del Huerto del Rey and more Euro-rock like the other spots along C. Fernán González. El Peregrino's mixed drinks (€5.50-6) can be pricey, so be the conservative pilgrim and order beers (€1.50).

✠ *From Pl. Santa María, to the left of the cathedral, go up the stairs and turn right onto C. Fernán González.* Ⓢ *Beer €1.50. Cocktails €5.50-6.* Ⓩ *Open Th-Sa 8pm-3am.*

ESSENTIALS
Practicalities

- **TOURIST OFFICES:** The **regional tourist office** has excellent maps that are necessary for navigating the city's jumbled streets. (Pl. Alonso Martínez, 7 ☎94 720 31 25 www.turismocastillayleon.com ✠ From the Burgos Cathedral, walk away from the Arco de Santa Maria up C. Fernán González. Take a very slight right, immediately followed by a slight left to continue onto C. Avellanos. Turn left onto Pl. Alonso Martínez. Ⓩ Open July 1-Sept 13 daily 9am-8pm, Sept 14-June 30 M-Sa 9:30am-2pm and 4-7pm, Su 9:30am-5pm.) The **municipal tourist office's** maps are a little more avant-garde, but it's closer to the cathedral. (Pl. Rey San Fernando, 2 ☎94 728 88 74 www.turismocastillayleon.com ✠ Take Pl. Rey San Fernando away from the Cathedral. Ⓩ Open summer M-F 10am-7:30pm, Sa-Su 10:30am-7:30pm; open rest of year M-F 10am-2pm and 4:30-7:30pm, Sa-Su 10:30am-1:30pm and 4:30-7:30pm.)

- **TOURS:** Tours of the cathedral and *centro histórico* are run during the summer by guides from the **Asociación de Guías Oficiales de Burgos** (☎ 65 926 83 21 www.guiasdeburgos.es); contact them directly or contact the tourist office for more information. There is also a **Tren Turístico** (☎ 94 710 18 88 www.chuchutren.com) that leaves from the cathedral and passes by more than 30 monuments and provides commentary in many languages; the train runs both during the day (Ⓢ €4.20, children €3.10 Ⓩ 45min.; July-Sept 18 daily 11am-9pm; Oct M-F 5 per day 3-7pm, Sa-Su and holidays 8 per day 11am-7pm; Nov-Dec M-F 4 per day 3-6pm, Sa-Su and holidays 7 per day 11am-6pm; Mar M-F 4 per day 3-6pm, Sa-Su and holidays 7 per day 11am-6pm; Apr-June M-F 5 per day 3-7pm, Sa-Su and holidays 8 per day 11am-7pm) and at night. (Ⓢ €5.20, child €3.10 Ⓩ 1hr.; July 1-Sept 15 daily 10:30pm, Sept 16-Sept 30 daily 9:15pm, Oct F-Su and holidays 8:15, Nov-Dec F-Su and holidays 7:15pm, Mar F-Su and holidays 8:15pm, Apr 1-May 15 F-Su and holidays 9:15pm, May 16-June 30 10:15pm.) Tickets are sold in a small window that is on the right of the Pl. Rey San Fernando if you are facing the cathedral.

- **CURRENCY EXCHANGE: Banco Santander** offers currency exchange and ATMs. (Pl. Mío Cid, 6 ☎94 726 91 25 www.bancosantander.es Ⓩ Open M-F 8:30am-2:30pm).

- **LUGGAGE STORAGE:** There are lockers available in the bus station. (C. Miranda, 4-6 ☎94 728 88 55 Ⓢ €2 per day.)

- **INTERNET ACCESS: Biblioteca del Teatro Principal** (Paseo del Espolón ☎94 728 88 73 Ⓩ Open M-F 9am-9pm, Sa 9:30am-2pm) and other public libraries have free Wi-Fi and computers with internet access. Many public areas and cafes have Wi-Fi as well.

- **POST OFFICE: Oficina de Correos** (Pl. de Conde de Castro, 1 ☎94 725 65 97 Ⓩ Open M-F 8:30am-8:30pm, Sa 9:30am-2pm.)

- **POSTAL CODE:** 09002.

Emergency

- **EMERGENCY NUMBERS: General Emergency.** ☎112. **Fire.** ☎080.
- **POLICE: Municipal Police.** (Av. Cantabria ☎092 ⇄ Take Av. Arlanzón along the river. Turn left onto Av. Cantabria.) **National Police.** (Av. Castilla y León, 3 ☎091 ⇄ From the intersection of Av. Paz and Av. Cantabria, take Av. Castilla y León.)
- **MEDICAL SERVICES: Hospital General Yagüe** (Av. Cid Campeador, 96 ☎94 728 18 00 ⇄ From Pl. Mayor, take C. Moneda, then turn right onto C. San Juan. Turn left onto Av. Cid Campeador. The hospital is on the right after about 10 blocks.)

Getting There

BY BUS

The cheapest way to get to Burgos is by bus. The **bus station** is located across the river from the cathedral. (C. Miranda, 4-6 ☎94 728 88 55 ⏰ Open daily 5:30am-1am.) **ALSA** (☎90 242 22 42 www.alsa.es) runs buses to Burgos from: Barcelona ($ €37-48 ⏰ 7¾-9hr., 6 per day 8:45am-10pm); Bilbao ($ €13 ⏰ 1¾-3¼hr.; M-F 11 per day 6:30am-8:30pm, Sa 8 per day 6:30am-7pm, Su 8 per day 6:30am-8pm); Carrión de los Condes ($ €5.67 ⏰ 1¼hr., M-F and Su 5:10pm); León ($ €15 ⏰ 2-3¼hr.; M-F and Su 3 per day 10:15am-9:15pm, Sa at 10:15am and 9:15pm); Logroño ($ €6 ⏰ 2½hr.; M-F at noon and 7pm, Sa noon); Madrid ($ €18-29 ⏰ 2¾hr.; M 19 per day 7am-1:30am, Tu-Th 18 per day 7am-1:30am, F 25 per day 7am-1:30am, Sa 17 per day 7am-1:30am, Su 24 per day 7:30am-1:30am); Salamanca ($ €17-24 ⏰ 3-4hr.; M-Th 3 per day 9:30am-2:45pm, F 4 per day 9:30am-4pm, Sa 3 per day 9:30am-2:45pm, Su 3 per day 9:30am-3:15am); San Sebastián ($ €17 ⏰ 2¾-3½hr., 7 per day 7:40am-12:30am); and Santiago de Compostela ($ €40 ⏰ 7-9hr., daily 2pm and 11:15pm).

BY TRAIN

The **train station** (Av. Príncipe de Asturias ☎90 224 02 02) is about 3mi. from the *centro histórico*. Trains arrive from: Barcelona ($ €58-81 ⏰ 5½-6½hr., 4 per day 9:30am-9:10pm); Bilbao ($ €23 ⏰ 2½hr.; M-F and Su at 8:57am and 5:10pm, Sa 8:57am); León ($ €24 ⏰ 2hr., 3 per day 1:12pm-12:12am); Logroño ($ €17-36 ⏰ 1¾hr., 3 per day 5:51pm-1:52am); Madrid ($ €21-42 ⏰ 2 ¼-4hr.; M-F and Su 6 per day 8:05am-6:55pm, Sa 4 per day 8:05am-4:05pm); Pamplona ($ €25 ⏰ 2hr., daily 1:17pm); Salamanca ($ €23 ⏰ 2½hr., daily 12:35am); San Sebastián ($ €24-29 ⏰ 3hr., 4 per day 8:42am-10:39pm); Lisbon ($ €61 ⏰ 10¾hr., daily 4:30pm); and Paris ($ €180 ⏰ 10hr., M-F and Su 6:53pm).

BY PLANE

The **Aeropuerto de Burgos-Villafría** (RGS; ☎90 240 47 04 www.aena.es) is about 2½mi. outside the *centro;* **Air Nostrum** operates daily flights from Barcelona (⏰ 1¼hr., M-F and Su 1pm.)

Getting Around

Burgos is a small city with an almost entirely pedestrian *centro histórico*, so the best way to get around is to **walk.** For sites outside the *centro*, the **bus** system (€0.95 if ticket bought on bus; €0.37 with *tarjeta monedero*, available for purchase at newsstands) is quick and easy to use. Most buses run through the Pl. España to the northeast of the *centro*. Buses #25 and #43 go from the Pl. España to the train station; bus #24 goes from the Pl. España to the **airport.** For **taxis,** call Radio Taxi Burgos (☎94 748 10 10 www.radiotaxiburgos.es).

gijón *xixón*

☎985

Gijón (or *Xixón*, in the local Asturian language) is the largest and most cosmopolitan city in the northern coastal region of Asturias. It's not the capital (that's Oviedo, a 30min. bus ride away), but Gijón doesn't mind—this confident, sea-facing city is perfectly happy to celebrate its past, enjoy its present, and toast its future, all with the sounds of seagulls overhead and a glass of the local *sidra* (alcoholic apple cider) in hand. The city has been inhabited since prehistoric times, but Rome put *Gigia* on the map as an important trading port. When the Romans packed up and left, they forgot their walls and part of their baths, both of which can be seen today. The city gained renewed importance in the 18th century as a port and in the 19th century as an industrial center. For many years, the *sidra* industry was the top dog in town; though the industry has declined in recent years, you'd never know from all the people pouring it (at an arm's length, to aerate it) in the cobblestone hills of the old town of Cimavilla and the lively *sidrerías* of El Llano, in the more modern part of the city. In the summer, tourists flock to Gijón's beaches to enjoy the sun and sand but also so they can tell their friends back home how they're helping the city's economy transition away from heavy industry toward tourism-centered services. Mostly for the sun and sand, though.

ORIENTATION

Gijón is a northern coastal city in the province of Asturias. The northernmost part of the city, *Cimavilla* (in Asturian, *Cimadevilla* in Spanish), is perched on the hill of a small peninsula extending into the Bay of Biscay. This is the heart of the *centro histórico*, which has several lively (but traffic-free) squares, including the **Plaza Mayor,** the **Plaza de Jovellanos,** and the **Plaza del Periodista Arturo Arias;** the **Plaza del Marqués,** at the bottom of the hill on the western side, serves as a gateway to the old town from the more modern part of the city. This modern part is considerably larger than the old town, yet it is still easy to walk between the two beaches on either side of the city: the **Playa de San Lorenzo,** to the east, and the **Playa de Poniente,** to the west. The bus and train stations are both located near the Playa de Poniente, a 15min. walk from the old town.

ACCOMMODATIONS

Gijón has lots of hotels, *pensiones*, and *hostales* in the *centro*, but most of these don't exactly fit into a student traveler's budget. The cheaper options are not located in any particular neighborhood, though the area around the bus station north of the Pl. de Europa has a particularly high concentration of more affordable establishments. The cheapest option, the youth hostel, is located in the suburbs.

▨ ALBERGUE JUVENIL PALACIO DE SAN ANDRÉS DE CORNELLANA   HOSTEL $
Camino de los Caleros   ☎98 516 06 73 www.alberguegijon.com
Palatial digs (literally) at backpacker prices await travelers a mere 20min. bus ride from the *centro* to the suburb of Contrueces. Gijón's only youth hostel is a late 17th-century palace that was renovated in 1992 to house five dorms, including a mammoth 18-bed dorm on the top floor. Those 48 beds weren't enough to meet demand, though, so an extension was built in 2001. The modern part of the building serves as a university dorm during the year but is part of the hostel during the summer; it has 4-person dorms with private bathrooms. The price is per person and indifferent to the size of the room, so you'll pay the same for a night in one of the new building's singles with private bathroom as you will in the 18-bed dorm of the old palace. Despite the hostel's distance from the city,

night owls need not worry—one of the city's night bus lines goes from the city center to the bus stop closest to the hostel.

*Bus #2, 12, 20, or Búho 3 to Ronda Exterior. From C. Ronda Exterior, turn right onto C. Río Narcea and walk uphill. The hostel is after the park, on the right. **i** Cash only. Reservations recommended in summer. Free Wi-Fi. Breakfast €2.80. Sheets €2.40. [$] Dorms €15.60. Dorm, breakfast, and dinner €23.90. Dorm and 3 meals €27.25. Reception 24hr.*

HOSPEDAJE DON PELAYO HOTEL $$$

C. de San Bernardo, 22 ☎98 534 44 50 www.hostaldonpelayo.com

Let's review: the bedroom is the one with the bed and the bathroom is the one with the bidet (whose function we're still not 100% sure of). This may seem obvious on paper, but when you walk into one of this hotel's rooms with a private bath, it can be disorienting—the bedrooms are big, and the bathrooms are just as large. If your band has a gig in Gijón, there's space for all, and maybe even a groupie or two, in the tighter but still uncramped room for five.

*From Pl. Mayor, proceed 3½ blocks on C. San Bernardo. **i** Free Wi-Fi. TV and laundry service available. [$] Doubles €30, with bath €40; triples €45; 5-person room €75. July €10 more, Aug €20 more. Reception July-Aug 24hr.; Sept-June M-F 10am-10pm, Sa-Su 24hr.*

HOSTAL RESIDENCIA PLAZA HOTEL $$

C. del Decano Prendes Pando, 2 ☎98 534 65 62 www.hostalresidenciaplaza.es

Just around the corner from the bus station, this *hostal* has simple but comfortable rooms with televisions and sinks. Unlike at many of Gijón's *hostales*, there are actually a few designated single rooms, so solo travelers won't automatically get a double bed. If you're in the market for a double (or they're out of singles), ask for a room with two beds, which tend to be larger than the rooms with double beds.

*From the bus station, turn right onto C. Llanes and right onto C. Infancia, which becomes C. Decano Prendes Pando. **i** Rooms with shared and private bath (sink in all rooms). Free Wi-Fi. TV available. [$] Singles €21-36; doubles €35-57. Reception 24hr.*

PENSIÓN GONZÁLEZ HOTEL $

C. de San Bernardo, 30 ☎98 535 58 63 www.pensiongonzalez.es

There are more pleasant places to stay in Gijón, but there aren't many cheaper ones. The beds here are fairly big, as is the shower in the shared bathroom, but these modest comforts come at the price of dark hallways and plastic floors. Still, one wonders how they keep the prices so low—especially since so much of the profits appear to go toward lining the hallways with assorted bric-a-brac.

*From the Pl. Mayor, with your back to the Casa Consistorial (and the water), turn left onto C. San Bernardo. **i** Some rooms with TV. Some rooms with Wi-Fi. [$] Singles €12-20; doubles €20-35. Reception 24hr.*

SIGHTS

Gijón's municipal museums (museos.gijon.es) are overseen by the city's government, which means potentially great deals if you plan to visit several museums. A **Bono de Entrada** (€6.50, students and seniors €4) provides admission to five museums: the **Muséu del Pueblu d'Asturies,** the **Termas Romanas de Campo Valdés,** the **Museo del Ferrocarril de Asturias** (Pl. Estación del Norte ☎98 530 85 75 [$] €2.50 Open Apr-Sept Tu-F 10am-7pm, Sa-Su 10:30am-7pm; Oct-Mar Tu-F 9:30am-6:30pm, Sa-Su 10am-6:30pm), the **Villa Romana de Veranes** (C. Veranes ☎98 518 51 29 [$] €2.50 June 16-Sept 15 Tu-Su 10:30am-7pm, Sept 16-June 15 Tu-Su 10am-3pm), and the **Parque Arqueológico de Campa Torres** (Cabo Torres, 3834 ☎98 518 52 34 [$] €2.50 Apr-Sept Tu-Su 10:30am-7pm, Oct-Mar Tu-Su 10am-5pm). A three-museum pass is also available (€4.50, students and seniors €3). Children under 16 get into museums for free, and admission is free for all on Sundays.

MUSÉU DEL PUEBLU D'ASTURIES (MUSEUM OF THE ASTURIAN PEOPLE) MUSEUM

Paseo del Doctor Fleming, 877 ☎98 518 29 60 museos.gijon.es

Getting to the neighborhood might be a little tricky, but once you're nearby, the Muséu del Pueblu d'Asturies is hard to miss. The modern building, with its slanted outer walls and exposed metal columns, represented the province of Asturias in the 1992 Universal Exhibition in Seville before moving to Gijón to house this thoughtful and varied museum dedicated to the history and ethnography of the people of the Asturian province. It's really a few museums in one. The modern building houses an exhibition on the domestic life of Asturians from 1800-1965. Wait, wait!—instruments for cooking and making clothes turn out to be surprisingly interesting. Outside of the main building is a variety of small pavilions. The three pavilions with farm equipment and primitive carriages are interesting, and the cider press is worth a look as well, but be sure not to miss the **Muséu de la Gaita** (Bagpipe Museum). If you've ever stayed awake at night because you didn't know the difference between the Western European and Eastern European bagpipe, you'll find your answers here. Though there are a few sections devoted to the Asturian bagpipe, this museum loves all bagpipes equally; its highly enjoyable collection has pipes from Scotland to Bulgaria, including a few that resemble animals (with faces and horns and a mouthpiece for a nose). The speakers in every room pump out Lady Gaga remixes (just kidding, it's bagpipe music).

⇞ Bus #1 or 10 to Las Mestas. Cross the street and walk along C. Óscar Muñiz toward the stadium. At the stadium, turn right and walk through the parking lot to the small bridge that crosses the Río Piles. The museum is at the other end of the bridge, on the left. ***i*** *Most signage is only in Spanish and Asturian. $ €2.50, students and retirees €1.40, under 16 free. Free on Su. ⏰ Open Apr-Sept Tu-F 10am-7pm, Sa-Su and holidays 10:30am-7pm; Oct-Mar Tu-F 9:30am-6:30pm, Sa-Su and holidays 10am-6:30pm.*

PARQUE DEL CERRO SANTA CATALINA PARK, SCENIC VIEW, RUINS

Northernmost tip of Cimavilla

The winds whipping in from the Cantabrian Sea make the grass look almost liquefied at the top of this park, situated at the northern tip of Gijón. Go ahead and brave the winds—the views from the top are worth it. Walk up the hill, make your way past the dogs, the couples making out, and the **Batería Alta de Santa Catalina** (the ruins of Gijón's Roman-era city walls), to the lookout point in front of Eduardo Chillida's sculpture *Elogio del Horizonte* (Praise of the Horizon). The incredible views include industrial areas on the far left, a bit of the city on the right, and the vast sea in between.

⇞ From the Pl. Mayor, walk 1 block on C. Acacia to Pl. Jovellanos. Proceed along C. Escultor Miranda Sebastián Miranda (to the right of the Museo Casa Natal) and walk up the stairs at the end. $ Free.

TERMAS ROMANAS DE CAMPO VALDÉS RUINS, MUSEUM

C. Campo Valdés ☎98 518 51 51 museos.gijon.es

Back when *Xixón* was the Roman city of *Gigia*, even the wealthy shared baths (take that, four-star hotels!). These Roman baths, discovered in 1903 and fully excavated between 1990 and 1994, were places to socialize and spend free time, as well as to take plunges into the cold *frigidarium* and piping hot *caldarium.* The museum's very low ceiling makes it hard to imagine the baths as they once were, but the hypothetical reconstructions on the wall and on video screens in front of each room help somewhat. If you start to get bath envy, just pop on your swim trunks and hop across the street to the Playa de San Lorenzo—the museum suggests that on a nice day even the Romans ditched the routine of the bath for a little fun in the sun.

⇞ From the Pl. Mayor, exit from the northeast corner and cross the street (the sea will be on the right as you exit). The stairs leading down to the entrance are on the left, halfway to the Iglesia de San Pedro. ***i*** *Signage in Spanish only. $ €2.50, students and seniors €1.40, under 16 free. Free on Su. ⏰ Open Tu-F 9:30am-2pm and 5-7:30pm, Sa-Su and holidays 10am-2pm and 5-7:30pm.*

MUSEO CASA NATAL DE JOVELLANOS MUSEUM

Pl. Jovellanos ☎98 518 51 52 www.jovellanos.net

This 14th-century house was the birthplace of the pride of Gijón, writer Gaspar Melchor de Jovellanos, but don't expect to see faded curtains and chamber pots—it now houses a fairly small art museum that features paintings and sculptures owned by Jovellanos, as well as a collection of modern works. Keep an eye out for the photograph-like Realist paintings of the late 19th century; Juan Martínez Abades' *Golpe de mar* looks exactly like the Playa de San Lorenzo at high tide.

From the Pl. Mayor, walk 1 block on C. Acacia to Pl. Jovellanos. ***i*** *Information on the wall in Spanish, but laminated translations in English, French, and Asturian are available in bins on the wall.* Ⓢ *Free. Spanish or English audioguide €1.60. Brochure €0.88.* *Open Tu-F 9:30am-2pm and 5-7:30pm, Sa-Su and holidays 10am-2pm and 5-7:30pm.*

BEACHES

During the summer, Gijón is a popular beach destination. The city has three beaches: the Playa de San Lorenzo, on the east; the Playa de Poniente, on the west; and the Playa del Arbeyal, even farther west. The metropolitan area has a total of nine beaches. Swimming season is May-Sept; at these times there are lifeguards on duty for most of the day, and information about water conditions is available in local newspapers at www.gijon.es and lifeguard stations.

PLAYA DE SAN LORENZO EAST OF CIMAVILLA

Across from C. Ezcurdia and Av. de Rufo García Rendueles

Asturia's most famous beach, this crescent-shaped stretch of sand extends 1.5km along Gijón's eastern shore. There are more than 15 staircases that take locals' and tourists' flip-flopped feet from the street, behind the stone wall, and down to the fine sand. Don't be alarmed if you find nothing but sea—at high tide, much of the beach is submerged as waves loudly crash into the stone wall. Don't auction off your towel just yet, though, since the eastern part of the beach (the opposite end as the Iglesia de San Pedro) usually sticks around all day.

From the Pl. Mayor, walk toward the river. Cross the street and turn right; for the next 1.5km there are stairs leading down to the beach. ***i*** *Bathrooms and showers available.* Ⓢ *Free.* *Lifeguard on duty May 11am-7pm, June-Aug 10am-9pm, Sept 1-Sept 15 10am-8pm, Sept 15-Sept 30 11am-7pm.*

PLAYA DE PONIENTE WEST OF CIMAVILLA

Across from C. de Rodríguez San Pedro

Gijón's "other beach" isn't as picturesque as Playa de San Lorenzo, nor is it quite as large. It's also not quite as real; in the mid-'90s, the city plopped some sand down in the Poniente neighborhood to increase the area of the city's beaches. During the summer, thousands of grateful sun-seekers flock to this beach to sunbathe, swim, and perhaps join in a pick-up game of beach volleyball on one of the courts near the east end of the beach. Unlike the Playa de San Lorenzo, this beach is essentially at street level, so it's easy to walk over to the nearby restaurants and food stands to get a sundae after the strenuous volleyball game or not-so-strenuous sunbathing.

From the Pl. Marqués, with the port on your right, follow the street next to the water, which becomes C. Rodríguez San Pedro. The stairs down to the beach are on the right, after the dock with the tourist office. ***i*** *Bathrooms and showers available.* Ⓢ *Free.* *Lifeguard on duty May-Sept.*

FOOD

Asturias is well-known throughout Spain for its *fabada* (a white bean stew with various meats) and its *sidra* (alcoholic apple cider). These local specialties, as well as the generally excellent seafood, can be tried at one of Gijón's many restaurants and *sidrerías*. The *casco viejo* is covered with relatively inexpensive places to eat, though some of these tend to be very tourist-oriented. The area around the Jardines de Begoña has some excellent *sidrerías*, especially on **Avenida de la Costa** and **Avenida de los Hermanos Felgueroso.** Ask at the tourist office for a *Ruta de la Sidra* map with some of the city's best-known *sidrerías*.

EL REQUEXU CIDER, ASTURIAN $$

C. del Rosario, 14 ☎98 517 67 97

If you enter from the front, you'd never know there was a bar, and if you enter from the back, you'd never know there were tables—indeed, there are both, and neither the food nor the *sidra* is to be missed. The excellent seafood dishes like the *revuelto de bacalao y espinacas* (scrambled eggs with cod and spinach, €10.50) and *navajas a la plancha* (grilled razor clams, €13) complement the seashells, (dead) fish, life rafts, and clock in the shape of a ship's steering wheel that decorate the wall. If that bottle of *sidra* opens your stomach a little too much for the modest portions, you can try to fill it up with the thick slices of brown bread or an order of ice cream.

🪧 From Pl. Marqués, proceed uphill on C. Óscar Olavarría. Take the 2nd right onto C. Vicaría and then the 2nd right onto C. Rosario. 💲 Menú del día €9.50 M-Tu and Th-Su noon-4pm. Cheeses €6. Entrees €10-20. Sidra €3. Wine by the bottle €10-20. ⏰ Open M-Tu noon-4pm and 7pm-midnight, W 7pm-midnight, Th-Su noon-4pm and 7pm-midnight.

ENOTECA MANDI ITALIAN $

C. Marqués de San Esteban, 11 ☎66 431 44 24

It might not feel right to eat Italian food when there are so many Asturian dishes still waiting to be tried, but any guilt will evaporate along with the steam from your pasta covered in the sauce of the day (€4, available M-F 1-3:30pm). Italian wines and beers are served and take center stage at night, when the restaurant becomes more of a bar and the food becomes less of a bargain.

🪧 1 block inland from the Playa de Poniente and the Puerto Deportivo, between C. Felipe Menéndez and C. Zamora. ℹ Gluten-free pasta available. 💲 Pasta €4, available M-F. Appetizers €3. Bruschette €3-8. Cheeses €7.50-14. Beer €2.50. Wine by the glass €2-3. Cocktails €4.50-5.50. ⏰ Open M-F 1-3:30pm and 7:30pm-midnight, Sa-Su 7:30pm-2am.

LA ZAMORANA SEAFOOD $$$$

Av. de los Hermanos Felgueroso, 38-40 ☎98 538 06 32 www.lazamorana.net

Stretching your budget is possible but worth it at this swanky seafood restaurant and *sidrería.* Ordering the €14 lunch *menú* or the plate of the day (€16-18) for dinner can keep your spending in check, but the allure of the more expensive options on the menu may help you become friends with the supermarket checkout lady over the next few days. The platter of grilled seafood and shellfish (€40) is a delicious experience you're unlikely to forget, and as long as you're breaking the bank, don't skip dessert—they're all homemade. The local *tarta gijonesa* is particularly delicious.

🪧 From the Jardines de Begoña (Av. Costa side), proceed 4 blocks along Av. Hermanos Felgueroso. 💲 Menú del día Tu-Sa €14 and Su €18 (served noon-5pm only). Dinner special of the day €16-18. Appetizers €14-28. Entrees €15-64. Desserts €5. ⏰ Open Tu-Su noon-5pm and 7:30pm-12:30am. Aug open daily noon-5pm and 7:30pm-12:30am.

TINO EL ROXU CIDER, ASTURIAN $$

Av. de la Costa, 30 ☎98 514 09 91 www.tinoelroxu.es

Those looking to get their *menú* on after dark will find a serviceable option at this *sidrería.* There's better food for similar prices during the day, but if €8 *raciones* of sardines aren't filling you up elsewhere, the two courses, bread, dessert, and water or wine served here certainly will. As the waiter pours your cider over a metal receptacle to catch the spill, compare his technique to that of the servers of yesteryear immortalized on the wall in photographs, drawings, wooden carvings, and stone plaques.

🪧 From the Jardines de Begoña (Av. Costa side), with the park on your right, proceed 4 blocks along Av. Costa. 💲 Menú €12. Raciones €6-20. Entrees €11-26. ⏰ Open M 11am-12:30am and W-Su 11am-12:30am.

NIGHTLIFE

Most of Gijón's nightlife is centered around the neighborhoods of **Cimavilla** (the old town) and **L'Arena,** as well as along **Calle de Rodríguez San Pedro** and **Calle del Marqués de San Esteban,** near the Playa de Poniente, and (in summer) along the **Playa de San Lorenzo.** Like in most smaller Spanish cities, things are slow during the week but pick up speed around Thursday.

BAMBARA BAR, CLUB

C. del Marqués de San Esteban, 9 www.bambara-gijon.com

During the week, this bar is a comfortable place to have a drink with friends, whether at the bar, a table, or in one of the lounge areas in the back, while listening to *tranquilo* tunes. On the weekend, however, it's goodbye tenor sax and hello Rihanna as the tables are whisked away and the bar becomes a *discoteca* open until 7:30am.

➜ From the dock with the tourist office, cross C. Rodríguez San Pedro and proceed 1 block on C. Felipe Menéndez, then take the 1st left onto C. Marqués de San Esteban. [$] Beer €2.20-3.50. Mixed drinks €5-6. ⏰ Open M-Th 8am-4am, F 8am-7:30am, Sa 5pm-7:30am, Su 5pm-4am.

BLOW-UP CLUB, BAR

C. de Rodríguez San Pedro, 3 www.blow-up.es

This nightclub's pink light and disco balls come with the matching tunes of Gloria Gaynor and the Village People. If all the *sidra* from dinner wasn't quite enough to get you doing the *i griega-eme-ce-a,* the bars are so large that it shouldn't be too hard to sidle up and ask for *una más.*

➜ Opposite the dock with the tourist office. From Pl. Marqués, walk with the river on your right and follow C. Rodríguez San Pedro. [$] Beer €4. Mixed drinks €6.50-12. ⏰ Open M-Th 10pm-5am, F-Sa 10pm-7:30am, Su 10pm-5am.

ESSENTIALS

Practicalities

- **TOURIST OFFICE: Municipal tourist office** (C. Rodríguez San Pedro ☎985 34 17 71 www.gijon.info ➜ Halfway down the big dock in Puerto Deportivo. ⏰ Open daily Apr 28-July 15 10am-8pm, July 16-Aug 26 10am-10pm, Aug 26-Nov 4 10am-8pm, Nov 5-Apr 28 10am-2:30pm and 4:30-7:30pm. Open 10am-8pm during Semana Santa.) There is a satellite office at the Playa de San Lorenzo. (⏰ Open June 1-July 6 10am-2pm and 4-8pm, July 7-Aug 26 10am-10pm, Aug 27-Oct 14 10am-2pm and 4-8pm.) The tourist office sells the **Gijón Card** ([$] 1 day €10, 2 days €12, 3 days €15), which provides discounts at certain establishments, free admission to the city's museums, and free unlimited use of city buses.
- **TOURS:** Audioguides for self-guided tours (in Spanish, English, and French) are available at the main tourist office for €2 plus a €10 deposit (free with Gijón card). Free PDF files of the routes and mp3s of the audioguide narration can be downloaded from the tourist office website, www.gijon.info. Four different tours are available: Gijón Cimavilla; Gijón, City of Sculptures; Enlightened Gijón; and Modernist Gijón. A tourist bus with commentary available in seven languages also runs between the major sights of the city; tickets can be purchased at the tourist office or on the bus. ([$] Adults 1 day €11, 2 days €16; children under 12 1 day €5.50, 2 days €8; children under 3 free. All tickets 50% off with Gijón Card. ⏰ Available daily June 25-Sept 2 every hour 10am-7pm, June 1-24 and Sept 3-30 available Sa-Su every hour 10am-7pm.)
- **CURRENCY EXCHANGE:** Any of the many banks along C. Corrida can change money, such as **BBVA.** (C. Corrida, 5 ☎985 35 79 40 ⏰ M-F 8:30am-2:15pm.) **El Corte Inglés Mall** (Ramón Areces, 2 ➜ Bus #10 or 15. ☎985 99 00 74 ⏰ Open M-Sa 10am-10pm) has longer hours, but is not centrally located.

- **INTERNET ACCESS:** Computers with internet access and free Wi-Fi are available at the **Biblioteca Jovellanos.** (C. Jovellanos, 23 ☎985 34 32 66 ➡ Between C. de León and Paseo de Begoña. ⏰ Open M-F 9am-9pm, Sa 10am-2pm and 4-8pm, Su and holidays 10am-2pm.) Free Wi-Fi is also available in many cafes and most hotels.
- **POST OFFICE:** Pl. Seis de Agosto (☎985 17 68 06 ➡ At the end of C. de la Libertad closer to the Jardines de Begoña. ⏰ Open M-F 8:30am-8:30pm, Sa 9:30am-2pm.)
- **POSTAL CODE:** 33206

Emergency

- **EMERGENCY NUMBER:** ☎112.
- **POLICE:** Municipal police at C. de San José, 2 ☎985 18 11 00. (➡ From Jardines de Begoña, proceed along Av. de los Hermanos Felgueroso and take the third left onto C. de San José.)
- **HOSPITAL:** Relatively close to the *centro* is a health center, the **Consultorio de Puerta de la Villa.** (C. de Donato Arguelles ☎985 14 30 30) The nearest hospitals, **Hospital de Jove** (Av. Eduardo de Castro ☎985 32 00 50 www.hospitaldejove.com) and **Hospital de Cabueñes** (C. de los Prados, 395 ☎985 18 50 00) are located well outside of the city center.
- **AMBULANCE:** ☎985 16 85 11.
- **PHARMACY:** A 24hr. pharmacy is located at C. José de las Clotas, 3. (☎985 34 28 61 ⏰ Open daily 24hr.) Other pharmacies are located throughout the city.

Getting There

BY BUS

The cheapest way to get to Gijón is by bus. The bus station (C. Magnus Blikstad, 1 ☎90 242 22 42 ➡ One block to the right of C. de Palacio Valdés as it curves sharply to the left) is near the center of the city. **ALSA** runs buses to Gijón from: Barcelona ($ €57-68 ⏰ 13hr., 4 per day 9am-10pm); Bilbao ($ €20-40 ⏰ 3½-5¾hr.; M-F 9 per day 6am-1:45am, Sa 7 per day 6am-1:45am, Su 10 per day 8:30am-1:45am); Madrid ($ €34-54 ⏰ 5½-7½hr.; M-Th 12 per day 8am-12:30am, F 19 per day 8am-12:30am, Sa 9 per day 8am-11:30pm, Su 16 per day, 8am-2:30am); Oviedo ($ €2.25 ⏰ 30min.; M-F 94 per day 6:30am-10:30pm, Sa 73 per day 6:45am-4:30am, Su 53 per day 5:30am-10:30pm); San Sebastián ($ €27-53 ⏰ 5¼-7¾hr.; M-F 6 per day 7:10am-12:20am, Sa 5 per day 9:10am-12:20am, Su 6 per day 7:10am-12:20am); Santander ($ €14-28 ⏰ 2¼-3¾hr.; M-Th 11 per day 7:15am-3:30am, F 14 per day 7:15am-3:30am, Sa 9 per day 7:15am-3:30am, Su 11 per day 8:30am-3:30am.), and Santiago de Compostela ($ €30-41 ⏰ 5¾-6¾hr.; M-F 4 per day 6am-6pm, Sa 3 per day 6am-6pm, Su 4 per day 6am-6pm). In Gijón, the information desk/ticket counter is across the street from the rest of the bus station.

BY TRAIN

Gijón is in the process of constructing a new train station; currently, both **RENFE** (national) and **FEVE** (regional) trains arrive at the **Estación Provisional de Sanz Crespo.** (C. Sanz Crespo; RENFE: ☎90 232 03 20 FEVE: ☎98 517 89 29 ➡ At the intersection of C. Carlos Marx and the Autovía del Cantábrico.) RENFE trains arrive from Barcelona ($ €75-99 ⏰ 11-12hr., 2 per day 9:20am and 9:10pm) and Madrid ($ €51 ⏰ 5½hr.; M-Sa 4 per day 7:30am-6:30pm, Su 3 per day 11am-6:30pm); FEVE trains arrive from Avilés ($ €1.70 ⏰ 40min.; M-F 32 per day 6:52am-10:30pm, Sa-Su 31 per day 7:26am-10:47pm) and Oviedo ($ €3.05 ⏰ 30min.-1½hr.; M-F 30 per day 6:35am-10pm, Sa-Su 19 per day 6:47am-9:47pm).

BY PLANE

The **Aeropuerto de Asturias** (OVD; www.aena.es) receives flights from ten national and international destinations operated by six airlines, including the budget airlines **EasyJet** and **Ryanair.** EasyJet has flights from London ($ €22-36) and Geneva ($ €30);

Ryanair has flights from Madrid (Ⓢ €16) and Barcelona (Ⓢ €16) The airport is about 25mi. outside of Gijón; ALSA runs buses from the airport to the city's bus station (Ⓢ €7.50 ⏰ 45min., 16 per day 7am-11pm) as well as buses from Gijón to the airport (Ⓢ €7.50 ⏰ 45min., 16 per day 6am-10pm.)

Getting Around

Walking is the cheapest and simplest way to get around Gijón and the only way to get around the *centro histórico*. Buses (€1.20, under 26 and over 65 €0.66, under 13 and with Gijón Card free) are an easy way to get to the occasional far-flung destination, like the youth hostel or the Muséu del Pueblu d'Asturies, and tickets can be bought on the bus (they will, in theory, make change up to €10). The city loans out bicycles for free at the **Palacio de Deportes** (Paseo del Doctor Fleming, 929 ☎98 518 17 50 ⚓ Bus #1 or 10 to Las Mestas. Continue in the direction of the bus along C. Ezkurdia, cross the river, and turn left onto the Paseo del Doctor Fleming), but make sure to get there early in the day. There are taxi stands all over the city, including at the Pl. de San Miguel and the south end of the Jardines de Begoña; alternatively, call Radiotaxi Gijón (☎98 514 11 11) or Radiotaxi Villa de Jovellanos (☎98 516 44 44).

santander ☎942

This sea-oriented city has always capitalized on its strategic peninsula location in the Bay of Biscay. For centuries, it was an important port for the Kingdom of Castile. Nowadays, since the port has moved to the 'burbs, the only ships arriving in Santander are ferries, which bring hordes of Europeans eager to bask on Santander's other great interface with the sea: beaches. Beaches are as much a part of Santander's history as its maritime past—the city became a popular beach resort when Alfonso XIII began spending his summers at the Península de la Magdalena—and they continue to draw visitors from Spain and abroad to this lively Cantabrian capital.

ORIENTATION

Santander sits on a peninsula jutting into the Bay of Biscay. The southern shore of the city forms the Bay of Santander and the eastern shore forms El Sardinero Cove. Along each of these shores are the city's two main neighborhoods: the *centro* and El Sardinero, respectively. The *centro* is home to most of the city's restaurants, nightlife, and budget accommodations, as well as the train and bus stations. El Sardinero has the city's most famous beaches. The city's most popular tourist attraction is the Península de la Magdalena, a peninsula on the southeastern tip of the city. The *centro* is fairly concentrated, but if you need to leave it, the excellent bus system will speedily take you where you need to go.

ACCOMMODATIONS

It's easy to find places to stay both in the *centro* and in El Sardinero, but budget travelers and revelers alike will prefer the *centro* for its lower prices and its proximity to most of the nightlife. For more information on accommodations, pick up a *Guía de Alojamientos* from the tourist office or from www.ayto-santander.es (click "Turismo" and then the "Alojamientos" image on the right).

🏨 **HOSTEL B&B&B**   HOSTEL $
C. Méndez Núñez, 6, 1st fl.   ☎942 22 78 17 www.hostelsantander.com
The only hostel in town not-so-humbly calls itself "B&B&B"—*bueno, bonito, y barato* (good, pretty, and cheap). It would be pretty brash if it weren't all so T&T&T (true, true, and true). The bunk beds are comfortable, and the pillows

are uber puffy. The included, decidedly modest, breakfast probably won't wow you, but the large common area with floor-to-ceiling windows looking out onto the Bay of Santander just might. The spotless four-, six-, and eight-bed dorms are all the same price, so take your pick—if it's available. Reservations are especially recommended on the weekends.

*‡ From the Estación de Autobuses, walk 1½ blocks on C. Méndez Núñez (the street opposite the main entrance, on the right). **i** Common area with TV. Kitchen. Free Wi-Fi. Free lockers. Towel rental €1. Laundry service €5. Printing €0.25 per page. Breakfast included. Shared bathrooms. [$] Dorms €19-21. ⏰ Reception 8am-1pm and 4pm-midnight, but guests get a key after leaving ID.*

PENSIÓN A-MADRID HOTEL $

C. Madrid, 21, 1st fl. ☎942 21 44 94 www.pensionensantander.com

You'll be hard pressed to find lower prices for a private room in the *centro*. A single is the size of a double at a lower price and is quite comfortable for a solo traveler, though the shower in the shared bathroom is somewhat small. And the owner's eagerness to chat at length? Free!

*‡ Upon exiting either train station, turn right onto C. Atilano Rodríguez. Cross C. Castilla, and take the second right onto the diagonal C. Madrid. **i** Free Wi-Fi. [$] Singles €18-20, doubles €30-40, triples €45-60. ⏰ Reception 24hr.*

HOSTAL CARLOS III HOTEL $$$$

Av. Reina Victoria, 135 ☎942 27 16 16 www.hostalcarlos3.com

A hotel named after a king on a street named after a queen doesn't exactly call out to the budget traveler, but if your heart is set on staying in El Sardinero, a night in this renovated building from the 1910s is among the cheaper options—and well worth the price. The dark, regal hallways, handsome wooden furniture, and well-kempt gardens will make you feel like you are living a life of luxury. The roomy doubles have plenty of space to walk around, while singles are a little smaller, and triples are essentially doubles with an extra bed squeezed in. Ask for the double; a spiral staircase leading to a small room with views of the bay will make you feel like a king for merely princely prices.

*‡ Bus 1, 2, 3, 4, 7, 13, or 15 to Luis Martínez. Proceed on Av. Reina Victoria with the bay to your right. Take the first left onto C. Luis Martínez and the first right onto what is also Av. Reina Victoria. **i** Open only Apr-Dec. Breakfast €3.90. TV. Free Wi-Fi. [$] June 21-July 10 singles €44, doubles €65; July 11-Aug singles €59, doubles €79; Apr-June 20 & Sept-Nov singles €36, doubles €55. Extra bed €12. ⏰ Reception 24h.*

PENSIÓN ANGELINES HOTEL $$

C. Atilano Rodríguez, 9, 1st fl. ☎942 31 25 84 www.pensionangelines.com

Big beds are squeezed into not-so-big singles at this *pensión* just steps away from the bus and train stations (the doubles have more standard proportions). Even if you have trouble getting out of your bed, you'll have no problems getting into a bathroom—there are five for the hotel's twelve rooms.

*‡ Upon exiting either train station, turn right onto C. Atilano Rodríguez. **i** TV. Free Wi-Fi. [$] Singles €18-25, doubles €28-38, triples €42-54. ⏰ Reception 24hr.*

HOSTAL LA MEXICANA HOTEL $$$$

C. Juan de Herrera, 3 ☎942 22 23 54 www.hostallamexicana.com

This *hostal*, with its three floors of well-lit, spacious singles and doubles, plus private bathrooms, sits just around the corner from the Ayuntamiento. Don't worry, you're probably in the right place, even if the lineup of armchairs in the living room next to reception makes it look like the site of a grandmothers' convention.

*‡ From the Ayuntamiento, turn left onto C. Isabel II and right onto C. Juan de Herrera. **i** TV. Free Wi-Fi. Breakfast €3. [$] July 1-Aug 31 (and Semana Santa) singles €46, doubles €64; Sept 1-15 singles €39, doubles €58; Sept 16-June 30 singles €29, doubles €44. ⏰ Reception 24hr.*

SIGHTS

PENÍNSULA DE LA MAGDALENA PALACE, BEACH, PARK

Península de la Magdalena ☎942 20 30 84 www.palaciomagdalena.com

One of the perks of being a king is that people give you lots of gifts. Alfonso XIII found this out in 1913 when the city of Santander formally presented him with the Palacio Real de la Magdalena—with its eclectic mixture of English and French architectural styles—as a gift and as an incentive to spend his summers in the city. Whether you, too, are here in summer or decide to come in the winter, you can visit the rooms of the palace, now open to the public and the highlight of the Península de la Magdalena (call the tourist office to book a free tour M-W). Santander's most visited tourist attraction, the peninsula also has pleasant parks, a small zoo, and the **Playa de los Bikinis,** supposedly the first place in Spain where the once-scandalous two-piece bathing suit was worn. The overpriced tourist "train" will take you by all of the peninsula's attractions, but walking is quite pleasant, even if it's somewhat hilly.

 # Bus #1, 2, 3, 4 7, 13, or 15 to La Magdalena. With the bay on your left, walk down Av. Reina Victoria and turn left down the hill; the entrance to the park is at the bottom of the hill. ***i*** *The inside of the Palacio de la Magdalena can only be visited as part of a guided tour, run by the Palacio de la Magdalena M-W 11am or noon, and by the tourist information office Sa-Su 10am (as part of a larger city tour). Reservations should be made in advance with the tourist information office for all tours. $ Park admission free. Tours M-W free, Sa-Su €10. Tourist train €2.10, under 10 €1.40. ⏰ Open summer 8am-10pm; winter 9am-8:30pm.*

MUSEO MARÍTIMO DEL CANTÁBRICO MUSEUM

C. San Martín de Bajamar ☎942 27 49 62 www.museosdecantabria.com/maritimo

So devoted to the sea that it's a bit hard to find from land, this museum explores all things maritime from multiple angles in a collection that spans three well-curated floors. Sailors and landlubbers alike will find something of interest because the artifacts are so varied: immense wooden model ships and 16th-century navigational instruments might interest some, while others might be more taken with the display of different fishing tools, including specialized nets and a particularly gruesome-looking rake used to collect shellfish. One of the most impressive items on display is a minutely detailed diorama depicting the construction of a wooden ship, from forest to seaworthy vessel, in an old Cantabrian shipyard. The aquarium on the bottom floor is a big hit with kids.

 # Bus #1, 2, 3, 4, 7, 12, 13 or 15 to González de Riancho. Walk down the stairs to Playa de los Peligros. With the bay on your left, walk along the beach and continue along C. San Martín de Bajamar. The museum will be on the left. ***i*** *All signs in Spanish, most also in French and English. $ €6; students, seniors, and under 12 €4. ⏰ Open May-Sept Tu-Su 10am-7:30pm; Oct-Apr Tu-Su 10am-6pm.*

MUSEO DE ARTE MODERNO Y CONTEMPORÁNEO DE SANTANDER Y CANTABRIA MUSEUM

C. Rubio, 6 ☎942 20 31 20

This museum's elegant building, constructed in 1909, clearly was not originally intended to house modern art. Walking up the stately, curved wooden staircase only to be greeted by *Glob*, a video of a whining green creature projected onto an amorphous white sculpture, could be somewhat jarring, but the juxtaposition of the traditional and the modern is actually quite charming. Señor Glob is the gatekeeper of the two floors that house the permanent collection of paintings, photographs, and sculptures by artists from Spain and around the world. Temporary exhibitions on the ground floor and basement rotate four times per year.

 # Bus #1, 2, 3, 7, 12, 13, 15 to Jesús de Monasterio. Turn right onto C. Florida and then right onto C. Rubio. ***i*** *Free guided tours available for groups; reservations required in advance. $ Free. ⏰ Open June 15-Sept 14 Tu-Sa 10:30am-1pm and 6-9pm, Su and holidays 11am-1:30pm; opens 30min. earlier Sept 15-June 14.*

CATEDRAL DE SANTA MARÍA DE LA ASUNCIÓN CATHEDRAL

Plaza del Obispo José Eguino y Trecu ☎942 22 60 24

This Gothic cathedral was constructed between the 12th and 14th centuries, but changes have been made to it over the years, particularly after it was damaged by a giant dynamite explosion in 1893 and a fire in 1941. It was built to replace a church that kept some relics that had been evacuated from the Muslim invasion of Spain. Despite this expansive history, though, it has thoroughly modern comforts: during one of the frequent masses, televisions and amplified sound ensure that there's not a bad seat in the house. A (free) peek is well worth it if you can find a time when mass isn't going on.

🚏 Bus #5, 6, 12, 13, or 15 to La Catedral. ℹ No visiting during worship. Free guided tours July-Aug; inquire at tourist office for hours. [$] Free. 🕐 Open M-F 10am-1pm and 4:30-7pm, mass at 11am and 6:30pm; Sa 10am-1pm and 4:30-8pm, mass at 11am, 5, and 8pm; Su and holidays 10am-1:30pm and 5-9pm, mass at noon, 1:30, 5, and 8pm.

THE GREAT OUTDOORS

Beaches fit for kings are one of Santander's main attractions. There are twelve beaches, but many of these are just subdivisions of larger stretches of sand. The most touristy are the **Playas de El Sardinero,** made up of the Primera Playa de Santander, the Segunda Playa de Santander, and the attached Playa de la Concha. Other beaches can be found both to the north and to the south of these (accessible by the Senda de Mataleñas to the north and by Av. Reina Victoria to the south).

★ **PLAYA DE MATALEÑAS** BEACH

Between Cabo Mayor and Cabo Menor

Just off the tourist map, both literally and figuratively, the Playa de Mataleñas is twice as beautiful and not quite as busy as the popular beaches of El Sardinero. Tucked in between the two imposing cliffs of Cabo Mayor and Cabo Menor, this beach might as well be on an island, as it is a stone's throw from any of the nearby cities. This seclusion has its advantages (fewer cars) but also has one big disadvantage: the beach is far from the ★**ice cream stands.** Though the beach is easily accessible by bus, walking from El Sardinero along the **Senda de Mataleñas,** while a bit of a hike, provides incredible views of the bay, the city, and the Cabo Mayor lighthouse.

🚏 Bus #15 to Mataleñas. Or from Plaza de Italia, walk with the bay on your right along Av. de Fernández Castaneda, which will turn into Av. del Stadium and Av. Manuel Garcia Lago. At the second traffic circle (shortly before the end of Playa de El Sardinero 2°), there will be a flight of stairs on the left that leads to the Senda de Mataleñas. After a 20 minute walk, there will be a flight of stairs on the right leading down to the beach. ℹ Showers available. [$] Free. 🕐 Lifeguard June-Sept daily 11:30am-7:30pm.

PLAYAS DE EL SARDINERO BEACH

Along Av. de Fernández Castaneda

The biggest and busiest beaches of Santander, these expansive stretches of sand make you understand why the Spanish king spent his summers in this city. The Segunda Playa de El Sardinero is the widest, which means more room for your towel but also more of a walk to the shower, bathrooms, and ice cream stands behind the beaches. The two beaches can be easily accessed from one another, but at street level they are separated by the well-kempt **Jardines de Piquio,** from which you'll get an incredible 180-degree panorama of sand and sea.

🚏 Bus #1, 2, 3, 4, 7, 13, or 15 to Plaza de Italia. Playa de El Sardinero 1° is down a marked flight of stairs off the plaza. Playa de El Sardinero 2° can be reached either by walking along El Sardinero 1° with the bay to your right or walking along Av. de Fernández Castaneda with the bay to your right, then down a marked flight of stairs. ℹ Showers available. Bathrooms (€0.30) on the boardwalk behind Playa de la Concha and on Av. de Fernández Castaneda behind El Sardinero 1°. [$] Free. Ice cream €2-3. Water €1 at nearby stands. 🕐 Lifeguard June-Sept daily 11:30am-7:30pm.

FOOD

Most of Santander's restaurants (and nightlife), can be found in the neighborhood bounded by the Paseo de Pereda, C. Sautuola, C. Santa Lucía, and C. Casimiro Sáinz. A few restaurants are also in El Sardinero near the Plaza de Italia; the **Barrio Pesquero,** on the #4 bus route, is well known for its restaurants. The best value option is almost always the *menú del día*, but this is only available during the afternoon; the price often rises on weekends. Many restaurants turn into bars at night.

EL SOLECITO — SPANISH $$

C. Bonifaz, 19 — ☎942 36 06 33 www.elsolecito.com

At first you may wonder why the African masks lining the blue and yellow walls have their eyes nearly popping out of their sockets. After your first bite of the *menú del día* (€11-13.50), you'll know: they're simply stunned at how good the food is for such low prices. The *crepes de verduras* taste like they should cost twice their price; even the bread and house wine taste much better than those at similarly priced establishments. If you're around in the evening, there's no *menú*, but the pizzas (€6-12.50) and other items on the à la carte menu are available all day. Even meat-lovers may swing vegetarian for a night with dishes like the *parrillada de verduras con salsa de mostaza* (grilled vegetables with mustard sauce; €12). If you simply can't get enough of the delicious, cheap food, you can always call for delivery to your hotel.

Proceed along the Paseo de Pereda with the bay on your right. Turn left onto C. Gandara and go 4 blocks, then turn right onto C. Bonifaz. ***i*** *Free delivery available by calling ☎942 32 51 18, minimum order €9.* [$] *Menú del día M-F €11, Sa-Su €13.50 (available noon-4pm). Appetizers €5.50-11. Entrees €6-13. Beer €2.25. Glass/pitcher of sangria €3.50/9.50.* 🕐 *Open Tu-Su noon-4pm and 8-11:30pm. Delivery hours M-Th 12:30-3:45pm and 7:30-11:30pm, F-Sa 12:30-4pm and 7:30pm-12:15am, Su 1:00-4:30pm and 7:30-11:30pm.*

LA PINCHERÍA — BAR, TAPAS $

C. Panamá, 2 — ☎685 77 17 76

Two wooden barrels herald the entrance to this haven of cheap prices among the tourist-oriented restaurants that line the beaches. It's an especially good deal for students, who only pay €6 for the *menú del día* (€10-12 for those without a student ID). If you order off the menu instead, be warned: compared to the prices at the bar, dishes are generally one euro higher if eaten at a table and two euros higher if eaten outside. The low prices are in spite of the restaurant's great location; it's not on the beach, but it's as close as any of the more expensive restaurants near the Casino.

From Plaza Italia, with the bay on your right, walk 1 block on Av. de Fernández Castaneda, then turn left onto C. Panamá. [$] *Menú del día €10-12, students with ID €6. Beer €1.50-2.* 🕐 *Open June-Sept daily 1-5pm and 9pm-midnight; open Oct-May M-Sa 1-5pm and 9pm-midnight, Su 1-5pm.*

EL PICÓN — MEXICAN $$$

C. Santa Lucía, 36 — ☎942 21 91 65

Despite the comically large sombrero and the kitschy plastic jalapeño arrangements hanging from the walls, this restaurant takes its Mexican food seriously—the waiter even sticks around to make sure that you fold your burrito correctly. Those flavorful, properly folded burritos and the enchiladas can be meals in themselves, but the tacos and quesadillas are considerably smaller. All water here is bottled, but if you're going to be drinking from a bottle anyway, you're better off with one of the ice-cold Mexican beers (€2.85-4.70). The ice cream with Kahlúa (€4.20) does double duty as a dessert and a warm-up for a long night at the bars and clubs right around the corner.

From Plaza Cañadío, walk uphill on C. López Doriga and take the first right onto C. Santa Lucía. [$] *Appetizers €3-3.50. Entrees €7-12. Menú del día €15 served 1-4pm. Tasting menu €18 (drink not included). Tequila shots €3-8.* 🕐 *Open daily 1-4pm and 8pm-midnight.*

LA GONDOLA CAFE $$

Plaza de Italia ☎942 27 10 52

If you want to find a cheap *menú* in the Plaza de Italia but would rather have workmen (not vacationing families) as your fellow diners, this is the place for you. The menu doesn't offer the best food in the neighborhood, but it's sufficient, cheap, and conveniently located so you can get back to the beach as soon as possible.

✦ *Bus #1, 2, 3, 4, 7, 13, or 15 to Plaza de Italia. Under the Casino.* ***i*** *Cash only. During the summer, à la carte menu is available in addition to the prix-fixe menu.* Ⓢ *Sandwiches €3.50-9. Entrees €10-16. Beer €1.50.* ☒ *Open daily 9am-11pm. Sometimes open later in the summer.*

NIGHTLIFE

Nightlife in Santander is largely confined to the small but energetic part of the *centro* that has most of the city's restaurants, bars, and clubs. The *noche santanderina* starts in the bars around the Plaza de Cañadío or along C. del Río de la Pila, with people spilling into the plaza or the street. People make their way to the clubs as the night progresses, and you're unlikely to find many partiers before 3am. Nightlife outside of the *centro* is accessible by one of the three nighttime buses, all of which go between the *centro* and El Sardinero before shooting off to different outer neighborhoods.

EL DIVINO CLUB

C. López Doriga, 5 ☎653 92 60 29 www.eldivinosantander.com

Even if you've had a few, this place is easy to find—it's just half a block away from the Plaza de Cañadío, up the hill with the massive crowd of students pregaming for a night out at this popular club. As the night goes on and the bottles start to empty, the crowd thins as people squeeze inside. Scantily clad bartenders behind the color-changing bar serve up pricey drinks, but most of the young crowd seems to be all set well before stepping inside.

✦ *From Plaza de Cañadío, walk uphill on C. López Doriga.* ***i*** *Ladies' night Th; women get voucher for 1 drink at entrance.* Ⓢ *Beer €3.50. Shots €3.50. Mixed drinks €5.50.* ☒ *Open July-Sept daily midnight-4:30am; Oct-May Th-Sa midnight-4:30am.*

INDIAN BAR, CLUB

C. Casimiro Sáinz, 10

Standing guard on the last big street of the nightlife neighborhood, this frontier outpost of revelry serves cheap drinks to a 20-something crowd. After a shot (€1), you might have the guts to notify the manager that the Rhode Island license plate on the wall doesn't really have anything to do with the club's Wild West theme, but your time would probably be better spent on the dance floor.

✦ *From Paseo de Pereda, turn left onto C. Casimiro Sáinz.* Ⓢ *Beer €2. Shots €1. Mixed drinks €4. Prices rise €2 at 3am.* ☒ *Open Th midnight-5am, F-Sa midnight-6am.*

MANDALA BAR

C. Pedrueca, 4 ☎942 76 43 09

A red glow illuminates this loud and lively religion-themed Asian bar. The Buddha looks on approvingly from the corner as patrons fight their way to the crowded bar for a cheap drink. The bathroom does double duty as a conversation starter—can we really say that Shiva was a woman?

✦ *From Paseo de Pereda, turn left onto C. Sautuola and right onto C. Pedrueca.* Ⓢ *Shots €1.50. Cocktails €4.* ☒ *Open M-Sa 4:30pm-4:30am, Su 5pm-4:30am.*

MALASPINA BAR, CLUB

C. Jesús Revaque Garea ☎942 31 39 39

Malaspina is a little calmer, drawing a slightly older crowd than many other bars in the neighborhood—at least at the beginning of the night. Around 3am, as the average age plummets, and the calm '90s music shifts to the likes of Rihanna.

⇟ From Pl. de Cañadío, walk 1 block up the hill on C. López Doriga, then turn right onto even steeper C. Jesús Revaque Garea, a dead end. ℹ 25+. $ Cover €6, F-Sa 1am-closing cover includes one drink. Beer €4. Shots €2.50. Mixed drinks €6. ⏰ Open June 15-Sept 15 Th-Sa 11pm-4:30am; Sept 16-June 14 Th 11pm-3:30am and F-Sa 11pm-4:30am.

ESSENTIALS

Practicalities

- **TOURIST OFFICES:** The **municipal tourist office** in the Jardines de Pereda provides tourist information, including a map of the city in English that is clearer than the Spanish-language map given out in hotels. (Jardines de Pereda ☎942 20 30 00 ⏰ Open June 15-Sep 15 daily 9am-9pm; Sept 16-June 14 M-F 9am-7pm, Sa 10am-7pm, Su 10am-2pm.) There is another municipal office at Plaza de Italia. (☎942 74 04 14 ⏰ Same hours.) The **regional tourist office** is in the Mercado del Este. (C. Hernán Cortés, 4 ☎942 31 07 08 ⇟ From the Banco Santander arch, take the second left. ⏰ Open daily 9am-9pm.)
- **TOURS:** Self-guided walking tours are available; a booklet provided at the tourist office outlines several routes. The **tourist office** runs tours (€10) that include the interior of the Palacio de la Magdalena on Sa and Su 10am; the Sa tour finishes in the *centro* while the Su tour visits the entire Península de la Magdalena and ends in El Sardinero. During July-Aug, there are several free tours of the *centro* with different themes on M-F. Free tours of various sights are available at other times of year; inquire at the tourist office.
- **CURRENCY EXCHANGE:** In the morning and early afternoon, most major banks in the *centro* exchange money, such as **Banco Santander.** (Paseo de Pereda, 9 ☎942 20 66 00 www.bancosantander.es ⏰ Open M-F 8:30am-2:30pm.) Outside of banking hours, the **El Corte Inglés** mall exchanges USD and GBP. (Plaza de Nueva Montaña ☎942 32 84 00 ⇟ Off of the S-10 highway. ⏰ Open M-Sa 10am-10pm.)
- **LUGGAGE STORAGE:** On the bottom floor of the **Estación de Autobuses.** (C. de Navas de Tolosa ⇟ Across the plaza from the train station. ☎942 21 19 95 $ Lockers €2.50 per day. ⏰ Storage available from 6am-midnight. Luggage office open M-F 8am-10pm, Sa 8am-1pm; at other times storage can be arranged with the information desk near the station entrance.)
- **INTERNET ACCESS:** Free Wi-Fi is available in the **Estación de Autobuses** and the Reference Room of the **Biblioteca Municipal** (C. de Gravina, 4 ☎ 942 20 31 23 ⇟ At the intersection with C. de Rubio, one block up the hill from C. de Jesús de Monasterio. ⏰ Open June 15-Sept 15 M-F 3:30-8:45pm, Sept 16-June 14 3:30-9:30pm).
- **POST OFFICE:** The most centrally located of Santander's five post offices is the one located near the Jardines de Pereda (C. de Alfonso XIII, 2 ☎942 36 55 19 ⏰ Open M-F 8:30am-8:30pm, Sa 9:30am-2pm). There is also a branch in El Sardinero (C. de Las Cruces, 6 ☎942 27 70 60 ⇟ From the Pl. de Italia, with the bay on your right, turn left onto Av. de los Infantes and right onto C. de Las Cruces. ⏰ Open M-F 8:30am-8:30pm, Sa 9:30am-1pm).
- **POSTAL CODES:** 39002 (C. Alfonso XIII); 39005 (C. de Las Cruces)

Emergency

- **EMERGENCY NUMBERS: General Emergency:** ☎112. **Ambulance:** ☎061. **Fire:** ☎080.
- **POLICE:** Municipal Police. (C. Castilla, 32 ☎092 ⇄ Proceed along the street to the left of the train station.)
- **HOSPITAL:** Hospital Universitario Marqués de Valdecilla. (Av. Valdecilla, 25 ☎ 942 20 25 20 ⇄ From the Ayutamiento, with the Ayuntamiento on your right, proceed along C. del Jesús de Monasterio, which will become C. de Burgos, C. de San Fernando, and Av. de Valdecilla.)
- **24HR. PHARMACY:** There are three 24hr. pharmacies, located at: Av. de los Castros, 153; C. Río de la Pila, 14; and C. Calvo Sotelo, 2.

Getting There

BY BUS

Buses are the cheapest way to get to Santander. The **bus station** (C. de Navas de Tolosa, 1 ☎942 21 19 95 ⇄ With the Ayuntamiento to your left, turn right onto C. de Isabel II, then right onto C. de Méndez Núñez) is close to the center of town, just a five minute walk from the Ayuntamiento. Buses arrive from: Barcelona ($ €52 ⏰ 10hr., 6 per day 10am-10:50pm); Bilbao ($ €6-14 ⏰ 1½hr., 27 per day 6am-1:45am); Oviedo ($ €12-25 ⏰ 2¼-3hr., 9-13 per day 7:45am-1am); San Sebastián ($ €13-24 ⏰ 3hr., 9-10 per day 7:10am-12:20am); and Madrid ($ €29 ⏰ 5½-6hr., 8 per day 8am-1:30am).

BY TRAIN

Two train systems serve Santander: **RENFE,** the national rail line, and **FEVE,** a regional train. Both train stations are in the same plaza that has the bus station. RENFE has service from Madrid, ($ €49. ⏰ 4½hr.; M-Sa 3 per day 8:30am-6:05pm, Su 2 per day 1:30pm and 6:05pm). FEVE has trains from Oviedo ($ €15 ⏰ 4¾hr., daily 7:05am and 3:35pm) and Bilbao ($ €8.25 ⏰ 3hr.; daily 8:02am, 1:02pm, and 7:30pm).

BY PLANE

If you are flying to Santander, you will probably fly into **Aeropuerto de Santander** (☎91 321 10 00) in nearby Camargo. **Ryanair** serves the airport, with flights from Madrid, Barcelona El Prat, Sevilla, Valencia, Málaga, and Palma de Mallorca. Buses to the airport leave the bus station every 30min. from 7am-11pm.

BY FERRY

Brittany Ferries (www.brittanyferries.com) operates **ferries** between Portsmouth, UK ($ €84 ⏰ 24hr.; Tu 5 pm, W 11am) and Plymouth, UK ($ €114 ⏰ 20hr., Su 3:30pm) and the Puerto de Santander. Reserve well ahead in summer.

Getting Around

The cheapest and easiest way to get around Santander is to walk, but while walking is well-suited to the compact *centro*, it's more of a trek out to El Sardinero. **Transportes Urbanos de Santander** operates the city's easy-to-use bus system (€1.20), and many lines go between the *centro* and El Sardinero. At night, these lines close and are replaced by three nighttime lines, all of which also run between the *centro* and El Sardinero (⏰ Sept-June F-Sa every 30min. until 3am, later July-Aug) There are also well-marked bike paths following the bay; tourists can rent bicycles using the vending machines of **TUSbic,** a bicycle rental service with numerous stations throughout the city. ($ For 1 day, €1+€0.60 per hour after the first hour; for 7 days, €5+€0.50 per hour after the first hour.)

PORTUGAL

LISBON

Portugal's capital is a mosaic, comprised of different neighborhoods that all come together to form the cohesive metropolis that is Lisbon. Each district has its own indelible character, from the graffiti-covered party that is Bairro Alto to chic Chiado and on to touristy Baixa and the crumbling tiles of Alfama—cross a single street or descend one steep staircase and you're someplace new. As is typical in Europe, the classic-to-the-point-of-cliché juxtaposition of ancient and modern holds here. But the true joy of Lisbon comes in peeling back the different layers of "old" that simultaneously exist. Pre-WWI tram cars run through the streets past buildings reconstructed after the earthquake of 1755. These are mixed in with remnants of the Renaissance, the Moorish invasion, and the Iron Age. Together, all of these layers form Lisbon, a city as full of surprises as it is of history. To experience its character to the fullest, get lost here. Let your nose lead you to *sardinhas assadas;* stumble through an alleyway to find an architectural marvel; talk to the locals at the hole-in-the-wall and take their advice. We promise you won't regret it.

greatest hits

- **GOING TOPLESS.** They say that the Igreja do Carmo (p. 461) lost its top in the 1755 earthquake, but we think it really happened at the awesome party the Igreja de São Roque (p. 461) threw the night before.

- **CHERRY BOMB.** Try *ginjinha*, Lisbon's trademark cherry liqueur, at Ginja d'Alfama. (p. 477)

- **LIMEY BASTARDS.** Get the most delicious caipirinhas at Bica Abaixo to tide you over between Bairro Alto and the waterfront. (p. 476)

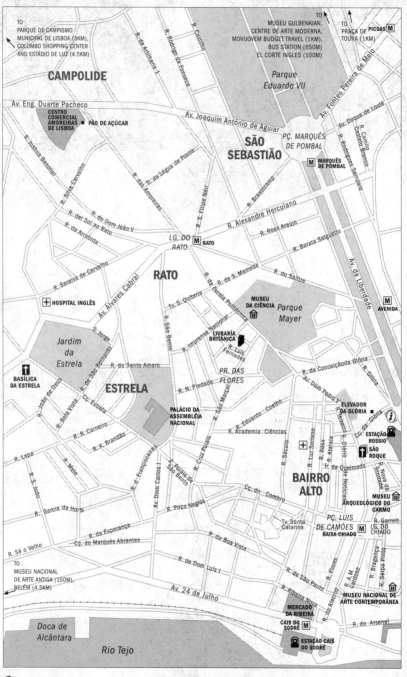

lisbon

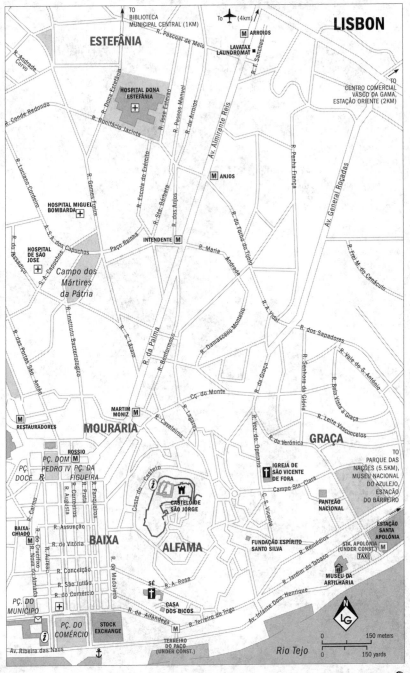

LISBON

ESTEFÂNIA

lisbon neighborhoods

MOURARIA

GRAÇA

BAIXA

ALFAMA

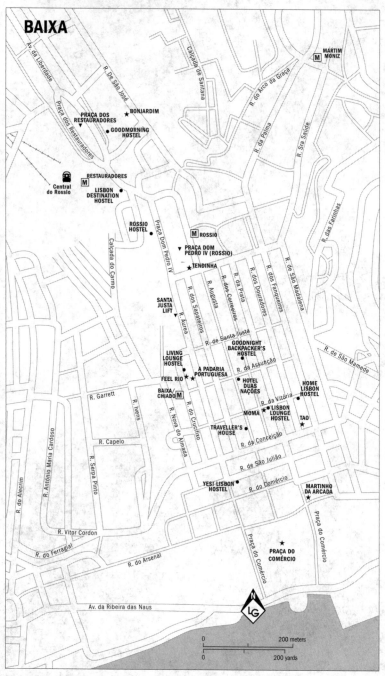

BAIXA

Av. da Liberdade
R. De São José
Calçada de Santana
R. do Arco da Graça
R. da Palma
R. Sta. Saúde

MÁRTIM MONIZ Ⓜ

R. das Farinhas

Praça dos Restauradores
★ BONJARDIM
● GOODMORNING HOSTEL
PRAÇA DOS RESTAURADORES ▽

Central do Rossio
RESTAURADORES Ⓜ
LISBON DESTINATION HOSTEL ●

Calçada do Carmo
Praça Dom Pedro IV

ROSSIO HOSTEL ●

Ⓜ ROSSIO
PRAÇA DOM PEDRO IV (ROSSIO) ▽
★ TENDINHA

R. das Portas de Santo Antão
R. dos Fanqueiros
R. de São Madalena

R. dos Correeiros
R. da Prata
R. dos Douradores
R. Augusta

SANTA JUSTA LIFT
R. Áurea ▽
R. dos Sapateiros

R. de Santa Justa
GOODNIGHT BACKPACKER'S HOSTEL
R. da Assunção
R. de São Mamede

LIVING LOUNGE HOSTEL ●
A PADARIA PORTUGUESA ★
FEEL RIO ★
HOTEL DUAS NAÇÕES ●
HOME LISBON HOSTEL

R. Garrett
R. Ivens
R. Nova do Almada
R. do Crucifixo

BAIXA/CHIADO Ⓜ
MOMA ★
R. da Vitória ★
LISBON LOUNGE HOSTEL ●
TAO ★

TRAVELLER'S HOUSE ●
R. da Conceição

R. António Maria Cardoso
R. Serpa Pinto
R. Capelo

R. de São Julião

YES! LISBON HOSTEL ●
R. do Comércio

MARTINHO DA ARCADA ★

R. do Alecrim
R. Vítor Cordon

R. do Ferragial
R. do Arsenal

Praça do Comércio
★ PRAÇA DO COMÉRCIO
Praça do Comércio

Av. da Ribeira das Naus

N
LG

0 ———— 200 meters
0 ———— 200 yards

lisbon

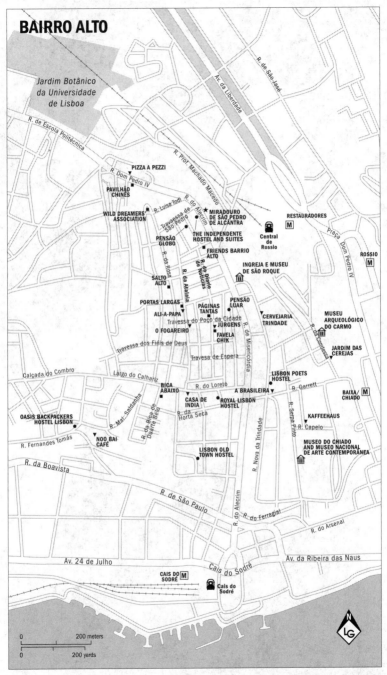

BAIRRO ALTO

Jardim Botânico da Universidade de Lisboa

R. de Escola Politécnica

R. Prof. Machado Macedo

Av. da Liberdade

R. de São José

PIZZA A PEZZI

R. Dom Pedro IV

PAVILHÃO CHINÊS

R. Luisa Todi

R. do Alecrim

WILD DREAMERS ASSOCIATION

Travessa de São Pedro

★ MIRADOURO DE SÃO PEDRO DE ALCÂNTRA

Central de Rossio

RESTAURADORES Ⓜ

PENSÃO GLOBO

THE INDEPENDENTE HOSTEL AND SUITES

FRIENDS BARRIO ALTO

R. do Diário de Notícias

INGREJA E MUSEU DE SÃO ROQUE

Praça Dom Pedro IV

ROSSIO Ⓜ

SALTO ALTO

R. da Rosa

R. da Atalaia

PORTAS LARGAS

PÁGINAS TANTAS

PENSÃO LUAR

ALI-A-PAPA

Travessa do Poço da Cidade

JÜRGENS

CERVEJARIA TRINDADE

MUSEU ARQUEOLÓGICO DO CARMO

O FOGAREIRO

FAVELA CHIK

R. da Misericórdia

R. da Condessa

JARDIM DAS CEREJAS

Travessa dos Fiéis de Deus

Travessa de Espera

Calçada do Combro

Largo do Calhariz

R. do Loreto

LISBON POETS HOSTEL

BICA ABAIXO

A BRASILEIRA ▼

R. Garrett

BAIXA/CHIADO Ⓜ

OASIS BACKPACKERS HOSTEL LISBON

R. Mar. Saldanha

R. da Bica de Duarte Belo

CASA DE INDIA

R. da Horta Seca

ROYAL LISBON HOSTEL

R. Nova da Trindade

R. Serpa Pinto

R. Capelo

KAFFEEHAUS

R. Fernandes Tomás

NOO BAI CAFÉ

MUSEO DO CHIADO AND MUSEO NACIONAL DE ARTE CONTEMPORÂNEA

R. da Boavista

LISBON OLD TOWN HOSTEL

R. de São Paulo

R. do Alecrim

R. do Ferragial

R. do Arsenal

Av. 24 de Julho

Cais do Sodré

Av. da Ribeira das Naus

CAIS DO SODRÉ Ⓜ

Cais do Sodré

0   200 meters

0   200 yards

N

LG

bairro alto

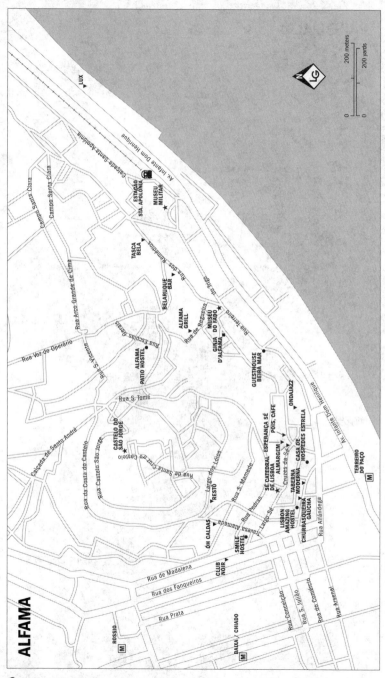

lisbon

ALFAMA

200 meters
200 yards

LUX

Av. Infante Dom Henrique

Calçada Santa Apolónia

ESTAÇÃO STA. APOLÓNIA

MUSEU MILITAR

Campo Santa Clara

Rua Arco Grande de Cima

TASCA BELA

Rua dos Remédios

BELARUQUE BAR

ALFAMA GRILL

Rua de Regueira

MUSEU DO FADO

Rua de São Vicente

Rua Escolas Gerais

Rua Voz do Operário

GINJA D'ALFAMA

Rua Terreira

ALFAMA PATIO HOSTEL

GUESTHOUSE BEIRA MAR

Rua S. Tomé

ONDAJAZZ

Calçada de Santo André

CASTELO DO SÃO JORGE

Rua da Costa do Castelo

Rua Castelo São Jorge

Rua de Santa Cruz do Castelo

ESPERANÇA CAFÉ

POIS. CAFÉ

SÉ CATEDRAL DE LISBOA

ALMARGEM

Largo dos Lóios

Cruzes da Sé

Rua S. Mamede

CASA DE HÓSPEDES ESTRELA

RESTÔ

TABERNA MODERNA

Av. Infante Dom Henrique

Rua das Pedras

Travessa Alameda

Largo Sé

TERREIRO DO PAÇO

M

LISBON AMAZING HOSTEL

CHURRASQUEIRA GAÚCHA

OH CALDAS

Rua Alfândega

SMILE HOSTEL

Rua de Madalena

CLUB NOIR

Rua dos Fanqueiros

Rua Conceição

Rua S. Julião

Rua do Comércio

Rua Arsenal

Rua Prata

ROSSIO

M

BAIXA / CHIADO

M

You'll find just as many tourists there, but Bairro Alto is a solid evening starting point for pretty much anybody under 30 in Lisbon. After that, most students migrate to the clubs by the riverfront, stopping at bars and smaller clubs along the way. You'll also find a good deal of students in the inexpensive Graça neighborhood.

orientation

Lisbon's historic center has four main neighborhoods: **Baixa,** where accommodations, shopping, and tourists abound; **Chiado,** where the shopping gets a bit ritzier; nightlife-rich **Bairro Alto,** still farther west; and ancient **Alfama,** on the east side of Baixa. The narrow, winding streets and stairways of Alfama and Bairro Alto can be confusing and difficult to navigate without a good map. The **Lisboa Mapa da Cidade e Guia Turístico** (€3) has nearly every street in these neighborhoods labeled and is a good investment if you're going to be exploring Lisbon for a few days. Even so, expect to spend some time aimlessly wandering, as even the most detailed of maps will have a hard time effectively detailing these neighborhoods. The maps at the tourist offices are reliable but do not show the names of many streets, particularly in Alfama and Bairro Alto. **Tram #28E** runs east-west, parallel to the river, and connects all these neighborhoods, with its eastern terminus in the inexpensive and off-the-beaten-path neighborhood of **Graça.** The palm-tree-lined **Avenida da Liberdade** runs north from Baixa all the way to the business district around the Praça do Marquês de Pombal, and on the far western edge of the city lies **Belém,** a neighborhood full of magnificent sights and delicious treats.

BAIXA

Baixa, Lisbon's old business hub, is the city's most centrally located neighborhood, and its streets are lined with accommodations and clothing stores. An oasis of order for travelers weary of getting lost in labyrinthine old cities, the entire neighborhood is flat and on a grid. The main pedestrian thoroughfare is the broad **Rua Augusta,** which runs from the massive riverside **Praça do Comércio** to Pr. de Dom Pedro IV, better known as **Rossio.** ⓂBaixa-Chiado has an entrance at the western end (to your right as you face the river) of R. da Vitória, which runs east to west and crosses Rua Augusta. Connected to Rossio's northwest corner is **Praça dos Restauradores,** a huge urban transit hub where the Rossio train station (for trains to Sintra) and tourist office can be found; it is also the main drop-off point for airport buses. From Pr. dos Restauradores, **Avenida da Liberdade** runs away from Baixa to the **Praça do Marquês do Pombal** and its surrounding business district.

BAIRRO ALTO AND CHIADO

Bairro Alto (literally, "High Neighborhood") is a hilly stretch of narrow cobblestone streets with graffiti-covered walls and laundry-lined balconies, best known for its unique nightlife and its *fado* (the Portuguese equivalent of soul music, if soul music made you weep like a little girl). The best way to get there is to take the Metro to Baixa-Chiado (Chiado exit), walk straight across Largo do Chiado, between the churches, and right up Rua da Misericórdia (it becomes R. de São Pedro de Alcântara) before heading left into Alto's daytime slumber or nighttime madness.

orientation

Chiado, slightly down the hill toward Baixa, is a little more clean-cut and cultured than its raucous neighbor to the west. The **Rua Garrett** cuts through the neighborhood, running between the **Largo do Chiado** and the stores and shopping center on R. do Carmo. The **Praça de Luís de Camões,** right next to Lg. do Chiado, connects the two neighborhoods.

ALFAMA

Alfama, Lisbon's hilly medieval quarter, was the only district to survive the 1755 earthquake, and those who have spent long, hot hours lost in its confusing maze of alleyways might sometimes wish it hadn't. Many alleys are unmarked and take confusing turns and bends; others are long, winding stairways known as *escadinhas;* still others are dead ends. Expect to get lost repeatedly—with or without a detailed map. The **Castelo de São Jorge** sits at the steep hill's peak, where you will find impressive views of all of Lisbon. The **Sé** (cathedral) is closer to the river and to Baixa. When in doubt, walk downhill to get closer to the river, where there is a flat, open area that will help you get your bearings. The **Mouraria** (the old Moorish quarter, more recently a multicultural neighborhood with immigrants from across the globe) is on the north and west slope of the hill, away from the river; and **Graça,** a slightly less confusing neighborhood, sits to the northeast.

GRAÇA

Graça, a hilly, residential district, is one of Lisbon's oldest neighborhoods. An easy tram ride on **28E** to the end of the line drops you off in **Largo da Graça.** On one side of the square is **Igreja da Graça,** a shady park, and a spectacular *miradouro* (viewpoint); the other side (where the tram stops) is a busy intersection lined with cheap eateries. It's an easy walk downhill from Graça into Alfama, or a less confusing tram ride back.

AROUND PRAÇA DO MARQUÊS DE POMBAL

The large Praça do Marquês de Pombal sits at the end of **Avenida da Liberdade,** opposite Pr. dos Restauradores. This is Lisbon's modern business district, full of department stores, shopping centers, office buildings, and some accommodations. But what space isn't taken up by commerce is lush and green, with multiple expansive parks. To the north of Praça do Marquês de Pombal is the **Parque Eduardo VII,** and to the northeast of that is the impressive **Museu Calouste Gulbenkian,** which is located in the **São Sebastião** district and has its own green space as well. Behind the shopping malls, the back streets of the area are quiet and contain small mom-and-pop shops where the prices tend to be a bit more reasonable than in more tourist-oriented areas.

baixa to praça do chiado

Want to get from sea-level Baixa all the way up to Praça do Chiado without breaking a sweat or spending a cent? Enter Ⓜ Baixa-Chiado at the western end of R. da Vitória in Baixa, take the escalators down into the station, walk straight through to the other side, and take the seemingly endless escalators up; you'll walk out of the station at Pr. do Chiado, with Pr. de Luís de Camões across the street in front of you.

accommodations

Lisbon has been an up-and-coming city for backpackers and other budget travelers alike in the last few years, which has led to an explosion in hostels and other cheap accommodations. Pair this trend with the recent recession, and it all works out in travelers' favor. The large number of hostels in **Baixa** and **Bairro Alto** means that there is cut-throat competition between them (one Let's Go researcher was even accused of being a spy for a different hostel), which keeps prices low and quality ever-rising. The hostels are all fairly similar—clean and brightly decorated, with mixed dorms, shared bathrooms, a common kitchen and living room, and free Wi-Fi and breakfast—but tend to differ slightly on amenities. That said, it can be difficult to go wrong when choosing a Lisbon hostel. Beds generally run €18-25 during the summer, with better rates for longer stays and larger groups.

Lisbon has many cheap hotels and *pensões* as well, but if you don't see your room before paying, you may wind up in a funky-smelling closet with a cot. These accommodations tend to cost more because the rooms are private, but the quality is not up to par with that of the hostels. If privacy is an important factor, many hostels have doubles that are cheaper than the *pensões*, so you can get higher quality for a lower price. Swanky hotels cluster around **Avenida da Liberdade,** while the less expensive rooms can be found in Bairro Alto and Baixa. Avoid the *pensões* on Rossio and the surrounding streets, where the rooms are overpriced; Baixa's **Rua da Prata, Rua dos Correios,** and **Rua do Ouro** have cheaper accommodations only about a 2min. walk from Rossio. Lodgings near the **Castelo de São Jorge** are quieter and closer to the sights but more difficult to find. You can usually find a room on little or no notice, but during mid-June the **Festa de Santo António** fills Lisbon's accommodations.

Camping is fairly popular in Portugal, but those who choose to pitch a tent can be prime targets for thieves. Stay at an enclosed campsite and ask ahead about security. There are 30 campgrounds within a 45mi. radius of the capital. The most popular, **Lisboa Camping,** is inside a 2200-acre *parque florestal* and has the highest rating given to campsites in Portugal. They also have a hotel for dogs with an on-site veterinary clinic. Seriously. (Parque Municipal de Campismo de Monsanto, Estrada da Circunvalação ☎217 62 82 00 www.lisboacamping.com ⇆ Bus #714 runs from Pr. do Comércio to Parque de Campismo. [$] July-Aug €7.30 per person, €6-8 per tent, €4.70 per car; May-June and Sept €6.25/5-7/4.20; Oct-Apr €5.75/4-6/3.70.)

BAIXA

Baixa doesn't offer much for the gourmand or party animal, but its location in the center of town and its easy navigability make it a prime spot for accommodations. It's hard to go wrong when almost all of Baixa's hostels manage to be both quirky and chic without runaway rates. Baixa's *pensões* are generally places of last resort, as they tend to be more pricey and devoid of the character found in the hostels.

👍 LISBON LOUNGE HOSTEL/LIVING LOUNGE HOSTEL HOSTEL $

R. de São Nicolau, 41 ☎213 46 20 61 www.lisbonloungehostel.com

R. do Crucifixo, 116 ☎213 46 10 78

These nearby hostels, under joint ownership, have large common spaces and spacious rooms with the best interior design around, hostel or not. While Living Lounge has individually decorated rooms, Lisbon Lounge features bright colors and amazing street art on common room walls. Both offer breakfast, loads of tours and activities (some free), and a delicious, traditional nightly dinner (€10) with endless wine.

🚏 Lisbon Lounge: From [M]Baixa-Chiado, take R. da Vitória exit, then immediate right onto R. do Crucifixo, then 1st left onto R. de São Nicolau, and walk 4 blocks. Living Lounge: From [M]Baixa-Chiado, take R. da Vitória exit, then immediate left onto R. do Crucifixo. ℹ Breakfast, towels, and linens included. Free lockers. Laundry €10. Kitchen. Free tours and activities. 💲 Lisbon Lounge: June 1-Sep 15 dorms €22; doubles €60. Apr 15-May 31 and Sept 16-Oct 14 dorms €20; doubles €60. Oct 15-Apr 14 dorms €18; doubles €50. Living Lounge: dorms and doubles same rates as Lisbon Lounge. Apr 15-Oct 14 singles €35; Oct 15-Apr 14 singles €30. ⏰ Reception 24hr.

👍 LISBON DESTINATION HOSTEL HOSTEL $

R. Primeira de Dezembro, 141, 3rd fl. ☎213 46 64 57 www.rossiopatio.com

Set in the top of the stunningly beautiful Neo-Manueline behemoth that is the Rossio train station, Lisbon Destination Hostel takes the cake for best common area in Baixa, if not Lisbon. With astroturf, tropical music, and a soaring ceiling of glass windows, it feels like you are closer to the Caribbean than the Tejo. The kitchen is just as spacious, and large stairs in the middle of the common room lead up to more rooms, some of which have great views of Rossio and Baixa.

🚏 [M]Restauradores. Walk away from the giant statue as you exit. The Rossio train station will be on your right. On the 3rd fl. ℹ Some doubles have private bath. Singles have shared bath. Linens, lockers, and breakfast included. Towels €1. Laundry €5. 💲 Dorms €18-23; singles €35-40; doubles €30-35; triples €25. ⏰ Reception 24hr.

GOODNIGHT HOSTEL/GOODMORNING HOSTEL HOSTEL $

R. dos Correeiros, 113, 2nd fl. ☎213 43 01 39 www.goodnighthostel.com

Pr. dos Restauradoes, 65, 2nd fl. ☎213 42 11 28

Green in Goodnight and teal in Goodmorning, these monochromatic color schemes (even the bathrooms haven't been spared) add to the ultra-modern decor of these two sister hostels. Iron beds and the occasional piece of funkadelic furniture add the finishing touches. Each hostel also has its own amenities—while Goodnight has a small but plush DVD room, Goodmorning has some great balconies and is located in the back of a tobacconist's shop. Don't miss out on the free tours, pub crawls, and the fresh bread that is delivered every morning for breakfast.

🚏 Goodnight Hostel: From [M]Baixa-Chiado, take the R. da Vitória exit and follow R. da Vitória for 4 blocks before turning left onto R. dos Correeiros. Goodmorning Hostel: [M]Restauradores. On east side of Pr. dos Restauradores (to your right as you face the long, tree-lined Av. da Liberdade); enter through Tabacaria Restauradores, next to Santander Totta bank. ℹ Breakfast and linens included. Lockers with €5 deposit. Towels €1. Kitchen. Shared baths. 💲 May-Sept dorms €18-22; doubles €25-28. Oct-Apr dorms €12-18; doubles €25. ⏰ Reception 24hr.

HOME LISBON HOSTEL HOSTEL $

R. de São Nicolau, 13 ☎218 88 53 12 www.mylisbonhome.com

The amenities that set this hostel apart are free laundry service (the Lisbon summer heat will make you go through clean clothes in record time), an elevator (it used to be called "Easy Hostel" for a reason), and Portuguese translations of useful English phrases painted on the common room wall (in case you left your dictionary at home). The rooms aren't huge but have classic wood floors and balconies with views over Baixa.

✲ *From ⓂBaixa-Chiado, take the R. da Vitória exit, then turn right onto R. do Crucifixo. Take the 1st left onto R. de São Nicolau; the hostel is 6 blocks down.* **i** *Breakfast, linens, and lockers included. Locks and towels available with a small deposit. Kitchen. Free laundry service. Elevator. Nightly dinner €10. Free daily walking tours.* Ⓢ *Dorms May-Sept €13-23; Oct-Apr €10-18.* ⚲ *Reception 24hr.*

TRAVELLERS HOUSE   HOSTEL $
R. Augusta, 89   ☎213 46 31 56, 210 11 59 22 www.travellershouse.com
Owned by the same people as Rossio Hostel, Travellers House has the same exposed wood decor and the same big selling point: its unbeatable location. Situated right on Rua Augusta, the main pedestrian street in Baixa, Travellers House is in the heart of the neighborhood and close to Lisbon's other major sights as well. With incredibly generous common areas and nightly activities, guests are exposed to multiple neighborhoods and get a balanced taste of Lisbon's culture.

✲ *ⓂBaixa-Chiado (Baixa exit). Exit onto R. da Vitoria. Take a right onto R. Augusta. Hostel is on the right.* **i** *Breakfast, linens, lockers, and towels included.* Ⓢ *Dorms €16-28; singles €30-40; doubles €25-40.* ⚲ *Reception 24hr.*

YES! LISBON HOSTEL   HOSTEL $
R. de São Julião, 148   ☎213 42 71 71 www.yeshostels.com
With 108 beds, this is one of the biggest hostels in Portugal, covering an elevator-serviced five floors of a building near the Pr. do Comércio. The ground floor is a large bar and lounge, and the wristband keys guests receive just add to the club-like atmosphere. Top 40 music blares, and the ubiquitous Yes! logo is stamped on just about everything. This is a natural habitat for those who like to follow a night out with an after-party instead of bed. The rooms are snug but the common areas are spacious.

✲ *From ⓂBaixa-Chiado, take the R. da Vitória exit, go 1 block on R. da Vitória, and turn right onto R. do Ouro. Walk 3 blocks and turn left.* **i** *Breakfast and linens included. Free lockers and towels. Kitchen. Dinner €10. Daily walking tours. Laundry service available.* Ⓢ *Dorms €13-20; doubles €50.* ⚲ *Reception 24hr.*

ROSSIO HOSTEL   HOSTEL $
Cç. do Carmo, 6   ☎213 42 60 04 www.rossiohostel.com
Smooth jazz drifts through the exposed wooden beams in this laid-back hostel. But fear not, Rossio Hostel is right in the heart of…Rossio! There is plenty of action going on in the center of Lisbon, and this hostel brings it all right to you. With nightly activities (sangria, anyone?) and hot breakfast included, Rossio Hostel offers a convenient and comfortable experience for a low price.

✲ *ⓂRossio. Head west (to your left as you face the theater, coming from the river) on Cç. do Carmo a few yards.* **i** *Breakfast, towels, and linens included. Free lockers. Kitchen.* Ⓢ *May-Sept dorms €20-25; doubles €50-70. Oct-Apr dorms €15-18; doubles €50.* ⚲ *Reception 24hr.*

DUAS NAÇÕES   HOTEL $$$$
R. da Vitória, 41   ☎213 46 07 10 www.duasnacoes.com
Like most *pensões* in Baixa, Duas Nações is pricey, but you are paying for privacy. Most rooms are small, although some have TVs and private baths. Larger rooms have balconies (rather, one balcony shared by many rooms—lock your window at night) over R. Augusta and R. da Vitória, two of Baixa's largest and most centrally located thoroughfares. Prices drop sharply in the low season.

✲ *ⓂBaixa-Chiado; take the R. da Vitória exit and follow R. da Vitória straight for 3 blocks.* Ⓢ *June-Sept singles €45, with private bath €65; doubles €55/75; triples with private bath €85. Oct-May €10-15.* ⚲ *Reception 24hr.*

BAIRRO ALTO AND CHIADO

Though not as centrally located as Baixa, the accommodations in the Bairro Alto and Chiado neighborhoods are closest to the nightlife and museums, making them a great pick for those who want to sightsee by day and pub crawl by night.

👍 LISBON POETS HOSTEL — HOSTEL $

R. Nova da Trindade, 2, 5th fl. ☎213 46 10 58 www.lisbonpoetshostel.com

Not just for the literary snob, this cultured hostel is luxurious enough to satisfy even the least poetic of travelers. The dorm rooms, named for famous poets, are large and clean, and the common room has space for you to write your own couplets in comfort. As the name suggests, a poetic theme prevails: writers' quotes line the walls, there's a small book exchange, and there's even a typewriter (but you'll need to fix it first if you want to use it). Activities ranging from city tours to *fado* nights to cafe crawls take place daily and are free for guests.

*‡ ⓂBaixa-Chiado; take the Pr. do Chiado exit, and turn right up R. Nova da Trindade. **i** Breakfast and linens included. Towels €1. Laundry €7. Free lockers. Kitchen. Shared bath. Elevator. Credit card min. €50. Ⓢ Dorms €18-22; private doubles €45-60. Discount with stay in Oporto Poets Hostel (min. 5 nights between the two). ⏰ Reception 24hr.*

👍 THE INDEPENDENTE HOSTEL AND SUITES — HOSTEL $

R. São Pedro de Alcântara, 81 ☎213 46 13 81 www.theindependente.pt

In an opulent white building right across from the gorgeous Miradouro de São Pedro, The Independente is quite luxurious for the price. A large staircase leads up to the generous common room looking out over the *miradouro*. Rooms are sizable and many have small balconies. And while a white motif pervades the entire establishment, all of the furniture looks like it's made from surprisingly stable plywood, just in case you started to feel a bit too posh.

*‡ ⓂBaixa-Chiado (Chiado exit). Take R. da Misericórdia until it becomes R. São Pedro de Alcântara. The hostel is on your left and shares a building with a cafe. **i** Breakfast and linens included. Towels €1.50. Lock and keycard €5 deposit. Ⓢ June-Sept dorms €17-20; suites €110. Oct-May dorms €13-18; suites €95. ⏰ Reception 24hr.*

LISBON OLD TOWN HOSTEL — HOSTEL $

R. do Ataide, 26A ☎213 46 52 48 www.lisbonoldtownhostel.com

Set off in a quieter area, this hostel has a nifty wall painted with images of backpackers and other travel-related goodness separating it from the road. Through the doorway are hardwood floors and some of the biggest rooms in the city, a quaint and welcoming living space. There are multiple common areas, and a kitchen is available for all to use.

*‡ ⓂBaixa-Chiado (Chiado exit). As you face the statue in the plaza, walk to the left on R. da Misericórdia. Take a right on Tv. de Guilherme Cossoul and a left on R. das Chagas. The hostel is behind the large wall with paintings of backpackers. **i** Breakfast and linens included. Towels €1. Laundry €6. Ⓢ June-Sept dorms €16-22; doubles €60. Oct-May dorms €14-20; doubles €44. ⏰ Reception 24hr.*

OASIS HOSTEL — HOSTEL $

R. de Santa Catarina, 24 ☎213 47 80 44 www.oasislisboa.com

Set aside in a quiet neighborhood just a few feet from the beautiful Miradouro de Santa Catarina, this hostel still packs quite a punch—it gives partygoers easy access to the bars in Bairro Alto and the flashy nightclubs in Cais do Sodré. It even has its own nightlife, with a private patio bar just off the street. Large and well-decorated rooms abound, and private doubles are located up the street and open onto a lovely courtyard.

*‡ ⓂBaixa-Chiado (Chiado exit). From Pr. de Luís de Camões, follow R. do Loreto (at far right side if entering plaza from direction of Metro station) 4 blocks, then left down R. Marechal Saldanha to the Miradouro de Santa Catarina (lookout point), then right; it's the big yellow house at the end of the street. **i** Breakfast, linens, and towels included. Kitchen. Free safe. Laundry €7. Ⓢ Dorms €12-26; doubles €25-66. ⏰ Reception 8am-midnight. Patio Bar open daily 6pm-1am.*

ROYAL LISBON HOSTEL
HOSTEL $

Pr. do Luís Camões, 22, 3rd fl. ☎218 00 67 97 www.royallisbon.com

Located in the main square in Chiado and right above the ever-bustling Brazilian consulate, Royal Lisbon Hostel is about as close to the action as you can get. It is also one of the cheapest hostels in the entire city, with rates falling beneath €10 in the winter. Many rooms have unparalleled people-watching potential, with large windows overlooking Praça do Luís Camões. Doubles and smaller dorms are located in a different building, but the hostel's location is certainly prime real estate.

✣ ⓂBaixa-Chiado (Chiado exit). Bus #758 or tram #28E. Head straight across the main square. *i* Breakfast and linens included. Laundry €3. Split between two buildings within the square. Ⓢ June-Sept dorms €14-18; doubles €35. Oct-May dorms €9.50-14; doubles €20. ⓩ Reception 24hr.

PENSÃO GLOBO
HOTEL $$$

R. do Teixeira, 37 ☎213 46 22 79 www.pensaoglobo-lisbon.com

This accommodation looks awfully enticing from its shady street (just about the only one in Bairro Alto with trees to its credit), but the rooms inside are a touch small. The location is what you're paying for here: quite close to the nightlife of Bairro Alto (you hardly have to go uphill to get there), but much quieter than its counterparts a few blocks farther south.

✣ ⓂBaixa-Chiado; take Pr. do Chiado exit, take a slight right out of the station, and go straight between the white churches toward Pr. de Luís de Camões, then right up R. da Misericórdia 7 blocks, left onto Travessa da Cara (where the park begins on the right) 1 block, then right onto R. do Teixeira. *i* Laundry service available. Ⓢ Singles and doubles €25-60; triples €75; quads €85. ⓩ Reception 24hr.

PENSÃO LUAR
HOTEL $$

R. das Gáveas, 101 ☎213 46 09 49 www.pensaoluar.com

This *pensão* is on one of Lisbon's busiest pedestrian streets, so it can get a bit noisy. It's full of beautiful *azulejo* tiling all over, and the rooms offer nonstop people-watching on the street below. Don't let the private baths fool you, though—they're private in that they're in your room, but they're only separated from the rest of the space (i.e., the bed) by thin sliding doors that don't come close to reaching the ceiling.

✣ ⓂBaixa-Chiado (Chiado exit) or bus #758 to Rua da Misericórdia. From Pr. de Luís de Camões, follow R. das Gáveas (to the left, off the center of the plaza if you're turned toward the 2 white churches that face each other and Pr. do Chiado) 3 blocks. *i* Laundry service available. Ⓢ Apr-Oct singles €15-60; doubles €45-65; quads €60-85. Nov-Jan singles €15-40; doubles €30-45; quads €50-65. Feb-Mar singles €15-50; doubles €35-55; quads €55-75. ⓩ Reception 24hr.

ALFAMA

Alfama's accommodations are expensive and limited but are perfect for those who can't resist the neighborhood's charm. The streets are steep and rarely well-marked, so leave a trail of bread crumbs or unwind a spool of thread as you head out. Just about the whole neighborhood is pedestrian, so if you usually go out, get smashed, and take a cab back to the hostel, Alfama's not for you.

SMILE HOSTEL
HOSTEL $

Tv. do Almada, 12 ☎96 373 66 83 www.smilehostel.com

You won't stumble across this tiny hostel as you walk through Lisbon. Even though it is just a few yards from Baixa, and even fewer from the cathedral, no signs indicate that it even exists. But luckily, you're in on the secret. Inside, the hostel is small and colorful, with cheerful paint and natural light to brighten up all of the rooms.

✣ ⓂTerreiro Paço, tram #28E, or bus #737 to Sé. From north side of Pr. Comércio, facing the river, take R. Alfândaga left and then turn left onto R. Madalena. Follow right at the Igreja da Madalena. *i* Breakfast, sheets, and towels included. Ⓢ May-Sept dorms €13-16, doubles €35; Oct-Apr dorms €18-22, doubles €50-60. ⓩ Reception 24hr.

accommodations

ALFAMA PATIO HOSTEL

HOSTEL $$

R. das Escolas Gerais, 3 ☎21 888 31 27 www.alfamapatio.com

It may seem like this hostel is out of the way, but that is part of its laid-back charm. In an alley off of the twisting Alfama roads, the Patio Hostel's common space is mainly outside—you guessed it—on the patio. Grilling, drinking, and general merriment abound, and after a hot day in the Lisbon sun, it's nice to come back and relax in this shady, secluded oasis.

✦ ⓂSanta Apolónia or tram #28E to R. Escolas Gerais. From Santa Apolónia, walk away from the river and take a left onto R. Remédios. Take a right at each of the next 2 forks onto R. Escolas Gerais, and finally a right onto Escolas Gerais. *i* Breakfast, sheets, and towels included. ⓈDorms €25-28; doubles €60-80. Prices lower in winter. ⓉReception 24hr.

LISBON AMAZING HOSTEL

HOSTEL $

Beco do Arco Escuro, 17 ☎21 888 00 54 www.lisbonamazinghostels.net

The rooms in this hostel certainly aren't the biggest, and the common area isn't the brightest, but the price and location are on the mark. Directly above one of the ancient neighborhood's arches, one block from the cheap restaurants on R. dos Bacalhoeiros and the cathedral, this hostel puts you right in the heart of Alfama. But, at the same time, it is secluded in one of Alfama's traditional alleyways, in a neighborhood much quieter at night than Bairro Alto, so you can actually get some sleep if you want.

✦ ⓂTerreiro Paço, tram #28E, or bus #737 to Sé. From the north side of Pr. Comércio (farthest from the river), facing the river, head left along R. Alfândega 3 blocks, then left on R. Bacalhoeiros, and then right through the arch and up the steps; follow signs for "LAHostels." *i* Breakfast, linens, and towels included. Laundry service €10. ⓈDorms €13-17; doubles €25-35, with bath €30-55. ⓉReception 24hr.

GUESTHOUSE BEIRA MAR

B&B $$

Lg. do Terreiro do Trigo, 16 ☎21 886 99 33 www.guesthousebeiramar.com

Definitely some of the best digs in Lisbon, this B&B houses seven airy and colorful rooms in a part of Alfama that's barely uphill from Baixa. The cozy common area allows travelers to be social without sacrificing their privacy. As an added bonus, some rooms have balconies with views of the water, while others look back onto Alfama. Enter on R. da Judiaria, 3, to shorten the climb if you're coming from uphill or to make it more scenic if you're coming from down below.

✦ ⓂSanta Apolónia, or bus #36, 732, 735, 759, 794 to Alfândega. From Alfândega bus stop, head 1 block away from river, then left to reach Lg. Terreiro do Trigo. *i* Breakfast, linens, and towels included. Free lockers. Kitchen. Cash only. ⓈDoubles €45-60; triples €45-60; 4-bed €60-90; 6-bed €85-120. Prices lower in winter. ⓉReception 24hr.

CASA DE HOSPEDES ESTRELA

HOTEL $$$

R. dos Bacalhoeiros, 8 ☎21 886 95 06

Clean, simple rooms, some with views of the water, sit near the Tejo River. It's very close to some of Alfama's sights—you can walk 2min. to the cathedral or, if you prefer, you can go Shawshank on the place and break through the wall into the neighboring 16th-century Casa dos Bicos.

✦ ⓂTerreiro Paço. From the north side of Pr. Comércio (farthest from the river), facing the river, head left along R. Alfândega 4 blocks, then left across the plaza; it's right next to Casa dos Bicos, the spiky building. *i* Linens and towels included. Cash only. ⓈSingles €25-40; doubles €30-45; triples €45-60. ⓉReception 24hr.

AROUND PRAÇA DO MARQUÊS DE POMBAL

LISBOA CENTRAL HOSTEL

HOSTEL $$

R. Rodrigues Sampaio, 160 ☎30 988 10 38 www.lisboacentralhostel.com

When it comes to tourists, this small and comfortable hostel knows exactly what it's doing. You have a question, they will have the answer. The wall also has maps of both Lisbon and the greater Lisbon area, each marked with dozens of sights, restaurants, markets, and anything else you could possibly need. A nice patio and three cozy common areas make this hostel a great place to curl up and take a break from the busy Lisbon streets.

✦ Ⓜ*Marquês de Pombal. Facing the statue from Av. Liberdade, turn right out of the circle. Then immediately turn right onto R. Rodrigues Sampaio.* ✦ *Breakfast, linens, and towels included. Laundry service €8.* Ⓢ *May-Sept dorms €20-24, doubles €64-72; Oct-Apr dorms €16-20, doubles €50-60.* ☪ *Reception 24hr.*

LISBON CHILLOUT HOSTEL
HOSTEL $

R. Nogueira e Sousa, 8   ☎21 246 84 50   www.lisbonchillouthostel.com

Lisbon Chillout Hostel is aptly named. The laid-back establishment is a relaxing get-away, but that doesn't mean the patrons here can't have fun! There are often theme nights and tons of activities for you and your hostel friends to enjoy. The patio is lovely, and frequent barbecues ensure that the space actually gets used.

✦ Ⓜ*Avenida. Walk down Av. Liberdade toward the statue. Turn right after 1 block, followed by a left after another 2 blocks. Then turn right onto Tv. Santa Maria (becomes R. Nogueira e Sousa). The hostel is on the right.* ✦ *Breakfast and linens included. Towels €1. Laundry €4.* Ⓢ *Dorms €13-17; doubles €50-60; singles €50-60.* ☪ *Reception 24hr.*

POUSADA DE JUVENTUDE DE LISBOA
HOSTEL $

R. de Andrade Corvo, 46   ☎21 353 26 96   www.pousadasjuventude.pt

This enormous hostel is a bit out of the way, but it's a good and reliably inexpensive alternative if the ritzier hostels in Baixa and Bairro Alto are all booked. Decorations and common space here are sparse, but it won't matter, since this is more a place to stay than it is a community. Thankfully, an elevator services the many floors of the hostel, so you can give your weary legs a rest after climbing all over Lisbon during the day.

✦ Ⓜ*Picoas, or buses #36, 44, 83, 91, 207, 727, 738, or 745. Exit* Ⓜ*Picoas onto R. de Andrade Corvo; the hostel is marked by a large banner on the same side of the street.* ✦ *Breakfast and linens included. Kitchen available.* Ⓢ *Dorms €15-18; doubles €43-46. Must have cartão de alberguista (€6).* ☪ *Reception open 8am-midnight.*

sights

Lisbon's history can be seen on every street in the city, stretching from the present back 3000 years. Moorish *azulejos* (painted and glazed tiles) line the ancient façades and interiors of **Alfama;** the fortress-like 12th-century Sé (cathedral) looms over the city with its imposing Romanesque presence; the 11th-century **Castelo de São Jorge** sits on a high hill over the center. **Graça** features the **National Pantheon,** an impressive domed building set against the backdrop of the Tejo. Monasteries are sprinkled throughout Lisbon as well, filled with breathtaking cloisters and sacred relics. And once you have gotten your fill of holier offerings, the plethora of art museums provides a more secular alternative as well. The diverse neighborhoods act as sights unto themselves; each has its own unique story and architecture, and they all come together to form the collage that is Lisbon. Those planning to do a lot of sightseeing in a few days should consider purchasing the tourist office's **Lisboa Card** for a flat fee based on the amount of days it is valid (€18.50-39). Keep in mind that many museums and sights are closed on Mondays, and are free before 2pm on Sundays and holidays.

BAIXA

Baixa doesn't have many historical sights—the whole neighborhood was leveled and rebuilt after the earthquake of 1755—but the pedestrian streets and *praças* have their own newer brand of beauty and offer excellent people-watching opportunities.

Around Rossio

Rossio, known more formally as **Praça de Dom Pedro IV,** is Lisbon's heart. The city's main square has been used as a cattle market, public execution stage, bullring, and carnival ground. Today, it is home to tourists and the large central statue of Dom Pedro IV, as well as circling drivers who treat the plaza as their own Indianapolis Motor Speedway. At the north end of the plaza is the magnificent Teatro Nacional de Dona Maria II, with a statue of Gil Vicente—Portugal's first great dramatist—peering down onto Baixa.

Around Praça dos Restauradores

In the long **Praça dos Restauradores,** just off the northwest corner of Rossio, a huge obelisk celebrates Portugal's independence from Spain, earned in 1640 after 60 years under the Spanish crown. The tourist office is in the Palácio da Foz on the west side of the plaza, and the gorgeous neo-Manueline **Estação Rossio** is in the southwest corner. From Pr. dos Restauradores, the long and straight tree-lined **Avenida da Liberdade,** modeled on Paris's Champs-Élysées, heads uphill 1mi. to **Praça do Marquês de Pombal.** There, an 18th-century statue of the Marquês watches over the city that he planned and put back together two and a half centuries ago.

Around Praça do Comércio

If you think all European cities have centers with small, narrow winding streets and ancient, crumbling buildings, then think again. The area between Rossio and the Rio Tejo is a **perfect grid,** built in the late 18th century after the earthquake destroyed what was there before. Many of the straight streets are named for the professionals once located on them: *sapateiros* (shoemakers), *douradores* (gold workers), and *bacalhoeiros* (cod merchants) all have their own avenues. At the end of R. de Santa Justa, in the northwest corner of the grid, is the **Elevador de Santa Justa,** a national monument that gives you a great view and takes you up the hill to Chiado at the same time (Rua Santa Justa, 103 ☎213 42 79 44 www.carris.pt $ €5 ⏰ July 13-Sept 30 7am-11pm; Oct 1-July 12 7am-10pm). The **Rua Augusta** runs through the center of Baixa, through the **Arco da Rua Augusta,** and into the enormous **Praça do Comércio,** at the edge of the Tejo. Dom João I watches over this huge, open space lined with shady colonnades; you can head down the steps that plunge right into the river and see the swarms of hungry fish at the banks. Just on the other side of the arch is the brand-new **Museu do Design e da Moda (MUDE),** which hosts exhibits of design and fashion history in a grand old bank building on the Rua Augusta (Rua Augusta, 24 ☎218 88 61 17 www.mude.pt $ Free ⏰ Open Tu-Th 10am-8pm, F-Sa 10am-10pm, Su 10am-8pm).

the ultimate cock block

Walking through the streets of Lisbon (and nearly every other Portuguese town), you may notice hundreds of images of Portugal's unofficial mascot: the rooster. According to legend, a rich landowner in Barcelos, a small town in the north of the country, accused a passing pilgrim of stealing his silver. His fate was left up to a judge, who was about to enjoy a roast cockerel dinner. The pilgrim claimed that if he was innocent, the rooster would stand up and crow. After he was sentenced to death, to the judge's surprise, the rooster stood up and crowed, and the pilgrim was saved. He returned years later to create a statue of the rooster that saved his life, thus sparking the image of the Galo de Barcelos (Barcelos Rooster), a national symbol of Portugal even today.

BAIRRO ALTO AND CHIADO

The culture per capita in Chiado is about as high as it gets in Lisbon, with museums and historic sights easy to come by. Neighboring Bairro Alto offers great views of the city from its *miradouros*.

MUSEU ARQUEOLÓGICO DO CARMO CHURCH, MUSEUM
Lg. do Carmo ☎213 47 86 29

Sick of those big, boring churches that all look the same? This archaeological museum is housed in a 14th-century Gothic church like any other, except it's **missing its roof.** The ruins became ruins in the 1755 earthquake and ensuing fire, and today they stand as an open courtyard under empty arches where the roof once stood. After you take in the cinematic setting, head inside to the museum—the collection spans four millennia and includes some pretty gruesome Peruvian mummy children. But even the sight of potentially undead South American kiddies can't trump the view from beneath the vaulted arches of the church.

⚐ Ⓜ*Baixa-Chiado (Chiado exit) or bus #758, or tram 28E. From Rossio, walk (steeply) up Cç. do Carmo to Lg. do Carmo.* Ⓢ *€3.50, students and seniors €2, under 14 free.* Ⓐ *Open M-Sa June-Sept 10am-7pm; Oct-May 10am-6pm.*

IGREJA E MUSEU DE SÃO ROQUE CHURCH, MUSEUM
Lg. Trindade Coelho ☎213 23 54 44 www.museu-saoroque.com

The Plague reached *Lisboa* in 1505, brought into the city on an infested ship from Venice. King Manuel I was not too happy about this and requested a relic of São Roque from the Venetians in return, as this saint was supposed to have powers that could ward off disease. That didn't work out, and thousands of Portuguese succumbed to the Black Death. Nevertheless, the Jesuits put up this church in the saint's honor in the 16th century. The alms box on the left side of the nave echoes the awestruck words of many who enter: "Jesus, Maria, Jose" ("Jesus, Mary, and Joseph"). The church is truly magnificent, with not a square inch untouched by the ornate decorations, so be sure to look up at the beautifully painted ceiling. The museum houses a collection of

sights

art and relics pertaining to the Jesuits as well as a collection of Eastern art that includes a dazzling chest with glimmering inlay from Macau.

✠ ⓂBaixa-Chiado (Chiado exit). Bus #758 or tram 28. From Lg. do Chiado, head uphill on R. da Misericórdia; the church is at the far side of the plaza on the right. Ⓢ Museum €2.50, students, under 14, and over 65 free; Su before 2pm free. ⌚ Church open M 2-6pm, Tu-W 9am-6pm, Th 9am-9pm, F-Su 9am-6pm. Museum open Tu-W 10am-6pm, Th 2-9pm, F-Su 10am-6pm.

MUSEU DO CHIADO AND MUSEU NACIONAL DE ARTE CONTEMPORÂNEA   ART MUSEUM
R. Serpa Pinto, 4   ☎213 43 21 48 www.museudochiado-ipmuseus.pt
This constantly updated museum has tons and tons of exhibition space but devotes only a small amount of it to its permanent collection (otherwise it wouldn't stay contemporary for very long, now would it?), which means the temporary exhibitions (four per year) get lots of room for full, comprehensive shows. Consequently, this museum is like a box of chocolates—you never know what you're gonna get. You might see abstract paintings or Portuguese photography or something completely different, but even if it's plastic containers (stacked artistically, rest assured), there will be something intriguing for you to ponder.

✠ ⓂBaixa-Chiado (Chiado exit). Bus #758, or tram 28E. From Lg. do Chiado, head 1 block toward Baixa (behind you as you exit the Metro station), then right down R. Serpa Pinto. Ⓢ €4, seniors €2, students €1.60, under 14 free; Su before 2pm free. ⌚ Open Tu-Su 10am-6pm.

MIRADOURO DE SÃO PEDRO DE ALCÂNTARA   PANORAMIC VIEWS
R. São Pedro de Alcântara
Offering one of the best views of Lisbon, this easily accessible park has a fountain, benches, and even a cafe that make things so perfect you will think you are in the middle of some awful rom-com set in Europe. But if you ignore Drew Barrymore lisping on about commitment and just grab a drink and soak in the scene, you won't want to leave. Baixa, the Castelo de São Jorge, and more are all under your domain (or at least in your line of sight). For a slightly more secluded experience, head down the stairs and sit beside the flowers on the less frequented lower tier.

✠ ⓂBaixa-Chiado (Chiado exit). Or bus #758 to Largo do Carmo. Head up R. São Pedro de Alcântara. The park will be on your right. Ⓢ Cafe coffee €1.40, sandwiches €3-5. ⌚ Cafe open daily 10am-10pm.

JARDIM BOTÁNICO DA UNIVERSIDADE DE LISBOA   GARDEN
R. da Escola Politécnica, 54   ☎213 92 18 00 www.mnhnc.ul.pt
Run by the Universidade de Lisboa and in partnership with the Natural History Museum next door, this expansive garden is a great place to get away from all of the noise and bustle of the urban jungle. Hundreds of diverse, labeled plants are interspersed throughout, but the butterfly house and impromptu encounters with wildlife (think baby ducks) make the experience truly rejuvenating. Get lost in this park and forget about the world around you.

✠ ⓂBaixa-Chiado (Chiado exit). Or bus #758 to R. da Misericórdia. Follow R. da Misericórdia until it becomes R. Dom Pedro V. The gate leading to the garden will be on your right. Ⓢ Adults €1.50, under 18 and over 65 free. ⌚ Open daily summer 9am-8pm; winter 9am-6pm.

ALFAMA

Castles, cathedrals, museums, oh my! Alfama is home to some of Lisbon's most significant and intriguing sights. Each encapsulates an important part of Lisbon's history and identity, and the architecturally ancient neighborhood is practically a sight in and of itself. Tram #28E is your friend here, making its way all the way to the top of the hill where the castle rests.

👍 CASTELO DE SÃO JORGE CASTLE, HISTORIC SITE, VIEWS

Castelo de São Jorge ☎21 880 06 20 www.castelosaojorge.pt

Built by the Moors in the 11th century on the highest point in Lisbon, this hilltop fortress was captured by Dom Afonso Henriques, Portugal's first king, in 1147. With one of the best views in Lisbon, the castle also acts as a one-stop shop for the entire historical Lisbon experience. Walk along the ramparts, see live images of Lisbon fed from an ancient periscope, feel like Indiana Jones at archaeological ruins dating from the Iron Age to the Renaissance (whip optional), and gawk at the seemingly random, yet stunningly beautiful, peacocks that strut about. At night, "Lisboa Who Are You?," a show exclusively comprised of images and Portuguese music, tells the story of Lisbon from beginning to end (€15).

➡ Bus #737, or trams #12E and 28E; follow signs to Castelo. $ €7, students and seniors €3.50, under 10 free. ⏰ Open daily Mar-Oct 9am-9pm, Nov-Feb 9am-6pm. Last entry 30min. before close. Museum has guided tours daily at noon and 4pm. Periscope 10am-5pm.

👍 SÉ CATEDRAL DE LISBOA CHURCH, MUSEUM

Lg. da Sé ☎21 886 67 52

Lisbon's 12th-century cathedral is massive and intimidating, built to double as a fortress, if needed. Its austere Romanesque style makes the few brightly-colored stained glass windows leap out of the walls, where the same ornamentation would be lost in a busy Gothic or Baroque church. The cloisters, an archaeological site perpetually under scaffolding, are well worth the cash, giving visitors a glimpse of the remains of Moorish houses, Roman sewers, and more. The treasury boasts relics, manuscripts, and lots of other shiny valuables.

➡ Bus #737, or tram #28E. From Baixa, follow R. Conceição east (to the left as you face the river) up past the church, then turn right onto R. Santo António da Sé and follow the tram tracks; it's the large, building that looks like a fortress. $ Free. Cloister €2.50. Treasury €2.50. ⏰ Church open M 9am-5pm, Tu-Sa 9am-7pm, Su 9am-5pm. Treasury open M-Sa 10am-5pm. Cloister open May-Sept M 10am-5pm, Tu-Sa 10am-6pm; Oct-Apr M-Sa 10am-5pm. Mass Tu-Sa 6:30pm, Su 11:30am.

MUSEU DO FADO MUSEUM

Lg. do Chafariz de Dentro, 1 ☎21 882 34 70 www.museudofado.pt

This bright pink museum tells the story of one of Lisbon and Portugal's greatest treasures: *fado*. Now on the UNESCO Cultural Heritage List, *fado* is intertwined with the Portuguese identity, and anyone who truly wants to understand Portugal must also understand this musical form. The museum offers a self-guided audio tour, available in multiple languages, and gives the complete history of the genre's role in Portuguese culture. Singing along inside the museum is not encouraged.

➡ ⓂSanta Apolónia. Follow the river west (to your left as you face it) from the station, right up C. Lingueta, and left onto R. Jardim do Tabaco. $ €5. ⏰ Open Tu-Su 10am-6pm. Last admission 30min. before close.

MUSEU MILITAR MUSEUM

Lg. do Museu da Artilharia ☎21 884 23 00 www.exercito.pt

Knights in shining armor, swords, cannons, and guns line the walls of this violent museum, seemingly out of place in peaceful Portugal. The exhibit covers the entirety of Portugal's military history, including relics from every period. There is a room dedicated entirely to the Portuguese involvement in World War I, but the coolest item on display is the sword of Portuguese explorer Vasco da Gama.

➡ ⓂSanta Apolónia. The museum is across the street from the station. $ €3. ⏰ Open Tu-Sa 10am-5pm.

GRAÇA

Graça is a charming neighborhood that lies a good distance from the center of the city. But don't be fooled; it still contains some massive monuments and churches that are certainly worth a look. Bring your walking shoes; Graça contains the highest point in the entire city (which, in Lisbon, is saying something).

PANTEÃO NACIONAL TOMBS, HISTORIC SITE

Campo de Santa Clara ☎21 885 48 39 www.igespar.pt

The Igreja de Santa Engrácia was started in the late 17th century, but once the architect died the king lost interest in the project and the funding dried up, leaving the church unfinished for some 250 years. The dictator Salazar rededicated the building as the National Pantheon, although it now, ironically, houses the remains of some of his staunchest opponents. Start at the ground level and see the tomb of the much beloved Amália Rodrigues, queen of *fado*, among others, then take the stairs leading all the way up to the top of the dome, a distinctive feature of the Lisbon skyline.

 # Ⓜ Santa Apolónia, bus #34, or tram #28E. Get off tram 28E at Voz do Operário stop in front of Igreja e Mosteiro de São Vicente de Fora, then follow Arco Grande de Cima (to the left of church), then take the 1st right, 1st left, and then another right. [$] €3, students and under 14 free, seniors €1.50. Su before 2pm free for all. ⏰ Open Tu-Su 10am-5pm.

IGREJA E MOSTEIRO DE SÃO VICENTE DE FORA CHURCH, MONASTERY

Lg. de São Vicente ☎21 885 56 52

The Church and Monastery of St. Vincent is grandiose, with impressive architecture, vaulted ceilings, and an extremely intricate altar. However, the recorded classical music (to make sure you experience the proper amount of reverence) is a bit much. The attached monastery—a beautiful site in its own right—has a small museum dedicated to the church's history, as well as lots of great features, such as a tiny Baroque chapel, an extremely old cloister, and access to the roof with a magnificent view of the surrounding area.

 # Ⓜ Santa Apolónia, bus #34 or tram #28E. Get off tram 28E in front of the massive white church at the Voz do Operário stop. [$] €4, students and seniors €2. ⏰ Open Tu-Su 10am-6pm. Last entry 1hr. before close.

MIRADOURO DA NOSSA SENHORA DO MONTE VIEWS

Cç. do Monte

The highest point in all of Lisbon, this is the one *miradouro* to rule them all. Unlike its brethren, there is no snack bar here, only a small monument in honor of Nossa Senhora and the best view you could possibly imagine. Sit at one of the benches under the shade of the tall trees and feel the pride of making it to the top while soaking in the city from this mini-Everest.

 # Tram #28E to Graça. Take a left out of the square. You are going in the right direction if you are walking uphill. [$] Free.

IGREJA E CONVENTO DA GRAÇA CHURCH

Lg. da Graça ☎21 884 39 73

This church is an oasis mostly safe from camera-swinging, fanny-pack-wearing tourists. It has all the gorgeous architecture and impressive ornamentation of a famous cathedral, yet it still feels like you could go here on Sunday for mass. Most of the people who frequent the pink, marbled interior of this church are locals and members of the church. If you come at the right time, you can stumble in on choir practice or a service in this comfortable space.

 # Tram #28E to Graça. Church is near the park in the square. [$] Free. ⏰ Open Tu-F 9am-12:30pm and 2:30-6pm, Sa 9am-12:30pm and 2:30-6pm, Su 9:30am-12:30pm and 5-8pm. Mass Tu-F 9:30am, Sa 4pm, Su 7pm.

MUSEU NACIONAL DO AZULEJO MUSEUM

R. da Madre de Deus, 4 ☎21 810 03 40 mnazulejo.imc-ip.pt

Enter this museum via its tranquil courtyard, passing by the incredible Manueline doorway of the Convento da Madre de Deus. The museum is devoted to the art of the *azulejo* (glazed and painted tile), one of Portugal's most famous and most ubiquitous forms of art. Some of the tiles are whimsical, others saucy, and others just impressive: the early-18th-century (pre-earthquake) panorama of the city of Lisbon is one of the world's largest works of *azulejo*. Ignore the tacky faux-*azulejo* boards with cut-outs to stick your face in for a photo-op, and move on to the incredible sanctuary to lift your spirits.

 # Take bus #794 from Santa Apolónia station bus stop (side closest to the river) to Igreja da Madre de Deus. $ €5, seniors €2.50, under 14 free. Su before 2pm free for all. ⏰ Open Tu 2-6pm, W-Su 10am-6pm. Last entry 30min. before close.

BELÉM

The Belém waterfront, a couple of kilometers west of Lisbon's center, is a majestic tribute to Portugal's Age of Discovery and its legendary seafaring spirit. This is where history-changing explorers Vasco da Gama and Prince Henry the Navigator left for distant lands, and the opulence of the new worlds they opened up can be seen today just a short tram ride from Baixa, in Belém. Equally as famous and almost as important as the historic sights is ★**Pasteis de Belém,** a pastry shop with a reputation as rich as its pastries. (R. Belém, 84-92 ☎21 363 74 23 $ Pastries €1.05 ⏰ Open daily 9am-11pm.) The easiest way to get to Belém is to take tram **15E** from Pr. do Comércio (dir.: Algés) to the Mosteiro dos Jerónimos stop, which is one stop beyond the one labeled Belém.

★ **MOSTEIRO DOS JERÓNIMOS** CHURCH, MUSEUM

Pr. do Império ☎21 362 00 34 www.mosteirojeronimos.pt

The Hieronymite Monastery was established in 1502 to honor Vasco da Gama's expedition to India. We're guessing the explorer's spirit is pleased with this ornate tribute. The Manueline building has the detail of its Gothic predecessors and the sweeping elegance of the oncoming Renaissance. In the 1980s, the monastery was granted World Heritage Site status by UNESCO and remains in pristine condition, both inside and out. The church contains tombs (both symbolic and actual) of Portuguese kings and bishops. Symbolic tombs (cenotaphs) include areas of tribute to Vasco da Gama and Luís de Camões, Portugal's most celebrated poet. Entrance to the cloister is not cheap (€7, but free Su before 2pm), but it's worth it to see one of Lisbon's most beautiful spaces, which somehow retains its charm despite being filled with hordes of tourists. Those on a shoestring budget can see the massive chapel for free, but the cloister is the real sight here.

 # Tram #15E or bus #28, 714, 727, 729, 743, 749, 751 to Mosteiro dos Jerónimos. $ Free. Cloister and museum €7, over 65 €3.50, under 14 free; Su before 2pm free. Combined ticket with Torre de Belém €10. ⏰ Open May-Sept Tu-Su 10am-6:30pm; Oct-Apr Tu-Su 10am-5:30pm. Last entry 30min. before close.

★ **TORRE DE BELÉM** DEFENSE TOWER, VIEWS

Torre de Belém ☎21 362 00 34

Portugal's most famous tower has risen out of the water (except at low tide, when it's connected to the shore by a narrow, sandy isthmus) from the banks of the Tejo for nearly 500 years, gracing visitors' memories and souvenir stores' postcards since its completion in 1519. Be prepared to relive childhood games (no, not The Floor is Lava) as you pretend to fire cannons on two different levels. Then head downstairs and check out the prison cells and ammunition area (hopefully this doesn't also remind you of your childhood). It's worth going up all the way to the top to see breathtaking panoramic views of Belém and the Tejo. There is also a rhinoceros carving in homage to the real rhino the king tried to bring back for the pope, because nothing garners favor from the pope like a large, horned animal.

From Mosteiro dos Jerónimos, take the unmarked underground walkway in front of the monastery (from entrance, head toward the river; it's a small stairway) to other side of road and tracks and walk west along the river (to the right as you face the water) about 15min. Alternatively, walk in the same direction on the monastery's side of the road and take the pedestrian walkway over the road at the tower. $ €5, over 65 €2.50, students and under 14 free. Su before 2pm free for all. Combined ticket with Mosteiro dos Jerónimos €10. Open May-Sept Tu-Su 10am-6:30pm, Oct-Apr Tu-Su 10am-5:30pm. Last entry 30min. before close.

MUSEU NACIONAL DOS COCHES MUSEUM

Pr. Afonso de Albuquerque ☎21 361 08 50 www.museudoscoches.pt

Not a showcase for uppity handbags, this museum actually holds dozens of ornate coaches previously owned by royalty. Unlike some museums that stall you for hours by trying to shove historical context down your throat, this one gets straight to the goods, diving into rooms lined with stagecoaches used by German, French, Spanish, and Portuguese aristocrats, as well as the pope. Obviously, you can't climb inside these historical treasures anymore. So although the luxurious coaches allow you to daydream about being greeted by throngs of your loyal subjects, you will have to do your best queen-wave from the museum floor.

From Mosteiro dos Jerónimos, exit facing the water and turn left. The museum will be past Pasteis de Belém and on the left. $ €5. Free Su before 2pm. Tu-Su 10am-6pm. Last entrance 30min. before close.

CENTRO CULTURAL DE BELÉM MUSEUM, THEATER

Pr. do Império ☎21 361 24 00 www.ccb.pt

This massive cultural center is a haven of clean, modern architecture on the otherwise overwhelmingly Manueline waterfront. A sizable auditorium and three pavilions host temporary works, while the **Museu Colecção Berardo** has an impressive collection of modern art, housing several extensive exhibitions by contemporary artists from around the world. Pieces range from thought-provoking (a mix of pictures of a woman's body and a day of revolution) to eye-rolling (two perpendicular blocks of wood). If modern art's not your thing, it makes for a nice air-conditioned stop on the way from the monastery to the *torre*.

From Mosteiro dos Jerónimos, walk toward the water (without crossing to the side of the highway closest to the river) and head right; the center is the big modern building. $ Free. Museum open daily 10am-7pm. Last entry 30min. before close.

SÃO SEBASTIÃO

MUSEU CALOUSTE GULBENKIAN ART MUSEUM

Av. de Berna, 45A ☎21 782 30 00 www.museu.gulbenkian.pt

Want an art history survey course for under €5? This museum has a large and eclectic collection of works from the ancient Mesopotamians and Egyptians to the Impressionists and beyond. The collection belonged to native Armenian and oil tycoon Calouste Gulbenkian, who came to Portugal on vacation in 1942 and never left. When he died, he gave his massive art collection to the state, which, like any good state, decided to charge people to look at it. The building itself is hideous, but the treasures inside are not—in particular the illuminated manuscripts from the Middle East to France seem to have been dunked in molten gold, and the dark, quiet room with a garden view is a lovely place to unwind.

[M]São Sebastião, or buses #96, 205, 716, 726, 746, 756. Exit [M]São Sebastião at Av. António Augusto de Aguiar (north exit) and go straight uphill along the avenue until you reach the massive Pr. Espanha, then turn right. It is NOT the building that looks like a castle in the park to the right; keep going along the avenue. $ €4, students under 25 and seniors €2, under 12 free. Temporary exhibits €3-5. Open Tu-Su 10am-6pm.

lisbon

on the down low

You've walked up the hill to the Castelo de São Jorge. You've seen the Torre de Belém rising up from the sea and on every souvenir shop postcard. But have you ever explored the sights that lie beneath Lisbon's streets? The answer is probably no, unless you've been around at the end of September, the only time that the Roman Galleries of Rua da Porta are open to the public. These ruins, discovered in 1771, are constantly flooded, but three days per year the city drains the passages beneath the streets of Baixa and allows visitors to explore these ancient structures on 20min. guided tours. The line to see this mysterious sight can run upward of 3½hr., and the visit is definitely not for the claustrophobic—to access the ruins, you must climb down a literal hole in the street, with cars and trucks still racing by on either side of you. However, it may be worth the wait and the slightly uncomfortable descent, as this anticipated yearly event is completely **free.**

CENTRO DE ARTE MODERNA MUSEUM

R. do Dr. Nicolau de Bettencourt ☎21 782 34 74 www.cam.gulbenkian.pt

Although it is overshadowed by its big brother up the street, the Centro de Arte Moderna (which is also a part of the Gulbenkian Foundation) deserves some love of its own. Filled with many temporary exhibits, the museum is like a box of chocolates—in the sense that it's awesome, and you would pay good money to enjoy it. Most exhibits indulge in it in some kind of multimedia experience, so the experience is typically more active and captivating than your more standard, stagnant art museum.

From Pr. Marquês de Pombal, take Av. Fontes Pereira de Melo. Make a left onto R. São Sebastião da Pedreira and keep left to stay on this street. Continue straight onto R. Dr. Nicolau de Bettencourt, the museum is on the right. $ *€4, students under 25 and seniors €2, under 12 free.* 🕘 *Tu-Su 10am-6pm.*

food

Lisbon has some of the best and most reasonably priced restaurants this side of the Rhine, and some of the finest wine to boot. Depending on the neighborhood, an average full dinner will usually run about €10-12 per person, with the *pratos do dia* often only €5-7. Some of the best and least expensive meals can be found in the ubiquitous **pastelarias.** Although the focus of these pastry shops are the counters, which contain mountains of treats, they also serve up tasty and well-priced meals. That said, don't skip the pastries: **pasteis de nata** are generally less than €1 and are the city's most popular sweet. The Portuguese love their coffee, but realize that when you order **café,** you are actually ordering a shot of espresso. You can order a "normal" coffee (*abatanado* or *americano*), but you might get some looks; many Portuguese think of it more as soup than real coffee. Local specialties include summertime *caracois* (small snails; look for a restaurant with a sign that says "Há caracois" in the window), *lombo de porco com amêijoas* (pork with clams, much tastier than it sounds), and the Portuguese staples *alheira* (smoked chicken sausage) and *sardinhas assadas* (grilled sardines). But the ultimate Portuguese food is **bacalhau** (codfish). Prepared in over 1000 different ways, cod is practically a religion here. A source of national pride, it can be found in almost any restaurant you visit. Some of the best deals, in terms of getting a lot for a little, are the *tostas*, large grilled sandwiches topped with melted butter that usually cost €2-3. The local traditional drink is **ginjinha** (pronounced "jee-JEE-nyah," also often called *ginja*), a sour cherry liqueur served ice-cold in a shot glass and meant to be sipped. If it's bad, it tastes like cough syrup, but if it's good, it's delicious and refreshing, particularly on hot Lisbon afternoons. It usually costs €1-1.50 and is sometimes served in a shot glass made of chocolate for a little extra dough.

BAIXA

Far from being a culinary paradise, Baixa is full of restaurants that are mostly forgettable. The eateries that line the pedestrian thoroughfares range from Italian (not exactly run by your *nonna*) to "traditional Portuguese" (accompanied by eyebrow-raising, multilingual menus) to places selling "American hamburgers." Look for establishments that have *pratos do dia* or lots of businessmen (generally locals on their lunch break who don't have time to go home and have no choice but to eat in Baixa).

MOMA
PORTUGUESE, ITALIAN $$

R. de São Nicolau, 47 ☎914 41 75 36

A white, simple, and clean aesthetic complements this delicious oasis of good food in the desert that is Baixa. Moma's chalk menu tells the story of Portuguese cuisine with an Italian twist. The dishes tend to be cool, light, and creative for the hot summer months, but heavier meals are here for the taking as well (the €9 veal filet is heaven on a plate). Outside is the best place to enjoy your meal; you will find yourself in the middle of the R. de São Nicolau but separated from the touristy madness by umbrellas and bamboo blinds.

✚ Ⓜ*Baixa-Chiado (Baixa exit). Exit Metro station onto R. da Vitória, then right 1 block, and then left onto R. de São Nicolau.* ⑤ *Entrees €6-9.* ⌚ *Open M-F noon-6pm.*

A PADARIA PORTUGUESA
BAKERY $

R. Áurea, 175 ☎213 46 80 30

This bakery, which draws you in with strategically placed baguettes in the windows, strikes both cute and modern notes with its chef's hats, comfy chairs, and split-level seating. Stop in for a delicious treat, a cup of coffee, or a generous soup-and-sandwich meal. Then sit upstairs and enjoy the Portuguese bread-based aphorisms on the walls. Don't miss the seemingly out-of-place yet stunningly refreshing pineapple juice.

✚ Ⓜ*Baixa-Chiado (Baixa exit). Exit onto R. da Vitória. Then left onto R. do Ouro/Aurea.* *i Free Wi-Fi.* ⑤ *Meals €3-6. Pastries €1-3.* ⌚ *Open daily 7:30am-8pm.*

so help me cod

Bacalhau (buh-kal-YOW), dried and salted codfish, is arguably the most popular ingredient in Portuguese cuisine—it is said that there are over 1000 recipes for this iconic staple. Here are some of the common variations you might encounter on your culinary travels through Lisbon.

- **BACALHAU COM TODOS.** Literally meaning "cod with everything," this traditional dish consists of *bacalhau*, vegetables, and hard-boiled egg boiled in the same pot and seasoned with garlic, olive oil, and white wine vinegar.

- **BACALHAU À GOMES DE SÁ.** This recipe—a casserole of *bacalhau*, potatoes, and onions—is considered to be one of the greatest variations of the ingredient in Portugal.

- **PASTÉIS DE BACALHAU.** The name means "codfish pastries," although fish and pastry don't seem like a likely combination. But these fried balls of cod, potato, egg, and parsley are perfect bites as an appetizer or main course.

MARTINHO DA ARCADA
Pr. do Comércio, 3

PORTUGUESE $$$
☎218 87 92 59

Although the prices are steep, the location and history make Martinho da Arcada a worthwhile stop if you can find the cash. Founded in 1782, this is Lisbon's oldest restaurant, and over the years it has been a hangout for writers and artists, including the celebrated poet Fernando Pessoa. Suits are common, but the Praça also welcomes plenty of tourists, so they won't throw you out for your tennis sneakers. Sit inside surrounded by traditional *azulejo* tile, or dine outside and enjoy the view.

✦ Ⓜ*Baixa-Chiado (Baixa exit). Follow R. da Vitória to R. Augusta, then turn right and follow R. Augusta to Pr. do Comércio; the restaurant is in the large yellow building on the left. i Reservations recommended for dinner on weekends.* Ⓢ *Entrees €14-25.* ☒ *Open M-Sa noon-3pm and 5-7pm.*

A TENDINHA
Pr. de Dom Pedro IV, 6

CAFE $
☎213 46 81 56

Frequented by older Portuguese natives, this tiny cafe has quite the rapport (it was founded in 1840). Not only is A Tendinha authentic and old, it also has prices that can't be beat: sandwiches cost €2 or less. Many people stand at the counter to eat, *pastelaría* style, although after sipping the bold espresso (€0.65) you might find yourself on the floor. The cafe also has a full service bar, and bottles of *ginja* line the walls. However, it isn't suited for drinking unless you enjoy the thought of getting retirement-home-wasted and going crazy with some dominoes.

✦ Ⓜ*Rossio. Exit to the left and follow around the praça passing R. Augusta. The cafe is on your left.* Ⓢ *Sandwiches €2. Coffee €1.* ☒ *Open M-Sa 7am-9pm.*

FEEL RIO
R. do Crucifixo, 108

SANDWICHES, JUICE BAR $
☎213 42 71 50 www.facebook.com/feelrio

This flamboyantly colored juice bar brings the energy of Rio to quickly serve the Portuguese. But the color doesn't stop at the decorations. More freshly squeezed and brightly colored juices than you could ever imagine line the menu (persimmon and fig, to name a couple). But the real treats are the Sucos Feel (€2-3 juice blends). Add a sandwich, and you will have yourself quite a meal. Feel Rio doesn't have much seating, but it is a great place to grab a bite on your way up to Rossio.

✦ Ⓜ*Baixa-Chiado (Baixa exit). Exit left onto R. do Crucifixo.* Ⓢ *Juice €2-4. Sandwiches €3-6.* ☒ *M-F 9:30am-9pm, Sa-Su noon-8pm.*

BONJARDIM
Tv. de Santo Antão, 12

GRILL $$$
☎213 42 74 24

A little bit past Rossio, this restaurant is just off the food-filled R. de Santo Antão and takes up almost an entire block to serve massive portions for animal lovers (i.e., not the PETA kind) to feast upon. Dine outside and enjoy your meal from the "king of chicken" while watching either crabs and lobsters duke it out in the window aquarium.

✦ Ⓜ*Restauradores or buses #36, 44, 709, 711, 732, 745, 759. Take Travessa de Santo Antão from the east side of Pr. dos Restauradores.* Ⓢ *Meals €10-30.* ☒ *Open Tu 6-11:30pm, W-Su noon-11:30pm. Outdoor seating until 10pm.*

TAO
R. dos Douradores, 10

VEGETARIAN $
☎218 85 00 46

This East Asian-themed dining room does not necessarily serve East-Asian cuisine. Rather, this quick restaurant runs the gamut of vegetarian options amidst a nation of meat-eaters. There is plenty of room to sit, but no matter where you go, you cannot avoid the gaze of one of the many Buddhas watching from various nooks and crannies.

✦ Ⓜ*Baixa-Chiado (Baixa exit). Follow R. da Vitória to R. dos Douradores, then turn right.* Ⓢ *Entrees €4-7.50.* ☒ *Open daily noon-midnight.*

food

BAIRRO ALTO AND CHIADO

The narrow streets of Bairro Alto are lined with international restaurants and *fado* houses sandwiched between the neighborhood's famous bars. Chiado's food tends toward the trendy, with sleek new restaurants and cafes. The side streets off Cç. do Combro (keep following R. do Loreto away from Pr. de Luís de Camões) have cheap, traditional hole-in-the-wall places, though most of the eateries in Chiado and Bairro Alto won't break the bank.

⬛ CERVEJARIA TRINDADE
PORTUGUESE $$$

R. Nova da Trindade, 20C   ☎213 42 35 06 www.cervejariatrindade.pt

Cervejaria Trindade is famous all over Lisbon for its *molhos*, beer-based sauces that were invented here. These savory and buttery sauces taste incredible on just about any meat you can think of, and eateries throughout the city will often offer a course "à trindade," named for this establishment. The restaurant is also famous for its history, as it was occupied by a convent as far back as the 13th century (the pulpit is still in the main dining room) and became one of Lisbon's first breweries at the start of the 19th century (don't skip the beer). The enormous dining rooms are covered with *azulejos* from this period, and the cloister of the convent is used for dining as well.

✈ From ⓂBaixa-Chiado, exit onto Lg. do Chiado, then take a sharp right up R. Nova da Trindade (to left of A Brasileira). Ⓢ Meat dishes à trindade €9-18. Pratos do dia M-F €7.50. ☼ Open daily 10am-2am.

⬛ KAFFEEHAUS
AUSTRIAN $$

R. Anchieta, 3   ☎210 95 68 28 www.kaffeehaus-lisboa.com

It's understandable if you didn't come to Lisbon to order in German, but this neo-Bohemian cafe has outrageously good food at great prices. The outdoor seats are on the narrow (and thus shady and breezy) street outside, while the inside of the cafe is air-conditioned and contemporary, with angular lamps and a single wall covered in posters. There is a comprehensive bar, but the real treats are the several refreshing homemade lemonades with unexpected but tasty additions such as ginger. Come on Sunday morning for their brunch options (€6.50-10).

✈ From ⓂBaixa-Chiado, exit onto Lg. do Chiado, take a very sharp right down R. Garrett 2 blocks, then head right down R. Anchieta. Ⓢ Sandwiches €4-6. Salads €5-10. Entrees €9-17. Vegetarian options €9-11. Coffees €1-3. ☼ Open Tu-Sa 11am-midnight, Su 11am-8pm.

O FOGAREIRO
PORTUGUESE $$

R. da Atalaia, 92   ☎213 46 80 59

As a visitor to Lisbon, it can be difficult to get traditional Portuguese food without stooping to the level of insanely touristy or ridiculously expensive. Luckily, O Fogareiro is there for you, with its tasty plates, its many reasonable *pratos do dia*, and most importantly, its lack of pushy waiters trying to lure you inside or to their sketchy, non-descript van. It really depends on the place. Order a bottle of wine, some olives, and *bacalhau* (Portuguese cod), and you will finally have the picturesque dinner you have been waiting for.

✈ ⓂBaixa-Chiado (Chiado exit), tram 28E, or bus #758 to Lg. do Luís Camões. From there, take R. do Loreto and turn right on R. da Atalaia. Ⓢ Entrees €9-12. Pratos do dia €7-9. ☼ M-Sa 8pm-2am.

ALI-A-PAPA
MOROCCAN $$

R. da Atalaia, 95   ☎213 47 41 43 www.aliapapa.com

Ali-a-Papa is a great place to fill your tank before you get tanked next door. But to call this restaurant a pit stop for booze-hounds does not do it justice. This Moroccan joint serves up delectable dishes with complex flavors, such as a couscous seffa (couscous, chicken, peanuts, sugar, and cinnamon; €10) that will leave you satisfied and full. They also offer vegetarian options that don't sacrifice flavor.

✈ ⓂBaixa-Chiado (Chiado exit), tram 28E, or bus #758 to Lg. do Luís Camões. From there, take R. do Loreto, and take a right on R. da Atalaia. Ⓢ Entrees €6-12. ☼ Open daily 7pm-midnight.

lisbon

JÜRGEN'S
BAR $

R. do Diário de Notícias, 68 ☎213 47 82 34

Despite the name, there is nothing German about this Bairro Alto drinking hotspot. Although it's a bar, the real treasure here is that during the early evening, this place is a cheap alternative to the more pricey restaurants that dominate the neighborhood. The *tostas*, or simple, grilled sandwiches with meat and cheese (€2-4), are cheap, enormous, and very tasty, and the drinks are reliably strong.

✦ Ⓜ*Baixa-Chiado (Chiado exit), tram 28E, or bus 758. From Pr. do Luís Camões, take R. do Loreto and turn right on R. do Norte. Then take the first left followed by the first right.* Ⓢ *Tostas €3-5. Wine €2. Cocktails €5.* ☼ *Open M-Th 3pm-2am, F-Sa 5pm-3am, Su 4pm-2am.*

CASA DA ÍNDIA
TRADITIONAL $$

R. do Loreto, 51 ☎213 42 36 61

Don't be fooled by the name—this restaurant serves Portuguese fare, not South Asian stuff. During more imperial times, the building was an integral part of the Asian trade, and the name stuck. Low-cost, high-quality Portuguese dishes make up for the nondescript interior. Be sure to come early, though, as seating is limited (even the counter fills up and leaves customers standing to eat).

✦ Ⓜ*Baixa-Chiado (Chiado exit). Take R. do Loreto a little over one block.* Ⓢ *Entrees €6-9.* ☼ *M-Sa 9am-2am.*

A BRASILEIRA DO CHIADO
CAFE $$

R. Garrett, 120-122 ☎213 46 95 41 www.cafe-abrasileira.com

This beautiful cafe has been around for over a century, serving coffee, pastries, and snacks in a gorgeous wood- and marble-filled space. It is most notable for being one of poet Fernando Pessoa's favorite haunts, and his statue sits outside today (with an extra bronze chair beside him, begging for cheesy photo-ops). If you are in a hurry, grab a *bica* (espresso; €0.70) and stand inside at the counter, taking in both the caffeine and the impressive scenery. But realize that cafe prices sneakily rise when you sit down, even more so if you sit outside.

✦ *Exit* Ⓜ*Baixa-Chiado (Chiado exit). Exit Metro station onto Lg. do Chiado, then turn right.* Ⓢ *Sandwiches €2-5. Entrees €8-20. Coffee €1-2.50.* ☼ *Open daily 8am-2am.*

NOO BAI CAFÉ
CAFE, VIEWS $

Miradouro do Adamastor (Santa Catarina) ☎213 46 50 14 www.noobaicafe.com

The food and drink here are perfectly fine, but few people come here on a culinary quest. Rather, it's the sweeping view of the Tejo, including the burnt-orange 25 de Abril bridge and the giant statue of Christ signaling an incomplete pass, that really brings the crowds. If you see an open table by the railing, leap for it and cling to it until sunset.

✦ Ⓜ*Baixa-Chiado (Chiado exit) or tram 28E to Santa Catarina. From Pr. de Luís de Camões, follow R. do Loreto (far right corner of plaza with your back toward Metro station) 4 blocks, then turn left down R. Marechal Saldanha to the miradouro.* Ⓢ *Sandwiches €4-6. Coffee €1-2.50. Beer €2-4.* ☼ *Open M-Th noon-10pm, F-Sa noon-midnight, Su noon-10pm.*

JARDIM DAS CEREJAS
VEGETARIAN, BUFFET $$

Cç. do Sacramento, 36 ☎213 46 93 08 www.jardimdascerejas.com

A lone island of vegetarian delights in a tumultuous sea of meat and fish. Of course, all-you-can-eat buffets are a great deal whether you're a vegetarian or not, and the fare here will satisfy meat-eaters as well. They also offer takeout for anyone in a rush or just trying to save a little money.

✦ Ⓜ*Baixa-Chiado. Exit onto Lg. do Chiado, then take a very sharp right down R. Garrett 3 blocks; turn left up Cç. do Sacramento.* Ⓢ *Lunch buffet €7.50. Dinner buffet €9.50. Takeout €6.50.* ☼ *Open daily noon-3:30pm and 7-11pm.*

food

PIZZA A PEZZI PIZZA, OPEN LATE $

R. Dom Pedro V, 84 ☎934 56 31 70

Just north of the major bar scene in Bairro Alto, Pizza A Pezzi is one of the few cheap and tasty places to refuel after or in the midst of a night on the town. This red and white tile pizza joint only offers takeout service, so most people aren't here to soak in the ambience anyway. Select from a large variety of slices (priced mostly by their weight), watch them go into the oven, and then get carbo-loading.

‡ [M]Baixa-Chiado (Chiado exit). Or bus #758 to Rua da Misericórdia. Follow R. da Misericórdia until it becomes R. Dom Pedro V. It is on the right. [$] €1-3 per slice. ⏰ Open daily 11:30am-2am.

ALFAMA

Alfama's maze of winding streets hides many small, traditional restaurants. The cheapest options tend to gather along **Rua dos Bacalhoeiros,** with the tastiest options located along **Rua de São João da Praça.**

★ **POIS, CAFE** CAFE $$

R. de São João da Praça, 93 ☎21 886 24 97 www.poiscafe.com

This Austrian-run cafe is quite comfortable, with couches, book-lined walls, and even a toy corner. Don't worry if it looks crowded inside; tables are shared. Almost everything on the menu has something inventive in it (e.g. apple and pesto on a veggie sandwich), although some more traditional options are available. Don't skip out on the custom lemonades, even though the coffee is almost as good.

‡ Tram #28E to Sé. From plaza in front of cathedral, walk to the right of cathedral; the cafe is on the right. [$] Lunch menu €5. Baked goods €2-7. ⏰ Open Tu-Su 11am-8pm.

★ **TASCA BELA** TAPAS, PORTUGUESE $$

R. dos Remédios, 190 ☎96 467 09 64

Tasca Bela deals only in *petiscos*, the Portuguese version of tapas. Come with friends and enjoy a myriad of reasonably priced small dishes for everyone to share. The restaurant is covered with old-time photos and Portuguese guitars, and they have *fado* multiple times per week. They are also open late, so it's a great place to fill up when you feel those 2am munchies coming on. Order the *chorizo assado* (€6) and watch it come out flaming. But beware, you might leave without your eyebrows.

‡ [M]Santa Apolónia. Head to the right of the Museu Militar, then left onto R. Remédios. [$] Petiscos €1-6. ⏰ Open daily 8pm-4am.

ESPERANÇA SÉ ITALIAN $$$

R. de São João da Praça, 103 ☎21 887 01 89

Although the food is a bit more expensive here, the ambiance is unbeatable. Given its location next to one of Lisbon's most frequented sights, the interior can afford to be minimalistic, with all white walls and solid black tables. Take advantage of this spot and sit at a candlelit table outside, where you can enjoy your pasta right next to the Sé Catedral. The romantic atmosphere is perfect for dining with your significant other and eating pasta Lady and the Tramp style—or sitting by yourself and watching other people do that…if you're into that kind of thing.

‡ Bus #737, or tram #28E. From Baixa, follow R. Conceição east (to the left as you face the river) up past the church, then turn right onto R. Santo António da Sé. Follow to the right past the cathedral. [$] Entrees €9-15. ⏰ Open M-F 8pm-2am, Sa-Su 1-4pm and 8pm-2am.

TABERNA MODERNA MODERN PORTUGUESE $$$

R. dos Bacalhoeiros, 18 ☎21 886 50 39

This restaurant sits close to the water, but that doesn't mean it's the same as all of its traditional Portuguese neighbors. As the name suggests, Taberna Moderna puts modern twists on Portuguese food by bringing in foreign influences, including Japanese and Italian. The dining room is wide open and minimalistic but gains personality from the giant nude painting adorning one of the walls.

✦ Ⓜ*Terreiro do Paço. From the north end of Pr. Comércio with the river behind you, take a right onto R. da Alfândega, then take a left after 3 blocks. The restaurant is on your right.* Ⓢ *Entrees €9-14.* Ⓞ *Open Tu-W 7:30pm-midnight, Th-Sa 7:30pm-2am.*

ALFAMA GRILL
PORTUGUESE $$

R. da Regueira, 26 ☎21 887 76 38

Alfama Grill is set back in a more secluded area of Alfama, away from the castle and the cathedral. With a stone interior and yellow walls, the area inside is a nice place to enjoy your *bacalhau*, but the large, outdoor patio is peaceful and serene. *Fado* is held multiple nights a week, and meals are reasonably priced.

✦ Ⓜ*Santa Apolónia. Follow the river west (to your left as you face it) from the station, right up C. Lingueta, and left onto R. Jardim do Tobaco. Take the next right and then another right at the end of the road. The restaurant will be on your left.* Ⓢ *Entrees €7-10.* Ⓞ *Open M-Sa 7pm-midnight.*

CHURRASQUEIRA GAÚCHA
GRILL $$

R. dos Bacalhoeiros, 26 ☎21 887 06 09

Here you will get tasty, traditional Portuguese fare in a simple but very large dining room. A tile mural and hanging lanterns make the place feel downright spiffy. The meat and fish stare at you from their display in a window on the street, so you can just walk by and pick what looks good, you cold-hearted meat-eater, you.

✦ *From Baixa, follow R. Comércio east (to the left as you face the water) until R. Madalena, then slight right onto R. Bacalhoeiros.* Ⓢ *Entrees €8-15.* Ⓞ *Open M-Sa noon-midnight.*

ÓH CALDAS
PORTUGUESE $$$

R. de São Mamede, 22 ☎21 887 57 11

This traditional restaurant (with an untraditional honeycomb design on the wall) has favorites like *sardinhas assadas* (grilled sardines), *alheira* (smoked chicken sausage), and an ever-changing three-course daily menu (€12). Its location on the scenic route between the Sé (cathedral) and the Castelo de São Jorge makes it a convenient Alfama stop.

✦ *From Baixa, follow R. Conceiçao east toward Alfama (to left as you face the river), just past the Igreja da Madalena. Head left up Tv. Almada for 3 blocks, then left onto R. São Mamede.* Ⓢ *Daily menu €12.* Ⓞ *Open daily noon-4pm and 8pm-midnight.*

ALMARGEM
PORTUGUESE $$

Tv. do Almargem, 4 ☎21 886 90 69

Down a small side street away from the cathedral and some of the pricier restaurants, Almargem has a tavern-like feel with two floors of seating and lots of wood. They serve massive and shareable portions of Lisbon classics like *porco com almêjoas* (pork with clams, €8). This place also has some of the best *fado* in town: Amália Rodrigues can usually be heard playing over the sound system on nights without a performance.

✦ *Take tram #28E to Sé, walk to right of cathedral, and head down a side street on the right, marked by a large sign.* Ⓢ *Entrees €7-10. Daily 3-course menu €8.50.* Ⓞ *Open M-Sa noon-3pm and 7-11pm.*

GRAÇA

The area around **Largo da Graça** is heaven for those looking for good, cheap meals. The *pastelarias* that line the square generally write their *pratos do dia* in magic marker on a paper tablecloth and post them outside; walk from one to the next and see what looks best and cheapest, though they all usually cost about €4-6. To get to Graça, take tram **28E** from the side of R. da Conceiçao that is closest to the river in Baixa all the way to the end of the line. If you're looking for a drink or a light lunch with an amazing view, try the **Esplanada da Igreja da Graca,** a lovely lookout point with carts that serve cheap sandwiches and drinks.

👍 HAWELI TANDOORI INDIAN $$
Tv. do Monte, 14 ☎21 886 77 13

A small island in a sea of *pastelarias* and other Portuguese cheap eats, Haweli Tandoori offers something that isn't found anywhere else in Graça: Indian food. Not only is it Indian, it's also delicious. The chicken tikka masala (€8) is savory, and the garlic naan (€1.50) is buttery and scrumptious. Naturally, plenty of vegetarian options are also available. And most surprisingly, the vast majority of the clientele is comprised of locals (everyone gets tired of codfish, eventually).

⇄ Take tram #28E to end of the line; walk down the street past the big church, and take a left onto Tv. do Monte. [$] Naan €1-2. Entrees €6-10. ⏰ Open M noon-3pm and 7-10:30pm; W-Su noon-3pm, 7-10:30pm.

O VICENTINHO PORTUGUESE $
R. da Voz do Operário, 1A

With a strikingly orange interior, O Vicentinho offers a comfortable place to sit down and enjoy a meal. Nice wooden tables give the ambience of a real restaurant at the prices of a *pastelaria*. Finally, you can enjoy your *Sande Mista* (ham and cheese sandwich, €2) without having to stand at a counter, staring at a blank, white, tile wall or pretending to text someone in order to avoid making awkward eye contact.

⇄ ⓂSanta Apolonia, bus #34 or tram #28E. Get off tram 28E in front of the massive white church at the Voz do Operário stop. [$] Sandwiches €2. Pratos do dia €6. ⏰ Open M-Sa 9am-7pm.

TASCA DO MANEL PORTUGUESE $$
R. de São Tomé, 20 ☎21 886 20 21

Black-and-white photographs line the walls of this traditional restaurant. The typical fare is on display, as are omelettes, so you can get your brunch on whenever the time is right. It's just down the road from Lg. da Graça toward Alfama, which makes it a very convenient stop. Expect a wait, as it's a local favorite.

⇄ From Lg. Graça, go to the small park in front of the church, next to the lookout point, then follow Cç. Graça straight; it becomes R. São Tomé after a small plaza (stay to the right of the kebab place). [$] Pratos do dia €6-9. Entrees €8-12. ⏰ Open M-Sa noon-3:30pm and 6:30-10:30pm.

lisbon

MATAS SNACK BAR SNACK BAR $
Lg. da Graça, 63A ☎21 887 95 82

With a brick interior and a bar declaring "we have snails" out front, Matas Snack Bar serves typical quick Portuguese food at good prices. It's the only restaurant in the square that has outdoor seating, so it's a great place to be on a nice day… unless you're a snail.

⇄ Take tram #28E to end of the line; it's near the park next to the big church. [$] Pratos do dia €5-8. ⏰ Open daily (closed W during summer and M during winter) 9am-midnight.

PASTELARIA ESTRELA DA GRAÇA PORTUGUESE, SWEETS $
Lg. da Graça, 98 ☎21 887 24 38

The pastry counter has more sweets than Lisbon has *pastelarias*, but don't get too distracted, as the daily specials are delicious and incredibly cheap. They usually come with all the fixings (rice, fries, small salad, sometimes an egg) and will leave you stuffed. But swallow your tears, man up, and get yourself some treats afterwards. A glass of the house wine costs less than €1 and is actually drinkable.

⇄ Take tram #28E to end of the line; it's across the street, next to the big church. [$] Pratos do dia €4-6. ⏰ Open daily 7am-10pm.

nightlife

Bairro Alto is one massive street party every night (even Sunday!) until 2am and is where just about everyone in town starts their evening. While some of the bars have charming character, most are just rooms that happen to serve alcohol, which is fine, since everyone takes their drinks outside to the steep streets to socialize on the sidewalk anyway. Drinks here tend to be cheap and strong; the best deals are the huge beers and caipirinhas, since you aren't rushed to finish them (you're outside, after all). The main nightlife area here is bordered by **Rua da Atalaia** to the west, **Travessa da Queimada** to the north, **Rua da Misericórdia** to the east, and the **Praça de Luís de Camões** to the south; the major streets for bars are **R. da Atalaia, Rua do Diário de Notícias,** and **Rua do Norte,** all of which run north-south through the neighborhood. After these bars close around 2am (a little later Friday and Saturday nights), there is a mass migration downhill toward **Cais do Sodré,** where bars gather under an overpass formed by **Rua do Alecrim.** On weekends, walking through R. do Alecrim is almost impossible, as people are packed in like sardines (which the Portuguese take very seriously). The bars here tend to be nicer, and plenty of clubs are open for dancing as well. If these clubs are too crowded, or if people are looking for something a little flashier, they'll head west along to river to **Santos** or even farther to **Alcântara** and the **Docas de Santo Amaro** at the foot of the 25 de Abril Bridge. The area near the Santa Apolónia train station also has a couple of newer clubs, including the famous **Lux.** Though Bairro Alto tends to be quite casual, don't expect to get into any of the clubs if you're still in your swim trunks and your flip-flops. Drinks inside range from expensive (€4-6 for beer, which can rise as dawn approaches) to aneurysm-inducing (double-digit cocktails), and there is often a cover for the best clubs (usually €5-15, depending on the time and how you look, though often free for women; the cover usually includes a couple of free drinks as well). Don't show up before midnight, when the places feel like seedier versions of middle school dances.

BAIRRO ALTO

ASSOCIAÇÃO LOUCOS & SONHADORES — BAR

Tv. do Conde do Soure, 2 ☎213 47 82 50

A few minutes away from the craziness of the Bairro Alto scene, the Crazies' and Dreamers' Association sits quietly in a non-descript building, with only a small, mysterious yet welcoming wooden sign on the door. Once inside, you will be glad that this gem is a well-kept secret. Dimly lit, this smoky bar is filled with clutter, paintings, and books. The chatter of friends and the smooth sounds of jazz somehow allow it to be simultaneously gritty, sophisticated, and sincere. Beer is cheap, bar snacks are on the table, and cigs are available at the bar.

[M]Restauradores. Cross the square and take a left onto Çç. da Gloria in the northwest corner, then take a right on R. São Pedro de Alcântara. Take a left onto R. Luisa Todi, which becomes Tv. do Conde do Soure. [$] Beer €1.10. Open Tu-Su 10pm-3am.

PAVILHÃO CHINÊS — LOUNGE

R. de Dom Pedro V, 89 ☎213 42 47 29

A little north of the main Bairro Alto scene, this nightlife spot is a bit more laid-back (and indoors) than its raucous neighbors, but it's hardly boring. A massive labyrinth, Pavilhão Chinês feels like a clash of the Victorian and the absurd, with thousands of figurines and odd paintings covering the place from floor to ceiling, while men in fancy blue vests tend the ornate wooden bars. There is a huge menu of teas and classic drinks, like the Sidecar (they're bringin' it back, baby) presented in a 50-page menu-cum-graphic novel.

Bus #758. From Pr. de Luís de Camões, follow R. da Misericórdia up toward the miradouro, and keep following the same street as it bends to the left and becomes R. de Dom Pedro V. [$] Beer €3. Tea €4. Drinks €6-9. Open M-Sa 6pm-2am, Su 9pm-2am.

PORTAS LARGAS
R. da Atalaia, 105

BAR, MUSIC
☎213 46 63 79

This staple of the Bairro Alto scene has live music every night (sometimes really good, other times unfortunate covers of '80s songs that are so bad they're good) and some of the biggest, strongest *caipirinhas* (the national cocktail of Brazil, made from sugar cane rum, sugar, and lime) and mojitos around (€5-7). True to its name, the large doors allow a good deal of traffic to make its way inside, but you can enjoy the music and drinks just outside if things get too crowded. Just don't expect to be able to loiter inside and enjoy the music without buying a drink.

✠ ⓂBaixa-Chiado (Chiado exit). Bus #758 or tram 28E. Walk up R. da Misericórdia 3 blocks from Pr. de Luís de Camões, then left for 5 blocks. Ⓢ Beer €4. Cocktails €5-7. ⌚ Open July-Sept M-Th 7pm-2am, F-Sa 7pm-3am, Su 7pm-2am; Oct-June M-Th 8pm-2am, F-Sa 8pm-3am, Su 8pm-2am.

BICA ABAIXO
R. da Bica de Duarte Belo, 62

BAR
☎213 47 70 14 www.bicaabaixo.blogspot.pt

This bar is located on the steep slope of the shiny, silver Elevador da Bica funicular, just to the south of the center of Bairro Alto. It's perfect for those making the trek down to the river or for those sick of Bairro Alto's cheaply made drinks—the native Brazilians who own and run this small bar make the best *caipirinhas* (€3.50) in town, crushed, mashed and mixed together right in front of you.

✠ ⓂBaixa-Chiado (Chiado exit). Or tram 28E to Calhariz-Bica. From Pr. de Luís de Camões, follow R. do Loreto (far-right corner of plaza, with your back to the Metro station) 3 blocks, then turn left down R. da Bica de Duarte Belo; the bar is on the left. Ⓢ Beer €1.50. Mixed drinks €3-4. ⌚ Open daily 9pm-2am.

FRIENDS BAIRRO ALTO
Tv. da Cara, 3

BAR, BOOK EXCHANGE
☎213 43 24 19

Recently moved to a new location, this hipster bar has a deep, dark secret: it is also a book exchange. Well, it isn't a secret to the earnestly apathetic 20-somethings mingling inside. They will tell you to trade a book in for a different one, or better yet, trade it in for a beer! Top 40 music blares, and traditional *azulejo* tile lines the lower wall (all ironically, of course), but this bar is all about a mellow and modern experience.

✠ ⓂBaixa-Chiado (Chiado exit). From Pr. de Luís de Camões, follow R. da Misericórdia 7 blocks, then turn left onto Tv. da Cara. The bar is on your left. Ⓢ Beer €1.50. Mixed drinks €3-5. ⌚ Open daily 3pm-2am.

FAVELA CHIK
R. do Diário de Notícias, 66

BAR, GLBT
☎967 07 67 39

Located on a busy street amidst a sea of bars, Favela Chik manages to catch the eye. Pink both inside and out, this bar matches its wild style with funky tunes, sometimes spun by local DJs. Seating is minimal, mostly because as the night goes on, the small bar gets packed as the crowd picks up and the drinks begin to flow. Be sure to try the sangria, which is a steal (€1).

✠ ⓂBaixa-Chiado (Chiado exit). From Pr. Luís de Camões, follow R. da Norte away for 3 blocks, then take a left, then a right on R. de Diário do Notícias. Ⓢ Sangria €1. Beer €1.25. ⌚ M-Th 8pm-2am, F-Sa 8pm-3am, Su 8pm-2am.

SALTO ALTO
R. da Rosa, 159

BAR
☎916 52 21 07

A new, hip bar that looks pretty much exactly how you would expect a new, hip bar to look: dim lighting, minimalist interior decorating juxtaposed with the occasional ornate mirror or chandelier (as a statement, of course), and shelves of backlit drinks behind a bar. It's usually a bit quieter (though by no means quiet) than the streets in the heart of Bairro Alto's a few blocks southeast, but this is still a happening place.

✢ ⓂBaixa-Chiado (Chiado exit) or tram 28E to Calhariz-Bica. From Pr. de Luís de Camões, follow R. do Loreto (far-right corner of plaza, with your back to the Metro station) 3 blocks, then turn right up R. da Rosa. Ⓢ Beer €2. Cocktails €3-5. ⌚ Open W-Sa 11pm-3am.

PÁGINAS TANTAS
JAZZ, LOUNGE

R. do Diário de Notícias, 85
☎917 60 03 29

This modern-day tribute to the Jazz Age is filled with images of famous jazz artists and even has an alto sax mounted atop the bar. Come inside and sit at one of the many tables for a more tame Bairro Alto experience. You'll come out feeling more cultured and determined to listen to more jazz (but just like last time, you won't remain determined for long). The impressive sound system blares jazz all night, but stop by on a weekday for a shot at hearing locals play the standards and more.

✢ ⓂBaixa-Chiado (Chiado exit). From Pr. de Luís de Camões, head up R. do Norte (to the right near the far side of the plaza if your back is to the Metro station) 1 block. Turn left, then right up R. do Diário de Notícias. Ⓢ Beer €2. Mixed drinks €5-6. ⌚ Open M-Th 8pm-2am, F-Sa 8pm-3am, Su 8pm-2am.

ALFAMA

Although not as renowned for its nightlife as Bairro Alto, Alfama can hold its own. With a fantastic mix of dives, bars, and nightclubs, a night in Alfama is full of possibilities. However, establishments aren't really centered in any one area in Alfama, so you will have to do a little legwork if you plan to hop from place to place.

▨ LUX
CLUB

Av. do Infante Dom Henrique
☎21 882 08 www.luxfragil.com

This club is known far and wide as one of the best clubs in Western Europe; Lisboans abroad will tell you that if you visit one *discoteca* in Lisbon, it has to be this one. The enormous riverside complex has three stories of debauchery, though you'll leave with a few more of your own Chill on the calm rooftop with amazing views, start to get schwasty at a slightly more intense bar on the floor below that, then descend into the maelstrom on the lowest level to find a raging disco, howling and shrieking with electronic music. Drinks are pricey (cocktails €8-12) and everything is cutting edge. "We cannot escape from each other" is written all around the main bar, giving creepy single guys a great segue into awful pickup lines. The bouncers tend to be very selective, so just act cool and try to get on their good side by being polite and speaking Portuguese. Dress well—only wear jeans or sneakers if the jeans are super-skinny and the sneakers are canvas high-tops, since the stylin' hipster look tends to play well.

✢ ⓂSanta Apolónia, bus #28, 34, 706, 712, 735, 759, 781, 782, 794. Just east of Santa Apolónia train station, on the side of the tracks closest to the river. Ⓢ Cover usually €12. ⌚ Open Tu-Sa midnight-6am.

▨ GINJA D'ALFAMA
GINJINHA

R. de São Pedro, 12

Hidden in the heart of Alfama, this tiny hole-in-the-ancient-wall bar specializes in *ginjinha*, Lisbon's native wild-cherry liqueur, and serves it up cheap and ice cold (€1). You can take it outside to the small tables around the corner, which are much cooler than the stifling bar itself. It's a great place to start the night, serving sandwiches for a good carbo-load before moving on to more raucous nightlife.

✢ Bus #28, 34, 706, 712, 735, 759, 781, 782, 794. Walk down R. São João da Praça, to the right of Sé Cathedral as you're facing it, and follow the same street (bear left at the fork 1 block past the cathedral) as it becomes R. São Pedro; it's a small store on the left side. Ⓢ Ginjinha €1. Sandwiches €1.50-2.50. ⌚ Open M 9:30am-midnight, W-Su 9:30am-midnight.

RESTÔ BAR, CIRCUS

Costa do Castelo, 7 ☎21 886 73 34 www.chapito.org

This bar has amazing views over Alfama and the Tejo, though they are best enjoyed during the daytime. At night, the outside patio comes alive with a carnival feel, and not without reason—it's on the grounds of Chapitô, a government-funded clown school. On most evenings, there are circus shows, with tightrope walkers and trapeze artists practicing aerial acrobatics over the party below. Go downstairs to enjoy the separate, dark and smoky bar that usually has live music, albeit fewer clowns.

🚏 Bus #737 to Costa do Castelo. From Baixa, it's a long walk uphill: follow R. da Conceição east toward Alfama (left as you face the river), past Igreja da Madalena, and up Tv. Almada to the left to R. São Mamede. Go up the steep and windy Tv. Mata, then left up Cç. Conde de Penafiel to Costa do Castelo, then right. $ Beer €2. Cocktails €5-7. ⏰ Open M-F noon-3pm and 7:30pm-1am, Sa-Su noon-1:30am.

ONDAJAZZ JAZZ CLUB

Arco de Jesus, 7 ☎21 888 32 42 www.ondajazz.com

This club has live performances every night, ranging from jazz and blues to poetry readings and open mic nights (Wednesdays). It has a cool coffeehouse feel, the sort you'd expect to find in Greenwich Village rather than traditional Alfama. The party often spills out onto the alley outside, one of Alfama's most beautiful, with a gorgeous *azulejo*-covered arch over the stairway. This club really is all about the music; everything directs your attention toward the stage. Many people dine here, but just having a few drinks is completely acceptable and frequently done.

🚏 Tram #28E to Sé. Facing cathedral, head down to the right of the cathedral and follow the street for 3 blocks; Ondajazz is down the alley to the right. $ Cover Tu, Th-Sa €4-7. ⏰ Open Tu-Th 8pm-2am, F-Sa 8pm-3am. Kitchen open until 11pm.

CLUB NOIR CLUB

R. da Madalena, 123 www.wix.com/club-noir

When you are sick of all the selective bouncers, the pricey drinks, and the bad house remixes of songs that should have been left in the '90s, it's time to move on to something else. Club Noir is here for you. A club dedicated to "alternative sounds," this nightclub/music venue is all about punk rock, hardcore, metal, and more. Expect to see a lot of leather and mohawks. Drinks are cheap and anyone can get in, so get your mosh on (if appropriate) and polish up on your punk discography; you just might fit in.

🚏 [M]Terreiro do Paço. From Pr. Comércio, walk to the right facing away from the water. Turn left onto R. da Madalena. $ Beer €1.50. Occasional cover €5. ⏰ Open F 11pm-4am, Sa 11pm-6am.

BELARUQUE BAR BAR

R. dos Remédios, 89 belaruque@gmail.com

With dirt cheap drinks (€1 shots) and a good location, Belaruque Bar is an ideal place to start the night. Grab some drinks and go chat in the streets with the locals. Mojitos (€3.50) are about one fourth of the price they will be at the night clubs, so load up now before you go hit the dance floor.

🚏 [M]Santa Apolónia. Head to the right of the Museu Militar, then turn left onto R. Remédios. $ Shots €1, mojitos €3.50. ⏰ Open daily 6pm-2am.

RIVERFRONT: CAIS DO SODRÉ, SANTOS, ALCÂNTARA, DOCAS

Once the bars in Bairro Alto close, the party walks down Rua do Alecrim to Cais do Sodré, where there are more than a dozen clubs. The area looks pretty unsavory from 7am-2am, but the lines for the clubs stretch around the block for the five hours in between. Many party enthusiasts then continue westward toward the **25 de Abril Bridge,** where the neighborhoods of Santos, Alcântara, and the newly redeveloped Docas de Santo Amaro have chic and exclusive clubs.

OP ART
Doca de Santo Amaro   ☎21 395 67 87 www.opartcafe.com   CLUB

During the daytime, this is a pleasant spot to sit by the water and watch the waves while listening to the hum of the cars passing over the bridge. On Friday and Saturday nights, it's a completely different story. Guest DJs rattle the panes of the all-glass structure, pumping hip hop, house beats, and more until the sun starts to rise over the Tejo. Stay all night and see the 25 de Abril Bridge (modeled after the Golden Gate Bridge) light up in the morning for the full experience.

   ✝ *Buses #28, 201, 714, 720, 732, 738 or trams #15E and 18E. Head toward the bridge along the waterfront. Ⓢ Cover €5-10; includes 1 drink. Beer €2.50. Cocktails €5-7. Ⓞ Open Tu-Th 3pm-2am, F-Sa 3pm-6am, and Su 3pm-2am.*

DOCK'S CLUB
R. da Cintura do Porto de Lisboa, 226   ☎21 395 08 56   CLUB

This disco near the bridge is famous for its Ladies' Nights on Tuesday (well, Wednesday morning), when women not only get in free but also get €14 in free drinks. Spare your friends the social commentary on this potentially sexist practice and enjoy the music blasting from the two different bars inside or the fresh air on the patio in back.

   ✝ *Buses #28, 201, 714, 720, 732, 738 or trams #15E and 18E. Ⓢ Cover €10-15. Beer €3. Cocktails €6. Ⓞ Open Tu midnight-6am, Th-Sa midnight-6am.*

MUSICBOX
R. Nova do Carvalho, 24   ☎21 343 01 07 www.musicboxlisboa.com   CLUB, LIVE MUSIC

This venue gets great indie and punk bands to play early in the night (sets usually start at 11pm), and the best local DJs spin from 2am until closing, which is shortly after dawn. The line is often so long you'll be surprised there's not a roller coaster waiting when you finally get to the door, but it's worth the wait. The space is small enough that 100 people will feel like a great crowd, but there will likely be even more than that.

   ✝ *Ⓜ Cais do Sodré or bus #28, 35, 36, 44, 706, 714, 735, 758, 760, 781, 782, 794 to C. Sodré. From Pr. Luís de Camões, walk all the way down R. Alecrim, then take a sharp right once you get to the bottom to double back under the bridge. Ⓢ Cover €6-10; usually includes 1 drink. Ⓞ Open W-Sa 11pm-7am.*

JAMAICA
R. Nova do Carvalho, 6   ☎21 342 18 59   CLUB

This bar in Cais do Sodré is fairly quiet before 2am, but once the crowd rolls down from Bairro Alto and an hour-long line forms around the block, it's suddenly the place to be. Known for playing music that's a little edgier than neighboring clubs—mostly rock, but also a lot of dub and reggae—this disco is perfect for those sick of Europop techno remixes. Come in and kiss the picture of Bob Marley before you do anything else, just to make sure Jah is on your side on the dance floor.

   ✝ *Ⓜ Cais do Sodré or bus #28, 35, 36, 44, 706, 714, 735, 758, 760, 781, 782, 794 to C. Sodré. From Pr. Luís de Camões, walk all the way down R. Alecrim, then take a sharp right once you get to the bottom to double back under the bridge. Ⓢ Cover €6-10. Ⓞ Open Tu-Sa midnight-6am.*

nightlife

CLUB VINTAGE CLUB

R. da Cintura do Porto de Lisboa, Armazém H ☎21 396 56 94 www.clubvintagelisboa.com

With its black leather chairs and hardwood everywhere, this club certainly has some vintage touches. But don't be fooled: this is a modern disco, with electronic dance music that blares well into the morning. The wide open dance floor means once things get going, there is nowhere to hide, so come prepared to boogy.

🚌 Buses 28, 201, 714, 720, 732, 738 or trams 15E and 18E. $ Cover €5-15. Beer €3. Cocktails €6-10. ⏰ Open W-Sa midnight-6am.

arts and culture

Although Lisbon might not be the first city that comes to mind when discussing art, it is actually packed with various museums and attractions, particularly those pertaining to design and modern art. Bullfighting reveals the edgier side of Portuguese culture, and *futebol* dominates the sporting scene. However, to experience the most authentic and distinct part of the Lisbon cultural experience, you have to turn to *fado*. This Portuguese soul music has moved hard-nosed men to tears, and even if you don't understand the words, the prevailing themes of love, loss, and Lisbon will be easily conveyed through the emotions of the performer.

FADO

A mandatory experience for visitors, Lisbon's trademark form of entertainment is traditional *fado*, an art form combining music, song, and narrative poetry. Its roots lie in the Alfama neighborhood, where women whose husbands had gone to sea would lament their *fado* (fate). Singers of *fado* traditionally dress in black and sing mournful tunes of lost love, uncertainty, and the famous feelings of *saudade* (to translate *saudade* as "loneliness" would be a gruesome understatement). However, many *fado* venues will have less melancholic songs and even some comical crowd-pleasers (if you understand Portuguese, at least). Many *fado* houses are located in Bairro Alto and in Alfama between the cathedral and the water, and finding one is not difficult, as you can hear snippets of songs drifting into the streets as you pass by (*fadistas* don't use microphones, but that doesn't mean you won't hear them). Almost all *fado* houses are rather touristy, but locals—especially older folk—still crowd in amongst the hordes of tourists. Expensive *fado* houses with mournfully high minimums include **Café Luso** (Tv. Queimada, 10 ☎213 42 22 81 www.cafeluso.pt $ €16 min. ⏰ Open daily 7:30pm-2am) and **Adega Machado** (R. Norte, 91 ☎213 22 46 40 www.adegamachado.pt $ €16 min. ⏰ Open Tu-Su 8pm-3am). There are also some well-marked and easy-to-find places on **Rua de São João da Praça** in Alfama, including **Clube de Fado,** with road signs pointing you in that direction all the way from Baixa. The places listed below are either free or truly worth the money.

A TASCA DO CHICO BARRIO ALTO

R. do Diário de Notícias, 39 ☎965 05 96 70

This Bairro Alto *fado* location is popular with locals and has no cover charge or drink minimum. You're going to want a cold drink, however, as everyone is packed in like *sardinhas* by the time the *fado* starts. Many choose to grab a spot at the open window and watch from the cool(er) street outside. Pretty much any amateur *fadista* who wants to take a turn can sing, so on any given night you can hear something you'd rather forget followed by the next big thing in *fado*.

🚌 Ⓜ Baixa-Chiado (Chiado exit). From Pr. Luís de Camões, head up R. Norte (to the right near the far side of the plaza if your back is to the Metro station) for 1 block, then take a quick left. Next, turn right up R. Diário de Notícias. $ Beer €1.50. ⏰ Open M-Sa 6pm-3:30am. Fado starts around 9:30pm, but arrive much earlier to get a seat.

VOSSEMECÊ

R. de Santo António da Sé, 18 ☎218 88 30 56 www.vossemece.com

This *fado* joint, conveniently located near Baixa, is housed in a beautiful, if oddly shaped, stable; arched ceilings and heavy stone columns run farther than the eye can see into the darkness of the surprisingly spacious restaurant. The *fadistas* rotate, each singing a couple of songs ranging from lively and funny to mournful and heart-wrenching. There's no cover charge or drink minimum, and the drinks are reasonably priced (€3.50-6.50) and quite good; however, the environment lends itself more toward sitting down for a nice meal with a bottle of wine (you will need it to cope).

✦ Ⓜ*Baixa-Chiado (Baixa exit), or tram #28E. Follow R. Conceiçao east toward Alfama (to the left as you face the river) past Igreja da Madalena; it's on the corner across the street to the left.* Ⓢ *Drinks €3.50-6.50. Entrees €10-15.* ⌚ *Open M-Tu noon-4pm and 8:30pm-midnight, Th-Su noon-4pm and 8:30pm-midnight. Fado performances 9pm-midnight.*

O FAIA

R. da Barroca, 54-56 ☎213 42 19 23 www.ofaia.com

There's no question that this swanky spot is a splurge, but it's a great place to come to see some of Lisbon's best *fadistas* sing their hearts out. There aren't many places with a €20 minimum that are worth the steep price, but this is one of them; so put on your Sunday best and have a night out on the town. If you are on a tighter budget and want a drive-thru experience, walk by and hear the sounds of *fado* as you proceed to the bar next door; it is owned by the same people, and the drinks are quite cheap.

✦ Ⓜ*Baixa-Chiado (Chiado exit). From Pr. Luís de Camões, head up R. Norte (to the right near the far side of the plaza if your back is to the Metro station) 1 block, then take a left and walk 2 blocks along R. Salgadeiras. Turn right up R. Barroca; O Faia is in front of you.* Ⓢ *Cover €20; includes 2 drinks. Entrees €25-35.* ⌚ *Open M-Sa 9pm-2am. Fado performances start at 9:30pm.*

BULLFIGHTING

Portuguese bullfighting differs from the spectacle practiced across the border in Spain in that the bull is not killed in the ring; it's butchered only afterward. In this version, it is the *cavaleiro* (the horseman who fights the bull first) who is the star of the show instead of the *matador*. Some *cavaleiros* are women, so you can have gender equality and social justice while you watch a creature get tortured for a couple of hours. At first blush, the Portuguese variety of *tauromaquia* seems a much fairer match between man and beast: rather than one *matador* with a sword, like in Spain, five unarmed *forcados* line up in front of the bull and take him down with their bare hands. However, once you remember that the bull has been poked, prodded, and stabbed for the previous 15-20min., the justness of the final battle becomes a little less impressive. Most bullfights take place on Thursday nights at the newly renovated **Praça de Touros de Lisboa** at Campo Pequeno (☎217 99 84 50 www.campopequeno. com Ⓢ €15-75). True fans of the sport, however, will want to make a pilgrimage to **Santarém,** Portuguese bullfighting's capital and home to the best matches. (Praça de Touros Monumental Celestino Graça, Campo Emílio Infante da Câmara ☎243 32 43 58 Ⓢ Tickets from €11. ⌚ 45min. by train. Trains run to Santarém from Lisbon's Santa Apolónia station 10-15 per day 8am-9:30pm.)

FUTEBOL *Soccer*

For many Portuguese, *futebol* (known in many Anglophone countries as "football," and in the United States as "soccer" or "that sport we care about for two weeks once every four years") is a way of life. The Portuguese returned from the 2006 World Cup as national heroes after reaching the semifinal round for the first time in 40 years. They had a strong showing in the 2010 World Cup as well, though they lost in the quarterfinal round to eventual champion Spain in a lackluster performance that left

arts and culture

many a Portuguese citizen in tears. If you're in Lisbon when Portugal is playing, head to one of the ■giant TV screens set up around town, usually located at **Praça do Marquês de Pombal, Praça da Figueira,** or just off **Praça dos Restauradores,** next to the Rossio train station. Two of the "big three" clubs that have dominated Portuguese soccer play in Lisbon: **Benfica** won the league championship in 2010, and **Sporting** last touched silverware in the '08-'09 League Cup and consistently finishes in the top three or four in the league. The two clubs have a combined total of 50 league titles. Benfica plays at **Estádio da Luz,** known to fans as the *catedral* (Av. General Norton de Matos ☎707 20 01 00 www.slbenfica.pt), and Sporting plays at **Estádio José Alvalade** (Av. Padre Cruz ☎707 20 44 44 www.sporting.pt). These two sides are bitter rivals, so be careful which team you're supporting and where. If you can't stand the thought of looking like a front-runner, or just want to see a match with a bit more character, **Estoril Praia,** who play just outside of Cascais at **Estádio António Coimbra da Mota** (R. Dom Bosco ☎214 661 002 www.estorilpraia.pt), were just promoted to the top league in 2012. Their stadium is a bit more cozy, seating just 5,000. The season begins in mid-August and ends in mid-May.

THEATER, MUSIC, AND FILM

Teatro Nacional de Dona Maria II in Rossio stages performances of classical and foreign plays. (Pr. Dom Pedro IV ☎213 25 08 00 www.teatro-dmaria.pt ⚓ ⓂRossio.) At Lisbon's largest theater, **Teatro Nacional de São Carlos,** opera and classical music hold sway. (R. Serpa Pinto, 9 ☎213 25 30 00 www.saocarlos.pt ⚓ ⓂBaixa-Chiado, tram #28E.) From the end of June to the end of July, this theater fills the neighboring **Largo de São Carlos** with free music and dance performances in the open-air Chiado evening. (Lg. São Carlos, www.festivalaolargo.com.) The **Cinema São Jorge** is one of Portugal's grandest and oldest movie theaters. (Av. Liberdade, 175 ☎213 10 34 00 www.cinemasaojorge.pt ⚓ ⓂAvenida.) Other cinema complexes can be found at the **Amoreiras** shopping center (Av. Engenheiro Duarte Pacheco ☎213 81 02 40 www.amoreiras.com ⚓ Bus #207 or 711), the **Colombo** shopping center (Av. Lusíada ☎217 11 36 36 www.colombo.pt ⚓ ⓂColégio Militar-Luz), the **Centro Vasco da Gama** (Av. Dom João II ☎218 93 06 01 www.centrovascodagama.pt ⚓ ⓂOriente), and **El Corte Inglés** (Av. António Augusto de Aguiar, 31 ☎213 71 17 00 www.elcorteingles.pt ⚓ ⓂMarquês de Pombal).

FESTIVALS

June in Lisbon is essentially one month-long festival, with food, drink, music, and dancing filling the streets from Bairro Alto to Graça and far, far beyond. The night of June 12 is the peak of the festivities, when Lisbon's adopted patron saint, Anthony, is celebrated during the **Festa de Santo António.** Banners, streamers, and colored lights criss-cross the streets and streetlamps, and confetti falls by the metric ton on the **Avenida da Liberdade** during the parade, where each of Lisbon's neighborhoods attempts to out-do the others with the finest display. Back at the Sé, a selective group of couples takes part in a joint marriage ceremony that is meant to bring great luck to their relationship. The crowded streets of Alfama, particularly around the **Igreja de Santo António da Sé,** erupt with zealous revelry, and everyone consumes *sardinhas assadas* (grilled sardines) and *ginjinha* (wild cherry liqueur). Brave souls try to walk all the way up the hill from the bottom to the Sé, stopping at each establishment along the way to have a beer. Decorations hang in Alfama for months after the **festas de Lisboa** end, and serve as reminders of the crazy month. For three days during the second week of July, the **Optimus Alive** music festival takes over the Algés waterfront, drawing some of the world's most popular artists and fans from across the globe (☎213 93 37 70 www.optimusalive.com).

shopping

All kinds of shoppers can find what they are looking for in Lisbon. For the high-end shoppers (or at least the fashionista window-shopper wannabes), **Baixa** and **Chiado** are lined with expensive designer clothing stores. Shopping centers can also be found along **Avenida da Liberdade.** But for the rest of the plebes (all you normal people), there are massive street markets that take place throughout the city.

FEIRAS *Markets*

Most of Lisbon's shopping districts and malls don't have anything that you couldn't find elsewhere, but the *feiras* can be great places to pick up one-of-a-kind souvenirs and other items on the cheap. *Feiras* that take place regularly include the **Feiras das Velharias,** antique fairs held in Lisbon's western suburbs (**Oeiras** and **São Julião da Barra** on the first Sunday of the month, **Caxias** on the second Sunday of the month, **Paço de Arcos** on the third Sunday of the month, and **Algés** on the fourth Sunday of the month), and the **Feira de Carcavelos,** one of the area's oldest (and cheapest) clothing markets, which takes place in Carcavelos every Thursday. The **Feira de Artesanato de Estoril,** a 30min. train ride west of Lisbon, takes place in front of the Estoril casino every July and August to celebrate Portuguese pottery.

🏛 FEIRA DA LADRA   GRAÇA
Campo de Santa Clara

Held in Graça near the edge of Alfama, the so-called "thief's market" is Lisbon's best known *feira.* The stalls at this market, which takes place every Tuesday and Saturday, stretch from the Mosteiro de São Vicente de Fora to the Panteão Nacional, with vendors selling treasures (ornate antique silverware), junk (used tennis balls), and everything in between (bootlegged kung-fu action movies). Prices are flexible, and bargaining is encouraged, but initially posing too low of an offer can be taken as an insult. Hawk-like vision may be necessary to spot the diamonds in the rough, but if you want anything worth having, get there early before the tour groups pick the place clean.

    ✠ *Take tram #28E to Igreja e Mosteiro de São Vicente de Fora, then walk to the left of the big white church.* ☒ *Open Tu and Sa 7am-2pm.*

MERCADO DA RIBEIRA   CHIADO/WATERFRONT
Av. 24 de Julio   ☎213 24 49 80 www.espacoribeira.pt

Although it is past its days of former glory as the dominant force in fruits and vegetables, Mercado da Ribeira is still a sight to behold. The massive, beautiful building hosts hundreds of vendors selling every kind of produce imaginable. But even more of a sight is the army of florists selling flowers in every hue and aroma. A warning: massive amounts of fruit get heavy; don't come hungry unless you bring your fruit-toting steed along with you.

    ✠ Ⓜ*Cais do Sodré, or bus #28, 35, 36, 44, 706, 714, 735, 758, 760, 781, 782, 794 to Cais do Sodré. From Pr. Duque da Terceira, while facing the river, take a left onto Av. 24 de Julio.* ☒ *Open Tu-Sa; food 5am-2pm, flowers 5am-7pm.*

shopping

essentials

PRACTICALITIES

- **TOURIST OFFICE: Main Tourist Office.** (Pr. Restauradores, 1250 ☎21 347 56 60 www.visitlisboa.com ✈ Ⓜ️Restauradores, or bus #36, 44, 91, 709, 711, 732, 745, or 759. On west side of Pr. Restauradores, in Palácio da Foz. 🕐 Open daily 9am-8pm.) The **Welcome Center** is the city's main tourist office where you can buy tickets for sightseeing buses and the **Lisboa Card,** which includes transportation and discounted admission to most sights for a flat fee. (R. Arsenal, 15 ☎21 031 28 10) The **airport branch** is located near the terminal exit. (☎21 845 06 60 🕐 Open daily 7am-midnight.) There are also information kiosks in Santa Apolónia, Belém, and on R. Augusta in Baixa.

- **TOURS: CARRIStur** provides 1½hr. tours of the historic center in pre-WWI tram cars. (Pr. Comércio ☎21 358 23 34 www.carristur.pt ✈ Ⓜ️Baixa-Chiado. Bus #28, 36, 44, 91, 92, 706, 709, 711, 714, 732, 745, 759, 760, 781,782, or 794. Or trams 12E, 15E, 18E, or 25E. Tour trams leave from Pr. Comércio, the giant plaza by the water at the end of R. Augusta in Baixa. Ⓢ €18, ages 4-10 €9. *i* Available in English, Dutch, French, German, Italian, Japanese, Portuguese, and Spanish. 🕐 Tours depart from Pr. Comércio daily every 30-40min. 10am-8pm.)

- **CURRENCY EXCHANGE: NovaCâmbios** in Rossio. (Pr. Dom Pedro IV, 42 ☎21 324 25 53 www.novacambios.com ✈ Ⓜ️Rossio. Bus #36, 44, 91, 709, 711, 732, 745, or 759. On west side of Rossio plaza. 🕐 Open M-F 8:30am-3pm.)

- **INTERNET: Biblioteca Municipal Camões** has free internet access. (Lg. Calhariz, 17 ☎21 342 21 57 www.blx.cm-lisboa.pt ✈ Ⓜ️Baixa-Chiado, tram 28E, or bus #58 or 100. From Pr. Luís de Camões, follow R. Loreto for 4 blocks. 🕐 Open July 16-Sept 15 M-F 11am-6pm; Sept 16-July 15 Tu-F 10:30am-6pm.)

- **POST OFFICE: Correios** main office is on Pr. Restauradores. (Pr. Restauradores, 58 ☎213 23 89 71 www.ctt.pt ✈ Ⓜ️Restauradores. Bus #336, 44, 91, 709, 711, 732, 745, or 759. 🕐 Open M-F 8am-10pm, Sa-Su 9am-6pm.)

EMERGENCY

- **POLICE: Tourism Police Station** provides police service for foreigners. (Pr. Restauradores, 1250 ☎21 342 16 24 ✈ Ⓜ️Restauradores. Bus #36, 44, 91, 709, 711, 732, 745, or 759. On west side of Pr. Restauradores, in Palácio da Foz next to the tourist office.)

- **PHARMACY: Farmácia Azevedo and Filhos** in Rossio posts a schedule of pharmacies open late at night, as do most other pharmacies; or just look for a lighted, green cross. (Pr. Dom Pedro IV, 31 ☎21 343 04 82 ✈ Ⓜ️Rossio. Bus #36, 44, 91, 709, 711, 732, 745, or 759. In front of metro stop at the side of Rossio closest to river. 🕐 Open daily 8:30am-7:30pm.)

- **HOSPITAL/MEDICAL SERVICES:** Lisbon's main hospital is **Hospital de São José.** (R. José António Serrano ☎21 884 10 00 ✈ Ⓜ️Martim Moniz. Bus #34, 708, or 760. 🕐 Open 24hr.) **Hospital de São Luis** is in Bairro Alto. (R. Luz Soriano, 182 ✈ Ⓜ️Baixa-Chiado. From Pr. Luís de Camões, follow R. Loreto 4 blocks, then turn right onto R. Luz Soriano. 🕐 Open daily 9am-8pm.)

GETTING THERE

By Plane

All flights land at **Aeroporto de Lisboa** (LIS; ☎21 841 35 00), near the northern edge of the city. The cheapest way to get to town from the airport is by **bus.** To get to the bus stop, walk out of the terminal, turn right, and cross the street to the bus stop, marked by yellow metal posts with arrival times of incoming buses. Buses #44 and 745 (Ⓢ €1.75. ⏰ 15-20min., daily every 25min., 6am-12:15am) run to Pr. Restauradores, where they stop in front of the tourist office. The express AeroBus #1 runs to the same locations (Ⓢ€3.50 ⏰ 15min., daily every 20min., 7am-11pm) and is a much faster option during rush hours. A **taxi** downtown costs €10-15, but fares are billed by time, not distance, so watch out for drivers trying to take a longer route.

By Train

Those traveling in and out of Lisbon by train are regularly confused, as there are multiple major train stations in Lisbon, all serving different destinations. The express and inexpensive **Alfa Pendular** line runs between Braga, Porto, Coimbra, and Lisbon. Regional trains are slow and can be crowded; buses are slightly more expensive but faster and more comfortable. **Urbanos** trains run from Lisbon to Sintra and to Cascais, with stops along the way, and are very cheap and reliable. Contact **Comboios de Portugal** for more information (☎80 820 82 08 www.cp.pt). Those who want to head south should go to the **Entrecampos** station. **Estação Cais do Sodré** is right at the river, a 5min. walk west from Baixa or a quick metro ride to the end of the green line. **Estação Rossio** is the gorgeous neo-Manueline building between Rossio and Pr. Restauradores and services almost all Lisbon suburbs, with lines ending in Sintra, Cascais, Azambuja, and Sado. **Estação Santa Apolónia** is one of the main international and inter-city train stations in Lisbon, running trains to the north and east. It is located on the river to the east of Baixa; to get there, take the blue Metro line to the end of the line. Trains run between Santa Apolónia and: Aveiro (Ⓢ €26 ⏰ 2½hr., 16 per day 6am-9:30pm); Braga (Ⓢ €32.50 ⏰ 3½hr., 4 per day 7am-7pm); Coimbra (Ⓢ €22.50 ⏰ 2hr., 20 per day 6am-10pm); and Porto (Ⓢ €24-30 ⏰ 3hr., 16 per day 6am-11pm). **Estação Oriente** runs southbound trains. The station is near the Parque das Nações, up the river to the east of the center; take the red Metro line to the end of the line. Trains run between Oriente and Faro (Ⓢ €21-22 ⏰ 3½-4hr., 5 per day 8am-8pm) with connections to other destinations in the Algarve.

By Bus

Lisbon's bus station is close to Ⓜ Jardim Zoológico but can be hard to find. Once at the Metro stop, follow exit signs to Av. C. Bordalo Pinheiro. Exit the Metro, go around the corner, and walk straight ahead 100m; then cross left in front of Sete Rios station. The stairs to the bus station are on the left. **Rede Expressos** (☎70 722 33 44 www.rede-expressos.pt) runs buses between Lisbon and: Braga (Ⓢ €20 ⏰ 4-5hr., 14-16 per day 7am-12:15am); Coimbra (Ⓢ €14 ⏰ 2hr., 24-30 per day 7am-12:15am); and Lagos (Ⓢ €19.50 ⏰ 5hr., 14-16 per day 7:30am-1am).

GETTING AROUND

Carris (☎21 361 30 00 www.carris.pt) is Lisbon's extensive, efficient, and relatively inexpensive transportation system and is the easiest way to get around the city, which is covered by an elaborate grid of subways, buses, trams, and *elevadores* (funiculars, useful for getting up the steep hills). Fares purchased on board buses, trams, or *elevadores* cost €1.75; the subway costs €1.15, but you must first purchase a rechargeable *viva viagem* card (€0.50). The easiest and most cost- and time-effective option for those who will use a lot of public transportation is the unlimited 24hr. **bilhete combinado** (€5), which can be used on any Carris transport and means you don't have to go into a Metro station to recharge your card before getting on a bus or tram. You can buy the *bilhete combinado* in any Metro station, and you can fill it with up to seven days' worth of unlimited travel.

By Bus

Carris buses (€1.75, €1.15 with *viva viagem* card) go to just about any place in the city, including those not served by the Metro.

By Metro

The Metro (with €1.15 *viva viagem* card) has four lines that cross the center of Lisbon and go to the major train stations. Metro stations are marked with a red "M" logo. Trains run daily 6:30am-1am.

By Tram

Trams (€1.75, €1.15 with *viva viagem* card) are used by tourists and locals alike to get around. Many vehicles predate WWI. Line 28E runs through Graça, Alfama, Baixa, Chiado, and Bairro Alto; line 15E goes from the Pr. Comércio to Belém, passing the clubs of Santos and Alcântara.

By Taxi

Taxis in Lisbon can be hailed on the street throughout the center of town. Good places to find cabs include the train stations and main plazas. Bouncers will be happy to call you a cab after dark. **Rádio Táxis de Lisboa** (☎21 811 90 00) and **Teletáxis** (☎21 811 11 00) are the main companies.

CASCAIS AND SINTRA

These two towns are usually tackled as daytrips from Lisbon—but that doesn't mean you won't want to stay for a week. Sintra has enough palaces to keep you living regal for days, and Cascais's beaches are tough to leave. Both are magical places—and we mean it, since we don't just throw around corny words like "magical" willy-nilly—full of quirky castles, sublime mountains, and, of course, sea, sun, and sand.

greatest hits

- **PALACES GALORE.** The Palácio da Pena (p. 496), Palácio Nacional (p. 496), Palácio da Regaleira (p. 495), and Monserrate (p. 496) will blow you away.

- **WIND-WHIPPED.** Try your hand at some extreme watersports at Praia do Guincho, near Cascais. (p. 490)

- **LIVE LIKE A KING. ACTUALLY.** Stay in a former royal residence: Residêncial Solar de Dom Carlos I in Cascais. (p. 489)

You'll find plenty of students escaping Lisbon for a day at the beach in Cascais, but these towns are hardly hubs of student activity.

cascais ☎214

A quick train ride (or really long swim) from Lisbon takes you away from the frenzied metropolis, past the historic sites of Belém and ritzier resort of Estoril, and into the beach town of Cascais. Once a strategic outpost for sea trade and defense, Cascais became popular with the Portuguese aristocracy at the end of the 19th century, and their palatial homes still dot the coastline. Changing times and multiple beaches mean there is now room on the sand for everyone, whether you came from 19th-century money or have only $19 to your name. Here in Cascais, locals and day-trippers alike seamlessly intermingle along the coast.

ORIENTATION

The Cascais **train station** is at the eastern edge of town; the **bus terminal** is beneath the large blue shopping center to the right as you exit the station. From here, head along Av. Valbom (just to the right of the McDonald's) to the end of the street to reach the **tourism office,** a yellow building with a sign reading *"turismo."* Facing the tourist office, head left down **Avenida dos Combatentes da Grande Guerra** to reach the beaches; **Praia da Ribeira** is the small one to the right, **Praia da Rainha** and **Praia da Conceiçao** are to the left. **Praça 5 de Outubro** and **Largo de Luís de Camões** are the town's main plazas (most of the restaurants are located here), both just west of Av. Combatentes da Grande Guerra. The streets around the beaches are full of tourists and shops selling schlock to them; those farther west and north tend to be quieter and are lovely to explore and get lost in.

ACCOMMODATIONS

Inexpensive accommodations are hard to come by in Cascais; it's far more practical to stay in Lisbon, a short and cheap train ride away. If you do want to spend the night, though, there are a few good options.

◪ AGARRE O MOMENTO

GUEST HOUSE $$

R. Joaquim Ereira, 458 ☎21 406 45 32 www.agarreomomento.com

Quite affordable and high in quality, Agarre o Momento is more like (brace yourself), home. The cliché is warranted, since you really are just staying in a nice house with a few other people. While Christina is the woman of the house and takes care of the logistics, the true overlord is Senhor Brownie, the Siamese cat who is watching your every move, so don't pull anything funny while you're here.

✠ *From the train station, head left onto Av. Marginal and continue onto Av. 25 de Abril. Turn right at Cidadela Hotel and continue until you see the guest house on the right.* ℹ *Breakfast €4. Linens included. Kitchen.* Ⓢ *Dorms €25-35; doubles €50-70.* ⚄ *Reception 24hr.*

PARSI

HOTEL $$$

R. Afonso Sanches, 8 ☎91 236 35 22

Large colorful rooms with walls covered in freshly painted designs overlook the Pr. 5 de Outubro and the beach. It can get a bit noisy in the evening when the pub downstairs fills up, but with a one-minute walk to the beach, the location can't be beat. The rooms are all different in terms of size and layout (one triple involves a kind of skewed bunk bed affixed to the wall), so ask to see all your options before choosing.

Just off Pr. 5 de Outubro, in the far left corner with your back to the beach. $ Singles with shared bath €30; doubles €40, with ensuite bath €50-80; triples with ensuite bath €60. Reception 24hr.

RESIDÊNCIAL SOLAR DE DOM CARLOS I HOTEL $$$$

R. Latino Coelho, 104 ☎21 482 81 15 www.solardomcarlos.net

This is your chance to live in a true palace: this former royal residence has massive rooms with bathrooms larger than many hostels' six-person dorm rooms. The triples are so called because they could easily host a three-ring circus; there's room to fit at least two extra beds (€15-20) in them comfortably. Although it isn't so assuming from the street, the royal flavor is obvious once you are inside. Breakfast is included in the huge, ornately painted dining area, but if that alone doesn't remind you you're staying in a palace, the extensive gardens (with a large and colorful parrot collection to match) certainly will.

From the tourist office, pick up the map you'll need to find this hotel, and take Av. Combatentes da Grande Guerra to the water, then turn right onto Pr. 5 de Outubro. Take the street to the left of the Câmara Municipal (on the far side of Pr. 5 de Outubre) onto R. Marquês Leal Pancada, then take a sharp right up R. Vitória and a quick left onto Tv. Vitória (1 block). Finally, veer right onto R. Latino Coelho. i Breakfast included. Laundry service available. Bicycle rental available. $ Singles €35-50; doubles €55-70; triples €60-100. Reception 24hr.

SIGHTS

BOCA DO INFERNO CAVE

At this massive open cave, you can supposedly hear the devil's whisper resounding from the crashing surf. If you record the sound and isolate the correct wavelength, then play it backward, you'll hear the Satanic message, "You have way too much free time on your hands." (Idle hands are the devil's playthings, as they say.)

Follow the road along the water west (to the right as you face the water) about 1km. $ Free.

MUSEU CONDES DE CASTRO GUIMARÃES MUSEUM

Av. Rei Humberto II de Itália ☎21 481 53 04

The Count Castro Guimarães had this house constructed in the latest style, which happened to be everything that has ever been in style in human history, all rolled into one. Thus, the house is somewhat disjointed stylistically, but it is still beautifully stunning in its own eclectic way. The top of the house is where the firearms collection is kept, and the second floor frequently has different temporary art exhibits. Please try to restrain yourself from using the displayed firearms on the temporary exhibits, regardless of how bad they are.

From Boca do Inferno, walk along the path back to Cascais. $ Free. Tu-F 10am-5pm, Sa-Su 10am-1pm and 2-5pm.

CASA DAS HISTÓRIAS PAULA REGO ART MUSEUM

Av. da República, 300 ☎214 82 69 70 www.casadashistoriaspaularego.com

This oddly shaped art museum (i.e., two red cones or Devo hats pointing skyward) is dedicated entirely to one artist: Paula Rego. Her versatility shines throughout the whole museum, as she expresses various emotions vividly and engages them in entirely different ways. The result is an art museum that is comprehensive in its scope and monographic in nature.

From the waterfront, head onto Av. Dom Carlos I, then turn right onto Av. República. The museum will be on the right. $ Free. Open daily 10am-7pm.

ASSOCIAÇÃO PORTUGUESA DE COLECCIONADORES DE ARMAS MUSEUM

Tv. do Poço Novo, 8 ☎21 483 23 21

This small museum, displaying weaponry from medieval times to the present day, has more guns than a Kentucky wedding; and it costs less than the Ring Pops exchanged at said wedding.

From Pr. 5 de Outubro, head up R. Afonso Sanches (far left corner, with your back to the beach), then turn left onto Tv. Poço Novo. $ €1, under 13 free. ⏰ Open Tu-Su 10am-1pm and 2-5pm.

THE GREAT OUTDOORS

Cascais has a few beaches more suitable for surfing than sunbathing. **Guincho,** a 25min. bus ride away, is located on the Atlantic coast. To call this beach windswept or even wind-battered would be an understatement: Guincho is wind-beaten-to-within-an-inch-of-its-life-and-left-for-dead. Gnarly waves and gale-force winds make it a major destination for all kinds of surfers: wind, kite, and regular. Lessons and rentals are available for all levels of experience. To get to Guincho, take **ScottURB** bus #405 (⏰ 1 per hr.; M-Sa 6:50am-7:50pm, Su 6:50am-6:50pm) or #415 ($ €3.20 ⏰ 1 per hr.; M-Sa 6:30am-8:30pm, Su 6:30am-7:20pm), which run from the Cascais bus terminal (below shopping center next to train station). From the Guincho bus stop, head to the right as you face the water to get to the beach.

Beaches

There are three main beaches in Cascais, all side by side near the city center. **Praia da Ribeira,** the westernmost of the three, is small but the most centrally located (right next to the Pr. 5 de Outubro) and tends to get packed. ★**Praia da Rainha** is also small, but it has interesting and beautiful rock formations that make it seem like a wild, undiscovered coastline, with hidden nooks and coves behind every boulder. It tends to attract a younger crowd and is better for socializing than swimming. **Praia da Conceição,** the easternmost of the three, is much larger and looks like any other beachgoer-filled shoreline. A stroll past the final beach will reveal even more beaches as visitors pass over into ritzier Estoril.

Surfing

GUINCHO SURF SCHOOL SURF SCHOOL

Praia do Guincho ☎91 753 57 19 www.guinchosurfschool.com

This surf school offers lessons for surfers of all ages and skill levels (€30). If conditions at Guincho are not suitable for surfing, instructors will take you to another beach free of charge. Longer sessions are available for those who are on holiday and want to learn from scratch (7 hours, €45).

Take ScottURB bus #405 or 415 to Guincho, then head to the right (as you face the water) to get to the beach; follow the sign down to the "Estalagem" and walk around it to the far side and continue down to the beach. The surf shop is in the same building, immediately to the left. i Reservations recommended; book a day in advance by 7pm. $ 1 lesson €30; 5 €100; 10 €150. ⏰ Open daily 9am-7pm.

GUINCHO SURF SHOP SURF SCHOOL, SHOP

Praia do Guincho ☎21 485 02 86 www.guinchosurfshop.com

Surfing, body-boarding, and kite-boarding schools plus a rental shop make Guincho your one-stop shop for all things gnarly. Longboards and other items that appeal to the beach-bum crowd are here as well. No siestas for these folks, who break the slacker-surfer stereotype.

Take ScottURB bus #405 or 415 to Guincho, then head to the right (as you face the water) to get to the beach; follow the sign down to the "Estalagem" and walk around it to the far side and continue down to the beach. The surf shop is in the same building, immediately to the left. ⏰ Open daily 9am-7pm.

FOOD

Restaurants line **Avenida dos Combatentes da Grande Guerra,** and cheap sandwiches and fast food can be found on the main drags running from beach to beach.

O VIRIATO PORTUGUESE $$$

Av. de Vasco da Gama, 34 ☎21 486 81 98

This locals-only joint in an otherwise tourists-only town is refreshing if you can endure the leering glances and whispered comments from the regulars. The food is traditional, which means you'll have to skin, gut, and bone your fish yourself unless you request otherwise—but everything's delicious. An interesting wooden wall with windows divides the patio seating area from the rest of the dining room, so if you get bored, you can always pretend that the people on the other side are in an aquarium.

From the tourist office, follow R. Alexandre Herculano (to the right of the office as you face it), which becomes Beco das Terras, then turn left onto Av. Vasco da Gama. $ Entrees €7.80-16. ⏰ Open M-Tu noon-3:30pm and 7pm-midnight, Th-Su noon-3:30pm and 7pm-midnight.

SHABU SHABU JAPANESE $$$

Edificio Baía Center, Loja 26, 2nd fl. R. do Regimento da Infantria, 19 ☎21 483 68 17

It may not be a traditional Portuguese meal (servers wear full Japanese garb), but for a raw taste of what's swimming just a couple of blocks away, try this restaurant's all-you-can-eat buffet—always a good deal for hungry travelers on a budget. In what is probably the most ingenious all-you-can-eat scheme ever, Shabu Shabu has you order a few dishes at a time, allowing them to prepare your sushi fresh as you stuff your face with more. Dessert is also included.

Upstairs on the side of Lg. Luís de Camões closest to the beach. $ All-you-can-eat lunch buffet €12.90, dinner buffet €15.90. ⏰ Open daily 12:30-3pm and 7-11pm.

RESTAURANTE DOM PEDRO I PORTUGUESE $$

Beco dos Inválidos, 32 ☎21 483 37 34

Sick of all the tourists and sunbathers on the beach and surrounding streets? Take a hidden alleyway off the Pr. do 5 de Outubre, and have a quiet lunch under the shade of a short but broad tree to escape the maddening crowds. Order some kind of dead animal (you're in Portugal after all), and wait for it to be brought out to your peaceful nook.

Take narrow Beco dos Inválidos from left side of Pr. 5 de Outubro, with your back to the beach. $ Entrees €8.50-11.50. ⏰ Open M-Sa noon-3pm and 7-10pm.

cascais

BANGKOK THAIMOODS THAI $$

R. das Flores, 18 ☎21 486 45 01 www.bangkokthaimoods.com

Located on one of the side streets that quickly fills during the nighttime, this Thai restaurant serves plenty of traditional favorites that incorporate a wide selection of meats, including duck, fish, pork, and more. Buddhist statues and velvet curtains fill the dining room, although the outdoor seating is also a nice place to enjoy your meal. Bangkok Thaimoods is above trying to fill its customers with bread before a meal; instead, it tries to fill them with rice cakes.

Exit left from the tourist center and turn right at the first road. Then turn right onto R. Flores. $ Entrees €9-12. ⏰ Open M 11am-3pm, Tu-Su 11am-3pm and 5pm-midnight.

B AND B RESTAURANTE PORTUGUESE $$$

R. do Poço Novo, 15 ☎21 482 06 86

A shiny and modern-looking restaurant in an otherwise old and classic part of town. Even though you can't see the water, the pastel-colored walls and the scent of freshly-cooked cod don't let you forget that you're at the beach. Of course, since it's Portugal, meat options are available as well, just in case you want to avoid those awkward conversations with the fish at the beach after eating one of their brethren.

Head up R. Afonso Sanches from Pr. 5 de Outubro (far left corner with your back to the beach), then take the 1st left, and then turn left onto R. Poço Novo. $ Entrees €10-14. ⏰ Open M-F noon-2:30pm and 7-9:45pm, Sa 7-9:45pm.

LUA DE MEL CAFE, PASTELARIA $

Av. 25 de Abril, 7B ☎21 484 65 57

A quick one-stop shop, Lua de Mel serves desserts, pastries, sandwiches, soups, and coffees. Essentially, it's a large and efficient *pastelaria* that is perfect for those who are in a hurry or just want a meal on the cheap. The *menús do dia* come with soup and a drink, but just coming in for an espresso is also perfectly acceptable.

From the tourist office, exit to the left. When you get to the circle, turn left onto Av. 25 de Abril. $ Menú €4.50-7. ⏰ Open M-Sa 7:30am-7pm.

RESTAURANTE DOM MANOLO GRILL $$

Av. dos Combatentes da Grande Guerra, 13 ☎21 483 11 26

This big *churrascaria* with tons of outdoor seating is right on the well-traveled tourist route from the train station and tourist office to the beach. A lot of the meat here is inexpensive, and Dom Manolo has declared himself the king of chicken—be sure to wait 30min. before swimming if you intend to test this claim.

Facing the tourist office, head left toward the beach. $ Entrees €8-14. ⏰ Open daily noon-midnight.

NIGHTLIFE

Nightlife in Cascais is simple: around 10:30pm, the bars along **Largo de Luís de Camões** fill up with partiers, and the few establishments compete with each other to be the loudest. If they're too crowded and you can't get in, try the back entrances on Av. dos Combatentes da Grande Guerra. **Praça 5 de Outubro** also has some action. At 2am, the party migrates down to the waterfront, where there are a couple of clubs along and just off **Avenida de Dom Carlos I.** These establishments are poppin' until 3 or 4am, but once these close, head back to **Largo de Luís de Camões,** where a couple of places are open until 6am—it will be obvious which ones.

O'LUAIN'S IRISH PUB $

R. da Palmeira, 4A ☎21 486 16 27

Cascais has a surprisingly large expat community, which becomes apparent when you step into this pub. While many bars like to put up an Irish flag and some green decorations and call themselves an Irish pub, O'Luain's is the real McCoy: the bartenders, the customers, and the musicians are almost exclusively Irish. So when you are tired of all that girly Sagres, get a proper pint of Guinness (€4.50) to put some hair on your chest.

Turn right out of tourism office. Turn right, and you should see a sign for an Irish pub. $ Beer €2. Pint of Guinness €4.50. ⏰ Open M 5pm-2am, Tu-Su noon-2am.

O POETA BAR $

R. Regimento 19 Infantaria, 55-61 ☎30 990 08 18 www.restauranteopoeta.com

Modern-looking furniture fills this snazzy black and white bar with the occasional splash of red. The bar plays music but doesn't attempt to keep up with the noise war raging around it outside.

From tourism office, exit to the left. Once you pass a line of restaurants, including a British-themed one, turn left; O Poeta is across the plaza. $ Beer €1.25. Cocktails €4-6. ⏰ Open daily noon-2am.

ARTS AND CULTURE

During the month of July, Cascais is filled with the syncopated notes of **Cascais Cool Jazz,** a month-long festival that in 2012 drew internationally renowned artists including Sting, Michael Kiwanuka, Lizz Wright, and Pat Metheny. Check the festival's website (www.cooljazzfest.com) for ticket prices (usually €20-30), schedules (most performances are usually concentrated at the end of the month), and locations (public parks throughout Cascais).

ESTORIL MUSIC FESTIVAL ESTORIL $

www.estorilfestival.net

This classical music festival takes place throughout the entire month of July each year. Concerts are held all over the Greater Lisbon area, but many are held specifically in Cascais and Estoril. Most concerts are free, although you need to get your hands on a ticket a few days in advance to get in.

[$] Typically free.

MUSA CASCAIS CARCAVELOS $

www.festivalmusa.org

An annual two-day music festival with a social conscience, MUSA aims to raise sustainability awareness through the rhythm of reggae music. Come get in touch with your inner rasta. This party is on the beach!

⯑ Take Av. Marginal to the water. You will run into Carcavelos. [$] 1 day €10, 2 days €12.

ESSENTIALS

Practicalities

- **TOURIST OFFICE: Informação Turística** has maps and information. (R. Visconde da Luz, 14 ☎21 482 23 27 ⯑ From train station, take Av. Valbom—to the right side of the McDonald's—straight to the end of the street. ⏰ Open daily 10am-1pm and 2-6pm.)
- **POST OFFICE: Correios** is a full-service post office. (Av. Marginal, 9302 ☎21 482 72 73 www.ctt.pt ⯑ While exiting the tourist office, look to the left. ⏰ Open M-F 8:30am-6pm.)

Emergency

- **PHARMACIES: Farmácia da Misericórdia** posts a schedule of pharmacies open late. (R. do Regimento da Infantria 19, 69 ☎21 483 01 41 ⯑ From Pr. 5 de Outubro, with your back to the beach, take the street from the far right corner straight 2 blocks; the pharmacy is on the left. *i* Wheelchair accessible. ⏰ Open M-F 8am-7pm, Sa 9am-2pm.)
- **POLICE STATION: Polícia de Segurança Pública** (R. Afonso Sanches, 29 ☎21 483 91 00 ⯑ Take a right at the fork before the train station. The police station is on the right.)

Getting There

Trains run to Cascais from **Lisbon's Cais do Sodré Station.** ([$] €2.05. ⏰ 30-40min., daily every 15-30min. 5:30am-1:30am.) ScottURB **buses** run from **Sintra.** ([$] €4. ⏰ 40min.-1hr.; M-F 11 per day 6:30am-7:25pm, Sa 12 per day 6:30am-8:35pm, Su 10 per day 7:45am-8:35pm.)

Getting Around

Cascais is a small town, and it's easy to get around on foot, but there are **free bike rental stands** (ID and hotel information required) that are available for the day in front of the train station and at the Cidadela Fortress's parking lot, along Av. de Dom Carlos I from Pr. do 5 de Outubre (get there early if you want a bike). (⏰ Apr-Sept daily 8am-7pm; Oct-Mar M-F 9am-4pm, Sa-Su 9am-5pm.) There is also a **taxi stand** outside the train station (☎21 466 01 01). **Buses** are necessary to get to Praia do Guincho.

sintra ☎219

The tiny town of Sintra sits at the foot of the mountains, a 45min. train ride west of Lisbon. Quirky romantic castles and ancient fortresses look down on the small city from the surrounding hillsides, with more palatial residences a couple kilometers away. The entire town is encompassed by a breathtaking national park, which, when combined with the fairytale castles, makes for a surreal experience. Although most visitors only come for the day, a longer stay in Sintra is both relaxing and rewarding, as the quaint town and natural landscape have a rejuvenating property that can't be found in nearby Lisbon. Sintra and the stretch of mountains just west of it are classified as a World Heritage Cultural Landscape by UNESCO, and castle-hopping visitors will surely understand why.

ORIENTATION

Sintra has three main neighborhoods: **Estefânia,** where the train station, bus stop, and several inexpensive restaurants and accommodations can be found; **São Pedro,** which is located a bit farther uphill and has some shops and government offices; and the **historic center,** where you'll discover most of the town's sights. To get to the historic center, take a left out of the train station onto **Avenida do Doutor Miguel Bombarda** and follow it 150m to the intersection, at which point the curving **Volta do Duche** veers to the left. This statue-lined road hooks around the valley between Estefânia and is about a 15min. walk to the center. Stay to the right for the **Palácio Nacional de Sintra** or keep straight to get to the **tourist office.** Sintra itself is small and easy to get around, but several sights lie outside of town and are best reached by bus or taxi.

ACCOMMODATIONS

Accommodations in Sintra tend to be pricey, especially in the historic center. The only inexpensive accommodations are near the train station, so you might as well stay someplace still less expensive in Lisbon and take a 45min. train ride. The tourist office in the center of town has a list of private accommodations that are usually about €5 cheaper than the *pensões* but are often located farther from both the train station and the center of town.

NICE WAY SINTRA PALACE   HOSTEL $

R. Sotto Mayor, 22   ☎21 924 98 00 www.nicewaysintrahostel.com

Although it isn't the size of a palace, this hostel sure has the feel of one, even if it is just a bunch of people sharing huge rooms in a very nice house. The mood is extremely laid-back, and no one here bothers to lock up their belongings. The common area has big doors that open onto a giant yard, which plays host to the occasional party. This hostel has relaxed vibes spilling out of the windows and doors.

> ⚡ *From Palácio Nacional, walk away from all of the restaurants, staying alongside the palace. After passing a large hotel, go down a hill and you'll see the hostel on the right.* **i** *Breakfast, linens, and towels included.* ⑤ *Dorms €16-21; doubles €25-35.* ⏰ *Reception 24hr.*

ALMÁA SINTRA HOSTEL   HOSTEL $$

Caminho dos Frades   ☎21 924 00 08 www.almaasintrahostel.com

Nestled in a secluded area, this hostel acts as a retreat from the outside world. Much of the seating inside includes simple pillows placed on the floor. Daily yoga takes place in a large tent outside, and an old water tank that sits in the garden is now used as a pool. Stop here to get away from it all and feel rejuvenated.

> ⚡ *From Quinta da Regaleira, go through the car park to the right and simply keep walking for about 500 yards. The hostel is on the left.* **i** *Breakfast, linens, and towels included.* ⑤ *Dorms €22-30; doubles €30-34.* ⏰ *Reception 24hr.*

CASA DE HÓSPEDES DONA MARIA PARREIRINHA HOTEL $$$

R. de João de Deus, 12 ☎21 923 24 90 www.dmariaparreirinha.com

This spotless *pensão* is well located and small enough to feel quite personal. The rooms are bright, with plenty of natural light, and functional, with a good amount of space and ever-so-delightful cable TV. It's close to the train station, but fortunately the noise from the tracks is blocked by the buildings in between.

 # On opposite side of tracks from train station exit; exit the station, turn left, and stay left around the station, but then veer right at the fork to go uphill on R. João de Deus. $ Singles €40-45; doubles €40-45. Extra bed €5. ⏰ Reception 24hr.

MONTE DA LUA HOTEL $$$$

Av. do Doutor Miguel Bombarda, 51 ☎21 924 10 29

Though still in Estefânia, this *pensão* is closer to the city center than any other inexpensive accommodation, and it's right across from the train station, which means you won't have to carry your bags more than a few meters. Rooms are not large but are clean and have TVs. The aesthetic isn't unrivaled, but the location, privacy, and price make it a worthwhile stay.

 # Right across the street from the train station entrance. $ Singles €40; doubles €50-60. Extra bed €10. ⏰ Reception 24hr.

SIGHTS

Sintra is full of fairytale castles and palaces that capture the imagination and lend the city to a great deal of sightseeing. There is also a smattering of museums that pale in comparison. Unfortunately, the sights can be quite far apart, but if walking is out of the question, the #434 and #435 buses can be caught at the tourism office and transport visitors to all the major attractions.

✓ PALÁCIO E QUINTA DA REGALEIRA PALACE, GARDENS $$

Quinta da Regaleira ☎21 910 66 56 www.cultursintra.pt

This UNESCO World Heritage Site was built in the first years of the 20th century for its eccentric owner, wealthy Brazilian capitalist António Augusto de Carvalho Monteiro, who wanted to create a magical and mysterious castle home. Italian architect Luigi Manini was certainly up to the task, and the finished product looks nothing short of fictional. Hidden mythological and occult motifs abound, and the library upstairs is possibly the **✓world's trippiest room.** The surrounding gardens are amazing enough to stand alone and are intended to be a transcendent microcosm of the universe—or something like that. You can explore an extensive tunnel system that goes below the castle and gardens or descend the spiral staircase 100ft. into the ground in the **Poço Iniciatico** (Initiation Well), which was inspired by the rituals of the Knights Templar and has alchemical references.

 # Bus #435 (€2.50) runs daily every 30min. and stops at the train station and historic center. On foot, turn right out of the tourist office and follow R. Consiglieri Pedroso as it turns into R. MEF Navarro; about a 15-20min. walk. $ €6, students and seniors €4, ages 9-14 €3, under 9 free. Guided visits €10, students and seniors €8, ages 9-14 €5, under 9 free. ⏰ Open daily Apr-Sept 10am-8pm (last entry 7pm); Oct 10am-6:30pm (last entry 6pm); Nov-Jan 10am-5:30pm (last entry 5pm); Feb-Mar 10am-6:30pm (last entry 6pm).

✓ CASTELO DOS MOUROS CASTLE $$

Parque de Sintra ☎21 923 73 00 www.parquesdesintra.pt

Not far downhill from the Palácio da Pena is this eighth-century Moorish castle, which looms over Sintra and offers fantastic views of the city and many of the nearby sights. The castle was abandoned and fell into ruin when the Moors were driven out in the 12th century, but Dom Fernando II fixed it up a bit and tore down some of the already decrepit Romanesque church to make a nice garden—very Victorian. The surprisingly large castle stretches along the ridge and looks like Portugal's own Great Wall from a vantage point along the ramparts. There are so many great views of the surrounding area that it is tempting to spread out your arms in an attempt at a cheeky *Titanic* reference, but do be careful—it's a long fall down the hill.

✚ Bus #434 (€3.50) runs from the tourist office to the castle daily every 15min., 9:15am-7:50pm. Ⓢ €7, students and seniors €6. ⓩ Open daily Apr-Sept 9:30am-8pm; Oct-Mar 10am-6pm.

▨ PALÁCIO DA PENA   PALACE $$$
Parque da Pena   ☏21 910 53 40 www.parquesdesintra.pt

Built during the 1840s on what was left of a medieval monastery by Prince Ferdinand of Bavaria and his wife Dona Maria II, this colorful royal retreat is one funky castle. It has Neo-just-about-any-style-you-can-think-of architecture, and the Neo-Mudejar entrance gate has **alligator gargoyles** at the top. On hot days, the fittingly strange "water room," which has holes in the walls that spit out water at seemingly random times, is a great place to be. The archway over the entrance to the purple building (not really purple; get a close look at the tiles) is spectacular in the weirdest, most ornate way, and views from the various terraces (the Queen's Terrace has the best) stretch all the way to Lisbon.

✚ Bus #434 (€3.50) runs from the tourist office to the palace daily every 15min., 9:15am-7:50pm; from entrance, either walk up to the palace or take shuttle bus. Ⓢ €13.50, before 11am €12.50, students and seniors €11. Guided tours additional €5. ⓩ Palace open daily Apr-Sept 9:45am-7pm (last entry 6:30pm); Oct-Mar 10am-6pm (last entry 5pm). Surrounding Parque da Pena open daily Apr-Sept 9:30am-8pm; Oct-Mar 10am-6pm.

MONSERRATE   VILLA, GARDENS $$
Parque de Monserrate   ☏21 923 73 00 www.parquesdesintra.pt

This palace looks like something Palladio would have come up with had he traveled extensively in India and had a little more flair for the flamboyant. Moghul-style arches clash wonderfully with Italian Renaissance-inspired domes and Far-Eastern eaves, which are all surrounded by lush gardens filled with exotic vegetation and enormous goldfish. Eclecticism meets Romanticism in a site visited by Lord Byron, who called Sintra a "glorious Eden." Keep an eye out for the arch that was brought over from India following the quelling of the colony's rebellion—because what's the point of subjugating people if you can't bring something nice home for the kids?

✚ Bus #435 (€2.50) runs daily every 30min., 9:45am-6:45pm, and stops at the train station and historic center. Ⓢ €5, students and seniors €4. ⓩ Open daily Apr-Sept 9:30am-8pm; Oct-Mar 10am-6pm.

PALÁCIO NACIONAL DE SINTRA   PALACE $$
Lg. da Rainha Dona Amélia   ☏21 910 68 40 pnsintra.imc-ip.pt

Once a summer residence for Moorish sultans and their harems, the Palácio da Vila was later taken over by the Portuguese; paintings of Portuguese noblemen gunning down Moorish soldiers stand as a testament inside. The palace and gardens were built in two stages: Dom João I built the main structure in the 15th century, and Dom Manuel I made it home to the world's best collection of *azulejos* (glazed tiles) a century later. The palace includes the gilded **Sala dos Brasões,** which houses some of the palace's greatest treasures—look up at the ceiling to see the royal coat of arms surrounded by the armorial bearings of 72 noble families, elaborately painted animals, and various other artistic flourishes. The palace is marked by an avian theme: doves symbolizing the Holy Spirit line the walls of the **Capela,** swans grace the **Sala dos Cisnes,** and on the ceiling of the **Sala das Pegas,** magpies represent ladies-in-waiting and hold a piece of paper proclaiming D. João I's motto, *"por bem"* ("for good").

✚ Exit the tourist office, go straight, and find the palace on the left. Ⓢ €7, students €3, seniors €4, under 14 free; Su before 2pm free. ⓩ Open M-Tu 9:30am-5:30pm, Th-Su 9:30am-5pm. Last entry 30min. before close.

MUSEU DO BRINQUEDO TOY MUSEUM $

R. do Visconde Monserrate, 26 ☎21 910 60 16 www.museu-do-brinquedo.pt

Feel like a kid all over again in Sintra's toy museum. The toys on display run the gamut, and some date back more than 100 years. Any toy enthusiast will appreciate the sheer size of the collection, which includes thousands of different model cars and figurines. There is an impressive array of toy soldiers, including many you might not have been exposed to as a child (think the Third Reich). Temporary themed exhibits also come through, such as a tribute to Disney.

➜ Turn left out of the Palácio Nacional. Look to the right when you get to the corner of the building. The museum is a few yards down. [$] €4, students and seniors €2. ⏰ Tu-Su 10am-6pm.

THE GREAT OUTDOORS

Sintra-Cascais Natural Park *Parque Natural de Sintra-Cascais*

The **Sintra-Cascais Natural Park** contains miles and miles of beautiful landscape, stretching from the *serra* on which Sintra sits all the way down to the coast, including Cabo da Roca, Europe's westernmost point. It has been a protected area for 30 years and contains many trails, though some are accessible only by car. One of the best hikes begins at the tourist office in **Cabo da Roca** and heads inland into the hills before coming back along the dramatic beach (about 10km total). There are many shorter hikes just around Sintra, which are by no means walks in the park. The 4.5km **Percurso da Pena,** which runs from the **Palácio Nacional da Sintra** up to the **Palácio da Pena,** will leave you a sweaty mess, but it goes up past the Igreja de Santa Maria, the Casa do Adro where Hans Christian Andersen once lived, the Convento da Santíssima Trindade, and the Castelo dos Mouros. A separate trail leads to **Convento dos Capuchos,** which is a small, cramped, and ancient convent in the midst of the park. The Sintra tourist office also has a map of 20.4km worth of bike itineraries in the area around the town.

FOOD

Pastelarias and restaurants crowd the end of **Rua de João de Deus** and **Avenida de Heliodoro Salgado.** In the old town, **Rua das Padarias** (near the **Palácio Nacional**) is lined with lunch spots. On the second and fourth Sundays of every month, take bus #433 from the train station to São Pedro (15min.) for the **Feira de São Pedro,** which features local cuisine, music, clothes, flowers, and antiques.

APEADEIRO CAFE, BAR $

Av. do Doutor Miguel Bombarda, 3A ☎21 923 18 04

This cafe offers a blend of tasty Portuguese food, low prices, and an interesting atmosphere (which can be hard to come by in Sintra). The faux-roof, with its traditional Portuguese red shingles, hangs over the bar acts as a reminder that the restaurant doesn't take itself too seriously but is still proud of its heritage. The creepy, animatronic little girl dressed as a mustachioed chef standing on the bar acts as a reminder that—well, that's still a little unclear.

➜ Left out of the train station and slightly down the hill. [$] Entrees €6-14. ⏰ Open M-W and F-Su noon-midnight.

PANISINTRA CAFE $

Av. de Dom Francisco de Almeida, 12 ☎21 923 30 00

Planning on getting to Sintra first thing in the morning to get an early start on your hike up to the Palácio da Pena? Or did you catch the early train without realizing that nothing opens before 9:30am? This cafe opens early and has delicious coffee as well as a huge selection of sugary pastries filled with energy. The best deal for a snack is an espresso plus a *pastel de nata* for only €1.20. Between the sugar and the caffeine, you will feel invincible—or at least ready to take on those dastardly hills. Don't order the fresh orange juice (€1.50) if you're in a hurry or if you advocate against the inhumane treatment of fruit, as you'll have to watch each orange get slowly and painfully juiced.

✦ *Just across from Palácio Nacional de Sintra. ⑤ Coffee €0.60-1.50. Pastries €1-2. ☒ Open M-Sa 7am-8pm, Su 8am-8pm.*

CAFÉ DA VILLA
RESTAURANT $$

Cç. do Pelourinho, 8   ☎96 709 13 96

This restaurant, which attempts to feature an Eastern theme but instead winds up with dimly lit acrylic-on-velvet paintings of the Dalai Lama, offers ample three-course meals at low prices. No such charming touches exist outside, but the food here is delicious, so let the discontinuity of the theme slide. The surprisingly large and very filling *tostas* (grilled sandwiches) are only €5 and come with a heaping plate of chips and a drink.

✦ *Entering the center from the train station, turn right just before the Palácio Nacional. ⑤ 3-course meals €8-15. Tostas combo €5. ☒ Open daily noon-2am.*

LEGENDARY CAFE
CAFE $

R. do Doutor Alfredo da Costa, 8   ☎21 924 38 25

A little farther away from the tourist hubbub but still close to the train station, this deceptively large cafe doesn't quite live up to its name. With its tea-cup-stenciled walls and alternative playlist, this cafe is nonetheless a nice place to grab a cheap meal. Try the *mazagram*, a refreshing mixture of ice, espresso, soda water, and lemon (€1), and drown your sorrows with Tori Amos and co.

✦ *With your back to the train station, turn left and walk down Av. Dr. Miguel Bombarda. Take the 1st right, then turn left onto R. Dr. Alfredo da Costa. The cafe is on the right. ⑤ Meals €5. Sandwiches €2-3. ☒ Open daily 9am-midnight.*

PURO SABOR
CAFE, ICE CREAM $

R. do Visconde Monserrate, 2

After making the hike to Palácio da Pena and back, gelato begins to seem less like dessert and more like the nectar of the gods. Get your personal ambrosia at Puro Sabor, where they have a selection of about 20 different flavors. Sandwiches, espresso, and more traditional cafe fare are also available, but once you see the words "crepe com gelato" on the menu, you will forget about any kind of real food.

✦ *With the Palácio Nacional at your back, head to the left. Puro Sabor is on the right. ⑤ Gelato €2.20. Crepes €3.50-3.80. ☒ Open daily 9:30am-7pm.*

A PÉROLA DE SINTRA
PORTUGUESE, AMERICAN $$$

Pr. da República, 12   ☎21 923 57 10

Funky chairs, a blue and pink motif, and '50s American rock and roll mesh together in this updated soda fountain. Surprisingly, the food served here is mostly Portuguese and of fairly high quality. Those looking to save can pick up sandwiches. Milkshakes also make an appearance on the menu, but Americans beware: they are probably not as thick as you are accustomed to.

✦ *Directly across the street from the Palácio Nacional. ⑤ Meal €10-15. Sandwiches €4-6. ☒ Open daily 9am-10pm.*

NIGHTLIFE

Since most visitors to Sintra are day-trippers, the town tends to be fairly sleepy at night. However, there is some action at the local watering holes, where you will find very few tourists, if any at all. There is no central location for bars within the historic center, so it is best to just go exploring.

FONTE DA PIPA
BAR $

Fonte da Pipa, 13   ☎21 923 44 37

Dedicating itself exclusively to nightlife, Fonte da Pipa is one of the busiest places in the historic center of Sintra on any given night. A cobblestone floor

cascais and sintra

and street lanterns almost make you forget that you're inside. Each room has different decor, and it is definitely not run-of-the-mill (note the African fertility statue eyeing you from the corner).

Go up the street across from the Palácio Nacional and after 1 block, turn right. $ Beer €1.25. Cocktails €4-5. ⏰ Open daily 10pm-3am.

ESTRADA VELHA BAR $

R. Consiglieri Pedroso, 16 ☎21 923 43 55

Although it serves food all day, this place becomes fairly packed when the night crowd rolls in. Two floors, each with its own bar, have booths and tiny cube seats for customers to sit on. Clean, red brick lines the walls, making the bar feel both casual and slightly sophisticated. This isn't a hoppin' place to meet singles, but is a nice bar where you can sit down with friends and pretend your life is a sitcom.

Pass the tourism office on the left. The bar is on the right. $ Beer €1.50. ⏰ Open daily 11am-2am.

XERTA BAR $

R. Consiglieri Pedroso, 2A ☎21 924 07 59

Head downstairs to this subterranean bar for a drink or two to start the night. Music blares, although it is more for atmosphere than it is for dancing. Stone walls and arches make this place feel colder than it actually is.

Head to the left of the tourism office. The bar is on the right, down a flight of stairs. $ Beer €2. Cocktails €4-7. ⏰ Open daily 10am-2am.

FESTIVALS

FESTIVAL DE SINTRA CITYWIDE

☎219 10 71 10 www.festivaldesintra.pt

Every June for the last half century, Sintra has been filled with the music, dance, and "counterpoints" (miscellaneous performances and exhibitions) of the Festival de Sintra. Events, which range from children's movies to avant-garde theater performances, often spill over on either end into May and July. Performances take place all over town, from public plazas to the massive *palácios* just up the mountain, and usually occur a few times a week.

i Events held at various venues throughout Sintra. $ Tickets for music and dance performances €15-20, under 18 and over 65 €10-12.50. Most other events under €10. ⏰ June.

SHOPPING

On the second and fourth Sundays of every month, the otherwise sleepy neighborhood of São Pedro, about a 30min. walk uphill from the historic center, comes to life for the colorful **Feira de São Pedro.** This bi-weekly market has been going on since the **Reconquista** and is a great place to shop for inexpensive wares and local cuisine, all while seeing a part of town most tourists usually miss. (Bus #433 runs from the train station to São Pedro.)

LANTERNA MÁGICA SINTRA CENTER

R. Consiglieri Pedróso, 15 ☎219 24 45 69 www.loja-lanternamagica.com

Filled with a mix of items both strange and glorious, this shop is stuffed with curiosities. Lots of great antiques are lying about, and the unexpected gems, such as a vinyl collection that includes Run DMC, wax seals, and Audrey Hepburn lunchboxes and tobacco tins make this place reminiscent of Diagon Alley (sans the Harry Potter magic). The space isn't very large, so it's easy to miss cool finds if you don't look carefully. If you are successful, this shop will provide you with a souvenir more memorable than one from any other place in town.

Pass the tourism office on the left side; Lanterna Mágica is on your left. ⏰ Open Tu-Su 10am-1pm and 2-7pm.

ESSENTIALS

Practicalities

- **TOURIST OFFICE: Posta de Turismo** is in the historic center, just up the street from the Palácio Nacional de Sintra. (Pr. República, 23 ☎21 923 11 57 www.cm-sintra.pt ⏰ Open daily 9:30am-6pm.) There is also a branch in the train station. (☎21 924 16 23 ⏰ Open daily 11am-6pm.)
- **INTERNET ACCESS: Sabot** offers Wi-Fi and has luggage storage and pizza. (R. Dr. Miguel Bombarda, 57 ☎219 23 08 02 🧭 Just across from the train station, to the right. $ €1 per 15min., €1.60 per 30min., €2.50 per hr. ⏰ Open M-Sa 1pm-midnight, Su 7pm-midnight.)
- **POST OFFICE: Correios** is on the way to the tourist office. (Pr. República, 26 ☎21 924 61 29 ⏰ Open M-F 9:30am-12:30pm and 2:30-6pm.)

Emergency

- **POLICE: Guardia Nacional Republicana:** (R. João de Deus, 6 ☎21 924 78 50 🧭 Exit the train station and keep left around the station; the Guardia Nacional building is across the street.)
- **PHARMACY: Pharmazul** is right across from the train station. (Av. Dr. Miguel Bombarda, 37 ☎21 924 38 77 ⏰ Open M-F 9:30am-7pm, Sa 10:30am-7:30pm.)
- **MEDICAL SERVICES: Centro de Saúde** (R. Dr. Alfredo Costa, 34, 1st fl. ☎21 924 77 70 🧭 Just across from the train station, to the left. ⏰ Open M-F 8am-8pm, Sa-Su 10am-6pm.)

Getting There

The easiest way to get to Sintra from Lisbon is by **train.** Trains run from Lisbon's **Rossio Station** in Baixa. ($ €2. ⏰ M-F every 15min. 6:08am-8:21pm, every 30min. 8:38pm-1:08am; Sa-Su every 30min. 6:08am-1:06am.) ScottURB runs **buses** from Cascais. (Bus #417 $ €4. ⏰ 40min.; every hr. M-F 6am-9pm, Sa 7am-8pm, Su 8am-8pm.)

Getting Around

The best way to get around within Sintra is by foot. To get to the sights, take a **bus** (#434, 435) from either the tourist office or train station. You can also take a 👍**horse-drawn carriage** from the Palácio Nacional de Sintra. (Sintratur, R. de João de Deus, 82 ☎219 24 12 38 www.sintratur.com $ Fixed rates of €30-70 depending on time and distance.) **Taxis** are also relatively inexpensive. (☎219 23 02 05 🧭 Stands in historic center across from Palácio Nacional and at train station.)

NORTHERN
PORTUGAL

Most tourists leave Lisbon and head south, but you're not most tourists. You're intrepid, you're fearless, and you can't get enough of that nasal Portuguese accent. So you head north to some of the country's less touristy but no less breathtaking cities. Coimbra's hilltop university is among Europe's oldest, and the rest of the student city isn't bad, either. Porto, at once gritty and beautiful, is home to dozens of port wineries, and its entire historic center is a UNESCO World Heritage Site (and it's not a small historic center, either.) Braga feels as authentically Portuguese as can be, and the nearby Parque Nacional de Peneda-Gerês on the Spanish border is a nature-lover's paradise on Earth. You don't just want booze and beaches (at least not yet). Leave the Algarve for later; head north.

greatest hits

- **IS THAT A CAR ON THE WALL?** Porto's Galeria de Paris restaurant is one quirky and delicious place. (p. 508)

- **NA NA NA NA NA NA NA NA...** Batman? Nope—real bats. Who eat bugs. Because those bugs eat books. Check it out at the Joanina Library at the University of Coimbra. (p. 523)

- **GET SOME AIR.** Enjoy the greatest of Iberia's great outdoors in the Parque Nacional da Peneda-Gerês. (p. 518)

porto *oporto* ☎22

Perhaps the most charming aspect of Portugal's second-largest city is its lack of veneer: crumbling buildings hang over tiny and confusing streets that are strung with drying laundry and echo with the conversations of residents. Here, the Mediterranean vibes of Lisbon are all but lost. Instead, the dark stone architecture that is prevalent throughout the city matches its cooler and wetter climate. The city's distinct flavor pervades the art, cuisine, and pace of everyday life, which is relaxed but still means business, staying true to its roots in industry and commerce. Though the historic center of Porto is a UNESCO World Heritage Site and the area right by the river is lined with shops and restaurants aimed at visitors, there's no question that the old city is more a living *bairro* than a pristine, Disney-esque tourist town. Porto has the gritty beauty of a city built and still thriving on commerce rather than tourism, and it's got the history (and port wine) to go along with it.

ORIENTATION

Porto's insane maze of steep streets can be very difficult to navigate; at times it seems a topographic map would be more useful than the flat ones available at the tourist offices. At the center of town is a massive, sloping plaza formed by **Praça da Liberdade, Avenida dos Aliados,** and **Praça do General Humberto Delgado.** East of this plaza is the **Rua de Santa Catarina, Mercado de Bolhão,** and the main shopping district; just off the southeast corner is the **São Bento train station,** and to the west is **Vitória,** a hilly, trendier area. The oldest part of town is the **Ribeira** district, which lies to the south of the city center and goes down to the banks of the **Río Douro,** where confusing streets contain many historic sights. The two-level **Ponte de Dom Luís** connects Porto to **Vila Nova de Gaia** on the other side of the river, where most of the port wine cellars can be found. The **Foz** district, several kilometers west of the center where the Douro meets the Atlantic, is a popular nightlife neighborhood, as is the area surrounding **Rua Galeria de Paris,** which is a few blocks northwest of the city center.

ACCOMMODATIONS

Since budget travel in Porto has seen a massive up-swing in the last few years, budget accommodations have also been on the rise. New hostels seem to spring up fairly frequently and *pensões* are also easy to come by. Unlike in some of Portugal's other cities, accommodations in Porto aren't centered around any one area but are instead spread throughout the city. Availability is typically high, with the exception of during large festivals and other peak times.

northern portugal

OPORTO POETS HOSTEL

HOSTEL $

R. dos Caldeireiros, 261   ☎22 332 42 09 www.oportopoetshostel.com

Although not as luxurious as its sister in Lisbon, Oporto Poets Hostel is still one of the top spots in the city. Each room is dedicated to a unique poet and has verses on the walls that may provide the literature-challenged with some decent pick-up lines. The dorms and reception are in a building on R. Caldeireiros (right behind the church with the tall tower) that has common spaces that will put your living room to shame, and the private rooms are located down an adjacent alley in a lovely little house with a patio, garden, cathedral views, and **hammock.**

✦ ⓜSão Bento. Bus #202 or 500 to Loios, or ZH, #305, 507, 601, 602, or 703 to Cordoaria. From ⓜSão Bento, walk up R. Clérigos past Torre dos Clérigos, then turn left down toward the river 2 blocks, then veer left onto R. Caldeireiros. *i* Breakfast included. Shared baths. Kitchen available. ⓢ Dorms €16-20; private rooms €42-50. 10% discount for stays of 5 nights or longer. ⌚ Reception 24hr.

ANDARILHO OPORTO HOSTEL

HOSTEL $

R. da Firmeza, 364   ☎22 201 20 73 www.andarilhohostel.com

You half-expect to be asked what the password is before you can enter this hidden hostel, but once inside this barely marked accommodation you'll find a beautiful, clean abode with a patio garden and comfortable living area. From the common areas to the rooms, everything is spacious in this hostel, and with a wall separating it from the busy street, you feel like you're in your own secluded palace without sacrificing location.

✦ ⓜBolhão or bus #302. From ⓜBolhão, head right on R. Fernandes Tomás 1 block, then turn left onto R. Santa Catarina, then right onto R. Firmeza; there is a small red door on the left side of the street with no sign. *i* Breakfast included. Laundry service. Kitchen available. ⓢ Dorms €15-16. ⌚ Reception 24hr.

PILOT HOSTEL

HOSTEL $

R. do General Silveira, 11   ☎22 208 43 62

This fresh-out-of-the-oven, brand-new hostel a few blocks from Porto's nightlife is one of the best deals in town. Rooms are dirt cheap, and the courtyard, common area, and bar are all large and in charge. The attempted theme appears to be minimalist/modern, but the stark gray walls combined with neon LEDs result in more of a warehouse-rave vibe. Fun quirks abound, such as the sign on the showers that reads "GET NAKED," in case you forgot how that whole "showering" concept works.

✦ ⓜAliados. Bus #207, 300, 302, 304, 305, 501, or 703. From Pr. Liberdade facing uphill, head up Av. Aliados, then turn left onto R. Fábrica. After the plaza, turn right onto R. Sá de Noronha. ⓢ Dorms €10-16. *i* Breakfast and linens included. Cash only. ⌚ Reception 24hr.

PORTO DOWNTOWN HOSTEL

HOSTEL $

Pr. de Guilherme Gomes Fernandes, 66   ☎22 201 80 94 www.portodowntownhostel.com

Overlooking the small but busy Pr. Guilherme Gomes Fernandes in the hip and hilly Vitória neighborhood, this hostel offers some of Porto's cheapest lodgings. Colorful and large spaces make this seem like an awesome, grown-up version of kindergarten, except this time you get to choose when nap time starts. The dorms are named after different colors and are painted accordingly. Most of the city (and ⓜAliados) is downhill from here; keep this in mind when debating whether to walk here with your luggage or take a bus.

✦ ⓜAliados. Bus #207, 300, 302, 304, 305, 501, or 703. From Pr. Liberdade facing uphill, head up Av. Aliados, then turn left onto R. Fábrica. Turn left onto Pr. Guilherme Gomes Fernandes. *i* Breakfast included. Free lockers. Kitchen and laundry service available. Shared baths. Cash only. ⓢ Dorms €12-15; triples €54. ⌚ Reception 24hr.

porto

INVICTUS HOSTEL

HOSTEL $

R. das Oliveiras, 73 ☎22 202 43 71 www.oportoinvictushostel.com

With its deep browns and other dark hues, this hostel acts as an extension of Porto's rustic atmosphere. Large windows overlook the streets below and are so big that you can stick your head out and gossip with the locals. Don't forget that local chit-chat requires you to stroke a cat whilst slandering others—although the hostel's pet policy isn't clear. Reasonable prices and comfortable rooms mean that Invictus Hostel is a great value. The location puts you a few blocks from Vitória and the nightlife area of town, making it a convenient place to stay.

✴ Ⓜ️Aliados. Bus #207, 300, 302, 304, 305, 501, or 703. From Pr. Liberdade facing uphill, head up Av. Aliados, then turn left onto R. Fábrica. After the plaza, turn right onto R. Sá de Noronha. *i* Breakfast and linens included. Ⓢ Dorms €14-18; doubles €40-50. 🕘 Reception 24hr.

PENSÃO DUAS NAÇÕES

HOTEL $

Pr. de Guilherme Gomes Fernandes, 59 ☎22 208 16 16 www.duasnacoes.com.pt

This *pensão* doesn't offer much beyond a TV and a bed, but it has some of the cheapest singles in town and is located in a convenient and inexpensive area. The plaza is only a block from Porto's main nightlife district, so even the most blundering drunks will be able to stumble their way home. The rooms are brightly decorated, and some even have views over the plaza. Every room is unique, so be sure to find out exactly what you are booking.

✴ Ⓜ️Aliados. Bus #207, 300, 302, 304, 305, or 501. From Pr. Liberdade facing uphill, head up Av. Aliados, then turn left onto R. Elísio de Melo, which becomes Pr. Filipa de Lencastre and then R. Ceuta. Then turn left onto Pr. Guilherme Gomes Fernandes. *i* Laundry service and TV available. Bicycle rental. Ⓢ Dorms €13-18; singles €15-20, with ensuite bath €26; doubles €27/32; triples €42/44; quads €52/54. 🕘 Reception 24hr.

PORTO RIAD

B&B $$$

R. de Dom João IV, 990 ☎22 510 76 43 www.portoriad.com

Though a slight schlep from the city's center, Porto Riad has an impressive and free breakfast buffet in a cool Middle Eastern dining room. This theme stretches throughout the whole B&B, even influencing the decor in the rooms. The small but pretty plaza across the street, however, reminds you that you aren't actually in the desert.

✴ Ⓜ️Bolhão. Bus #206, 302, or 303. From Ⓜ️Bolhão, head right on R. Fernandes Tomás 3 blocks, then left up R. Alegria 4 blocks uphill. *i* Breakfast included. Kitchen available. Private baths in private rooms. Laundry service available. Ⓢ 4-bed dorms €20-22; singles €40-50; doubles €55-70. Extra bed €15-20. 🕘 Reception 24hr.

SIGHTS

You can discover part of Porto's incredible character by simply wandering the streets and taking in the striking architecture. But that's not to say that there aren't specific sights to be seen. Most sights can be found near the twisting streets of Ribeira, alongside the river, or near the São Bento train station.

🏛 PALÁCIO DA BOLSA

HISTORIC SITE

R. de Ferreira Borges ☎22 339 90 00 www.palaciodabolsa.pt

The enormous and elegant Palácio da Bolsa (stock exchange) sits over Ribeira's main plaza and is one of Porto's most visited sites. Upon entering, visitors walk into the massive, bright, and beautifully decorated market floor, which contains paintings that represent Portugal's biggest trade partners. You can then continue up the granite stairs whose construction delayed the building's completion by almost half a century. The whole building radiates opulence, but not in a Donald-Trump-creepy-comb-over kind of way. More spectacular than any of the area's churches and entirely dedicated to commerce, the Palácio encapsulates where Porto's interests truly lie. One room has a table with an intricate wooden inlay, done entirely with a pen-knife, while another looks to be decorated with wood, bronze, and marble but is actually all just painted plaster, designed to show off the local painters' craftsmanship. The Palácio da Bolsa's most spectacular room is the Sala Árabe, whose sole purpose was to impress foreign businessmen who were received there. Perhaps the most incredible room in all of Portugal, any visitor will have to admit that it accomplishes its goal. Its walls and ceilings proclaim the odd combination of the phrases "Glory to Allah" and "May Allah protect Dona Maria II," Portugal's Catholic queen.

⇞ [M]São Bento. Bus ZH or ZM. From [M]São Bento, follow R. Mouzinho da Silveira downhill to Pr. Infante Dom Henrique—it's the massive building on the right side of the plaza. ℹ Guided tours available in English. [$]€7, students and seniors €3. ⏰ Open daily Apr-Oct 9am-7pm; Nov-Mar 9am-1pm and 2-6pm. Last tour 30min. before close.

IGREJA DE SÃO FRANCISCO CHURCH

R. do Infante Dom Henrique ☎22 206 21 00

This is a special treat for those passionate about gilded wood, although it is also perfectly enjoyable for people who just like pretty things. The gilded wood is beautiful, and this church has a ton of it, almost literally—there was at one time about 1000lb. of gold decorating the chapel's walls and altar, all donated by wealthy residents of Porto, who no doubt did it only out of the good of their own hearts—not because they wanted to buy their way into eternal paradise or anything. But let their deep-seated guilt become your traveling pleasure as you marvel at the workmanship inside the church. The museum next door has a collection of fairly generic religious artwork and a mass burial ground in the basement.

⇞ [M]São Bento. Or bus ZH or ZM. From [M]São Bento, follow R. Mouzinho da Silveira downhill to Pr. Infante Dom Henrique, then turn right along the street at the far side. [$] €3, students and seniors €2.50. ⏰ Open daily June 9am-7pm; July-Aug 9am-8pm; Sept-Oct 9am-7pm; Feb-May 9am-6pm.

SÉ (CATHEDRAL)
CHURCH

Terreiro da Sé ☎22 205 90 28

With fabulous views of the city from the plaza in front of it, the old Romanesque Sé (short for *Sede Episcopal*) is one of Porto's more formidable buildings, with a large, dark, fortress-like appearance and a statue of a knight out front for good measure. But just like that guy with the mohawk that you tried to bring home once; it really is nice if you just take the time to get to know it. The cathedral was built in the 12th and 13th centuries, with the tiled Gothic cloister added 100 years later. The interior is simple, and the cool shade is quite nice after the climb uphill to the site.

✝ ⓂSão Bento. Or bus ZH. From ⓂSão Bento, follow Av. Vimara Peres toward the river (left with your back to the train station) and bear right uphill. Ⓢ Free. Cloister €3, students €2, under 10 free. ☒ Cathedral open daily Apr-Oct 9am-12:30pm and 2:30-7pm; Nov-Mar 9am-12:30pm and 2:30-6pm. Cloister open daily Apr-Oct 9am-12:15pm and 2:30-6:30pm; Nov-Mar 9am-12:15pm and 2:30-5:30pm.

MUSEU NACIONAL DE SOARES DOS REIS
MUSEUM

R. de Dom Manuel II, 44 ☎22 339 37 70 mnsr.imc-ip.pt

For the seven people who wrote their thesis about the impact of Portuguese art on the aesthetic understanding of the Iberian Peninsula but now only get to recreate their favorite pieces in the foam of your cappuccino, this museum is heaven. For the rest of us, it's an education on some under-appreciated domestic talents who deserve some love. This historic 18th-century palace houses the country's museum of Portuguese art and has pieces ranging from paintings to sculptures to fine china. Don't go if you are in a hurry—the passionate volunteers want to make sure you fully appreciate each piece before you can leave.

✝ Bus #200, 201, 207, 303, 501, 601, or 602. From ⓂSão Bento, head up R. Clérigos, go right past the church and tower, head straight toward Hospital Santo António, then go around it to the right, then go straight on R. Dom Manuel II. Ⓢ €5, students and seniors €2.50, under 14 free; free to all on Su before 2pm. ☒ Open Tu 2-6pm, W-Su 10am-6pm.

IGREJA E TORRE DOS CLÉRIGOS
CHURCH, VIEWS

R. de São Filipe Nery ☎22 200 17 29

The Torre dos Clérigos is one of Porto's most recognizable landmarks and Portugal's tallest tower, rising over the city and dwarfing everything around it. The church inside is also actually distinguishable from the millions of other European churches, since it is shaped like an oval, making it an intriguing novelty. The view from the top is spectacular but requires the strength to climb the 225 dizzying spiral steps (you may wonder as you climb why *they* didn't pay *you* the €2 entrance fee) or a harness and pickaxe to go up the outside. (*Let's Go* strongly discourages climbing up the outside.)

✝ ⓂSão Bento. Or bus ZH, 22, 202, 303, 500, 501, 507, 601, or 602. From ⓂSão Bento, head straight up R. Clérigos. Ⓢ Free. Tower €2. ☒ Church open M-Sa 8:45am-12:30pm and 3:30-7pm, Su 10am-1pm and 9:30-10:30pm. Tower open daily Apr-July 9:30am-1pm and 2:30-7pm; Aug 9:30am-7pm; Sept-Oct 9:30am-1pm and 2:30-7pm; Nov-Mar 10am-noon and 2-5pm. Last entry 30min. before close.

JARDINS DO PALÁCIO DE CRISTAL
PARK

R. de Dom Manuel II ☎22 543 03 60 www.portolazer.pt

The Palácio de Cristal (Glass Palace) is not made of glass, but its surrounding gardens are sufficiently garden-like to avoid the tag of complete misnomer. The space is surprisingly large for being in the middle of such a big city, and it is a great place to kick back and relax with nature. There also happen to be those cute little old-people exercise stations, just in case you feel like getting your modified push-ups on. Walk down to the end of the park opposite the entrance for fantastic views and an equally impressive wine cafe, but do not tease the peacocks because they can get a tad bitey.

🚌 *Bus ZM, 200, 201, 207, 303, 501, 601, or 602. From Ⓜ São Bento, head up R. Clérigos, go right up R. Carmelitas, head straight toward Hospital Santo António. Go around the hospital to the right, then straight on R. Dom Manuel II; the park is on the left.* **i** *Do not provoke the peacocks. They will bite.* Ⓢ *Free.* 🕐 *Open daily Apr-Sept 8am-9pm; Oct-Mar 8am-7pm.*

CASA DO INFANTE DOM HENRIQUE   MUSEUM, ARCHIVE
R. da Alfândega, 10   ☎ 22 206 04 00 www.cm-porto.pt

Once an old customs house and said to be the birthplace of Prince Henry the Navigator, this building now houses a museum and historical archive. The customs house has since moved, but that doesn't have to stop you from putting on a thick British accent and pretending to be in the port trading business. Although some of the information here is about Prince Henry, much of the museum tends to focus on the history of Porto as a whole.

🚌 *Ⓜ São Bento. Bus ZH or ZM. From Palácio da Bolsa, walk toward the river. The house is on the left.* Ⓢ *€2.20.* 🕐 *Museum open Tu-Su 10am-1pm, 2-5:30pm.*

WINERIES

If you're in Porto, at least one visit to a winery is mandatory. They're either free or very cheap (under €5), and tours usually run about 30-40min. Most of the tasting occurs across the Douro in **Vila Nova de Gaia** and its 17 massive **port** lodges, and the best way to get to this port authority is to walk across the bottom level of the Ponte de Dom Luís from Ribeira.

TAYLOR'S   GAIA
R. do Choupelo, 250   ☎ 22 374 28 00 www.taylor.pt

This almost ancient winery has been graced by the likes of many Latin American presidents (might as well stop by for some good port on the way home from Spain, right?), and for good reason. Inside, the ceiling of the lobby is like a big circus tent, but this place is no joke. For three euro you can try three wines, including an LBV (Late Bottled Vintage), which is high-quality and not usually given out at tastings.

🚌 *Ⓜ Jardim do Morro. Or bus #900, 901, or 906. From Gaia waterfront, take R. Dom Alfonso III and follow signs to Taylor's.* Ⓢ *Tour and tasting (3 wines) €3.* 🕐 *Open M-F 10am-6pm. Last tour 1hr. before close.*

CROFT   GAIA
Lg. de Joaquim Magalhães, 23   ☎ 22 374 28 00 www.croftport.com

This rustic-looking winery lets you sip three different varieties of port while sitting atop tiny wooden chairs shaped like wine-barrels. Croft has been around since 1588, and they know their stuff; visitors will leave feeling like port connoisseurs. Visits must be guided, lest tourists attempt to make off with one of the massive aging vats.

🚌 *Ⓜ Jardim do Morro. Or bus #900, 901, or 906. From Gaia waterfront, follow R. Dom Alfonso III 2 blocks, then turn right.* Ⓢ *Tour and tasting (3 wines) €3.* 🕐 *Open daily July-Aug 10am-8pm; Sept-June 10am-7pm. Last tour starts 45min. before close.*

SANDEMAN   GAIA
Lg. de Miguel Bombarda, 3   ☎ 22 374 05 33 www.sandeman.eu

Founded by a Scottish merchant at the end of the 18th century, this winery offers inexpensive tours and tastings. The interior attempts to exemplify the winery's sensual and contemporary marketing themes, but once you step into the cool cellars and the scent of port and oak hit your nostrils, you will forget all about marketing. Dusty bottles of vintage wine bottled over 100 years ago sit, still waiting to reach their full potential. Their trademark caped don lurks in the shadows behind the casks.

🚌 *Ⓜ Jardim do Morro. Or bus #900, 901, or 906. On the Gaia waterfront 3 blocks west of the iron bridge.* Ⓢ *Tour and tasting (2 wines) €4.50.* 🕐 *Open daily Mar-Oct 10am-12:30pm and 2-6pm; Nov-Feb 9:30am-12:30pm and 2-5:30pm. Last tour 45min. before close.*

porto

CÁLEM GAIA

Av. Diogo Leite, 344 ☎22 374 66 60 www.calem.pt.

Although it came a bit late to the game (founded in 1859, the young gun), this winery has still managed to put out some high-quality and award-winning wines. The stone arches ooze classiness along with the rest of the decor, allowing visitors to at least pretend that they enjoy the finer things in life. The tours are both informative and brief, which is good, because nothing is worse than someone getting between you and your wine.

 # [M]Jardim do Morro. Or bus #900, 901, or 906. On the Gaia waterfront 1 block west of the iron bridge. [$] Tour and tasting (2 wines) €4.50. ⏰ Open daily May-Oct 10am-7pm, Nov-Apr 10am-6pm.

FOOD

The areas around **Praça da Batalha** and uphill west of Av. Aliados have cafes offering inexpensive meals, as do the tiny restaurants that line the waterfront in **Ribeira.** That said, a good way to find the best deal is to wander a few blocks away from all of the touristy restaurants. The local (and cheap) cafes tend to be located near, but not in, the tourist trap areas. The biggest bang for your buck is a *francesinha:* a cheap sandwich available at most cafes that includes several types of meat smothered in cheese and a tomato-like gravy and squeezed between two pieces of bread. Order it *especial* and get a sunny-side-up egg on top. Your cardiologist won't love you, but your taste buds will.

BRASA DOS LEÕES GRILL $

Pr. de Guilherme Gomes Fernandes, 7 ☎22 205 11 85

Big appetite? Small budget? The *pratos do dia* here are cheap, and the heaping servings certainly won't leave you hungry. For the best deals, bring a friend and split *1 dose*, or "1 portion," which is actually enough to feed a family of starving lions. There is also outdoor seating on a shady plaza just up the street from the Torre dos Clérigos.

 # [M]Aliados. Or bus #207, 300, 302, 304, 305, or 501, 703. From Pr. Liberdade facing uphill, head up Av. Aliados, then left onto R. Elísio de Melo, which becomes Pr. Filipa de Lencastre and then R. Ceuta. Turn left onto Pr. Guilherme Gomes Fernandes. [$] Entrees €4-7. ⏰ Open daily 10am-10pm.

GALERIA DE PARIS CAFE, BAR $$$

R. da Galeria de Paris, 56 ☎22 201 62 18

The vintage paraphernalia that lines the shelves behind the bar and scattered throughout this restaurant fall somewhere between kitsch and awesome, while the atmosphere is decidedly cool. Tables are cramped and candlelit, meaning things get intimate. There's an entire vintage car just hanging on one wall and a host of bicycles suspended from the ceiling downstairs near the bathrooms. The food isn't cheap, but it's delicious. There's frequently entertainment at night, including live music and a cross between a mime and Alan Rickman swinging cats about on ropes—we don't ask questions.

 # [M]São Bento. Or bus #200, 201, 207, 300, 302, 304, 305, 507, 601, or 602. From [M]São Bento, head up R. Clérigos, then right up R. Carmelitas, then right up R. Galeria de Paris. [$] Daily special €10. Entrees €8-13. ⏰ Open M-Sa 9am-2am, Su 7-9pm.

CAFE D'OURO CAFE $

Pr. de Parada Leitão, 55

This student hotspot has nifty, all glass *esplanades* outside, so you can sit and take in the sun without frying beneath it. Many come here just to snack and shoot the breeze, but full-blown meals are also available. The cardiac-arrest-inducing *francesinha* (€8) sits as the centerpiece of the menu.

 # [M]Aliados. Or bus #207, 300, 302, 304, 305, 501, or 703. From Pr. Liberdade, while facing uphill, head toward the large tower on the left. Once you reach the tower, turn right. The cafe is just beyond the fountain with the lions. [$] Entrees €4-10. ⏰ Open daily 9am-2am.

CAFÉ MAJESTIC

CAFE $$

R. de Santa Catarina, 112   ☎22 200 38 87 www.cafemajestic.com

This *Titanic*-esque restaurant is a Porto landmark, with outdoor seating on the R. Santa Catarina and an interior that perfectly replicates turn-of-the-century extravagance. Sitting inside and soaking in the almost overwhelming ambience is recommended. Comfy leather banquettes and an Art Nouveau decor that can't be beat make a great setting for the whipped-cream-filled *café bombom* (€3.75), the local favorite. For the proper early-20th-century treatment, spring for the "Majestic Afternoon Tea" (€12), which includes a drink, smoked salmon, cucumbers with cream cheese, scones, and even more delights to fill you with condescending feelings toward the underlings. And while it is tempting to get into character, please don't take the last name of your waiter immediately after meeting him or ask him to paint you like one of his French girls—unless he looks like Leonardo DiCaprio.

✠ Ⓜ*Aliados; bus #302. From Pr. Liberdade, head 2 blocks uphill, then turn right onto R. Dr. Magalhães Lemos, which becomes R. Passos Manuel, then turn left onto R. Santa Catarina.* Ⓢ *Entrees €8-16. Sandwiches €5-13. Pastries €4-6. Coffee €1.50-4.* ⌚ *Open daily 9:30am-midnight.*

O CARAÇAS

PORTUGUESE $

R. das Taipas, 27   ☎22 017 45 05

There's not much in the way of food in this area beyond seedy bars, but this very inexpensive restaurant attracts a local crowd. Much of the food is grilled on the patio in the back, but the interior has a clean-cut feel. Even though this restaurant is only a few hundred meters from the water, Porto is not in tourist-town, so you are going to want to do your best to blend in (leave your water-wings and fanny-packs in the hostel). They do a great *alheira*, or chicken sausage (€5.50), and you can't go wrong with the seafood dishes.

✠ Ⓜ*São Bento; bus ZH. Head down R. Mouzinho da Silveira, then turn right onto R. Belomonte, then right up R. Taipas.* Ⓢ *Entrees €3.50-6.50.* ⌚ *Open M-Sa 11:30am-2:30pm and 7-10pm.*

ARROZ DE FORNO

PORTUGUESE $$

R. Mouzinho da Silveira, 203   ☎22 200 74 65

As the name would suggest, this place does rice, and they do it right. The menu can be a bit deceptive at first, since there don't seem to be any obvious rice dishes; but anything you order will reap some of the grainy goodness on your plate. Mostly filled with local suits on their lunch break, this is a great place to get a quality meal for the same price you would pay for a crappy one on the river. It's right on the way downhill to Ribeira if you're coming from the center of town, and it's a good place to stop and catch your breath if you're heading in the opposite direction.

✠ Ⓜ*São Bento; bus ZH. Head down R. Mouzinho da Silveira from* Ⓜ*São Bento.* Ⓢ *Daily specials €5-6.50. Entrees €6.50-13.50.* ⌚ *Open M-Sa noon-4pm and 7pm-midnight.*

ADEGA SÃO NICOLAU

PORTUGUESE $$

R. de São Nicolau, 1   ☎22 200 82 32

This small seafood restaurant on a sloping alley just up from the Douro gets packed quickly, so try to get here on the early side. When you sit down, be sure to mention that you don't want the €1 fish croquette that will be otherwise foisted on you, unless of course you want the €1 fish croquette (decisions, decisions). Much of the fish waiting to enter your stomach is on display over ice inside the restaurant, so you can see what looks good from today's catch before deciding what to order. The seating is jammed in a tiny alleyway away from the river, so while you will get seclusion and privacy, you may also be sitting fairly close to a neighbor's drying laundry. But anything on the menu under *mariscos* or *peixes* is certain to be delicious and worth the lack of personal space.

✠ Ⓜ*São Bento. Or bus ZR, 900, 901, or 906. From Pr. Infante Dom Henrique (in front of Palácio da Bolsa), head down toward the water along R. Alfandega 1 block, then turn right, then right again.* Ⓢ *Entrees €6-12.* ⌚ *Open M-Sa noon-3pm and 7-11pm.*

porto

POSTIGO DO CARVÃO DA RIBEIRA
R. da Fonte Taurina, 24

PORTUGUESE $$$

☎22 200 45 39

Something a little nicer than the dime-a-dozen holes-in-the-wall that line the Ribeira alleys but still well within your budget, this traditional restaurant has a fairly inexpensive menu and a large selection of both meat and fish dishes. Each meal includes a pleasant surprise: a refreshing aperitif on the house. You could fill up on the smorgasbord of table appetizers (which are not so free) alone.

✦ Ⓜ São Bento. Or bus ZR, 900, 901, or 906. From Pr. Infante Dom Henrique (in front of Palácio da Bolsa), head down toward the water along R. Alfandega 1 block, then turn left onto R. Fonte Taurina. Ⓢ Entrees €8-12. ☼ Open daily 8am-2am.

CAFE JAVA
Pr. da Batalha, 97

CAFE, RESTAURANT $$

☎22 200 51 44

This cafe offers good cheap food all day long and well into the night. The *francesinha* is a good call (€8), but skip the very hit-or-miss wine. With a large variety of cheap eats, the menu gives a look into the diet of one of Porto's many university students who frequent the cafe. Home to some of the world's strangest pricing, the 20mL beer is a steal for €1, but double the volume and the price jumps to €2.20, so make sure to specify the size when you order.

✦ Ⓜ São Bento. Bus #200, 202, 207, 301, 303, 305, ZH, 500, 900, 901, 904, 905, or 906. From Ⓜ São Bento, facing the station, head to the left of the station up R. 31 de Janeiro, then turn right onto Pr. Batalha. Ⓢ Entrees €6-11. ☼ Open daily 7am-2am.

NIGHTLIFE

Porto's best nightlife is mostly centered in **Vitória,** particularly along **Rua Galeria de Paris.** The **Ribeira** district down by the river also has some bars, though these aren't as relevant as they used to be. After 2am, the scene moves farther afield to **Foz,** along the riverfront and the industrial areas farther inland near Ⓜ Viso. Public transportation to these areas does not run after 1am, which means you can't get there when you want unless you take a cab (€5-6) or have a car. **Gaia,** just across the river, is a much more easily accessible option; just cross the Ponte de Dom Luís from Ribeira or take a €3 cab.

⬛ PLANO B
R. Cândido dos Reis, 30

BAR

☎22 201 25 00 www.planobporto.com

Almost like a more chilled out version of Moulin Rouge (and completely unrelated to birth control—unless we're missing something), Plano B makes you expect burlesque dancers to come out at any moment. The atmosphere is decidedly melodramatic and vintage, with loads of old furniture and leather couches juxtaposed with a gigantic disco ball and a bubble chandelier. This was the spot where everyone raged until sunrise before local laws changed, forcing the bar to close at 4am. However, Plano B still brings the party, with a huge space for dancing that is just begging to be used.

✦ Ⓜ São Bento. Or bus #200, 201, 207, 300, 302, 304, 305, 507, 601, or 602. From Ⓜ São Bento, head up R. Clérigos, then right up R. Carmelitas; turn right up R. Cândido dos Reis. Ⓢ Beer €2. Cocktails €6. ☼ Open Tu-Sa 10pm-4am.

⬛ CAFE AU LAIT
R. da Galeria de Paris, 44

BAR

This spot on R. Galeria de Paris is populated almost exclusively by local students who happen to be many of the bartenders as well. The decor is minimalistic, with dim incandescent bulbs hanging down from the ceiling on wires, giving the bar an almost eerie feeling. Bring friends or strike up a conversation with one of the students, almost all of whom speak great English.

✦ Ⓜ São Bento. Or bus #200, 201, 207, 300, 302, 304, 305, 507, 601, or 602. From Ⓜ São Bento, head up R. Clérigos, then turn right up R. Carmelitas, then right up R. Galeria de Paris. Ⓢ Beer €1.50. ☼ Open M-F 10pm-3am, Sa-Su 10pm-4am.

RENDEZ VOUS

R. Cândido dos Reis, 77

BAR

www.rendezvousporto.com

This bar knows where the party is at: outside. That's why they have an additional bar facing the street. Consider it the drive-through of cocktail bars. The place bills itself as an "electro-rock cafe," and while it is still yet to be seen exactly what that means, a few things are certain: big crowds, loud music, and flashing lights. Head out onto the street and join the party.

✝ Ⓜ São Bento. Or bus #200, 201, 207, 300, 302, 304, 305, 507, 601, or 602. From Ⓜ São Bento, head up R. Clérigos, then right up R. Carmelitas, then right up R. Cândido dos Reis. Ⓢ Shots €1. Caipirinhas €2.50. ☼ Open W-Sa 10pm-4am.

ITAIPÚ

R. da Galeria de Paris, 91

BAR

☎22 200 29 38

So many people crowd Itaipú that the tropical theme becomes believable as temperatures rise; they even have a large Brazilian flag in Luso-solidarity. The specials here are a variety of different fruit-flavored caipirinhas (€3.50), which in reality means alcoholic smoothies. It doesn't matter whether it's strawberry, peach, or kiwi—these drinks are absolutely delectable and refreshing, giving you the energy to face the streets of Porto once again.

✝ Ⓜ São Bento. Or bus #200, 201, 207, 300, 302, 304, 305, 507, 601, or 602. From Ⓜ São Bento, head up R. Clérigos, then right up R. Carmelitas, then turn right up R. Galeria de Paris. Ⓢ Caipirinhas €3.50. ☼ Open M-Sa 10pm-2am.

SAHARA

Cais da Estiva, 4

BAR

☎96 920 60 37

A fairly obvious North-African theme pervades this loungey bar by the river, marked by its cushioned seats and Near-Eastern rugs. The *não fumadores* sign and the hookahs inside make for an odd paradox, as if the owners just wanted to nominally stick it to the man. If you don't feel like kicking back with a bowl of shisha, the creative coffees will give you the boost of caffeine you need for the rest of the night.

✝ Ⓜ São Bento. Or bus ZR, 900, 901, or 906. From Pr. Infante Dom Henrique (in front of Palácio da Bolsa), head down toward the water along R. Alfandega, then turn left at the waterfront. Ⓢ Coffee €1-3. Mixed drinks €2-6. ☼ Open daily 3pm-2am.

O CAIS

R. da Fonte Taurina, 2A

BAR

☎91 452 36 72

This feels like a 19th-century smoking room but with stronger drinks. Dark and somewhat mysterious, with leather furniture and wood paneling, the decor makes everything seem more manly. Before you know it, you will be boxing shirtless with a handlebar moustache. It gets very lively after 2am, when many of the neighboring bars close.

✝ Ⓜ São Bento. Or bus ZR, 900, 901, or 906. From Pr. Infante Dom Henrique (in front of Palácio da Bolsa), head down toward the water along R. Alfandega 1 block, then turn left onto R. Fonte Taurina. Ⓢ Beer €2. Mixed drinks €2.50-7. ☼ Open daily 9pm-3am.

BAR PRIORIDADE

R. da Lada, 76

BAR, DIVE

This bar is behind an arch that separates it from the water, quite at home among several other similarly inexpensive drinking holes. But just because it is set aside doesn't mean it's a secret; this is probably one of the loudest and busiest bars down by the river on a nightly basis. This isn't a destination for dancing, but it is a good spot to knock back drinks late into the night.

✝ Ⓜ São Bento. Or bus ZR, 900, 901, or 906. Head along the waterfront on C. Ribeira toward Ponte de Dom Luís (the iron bridge), then turn left through the arches; there are signs for the bars here. Ⓢ Shots €1. Beer €1-2.50. ☼ Open daily 9pm-2am.

LA BOHÈME

R. da Galeria de Paris, 40

BAR

This crafty-looking bar is a good place to start the night. La Bohème mainly deals in *petiscos*, a more casual Portuguese version of tapas, and they back it up with a lengthy list of wines. As the night rolls on, it turns into more of a typical bar. Ever resourceful, the bartenders set up shop outside as the crowd grows in the street, with makeshift bars placed on top of the pillars that are meant to stop cars from riding on the sidewalk.

⚲ ⓂSão Bento. Or bus #200, 201, 207, 300, 302, 304, 305, 507, 601, or 602. From ⓂSão Bento, head up R. Clérigos, then turn right up R. Carmelitas, then right up R. Galeria de Paris. ⓢ Beer €1.50-2. Mixed drinks €2.50-6. ⓩ Open M-F 8:30pm-2am, Sa 3pm-2am.

FESTIVALS

As Portugal's second-largest city, Porto has plenty of parties to enjoy. However, **Noite de São João,** the celebration of their patron saint, is hands-down the biggest night of the year. For information about upcoming events, head to www.cm-porto.pt, the city's official website.

◤ NOITE DE SÃO JOÃO

CITYWIDE

On the evening of June 23 each year, the citizens of Porto run through the streets hitting complete strangers on the head with leeks (not what they look like when you eat them—these are long stalks with round purple flowers at the end) and toy mallets while stopping at bars and restaurants to eat entire schools of grilled sardines and whole herds of baby goats. Every few hundred yards, another stage can be found, with bands playing Portuguese music and hordes of people dancing through the night. Carnival rides and street vendors selling delicious chocolate-filled churros that go straight to your thighs abound. At midnight, the

northern portugal

town goes down to the riverside to watch the fireworks, after which the under-25 population walks 8km to the beach to hit the temporary open-air nightclubs that blast house music until the sun comes up. Celebrants jump over bonfires for luck, and women roll in the morning dew to ensure fertility. The next day is much sleepier, but there is a sailboat race in the early afternoon between all the port wineries from the mouth of the Douro to the city; the competition was originally meant to determine which winery had the fastest boats and could thus ship the most port.

Ⓢ *Mallets €1-4. Churros €1.50 and heaps of regret.* Ⓩ *June 23-24, with festivities and free events throughout June.*

FESTIVAL INTERNACIONAL DE TEATRO DE EXPRESSÃO IBÉRICA   CITYWIDE
R. do Paraíso, 217, 2nd fl., Room 5   ☎222 08 24 32 www.fitei.com

Running from the end of May through the first week of June, this festival features free Spanish and Portuguese theater performances staged throughout the city in various public spaces, from Metro stops to the Palácio da Bolsa. Similarly, performances happen at all hours, from early in the morning to midnight. Check the festival's website for schedule and locations.

⚑ *Performances in public spaces throughout city.* Ⓢ *Most performances free.* Ⓩ *Usually end of May.*

SHOPPING

Porto's main shopping area is around the **Rua de Santa Catarina,** which is lined with stores and has the Via Catarina shopping center for those pining for an American-style mall. Stores also line **Praça da Liberdade** as well as the area leading down to the river.

🕮 LIVRARIA LELLO E IRMÃO   BOOKS
R. das Carmelitas, 144   ☎22 201 81 70 www.lelloprologolivreiro.com.sapo.pt

This magnificent Art Nouveau bookstore on R. Carmelitas is a Mecca for book-lovers. The white façade draws tourists and pilgrims alike to ornate wooden shelves holding books from every genre and era. A twisting staircase leads to a second floor, where there are more books, a cafe, and memorabilia from the bookstore's history. But don't even think about pulling your camera out, lest you be reprimanded by an ever-vigilant employee: no photos here. Don't forget to look up at the marvelous stained-glass on the ceiling.

⚑ Ⓜ*São Bento. Or bus #200, 201, 207, 300, 302, 304, 305, 507, 601, or 602. From* Ⓜ*São Bento, head up R. Clérigos, then turn right up R. Carmelitas.* Ⓩ *Open M-F 10am-7:30pm, Sa 10am-7pm.*

MERCADO DO BOLHÃO   MARKET
R. Formosa   ☎22 332 60 24 www.cm-porto.pt

Fresh produce, flowers, handicrafts, and more line the stalls of this enormous two-story market. Vendors know each other and socialize in the narrow alleys between the stalls. Some of the best deals are the baked goods and produce, which are much fresher (and cheaper) than what you'll find at supermarkets. Come early when everything is at its freshest; most vendors tend to leave an hour or two before closing time.

⚑ Ⓜ*Bolhão. Or bus #55, 69, 70, 94, 401, or 800. From Pr. Liberdade, head uphill along Av. Aliados, turn right onto R. Dr. Magalhães Lemos, then turn left onto R. Sá da Bandeira.* Ⓩ *Open M-F 7am-5pm, Sa 8am-7pm.*

MUNDO ASTRAL   OCCULT
R. de José Falcão, 14   ☎22 208 18 55

When you are done with all of your cathedral and church visits, take a not-so-Vatican-approved trip to Mundo Astral, a tiny shop dealing in all things occult. Tarot cards and crystal balls fill the shelves, letting the imagination wander, although it could just be the incense getting to your head. But Jesus fans need not despair! There are also figurines of the Virgin Mary and the big

porto

guy himself. They just happen to be lined up next to Buddha, Vishnu, and a handful of other exotic deities.

�∅ ⓜAliados. Or bus #207, 300, 302, 304, 305, 501, or 703. From Pr. Liberdade facing uphill, head up Av. Aliados, turn left onto R. Elísio de Melo, which becomes Pr. Filipa de Lencastre and then R. Ceuta. Turn left onto Pr. Guilherme Gomes Fernandes. 🕐 Open daily 10am-1pm, 2:30-6:45pm.

A VIDA PORTUGUESA   SOUVENIRS
R. da Galeria de Paris, 20   ☎22 202 21 05 www.avidaportuguesa.com

Found on the second floor of a beautiful Vitória building, A Vida Portuguesa sells all of the things that make Portugal, well, so Portuguese. That includes domestic wines and liqueurs, specialty sardines, toy hammers in time for São João, and more. Even if you aren't interested in buying anything, come inside just to see the impressive wood interior and drool over some Portuguese candies.

�∅ ⓜSão Bento. Or bus #200, 201, 207, 300, 302, 304, 305, 507, 601, or 602. From ⓜSão Bento, head up R. Clérigos, then turn right up R. Carmelitas. 🕐 Open M-Sa 10am-8pm.

ESSENTIALS
Practicalities

- **TOURIST OFFICES: Postos de Turismo Municipais** are located throughout the center of town and sell **Porto Cards,** which give discounts at museums, monuments, shops, and restaurants and provide unlimited access to public transportation systems. **Centro.** (R. Clube dos Fenianos, 25 ☎22 339 34 70 �∅ ⓜAliados; bus #904. From Pr. Liberdade, walk up left side of Av. Aliados 3 blocks. 🕐 Open daily June-Sept 9am-8pm; Oct-May 9am-7pm.) **Ribeira.** (R. Infante Dom Henrique, 63 ☎22 206 04 12 �∅ ⓜSão Bento. Or bus ZR, 900, 901, or 906. On side of Pr. Infante Dom Henrique closest to the river. 🕐 Open daily June-Sept 9am-8pm; Oct-May 9am-7pm.) **Sé.** (Terreiro da Sé ☎22 332 51 74 �∅ ⓜSão Bento; bus ZH. Next to cathedral. From ⓜSão Bento, follow Av. Vimara Peres toward the river (left with your back to the train station) and bear right uphill. 🕐 Open M-F 10am-6pm.)

- **CURRENCY EXCHANGE: Novacâmbios** has an office in São Bento train station. (🕐 Open M-F 8:30am-7:30pm, Sa 10am-7pm, Su 10am-6pm.)

- **LAUNDROMATS: Lavandaría Oimpica** washes and dries clothes for €3/kg. (R. Miguel Bombarda, 100 �∅ ⓜAliados. Walk uphill from the plaza and turn left onto R. Ricardo Jorge. At the end of the road, turn right and take an immediate left. 🕐 Open M-F 9am-1pm and 2:15-7:30pm, Sa 9am-1pm.)

- **INTERNET: McDonald's** has free Wi-Fi. (Pr. Liberdade, 126 🕐 Open daily 8:30am-midnight.)

- **POST OFFICES: Correios** has a **Poste Restante.** (Pr. General Humberto Delgado ☎22 340 02 00 �∅ ⓜAliados; bus 904. From Pr. Liberdade, walk up right side of Av. Aliados 3 blocks. 🕐 Open M-F 8am-9pm, Sa 9am-6pm.)

Emergency

- **POLICE: Polícia Municipal** are located uphill from Pr. Liberdade. (R. Clube dos Fenianos, 11 ☎22 208 18 33 �∅ ⓜAliados; bus #904. From Pr. Liberdade, walk up left side of Av. Aliados 3 blocks.)

- **PHARMACY: Farmácia Santa Catarina** posts a 24hr. pharmacy schedule. (R. Santa Catarina, 141 ☎22 606 92 36 www.fscatarina.com �∅ ⓜBolhão; bus #302. Just up R. Santa Catarina from Pr. Batalha. 🕐 Open M-Sa 9am-8pm, Su 10am-7pm.)

- **HOSPITALS/MEDICAL SERVICES: Hospital Geral de Santo António.** (Lg. Profesor Abel Salazar ☎22 207 75 00 �∅ ⓜSão Bento. Or bus #18, 200, 201, or 207. From ⓜSão Bento, walk up R. Clérigos, then turn right onto R. Carmelitas, then straight along R. Carmo.)

Getting There

BY PLANE

Aeroporto Francisco de Sá Carneiro (OPO; ☎22 943 24 00) is 13km from downtown. The Metro E (violet line) goes to the airport and is the fastest and cheapest option. (Ⓢ €1.45 ☒ 25min.) Bus #601 runs from the airport to R. Carmo but makes multiple stops. (Ⓢ €1.85 ☒ 1hr.) Taxis are even faster but are predictably more expensive. (Ⓢ €20-25. ☒ 15-20min.) **Ryanair** (www.ryanair.com) and **easyJet** (www.easyjet.com) offer some of the most affordable flights into Porto.

BY TRAIN

Trains to Porto arrive at **Estação de Campanhã** (Pr. Almeida Garrett ☎80 820 82 08 www.cp.pt); some trains continue on to **Estação de São Bento** in the center of town. Otherwise, you can transfer to a free train that does so. Trains arrive at São Bento from Braga (Ⓢ €3 ☒ 1hr., 29 per day 4:30am-11:30pm). Trains arrive at Campanhã from Coimbra (*i* Requires transfer in Aveiro. Ⓢ €16 ☒ 2hr., 22 per day 5:45am-10:20pm) and Lisbon (Ⓢ €24-30 ☒ 3hr., 18 per day 6am-9:30pm).

BY BUS

There are several bus companies that operate in the downtown area. Try to find out ahead of time where your bus will stop, since there is no central bus terminal. **Internorte** (Pr. Galiza, 96 ☎22 605 24 20 www.internorte.pt) runs buses from Madrid (Ⓢ €41-46 ☒ 10hr., 1-3 per day). Book at least 3 days in advance. **Rede Expressos** (R. Alexandre Herculano, 366 ☎707 22 33 44 www.rede-expressos.pt) runs buses from: Braga (Ⓢ €6 ☒ 1hr., 20-25 per day 5am-11:30pm); Coimbra (Ⓢ €12.50 ☒ 1½hr., 11-13 per day 7:30am-3am); and Lisbon (Ⓢ €19 ☒ 3½hr., 20-24 per day 6:15am-12:15am). **Renex** (Campo Mártires da Pátria, 37 ☎22 200 33 95 www.renex.pt) runs express buses from Lagos (Ⓢ €30 ☒ 4½hr., 8 per day 5:30am-12:30am).

Getting Around

Though Porto is a large city, it's quite walkable, and many streets in the old part of town are pedestrian-only. The main issues with walking around Porto are the steep hills; many prefer to walk downhill and take public transportation uphill. The metro system is mostly for transport between Porto and its suburbs. The only line that is particularly useful for visitors is the D (yellow) line, which stops at **Avenida dos Aliados** and **São Bento** and covers most of the main sights in the city. With service to just about every corner of the city, the bus and tram system is massive and one of the best ways to get across town. You can pick up a detailed bus and Metro map from the tourist offices. If you take a taxi, make sure it has a meter; otherwise you may get ripped off.

braga   ☎253

Braga is the largest city in Minho, the region responsible for the beginnings of Portugal and its culture. Formerly known as Bracara Augusta, this city was an important part of the Roman Empire on the Iberian Peninsula, and it still has plenty of ancient ruins lying around to prove it. Previously a destination for the AARP crowd, who rolled in on buses to look at the dozens of churches littered throughout town, Braga is finally beginning to see budget travelers arrive in numbers. The downside to the timing of this development is that backpacker infrastructure (e.g., hostels and nightlife) is still in its crawling stages, but the upside is that you won't be assumed to be a tourist until proven otherwise, and the natural rhythm and flow of Portuguese life isn't covered in a touristy sheen. The city is small enough to be manageable but big enough to be interesting, allowing for excellent wandering opportunities as well as a great launching point for a visit to the nearby Parque Nacional da Peneda-Gerês.

ORIENTATION

Braga's center is mostly pedestrian and fairly easy to navigate, with the **Rua do Souto** cutting east-west through the city center with smaller streets leading off it. The pleasant **Jardim de Santa Bárbara** and the **Praça do Municipio** lie to the north, and the **Cathedral** lies to the south. At the east end of R. Souto is the **Largo Barão de São Martinho,** a massive plaza from which the store-lined **Avenida Central** leads east and the pedestrian thoroughfare **Avenida da Liberdade** leads south. The **tourist office** is at this intersection, and the **bus station** is a few blocks north of the oldest part of town. To get from the bus station to R. Souto, turn right onto **Avenida de General Norton de Matos,** then right again onto **Rua de Gabriel Pereira de Castro,** and then a slight left at **Rua do Carmo.** From the **train station** a few blocks west, take **Rua de Andrade Corvo** past the plaza and through the old gate.

ACCOMMODATIONS

Budget travel is a new development in Braga, so hostels are rare. Most worthwhile accommodations are located in the city center, although there are quite a few just outside along **Avenida João XXI.**

⬛ BRAGA POP HOSTEL
HOSTEL $

R. do Carmo, 61, 3rd fl.   ☎25 305 88 06

Hands-down the best budget accommodation in the city, this 20-bed hostel is cozy but still a load of fun. The "Pop" part of the name doesn't refer to music so much as the art along the walls, which you are completely welcome to add to. The small number of inhabitants means that the hostel is very social; there are plenty of great places to chat, from the hammock on the balcony overlooking the city to the common room with colorful furniture and a wide selection of movies. The snarky signs along the three flights of stairs leading to the hostel let you know that you will have fun here. You have no choice in the matter.

⚑ *From Lg. Barão de São Martinho, walk away from Av. Liberdade and under the flashing sign over the Irish pub. At the end of the path, turn right. The hostel is on the left.* ℹ *Breakfast and linens included.* Ⓢ *Dorms €16-19; doubles €45.* 🕐 *Reception 24hr.*

LIBERDADE GUESTHOUSE
GUESTHOUSE $$$

Av. da Liberdade, 696, 3rd fl.   ☎93 619 53 55

Located right on the main avenue in the city center, this guesthouse is a little pricey, but only because you are getting both privacy and a stellar location. The rooms are fairly large and the modern decor makes them seem a bit posh, so feel free to act like an elitist in your new home ("Why yes, the masses *are* revolting, darling"). And since the location is still on the pedestrian portion of the avenue, most days things are quiet and peaceful without sacrificing convenience.

⚑ *From Lg. Barão de São Martinho, take Av. Liberdade. The guesthouse is on the left.* ℹ *Breakfast included.* Ⓢ *Doubles €38-40; triples €55.* 🕐 *Reception 24hr.*

TRUTHOSTEL
HOTEL $

Av. da Liberdade, 738, 3rd fl.   ☎25 360 90 20   www.truthostel.com

A *pensão* in hostel's clothing, this place recently underwent rebranding in an attempt to "get hip to the kids' trends these days." But just like when your dad tries to verbalize OMG, you can see right through the façade: they slapped a new logo on the *pensão* and offer a few rooms where you can rent by the bed. But this doesn't mean that it isn't worth the stay. Right next to the tourist office in the center of town, this is Braga's easiest place to find. The rooms have balconies over the broad Av. Liberdade, which is a bonus, except during loud festivals. With breakfast included, shower water hot enough to boil pasta, and TVs with more channels than you can shake a remote at, Truthostel is quite the backpacker's steal—just be wary of the private baths, which are more ad-hoc cubicle structures in the corner of rooms than ritzy washrooms.

⚲ On Av. Liberdade, next to tourist office. 𝒊 English spoken. Elevator closed midnight-8am. Ⓢ Dorms €10; singles €25; doubles €36; triples €50. ⓒ Reception 24hr.

HOTEL SÃO NICOLAU
HOTEL $$

Av. João XXI, 732   ☎23 632 19 18 www.hotelsaonicolau.com.pt

Hotel São Nicolau provides simple, inexpensive rooms in a newer part of town just a short walk from the pedestrian center and even closer to the town's Roman ruins. Also, its name rhymes. *Let's Go* enjoys rhymes—especially in foreign languages.

⚲ Follow Av. Liberdade away from Lg. Barão de São Martinho 4 blocks, then turn left onto Av. João XXI. Ⓢ Singles €25-28; doubles €30-35; triples €35-40. ⓒ Reception 24hr.

POUSADA DA JUVENTUDE (HI)
HOSTEL $

R. de Santa Margarida, 6   ☎25 361 61 63 www.movijovem.pt

Braga's least expensive option for accommodations is this youth hostel, offering rooms for €10 a night—plus an extra €6 for a Hostelling International card if you don't already have one. The location is a bit out of the way, but only relative to other accommodations smack in the middle of the city. The private doubles (€25) are bigger than what you'll find in most *pensões* and though the dorm-style shared rooms are a bit cramped, the common room is spacious and has a pool table and sofas around a TV.

⚲ From Lg. Barão de São Martinho, follow Av. Central (with the park in the middle) to Lg. Senhora-a-Branca, then turn left onto R. Santa Margarida. 𝒊 Breakfast included. Kitchen, common room with TV, and pool table. Must have Hostelling International membership or jovem card for 15% discount. Ⓢ 8- to 10-bed dorms €11-12; doubles with ensuite bath €25-27. ⓒ Reception 8am-midnight.

SIGHTS

Braga's sights tend to fall into one of two camps: religious or Roman. Dozens of churches (with competing hourly bells) mean that the religiously-inclined will never get bored, while the city's long history as part of the Roman Empire means that there are more ruins than in a gingerbread village the day after Christmas.

SANTUÁRIO DO BOM JESUS DO MONTE
CHURCH

How many times have you put the words "thrilling" and "sanctuary" together in the same sentence? You can now, as you ride on a funicular from 1882 (the closest the Catholic Church has come to building a wooden roller-coaster) all the way to the top. Putting your hands in the air and screaming is completely optional (and perhaps even encouraged for the shameless). Though the current church was built in the 18th century, this hilltop site overlooking Braga has been a holy pilgrimage destination since the Middle Ages. The long, zigzagging stairway to the church at the top is also worth seeing, but it is quite a climb, so your best bet is to take the roller-coaster (read: funicular) to the top and the stairs back down.

⚲ Take bus #2 from Av. Liberdade (between R. 25 de Abril and R. Raio) to Bom Jesus. Ⓢ Free. Funicular €1.20, round-trip €2. ⓒ Open daily 8am-7pm.

CATEDRAL DE SANTA MARIA DE BRAGA
CHURCH, MUSEUM

R. do Cabido   ☎25 326 33 17 http://se-braga.pt

Braga's cathedral, *Sé de Braga*, founded in the late 11th century, is the oldest in Portugal, meaning it has enormous cultural and religious significance. Its twin spires are typical of the Portuguese style seen throughout Braga. The interior of the church is lovely, although the iron-gate-covered porticos out front give off a definite prison vibe. But just because it's from the 11th century doesn't mean that it hasn't been touched since then. Drop in on Sundays and listen as the sounds of mass fill the sparkling (and definitely not 11th-century) Baroque interior.

From Lg. Barão de São Martinho, follow R. Souto 5 blocks, then turn left. $ Cathedral free. Museum €3. ⏰ Cathedral open daily 8am-6:30pm. Museum open Tu-Su 9am-12:30pm and 2-6:30pm.

MUSEU DOS BISCAINHOS PALACE, MUSEUM

R. dos Biscainhos ☎25 320 46 50 www.ipmuseus.pt

Take a tour of this 16th-century palace right in the heart of Braga and witness how the rich and powerful lived back in the day. Some guides aren't the best at English, but they still give it the good ol' college try. Luckily, laminated sheets in each room give information on what in the world you are actually looking at. They even pull out some esoteric words that will baffle even the most expansive vocabularies (who knew you could "japan" a cabinet?). The Eastern and Moorish influence sets this museum apart, as does the garden outside with a massive, 200-year-old tree.

Facing the cathedral, take the road behind it to the left. Turn right onto R. Biscainhos. $ €2. ⏰ Open Tu-Su 10am-12:15pm and 2-5:30pm.

FONTE DO ÍDOLO ROMAN RUINS

R. do Raio ☎25 321 80 11

The slightly misleading name makes it sound like visitors will be approaching a mystical fountain in the middle of the city, where they can frolic in the water and achieve ever-lasting life. Not so fast. In reality, it's a first-century Roman ruin of a sacred fountain that is nicely displayed in a new museum. So it's a "no" on the frolicking, but that doesn't mean it isn't worth seeing. The English version of the accompanying video has great neologisms and combinations of words, like "musealized." If you can get past the weird language, the video does show some pretty impressive reconstructions of what the fountain might have looked like, and this sight is worth a half-hour visit.

Follow Av. Liberdade away from Lg. Barão de São Martinho and turn right onto R. Raio. $ Free. ⏰ Open Tu-F 9am-12:30pm and 2-5:30pm, Sa-Su 11am-5pm.

MUSEU REGIONAL DE ARQUEOLOGIA MUSEUM

R. dos Bombeiros Voluntários ☎25 327 37 06 http://mdds.imc-ip.pt

The Archaeological Museum's austere building displays artifacts from Bracara Augusta, the Roman settlement that once stood where Braga's center is today. The exhibits are fairly large, but are not exactly the most interesting, as they mostly boil down to a bunch of old stones (with the unique exception of the house recreated in the basement). They can give you information on where to see other *in situ* Roman remains throughout the city, but generally the place is pretty dry for anyone but the classical archaeologist.

Follow R. Souto away from Lg. Barão de São Martinho through the gate, turn left onto R. Matadouro, then turn right onto R. Bombeiros Voluntários. $ €3, over 65 €1.50, under 14 free. All free Su 10am-2pm. ⏰ Open Tu-Su 10am-5pm.

GREAT OUTDOORS

PENEDA-GERÊS NATIONAL PARK PARK

www.geira.pt

Portugal's only national park, Gerês is 271 sq. mi. of pure beauty. Filled with varying landscapes, the park contains massive rocky hills, lush green forests, and stunning **waterfalls.** Sadly, funding is not very easy to come by, so the maps are bad, trails are poorly marked, and even most Portuguese citizens don't know about all the wonderful treasures that the park holds. Unfortunately, the park doesn't receive nearly as many visitors as it should, but the silver lining to this dark cloud is that you will run into almost no one: it is just you and nature.

Because of this, it is recommended that travelers take a tour or visit the park with someone else who knows the area. Otherwise, the park is massive and finding specific locations is near impossible, so many visitors unnecessarily go home in frustration. The flora is great, but the fauna is even better, with **wild horses,** cattle, and goats roaming around everywhere, completely unfazed by humans. Certain sites, such as the **Blue Lagoon,** are beautiful to the point of surreal, with water that is crystal clear.

Oporto Adventure Tours (www.oportoadventuretours.com) is the first and only group to give tours of the park. The typical tour is an all-day affair that includes transportation from Braga (or Porto) to and from the park, visits to (and swimming beneath) multiple waterfalls, horseback riding in a local village, lunch, hiking, and a visit to the Blue Lagoon all for €75. More adventurous options, including canyoning (a mix of rappelling and jumping down waterfalls) are also available.

The park is about 1hr. north of Braga and abuts the Spanish border to the north. Empresa Hoteleira do Gerês (☎25 361 58 96 www.ehgeres.com) runs buses from Braga to Gerês M-F 10 per day 7:10am-7:10pm, Sa 6 per day 7:55am-7:10pm, Su 4 per day 9:15am-7:10pm; last bus back to Braga leaves M-F 6pm, Sa-Su 5pm. $ Adventure tour €75. ⏰ Adventure tour May-Oct 8am-8pm.

FOOD

There are dozens of cafes and pastry shops that serve inexpensive meals scattered throughout the pedestrian part of town along **Rua do Souto** and **Rua de Dom Afonso Henriques.** The **Campo das Hortas,** just beyond the gate at the far west end of R. Souto, is lined with restaurants, and the **Parque do Conde de Agrolongo** (Head away from Lg. Barão de São Martinho on R. Souto 3 blocks, then turn right onto R. Cidade do Porto 1 block past the garden, then left) has some reasonably priced options as well.

BRAC

RESTAURANT $$$

Campo das Carvalheiras ☎25 361 02 25 www.brac.com.pt

Sometimes even backpackers need to splurge, and this is the place you should do it. Whether it is the appetizers, the white sangria, the main courses, or the desserts, everything that hits your lips has a chance of being the best you have ever tasted. The food is pricey, but is of such high caliber that it is still a great value for the cost. Trying to decide what to order is like picking out the perfect Rolls-Royce: you're splitting hairs. The dining area actually lives up to the adjective "chic," with its comfortable white chairs and sharp, modern angles on everything else. The strange artwork on the ceiling that includes larger than life nude/robot-looking women is the work of a photographer based down the street.

Follow R. Souto away from Lg. Barão de São Martinho all the way through the arch, then turn left to get to Campo das Carvalherias. $ Entrees €13-20. ⏰ Open M-Sa 5:30pm-1am.

ADEGA MALHOA

TRADITIONAL $

R. de Dom Paio Mendes, 19 ☎96 400 59 71

This colorful, dimly lit den serves an €8 menu that includes two courses, bread, wine, and coffee. The decor might be referred to as "everything and the kitchen sink," since postcards, football scarves, kids' drawings, and just about anything else cover the walls. House specialties are traditional regional dishes like *rojões à moda do Minho* (spiced and marinated cubes of pork, €6) and various *bacalhau* (cod) dishes. A few cents short when it comes time to pay? Grab one of the hundreds of pennies placed on the stones that make up the walls.

Follow R. Souto 6 blocks away from Lg. Barão de São Martinho. Turn left in front of the Catedral, then turn right onto R. Dom Paio Mendes. $ Entrees €6-9. Daily menu €8. ⏰ Open Tu-Su noon-3pm and 6-10pm.

CONFEITARIA CHRISTINA CAFE $

Pr. do Conde de Agrolongo, 71 ☎25 327 78 49 www.confeitariachristina.com

After traveling for a while in Portugal, just hearing the word "salad" can make your mouth water. If only you could get your hands on some fresh, cheap produce without scrounging through the local market. Now you can. Confeitaria Christina offers quite tasty sandwiches and pastries, but the real deal is the quality salads (€4) with fresh fruit, which is not an easy thing to come by in these parts. A long list of infusion teas and hot chocolates (€2) makes Confeitaria Christina a nice place to relax for a while, even if you aren't interested in a meal.

➜ From Lg. Barão de São Martinho, walk away from Av. Liberdade and under the flashing sign over the Irish pub. At the end of the path, turn left, followed by a right onto the plaza. The cafe is on the left. $ Sandwiches €2. Salads €4. ⏰ Open daily 7am-8pm.

LUSITANA CAFE, SWEETS $$

R. de Cidade do Porto, 54 ☎25 326 26 31 www.lusitanapastelaria.blogspot.com

Not to be confused with the *Lusitania*, the British ocean-liner sunk by U-boats (because it's easy to get them mixed up, you know?), Lusitana is one of many *pastelarias* that line the streets of the old city. It is located just around the corner from the beautiful Jardim de Santa Bárbara and has outdoor seating on a wide, pedestrian street that's perfect for people-watching. Those who keep to themselves can sit inside, which is perfect for pastry-watching. Lusitana serves simple but tasty meals and make their bread and pastries on site.

➜ Follow R. Souto 3 blocks away from Lg. Barão de São Martinho, then turn right onto R. Cidade do Porto. $ Pastries €1-3.50. Entrees €2.50-6.50. ⏰ Open daily 8am-8pm.

BACALHAU PORTUGUESE $$

Campo das Hortas, 18 ☎25 326 90 30

In all honesty, this restaurant does not have the highest quality food that you will ever taste. What it does have, however, is a high-value menu (bread, soup, wine, main course, dessert, and coffee for €10) that is a must for the hungry traveler. For those looking to save but who don't want to cook their own food, try eating around 4pm and let this feast be your daily meal (not doctor-recommended). The dining area is cozy and the plates are traditional. The house wine is memorable, but not for the right reasons.

➜ Facing the cathedral, turn left onto R. Dom Paio Mendes and keep walking. The restaurant is on the left. $ Entrees €7-10. Daily menu €10. ⏰ Open M-Sa 11am-11pm.

NIGHTLIFE

If you are the party-hardy type looking to go boozin' and floozin' across the land, we will level with you: Braga is not the place for you. But nightlife is up and coming, and if you like more relaxed bars where you can chat with friends long into the night, here are some suggestions.

👍 **COLINATRUM CAFÉ** CAFE, BAR $$

R. Damião de Góis, 11 ☎25 321 56 30 www.colinatrum.com

With some top-notch views of the city, this structure sits atop a hill and has all-glass walls. Cafe by day and bar by night, the mood switches from relaxed to gregarious as the day wears on. On weekend nights, the entire place is packed with students and locals having a beer and chatting over the many small tables that fill the cafe. Try to get there early if you want to grab prime real estate (i.e., a seat outside with an impeccable view of the city).

➜ Facing the cathedral, turn left and then another left 4 blocks later. Follow straight for a few hundred meters; the bar is on the right. $ Beer €1-2. ⏰ Open daily 8am-2am.

ESTÚDIO 22 CAFE, BAR $$

R. Dom Paio Mendes, 22 ☎25 305 37 51

This bar is a cafe that serves tapas next to the Sé during the day, but it becomes a hotspot for students and young adults at night. It might be right next to the cathedral, but at night it plays the devil's music. Weekends feature indie and rock bands, among other styles, although those nights typically include a €3 minimum consumption. The bar is small, making it perfect for intimate performances, and much of the focus is directed toward the stage.

Walk directly away from the cathedral. The bar is on the left. [$] Beer €2. Weekend nights have €3 min. ⏰ Open daily 8am-1am.

TABERNA SUBURA BAR $

R. Dom Frei Caetano Brandão, 101 ☎96 425 41 44

Although the name hearkens back to the time of the Roman Empire (stylized TABERNA SVBVRA), the theme comes to an abrupt halt there. However, you are welcome to pick up where they left off and come in your finest of togas. This is a great local joint where beer is cheap and conversation is free. On occasion, local musicians come and play regional favorites, and the bar is packed with *bracarense* singing along to every word. The door is frequently closed—which is odd in Portugal—to keep out the cold of the Braga night, but don't be afraid to open it up and join in on the party.

Walk directly away from the front of the cathedral and turn right at the first real street. The bar is on the right. [$] Beer €1.40. ⏰ Open daily 2pm-midnight.

ESSENTIALS

Practicalities

- **TOURIST OFFICE: Posto de Turismo.** (Av. Liberdade, 1 ☎25 326 25 50 www.cm-braga.pt At intersection of R. Souto, Av. Liberdade, and Av. Central. ⏰ Open M-F 9am-1pm and 2-6:30pm, Sa-Su 10am-12:30pm and 2-4:30pm.)
- **LAUNDROMAT: Lavandería Bracarense.** (R. São Marcos, 117 ☎25 311 35 54 On the right side of Lg. Barão de São Martinho if you are facing down Av. Liberdade. [$] 4kg wash and dry €12. ⏰ Open M-F 8am-7:30pm, Sa 8am-2pm.)
- **POST OFFICE: Correios.** (Tv. Praça da Justiça ☎25 320 83 30 From Lg. Barão de São Martinho, take the walking path away from the square. Turn right and then left at the church. ⏰ Open M-F 9am-12:30pm and 2-5:30pm, Sa 9am-1pm.)

Emergency

- **POLICE: Polícia Municipal.** (Lg. Rossio da Sé, 12 ☎25 360 97 40 From Lg. Barão de São Martinho, follow R. Souto 5 blocks, then turn left.)
- **MEDICAL SERVICES:** The **Centro de Saúde de Braga I** offers healthcare services. (Lg. Mercado do Carandá ☎25 320 15 00. On the right side of Lg. Barão de São Martinho if you are facing down Av. Liberdade.)

Getting There

Rede Nacional de Expressos (☎25 320 94 01 www.rede-expressos.pt) runs buses from: Coimbra ([$] €14 ⏰ 3hr.; M-Sa 10 per day 8:30am-3am, Su 8 per day 10am-3am); Lisbon ([$] €20 ⏰ 5hr., 13 per day 7am-12:15am); and Porto ([$] €6 ⏰ 1hr.; 20-33 per day M 8:45am-4:30am, Tu-Sa 10am-4:30am, Su 10:30am-4:30am). **CP** (www.cp.pt) runs trains from Porto ([$] €3 ⏰ 45min., 30 per day 6:15am-12:15am). **Alsa** runs buses from Santiago de Compostela ([$] €30 ⏰ 3hr., daily at 11am) via Pontevedra and Vigo.

Getting Around

Since the city isn't large and most of it is accessible only to pedestrians, the best way to get around the old part of Braga is to **walk.** There is a **bus** system (www.tub.pt) and a 24hr. **taxi** service, **Braga Táxis** (☎25 325 32 53).

coimbra   ☎239

Coimbra is best known for its hilltop university and its famous **fado,** traditional folksongs. The **University of Coimbra** has been around for over 700 years, and Coimbra's mournful *fado*, whose distinct northern brand is usually sung by men, sounds something like a musical embodiment of death, but in the most beautiful way possible. Tradition is a large part of Coimbra's identity, as the ancient university plays an important role in the city; students wear capes for special events and burn ribbons at others, and all these traditions are well-known and revered city-wide. The vibe of the city can vary significantly as you move about the hill, but Coimbra is to a certain extent the epitome of a typical Portuguese city. The city is large, but except for those who come to see the university there are few tourists, so the Portuguese lifestyle can be observed at a more natural pace. Unlike many cities, which are at their liveliest in the summer months, Coimbra is at its most vibrant during the school year, when students run wild.

ORIENTATION

Coimbra's historic upper city, **Alta,** once reserved for students by royal decree, has steep streets and stairways, with the university at the top; the lower part of town forms a crescent around the upper city's hill. Maps don't do the city justice because of the drastic changes in altitude, but walking uphill to the university will help you get your bearings. In **Baixa,** the lower part of Coimbra, the **Coimbra-A train station** is right on the river. From the station's main entrance, head left one block to reach the wide **Avenida de Fernão de Magalhães,** which runs parallel to the river; take the same route from the **bus terminal.** To the right, Av. de Fernão de Magalhães becomes the narrower R. da Sota and goes to **Largo da Portagem,** a big plaza where a **tourist office** is located. Continuing along the river is a park with some restaurants and accommodations across the street. In the other direction, the pedestrian **Rua de Ferreira Borges** goes from Lg. da Portagem straight to the **Praça 8 de Maio,** with two sets of stairs along the way on the left side that lead down to **Praça do Comércio.** This street and these two plazas are the heart of Baixa, with narrower capillaries leading off them. Continuing to the right after Pr. 8 de Maio will take you around the old city's hill to the huge, tree-lined **Avenida Sá da Bandeira,** which ends at the **Praça da República.**

ACCOMMODATIONS

Most accommodations are packed along the **Avenida de Fernão de Magalhães** and the streets just off it around the **Coimbra-A train station,** while the pair of hostels is a 30min. walk (largely uphill), 10min. bus ride, or €4 cab ride away from the station.

🏠 GRANDE HOSTEL DE COIMBRA   HOSTEL $
R. Antero de Quental, 196   ☎23 910 82 12 www.grandehostelcoimbra.com

A massive house set aside in a quieter area of Coimbra, Grande Hostel really does live up to its name. This three-floor hostel has multiple patios, balconies, and common spaces, so you won't feel like cattle simply shuffling to and from your dorm room. Outside, there is a mysterious painting of a man with a panda head swinging away, but fear not, the rest of the hostel does not keep up with this level of quirkiness. We like quirky, but we know where to draw the line.

Rooms are good-sized and many have breathtaking views of the city, aided by the hostel's high vantage point.

🏃 *From Pr. 8 de Maio, head to the left of the church and follow the main road toward Pr. República. Just before the Pr. República, make a sharp left up R. Tenente Valadim, then turn left at the end of that street onto R. Antero de Quental. The hostel is on the right.* *i* *Breakfast, linens, and towels included.* Ⓢ *Dorms €18; privates €40. Cash only.* 🕐 *Reception 24hr.*

RESIDÊNCIAL VITÓRIA   HOTEL $$

R. da Sota, 11   ☎23 982 40 49

Vitória has inexpensive rooms on a busy, narrow street just two blocks from the train station and the river. Rooms are simple but come with A/C and TV. The place is rather shiny and up-to-date for a *pensão*, and rooms have their own private bathroom, but they need to impress you: it's located next to about 30 other *pensões*, all of which are vying for your hard-earned cash.

🏃 *From Coimbra-A train station, head 1 block away from the river to Av. Fernão de Magalhães, then turn right to reach R. Sota.* *i* *Breakfast, linens, and towels included.* Ⓢ *Singles €30-40; doubles €50-60; triples €60.* 🕐 *Reception 24hr.*

PENSÃO SANTA CRUZ   HOTEL $

Pr. 8 de Maio, 21, 3rd fl.   ☎23 982 61 97 www.pensaosantacruz.com

This *pensão* is a bit worn down, so if you're looking for someplace shiny and new, keep lookin'. That said, the views of the Igreja de Santa Cruz directly across the plaza and the low prices make the small rooms and run-down furniture all worth it. From this *pensão*, you have easy access to most of the sights and areas of Coimbra you want to visit. The plaza it faces is right in the heart of things, with occasional performances and markets taking place right outside the front door.

🏃 *On Pr. 8 de Maio, directly across from Igreja de Santa Cruz.* Ⓢ *Singles €18-22, with bath €25-35; doubles €23-27/30-40; triples €28-32/35-45.* 🕐 *Reception 24hr.*

POUSADA DE JUVENTUDE (HI)   HOSTEL $

R. do Doutor Henriques Seco, 14   ☎23 982 29 55 www.pousadasjuventude.pt

This hostel, which boasts the only single room in the Portuguese youth hostel system (take out your HI card and say five Hail Marys), has rooms of four and six beds, with floors divided by sex. Although it's not terribly different from its HI counterparts, it's in a huge old home on a shady, residential street uphill from the Pr. República and has a cozy common space downstairs. It is also close to the supermarket—surprisingly an elusive commodity for Portugal's fourth-largest city.

🏃 *From Pr. República, follow R. Lourenço de Almeida Azevedo uphill along the left side of Jardim da Sereia for 4 blocks, then turn right onto R. Doutor Henriques Seco. Buses #6, 7, and 29 run to R. Augusto Rocha; from bus stop, head down R. Augusta Rocha and turn left at the fork onto R. Doutor Henriques Seco.* *i* *Breakfast and sheets included. Towels not included. Kitchen available.* Ⓢ *Dorms €11-13; singles with bath €18; doubles €26-28, with bath €28-30. Must have HI card (€6) or Jovem card (€8).* 🕐 *Reception 8am-midnight.*

SIGHTS

Coimbra is an ancient city, so it is not lacking in sights. However, the university stands out above all others as the must-see attraction, partly because multiple museums can also be found in and around campus.

▩ **UNIVERSIDADE DE COIMBRA**   UNIVERSITY

Lg. da Porta Férrea   ☎23 985 98 84 www.uc.pt

The walk to the university from Baixa takes you through the ancient part of town, up streets that were clearly meant to be conquered via mule. The university, for centuries the country's only one and still among its most prestigious, is at the very top of the hill. The ▩**Biblioteca Joanina,** a Baroque library (Portugal's oldest) whose building dates from the start of the 18th century but whose collection goes back centuries earlier, seems like it came out of a book itself, trimmed with gold and filled with three stories of ancient tomes. Listen for the squeaks of the **bats** that live here and protect the collection by feasting on evil papyrophagi (paper-eating insects). Beneath the library is the **academic prison,** which was used to punish students found guilty by the school's own special courts and very well might have been inspiration for "The Chokey" in *Matilda.* Next door, the **Capela de São Miguel** is a Manueline masterpiece, with incredible decorations and a 3000-tube organ from 1737 that is played often, even when visitors are coming through. The **Sala dos Capelos** (Room of Cowls, a reference to the academics' garb), also known as the Sala dos Actos (Room of Acts), is one of the university's most important rooms, in which doctoral candidates take their examinations and later (fingers crossed) receive their caps and velvet cowls. This room was once the Royal Palace's **throne room,** where the first kings of Portugal held court from 1143-1383.

*⇟ Buses #1A, 34, 60, 103, or market elevator from Mercado de Dom Pedro V. **i** Tickets can be purchased in the Biblioteca Dom João V, on Pr. Porta Férrea. $ Combined admission (includes visit to Biblioteca Joanina, Sala dos Capelos, Capela de São Miguel, and Academic Prison) €7, students and seniors €5.50, under 12 free. 🕐 Open Apr-Oct daily 9am-7:30pm; Nov-Mar M-F 9:30am-5:30pm, Sa-Su 10:30am-4:30pm.*

SÉ VELHA DE COIMBRA — CHURCH

Lg. da Sé Velha ☎23 982 52 73

This 12th-century Romanesque fortress-cathedral (built on the remains of a 10th-century basilica whose foundation stone is inside) looms over Coimbra from the hillside below the university. In typical Romanesque fashion, it is as intimidating as it is beautiful. A curtain is drawn in front of the doors to keep the light and noise from the outside world at bay, lest the place get brightened up a bit. Inside to the left, the walls are covered with gorgeous 16th-century *mudéjar* tiles from Sevilla, and tombs of bishops and royalty line the walls. The fairly austere interior is punctuated by the bright colors of the stained-glass windows, which jump out from the dark walls.

⇟ From R. de Ferreira Borges, head up past Arco de Almedina and up the be-staired R. Quebra-Costas. $ Free. Cloister and gardens €2. 🕐 Open for tourist visits M-Sa 10am-6:30pm. Open daily 10am-7pm.

IGREJA DE SANTA CRUZ — CHURCH

Pr. 8 de Maio ☎23 982 29 41

This church, begun in 1131 but with a tremendous façade from the 16th century, looms large over the Pr. 8 de Maio as Baixa's magnificent centerpiece. The detached and more playful triumphal arch was added a few centuries later. The vaulted arches and striking organ make the interior just as memorable as the façade. The *azulejo*-covered sacristy contains the tombs of Portugal's first kings, Alfonso Henriques and Sancho I.

⇟ On Pr. 8 de Maio; from tourist office at Lg. da Portagem, follow R. de Ferreira Borges straight to Pr. 8 de Maio. $ Free. Cloisters and sacristy €2.50, students and seniors €1.50. 🕐 Church open M-F 7:30am-6:30pm, Sa 7:30am-12:30pm and 2-7:30pm, Su 8:30am-12:30pm and 4-7:30pm. Cloisters open M-Sa 9am-noon and 2-5:30pm, Su 4-6pm. Sacristy open M-Sa 9am-noon and 2-5pm, Su 4-5pm.

MUSEU NACIONAL DE MACHADO DE CASTRO — MUSEUM

Lg. do Doutor José Rodrigues ☎23 982 37 27 www.mnmachadodecastro.imc-ip.pt

This museum has an extensive collection of fine art featuring paintings, jewelry, ceramics, and more. But the real fun is in the ancient Roman cryptoporticus, which was built as a foundation for the Roman forum. The base still stands, almost completely intact, and you can aimlessly wander in its maze (well, you can't technically, but it's fun regardless). Walking through the cool stone halls brings the ancient history to life and, in the meantime, sheds some light on Coimbra's illustrious past.

⇟ Buses #1A, 34, 60, 103, or market elevator from Mercado de Dom Pedro V. $ €5, students and seniors €3.50. 🕐 Open Apr-Sept Tu-Su 10am-6pm; Oct-Mar Tu-Su 10am-12:30pm and 2-6pm.

ARCO DE ALMEDINA
ARCH

This arch, built later than the two turrets that constitute its supports on either side, is part of the original town wall from when Coimbra was ruled by the Moors. The tower now serves as the municipal archives, although it has had many uses over the centuries. The street leading away from the arch translates to "Backbreaker Street," which is sadistically fitting. This was the main point of access going to and from the city. As anyone who looks at it can imagine, there were some serious bottleneck issues.

✦ *Head up R. de Ferreira Borges from Lg. da Portagem, then turn right up narrow street and stairs.*

MUSEU DA CIÊNCIA
MUSEUM

Lg. Marquês de Pombal ☎23 985 43 50 www.museudaciencia.org

Sitting in what used to be the chemistry lab, which can make finding the museum a confusing ordeal, the science museum offers a wide range of exhibits, many of which are hands-on. The museum addresses a great deal of scientific concepts in a way that is fairly easy to understand and presents them in an intriguing multi-media fashion. If science isn't your thing, or your brain begins to hurt, head on over to the cafe and grab a coffee.

✦ *From Pr. da República, turn left while facing McDonald's and then turn left again when you see Associação Académica. Follow this road up to the campus and you will see the museum on your left.* ⓢ *€4, students and seniors €2.* ☐ *Open Tu-Su 10am-6pm.*

coimbra

FOOD

The side streets off Pr. do Comércio and Pr. 8 de Maio tend to be good locations for inexpensive meals, as is the area around Pr. da República on the other side of the hill. Local specialties include gamey but tasty *cabrito* (kid goat) and the not-terribly-appetizing-looking *arroz de lampreia* (rice with lamprey eel). The **Mercado de Dom Pedro V** on R. Olímpio Nicolau Rui Fernandes (🕐 Open M-Sa 8am-1pm) is a great place for fresh bread, produce, and just about everything else, with the fish in a separate room so the whole place doesn't stink by the afternoon; but understand that this is a market with individual vendors, rather than a large convenience store. The supermarket, **Pingo Doce,** is at R. de João de Ruão, 14, a 3min. walk up R. da Sofia from Pr. 8 de Maio. (☎23 985 29 30 🕐 Open daily 8:30am-9pm.)

👍 **ADEGA PAÇO DO CONDE** GRILL $

Tv. Paço do Conde, 1 ☎23 982 56 05

This restaurant, which has indoor and outdoor (well, tin-roof-covered) seating, is loved by locals and budget travelers alike. The white, blue, and red arch over the doorway lets you know that you are stepping into a serious chow-zone. You can get huge portions for €5-6—the shareable *costeleta de porco* (pork ribs/chops) is a great deal for €5.50 and comes with tons of fries, rice, and salad, although it is difficult to go wrong here since almost everything is so reasonably priced.

➤ From Pr. Comércio, take R. Adelino Veigo (directly across from Igreja de São Tiago) 2 blocks, then turn right. $ Entrees €5-10. 🕐 Open M-Sa noon-3pm and 7-10pm, Su noon-3pm.

👍 **FUGAS** BAR, ITALIAN $

R. António Vasconcelos, 17 ☎23 982 71 95

With signs for bathrooms and departures that look like they were lifted from the local airport and coffee table books about international destinations at each place (sorry, none about coffee tables), Fugas puts the emphasis on the international. Its drink selection follows suit, with Danish beer and Swedish cider on tap. But when it comes to food, almost everything is Italian or Portuguese, and everything is delicious. Don't even bother looking at the menu—just order the daily special (€5.50), which will have generous portions and comes with a drink of your choice.

➤ From Pr. República, take the road to the left of McDonald's and then turn left at the end of the road. Walk for 5min. and you will see Fugas on the right. $ Pratos do dia €5.50. 🕐 Open daily 11am-2am.

CAFÉ SANTA CRUZ CAFE $$

Pr. 8 de Maio ☎23 983 36 17 www.cafesantacruz.com

Coimbra's most famous cafe sits on the Pr. 8 de Maio next to Igreja de Santa Cruz and is itself housed in a former church (the apse is at the back). The coffee is fine, but the atmosphere is what people actually come for. The terrace has pleasant views of the plaza, though the arches that give the cafe away as an old church are much more memorable. There's free *fado* on some summer weekends as well.

➤ On Pr. 8 de Maio just to right of Igreja de Santa Cruz. $ Coffee €0.60-2.50. Pastries €1-2. 🕐 Open daily 7am-2am.

CALADO AND CALADO PORTUGUESE $$$

R. da Sota, 14 ☎24 982 73 48

Though by no means small, this place tends to fill up, so you might have to wait a little while for your food, but it's well worth the wait. The exterior makes you remember the Alamo, but the food inside is anything but Texan. The *arroz de pato* (rice with duck, €10) is delicious and easily feeds two, which is a fairly common feature of the menu here.

➤ On R. Sota between Lg. Portagem and Av. Fernão de Magalhães. $ Entrees €7-16. 🕐 Open daily noon-3pm and 7-11pm.

PORTA ROMANA RESTAURANT $$

R. Martins de Carvalho, 8 ☎23 982 84 58

Tucked in a narrow street just off the Pr. 8 de Maio, Porta Romana serves up inexpensive, large meals. Heaping plates of pasta run around €6.50, and the daily specials are €5.50-8. While many restaurants have outdoor seating in Praça 8 de Maio, Porta Romana is exclusively indoors, so you can enjoy one of the wines from their extensive collection in peace and away from the madding crowd.

⇞ Just up the street to the right of Café Santa Cruz, off Pr. 8 de Maio. [$] Entrees €6.50-15. ⏰ Open July-Aug daily noon-3:30pm and 7pm-midnight; Sept-June Tu-Su noon-3:30pm and 7pm-midnight.

FEBRÉS INDIAN, PORTUGUESE $$

R. do Corvo, 8 ☎23 982 31 24

Believe it or not, the tandoori side of the menu is not a part of the local *conimbricense* (Coimbran) cuisine, but this cafe has something to offer everyone. You can take either the Indian or the Portuguese menu, and while the Portuguese meals are quite reasonable (€5-6), the Indian menu features kebabs that are downright dirt-cheap (€4, comes with fries).

⇞ Just off far left corner of Pr. 8 de Maio with your back to Igreja de Santa Cruz. [$] Entrees €7.50-12.50. Pratos do dia €5.50. Kebabs €3-5. ⏰ Open daily 1-3pm and 8pm-midnight.

MONDEGO IRISH PUB SANDWICHES, LIVE MUSIC, PUB $

Parque Verde do Mondego ☎23 983 70 92 www.mondegoirishpub.pt

This bar has outdoor seating right next to the Río Mondego, with beautiful sunset views in the evenings. While it doesn't have much in the way of a full dinner, it has a good and reasonably priced snack menu, which is full of sandwiches that aren't really Irish but are still tasty. The food is much better than the significantly more expensive Italian place along the river closer to the center of town. Both the indoor and outdoor seating areas are quite large, and sitting on the river with your sandwich and a Guinness is recommended. Live music late at night makes this a happening nightlife spot as well.

⇞ Enter park across from Lg. Portagem and follow river about 500 yards. [$] Sandwiches €2.90-5.80. ⏰ Open M-Th noon-3am, F-Sa noon-4am, Su noon-3am.

NIGHTLIFE

Coimbra's nightlife is at its best from October through June, when the students are around to keep the party going. The bars below the university around Pr. da República tend to be good spots earlier in the night, with the bars and clubs on the hill on the other side of R. Sá da Bandeira becoming more popular, as well as the new side-by-side bars along the Río Mondego. However, there is no one hotspot in town for nightlife, so aimlessly wandering until you hear loud music is always a viable option. Many choose to take a train to Figueira da Foz, an hour away on the coast, and party all night before heading back on the first train in the morning.

A CAPELLA FADO

R. do Corpo de Deus ☎91 811 33 07 www.acapella.com.pt

Built as a 14th-century church, this small chapel now houses a smoky *fado* club with professional *fadistas* and loads of tourists. Set aside from all the other nightlife and all the other everything, for that matter, this club is typically customers' only destination for the night. The acoustics are phenomenal, and anyone who has ever visited a stone church during a service and had to sneeze will understand why. There is also a cafe with outdoor seating on the cobblestone plaza in case "smoky *fado* joint" begins to feel more like "brick oven."

⇞ From Pr. 8 de Maio, head toward Lg. Portagem along R. Visconde da Luz, then take the 1st sharp left up R. Corpo de Deus; it's on the left after a small plaza. [$] Cover €10; includes 1 drink. ⏰ Open daily 9pm-2am. Performances typically start at 10pm.

DILIGÊNCIA BAR FADO

R. Nova, 30 ☎23 982 76 67 www.diligenciabar.com

This is a pretty touristy joint, in case the signs in English out front don't tip you off, but it's easy to get to and has a nice, traditional feel inside. Set in a secluded alley, the bar is small and has dim lighting, making it as intimate as *fado* should be. Much of the *fado* performed here is sung by caped students (part of their traditional university uniform, not super-hero related) or by nightly regulars.

 # From Pr. 8 de Maio, head along R. Direita (far-right corner with your back to Igreja de Santa Cruz) 1 block, then turn right onto R. Nova. $ Cover €5. Entrees €9.50-13.50. Sangria €10 per jug. Credit card min. €5 ⏰ Open daily 7pm-2am.

ROCK CAFE BAR, MUSIC

Parque Verde do Mondego ☎23 983 70 92 www.rockcafecoimbra.pt

As is to be expected, electric guitars adorn the walls. A little more surprising, however, is the upside-down drum set hanging from the ceiling. Rock out on the still banks of the Mondego, where the side-by-side bars make the night echo with live music. Rock Cafe is known for having some of the best music and drinks in Coimbra, but other similar establishments are essentially interchangeable. The space is huge for a bar in Coimbra, and there is an extra tap outside just in case you don't want to go through the trouble of wandering back inside for your next beer.

 # Cross into park from Lg. Portagem, then left along the river. $ Food €2-7. ⏰ Open M-Th noon-3am, F-Sa noon-4am, Su noon-3am.

COIMBRA COCKTAIL BAR BAR

Av. Sá da Bandeira, 7 ☎91 043 64 71 www.coimbracocktailbar.com

Don't let the name fool you—this tavern-esque upscale bar seems to be more about beer than cocktails. Flat screen TVs show the latest games, and one is even played on an exterior window so you can watch from the street. This bar isn't so much about dancing as it is about having a beer with friends.

 # From Pr. República, head toward Baixa on Av. Sá da Bandeira. The bar is on the right. $ Beer €1.70. ⏰ Open daily 8pm-4am.

SEV7N BAR

R. do Doutor António de Vasconcelos, 23 ☎91 261 30 73

The racing-arrows design that can be found all over this bar is quite fitting, because you will be rushing through cheap shots to get as much bang for your buck as possible. A long list of shots is posted on the wall, but beware: the best deals are all about buying in bulk, so make sure to bring a few friends along. Sev7n is mostly a hang-out spot for students who grab the deals and then just roll right back down to Baixa.

 # Head up R. Manutenção Militar from Av. Sá da Bandeira (about midway between Pr. 8 de Maio and Pr. República; on the left heading up from Pr. 8 de Maio, on the right heading down from Pr. República), then take a sharp right onto R. Doutor António de Vasconcelos. i 5 shots €5, 12 shots €10. $ Beer €1. Mixed drinks €1.50-2.50. ⏰ Open M-Sa 11pm-4am.

CAFÉ TROPICAL BAR

Pr. da República, 35

Rock legends such as Jim Morrison adorn the walls of this two-story bar-cafe hybrid. A great place to sit down and have a few drinks with friends, this bar plays loud rock music but is still intended for chilling out rather than raging all night. You can also sit outside and watch the cars race by to see who can crash in a fiery explosion first as they whiz around the plaza. Some of the staff have an uncanny ability to open beer bottles on their necks.

 # Pr. República on the side opposite the post office. $ Beer €1.30. ⏰ Open daily 8am-2am.

FESTIVALS

JAZZ AO CENTRO JAZZ

www.jazzaocentro.pt

Concerts, short films, and art exhibits fill Coimbra from the end of May to the beginning of June as Jazz ao Centro draws artists and fans from around the globe. The events take place in different venues throughout the city, and there is a focus on the international, with artists representing many different styles of jazz. All tickets are cheap or free, so the performances are something the whole community can enjoy.

$ Free to €8. ⏰ Late May to early June.

SHOPPING

The tiny streets around Pr. do Comércio and Pr. 8 de Maio are full of clothing and shoe stores; there are more stores along Av. Sá da Bandeira as well. Shops labeled **Tecidos de Coimbra** sell a myriad of goods and tend to have bottom-of-the-barrel quality and prices.

ANTIQUES FAIR FLEA MARKET

Pr. do Comércio

The Pr. Comércio gets completely packed with vendors selling everything from 18th-century books to gramophones. Prices are very low and drop significantly lower if you bargain. Coming early is always advised in order to find the best items as well as the best values.

⏰ 4th Sa of every month 9am-7pm.

SÉ VELHA MARKET FLEA MARKET

Lg. da Sé Velha

Stretching from the famous arch all the way to the cathedral, this market is a bit of a free-for-all. Toward the bottom, vendors sell handmade crafts and the occasional antique. As you start to climb, more fruit and vegetable vendors arise. By the time you reach the cathedral, people are just selling random junk they found anywhere and everywhere. So if you are looking for a new painting or an old, useless muffler, this is your market.

⏰ 3rd Sa of every month 9am-4pm.

ESSENTIALS

Practicalities

- **TOURIST OFFICE: The Regional Office** has information about Coimbra, though it specializes in information about the region rather than the city itself. (Lg. Portagem www.turismo-centro.pt 🚶 From Estação Coimbra-A, walk along the river with the water to your right until Lg. Portagem; the office is on the far side. ⏰ Open June-Sept M-F 9am-6pm, Sa-Su 9am-1pm and 2:30-6pm; Oct-May M-F 9am-5pm, Sa-Su 9am-noon and 2:30-5pm.) The **Municipal Office** has a desk in the Biblioteca de Dom João V at the University. (Pr. da Porta Férrea ☎23 983 41 58 ⏰ Open M-F 10am-5pm, Sa-Su 10am-6pm.)
- **CURRENCY EXCHANGE: Montepio** will exchange money under €50 commission-free. (Lg. Portagem ☎23 985 17 00 ⏰ Open M-F 8:30am-3pm.)
- **LAUNDROMAT: Lavandaria Lucira.** (Av. Sá da Bandeira, 86 ☎23 909 06 15 $ Wash and dry 6kg for €6. ⏰ Open M 9am-7pm, Tu-F 9am-8:30pm, Sa 9am-5:30pm.)
- **INTERNET ACCESS: Esp@ço Internet** is a city-run service on the Pr. 8 de Maio that offers free internet access. (Pr. 8 de Maio, 38 www.integrar.org ℹ ID required. ⏰ Open M-F 10am-8pm, Sa-Su 10am-10pm.)

- **POST OFFICE: Correios.** (Lg. Mercado Municipal de Dom Pedro V ☎23 985 18 70 ⏰ Open M-F 8:30am-6:30pm, Sa 9am-12:30pm.)

Emergency

- **POLICE: Polícia Municipal** (Av. Sá de Bandeira, 106 ☎23 985 44 10 🚶 From Pr. 8 de Maio with the church to your right, head right and cross the street.)
- **HOSPITAL: Hospital da Universidade de Coimbra** (☎23 940 04 00 🚶 At Pr. do Professor Mota Pinto and Av. do Doutor Bissaya Barreto. Take bus #6, 7, 7T, 29, 35, 36 or 37.)
- **LATE-NIGHT PHARMACIES: Farmácia Universal** is right on the Pr. 8 de Maio and has a schedule of pharmacies open at night and on Sundays in the window. (Pr. 8 de Maio, 35 ☎23 982 37 44 ⏰ Open daily 8am-7pm.)

Getting There

BY TRAIN

There are two train stations in Coimbra. **Estação Coimbra-A (Nova)** is right beside the river near the center of Baixa; **Estação Coimbra-B (Velha)** is 3km northwest of town. (www.cp.pt) All trains stop at Coimbra-B, but long-distance trains do not continue on to Coimbra-A. If your train will not go to Coimbra-A, get off at Coimbra-B and take a free connecting train to Coimbra-A to reach the city. Trains arrive from: **Lisbon's Sta. Apolónia Station** ($ €22.50 ⏰ 2-3hr., 16 per day 6am-8pm) and **Porto's Campanhã Station** ($ €8.15 ⏰ 1-2hr., 25 per day 5:47am-8:47pm), although trains from Porto typically transfer in Aveiro.

BY BUS

Buses (www.rede-expressos.pt) arrive at the river, next to Estação Coimbra-A from: Braga ($ €14 ⏰ 3hr., 9-12 per day 6am-11:30pm); Lisbon ($ €14 ⏰ 2½hr., 25-30 per day 7am-12:15am); and Porto ($ €12.50 ⏰ 1½hr., 12-15 per day).

Getting Around

The **bus** system is the easiest way to get to the university without breaking a sweat. **SMTUC** buses (www.smtuc.pt) cost €1.60 for a one-way ticket purchased on the bus. ($ 1-day ticket €3.50, 3-trip ticket €2.20, 11-trip ticket €6.40.) These can be purchased at vending machines in Lg. Portagem, Pr. República, and small shops throughout town. There is a **taxi** stand outside Estação Coimbra-A, or call **Politáxis** (☎23 949 90 90 or 23 982 22 87).

SOUTHERN PORTUGAL

Some come down here for sunny peace and quiet. Some come to smell the fragrant almond blossoms that accent the Algarve region. But, if you're reading this, chances are you want to get smashed on the beach. We've got you covered, with the best nightlife (and everything else, of course) in Lagos and its neighbors on the southern coast. And if you fall on the looking-for-peace-and-quiet end of the spectrum, you're all set, too. Sightseeing attractions include a church full of bones and some awesome old forts. Though, should you decide to hop on the booze cruise, you know where to look.

greatest hits

- **WHAT THE WHAT.** Don't worry, those aren't real bo...nope, never mind, they're real. Real bones cover the walls of the Capela dos Ossos in Faro. (p. 546)

- **PUN INTENDED.** Stay and party at the Rising Cock hostel in Lagos. (p. 532)

- **TO THE ENDS OF THE EARTH.** Stand at the end of the Cabo de São Vicente and look out over the overwhelmingly vast Atlantic. (p. 541)

student life

The student life along Portugal's southern coast consists mainly of American, British, and Aussie students getting wasted together.

lagos ☎282

You'll have some insane memories from Lagos...if you can remember your time there. This tiny beach town in the south of Portugal proves that life's a beach and a party. Practically Australian sovereign territory, this city is full of (and mostly caters to) English-speaking tourists. Many a proprietor came to Lagos on holiday and simply never left. Stunning grottoes are waiting to be explored, and the long white-sand beaches give you ample space to soak up the sun. If lounging isn't your idea of fun, there are dozens of recreational activities to keep you busy, including sailing, scuba diving, surfing, and biking. Once you've worked up an appetite, you'll be happy to discover the wide array of cuisines and giant portions of food served up throughout the city. After-meal naps are a good call: once you hit Lagos's raging bars and nightclubs, you won't be sleeping any time soon.

ORIENTATION

From the train and bus stations, the center of town is a 10min. walk south. You'll know you're there when you see the children's carousel and clothing shops. From there, you will see **Praça Gil Eanes,** which has a funny-looking statue in the middle. Follow the **Rua 25 de Abril,** on the left (it changes names multiple times) to walk through the main area of town, clustered with shops, restaurants, and bars. A little past the center of town (about a 2min. walk) you will find the city's most crowded beach, **Batata.** To get to more secluded beaches like beautiful **Pinhão,** walk along the cliff road and make your way down when you see direction signs. Alternatively, you can take the tiny ferry across the channel to **Meia Praia,** the area's largest beach.

ACCOMMODATIONS

Although Lagos is a small town (only 30,000 inhabitants), it has more hostels than you might expect. Spread throughout the historic center, all have easy access to the area's sights, restaurants, and beaches. Be aware that prices in Lagos soar in August.

RISING COCK HOSTEL $$

Tv. do Forno, 14 ☎96 875 87 85 www.risingcock.com

We don't mean to be "fowl," but with signs like "Are you wet?" and a name like Rising Cock, you know you'll have a good time here. Come to this legendary party hostel for a rowdy, messy time. A former preschool, the Rising Cock has colorful rooms (think lime-green walls and Thomas the Tank Engine sheets), as well as crowds of raucous backpackers and students ready for a good time. If you're looking for a restful night's sleep, don't come here. Guests begin drinking on the outdoor patio whenever they happen to wake up and come stumbling home at all hours of the night. On Wednesdays and Saturdays, almost everyone heads out on an all-day booze cruise (€45). If you're of the fairer sex, check out the girls-only "Hen House" down the street. The beloved "Mama" of the house, Mrs. Ribero, makes crepes and "magic juice" for breakfast. As one sign in the hostel puts it, "We're not leaving 'til we're heaving!"

From the bus station, walk along the waterfront and cross the street when you see the carousel. Continue past the carousel and turn left onto R. 25 de Abril. Once you see the hospital, turn right. The hostel is on the right. ***i*** *Breakfast and linens included.* *$ Dorms €22-28.* *Reception 24hr.*

[icon] STUMBLE INN — HOTEL $$

R. Soeiro de Costa, 10-12 ☎28 208 16 07 www.stumbleinnlagos.com

Perfectly located among Lagos's beaches, restaurants, and nightlife, the Stumble Inn is a *hostal* developed from a row of converted Portuguese houses, but some of its old qualities have carried over. With only triples and quads, you'll feel like you're living in a room in a home rather than in an overcrowded, messy hostel. While not as raucous or social as some other nearby options, it's a great place to come back and recuperate after a hard day's night of bar-hopping. Shepard Fairey artwork adorns the cabinets, and the common areas offer calm and relaxing spaces with plenty of natural light. The owner, Jamie, is one of the nicest guys in Lagos, and he's full of suggestions for excellent restaurants and bars.

🚏 From the information office, walk away from the water down R. 25 de Abril, then turn right onto R. Soeiro da Costa. $ Dorms €20-30. ⏰ Reception 24hr.

ESCAPE HOSTEL — HOSTEL $$

R. Gil da Vicente, 23 ☎28 276 73 47 www.lagos-escape-hostel.com

Quiet and serene but still close to the action, Escape Hostel allows you to find your inner Zen—or at least to get a good night's sleep. Images of the Buddha are everywhere, alongside words such as "dedication" and "love," as if the round-bellied guy himself is urging you to take a break from the crazy nightlife outside. A decadent breakfast (featuring omelettes) is served daily on the rooftop terrace, giving guests an opportunity to socialize over great food.

🚏 From Pr. Gil Eanes, take R. 25 de Abril to the hospital, then turn right. From there, take the 2nd right, followed by an immediate left, a right (following Three Monkeys), and then the 2nd left. ℹ Breakfast and linens included. $ Dorms July-Aug €25-28; Sept-June €11-20. ⏰ Reception 24hr.

CLOUD 9 HOSTEL — HOSTEL $

R. Soeiro da Costa, 9 ☎28 218 33 55 www.cloud9hostel.com

Cloud 9 Hostel is fun and social, with weekly sangria and barbecue nights, but don't worry—it's not raucous and crazy all day long. Plenty of natural light keeps things from seeming too cramped, and some rooms have small balconies overlooking the street below.

🚏 From the tourist information office, walk away from the water down R. 25 de Abril, then turn right onto R. Soeiro da Costa. ℹ Linens included. $ Dorms €16-25. ⏰ Reception 24hr.

CARLOS HOUSE — GUEST HOUSE $$$

R. Jogo da Bola, 8 ☎91 659 42 25 www.carloshouse.lagoshostels.com

If you didn't come to Lagos to rage all day and night, Carlos House is for you. A 10min. walk uphill from the center of town, Carlos House is far enough from the boisterous nightlife to let you get some peace and quiet. Because of its private-room-only set-up, it's ideal if you come with friends or family. The large terrace is perfect for catching some sun and kicking back with sangria.

🚏 From Pr. Gil Eanes, take R. Gil Eanes away from the water. Continue straight as the road becomes R. Paiol, and turn right when the road ends. The house is on the right. $ Doubles €34-52. Rooms with private bath more expensive.

INTERNATIONAL YOUTH HOSTEL (HI) — HOSTEL $

R. Lançarote de Freitas, 50 ☎28 276 19 70 www.hihostels.com

One of the cheapest options in Lagos, the International Youth Hostel features a large outdoor common space surrounded by two stories of basic rooms. Between the patio and the colored walls, this hostel feels much less sterile and much more personal than many of its other HI counterparts. Although the price is right, you will need a member card (€6.50) to stay here.

🚏 From the hospital on the waterfront, walk up the street and take the 2nd right, followed by an immediate left. The hostel is on the right. $ Dorms €13-20. ⏰ Reception 24hr.

SIGHTS

Lagos is known more for its surf, sand, and parties than for its sights. However, there are still things to see here, with many vestiges of the Age of Discovery still standing throughout the city. The sights, like most anything else travelers seek in Lagos, are grouped in the historic center.

IGREJA E MUSEU DE SANTO ANTÓNIO CHURCH, MUSEUM

R. General Alberto da Silveira ☎28 276 23 01 radix.cultalg.pt

This museum tells the story of Lagos and the Algarve from ancient history until today. Along the way, they have amassed a collection of ancient artifacts from the past millennia. The exhibit ends in what used to be a church; the unmistakably Baroque chapel is covered in so much decoration that it is almost impossible to take it all in.

➜ From Pr. Gil Eanes, walk along R. 25 de Abril until you see the large church. This also houses the museum. $ €3, students and seniors €1.50. ⏰ Open Tu-Su 10am-5:30pm.

FORTA DA PONTA DA BANDEIRA FORT

Av. dos Descobrimentos, 8600 ☎28 276 14 10

The former barracks of this naval fortress now tells the history of the fort within the context of the Age of Discovery. A short movie plays in a theater to the left. Running around on top of the fort and pretending to fight off invaders provides for classic photo-ops.

➜ Walk south along the waterfront (to your right as you face the water) until you see the large fort. You can't miss it. $ €3, students and seniors €1.50. ⏰ Open Tu-Su 10am-6pm. Last entry 30 min. before close.

MERCADO DE ESCRAVOS MUSEUM

Pr. do Infante Dom Henrique

This former slave market looks like it came straight out of a world history textbook. The arches outside open the imagination to the immense suffering that took place in this very plaza. Inside, the one-room museum offers some historical context as well as a few artifacts related to the colonial slave trade.

➜ Walk along R. 25 de Abril toward the church. The museum is on the left. $ €3, students and seniors €1.50. ⏰ Open Tu-Su noon-6pm.

GREAT OUTDOORS

Lagos is surrounded by dazzling coves, sparkling beaches, and in some spots, nearly transparent water. Boat tours take visitors into grottoes where they can find the perfect photograph to take home. Families and hung-over students lie on the beach, either relaxing or recovering. The main beaches are fairly obvious and are there for the taking. However, the best way to find spectacular views might just be to explore, meandering up and down the coast, uncovering small, deserted beaches as you go.

Beaches

BATATA SOUTH OF CITY CENTER

Av. dos Descobrimentos

The closest beach to the center of town is unsurprisingly also the most popular, teeming with tourists and locals staking out their piece of sand. Many families come here during the day, so don't expect a boozin' party. Beach-goers are warned to stay away from the cliffs, which can have occasional rock slides. Waves here aren't suitable for surfing, but swimming is definitely welcome. If you are looking to be rebellious, you can head to the snack bar and wait fewer than 30min. before jumping back into the water.

➜ 2nd beach past the Lagos fortress.

MEIA PRAIA

Estr. de São Roque

Although it can be trickier get to than the other beaches, the expansive sands of Meia Priaia make it worth your while. To get here, take the tiny ferry across the harbor or just walk across the footbridge toward the train station. Much larger than the other beaches in the area, Meia Praia has room for everyone to spread out and is only crowded on the busiest of days.

⚓ Walk toward the harbor, where you'll see the tiny ferry that takes you to the beach.

PINHÃO

Av. dos Descobrimentos

Climb down hundreds of steps and past wall after wall of graffiti to this secluded little beach. On certain days, you can have the whole beach to yourself if you're lucky. With a short stretch of shore and high, crumbling cliffs all around, this isn't the best place for tanning, but the clear green-blue waters and small alcoves make it perfect for snorkeling or swimming.

⚓ Walk along the main street past Batata beach. There is a sign that points you toward Pinhão on the left.

Water Sports

SURF EXPERIENCE

SURFING

R. dos Ferreiros, 21
www.surf-experience.com

If you want to spend your vacation riding the waves but have no idea where to start, begin at Surf Experience. The company offers week-long surf camps for all levels of experience. Rather than simply taking day lessons, surfers here eat, sleep, and surf together in this all-encompassing extreme vacation. And if the

lagos

beaches at Lagos aren't ideal on a given day, Surf Experience will take you to the perfect beach elsewhere.

From Pr. Gil Eanes, head back toward the bus station. The shop is on the left. $ 1 week Apr-Oct €467; Nov-Mar €428. ⏰ Reception 24hr.

THE BOOZE CRUISE BOATING

Leaves from Travessa do Forno, 11 ☎96 875 87 85

For a water sport of a different sort, go on the booze cruise—basically, a frat house full of Australians on the water. Hours of alcohol consumption in small quarters under the sun mean that debauchery is at its maximum. Be prepared to chug (or "skull," as the Aussies call it) your beer or sangria if you don't comply with the cruise rules—like drinking only with your left hand—or you'll get pegged with a clothespin. Midway through the trip, anchor drops and partygoers jump into the water for a not-so-sober swim. (Note: Let's Go does not recommend drowning.) The cruise meets up and leaves from Nah Nah Bah (see **Food**).

Groups rendezvous at Nah Nah Bah. $ €45. ⏰ Typically every W and Sa. Check hostels for times.

GROTTO TOURS TOUR

As you walk along the waterfront that stretches out away from the bus station, you will see sign after sign for groups offering boat tours. Since there are so many companies offering multiple tours a day, groups typically remain very small. Definitely a must-see while you're in Lagos, the tiny tour boats take you on a 30min. trip along the Lagos coastline, sailing into some of the caves and grottoes. Prepare for absolutely stunning views of crystal clear waters and striking rock formations.

$ Around €15. ⏰ Boats typically leave every hour.

FOOD

Traditional Portuguese food is available in Lagos, but between all the old expats and fresh-faced travelers, most of the culinary gems in Lagos are based off of American and other international cuisines. Restaurants can be found up and down **Rua 25 de Abril** and **Rua Silva Lopes.**

NAH NAH BAH SOUL FOOD $$

Tv. do Forno, 11 ☎96 620 77 02 www.risingcock.com/nahnahbah

As it turns out, one of the world's top-rated burger joints is nestled in Lagos. Nah Nah Bah has a tropical theme, with plenty of Bob Marley to go around, but its food is all-American, with gigantic burgers and delightful fries that will leave you both a complete mess and completely satisfied. If you can complete the "Kilo-Burger Challenge," you get the burger for free (otherwise €31.50). At night, things start to get rowdy, as €1 shots are sold for an hour before the place shuts down at midnight. Whether it is from a failed attempt at the challenge or too many €1 shots, you will probably have to be carried out of here.

From the hospital, walk away from the water. Once you pass the Rising Cock, Nah Nah Bah is on the left. $ Entrees €8-15. ⏰ Open daily 6pm-midnight.

CAFE ODEON BREAKFAST, CAFE $

R. do Castelo dos Governadores, 10 ☎28 208 21 60 www.cafeodeon.com

The ultimate cure to last night's hangover, Cafe Odeon serves up a complete American breakfast (two eggs, two pieces of toast, two slices of bacon, and two hash browns) for a mere €3. And if that wasn't already beautiful enough to bring you to tears, listen to this—you can get it **all day long.** That's right, breakfast for dinner (or, "brinner") is this cafe's specialty. And while there are other options on the menu, the breakfast is so good there's no reason to try anything else.

From Pr. Gil Eanes, take R. 25 de Abril until you reach the fork. Turn left and follow the road up past the hospital. The cafe is on the right. $ Breakfast €3. ⏰ Open daily 8am-8pm.

MEU LIMÃO TAPAS $$

R. Silva Lopes, 40-42 ☎28 276 79 46

With octopus salad, *piri-piri* chicken, and more, Meu Limão offers up an excellent variety of various Portuguese tapas dishes. The fresh-squeezed house lemonade is refreshing, tart, and has so much pulp you could probably eat it with a spoon. *Fado* drifts through the semi-casual dining area, but those who want to enjoy the weather can sit outside and people-watch on the pedestrian thoroughfare. The specialty here is a 0.5kg dish of mussels, which can be ordered with different seasonings and is not to be missed.

 # Follow R. 25 de Abril and turn right at the hospital. $ Tapas €4-6. ⏰ Open daily 10am-midnight.

CROISSANTERIA 29 CAFE $

R. da Estrema, 29 ☎28 276 85 90

This cafe has sandwiches at dirt-cheap prices, which isn't too unusual, except for the fact that they are served on flaky, scrumptious, freshly baked croissants. The most expensive sandwiches barely exceed €2, and dessert variants are available as well, including the banana-chocolate croissant. The decor is nothing special, but the fresh croissants make this cafe one of the top quick-service stops in the city.

 # Walking down R. 25 de Abril, turn right onto R. Estrema. The cafe is on the left. $ Croissants €1-2.30. ⏰ Open M-Sa 8am-7pm.

ROCKEFELLA'S AMERICAN, DINER $$

R. 25 de Abril, 91 ☎28 279 86 34

Rockefella's feels like a 1950s American diner reincarnated in Lagos. Checkered patterns on the wall and loud '50s rock 'n' roll set the mood, while the leather-clad mannequin in the corner is just plain scary. Intense burgers and sandwiches with interesting names (e.g., The Chuck Norris) fill out the menu, and a variety of special sauces with equally creative names (e.g., An Epi Pen) are available to add to any order.

 # On the left side of R. 25 de Abril, walking away from Pr. Gil Eanes. $ Entrees €8-12. ⏰ Open daily noon-midnight.

NIGHTLIFE

Calling Lagos's nightlife wild would be a dramatic understatement. Although large *discotecas* are not prevalent, the bars do more than enough to make up for their absence. Almost every night the bars, which can mostly be found within a few blocks of **Rua 25 de Abril,** are packed with partiers, and drinking and dancing go on late into the night. The debauchery is turned up to 11 here, with beer funnels, table-top dancing, and fish bowls all making frequent appearances.

THREE MONKEYS BAR

R. Lançarote de Freitas, 26 ☎28 276 29 95 www.3monkeys.me.uk

With rock 'n' roll music and cheap drinks, Three Monkeys brings the party early in the evening: get two-for-one cocktails from 7-11pm. As the night rolls on, things start to get crazy. A certain bartender is known to wear dresses and booty shorts, the bar is frequently lit on fire, and beer bongs are plentiful. Make sure you finish your funnel, or the remnants will be poured out all over you.

 # From the hospital, turn right, walking away from the water. Take the 2nd right and as you approach the next intersection; the bar is on the left. $ Pint of beer €3. Cocktails €5-6. ⏰ Open daily 1pm-2am.

JOE'S GARAGE BAR

R. de Maio, 1 www.risingcock.com/joes

With a name like Joe's Garage, you'd expect a manly vibe, and that's what you'll get. Get cocktails and pints until 11pm for €2. The decor is obviously automobile-oriented, with license plates and rims all over the walls, but a few drinks in, the decor ceases to be relevant. Once the night gets going, Joe's becomes a hot and sweaty dance-club hotspot complete with girls dancing on tabletops. The split-level dance floor leads to twice the debauchery, as dancers on the upper floor lean over the railings. Be forewarned: this place doesn't have A/C, so the dance floor becomes a sauna fast.

⇟ Walking away from Pr. Gil Eanes, turn right onto R. Estrema and keep walking until you hit a dead end. Turn right and Joe's is on the right. $ Beer €3. Cocktails €5-7. ⏰ Open daily 9am-2am.

INSIDE OUT BAR

R. Cândido dos Reis, 119 www.insideoutbar.com

Few come here sober, and those who do certainly don't leave that way. Inside Out gets packed around midnight, and the shots are passed around as quickly as the bartenders can pour them out. The bar pumps loud music onto the dance floor late into the night. A popular drink is the fish bowl (€25), which is an actual fish bowl filled to the brim with a mysterious mixture of alcohols and served with a multitude of 2ft. straws.

⇟ From Pr. Gil Eanes, follow R. Gil Eanes away from the water, then turn left onto R. Cândido dos Reis. Inside Out is on the left. $ Shots €3-3.50. Beer €3-4.50. Mixed drinks €5-6.50. ⏰ Open daily 8pm-4am.

GRAND CAFE BAR, CLUB

R. Senhora da Graça, 7 ☎28 276 26 22

Transitioning from sophisticated bar to sloppy mess as the night proceeds, Grand Cafe is the place to be in town after 3am. The space itself is massive, with different areas that each have their own feel, from the bumpin' dance floor to the more laid-back patio. Although the crowd gets going a little later than other bars, once things are rolling, they are out of control. The best action happens on the second floor, where DJs spin Top-40 hits and house music. Like all the nightlife spots in Lagos, when this place heats up, it does so literally, leaving you in a blanket of sweat on your way out. If you've had a bit too much drinking and dancing for one night (or want to take a break before partying some more), sober up at the excellent kebab shop across the street.

⇟ Take R. 25 de Abril away from Pr. Gil Eanes. The bar is on the left. $ Beer €2. Cocktails €6. ⏰ Open daily 9pm-4am.

THE RED EYE BAR

R. Cândido dos Reis, 119 www.redeyebarlagos.com

Filled with Anglophones from across the globe, The Red Eye is a great place to grab some cheap drinks and strike up a conversation with someone else almost undoubtedly on holiday. Don't be fooled: this bar isn't quiet, it just isn't as insane as some of its Lagos counterparts. Two-for-one cocktails, a pool table, and the surfboards adorning the walls make this a good place to start the night. Be sure to get your free house shot with your first drink.

⇟ From Pr. Gil Eanes, take R. Gil Eanes away from the water, then turn left onto R. Cândido dos Reis. Red Eye is on the left. $ Shots €2.50. Pint of beer €3. Mixed drinks €4. ⏰ Open daily 8pm-2am. Happy hour 8-10pm.

ARTS AND CULTURE

CENTRO CULTURAL DE LAGOS CULTURAL CENTER

R. Lançarote de Freitas, 7 ☎28 277 04 50 www.centroculturaldelagos.wordpress.com

The source of all things cultural in Lagos, this building serves a multitude of purposes. Throughout the year, it hosts exhibits for various local artists. It also acts as a performance center where you can see anything from classical music to jazz artists to magicians. Although there aren't any huge annual festivals in Lagos, there are plenty of smaller events happening all the time.

⇟ Walking away from the plaza on R. 25 de Abril, turn right at the fork. The Cultural Center is a large building a few blocks away. $ Ticket prices vary. ⏰ M-Sa 11am-7pm.

ESSENTIALS

Practicalities

- **TOURIST OFFICE:** Largo Marquês de Pombal ☎28 276 41 11 ⏰ Open daily 9am-5pm.
- **CURRENCY EXCHANGE: Cotacâmbios.** (Pr. Gil Eanes, 11 ☎28 276 44 52)
- **LAUNDROMAT: Lavanderia Míele.** (Av. Descobrimentos, 27 $ Wash and dry €8 per 5kg. ⏰ Open M-F 9am-1pm and 3-7pm, Sa 9am-1pm.)
- **INTERNET ACCESS:** Hotspot available for free in **historic center** of town.

Emergency

- **POLICE: Guarda Nacional Republicana.** (Pr. Gil Eanes ☎28 276 29 30)
- **HOSPITAL/MEDICAL SERVICES: Unidade Hospitalar de Lagos.** (R. Castelo dos Governadores ☎28 277 01 00 www.chbalgarvio.min-saude.pt)
- **LATE-NIGHT PHARMACIES: Farmácia Silva.** (R. 25 de Abril, 9 ☎28 276 28 59 ⏰ Open daily 9am-8pm.)

Getting There

To reach Lagos from northern Portugal, you must go through Lisbon; trips originating in the east generally transfer in Faro. Coming by train is not recommended, as there is no regular train service from Lisbon to Lagos, and travel usually requires multiple transfers. The **EVA bus station** (Av. Descobrimentos ☎28 276 29 44) has buses that arrive from Lisbon ($ €19.50 ⏰ 5hr., 12 per day 7:30am-8:30pm) and Sagres ($ €4 ⏰ 1hr., 15 per day 7:15am-8:30pm).

Getting Around

You can reach anything in Lagos on foot. If you have a lot of luggage, you might want to get a taxi from the bus or train station, but once you are situated, nothing worth seeing is more than a short walk away. **Taxis** can be found right outside the station and also line the main drag along the water.

sagres ☎282

The epitome of quaint, Sagres is a tiny beach town of about 2,000 that sits at the end of the world—or at least the southwest corner of Portugal. Small white houses with blue trim line the handful of roads that meander toward the coast. The residents all know one another and converse in the street about their families and lives in this Portuguese Pleasantville. Although Sagres is a tad sleepy, it is also a surfer's paradise, with most of its visitors coming to learn how to take on the Atlantic's mighty waves. The town was important during the Age of Discovery, and a few sights stand as a testament to that fact. Time here, however, is best spent at the beach, whether that means riding the waves or soaking up the sun.

ORIENTATION

It isn't hard to get around Sagres, as there isn't much of it. Almost all of the city's best restaurants and bars are on the main street, **Avenida Comandante Matoso,** which runs from the roundabout near the tourist center to the harbor and can be traversed in 15min. or less. It is intersected by **Rua da Fortaleza,** which runs south to the old fort, a remnant of the Age of Discovery and the days of Portuguese naval power. Anything outside these areas is almost exclusively residential.

ACCOMMODATIONS

Hostels aren't particularly common in Sagres, though there are a few. If all of the typical accommodations are booked up, your best bet is to just walk up and down **Avenida Comandante Matoso** and keep an eye out for signs that say "rooms," "*quartos*, " or "*zimmern.* " Many residents rent out rooms in their houses, which can be quite nice and are an interesting change of pace from the typical hostel scene.

CASA AZUL GUEST HOUSE $$

R. de Patrão António Faustino ☎28 262 48 56 www.casaazulsagres.com

You can't miss this shockingly blue guest house close to the harbor. Inside, the color doesn't stop: each room is assigned its own hue, which is listed on the door in case you continue to struggle with the color wheel. The rooms are luxurious, with large windows, private bathrooms, TVs, and refrigerators. But watch when you are visiting, as prices are criminal in both directions: in winter they're a steal, while in summer they are armed robbery.

⇄ While walking down Av. Comandante Matoso, look to your left as you approach the harbor. The guest house is on the side of the street closer to the water. $ May-Sept doubles €65-120, triples €85-156; Oct-Apr doubles €42-48, triples €55-63. ⏰ Reception 24hr.

GOODFEELING HOSTEL $

Raposeira, Vila do Bispo ☎91 465 88 07 www.thegoodfeeling.com

A great place to crash after a long day of surfing, Goodfeeling's hammocks and patios allow guests to kick back in peace and quiet. A 15min. bus ride from Sagres makes it a little inconvenient to get to the beach, but it's not as if there are loads of hostels sitting in downtown Sagres. Moreover, many of the surf camps (which is what most travelers are here for in the first place) will come and pick up students each morning. At night, the hostel owners make a delicious dinner (€4) and often take group trips to get coffee at the bar down the road or drinks in Sagres.

⇄ From the Raposeira bus stop, walk away from the plaza and the hostel is on the right. $ Dorms June-July €20; Aug €22; Sept €20; Oct-May €15. Doubles €25/30/25/17.50. ⏰ Reception 8am-midnight.

CASA MARIANA GUESTHOUSE $$

Av. Comandante Matoso ☎93 313 15 88 anagoulãodias@sapo.pt

At first, Casa Mariana appears to be a residential house—that's because it is. However, the family here has a few surprisingly nice rooms that they rent out at bargain prices. Private rooms this spacious and comfortable would cost much more elsewhere; between the price and prime location just minutes from the beach, Casa Mariana is a sweet deal.

⇄ From the inter-city bus stop, walk down Av. Comandante Matoso. The house is on the right. $ Doubles €30.

MARETA BEACH BED & BREAKFAST B&B $$$$

Pr. da República ☎28 262 00 40 www.sagresholidays.com

Near the tourist office and in the heart of Sagres, this B&B has a bright blue interior accompanied by modern and minimalist decor. Visitors will find themselves in the lap of luxury, as each room has A/C, a plasma TV, and an ensuite bathroom. The B&B is very close to the beach, and many rooms have balconies with views of the water and surrounding area.

⇄ From the inter-city bus stop, walk toward the roundabout. The B&B is across the intersection. $ Singles June-July €60-89; Aug €117.50; Sept €60-89; Oct-Apr €41-60. Doubles €65-99/127.50/65-99/46-65. ⏰ Reception 24hr.

SIGHTS

Visitors are not usually drawn to Sagres for the sights, but there are a couple that are worth seeing if the waves aren't prime. These sights, just like Sagres, are deeply tied to the country's past years of naval glory. While the fort is a short walk to the southern edge of town, the cape is best reached by bus.

CABO DE SÃO VICENTE LIGHTHOUSE, VIEWS

Considered "the end of the world" before Columbus realized there were people living in a little place called America, St. Vincent's Cape is the main attraction in Sagres. The cape has been famous since the Age of Discovery and is a landmark on the sea routes linking Europe, Africa, and Asia. The wind-battered cliffs offer spectacular views that will give you chills, particularly around sunset. A small museum is here as well, but the cape is honestly all about the view. Although it is tempting to get the perfect Kodak moment on the edge of the cliffs, let the memorial stone serve as a reminder that the crumbling rocks are not to be tested.

Two buses generally transport tourists from the main bus stop in Sagres to the cape. Ask at the tourist office for times. [$] Cape free. Museum €1.50. ⏰ Museum open daily May-Sept 9:30am-8pm; Oct-Apr 9:30am-5:30pm.

FORTALEZA DE SAGRES FORT

R. da Fortaleza

Allegedly the site of Henry the Navigator's naval school (which is now believed to never have existed), this fort was built during the Age of Discovery to help give Portugal the necessary naval infrastructure to explore the new world as well as protect the country's coasts. Less crowded than St. Vincent's Cape, this is a great place for snapping pictures without other tourists milling about. On the way, you'll also see a bizarre, large, geometrical sand design dating back to Henry's days called "Wind Rose." Nobody knows what it means (a compass rose? a sun dial?), but it gets the people going.

[$] €3, under 25 and retired €1.50, youth cardholders €1.20. Free 30min. guided tours at noon, 4, 5pm. Max. 20 people. Meet near Wind Rose. ⏰ Open daily May-Sept 9:30am-8pm; Oct-Apr 9:30am-5:30pm.

THE GREAT OUTDOORS

A wide selection of beaches, each surrounded by intimidating (and sometimes crumbling) cliffs, makes Sagres a great location for both relaxation and surfing. More adventurous sorts should head to one of the area's surf shops, where you can rent bikes, boards, kayaks, and more. **Surf schools** line **Avenida Comandante Matoso,** but don't waste your time shopping around for the best-priced: they are almost all exactly the same.

Take **Rua Infante Dom Henrique** to the water from the tourist center to reach **Praia da Mareta,** the best beach for relaxing or swimming in the ocean. **Rua de São Vicente** will take you in the right direction toward **Praia do Tonel,** which is mostly a surfer's beach, with its large waves and shallow shoreline. However, you will have to follow the signs once you reach the roundabout to get there. For a smaller and more private beach, Avenida Comandante Matoso runs all the way to the harbor, which sits right next to **Praia da Baleeira.**

SURF PLANET

Pr. da República ☎28 262 47 27 www.surfplanet.pt

With beachwear galore—wetsuits, body boards, swimming fins, kayaks, surfboards, skim boards, and more, Surf Planet is a one-stop shop for everything you need to be ocean-bound. Like most of the other surf shops in the area, this place gives lessons, but its week-long surfing camps for beginner and intermediate surfers are what make Surf Planet unique.

Across the intersection from the bus stop and tourist center. [$] Lessons €55 per day; includes board, wetsuit, and transportation. Lower rates for multi-lesson packages. ⏰ Open daily 9:30am-1:30pm and 3:30-6:30pm.

FOOD

With the exception of the occasional beach-side restaurant, everything in Sagres is on **Avenida Comandante Matoso.** The town mostly caters to travelers, but there is still a healthy mix of traditional Portuguese and more international offerings.

O TELHEIRO DO INFANTE SEAFOOD $$$

Praia de Mareta ☎28 262 41 79 www.telheirodoinfante.com

This slightly snazzy seaside restaurant has a wide wine selection and a top-notch view of the ocean. Sit out on the balcony and enjoy their menu of fresh seafood, including the lobster rice-pot, monkfish and shellfish *cataplana*, and special Sagres fish. It isn't exactly a local hotspot, but that doesn't mean the fresh fish isn't delicious. Although this restaurant is a bit out of the way, there are signs on the major street pointing you in the right direction.

From the tourist office, follow the many signs pointing to the restaurant. $ *Fresh fish €10-20. House specials for 2 €30-45. Mixed salads, cold dishes, eggs, spaghetti, fish, and meat €10-20.* ⏰ *Open M and W-Su 10am-10pm.*

VILA VELHA PORTUGUESE $$$

R. Patrão António Faustino ☎28 262 47 88 www.vilavelha-sagres.com

Set aside off of the main road (as if things could get any quieter), Vila Velha is one of the fancier restaurants in the area. It's hard not to splurge once you are seated in the dining area, surrounded by white tablecloths and delectable smells. Vegetarian options are available, but for everyone else it is advisable to go big or go home and order the chef's special four-course meal (€25).

From the bus station, walk east toward the harbor on Av. Comandante Matoso. Turn right onto R. Patrão António Faustino. $ *Entrees €13-20.* ⏰ *Open daily 6:30-midnight.*

BOSSA NOVA PIZZERIA, MEDITERRANEAN $$

R. da Mareta ☎28 262 45 66 www.dromedariosagres.com/bossa-nova

Hidden behind Dromedario, Bossa Nova has a shady patio area that allows visitors to munch on delectable pizzas and take a break from the relentless sun. The large menu also has Mediterranean offerings such as lighter pasta dishes. The canopy and the secluded location make Bossa Nova feel like a private getaway or your own special secret. But don't get too excited—others are bound to smell the pizza and be drawn inside as well.

Heading down Av. Comandante Matoso, turn left onto R. da Mareta after passing Dromedario. $ *Pizza €7-9.* ⏰ *Open daily 7-11pm.*

CAFFE ESPRESSO CAFE $

Pr. da República ☎28 262 00 40

If you need a break from Sagres's surf and sand, get your coffee fix at Caffe Espresso, steps away from the main beach. They get creative with their coffee here, with options that range from coffee with gelato to coffee with liquor. *Tostas*, paninis, and salads are all available in what is one of the more reasonably priced restaurants in town. The dining area is set up more like a modern cafe than the typical Portuguese variant, with a big-screen TV and free Wi-Fi.

From the bus station, turn right and walk 2min. $ *Entrees €5-10.* ⏰ *Open daily 8am-10pm.*

NIGHTLIFE

The main bars in Sagres actually sit in a line, one after the other, making for what might be one of the easiest pub crawls of all time. This isn't a party town, however, so most bars don't come anywhere close to hitting capacity most nights, and only the decor really distinguishes one establishment from the next.

MITIC BAR

Av. Comandante Matoso ☎96 413 93 50

One of the newest in the series of bars lining Av. Comandante Matoso, Mitic blares music all day long, whether the crowd is one or 100. Purple is everywhere, from the bar to the seats to the walls, and a bamboo ceiling ties together the entire attempt at the modern look. Sit out on the second-floor terrace for great views of the beach. With a huge selection of smoothies, fresh-squeezed juices, coffees, teas, beers, and cocktails, Mitic has pretty much every drink you could want for any time of day. If you're hungry, the hamburgers are surprisingly tasty. At night, Sagres residents and tourists gather here to watch the game or listen to live music. Try their tequila sunrise (€6), made with fresh-squeezed orange juice and a lot of liquid courage.

⇆ From the bus station, walk down Av. Comandante Matoso. The bar is on the left. $ Beer €1.70. Cocktails €5-6. ⏰ Open daily 10am-3am.

DROMEDARIO BAR

Av. Comandante Matoso ☎28 262 42 19 www.dromedariosagres.com

Established in 1985, Dromedario is one of Sagres's oldest favorites. Despite the Moorish arches, camel mascot, and all-around Arabian theme, Dromedario is more of an oasis than a desert, serving up a myriad of ice-cold cocktails that come with tropical touches, such as fruit slices and leaves. During the day, come for a bite of the mouth-watering snacks, crepes, and hamburgers; by night, come for the big fruity mixed drinks.

⇆ From the bus station, walk down Av. Comandante Matoso. Bar is on the left. $ Beer €1.70. Cocktails €6. ⏰ Open daily 10am-3am.

LAST CHANCE SALOON BAR

Praia da Mareta ☎28 262 40 61

Hang up your six-shooter after high noon and have a drink at this spaghetti Western-themed bar. Sitting above the beach with a satisfying view of the ocean, this bar lives up to its name—it actually is the last place you can get a drink before wading off into the Atlantic. Although admittedly not the roughest and toughest of drinks, a cold bottle of cider (€2.50) or a pitcher of sangria makes this the perfect relaxation spot after a long day at the beach.

⇆ Head toward Praia da Mareta. You will see the bar as you head down to the shore. $ Beer €1.30. ⏰ Open daily 2pm-2am.

ÁGUA SALGADA BAR

Av. Comandante Matoso ☎28 262 42 97

The trippy walls in Água Salgada make you feel like you have unknowingly walked into an aquarium, and a turtle gives you the evil eye as you walk through the door. Kick back with a huge, strong cocktail or fruity drink. Locals love the crepes, and the copious amounts of whipped cream and syrup will satisfy even the most intense sweet tooth. They also have a wide selection of creative caipirinhas (€5) that include all kinds of new ingredients, like pineapples. Head to the upper level, sandwich in hand, and take advantage of the free Wi-Fi and computers.

⇆ From the bus station, walk down Av. Comandante Matoso. The bar is on the left. $ Beer €1.70. Cocktails €5-6. ⏰ Open daily 10am-3am.

PAU DE PITA BAR

Av. Comandante Matoso ☎28 262 49 03

Known to occasionally host live music on the weekends, Pau de Pita is open all day and has an expansive menu for those who are simply looking for lunch as well as those who want to throw a few back at the bar. On a summer night, this place is packed with young travelers and locals alike. During the winter, it is a cozy option, especially when they light the fireplace.

⇆ From the bus station, walk down Av. Comandante Matoso. The bar is on the left. $ Beer €1.70. Cocktails €5-6. ⏰ Open daily 10am-2am.

ESSENTIALS

Practicalities

- **TOURIST OFFICE:** R. Comandante Matoso ☎28 262 48 50 ⇆ To your left when you get off the bus. ⏰ Open daily 9am-6pm.
- **INTERNET ACCESS:** Free **Wi-Fi** is available at **Água Salgada** and neighboring **Dromedário.** (See Nightlife.)
- **POST OFFICE:** R. Comandante Matoso ⏰ Open M-F 9am-12:30pm and 2-5:30pm.

Emergency

- **PHARMACY:** R. Comandante Matoso ⏰ Open M-F 9am-7pm.

Getting There

EVA buses (☎28 289 97 00) run from Lagos. ($ €4. ⏰ 1hr.; M-F 14 per day 7:15am-8:30pm, Sa 9 per day 7:15am-8:30pm, Su 7 per day 7:15am-8:30pm.) Buses also run to Lisbon during the summer. ($ €4. ⏰ 5hr., July-Sept daily 7:30am.)

Getting Around

Getting around Sagres is easy and is best done on foot, as almost all of the city's bars and restaurants center around the main street, **Avenida Comandante Matoso,** just steps away from the beach. If you're staying in a different area, check the tourist office (right next to the bus station) for **bus** times. If it's too late and the last bus has left, you can call **Táxis Salmonete** (☎28 262 44 50). **Bike** rentals are available at Surf Planet (€5 per hr., €10 for 4hr., €15 for 8hr.) and many other surf shops.

faro ☎289

Many a traveler is surprised to find that Faro, though it sits right on the water, isn't much of a beach town. But even though the sand is far away, Faro still manages to retain the charm of the Algarve. Ancient stone walls enclose the old city, which holds Faro's history in its many sights; the harbor is packed with boats, illustrating the city's symbiotic relationship with the ocean. All of the things that make the Algarve unique can be found here. Taste some regional almond sweets...and try to keep them down at the morbid **Chapel of Bones.**

ORIENTATION

Faro is a bit more difficult to navigate than most coastal towns because the water is not a particularly helpful reference, as it borders the town from both the south and west. The southernmost part of the city is the **old city,** which contains many of the sights visitors come to see and can be easily identified by the ancient stone walls surrounding it. **Rua do Comandante Francisco Manuel** borders the old city near the water. Exiting the old city via this street leads to **Jardim Manuel Bívar,** a long park area downtown that hosts many events. From the park, continuing left will take you to **Avenida da República,** which runs to the **bus and train station,** while heading to the right will take you to a mess of pedestrian streets lined with cafes and clothing stores.

ACCOMMODATIONS

Faro tends to be more of a day-trip destination than a long-term stop in most travelers' itineraries. While this means that hostels are not plentiful, accommodations are still available for those looking to travel on a budget. If you roll into town late and need to find a place to stay fast, fairly reasonable *pensões*, which typically have high availability, line the pedestrian streets behind the harbor.

⊠ CASA D'ALAGOA · HOSTEL $$

Pr. Alexandre Herculano, 27 · ☎28 981 32 52 · www.farohostel.com

The top dog of budget accommodations in Faro, Casa D'Alagoa was an awesome old house that has been transformed into a hostel. With super-tall door frames and a wide staircase, it's obvious this used to be a play-thing for the rich, but now it is open for your enjoyment. The rooms are enormous, and second-floor terraces have ample space for soaking up the sun and pretending to be posh, perhaps with a highball in hand and your finest monocle in eye. This hostel also likes to have fun: sangria is made by the bucket and drinking games with the owners go late into the night.

☞ *From the tourism office, follow R. Misericórdia away from the water; this becomes R. Alexandre Herculano. Take a left at the plaza with a garden running through the center: this is Pr. Alexandre Herculano. The hostel is on the right.* ⓘ *Linens, towels, and breakfast included. Cheapest rates available through website.* ⓢ *Dorms €25-29. Private rooms €30-40.* ⌚ *Reception 24hr.*

INTERNATIONAL YOUTH HOSTEL (HI) · HOSTEL $

R. da Polícia de Segurança Pública · ☎28 987 80 90 · www.hihostels.com

Located within a short walk of the old city, this HI branch is a cheap place to kick back and relax. All of the rooms, which are average-sized, sit on the second floor, some with views of the neighboring park. The common area is indoors but feels like a patio, with natural light filtering through the ceiling. A strange metal catwalk leading to the bathrooms hangs over the reception; work on your runway form and accompanying pout before arriving.

☞ *From the tourism office, head away from the water. Bear right at the fork onto R. Albergue, then take the 2nd left onto R. Teresa Ramalho Otrigão and follow it for about 500m. Finally, turn right onto R. PSP (Polícia de Segurança Pública) at the large garden. The hostel is on the left.* ⓘ *Linens included.* ⓢ *Dorms €13. Doubles €28. Prices slightly higher without membership card (€6).* ⌚ *Reception 24hr.*

RESIDENCIAL OCEANO · HOTEL $$

R. Ivens, 21 · ☎28 982 33 49

Although Faro is one of the flattest cities in Portugal, the thoughtful people at Residencial Oceano thought they would give you the full Portuguese experience by letting you climb a flight of stairs before finding the reception. But everything is roses from there. A small living room offers a computer for everyone to use, and all of the rooms have private bathrooms, TVs, and air-conditioning. Sitting on a pedestrian thoroughfare, this *pensão* puts you a few meters away from the majority of Faro's shops and cafes.

☞ *From the tourism office, head up the right side of the park, and turn right just before Hotel Faro. Follow the road to the left and you will see the pensão on the right.* ⓘ *Linens and towels included.* ⓢ *Singles €32; doubles €42; triples €48.* ⌚ *Reception 24hr.*

faro

SIGHTS

Faro, whose own origins stretch back to the Roman Empire, is rich with history. This legacy means that plenty has been left behind for the travelers to explore. Most of the important sights are found within the ancient walls of the old city, but some of the highlights are scattered throughout newer portions of the city, too.

[✓] CAPELA DOS OSSOS — CHAPEL

Lg. do Carmo ☎28 982 44 90

Behind the mighty church that sits in Lg. Carmo is a tiny chapel. That sounds quaint, until you realize that **the walls are covered with the bones of dead monks.** Skulls, arms, legs...if you can touch it when Simon says, it is probably on the wall. Perhaps the most depressing thing about this simultaneously grotesque and captivating sight is that it isn't even the only bone chapel in Portugal: another lies to the north in the city of Évora. You can walk right up and touch the bones, and there is hardly anyone around to judge you, so sidle up next to your favorite skull and get that new profile picture you've been waiting for.

⇆ From the bus station, turn right onto Av. República, then a left onto R. Primeiro de Maio, and follow the signs to Igreja do Carmo. $ Bone chapel €1. ⏰ Open M-F 10am-1pm and 3-5pm, Sa 10am-1pm.

SÉ CATEDRAL DE FARO — CATHEDRAL

Lg. da Sé

Built in the 13th century on top of the former Roman forum, this cathedral sits in an idyllic plaza lined with orange trees. There is a small museum holding the church's treasures, and the church itself is beautiful, but some of the best parts of the visit are less obvious. The ornate and stunning red-and-gold organ sits above the congregation on a balcony and looks strikingly East Asian. Stairs also

southern portugal

lead to the roof of the cathedral, where on nice days you can see crystal-clear views of the city and its barrier islands off of the coast.

Take a left out of the tourism office and another immediate left. Follow this road through the old city walls to the plaza with the cathedral. [$] €3. ⏰ Open in summer M-F 10am-6pm, Sa 10am-1pm; in winter M-F 10am-5pm, Sa 10am-1pm.

MUNICIPAL MUSEUM OF FARO MUSEUM

Lg. Afonso III, 14 ☎28 987 08 29 www.cm-faro.pt

Judging by its name alone, this museum sounds about as fun as listening to a radio broadcast of the National Rock Paper Scissiors Championship, but don't be fooled: this Municipal Museum of Faro packs quite a punch. Acting as a kind of catch-all grab-bag of museums, it hosts multiple exhibits of very different natures. The most outstanding part is far and away the archaeological exhibit, which brings the Roman Empire back to life through its collection of ruins and artifacts. Other areas include a permanent exhibit of oil paintings and temporary exhibits by local artists.

From the cathedral, take R. Trem away from the square and take the 1st left. The museum is on the right. [$] €2. ⏰ Open Tu-F 10am-7pm, Sa-Su 11:30am-6pm. Closes 1hr. earlier in winter.

MARITIME MUSEUM MUSEUM

R. da Comunidade Lusíada ☎28 989 49 90

This museum is small, but anyone who has any interest in the high seas should make a point to stop by. Some of the displays explain the methods of and pay tribute to the seafaring ways of the Algarve's fishermen. The model ships reach extremely large sizes and are meticulously detailed, but perhaps the most fun activity is standing at the nautical wheel in the lobby and pretending to weather the oncoming storm on your 3hr. tour.

Take a right out of the bus station, then take the 1st right and walk toward the water. The museum is on the right. [$] €1. ⏰ Open M-F 9am-noon and 2:30-5pm.

FOOD

Faro isn't the most tourist-oriented of cities. Pair that with its location on the water and you get some amazing traditional Portuguese seafood. Loads of restaurants and cafes line the pedestrian streets behind the marina, but be wary of multilingual menus and fake-smiling chefs standing out front: the food might still be good, but the prices will probably be unappetizing.

BIJOU PASTELARIA $

R. Vasco da Gama ☎28 931 57 02

A *pastelaria* upgraded to the 21st century, Bijou offers cheap, yummy Portuguese options. While many of these kinds of cafes blend together and become virtually indistinguishable, Bijou sticks out with its bright red furniture and sleek look. The *tostas* are so scrumptious and buttery that you almost feel bad paying so little for them (€2-4). If you are feeling really adventurous or are just slightly insane, try the *tosta á casa* (€3), full of cheese, cinnamon, and mysterious sugary substances.

From Jardim Manuel Bívar, take R. Primeiro de Maio away from the park. Turn right when you see the military recruitment center onto R. Vasco da Gama. [$] Sandwiches €2-4. ⏰ Open daily 8am-11pm.

SOL E JARDIM PORTUGUESE $$

Pr. Ferreira de Almeida, 22 ☎28 982 00 30

From the exterior, Sol e Jardim looks just like just another Portuguese restaurant. But stepping inside feels like entering another world. The restaurant has an outdoor covered courtyard that is completely secluded from the street outside. Sit down and enjoy the weather in peace while admiring the lush vegetation, but realize you won't be eating any of it: this restaurant serves up large, carnivorous portions of meat and fish. For a particularly tasty treat straight from the sea, try the warming *arroz com polvo* (rice with octopus, €8.90).

➜ From Jardim Manuel Bívar, take R. Primeiro de Maio away from the water to Pr. Ferreira de Almeida; it's at the far right corner of the plaza. $ Meals €7-13. ⏰ Open M-Sa noon-3pm and 6-10pm.

CIDADE VELHA PORTUGUESE $$

R. Domingos Guieiro, 19 ☎28 982 71 45

Although it isn't the only outdoor cafe within the old city walls, Cidade Velha is probably the cheapest. The *pratos do dia* (€6-9) are reasonably priced, and the sweets and milkshakes (try the banana) can really hit the spot. The outdoor seating area puts you right next to the cathedral, and although it is a popular tourist attraction, the atmosphere is remarkably relaxed, so you can eat your meal without a billion fanny-packed tourists running into your table. If things get too hot, opt to go inside to Cidade Velha's air-conditioning, which is not too common in these parts.

➜ From Sé Catedral, exit to the right and continue as if you were to leave the square. You will see the restaurant on the right. $ Pratos do dia €7.50. ⏰ Open daily 8am-8pm.

CAFÉ DO CORETO PIZZERIA, CAFE $$

Jardim Manuel Bívar ☎28 982 29 64

When you are tired of all the Portuguese staples, or if you think that cod has been a bit played out (don't dare say that out loud), you might want something a bit more familiar. Café do Coreto offers the typical Portuguese cafe favorites, but it also offers a plethora of pizzas fresh out of the oven. Some of them get downright weird, with toppings like apple, banana, and tomato all on the same pie. The building looks very fashion-forward, as the walls are almost all glass, which means you can enjoy the seaside view from the comforts of the interior.

➜ From Jardim Manuel Bívar, head toward the marina. The restaurant is on the side of the road closest to the water. $ Pizzas €9-12. ⏰ Open daily 8am-midnight.

NIGHTLIFE

Faro has a large student population, so even though the town isn't huge, its nightlife is still worthwhile. The nightclubs tend to be open only on weekends, while the bars are usually open every day. Students wander down toward the water at midnight or later and stay out all night. Most of the popular bars and nightclubs can be found on **Rua do Prior** or on the adjacent streets near the bus station.

CHE60 BAR

R. do Prior, 24 ☎93 119 43 14

Pronounced "Chessenta," Faro's hippest bar also happens to be its most 👍**communist.** To each according to his ability, to each according to his mead… or something like that. There is nothing revolutionary here, just good music and cheap drinks. Iconic images of Ché line the walls in this two-floor hang-out spot. DJs spin most nights, and the crowds really pick up around 1am. Although for a communist bar, they sure do seem to be making a good deal of cash…

➜ From Jardim Manuel Bívar, follow R. Primeiro de Maio away from the water and turn left onto R. Prior. The bar is on the right. $ Beer €2. Cocktails €4.50-7. ⏰ Open daily 9pm-4am.

COLUMBUS BAR COCKTAIL BAR

Jardim Manuel Bívar, 13 www.barcolumbus.com

Both the bougiest and busiest bar in town (at least at the start of the night), Columbus Bar focuses on cocktails. A huge front porch with modern (read: somewhat uncomfortable) seating and an interior filled with black leather, it seems that the decor is trying to make the bar appear more upscale (and it's working). Hold any of the tall and colorful cocktails in your hand and you earn instant sophistication points. One of the most intriguing items on the extensive menu is the Algarve Cocktail (€5), whose recipe is a house secret.

From Jardim Manuel Bívar, walk away from the marina and to the right. $ Cocktails €5-7. ⏰ Open daily 11am-4am.

ROCKLINE BAR

Tv. dos Arcos, 5 ☎96 617 95 58

A down-to-earth everyman's bar, Rockline is where that sitcom about you and your three best friends should probably take place. Drinks are quite cheap, especially in bulk, so the show should have a decent-sized cast of tertiary characters. Loads of wind chimes, dreamcatchers, and other trinkets hang from the ceiling. Unsurprisingly, rock music is the genre of choice, but it isn't edgy enough to make anyone want to leave.

From Jardim Manuel Bívar, take R. Primeiro de Maio away from the water. Turn left at the McDonald's, then the following right. $ Beer €1.30. ⏰ Open daily 9pm-4am.

UPA UPA BAR BAR, CAFE

R. do Conselheiro Bívar, 57

With plenty of seating outside to gawk at the drunk passersby, Upa Upa Bar carries its cafe image well into the night. There is noisy rock music and dark wooden furnishings inside, but almost everyone takes their drinks to the tables out in the street. The bar sits across the street from a late-night snack shop, so you can fill up on pizza before you move on to bigger and louder things.

From Jardim Manuel Bívar, walk away from the marina. After you see McDonald's, turn left onto the next street. The bar is on the left. $ Beer €1.50. ⏰ Open daily 9pm-2am.

ARTS AND CULTURE

Although not renowned for its musical prowess or high-brow culture, Faro holds a great deal of cultural events year-round, especially for a city of its size. The best place for information on festivals and cultural events is the city's website (www.cm-faro.pt).

FARO INTERNATIONAL MOTORCYCLE RALLY DOWNTOWN

☎28 982 38 45 www.motoclubefaro.pt

Every summer for four days, Faro turns into Europe's biker Mecca. Thousands of bikers take their rides straight through downtown for everyone to see. For those involved, there are also big-name live bands and entertainment all week long.

$ Contact club for packages. ⏰ Late July.

FESTA DA RIA FORMOSA LARGO DA SÉ

☎28 987 08 70 www.cm-faro.pt

Almost directly after the bike rally, Faro switches gears and heads into an all-out seafood extravaganza. Chefs come in from the world over, and many gastronomical exhibitions are put on. Seafood is also obviously everywhere, with vendors selling more fish than you could ever dream of.

⏰ Late July to early Aug.

SHOPPING

The pedestrian streets behind the marina, particularly **Rua de Santo António,** are filled with all kinds of clothing stores, from designer to discount. The streets just beyond that area also have some various strip malls and stores, but not to the same extent. Antique and general flea markets occur in **Montenegro** (1st Su of month), **Estoi** (2nd Su of month), and by Faro's **Municipal Theater** (3rd Su of each month). These markets run the gamut from food vendors to antique hoarders to people just trying to sell junk. As always, go early for the best picks.

ESSENTIALS

Practicalities

- **TOURIST OFFICE:** R. Misericórdia, 8 ☎28 980 36 04 ⇄ From the bus and train station, turn right and follow Av. República along the water. Continue to follow the water as you pass Jardim Manuel Bívar; turn left after the Jardim onto R. Misericórdia. ⏰ Open daily 9:30am-5:30pm.
- **CURRENCY EXCHANGE: Cotacâmbios.** (Av. República, 16 ☎28 982 20 44 ⏰ Open daily 9am-10pm.)
- **INTERNET ACCESS:** Free Wi-Fi at **McDonald's.** (R. Conselheiro Bívar, 23 ☎28 987 89 60 ⏰ Open daily 10am-midnight.)
- **POST OFFICE:** Lg. Carmo ⏰ Open M-F 8:30am-6:30pm.

Emergency

- **POLICE:** Rua PSP, 32. ☎28 989 98 99
- **MEDICAL SERVICES: Hospital de Faro.** (R. Leão Penedo ☎28 989 11 59)
- **PHARMACY: Farmácia Montepio.** (R. Santo António, 55 ☎28 982 36 36 ⏰ Open daily 9am-8pm)

Getting There

Hordes of travelers fly into **Faro International Airport** (FAO ☎289 80 08 00 www.faro-airport.org), mainly because of the ridiculously cheap flights offered by **Ryanair** (www.ryanair.com). The **Urbana #14 and 16** buses and **taxis** can be taken into the city. **Trains** run from the Lisbon Entre Campos station to Faro. ($ €21-22. ⏰ 3-4hr., 5 per day 8:30am-6:30pm.) **Rede Expressos buses** are available from Lisbon ($ €19.50-20 ⏰ 3-4hr., 10-15 per day 7am-1am), and **EVA buses** are available from Lagos ($ €5.80 ⏰ 2hr., 6 per day 6:50am-5:15pm).

Getting Around

Faro is not a large city, so most choose to get around on foot. However, the beach and a few other locations are accessible by **bus** if you don't feel like breaking a sweat. There are only a few bus routes, the most useful being the **Urbana #14 and 16.** ($ €1.90. ⏰ M-F 7:00am-10:05pm, Sa-Su 7:00am-7:30pm.) Both can be picked up at Av. República and run all the way out to the airport and the beach. **Taxis** (☎28 982 41 86) are available near the bus station, but are used almost exclusively for transport to and from the airport.

ESSENTIALS

You don't have to be a rocket scientist to plan a good trip. (It might help, but it's not required.) You do, however, need to be well prepared, and that's what we can do for you. Essentials is the chapter that gives you all the nitty-gritty you need to know for your trip: the hard information gleaned from 50 years of collective wisdom and several months of furious fact-checking. Planning your trip? Check. Where to find Wi-Fi? Check. The dirt on public transportation? Check. We've also thrown in communications info, safety tips, and a 🔖phrasebook, just for good measure. Plus, for overall trip-planning advice from what to pack (money and as little underwear as possible) to how to take a good passport photo (it's physically impossible; consider airbrushing), you can also check out the Essentials section of www.letsgo.com.

So, flick through this chapter before you leave so you know what documents to bring, while you're on the plane so you know how you'll be getting from the airport to your accommodation, and when you're on the ground so you can find a laundromat to cater to all your 3am stain-removal needs. This chapter may not always be the most scintillating read, but it just might save your life.

greatest hits

- **GET A PASSPORT.** Get one or don't plan on getting in. (p. 552)

- **MO' MONEY, FEWER PROBLEMS.** Credit, debit, ATM, traveler's checks. They all have their merits, but you don't want to be stuck exchanging money at a horrible rate because you didn't plan ahead. (p. 555)

- **USE SKYPE TO STAY IN TOUCH.** So free, but only if you can teach your parents how to use it. (p. 562)

- **BUY A RAIL PASS** Want to traipse all over the country with no pesky reservations? (p. 559)

- **SHIP SOUVENIRS HOME BY SURFACE MAIL.** Our scintillating "By Snail Mail" section will tell you how. You'll laugh, you'll cry. (p. 563)

planning your trip

DOCUMENTS AND FORMALITIES

You've got your visa (especially if you're studying abroad) and your work permit, just like Let's Go told you to, and then you realize you've forgotten the most important thing: your passport. Well, we're not going to let that happen. **Don't forget your passport!**

Visas

EU citizens do not need a visa to globetrot through Spain and Portugal. Citizens of Australia, Canada, New Zealand, and the US do not need a visa for stays of up to 90 days, but this three-month period begins upon entry into any of the countries that belong to the EU's **freedom of movement** zone. For more information, see **One Europe** (below). A visa allows the holder to spend six months in Spain or Portugal.

Non-EU citizens who are going to be studying abroad in Spain or Portugal, and who will thus be staying for more than three months, will need a visa. Obtaining a student visa will allow you to spend up to six months in the country. Student visas for study in Spain cost $100 for American students and $80 for students from most other countries. Student visas for study in Portugal are less expensive, typically costing around $45. Visas can be purchased at the Spanish Consulates in (US) Boston, Chicago, Houston, Los Angeles, Miami, New York City, San Francisco, Washington DC, (Canada) Edmonton, Halifax, Montreal, Ottawa, Quebec, St. John's, Toronto, Winnipeg, (Australia) Canberra, Melbourne, Sydney, (New Zealand) Christchurch. Portugal's consulates are located in (US) Boston, Chicago, Honolulu, Houston, Los Angeles, Newark, New York, Philadelphia, San Francisco,

essentials

Washington DC, (Canada) Ottawa, Toronto, (Australia) Canberra, Sydney, (New Zealand) Auckland, Wellington.

Double-check entrance requirements at the nearest Spanish or Portuguese embassy or consulate (listed below) for up-to-date information before departure. US citizens can also consult http://travel.state.gov. For more information on studying abroad, see the **Beyond Tourism** chapter.

spanish consular services

- **SPANISH CONSULATE IN AUSTRALIA: Consulate General.** (Level 24, St. Martin's Tower, 31 Market St., Sydney NSW 2000 ☎+61 2 9261 2433 ⌚Open M-Tu 9am-2pm, W 9am-4pm, Th-F 9am-2pm.)

- **AUSTRALIAN EMBASSY IN SPAIN: Embassy.** (Torre Espacio, Paseo de la Castellana, 259D, 24th fl., Madrid 28046 ☎+34 91 353 6600 www.spain.embassy.gov.au ⌚ Open M-F 8:30am-4:30pm.)

- **SPANISH EMBASSY IN CANADA: Embassy.** (74 Stanley Ave., Ottawa, Ontario, Canada, K1M 1P4 ☎+1 613-747-2252 www.maec.es/subwebs/Embajadas/Ottawa ⌚ Open M-F 9am-1pm.)

- **CANADIAN EMBASSY IN SPAIN: Embassy.** (Torre Espacio, Paseo de la Castellana, 259D, Madrid 28046 ☎+34 91 382 8400 www.canadainternational.gc.ca/spain-espagne ⌚ Open M-Th 8:30am-1pm and 2-5:30pm F 8:30am-2:30pm, during August M-F 8:30am-2:15pm.)

- **SPANISH EMBASSY IN IRELAND: Embassy.** (17A Merlyn Park, Ballsbridge, Dublin ☎+353 1 26 91 640 www.mae.es/Embajadas/dublin ⌚ Open M-F 9:30am-1:30pm.)

- **IRISH EMBASSY IN SPAIN: Embassy.** (Ireland House, Paseo de la Castellana 46-4, Madrid 28046 ☎+34 91 436 4093 www.irlanda.es ⌚ Open M-F 10am-2pm.)

- **SPANISH EMBASSY IN NEW ZEALAND: Embassy.** (Level 11 BNZ Trust House Bldg., 50 Manners St., Wellington 6142 ☎ +64 4 802 5665 www.mae.es/Embajadas/wellington ⌚ Open M-F 10am-1pm.)

- **NEW ZEALAND EMBASSY IN SPAIN: Embassy.** (Pinar 7, 3rd fl., Madrid 28046 ☎+34 91 523 0226 wwww.nxembassy.com/spain ⌚ Open Sept-June M-F 9am-2pm and 3-5:30pm, July-Aug M-F 8:30am-1:30 and 2-4:30pm.)

- **SPANISH EMBASSY IN BRITAIN: Embassy.** (39 Chesham Pl., London SW1X 8SB ☎+44 20 7235 55 55 www.maec.es/Embajadas/Londres ⌚ Open M-F 9:30am-noon.) **Consulate General.** (63 North Castle St., Edinburgh EH2 3LJ ☎+44 780 137 1704 www.maec.es/consulados/Edimburgo ⌚ Open M-F 9am-2pm.)

- **BRITISH CONSULATE IN SPAIN: Consulate-General** (Torre Espacio, Paseo de la Castellana 259D, Madrid 28046 ☎+34 91 334 2194 http://ukinspain.fco.gov.uk ⌚ Open M-F 8:30am-1:30pm.)

- **SPANISH EMBASSY IN US: Embassy.** (2375 Pennsylvania Ave. NW, Washington DC 20037 ☎+1 202-452-0100 www.maec.es/embajadas/Washington ⌚ Open M-F 9am-5pm.)

- **US CONSULATE IN SPAIN: Consulate General.** (Paseo Reina Elisenda de Montcada 23, Barcelona 08034 ☎+34 93 280 22 27 http://barcelona.usconsulate.gov ⌚ Open M-F 9am-1pm.)

- **PORTUGUESE EMBASSY IN AUSTRALIA: Consulate General.** (55 Clarence St., Sydney NSW 2000 ☎+61 2 926 221 99 www.secomunidades.pt/web/sydney 🕐 Open M-F 9am-1pm.)

- **AUSTRALIAN EMBASSY IN PORTUGAL: Embassy.** (Av. da Liberdade, 200, 2nd fl., Lisbon 1250-147 ☎+351 21 310 1500 www.portugal.embassy.gov.au 🕐 Open M-F 9am-5pm.)

- **PORTUGUESE EMBASSY IN CANADA: Embassy.** (645 Island Park Dr., Ottawa, Ontario K1Y 0B8 ☎+1 613-729-0883.)

- **CANADIAN EMBASSY IN PORTUGAL:** **Embassy.** (Av. da Liberdade, 198-200, 3rd Fl., Lisbon 1269-121 ☎+351 21 316 4600 www.canadainternational.gc.ca/portugal 🕐 Open M-Th 8:30am-12:30pm and 1:30pm-5:30pm, F 8:30am-2pm.)

- **PORTUGUESE EMBASSY IN IRELAND: Embassy.** (15 Leeson Park, Dublin 6 ☎+34 01 412 7040 www.embaixadaportugal.ie.)

- **IRISH EMBASSY IN PORTUGAL: Embassy.** (Av. da Liberdade 200, 4th fl., 1250-147 Lisbon ☎+351 213 208 200 www.embassyofireland.pt 🕐 Open M-F 9:30am-1-2:30pm.)

- **PORTUGUESE CONSULATE IN NEW ZEALAND: Consulate.** (16 Fisher Crescent, Mt. Wellington, Auckland, PO Box 305 ☎+64 9 259 4014 🕐 By appointment.)

- **NEW ZEALAND EMBASSY IN PORTUGAL:** Represented by the New Zealand Embassy in Rome, **Italy.** (Via Clitunno 44, Rome 00198 ☎+39 06 853 7501 www.nzembassy.com/italy 🕐 Open M-F 8:30am-12:30pm and 1:30-5pm.)

- **PORTUGUESE EMBASSY IN BRITAIN: Embassy.** (11 Belgrave Sq., London SW1X 8PP ☎+44 020 7235 5331 www.portuguese-embassy.org.uk 🕐 Open M-F 8:30am-1pm.)

- **BRITISH EMBASSY IN PORTUGAL: Embassy.** (Rua de São Bernardo 33, Lisbon 1249-082 ☎+351 21 392 4000 http://ukinportugal.fco.gov.uk/en 🕐 Open M-F 9am-1pm and 2:30-5pm. Consular services available M-F 9:30am-2pm.)

- **PORTUGUESE EMBASSY IN US: Embassy.** (2012 Massachusetts Ave. NW, Washington, DC 20036 ☎+1 202-332-3007 www.embassyportugal-us.org 🕐 Open M-Th 8am-3pm, F 9am-1pm.)

- **US EMBASSY IN PORTUGAL: Embassy.** (Av. das Forças Armadas, Lisbon 1600-081 ☎+351 21 727 3300 http://portugal.usembassy.gov 🕐 Open M-F 8am-5pm.)

Work Permits

Admittance to a country as a traveler does not include the right to work, which is authorized only by a work permit. For more information, see the **Beyond Tourism** chapter.

TIME DIFFERENCES

Spain is 1hr. ahead of Greenwich Mean Time (GMT) and observes Daylight Saving Time. During the summer, from the end of March until the end of October, time is shifted forward 1hr. (GMT +2). This means that it is 6hr. ahead of New York City, 9hr. ahead of Los Angeles, 1hr. ahead of the British Isles, 8hr. behind Sydney, and 10hr. behind New Zealand.

essentials

Portugal is on Greenwich Mean Time (and is thus 1hr. behind Spain) and observes Daylight Saving Time. During the summer, from the end of March until the end of October, time is shifted forward 1hr. (GMT +1).This means that Portugal is 5hr. ahead of New York City, 8hr. ahead of Los Angeles, the same time as the British Isles, 9hr. behind Sydney, and 11hr. behind New Zealand.

money

GETTING MONEY FROM HOME

Stuff happens. When stuff happens, you might need some money. When you need some money, the easiest and cheapest solution is to have someone back home make a deposit to your bank account. Otherwise, consider one of the following options.

Wiring Money

Arranging a **bank money transfer** means asking a bank back home to wire money to a bank in Spain or Portugal. This is the cheapest way to transfer cash, but it's also the slowest and most agonizing, usually taking several days or more. Note that some banks may only release your funds in local currency, potentially sticking you with a poor exchange rate; inquire about this in advance. International bank transfers normally take 2-4 days to complete. Money transfer services like **Western Union** are faster and more convenient than bank transfers—but are also much pricier. Western Union has many locations worldwide. To find one, visit www.westernunion.com or call the appropriate number: in Australia ☎1800 173 833, in Canada ☎800-235-0000, in the US ☎800-325-6000, in the UK ☎0800 735 1815, in Spain ☎900 983 273 and in Portugal ☎800 832 136. To wire money using a credit card in the US and Canada, call ☎800-CALL-CASH; in the UK, ☎0800 731 1815.

US State Department (US Citizens Only)

In serious emergencies only, the US State Department will forward money within hours to the nearest consular office, which will then disburse it according to instructions for a US$30 fee. If you wish to use this service, you must contact the Overseas Citizens Services division of the US State Department. (☎+1 202-501-4444, from US ☎888-407-4747)

pins and atms

To use a debit or credit card to withdraw money from a cash machine (ATM) in Europe, you must have a four-digit Personal Identification Number (PIN). If your PIN is longer than four digits, ask your bank whether you can just use the first four or whether you'll need a new one. Credit cards don't usually come with PINs, so if you intend to hit up ATMs in Europe with a credit card to get cash advances, call your credit card company before leaving to request one.

Travelers with alphabetic rather than numeric PINs may also be thrown off by the absence of letters on European cash machines. Here are the corresponding numbers to use: 1 = QZ; 2 = ABC; 3 = DEF; 4 = GHI; 5 = JKL; 6 = MNO; 7 = PRS; 8 = TUV; 9 = WXY. Note that if you mistakenly punch the wrong code into the machine multiple (often three) times, it can swallow (gulp!) your card for good.

money

TIPPING AND BARGAINING

Native Spaniards rarely tip more than their spare change, even at expensive restaurants. However, if you make it clear that you're a tourist—especially an American one—they might expect you to tip more. Don't feel like you have to tip; servers' pay is almost never based on tips. At many restaurants, the tip is simply included in the bill and if you order the *menú del día*, no tip is necessary. No one will refuse your money, but you're a poor student so don't play the fool.

In Portugal, the natives almost never leave tips. If you do tip a waiter, don't tip more than 5% and try to be discreet about it. As a general practice, though, don't leave tips. Your money will likely not be refused, but it is not at all necessary or expected.

Bargaining is common and necessary in open-air and street markets in Spain and Portugal. Especially if you are buying a number of things, like produce, you can probably get a better deal if you haggle. Don't try to lowball vendors, though, because it can be taken as offensive. Do not barter in malls or established shops.

---

the euro

Despite what many dollar-possessing Americans might want to hear, the official currency of 16 members of the European Union—Austria, Belgium, Cyprus, Finland, France, Germany, Greece, Ireland, Italy, Luxembourg, Malta, the Netherlands, Portugal, Slovakia, Slovenia, and Spain—is the euro.

Still, the currency has some important—and positive—consequences for travelers hitting more than one eurozone country. For one thing, money-changers across the eurozone are obliged to exchange money at the official, fixed rate (below) and at no commission (though they may still charge a small service fee). Second, euro-denominated traveler's checks allow you to pay for goods and services across the eurozone, again at the official rate and commission-free. For more info, check a currency converter (such as www.xe.com) or www.europa.eu.int.

TAXES

Both Spain and Portugal have a value added tax (*IVA*) on all restaurant services and accommodations. In Spain, the tax is 10%, whereas in Portugal it is 13%. The prices listed in Let's Go include IVA unless otherwise mentioned. Retail goods bear a high 21-23% IVA, although the listed prices generally include this tax. Non-EU citizens who have stayed in the EU fewer than 180 days can claim back the tax paid on purchases at the airport. Ask the shop where you have made the purchase to supply you with a tax return form, but stores will only provide them for purchases of more than €50-100. **Taxes,** presently 23%, are included in all prices in Portugal. Request a refund form, an *Insenção de IVA*, and present it to customs upon departure.

safety and health

GENERAL ADVICE

In any type of crisis, the most important thing is to **stay calm.** Your country's embassy abroad is usually your best resource in an emergency; registering with that embassy upon arrival in the country is a good idea. The government offices listed in the **Travel Advisories** feature at the end of this section can provide information on the services they offer their citizens in case of emergencies abroad.

Local Laws and Police

Travelers are not likely to break major laws unintentionally while visiting Spain or Portugal. You can contact your embassy if arrested, although they often cannot do much to assist you beyond finding legal counsel. You should feel comfortable approaching the police, although few officers speak English. There are several types of police in Spain. The **Policía Nacional** wear blue or black uniforms and white shirts; they guard government buildings, protect dignitaries, and deal with criminal investigations (including theft). The **Policía Local** wear blue uniforms, deal more with local issues, and report to the mayor or town hall in each municipality. The **Guardia Civil** wear olive-green uniforms and are responsible for issues more relevant to travelers: customs, crowd control, and national security. Catalonia also has its own police force, the **Mossos d'Esquadra.** Officers generally wear blue and occasionally sport berets or other interesting headgear. This police force is often used for crowd control and deals with riots. In Portugal, the **Policía de Segurança Pública** is the police force in all major cities and towns. The **Guarda Nacional Republicana** polices more rural areas, while the **Brigada de Trânsito** is the traffic police, who sport red armbands. All three branches wear light blue uniforms.

Drugs and Alcohol

Recreational drugs are illegal in Spain and Portugal, and police take these laws seriously. In Portugal, however, recreational drug use has been decriminalized, so instead of jail time and fines, perpetrators face community service and government-imposed therapy. The legal minimum drinking age in both countries is 16. Spain and Portugal have the highest road mortality rates in Europe, and Spain has one of the highest rates of drunk driving deaths in Europe. Recently, Spanish officials have started setting up checkpoints on roads to test drivers' blood alcohol content (BAC). Look for new cautionary signs on the highways that display how many Spaniards have died recently from drunk driving. Do not drive while intoxicated and be cautious on the road.

SPECIFIC CONCERNS

Terrorism

Until very recently, **Basque terrorism** was a serious concern for all travelers in Spain. A militant wing of Basque separatists called the *Euskadi Ta Askatasuna* (**ETA;** Basque Homeland and Freedom) continued to have an active presence well into the 2000s, but has recently taken a more dormant stance. Historically, ETA's attacks have been politically targeted and are not considered random terrorist attacks that endanger regular civilians. In January 2011, ETA declared a "permanent and general cease-fire," and at this point many of ETA's leaders have been arrested. The group has also announced a "definitive cessation of its armed activity."

safety and health

The following government offices provide travel information and advisories:

- **AUSTRALIA: Department of Foreign Affairs and Trade.** (☎+61 2 6261 1111 www.smartraveller.gov.au)

- **CANADA: Department of Foreign Affairs and International Trade.** Call or visit the website for the free booklet *Bon Voyage, But...* (☎+1 800-267-6788 www.international.gc.ca)

- **NEW ZEALAND: Ministry of Foreign Affairs and Trade.** (☎+64 4 439 8000 www.safetravel.govt.nz)

- **UK: Foreign and Commonwealth Office.** (☎+44 845 850 2829 www.fco.gov.uk)

- **US: Department of State.** (☎888-407-4747 from the US, +1-202-501-4444 elsewhere http://travel.state.gov)

PRE-DEPARTURE HEALTH

Matching a prescription to a foreign equivalent is not always easy, safe, or possible, so if you take **prescription drugs,** carry up-to-date prescriptions or a statement from your doctor stating the medications' trade names, manufacturers, chemical names, and dosages. Be sure to keep all medication with you in your carry-on luggage.

Pharmacists in Spain and Portugal often speak very good English and can help you find common over-the-counter drugs. The names for such drugs in Spanish are also quite similar to those in English. One difference you will notice is that the Spanish are fond of effervescents—drugs are often delivered in powder form, which you dissolve into water.

Immunizations And Precautions

Travelers over two years old should make sure that the following vaccines are up to date: MMR (for measles, mumps, and rubella); DTaP or Td (for diphtheria, tetanus, and pertussis); IPV (for polio); Hib (for *Haemophilus influenzae* B); and HepB (for Hepatitis B). If you are reading this and are under the age of two, congratulations, you don't need vaccines and are entirely too literate for your age. For recommendations on immunizations and prophylaxis, check with a doctor and consult the **Centers for Disease Control and Prevention (CDC)** in the US or the equivalent in your home country. (☎+1 800-232-4636 www.cdc.gov/travel)

getting there

BY PLANE

When it comes to airfare, a little research can save you a bundle. Courier fares are cheapest for those whose plans are flexible enough to deal with the restrictions. Tickets sold by consolidators and standby seating are also good deals, but last-minute specials, airfare wars, and charter flights often beat these fares. The key is to hunt around, be flexible, and ask about discounts. Students, seniors, and those under 26 should never have to pay full price for a ticket.

Airfares to Spain and Portugal peak between the end of May and early September, and holiday periods are also expensive. The cheapest times to travel to the Iberian

essentials

Peninsula are typically between December and February. Midweek (M-Th morning) round-trip flights run a bit cheaper than weekend flights, but they are generally more crowded and less likely to permit frequent-flyer upgrades. Not fixing a return date ("open return") or arriving in and departing from different cities ("open-jaw") can be pricier than round-trip flights. Patching one-way flights together is the most expensive way to travel. Flights between Spain and Portugal's capitals or regional hubs—Madrid, Barcelona, Lisbon—will tend to be cheaper.

BY TRAIN

You can either buy a railpass, which allows you unlimited travel within a particular region for a given period of time, or rely on buying individual point-to-point tickets as you go. Almost all countries give students or youths (usually defined as anyone under 26) direct discounts on regular domestic rail tickets, and many also sell a student or youth card that provides 20-50% off of fares.

Railpasses were conceived to allow you to jump onto any train in Europe, go wherever you want whenever you want, and change your plans at will. In practice, it's not so simple. You still must stand in line to validate your pass, pay for supplements, and fork over cash for seat and couchette reservations. More importantly, railpasses don't always pay off. If you plan to spend extensive time on trains hopping between big cities, a railpass will probably be worth it. But in many cases, especially if you are under 26, point-to-point tickets may prove a cheaper option. It may be tough to make your railpass pay for itself in Spain and Portugal, where train fares are reasonable, distances short, and buses often preferable.

Eurail

Eurail is valid in much of Europe: Austria, Belgium, Bulgaria, Croatia, Czech Republic, Denmark, Finland, France, Germany, Greece, Hungary, Italy, Luxembourg, the Netherlands, Norway, Portugal, the Republic of Ireland, Romania, Slovakia, Slovenia, Spain, Sweden, and Switzerland. It is not valid in the UK. Eurail Global Passes, valid for a given number of consecutive days, are best for those planning on spending extensive time on trains every few days. Global passes valid for any 10 or 15 (not necessarily consecutive) days within a two-month period are more cost-effective for those traveling longer distances less frequently. Eurail Pass Saver provides first-class travel for travelers in groups of two to five (prices are per person). Eurail Pass Youth provides parallel second-class perks for those under 26. Passholders receive a timetable for major routes and a map with details on possible bike rental, car rental, hotel, and museum discounts. Passholders often also receive reduced fares or free passage on many boat, bus, and private railroad lines. The Eurail Select Pass is a slimmed-down version of the Eurail Pass: it allows five, six, eight, 10, or 15 days of unlimited travel in any two-month period within three, four, or five bordering countries of 23 European nations.

Eurail Passes are designed by the EU itself and can be bought only by non-Europeans almost exclusively from non-European distributors. These passes must be sold at uniform prices determined by the EU. However, some travel agents tack on a handling fee, and others offer certain bonuses with purchase, so shop around. Also, keep in mind that pass prices usually go up each year, so save cash by purchasing before January 1 (you have 6 months from the purchase date to validate your pass in Europe). Because only a few places in major European cities sell them, and at a marked-up price, it is best to buy your pass before leaving. You can get a replacement for a lost pass only if you have purchased insurance under the Pass Security Plan (€10). Eurail Passes are available through travel agents, student travel agencies like STA, as well as Rail Europe (www.raileurope.com) or directly from Eurail's website, www.eurail.com.

getting there

Other Multinational Passes

If your travels will be limited to one area, regional passes are often the best value. Visit www.raileurope.com and www.eurail.com for Portugal-Spain Pass options. If you have lived for at least six months in one of the European countries where **InterRail Passes** are valid, they prove an economical option. The InterRail Pass allows travel within 30 European countries excluding the passholder's country of residence. The Global Pass is valid for a given number of days (not necessarily consecutive) in a 10-day to one-month period. The One Country Pass limits travel to one European country. Passholders receive free admission to many museums as well as discounts on accommodations, food, and ferries. Passes are available at www.interrailnet.com as well as from travel agents and at major train stations throughout Europe.

getting around

BY PLANE

Many national airlines offer multi-stop tickets for travel within Spain and Portugal. These tickets are particularly useful for travel between the Spanish mainland and the Balearic and Canary Islands. Outside of the peninsula, the recent emergence of no-frills airlines has made hopscotching around Europe by air increasingly affordable and convenient. Though these flights often feature inconvenient hours or serve less-popular regional airports, it's never been faster or easier to jet across the Continent.

The **Star Alliance European Airpass** offers economy-class fares for travel within Europe to more than 200 destinations in 44 countries. The pass is available to non-European passengers on Star Alliance carriers, including ANA, Austrian Airlines, BMI, LOT Polish Airlines, Lufthansa, Scandinavian Airlines, SWISS, TAP Portugal, Turkish Airlines, and US Airways. See www.staralliance.com for more information. In addition, a number of European airlines offer discount coupon packets. Most are only available as tack-ons for transatlantic passengers, but some are stand-alone offers. Most must be purchased before departure, so research in advance.

All major international airlines offer service to Madrid and Barcelona, most serve the Balearic and Canary Islands, and many serve Spain's smaller cities. **AirEuropa** (☎+34 902 401 501 www.aireuropa.com) flies between major European cities. **Iberia** (Canada and US ☎+1 800-772-4642, Spain ☎902 40 05 00, UK ☎+44 870 609 0500 www.iberia.com) serves all domestic locations and all major international cities.

budget airlines

- **EASYJET:** (☎+44 871 244 2366 www.easyjet.com). Serves 78 destinations across Europe and northern Africa.

- **RYANAIR:** (☎+353 1 249 7791, UK ☎0871 246 0000 www.ryanair.com). Serves over 100 airports across Europe and northern Africa.

- **VUELING:** (☎+34 902 33 39 33 www.vueling.com). Based in Barcelona, Vueling serves major cities in Spain and the rest of western Europe.

- **IBERIA:** (☎+1 800-772-4642 www.iberia.com). Offers discount airfare to and within Spain and Europe.

essentials

Most major international airlines serve Lisbon; some serve Faro, the Azores, Madeira, and Porto. **TAP Air Portugal** (US and Canada ☎+1 800-221-7370, UK ☎+44 845 601 0932, Lisbon ☎707 20 57 00 www.tap.pt) is Portugal's national airline, serving all domestic locations and many major international cities.

BY TRAIN

Trains in Spain and Portugal are generally comfortable, convenient, and reasonably swift, and second-class compartments are great places to meet fellow travelers. Make sure you are on the correct car, as trains sometimes split at crossroads. Towns listed in parentheses on European train schedules require a train switch at the town listed immediately before the parentheses.

You can either buy a **railpass,** which allows you unlimited travel within a particular region for a given period of time, or rely on buying individual **point-to-point** tickets as you go. Almost all countries give students or youths (under 26, usually) direct discounts on regular domestic rail tickets, and many also sell a student or youth card that provides 20-50% off all fares for up to a year.

RENFE dominates the train services in Spain and Portugal and offers great rates if you book ahead on the web. (☎+34 902 320 320 www.renfe.com.) Beware though, RENFE's English website is not as good as its Spanish version, and can often be difficult to navigate. You may be better off purchasing your ticket at the station.

BY BUS

Though European trains and railpasses are extremely popular, in some cases buses prove to be a better option. The bus network in Spain and Portugal is much more comprehensive than the train network and is often the best way to get to more rural destinations. Often cheaper than railpasses, **international bus passes** allow unlimited travel on a hop-on, hop-off basis between major European cities. **Busabout,** for instance, offers three interconnecting bus circuits covering 29 of Europe's best bus hubs. (☎+44 845 026 7 514 www.busabout.com) **Eurolines,** meanwhile, is the largest operator of Europe-wide coach services. We get misty-eyed just thinking about their unlimited 15- and 30-day passes to 41 major European cities. (www.eurolines.com $ High season 15-day pass €350, 30-day pass €460; under 26 €295/380. Mid-season €245/335; under 26 €210/275. Low season €210/315; under 26 €180/245.)

Bus routes, far more comprehensive than the rail network, provide the only public transportation to many isolated areas, and almost always cost less than trains. They are generally quite comfortable, though leg room may be limited. For those traveling primarily within one region, buses are the best method of transport. We list below the major national companies, along with the phone number of their Madrid office; you will likely use many other companies. For more information, see the Getting There section for your destination.

In Portugal, buses are cheap and frequent. They connect just about every town in Portugal. **Rodoviária** (☎212 94 71 00 www.rodotejo.pt), the national bus company, was recently privatized. Private regional companies also operate. Be wary of non-express buses in small regions like Estremadura and Alentejo, which stop every few minutes. Express coach service *(expressos)* between major cities is especially good; inexpensive city buses often run to nearby villages. Schedules *(horarios)* are usually printed and posted, but double-check with the ticket vendor to make sure they are accurate.

keeping in touch

BY EMAIL AND INTERNET

Hello and welcome to the 21st century, where you can check your email in most major European cities, though sometimes you'll have to pay a few bucks or buy a drink for internet access. Although in some places it's possible to forge a remote link with your home server, in most cases this is a much slower (and thus more expensive) option than taking advantage of free **web-based email accounts** (e.g., 🗹**www. gmail.com**). **Internet cafes** and the occasional free internet terminal at a public library or university are listed in the **Practicalities** sections of cities that we cover. For lists of additional cybercafes in Spain and Portugal, check out www.cybercafes.com and www.andalucia.com/internet/cybercafes/home.htm for Andalucía specifically. Also, sometimes you can steal Wi-Fi from hostels—just look like you're staying there and chill in the common area.

BY TELEPHONE

Calling Home From Spain/Portugal

Prepaid phone cards are a common and relatively inexpensive means of calling abroad. Each one comes with a Personal Identification Number (PIN) and a toll-free access number. You call the access number and then follow the directions for dialing your PIN. To purchase prepaid phone cards, check online for the best rates; www.callingcards.com is a good place to start. Online providers generally send your access number and PIN via email, with no actual "card" involved. You can also call home with prepaid phone cards purchased in Spain or Portugal.

If you have internet access, your best—i.e., cheapest, most convenient, and most tech-savvy—bet is probably our good friend **Skype.** (www.skype.com) You can even videochat if you have one of those new-fangled webcams. Calls to other Skype users are free; calls to landlines and mobiles worldwide start at US$0.021 per minute, depending on where you're calling.

Another option is a **calling card,** linked to a major national telecommunications service in your home country. Calls are billed collect or to your account. Cards generally come with instructions for dialing both domestically and internationally.

Placing a collect call through an international operator can be expensive but may be necessary in case of an emergency. You can frequently call collect without even possessing a company's calling card just by calling its access number and following the instructions.

Cellular Phones

The international standard for cell phones is **Global System for Mobile Communication (GSM).** To make and receive calls in Spain and Portugal, you will need a GSM-compatible phone and a **SIM (Subscriber Identity Module) card,** a country-specific, thumbnail-sized chip that gives you a local phone number and plugs you into the local network. You can buy additional cards or vouchers (usually available at convenience stores) to "top up" your phone. For more information on GSM phones, check out www.telestial.com. Companies like **Cellular Abroad** (www.cellularabroad.com) and **OneSimCard** (www.onesimcard.com) rent cell phones and SIM cards that work in a variety of destinations around the world.

essentials

international calls

To call Spain/Portugal from home or to call home from Spain/Portugal dial:

1. THE INTERNATIONAL DIALING PREFIX. To call from **Australia,** dial ☎0011; **Canada** or the **US,** ☎011; **Ireland, New Zealand,** or the **UK,** ☎00; **Spain,** ☎00; **Portugal,** ☎00.

2. THE COUNTRY CODE OF THE COUNTRY YOU WANT TO CALL. To call **Australia,** dial ☎61; **Canada** or the **US,** ☎1; **Ireland,** ☎353; **New Zealand,** ☎64; the **UK,** ☎44; **Spain,** ☎34; **Portugal,** ☎351.

3. THE CITY/AREA CODE. *Let's Go* lists the city/area codes for cities and towns in Spain and Portugal opposite the city or town name, next to a ☎, as well as in every phone number. If the first digit is a zero (e.g., ☎0981 for Santiago de Compostela), omit the zero when calling from abroad (e.g., dial ☎981 from Canada to reach Santiago de Compostela).

4. THE LOCAL NUMBER.

BY SNAIL MAIL
Sending Mail Home From Spain or Portugal

Airmail is the best way to send mail home from Spain or Portugal. **Aerogrammes,** printed sheets that fold into envelopes and travel via airmail, are available at post offices. Write "airmail," "par avion," "por avión," "por avião," or "via aerea" on the front. In Spain, airmail usually takes from five to 10 business days to reach the US or Canada. Express mail may be the most reliable way to send a letter or parcel, and takes four to seven business days. Mail in Portugal can be inefficient—airmail can take from one to two weeks longer to reach the US. Note that most post offices will charge exorbitant fees or simply refuse to send aerogrammes with enclosures. **Surface mail** is by far the cheapest (and slowest) way to send mail. It takes one to two months for items to cross the Atlantic and one to three to cross the Pacific—good for heavy items you won't need for a while, like tacky souvenirs that you've acquired along the way.

Sending Mail To Spain or Portugal

In addition to the standard postage system whose rates are listed below, **FedEx** handles express mail services from most countries to Spain or Portugal. (☎+1 800-463-3339 www.fedex.com.) DHL serves the same purpose but serves more cities. (☎+1 800-225-5345 www.dhl.com.) Sending a postcard from Spain costs as little as €0.78 while sending letters up to 20g domestically costs €0.34. Sending a postcard from Portugal costs €1.85 while sending a letter domestically costs €0.32.

There are several ways to pick up letters sent to you while you are abroad. Mail can be sent via **Poste Restante** (General Delivery; *Lista de Correos* in Spanish and *Posta Restante* in Portuguese) to almost any city or town in Spain or Portugal with a post office, but it is not very reliable. Address Poste Restante letters like so:

Salvador DALÍ	Amália RODRIGUES
Lista de Correos	Posta Restante
postal code	postal code
City, Spain	City, Portugal

The mail will go to a special desk in the central post office, unless you specify a post office by street address or postal code. It's best to use the largest post office, since mail may be sent there regardless. It is usually safer and quicker, though more expensive, to

keeping in touch

send mail **express or registered.** Bring your passport (or other photo ID) for pickup. If the clerks insist that there is nothing for you, ask them to check under your first name as well. *Let's Go* lists post offices in the **Practicalities** section for each city.

American Express has travel offices throughout the world that offer a free **Client Letter Service** (mail held up to 30 days and forwarded upon request) for cardholders who contact them in advance. Some offices provide these services to non-cardholders (especially AmEx Travelers Cheque holders), but call ahead to make sure. For a complete list of AmEx locations, call ☎+1 800-528-4800 or visit www.americanexpress.com/travel.

climate

Much of Spain and Portugal has a Mediterranean climate, with hot dry summers and relatively mild winters. Northern Spain and Portugal have an Atlantic climate that is wetter and cooler than the south. The far northeast corner of Spain near the Pyrenees Mountains has an alpine climate.

AVG. TEMP.(LOW/ HIGH), PRECIP.	JANUARY			APRIL			JULY			OCTOBER		
	°C	°F	mm	°C	°F	mm	°C	°F	mm	°C	°F	mm
Madrid	2/9	35/49	39	7/18	54/65	48	17/31	63/88	11	10/19	50/66	53
Barcelona	6/13	43/56	31	11/18	52/65	43	21/28	70/83	27	15/21	59/70	86
San Sebastián	6/11	44/51	91	9/14	47/57	107	16/22	61/71	63	13/18	55/65	110
Málaga	2/7	37/46	63	2/7	37/46	63	2/7	37/46	63	2/7	37/46	63
Santiago de Compostela	5/11	41/52	153	7/16	44/60	110	13/24	56/76	27	10/18	50/64	171
Lisbon	8/14	47/57	92	11/19	52/66	54	18/28	64/83	5	15/22	59/72	96

To convert from degrees Fahrenheit to degrees Celsius, subtract 32 and multiply by 5/9. To convert from Celsius to Fahrenheit, multiply by 9/5 and add 32. To learn how to multiply and divide, we recommend a math book or the Google.

°CELSIUS	-5	0	5	10	15	20	25	30	35	40
°FAHRENHEIT	23	32	41	50	59	68	77	86	95	104

measurements

Like the rest of the rational world, Spain and Portugal use the metric system. The basic unit of length is the meter (m), which is divided into 100 centimeters (cm) or 1000 millimeters (mm). One thousand meters make up one kilometer (km). Fluids are measured in liters (L), each divided into 1000 milliliters (mL). A liter of pure water weighs one kilogram (kg), the unit of mass that is divided into 1000 grams (g). One metric ton is 1000kg.

MEASUREMENT CONVERSIONS	
1 inch (in.) = 25.4mm	1 millimeter (mm) = 0.039 in.
1 foot (ft.) = 0.305m	1 meter (m) = 3.28 ft.
1 yard (yd.) = 0.914m	1 meter (m) = 1.094 yd.
1 mile (mi.) = 1.609km	1 kilometer (km) = 0.621 mi.
1 ounce (oz.) = 28.35g	1 gram (g) = 0.035 oz.
1 pound (lb.) = 0.454kg	1 kilogram (kg) = 2.205 lb.
1 fluid ounce (fl. oz.) = 29.57mL	1 milliliter (mL) = 0.034 fl. oz.
1 gallon (gal.) = 3.785L	1 liter (L) = 0.264 gal.

essentials

language

SPAIN

Spanish *castellano*

Castilian or **Spanish** is the official language of Spain. During the *Reconquista*, the kingdom of Castile (centered around modern-day León and Burgos) conquered the central part of the country, along with the key cities of Toledo and Sevilla. When the capital was subsequently established in the Castilian city of Madrid, *castellano*'s place as Spain's primary language was cemented. Spain's Spanish is distinct from its Western Hemisphere counterparts in its hallmark lisp of the *z* and soft *c* and its use of the *vosotros* form (second-person plural).

PRONUNCIATION

All of the phonetic sounds in Spanish are found in English but are represented differently. The *h* is silent in all words. An accent on a letter indicates that the emphasis of the word should be placed on that letter.

PHONETIC UNIT	PRONUNCIATION	PHONETIC UNIT	PRONUNCIATION
a	ah, as in "bra"	u	oo, as in "boo"
e	ey as in "ray"	ll	y-, as in "year"
i	ee as in "fee"	j	h- as in "hat"
o	oh as in "oval"	v	b- as in "boy"

PHRASEBOOK

ENGLISH	SPANISH	PRONUNCIATION
Hello!/Hi!	¡Hola!	OH-lah!
Goodbye!	¡Adiós!	ah-dee-OHS!
Yes.	Sí.	see.
No.	No.	samesies
Please.	Por favor.	pohr fa-VOHR
Sorry!/Excuse me!	¡Perdón!	pear-DOHN!
Good morning	Buenos días	BWAY-nos DEE-ahs
Good evening	Buenas noches	BWAY-nas NO-cheys
How are you?	¿Cómo estás?	CO-mo ehs-TAS?
I'm fine, thanks, and you?	Bien, gracias, ¿y tú?	bee-EN, GRAH-thee-ahs, ee too?
What time is it?	¿Qué hora es?	kay OH-rah ehs?
It's 5 o'clock	Son las cinco.	sown las SEEN-koh
Wait!	¡Espera!	ehs-PEAR-ah
EMERGENCY		
Go away!	¡Vete!	VAY-tay!
Help!	¡Socorro!	So-COHR-ro!
Call the police!	¡Llama la policia!	YAH-mah lah po-LEE-see-ah!
Get a doctor!	¡Llama el médico!	YAH-mah el MEY-dee-koh!
FOOD AND DRINK		
Waiter/waitress	camarero/a	ca-ma-RAY-roh/rah
I'd like...	Me gustaría...	may goost-ah-ree-ah...
Is there meat in this dish?	¿Tiene carne este plato?	tee-YEN-ey CAR-nay EHS-tay PLA-to?
salad	ensalada	try this one on your own
wine (sherry)	vino (jerez)	BEE-no (hay-RAYTH)
shots	chupitos	choo-PEE-tohs
Spanish cured ham	jamón serrano	ha-MOAN ser-RAH-no

| Can I buy you a drink? | ¿Te compro una copa? | tay KOM-pro OO-nah KO-pah? |
| Is the bread free? | ¿Está gratis el pan? | es-TAH GRAH-tees el pahn? |

ENGLISH	SPANISH	ENGLISH	SPANISH
I am from (the US/ Europe).	Soy de (los Estados Unidos/Europa).	What's the problem, sir/ madam?	¿Cuál es el problema, señor/señora?
I have a visa/ID.	Tengo una visa/identifi- cación.	I lost my passport/ luggage.	Se perdió mi pasaporte/ equipaje.
I will be here for less than three months.	Estaré aquí por menos de tres meses.	I have nothing to declare.	No tengo nada para declarar.
How much does a bed in the dorm (a single/ double/triple/quad roo) m cost?	Cuánto vale una cama en el dormitorio (una habi- tación individual, doble, triple, cuádruple)?	Are the towels/linens free?	Está gratis el uso de las toallas/las sábanas?

Catalan *català*

Along the Mediterranean coast from Alicante up to the French border, the main language spoken is **Catalan,** along with its close relative **Valencian.** Throughout the regions of **Catalonia**, **Valencia**, and the **Balearic Islands**, as well as parts of Aragon, this Romance language sounds to most ears like a combination of Spanish, Italian, and French. It's perhaps most closely related to the southern French Provençal and Occitan, the languages of medieval troubadours. The language experienced a literary renaissance, the *Renaixença*, toward the end of the 19th century, was suppressed by Franco in the 20th, and has returned once more to regional dominance. It's also the official language of the small principality of Andorra. Never imply that Catalan is a dialect of Spanish—this is untrue and will turn the entire nation of Andorra against you.

PRONUNCIATION

Vowel sounds in Catalan vary depending on whether or not they are the stressed syllable in the word (for example, the stressed vowel in "Barcelona" would be "o"). An accent on a letter indicates that the emphasis of the word should be placed on that letter. Otherwise, the accent falls on the second-to-last syllable in words ending in a vowel or "s," and on the final syllable in almost all other cases. Valencian dialects have pronunciation nearly identical to that of Spanish.

PHONETIC UNIT	PRONUNCIATION	PHONETIC UNIT	PRONUNCIATION
a (stressed)	ah, as in "far"	ll	y, as in "yet"
a (unstressed)	ah, as in "body"	l·l (sometimes written l.l)	l-, as in "pillow"
c (before a, o, u, or consonant)	k- as in "code"	ny (at end of word)	ny(uh), as in "canyon"
c (before e or i)	s- as in "sun"	o (stressed)	oh, as in "oval"
e (stressed)	eh, as "end"	o (unstressed)	oo, as in "food"
e (unstressed)	ah, as in "body"	r (at end of word, pre- ceded by vowel)	silent
g (before a, o, u, or consonant)	g-, as in "go"	r (elsewhere)	same as in Spanish
h	silent	s (not between vowels)	s-, as in "sun"
i	ee, an in "fee"	s (between vowels)	z-, as in "lazy"
ig	-ch, as in "beach"	u	oo, as in "food"
ix	-sh, as in "fish"	v	b-, as in "bed"
j	j-, as in "regime"	x	gs-, as in "example"

essentials

ENGLISH	CATALAN	PRONUNCIATION
Please.	Si us plau. (Sisplau.)	sees-PLOW
Sorry/Excuse me.	Perdó.	pahr-DOH
Good morning/good day.	Bon dia.	bohn DEE-ah
Good afternoon.	Bona tarda.	BOH-nah TAHR-dah
How are you?	Què tal?	keh tahl?
Where are the toilets?	On són els lavabos?	ohn sohn als la-BAH-boos?
How do I get to the Carrer dels Banys Vells?	Cóm s'arriba al Carrer dels Banys Vells?	kom sah-REE-bah ahl kah-RREH dahls bahny(uh)s bays?
What time is it?	Quina hora és?	KEE-nah OH-rah ehs?
It is five thirty.	Són dos quarts de sis. (literally, "it is two quarters of six")	sohn dohs kwarts dah sees
Don't shoot, I'm an American!	No dispari, sóc un nord-americá/ una nord-americana!	noh dees-PAH-ree, sohk oon nohrd-ah-mah-ree-KAH / OO-na nohrd-ah-mah-ree-KAH-nah
It is too expensive.	És massa car.	ehs MAH-sah kahr
I was born in New York.	Vaig néixer a Nova York.	bahch NEH-shah ah NOH-vah york
They told me it never rained in Barcelona. Where can I buy an umbrella?	M'havian dit que mai plou a Barcelona. On puc comprar un paraigües?	mah-BEE-ahn deet kah my ploh ah bahr-sah-LOH-nah. ohn pook koom-PRAH oon pah-RYE-gwahs?
The brothel is right next to the church.	El bordell és al costat de l'església.	ahl boor-DEY ehs ahl koo-STAHT dah lahs-GLEH-zee-ah
My hovercraft is full of eels.	El meu aerodeslizador està ple d'anguiles.	ahl MEH-oo eh-roh-dehs-lee-zah-DOH eh-STAH pleh dahn-GWEE-lahs
It/that hashish/your child is not mine.	Això/aquell haixix/el teu nen no és meu.	ah-SHOH / ah-KAY ah-SHEESH / ahl TEH-oo nehn noh ehs MEH-oo

Basque *euskara*

Basque has stumped linguists for ages—it cannot be connected to any other known language, living or dead, although best guesses are that it's an original tribal language from before the Romans. The language looks extraterrestrial—full of *z*'s, *x*'s, and *k*'s—but the Basques don't care how pretty their language looks; they just care about preserving it. After decades of concerted efforts by Franco to wipe *euskara* out, it is still the official language of about 600,000 people, though you won't need to know a word of it to get by in País Vasco's main cities.

Galician *galego*

Somewhere between Spanish and Portuguese falls Galician, spoken in **Galicia,** in the northwest corner of the peninsula. As with Basque, you won't need your Spanish-Galician dictionary to get by, though it'll probably help with most menus.

Other Languages

In the British territory of Gibraltar, **English** is spoken, of course, though the locals also speak a creole known as **Llanito.** Languages you're less likely to come across in your travels include **Asturian,** spoken along parts of the northern coast; **Leonese,** in the area around **Astorga; Extremaduran,** in Extremadura; **Aranese,** in the valley around Vielha; **Aragonese,** in the mountains of Aragon north of Huesca; and **Caló,** spoken by the Romani or gypsy community across Spain.

language

PORTUGAL

Portuguese *português*

Despite sharing a peninsula of origin and many linguistic similarities, Portuguese is nonetheless distinct from Spanish. The Portuguese are very proud of their linguistic heritage and will only begrudgingly understand if you speak to them in Spanish, so it might be better to just use English.

PRONUNCIATION

Portuguese words are often spelled like their Spanish equivalents, although the pronunciation is different. In addition to regular vowels, Portuguese, like French, has nasal vowels: those with a *tilde* (*ã*, *õ*, etc.) or before an *m* or *n* are pronounced with a nasal twang. At the end of a word, *o* is pronounced "oo" as in "room," and *e* is sometimes silent (usually after a *t* or a *d*). The consonant *s* is pronounced "sh" or "zh" when it occurs before another consonant. The consonants *ch* and *x* are pronounced "sh," although the latter is sometimes pronounced as in English; *j* and *g* (before *e* and *i*) are prounounced "zh"; *ç* sounds like "s." The combinations *nh* and *lh* are pronounced "ny" as in "canyon" and "ly" as in "billion." The masculine singluar definite article is "o" and the feminine singular definite article is "a."

PHRASEBOOK

ENGLISH	PORTUGUESE	PRONUNCIATION
Hello!/Hi!	Olá!	oh-LAH!
Goodbye!	Até logo!	ah-TEH low-goo!
Yes.	Sim	see
No.	Não.	now
Please.	Por favor.	pohr fa-VOHR
Thank you.	Obrigado/a.	oh-bree-GAH-doo/dah
Sorry!/Excuse me!	Desculpe!	dish-KOOL-puh!
Good morning	Bom dia	bohm DEE-uh
Good evening	Boa noite	BO-ah NOY-tuh
How are you?	Como vôce está?	KO-mo voh-say 'sh-TAH?
I'm fine, thanks, and you?	Eu bem, obrigado/a, e vôce?	eh-oo BAYM, obrigado/a, eh vo-say?
What time is it?	Que horas são?	kay OH-rash sao?
It's 5 o'clock	É cinco horas.	ay SEEN-ko oh-rahs
Wait!	Aguarde!	ah-GWAR-duh!
EMERGENCY		
Go away!	Vá embora!	VAH ehm-BOR-uh!
Help!	Socorro!	so-COH-hoo!
Call the police!	Chamar a polícia!	shah-MAR ah po-LEE-see-ah!
Get a doctor!	Chamar um doutor!	shah-MAR oom doh-TOR!
FOOD AND DRINK		
waiter/waitress	garçom/garçonete	gar-SOHM/gar-sohn-EH-tuh
I'd like...	Gostaria...	goh-shtuh-REE-uh...
Is there meat in this dish?	Este prato tem carne?	ESH-tuh PRAH-too tehm KAR-neh?
salad	salada	try this one on your own
wine (sherry)	vinho (xerez)	VEEN-yoo (shuh-RAYZH)
shots	doses	do-says
seafood	frutos do mar	FROO-toos doo mahr
Is the bread free?	Este pão é grátis?	ESH-tuh pow eh GRAH-tees?

ENGLISH	PORTUGUESE	ENGLISH	PORTUGUESE
My name is...	O meu nome é...	Do you speak English?	Fala inglês?
What's your name?	Como se chama?	I don't understand...	Não entendo.

How much does this cost?	Quanto custa?	Where is...?	Onde é...?
Who/what	quem/que	How do you get to...?	Como chego á...?

glossary

SPAIN

abadía: abbey
abierto: open
ayuntamiento/ajuntament (C): city hall
alcázar: Muslim palace/fortress
billete: ticket
cambio: currency exchange
casco antiguo/ciutat vella (C): old city
consigna: luggage storage
Correos: post office
corrida: bull fight
encierro: runining of the bulls
estanco: tobacco, stamp shop
fuente/font (C): fountain
gitano: Gypsy
judería/call (C): Jewish quarter
llegada: arrival
madrileño: Madrid resident
manchego: from la Mancha (especially cheese)
mezquita: mosque
mirador: lookout point
mudéjar: Muslim architectural style
paseo, Po./passeig, Pg. (C): promenade
playa/platja (C): beach
rastro: flea market
real: royal
sala: room, hall
salida: departure, exit
Semana Santa: Holy Week, leading up to Easter Sunday
Siglo de Oro: Golden Age
zumo: juice

PORTUGAL

açorda: thick soup with bread and garlic
adega: wine cellar, bar
aguardente: firewater
alface: lettuce
almoço: lunch
arrufada de Coimbra: raised dough cake with cinnamon
carioca: American coffee
churrasco: barbecue
conta: bill
doce: sweet
ementa: menu
frango: chicken

gelado: ice cream
jantar: dinner
lula: squid
pequeno almoço: breakfast
posta: slice of fish or meat
prato do dia: dish of the day
queijo: cheese
sande/sanduíche: sandwich
sobremesa: dessert
suco: juice
tasca: bistro/cafe
vinho verde: young white wine, often sparkling

let's go online

Plan your next trip on our spiffy website, www.letsgo.com. It features full book content, the latest travel info on your favorite destinations, and tons of interactive features: make your own itinerary, read blogs from our trusty Researcher-Writers, browse our photo library, watch exclusive videos, check out our newsletter, find travel deals, follow us on Facebook, and buy new guides. Plus, if this Essentials wasn't enough for you, we've got even more online. We're always updating and adding new features, so check back often!

essentials

SPAIN 101

Spain is, all at once, extremely radical and incredibly conservative. Sound impossible? Well, you aren't the first to think that. As one may expect, the clash of these two elements that have defined Spanish culture has created a history that could rival the most war-torn nations. Yet, even after thousands of years of political strife, war, and general debauchery, Spain has not only managed to stay together as a country, but has also allowed the individual states within the country to flourish. This country's got more cultural diversity to offer in one nation than practically the entire continent of North America.

facts and figures

- **BAR TO PERSON RATIO:** 1:129
- **YEAR THAT SPAIN APPROVED GAY MARRIAGE:** 2005
- **KILOMETERS OF BEACHES:** 8000
- **HOW MANY TIMES THE BULL HAS WON IN A BULLFIGHT:** 52

history

WHEN IN ROME'S EMPIRE (300 BCE-711 CE)

3RD CENTURY BCE
The name Spain derives from the Roman word for the Iberian Peninsula: Hispania. How's that for staying power?

Although Spanish history doesn't really get exciting—and by exciting we mean recorded—until the Romans, there is a bit to tell about the early tribes on the Iberian Peninsula. The pre-Roman inhabitants consisted mostly of Greeks in the south along the Mediterranean and Celts in the north, with various Iberian tribes scattered throughout. The Romans rolled into Spain in the third century and conquered the peninsula with just the teensiest bit of difficulty. The Basque tribes in the northeast kept up the fight for a good 200 years after the rest of Iberia was conquered. (Think *Braveheart*: the Spanish version.) Although the Romans were incredibly oppressive and attempted to wipe out most Iberian cultural traditions, they did leave a few positive impressions on the country. Organized government and a powerful economy greatly improved the general living standards of the peninsula's residents, with a lasting effect. Many aspects of modern Spain can be traced back to the Roman Empire's religion, laws, and language. Where do you think the term Romance language came from? (Besides Catalan's unquestionably romantic nature, of course.)

1480 CE
In a totally unexpected move, the Spanish Inquisition demands that all those of Jewish or Muslim faith leave the country or convert.

When the Roman Empire collapsed in the fifth century Spain was once again up for grabs. Germanic tribes invaded Spain in full force, with the super-Christian Visigoths ultimately taking control; the Visigoths ruled from the fifth to the eighth century.

TELL ME MOOR, TELL ME MOOR (711-1492)

1492-1700
Centuries of inbreeding finally catch up to the royals, giving them that Hapsburg chin and the subsequent Hapsburg lisp. Since the royals are never wrong, the legend goes, the whole country begins to emulate them.

The rapid spread of Islam and its empire across northern Africa would bring another change to the Iberian Peninsula. After all, it's just a hop and a skip from northern Africa to Spain: it was bound to happen. The Moors invaded in 711: once they gained control, Spain experienced one of its least violent and most prosperous periods ever. Though the caliphate's capital lay in Damascus, *Al-Andalus*, as Spain became known, was one of the most important parts of the empire. Though the Muslim-controlled land was relatively conflict free, they did have to deal with the constant threat of the Christian *Reconquista*, the gradual reconquest of the peninsula from the north by the Christians who held out in the mountains, never conquered.

A GOLDEN AGE OF IGNORANCE (1492-1715)

After eight centuries of warfare, **Ferdinand and Isabella** finally succeeded at driving the Muslims from the Iberian Peninsula, capturing the last stronghold of Granada in 1492. Oh, and that year Columbus just happened to discover America. All of a sudden, boom! Spain's back on top. The royals' objective was to expand and conquer, and with the best land army in the world and a God-sent armada, expand and conquer they did. They threw huge amounts of manpower and money into acquiring more manpower and money. More specifically, they threw all of their energy into acquiring gold from the Americas. The conquistadors pretty much took care of (and we use "took care of" here in the North Jersey sense of the word) any indigenous peoples who got in their way and sent all their plunder back to Spain. This turned out to be pretty awesome for the Spanish nobility, for whom this period is appropriately called the Golden Age. This Golden Age quickly lapsed into decadence, however, as Spain's riches flowed right through the Iberian Peninsula and into the rest of Europe to pay down Spain's massive debts. Facing a serious crisis and clearly unaware of the dangers of circular reasoning, Charles V decided to go to war to get money to pay his soldiers. In a completely expected and predictable twist, this led to the collapse of the Hapsburg Dynasty. What happens when a dynasty collapses? You guessed it. A little bit of war.

It was at this point that Spain stopped being a player on the world stage and started getting played. The **War of Spanish Succession,** which lasted from 1700-1715, saw France attempting to place their own ruler on the Spanish throne. While this was clever thinking on France's part, there was no way Austria, the Netherlands, and Britain were going to let France obtain that kind of power. With everyone trying to put their own puppet king in place, Spain became a country to be dominated, not feared. In the end, France got their royal Frenchman, Philip V, on the Spanish throne. Completely exhausted from the war, however, it would be a stretch to call this a victory for France.

GETTING CONQUERED: THE SPAIN STORY (1716-1897)

A relatively peaceful era of postwar lull was short-lived. One **Napoleon Bonaparte** was on the move, and Spain had to pick a side. Napoleon already had a fair amount of land conquered—all of the rest of continental Europe, basically, plus a bit more elsewhere—and was looking to scoop up Portugal while he was rolling. Spain was on board with this plan. What he didn't tell Spain, as he was moving 100,000 troops through their country "to Portugal," was that he planned to pick up Spain along the way. In April 1808, on his casual conquering trip to Portugal, Napoleon deposed the Spanish monarch and placed his brother, Joseph Bonaparte, in charge of Spain. While the deposing and re-monarching of Spain was pretty easy, quelling the ensuing Spanish revolution was not. With Britain's support, the Spaniards proceeded to give 'em hell, and in 1814, they successfully drove the French out. However, this sparked yet another war of Spanish succession that raged on and off during the 19th century. This time period saw three different rulers, and, just for a bit of spice, the creation of the First Spanish Republic (1873-74). Needless to say, Spain was a hot mess (wouldn't be the first time), and things were only going to get worse.

JULY 1506
Queen Juana la Loca travels around the city with a glass coffin containing her dead husband, periodically kissing him on the lips. Let's just say it was a well-deserved nickname.

1914-1945
Spain does not participate in any World Wars. Not for any noble reason: they are just too busy fighting with themselves.

1936-39
Over 500,000 die during the Spanish Civil war, not including the hundreds of thousands more that Franco kills during his reign from October 1936 to his death in November 1975.

1988
World-famous director Pedro Almodóvar's film, *Mujeres al Borde de un Ataque de Nervios (Women on the Verge of a Nervous Breakdown)* is an international success. Real housewives everywhere are inspired.

history

THE DISASTER OF 1898

As bad as things were in Spain, they were still worse in its colonies. Spain had, over the preceding century, lost most of its American possessions as they became independent nations. Cuba, too, was unhappy with Spain's state of affairs, and the United States was unhappy with Cuba's. Fortunately for Spain, the United States had expressed little interest in going to war with Spain, and the Cuban revolution was an easily fixable situation. Unfortunately for Spain, they messed everything up so badly that most Spaniards still refuse to talk about the **"Disaster of 1898."** The USS *Maine*, (obviously an American ship) was "mysteriously" blown up on a friendly trip to Cuba. The United States, a nascent superpower, had been more than willing to stay out of the conflict until that moment. Apparently, the US takes the whole sinking ships thing seriously (World War I, anyone?), and proceeded to invade and liberate Cuba, Puerto Rico, and the Philippines, effectively wiping out any presence Spain had left in the New World.

Besides being embarrassing for Spain, the Disaster of 1898 was a wake-up call: they were stuck in the past. It took the loss of their colonies to make Spain realize that it was no longer an empire or even a world player. And so began Spain's shift from authoritarian monarchy to polarized left- and right-wing radical thinking.

A CENTURY OF TURMOIL (1900-2000)

With WWI on the horizon, Spain had a chance, once again, to get ahead in the geopolitical race. With enough political strife to keep themselves occupied in their own country, the Spanish stayed neutral for the entirety of the war. So neutral, in fact, that they sold supplies to both sides, making a huge profit. Most of the money went to paying off national debt, but, hey, at least Spain had a chance to get itself back on track. The only thing slowing it down? The ridiculous amount of political tension in the country. Spain was divided between extreme conservatives and leftist radicals. Alfonso XIII, a very conservative king, ruled Spain from 1902 until 1923. His harsh treatment of radicals and prevention of liberal reforms led to a successful coup under the leadership of Miguel Primo de Rivera in 1923. Miguel, the "liberal," established martial law, censorship, and suspended the constitution, all the while promising to end political corruption in Spain—a pretty impressive feat of hypocrisy. With his authoritarian rule, Primo de Rivera pushed Spain too far. The Spanish people decided that it wasn't working for them and ousted him in 1930. The leftists (i.e., anarcho-syndicalists and communists) won in the 1930 elections, but did a terrible job of governing, and the conservatives won control of the government in 1934 as a result. In reaction, anarchist riots erupted in cities across the country, leaving the military, led by one **General Francisco Franco,** to quell the rebellions. Two years later, the left made some gains in national elections, and Franco dropped the hammer, initiating a civil war that continues to tear the country apart even today, 74 years after its supposed conclusion.

Though the Republicans were technically in control of the government—we use the term "in control" loosely—and had fairly broad-reaching support, they were fractured in their political ideologies. The anarchists, communists, and socialists just couldn't get along—shocking. Franco's fascist supporters, on the other hand, were disciplined and well organized and had the support of Mussolini's and Hitler's powerful governments. The clash between the Republicans and Franco's fascists led to three years of civil war from 1936-39, which saw the loss of hundreds of thousands of lives, many of them civilians, followed by 50 years of brutal dictatorship under Generalísimo Franco.

Even today, Spain is divided over Franco's rule. Some call it the National Tragedy, probably due to the mass amounts (estimated at more than 150,000) of people killed. Local languages and traditions were suppressed in favor of one language and one flag, in the name of nationalism. Yet, under Franco's rule, Spain had one of its longest periods of political stability. After the decline that Spain had experienced over the previous centuries, it's not hard to understand how some people found peace under Franco.

With Franco's death in 1975, Spain transitioned to a constitutional monarchy, once again lagging far behind its European counterparts. Today, Spain is a flourishing liberal country, though just as culturally divided as it's always been. Though considered something of a Eurozone liability in economic terms, along with Italy and Greece, modern-day Spain is nevertheless an integral part of the European Union.

customs and etiquette

WHEN IN SPAIN...BE LATE

When it comes to this category, it's probably best to fully adapt to "Spanish time," or you might end up missing out on most of what Spain has to offer. Besides the little things, like being 15-20min. late for meetings or events, the Spanish basically overhaul their entire day's schedule to better fit their night-owl lifestyle. A prime example: meals. Lunches don't happen before 1pm; most occur often around 2pm and are usually followed by a siesta, during which most businesses will close. As for the evening, Spain is not constrained by any of the Puritan influences that Americans have to deal with—nothing closes at 2am (looking at you, Boston). How does this work, you might wonder? Let us walk you through a normal day. Wake up around 9am and eat a light breakfast. Work until lunch around 2pm, take a siesta, then head back to work from around 4 or 5pm until 8 or 9pm. Dinner is usually around 10 or 11pm. For the younger crowd, the bars only get interesting around midnight or 1am. Go drink for a few hours, until the bars kick you out around 3am and the nightclubs open. Dance until 5 or 6am, stumble home to your (or a) bed, and get ready to wake up at 9am to do it all over again.

HOW TO AVOID GETTING PUNCHED

You've probably realized by now that Spain is a pretty divided country, meaning that Spaniards have a huge sense of pride in their home neighborhoods and provinces. In fact, many of them would probably be pretty insulted that we keep writing "Spaniards." Consider them Catalans/Basques/Andalusians/Romani/Madrileños first and Spaniards second. Another tip? Avoid discussing the Spanish Civil War unless you know for sure which side the family of the person to whom you are speaking was on. The wrong comment could bring up some relatively fresh wounds. Same goes for soccer. Unless you know with certainty that your audience is full of Barça supporters, you might want to hold off on describing Messi's most recent goal in excruciating detail.

DON'T PACK YOUR SWEATS

Spaniards are very clothing-conscious: don't expect to see anyone out in old sweats doing their errands. For tourists, these guidelines might not matter as long as you don't mind being pegged as an out-of-towner. Proper church attire is a must. Wearing shorts or miniskirts while visiting churches and cathedrals is often not allowed and is always just plain rude. Women must have their shoulders covered, which may be the only real reason to ever wear a shrug. As a rule, keep it classy.

food and drink

Meals in Spain are nothing to joke about. The Spanish eat late, and they're serious about their food. Given the schedule that Spaniards keep, breakfast is rarely eaten at home and is hardly considered a meal. To make up for it, lunches and dinners are practically small holidays. Expect constant conversation and a lively atmosphere. Like everything else Spanish, the cuisine depends largely on what region of Spain you're in. So sit back, pour yourself some *tinto*, and prepare to drool at the best that Spain has to offer.

FOOD

You've probably been to a **tapas** bar, but you might not have known that tapas is not a type of food—it simply refers to the way the food is presented. The bite-sized portions served at the bar are not to be mistaken with appetizers. Spaniards eat tapas most commonly after work, well before dinner, or while just out drinking. *Pinxtos*, the Basque equivalent, are served on toothpicks.

If you're in Spain during the summer, you will most likely end up getting **gazpacho**, a chilled tomato soup. One thicker variety of gazpacho is salmorejo; think of it as the delicious lovechild of normal tomato soup and traditional gazpacho.

On a budget? Probably, given that you're using *Let's Go* as a travel guide. No worries, Spanish peasants had years to try and make their measly amount of ingredients taste good—cue **paella.** Common at village festivals, this rice-based dish can be flavored with pork, seafood, veggies, snails, and whatever mystery meat is found in the freezer that week—it really doesn't matter. Just cook up some rice, let it marinade for forever (at least all day) with whatever flavoring suits you best, and you're done!

If you've got cash to blow, your primary goal in Spain should probably to get your hands (and tongue) on some *jamón ibérico*. In simple terms, it's Spanish ham. But there is so much more to it than that. The *ibérico* pigs are treated like royalty, allowed to roam the countryside stuffing their fat faces with acorns for two years. After being butchered, the ham is salted and cured for two years, during which time it loses at least 20% of its weight and gains about 400% of its monetary value. Make it your life goal to find some of that thinly sliced piece of heaven.

DRINKS

Wine

Sangria is Spain's drink much the same way that a vodka Red Bull is America's—it gets you drunk, and most people would never drink it in the light of day. It's made by mixing wine with fruit juice and whatever cheap liquor one can easily acquire. Usually it's rum, bourbon, and whiskey. Yes, we meant to say "and," not "or." Think of it as the Spanish version of frat boy punch. Another way to utilize bad wine? *Tinto de verano*—"red wine of summer." Just take the old/cheap/bad-tasting wine you have/found/made and mix it with some lemon soda. Mix it with Coke, and you have a **kalimotxo.** The hotter the day, the more mixer you use, and you've got yourself a refreshing summer drink.

Beer

If beer is more your thing, Spain isn't famous for its selection. Most bars will just have one beer on tap, and it will most likely be a **Mahou,** though Cruzcampo and San Miguel are also popular. In Catalonia the standard is **Estrella Damm,** which is by far Let's Go's favorite.

sports

Spain, like any other normal European country, does the usual when it comes to European sports—skiing in the mountains, playing soccer on any flat surface, and ignoring American football. As in France, cycling and handball are popular spectator and recreational sports. Basketball, too, is quite popular: several Spaniards have made their way into the NBA. Yet there are a few sports that are considered quintessentially Spanish.

NOT TO BE CONFUSED WITH THE RUNNING OF THE BULLS

Bullfighting, Spain's oldest sport, has historically been its most controversial (unless you consider the Inquisition a sport). Apologists consider it more of an art and a tradition than a sport. Critics call it a horrid spectacle of bloodsport and violence. Either way, it garners attention. Matadors can achieve the same level of celebrity as actors and soccer stars. So how does bullfighting work, exactly? It's divided into three stages, with three different players for each stage: the *picadores*, the *bandilleros*, and the shiny-panted men, more officially known as matadors. First, the *picadores* come out on horseback and stab the bull many times with a lance to tire and wound it. Then the *bandilleros* come out and stab the bull in the back of the neck with colorful spears. Finally, the matador arrives to much fanfare, toys with the bull for a little while, and kills it by stabbing it in the neck. This ritual is then repeated five more times in a *corrida*. The Canary Islands and Catalonia have banned the practice of the sport.

THE FAVORITE CHILD

Bullfighting may be Spain's oldest sport, but **football** (the European kind) is Spain's universally adored younger child. Spaniards live and breathe for their teams, the most famous and successful being Real Madrid and ❚FC Barcelona. La Liga, the Spanish premier league, is arguably the best in the world, though the argument depends on how British you are. Games run from August until May, with league games generally played on the weekends and Copa del Rey (an open tournament for all Spanish teams) and Champions League (comprised of the best clubs in Europe) games during the week.

THE GAME OF A THOUSAND THRILLS

The Basques, ever fiercely independent, have their own sport, too. **Jai alai,** or *pilota*, is sort of like racquetball, only the players wear baskets on their hands and the ball might as well be live ammunition. Called the fastest game in the world, the ball can reach speeds of 180mph. While that may not be as fast as a bullet, it is fast enough to do some serious damage to those who get in its way. Basically, the two players hurl the ball at the wall in an attempt to either score a point or decapitate their opponent. Although the decapitating part is not in the official handbook, from empirical observation one can only assume that it's one of the main objectives of the game.

art and architecture

ARCHITECTURE

Spanish architecture, with just as many influences as the rest of Spanish culture, is all over the place. You'll find traces of Roman, Celtic, Islamic, Romanesque, Gothic, Renaissance, Baroque, Modernist, and postmodern architecture all over the country, in various combinations.

Islamic Architecture

All over Andalusia you'll find remnants of the era of Muslim rule. The most astounding examples that still stand are the **Alhambra** in Granada, the **Alcázar de Sevilla**, and the mosque (now **Cathedral**) of Córdoba—architecture that all dates from the eighth to 15th century.

Romanesque and Gothic

Most of the churches you'll come across in your Spanish travels will fit into one of these categories. **Romanesque** architecture is characterized by semicircular arches, heavy stone walls with small windows, and simple interiors; many of the most austerely beautiful spaces in Spain are in this style. **Gothic** architecture is probably a bit more familiar—pointed arches, huge stained-glass windows, and the famous flying buttresses. Though there is some overlap, Romanesque architecture generally precedes Gothic, with the transition occurring in around the 13th or 14th centuries in most places.

Mudéjar

As conquering Christian forces drove south, the Spanish adopted many aspects of Islamic architecture and incorporated it into a new hybrid style called the **mudéjar** style. This originated on the Castilian plain, most likely in the town of Sahagún, and spread all across the regions of Castile and Aragon. Some chief characteristics of this style are intricate, patterned brickwork as the chief material, with some Islamic-inspired ornaments and motifs, including glazed tile or *azulejo*. Prime examples include Sevilla's **Plaza de España** and Barcelona's **Arc de Triomf**.

Modernisme

Limited mainly to Barcelona and nearby cities during the final decade of the 19th century and the first of the 20th, the **modernista** movement threw splashes of color and trippy architectural motifs all over Catalonia. Its most famous innovator is undoubtedly **Antoni Gaudí.**

PAINTING

Diego Velázquez: court painter, architect, lady-killer. At least, this is what we gather from his famous self-portrait on the left margin of *Las Meninas*. It calls attention to his long hair, impressive moustache, and piercing gaze. Influenced by Spanish and Flemish realism, Velazquez is best known for his naturalistic paintings, such as *Las Meninas* and *The Water Carrier of Seville*. Also operating in the early 1600s was **El Greco**, real name Doménikos Theotokópoulos. No wonder they gave him a nickname. For those who haven't guessed yet, his name means the Greek. Less of a lady-killer than Velázquez (he was bald), El Greco made up for it with his vivid and emotional paintings. Said to reflect the Counter-Reformation in Spain, his strong color contrasts and elongated human figures can be pretty creepy, but beautifully vivid.

Moving on to the 18th century, we stumble upon **Francisco Goya,** affectionately called the Father of Modern Art. Also a court painter, his best work was done outside of his courtly duties. His frank, emotional technique created a whole new style of painting, refreshing to the Spanish people. It was a bit too refreshing for the Spanish Inquisition, however. Goya was detained and questioned for his painting, *The Naked Maja*, one of the first paintings of a nude woman in Spain. Released relatively unscathed, Goya lived on to do some of his best works exposing the French atrocities during Napoleon's rule of Spain. The most famous of these, *The Third of May 1808*, depicts the slaughter of Spanish civilians by the French army. His Black Paintings are also seriously weird.

From there, we move into more modern styles and the inevitable **Pablo Picasso.** Volatile, emotional, always in need of a muse, Picasso is everything we expect a painter to be. Picasso is credited with starting the Cubism movement, commonly called the "What the heck is happening in this painting?" movement, and made a tremendous political statement with *Guernica* in 1937, depicting the bombing of civilians by fascists during the Civil War.

Heavily influenced by Picasso, **Joan Miró** moved the 20th century into Surrealism. An unsmiling man always dressed in somber suits, he took his work very seriously. Not that one could really tell. His playful colors and simple forms bring to mind children's artwork. Look closely though, and there is a certain dark feeling to his work that stays with you.

There's no way to have a conversation on surrealism without the movement's star: **Salvador Dalí.** With a moustache to die for, greased back hair, and always in a suit, Dalí was a character whose ultimate goal was to get at the greater reality of man's subconscious. Most famous for his painting *The Persistence of Memory,* (a dorm room favorite) Dalí did much more than paint. He did everything from sculptures to book illustrations to jewelry design. Judging by all the photos we found of him, he also enjoyed intensely staring people down and walking his pet anteater and his ocelot, Babou.

LITERATURE

Although not always renowned for its literary genius, Spain does have a few key authors to mention. While Miguel de Cervantes's name might not trigger a memory, his world famous opus, *Don Quixote*, certainly should. Born in 1547, Cervantes's life is almost more interesting than anything he could ever have written: it involves getting kidnapped by pirates and enslaved in Algiers for two years.

Another groundbreaking work of Spanish literature, *The Life of Lazarillo de Tormes and His Fortunes and Adversities*, came in quite low in the shortest title competition. In the mystery category, however, it ranked quite high. It was published anonymously in 1554 and then outlawed by the Spanish Inquisition for heresy (hence the anonymity of the author). Then again, what wasn't? One of the first Picaresque novels, *Lazarillo de Tormes* was highly critical of Spanish society and greatly advanced the genres of the satire and the novel in one blow.

Federico García Lorca wore many hats during his lifetime. As a poet, dramatist, and theater director, Lorca gave the world insight into 20th century Spain. Right smack dab in the middle of corruption and coup, Lorca's work reflects the decades of violence, but also dabbled in themes of love and passion. Considered too liberal by conservative nationalists, Lorca was shot and buried in an unmarked grave in 1936 at the start of the Civil War.

FLAMENCO

Most likely drawing from Jewish, Muslim, and Roma culture, Flamenco may be Spain's most stereotypically known art form. Most people only think of flamenco as shapely ladies in tight polka-dotted dresses, but it actually originated as a musical genre, with the dancing added on later to complement the pairing of guitar and vocals. Flamenco is violent and emotional; you sort of need to see it to get it.

art and architecture

holidays and festivals

With a brief reminder that Spain is 94% Roman Catholic, can you guess what roughly 94% of the holidays and festivals are based on? Now before you go thinking that these Roman Catholic holidays are going to be all church, stop. Spaniards know how to celebrate, and we really do mean celebrate, their faith.

HOLIDAY OR FESTIVAL	DESCRIPTION	DATE
Three Kings Day	Three men dress up as kings and parade around town giving sweets to children.	January 6
Carnaval	People spend months preparing fancy clothes and masks for this festival. There are floats and parades all week, and prizes are given out to the best costumes.	February 7-17
Semana Santa and Easter	Cities all across Spain host processions in which wood and plaster sculptures of Jesus and the Virgin Mary are carried through the streets, all leading up to the celebration of Easter Sunday.	March 22-31
Dia de Sant Jordi	Similar to Valentine's Day, lovers exchange roses and books to show their affection.	April 23
Fiesta de San Juan	Spaniards celebrate by camping out on beaches and making bonfires. It's said one must wash their face at midnight to wash away their sins and then jump over a bonfire three times.	June 23-24
Spain's National Day	Commemorates Columbus's discovery of America. October 12th is also Spain's Day of the Armed Forces, which includes a military parade in Madrid.	October 12
Constitution Day	Celebrates the national referendum to approve Spain's most recent constitution.	December 6
Día de la Inmaculada Concepción	A day to commemorate the Immaculate Conception of the Virgin Mary. More likely, the Spaniards wanted an excuse for a long weekend. Coupled with Constitution Day, most businesses take an extra three days off.	December 8
Christmas	Spain takes Christmas very seriously. With the Virgin Mary as the country's patron saint, the Christmas season begins on December 8th, the feast of the Immaculate Conception. Jota, a traditional Christmas dance, is performed after the Midnight Mass on Christmas Eve.	December 25

PORTUGAL 101

A small country with a turbulent history, Portugal is daily becoming a more popular destination for tourism. In this chapter, we'll teach you how to navigate its rich culture and tradition, from the seafood meccas of the Atlantic coast to the unique (and borderline bizarre) days of reverie in the central provinces. Armed with a pair of soccer cleats and your best table manners, you'll learn to pick out *fado* among the bustling streets of Lisbon and to wine and dine like a true local.

facts and figures

- **NUMBER OF DIFFERENT GOVERNMENTS BETWEEN 1910-1945:** 45
- **DIAMETER OF PRINCE HENRY'S PERSONAL COMPASS:** 141 feet
- **YEARS SINCE TOP 3 WORLD CUP FINISH:** 47
- **VOLUME OF WINE PRODUCED PER YEAR:** 8 million hectoliters

history

219 BCE
The Romans decide that they would like to have Portugal.

469 CE
The Moors encourage reading with introduction of linen paper and books.

1250
A unified Portugal emerges from the ruins of the Reconquista.

1386
The Treaty of Windsor establishes lasting relations between the Portuguese and the British.

1492
Chris Columbus "discovers" the "New" "World" for Spain; Portugal goes green with envy.

GET TRIBAL: EARLY YEARS (8000 BCE-469 CE)

Starting around 8000 BCE, Neolithic peoples from the Iberian Peninsula began to colonize and settle in the area that would eventually become Portugal. This land would turn out to be hot real estate in the first millennium BCE, seeing the immigration of Celts from Central Europe and the subsequent creation of innumerable (and unpronounceable) mixed-race tribes. The first six or seven centuries BCE saw quintessential Mediterranean civilizations like the Carthaginians, the Phoenicians, and the Greeks come and go. Wearing bedsheets and wielding pointed sticks, the Romans invaded during the second and third centuries and (surprise!) quickly took over the whole region.

TELL ME MOOR! (469-1250)

By the early fifth century, Rome had made the classic mistake of empires, spreading its forces too thin and wide, and began to succumb to Germanic tribes. After a relatively brief stint by the Visigoths, the Moors stole the spotlight and took center stage in Portugal. Who were the Moors? As Islam spread from the Arabian Peninsula, Muslim forces moved through North Africa and up into Iberia, settling in Portugal and establishing a thriving culture there. While their name lends itself to bad puns, the Moors left a rich tradition of agricultural infrastructure and architecture—look for colorful ceramic tiles and ornaments that decorate buildings even today.

IT'S A BOY: A NATION IS BORN (1139-1415)

From the 12th to the early 15th century CE, the inhabitants of Portugal fought simultaneously for both their independence and for their religion. The Spanish *Reconquista* ultimately drove the Moors out of Iberia, and after a series of power grabs typical of early monarchies, single rule fell into the hands of Afonso I. Afonso and his successors slowly began to reclaim and consolidate lands previously controlled by the Muslims. The gleaming, shiny, final product emerged in 1250—a unified and independent nation. A series of territorial scuffles with Spain under João I set the framework for a future soccer rivalry between the two nations.

SUGAR AND SPICE AND, ER...SOME THINGS NICE (1415-1755)

Portugal's **Age of Discovery** began in the 15th century with advances in sailing technology and the reign of **Prince Henry the Navigator.** While their Iberian kingdom may have been small, the Portuguese expanded their overseas empire massively over the next two centuries, gaining control of a large and wealthy empire that spanned the New World and extended into Asia. Countless famed explorers like Vasco da Gama, Bartolomeu Dias, and Ferdinand Magellan (whom you may remember from grade school) discovered and claimed huge chunks of territory for their nation and brought back shiploads of spices, gold, and other similar bling. This Golden Age peaked with the reign of Manuel I the Fortunate, and while he was indeed fortunate, his successors would not be—as competition, piracy, domestic issues, and eventual Spanish rule diminished Portugal's wealth and international prestige.

FRENCH FRIED (1755-1910)

The poor luck continued into the 1700s, climaxing in the mid-18th century with the great **Earthquake of Lisbon.** The quake, the accompanying fires, and a tsunami destroyed much of the city, but remarkably, it was rebuilt fairly quickly and successfully under the guidance of the Marquês de Pombal. After this brief stint of optimism, the Portuguese found themselves in a world of trouble as European foreign policy went south. Before they knew it, the nation was on the defensive once again as Napoleon's forces invaded and pillaged the country Viking-style. It was only with the help of the Brits that Portuguese leaders were able to drive out the petit Frenchman and re-establish some semblance of order for the following decades.

A POLITICAL POTLUCK (1910-1986)

Portugal was to have its fair share of radicalism, as the monarchical regime was overthrown early in the 20th century for a weak republic. This was indeed too good to be true, and the republic quickly degenerated into an incredibly unstable political climate. With a turnover rate approaching that of a fast food restaurant, Portugal saw 45 (yes, 45) different regimes from 1910-1945. Eventually, this power vacuum sucked up the powerful dictator Antonio Salazar, who would rule the country with an iron fist and a ruthless secret police for almost 40 years. With his death in 1968, the Portuguese people let out a sigh of relief, only to find themselves increasingly strained and drained by unpopular colonial wars. The pot boiled over in April of 1974 with the **Carnation Revolution,** sending the dictatorial dynasty out the window and ushering in an era of Marxist reforms and release of colonial possessions. In the following decade, Portugal would slowly stabilize economically and politically, joining a proto-EU in 1986.

A MIXED MODERNITY (1986-PRESENT)

With monetary assistance from the EU, Portugal's economy progressed and its democracy solidified after nearly a century of instability. Beginning in the mid-1990s, however, its finances once again began to lag and earned the nation a place in the acronym PIGS (Portugal, Italy, Greece, and Spain—all countries that have remained economically unstable).While the Portuguese do like sausage, they've deemed this swiney acronym offensive, so don't use it publicly. The last of the

1494
Through the Treaty of Tordesillas, Spain and Portugal reluctantly agree to split the undiscovered world in half.

1523
One of Magellan's ships completes its circumnavigation of the globe (sans Magellan).

1755
The great quake shakes Lisbon like a Polaroid picture.

1939-45
Estoril Casino becomes an alleged meeting spot for espionage agents during WWII; it will later provide inspiration for the classic Bond novel *Casino Royale.*

1974
Flower shops around Portugal make record profits as the Carnation Revolution topples Salazar's dictatorship.

history

former empire was finally pried from Portugal's rusty colonial grip in 1999 with the cession of Macau and its slot machines as well as East Timor in 2002. While economic struggles and inequality still exist around the country (especially in the wake of the most recent financial crisis), Portugal has played host to a number of high profile sporting events in the last decade and held the presidency of the European Commission in 2004.

customs and etiquette

HELLO, MY NAME IS

Introductions are incredibly important in Portugal. In pretty much all social interactions, make sure to keep both politeness and formality in mind. Handshakes are standard for most first time greetings, with a slightly relaxed grip the norm (just don't go limp fish). Among women or younger Portuguese, light touches or a kiss on each cheek is also customary.

DO YOU EXPECT ME TO TALK?

In general, the Portuguese are very open to foreigners, and, unlike the French, they appreciate attempts to speak the native language. Although the person you're addressing probably speaks Spanish, don't assume they do: this might be taken offensively and mark you as culturally insensitive. Portuguese often speak loudly and quickly—don't be intimidated; this is normal and doesn't indicate any anger or irritation (usually).

PLEASE, SIR, CAN I HAVE SOME MORE?

Probably not, unless you want to pay for it. Portuguese restaurants often charge for what might seem to be freebies—for example, the cheese, bread, and olives served at the beginning of the meal. Expect to pay a few euros for these small appetizers. Don't forget a five to 10% tip if the service charge is not already included.

food and drink

SOMETHING'S FISHY

The Portuguese take their food seriously—especially **fish.** The national and easily the most prevalent dish throughout the country is *bacalhau,* a salted cod with origins in the sea voyages of the 15th and 16th centuries. While you may be sick of it after a few days, the Portuguese won't be—it is said that a different recipe exists for each day of the year. Fresh seafood, though, is more than available—particularly in coastal regions like Algarve, *peixe espada* (swordfish), *polvo* (octopus), *lulas grenhadas* (grilled cuttlefish), and a wide variety of shellfish are inescapable.

TERRESTRIAL TREATS

Meat and pastries are also staples of Portuguese cuisine. For a manly meal, head inland to ranching regions like Alentejo, where hearty meat stews *(cozida)* are standard fare. For more adventurous travelers (and those on Team Edward), ask for *cabidela,* a dish made with the blood of pigs or chickens. Portuguese foods are not without their delicacy, though, as evidenced by the ever-popular croissant. While one might not normally associate croissants and the Catholic church, the rich tradition of pastries in Portugal dates back to the monasteries of the Middle Ages—explaining today's *barriga de freira* (nun's belly) and *papos de anjo* (angel's chins).

NO WINING

Portuguese wine is the famous grandfather of all alcoholic beverages, known for its quality since ancient Roman times. Most well-known, especially nowadays, is port—a sweet wine grown in the Douro valley often served as an appetizer drink or as a dessert wine. You may just be looking for a buzz, but stop to appreciate what goes into a glass of port—a specialized wine institute certifies quality and production methods. Your high school Spanish may be good, but don't get caught looking like a tourist—*vinho verde* isn't a green wine but a young, un-aged wine often served sparkling. For other drinks, try **ginjinha,** a sour cherry liqueur native to Lisbon.

OTHER USEFUL INFO

Given its impressive colonial history, Portugal's cuisine is underrepresented outside its own borders. As the Portuguese people are more than happy to make clear, their Mediterranean-inspired style is similar to that of Spain's upon first glance but is, in fact, quite distinct. External influences are everywhere—a unique blend of exotic spices often used in even the most basic dishes reflects the nation's past in the far east, while other dishes show traces of religious diversity and the Judeo-Christian mixture within Portugal itself. Cuisine varies from region to region, but meat and seafood pairings and a rich, filling, full-flavored cuisine is constant throughout. Breakfast is a light affair in Portugal—pop a small pastry or toast and some OJ for your hangover. Meal times are slightly shifted from the American norm—lunch *(almoço)* is served a bit later in the afternoon and dinner *(jantar)* is served late, from about 8pm on.

sports and recreation

Eventually, you might get tired of museums and hunger for a little action (that is, if you aren't too full on yummy seafood). Whether playing some pickup soccer with local kids or shredding the Atlantic coastal waves, these activities are not just good for burning off those pastries but also for connecting with locals, even if you don't speak the language.

Portuguese athletes have garnered major achievements in the areas of track and field and running—but to be honest, you probably didn't come to Portugal to find a jogging buddy. There are a number of more interactive and culturally involved sports, and yep, you guessed it—*futebol* is the most popular. The country has been graced with a number of major stars in the past, such as Eusebio, Luis Figo, and Nani, not to mention today's all-star and cover boy, Cristiano Ronaldo. Although one of the top-ranked European teams, Portugal's national side doesn't often win major competitions and historically has had disappointing results in the World Cup. That being said, the locals are obsessed with the sport and will gladly welcome you into the cheering section at the local bar—just make sure you don't mention the success of neighboring Spain. If you can't tell a punt from a corner kick, don't worry—there are tons of other options for recreation. Not for the faint-hearted, bull fighting occurs around the country but differs substantially from the Spanish version in that the men face the bull completely weaponless. In coastal regions like Algarve, fishing and water sports like surfing, scuba diving and snorkeling, windsurfing, and sailing are all options. Who knows, if your moves are good enough, the fish might not be the only thing around to catch.

music

You are almost guaranteed to encounter *fado*, a traditional genre of music generally characterized by mournful tunes and haunting lyrics. This may sound a bit depressing for your riotous Euro-trip, but in Portugal, you're bound to run into it either in restaurants or on the street. The two main centers for *fado* are Lisbon and Coimbra, a small university city in the center of the country. Despite some regional differences, the two styles share much in common: all *fado* is meant to embody a sense of *saudade*, most approximately translated into English as a feeling of permanent loss and the emotional damage it causes (cheery, no?). Typically, this manifests itself through romantic, tragic lyrics and tearful melodies. Singers can be male or female (men are more frequent singers up north) and are often accompanied by the twang of a traditional Portuguese guitar. *Fado*'s origins are unclear—some trace it back to the early 1800s as the music of the urban poor, while others claim that the genre arose in the 15th century among the lonely wives of men at sea. In any case, the tradition remains strong and has given rise to a number of internationally recognized stars, the most beloved being Amália Rodrigues. Whether you're interested in learning more about Portuguese culture or just need a good cry (we all do sometimes), seek out some *fado* in Lisbon or Coimbra.

holidays and festivals

Like any good Catholic country, Portugal celebrates classic holidays like Good Friday and Christmas, albeit with their own special twist. However, you didn't come all this way to hunt for Easter eggs. The holidays and festivals listed below are unique to Portugal, so you can get the enlightening, cultural travel experience you came for.

HOLIDAY OR FESTIVAL	DESCRIPTION	DATE
Festa das Chouriças	Honor São Luís, patron saint of animals, as you sample the best smoked pork sausages in Algarve. Brings a new meaning to sausage fest.	January 21-22
Carnaval	Nationwide festival, similar to Mardi Gras, celebrating the end of winter. Mix of ancient and tropical themes. Expect floats and lots of body paint.	February 21
Dia da Liberdade	"Freedom Day"—because ending a dictatorial regime is worth celebrating!	April 25
Dia de Camões	"Portugal Day"—every good country has a national epic. This day marks the death of Luís Vaz de Camões, the author of the Lusiads.	June 10
Festa de São António	Essentially the largest block party to hit the Lisbon streets, the city overflows with partygoers celebrating Lisbon's patron saint with parades, music, dancing, fireworks, drinks, and food (especially sardines).	June 12-13
Festa de São João	A riotous night of jumping over bonfires, fireworks, sardines, and being hit over the head with leek stalks, this festival celebrates Porto's patron saint with nothing short of enthusiastic vigor.	June 23-24
Festa de São Pedro	In honor of the patron saint of fishermen and widows, bonfires are lit in one of the more tame festivals celebrated in June.	June 28-29
Festa da Ria	The Festival of the Estuary in Aviera (central Portugal) celebrates the river and the harvest of seaweed. No, you still can't smoke it.	Mid-July
Festival do Marisco	Festival of the sea dedicated primarily to celebrating local shellfish. Perhaps not the most kosher of holidays.	August 10-15

BEYOND TOURISM

If you are reading this, then you are a member of an elite group—and we don't mean "the literate." You're a student preparing for a semester abroad. You're taking a gap year to save the trees, the whales, or the dates. You're an 80-year-old woman who has devoted her life to egg-laying platypuses and what the hell is up with that. In short, you're a traveler, not a tourist; like any good spy, you don't just observe your surroundings—you become an active part of them.

Your mission, should you choose to accept it, is to study, volunteer, or work abroad as laid out in the dossier—er, chapter—below. We leave the rest (when to go, whom to bring, and how many changes of underwear to pack) in your hands. This message will self-destruct in five seconds. Good luck.

greatest hits

- **DANCE** through classes like "Anthropology of Flamenco". (p. 590)
- **DIVE** into the sea on a conservation trip. (p. 592)
- **DAYDREAM** while spending your afternoons supervising an intensive English camp. (p. 593)

studying

So you're bored with your own university? Less than entertained by the local nightlife scene these days? Sick of the same pizza and burritos? Craving a semester- or year-long adventure? No worries! We've got you covered. Whether you're still in the process of planning your trip to the Iberian Peninsula or have already made your way to one of Spain or Portugal's many exciting cities, we are here to help you find an exciting new university to call home. And the best part is you don't even have to speak the language, as most classes are taught in English. Of course, if you want to learn the local tongue, we've got you covered there, too.

visa information

If you are planning to study in Spain or Portugal for more than 90 days, you will need to apply for a visa. In order to do this, students must bring the following documents to the nearest Spanish/Portuguese Embassy or Consulate: a passport, three additional passport-sized photos, proof of US residence, a letter of acceptance into a study abroad program (and, if applicable, any scholarship letters), proof of payment for the program, an electronic receipt of round-trip air ticket, a letter from the home university confirming sufficient healthcare insurance coverage to participate in a study abroad program, and proof of the financial means to live and study in the country. Students applying for a Portuguese visa must also fill out an application which can be found online. Getting the visa can take several months, so it is best to start the process as early as possible.

UNIVERSITIES

International Programs

UNIVERSITY STUDIES ABROAD CONSORTIUM: UNIVERSITY OF ALICANTE

Carretera San Vicente del Raspeig, Alicante, Spain ☎+34 96 590 34 00 http://usac.unr.edu

Spend Monday through Friday immersed in Spanish and European studies and enjoy your weekends relaxing on the beautiful beaches of Alicante. The city is nestled right on the Mediterranean Sea, with sunny weather, busy cafes, bustling nightlife, and abundant street markets that will be sure to make your semester here more than enjoyable.

i Minimum 2.5 GPA. Courses taught in English and Spanish. $ $7780 per semester.

GLOBAL LEARNING SEMESTERS: UNIVERSITAT AUTÒNOMA DE BARCELONA

Cerdanyola del Vallès, Spain ☎+34 93 581 11 11 www.globalsemesters.com

Occupy Wall Street got you all hot and bothered? Whether you're looking to catapult yourself into the 1%, or fight for economic redistribution, you can study any aspect of business and economics at this university. When you're taking a break from your studies, downtown Barcelona is just a stone's throw away.

i Students housed in same-sex apartments. Minimum 2.5 GPA required. $ $13,250 per semester.

ACADEMIC PROGRAMS INTERNATIONAL: POMEPU FABRA UNIVERSITY

C. Mercè, 10, Barcelona, Spain www.apistudyabroad.com

If you often find yourself sitting in the back of a movie theater watching indie films and informative documentaries, then this program is for you. A semester here will leave you poised to make a documentary almost as amazing as *March of the Penguins*.

i *Students live with host families. Minimum 3.0 GPA. Courses taught in English and Spanish* Ⓢ *$5600.*

ACADEMIC PROGRAMS INTERNATIONAL: UNIVERSITY OF DEUSTO

Av. Universidades, 24, Bilbao, Spain ☎+34 94 413 90 00 www.apistudyabroad.com

The University of Deusto is perfect if you daydream about being a leading advisor in the Department of State or jetting around the world as a United States Ambassador. If you can pull yourself away from these thoughts of grandeur long enough, you might just find yourself one step closer to the real deal and on a flight to Bilbao to study international relations.

i *Students live with host families. Minimum 2.75 GPA. Courses taught in Spanish and English.* Ⓢ *$12,600 per semester.*

ACADEMIC PROGRAMS INTERNATIONAL: UNIVERSITY OF THE BASQUE COUNTRY

Leioa, Spain ☎+34 94 601 20 00 www.apistudyabroad.com

If you thought studying abroad was only for people interested in hitting the books, we are here to tell you that you are mistaken. In a country known for having some of the most notable artists, it shouldn't come as a surprise that there would be a study abroad program allowing you to indulge in your passion for studio art. Just remember who your real friends are when you become the next Picasso or Dalí.

i *Students live with host families. Minimum 2.75 GPA. Two semesters of college Spanish required.* Ⓢ *$10,400 per semester.*

ACADEMIC PROGRAMS INTERNATIONAL: UNIVERSITY OF GIRONA

Pl. Sant Domènec, 3, Girona, Spain www.apistudyabroad.com

Get ready to hit the history books with this program. Here, you can focus on Hispanic Studies or the history of Jews in Spain. Either way, you'll be sure to return home a Spanish history buff of sorts.

i *Students live in dorms. Minimum 2.75 GPA. Classes taught in Spanish and English.* Ⓢ *Summer program $5400.*

ACADEMIC PROGRAMS INTERNATIONAL: ANTONIO DE NEBRIJA UNIVERISTY

C. Pirineos, 55, Madrid, Spain ☎+34 90 232 13 22 www.apistudyabroad.com

Not quite sure what you want to study? This university offers a wide array of courses, ranging from International Marketing to the Contemporary World to the Roles of Women.

i *Students live with host families. Minimum 2.75 GPA. Classes taught in English in Spanish.* Ⓢ *$14,000 per semester.*

SUFFOLK UNIVERSITY

C. Viña, 3, Madrid, Spain www.suffolk.edu

This program gives you the chance to study abroad at an American university. Suffolk offers a broad liberal arts program at its Madrid campus, with courses in subjects such as philosophy, journalism, sociology, business, and many more.

i *Students live with host families or in apartments. Minimum 2.75 GPA. Classes taught in English.* Ⓢ *$18,000 per semester.*

CIEE: UNIVERSITAT DE LES ILLES BALEARS

Edifici Sa Riera 2, Palma, Spain ☎+34 97 117 30 00 www.ciee.org

Here in Palma de Mallorca, you can satisfy any one of your diverse interests. Environmental Studies, Mediterranean Studies, Hotel Management, and Tourism are just a few areas in which you can concentrate during your semester or year abroad.

i *Students live with host families. Minimum 2.75 GPA and 5 semesters of college-level Spanish.* Ⓢ *$12,600 per semester.*

studying

ACADEMIC PROGRAMS INTERNATIONAL: PABLO DE OLAVIDE UNIVERSITY

Carretera de Utrera, Km 1, Sevilla, Spain ☎+34 95 434 92 00 www.apistudyabroad.com

Interested in learning more about the culture of southern Spain? At this university you can take classes on just that, such as "Anthropology of Flamenco".

i *Students live with host families. Minimum 2.75 GPA. Classes taught in English and in Spanish.* Ⓢ *$4680 per semester.*

UNIVERSIDADE NOVA DE LISBOA

Campus de Campolide, Lisbon, Portugal ☎+351 21 371 56 00 www.ciee.org

At this public university in Lisbon, you can choose from a wide array of courses, including cinema studies, music, and literature. Excursions into the city are incorporated into many of the classes in order to give students a greater understanding of the material.

i *Minimum 2.75 GPA. Classes taught in English and Portuguese.* Ⓢ *$12,300 per semester.*

UMASS IN LISBON

285 Old Westport Road, Dartmouth, MA, USA ☎1-508-999-8000 www.umassd.edu

UMass Dartmouth is the only major American university to offer a residential study program in Portugal. Students mostly study Portuguese politics, along with options in economics, management, and business.

Ⓢ *$16,060 per semester.*

GEORGIA STATE UNIVERSITY

Atlanta, GA, USA ☎1-404-413-8245 www.gsu.edu

Georgia State accepts on average 10-20 students for their summer programs. The current featured program focuses on the Portuguese education system.

i *Students live in dorms. Classes taught in English.* Ⓢ *$2920 per semester.*

UNIVERSITY OF WISCONSIN—MADSION

500 Lincoln Dr., Madison, WI, USA ☎1-608-265-6998 www.wisc.edu

Students are given the opportunity to study Portuguese culture at one of Portugal's finest universities, the Universidade de Coimbra. Students advanced enough in the language are allowed to enroll in humanities and social science courses at the university.

i *Students live in apartments. Must be a junior or senior. Minimum 2.5 GPA overall, 3.0 GPA in all Portuguese language courses.*

LANGUAGE SCHOOLS

As renowned novelist Gustave Flaubert once said, "Language is a cracked kettle on which we beat out tunes for bears to dance to." While we at Let's Go have absolutely no clue what he is talking about, we do know that the following are good resources for learning Spanish and Portuguese.

ACADEMIC PROGRAMS INTERNATIONAL: UNIVERSITY OF CÁDIZ

C. Ancha, 16, Cádiz, Spain www.apistudyabroad.com

For those who already speak Spanish and are looking to become more advanced, this local university offers intensive language classes throughout the year. By enrolling in the language program during the academic year, you can also choose to enroll in other classes at the university, which are taught in Spanish.

i *Students live with host families. Minimum 2.75 GPA.* Ⓢ *Summer program $3990; $10,200 per semester.*

ACADEMIC PROGRAMS INTERNATIONAL: UNIVERSITY OF GRANADA

Av. Hospicio, 0, Granada, Spain www.apistudyabroad.com

This university program is open to students who are looking to learn the local lingo. Providing up to 300 contact hours, you'll be sure to leave the university having advanced at least two levels in your Spanish studies.

i *Students live with host families. Minimum 2.75 GPA.* Ⓢ *$10,880 per semester.*

UNIVERSITY OF SALAMANCA

C. Libreros, 1, Salamanca, Spain ☎+34 92 329 44 00 www.aifs.com

One of the most renowned universities in the Spanish-speaking world opens its doors to students eager to learn Spanish as a second language. Spending a semester here will have you speaking like Castilian locals in no time. Not to mention the program fee includes exciting excursions to various other cities.

i Minimum 2.5 GPA. Ⓢ $13,500 per semester.

UNIVERSITY OF SEVILLE

C. San Fernando, 4, Sevilla, Spain ☎+34 95 455 10 00 www.apistudyabroad.com

Intensive Spanish classes are offered here for advanced speakers. They also offer Arabic for students at any level.

i Students live with host families. Minimum 2.75 GPA. Ⓢ $4680 per semester.

NIKITAS LANGUAGE ABROAD

☎1-646-580-8677 www.nik-las.com

With Spanish programs in Barcelona, Cadiz, Granada, Madrid, Malaga, Marbella, Salamanca, and Sevilla, and Portuguese programs in Lisbon and Faro, it shouldn't be hard to find a class that suits your fancy. You have the flexibility to choose how long and how many hours you want your program to be, and the school can also arrange *intercambios* for you, which are an opportunity to meet locals to improve your language skills. This organization is also known for offering up to a 20% discount for booking at least 65 days in advance.

Ⓢ *$345-2305.*

EUROCENTRES

☎1-866-869-3520 www.eurocentres.com

Through this organization you can take general language courses, business courses, or long-term courses in Spanish. Classes are offered in Barcelona, Marbella, and Valencia.

i Students live in apartments or homestays. Ⓢ $410-3054.

FARO PORTUGUESE SCHOOLS

R. Almeida Garrett, 44, Faro, Portugal www.amerispan.com

Located in the heart of the city near the beautiful waterfront and popular shopping streets, this school's location supplements its quality language classes. Portuguese classes are offered five days per week for three hours per day and will leave you well prepared to barter for knick knacks after class.

i Students live with host families. Ⓢ $670 per week.

EUROLINGUA

www.eurolingua.com

Through Eurolingua, students are placed in homestays with tutors who help them learn the language. Studying Portuguese in this way provides great flexibility and allows students to live in a variety of cities such as Portimão, Leiria, Matosinhos, Cascais, and many more.

i Students live in homestays. Ⓢ $1185-6215.

A2Z LANGUAGES

☎1-888-417-1533 www.a2zlanguages.com

Offering Portuguese programs in Lisbon, Faro, and Porto as well as Spanish programs in Barcelona, Granada, Madrid, Málaga, Mallorca, Marbella, Salamanca, San Sebastián, Sevilla, Tenerife, Valencia, and Vejer, A2Z Languages specializes language based on cultural immersion.

i Students live in homestays. Ⓢ $660-6320.

studying

volunteering

So you've got a bleeding heart, and we have a Band-Aid. No matter what cause has you fired up and ready to go, there's a little something for everyone on the Iberian Peninsula. Plan ahead or start volunteering on a whim; either way, the world will be happy you did. And you'll probably feel a little better about yourself, too.

COMMUNITY OUTREACH

FUNDACION TOMILLO

C. Serrano, 136, Madrid, Spain   ☎+34 91 562 26 04   www.tomillo.org

The goal of this organization is to help the community in any way possible. You can help, too. Become a volunteer, working to train and guide youths towards careers, organizing community activities, training the unemployed to become gardeners, and taking care of the old and disabled.

GLOBAL VOLUNTEERS

Beja, Portugal   www.globalvolunteers.org

Become a volunteer teacher in classrooms and learning centers in Beja and surrounding villages. You will teach English to both children and adults and help to enhance the community.
⑨ $2595-2795.

FUNDACION INTERVIDA DE ESPAÑA

☎+34 90 219 19 19   www.intervida.org

Committed to sustainable human development, this organization is looking for willing and dedicated volunteers to help with awareness campaigns involving the improvement of living conditions for the most disadvantaged communities.

HISTORICAL RESTORATION

GLOBAL WORKS

☎1-303-545-2202   www.globalworkstravel.com

Travel to Andalucia and complete 20-30 hours of service while being immersed in the language and culture. Choose from a variety of activities, including teaching English, working in an organic garden, and restoring historic buildings, all while seeing the beautiful sites of Madrid and Granada.
⑨ $4495.

CADIP

☎1-310-882-7400   www.cadip.org

Travel to the village of Granja do Ulmeiro to paint, rebuild, promote local festivals, facilitate intercultural exchange, and clean streets. When you're not dedicating your time to making the world a better place, have some fun traveling through the region to see the city of Coimbra and the beach of Figueira-da-Foz.
i Group living. Must be 18-30, Canadian or American. ⑨ $290.

ENVIRONMENTAL CONSERVATION

BTCV

www.btcv.org

Go on a conservation journey from the peaks of Alvao, through the Douro valleys, to the sandy dunes of Litoral Norte, finishing your journey with scuba diving in the sea. Volunteers will mainly spend their time removing harmful invasive plant life from the nature reserves.
i 18+. ⑨ $590.

SOCIAL ACTIVISM

ARSIS FOUNDATION

C. Ramon Turó, 10B, Barcelona, Spain ☎+34 93 187 38 35

This non-profit in Barcelona is determined to provide education, culture, arts, and sports for children and adolescents through activities and workshops. They are often looking for several volunteers to work with their teachers to further these goals.

APAV

Portugal www.apav.pt

The Portuguese Association for Victim Support accepts volunteers who are interested in providing confidential and free services and support to victims of crimes. Those interested in volunteering can apply online.

EXPERIMENT IN INTERNATIONAL LIVING

☎1-800-345-2929 www.experimentinternational.org

Through this program, you will have the opportunity to travel all over Spain, beginning in Madrid. Participants go from city to city, living in homestays and volunteering to help integrate immigrants into society.

i 2 years of Spanish required. 4 weeks. $ $7000; airfare from New York included.

FOR THE UNDECIDED ALTRUIST

INTERCOINED

☎1-800-897-9631 www.intercoined.org

This organization allows travelers over the age of 18 find various volunteer opportunities in the fields of education, health, and community development. Volunteers can help keep children from dropping out of school, teach English to disadvantaged people, raise awareness about rare diseases, help people with disabilities, build the self-esteem of children, and more.

PORTAL DA JUVENTUDE

www.juventude.gov.pt

This is an online portal that can help you find volunteer opportunities in Portugal based on your interests and where you would like to volunteer. Go to juventude.gov.pt to start your search.

working

They say money can't buy happiness, but working abroad can certainly earn you the spending money to enjoy the exhilarating nightlife and historical wonders of Spain and Portugal. Here at Let's Go we know you can't put a price tag on memories, but, hey, the drinks aren't free, so unless you can flirt your way through a free night on the town, we suggest you look into getting a job. And this new addition to your resume can't hurt, right?

LONG-TERM WORK

Teaching English

Finding a teaching job in Spain will be relatively easy. The certification requirements make job-hunting in Portugal a much harder task, as teaching English in Portugal requires TEFL/TESOL certification. The easiest way to receive certification is through an online course, like the one offered by the **TEFL Institute** (☎1-773-880-5141; www.teflinstitute.com. 150 hours online, $1350). Spain, on the other hand, does not have these requirements, making it the perfect place to spend some time helping the natives learn

English. Even better, Spain is home to an endless amount of homestays that will make living and working in Spain that much easier and more enjoyable.

CIEE TEACH ABROAD

☎1-800-40-STUDY www.ciee.org

With CIEE you can find yourself working in urban or pueblo locations throughout Andalucia. There are a variety of different programs where you can teach, whether in a classroom, an immersion program, or even in a professional training setting, depending on your level of Spanish.

$ €700 per month.

GEOVISIONS

☎1-877-949-9998 www.geovisions.org

GeoVisions provides native English speakers with a chance to teach the language to others in a variety of settings, including to children, families, and in the classroom. Typically, those that apply will live with a family and teach them English.

i Must teach for 20 hours per week. 18+. Basic Spanish required. $ $55 per week.

LANGUAGE CORPS

☎1-978-562-2100 www.languagecorps.com

Through this program you will receive TESOL Certification and job placement in Spanish schools. Participants in the program can choose to finish their training at prestigious universities in Barcelona or Sevilla and will complete over 140 hours of classroom time.

$ Barcelona $1895; Sevilla $2295. EFL teacher's salary €900-1300 per month.

LANGUAGE LIVING

☎1-512-469-9089 www.languageliving.com

This program offers free room and board in exchange for 15-20 hours of teaching per week. When not teaching English, you will be free to roam the cities or go on weekend excursions around the country. You are also offered the option of completing TEFL certification online for a small fee.

CONVERSATION ASSISTANT PROGRAMME FOR SCHOOLS (CAPS)

www.goabroad.com

Designed by the organization Home-to-Home, this a program is for young people looking to spend a year abroad and work in a school in Catalonia. Conversation

more visa information

If you are planning to work in Spain, you will need a work permit. If you are already in the country, you can apply at the Foreigner's Office or the provincial Ministry of Labour. If you have not yet arrived in Spain, you must apply at the nearest consulate. When you apply, you will need: a valid passport, certificate of criminal records, official medical certificate, three passport-sized photos, fiscal registration number and Social Security registration number of the employer, offer of employment containing labor conditions, and a description of the job. Also note that there are different permits depending on the type of work: Type A is for seasonal work; Type B is initial, which is valid for one year in a specific profession and can be renewed; and Type C, which is issued after Type B renewed has expired. For a Portuguese working visa, you must bring the completed employment visa form, two passport photos, valid resident visa, health insurance confirmation, current bank statement, reference letter from employer and all fees to the nearest Portuguese consulate or embassy.

Assistants (CAs) are assigned to students between the ages of three and 16 and will work with them to improve their English.

i *25 hours per week.* Ⓢ *€50 per month, accommodations, and transportation.*

ESL EMPLOYMENT PORTUGAL

eslemployment.com

If you already have teaching experience and are TEFL/TESOL certified, this search engine will help you to find job openings all over Portugal for ESL teachers.

Ⓢ *€800-1200 per month.*

Au Pair Work

Finding an au pair job in Spain might be easier than in Portugal. With numerous agencies looking to help you out, you won't have to learn the ropes on your own while escorting a gaggle of googley-eyed rugrats through Madrid or Barcelona. Portugal, on the other hand, lacks these agencies. So although there are families looking to hire, you'll have to find them on your own through various search engines rather than having a professional do it for you. But then again, there's something to be said for having the freedom to choose the right family for you.

AU PAIR SPAIN

C. Ter, 22A Chalet 43, Villaviciosa de Odón, Spain ☎+34 93 508 81 05 www.aupairspain.com
With Au Pair Spain, you are expected to become a member of the family. As an au pair, you will enjoy accommodations and food provided by your family, as well as monthly pocket money, at least one day a week off, and a five-hour work day.

i *Must speak Spanish.*

PLANET AU PAIR

Av. Ausias March, 32, Pta. 4, Valencia, Spain ☎+34 96 320 64 91 www.planetaupair.com
Planet Au Pair allows you to choose to work for anywhere from one to 12 months at a time. Not only will you find a new family, but you will be given the contact information for other au pairs in the area should you choose to meet them. And although you will be working as domestic help, the primary purpose of this program is cultural exchange.

i *2 days free per week. 2 weeks paid vacation per 6 months.* Ⓢ *€70-100 per week.*

AU PAIR IN SPAIN

☎+34 64 456 85 98 www.aupairinspain.com
Putting children first is the main goal of this organization, and Au Pair in Spain only accepts the best applicants for their au pair service. However, if you are selected, the company is more than accommodating, offering help every step of the way.

i *Must be 18-27. Must speak some Spanish. Free Spanish lessons.* Ⓢ *€65-75 per week.*

NEW AU PAIR

www.newaupair.com

This site allows you to search through Portuguese families looking to hire an au pair. Finding a job in this way gives you the freedom to choose a family that you think suits your personality and goals as an au pair.

AUPAIR.COM

www.aupair.com

This is another site that will allow you to look through families in Portugal and decide which one you would like to work for.

working

Other Long-Term Work

If you are a gap-year teen or college student looking to spend time abroad, you'll likely find long-term work in the form of internships. Lucky for you, between Spain and Portugal, there's an internship for every interest under the sun.

IAESTE SPAIN

Camino de Vera, Bldg. 8k, Valencia, Spain   ☎+34 96 369 94 80 www.iaeste.es

The International Association for the Exchange of Students for Technical Experience provides training opportunities abroad. Positions are available in industry, research institutes and universities, consulting firms, labs, and more. Jobs are available for eight to 12 weeks in the summer and longer placements during the year.

i *Must be 19-30, currently enrolled full-time in Bachelor's or Master's program.*

WORLD ENDEAVORS SPAIN

Valencia, Spain   ☎1-612-729-3400 www.worldendeavors.com

If you're interested in a unique internship experience, this is the program for you. In Valencia, you will find opportunities in business, public relations, journalism, culinary arts, and many more.

i *Housing is provided.* Ⓢ *$4490-6700.*

GLOBAL EXPERIENCES

Barcelona, Spain   ☎1-877-GE-ABROAD www.globalexperiences.com

Barcelona awaits you with these internships. Whether you're interested in accounting, advertising, business, event planning, hospitality, IT, law, or video production, Global Experiences has at least one internship for you, usually more.

i *Must be 19-30. Some Spanish required. Housing provided.* Ⓢ *$7990-8990.*

WWOOF

www.wwoof.org

World Wide Opportunities on Organic Farms places volunteers on organic farms in both Spain and Portugal. Workers get free room and board in return for their help on the farms.

XPAT JOBS

www.xpatjobs.com

This search engine allows you to browse through job openings in Spain and Portugal. You can limit your search based on fields you are interested in. Your dream job awaits.

EUROYOUTH PORTUGAL

Calçada do Garcia, 29, Lisbon, Portugal   ☎+351 21 887 00 30

This company will help you find an internship or job in Portugal. EuroYouth offers support in a variety of fields, including education and culture.

IAESTE PORTUGAL

Av. Rovisco, Lisbon, Portugal   ☎+21 841 73 62

The International Association for the Exchange of Students for Technical Experience provides traineeship opportunities abroad. Positions are available in industry, research institutes and universities, consulting firms, labs, and more. Jobs are available for eight to 12 weeks in the summer and longer placements during the year.

i *Must be 19-30 and currently enrolled full-time in Bachelor's or Master's program.*

SHORT-TERM WORK

Unfortunately, making the few extra bucks to continue living abroad may be more complicated than you think. Work permits are required for most jobs, even short-terms ones, and this long and tedious application process needs to be done well in advance of your wallet running out of dough. Fortunately, there are some jobs that will pay workers under the table or allow you to work in exchange for room and board. For most of these jobs, though, you'll have to ask around or keep an eye out for the oh-so-identifiable "Help Wanted" sign. The following listings will help you get started.

PUEBLO INGLÉS

☎+34 90 210 37 37

Essentially, you'd be working at an intensive English camp right outside Salamanca for a week. There's no pay, but the program allows you to stay on site for free, so long as you agree to speak only English to the guests.

LOQUO

www.loquo.com

When you're looking for some quick cash at home, you'd probably check out Craigslist for some short-term gigs. Well, Spain has one of those, too. It's www.loquo.com, and it can help you find listings for short-term opportunities while you're traveling throughout the country.

TRANSITIONS ABROAD

www.transitionsabroad.com

This site offers job listings of every type in both Spain and Portugal, although many are seasonal. Perfect for someone looking to work only a few days or weeks.

WORKAWAY

workaway.info

Workaway.info is a website that allows you to find short-term work and occasionally long-term work. Some of the jobs include working at hostels in exchange for room and board, working at music festivals, working on farms, teaching English, and more. Opportunities are always changing, so check back often.

working

tell the world

If your friends are tired of hearing about that time you saved a baby orangutan in Indonesia, there's clearly only one thing to do: get new friends. Find them at our website, www.letsgo.com, where you can post your study-, volunteer-, or work-abroad stories for other, more appreciative community members to read.

INDEX

index

index

index

MAP INDEX

map index

LET'S GO!

THE STUDENT TRAVEL GUIDE

Available at bookstores and through online retailers:

EUROPE
Let's Go Budget Amsterdam, 1st ed.
Let's Go Amsterdam & Brussels, 1st ed.
Let's Go Budget Athens, 1st ed.
Let's Go Budget Barcelona, 1st ed.
Let's Go Budget Berlin, 1st ed.
Let's Go Berlin, Prague & Budapest, 2nd ed.
Let's Go Budget Florence, 1st ed.
Let's Go France, 32nd ed.
Let's Go Europe 2013, 53rd ed.
Let's Go Europe Top 10 Cities, 1st ed.
Let's Go European Riviera, 1st ed.
Let's Go Germany, 16th ed.
Let's Go Great Britain with Belfast and Dublin, 33rd ed.
Let's Go Greece, 10th ed.
Let's Go Budget Istanbul, 1st ed.
Let's Go Istanbul, Athens & the Greek Islands, 1st ed.
Let's Go Ireland, 14th ed.
Let's Go Italy, 32nd ed.
Let's Go Budget London, 1st ed.
Let's Go London, Oxford & Cambridge, 3rd ed.
Let's Go Budget Madrid, 1st ed.
Let's Go Madrid & Barcelona, 1st ed.
Let's Go Paris, 17th ed.
Let's Go Budget Paris, 1st ed.
Let's Go Paris, Amsterdam & Brussels, 1st ed.
Let's Go Budget Prague, 1st ed.
Let's Go Budget Rome, 1st ed.
Let's Go Rome, Venice & Florence, 2nd ed.
Let's Go Spain & Portugal, 27th ed.
Let's Go Western Europe, 10th ed.

UNITED STATES
Let's Go Boston, 6th ed.
Let's Go New York City, 19th ed.
Let's Go Roadtripping USA, 4th ed.

MEXICO, CENTRAL & SOUTH AMERICA
Let's Go Buenos Aires, 2nd ed.
Let's Go Central America, 10th ed.
Let's Go Costa Rica, 5th ed.
Let's Go Costa Rica, Nicaragua & Panama, 1st ed.
Let's Go Guatemala & Belize, 1st ed.
Let's Go Yucatán Peninsula, 1st ed.

ASIA & THE MIDDLE EAST
Let's Go Israel, 6th ed.
Let's Go Thailand, 5th ed.

Exam and desk copies are available for study-abroad programs and resource centers. Let's Go guidebooks are distributed to bookstores in the U.S. through Publishers Group West and in Canada through Publishers Group Canada. For more information, email letsgo.info@perseusbooks.com.

ACKNOWLEDGMENTS

MALLORY THANKS: Our RWs for their brave, bold, and badass attitude. Mark for not judging country music (or doing it quietly) and for helping me eat ALL the sushi. Clemmie for never spilling your water on my side and for being the RM to my Ed through the good, the bad, and the manstores. Michael for delicious duck, comfy beds, and a place to rest my head when silly-time rolled around. Claire for your celebrity scoops and for making me laugh over copyflow and salads. Haley for talking to strangers on buses (no wait, that's not okay). Mariel for tweets and frozen grapes. And everyone at Let's Go for a wonderful summer. Mom, Dad, Jack, and Jay for always making me laugh (LBI next year, I promise). Demetrio for a summer of country music (and we do). And all my friends scattered about for all the silliness and support.

CLEMMIE THANKS: Mark, my faithful ME, for always being there to take the weight off of our shoulders, whether with a helping hand or an off-the-cuff joke. You always make me smile. Mallory for being the most reliable, savviest editor ever and always brightening the mood. My awesomely adventurous RWs, who took everything in stride and allowed me to live vicariously through them this summer. Trailblazers. For real. Roland and Faith for prodding us along and putting up with the chaos. Michael, Haley, Claire, Lauren, Mariel, and Jess for being great at what they do and making the office a lighthearted and fun, yet productive place. Sara for holding it all together. **Bassnectar, Dillon Francis,** and **Zeds Dead** for keeping me thoroughly entertained when monotony hit. Thanks Paul for keeping me happy. Finally, thanks to **the moms.** I love you, Mum!

DIRECTOR OF PUBLISHING Sara Plana
MANAGING EDITORS Michael Goncalves, Mark Warren
PRODUCTION AND DESIGN DIRECTOR Roland Yang
DIGITAL AND MARKETING DIRECTOR Lauren Xie
PRODUCTION ASSOCIATE Faith Zhang
MARKETING ASSOCIATES Zi Wei Lin, Mariel Sena, Jess Stein

DIRECTOR OF IT Calvin Tonini
PRESIDENT Kirk Benson
GENERAL MANAGER Jim McKellar

ABOUT LET'S GO

THE STUDENT TRAVEL GUIDE

Let's Go publishes the world's favorite student travel guides, written entirely by Harvard students. Armed with pens, notebooks, and a few changes of clothes stuffed into their backpacks, our student researchers go across continents, through time zones, and above expectations to seek out invaluable travel experiences for our readers. Because we are a completely student-run company, we have a unique perspective on how students travel, where they want to go, and what they're looking to do when they get there. If your dream is to grab a machete and forge through the jungles of Costa Rica, we can take you there. If you'd rather bask in the Riviera sun at a beachside cafe, we'll set you a table. In short, we write for readers who know that there's more to travel than tour buses. To keep up, visit our website, www.letsgo. com, where you can sign up to blog, post photos from your trips, and connect with the Let's Go community.

TRAVELING BEYOND TOURISM

We're on a mission to provide our readers with sharp, fresh coverage packed with socially responsible opportunities to go beyond tourism. Each guide's Beyond Tourism chapter shares ideas about responsible travel, study abroad, and how to give back to the places you visit while on the road. To help you gain a deeper connection with the places you travel, our fearless researchers scour the globe to give you the heads-up on both world-renowned and off-the-beaten-track opportunities. We've also opened our pages to respected writers and scholars to hear their takes on the countries and regions we cover, and asked travelers who have worked, studied, or volunteered abroad to contribute first-person accounts of their experiences.

FIFTY-THREE YEARS OF WISDOM

Let's Go has been on the road for 53 years and counting. We've grown a lot since publishing our first 20-page pamphlet to Europe in 1960, but five decades and 60 titles later, our witty, candid guides are still researched and written entirely by students on shoestring budgets who know that train strikes, stolen luggage, food poisoning, and marriage proposals are all part of a day's work. Meanwhile, we're still bringing readers fresh new features, such as a student-life section with advice on how and where to meet students from around the world; a revamped, user-friendly layout for our listings; and greater emphasis on the experiences that make travel abroad a rite of passage for readers of all ages. And, of course, this year's seven titles are still brimming with editorial honesty, a commitment to students, and our irreverent style.

THE LET'S GO COMMUNITY

More than just a travel guide company, Let's Go is a community that reaches from our headquarters in Cambridge, MA, all across the globe. Our small staff of dedicated student editors, writers, and tech nerds comes together because of our shared passion for travel and our desire to help other travelers get the most out of their experience. We love it when our readers become part of the Let's Go community as well—when you travel, drop us a postcard (67 Mt. Auburn St., Cambridge, MA 02138, USA), send us an email (feedback@letsgo.com), or sign up on our website (www. letsgo.com) to tell us about your adventures and discoveries.

For more information, updated travel coverage, and news from our researcher team, visit us online at www.letsgo.com.

quick reference

YOUR GUIDE TO LET'S GO ICONS

✎	*Let's Go* recommends	☎	Phone numbers	⇄	Directions
i	Miscellaneous info	$	Prices	⏰	Hours

PRICE RANGES

Let's Go includes price ranges, marked by one through four dollar signs, in accommodations and food listings. For an expanded explanation, see the chart in How To Use This Book.

SPAIN	$	$$	$$$	$$$$
ACCOMMODATIONS	under €23	€23-35	€36-50	over €50
FOOD	under €9	€9-16	€17-25	over €26

PORTUGAL	$	$$	$$$	$$$$
ACCOMMODATIONS	under €21	€21-30	€30-45	over €45
FOOD	under €7	€7-14	€15-22	over €22

IMPORTANT PHONE NUMBERS

SPAIN EMERGENCY: POLICE ☎092, FIRE ☎080, MEDICAL ☎112			
US Consulate in Madrid	☎+34 91 587 22 00	US Embassy in Barcelona	☎+34 93 280 22 27
International Operator	☎1008	Directory Assistance	☎1003

PORTUGAL EMERGENCY: POLICE ☎112, FIRE ☎112, MEDICAL ☎112			
US Embassy in Lisbon	☎+351 21 727 33 00	US Consulate in Ponta Delgada	☎+351 29 628 22 16
International Operator	☎00 35 11 18	US State Department	☎+1 317-472-2328, ☎+1 202-647-4000 (after hours)

USEFUL SPANISH AND PORTUGUESE PHRASES

ENGLISH	SPANISH	PORTUGUESE
Hello.	Hola.	Olá.
Good morning/afternoon/night.	Buenos días/Buenas tardes/Buenas noches.	Bom dia/Boa tarde/Boa noite.
Please.	Por favor.	Por favor.
Thank you.	Gracias.	Obrigado/a.
You're welcome.	De nada.	De nada.
How much is...?	¿Cuánto es...?	Quanto é...?
Where is...?	¿Dónde está...?	Onde é...?
Help!	¡Socorro!	Socorro!

TEMPERATURE CONVERSIONS

°CELSIUS	-5	0	5	10	15	20	25	30	35	40
°FAHRENHEIT	23	32	41	50	59	68	77	86	95	104

MEASUREMENT CONVERSIONS

1 inch (in.) = 25.4mm	1 millimeter (mm) = 0.039 in.
1 foot (ft.) = 0.305m	1 meter (m) = 3.28 ft.
1 mile (mi.) = 1.609km	1 kilometer (km) = 0.621 mi.
1 pound (lb.) = 0.454kg	1 kilogram (kg) = 2.205 lb.
1 gallon (gal.) = 3.785L	1 liter (L) = 0.264 gal.

HELPING LET'S GO. If you want to share your discoveries, suggestions, or corrections, please drop us a line. We appreciate every piece of correspondence, whether a postcard, a 10-page email, or a coconut. Visit Let's Go at **www.letsgo.com** or send an email to:

feedback@letsgo.com, subject: "Let's Go Spain and Portugal"

Address mail to:

Let's Go Spain and Portugal, 67 Mount Auburn St., Cambridge, MA 02138, USA

In addition to the invaluable travel advice our readers share with us, many are kind enough to offer their services as researchers or editors. Unfortunately, our charter enables us to employ only currently enrolled Harvard students.

Maps © Let's Go and Avalon Travel
Design Support by Jane Musser, Sarah Juckniess, Tim McGrath

Distributed by Publishers Group West.
Printed in Canada by Friesens Corp.

ISBN-13: 978-1-61237-031-6
Twenty-seventh edition
10 9 8 7 6 5 4 3 2 1

Let's Go Spain and Portugal is written by Let's Go Publications, 67 Mt. Auburn St., Cambridge, MA 02138, USA.

Let's Go® and the LG logo are trademarks of Let's Go, Inc.